The United States Since 1865

By
LOUIS M. HACKER

Professor of Economics, Columbia University
Harmsworth Professor of American History
Oxford University

and

BENJAMIN B. KENDRICK

Late Professor of History, The Woman's College
The University of North Carolina

with the collaboration of
HELENE S. ZAHLER

FOURTH EDITION

APPLETON-CENTURY-CROFTS, Inc.
New York

Copyright 1949, by
APPLETON-CENTURY-CROFTS, INC.

Copyright renewed, 1960, 1962, by
Louis M. Hacker, Benjamin B. Kendrick, Janet K. Buckley,
John W. Kendrick, and Margaret K. Horney

All rights reserved. This book, or parts thereof, must not be reproduced in any form without permission of the publishers.

612-6

COPYRIGHT, 1932, 1934, 1939, BY
LOUIS M. HACKER AND BENJAMIN B. KENDRICK

MANUFACTURED IN THE UNITED STATES OF AMERICA

Editor's Foreword

GENERALLY speaking, the historical facts of a decade or a quarter-century since are the vaguest in our understanding. We have a vivid notion, though confused, of what happened yesterday, for the headlines are still fresh in our personal memories; what happened many years ago is neatly analyzed and schemed into a formal doctrine by the standard histories. But the life-time of our fathers has usually been to us neither history nor experience. And personal observation turns out to be a treacherous chart to the important tendencies of our own day, made up as it is of haphazard impressions shaped by the accidents and prejudices of an individual's course through a tiny part of the world's life. Educational theorists, surrendering to such difficulties, once thought "recent history," if not a contradiction in terms, at least practically unteachable. A learned committee of the National Education Association, reporting on the school curriculum in 1895, declared that, "The formation of the Constitution, and a brief study of the salient features of the Constitution itself, conclude the study of the portion of the history of the United States that is sufficiently remote to be treated after the manner of an educational classic," and advised that nothing be done about the century and more that had since transpired.

Now we are under a different dispensation; the governing theory is that history is chiefly useful to explain the present, and that the present cannot be explained without a special emphasis upon those events which are immediately back of it and have, as it were, given the final push that has brought it into being. In obeisance to this theory recent histories have been written, but almost all have failed to focus clearly on the present they set out to explain. It is the peculiar feature of this book, and in the light of governing theory a great merit, that as it approaches the present it becomes constantly more thorough in discussion and richer in detail. Not only is as much space given to the thirty years of the twentieth century as to the forty which preceded it, but within these thirty years the emphasis is upon the last fifteen, ending with incisive treatment of the unfinished business of this very year. Economic forces are kept in near view throughout.

Though a long book, much is omitted which has often been regarded as the staple of history. The technical maneuvering of party forces, the *game* of the professionals, has been summed up as briefly as possible, to make room for realistic study of the changes which politicians rarely brought about and which many of them ignored as long as they could. The real problems, such as: the restoration of nationality after the Civil War; the monetary confusion that resulted from financing that conflict; the removal of routine administration from the sphere of party contests, that is, Civil Service reform; the attempts at hegemony in the Western Hemisphere; the struggles of the American agricultural order to find a proper place for itself in the domestic economic scheme; the nation-wide organization of capital, of industry, and of labor, with the various political reverberations; the imperialism of territorial expansion and the more significant imperialism of financial penetration throughout the world; the social politics of Roosevelt and Wilson; the painful discovery in 1917 that we were a part of the world, the mighty regimentation of the American people to play a necessary rôle in its critical affairs, and then the resolute attempt to secede from it again;—all these, though there is a rough chronological plan, are discussed topically. But this is historical reason disentangling for our comprehension fibers which as they grew day by day conditioned one another and were closely matted in the general experience of the nation. Inevitably, therefore, it is necessary now and then to mention subjects which must await a full development later in the book, a consideration the reader may well recall when, as he reads, he thinks some topic too summarily disposed of.

Few if any college textbooks rival this in the space devoted to such matters as philanthropy, religion, learning, the arts, taste, the influences shaping opinion, and the like, in our modern American life. If the student misses the names of some Cabinet secretaries he may remark for the first time those of Robert A. Woods, Charles S. Peirce, Thomas Eakins, and Frank Lloyd Wright. But though names are listed, most of them become much more than names. We read, for example, that John Singer Sargent's later life never fulfilled the promise of his youth, that Emily Dickinson was the greatest poet of her day. This is not the usual perfunctory mention, guarded against controversy, but lively comment compelling curiosity, possibly stirring the pervious student mind to check the judgment in the library or even the gallery.

If a textbook should say nothing that could not be endorsed by every literate American, if it must content itself with rehearsing only that orthodoxy that overlaps the corners of all individual opinion, in other words, if the teacher, the student, and the student's father must each agree with every judgment, then this work cannot qualify as a textbook. For while the authors conscientiously attempt to set forth facts with all fairness, their pronouncements on them are not intended to be memorized as dogma, but rather to provoke reflective thinking. The college professor who will tolerate intelligent debate in his classroom will find many bases for it in each chapter. Andrew Carnegie is described as promoting peace with one hand while he made armor plate for battleships with the other. It does not do to lose one's temper at such a collocation; it is better to decide which fact was more significant in American history. If, as a class discusses the background of America's entry into the war against Germany, the majority decides the book is wrong, that day will have at least as memorable a value in the student's education as if it had been proved right. Only the timid teacher, who, having no personal grasp of his subject, desires his class to recite on passages learned by rote from an "authority," need shun a book which dares to argue; most textbooks do not present discussable matter in a way that it can be discussed. What would be inappropriate in a text for high school adolescents is invaluable for men and women sufficiently mature to be in college.

American history is seen in this account from the points of view of the farmer, the village tradesman, and the mill hand, points of view which Professor Kendrick has for many years made deeply interesting to students at Columbia University and at The Woman's College of The University of North Carolina. Mr. Hacker, who has spent his life in New York City, gained a sympathetic understanding of this view while an undergraduate and then a graduate student at Columbia a dozen years ago. In the meantime, as a journalist and working economist, he has seen aspects of American life not so clear to those immured in academic studies. The text is largely his. Professor Kendrick has written chapters dealing with the Civil War and its immediate aftermath; but his counsel, based on many years of teaching experience, and his substantial revisions have affected the work throughout.

The historian's telescope is here swung from new watch-towers. Not only because of the abundance and unconventionality of its data but because of this fresh evaluation the book will, it is thought, pay large returns from the student's attention.

DIXON RYAN FOX

Introduction

THE PRESENT is the fourth edition of *The United States Since 1865*, which first appeared in 1932. Originally, it was a rather bold venture; and it continues to be so. For any work that seeks to give the backgrounds of contemporary events, as well as the events themselves, runs the risks of incorporating those judgments and prejudices that personal involvements must produce. I am simply saying that citizenship in a democracy means participation; and to this extent so-called objectivity is emotionally and intellectually impossible. For good or ill, the authors have expressed their own convictions about many of the things of which they have written.

This edition has been prepared in the same spirit that characterized the first and the level of analysis continues the same. It is written for the intelligent student of national affairs rather than the specialist. I have always believed that adult readers are capable of handling economic, legal, and intellectual questions maturely; and the reception this book has had over the years justifies that confidence. For that reason, too, I have given a good deal of attention to economic matters. That does not mean I believe in economic causation; quite the reverse. But we cannot understand the institutional character of this highly complicated modern world in which we live unless we understand the significant parts played by money and banking, capital formation, outlays and movements, prices, wages, and the like. In addition to being a political, social, and diplomatic history of the United States, this book therefore is also an economic history. And it is an economic history with the proper balance, for it seeks to reveal the links between economic interests and public policy.

Thus, the essential qualities of the original book have been preserved. But this edition is more than a revision in the usual sense; for the whole work has been re-examined and completely reset in a more attractive format. There are fresh illustrations and maps; the bibliography has been brought up to date to include the latest works in scholarly research. The index is new and fuller.

At only one point have earlier judgments been modified. I have been less dogmatic in my attitude toward the first generation of industrial capitalists who came out of the Civil War. They were—many of them—bold and unscrupulous businessmen; but they were great innovators, and their ingenuity made possible the creation of an industrial machine whose achievements have been the wonder of the world. Today, that industrial power is about the only means mankind has of saving civilization. I have not swung to the opposite pole and engaged in apologetics. But I have tried to explain the contributions of these captains of industry to the making of modern America a little more carefully than was done in the first edition. To this extent, the longer perspective of an additional fifteen or so years has been helpful.

When this book was first written, two themes seemed to express the recent history of the United States. The first was the submergence—politically and economically—of the agrarian interest; the second was the emergence of the United States as an imperial power. Since that writing, the outlines—and horizons—have widened. In the almost one hundred years that have passed since the beginning of the Civil War, in addition to the two themes already mentioned, two others have appeared. They are: first, the state interventionism that the New Deal marked; and second, the world leadership of the United States. In effect, the American destiny, which began to unfold during the Civil War, has been now fulfilled with all its promise and risk: for the triumph of industrialism at home sooner or later required a fuller participation abroad in the economic and political programs needed for peace and progress.

Just as the Civil War marked a revolution in our course, so did the New Deal. The New Deal demonstrated many things: the instabilities that are basic to a complex industrial civilization; the need for state intervention through fiscal policy and other devices to maintain the economy on an even keel; the desirability—in fact, the necessity—on the part of the state of concerning itself constantly with the question of redistribution of wealth and income if balances and compromises are to be maintained in a democracy. In working out programs along these lines the New Deal created the Big State and Big Labor. These were inevitable and these brought real problems in their train. For with power comes responsibility. These developments and questions in the domestic sector have been the focal point of a large part of the new writing in this edition. All these subjects are treated in considerable detail.

The same has been true of our place in the outside world. Nazism and today Communism, because both have been based on theories of conquest, have menaced our internal well-being, for they have questioned our legitimate rights to expand economically and politically. The United States accepted the challenge of Nazism and its allies and entered World War II. To make the peace effective, to restore war-torn Europe, to reopen the world channels of trade, the United States has been compelled to accept the challenge of Communism. Here again, power and responsibility are the two sides of the same coin. Much of the new writing has been concerned with an exposition of these developments. There are therefore to be found extended discussions of World War II, the creation of U.N., and the prob-

INTRODUCTION

lems of the peace here and outside our shores. The outcome of the Presidential election of 1948 is also included.

The first edition was written in the midst of the Great Depression: it was perfectly natural that its tone—as the authors regarded the immediate future of America—should be somewhat muted. Americans survived the depression and World War II. They came through both events richer in experience and understanding and soberer, too. They face today a world of turmoil and danger; but they do so with more confidence. They continue committed to their ancient ideals: men must be free to live their own lives and make their own institutional arrangements; and men must not be thwarted from their quest for the attainment of human and social welfare. Americans realize this as well: that they themselves cannot live in peace at home unless all peoples the world over have similar assurances. This is the meaning of our twin responsibility: to keep our own house in order and to help the rest of the world achieve the goals we have set for ourselves. The perspective and happenings of the last decade and a half therefore have had another influence on this book which this edition seeks to capture.

Since the appearance of the previous edition, my old friend, teacher, and collaborator Benjamin B. Kendrick has passed away. This time I do not have the benefit of his wise advice and counsel. He may have disagreed with my analysis at some points; in any case, the responsibility for this edition is mine entirely. Miss Helene S. Zahler has helped me in many ways: she has collected much of the material I have employed for the writing of the new chapters; many of the judgments in the last chapter are hers and I have used them because they seem to me so shrewd; she has drawn up the new bibliography and index, helped to prepare the new graphic materials, and read most of the proofs. I am pleased to acknowledge my debt to her here and on the title page.

LOUIS M. HACKER

Contents

Part One: THE HUMBLING OF THE FARMERS

Section I: THE FRUITS OF THE CIVIL WAR

Chapter		Page
1.	**THE SMOLDERING EMBERS OF WAR**	
	An Age of Hate	3
	Abraham Lincoln and the South	7
	Andrew Johnson and the South	11
	Congress Versus President	15
	The Triumph of the Radicals	20
	The Impeachment of Johnson and the Election of 1868	23
2.	**AFTERMATH OF VICTORY**	
	A New Birth of Freedom	28
	Closing Phases of Reconstruction	32
	Foreign Affairs During Reconstruction	37
3.	**PASSING OF THE SOUTHERN QUESTION**	
	Grantism	44
	The Election and Administration of Hayes	50
	Emergence of the New South	54
	The Political, Civil, and Social Status of the Negro	56

Section II: PARTY GOVERNMENT AND PUBLIC AFFAIRS

4.	**THE EMBATTLED POLITICIANS**	
	The Party Hosts and Their Chieftains	61
	Garfield and Arthur	65
	The Return of the Democracy	69
	Benjamin Harrison in Office	73
	Cleveland Again President	76
5.	**THREE LEADING QUESTIONS BEFORE THE POSTBELLUM PARTIES**	
	The Protective Tariff	78
	Civil Service Reform	84
	Spending the Surplus and Rewarding War Veterans	87
6.	**RELATIONS WITH THE OUTSIDE WORLD, 1876–1896**	
	Character of American Foreign Policy	91
	The United States and Latin America	92

Chapter	Page
The United States and Great Britain	93
The United States in the Pacific	99
The Territory of Hawaii	100
The Territory of Alaska	103
The New Navy	105

Section III: THE MAKING OF MODERN AMERICA

7. SETTLING THE CONTINENT

The Growth of Population	108
The West and the Passing of the Frontier	109
The Public Domain	110
The Cow Country	113
The Indians	115
The Waves of Immigration	117
Reasons for Immigration Restriction	120
Restriction Legislation	121

8. BUILDING THE RAILROADS

The Railroad Net	124
The Great American Rail Systems	126
Financing the Railroads	135

9. THE NEW AGRICULTURE

The Characteristics of the New Agriculture	138
Wheat	141
Cotton	143
The American Farm Surpluses	146
Science Routs the Old-Fashioned Farmer	148
The Farmers' Dilemma	151

Section IV: THE PROCESSES OF INDUSTRIALIZATION

10. THE NEW INDUSTRIALISM

What Made the New Industrialism Possible	155
How American Industry Grew	157
Steel	160
Economic Laissez-Faire and the Supreme Court	165

11. MONEY AND TRADE

The Resumption of Specie Payments	171
The National Banking System	173
Silver	176
Foreign Trade	182
The Decline of the Merchant Marine	185

12. THE ORGANIZED WORKERS

General Characteristics	188
Trade Unionism in the Sixties and Seventies	188
The Knights of Labor	190

	Page
Chapter	
Craft Unionism	195
Violence	197

13. AMERICAN LIFE, LETTERS, AND ART, 1865–1900
Characteristics of the Social Scene	202
Some Aspects of American Society	205
The Intellectual Life	210
Letters, Art, and Architecture	215

Section V: AGRARIAN DISCONTENT

14. CURBING THE RAILROADS: THE INTERSTATE COMMERCE ACT OF 1887
The Springs of Western Unrest	223
Railroad Abuses	224
State Regulation and the Supreme Court	228
The Evolution of Federal Control	230
The Frustration of the Interstate Commerce Commission	235

15. THE SHERMAN ANTITRUST LAW
The Processes of Concentration	238
The Standard Oil Company	241
The Common Law and State Action	246
The Writing of the Sherman Antitrust Law	246
The Enforcement of the Law	248

16. THE AGRARIAN REVOLT: GREENBACKISM, POPULISM, THE ELECTION OF 1896
What Populism Implied	252
The Greenback Movement	253
Populism	255
The Battle of 1896: The Gathering Forces	264
The Battle of 1896: The Campaign	269
Aftermath of the Free-Silver Controversy	272

Part Two: THE EMERGENCE OF IMPERIAL AMERICA

Section VI: EXPANSION OVERSEAS

17. REPUBLICANISM TRIUMPHANT
The McKinley Administration	277
Political and Economic Interests in Cuba	281
Events Leading up to the War with Spain	286

18. A SHORT AND GLORIOUS WAR
War Preparations	292
Attitude of the European Powers	294

CONTENTS

Chapter	Page
The Conduct of the War	295
The Peace of Paris	298
The Election of 1900	303

19. A WORLD THEATER

Imperialism in the United States Before World War I	306
The United States in the Philippines	308
The United States in Puerto Rico	314
The Constitution and Our Island Dependencies	317
The United States in Cuba	319
Secretary Hay and China	323

Section VII: THEODORE ROOSEVELT AND REFORM

20. THEODORE ROOSEVELT AND WILLIAM HOWARD TAFT

The First Roosevelt Administration	326
The Second Roosevelt Administration	330
The Presidency of William Howard Taft	333

21. ROOSEVELTIAN POLICIES AT HOME

The Trust Problem	340
The Money Power	344
Railroad Legislation	346
Conservation	349

22. THE TRIUMPH OF REFORM

Factors Influencing the Reform Movement	352
Political Reform	355
Social and Economic Legislation	358
Socialism in the United States	363

23. ROOSEVELTIAN POLICIES ABROAD

Roosevelt in Venezuela and Panama	367
The Roosevelt Corollary of the Monroe Doctrine	372
Roosevelt and the Far East	374
Roosevelt and Europe	376
Dollar Diplomacy	378
Navalism	380

Section VIII: WOODROW WILSON AND WORLD WAR I

24. THE NEW FREEDOM

The Election of 1912	384
Woodrow Wilson, President	389
The Tariff Act of 1913	391
The Federal Reserve System	394
Trust Legislation	397

CONTENTS　　　　　　　　　　　　　　xvii

Chapter　　　　　　　　　　　　　　　　　　　　　　　　　　*Page*

　　Agrarian Legislation 402
　　Other Legislation 404

25. FOREIGN AFFAIRS IN THE WILSON ADMINISTRATIONS
　　Woodrow Wilson and Mexico 405
　　Woodrow Wilson and the Caribbean 410
　　The Peace Movement 412
　　American Neutrality: The British Blockade 414
　　American Neutrality: Submarine Warfare 419

26. THE UNITED STATES ENTERS WORLD WAR I
　　Interlude: The Election of 1916 423
　　Why We Fought: The Background 425
　　Why We Fought: Direct Causes 429
　　Mobilizing Men and Money 432
　　Mobilizing Industry and Labor 435
　　Mobilizing Opinion and Morale 440

27. THE OUTCOME OF THE WAR
　　On the Western Front 444
　　Armistice 448
　　The Congressional Elections of 1918 449
　　The Peace Conference and the Treaty of Versailles . . . 450
　　The Rejection of the Treaty by the Senate 454
　　The Collapse of Wilsonism 456

Section IX: THE GOLDEN TWENTIES

28. POLITICS IN THE NINETEEN TWENTIES
　　The Election of Harding 460
　　The Administrations of Calvin Coolidge 464
　　The Engineer in Politics 470

29. LEADING LEGISLATIVE PROBLEMS OF THE NINETEEN TWENTIES
　　The Tariff Acts of 1922 and 1930 473
　　Creating a Merchant Marine 476
　　The Railroad Problem 478
　　The Public Debt and Tax Reduction 480
　　Providing for the War Veterans 481
　　The Regulation of Power 482

30. AMERICA IN TWO HEMISPHERES
　　The United States and Latin America 486
　　Renewal of the Peace Movement 492
　　Naval Limitation 495
　　Interallied Debts and Reparation Payments 497
　　Russian Relations 500

CONTENTS

Section X: IMPERIAL AMERICA IN THE MACHINE AGE

Chapter

31. **CAPITAL AND LABOR**
    - The Growth of Population 503
    - The Growth of Industry 504
    - Mass Production 507
    - Productivity 508
    - The Position of Labor 509
    - The Supreme Court and Property 515
    - Mergers and Antitrust Legislation 517

32. **THREE OUTSTANDING PROBLEMS OF THE TWENTIES AND THIRTIES**
    - Prohibition 520
    - Immigration Restriction 523
    - The Decline of Agriculture 526

33. **ECONOMIC IMPERIALISM**
    - Origins in America 535
    - Imperialist Foreign Policy 536
    - America as a Creditor Nation 538
    - Foreign Trade 542

Part Three: AMERICA AND WORLD LEADERSHIP

Section XI: AMERICA FIGHTS DEPRESSION

34. **THE NEW DEAL**
    - From an Old to a New Deal 551
    - Theory and Tactics 554
    - The Bases of New Deal Policy 556
    - Programs of Action 558
    - The New Deal Agencies 561

35. **CHALLENGES TO THE NEW DEAL**
    - The Election of 1936 572
    - The Supreme Court Fight 573
    - The Recession of 1937 to 1938 574
    - Slowing Down of the New Deal 576
    - Deficit Financing 578
    - Toward a Critique of the New Deal 579

CONTENTS

Section XII: WORLD WAR II AND ITS CONSEQUENCES

Chapter		Page
36.	**THE STRUGGLE FOR NEUTRALITY**	
	The International Economic Policy of the New Deal	583
	Latin-American Affairs	585
	Neutral Rights and Philippine Independence	589
	Naval Construction	591
	Fascist Aggression	592
	The New Preparedness	594
	The Third-Term Contest	595
	Lend-Lease	596
37.	**THE SHOOTING WAR**	
	The Road to Pearl Harbor	599
	The War in the Far East	602
	The War in Europe	605
	The Peoples' War	612
	The United Nations	614
38.	**DOMESTIC PROBLEMS OF WARTIME AMERICA**	
	Mobilization of Men and Resources	618
	Mobilizing Science	622
	Mobilizing Morale	624
	Economic Impacts of the War	625
	Fiscal Issues and Inflation	632
	The Election of 1944	634
	America's Contribution to the War Effort	637
39.	**POSTWAR RECONSTRUCTION**	
	Problems of International Economic Reconstruction	638
	International Political Problems	640
	The Marshall Plan	644
	The U.N.	646
	The Postwar Political Climate	649
	The Presidential Election of 1948	654
	Problems of Reconversion	657
	The Postwar Boom	658
40.	**LIFE, LEARNING, AND THE ARTS BETWEEN WORLD WARS**	
	Aspects of the American Scene	665
	Scientific Advance	673
	Education and the Social Disciplines	675
	Music, Painting, and Architecture	679
	Literature Between the Wars	681
	The Level of Popular Taste	684
	The New America	685
BIBLIOGRAPHY		691
INDEX		723

Tables

	Page
The Negroes in the American Population, 1850–1940	59
Percentage of Population Negro in Certain Southern States, 1900, 1940	60
Leading Wheat Producing States, 1859–1929	142
Production of Cotton in Leading Cotton-Growing States, 1859–1929	145
Growth of Manufactures in the United States, 1849–99	158
Mineral Production, 1880, 1900, 1947	160
Domestic Exports, by Groups, 1870–1900	184
Domestic Exports for 1870 and 1900	185
Vote in House on McCrary Bill, 1874	232
Vote in House on Reagan Bill, 1878	233
Ordinary and Naval Expenditures, 1890–1914	381
American Naval Establishment in 1914	382
Index Numbers, 1914–18	439
America's Economic Interest in the Caribbean, 1913–29	490
The Refunding of the War Loans, 1923–30	498
Growth of Manufactures in the United States, 1899–1929	506
Immigration by Countries of Origin, 1901–47	526
Index of Farm Prices, 1896–1914	527
Condition of Agricultural Real Estate, 1914–33	529
Interest and Dividends Paid by Americans and Foreigners, 1921–39	542
Exports and Imports of Merchandise, 1901–39	542
Production of Movable Goods and Proportion Exported, 1899–1939	543
Leading Exports, 1926–30	543
Percentage of Product of Certain Industries Exported, 1914–39	544
Geographic Distribution of Export Trade, 1896–1939	545
Dependence of American Industry on Certain Imports, 1925–29	546
Geographic Distribution of Import Trade, 1896–1939	547
Indexes of Production, 1940–45	627
Consumer Price Indexes, 1939–41	628
Real Wages, 1939–45	628
Income Distribution, 1935–36, 1942, 1945	628
National Income by Distributive Shares, 1939–45	629
Disposition of Personal Income, 1939–45	629
Index of Income Payments, 1940–45	634
Share of National Income Received by Spending Units, 1935–36—1946	660

Illustrations

WORLD LEADERSHIP
Opening of the United Nations Security Council, New York City, March 25, 1946 . . . . *Frontispiece*

                                                                                                      Page

THE IMPEACHMENT TRIAL OF ANDREW JOHNSON
In the Senate Chamber, March 13, 1868 25

FUNCTION AND FAÇADE IN AMERICAN ARCHITECTURE
Guaranty Building, Buffalo, 1894–95
The Court of Honor at the World's Columbian Exposition, Chicago, 1893 221

A MEETING OF THE GRANGERS
Near Winchester, Scott County, Illinois 231

A TRIFLE EMBARRASSED
Cartoon on Spanish-American War 301

ELECTION CIRCUS, 1912
Cartoon of Theodore Roosevelt 387

TWO POINTS OF VIEW
Cartoon of Alfred E. Smith 471

IT LOOKS AS IF THE NEW LEADERSHIP WERE REALLY GOING TO LEAD
Cartoon of Franklin D. Roosevelt 555

ATOM BOMB PLANT
Oak Ridge, Tennessee 623

THAT'S OKAY, JOE—AT LEAST WE CAN MAKE BETS
Cartoon on the Soldier Vote, 1944 635

Maps and Charts

MAPS

	Page
The Processes of Reconstruction and Redemption in the South	53
Closing the Frontiers, 1889–1912	111
The Sectional Division on the Free Silver Issue, 1886	179
Populism in 1892 and 1896	271
The American Army in France: World War I	447
The United States in the Caribbean	489
American Investments Overseas, 1933	539
World War II: Pacific Phase	603
World War II: On the Western Front	609

CHARTS

Party Fortunes, 1928–48	651
Gross Government Debt and National Income, 1913, 1922, 1932, 1940 and 1945	663
Liquid Asset Ownership by Individuals and Businesses, 1940–50	663
Industrial Production, Freight Carloadings, Agricultural Prices Paid and Received, 1920–48	664
Trends in Employment, Working Hours, Output per Man-Hour and National Income, 1850–1960	686
Changing Composition of American Labor Force, 1870–1940	687

Part One

THE HUMBLING OF THE FARMERS

> Section I
> THE FRUITS OF THE
> CIVIL WAR

· 1 ·

The Smoldering Embers of War

AN AGE OF HATE

FOURSCORE and ten years have elapsed since the War between the States, a span of years already greater than the biblical allotment of life to man. Until recently survivors of either the Union or the Confederate armies—the wearers of the blue or the gray—were conspicuous citizens in nearly every American hamlet. From among these former soldiers for fifty years the American people elected Presidents, Senators, Congressmen, Governors and lesser state officials, county and municipal officers. Oftentimes, a candidate for office in the North was at a disadvantage unless he belonged to the G.A.R., as the veterans of the Union armies familiarly spoke of their organization, the Grand Army of the Republic. In the South it was equally unfortunate for a politician not to be an active member of the United Confederate Veterans. So numerous did the veterans of the Confederate armies come to be in the Congress of the United States during the last quarter of the nineteenth century that they were frequently referred to by their opponents, with thinly veiled contempt, as "the Confederate Brigadiers." For a half-century the American people did not permit themselves to forget the Civil War.

Perhaps no war in history was preceded, accompanied, and followed by so much hate. The explanation of this phenomenon does not lie so much in the generally accepted statement that "civil wars are ever bitter wars" as in the fact that it was to the apparent advantage of the politicians both North and South, whether they were participants in the war or not, to keep alive sectional antipathies. Much of the history of the United States from the middle of the nineteenth century to its close cannot be read aright unless this fact is borne constantly in mind. Indeed, it is not overemphasizing the point to say that in the last analysis the war itself was precipitated out of the exigencies of the political situation in the decade of the eighteen fifties.

In the South of 1850, particularly the lower South, the dominant articulate political group had come to be the slave-owning planters who had convinced themselves that their prosperity depended upon the maintenance of the system of Negro slavery. Since ultimately men's standards of right and wrong are deeply influenced by what they regard as being to their advantage or disadvantage, the slave-owning southerners and their satellites had come to sanction Negro slavery as morally good and in accordance with natural law, reason, and religion. Hence for a politician to be elected to office he must chant a paean of praise to slavery and sing a hymn of hate to its opponents. Even ministers of the gospel prayed for the safety and perpetuation of the South's "peculiar" institution.

In the North the situation was partly but not wholly reversed; but the tendency as time went on was toward complete reversal. Slavery had never taken firm root north of the Mason and Dixon line and the Ohio River, originally because of the relatively short growing season and the nature of the agricultural crops cultivated. In a system of self-sufficing agriculture and grain-growing, slave labor was unprofitable. As manufacturing establishments arose in New England and the Middle Atlantic states in the first four decades of the nineteenth century, an ample supply of cheap labor was at hand in the surplus farm population of the countryside. As the plants became larger and more numerous, between 1840 and 1860, and the demand for labor threatened to outrun the native supply, the deficiency was more than made good by foreign immigration, which attained considerable proportions during those twenty years. In the Northeast no single group dominated the political and social life as the planters did in the South, although the commercial and manufacturing interests usually had their way. In the Middle West the wishes of the farmers were generally respected by the politicians, but in the last decade before the Civil War the rising manufacturing and commercial groups were rapidly gaining ground and, as we shall see, were destined to put the embattled farmers to rout before the end of the century.

Since slavery was not profitable in the Northeast and Middle West, it ceased to exist. It also became immoral as a result of the growing hostility of the North's churches to it. But wars are not generated wholly by moral issues, however much the combatants on both sides may be sustained in the heat and weariness of the fray by lofty ethical ideals. The fact of the matter is, the southern plantation slave system seemed to stand in the way of, and in fact its champions did challenge at every point, the ambitions of the manufacturing, commercial, small-farming Northeast and Middle West to grow economically and to expand into the trans-Mississippi West.

Bargains, called compromises, delimiting the territory into which the two competing systems might expand, had been made in 1820 and in 1850, but subsequently extremists on both sides, believing they had been bested by their opponents, regretted these agreements and were ready to take advantage of whatever opportunity might offer to steal a march on their rivals. In 1854, a few of the southerners' northern allies, who had political and economic axes of their own to grind, presented such an opportunity to the South's leaders. This was the Kansas-Nebraska bill, which terminated the earlier bargains and nominally opened to slavery all of the trans-Mississippi territory that had not yet been admitted into the Union as states. It was a Pyrrhic victory. The small farmers of the Middle West were particularly aroused. Under the leadership of ambitious and clever politicians the Republican party was formed with the avowed single purpose of resisting the overgrown pretensions of the slave interests.

Heretofore more often than not western farmers had acted politically in alliance with the southern planters, with whom they had many common interests, but now they invited the co-operation and assistance of the political leaders of the eastern industrialists and commercialists. Some of the easterners accepted the invitation with alacrity. They had many old scores of their own against the planters which they were desirous of settling. For the southerners, from the close of the thirties until the eve of the Civil War, dominated the central government. During this time they had swept away the last remnants of Hamilton's financial program, which had assured fiscal stability and a sound monetary system; they had discomfited the manufacturers by gradually lowering the protective tariff which had been fathered by Hamilton and given new life by Clay; they had opposed the building of transpacific railways; and in 1857 they had gained their signal (and last) triumph by diminishing the protective features of the tariff almost to the vanishing point. It was this planter victory which induced many wealthy easterners, who had not been particularly moved by the Kansas-Nebraska bill, to join with the westerners, the more so since the latter held out the seductive bribe of a high protective tariff—a policy heretofore opposed by many of them.

Previous to 1854 the fight of the planters for the westward extension of slavery was for something tangible, although they had established it in at least one state in which it throve but ill, Missouri, and it was losing ground in the older states of Delaware, Maryland, and Kentucky. Moreover, it had never been firmly established in mountainous and submontane regions of a number of states located farther south. By this time the southerners should have known that the extension of slavery was not determined by bargains and bills but by altitude and latitude. If anything was wanting to teach the lesson, the action of the California pioneers should have demonstrated it beyond a shadow of doubt. Hardly was the ink dry on the Treaty of Guadalupe Hidalgo, which ended the Mexican War, before that fairest territory in the Mexican cession was knocking at the door of Congress, asking for admission as a free state. California was not adapted to slavery and the settlers there knew it; hence they organized a government under a free-state constitution despite the fact that many of the members of their constitutional convention were of southern origin. If the conduct of California did not suffice, the speech of Daniel Webster on the Compromise bill of 1850 should have been conclusive when in effect he said it did not matter whether slavery were permitted or prohibited by law in New Mexico and Utah; the nature of the country would make them free in any case. Likewise, as has been said, the Kansas-Nebraska bill was a costly victory. Although it opened all the remaining trans-Mississippi lands to slavery, and although three years later the Supreme Court in the Dred Scott case decided that Congress had no constitutional power to prohibit slavery in any territory, events soon demonstrated that even in Kansas, the only region in which slavery might hope for success, the further extension of the institution was impossible.

In the meanwhile opposition to slavery had become popular in the North. Not everyone by any means regarded the institution as immoral, but it had no friends and many enemies; nor were political leaders slow in sensing this. So Lincoln could declare that "a house divided against itself cannot stand" and Seward could speak of the "irrepressible conflict," as though men in the same political dwelling had never previously been divided. But there was this difference. Usually such controversies set off classes and groups in the same area; in that case they are generally decided peaceably or the people live in relative amity without ever resolving the question one way or the other. But in the dispute over slavery the dividing line was geographical. In the South no politician or even private citizen would, or could with safety, present the northern point of view. If a man were sound on the paramount issue, he could be forgiven vulgarity, narrow-mindedness, ignorance, and dishonesty. In the North the situation was not far different. Although in the South cotton, the child of slavery, was king, in the North there was none so poor to do him homage. Moderate men with some capacity to see the southern point of view were being retired to private life. The extremists were coming to the fore. Some of them were dishonest intellectually and otherwise, but if they, too, were sound on the paramount issue, they were honored with public office. An impasse had been reached. What had been economic and political questions had largely passed or were unreal. Moral issues were the order of the day. Deadly hatred spread over the land: hatred, sublimated in the North as love of the Union and liberty; hatred, sublimated in the South as devotion to states' rights and, ironically enough, liberty, too. Men fought, and although it was on all lips that the time for argument to cease had come, controversy was not stilled. Four years of bloody war and incessant argument fed the ancient grudge seventy times sevenfold. It was on this scene of hatred and war's desolation that the era of reconstruction commenced.

ABRAHAM LINCOLN AND THE SOUTH

There were a few men in both sections who, while taking sides in the conflict, nevertheless kept themselves comparatively free from hatred; not the least of these was Abraham Lincoln, President of the United States. Lincoln seems never to have harbored any animosity toward the southern people, and this despite the bitter terms of opprobrium in which he was commonly spoken of by southerners. At the outbreak of the war, Lincoln evolved his "border state" policy, a policy which was calculated to hold in the Union Maryland, Kentucky, Missouri, Arkansas, Virginia, North Carolina, and Tennessee. In a word, this program denied that the war was intended to abolish slavery; rather, it was solely for the purpose of maintaining the nation intact. It is true that four of these states quit the Union when offered the alternative of fighting for or against the seven lower southern states which had already seceded. However, the western third of Virginia split off from the Old Dominion and in 1863 was admitted into the United States as West Virginia. In the other three, almost all the people in the mountain regions as well as considerable numbers elsewhere either remained loyal to the Union or were lukewarm in their attachment to the Confederacy. From the first of the war Lincoln as well as other leaders of his party had believed that slavery could not withstand the shock of a prolonged war fought on southern soil, but it was appreciated that the handling of the question required patience and skill. Until everyone had definitely taken sides, it was a dangerous matter with which to deal.

In July, 1861, the Republican Congress solemnly resolved that the object of the war was to preserve the Union and not to abolish slavery. A year later most Republican leaders (who called themselves Radical Republicans and who were becoming increasingly critical of Lincoln) were ready to make of the war an abolitionist crusade. Lincoln held back because he still feared the effect of such a change of objective on the southern loyalists as well as on thousands in the North who were not yet ready to fight for the freedom of the Negro race. Yet the insistence of the Radicals as well as the exigencies of the international situation made it dangerous not to act. Accordingly in September, 1862, following the by no means glorious Union victory at Antietam, Lincoln issued his preliminary Emancipation Proclamation. In it he stated that unless opposition to the federal authority had ceased by January 1, 1863, all slaves within the Confederate military lines would be proclaimed free. When the new year arrived the southern states were still in rebellion and consequently the Emancipation Proclamation was issued. As the Union armies gradually advanced into the Confederacy during the two and one-third remaining years of the war the slaves were freed in fact as well as in name. Before the close of the war they had been freed by state action in Missouri, Maryland, and West Virginia. On December 18, 1865, the Thirteenth Amendment to the Constitution, which had been passed by Congress early in the year, and had been ratified by three-fourths of the states, was proclaimed in effect. What should be the legal, economic, and social status of the ex-slaves had not been determined either by state or by federal action when the Confederacy came to an end in April, 1865, although the government had made an initial attack on the problem by creating in March, 1865, a Freedmen's Bureau.

In the autumn of 1863 Lincoln began to give consideration to the problem of the restoration of the seceded states to their normal relations with the United States government. By this time five of these states, Virginia, Tennessee, North Carolina, Arkansas, and Louisiana, were in greater or less part subjugated. Acting under authority of Congress, Lincoln had appointed a military governor for each of them except Virginia,[1] but even within the Union lines the authority of these military governors did not amount to much except in Tennessee where the vigorous Andrew Johnson held the office. In three of these states, however, namely, Arkansas, Louisiana, and Tennessee, these governors did serve as the agents of the President in carrying into effect the preliminary steps in the policy of reconstruction which he outlined in a proclamation on December 8, 1863.

In this, Lincoln announced as the conditions necessary for his recognition of a state "the completion of an organization by persons who have subscribed to the Constitution of the United States, and who have pledged themselves to support the acts and proclamations promulgated during the war with reference to slavery." Anyone was allowed to take the oath of allegiance except certain high military and civil officials of the Confederacy and a few others who had rendered themselves especially obnoxious to the federal government. Full amnesty and pardon were granted to all who should take the oath. The President further specified that whenever as many as 10 per cent of the qualified voters of 1860 should take the oath of allegiance they might proceed with the organization of a government loyal to the United States; and when such government should have been organized, the executive branch of the federal government would recognize such a state as having resumed its proper relations with the Union. Representation in Congress, the President admitted, was a matter for the two branches of that body to decide for themselves. The President's object in this so-called "10-per-cent" plan was further to divide the southern people by forming a nucleus around which the loyal people in the seceded

---

[1] Virginia was excepted because there existed in that state a sort of "vest-pocket" loyal government, with headquarters at Alexandria, which had been recognized by the federal government principally for the reason that the consent of some authority calling itself "Virginia" was necessary to accomplish the separation of West Virginia and at the same time nominally conform to constitutional requirements.

states could collect. In his opinion the measure would materially shorten the war—hence he supposed it to be good strategy.

As a matter of fact, it does not appear to have had any such effect. During the year 1864 the plan was put into operation in only two states, Louisiana and Arkansas. In both states the number of voters participating in the organization of loyal state governments barely came within the 10-per-cent limit and many believed that a considerable proportion of those who participated were not bonafide citizens of their commonwealths. Their numbers were not materially increased before the end of the war. Indeed, it was not until the war was virtually ended that a loyal government was organized in Tennessee. Nowhere else was the plan ever put into operation. Meanwhile Congress had taken a defiant attitude with regard to the assumption by the President that the restoration of the rebel states was a matter to be handled entirely by the executive branch of the government.

In June, 1864, just before the adjournment of the first session of Congress, that body passed a reconstruction measure known as the Wade-Davis bill. Lincoln had always maintained that the states were not out of the Union but simply out of their proper relation to it. This bill, at first in specific terms, and by implication later as amended, held that the states were in fact out of the Union, that essentially they occupied the status of territories, and therefore it was the business of Congress to provide the conditions upon which they might be readmitted. This was the theory of reconstruction as the Radicals had developed it; more particularly, it was the work of Senator Charles Sumner of Massachusetts. The bill then proceeded to state the Congressional terms. In the first place, whatever the President had done in the matter of restoration was to be set aside as incompetent. Second, when a state should become entirely conquered, a census of the white men was to be taken under the authority of a provisional governor. And third, when a majority of these had taken the oath of allegiance, they were authorized to elect delegates to a state convention. Such a convention must disfranchise practically all high civil or military officers of the Confederacy, abolish slavery, and repudiate all debts contracted by the rebel state government. After such a constitution had been adopted, the President, under the authority of Congress, might recognize the state and permit it to elect regular state officers, representatives to Congress, and Presidential electors.

Lincoln disposed of the Wade-Davis bill by a pocket veto on July 4, 1864. A few days later he issued a statement explaining the reasons for his action. The Presidential letter ran: It was fatal to admit that the states were out of the Union as the bill did. Congress had no power to prescribe the abolition of slavery in the states, although as a military measure he himself had abolished it in most of them a year and a half earlier. He was unwilling to set aside what had been accomplished in Louisiana and

Arkansas or to commit himself to any one plan of reconstruction. He was ready to aid any state which preferred to follow the Congressional plan rather than his own (knowing, of course, how improbable it was that any state would choose a harder road when an easier one was open). The authors of the Congressional scheme for reconstruction struck back almost at once.

Early in August, Senator Wade of Ohio and Representative Davis of Maryland issued a biting manifesto, and this despite the fact that the Presidential election was only three months off:

> This rash and fatal act of the President [said they] is a blow at the friends of his administration, at the rights of humanity and the principles of republican government. . . . But he must understand that our support is of a cause and not a man; that the authority of Congress is paramount and must be respected; . . . he must confine himself to his executive duties—to obey and to execute, not make the laws, and *leave political reorganization to Congress.*

In the light of future events, this statement was prophetic. For the time being, however, the question of reconstruction was subordinated to that of winning the war and preserving the Union. On that issue the Union-Republican party was triumphantly returned to power and Lincoln was re-elected to the Presidency, Andrew Johnson, a loyal Unionist from Tennessee, to the Vice-Presidency, and over two-thirds of the seats in both houses of Congress were captured by Union-Republicans. In a little more than a month after Lincoln and Johnson were inaugurated the Confederacy collapsed. The war had come to an end and not a single plan of reconstruction had been adopted. For better or worse Lincoln had had his way. But he did not live to face the real test, for on April 14, 1865, he met his death at the hand of John Wilkes Booth.

Whether or not Lincoln could have continued to dominate the Congress is a question frequently debated by historians; a certain answer is not easy. That he would have been obliged to modify his reconstruction policy in some particulars to insure its acceptance by Congress is certain. That he would have done so is also likely, for Lincoln possessed political astuteness to a high degree and knew when to yield minor points in order to obtain major objectives. Such tactics probably (but only probably) would have won the day. As has been suggested, it was a time when passion ran high. Nor can one disregard the great political and economic prizes at stake. The lusty young capitalists, their appetites fairly whetted by the extraordinary profits which had poured in upon them during the war and the way open now to great economic expansion, were not inclined to allow their ancient antagonists, the southern agrarians, again to assume their wonted place of power in the affairs of the nation. Similarly, it was hardly to be expected that their allies and spokesmen, the Union-Republican politicians, having feasted for four years from the fleshpots of public office, would tamely give room at the table to their hated foes, the ex-rebels and the Democrats. And it appeared to them that Lincoln's policy was nothing short of an open-armed welcome to the prodigals. Even their own Wade-Davis bill now seemed much too mild, and in their hearts they must have been thankful for Lincoln's pocket veto.

ANDREW JOHNSON AND THE SOUTH

It has generally been accepted that Lincoln's successor, Andrew Johnson, in formulating his own reconstruction policy, patterned it upon that of his illustrious predecessor. But only to a partial extent is this true. It is more nearly correct to say that he adhered to Lincoln's program as it would have been modified had the Wade-Davis bill become law. Even here, a reservation is necessary. In most details, Johnson's guide was the Wade-Davis bill; however, it was Lincoln whom he followed when he assumed that the business of reconstruction was an executive and not a legislative function. And in the end it was this attitude which proved his undoing.

At the beginning of his administration the Radicals were not insistent that Johnson should call Congress in extra session and have that body draw up a reconstruction law for his direction. There were two reasons for this. In the first place, the Radicals were not at all sure that they could muster a sufficient majority in Congress to write a law to their liking. In the second place, they had every reason to believe that Johnson was one of them and that if left to his own devices he would accomplish their purposes even better than if he called upon Congress for aid. Indeed, everything in Johnson's early career pointed to the validity of such an assumption.

Andrew Johnson was a North Carolinian by birth. He was white, of course, and poor, but it is hardly correct to call him a "poor white" as that phrase is commonly understood today. In the pre-Civil War South there were millions of people who had no direct economic interest in slavery and who were poor in this world's goods, but who in no sense deserved to be reproached with the invidious term so generally (and incorrectly) used by many persons discussing prewar southern society. In this class of humble Americans—stalwart, intelligent, possessing high moral rectitude—Andrew Johnson was born. In his native city of Raleigh he learned the tailoring trade by the only means available, that is to say, apprenticeship. Before he was fully grown he moved to Greenville in eastern Tennessee, a section of the South where geographical conditions tended to prevent slavery from becoming important economically. Here Johnson established himself as a tailor and a politician. His occupation was as honorable as any, and he quickly gained the respect of his neighbors. Yet his rise politically was little short of phenomenal when it is considered that he had no formal schooling. During the thirty years between 1830 and 1861 Johnson was almost continuously in public office, holding successively the positions of alderman, mayor of Greenville, member of the Tennessee legislature, member of the United States House of Representatives, governor of Tennessee, and United States Senator. When the Civil War broke out, he had been a member of the Senate for four years, and despite his long public career he was still only fifty-two years old. Although a lifelong Democrat and a supporter of slavery, Johnson did not resign his seat in the Senate when his state seceded; in fact, he became an outstanding opponent of secession. In this respect he was in accord with the majority of the people of his section of Tennessee. In 1862, President Lincoln appointed him military governor of Tennessee and when he relinquished that office in February, 1865, he had, under Lincoln's plan of restoration, almost completed the organization of a loyal state government.

Johnson proved himself to be a capable administrator and a loyal citizen of the Union; he boldly attacked secessionists, did not hesitate to call them traitors in a section of the country where such conduct required a high degree of moral and physical courage, and openly advocated death as the only fitting penalty for disloyalty. As Vice-President, and indeed after having assumed the office of President, he continued to speak in the same vein. As an earnest of his sincerity, he offered rewards for the capture of Jefferson Davis and other high officials of the late Confederacy. He went so far as to express a desire for the arrest and punishment of General Lee. He permitted the trial and conviction of Booth's confederates by a military commission, before which their opportunity for having their elementary legal rights safeguarded was, to say the least, inadequate. Johnson was not personally responsible for the mockery attending this trial, yet he did nothing to assure that the proceedings would be conducted in a straightforward and orderly fashion. It must not be assumed that Johnson was cruel and vindictive: it was only that he, along with so many others of his generation, had been wrought up to a high pitch of honest hatred for rebels in general and the "arch-conspirators" in particular.

Yet the Radicals in Congress made one mistake: they believed that because Johnson was not inclined to be merciful toward the southern leaders he, like them, was prepared to subject the South to Negro suffrage. After all Johnson was a southerner. His detestation of the secessionists was not so much due to the fact that he was not socially one of the large planter group, as is often said. Rather, it was because, being identified with a section of the South whose economic and social interests were alien to the planter economy, he had everything to lose and nothing to gain from secession. It is possible that Johnson felt as he did toward the southern leaders for the reason that with a very small change in the east Tennessee situation he might have been one of them. Hatred may have been an unconscious part of his self-justification for his apostasy.

Thus, Johnson was willing to travel with the Radicals fully as far as they themselves had gone in the Wade-Davis bill. For those looking for a key to Johnson's policy, it is well to ponder a sentence in a letter which he wrote to his wife while he was still military governor of Tennessee. "I intend," said he, "to appropriate the remainder of my life to the redemption of my adopted home, east Tennessee." East Tennessee was a country of small independent farmers. Of such was the great majority of the southern white population composed, but while in east Tennessee these were in a compact body with very few large planters and Negroes among them, in the rest of the South the small farmers were overwhelmed by the large planter element on the one hand and the fear of free Negro competition on the other. This small-farmer element Johnson undertook to make the basis of political power in the southern states.

Accordingly, on May 29, 1865, President Johnson issued an amnesty proclamation. In this he granted pardon to all ordinary persons who had participated in the rebellion on their taking an oath of allegiance to the United States. Persons who had occupied positions of leadership in the South before and during the war and who had taken part in the rebellion, as well as all others worth over $20,000, were not permitted to take the oath, but were required to apply individually to the President for clemency. The President treated such petitions with indulgence, with the result that the year following the close of the Civil War saw very few men in the South still unpardoned. Before the end of 1865 all individuals who had been arrested for their participation in the rebellion, with the exception of Jefferson Davis, had been released from prison. Davis was eventually released on bail and was never tried; but neither was he granted nor did he sue for pardon, and he died, technically, a man without a country.

The grant of citizenship rights to the southern people was not, however, the only thing needed to restore the southern states to their former places in the Union. As we have seen, in four of the late Confederate states, namely, Arkansas, Louisiana, Tennessee, and Virginia, there existed at the end of the war, state governments which were loyal to the United States. These Johnson recognized as regular and entirely legal. In the other seven states only military government existed, but between May 29 and July 13 Johnson issued proclamations appointing a provisional governor for each of these. In each case the governor was instructed to call a constitutional convention of delegates who had taken the oath of allegiance or had received special pardon from the President. Only white men who had obtained amnesty were to be permitted to participate in the election of the delegates, despite the fact that the Radicals had hoped and apparently expected that the President would extend the franchise to the Negroes. The President believed that the extent of his authority was to see that the state conventions should recognize the purposes for which the war had avowedly been fought: that is, the preservation of the Union and the abolition of slavery. Consequently, Johnson let it be known in each instance that the central authorities would expect the convention to repeal or declare null and void the ordinance of secession that had been passed by a similar convention in 1860 or 1861; to repudiate such part of the state's debt as had been contracted for the purpose of carrying on the war; and to insert into the state constitution a provision for the abolition of slavery. For the most part these requirements were met by the conventions when they gathered in the summer and autumn of 1865. Soon after the conventions adjourned the state legislatures, which had been elected, assembled, and they were virtually required to ratify the Thirteenth Amendment to the Constitution of the United States. A sufficient number of states, loyal and ex-Confederate, having done this by December 18, Secretary of State Seward issued a formal proclamation declaring the Thirteenth Amendment a part of the Constitution. The institution of slavery was dead forever.

Though the southern states were now redeemed and were again, presumably, sovereign commonwealths, they did not have a free hand in dealing with the Negro situation. A number of reasons existed for this anomalous state of affairs: 1. The United States Army had not been entirely withdrawn from the South; the fact is, many of the soldiers in blue were Negroes. The presence of the military quite effectively tied the hands of southern civil officers. 2. The Freedmen's Bureau was still in operation. While the general function of the agency was philanthropic, not a few of its local representatives, appreciating that a time might come when the blacks would be invested with the franchise, busied themselves with building up a following among their wards. To this end Union League clubs were organized among the Negroes and in these they were taught that only from the Union-Republican party might they expect to have their rights as free men respected and protected. 3. The general economic situation in the South militated against a rapid adjustment to the new order. Although the President, during the summer, had proclaimed the opening of southern domestic and foreign trade, the truth is that the southern people had little to sell, no money, and very little credit with which to buy. They could not, if they would, pay the Negroes in cash; share tenancy was the best they could offer their former laborers. Many of the Bureau agents, either not understanding the situation or deliberately shutting their eyes to it, led the Negroes to believe that they were about to be swindled, thus kindling the flames of a deep-seated racial antagonism. 4. The poorer whites, who had always supported slavery on racial rather than on economic grounds, now had their worst fears realized when they beheld the Negro as free, and quite as well off economically, as they themselves were. That racial antagonism should follow was not surprising.

These manifestations Radical leaders regarded uneasily. The South was apparently still unrepentant; the fruits of victory were still ungarnered. And when southern legislatures began to enact "black codes" whose sole intent was to keep the Negroes at work, northern politicians saw their fears confirmed. Before Congress assembled in December, 1865, there had appeared a party among Union-Republican legislators which was committed to the exaction of the most solemn and far-reaching guaranties from the South before it would be willing to readmit the section into the councils of the nation.

CONGRESS VERSUS PRESIDENT

Johnson's hope that his conciliatory policy would gain support among the moderate elements of the Union-Republican party soon turned out to be illusory. When the Thirty-ninth Congress opened it was at once apparent that both Conservative and Radical Republicans regarded the President's work with suspicion. The Conservative program centered in these two demands: the passage of a Constitutional amendment under which the Negroes were to have equal civil (though not necessarily political) rights; and the passage of another amendment by which states denying the Negroes suffrage were to suffer reductions in their representation in the lower house of Congress and their votes in the electoral college. The Radicals, led by Thaddeus Stevens of Pennsylvania in the House and Charles Sumner of Massachusetts in the Senate, were entirely at odds with the Presidential plan, their desire being to undo Johnson's work altogether and to create new southern state governments on the basis of universal Negro suffrage and a wholesale disfranchisement of the southern whites. Because, however, they feared the hostility of their constituencies, for the time being they delayed, giving support to the Conservatives and joining with them in setting up a Joint Committee of Fifteen on Reconstruction, drawn from both houses, to which were referred all matters bearing on suffrage and southern representation in Congress. For six months this committee carried on its discussions, while southern Senators and Congressmen were denied the right to take their seats.

In an initial test of strength between President and Congress, Johnson came off triumphant. He vetoed a bill extending the life and enlarging the functions of the Freedmen's Bureau, mainly on the ground that Congress had no right to legislate for the southern states while they were still unrepresented, and in this he was upheld by a large enough group of Senators.[2] On a second measure Johnson was less successful. His veto of

[2] It is to be noted, however, that later in the session another Freedmen's Bureau bill was passed, this time over Johnson's veto, and that agency continued to function until 1872.

the Civil Rights bill, which was designed to nullify the "black codes" by guaranteeing the Negroes the equal protection of all laws and vesting the federal courts with jurisdiction, was not sustained and the bill became a statute through repassage in both houses by a two-thirds vote. Johnson refused to acknowledge defeat; he looked forward to trying the issue at the polls in the Congressional elections of 1866.

In the meantime the Joint Committee of Fifteen had submitted its report. Insisting that ultimate control in the matter of reconstruction belonged to Congress and denying, by implication, the legality of the southern state governments, this body recommended to Congress the submission to the states of an amendment incorporating only a part of the Radical program. This amendment, the Fourteenth, was passed by the necessary majorities in both Houses and sent to the states for ratification before the first session of the Thirty-ninth Congress adjourned in July. Unlike all previous amendments to the Constitution, the Fourteenth contained more than one proposition. Section 1 included the heart of the Civil Rights bill and also declared the Negro to be a citizen of the United States—something which the Supreme Court had denied in the Dred Scott decision. Section 2 provided that if any state denied the Negroes the right to vote, its representation in Congress was to be cut in the proportion that the number of its Negroes bore to the total population. Section 3 made certain classes of former Confederates ineligible for office until their disabilities were removed by Congress (thus putting the pardoning power in Congress' and not the President's hands). Section 4 asserted the validity of the debt of the United States, outlawed the Confederate debt, and denied the legality of all claims arising out of the emancipation of the slaves.

With the exception of its first section, the Fourteenth Amendment was a shrewdly conceived political platform, especially designed to catch votes in the forthcoming Congressional elections of 1866. Particularly was this so of the section relating to representation. One must recall that from the original organization of the federal government to the Civil War, the South had been permitted to count, for purposes of representation, three-fifths of its slaves. By 1860 this three-fifths provision gave the slave-holding states eighteen more Congressmen (as well as votes in the electoral college) than would have been theirs had representation been based on white population alone. With the Negroes free and the three-fifths provision no longer operative, the southern states were to have twelve additional Congressmen after the next census (1870). So, altogether, the southern states would have thirty additional representatives for their Negro population. Yet not a Negro could vote in any of them! In effect, therefore, Congress was threatening the South with the loss of these thirty Congressmen unless the Negroes were enfranchised. Of course the North (for by 1866 but six states had given the ballot to the Negro) was to suffer the

SMOLDERING EMBERS OF WAR

same penalties—on paper. Actually, in no northern state was the colored population large enough to affect Congressional apportionment in the event that the right of suffrage was withheld.

It was small wonder that the North hailed the proposed arrangement as being eminently a fair one. Nor, on the score of political expediency, could it be expected that the North would consent to see the South gain in power so long as means were at hand to prevent it. Roscoe Conkling, typical Radical Republican spokesman in the lower house, phrased the thought of many political leaders when he said:

> Shall the death of slavery add two-fifths to the entire power which slavery had when slavery was living? Shall one white man have as much share in the government as three other white men merely because he lives where blacks outnumber whites two to one? Shall this inequality exist, and exist only in favor of those who without cause drenched the land with blood and covered it with mourning? Shall such be the reward of those who did the foulest and guiltiest act which crimsons the annals of recorded time? No sir; not if I can help it.

It seems strange to us now that Andrew Johnson, practical politician though he was, could not appreciate that his own scheme of reconstruction would be voted down in favor of that of Congress when the excited northern electorate was appealed to in such language as Conkling's. Had he from the first seen that the North would be unwilling to have the South restored before the Negroes were guaranteed equal civil rights with the whites and especially until the basis of representation had been changed, he might have come to an understanding with the Conservative Republicans and thus have avoided the worst phase of reconstruction. For the Radicals did not intend that the Fourteenth Amendment should be a final plan of reconstruction; it was merely to be the preliminary step in a much more drastic scheme.

It is in this fact that we can see the significance of the punitive section of that amendment. It is important to remember that the Fourteenth Amendment was to be presented to the southern states, not as terms of peace imposed on a conquered nation but as a policy to be accepted freely by them in their capacity of sovereign commonwealths. Therefore, by voluntarily consenting to invest the Negroes with equal civil rights under pain of a reduction of representation in Congress and by allowing the disqualification of their most important leaders, the southern legislatures were being asked to stultify themselves. Nor was this all. The South, doubtless, would have consented had no other alternative been presented and had it been plainly told that only on acceptance of the Fourteenth Amendment would southern Senators and Representatives be allowed to take their seats in Congress. But President and Congress were divided, for one thing; for the second, the Radical Republicans were secretly hoping that the terms of the amendment would be regarded with so much distaste that its rejection must be assured. So they insisted upon the punitive sections, for they sensed, and correctly, that with the defeat of the amendment in southern legislatures Conservative Republicans in Congress could be forced to support an even more Carthaginian program.

In such an atmosphere the campaign of 1866 took place. Johnson, the Democrats, and a small number of Conservative Republicans sought to convince the country that the Presidential plan of restoration was both sufficient and wise. But in vain. The Radicals were victorious and there was elected to the Fortieth Congress an even greater Republican majority than that party had had in the Thirty-ninth.

It was not the new Congress, however, which met in December, 1866; it was the old one for its short term. As the Radicals had expected, all the southern states except Tennessee rejected the Fourteenth Amendment.[3] The President, to a large extent, was responsible for the fatal error. Instead of bowing before the inevitable and, even at that late date, seeking to effect an alliance with Conservative Republicans (who did not wish to go any further than the Fourteenth Amendment), Johnson actually urged the South to vote down the amendment. Thus southern states, the President, and the Conservative Republicans had been delivered into the Radicals' hands. With some show of reason that rising young Ohio politician, James A. Garfield, could say: "The last one of the sinful ten with scorn and contempt has flung back into our teeth the magnanimous offer of a generous nation." The way was now open for the enactment of the Radical reconstruction plan.

Conditions in the South lent color to the Radical claim that the former Confederate states were still unregenerated. During the late summer and autumn of 1866, at New Orleans and Memphis, large-scale riots had occurred in which several hundred Negroes and a few white men had lost their lives. Numerous murders had been committed elsewhere and cases of flogging and other outrages had taken place. Radical politicians and newspapers cried out that white men were assaulting Negroes and loyalists simply because the latter were good Union men; it was charged that the southern states were making little if any effort to bring the offenders to justice.

Few in the North appreciated that such assaults as took place on the Negroes were almost entirely for personal reasons, rarely for political ones. Under the tutelage of Freedmen's Bureau agents and other northern philanthropically inclined persons, the Negroes were being taught that they must assert their rights to equality, and claim all the prerogatives of

---

[3] It is to be noted that Tennessee ratified the Fourteenth Amendment before the first session of the Thirty-ninth Congress had been adjourned. In considerable measure this was due to the fact that Tennessee's constitution, adopted during the war, had virtually deprived all ex-Confederates of the right to vote.

free men. Although only a relatively small number of Negroes acted upon this advice, there were enough of them whose deportment filled the whites with resentment. Particularly was this true of the white masses of the South, who had never belonged to the slave-holding aristocracy. The most perceptible differences between these and the Negroes, before the war, had been their legal status and the color of their skins. Civil inequalities had now been eliminated; but the white masses refused to regard this as a warrant for the assumption of social equality by the blacks. Economic distress only made tempers the more ugly. The crops of 1866 had been everywhere bad, because of unfavorable weather and the fact that both whites and Negroes had shown themselves none too much inclined to work in the midst of such uncertainty. It was inevitable that hard times should nourish race conflict; the wonder was that desperate whites did not resort to greater disorders as a sign of their despair.

This was the setting for the introduction in Congress of the Radicals' first reconstruction measure. The intentions of its sponsors were: to re-establish military rule in the South; to set up new state governments on the basis of universal Negro suffrage; and to assure the primacy of the Republican party in the political life of the section. The bill incorporated the following six provisions: 1. new state conventions were to be called; 2. all male citizens, except such ex-Confederates as were disqualified from holding office by the Fourteenth Amendment, were to vote for members of these conventions and be eligible for election to them; 3. all conventions were to incorporate into state constitutions provisions guaranteeing Negroes the right to vote; 4. constitutions were to be submitted to the electorate for their approval; 5. the new state legislatures were to ratify the Fourteenth Amendment; 6. the frames of government thus prepared by such constitutional conventions were to be submitted to Congress for its examination. Only after Congressional approval were the military governments to be removed, the South's Senators and Representatives reinstated in their seats, and the once-Confederate states declared to be in their regular relations with the United States government. Conservative Republicans were still inclined to be merciful and objected to the disqualification of former Confederates from voting and taking part in the deliberations of the constitutional conventions. The Democrats, on the other hand, hoping to make the whole bill obnoxious, voted for the retention of the disfranchising section. But their strategy was of no avail. Congress passed the bill; Johnson vetoed it; the measure was carried over the President's veto, and on March 2, 1867, two days before the end of the Thirty-ninth Congress, the Radicals' first Reconstruction Act had become a law.

Thus, almost two full years after the war's close, ten of the eleven former Confederate states found themselves exactly where they had been when

Lee surrendered: under the military rule of the conquerors. Those state governments which Johnson had called into being and which, for a year and a half, had been regularly operating were not abolished in so many words. They were declared, however, to be "provisional" only and in all respects were actually subject to the paramount authority of Washington. Henceforth they were but the mere shadows of governments and eventually all were superseded.

THE TRIUMPH OF THE RADICALS

In the ordinary course of events the Fortieth Congress would not have assembled until December, 1867; nor was there any reason to believe that the President would call it in special session before that time. Consequently, before the adjournment of the Thirty-ninth Congress, that body had provided that its successor should assemble immediately upon its own expiration. There were two reasons for this unusual step. In the first place, the Radicals professed to fear that if left to himself Johnson would not faithfully enforce a law to which he was so bitterly opposed. His power had already been greatly curtailed by the passage of the Tenure of Office Act (March 2, 1867) under which the President, in making removals from office, was required to obtain the consent of the Senate. In doing this, Congress was not prompted by high ideals of Civil Service reform, but by a general desire to maintain in office all officials who sided with the Radicals in the controversy between Congress and the President. Particularly was this true of the Secretary of War, Edwin M. Stanton, who, the Radicals knew, was hostile to his chief's program. Moreover, Congress had inserted a section into the Army Appropriation Act forbidding the President to issue military orders except through the General of the Army, U. S. Grant. The violation of either of these statutes was made a misdemeanor for which the President might be impeached. It was expected, and indeed hoped, that Johnson would disregard one or the other of these acts and leave himself open to impeachment proceedings. For this reason, Congress wished to be at Washington.

In the second place, the Reconstruction Act of March 2 had not provided the machinery necessary to the assembling of the state conventions nor the freeing of the southern states from military rule once the provisions of the law had been complied with. The Radicals did not look for the early summoning by southern governors of these bodies, in which they and other leaders of the South were, for the most part, ineligible to participate and where they must act as instruments in the initiation of a policy of universal Negro suffrage. Indeed, the Radicals were as much prompted by the wish to see the situation taken out of the hands of the southern native whites and placed in those of their own puppets.

The Fortieth Congress proceeded to carry out this program at once. On March 23, there was passed what was called a Supplementary Reconstruction Act under which the generals in command of the five military departments into which the ten former Confederate states had been divided, were charged with the enforcement of the law of March 2. They were, in short, to supplant the southern governors; that is to say, enroll the voters, hold the elections for delegates to the constitutional conventions, call the conventions into session, summon the voters to pass on the ratification of the constitutions thus prepared, and finally submit such constitutions to the President for his transmission to Congress.

In order to insure the disqualification of as many whites as possible, another such Supplementary Reconstruction Act, passed July 19, conferred additional powers of appointment and removal on the General of the Army (by implication denying those powers to the President). As a result of these measures, when registration figures were completed, it was seen that the Negro electors were in the majority in six of the ten states, although in but two of them did they constitute an actual majority of the population. In the other four states, namely, Virginia, Arkansas, Texas, and North Carolina, the whites made up the larger part of the registered voters. It is to be noted, however, that in each of these there was a sizable party of whites, particularly in the mountain sections, who had bitterly resented secession and who therefore tended to act with the Republicans against their old antagonists, the former slave owners. This circumstance, together with the fact that the election officials appointed by the military were all men who could take the so-called "ironclad" oath (to the effect that they had never voluntarily given aid or comfort to the rebellion), insured a Republican preponderance in all the conventions except that of Virginia.

These assemblies were an interesting study in democracy under the new dispensation. The more conspicuous members of the majority party were men whom southern whites had contemptuously dubbed "Carpetbaggers" because they had appeared in the South after the war with, it was alleged, all their worldly goods packed in a single carpetbag. Most of them had been Freedmen's Bureau agents, members of the Union armies or federal Treasury officials; a few had come prompted by a real wish to aid the Negro; some were common adventurers. Another element in the majority group was made up of native southern whites who came to bear the sobriquet of "Scalawags," though the title was not fairly applicable to all of them, particularly to those whites who had come from regions where secession had been opposed. Finally, there was in each convention a scattering of Negroes: in South Carolina, in fact, the blacks were actually in the majority. Against these there was pitted a small party of whites, few of whom had been conspicuous in the life of the prewar South but all of whom were deeply hostile to rule by Carpetbaggers, Scalawags, and Negroes. In the face of the rising tide of Radicalism these were entirely helpless.

Lacking as they were in political experience, the members of these southern constitutional conventions copied almost literally the frames of government in force in northern states. Massachusetts' constitution, in particular, served as such a model. In almost every detail these new fundamental laws left nothing to be desired. The constitutions provided for universal manhood suffrage (with the exception of the disabilities placed on certain classes of ex-Confederates); granted equal civil rights to Negroes; provided for a system of public education; reorganized the judiciary on a popular basis and created a more equitable tax system; and instituted democratic reforms in the machinery of local government. In the abstract, all these innovations were highly commendable. But whatever southern whites may have thought of the changes in themselves, they opposed the constitutions because these documents were designed to insure for the future a large participation of the Negroes in the functions of government. Before this fear, all other questions were subordinated; and the Negroes became the focus of a growing contempt and hatred. To a very real degree the blacks were the innocent victims of an economic program fathered by the Radical Republicans of the North and carried out, in its political details, by their tools and agents, the Carpetbaggers of the South.

At first blush it must seem strange that the Republican party, spokesman for the large vested interests of the North, was willing to place in control of the South a group whose economic status was so humble. Was there not the danger that the Negro would become class-conscious and in time learn to oppose the designs of financiers and industrialists? Yet the Radical Republicans read the minds of the former slaves with extraordinary insight. In the first place the older Radicals were honest and passionate equalitarians. But the newcomers to their ranks sensed that by offering the Negroes civil and political liberties, by dangling before them the promise of social equality with the once ruling white classes, in brief, for a small mess of pottage, they would be able to obtain the support of the Negroes to a ramified scheme whose whole intent was the establishment of the supremacy of the rising industrial class of the North over the affairs of the nation. Nothing was to be feared from the Negroes themselves; and with Negro aid the former large planter class, which for so long had thwarted the expansion of northern industry and finance, could be reduced to impotence. In these facts must we read the real motives of the Radical Republicans; abstract ideals concerning the rights of man played a part, but they were also used as screens behind which the victory on the battlefield was made secure and lasting.

There is no need, here, for examining in detail the processes of reconstruction as they were worked out in the individual southern states. Suffice it to say that in all the ten states put under military control in 1867 new constitutions were adopted either in 1868 or in 1870; that Carpetbag rule, characterized by rather more than the average corruption which seemed to attend the functionings of democratic government at that time, continued to operate in some of these states until 1877; that by the time the native whites, by fair means or foul, were able to regain the ascendancy in the South, the power of the old plantation owners had been so completely destroyed that they never again seriously threatened the dominance of the new captains of industry. This was the nature of the triumph of the Radicals; there could be no question of its completeness.

THE IMPEACHMENT OF JOHNSON AND THE ELECTION OF 1868

Andrew Johnson occupies the unique distinction of being the only President of the United States against whom impeachment proceedings were ever brought. During the whole of 1867 Johnson's enemies were seeking a lever by which to force his removal and, in fact, a committee of the House of Representatives made a searching examination not only into his political acts but into his private and personal affairs as well. Although more than one thousand pages of evidence were gathered, none of it yielded a single incident upon which proceedings might be instituted against the President. However, the House committee voted that sufficient cause did exist and on February 24, 1868, it was sustained by the House. But only because a new factor had been brought into the situation. This was Johnson's removal of his Secretary of War Stanton in the face of the provisions of the Tenure of Office Act.

From the beginning of his contest with Congress, Johnson had suspected that Stanton was in secret alliance with the Radicals. Why he did not demand the resignation of the disloyal Secretary before March, 1867, is a mystery to which the key has not been furnished. It will be recalled that the Tenure of Office Act provided that no person might be removed from office without the consent of the Senate. It further declared that the President could suspend an officer during the recess of the Senate; but upon the reconvening of that body he was to submit to it the reasons for his act. If the Senate did not concur, the suspended officer was to be returned to his former position. During the summer of 1867 Stanton became such a thorn in the side of Johnson that he relieved him of his post and appointed General Grant in his stead, with the understanding, however, that if the Senate rejected the President's explanation, Grant was to place the office at the disposal of the President instead of turning it back to the ousted Secretary. Johnson's object in exacting this promise from Grant was to force Stanton to bring suit for the office and thereby have the courts pass upon the constitutionality of the Tenure of Office Act. As Johnson expected, the Senate did not concur in his reasons for the suspension of Stanton when it reconvened. The formal vote was taken on January 13, 1868. Immediately upon being notified of the Senate's action, Grant, contrary to his understanding with Johnson, surrendered the office to Stanton and thereby thwarted the President's plan of having the matter tested in the courts. Whether Grant was guilty of bad faith or whether he did not appreciate the significance of the agreement has never been clearly determined. Some sharp notes passed between him and the President and they parted bitter enemies, Grant going over completely to the Radical Republicans.

Johnson's position was now intolerable. The Senate had forced back into his immediate political family a man with whom the President was not on speaking terms, and had done so for no reason save to embarrass him. Johnson's only way out of the dilemma required that he lay himself open to a charge of having committed a misdemeanor under the terms of the Tenure of Office Act. He did not flinch from the test, however, and on February 21 he removed Stanton and appointed General Lorenzo Thomas in his place. Stanton refused to yield the office to Thomas; the Senate passed a resolution stating that Johnson had no right to dismiss Stanton; and on February 24 the House, by a strict party vote, brought resolutions of impeachment against the President. The trial was set for March 13, thus giving Johnson less than three weeks to prepare his defense.

Although the Senate had quickly condemned Johnson, it was found on investigation that there was grave doubt after all as to whether he had really violated the Tenure of Office Act. For the Act provided that, with respect to Cabinet members, their stay in office was limited to "the term of the President by whom they may have been appointed and for one month thereafter." Ironically enough, this excluded Stanton from the protection of the statute, as he had been appointed in 1862 by Abraham Lincoln and had simply remained in Johnson's Cabinet without formal reappointment. When this fact became apparent, fair-minded men appreciated that if Johnson were to be convicted at all, it would not be for any crime but purely on considerations of party expediency. While most of the Radical Republican Senators were quite ready to proceed to the bitter end, a party of seven Senators, who had heretofore acted with them with some reluctance, now voted with the Democrats against Johnson's conviction. The vote on the question of the President's guilt stood 35 yes and 19 no. Since this was one vote less than the two-thirds majority constitutionally required in cases of this sort, Andrew Johnson was allowed to serve out the remaining months of his term.

By the time the impeachment trial was concluded, the Presidential cam-

THE IMPEACHMENT TRIAL OF ANDREW JOHNSON

In the Senate Chamber, March 13, 1868

From *Frank Leslie's Illustrated Newspaper*

paign of 1868 was under way. Much to Johnson's disappointment, the Democratic party (with which he had been formerly affiliated) was not prepared to assume the responsibility for his general unpopularity and it passed him over for a more "available" candidate. The nomination fell to Horatio Seymour, war governor of New York, who was known to be hostile to prevailing currency "heresies." For the Vice-Presidency, the Democrats chose General F. P. Blair of Missouri. In their platform the Democrats endorsed the reconstruction policies of President Johnson and denounced the Radical Republican acts as "unconstitutional, revolutionary and void." Since, however, seven of the ten former Confederate states had already been readmitted into the Union, the Democrats did not venture to say what they proposed to do about the matter. On the one hand, they refused to underwrite the position of Blair that it was the duty of a Democratic administration, if elected, to overthrow by force the Carpetbag governments. On the other hand, they turned a deaf ear to the demands of their western delegates that the question of reconstruction be subordinated to a financial issue and in particular the redemption of the war bonds in greenbacks instead of gold. While this so-called "Ohio Idea" was incorporated into the Democratic platform, the naming of Seymour for the Presidency guaranteed its ultimate rejection in the event of victory. Thus, as was so often to be the case in its later history, the Democratic party entered the campaign of 1868 handicapped by a lack of unity in purpose and rent by factional dispute.[4]

It is doubtful whether the Democrats could have carried the election in any case, for the Republicans had chosen as their standard-bearer the great northern hero of the war, General U. S. Grant. Since his break with Johnson in the early part of the year, Grant had forsaken leniency and had thrown in his lot with the Radicals. At their convention in May the Republicans nominated Grant unanimously, picking for second place on the ticket the Speaker of the House, Schuyler Colfax of Indiana. The Republicans, in their platform, were no more plain-spoken than their opponents. Since their party had imposed Negro suffrage on the South, friends of the emancipated slaves expected a plank in the platform calling for another constitutional amendment forbidding any state to disfranchise the Negro because of his race, color, or previous condition of servitude. Indeed, many Radicals favored such a pledge; but they were embarrassed by the fact that, only recently, a number of northern states had refused to grant the Negroes the ballot. The platform, therefore, spoke in a language that was a model of political circumlocution: "The guarantee by Congress of equal suffrage to all loyal men in the South was demanded by every consideration of public safety, of gratitude and of justice, and must be main-

---

[4] The financial controversies of the post-Civil War period are discussed in greater detail below. See Chapter 11.

tained; while the question of suffrage in all the loyal states properly belongs to the people of those states." On the financial issue, the party was even less direct, with the result that western "cheap" money men were permitted to gain the impression that they might look for relief to a Republican administration, while eastern bondholders were told that the Republican nominee favored the paying of principal and interest of the national debt in gold. More than anything else, however, Republican orators pointed to their party's reconstruction triumphs, sang the praises of their candidate, and made much of the concluding words to be found in Grant's letter of acceptance: "Let us have peace."

The magic of Grant's phrase could not be denied. The American people were ready to believe that after four years of war and more than three and a half years of succeeding political strife, the strong, silent man on horseback, who had brought a sanguinary war to a successful close, could also bring peace to a country distracted by faction. Grant was elected; but his victory was not so overwhelming as the electoral vote seemed to indicate. In the electoral college, Grant received 214 votes; Seymour, 80. Grant carried twenty-six states; Seymour but eight, as follows: New York, New Jersey, and Oregon in the North; Kentucky, Delaware, and Maryland, among the border states; and Louisiana and Georgia in the South. Altogether Grant's popular majority was only 309,500 out of a total of 5,716,000 ballots cast; he barely won California, Connecticut, and Indiana. Ulysses Simpson Grant, obscure army officer, unsuccessful small businessman, General of the Army, was now President of the United States.

· 2 ·

Aftermath of Victory

A NEW BIRTH OF FREEDOM

The surrender of Lee to Grant at Appomattox in April, 1865, marked the close of the military conflict; the elections of 1866 and 1868 sealed the victory of the industrial North over the agricultural South; the triumph of the Republicans in 1868 terminated the political struggle. The eight years of Grant's administrations were spent in consolidating these gains and when, on March 4, 1877, the General's carriage rolled out of the White House grounds for the last time the forces of industrialism were everywhere in the ascendancy. In the famous closing of his Gettysburg address, Abraham Lincoln had said: "We here highly resolve that these dead shall not have died in vain—that this nation, under God, shall have a new birth of freedom—and that government of the people, by the people, for the people, shall not perish from the earth." The half-century after the close of the Civil War was to signalize a new birth of freedom indeed— but not for the Negroes alone. For the industrialists, the financiers, the railroad builders, all those whose expansion had been held in check during the period of the planters' power, were now to wax and grow to undreamed-of proportions. And as they individually prospered, they also converted America from an agricultural into a great industrial nation.

All this was made possible because the Radical Republicans, by holding the South in bondage for fully a decade, were able to prevent a union of the agrarian sections of the nation. The West by itself—antiprotectionist; foe of the "sound" money advocates, the railroads, the monopolists, the exploiters of the country's natural resources—was unable to resist successfully. By the time reconstruction was over and the southern states were once again functioning normally, opposition had been rendered harmless. Industrial capitalism, without fear of agrarian interference and with the blessing of government, was dominating the economy of the nation. Thus were the fruits of victory of the Civil War gathered, but only at the expense of the willful humbling of the vanquished section over a long period of years.

No sooner was Grant's administration installed than the Forty-first Congress, called in special session on March 18, 1869, passed a resolution pledging the faith of the United States to pay in coin all its bonded indebtedness. In the next few years, refunding laws were enacted to set the machinery in motion. All those persons who had purchased the war issues in a depreciated currency, the bankers who had acquired them at generous discounts, that whole group in the North that had had a financial stake in the successful outcome of the Civil War—these were now to reap their reward. At the same time, of course, the fiscal soundness of the government was guaranteed. With one class of creditors protected, it was natural that similar safeguards should be erected for all the others. The danger of continued inflation was a real threat and the resumption of specie payments was the only sure way to check its growth. Accordingly, on January 14, 1875, a Resumption Act was passed and America's rentiers were left assured that their investments in farm mortgages, railroad bonds, state and municipal securities would, if anything, increase in value through the maintenance of a dear dollar.

Nor was this the only legislation definitely in the interests of the rising new middle class. During the war, to raise the needed revenues, Congress had resorted to a complex series of internal revenue taxes, many of which bore heavily on ordinary commercial operations. Partly as compensation for these onerous duties (though as much, as we shall have occasion to note, because the way was now open for the revival of the early protective system of Hamilton and Clay), manufacturers had agitated for higher tariff walls to protect their wares from the competition of foreign products. With the war over, the Radical Congresses made haste to repeal all these internal taxes except those on alcoholic liquors and tobacco; also, the well-to-do were relieved of an additional burden when the income-tax law was withdrawn in part in 1867 and entirely in 1872. But the tariff remained; and the principle of protection became a foundation stone upon which the new industrialists were able to build.

President Johnson had merely echoed the sentiments of small farmers throughout the country when, in his first Congressional message, he expressed himself thus on the question of monopoly:

> Monopolies, perpetuities and class legislation are contrary to the genius of free government. . . . Wherever monopoly attains a foothold, it is sure to be a source of danger, discord and trouble. . . . The government is subordinate to the people; but, as the agent and representative of the people, it must be held superior to monopolies; which in themselves ought never to be granted and which, where they exist, must be subordinate and yield to the government.[1]

---

[1] "Monopoly" in the sixties and seventies meant corporate enterprise that received the assistance of government by land grants, charters, or privileges and immunities of one kind or another. Our vocabulary has changed somewhat during the intervening years and today the term has a more specific economic meaning. For the old "monopoly," later American generations have substituted the words "the interests" and "privilege." The connotation, in all three cases, has always been the same.

But Johnson, by himself, was powerless to act and his opposition to governmental assistance for railroads and the opening of the public lands for exploitation by mineral and timber interests was of no avail. Monopoly, encouraged by the Radical Republicans (many of whom were personally interested in railroad, coal, and land companies), flourished, and before Grant's administrations were over it had received more than three times as many acres out of the public domain as had all the homesteaders put together!

Nothing indicated more plainly the true nature of the new dispensation than the careers of the railroad builders and financiers. The end of the Civil War opened a new era in railroad building; reconstruction, too, witnessed the beginnings of consolidation. In these two fields the promoters of the new lines reaped a rich harvest. Particularly were they able to take advantage of the fact that the absence of southern representatives from the councils of the nation now made possible the laying down of the great line across the western plains and mountains that southern statesmen had so long successfully thwarted. In 1862, Congress chartered the Union Pacific Railroad Company to build a railroad from Omaha, Nebraska, to the California boundary and, because the resources of private capital were far too limited for the undertaking, the federal government gave public lands, timber, stone, and earth rights and finally financial aid. To the Central Pacific Railroad Company, a California corporation, similar generous subsidies were paid.

Railroad promotion, with its rich prizes from the public domain, did not alone content the new entrepreneurs. Other sources of profit were to be quickly discovered, particularly from the creation of dummy construction companies and from railroad consolidations. The history of the Crédit Mobilier, as the construction company which built a large part of the Union Pacific was called, was merely the best known of many similar ingeniously devised frauds. In this case, the controlling stockholders in the Union Pacific organized a construction company and awarded themselves a contract at such terms that before the road was completed they were in possession of practically all the assets of the property, in other words, land, bonds, and stock. One of the chief beneficiaries was a Radical Republican Congressman from Massachusetts, Oakes Ames by name, who voted regularly with his fellow Radicals to assure the newly enfranchised Negroes their possession of their political and civil rights—and who gained Congressional friends for the Union Pacific and the Crédit Mobilier by a judicious distribution of stock shares, "where," as he later said, "they would do us the most good." Speaker of the House, Schuyler Colfax of Indiana, Senator Henry Wilson of Massachusetts, Representative James A. Garfield of Ohio, were some of Ames's colleagues who were permitted to subscribe for shares of the Crédit Mobilier at par without being called upon to put up any money, Ames obligingly carrying their stock for them. All these statesmen were stanch Radicals; all were to be subsequently honored by their fellow citizens—Colfax and Wilson as Grant's Vice-Presidents during his first and second terms, Garfield as President of the United States in 1880.

In the East and Middle West, the period of reconstruction was at the same time one of railroad consolidation and stock-watering on a grandiose scale. We shall have occasion to examine the accomplishments of the captains of the rails in another connection, but it is proper to point out in this place that many of the darker phases of the country's railroad growth had their beginnings in those years when Executive and Congress preoccupied themselves so earnestly on behalf of the freedmen. A significant financial discovery, made by Jay Gould and Jim Fisk (who figured in the destinies of the Erie Railroad), Cornelius Vanderbilt (responsible for the consolidation of the New York Central) and the Garretts (who created the Baltimore and Ohio system), revealed that the value of corporate stocks, in amalgamations, could be made to depend not so much on the physical assets of the individual properties they linked together as on their combined earning power. Needless to say, the rewards realized from such operations were well-nigh incalculable; it was no wonder that America's greatest fortunes were built from the rails.

Gould and Fisk pushed their ingenuity even further: They saw the possibility of marketing railroad securities at more than their earning power, provided the investing public could be persuaded that the near future would witness a great rise in the profits of their lines. In 1869, these two launched a bold enterprise whose purpose was to send up the stock values of their heavily watered Erie Railroad system and at the same time afford them an opportunity to make a killing in the gold market.

It will be remembered that the ordinary circulating medium of the country, up to the close of the seventies, was the Treasury certificate or greenback. Gold was used, mainly, for four purposes: to pay import duties; to settle adverse foreign balances; to satisfy accounts whose contracts specifically called for gold payments; and for speculation. In addition, the federal government paid the interest on its debt in gold. In view of the fact, however, that the amount of the metal obtained from import duties was usually in excess of the total needed to meet interest charges, the Treasury from time to time sold gold in the open market. In 1869, it took, ordinarily, $133 in greenbacks to buy $100 in gold. But what did all this have to do with Gould and Fisk? The connecting links were the following circumstances: The Erie Railroad was one of the largest movers of western wheat, but because the price of the grain, at the opening of the harvesting season, was relatively low the wheat growers had shown a disposition to hold their stocks on the farms. If, reasoned the promoters of Erie, the value of gold in relation to the greenbacks might be induced to rise, then commodity prices generally and wheat in particular would increase, the farmers would release their stocks, the freight business of the Erie would improve, so would its earnings, and a market would at once appear for these securities they desired to unload on a gullible investing and speculating public. Obviously, then, a corner in the gold market was the first operation in the grand maneuver.

Success almost crowned their efforts. Obtaining what they thought was a promise from President Grant that the federal Treasury would refrain from selling gold for a whole season, the bold speculators appeared on the exchange and proceeded to bid up the price of gold until, on Friday, September 24, 1869, it stood at 162. Fisk confidently predicted that the metal would soon reach 200 and it might well have, had not two events occurred to prick the bubble. The first was, that Gould began to sell gold secretly; the second, that the Secretary of the Treasury, who, apparently, had not been informed of Grant's pledge to the conspirators, released on the market four million dollars' worth of gold. The corner, of course, collapsed, the price of gold settled to its normal figure, and hundreds of men who had unwittingly lent themselves to the plot were ruined. Not so Fisk, who saved himself from bankruptcy by simply repudiating his contracts.[2]

Such was the nature of some of the chapters in the history of American business as the reconstruction program of the Radical Republicans was being evolved. It must be plain that by overt acts and through their unwillingness to interfere, the statesmen who ruled the destinies of the Republic from 1865 to 1877 did much to assure the railroad promoters, bankers, and industrialists a free hand in their careers of expansion and exploitation.

CLOSING PHASES OF RECONSTRUCTION

When General Grant concluded his speech of acceptance in 1868 with the memorable words, "Let us have peace," there could be no doubt of his sincerity. Like Lincoln, he entertained no bitter feelings against his antagonists; and until his break with Johnson he favored a lenient course toward the fallen foe. There is little reason to believe that he understood

---

[2] It is beside the point to recount here how Grant was caught in the toils of the conspirators. He easily succumbed to their flattery and was quickly convinced, it would seem, that Gould and Fisk had devised a working plan for the relief of the hard-pressed farmers! The whole episode, which came to be known in the annals of the time as "Black Friday," received the attention of a Congressional investigating committee. Although the legislators collected enough evidence to warrant the indictment of Gould and Fisk and although their report declared that "for many weeks the business of the whole country was paralyzed" and the "foundations of business morality were rudely shaken," neither New York State nor the United States government took any action against the offenders.

that stern political measures were being employed to cloak an economic policy with widespread ramifications. After the Reconstruction Acts had been passed and put into force he still did not realize their revolutionary character. It was his understanding that as soon as all the southern conventions had completed their work and the constitutions had been accepted by the electorates, after civil governments had been established and the southern representatives admitted to their places in Congress, the Union would be as it had always been—except for the abolition of slavery. That there was to be no peace and that Grant was to become the agent of those Radicals who saw that southern debasement and their own victory in the economic field were both aspects of the same question, the events of the following years were to disclose.

Before Grant entered the White House on March 4, 1869, seven of the ten states that had been placed under military rule in the spring of 1867 had been able to obtain release by complying with the requirements of the Reconstruction Acts. They had then been readmitted to equal standing in the Union. With their ratification of the Fourteenth Amendment, the necessary three-fourths majority of the states had been secured and thenceforth the civil rights of the Negroes were safeguarded beyond any possibility of hostile action by the states themselves. The fear on the part of the Radical Republicans, that sooner or later native southern whites might again return to power and repeal those provisions of their constitutions that forever guaranteed the right of the Negroes to vote, prompted Congress, when it reconvened in December, 1868, to enact the Fifteenth Amendment. This provided that no person was to be deprived of the franchise because of race, color, or previous condition of servitude. There was much uncertainty about the new amendment receiving the approval of three-fourths of the state legislatures necessary for adoption. Consequently, still another Supplementary Reconstruction Act was passed applying to the three states in the South that had not yet completed the process of reconstruction, namely, Virginia, Texas, and Mississippi, by which it was provided that they were to ratify both Fourteenth and Fifteenth Amendments before their representatives might seek readmission to Congress and the military forces be withdrawn. In 1870, these, too, had complied with all the conditions laid down by Congress, and political reconstruction was thus nominally ended.

In the meantime, however, the native whites had gained partial control of the government of Georgia as a result of the election of 1868. They had then proceeded to take advantage of a technicality in the constitution framed by the "black and tan" [3] convention and had ejected all the Negro

---

[3] This term of opprobrium was applied quite extensively by the native southern whites to the conventions that had been called in the ten southern states affected by the Reconstruction Acts of 1867.

members of the state legislature, on the ground that the right to hold office had not been specifically bestowed on the newly enfranchised freedmen. The clever trick gained as its reward a declaration by Congress that Georgia did not have a republican form of government; its representatives in Congress, therefore, were denied their seats and the state once more was remanded to military government. Before being readmitted to full fellowship Georgia was forced to comply with that provision of the Supplementary Reconstruction Act that called for ratification of the Fifteenth Amendment as a condition precedent to complete restoration. This proceeding with respect to the supposedly sovereign state of Georgia is worthy of more than passing notice. In the first place, it may some day serve as a precedent for the federal executive and Congress to place a state under military rule should one of the forty-eight exercise its right to establish a form of government obnoxious to the dominant political group in the country as a whole. In the second place, it marked the beginning of a policy pursued throughout the eight years of the Grant administrations, namely, of interfering in the South when matters seemed to be going contrary to the wishes of the Radical Republican leaders.

Thus, peace was as distant as ever. Nor did developments in the southern section itself point to a quick termination of this unhappy state of affairs. As early as the election of 1868, it was generally believed in the North that southern whites were bent upon preventing their former slaves from exercising the full enjoyment of the voting privilege. Secret organizations, of which the Ku Klux Klan gained the greatest notoriety, were set up in the South for the avowed purpose of preventing their section from becoming thoroughly Africanized and for re-establishing Anglo-Saxon supremacy. In their behavior toward the Negroes the Klansmen first resorted to intimidation and corporal punishment and then, when the terror they had first occasioned had spent itself, to more drastic measures among which hanging was a not infrequent occurrence. The upshot was, Carpetbag governors, having no local militia upon which they could rely, appealed to the President for soldiers, and such demands were usually complied with, particularly when elections impended. The presence of federal troops at the polling places was sufficient, as a rule, to guarantee a Republican victory. But to make assurance doubly sure, a second expedient was hit upon. A board was organized in each state, known as the canvassing or returning board, in which power was vested to examine and recount the votes and throw out all those ballots that, supposedly, had been fraudulently cast. Needless to say, the rejected ballots were more often those of Democratic voters than of Republican. Finally, to legalize Grant's action in dispatching troops to the southern polls, as well as to strengthen the power of the federal courts as far as reconstruction was concerned, Congress in 1870 and 1871 passed a series of measures known as Enforcement Acts and Federal Election Laws. We shall have occasion to note how the southern returning boards and these acts of 1870 and 1871 played their parts in the passing of the southern question, before the decade of the seventies was over.

In less than six months, Grant had fallen entirely under the domination of a group of younger Radical Republicans, of whom Senators Conkling (N.Y.), Cameron (Pa.), and Morton (Ind.), Representative Benjamin F. Butler (Mass.), and two members of his own Cabinet, Williams and Boutwell, were the most conspicuous. Some of these men, notably Conkling and Cameron, were spokesmen par excellence for the railroads and other vested interests of the country; all of them were political leaders of the customary factional stamp. Although it is not a matter of record that any one of these statesmen (unlike the older Radicals) ever gave serious consideration to any project designed to elevate the Negroes (or, for that matter, any other members of the poorer classes of the country), all early found it expedient to urge upon the President and their fellow legislators the necessity for maintaining in power, by force if need be, the Carpetbag southern governments. Their ostensible purpose was the need for guaranteeing to "our loyal allies" the rights and privileges which the war amendments were designed to secure to them; actually, their course was dictated by quite different motives. For one, by keeping alive the southern question and constantly reminding Americans of the "foul crimes of unrepentant rebels"—waving the bloody shirt, as the practice was aptly called—they could divert attention from their own questionable political practices and particularly from their habit of voting in the interests of industrial capitalism on every question that presented itself for the consideration of Congress. Again, the Republican party needed the votes of southern states to make sure of carrying the Congressional and Presidential elections; and the only way to obtain these was the maintenance in power of the Carpetbag governments in as many southern states as possible. Thus, in the election of 1870, slightly more northern and border state districts elected Democratic Congressmen than Republican, with the result that the slim majority the Republicans were able to claim in the House during the last two years of Grant's first term was due to the preponderance of Republican representatives from the ten recently reconstructed states.

Yet, despite enforcement acts and election laws, each biennial election in the South saw the "redemption" of one or more of the late Confederate states by native whites. We must examine, in some detail, how this turn of affairs came about.

During 1869, 1870, and 1871, over two hundred cases occurred where federal troops were sent into one locality or another of the South to aid federal or state civil authorities in the enforcement of laws. By one of the enforcement acts, the President was authorized to declare whole areas in a state of insurrection and to suspend the writ of habeas corpus. Indeed, on one occasion, in 1871, Grant did suspend the writ in nine counties of South Carolina and detachments of federal troops arrested several hundred persons accused of belonging to the Ku Klux Klan and fomenting rebellion against the United States. A number of the arrested men were brought to trial before the federal courts; some were convicted. The evidence revealed the existence of widespread disorders and not a little barbarity on the part of the whites against the Negroes. But it failed to prove the main charges that the crimes were of more than a local nature and that their perpetrators were in rebellion against the federal government. The suit acted as a boomerang; there was no further denial to southerners of the right to protection under the habeas corpus; and intelligent northerners began to scrutinize more closely the policy being pursued by President and Congress.

In fact, the President became aware of this growing unfriendliness and he was more and more reluctant to send federal troops into the South to bolster up the Carpetbag governors. Not the least among the reasons for this change of tune was the appearance of the so-called Liberal Republican movement with its threat against Grant's re-election in 1872. Here, we need simply point out that the diminishing use of federal troops gave the southern whites a better opportunity to control the Negroes than they had had before.

But southern whites were perfecting their technique, too: there was less use of direct force and more of economic pressure. The Freedmen's Bureau went out of existence in 1872 so that the Negroes could no longer rely on that agency for subsistence in an emergency. Therefore, the blacks were compelled to stay on the land, in most cases as the tenants of the native whites; and by threats of ejection, white landlords found it not difficult, in many instances, to force their Negro laborers and share croppers to refrain from political activity. Where there was any industrial enterprise, the power of the employer over his workers was utilized to the same end. The gradual realization, too, on the part of many Negroes that they might expect more personal kindness from their former white masters than from the Carpetbaggers led to a tacit acceptance of the program of "redemption."

The southerners found their hands further strengthened when Congress, in 1872, lifted the civil disabilities, imposed by the Fourteenth Amendment, from all but a very small remnant of the former Confederate soldiers and statesmen. This enabled the old and tried southern leaders to take charge, once more, of the Democratic party and to relegate to the background many of the more headstrong men who had directed party affairs since the beginning of Reconstruction. Their method was twofold: they refrained from such overt acts as would be likely to bring on Presidential intervention; and they followed the ancient precept of "divide and rule." As was to be expected, the varied host which had descended on the South sooner or later began to reveal internal dissensions over the division of the spoils. Such quarrels the returned leaders assiduously encouraged; nor was it long before, by union with the more moderate elements, they were able to bring the situation under their own control. By 1876, when Grant's second term was coming to a close, all but three former Confederate states, to wit, South Carolina, Florida, and Louisiana, had been redeemed and the entire machinery of government was in the hands of the native white party. As we shall see, the three remaining states were also won back in 1877 and they, together with the other eight states which once made up the Confederacy, formed that political bloc known as the "Solid South." Until the Presidential election of 1928, the Republican party was never able, seriously, to split it.

FOREIGN AFFAIRS DURING RECONSTRUCTION

A time-honored device, whereby an administration harassed with domestic difficulties is enabled to distract attention from its unpopular course, is the pursuit of a vigorous foreign policy. The aspect of American foreign relations at the close of the Civil War gave first Andrew Johnson and afterwards General Grant an opportunity to take advantage of this expedient. That in America's controversies with France and Great Britain, during the period, neither man resorted to this maneuver is to the credit of both.

When the Civil War began, France was in that stage of her political history known as the Second Empire. A nephew of the great Napoleon, Louis Napoleon Bonaparte, had first succeeded in gaining the presidency of France following the revolution of 1848 and then, during the next few years, was able to transform the republic into an empire with himself at its head. Lacking the military genius and the larger statesmanship of his illustrious uncle, he nevertheless achieved more than a temporary success by means of the arts of the clever politician. Opposition, however, was not altogether stilled and there existed in the country two important factions whose hostility toward Napoleon III was marked. One of these was the clericals, made up of the Catholic hierarchy and the more ardent laymen; the other was the republicans, who counted among their numbers many of the rising French industrialists and financiers. In general, the two factions were mutually antagonistic and a policy designed to appease the one was likely to alienate the other. Napoleon's interference in Italian affairs in the late fifties had not enhanced his prestige with either party, with the result that the emperor was compelled to cast about for some adventurous enterprise to restore him in the good graces of both. The situation in Mexico, coupled with the fratricidal strife just beginning to rage between the states of Mexico's great northern neighbor, seemed to offer Napoleon the very opportunity he was seeking.

Since becoming independent in the eighteen twenties, Mexico had been a tempting morsel to the insatiable appetites of imperialistic nations. Rich in natural resources but ever possessing a weak and unstable government, that hapless country was in no position to offer resistance to any despoiler who might feel inclined to descend on it. But for the existence of our own Monroe Doctrine it might have been invested long before 1861; even then, that doctrine had not saved the northern provinces from being appropriated by the United States in the eighteen forties. During the thirteen years between the close of our war with Mexico and the outbreak of the Civil War, Mexico had possessed no government worthy of the name. Each successive adventurer who had sat in her presidential chair had been principally bent upon enriching himself while the opportunity lasted, more frequently than not at the expense of the wealthy Catholic church. Such interference with the "liberties" of the church was a matter of grave concern to devout Catholics in other lands, and nowhere more than in France. Hence Napoleon's intervention, pledging as it did the protection of the church from further despoliation, appealed strongly to the French clerical party. At the same time, the opportunities offered for French trade and investment in Mexico attracted the middle-class republicans. On the Mexican question, therefore, the emperor, who was very much in the position of a circus equestrian attempting to ride two horses, each of which was determined to run in a contrary direction, seemed for once to have the situation under control.

The opportunity for intervention came when the irresponsible Mexican government declined to pay the interest on its indebtedness to foreigners. At first England and Spain joined with France to coerce Mexico into making a settlement with their nationals. Having secured a satisfactory arrangement with Benito Juarez, the momentary titular head of Mexico, the Spanish and English withdrew. Not so Napoleon. He declared war on Juarez, sent over some 35,000 French troops, and compelled the native chieftain to flee from Mexico City and retire into the fastnesses of the northern mountains. Napoleon then arranged for a hand-picked Assembly of Notables, which changed the government into an hereditary monarchy and called Maximilian, brother of the Austrian Emperor, to the throne. The Mexican people as a whole, despite their internal differences, did not welcome the change, and Maximilian was able to maintain his rule only with the support of the French troops. First and last, the Mexican adventure cost the French treasury some $40 million. The compensating advantages to the French nation did not seem to warrant such a huge outlay and by the time the American Civil War was over, French sentiment, which at the start had been favorable to the enterprise, was beginning to turn against it. Napoleon knew that the failure of the Confederacy meant the eventual withdrawal of his support of Maximilian unless he was willing to risk hostilities with the North. This Napoleon was reluctant to do, more particularly since the European international situation was assuming an aspect which might well involve France in difficulties on the Continent at any time. Consequently, he was anxious to find some graceful means of retiring from a position fraught with so much danger.

It was at this point that Andrew Johnson had his opportunity to turn American attention from his reconstruction policy to a war that could hardly result otherwise than in success. Grant and other Union generals championed a bold stand against Napoleon. Such an attitude, undoubtedly, would have had the approval of the majority of the American people. But Johnson was no Bismarck or Beaconsfield. His Secretary of State, William Henry Seward, wished to settle the matter peacefully, at the same time securing an American diplomatic triumph, and in this he had the encouragement of the President. Using tact and being careful not to offend the French national honor, Seward succeeded in obtaining a pledge from Napoleon that the French troops would be withdrawn in detachments between November, 1866, and November, 1867. A rupture was again imminent when the earlier date arrived and no troops were embarked for home; but Napoleon then promised that he would recall all the French forces at one time in the spring of 1867. And this was done. Maximilian refused to relinquish his throne but without French support found himself utterly unable to hold it. He was captured by the Juarez followers in June and, despite some effort on the part of Seward to save him, was almost immediately executed by the Mexicans. Thus Seward and his chief gained an outstanding diplomatic victory. It is an interesting commentary on human nature that the whole affair was much too tame to succeed in stemming the tide of unpopularity that had already set in against the Johnson administration.

Against England, there was a great deal more adverse American sentiment as a result of its attitude during the Civil War. This was occasioned not by virtue of the fact that England had been less strict in the observance of neutrality than had France, but because the North felt that since the English for over a generation had been committed to the cause of abolition, the war against slavery deserved their sympathy. That, however, the English upper classes and governmental circles almost unanimously favored the South quickly became apparent. Two official British policies, in particular, stirred resentment in the North. The first was the recognition by Great Britain, very early in the conflict, of southern belligerency.[4] On

---

[4] This indicated the acceptance by neutrals of the existence of a state of war, as opposed to insurrection or rebellion.

this score there could be no real ground for complaint; nevertheless, the North did complain, and at the close of the struggle one of the extreme indictments made against the English by certain American statesmen, in particular Senator Charles Sumner, the chairman of the Senate Foreign Relations Committee, was that they had thus doubled the duration of the war and should pay the United States something like two billion dollars in consequence.

A more just grievance was England's failure to enforce strictly its neutrality laws, especially with respect to permitting to be built in English dockyards cruisers that were plainly meant for Confederate use. The best known of such warships was the *Alabama,* and the destruction caused by this and other men-of-war of the same type, in preying upon American merchant vessels on the high seas, amounted to a sum totaling some $15,500,000. Such, at any rate, were the direct losses sustained by American shippers. Men like Sumner, however, maintained that the higher insurance rates, the transference of American ships to foreign registries, and particularly the decline of the American merchant marine were due to the ravages of the Confederate cruisers and that the damages thus suffered indirectly came to ten times the sum of the direct losses. That British shipowners, ever jealous of any other maritime power, were well pleased to have American competition eliminated, cannot be gainsaid, and there is little doubt that part of the laxity of the British government was due to its responsiveness to these powerful interests.[5]

Thus matters stood at the end of the Civil War. American opinion would have supported a war with Great Britain on almost any ground. A pretext could have been found in the Fenian movement for the liberation of Ireland, which in its American aspect took the form of an attempted invasion of Canada by bands of Irish-Americans. The whole affair was a fiasco, but had Johnson and Seward been so inclined they might have dignified it with the respectability of belligerency and thus brought on war with England. Again they chose the path of peace. Seward made a number of attempts to have the "*Alabama* Claims," as the losses caused by all the English-built Confederate cruisers came to be called, adjusted. At first, Downing Street was disinclined to bring its official acts during the war into discussion, but the threatening aspect of European affairs finally caused the government to adopt a more conciliatory attitude. The result was that Reverdy Johnson, whom Andrew Johnson had appointed ambassador to the Court of St. James's, was able to conclude a treaty late in 1868 with Lord Clarendon, the British Minister of Foreign Affairs. This convention called for the submission of the claims of the citizens of either country against the other to a joint high commission. But the United States

[5] See below, pages 185–87, for a discussion of the reasons for the decline of the American merchant marine.

Senate was plainly hostile to the settlement; it opened its deliberations to the public; it permitted the broadcasting of the extravagant demands of the extremists, Sumner's in particular; and it proceeded to reject ratification, a short month after the close of Johnson's term, by a vote of 54 to 1. Since the new Grant administration had not taken any official stand with regard to the *Alabama* Claims and the alleged indirect losses, Sumner's utterances were looked upon as official. It was apparent that a crisis had been reached.

Had Grant been so inclined, he could have seized the opportunity to add further laurels to his martial fame by involving the nation in a costly and sanguinary conflict. Like Johnson and Seward, however, he and his Secretary of State, Hamilton Fish, desired peace. Their task was rendered very difficult by reason of the fact that Sumner presently became a bitter critic of the Grant administration and insisted that no settlement should be made which did not include the indirect losses. For these, the only compensation at all satisfactory must be the withdrawal of Great Britain from the Western Hemisphere! It was natural that British opinion should regard such a proposal as in the nature of a demand for a war indemnity; nor could any British government supinely consent to discussions on this basis without suffering at once the displeasure of its electorate. Appreciating this, and angered further by Sumner's denunciation of his Santo Domingo policy (to be noted presently), Grant brought all possible pressure to bear to depose Sumner from his chairmanship of the Foreign Relations Committee. In this he was successful in March, 1871. Henceforth, matters moved with greater smoothness and dispatch. On May 8, 1871, the Treaty of Washington was signed by Fish and Sir John Rose, the special commissioner whom the British government had sent to Washington for that purpose. And on May 24, the Senate ratified the convention, although its terms were not essentially different from those of the earlier Johnson-Clarendon agreement.

By the provisions of this treaty, the *Alabama* Claims were to be submitted to a tribunal of arbitration, which was ultimately composed of one representative each from the United States, Great Britain, Italy, Switzerland, and Brazil. This international commission met at Geneva, Switzerland, on December 15, 1871, and continued to sit for over eight months, the chief reason for the prolongation of its sessions being the unexpected submission by the United States of the indirect claims arising out of the war. This was not really a violation, on the part of Secretary Fish, of the understanding reached between him and Sir John Rose; it was occasioned by a desire to silence Sumner and his followers and to have settled once and for all a subject that must otherwise long exist to trouble Anglo-American relations. Fish's motives were not at first understood by the British, with the result that the conference threatened to end in failure.

But the air was cleared when the arbitral tribunal itself eliminated the indirect claims. From this time on, the deliberations proceeded to a speedy close, and on August 25, 1872, the decision was made public. It declared Great Britain negligent in her duty as a neutral in allowing three of the Confederate cruisers, the *Alabama,* the *Florida,* and the *Shenandoah,* to leave British ports during the war, and it ordered the payment of $15,500,000 to the United States in compensation for the direct damages that American citizens had sustained through the depredations of the three ships. The British government accepted its diplomatic defeat, quickly paid over the money, and a major cause for friction between the two powers was removed.

In addition to the controversies with France and England, three other matters relating to foreign affairs came up for consideration during the administrations of Johnson and Grant. The first of these was the purchase of Alaska from Russia. During the war, the czar had been distinctly friendly to the northern cause and when, in March, 1867, the Russian minister at Washington approached Seward with an offer to sell the entire tract to this country the Secretary of State accepted the offer promptly. The terms of the purchase were fixed at $7,200,000. Despite the hostility of the Senate to the Johnson administration, it ratified the treaty with alacrity on April 9. For this, there were a number of cogent reasons. Russia had not supported the Confederacy during the war. There was now presented an opportunity to further the rounding out of our possession of the entire North American continent and to rid it of one more European power. The richness of Alaska's natural resources was not entirely unsuspected. Finally, there is considerable reason to believe that the czar's minister used not a small part of the extra $200,000 of the purchase money as *douceurs* where he considered they would best smooth the way for ratification.[6]

Soon after his election, Grant was presented with an opportunity to annex Santo Domingo by the president of the little Negro republic, one Baez, who doubtless looked forward to improving his own personal fortunes from the transaction. Grant took the proposal seriously and sent his private secretary, Babcock, to Santo Domingo to investigate conditions. Babcock reported favorably; was authorized to make a treaty of annexation; and returned with a convention, which was submitted to the Senate. The President left no stone unturned in order to obtain a favorable vote by the Senate and went so far as to call personally on Sumner in an effort to enlist his support. Though Grant had understood that he had won over the chairman of the Senate's Foreign Relations Committee to his side, when the matter came up for debate Sumner delivered one of his characteristic philippics against the treaty. This action and the doubts he threw on

[6] See memorandum of a conversation between Andrew Johnson and W. H. Seward, Johnson Papers, Library of Congress, Washington.

ntegrity of Grant's motives led to a falling out between the two men further contributed to Grant's determination to see Sumner forced his ranking position in the Senate. Though the President won here, as we have seen, he could not gain his point on the matter of Dominican annexation and the little revolution-ridden republic was permitted to go on its independent way for another generation.

Another question to claim the attention of Grant and his able Secretary of State was that of Cuban independence. At the close of the sixties, rebellion had broken out in Cuba against the authority of the mother country, Spain. Although the Cuban insurgents were making small progress, they and a number of their American sympathizers, including the Secretary of War, General John A. Rawlins, called upon the United States to accord them the rights of belligerents. Grant, influenced partly by Rawlins and partly by a desire to punish Spain for having recognized Confederate belligerency, was inclined to submit to the request. He went so far as to sign a proclamation to this effect and ordered Fish to seal and issue it. The Secretary, knowing that the condition of the Cuban rebels could in no way be considered comparable to that of the Confederates when Spain had acted in their favor, neglected to obey the mandate of his chief. Grant did not press the matter and a year later, when the United States officially proclaimed a policy of nonintervention, he thanked Fish for his disobedience. Nevertheless, the conflict in Cuba dragged on, accompanied by a number of cruel acts of reprisal on both sides. A particularly reprehensible one was that perpetrated by the Spaniards in connection with the ship the *Virginius* in 1873. The *Virginius,* flying the American flag and carrying troops and arms to the rebels, was captured by a Spanish man-of-war. Fifty-three of the passengers and crew were almost immediately executed at Santiago, eight of the victims being American citizens. Cries for war were heard on every side, but Fish was not to be stampeded. He demanded reparation of the Spanish government and, after some delay, Spain agreed to restore the *Virginius* and her survivors to the United States authorities and to punish the officials responsible for the executions. It was later learned that the *Virginius* had had no right to fly the American flag as her owners had obtained her registry by fraud. And so Cuba was to wait another twenty-five years before being transformed from a Spanish possession into a virtual American protectorate.

· 3 ·

Passing of the Southern Question

GRANTISM

The peaceable resolution of the difficulties with England and Spain by Secretary Fish brought to the Grant administrations their only honorable distinction. We have already noted the disastrous effects produced by Grant's southern policy and how, in dealing with the new problems arising from the rapid expansion of the country's industry and commerce, his government threw all its influence on the side of the new business interests. In carrying on the ordinary functions of state, the administrations were characterized by nepotism, favoritism, inefficiency, and corruption. Part of this is attributable to the low private and public morality which seems to follow inevitably upon the heels of any war of major proportions; part of it must be laid to the incompetence of Grant himself. Hence, it is not altogether unfair to designate the many unsavory incidents that are associated with his stay in office by the term Grantism.

It is particularly unfortunate for Grant's place in history that he ever allowed himself to become the tool of the Radical Republicans in 1868. As a soldier he had displayed qualities of leadership of a high order and, although in some respects he had been favored by fortune, on the whole he deserved the extraordinary esteem in which he was held by the people of the North for his part in bringing the war to a successful termination. He bore his great military honors modestly; knew how to take orders from his superior, the President; and knew how to give them, too, without arousing resentment or antagonism—qualities that the majority of his predecessors in command had not possessed. After the assassination of Lincoln, Grant continued to give to Lincoln's successor, Andrew Johnson, that same obedience and respect which he felt was the President's due as commander-in-chief of the Army. This, at any rate, was his attitude toward Johnson until the break took place between them over the removal of Stanton as Secretary of War in January, 1868. From that time on no Radical was more contemptuous of Johnson or more desirous of seeing the impeachment proceedings terminate successfully. Henceforth, Grant was transformed from a manly, first-rate soldier into a time-serving, third-rate politician.

The metamorphosis gradually made itself apparent. In the appointment of many of the members of his Cabinet, Grant permitted himself to be guided by personal considerations. He also named to many lesser offices a large number of his own and his wife's relatives, as well as personal friends who in one way or another he felt had claims upon him. He quickly showed his partiality toward men of wealth. Himself a complete failure financially when he re-entered the Army in 1861, he had an unbounded admiration for men who had built up imposing fortunes. Thus, he was not above associating with Fisk and Gould; and he named to his Cabinet A. T. Stewart, a rich New York merchant, and Adolph E. Borie, a wealthy Philadelphian, as heads of the Treasury and Navy Departments respectively. The former the Senate failed to confirm and the latter soon retired from public life; nevertheless, Grant continued to allow the very rich to cultivate his acquaintance and to influence his policies on finance, currency, tariff, and other public questions. Before the first administration was half over, the politician had been fully formed; he had learned to manage Congress less as the military commander and more as the party chief; and he gave ready ear to that small group of Radical leaders who were shaping the government's reconstruction policies.

Before 1870, the electorate of the North had never had a clear-cut opportunity to pass judgment on the questions of Negro suffrage and the other aspects of the reconstruction program. In the Congressional elections of that year, however, the issue was squarely joined. The results showed that the voters of the North and the border states by no means completely approved of the course of the Radicals, for fully as many Democrats were returned as were Republicans from these areas. While the Republican party continued to maintain its control over the House, because of the fact that many Republican Congressmen were elected from the reconstructed South, the party was being confronted by a growing unrest in its own ranks. This dissatisfaction was, in 1872, to break out into open revolt.

The Liberal Republican movement had its origin in Missouri, where, during the war, the persons loyal to the Union had passed drastic disfranchisement laws against all southern sympathizers. Fully one-third of the state's population had suffered under these disabilities and the continued disfranchisement of so large a part of the normal electorate, long after the war's close, had served to arouse the concern of a faction in the local Republican party. In alliance with the Democrats, this group gained the ascendancy in 1870 and immediately succeeded in restoring full political and civil rights to all citizens of the state. Chief among the Missouri Liberal Republicans was Senator Carl Schurz who, at the close of the war, had been an ardent avocate of Negro suffrage but who was soon to couple this doctrine with a plea for universal amnesty. During 1871 and 1872, as the climax of southern reconstruction was reached, the Liberal Republicans attracted many notable persons to their ranks. By the latter year, a program had taken form based on the following tenets: the cessation of the administration's high-handed methods in the South, the reform of the Civil Service, and tariff revision.

In January, 1872, the Missouri Liberal Republicans issued a call for a national convention. They met with a widespread and enthusiastic response, with the result that their leaders had every reason to believe that their candidate would gain the indorsement of the Democrats and at the same time attract the support of reforming groups generally. Indeed, the two Liberal Republicans most prominently mentioned for the nomination were "available" in every sense. The first was Lyman Trumbull of Illinois, remembered as one of the seven Republican Senators who had voted against the conviction of Johnson in 1868. The other was Charles Francis Adams of Massachusetts, son of one President and grandson of another, and distinguished in his own right for the services he had rendered his country as ambassador at the Court of St. James's during the troublous days of the Civil War. Either of these men would have been acceptable to the rank and file of the Democrats. But the convention, which met at Cincinnati on May 1, 1872, was unable to unite on either and on the sixth ballot named Horace Greeley of New York for the Presidency. The Vice-Presidential nomination went to Gratz Brown of Missouri. A worse nomination than that of Greeley could not have been made. Although he ardently desired the termination of misrule in the South and the restoration of the civil and political rights of all former Confederates, he was known to be a devotee of the spoils system in politics and a defender of the high protective tariff. Moreover, despite his abilities as editor of the *New York Tribune*, he was erratic and capricious in his judgments of men and policies. But the most unfortunate aspect of the nomination was the fact that Greeley had been a lifelong foe of the Democracy and all its works. Such was the man whom Democrats were expected to indorse.

Paradoxical as it may seem, not only did the Democracy accept Greeley when it assembled in convention at Baltimore on July 9, but it also gave its approval to the Liberal Republican platform. This campaign document severely arraigned the conduct of the administration in the South, promised the reform of the Civil Service, approved the grant of civil and political rights to the Negroes and opposed the reopening of the questions that had been settled by the Thirteenth, Fourteenth, and Fifteenth Amendments. It will be remembered that but four years earlier the Democratic platform had denounced the Reconstruction Acts as "unconstitutional, revolutionary, and void." This "new departure" (as it was called) on the part of the Democrats meant their abandonment of wartime issues and their acknowledgment that Negro suffrage was an accomplished fact.

Greeley, however, was too much for many Democrats and Liberal Republicans to swallow, with the result that Grant, who as a matter of course had received the regular Republican nomination, was re-elected by an impressive majority. Nevertheless, the appearance of the Liberal Republicans on the scene had two salutary results: the Radicals were frightened into removing most of the remaining disabilities under which former Confederates had been placed by the punitive section of the Fourteenth Amendment; and Grant came to use federal troops at southern elections less frequently. With the screws thus removed, southern whites found it less difficult to regain control over their state governments, as we have seen.

Hardly had Grant been formally reinstalled in the Presidency, on March 4, 1873, when two series of events occurred which were to add further to the long bill of particulars drawn against the Radicals and their titular head, the President. One of these was the panic and industrial depression of 1873; the other was the beginning of revelations of misconduct in office by persons high in the Republican party councils and frequently very close to the President himself. The depression was a typical postwar reaction, aggravated by overexpansion of the railroad net and the absence of central banking control. This permitted banking reserves accumulating in New York to flow into security speculation. The rapid opening of new lands in the West had resulted in the growing of more agricultural staples than could be sold either at home or abroad at profitable prices. The declining purchasing power of the farmers had its repercussions on manufacturing and merchandising, so that boom times in industry suddenly ended. The cessation of railroad construction and the collapse of railroad securities, when the investing public discovered that much of the building from 1865 to 1873 had been speculative, shook the general confidence. Another important reason for sharp recession was the combined facts that the United States, until 1873, had an unfavorable balance of trade and at the same time was a debtor nation. In short, borrowings from Europe paid for imports.

The signal that the panic had arrived in full force was given when on September 8, 1873, the banking house of Jay Cooke and Company announced its bankruptcy. This firm was a heavy investor in the securities of the Northern Pacific Railroad and had resold millions of dollars' worth of bonds to small investors by the same methods it had employed during the war for marketing the government issues. Jay Cooke himself was an unusually pious man and in the eyes of good people throughout the country stood apart markedly from the customary type of Wall Street investment banker. If a person of such sterling qualities could fail, how sound were other houses? The panic's lightning now struck everywhere and for ten days, at the end of September, the New York Stock Exchange was compelled to close its doors. Manufacture and trade fell to about two-thirds of their former level and for five years depression held the country in its grip. The national government did virtually nothing beyond the releasing of some $13 million through the repurchase of government bonds.

The Democrats were quick to take advantage of the situation. With considerable truth, they maintained that the panic had been caused by the orgy of speculation that their opponents had done nothing to prevent but, in fact, had encouraged. Moreover, they rang the changes on misgovernment in the South and they denounced Grantism for its centralizing tendencies and its continued interference in the affairs of some of the as yet "unredeemed" southern states. The exposure of corruption, involving high Republican officials, strengthened the hands of the Democratic critics. It was divulged that Secretary of the Treasury Richardson, in collusion with Representative B. F. Butler, had granted contracts for the collection of a large part of the federal revenues in Massachusetts to one Sanborn, a friend of Butler. Most of the money would have come into the Treasury through the ordinary channels; nevertheless, Sanborn was allowed a commission of 50 per cent for his pains. It was generally believed, though not proved, that both Butler and Richardson shared in the spoils and the gossip attending the disagreeable affair forced Richardson's retirement. In the District of Columbia a somewhat similar tale was disclosed. Here a clique, under the leadership of an official named Shepherd, was found guilty of extravagance, corruption, and oppression. The result was the abolition of the territorial form of government in the District and the establishment of direct Congressional control. It is not insignificant to note, as a commentary on the state of public morality, that Richardson, Butler, and Shepherd continued to enjoy the friendship of Grant.

The Democrats, however, could not plead that their own house was entirely in order, for the affair of the "Tweed Ring," in New York City, was by this time generally known. Tweed, the boss of Tammany Hall (as the Democratic organization in the metropolis had long been called), and his confederates, between 1868 and 1871, stole directly from the city treasury a sum variously put at between $50 million and $100 million. In 1871, the operations of the Ring were revealed with the result that a number of the leaders, Tweed among them, were jailed. Fortunately for the Democrats, punishment for this scandal had been visited on the party in the election of a local reform administration. By 1874, therefore, popular indignation ran much higher against the Republicans so that, in the Congressional elections of that year, the Democrats succeeded in capturing the lower house. Besides, they were victorious in the state elections in such usually Republican strongholds as Pennsylvania, Ohio, and Massachusetts. Because only one-third of the Senate's members were up for re-election, the

Republicans retained their control in that chamber; this circumstance, as we shall see, had a direct bearing on the ultimate determination of the Presidential election two years later.

With the assembling of the Forty-fourth Congress, in December, 1875, the Democratic House set assiduously to work to prepare for the election of 1876. That is, it turned its searchlight on the activities of Republican officialdom, gaining not a little aid from the zeal for ferreting out wrongdoing displayed by a member of Grant's own administration. This was Secretary of the Treasury Bristow, who had succeeded the discredited Richardson. In the spring of 1875 Bristow discovered evidence that there existed in the city of St. Louis a "Whiskey Ring" which had defrauded the government of millions of dollars in internal revenue. The chief accomplice of the ring was a disreputable politician, John McDonald by name, whom Grant had appointed to a responsible position in the internal revenue service in 1870 over the protest of both the Senators from Missouri. While in St. Louis in 1874, when the depredations of the gang were at their height, Grant had been lavishly entertained by McDonald and had accepted a fine pair of horses from him as a present. McDonald, along with a large number of other revenue officials, was convicted, the chief defense of some of the lesser fry being that most of their ill-gotten gains had gone as virtually forced contributions into the Republican campaign fund. Bristow further found that the President's own private secretary, Babcock, was seriously implicated in the affair. Babcock was put on trial but the President placed such obstacles in the way of the prosecution that the verdict of the jury was "not guilty." Although the evidence brought out in the proceedings clearly showed that Babcock had been on intimate terms with McDonald and the others, the President sent to St. Louis a sworn deposition in which he stated that he knew of no wrongdoing by the accused and of nothing suggesting it!

Another scandal, which reflected even more directly on the administration, was one in which the Secretary of War, W. W. Belknap, was the central figure. In this case disclosures made by an investigating committee of the House showed that the Secretary had been guilty of receiving indirectly several thousand dollars each year, since 1870, from an Indian Territory trader for the privilege of retaining a lucrative concession at Fort Sill. The committee recommended that articles of impeachment be brought against the offending officer and the recommendation was unanimously adopted by the House. But before this action was taken Belknap offered his resignation to the President, who accepted it with an alacrity that could only show Grant's sympathy with the offender. Nevertheless, the Senate proceeded with the trial and Belknap was acquitted, not, it seems, because two-thirds of that body were not convinced of his guilt, but rather because a number of Senators felt that they no longer had jurisdiction. Grant's attitude in the Babcock and Belknap cases was not one of regret that men so close to him personally and politically should be found guilty of malfeasance in office. Rather, he regarded the investigations by the Democratic House and by the more honorable members of his own party as propaganda against himself and his Radical friends. He put a similar interpretation on the numerous other exposures made public during the spring and summer of 1876. These proved extravagance, inefficiency, favoritism, and jobbery in nearly every department of the government. When Bristow, in the Treasury, and Jewell, in the Post Office, attempted to clean house, Grant dropped them for their pains—Bristow by a forced resignation, Jewell by open dismissal.

Amid such alarms and excursions, the Presidential canvass of 1876 took place.

THE ELECTION AND ADMINISTRATION OF HAYES

To carry their standard in the Presidential contest of 1876, the Republicans chose Rutherford B. Hayes, a compromise candidate, yet in many ways a thoroughly acceptable one. He came from a pivotal state (Ohio) and had proved his political mettle by three times wresting gubernatorial contests from popular Democrats. He was a Civil War brigadier who had seen one hundred days of actual fighting and had been wounded four times. He was for hard money in a region where inflation was popular. He was a regular party man and when in Congress (1865–67) had voted with his party chiefs for their reconstruction program and had busied himself in pension matters on behalf of Ohio constituents. His public and private life was impeccable, his wife was popular, and the breath of scandal had never touched his name. He was soon to show that he was a man of only average capacity with a conventional cast of mind. But his very mediocrity was attractive, and though he had no loyal friends and no real enemies, his fellow countrymen, after the scandals of the Grant administration, warmed up to him. Hayes was fifty-four years old at the time of his nomination.

The Democrats, as in 1868 and 1872, turned to New York for their candidate and nominated Samuel J. Tilden. He was known as a reformer, had joined in the fight on the Tweed Ring in New York City, and had served a term as governor of New York State. He was one of the most astute and successful lawyers of his day, had done yeoman work in bringing about railroad consolidations, and had become wealthy in the process. He was Hayes's antithesis in many ways: he was a highly cultured person, something of a political theorist, cool, calculating, and secretive as against Hayes's kindliness and simplicity. Though Tilden was perfectly willing to accept the mantle of reform there is no question that during the campaign, as was subsequently revealed by a Congressional investigation, he was aware of dishonorable practices going on about him. He was sixty-two years old when nominated.

The Presidential election of 1876 ended in uncertainty. Tilden carried New York, New Jersey, Connecticut, and Indiana and apparently all the southern states, and appeared to be elected by a comfortable majority in the electoral college. It soon became evident that fraud and violence had been employed in parts of the South, particularly in Louisiana, Florida, and South Carolina. The uneasiness of the ensuing months of November, 1876, to March, 1877, was dissipated only slowly. While there seemed to be Democratic majorities in the three southern states, the electoral offices were controlled by Republicans and they proceeded to attest the certificates of the Republican electors. In South Carolina, this procedure was probably correct; in Florida and Louisiana there was slight legal justification for such action. However, strong pressure was brought to bear on the Florida and Louisiana election or returning boards by a group of northern "Visiting Statesmen." Money was not passed (though all the election boards of the three states at one time or another were for sale) but political promises were given and the probability is, too, that a bargain was made between Democrats and Republicans. Certainly, leading politicians in both camps were engaged in conversations looking toward the complete restoration of white rule in the South in December of that fateful year.

Congress was thus confronted by two sets of returns from Louisiana, South Carolina, and Florida. (There was, too, a contest over a single electoral vote from Oregon.) Congress, with a Republican Senate and Democratic House, found a way out of the dilemma by setting up an electoral commission of fifteen members, made up equally from the House, the Senate, and the Supreme Court bench. It was originally hoped that the commission would stand seven Republican, seven Democratic, and one Independent, and thus permit a settlement of the question on its merits. However, the Independent (Supreme Court Justice Davis) counted upon to hold the balance, suddenly became unavailable with the result that the fifteenth member chosen turned out to be a Republican. The commission easily disposed of its leading difficulty: it resolved not to go back of the returns but to concern itself with determining only which of the two sets of electoral votes had been legally certified. Then by a strictly partisan vote of 8 to 7 in each instance, the electoral commission accepted the certificates of the Republican electors from Louisiana, Florida, South Carolina, and Oregon. On March 2, the final count was taken and Hayes was declared the President by an electoral vote of 185 to 184. There is no question that trouble was averted only by the tender, to southern Democrats, of the most categorical assurances that Hayes would withdraw federal troops from Louisiana and South Carolina, if no dilatory tactics were attempted in the Congress.

Whether it was in fulfilment of this bargain or because he was prompted by an honest desire to end Radical reconstruction of the southern states, Hayes's first concern as President was to withdraw federal troops from the capitals of Louisiana and South Carolina. On April 10, the federal garrison quitted Columbia, S.C., and the northern Carpetbagger who was the governor of the state entrained for the North. On April 24, the same story was repeated in New Orleans, and Louisiana, too, was purged. By these acts, all former Confederate states were once again under white Democratic control, but much of the Radical reconstruction legislation still remained on the federal statute books as a remote but none the less possible threat to such domination.

The lower house of the Forty-fifth Congress (1877–79) was controlled by the Democrats, while in the Senate the Republicans maintained with difficulty a slight lead. The Forty-sixth Congress (1879–81) had Democratic majorities in both houses for the first time in twenty years. In this situation it was natural that the Democratic Congress should make the Enforcement Acts the chief points of its attack. Particularly objectionable were those laws which gave the federal deputy marshals and supervisors the power to regulate elections and to resort to the federal courts in cases of fraud. The best way to embarrass the President was to attach riders to appropriation bills, which the Democratic House proceeded to do, singling out the Army bill as the most vulnerable. In 1877, the Republican Senate refused to accept one such bill and the Army went unprovided for. In 1878, however, Hayes was compelled to capitulate and to put his signature to an Army appropriation bill that took away from the President, at the same time, the right to use troops in election contests. Congress returned to the attack in the next two years and sought to put an end to the use of deputy marshals in elections, passing eight laws that concerned themselves with various aspects of the problem. But Hayes vetoed all these measures and the inability of Congress to muster the two-thirds vote necessary to overcome the Presidential veto left this phase of the Enforcement Laws untouched. It remained for the United States Supreme Court and the Congresses of the eighteen nineties to eradicate the last vestiges of Radical reconstruction legislation.

The most important law passed during the Hayes administration was the Bland-Allison Act of 1878, which called upon the Treasury to purchase between $2 million and $4 million in silver each month. Hayes, true to his "sound" money principles, vetoed the bill, but Congress overrode the Presidential veto. In 1879, Hayes put his signature to the Arrears of Pensions Act, a frank piece of class legislation designed to enrich Civil War veterans and their dependents in the sum of almost a quarter of a billion dollars. In

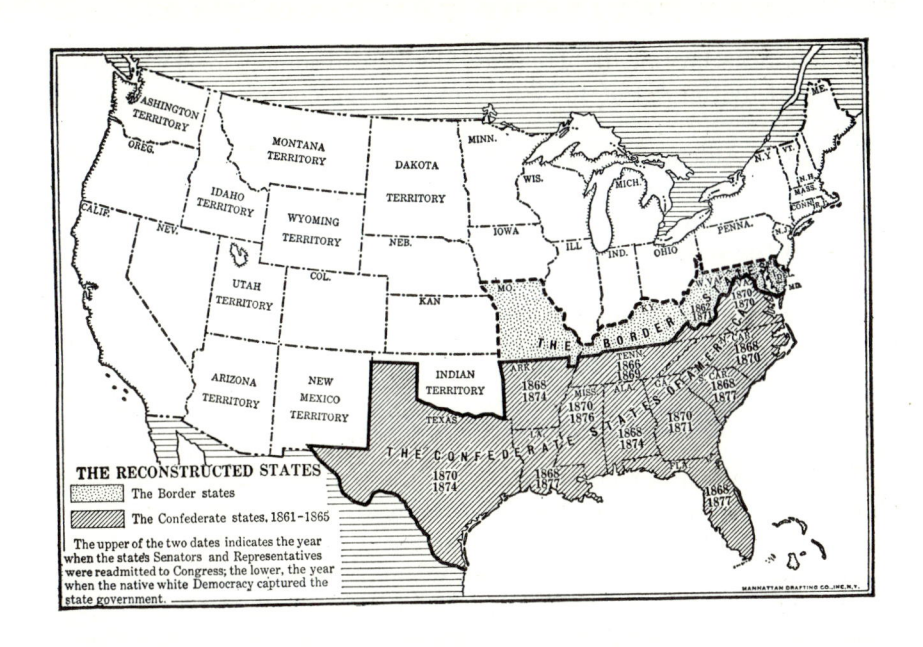

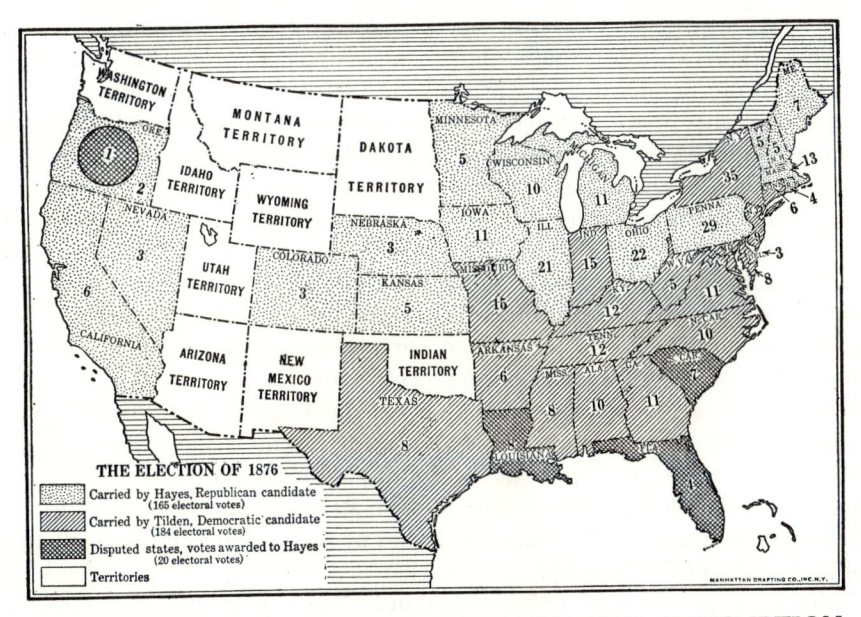

THE PROCESSES OF RECONSTRUCTION AND REDEMPTION
IN THE SOUTH

1879, too, Secretary of the Treasury Sherman resumed specie payments, as directed by the Act of 1875, thus putting the country again on a gold basis.

Hayes's Presidential term ended auspiciously. Governmental scandals were things of the past, the South was now going its own way, party feuds were less rampant. Hayes had indicated his lack of interest in a second term with the result that Republican leaders, generally, failed to include him in their councils. But his reputation was secure, for he had been an important agent in closing those wounds that politicians had kept open a full ten years after the Civil War's end.

EMERGENCE OF THE NEW SOUTH

The Civil War and reconstruction left the old South broken, it seemed almost beyond repair: victorious Northern armies had destroyed whole sections of the countryside; railroads were run down and their equipment was antiquated; at least one-fourth of white southern manhood had been slain; as a result of the promises of the Carpetbaggers, the laboring population—the Negroes—had been left recalcitrant and indisposed toward regular employment. Forty years had to go by before southern property was again worth what it had been in 1860. Not until the late seventies were southern cotton farmers able to raise as large a crop as had been harvested in the year before war broke out. In time, the normal round of living was once more restored; but the old South, as a way of life, had slipped into the past, along with Emerson's Concord of the Middle Period.

A new South emerged, new in many different and curious ways. For one, the section's dominance in the political and economic spheres was never to be regained. All those policies that the South of the antebellum period had steadfastly opposed were firmly written into the scheme of the national system by 1877: the opening of the free lands of the West, the protective tariff, federal support of great railroad projects, a governmentally sustained banking system. The South was eclipsed politically through the carving of new states out of the western territories; it was eclipsed economically when wheat and meat products supplanted cotton as the country's leading export. The South had become a minor geographical division of the United States; indeed, its representatives were to be found less frequently at the council tables of the nation than those of any other portion of the country.

Slowly, new industrial activities began to make their appearance. First, cotton mills sprang up in increasing number; railroad building was resumed; lumbering and the manufacture of furniture took on importance; tobacco factories (in North Carolina and Virginia) and iron and steel plants (in the Chattanooga-Birmingham district) **came to figure promi-**

nently in the South's new economy. By 1900, almost $1 billion was invested in southern manufacturing establishments. The new industrialists, in the beginning, were not northern men, nor were they financed by northern capital: many were members of the old planter aristocracy, many were younger sons compelled to seek their fortunes in trade, a considerable number were professional men from whose savings the funds were obtained for the inception of these enterprises. These local enterprisers and capitalists gradually consolidated their economic and political power so that, by the nineties, they had formed important financial connections with the North and were, too, in control of the seats of government. The rule of this so-called "Bourbon Democracy" had two significant results.

Imperceptibly, the cultural life of the South underwent a transformation as the area came to be joined economically to the Middle Atlantic and East North Central states. Just as the greater weight of northern arms and dollars had been able to crush the old South's economic system, so the more vigorous habits of living of the North could not be denied. The antebellum South lingered in the memories of the womenfolk and in the romantic writings of a Cable or a Page. The traditions of chivalry and old-world hospitality and of a cultural affinity with Georgian England now and then were spoken of as though still alive; but those days were irretrievably gone. Everywhere, the South gave way before the onrush of the North: in manners, in taste, even in architecture. The saddest phase of the South's defeat was its cultural submergence. It would not be stretching the facts too much to say that before the nineteenth century had closed the South had become merely an appanage of New York and the Ohio Valley.

In this way the Bourbon Democracy, unconsciously or not, achieved an outstanding success; in the political arena, however, its supremacy was to be contested by an uprising of the southern white masses. As the last decade of the nineteenth century opened, the small independent white farmers of the up-countries of many of the southern states entered the political lists to wrest control from the conservative white masters of the South. Their grievances were many. They resented the sway of the Bourbon Democracy over government and in economic life. They suffered from a stringency of credit, heavy mortgage debts, the depredations of the railroad managers. They were compelled to bear a disproportionate share of the public debt burden. They were alarmed at the way in which the Negro voters were regularly being used by the liquor interests to defeat state programs for local option.

What happened in South Carolina was typical of the triumphs which the white masses won in most of the other states of the cotton and black belt. In 1890, this faction captured the Democratic party of South Carolina, elected its chief, Benjamin R. Tillman, governor, and refused to return to the United States Senate the leader of the local Bourbons, though he was none other than General Wade Hampton, who had won the state from Carpetbag rule in 1876 to 1877. It then proceeded in this and the succeeding years to make its victory secure by the enactment of legislative measures and the writing of a new constitution. Most important among the reforms effected were the following: the vesting in the state railway commission of the power to fix rates; a more equitable distribution of taxes; the funding of the state debt; the decentralization of government, with greater powers placed in the hands of the counties; a decrease in the representation of the low country in the state legislature; greater public expenditures for education; the creation of a state monopoly over the sale of alcoholic beverages; the legal disfranchisement of the Negro, and the adoption of the direct primary. These last two expedients were resorted to in order to end the manipulation of the Negro vote by the Bourbons and the foes of Prohibition. In 1894, Tillman was elected to the United States Senate, where, in time, he was joined by other southern Senators representing similar constituencies.

Nor did the white masses move against the local Bourbon Democracy alone. They joined hands, in the same decade, with the farmers of the West, repudiated the leadership of Cleveland, and in 1892 helped in the formation of the Populist party. Though Populism, as we shall see, soon passed from the national scene, it lingered on in the southern states until the first world war, generally as a faction in the Democratic party, and its outstanding accomplishment was that it made certain the overthrow of the old aristocratic tradition. Since World War I, southern state governments have been dominated in the main by commercial, industrial, and financial interests and the old agrarian Populist faction has suffered almost total eclipse.

THE POLITICAL, CIVIL, AND SOCIAL STATUS OF THE NEGRO

The re-establishment of white mastery in the southern states was effected by a number of devices which ranged from terrorism and economic pressure to solemn constitutional enactment. The Ku Klux Klan, in the first decade after the Civil War, sought to keep the Negroes from the polls forcibly; the use of poll taxes, the familiar methods of machine politics, the Negroes' apathy, and the indifference of Republican politicians—all these were factors in the further attainment of the desired result.

Beginning with the eighteen nineties, the commonly existing Negro disfranchisement was given the sanction of law. First in Mississippi in 1890, and then later in most of the southern states, largely to prevent the Negro vote from being employed in contests between white groups, new constitutional provisions were written to make the exercise of the suffrage dependent upon a series of qualifications that most Negroes did not possess. The so-called "grandfather clause," which was to be found generally in these constitutions, established a privileged body of voters who were not called upon to comply with any other requirements. In effect, these laws permitted the registration on a voting list, to be open for varying lengths of time, of those persons who had served in the armies of the United States or the Confederacy, or who were the descendants of such soldiers, or who had had the right to vote in the state of their residence before January, 1867. Obviously, most whites automatically qualified and most Negroes did not. For such as were not able to register under the "grandfather clause," the satisfaction of the following tests was demanded: 1. a fairly long term of residence, usually two years in the same state; 2. the payment of a poll tax; 3. the ability to read and write any section of the state or federal constitution and to indicate to the registration officials an understanding of its significance. As an alternative to this last, which came to be called the "understanding clause," the applicant for voting privileges might submit proof of the possession of a small amount of property, usually to the value of $250.

The "grandfather clauses" were permitted to stand on the statute books of the southern states, without judicial interference, until they had run their terms. When, however, Oklahoma, in its constitution of 1910, sought to establish a permanent body of privileged voters by providing that a registration list of the kind described was to be kept open indefinitely, the Supreme Court in 1915 intervened and declared the section in violation of the Fifteenth Amendment.

The creation of the white primary made white rule doubly certain. Through the passage of enabling acts by southern state legislatures, political parties were given the right to fix their own rules for party membership and for participation in primary elections. The elimination of the Negro has been easy, therefore, in those states where the Republican party exists only nominally and where all election contests are settled in the Democratic primaries. Even in those southern states where the Republican party can gather a respectable minority, white members control. Thus, the North Carolina state Republican platform of 1922, for example, carried this pledge: "We deplore the attempts of the Democratic party to drag the Negro question into any campaign. The Republican party of North Carolina is an organization of white men and women. It has no intention of appointing Negroes to office within the state." [1]

---

[1] Such members of the Republican party are known as "lily-white" Republicans. In the case of the white primaries, it should be borne in mind that Negro disfranchisement is effected not through legislative fiat but by party rule. Texas was the only one among the southern states to establish the white primary by law (1923); but four years later the Supreme Court found the statute unconstitutional on the ground of violation of the Fourteenth Amendment.

No real efforts were made by the federal government to continue as the guardian over the Negro's civil rights from 1877 to 1890. In the latter year the Republican party made a last unavailing attempt to put teeth once more into the Civil Rights Laws of reconstruction days. The only important effect of this belated Federal Election or Force bill was to strengthen the hands of those southerners who were urging their fellow citizens to place Negro disfranchisement in the state constitutions. In a sense the southern state constitutional amendments, already noted, were the southern answers to this bill. Meanwhile, the Supreme Court had made the enforcement of the laws next to impossible, for, in a group of decisions handed down in the seventies and eighties, the Court, in defining the status of the blacks under the Thirteenth, Fourteenth, and Fifteenth Amendments, held that relief against oppression, when practiced by individuals or groups, was to be found only in state agencies. Thus, it was a recognition of the southern doctrine that political rule properly belonged in the hands of the white citizenry. In 1894, the Democracy, for the first time since the Civil War in control of all branches of the federal government, gladly accepted this circumscription of federal powers and repealed what was left of the Reconstruction Acts. Thus, it devolved upon southern lawmakers to guarantee the Negro equality before the laws. To a very large extent this has been effected and, except for the denial of the right to serve on juries and in cases where attack upon a white woman [2] by a Negro is charged, the Negroes of the South receive about as much civil justice as do whites of the same economic class.

Social equality, however, the Negro does not possess and "Jim Crow" laws and segregation acts are to be found on the statute books of all the southern states. Under these, southern Negroes are compelled to use separate hotels, restaurants, and street and railway cars and to abstain from making their residence in certain localities. The same is true of schools and colleges. In 1875, to check segregation of this sort, Congress passed a law guaranteeing the Negro against social disabilities by the southern states and municipalities; but in 1883 the Supreme Court found the act unconstitutional on the ground of undue interference with the rights of the states. Since 1915, however, the Court has been moving against housing segregation. State statutes and municipal ordinances to this effect have been held in contravention of the Negro's constitutional rights; in 1948, the Court declared private "restrictive covenants" barring Negroes from residence or purchase in certain areas to be nonenforceable in the federal courts. During the nineteen thirties and forties, in fact, the Court stood steadfast in its determination that Negroes were to possess equal civil rights and educational facilities. In 1944, the Court found the "white

[2] The southern practice of lynching Negroes charged with this and certain other crimes has declined: recorded lynchings dropped from 106 in 1900 to 20 in 1930, the total for the period 1940 to 1947 was 26.

primary" unconstitutional and later barred evasion of that judgment by state laws divorcing party practices from official election machinery. The number of Negroes voting in the South tripled between 1938 and 1946; and schools and other public facilities were improving.

The Negro population in the United States presents several curious demographic aspects. From 1860 to 1900, the total number of Negroes in the country exactly doubled; from 1900 to 1940, their increase was but one-third as much again. Over the same periods, the relative numerical importance of the group seriously declined. In 1790, the Negroes made up one-fifth of the country's total population; by 1860, they represented one-seventh; by 1900, one-eighth; by 1940, less than one-tenth. The increase of the white population through immigration almost entirely accounted for the proportionate outnumbering of the Negroes. But with the raising of bars against newcomers, beginning with the nineteen twenties, and with the birth-death ratio very much the same for both whites and blacks, the Negro's numerical strength in the population will probably not dwindle. The following table presents the relative increases for both racial groups since 1850.

THE NEGROES IN THE AMERICAN POPULATION

Year	Per Cent Increase Over Preceding Decade Whites	Negroes	Per Cent of Population Negro	Negroes per 1000 Whites
1850	37.7	26.6	15.7	186
1860	37.7	24.2	14.1	165
1870	27.5	21.4	13.5	157
1880	26.4	23.2	13.1	152
1890	26.7	16.2	12.3	142
1900	21.2	17.1	11.6	132
1910	22.3	11.5	10.7	120
1920	16.0	6.3	9.9	111
1930	15.7	13.6	9.7	109
1940	7.2	8.2	9.8	107

The Negro continued to be largely a resident of the South although the proportion of southern Negroes to whites showed steady decreases. In 1860, 92.9 per cent of all Negroes in the country lived in the southern states; in 1900, the proportion was 89.7 per cent; by the end of the nineteen thirties, almost 25 per cent of the nation's Negroes were living outside the South. The following states had large Negro groups in their populations at the turn of the century. It will be observed how markedly the percentage of Negroes in them declined over the period 1900 to 1940.

PERCENTAGE OF POPULATION NEGRO IN CERTAIN SOUTHERN STATES

	1900	*1940*
Alabama	45.2	34.7
Florida	43.7	27.1
Georgia	46.7	34.7
Louisiana	47.1	35.9
Mississippi	58.6	49.2
South Carolina	58.4	42.9
Virginia	35.6	24.7

The years since emancipation have seen four considerable movements of Negro population, namely: to the Southwest, to the cities of the South, to the metropolitan centers of the North, and, during the period 1941 to 1948, to smaller industrial cities in the mid-West and to the Pacific Coast (of the 700,000 Negroes moving to war industry centers, 250,000 went to Los Angeles, San Francisco, and the Portland-Vancouver area). The first movement took place mainly between 1870 and 1895, when new cotton lands were being opened up in Arkansas, Texas, and Oklahoma. For the most part, the Negroes were taken along as hired laborers by white southern farmers who were migrating there at that time. The second movement was a part of the general urbanization that began in the South in the eighties and gained momentum from the low price of cotton prevailing in the nineties. The third movement received its initial impetus from the labor shortage existing in the large northern cities during World War I and continued with only slight abatement during the next twenty years. The general line of movement was from southern rural areas to southern cities, thence to the northern metropolises and other industrial centers. By 1947, a majority of the Negro population (estimated at more than 14,000,000) was, for the first time, living in urban areas like Mobile and Birmingham in the South and New York, Chicago, Philadelphia, Detroit, and Cleveland in the North.

> Section II
> PARTY GOVERNMENT AND
> PUBLIC AFFAIRS

· 4 ·

The Embattled Politicians

THE PARTY HOSTS AND THEIR CHIEFTAINS

THE political record of the post-Civil War period is perhaps the most unsatisfactory one to contemplate in American history. It was not petulance, but the sober judgment of years of detachment which made Henry Adams, writing in 1905, say of it: "One might search the whole list of Congress, judiciary, and executive during the twenty-five years 1870 to 1895, and find little but damaged reputation. The period was poor in purpose and barren in results." Never in American history was politics quite so divorced from reality. The stage was set for the enactment of a great drama. The generation following the Civil War saw the final subjugation of a vast continent and its settlement by an extraordinary mélange of peoples, many unfamiliar with Anglo-Saxon institutions; it witnessed the conversion of a handicrafts culture into an industrial civilization; it beheld the transformation of a rural economy into an urban life; it lived in a day when there began to develop an awareness of the outside world which only Jefferson and his contemporaries had felt.

In the contests of the political parties one might have expected leadership in the shaping of these forces. Yet statesmanship was never quite so uninspired, nor statesmen so inadequate. The Republican party, by 1870, had attracted to itself all those elements which regarded it with suspicion in 1860; by opposing inflation, by championing the high-tariff interests, by maintaining an attitude of detachment in the face of the depredations of the railroads and the exploitation of the country's natural resources, it had become the party of industrial capitalism. But, so, too, had the Democratic party. If Harrison was a corporation lawyer and, on the face of his record, entirely satisfactory, to large business groups, so was Tilden. If Hayes was a "hard" money man and opposed to all schemes of inflation, so was Cleveland. If Blaine and McKinley could be trusted on tariff matters, so, too, could Democratic leaders like Gorman and Hill. The key to the situation is this fact: political parties had become institutionalized, quite as much, let us say, as had the churches, organized philanthropy, or corporate business. They owned buildings, operated newspapers, had by every known tie of loyalty attached to themselves great bodies of paid retainers, appreciative friends, and economic groups which sought and had already obtained franchises, licenses, privileges, and immunities. The two parties were vested interests—and a vested interest cannot afford to be intransigent. Regularity was a necessity; irregularity meant obscurity and the end of political careers. In short, the two great parties that dominated American political affairs after the Civil War would not move with American life because everything was to be gained by standing still.

By 1874, two definite factions had appeared in the ranks of the Republican party, struggling for the control of the organization. The so-called "Stalwarts" were led by Conkling, Cameron, Logan, and Morton, and their common characteristic was that they were the political friends of Grant. The so-called "Half-Breeds" were led by Blaine, Sherman, Garfield, and Hoar, standing together in their opposition to their titular chief. It is a mistake to believe that at any time was either of these groups actuated by a definite body of political convictions—let alone economic principles. The members of the factions were individuals loosely banded together for partisan purposes and their own personal advantage. It is worth while pausing to examine the careers of those two men who, beyond all others, stood for the Republicanism of the day.

James G. Blaine was born in Pennsylvania in 1830 and, at the age of twenty-four, already married, moved to Augusta, Maine, where by the aid of his wife's relatives he set himself up as the publisher and editor of a small local newspaper. From 1861 until his death in 1893 he made politics his leading interest and his chief economic support. He was successively a member of the Maine House of Representatives (1861–62), a member of Congress (1862–76), Speaker of the House (1869–75), Senator from Maine (1876–81), Secretary of State under Garfield and Harrison, and once the standard-bearer of the Republican party (1884). From 1876 until he died he was ever seriously regarded as a contender for the Republican Presidential nomination and if it had not been for an unsavory scandal in which he figured, he might have graced the Presidential chair. It is an interesting commentary on the period that despite the fact that his name cannot be associated with a single piece of legislative work of any importance or a political precept no matter how obvious (except, possibly, his desire to see closer relations established with Latin American nations), the figure of Blaine to his contemporaries was cast in an heroic mold. He was undoubtedly the most popular personage of his generation. He dazzled college presidents, financiers, workingmen, and farmers and numbered among his admirers even Andrew D. White and Harry Thurston Peck! When he was called

THE EMBATTLED POLITICIANS 63

a plumed knight by Ingersoll, the name stuck and nobody saw anything comic in such a designation for a man who as late as the eighties could still fan the flames of sectional hatred for political advantage and who had openly been proved to have used his office for financial gain. From the point of view of political principle, there was nothing to distinguish him from a thousand party hacks. He voted the straight party reconstruction program, favored the impeachment of Johnson, was a "sound" money man, championed the protective tariff, was not averse to twisting the British lion's tail, and was the vocal friend of the Civil War veteran. The key to his prominence is undoubtedly to be found in the fact that everything he did was so exciting. He was, in brief, a popular hero and in the same line of American idols that has included Admiral Dewey and Theodore Roosevelt. Blaine's lifelong quarrel with Conkling was watched with sympathetic interest by thousands who had not the slightest suspicion of what it was about; his vindictive attack on Jefferson Davis in 1876 was cheered to the echo by a whole section of the nation; he made international affairs a subject of household debate in 1881 and people once more began to regard England as the traditional foe just because it would not give way before him. Blaine always wanted to be President and, never having attained that goal, he died a disappointed man.

Roscoe Conkling of New York was his opposite in almost every way. Where Blaine was charming, scintillating, the proud possessor of hosts of friends, Conkling was arrogant and cruel. He had built up a great personal political machine in New York and had been elected to Congress and the Senate because he knew how to cultivate all the more obscure arts of politics. In 1858, when he first took his seat in the House, he was only twenty-nine years old. In 1867 he went to the Senate where he remained until 1881, when Garfield and Blaine were responsible for his retirement from public life. He figured prominently in the work of the Joint Committee of Fifteen on Reconstruction and was the first one publicly to divulge that the Fourteenth Amendment was written as much in the interests of private property as to protect the civil liberties of the Negro.[1] Politically, there was not much to distinguish him from Blaine. He was for high tariffs and the contraction of the currency, waved the bloody shirt, and believed implicitly in the spoils system. Civil service reform was "snivel service" to him and G. W. Curtis, its leader, was a "man-milliner in politics."[2] In 1876, he was a seeker after the Republican nomination and in 1880 he led the Grant third-term forces. Because he hated Blaine, he was cool toward Garfield and gave support to the Ohioan's candidacy only reluctantly.

[1] See B. B. Kendrick, *Journal of the Joint Committee of Fifteen on Reconstruction* (1914).
[2] Because Curtis regularly wrote for *Harper's Bazaar*, a popular women's magazine,

Outside of the two factions led by Blaine and Conkling, in an erratic orbit moved a group at different times denominated Independent Republicans, Liberal Republicans, and Mugwumps. They represented the reformers in the party and had little influence in party councils. In 1872, they seceded and supported Greeley as against Grant, forcing their candidate on the distraught Democratic party. In the preconvention contest of 1876, they backed Bristow but did not fight Hayes when he received the nomination. In 1880, they stood resolutely against Grant's renomination and compelled the choice of Garfield as a compromise candidate. In 1884, they opposed Blaine in the convention and when he was nominated some of them supported Cleveland.

The Democratic party was less torn by faction, largely because its long exile from the seat of the national government had militated against the appearance of personal rivalries. Such leaders as it had were prominent state politicians, like Tilden and Cleveland of New York, Thurman of Ohio, and Hendricks of Indiana. In national contests the Democrats could count only upon the South, which by 1880 was hardened solid. Strong local organizations in New York, New Jersey, and Connecticut, and disaffection among the farmers of the Ohio Valley, particularly in Indiana and Ohio, occasionally led these states to return Democratic electors. The Republican party, on the other hand, could normally count on the industrial East and the agrarian West. To the East, it posed as the protector of industrialism, the destroyer of the slave power of the South and the defender of economic laissez-faire; to the West, it could say justly that it had passed the Homestead Act of 1862 and thus had given the western farmers their free lands.

Generally speaking, the sections voted in national elections along the lines indicated above, but when it came to economic legislation party ties were held very lightly indeed. Throughout the seventies and the eighties almost every piece of Congressional legislation that had important economic implications was passed by votes that cut across parties. On such matters as the currency and banking, the tariff, public lands, internal improvements, regulation of railways, control of trusts, and immigration, there were sectional divisions, irrespective of party loyalties, with the West and South generally arrayed against the North and East. Sectionalism, in American history, was of course no new phenomenon. Ever since the Colonial interior counties had taken their common stand against the tidewater, sectionalism has played an important role in American life. But in this period particularly, because of the bankruptcy of party leadership, sectional antagonisms were especially marked. The agricultural West and South, loaded with debt and exploited by railroads, banks, and land speculators, were joined by common bonds of interest against the industrial and capitalistic North and East. We shall have occasion to see, in the discussions of legislation affecting the tariff, banking and currency, and railroads, something of the character of the sectional antipathies that existed in the period following the close of the Civil War.

GARFIELD AND ARTHUR

The Stalwarts, who came to the Republican convention of 1880 determined to nominate Grant once more, had won the first maneuver in forcing the choice of Cameron of Pennsylvania as chairman of the Republican National Committee. Conkling had gained control over the New York delegation; Logan came with Illinois pledged; and Pennsylvania was prepared to follow Cameron. Blaine and Sherman were the choices of the Half-Breeds; the Independents were supporting Senator Edmunds of Vermont. Garfield was a prominent figure in the early proceedings, as Sherman's manager and as general conciliator in the interests of party harmony. But Conkling met his first defeat when the convention, following Garfield and not himself, refused to accept his resolution committing the states to the observance of the unit rule. On the thirty-sixth ballot, when it was apparent that neither Grant nor Blaine could possibly be nominated, the delegates turned to the man who had served his party best in the stormy proceedings—by his temperance, his good humor, his conciliatory and wise spirit—and selected not Sherman but his friend and colleague James A. Garfield. Chester A. Arthur of New York, ousted Collector of the New York Port, friend of Conkling and Stalwart politician, received the nomination for the Vice-Presidency in the hope that Conkling and Grant would support the national ticket.

Garfield of Ohio appeared to be a model candidate. He was a handsome man with a massive head and a rough strong face. He had early learned the arts of oratory (as lay preacher and teacher) and was known far and wide for his forensic skill in a day when the forms of mass entertainment were limited and listening to orations ranked with the major amusements. His parents had migrated from Massachusetts to Ohio where Garfield had been born in a log cabin in 1831. His boyhood had been one of toil, and education had been wrested only by dint of the greatest sacrifice. He had taught school and at twenty-six was the principal of the Hiram Eclectic Institute from which he had graduated. Admitted to the bar in 1859, he relinquished thoughts of a legal career to volunteer with the outbreak of the Civil War. He became a brigadier general, served as a staff officer under Rosecrans in the Tennessee campaigns and was mustered out a major general in 1863, when he was elected to a seat in the House. From 1863 to 1880 he served his party faithfully. He was successively chairman of the Military Affairs Committee, the Banking and Currency Committee, and the Appropriations Committee. In 1876, in the interest of Hayes's election, Garfield was one of the Republican "Visiting Statesmen" to New Orleans, where he stayed for eighteen days and did yeoman service. Then he returned to Washington to sit on the electoral commission which chose Hayes. During the Hayes administration he was the minority leader of his party in the lower house. Considering himself a scholar and a student of English political economy, Garfield had elaborated a set of convictions that made him an eminently satisfactory representative to the industrial constituency which he served. He favored a tariff that protected infant industries. In 1866, he evolved a curious formula whose basis was "that free trade which can be reached only through protection," and though in the Presidential campaign he was to follow the dictates of the party leaders and say nothing about a fine balance between protection and free trade he still prided himself upon having held "that equipoise." To his contemporaries, Garfield was a cultured person: Hayes thought he might have been a successful "metaphysician"; Hoar believed he "could have attained greatness as . . . a mathematician, in any of the exact sciences, as a linguist. . . ." Actually, he knew next to nothing about music, art, and science, and while his intellectual interests were wide, apparently none of them was based on profound knowledge. He had many friends, Blaine, Sherman, and Hoar among them. Yet none appeared really to trust him. Long after he had fallen by an assassin's bullet, they spoke of him as a timid, vacillating, time-serving person (these are Hoar's words); who easily changed his mind (so said Sherman); who was not a moral force (so said Hayes). Conkling disliked him; Grant was openly disdainful.

To the Democrats, meeting shortly after the Republican convention, Tilden was no longer available. The wily Republican politicians had robbed him of his halo of martyrdom when a House investigating committee in 1878 made public a group of telegrams that proved, by implication, that Tilden must have been aware of efforts to sell southern electoral votes to his managers. In view of the fact that the Democratic campaign had been run from his own home and a close relative figured in the interchange of the damaging dispatches, the inference was inevitable. Tilden was eliminated and the choice fell on General Winfield S. Hancock of Pennsylvania. He had had a distinguished Civil War career, came from a manufacturing state, and at the same time had made many friends in the South because of the mildness of his rule as the military commander of the reconstructed states of Louisiana and Texas.

The management of the Garfield campaign was largely in Blaine's hands, though, ironically enough, Conkling and Grant saved the day for the Republican candidate. The course of the campaign saw Garfield's character besmirched: the country was reminded that Garfield had figured in the Crédit Mobilier scandal and that he had received an excessive fee of $5000 in a paving-contract fraud of which the city of Washington was the victim. He was cool toward Civil Service reform and backed up the attempts of his managers to force campaign contributions from the federal officeholders. The September Maine election resulted in the victory of a Greenback governor. Only then, with Ohio and Indiana imperiled, did the sulking Conkling and Grant yield to importunities. Conkling spoke in New York; Grant and Conkling went to Ohio; and Conkling took charge of affairs in Indiana, a Greenback state, where, by using all those political devices of which he was past master, he succeeded in holding Indiana for the Republican party. Indiana went Republican by 7000 votes and Ohio by 23,000 in the elections which took place in October. Garfield's election was assured. In November it was seen that he had defeated Hancock by an electoral vote of 214 against 155 and that he had carried every northern state, except New Jersey, and the whole West and Far West, with the exception of Nevada and a part of the electoral vote of California. Nearly ten million votes were cast, five-sixths of the total possible vote. Despite the fact, too, that the whole contest was devoid of a single issue, less than 4 per cent of the electorate voted for a protest candidate (General Weaver of the Greenback party). The Forty-seventh Congress, elected at the same time, had a sizable Republican majority in the lower house.

After Conkling's first address in Ohio, Garfield had said to him: "Conkling, you have saved me! Whatever man can do for man, that will I do for you!" But Blaine dominated the administration, the Cabinet, and the distribution of the Presidential rewards. Blaine was chosen Secretary of State, William Windom received the Treasury, Robert T. Lincoln (Abraham Lincoln's son) was given the War Department. The only concession made to the Stalwarts was the selection of the Postmaster-General, who came from New York and who was a lieutenant of Conkling. However, small comfort was to be had in the appointment in view of the fact that this Cabinet officer was an avowed Civil Service reformer. The gage of battle was thrown down quickly by Blaine and Garfield when the President, in the list of the Presidential appointments submitted to the Senate, included the name of W. H. Robertson, Conkling's most prominent personal and political enemy in New York, for the post of New York Port Collector. The battle raged for two months and then Conkling and his colleague Platt, seeing that the Senate was prepared to uphold the President on the issue of the control of the patronage, resigned their seats and returned to Albany to seek vindication at the hands of the New York legislature.[3] Fifty-six ballots were taken before Conkling and Platt were willing to concede defeat. They were not returned; Conkling was definitely through with politics; and Grant was led to remark contemptuously: "I will never again lend my active aid to the support of a

[3] At that time Senators were elected by state legislatures.

Presidential candidate who has not strength enough to appear before a convention as a candidate.... Garfield has shown that he is not possessed of the backbone of an angleworm." The fight that Hayes and Garfield had made against the Senate on the patronage issue marked the doom of the Tenure of Office Act of 1867, and in 1886 the law was repealed.

It was the lot of Garfield to reap the harvest he had sown. Having made politics his lifework, and being thus dependent upon the good wishes of hosts of persons, he found his days filled listening to the claims of hungry office seekers. It was the contemporary belief that the President found it necessary to give up one-third of his working time to the patronage. In the midst of these irksome tasks, and with the tale of scandal already sounding in his ears because of the exposure of frauds in the Post Office, Garfield met his fatal wounding at the hands of a demented assassin, July 2, 1881. On September 19 he died and Chester A. Arthur was President of the United States.

Arthur was a college graduate, a successful lawyer who had demonstrated his ability in the difficult post of quartermaster-general of New York State during the Civil War, and a tactful and wise politician. He was Conkling's perfect lieutenant, and while his chief used the weapons of scorn and terror, he held the loyalty of men by the ties of friendship. That he was a machine politician was unquestionably true. But he was no more rapacious in the manipulation of the New York custom house offices than had been De Witt Clinton or Martin Van Buren. That he felt the Presidential displeasure in 1877, which resulted in his removal, was due to an obscure intrigue and not entirely to Hayes's zeal for reform. For Hayes was perfectly willing to reward the members of the Louisiana returning board for their good work in his behalf in 1876, and he accepted complacently the levying of assessments on the federal officeholders. Arthur had severe handicaps to labor under. It is to his credit to say that he emerged with flying colors. His administration was quietly conducted, his old political friends were unostentatiously put in their places, and he left office with a series of distinct achievements to his credit. During his administration was passed the first Civil Service law, the Chinese immigration question was definitely settled, and the first ships of the modern American Navy were authorized. In 1882, he dared to put his veto on a rivers and harbors bill that carried appropriations of $18 million.

Foreshadowing change to come, the Forty-eighth Congress, elected in 1882, had a large Democratic majority in the lower house. The same year saw a Democratic resurgence in the states, where nine normally Republican commonwealths chose Democrats as governors. Among the more prominent of these was Grover Cleveland of New York.

THE RETURN OF THE DEMOCRACY

In June, 1884, the Republican national convention named Blaine as its candidate with General John A. Logan, Illinois Stalwart, as his running mate. The Democratic standard was placed in the hands of Grover Cleveland, "available" for many reasons: he was from New York, a large and doubtful state; he had been a reform governor and a foe of Tammany Hall; he was a Presbyterian; a conservative; and a straight-party man. The Independent Republicans were torn between conflicting emotions. They had opposed Blaine's nomination in the preconvention contest, but at the convention they had been compelled to watch helplessly as the delegates were stampeded by the friends of that incomparable politician from Maine. The Independent Republicans represented the best talents in the party: many of them were earnest, sincere, not entirely unambitious younger men, who vainly hoped that party contests might be raised to planes of greater dignity, if not thoughtfulness. Curtis, Schurz, the militant preacher Henry Ward Beecher, the college presidents White of Cornell and Eliot of Harvard, those scions of respectable American families, Theodore Roosevelt of New York and Henry Cabot Lodge of Massachusetts, were the leaders of the Independents who sought to purge Republicanism of Blaine and machine politics. But Blaine was nominated by a turbulent and enthusiastic host and exile surely awaited those who did not stay regular. Roosevelt and Lodge campaigned for Blaine, hoping for more propitious times; Curtis, Beecher, Schurz, Eliot, and some of the lesser lights drank the poisoned cup—they supported Cleveland. For this act of courage, they were ridiculed roundly (Dana of the *Sun* called them "Mugwumps," and because the name was such an amusing one it clung), and they lived to see themselves disregarded by the party they had rallied to and forgotten by the party they had deserted.

There were no issues in the contest of 1884. The inevitable result was that the campaign degenerated into one of personal vilification which left none of the principals involved unsullied. It was discovered that Cleveland was the father of an illegitimate child. Cleveland admitted the truth of the charge, while his supporters were quick to point out that he had properly provided for both the victims of a youthful indiscretion. The Democrats, on their side, charged that Blaine had never satisfactorily cleared up his relationship with the Union Pacific Railroad in the matter of the defunct Little Rock and Fort Smith Railroad. It was this scandal that dogged Blaine's footsteps until the day of his death. In 1876, Blaine had cleverly obtained possession of a collection of letters held by one Mulligan, which unmistakably showed that Blaine had indulged in some sharp practices of which his friends in Maine had turned out to be the victims. He had sold them bonds in the landgrant Little Rock and Fort

Smith Railroad; when that road had failed to pay its obligations, he had been compelled to reimburse his friends; he had then turned around and sold his worthless bonds for $64,000 to the Union Pacific. In 1876, reading excerpts to Congress from the captured Mulligan letters, Blaine had for the nonce triumphantly vindicated himself. Nevertheless, the story had stood in his way in 1876 and in 1880, and was to contribute toward his defeat in 1884, for the Democrats printed not Blaine's version but the original letters themselves. They, alas, proved Blaine's guilt.

Tired, probably dispirited, Blaine, in the last days of the campaign, permitted an utterance to be made in his presence that broke another storm about his head. A visiting Baptist clergyman named Burchard rhetorically condemned the Democracy as the party of "Rum, Romanism, and Rebellion." Blaine failed to rebuke the pastor and the next day it was already too late: Catholic New York City was alienated. New York went Democratic by only 1149 votes of the total of one million cast in the state; Blaine lost as well the pivotal states of New Jersey, Connecticut, and Indiana. The final electoral vote showed 219 for Cleveland and 182 for Blaine. The popular vote showed a scant Cleveland plurality of 23,000 out of more than ten million ballots cast. The Democrats also carried the lower house, though the Senate still remained Republican. The Democracy had returned to power after the lapse of a quarter of a century.

Cleveland was forty-eight years old when he took the oath of office. He had been born in Caldwell, New Jersey, the son of a Presbyterian minister who died soon afterward; he had an early life of toil, no formal education, no inspiring friendships. At the age of fourteen he was a clerk in a small country grocery store; at the age of seventeen he was living in Buffalo seeking his fortune. Befriended by an uncle, he was induced to study for the bar, and in 1859 he was a practicing lawyer. Politics opened the door to a small career and the emoluments of office offered those slight returns that were enough to provide for the wants of an unmarried young man with a widowed mother to support. In 1863, Cleveland held the post of assistant district attorney of Erie County; during 1870 to 1873 he held the elective office of sheriff. In 1881, he was elected mayor of the city of Buffalo and in 1882 he received the gubernatorial nomination of his party. Because he had obtained the reputation in his city of being a safe, sane, everyday citizen, and because Republican factionalism had turned that party, for the time being, into a cockpit, middle-class persons generally supported Cleveland and he was elected governor by a great majority. In office he used his veto power unsparingly and checked legislative extravagances. He showed himself to be a prodigious worker, gave of his time unstintingly to the details of his office, was unostentatious in his personal life, and sought his friendships among the humbler walks of society.

As President, Cleveland's virtues and defects were magnified a thousandfold. His independence of mind often took on the aspect of perversity. His distrust of advice necessitated laborious hours spent in the mastery of simple subjects that he might have learned of easily secondhand. His brusqueness antagonized party politicians; his lack of imagination was the despair of his quicker friends; his indecision sometimes rendered his final actions ludicrous. He was firm, for example, in his objections to the Dependent Pension bill of 1887 and scrutinized private pension bills carefully, yet he signed more individual pension bills than had all his predecessors since Johnson put together. He spurned the Republican treaty for the annexation of Hawaii in 1893, yet the very next year he recognized a republic in the islands controlled by the very men who had set up the earlier provisional government. His political principles were grounded in the prevailing economic doctrine of the day (he was a thorough-going "hard" money man, for example) and the rule of the people got no nearer to realization as a result of his administration than it had under Grant, Hayes, Garfield, and Arthur or was to get under Harrison and McKinley. Withal, Cleveland was honest, solid, a plain man of the people, a true representative of the humbler folk who made up the America of the day.

Cleveland's first administration was devoid of serious achievement. The make-up of his Cabinet showed that it was his intention to lead his party. He paid off election scores by appointing the financial manager of his campaign Secretary of the Treasury and by turning over the Post Office to the chairman of the Democratic National Committee. The Navy office, however, he gave to William C. Whitney of New York, wealthy reformer and enemy of Tammany, who was to do yeoman work in the building of the new navy. The Department of the Interior was headed by the capable Mississippi Senator, Lucius Q. C. Lamar, who guarded the public lands zealously. Cleveland early antagonized party hacks by refusing to permit them to despoil the Civil Service and then infuriated his Mugwump supporters by the thoroughness with which he did the job himself. In the first sixteen months of his Presidency Cleveland removed 90 per cent of the previous Presidential appointees and 68 per cent of the unclassified employees of the Department of the Interior. As we shall have occasion to see, Cleveland was not particularly successful, either, in disposing of the Treasury surplus or in effecting any tariff reform. He was too earnest to be popular, had never learned how to soothe hurt vanity or to placate injured friends, and his handling of most of the domestic questions of the day left him with many enemies and few wholehearted supporters.

The result was that the year 1888 saw Cleveland regarded with suspicion by many groups of powerful interests: the Civil War veterans, the manufacturers in the protected industries, the exploiters of the country's natural resources, the organized farmers of the West and the South. But despite the opposition of Tammany Hall and some other disgruntled factions, Cleveland received the Democratic nomination on the first ballot by acclamation. Thurman of Ohio, a tried party leader, was given the Vice-Presidential nomination. The proceedings of the Republican party convention in 1888 were characterized by uncertainty. Blaine, ill and prematurely old, was in Italy, seeking to regain his health. He had written publicly that he would not run in 1888, and at the same time he recommended that the nomination go to former Senator Benjamin Harrison of Indiana. The convention received the suggestion favorably and Harrison was nominated. His running mate was the New York banker, Levi P. Morton.

Harrison was the proper candidate for the Republican party in the campaign of 1888. For the Republican party now openly espoused the interests of industrial capitalism, and Harrison himself was a successful man of affairs, grown wealthy in the service of corporate industry. He had been born in Ohio in 1833, the son of a prosperous farmer and the grandson of General William Henry Harrison. At the age of twenty-one he had begun the practice of law in Indianapolis, only to put aside an already promising career to enlist in the Civil War. He had been commissioned a colonel of volunteers in 1862 and had been mustered out a brigadier general in 1865. Returning to Indianapolis, he took up the law where he had left it and was soon defending many of the outstanding corporations of the Middle West, the railroads prominent among them. From 1881 to 1887 he represented his state in the Senate where he voted with his party for a big navy, Civil Service reform, and Civil War pensions, and against inflation and tariff tinkering. His outstanding achievement as a legislator had been the support of a bill to give the dependency of Alaska a frame of government.

The Republicans left no stone unturned to assure victory. They dragged out the bugaboo of free trade and accused Cleveland of trying to sell out the American manufacturer to British industry; they terrorized the American workingman with thoughts of the competition of European pauper labor; knowing of the hatred of Tammany Hall for Cleveland, they induced it to knife its national leader and promised in return support of Hill for re-election to the governorship. Senator Quay of Pennsylvania, as chairman of the Republican National Committee, for the first time developed on a grandiose scale new sources of revenue, and on the basis of promised tariff protection sought and obtained large contributions from industrialists. Money was lavishly poured into Indiana, Harrison's own state, despite the fact that the candidate stayed at home, prepared to address visiting delegations on every conceivable topic from the sealing industry of Alaska to the rights of the Red Man. Harrison delivered some ninety felicitous little speeches that sent all his Republican auditors back to their homes, reassured and happy. Even fraud was resorted to, and a forged letter was addressed to the British minister in the United States in an effort to obtain a statement from him showing British friendliness for the Democratic candidate. The British minister rose to the bait and, replying to what he thought was the honest inquiry of a naturalized Englishman, wrote saying that Cleveland was more likely to be kindly disposed toward the mother country than Harrison. The letters were published and helped to embarrass Cleveland, particularly when Blaine used them with telling effect before Irish audiences.

Republican strategy was successful and Cleveland lost the pivotal states of New York and Indiana, though he carried New Jersey and Connecticut. The electoral vote was: Harrison 233; Cleveland 168. Though Cleveland again obtained a plurality of the popular votes cast, as he had in 1884, this time he was the defeated candidate and retired on March 4, 1889, to make way for his Republican successor.

BENJAMIN HARRISON IN OFFICE

Harrison's Cabinet, except for one or two good appointments, had the customary political stamp. Blaine, still the outstanding Republican, was named for the State Department and for nearly four years had a free hand in pursuing those policies of which only a hint had been given in the short time he held the same portfolio under Garfield. Windom of Minnesota was given the Treasury office; Tracy of New York was put in charge of the Navy Department, where he continued the work begun by Chandler and Whitney. The promoted Department of Agriculture (for the first time of Cabinet rank) was headed by J. M. Rusk of Wisconsin. John Wanamaker, merchant prince of Philadelphia and philanthropist (he was an early supporter of the new Y.M.C.A. movement and he had helped Quay nobly in rounding up contributions for the Republican campaign chest), was placed in charge of the Post Office. W. H. H. Miller of Indiana, former law partner of the President, was named the Attorney-General. Young Theodore Roosevelt was appointed to the Civil Service Commission.

The political accomplishments of the Harrison administration may be quickly summarized. In the single year 1890, by the enactment of pension and prohibitive tariff legislation, the Republicans effectively disposed of the problem that had given Cleveland so much serious concern, that is to say, the Treasury surplus. The Sherman Silver Purchase Act was passed, so was the Sherman Antitrust Law, and Idaho and Wyoming (with sparse populations but bound to add to Republican strength in the electoral college) were admitted to statehood. The lower house, too, tried for the last time to break the Democratic Solid South by passing a Federal Election bill to place federal marshals at Congressional polling places. Henry

Cabot Lodge, cutting his political teeth in Congress, led the support for the bill; it died, however, in the Senate.[4]

But the outstanding political event of the period was the reduction of the lower house to an unimportant deliberative assembly, achieved by the investing of its Speaker with the full powers of absolutism. The Speaker recognized or could refuse to recognize private members; he was a member of the Rules Committee; he named the committee chairmen. For twenty years the House's presiding officer ruled with a rod of iron and though, in 1910, the Speaker was dethroned, so effective had been the work of Thomas B. Reed and his successors that the House of Representatives never again climbed back to the high estate it had held up to the eighties. Thomas B. Reed of Maine had been a member of Congress for twelve years when he was elected its Speaker in 1889. Immediately the sobriquet of "Czar" was bestowed upon him. Confronted by a large and pugnacious Democratic minority in the Fifty-first Congress, he, with the ready support of his Republican colleagues, evolved a new set of rules that once and for all deprived the minority, and a private member as well, of the rights of opposition. The Speaker, by this revised code, was given the power to refuse to entertain motions which, in his own opinion, could be considered dilatory. He was permitted to direct the clerk to include among those present all persons who, while in the chamber, refused to vote on the roll call. (This latter expedient was devised to prevent the claim of "no quorum" by a large minority.) The quorum for the Committee of the Whole was arbitrarily fixed at one hundred. The order of business in the House was drastically changed and great power was placed in the hands of the Speaker in disposing of routine matters. The Republican majority complacently accepted the new rules and as complacently obeyed the crack of the party whip when it passed the party legislative program of 1889 to 1891.

Retribution swiftly visited the Republicans, for in the fall elections of 1890 they carried only 88 out of the 332 seats in the lower house. Even Representative McKinley, author of the tariff bill of 1890, was swept into the discard and had to console himself with the Ohio gubernatorial chair. The Republican majority in the Senate was reduced from fourteen to six. There also appeared in the legislative halls a host of new faces, some of them members of a new political group, for the Farmers' Alliance returned nine Congressmen and two Senators (from South Dakota and Kansas) in this election. And not among the least of the junior members was a young Nebraskan Democrat, William Jennings Bryan. No serious business could be trans-

[4] As a result of a bargain made with southern Senators by which, for their support of the McKinley tariff bill, they were promised that the Federal Election bill would not be pressed.

acted in a Congress thus divided and the time was given up largely to speeches devoted to the tariff and free silver.

In 1892, Blaine made a last effort to obtain the honor he had so long coveted. He resigned from the State Department and in thus parting with his chief of four years plainly indicated his intentions: he would accept the Republican nomination if it were offered. Harrison, however, was named on the first ballot and Blaine's day was over. "The gentleman from Maine" died in January, 1893, knowing that Cleveland once more would be President of the United States. The Republican platform extolled the Tariff Act of 1890, denounced trusts and the Solid South, and hedged on the free-silver issue.

The Democrats again turned to Cleveland, though the distaste with which the party managers regarded him was openly known. Cleveland, like Harrison, received his party's nomination on the first ballot. The Democratic platform was for an out-and-out tariff for revenue; the trusts were charged to the protective tariff; the Sherman Silver Purchase Act, that Republican bait which had been set to catch the easy-money men of the West, it stigmatized as "a cowardly makeshift."

The Socialist Labor party and the People's party (substantially the same group which had elected such a sizable bloc to the Congress of 1891 to 1893) also named candidates. In view of the fact that Populism is given extended treatment below, mention of its interesting platform need not be made now. Suffice it to say that Populism contributed largely to Harrison's defeat, for in the normally Republican states of Kansas, Colorado, Idaho, Wyoming, Nevada, and North Dakota the Democrats named no electors but indorsed the Populist ticket.

The campaign itself was unexciting. Both parties avoided free silver and talked tariff. The Democrats were able to make political capital out of the Homestead (Pa.) strike, which had been precipitated when the Carnegie Steel Company had sought to cut wages. The end of the contest saw Cleveland sweeping the country. Not only did he carry the Solid South and the doubtful states of Connecticut, Indiana, New Jersey, and New York, but he also won the Republican states of California, Illinois, and Wisconsin. Cleveland's total electoral vote was 277 and his popular vote was 5,556,000. Harrison's electoral total was only 145. His popular vote, not strategically placed, was 5,175,000. Weaver, the Populist candidate, carried the states of Colorado, Kansas, Idaho, and Nevada and got electoral votes in Oregon and North Dakota for a total of 22 electoral votes and 1,041,000 popular votes. The Democrats also obtained safe majorities in both houses of Congress. The Populists elected ten Representatives to the lower house as well as five Senators.

CLEVELAND AGAIN PRESIDENT

The shadow of 1896 lay across the four years of Cleveland's second administration. Fierce industrial strife; financial panic, bad depression, and the continued contraction of the currency; agricultural distress; the bankruptcy of party leadership: all these made the ascendancy of the West and the leadership of Bryan inevitable. Cleveland's very Cabinet appointments showed plainly that he had no sympathy with the insurgency in his party. Before 1893 had rounded its course, Cleveland's party had repudiated his leadership. Cleveland had assumed the Presidential chair with safe majorities in Senate and House (the first year since 1853 to witness such a Democratic triumph); his election had been a personal vindication; everything was propitious for the enactment of the legislative program that would have definitely stamped the Democratic party as the party of the people. But Cleveland (impressed by the dialectics of his conservative eastern friends) chose to regard the Sherman Silver Purchase Act as the source of all economic evil. He called a special session of Congress in August, 1893, and asked the legislators for the law's repeal. The act was withdrawn despite a bitter fight led by western Democrats; this was achieved only through the almost unanimous support given the President by Republican Congressmen. Here Cleveland had scored over the radical branch of his party; on the tariff he was to go down to defeat—at the hands of the conservative wing. The House, following Cleveland's leadership, soon passed the Wilson Tariff bill, a measure really protective in principle though it did bring revision into the raw-material schedules. In the Senate, the House bill was rewritten by Democratic Senators from industrial states with the result that the final act to emerge did not in most particulars differ from characteristic Republican tariff measures. Cleveland was indignant, yet allowed the bill to become a law without his signature in August, 1894.

Popular support of the President increasingly became alienated as a result of his hostility to veteran pension legislation, the hard times that followed the panic of 1893, the federal interference in the railroad strike of 1894, and the sale of gold bonds to private bankers by Secretary of the Treasury Carlisle. The Congressional elections of 1894 resulted in the repudiation of the President, for the Republicans obtained a great majority in the House and a safe lead in the Senate. The West turned to the Populists, and besides electing some five hundred state officers, sent seven Congressmen to the lower house and six Senators to the upper chamber from that party. The next two years were necessarily barren of significant legislative accomplishment. Cleveland continued to sell gold bonds. He brought the country to the verge of war with Great Britain in 1895 when he insisted upon the recognition of the peculiar interest of the United

States in the settlement of the Venezuelan boundary dispute. His handling of the Hawaiian question was not above serious criticism. On all these matters Cleveland found himself moving farther and farther away from public opinion and the sympathies of the man in the street, with the result that when 1896 approached his desertion by his party was received without any real protest.

· 5 ·

Three Leading Questions Before the Postbellum Parties

THE PROTECTIVE TARIFF

THE present American high protective tariff system grew out of the Civil War. Partly by design, partly by chance (for furnishing the sinews of war was an ever serious concern), the War Congresses by a series of measures wrote a tariff act that once and for all put the stamp of protection on American domestic policy. The original bill of 1861, fathered by Morrill of Vermont, was passed in the last days of the Buchanan administration. Its rates were only mildly protective—indeed it is not hard to believe that Morrill spoke the truth when he declared, later, that it was his intention to restore the revenue duties of the 1846 tariff law. The chief interests of this early protective tariff were the iron and wool schedules, and into the twentieth century iron and wool have been the pivotal points about which tariff-making has revolved. The Civil War tariff was seen through its various transformations—it was amended in 1862 and again in 1864— by Morrill and Stevens of Pennsylvania, and each time its amendment was sought the single justification advanced was the following: the country, in its dire need for revenue, has been compelled to raise, by heroic efforts, funds wherever it could find them. This had placed a great burden upon domestic manufacture which was finding it increasingly difficult to meet the competition of foreign industry. The tariff rates were needed, therefore, as an offset to permit once more American producers to compete with foreign manufacturers on terms of equality. So familiar had become the ring of this argument that in 1864, without any real dissent, and in four days, new schedules incorporating still higher rates received the sanction of Congress. By the time the War Congresses had finished their work they had raised the average on dutiable goods from 18.8 per cent (1861) to 40.3 per cent (1866).

The years that followed saw the quick adjustment of industry to the high rates. What had been a war measure and therefore only a temporary expedient, not even having been accorded the honor of serious debate, became quickly the keystone of the whole structure of American industrialism. Prices were adjusted to take permanent account of the additions fixed by the duties; organizations were formed to keep ever before the federal legislators the needs of particular industries; Congressmen and Senators found it wise to make their sentiments known on the subject of protection. The tariff had, before the Civil War, been one of the major points of departure which distinguished the Federalists–Whigs from the Jeffersonian and Jacksonian Democrats. The period 1865 to 1895 (except once in 1888) saw Democrats and Republicans in substantial agreement. Protection for American industry, and American workingmen incidentally, had much to do with American prosperity and should be continued, was the expressed shibboleth of the Republicans. Silence on the part of the Democrats could only mean assent.

The Tariff Act of 1870 incorporated some reductions and decreased the duties on tea, coffee, wines, sugar, and molasses. Yet it did no violence to the protective principle, for rates were raised on a number of protected industries, chief among them steel rails. The House tariff bill of 1872 did seek to come to grips with protection. Frightened by western clamor and in the face of large Treasury surpluses, the House Ways and Means Committee brought in a bill which proposed to cut duties on iron, wool, coal, salt, and lumber. The method employed was that of a horizontal reduction of 20 per cent from prevailing duties. The Senate was steadfast, however, in its refusal to yield and, aided by Speaker Blaine, forced on the House tariff reformers reluctant acceptance of a bill which carried, generally, a horizontal reduction of 10 per cent. The 10 per cent reduction affected cotton goods, wool, iron, steel, metals, paper, glass, leather. These were the great protected industries and the small reduction changed their status little. The only tangible result was a shrinkage of $53 million in federal revenues. In 1875, because of the panic of 1873 and the resulting decline in governmental revenues, the 10 per cent cut was quietly restored and the Civil War tariff again continued its beneficent operation.

Between 1875 and 1883 two attempts at tariff reform were made, in both instances by Democratic Houses. Morrison of Illinois, an honest tariff reformer, in 1876 presented a tariff bill, but it never was reported out of the Committee of the Whole. The tariff bill of 1878 was also a Democratic measure, introduced to satisfy the campaign pledges of 1876, but the bill never got out of the House, the indifference of its friends and the scorn of its foes being too great a handicap.

The campaign of 1880 heard much of the tariff. In their platform, the Republicans promised revision, but with a continuance of protection in the event of victory; their orators went out of their way to ridicule General Hancock, the Democratic candidate, for calling the tariff a local issue, which, in the light of sectional demands, it unquestionably was. Accordingly, in 1883, a Republican Congress wrote a new tariff measure and President Arthur signed it. The train of events leading to this act is worth tracing. By act of Congress in 1882 the President was authorized to appoint a tariff commission to investigate the needs of American industry and to submit new schedules of duties, so drawn as to take the tariff out of politics. That, at any rate, was the hope of the original sponsor of the measure, a hope which evidently would not die easily in American political economy. The commission was frankly "packed," its chairman being the paid employee of the Wool Manufacturers' Association. The iron, wool-growing, and sugar-raising industries also had official representatives. Still, the commission was not immoderate. After lengthy hearings in many cities it sent to Congress a report which carried with it a bill incorporating substantial reductions. But the commission's report got small consideration.

The Tariff Act of 1883 was written by a Conference Committee of both houses, and practically every man on it was a high protectionist. Some duties, for example those on raw materials like wool and pig iron, were slightly cut; others, like that on iron ore, were raised. On finished goods, where reductions were made, they were largely nominal. On certain classes of woolens, and also on cotton goods, the rates were changed upwards. While the tariff as a whole was not particularly higher than previous measures, this judgment, at any rate, is indisputable: the 1883 tariff was in direct line of succession of the protection policy established during the Civil War. That the early explanations of tariff duties as offsets for revenue taxation no longer had validity can be seen in the fact that such onerous internal revenue devices as had not already been eliminated were now lifted. The 1883 Tariff Act abolished the tax on bank deposits and capital, the two-cent stamp on bank checks, the duties on proprietary medicines and cosmetics, the taxes on matches, all of these made necessary in the conduct of the war. The high duties of 1864 had been a compensatory device but the Congress of 1883 apparently decided that apologies for protection were no longer necessary.

In 1884 and 1886, Democrats again controlled the lower house, and in both of these Congresses Morrison introduced tariff bills looking toward reductions. Both measures were killed on routine motions. The vote on the 1884 bill was on the motion to strike out the enacting clause and stood 159 yeas, 155 nays, and 10 not voting. The following was the division: for the motion, 118 Republicans and 41 Democrats; against the motion, 4 Republicans and 151 Democrats. Of the 41 Democrats who voted for the motion (and hence against their party's tariff bill), 12 came from Pennsylvania, 10 from Ohio, 6 from New York, 4 from California, 3 from New Jersey, and 1 each from Illinois, Connecticut, Virginia, West Virginia, Maryland, and Louisiana. It is evident from this division that Congressmen were following the economic interests of their constituencies rather than their supposed political allegiances. Pennsylvania Democrats rose in defense of their state's iron, coal, and steel interests; Ohio Democrats voted to protect ironmasters and woolgrowers; New Jersey Democrats voted in the interests of pottery works; the Virginia Democrat thought of iron ore; the West Virginia Democrat of coal; the Louisiana Democrat of sugar; and the New York Democrats of cotton and woolen goods, collars and shirts, and other manufactured articles. In the 1886 Congress, the House defeated a motion that it go into Committee of the Whole to consider revenue bills (i. e., the new Morrison tariff proposal). The division was 140 yeas, 157 nays, 27 not voting. Of the 140 for the motion, 136 were Democrats and 4 were Republicans; of the 157 against the motion, 122 were Republicans and 35 Democrats. The 35 Democrats were from states particularly interested in high tariffs. Again, it was the agricultural South and West against the manufacturing North and East.

For a single brief period Democratic leadership asserted itself. In a message to Congress in December, 1887, which was entirely devoted to tariff revision, Cleveland cracked the party whip. He called upon the Democratic majority in the lower house to reduce the tariff rates of 1883. The surplus in the Treasury worried him: it had reached more than $100 million. The Mills tariff bill, introduced in the lower house in 1888, was passed by a straight party vote, only 4 of the 169 Democrats voting against it. This bill sought to reduce duties on pig iron and cotton and woolen goods and placed on a free list: salt, tin plate, hemp, flax, lumber, and wool. The Senate of 1888 was Republican, however, and under the leadership of Allison (ably assisted by Aldrich of Rhode Island) it wrote a high tariff measure which the House Ways and Means Committee promptly buried. The way was thus clear for the Presidential contest of 1888 and Cleveland had given the jubilant Republicans a clear-cut economic issue for the first time since the Civil War.

The Republican victory, with the election of Harrison and majorities in both houses, was interpreted as a triumph for the protection principle, and McKinley, now heading the House Ways and Means Committee, sat down to write a tariff bill which his admirers in the Industrial League, the Iron and Steel Association, and the National Association of Wool Manufacturers could not but approve. The McKinley Tariff Act, as finally completed and signed in October, 1890, was protection undisguised. It is true there were political gestures made to conciliate the farming interest: wheat, corn, potato, and egg duties were raised. But in view of the fact that imports in these commodities were nonexistent and that overproduction in the first two staples had helped in the depression of world prices, their inclusion was not to be taken seriously. The wool and woolens schedule, the heart of the tariff, was strengthened; the rate on tinplate was raised. The duty on refined sugar, a domestic monopoly entirely controlled by the

Havemeyer interests (American Sugar Refining Company), was placed at one-half cent a pound. Raw sugar was put on the free list, but to placate the Louisiana cane-sugar growers, who produced 10 per cent of the domestic consumption, a bounty of two cents a pound was offered.

Older Republican leaders, Secretary of State Blaine among them, were disquieted. The rumblings in the West, in normally safe Republican states, presaged ill for the future. The American foreign trade, just beginning to assume a place in the economic life of the nation, was threatened by the prohibitive rates. If we shut out all the manufactured articles of Europe, who would buy our great surpluses of wheat, beef, and pork products? At Blaine's insistence, the Senate accepted an amendment to its bill including a reciprocity or penalty clause by which the President was given the power to impose duties on sugar, molasses, tea, coffee, and hides if he thought that the nations exporting these articles were levying discriminatory duties on American goods. In 1892, Blaine did write a number of reciprocity treaties with Latin-American nations assuring foreign markets for surplus American agricultural products, but these conventions lapsed with the Tariff Act of 1894.

The Republicans in 1890 lost the lower house, and in 1892 the Presidency and both houses of Congress. With Cleveland re-elected in 1892 and with a comfortable majority in the lower house and a working majority in the Senate, the Democrats were in a position to redeem campaign pledges. The Democratic resolutions committee had written a straightforward revenue-tariff plank into the Democracy's platform in 1892. Cleveland in his acceptance speech was more circumspect, promising free raw materials and "a careful distribution of necessary tariff burdens rather than the precipitation of free trade." The Wilson tariff bill, when it left the House on February 1, 1894, was no radical measure and Democratic tariff reformers were plainly disappointed. To appease the South and West, the bill carried an income tax of 2 per cent on all personal incomes in excess of $4000.

The Democratic party machine, for a second time, worked efficiently and the House passed the Wilson bill by a vote of 204 to 110, only 17 Democrats voting in the negative. The Senate was not so easily controlled. Cleveland had some old enemies in the upper chamber, who had been antagonized by slights administered in the making of Presidential appointments; the Louisiana Senators could not be counted on because of sugar, the Alabama and West Virginia Senators because of coal and iron ore; there was soreness because of the repeal of the Silver Purchase Act in 1893 (discussed below). The lineup, at best, offered small comfort, with 44 Democrats, 38 Republicans, and 3 Populists in the chamber. The upshot was the emasculation of the Wilson bill with Democratic Senators taking the lead, Gorman (Md.), Hill and Murphy (N.Y.), Smith (N.J.), Brice

(O.) being its chief foes. A protective measure was written in the Senate. The House had put coal and iron ore on the free list; the Senate put duties on both, lower, it is true, than the 1890 rates, but still prohibitive. The duties on pig iron and steel rails were lowered, but as a result of technological improvements in both industries the duties were also prohibitive. A revolution was effected in the placing of raw wool on the free list, but the farmers and not the industrialists were the ones to suffer. Another schedule to be manipulated was that of sugar. The House bill put raw sugar on the free list and removed the bounty, too. The House also defied the Havemeyers and put refined sugar on the free list. The Senate put a 40 per cent ad valorem duty on raw sugar and a specific duty of one-eighth of a cent a pound on refined sugar. It also ordered an extra duty of one-tenth of a cent a pound on refined sugar coming from countries giving an export bounty. Germany's newly developed beet sugar industry was aimed at here. In all, the Senate made 334 changes in the House bill and then passed the measure on July 3 by a vote of 39 to 34.

The House was indignant but had to accept the Senate bill. Cleveland was unwise enough to denounce Gorman publicly; he then had to swallow his words by permitting the Wilson tariff measure to become a law August 27, 1894 (without his signature, it is true). Cleveland's intimations that the sugar schedule was manipulated by speculating Senators were later substantiated when Senators Quay and McPherson admitted to a Senate investigating committee that they had dealt in sugar stocks. Popular rumor associated other prominent tariff makers with the scandal (Aldrich in particular was named) but the matter was never pressed. The Democrats were further humiliated when the income tax section of their act, which the Senate had not molested, was declared unconstitutional by the Supreme Court on May 20, 1895.[1]

The Democrats' brief day in power thus ended ingloriously. The party had definitely belied its own pretensions to being a free-trade party: its parting with its past was complete. It had turned on its chief executive and party leader when he sought to form its lines on a clear-cut issue and had discredited him. In 1896, the western and southern wings tried once more to establish the Democracy, as the party of the opposition, on the issue of inflation. Defeat, once again, was its portion, as we shall see. By upholding protection, by rejecting inflation, by a refusal or an inability to cope with railroad abuses, the central government had shown its willingness to underwrite the doctrines of industrial capitalism. The keystone of the structure was the protective tariff, and how securely that device had been fitted into its proper place the events of 1861 to 1895 plainly showed.

[1] See below, page 170.

CIVIL SERVICE REFORM

The influences which effected the reform of the Civil Service in the generation after the Civil War were diverse. The outstanding one was, perhaps, the impact of European institutionalism upon the American consciousness. Charles Sumner of Massachusetts, as a result of his familiarity with English political life, was quick to see that one of the reasons that rendered the position of his English political friends so much more dignified was their aloofness from the common business of political jobbery. Their political fortunes were not dependent upon their ability to keep satisfied great hordes of hungry officeseekers. The performance of the routine functions of the state, in England, was in the hands of trained persons who attained their positions by competitive examinations. John Bigelow, Johnson's minister to France, returned to the United States similarly impressed by the importance, in the French public life, of the civil servant. Carl Schurz, who knew his native Germany as well as his adopted Missouri, was an admirer of those German bureaucracies which functioned so satisfactorily. These men were prominent in American public life, and their opinions on matters affecting the Civil Service were given respectful attention.

A second outstanding influence was the propaganda carried on by organized reform organizations. The New York Civil Service Reform Association was organized in 1877 and the National Civil Service Reform League was formed in 1881. Led by independents in politics, these groups (and others like them) made up for their smallness in numbers by their earnestness and persistence, employing every form of appeal to enlist the support of public opinion. The founder of the National Civil Service Reform League was George William Curtis, political editor of *Harper's Weekly* and an Independent Republican whose refusal to remain in the organization earned the abiding disgust of regulars like Conkling, Grant, and Logan. Carl Schurz, too, became an active worker for the League. Others associated with its activities in the generation following the Civil War were Dorman B. Eaton, Everett P. Wheeler, and Charles J. Bonaparte. The support of the cause of reform by these gentlemen carried particular weight with respectable citizens because these men were, at the same time, so sound on all economic and financial questions.

The political scandals which rocked the seventies, the assassination of President Garfield in 1881 by a disappointed officeseeker, the entrance into politics of new blood like Roosevelt and Lodge, the development of a surer method of financing political organizations than the meager and reluctant contributions of officeholders, all aided in the shaping of public policy. Beginning with the seventies, the reform of the federal Civil Service became a recognized public problem to whose resolution successive Presidential aspirants found it necessary to commit themselves.

In 1864, Charles Sumner introduced a bill in the Senate providing for the creation of a board of examiners and the appointment of federal officeholders by competitive examination, with promotion by seniority and removal for cause only. In 1865, a bill along similar lines was introduced in the House. In 1871, at the request of President Grant, Congress appropriated $25,000 to be expended in the creation of a machinery to put the Civil Service on a classified basis. An advisory board of seven was established and Curtis was named to head it. But Curtis' association with the Liberal Republicans in 1872 displeased Republican Stalwarts and in 1873 Congress failed to renew the appropriation. In 1876 and 1877, Hayes, in his letter of acceptance, inaugural address, and first message to Congress, lined himself up with the Civil Service reformers. He appointed Schurz to the Department of the Interior, made Eaton a special commissioner for the purpose of studying the British civil service system, encouraged his Secretary of the Treasury (Sherman) to clean up the custom houses, and issued an executive order calling a halt upon the levying of political assessments on federal officeholders. His interest led to the placing of a number of positions in the New York Custom House and Post Office on a competitive basis. On the other hand, Hayes made no attempt to interrupt the financial solicitation of officeholders both in the Congressional campaign of 1878 and in the Presidential campaign of 1880.

The tragic end of Garfield and the events immediately preceding his death—the exposure of frauds in the Post Office Department and the knowledge that Garfield's brief life in office had been harassed by importunate job hunters—were the immediate causes of the passage of the Pendleton Act (1883). The measure provided for the appointment by the President, with the consent of the Senate, of a Civil Service Commission of three persons who were to draw up rules for competitive examinations for positions already classified or which in the future might be classified by executive order or act of Congress. Certain places in the Treasury Department and the Post Office were ordered classified, the largest single group consisting of those post offices that had more than fifty employees. The Civil Service rules were to exclude drunkards, give military and naval veterans preference, establish a fair apportionment of Washington positions among the citizens of the various states, and protect civil servants against political assessments. Eaton was chosen by Arthur to head the first commission, and before Arthur's term was over some 16,000 federal officeholders had been assured permanency of tenure by being placed on the classified Civil Service list. The reform was significant, though there were still approximately 100,000 federal officeholders whose heads could fall at the Presidential caprice.

The history of the Civil Service after 1884 must be read in the light of the dual nature of the Presidential position: the President is the chief executive officer of the nation and as such is interested in the efficient and economical conduct of the nation's business; he is, too, the head of his party, and as such is concerned over the perpetuation of the organization which made his election possible.

All Presidents, from Cleveland to Truman, expanded the classified list: Cleveland, in his first administration, added the railway mail clerks; Harrison put some 10,000 positions under the protecting wing of the Civil Service Commission; Cleveland, in his second term, widely extended the whole system as well as improving and simplifying it. Theodore Roosevelt was responsible for notable improvements, chief of which was the placing of all fourth-class postmasters in the fourteen states north of the Ohio and east of the Mississippi under Civil Service regulations. Taft extended the classified service to include assistant postmasters of first- and second-class offices and all those fourth-class postmasters not affected by the Roosevelt order. In 1917, Wilson directed the Postmaster-General to fill vacancies in the first-, second-, and third-class postmasterships from lists to be prepared by the Civil Service Commission. At the conclusion of the Coolidge administrations, three-fourths of all federal employees were on the classified lists. Although the unclassified service reached a high point of 308,591 excepted positions in 1937, an Executive Order of 1939 put all but policy-determining officials and those excepted by statute into the classified service. The war emergency of the forties again swelled the list of excepted positions. By 1947, these were reduced to 151,213 (of which about a fifth were in presumably temporary agencies). Nevertheless, the President can fill more than 130,000 posts: these jobs represent the power of the President as his party's dispenser of patronage.

Another significant reform was the extension of the classified service to the State Department. In 1906, the consular service was placed under Civil Service rules; in 1909, the lower ranges of the diplomatic service were similarly treated. Finally, by the Rogers Act of 1924 the two services were merged under the title "The United States Foreign Service." By the act, the service was divided into classes; admission into it was to be by examination; promotion was to be based on merit; and a Foreign Service School was created to give preliminary training to those candidates who had already passed their initial examinations. The intention was to make possible the development of careers in the foreign service and Presidents Coolidge, Hoover, and Franklin D. Roosevelt recognized the principle by selecting a number of their ambassadors and ministers—to lesser countries, it is true—from among the men who had come up from the ranks.

SPENDING THE SURPLUS AND REWARDING WAR VETERANS

Another public question to agitate the generation after the Civil War was the presence of a large surplus in the federal Treasury. It was generally recognized that a surplus was as uncomfortable a phenomenon in public finance as a deficit. Economists, particularly, inveighed against it because it withdrew from circulation a sizable part of the liquid capital of the country. In 1867, the surplus was $116,117,000. Except for the single year 1874, when there was a slight deficit, there continued to be an average annual surplus of almost $100,000,000 up to the year 1890. During the decade of the eighties, particularly, the disposal of the surplus was almost continuously before the public attention and a large part of the work of the first Cleveland administration centered in the problem it presented. It remained for the Republican administration of Harrison, in the single year 1890, to cut the Gordian knot. The Republican Congress and President adopted two expedients, both sensationally successful: they passed the McKinley Tariff Act, which in two years reduced customs revenues from $229,600,000 (1890) to $177,400,000 (1892); they also passed a Disability Pension Act, which in 1892 accounted for the expenditure of $141,000,000. The result was that in 1891 the surplus melted away to $37,240,000 and in 1892 to $9,914,000. When Cleveland once more became President in 1893 the surplus had disappeared almost to the vanishing point. In 1894, there was a deficit of $69,802,000 in the Treasury to worry him.

The surplus was built up, over the period 1866 to 1890, by the refusal of Congress to wipe out at once the internal revenue taxes created to finance the Civil War, and by the imposition of high duties in the series of postwar tariffs which it wrote. The withdrawal of the wartime revenue acts was only a gradual process. In 1866, 1867, and 1868, the taxes on coal and pig-iron production, corporations, cotton, advertisements, and manufactures generally were repealed so that internal revenues were reduced from $309,200,000 in 1866 to $184,900,000 in 1870. In 1872, the income tax was repealed. In 1883, Congress cut the duty on tobacco in half and abolished the taxes on friction matches, patent medicines and perfumery, bank checks, commercial and savings bank deposits and bank capital. The result was that in 1885 the internal revenues brought in only $112,500,000. By the last decade of the century, therefore, the three chief supports of the internal-revenue system were again tobacco, spirits, and fermented liquors.

Serious efforts were made, before the Republicans by reduction of tariff receipts gave the surplus away in 1890, to formulate a statesmanlike program for its disposal. One device perfected was the reduction of the public debt. In 1865, the public debt had stood at $2,758,000,000; by 1890, it had been reduced to $891,000,000. The upshot was that whereas in 1870 interest on the national debt ate up 44 per cent of the federal expenditures, and pensions, by contrast, only 9.6 per cent; in 1885, interest made up only 19.7 per cent of total expenditures as against 21.5 per cent for pensions; and in 1893, interest's proportion of the total was 7.1 per cent as against the proportion for pensions of 41 per cent. Debt refunding was the only attempt at any sort of program to cope with the surplus and, as we shall see, led to contraction and serious economic damage.

Numerous other proposals for ridding the federal Treasury of its incubus were advanced, but in the end Congress found that the simplest way of all, and politically the most satisfactory, was to spend the surplus, largely by pensioning Civil War veterans.

It is a common error to say Congress recklessly indulged in large appropriations for rivers and harbors bills. While these expenditures mounted, the sums voted dwindle into insignificance when compared with pension appropriations. In 1866, $300,000 was voted for the improvement of rivers and harbors; in 1870, $3,500,000; in 1890, $11,700,000. On the other hand, in 1866 there was disbursed on federal pensions (exclusive of administrative costs) $15,450,000; in 1870, $29,351,000; and in 1890, $88,842,000. In 1895, pensions were costing the government $139,812,000. If the "bloody shirt" issue of the Civil War disappeared from American politics after 1884, the Civil War veteran did not, and a public solicitude for him and his dependents cost the American government, during 1866 to 1917, more than $5,000,000,000.

The first far-reaching Civil War pension legislation was enacted in 1862 and this law continued as the basis of pension grants until 1890. It was a service-disability-pension law, for it made it incumbent upon the claimant or his dependents to prove that disability was incurred as the direct consequence of the performance of military duty. Disabled veterans received federal pensions if they could establish invalidity as a result of gunshot wounds or disease. Widows of soldiers, dependent children, and other dependent relatives were entitled to pensions if they could prove death of the soldier in action or from causes directly traceable to wounds or disease contracted while in the military service. Over the period 1864 to 1904 almost every year saw the passage by Congress of amendments to this fundamental law for the purpose of increasing the disability benefits. Thus, by the act of 1862, a man who had lost both his hands in action got $8 a month; by 1890 he would be getting $100 a month. Under this legislation in 1866 there were 126,722 pensioners on the rolls; and in 1890, 537,944. In the next decade the numbers increased enormously as a result of the change in the fundamental law. In 1891, there were 676,160 pensioners; in 1895, 970,524; and in 1900, 993,529.

Early in the eighties the lobbyists of the G.A.R. began to agitate for a pension scheme based on service pure and simple. In 1887, both houses of Congress passed a measure that provided just a little less than that sought by the G.A.R. In other words, the bill granted pensions to veterans who were dependents or public charges due to mental or physical disability and not necessarily arising out of war service. Cleveland had the courage to veto it, in the face of a surplus of more than $100 million. The House sustained him and the bill was lost.

In the debate on the Mills tariff bill of 1888, Republican orators laid their preparations for the Presidential campaign of the fall: Cleveland had vetoed the new pension bill because only tariff reductions would satisfy him as a solution to the surplus problem; the war veterans had the very first call on the nation's bounty, all other expenditures being secondary; Cleveland had proved his niggardliness in vetoing special pension legislation. McKinley, Reed, and Cannon all spoke in this vein. Harrison, in the Presidential campaign, followed his party leaders and said that it was "no time to be weighing the claims of old soldiers with apothecary's scales." The result was the defeat of Cleveland, as much due to the hostility of half a million members of the Grand Army of the Republic as to the alarm of the protectionist interests.

Harrison redeemed his campaign pledges in two ways. In the first place, he appointed, to the Pension Office, Corporal James Tanner, a G.A.R. lobbyist and claim agent, who proceeded to rerate pensions upwards and to pay arrears, too, often without the solicitation of the beneficiaries. Tanner's resignation was forced before he had finished a year in office, but his successor showed an almost equal liberality. In the second place, Harrison gave his complete approval to the Disability Pension Act, which was passed by Congress in 1890 with the support of Sherman, McKinley, and Reed. The measure was a disability pension law in name only; actually, it was a service pension act, for it prescribed pensions for all veterans of ninety days' service who could lay claim to any physical or mental disability, regardless of origin, which interfered with the gaining of a livelihood by *manual* labor. Such pensions were to range from $6 to $12 monthly. In addition, pensions were to be granted to widows, without regard to the cause of the husband's death, if the marriage had taken place prior to 1890. In short, disability did not have to grow out of military service; it did not have to interfere with the earning of an income as a legislator, lawyer, banker, clerk, or merchant; it did not matter whether the beneficiary was rich or poor. As for the widows, they might even have been born after the Civil War's close.

In March, 1904, by the action of President Roosevelt, this disability pension law became a straightforward service pension measure. With a Presidential election in the offing, Roosevelt issued an executive order which placed all Civil War veterans, of ninety days' service and over 62 years of age, on the pension rolls. Allotments were to range between $6 and $12 monthly, depending on the ages of the pensioners. In 1907 Roosevelt's order received statutory sanction when Congress enacted the Service Pension Act.

The results of the pension legislation of 1890 were diverse, but all were happy. During the nineties, the average annual number of pensioners receiving grants was 900,000 and the average annual disbursement was $138,000,000. The act of 1890, from the year of its passage until World War I, cost the American people more than $2,250,000,000. Finally, Republican campaign pledges to the Grand Army of the Republic were redeemed; the surplus was got rid of; a strong argument in favor of tariff tinkering was entirely eliminated; and the Republican party, every four years, continued to receive the grateful recognition of the veterans and their families. In the twenties and forties of the next century, when legislators came to contemplate the needs of a new host of returned soldiers, they had before them as a signpost the examples of Harrison, McKinley, Sherman, Reed, and Cannon. And Congressmen after World Wars I and II followed closely along the way already blazed by these earlier statesmen: they, too, gave earnest heed to the representations of veterans' organizations and they, too, proceeded to make lavish grants out of the federal Treasury.

· 6 ·

Relations With the Outside World 1876–1896

CHARACTER OF AMERICAN FOREIGN POLICY

It has not infrequently been said that it was the peculiar distinction of the last generation living in the nineteenth century to witness the lowest level in American diplomatic relations. Certainly, this indictment might have much support: for between Fish (Grant's Secretary of State) and Hay (Roosevelt's Secretary) a succession of politicians sat at the right hand of American Presidents who directed the nation's foreign affairs without steady plan or purpose. The record was not altogether a happy one. We almost blundered into a war with Great Britain; we were on the point of gaining—and then almost completely lost—the enduring friendship of the Latin-American republics; we were about to undertake the building of an Isthmian canal by honorable means—and then launched on a doubtful adventure from whose ill effects we still suffer.

Nevertheless, the obverse side of the medal had a nobility about it which has been too often overlooked. Our economy was essentially agricultural and American insularity was definitely a state of mind. The United States had a continent to break and make fruitful; that task left small room for serious concern with the consequences of European scrabbles for power. American statecraft may have been unimaginative and unambitious, but it was for the most part honest, rugged, and peaceful in its intentions. We may have had no foreign policy nor brilliant foreign secretaries; neither, on the other hand, were we compelled to scan anxiously every distant horizon lest discord in some foreign land endanger the commercial and financial interests of our nationals. It remained for the succeeding generation to raze the walls that shut us off from the outside world. As we grew more powerful economically, our foreign policy took on definite form: we belonged in the van of the mighty nations of the earth, and with leadership, naturally, came responsibility. So Theodore Roosevelt, as we shall have occasion to observe, directed our destiny along strange paths.

THE UNITED STATES AND LATIN AMERICA

The first American Secretary of State to turn serious attention to Latin America was Blaine, Garfield's Secretary. His interests were twofold, the first political and the second economic. Blaine prided himself upon his resemblance to Henry Clay and sought to continue his great predecessor's foreign policy of "America for the Americans." Like Clay, Blaine was dissatisfied with the purely negative features of the Monroe Doctrine; to him the United States' function was greater than merely being guarantor of the territorial integrity of the nations of the Western Hemisphere against European aggression. He would unite the peoples of the Western Hemisphere into a loosely defined union with our country playing the role of "elder sister"; he would maintain peace among them through the continuous exercise of the good offices of the United States; he would have them meet regularly in formal conference for the purpose of planning policies of mutual advantage; he would make them Americans and not Europeans, in culture, sympathies, world interests. That Blaine, too, had already faint glimmerings of America's imperial might is not to be overlooked. Already a small number of American industries were producing surpluses of manufactured goods for which foreign markets were necessary. Great Britain's hold on South America was becoming increasingly apparent, and here, as into the United States only a short period before, were going British capital and British textiles and machinery. Already, the Argentine surpluses of wheat and meats were threatening American markets in Europe. Such, in brief, was Blaine's economic interest in the development of a Latin-American policy.

His first Secretaryship of State he held during March to November, 1881. In that brief interval his presence was to be felt in all disputes that involved the nations of Latin America, both among themselves and with European powers. Blaine, too, laid the plans for the meeting of a Pan-American conference at Washington, and the Department of State already was in receipt of a number of acceptances to his invitations when his successor, Frelinghuysen, with President Arthur's approval, canceled the proceedings.

In 1889, Congress having authorized the proceedings by legislative enactment, and with Blaine once more Secretary of State, the first Pan-American Conference was finally held. On October 2, 1889, there assembled in Washington the delegates from seventeen of the eighteen Latin-American nations. Blaine, as chairman, called for closer ties among the nations of the Western Hemisphere—the elimination of force in the settlement of disputes, the development of railroads and waterways, the fostering of commercial relationships, the breeding of good will. His doctrine of "America for the Americans" was listened to courteously; it did not, however, receive general approval. The first Conference did underwrite one solid achievement. It gave its consent to the establishment at Washington of a bureau of information of the International Union of American Republics, which today functions under the name of the Pan–American Union and is housed in the capital city in an impressive structure erected through the benevolence of Andrew Carnegie. On two important measures the Conference turned a cold shoulder: it refused to adopt a convention calling for the promotion of peace by arbitration, and it would not underwrite Blaine's economic policy of trade reciprocity.

These tentative efforts at the creation of a sound Pan-American policy bore little fruit until the nineteen thirties and nineteen forties. There were to be subsequent Pan–American Conferences and further American protestations of friendship for the peoples of Latin America. But while our statesmen were to proclaim eloquently their desire to join the nations of the Western Hemisphere in a union founded on common sympathy and respect, they were not to be halted from seizing the Panama Canal site, acquiring Puerto Rico and the Virgin Islands, turning the Caribbean into an American lake, and establishing virtual protectorates over Cuba and Panama. With new threats to our leadership, however, a new understanding emerged. And before the nineteen forties were over, there were evidences that the countries of the Western Hemisphere were prepared to understand that on matters of defense, at least, union was necessary.

THE UNITED STATES AND GREAT BRITAIN

Anglo-American relations, during the eighties and nineties, were distinctly unfriendly. The reasons for continued anti-English feeling in the United States were many and diverse. These were among the more important: 1. The hostile tone of most American school histories, which brought up young Americans to regard Englishmen as the past and ever-present foes of American liberty, was probably the most potent reason. 2. England's threatening attitude during the Civil War was not forgotten by postwar American politicians, despite the fact that important sections of the British public had favored the North. 3. The ceaseless agitation of the Irish-Americans, living for the most part in the large cities and representing therefore influential political minorities, had its effect. Blaine cultivated the Irish all the time and a number of his diplomatic notes to the British Foreign Office were written largely for their eyes. 4. The emergence of a new national sensitivity made the American people resent the critical and amused attitude of the British upper classes. American self-confidence had waxed as a result of the outcome of the Civil War, the conquest of a great continental domain, the appearance of an urban life on a grand scale. The result was that the educated classes in America took in ill part the strictures of those cultivated Englishmen who visited us during the period and then returned home to write urbane—and highly unflattering—travel books. Herbert Spencer, Matthew Arnold, E. A. Freeman, and Rudyard Kipling were among the chief offenders on this score. Not until the turn of the century did British travelers in America show anything approaching a real understanding of American problems or a desire to further the friendship of the two great English-speaking nations.[1]

This ill will found its public expression in the relations between the two nations during the period. On four different matters the United States and England were in disagreement, and the settlement of these difficulties was encompassed only with the greatest travail. The four points at issue were: the control of an Isthmian canal; the right to fish in Canadian waters; the Bering Sea dispute; the Venezuela boundary controversy.

The question of an Isthmian canal first received American attention, in the period following the Civil War, in 1879 when the Frenchman De Lesseps, having successfully completed the Suez Canal, turned his eyes on Panama. The rumor persisted, despite an official French disclaimer, that the European powers were considering a joint guarantee of such a canal's neutrality, with the result that in 1881 Blaine sent an identical letter to the American ministers in the European countries informing them that any interference in American-Colombian relations would be regarded as an unfriendly act. Great Britain's reply was disconcerting: it pointed to the Clayton–Bulwer Treaty of 1850 and insisted that that convention covered every aspect of the question. The fact is, the treaty, at the time of its writing, had been a diplomatic triumph for the United States. Under it, Great Britain, then the world's most powerful nation, had deferred to American wishes and had agreed not to establish exclusive control over any Isthmian canal it might in the future construct. The American State Department had delivered a similar pledge. Despite the plain provisions of this understanding, however, Blaine insisted upon entering into an acrimonious correspondence with the British Foreign Office. The none too skilful arguments of our State Department were easily answered by the British Foreign Secretary; and there the matter stood, with occasional bickerings, until 1902 when both powers formally exchanged ratifications of the Hay–Pauncefote Treaty and Great Britain definitely recognized the United States' primacy in the Western Hemisphere.

During 1885 to 1888, feeling ran high between the two countries over the right of American fishermen to fish in Canadian waters. A series of short-term conventions, the last written in 1871, regulated the rights of

---

[1] This criticism of the attitude of British travelers does not, of course, apply to James Bryce, who was sincerely interested in the establishment of amicable Anglo-American relations.

American fishermen to fish within the three-mile limit of the British North American waters. The convention having terminated in 1885, Cleveland asked Congress for its approval of the appointment of a commission to draw up a new treaty. But because Cleveland had declared that he would support the Canadians in their claim for a greater measure of reciprocity and would approve of the admission of Canadian prepared-fish into the United States duty-free, he antagonized the New England fishing interests. The result was that the Republican Senate refused to pass the necessary legislation. American fishermen were thus left without treaty protection and began to feel the weight of Canadian displeasure. A number of American fishing smacks were seized for technical violation of the old 1818 treaty. The State Department complained to London but met with little satisfaction. Congressional indignation ran particularly high and a number of retaliatory measures were introduced for the purpose of putting an end entirely to all commercial intercourse between the United States and Canada. In fact, in 1887 an act was passed giving the President the discretion to deny all Canadian vessels the right of entry into American ports and to prohibit the importation of Canadian products.

On his own responsibility, Cleveland's Secretary of State Bayard appointed a commission to confer with British representatives, and on February 15, 1888, the so-called Bayard–Chamberlain Treaty was submitted to the Senate for its approval. But because this treaty contained reciprocal tariff privileges, the Senate voted down the agreement by a straight party vote. The State Department did, however, effect an informal modus vivendi which put an end to most of the difficulties; and this understanding continued to operate until 1910, when a formal convention was finally written.

In the adjudication of the Bering Sea dispute the United States came off with less success. In 1870, there had been granted to the Alaska Commercial Company the exclusive monopoly to kill bachelor seals on their breeding grounds off the Pribilof Islands (part of the newly acquired Alaska). But the habit of the seals of cruising far out into the waters of the Bering Sea turned that body of water into a general hunting ground and led to the indiscriminate slaughter of the herds. The government, to protect the American monopoly and prevent the extermination of the Alaskan seals, took forcible measures and in 1886 a number of British ships were seized. In 1888, Bayard sought to protect the herds through an international convention, but the Canadians, aroused over the Senate's rejection of the fisheries treaty, induced the British Foreign Office to withdraw from the proceedings. In 1889, Blaine took up his old controversy with Great Britain, this time in the interest of the seals. He carried on a curious and at times ill-natured correspondence with Lord Salisbury in which he advanced the doctrine that the Bering Sea was a *mare clausum* (though the United

States itself had denied this when Russia had propounded the thesis); that the seals were not *ferae naturae* (which of course they were); and that it was in the interest of public morals that the Alaskan herds be preserved from extinction. Salisbury took considerable pains to point out Blaine's historical, legal, and ethical errors with the result that good feeling did not gain by the interchange. Failing diplomatically, Blaine wrote to Salisbury that American revenue cutters would be instructed to capture British sealing ships when found in the Bering Sea. When Salisbury replied that the British Navy would be used to resist the revenue cutters, the time for arbitration had come. In 1892, a treaty was signed which placed the controversy before an arbitral court and in the next year a decision was rendered which ruled against the United States on every point. Some further efforts were made to save the seals but not until 1911, when most of the damage was already done, was there signed an international convention putting a stop to pelagic sealing for fifteen years.

It was the Venezuela boundary dispute which almost precipitated a war between the two countries. The difficulty arose out of the long-unsettled boundary between British Guiana and Venezuela. In 1876, Venezuela had appealed to the United States for its good offices but Secretary of State Fish had shown no more than a friendly interest. The discovery of gold in the contested region made for a redoubling of effort on the part of the British; the Venezuelan claims on the other hand became excessive; threats were exchanged. The inevitable result was that in 1887 diplomatic relations between the two countries were broken off. Bayard in 1886, Blaine in 1890, and Gresham in 1894 had all tendered the services of the United States as mediator, only to have their proffers rejected. Suddenly the air became charged with danger. On December 17, 1895, Cleveland placed before Congress, and before the American public at the same time, a series of notes that had been exchanged between Olney, his new Secretary of State, and Salisbury, the English Foreign Minister. It is important that the steps of the controversy be retraced in some detail.

Olney's original note was sent to Salisbury on July 20, 1895. In it he expounded the following two principles: first, because of the Monroe Doctrine, the United States must resist any designs on the territorial integrity of Venezuela on the ground that the arbitrary rectification of the disputed boundary by Great Britain was in reality an extension of European dominion in the Western Hemisphere; second, there was but one way of settling the dispute, namely, by "peaceful arbitration." But the corollaries deduced from these principles were quite novel. European colonialism in the Americas was but a transitory phenomenon. Said Olney: "That distance and three thousand miles of intervening ocean make any permanent political union between a European and an American state unnatural and inexpedient will hardly be denied." Again, it was inevitable that we should assume a position of superiority in all affairs affecting the nations of the Western Hemisphere. Here, Olney said:

> Today the United States is practically sovereign on this continent, and its fiat is law upon the subjects to which it confines its interposition. Why? It is not because of the pure friendship or good will felt for it.... It is because, in addition to all other grounds, its infinite resources combined with its isolated position render it master of the situation and practically invulnerable as against any or all other powers.

It would seem that for Blaine's shibboleth of "America for the Americans," Olney was prepared to substitute the cry "America for the United States." It is imperative to point out here that such a doctrine was disquieting not only to European nations with interests in the Western Hemisphere but to the nations of Latin America, to whom the talk of American fiat had an ominous ring.

Salisbury did not reply until November 26. Then he sent two notes: the first rejected the American demand for arbitration; the second denied the applicability of the Monroe Doctrine to this particular dispute. Salisbury developed Olney's theses to their inevitable conclusion. If the United States was to stand in the role of protector over the Latin American nations, then:

Such a claim would have imposed upon the United States the duty of answering for the conduct of these states, and consequently the responsibility of controlling it. It follows of necessity that if the Government of the United States will not control the conduct of these communities, neither can it undertake to protect them from the consequences attaching to any misconduct of which they may be guilty towards other nations.[2]

It is undoubtedly true that the English minister underestimated the seriousness of the situation. He had every reason to feel sure of his ground: abstract justice was on his side; the Monroe Doctrine had never received international sanction. The irritating character of Salisbury's logic—because it was so sound—was not calculated to soothe Cleveland's ruffled feelings.

On December 17, Cleveland made public the notes which had passed between Olney and Salisbury. Accompanying them was his own message. It was now necessary for the United States to ascertain the true boundary through the agency of an American commission. He wanted Congressional approval and the voting of an appropriation to defray the costs of the commission's work. And after the commission had done its work and rendered its report? Then: "... it will in my opinion be the duty of the

---

[2] It is important to note that Theodore Roosevelt accepted these implications in 1904 when he enunciated his so-called Corollary of the Monroe Doctrine. See below, page 373.

United States to resist by every means in its power as a wilful aggression upon its rights and interests the appropriation by Great Britain of any lands or the exercise of governmental jurisdiction over any territory which after investigation we have determined of right belongs to Venezuela."

This was the sequence of events that suddenly whipped American public opinion into a frenzy. Theodore Roosevelt, Chauncey M. Depew, William C. Whitney, Andrew D. White, John W. Foster, all publicly applauded the President for his courage. Of twenty-eight governors whom the *New York World* reached, twenty-six gave the President their solemn and patriotic support. Civil War veterans offered their services; school children (at Roosevelt's suggestion) began to commit to memory the truculent last paragraph of the Presidential message; Dana of the *Sun* carried the headline "War if Necessary."

Fortunately, however, a number of circumstances, many of them fortuitous, intervened to prevent trouble. There was no war, and the incident closed, strangely enough, with the completing of the groundwork of firm Anglo-American friendship. Perhaps the most important single agency in the cause of peace was Joseph Pulitzer who, through the medium of the popular *New York World,* worked unceasingly to bring American and English public men to their senses. Pulitzer was our first modern American journalist in the sense that he had an uncanny instinct for the timely. He cabled, for example, to those Englishmen whose opinions carried weight in the United States, obtained from them messages of peace to the American public, and printed these prominently in his paper. Another factor was a Wall Street panic caused by the dumping of American securities on foreign stock exchanges. Wall Street was alarmed by the depreciation of something like $400 million in the values of American stocks, with the result that chambers of commerce and businessmen generally began to regret their impetuosity. Chauncey M. Depew now publicly recanted and appealed to the President to leave no stone unturned in the cause of peace. Again, the clergy were almost unanimously opposed to war with Great Britain and their sermons helped bring Americans to their senses. On the other side, second thoughts were much calmer, too. Englishmen, contemplating their nation's foreign relations, suddenly awoke to the fact that their country had permitted itself to become isolated in world politics. In the Nile and Niger valleys, in Persia and China, in South Africa, Englishmen found themselves actively opposed by the French, Russians, and Germans and their schemes of empire thwarted or hampered. Certainly it was not desirable to add the United States to this hostile array. There followed a kindlier tone when public mention was made of the American people. Finally, events a little nearer at home turned English attention to another and probably more exciting subject. The Kaiser had had the temerity to send to President Kruger of the Boer Republic a telegram congratulating him on the capture of the Jameson raiders, and British politicians and public turned to a consideration of the iniquities of Germany's new young ruler. The result was that hard feelings had almost completely vanished by January, 1896, when Cleveland appointed his Venezuelan boundary commission. The commission began its work under happy auspices, for the English Foreign Office quickly complied with a request for all pertinent data in its hands. On February 2, 1897, a treaty was signed referring the entire dispute to an arbitral tribunal and when the arbitrators met in Paris in 1899 they made a series of decisions which largely supported the original British contentions. Henceforth relations between the two countries steadily improved.

THE UNITED STATES IN THE PACIFIC

During the period under examination, American interests in the Pacific were becoming an important part of American foreign policy. It must be appreciated that here, as well as in our preoccupations with other extraterritorial concerns, there was no conscious planning on the part of statesmen evident; the absence, too, of public discussion showed plainly that up to the war with Spain in 1898 the American people were not thinking in imperialistic terms. It had become apparent, however, by the seventies and eighties, that American life revolved on two axes, an Eastern and a Western one. To the opening of California and the whole Pacific Coast, the life of the nation revolved about the East. The Middle West was, in large part, a New England colony. As far west as the Great Plains, the people of the country looked to the eastern seaboard for their inspiration. But with the acquisition of Oregon (1846) and California (1848) there began to develop a life on the Pacific which became more or less self-centered. More than two decades elapsed before Far West and East were united by the iron bands of the transcontinental railways; another two decades were to round their course before West and East became integral parts of the same whole, through the disappearance of the frontier. In those forty years it was inevitable that Far West and East should have developed different interests and attitudes that did not originate from the same sources or indeed contemplate the same ends. The Far West had its eyes turned west over the wide expanses of the Pacific Ocean, just as the Atlantic seaboard and the Middle West looked across the Atlantic to Europe.

The United States began to figure prominently in the Samoan Islands, in the distant South Seas, in the seventies. In 1872, the American consul in the islands obtained harbor privileges for American ships; six years later, the United States was signatory to a treaty by which we were accorded the exclusive right to use the harbor of Pagopago. In return the American State Department promised to employ its good offices in the event of disputes between the Samoan king and other nations. We played a part in Samoan affairs, along with Great Britain and Germany, in 1886 and in 1889. In the earlier year, the American consul proclaimed an American protectorate over Samoa, only to have the State Department disavow the act. In the later year, international complications for a time seemed imminent, when Germany sought to impose its domination on the native chieftains. There were soon gathered in the harbor of Apia the warships of the three powers, but a tropical hurricane blew up and soon all but one of the ships were wrecked (March 16, 1889). The common distress drove away all thoughts of hostilities. Later in the year, at Berlin, representatives of the United States, Great Britain, and Germany signed a convention which resulted in one of the rare instances of American formal participation in foreign affairs in the company of other powers. The three nations recognized the independence of Samoa but placed authority in the hands of a chief justice and the Apian municipal council, the members of which were to be chosen by the British, the Germans, and ourselves. With the conclusion of the Spanish-American War, and the appearance of a definite colonial outlook in our foreign relations, we openly abandoned our former policy of scrupulous observance of native rights. On December 4, 1899, a treaty was signed by which the Samoan Islands were partitioned between Germany and the United States, the American share being the Island of Tutuila (with its harbor of Pagopago). American insular possessions in the Pacific were further rounded out by the acquisition of Wake Island and Midway Island, both situated in the Northern Pacific and valuable as naval stations—as events of World War II clearly demonstrated.

THE TERRITORY OF HAWAII

The Hawaiian Islands, lying in the lower end of the North Pacific Ocean and but 2100 miles from America's Pacific coast, began to figure prominently in American annals as early as the twenties of the nineteenth century. To this sunny land had come a small band of Boston missionaries in 1820, and in a short time their influence was to be deeply felt. They introduced schools, built churches, established newspapers, and brought modern medical care into the islands. Yankee ship captains, dropping into Hawaiian harbors after their fur-trading expeditions on the North Pacific coast of America, found that the islands' sandalwood was prized in China. As a result there soon developed a thriving three-cornered trade, Hawaiian sandalwood paying for Chinese silks, spices, and chinaware for the American market. The stripping of the sandalwood forests (by the thirties) did not end American interest in the islands. Whales were found in the Pacific, and American ships continued to be attracted to Hawaii, in whose ports they could provision, make repairs, and take on additional seamen. During the twenty years 1840 to 1860 as many as four hundred American whalers annually visited the islands. As early as the forties it was found that Hawaii could grow sugar on a grand scale, and this development forged another link in the close bonds already uniting the islands with the United States. The end of the Civil War saw the decline of the American merchant marine and the discovery of natural gas and oil (for kerosene) in the United States, with the result that the whaling industry languished. Sugar remained, and it was Hawaiian sugar that brought the islands under the control of the United States at the end of the nineteenth century.

As early as 1851 sugar planters in the islands (Americans for the most part and the sons of American missionaries and traders) sought an American protectorate—partly as relief from continuous foreign molestation at the hands of British and French Far Eastern officials; largely, however, to escape the heavy duties of the American tariffs. In 1875 the sugar planters gained a signal victory with the signing of a treaty of reciprocity between the islands and the United States by which Hawaiian sugar was given most-favored-nation treatment. Sugar growing boomed, Hawaiian planters and American refiners benefiting magnificently thereby. Whereas in 1875 some 18 million pounds had been sent into the United States, by 1890 the export of sugar totaled 260 million pounds and was valued at $12 million. The 1875 treaty was terminable after seven years, but in 1884 an extension was obtained, not without considerable profit to the United States, for by this Hawaii ceded to America the exclusive rights to enter and maintain a naval station in Pearl Harbor.

The Tariff Act of 1890 burst the bubble of Hawaiian content. To dispose of the American Treasury surplus, it placed all sugar on the free list, while giving a bounty of two cents to American growers. In one year the price of Hawaiian sugar was cut in half and the American minister to the islands estimated the loss to the native planters and mill owners at not less than $12 million. America's annexation became the only remedy that could restore the old prosperity to the American-owned plantations in Hawaii.

It is important to note how deeply the Americans in the islands had entrenched themselves. Previous to 1848, land in the archipelago had been held under a native feudal system whose center was the king. During the fifties and sixties, as a result of the influence of western institutions, a division of the lands had taken place with the crown, the government, and the chiefs being the only beneficiaries. Private property in land gave foreigners their opportunity, and they found it easy to buy up and lease large tracts, for the chiefs and the crown had fallen heavily into debt. In 1893, there were 1,800,000 acres of private lands of which Americans and

Europeans owned 1,050,000 acres. In addition, the greater portion of the 915,000 acres owned by the crown was leased to planters and was under sugar. At this time the total value of the private plantations was $32 million, of which Americans owned 74 per cent.

It was inevitable that such a heavy economic stake should lead to concern over the archipelago's political stability. The native rulers were induced to promulgate a series of constitutions during 1847 to 1877 which abolished the guarantee of the franchise (for the natives), placed a property qualification on voting for the house of nobles, and extended the right of suffrage to resident foreigners of American and European birth or descent. The American party in the islands actively entered politics and backed the candidacy of Kalakaua, who was chosen king in 1874 over Queen Emma (who had the support of the natives and the British interests). The reciprocity treaty of 1875 followed, bringing in its train the problem of a large Asiatic population imported under contracts to till the sugar fields. From 1874 to 1878 the American party had the situation in hand. Then it slipped from their grasp as the king increasingly showed that his sympathies were with the aspirations of the natives and Asiatics.

In 1887, the American party again sought to gain control. A revolution took place and a new constitution was wrested from the king which placed propertied men at the head of the government. But by 1890 the small group of influential Americans—not numbering more than a few thousand persons—was again driven from power, this time by a union of the native party with the white laborers, who were opposed to the coolie labor policy of the planters. The death of Kalakaua in 1891 and the succession of his sister Liliuokalani, who detested the foreign domination and was committed to the extension of native rule, brought the whole matter to a head.

The foreign capitalists organized a Committee of Safety headed by Sanford B. Dole, the native-born son of an American missionary, obtained the promise of support of the American minister, J. L. Stevens, and on January 17, 1893, in the presence of American marines (who were ostensibly landed to protect American property), terminated the Hawaiian monarchy. Stevens recognized the new provisional government before the queen's surrender, thus forcing her submission. The American minister, without having received the consent of the State Department, ran up the American flag on the government building and an American protectorate remained in force until March 31, 1893. An Hawaiian commission at once repaired to Washington where on February 14, 1893, there was signed a treaty annexing Hawaii to the United States. The Senate failed to act before Cleveland's inauguration with the result that Cleveland, suspecting that the revolution had not been altogether spontaneous, withdrew the treaty and sent at once a special commissioner to the islands to make a first-hand investigation.

It was this commissioner, J. H. Blount, who ordered the lowering of the American flag. Blount reported to Cleveland that the revolution could not have been effected without Stevens' aid and that it was not a native uprising but entirely a movement of the American and European planters and capitalists. The new American minister was ordered to negotiate with the provisional government and with the queen: the first was to be asked to restore the monarchy, the second to grant a general amnesty to the "revolutionists." But Dole, as leader of the provisional government, refused to yield and in 1894, while Cleveland temporized, a republic was proclaimed and Dole was named its first president. Cleveland at once wrote a formal letter of recognition in which he was quickly followed by the foreign offices of other nations; an unsuccessful native insurrection in the next year forced the queen's abdication and Hawaii thus had joined the roll of republican states.

On June 16, 1897, McKinley, in office but three months, ordered the signing of a new treaty of annexation with the island republic. But colonialism had not yet become accepted American currency, and as the Senate debated a heated war of pamphlets took place. The Little Americans exposed the facts of the ruling foreign oligarchy and the domination of sugar and pointed out that the national Hawaiian debt of $4 million, which the treaty accepted, was held by speculators. The Big Americans talked of hostile powers in the Pacific, Japan in particular, quoted Captain Mahan, America's great naval authority, on the strategical value of the islands, and declared that annexation would secure to the United States the commerce and carrying trade of Hawaii. The Little Americans prevailed and the treaty was rejected. In the heat of the War with Spain, however, Congress passed a joint resolution annexing the islands to the United States, and on July 7, 1898, President McKinley affixed his signature and Hawaii was ours. On April 30, 1900, Hawaii received the full status of a territory and Dole, the island's first president, was appointed the territory's first governor. Not only were a territorial legislature and a judicial machinery at once set up but, unique among territories, Hawaii was given the administration and revenue of its public lands.

Under American rule, Hawaii continued to thrive. Investments were sizable; standards of living rose; and the islands became an important American pleasure resort. Continued efforts to grant the islands statehood, however, were unavailing, the latest such serious attempt being rejected in 1948.

THE TERRITORY OF ALASKA

From 1867 to 1884 the land of Alaska with its 590,000 square miles of territory was popularly referred to as "Seward's Folly" and had the studied neglect of American statesmen. The Army and a customs collector ruled it for the first eleven years; a naval officer was in charge during 1879 to 1884. To such Americans as were aware of Alaska, that distant and frozen land was merely a seal rookery from which a bare $300,000 annually might be obtained through the lease of the sealing rights to a trading company. By the eighties, there were only 1000 whites, some 5000 half-breeds, and 30,000 natives living in the country. In 1884, Congress passed a law giving Alaska some rudiments of civil government. A governor and a group of commissioners were to be appointed by the President, as was also a district court judge. But there were to be no Congressional delegate, no legislative assembly, no constitutional oath, and no scheme of taxation for a number of years to come.

In 1896, gold was discovered on the Canadian side of the boundary; the next year prospectors had found gold in the Yukon Valley; soon they were to come across the precious metal in the sands around Nome. By the end of the nineteenth century 50,000 white stampeders had made their way into Alaska. The gold craze was followed by others—by copper, coal, and oil—and Alaska began, in Congressional eyes, to seem a desirable possession. In 1898, a Transportation and Homestead Act was passed; in 1899, Congress wrote a criminal code for the territory; in 1900, a civil code was enacted; in 1903, a generous homestead law was written; in 1906, Alaska got its delegate in Congress. The criminal and civil codes made possible the erection of local governmental machinery and five cities shortly availed themselves of the right to incorporate.

The struggle for the control of the territory's coal fields set off a whole new train of events. Theodore Roosevelt, developing his conservation policy, withdrew from entry all of Alaska's coal lands in 1906. In the same year there appeared the Alaska Syndicate, a private corporation backed by powerful American financial interests and formed to exploit the country's natural resources. Starting first with copper, this group soon was figuring prominently in steamship transportation, the salmon industry, and railroading. Its ever-present lobby at Washington steadily blocked home rule for the district and succeeded in keeping at arm's length potential railroad rivals. When, during the Taft administration, the Alaska Syndicate sought to push its activities into the coal lands it brought to a head the whole conservation conflict. Taft gave way only reluctantly, but by 1912 he was prepared to acknowledge his defeat. That year saw the enactment of legislation giving Alaska territorial status with a legislative assembly and other civil officers, the establishment of a policy of coal leases, and the approval of plans for a trunk-line railroad to be constructed and owned by the national government. The Wilson administration witnessed the leasing policy extended to the oil lands and waterpower sites. Under Wilson, too, was begun the Alaskan railway, the main line of which was finished in 1923.

Despite the extraordinary richness of Alaska's mineral resources, the fisheries continue to be the territory's chief industry, the annual yield being worth as much as the output of all the other industries combined. Copper mining is the chief mineral activity, having supplanted gold. Oil, too, has been found, as well as lead, tin, tungsten, natural gas, marble, platinum, sulphur, and, of course, large fields of sub-bituminous and lignite coal. Under wise governmental supervision to check exploitation, Alaska must sooner or later turn out to be one of the most fortunate acquisitions made by the United States. During and after World War II it was found that Alaska has great strategic significance: it turned out to be an important American outpost on the Pacific and Arctic Oceans.

THE NEW NAVY

From 1865 to 1880 the American Navy consisted of a collection of rotting wooden ships, the great majority unavailable for immediate service or incapable of carrying guns. While the European powers, impressed by the lessons of the Civil War, experimented with and developed rifled guns, torpedoes, steel armaments, and the use of steam, Americans derived comfort from their isolation and believed that at the threat of danger the necessary elements of ships and men could be obtained from the nation's merchant marine. The year 1880 saw 142 vessels in the American Navy; but a chromo of the period, depicting the President reviewing the fleet, could muster only a round dozen presentable ships, all of wood, and among which were to be found the ancient frigate *Constitution* and the side-wheeler steamer, the *Powhatan* (laid down in the forties)! At the door of that restless spirit Blaine is to be laid the credit for the development of a new naval policy, just as one must concede him the responsibility for having turned the attention of the America of the eighties to the world which lay outside its door. His interest in the Isthmian canal, his preoccupation with Hawaiian affairs, his concern over the safety of the country's long Pacific coast line appear to have had their influence on fellow Cabinet members, for Garfield's Secretary of the Navy adverted to all these when he called Congress' attention to the deplorable state of the Navy. Another Secretary, in addressing Congress in 1883, already could speak openly of a need for new armaments "to assert at all times our natural, justifiable and necessary ascendancy in the affairs of the American hemisphere."

From 1882 to the end of the century events moved swiftly. A Naval Advisory Board was set up and it proceeded to bombard Congress with requests for large naval appropriations. In 1883, after considerable debate, Congress yielded to the extent of authorizing the Secretary of the Navy to construct four steel vessels in American yards, "said vessels to be provided with full sail power and full steam power." Thus the new Navy definitely emerged. These four vessels were the nucleus of that White Squadron which played such a prominent role in the life of the America of the eighties and nineties. They were small unarmored craft, the largest having a displacement of but 4500 tons and a sea speed of 14 knots. Almost every year thereafter saw the authorization of new steel vessels; in 1886, came the *Texas,* the first ship to carry armor plate; in 1887, two more cruisers were sanctioned; in 1888, six cruisers were added; and in 1890, the initial first-class battleship was contracted for. To allay hostility, lest all this might mean elaborate preparations for offensive war, the new fighting ships were officially denominated "sea-going coastline battleships." By 1900, the American Navy (launched, in building, or authorized) consisted of fifteen battleships of the first class, one battleship of the second class, five armored cruisers, one armored ram, twenty-four protected and unprotected cruisers, twenty-three coast-defense ships, eighteen gunboats and fifty-three torpedo-craft. The cost of these ships was approximately $275,000,000. The government also owned twenty-three navy yards, valued at $100,000,000, for their service. The ships were manned by a personnel of more than 20,000 officers, seamen, and apprentices. In 1880, the United States had spent on its navy the sum of $13,500,000; in 1900, naval expenditures were $55,953,000. Whereas in 1880 the United States ranked as the world's twelfth naval power and it was commonly said that its wooden hulks could be no match for Chile's modern fleet of two cruisers, by 1893 the country had moved to fifth place and by 1900 to third. Only Great Britain and France outranked America as the twentieth century opened.

A number of interesting consequences of this preoccupation with naval matters are to be noted. The impetus given to the development of the country's steel industry by the Congressional mandate that only domestic steel be employed in the construction of the ships was decided. Because of the insistence of Cleveland's Secretary of the Navy, William C. Whitney, that the armorplate required for the ships be of American manufacture, the Bethlehem Iron Company and the Carnegie Steel Company turned to its production, the Carnegie plant in 1890 alone making 6000 tons. It is a curious commentary on men and events that Carnegie, in his autobiography, gives considerable space to his philanthropies and none at all to the new American Navy which he helped to build. In 1885, the Naval War College was established at Newport and to this event may be directly attributed much of the significance of naval armaments in the history of the modern world of the twentieth century. The College's president invited a middle-aged naval officer to join his staff as lecturer on naval history. Out of this academic exercise emerged the work of Captain (later Admiral) A. T. Mahan. In 1890, Mahan published his *Influence of Sea Power upon History;* in 1892, his *Influence of Sea Power upon the French Revolution and Empire* appeared; in 1905, came his *Sea Power in Its Relations to the*

War of 1812. Mahan was a propagandist as well as an historian and a great number of magazine articles, counseling naval preparedness, poured from his prolific pen. These books and articles at once obtained world-wide recognition, hastened the construction of the modern German and Japanese fleets, and strengthened Great Britain in its conviction that in its fleet lay its power and security. Mahan taught his generation to think in imperialistic terms; he spoke of dreadnoughts and not of cruisers, of fleets as opposed to single ships, of preparing for offensives, and of the control of the seas as against coast defense. Shortly after the appearance of his work American Congresses stopped talking of "sea-going coastline battleships." The words "a navy second to none" were more frequently to be heard.

Section III
THE
MAKING OF MODERN AMERICA

· 7 ·

Settling the Continent

THE GROWTH OF POPULATION

WITHIN the life of a single generation, that is to say between 1870 and 1900, the population of the United States doubled. The census of 1870 showed that in the continental United States there were living 38,558,000 persons; by 1900, their numbers had increased to 75,994,000. The process of industrialization filled the older sections of New England, the Middle Atlantic, and the East North Central states; it was the growth of the cities and the heavy influx of European immigrants that made for this development. On the other hand, the West grew amazingly, as millions of farming families penetrated beyond the Mississippi River to fill up the public lands. The western sections of the country showed the greatest proportionate gains in these thirty years.

A significant demographic tendency of the period was the settlement of the cities. In 1870, but one-fifth of the country's population was urban (living in places of 8000 or more population); by 1900, the proportion was almost one-third. In the North Atlantic states, by the turn of the century, more than one-half of the population had become industrialized and its breadwinners were working in factories and in mercantile pursuits; in the North Central states the industrial and mercantile population had grown to 30 per cent of the total; in the western states, the proportion had climbed to 31 per cent. Also, in the thirty years the great metropolis had definitely emerged. In 1870, there had been but seven cities having 200,000 inhabitants or more, and their combined population had been 3,356,000, or less than 9 per cent of the country's total. In 1900, the cities of this class had grown to nineteen in number and had a combined population of 11,796,000, or 15.5 per cent of the country's inhabitants. Particularly marked had been the development of the cities of the North Central states. Whereas Boston in the thirty years had shown a gain of only 124 per cent and Baltimore only 90 per cent, Chicago had gained 470 per cent, Cleveland 310 per cent, Minneapolis 1460 per cent, and Omaha 536 per cent.

We may observe the other outstanding characteristics of the country's population: The proportion of Negroes was on the decline. By the census of 1860 (more reliable than that of 1870) the Negroes had made up 14.1 per cent of the country's total population; in 1900, they made up but 11.6 per cent. The size of the foreign-born group showed a slight decrease, proportionately. But the native-born whites of foreign parentage showed a great increase. In 1870, this group represented 15.9 per cent of the population; by 1900, it had increased to 23.4 per cent. In point of age, the population of the United States had definitely the characteristics of a pioneer and immigrant people, and it was a young nation that settled the West, built the railroads and laid the foundations of America's industrial greatness. So, in the age groups under 45 years, 85 per cent of the population was to be found in 1870; 82 per cent in 1900; 79.1 per cent in 1920; and 73.5 per cent in 1940.

THE WEST AND THE PASSING OF THE FRONTIER

The West has always been a relative term in American history. It is a condition of development and, as F. J. Turner has so brilliantly pointed out, a frame of mind. In the thinning lines of settlement, where the simple matter of living is accompanied by so much travail and uncertainty, there have developed traits and mental attitudes which have ever been the peculiar characteristics of a frontier society. The frontiersman has been an individualist; impatient of the restraints of an ordered group life; credulous and superstitious because life does hang on a thread; a believer in easy panaceas because his own single-handed victory over nature has led him to feel that for every difficulty a key can somewhere be found. The man of the West has been deeply religious but his religion has often taken strange forms. He has believed in government but has refused to invest civil codes with the sanctity which tradition builds about them. He has believed in the rights of private property but it has been a property of land, kine, and buildings: the private property of good will, franchise rights, depreciation values, patents, and royalties, he has always suspected. Art, leisure, the orderly habits of a settled life that has grown introspective —what we sometimes call civilization—these have not been of the West. In other words, the West is youth, and because it has always grown older it, in turn, has come to regard with suspicion newer Wests.

The sweep toward the West had not gone on inexorably: there had been temporary setbacks and heartbreaking interludes which filled the older communities with broken men and women. The prairies were not finally conquered until the fifties; the Great Plains of Kansas and Nebraska did not yield to the persistence of the American pioneer before the nineties; there are still indomitable souls battling against the fierceness of nature in the deserts of western California, Utah, Nevada, and Arizona. Nevertheless, the process slowly continued and by the end of the century the frontier was no more: East had joined West, and in so doing had written the conclusion to the great American epic of settlement.

What had contributed toward this miraculous growth? These factors stand out as the most important reasons for the peopling of the Far West: 1. the easy entry of the lands in the public domain; 2. the growth of the railroad net; 3. the propaganda, in Europe, of the transatlantic steamship companies; 4. the activities of European immigration agents of a number of the western states; 5. the cattle boom on the Great Plains; 6. the discovery of gold in the Black Hills of the Dakotas; 7. the bad harvests which hit almost all the wheat-growing regions of the world in the seventies and which sent European peasants and eastern farmers into the West to open new wheat lands; 8. the series of wars in which European nations were involved during the period, and which accounted for heavy European emigrations of men sick of military service.

By thousands of families, every day saw new settlers forcing their stubborn way into the unhabited territories of the Far West. They came with small capital, little household furniture, and none of those simple comforts of life which make existence supportable. Because of the scarcity of timber, they lived in dugouts or sod houses. Indians, prairie fires, blizzards, locusts, and droughts, not to speak of the depredations of their fellowmen, made the life of the pioneers on the plains one of frequent suffering. Added to all this, communities, except in the case of religious groups, were rare; methods of communication were primitive. The population was heterogeneous, coming from many lands, different states, speaking numerous languages, and worshiping God in a great variety of ways. Yet, houses were finally built, communities were welded together, schoolhouses rose, the Indian was pushed farther and farther back. Inventions appeared to make the agricultural round less arduous, and agricultural colleges sprang up in the western states to bring science to the aid of the struggling farmer. In time nature was conquered. But the pioneers of the West met defeat at every turn when they sought to overcome human obstacles. The uprising of the West was the fitting climax of the drama of western settlement and the history of this short period, as we shall see, marks one of the great epochs in American annals.

THE PUBLIC DOMAIN

The western settler, seeking a farm to till, could obtain a homestead in one of a variety of ways. He might buy a farm outright from the national government as a result of the operations of the Pre-emption Act of 1841. This law, passed largely to protect the squatter rights of the early settlers

**CLOSING THE FRONTIERS
1889-1912**

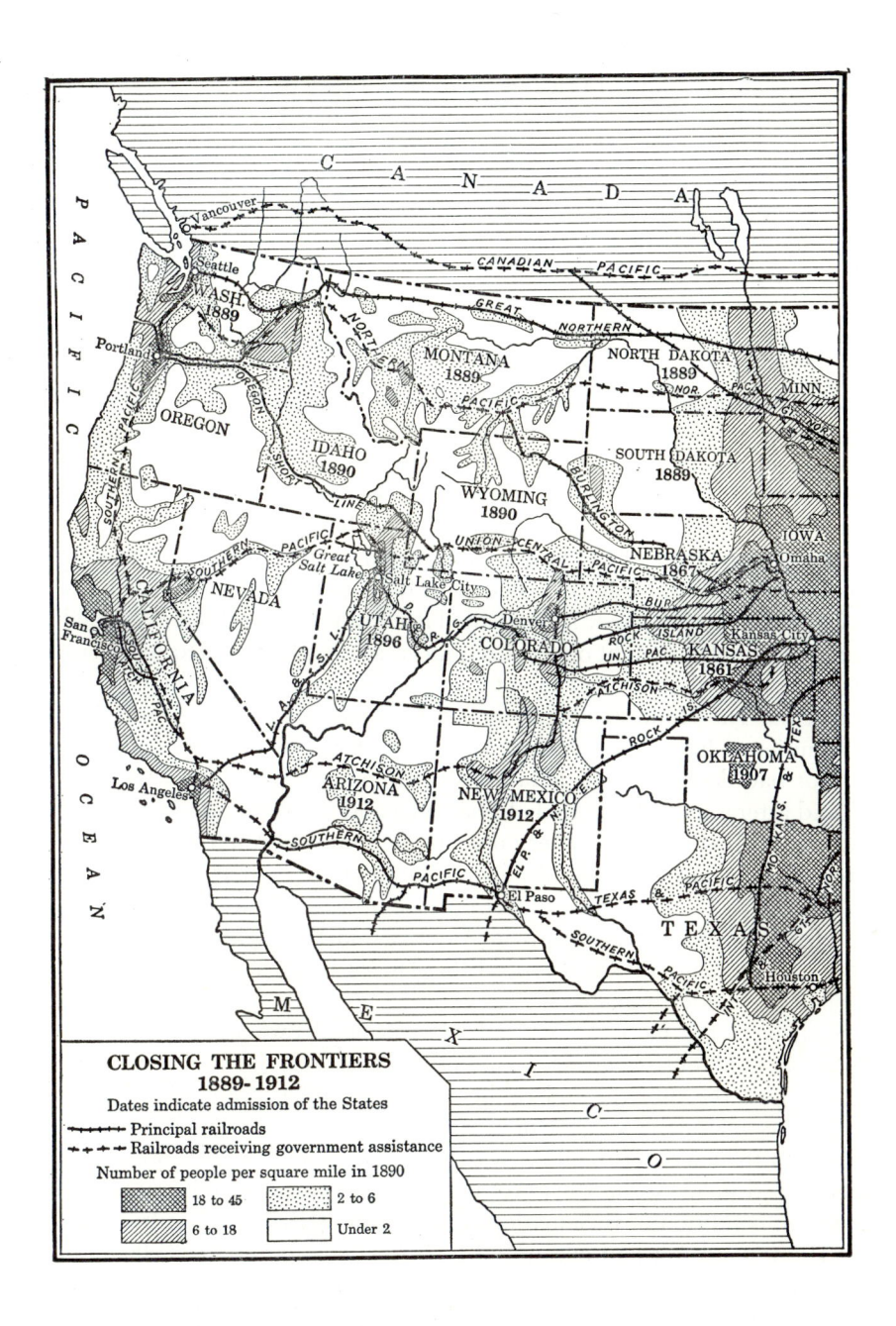

Dates indicate admission of the States

- ┼┼┼┼ Principal railroads
- ┼─┼─┼ Railroads receiving government assistance

Number of people per square mile in 1890

- 18 to 45
- 2 to 6
- 6 to 18
- Under 2

in the Middle West, made possible the purchase of a quarter section of 160 acres at the nominal price of $1.25 per acre. The statute continued in force until 1891, being rescinded only after it had become apparent that reckless speculation had been carried on under it. Again, he might purchase his quarter section from one of the many land-grant railroads. The federal government had made its first land grants from the public domain, for the purpose of encouraging railroad building, in 1850. Then, beginning with 1862, when the Union Pacific Railroad had been incorporated by Congress, and ending in 1871 the federal government had chartered a group of great railroad corporations to which it had given bountifully from the public domain. As a third alternative, the farmer might purchase his quarter section from any one of the states in the Union. As far back as the beginnings of the American nation, the federal government had begun the practice of making grants from the public domain to the individual states to encourage internal improvements and the establishment of common schools. In 1862, these state holdings had been enormously increased through the passage of the Morrill Act, which gave every state establishing a public agricultural college 30,000 acres for each representative that it had in Congress. In time every state availed itself of the federal bounty. Finally, the western settler might obtain his quarter section free of charge by entering the public domain and maintaining a residence on his homestead for five years. The Homestead Act, signed by Lincoln in 1862, gave to heads of families or individuals twenty-one years of age or over, who were citizens or had declared their intentions of becoming such, a quarter section of land after a five-year period of residence and cultivation. A homesteader was allowed, at any time after entry, to commute his quarter section into a pre-emption and thus buy his farm outright at the regular price. It should be noted that the great majority of entries, up to 1900, were completed by purchase. But land was cheap in America—in the eighteen seventies as little as $5 an acre in Kansas—and the American pioneer was able to become a freeholder quickly.

Such were the methods devised to make land ownership easy for the settler. A generous Congress passed other measures, during the period, to throw open the mineral and timber lands. In 1864, pre-emption of coal lands was made the subject of a special law; a timber culture act was passed in 1873; a desert land act was passed in 1877; a timber and stone act was passed in 1878; the Cary Act of 1894 made desert-land grants to the states on condition of reclamation. From 1868 to 1880, final entries under the Homestead Act had accounted for the alienation of 19,265,000 acres; by 1927, alienation had accounted for 228,742,000 acres (1,400,443 entries), making an average per year of 23,340 entries and 3,812,000 acres. The public domain of the continental United States had at one time or another included an area of 1,442,200,320 acres and had taken in the whole territory of the country with the exception of the thirteen original states and the lands within the confines of Maine, Vermont, Kentucky, Tennessee, Texas, and West Virginia. By June 30, 1930, the area of unreserved and unappropriated lands had shrunk to 179,000,000 acres. Moreover, such unappropriated lands as now remain are unavailable for tillage, and so to all intents and purposes the public domain is exhausted.

The whole system of land disposal soon became honeycombed with fraud. There was fraud in the filing of homestead entries and in the purchase of land under the Pre-emption Act; there was open theft of the public lands through illegal enclosing, particularly by the cattlemen; timber and mineral lands were illegally pre-empted. The land-grant railroads were notoriously culpable: they sought to maintain possession of their sections without troubling to comply with the terms of the awards; and even after they had laid down their tracks, many continued to hold out the choicest sections for their speculative values.

In 1879, a commission recommended that new classifications be created for the alienation of agricultural, grazing, timber, and mineral lands. It suggested the repeal of the Pre-emption Law of 1841; urged the disposal of the western lands through the Homestead Law exclusively; called for the sale of timber lands apart from the surface; and recommended the repeal of the Timber and Stone Act. Cleveland was the only President, before Theodore Roosevelt, to take serious measures looking toward the recapture of lands that had been illegally entered. It was not until the twentieth century, however, that there began to emerge glimmerings of an intelligent national policy for the management of the public lands and the conservation of the country's natural resources. America's lands and resources were given away with a reckless hand; yet in the process America was settled and its industrial greatness assured. Could a balance have been struck? It is hard to say.

THE COW COUNTRY

The cow country of the Far West provided another chapter in the later history of the American frontier. For some two centuries longhorn cattle, which had been known to the Southwest since the early days of the Spanish occupation, had been bred on the Texas plains largely for their hides. The coming of the Union Pacific and the Kansas Pacific into the Western country opened the eyes of Texas cattlemen to the possibilities of the meat market of the East.[1] They crossed the longhorn cows with imported sires and produced a variety of prime beef which was welcomed in the markets of the East and of Europe, particularly because of the crop failures through-

---

[1] There were other influences, of course, in the development of the cattle industry, among which the perfection of the refrigerator car and the growth of the canning factories were the more important.

out the world in the late seventies. The unfenced plains of the public domain, where pasturage was bountiful and free for the taking, gave the industry every opportunity to develop. Great herds of cattle soon filled the Texas country from the Rio Grande to the Red. In the seventies there were as many as 5,500,000 head of cattle roaming the Texas plains. In the spring, the cattlemen rounded up the cows and their calves and branded the young animals with the distinctive marks of their owners. Then commenced that long drive which, in a short time, stretched from Texas clear to the Canadian border. The yearlings were usually turned over to feeders or drovers and, guarded and tended by the cowboys, they were driven across the Great Plains to railroad stations or to the northern ranges. In the seventies, the long drive went through the Panhandle, the Cherokee country, Kansas, and Nebraska. Dodge City (Kansas) on the Kansas Pacific and Ogallala (Nebraska) on the Union Pacific were two of the earliest shipping points. Here the cattle were usually loaded on the trains and sent to Kansas City or Chicago stockyards. As the industry became popular and more and more persons participated in it, it turned into a duel between the commission men and the growers. The cattlemen found that the herds could winter on the northern plains as comfortably as they had done in Texas, and that in this fact they had a weapon with which to fight the eastern markets. In other words, it was not necessary to entrain the animals on the cars at the very first railroad station reached and thus be compelled to accept the prices offered by the eastern buyers.

Thus the long drive lengthened. The herds were driven into northern Colorado, Dakota, Wyoming, and Montana. Here they were pastured on the public domain, usually on great ranches illegally enclosed with barbed wire and often around streams and waterholes, where their owners held their stocks until the time was ripe for shipment east. The first shipment of cattle from Wyoming eastward over the Union Pacific took place in 1870. In 1879, 100,000 longhorns got by the Wyoming buyers and trailed north into Montana. From 1865 to 1885, the number of cattle that were driven north to be fattened on the ranges and then shipped over the railroads to the stockyards totaled 5,714,000—an average of 285,700 for each year.

The cattle business witnessed boom times in the eighties and foreign capital poured into the country to permit of operations on a large scale. From Glasgow, London, Boston, and New York offices stock prospectuses went forth to middle-class homes to excite small investors with dreams of wealth. Yet the end of the decade saw the whole thing as flat as a pricked bubble. It is enough for our purposes here to recite the causes of the collapse of the western cattle industry: The same railroads which furnished facilities for the shipment of the cattle east brought the homesteaders to the West. The fencing of the western farms put an end to the open range and thus deprived the industry of its feeding grounds. The boom brought crowded ranges and the presence in the field of the stock companies necessitated the production of quick profits. As a result, prices dropped steadily until from a peak of $4.25 per hundredweight in April, 1883, they reached $1.00 in the winter of 1887 (Chicago market). For sanitary and economic reasons, western states and European nations began to place quarantines on the plains cattle. Kansas, Nebraska, and Colorado enacted laws in the eighties against the driving of foreign cattle across their borders and the cowboys were met by embattled farmers armed with shotguns. Western Europe closed its ports to plains cattle and the federal Bureau of Animal Husbandry, founded in 1884 (for the inspection of the cattle), came too late to repair the damage. The illegal fencing of the range by the northern cattlemen forced governmental agencies to move against them. The cattlemen had become particularly unpopular because they had pre-empted the few watercourses in an arid country. The East began to compete with the West and to send its yearlings to be fattened on the plains, too. The industry tempted the farmers of the Middle West and soon there began to appear on the western ranges the barnyard stock of Illinois, Wisconsin, Michigan, Iowa, and Missouri. This further aggravated the processes of overexpansion. Sheepmen began to raise their heads in the West, to compete for grazing lands and watering places.

As a result of the general depression of the late eighties and early nineties, because of the strangle hold that the railroads, commission men, and packers had on the situation, and with the larger competition of barnyard growing, the cattlemen of the open plains found themselves trapped and soon gave up the unequal struggle. The northern plainsmen leased or bought land, fenced it, grew hay, and finally turned to sheep because they were easier to breed. The cowboy had lived his brief, colorful day, the range was closed, and another episode in the history of the American frontier was ended. But the stockyards, which had grown with the cow country, did not languish. The Union Stockyards of Chicago, first opened in 1865, continued to flourish, and the men who had made their fortunes by cultivating the western cattlemen remained to tighten their grip on the American provisions industry.

THE INDIANS

The policy of concentrating the Indian tribes on reservations was not a new one. As early as 1804 the first such treaty had been drawn; in 1825, the Indian Territory had been acquired and by 1840 the "Five Civilized Tribes" had all been settled on its lands. Beginning with the middle of the nineteenth century, for almost fifty years the Indians of the Middle and Far West waged an unequal struggle to keep their open hunting grounds. But the westward progress of the white man was not to be stayed and by the end of the century the Indians were all safely confined on reservations.

It may be said that nothing contributed more to their final reduction than the program of pauperization employed by the federal Bureau of Indian Affairs. As wards of the nation, the Indians were fed, clothed, and housed at governmental expense; no efforts were exerted to make them self-sufficing. One cannot regret too deeply the methods employed in making the western plains safe for white habitation. The federal agents at the Indian reservations were as a rule ignorant and grasping men; many army generals capitalized their presence in the Far West to build up their reputations; the Washington officials employed all the devices of a cruel penology to break the spirit of the tribesmen, the most frequent one being exile to the swamps of Florida. To study patiently the problems of the Indian; to seek to smooth the way for his adjustment to a newer and higher civilization; to help preserve an ethnic consciousness which might have made the Indian happy in his bondage; by education to teach the Red Men to stand on their own feet and to find in economic independence one form of release: all these did not come until the American chronicle had become spotted with unnecessary Indian wars, the illegal entry of Indian reservations and the breaking of the spirit of the few free tribesmen who sought to remain on their ancestral lands.

As the War Department, during the seventies and eighties, pursued its own relentless way, "pacifying" the Indians by exterminating them, wiser policies slowly began to take shape at Washington. In 1869, an unpaid Board of Indian Commissioners was set up to give the benefit of its advice to the Indian Bureau. In 1871, Congress ended the farce of treaty writing with the Indians and took the tribes under its complete supervision. The seventies, too, saw the evolution of a governmental educational program and the establishment of Indian boarding schools removed from the reservations. It was not until considerably later that the enlightened decision was made that the proper place for the Indian child was at the side of his small white neighbor, or in day reservation schools which could serve as community centers. (At the present time two-thirds of the Indian children attend ordinary public schools.) In 1887, Congress took the first serious step toward solving the Indian land problem. The Dawes Act of that year sanctioned the division of the tribal lands among the individual Indians, granting to each head of family an allotment of 160 acres and to each adult single person 80 acres. The surplus lands were to be sold and the receipts held in trust by the government for the entire community. These homesteads, however, were to be maintained as trusts for twenty-five years, were inalienable and were to be exempt from taxation. Also, such homesteaders were to be invested with citizenship rights. The original law underwent a series of modifications: allotments came to be made to all persons; the prohibition against inalienability was gradually lifted and land leasing was permitted; the grant of citizenship was delayed until 1924. In 1934, laws denying civil rights to Indians were repealed, and the Indian Reorganization Act attempted to reverse past trends, and to preserve tribal organization and tribal land.

Governmental trusteeship of the Indians has made for a number of ironical situations: the Indians today are landed proprietors whose homesteads are being cultivated in some areas by a white tenantry; inalienability, too, has prevented the expropriation of the rich oil and mineral lands of the Oklahoma and Dakota Indians. The Osage Indians of Oklahoma, for example, numbering fewer than 3000 souls in all, own oil fields to the value of almost $3,250,000,000. The total value of other Indian properties in the United States was estimated at more than $2,000,000,000 in the late nineteen forties. Thus a sort of rough compensation has made its appearance, and today many an Indian is richer than his so-called superior white brother who toils in the factories and mines. In addition, the Indian has a fair degree of economic security and the watchful care of a solicitous officialdom which is trying to preserve his cultural integrity rather than to force him into white patterns of thought and behavior. It should be noted, too, that for the last sixty years, the Indian has been thriving under this policy. Whereas in 1887 the Indian Affairs Bureau estimated the total number of Indians in the country at 243,000, the 1940 census counted 333,969, and the proportion of female births indicated that the Indian is by no means on the way to extinction. Dilution and absorption will probably be his lot, none the less, as it has always been that of a conquered people, from the ancient Etruscans to the contemporary Hawaiians.

THE WAVES OF IMMIGRATION

From 1820 to the end of the century, almost 20,000,000 immigrants poured into the United States. The stream was a steady and apparently an inexhaustible one: it flowed from every European country and from almost every Oriental land. By the time its course had been checked, at the end of the nineteen twenties, it had filled the American continent with a congeries of peoples whose ways of life and modes of thought would have been bewildering even to a Benjamin Franklin, cosmopolitan though he was.

In the nineteenth century, government and industry welcomed the immigrant gladly. In 1864, the federal government took the first step to encourage immigration officially: it set up an Immigration Bureau at Washington, and Congress wrote a law giving legal sanction to the importation of contract laborers from Europe and China. It is to be noted, too, that the federal courts declared unconstitutional a series of New York and

Massachusetts enactments which sought to place some of the burdens of immigration regulation on the steamship companies. In other words, not only did the federal government refuse to check the immigrant flow but it opposed any action on the part of the states to shift the duties of inspection and housing of immigrants to private individuals or corporations. Then, too, many of the western states, notably Wisconsin and Minnesota, maintained immigration bureaus and foreign agents for the purpose of encouraging European settlers.

To fill the holds of the newly formed steamship companies, to take up homesteads, to purchase the surplus acres of the railways in the West, and to supply the man power that expanding American industry needed—these were the prime motives at the back of governmental and private encouragement of immigration. It is true that the misery and squalor of European slums and tenant farms made the break with home ties easy for many; that the official oppression of minorities in Hungary and Russia added their thousands to the immigrant stream; that desire to escape military service in the growing military and naval establishments of Western European nations drove many young men into flight; that assisted immigration by Ireland, Great Britain, Switzerland, and philanthropic agencies in Germany and France smoothed the way for many others. The glowing pictures painted by the agents of the railroad and steamship companies and the letters and stories of immigrants already here and those who had gone back, helped to create an illusion whose pull was irresistible. America was the golden land of opportunity and the haven of the oppressed. In addition, transportation was cheap, farm lands were to be had for the asking, wages by European standards were high, there was freedom of religious worship, no military service, no ruling castes, nothing to stand in the way of aspiring and ambitious peoples who, by work alone, might lift themselves out of the social degradation in which Europe had kept them for centuries. So they came—first the Irish, Germans, Swedes, and Danes, and then the Italians, Jews, Poles, Finns, Croats, Rumanians, Czechs, Ruthenians, Latins, Turks, Greeks. The Germans, Swedes, Finns, and Czechs went on the farms of the old Northwest and helped populate Wisconsin, Michigan, Minnesota, Nebraska, and the Dakotas; the Irish went into the cities of the North; the Jews filled the sweat-shops of New York, Boston, Philadelphia, and Baltimore; the Italians became the day laborers of our growing metropolises; the Poles, Croats, Slovenes, Rumanians went to labor in the stockyards of Chicago and Kansas City, the coal mines of Pennsylvania and Illinois, the textile mills of Fall River, Lowell, and Paterson, the steel mills, the iron foundries, the salt, copper, and lead mines of North, East, South, and West. The giant strides which American industry took in the decades after the Civil War were made possible by a combination of American initiative, British, German, and Dutch capital, high protective tariffs, and the unending toil of millions of immigrant men, women, and children in mills, factories, and coal pits.

It has been said that from 1820 to 1900 almost 20,000,000 immigrants entered American ports. It is not possible to record the number that returned to European and Oriental homes, but it is safe to estimate that from two-thirds to three-fourths remained permanent residents of the United States. In the decade of the forties the total of immigration was 1,713,000; in the decade of the fifties, the total was 2,600,000; in the decade of the sixties, it was 2,314,000; in the decade of the seventies, the total was 2,812,-000; in the decade of the eighties, the total reached the unprecedented figure of 5,246,000; in the nineties, it was 3,687,000. The high point attained in the post-Civil War era was in 1882 when almost 800,000 immigrants landed on American shores. It was not until 1903 that this figure was to be exceeded and not until 1905 that more than 1,000,000 foreigners were to leave Europe and the Near East for America.

The decade of the eighties was to see not only new immigration records being established but a profound change making itself evident in the national origin of the new arrivals. Up to the eighties, three-fourths of all the persons who migrated to the United States came from the Celtic and Teutonic countries of Northern and Western Europe; from that decade on, immigrants from Southern and Eastern Europe and from the Near East took their places. In the decade of the eighties, the immigrants from Italy, Austria-Hungary, and Poland made up 19 per cent of the total; in the decade of the nineties they made up 49 per cent of the total; in the first decade of the twentieth century they made up 66 per cent of the total.

To a certain extent, the immigration from Eastern and Southern Europe was not voluntary: it was induced or aided by American industrialists and by European philanthropists. The Slovaks and Slavs of the Austro-Hungarian monarchy were recruited by the labor agents of the mine operators, railroads, and mill owners of the new American industrialism. The Italian unskilled laborers were brought in by their own *padroni,* who herded them, in great numbers, into the new construction camps of American railroads, roads, and public works. Some Jews from Russia, Austria, and Rumania had their passage paid for by German and French philanthropists, moved by the suffering of their kinsmen in the ghettos of the Old World. As has been said, these newer immigrants peopled the American cities, created the labor reserve for the factories and mines, and furnished the man power that made American industrialism a reality. But their introduction into the country in large numbers transformed the attitude of the government and the ruling groups from one of welcome to one of hostility. With the eighties, not only did the character of our immigrant stocks change but there also began to appear a movement to restrict the flow of immigration, first by selection and then by definite exclusion.

REASONS FOR IMMIGRATION RESTRICTION

In discussing the arguments advanced for restrictive legislation, it is well to distinguish between the social and the economic reasons. Among the former type were such familiar ones as the following. The aliens, particularly those from regions other than the northern and western parts of Europe, were polluting the native American stock and were making, therefore, undesirable citizens. The greater fecundity of the aliens tended to cause the ultimate disappearance of the original native groups. The slums of the cities, breeding places for crime and pauperism, were vexing community problems that could be justly laid at the door of the newcomers. The economic reasons for the hostility displayed toward the newer immigrants deserve a more extended examination.

In the first place, the immigrants were tending to espouse radical and destructive doctrines. This was true of a small group who brought the theories of socialism and anarchism into America; but they were vocal, and their espousal of these causes led to the mistaken assumption that most immigrants were radical. The first American socialist movements were organized by Germans; violence and the doctrines of anarchism were preached by aliens in the eighties; the co-operative schemes of the Knights of Labor were of European origin. The Chicago Haymarket riot of 1886 and the turbulence which characterized most of the strikes of the seventies and eighties convinced American industrialists that this incendiarism was due almost entirely to the foreign leaven in the American population. "Keep the undesirables out," ran the thought of these persons, and there would be no labor difficulties. In other words, the very persons who before had made for the extraordinary immigration development of the nation were now seeking some means of undoing their own handiwork. Chauncey M. Depew, in a Fourth of July address in 1887, called for restriction of immigration and had this to say of those aliens whom the railroad corporations he was representing had brought into the country: "The ranks of anarchy and riots number no Americans. The leaders boldly proclaim that they come here not to enjoy the blessings of our liberty and to sustain our institutions but to destroy our government, cut our throats and divide our property." Henry Cabot Lodge looked with alarm, too, on those foreign societies which were "dangerous to law and order and hostile to every theory of American institutions." The Immigration Restriction League, organized in Boston in 1894, adopted the above arguments in its efforts to convince the government that legislation was necessary.

In the second place, the country's laboring people themselves regarded with dismay the continuous expansion of their ranks, for the new immigrants were being employed as a labor reserve to break strikes and depress wages. Dispute after dispute had been successfully terminated by factory owners merely by filling the places of the striking workers with cheap and docile men from the boats which ever thronged the Atlantic and Pacific harbors. Labor had first felt the dread effects of cheap competition on the Pacific coast where the Pacific railroad workers, on reaching San Francisco and Los Angeles, had found Chinese coolie labor, with its low standards, frugality, and industry, ready to take the bread out of their mouths. Eastern workers, too, were able to witness the cruel results of the introduction of Chinese labor when they saw coolies taking their places at North Adams (Mass.) in 1870 and at Beaver Falls (Pa.) in 1877. In the latter year, too, the railroad managers had brought the first cargo of Magyars into the country to help break the strikes of the trainmen. The same period saw the importation of French Canadians into Massachusetts mill towns with the result that here in seven years wages already low were cut almost one-half. Similarly, as strikebreakers, Slavs were introduced into the coal fields of Pennsylvania; Poles were brought into Cleveland to replace strikers in the local wire mills; Italians and Poles took the places of Irish and Welsh miners, first in Illinois and later in Kansas; Slovaks, Ruthenians, and Poles brought to an unsuccessful conclusion the strike of the Irish and American coopers in the largest oil refining plant of Bayonne (N.J.). All this had been driven into the consciousness of American workingmen in the late seventies and early eighties.

Unions were imperiled, all the efforts of workingmen for higher wages, shorter hours, and better working conditions were as naught when plant managers, with a scratch of the pen, were in a position either to deprive them of jobs altogether, or to fill the adjacent benches with recently arrived immigrants whose very newness (and incidentally, unfamiliarity with the English language or indeed the dialects of one another) made them impervious to the cajoling of union organizers or the arguments for labor solidarity. It is no wonder that one of the labor leaders of the period could say bitterly, "Our living is gauged by immigration; our wages are based on immigration; the condition of our family is gauged by immigration. It is governed by the fellow who is competing with us for the job." Such were some of the pressures that forced a re-examination of America's traditional and free immigration policy.

RESTRICTION LEGISLATION

The first successful move for restriction was aimed at the Chinese coolie labor of the Pacific coast. The gold rush and railroad construction had brought the Chinese, in great numbers, into the Californian cities: they had come first as the cooks and laundrymen of the gold camps; they had then, in the sixties, been imported as contract laborers by the financiers who were constructing the Central Pacific Railroad. The federal government, too, was benevolently inclined. In 1868, the State Department negotiated the Burlingame Treaty with the Chinese government by which we pledged ourselves not to interfere with the goings and comings of the Chinese; in fact, they were to be accorded the treatment received by citizens of most-favored nations. By 1870, out of a total of 56,000 Chinese in the United States, all but 467 lived west of the Rocky Mountains.

The completion of the Central Pacific, and the arrival in the Pacific cities of the white labor gangs that had built the Union Pacific, in the early seventies, brought those inevitable race antagonisms which immediately show themselves when there are not enough jobs to go around. An early race riot (in 1871) in Los Angeles resulted in the lynching of fifteen Chinamen. In 1877, the anti-Chinese agitation came to a head with the creation of a workingmen's party in California, which was soon exerting a leading influence in the affairs of the state. California's new state constitution delegated to the municipalities the power of regulating the lives of the Chinese. The question of Chinese immigration was brought to Congressional attention, with the result that a law was passed ordering President Hayes to abrogate the Burlingame Treaty. This the President refused to do; but he did send a mission to China to sound out the Manchu government. The report that Peking was not the slightest bit interested in the civil rights of the coolies in America made restriction inevitable. In 1882, therefore, an exclusion bill was enacted which barred from entry Chinese laborers for ten years; provided for the issuance of return certificates to resident Chinese who wished to make short visits to their native land; and made exceptions in the cases of visiting teachers, students, merchants and travelers. This last provision of the act was interpreted literally by the courts and immigration officials, with the result that skilled artisans and professional groups were excluded as well as the day laborers.

In 1888, because of the fraudulent transfer of return certificates, this privilege was revoked completely. In 1892, the ban on Chinese immigration was renewed for another ten years. Two years later, the whole procedure received the sanction of international law with the writing of a new Chinese treaty. The Chinese government formally accepted our exclusion policy with the proviso that return certificates were to be issued to resident Chinese, for purposes of visit, who had families in this country or who owned property to the value of $1000. Finally, in 1902, the exclusion edict against the Chinese was made perpetual in duration; the same act prohibited Chinese immigration to the United States from our own island possessions (Hawaii and the Philippines).

The second important restriction measure was the passage, in 1885, of the law prohibiting the entry of laborers under contract. This practice, which had contributed to the extraordinary increase of immigration from Southern and Eastern Europe, had received direct governmental sanction during the four years 1864 to 1868 and had been winked at in the years following. It had become the target of attack on the part of the Knights of Labor, and it was largely due to the pressure of this powerful workingmen's group that the law of 1885 was finally written. Congress strengthened the law in 1891 when it prohibited, under penalty of fine, the advertising for and the direct solicitation of immigrants by American factory owners. From that time on, the number of aliens turned back at ports of entry, because they were contract laborers, dwindled.

The decades of the eighties and nineties saw the first efforts being made by the federal government to close the gates to undesirables and the list of such prohibited persons steadily grew.[2] In 1891, an act imposed a head tax of fifty cents on each immigrant, created the office of Superintendent of Immigration, and for the first time placed complete control of the immigration processes in the hands of the federal government. This law thus marked the appearance of the federal inspection service and made selection of immigrants a reality.

Before the decade closed one further attempt was made to raise higher the restriction bars. In 1891, H. C. Lodge, in the House of Representatives, introduced a measure calling for a literacy test for all new arrivals. In 1896, Lodge, by this time the junior Senator from Massachusetts, introduced his bill in the upper chamber. It demanded the exclusion of all immigrants between the ages of fourteen and sixty who could not read and write English or some other language. So familiar had the nation become with the demands of the restrictionists that there was no difficulty in mustering majorities for the measure in both houses, and in 1897 the bill was sent to the President. On March 2, two days before his official retirement, Cleveland vetoed the bill.

By the end of the century the program of the restrictionists centered in four chief demands: they wanted an increase of the head tax, some favoring one as high as $100; they sought the imposition of the literacy test; they called for the examination and certification of immigrants by American officials before visas were granted. This examination was to cover not only medical fitness but political fitness as well. Lodge wanted to keep out those persons he called "ultrasocialists." Finally, the immigrant ought to be in possession of a sizable sum of money. This, it was believed, would prevent pauperization. We shall see, below, how this program in its main essentials was realized in the next two decades and how the failure to achieve any appreciable effects through selection led to the definite stoppage of immigration in the decade of the nineteen twenties.

[2] Paupers, criminals, convicts, and the insane were specifically excluded in 1882, and the onus was placed on steamship companies which had to take such persons back at their own expense. The law of 1891 further augmented the list of undesirables to include prostitutes, idiots, polygamists, and persons suffering from contagious or loathsome diseases.

· 8 ·

Building the Railroads

THE RAILROAD NET

THE story of America since the close of the Civil War is the story of its public lands, its growing wheat country, its immigrant hosts, its industrial cities and, not the least in the array, its mighty railroads. If the generosity of the government made the expansion of the agricultural areas possible, the railroads brought the free lands their settlers; if the new industrialism opened fresh mines, built countless mills and factories, and filled the land with thousands of flaming forges, the railroads joined the raw materials with the seats of fabrication, sought out the local centers of consumption and reached the outlets to the sea so as to make foreign markets for America again a reality; if the ocean liners entered American ports with their hundreds of thousands of foreign laborers, the railroads quickly distributed them among the textile mills of New England, the steel and iron foundries of the Pittsburgh area, the sheep ranches of Wyoming, and the coal mines of Illinois and Kansas. The essential pattern of the rails was woven into the fabric of the American life. Public aid, bestowed with a generous and a reckless hand, private enterprise, genius, imagination, and foreign capital built the American railroad system and in seventy years made the United States the greatest rail power in the world.

Between 1831 and 1861, some 30,000 miles of railroad had been built. The Civil War checked the expansion, though in the old Northwest, removed from the theater of war, building went on. During the five years 1868 to 1873, something like 28,000 miles were added to the country's trackage. But other phases of development were even more notable. The drop in the price of steel rails made the adoption of the heavier rail a certainty, and the year 1880 saw one-third of the railroads using steel. There was, too, a movement toward the general acceptance of the standard gauge. Most important of all, the era of consolidation that set in made possible long unbroken hauls, through passenger journeys, and falling railroad rates.

In 1880, there were 93,000 miles of track in the country. So great had been the expansion following the Civil War that this year saw Ohio and Illinois each having more miles of track than all of New Engand together. Railroad building was increasing about two and one-half times as fast as the population. In 1860, there were 985 miles of road per one million of inhabitants; twenty years later the ratio had doubled, and in another ten years it had almost tripled. The ten years 1881 to 1890 marked the peak of achievement in railroad history in the United States. In this decade 73,000 miles of track were laid down. The single years 1883 and 1887 saw the construction of 11,569 miles and 12,983 miles respectively. Previous to 1880 the average of railroad construction for a single year had been 2000 miles.

Other significant developments are to be noted: 1. The renewal of rate wars among the trunk lines, ending in the creation of agreements or pools which were tantamount to the division of traffic among competing lines as well as the fixing of rates. 2. The definite eclipse of water transportation. 3. Perfection of real economies in railroad management, made necessary by the decline in revenues because of the permanent reduction of rates. 4. The building of speculative lines, prompted largely by the hope that carriers originally serving the area would be forced to buy out these new competitors. 5. The march of manufacturing plants into the country's interior. The railroads made possible the location of great industrial centers in Ohio, Indiana, Illinois, and Michigan. 6. The development of the Gulf ports of New Orleans and Galveston, particularly as the wheat outlets of the country. In 1900, these two together were exporting more wheat than New York City. 7. The union of railroads with industry, in a hundred and one different and subtle ways. The Pennsylvania Railroad bought heavily of Pennsylvania coal lands, the Great Northern Railroad owned some of the richest ore fields of the Northwest, the Southern Pacific and the Northern Pacific railroads were the possessors of mighty fleets of coastwise and transpacific boats. The directors of industrial corporations sat on the boards of railroads, favors were exchanged, and there grew up a system of pernicious discriminations by which the large shippers were aided in their efforts to strangle the small. 8. The coming of federal regulation, as a result of countless railroad abuses and because of the Supreme Court's denial of state power. In 1887, the Interstate Commerce law was enacted. Laissez-faire, as an economic doctrine, was on the way to being seriously abridged.

From the zenith of the eighties the railroads touched their nadir in the nineties. That decade saw the addition of but 30,000 miles of road as well as the bankruptcy and the reorganization of some of the country's greatest systems. In 1900, there were 193,000 miles of road in the United States; this was more than the combined mileage of all the European nations and in fact represented 40 per cent of the total mileage of the world. Subsequent years have seen only slight additions: in 1910, the total mileage of the country was 240,000; in 1920, it was 252,800; at the end of the nineteen forties it was about 250,000.

Before the nineteenth century had run its course, the American train of modern times with its speed and comforts was already a familiar institution. Steel rails were being used universally at the end of the eighties, and the conclusion of the same decade witnessed the common employment of the standard gauge. The dining car and the Pullman sleeper were in general service soon after the Civil War. So were the Westinghouse airbrake and the block signaling system. First gas and then electricity took the place of kerosene and coal for illumination and heating. New and larger locomotives were being used and the freight cars were carrying from fifteen to twenty tons. The railroads were the first agencies to span the great rivers, the first Mississippi bridge south of St. Paul, for example, being built by the Chicago and Rock Island in 1856. In 1883, the railroads of the country made a signal contribution toward the unification of the country's economic life when they adopted a convention for the standardization of time. They divided the nation into five time zones centered at the 60° (Colonial Time), 75° (Eastern Time), 90° (Central Time), 105° (Mountain Time), and 120° (Pacific Time) meridians. It was not until 1918 that the federal government took official recognition of the act. Too, the rapid expansion of the railroad net made for the quick development of the country's telegraph system, and by 1883 all the wires were being controlled by a single corporation, the Western Union. Even the railroad executive underwent a complete metamorphosis. The financiers and speculators who had built the country's early lines and figured in the first consolidations found themselves supplanted by the practical railroad men, who usually were trained from early manhood in the hard school of railroad operation and came to their posts interested only in efficient management and the returns that could be achieved by intelligent promotion and competition.

THE GREAT AMERICAN RAIL SYSTEMS

It was Cornelius Vanderbilt, already at the age of sixty-six years and in possession of a fortune made in steamboats, who first foresaw the possibilities of large railroad combination. In 1853, eleven short lines along the route from Albany to Buffalo had been consolidated by their local owners, and the system under the name of the New York Central was being operated from Albany. In addition, two lines were, together, binding the cities of New York and Albany: the New York and Harlem and the Hudson River Railroad. But shipments from New York to Buffalo were possible only with difficulty: the Hudson had to be ferried and a number of train changes were necessary. Cornelius Vanderbilt entered railroading in 1860, when he began to buy up the shares of the New York and Harlem. He was impressed by the possibilities of a line that could tap the Great Lakes region and bring its produce to its natural outlet—New York City; he also sensed that the speculative values of the rails were incalculable. In the operations of all the great rail masters from Vanderbilt to Harriman these two motives were intertwined and indeed inseparable: the railroads had an important role to play in linking vast areas with their natural markets and they had financial possibilities whose rewards could not be measured by any of the standards then known. The fact is, the first great American fortunes of modern times were built up on the rails. Vanderbilt, then, opened up new financial horizons in the United States when after trading on the exchange for a brief four years he succeeded in running up the shares of the New York and Harlem from 32 to 285. In 1864, he had acquired the first unit in his Great Lakes-to-ocean railway and had made a fortune besides. By 1867, Vanderbilt had completed the primary operations of his masterly performance, for he had by then gained possession, too, of the Hudson River Railroad and the New York Central. In 1869, he consolidated his holdings, incorporating them under the name of The New York Central and Hudson River Railroad and at a capitalization of $86 million (by this single stroke adding a book value of $42 million to the properties of the railroad). But in addition to being a shrewd speculator, Vanderbilt was a far-sighted railroad manager: he double-tracked his lines, led the way for the general use of steel rails, threw modern bridges of steel across embankments and rivers, and acquired for his railroad the Grand Central Terminal at New York City. Other maneuvers could not so easily be defended, notably his struggle with Drew and Gould for the control of the Erie, during the course of which politicians, judges, and legislators were bought and sold with a cynicism that only the post-Civil War generation knew.

Vanderbilt's work was not finished with his death. His son, W. H. Vanderbilt, continued the processes of expansion and consolidation. By 1885, the New York Central system had acquired control of the Lake Shore and Michigan Southern (linking Buffalo and Chicago), the Michigan Central (linking Detroit and Chicago), the Canadian Southern Railway (linking Detroit and Toronto) as well as eight hundred miles of other lines in Ohio, Indiana, Michigan, and Pennsylvania. It had bought up the competing West Shore and was figuring prominently in the competing Nickel Plate. In 1885, the House of Morgan began to shape the destinies of the New York Central, when the younger Vanderbilt, more sensitive than his father, bowed to the popular clamor against his vast holdings and employed J. P. Morgan and Company to sell $25 million of New York Central stock to English investors. But the growth of the system went on unchecked, and before the twentieth century opened New York Central lines had terminals in New York, Buffalo, Cleveland, Detroit, Chicago, St. Louis, Cincinnati, Indianapolis, and Boston. The system successfully weathered the storm of 1893 when one-sixth of all the railroad mileage of the country went into the hands of receivers. By the end of World War I, the Vanderbilt lines had grown from the 850 miles of the first consolidation to 13,000 miles of main track and 5000 miles of extra track and from the first capitalization of $86 million to a value in excess of $1 billion.

The Pennsylvania system was built up to become the most important railroad and in fact one of the outstanding business enterprises in the country. The fraud which made the history of many of the rails a byword in American economic life was unknown to its annals; the stock manipulations of the Vanderbilts never had their parallel in its steady growth. Its founders saw, as did Vanderbilt, the importance of bringing the Middle West to the Atlantic seaboard, with the result that by 1858 they had a through line running from the Pittsburgh area to Philadelphia. Under J. Edgar Thomson, T. A. Scott, and G. B. Roberts, the three men who managed the Pennsylvania lines from the Civil War until 1897, the system spread its network of rails into the most important Middle Atlantic and North Central industrial centers. By 1869, the railroad was operating 1000 miles in Pennsylvania and was reaching Lake Erie through New York State; the next year, through the control of the Pittsburgh, Fort Wayne and Chicago, it was in the middle western metropolis; in 1871, its fingers were touching Cleveland, Cincinnati, and St. Louis. It was tapping, as well, the great Pittsburgh area, the newly discovered oil fields of western Pennsylvania, and the bituminous coal lands of Ohio and Indiana. Its achievements in operation were not to be matched: it was the first road to lay rails made by the Bessemer process; it was the first to put the steel firebox under the locomotive boiler; it was the pioneer road to experiment with the airbrake and the block signal system. It was a profitable road from the start, and from 1860 on never failed to pay a dividend. During the decades of the eighties and nineties the Pennsylvania system spread south and north and reached Wilmington, Baltimore, and Washington as well as Lake Michigan and Lake Ontario.

The twentieth century was to see the rounding of the circle, when under the presidency of A. J. Cassatt, the Pennsylvania Railroad came into New York City. The fact that it was on the wrong side of the river was a serious obstacle and had to be overcome. The difficulties were meet at great cost and the success of the feat must remain one of the great monuments to American business enterprise. The Hudson River was tunneled; so was the East River; the Pennsylvania Station was erected in New York City; the valuable Long Island Railroad was acquired when New York City suburban developments were still real estate promoters' dreams; and in a brief period the Pennsylvania was sharing with the New York Central the rail control of the greatest harbor in the world. Cassatt's New York terminal project had cost $100 million: never was a bold coup more richly rewarded.

If the history of the Pennsylvania epitomized many of the virtues of capitalistic daring, then the tale of the Erie summed up on a single black page all its vices. The New York and Erie Railroad, which had been chartered in 1832, was in 1851, after a number of early financial failures, operating 460 miles of line from the Hudson River to Lake Erie. Stock market manipulators had already begun to make the road a speculative football, for though it had been constructed at a cost of $15 million at the beginning of the fifties, its capital obligations totaled $26 million. From 1851 to 1868 the Erie was dominated by Daniel Drew, one of the most disreputable figures in American finance. He manipulated his own stock on the exchange, at one time depressing the price from 90 to 50; he used the printing presses to flood the market with 50,000 additional unauthorized shares; and in 1868, to thwart Vanderbilt's effort to gain control of the Erie for the purpose of consolidating it with the New York Central, he sent his ally Jay Gould to Albany to buy up the New York legislature. It was to be Gould's purpose to get measures enacted legalizing the emission of the unauthorized stock and stopping Vanderbilt's efforts to combine the two railroads. Gould spent half a million dollars in bribes and Drew's laws were passed. The Erie emerged with a capitalization of $60 million; Vanderbilt was bought out; and Jay Gould quickly succeeded his accomplice as the president of the Erie.

Gould's presidency from 1868 to 1874, in its short life, made use of all the devices known to financial roguery. There was, in short, one continuous round of bribery, chicanery, and fraud to the accompaniment of injunctions, court orders, and arrests. In 1875, the Erie went into the hands of receivers; in 1885 and 1886, it was again in financial difficulties; in the panic of 1893 it was one of the first roads to go under. In 1894, the House of Morgan, backed by English investors, reorganized the Erie, but at a great sacrifice on the part of security holders, for only in this way could the water be pumped out of the road. With the beginning of the twentieth century the system entered on the first real chapter of its legitimate function, i. e., railroading. Presidents E. B. Thomas and F. D. Underwood double-tracked the line from New York to Chicago and turned their attention to cultivating the hard-coal and soft-coal centers of Pennsylvania, Ohio and Indiana. Before long the Erie freight trains were averaging heavier train loads than those of the successful New York Central, and the end of World War I saw the Erie system among the first great trunk lines of the country. But it had taken forty years of bankruptcy and the mulcting of thousands of small investors to do it.

Of the financial history of the other great northeastern and middle western systems, of which the New York, New Haven and Hartford and the Baltimore and Ohio are the most important, it is not necessary to speak further than to say that their process of consolidation followed more or less closely one or another of the three systems whose history has been given.

The building of the Union Pacific, the first of the transpacific railroads, became possible only as a result of the direct aid its promoters received from the federal government. In 1862, by Congressional enactment, the company was granted a charter to run a line from Nebraska to the eastern boundary of California. At the same time the Central Pacific (a California corporation) was to build eastward from the Pacific coast for the purpose of effecting a juncture with the Union Pacific. Both companies were the recipients of the governmental bounty: not only were they to have the rights of way and the free use of timber, earth, and stone from the public lands but they were to get twenty sections of free government land for every mile laid down, as well as a government loan, secured originally by a first mortgage but soon converted into a second. The federal government committed itself to lending the railroad builders $16,000 for every mile built in level country, $32,000 for every mile built in the foothills and $48,000 for every mile constructed in the mountain regions. But construction was not begun seriously until 1866, and by July of that year only some three hundred miles of track had been laid down. The railroad builders needed additional rewards before they were prepared to undertake their work in earnest. The device which built the first transpacific railroad was the dummy construction company, owned by the very persons who possessed the charters for the railroads. In other words, Durant and the Ameses, who were to build the Union Pacific, and Huntington, Stanford, Hopkins, and Crocker, who were to build the Central Pacific, became possessed of dual personalities: as the Doctor Jekylls they were the courageous and respected railroad financiers assuming the long chance of the roads' ever becoming profitable and being able to pay dividends on their common stock; as the Mr. Hydes they were the covetous railroad construction contractors who sweated labor, bribed Congressmen, and lined their own pockets with exorbitant profits which they were able to take immediately. The Union Pacific, then, was built by the Crédit Mobilier, a Pennsylvania corporation organized in 1867 at a capitalization of $3,750,000. In the single year 1868, for example, the owner of a single share (with a book value of $100) obtained in dividends, made up of first mortgage bonds, common stock, and cash, a total of $341.85. Of course the bonds could not be sold at par, the common stock had only a speculative value, and funds were poured profligately into secret channels where aid and encouragement might be expected. We have seen, for example, how Garfield, to mention but one prominent politician, was caught in the meshes of the web spun by the Crédit Mobilier, as were indeed many other public figures.

A Congressional committee in 1888 estimated that the Union Pacific actually cost $50 million; but by the time the Crédit Mobilier had completed its work the obligations of the road were in the neighborhood of $94 million. Similarly, the Crocker Company, which built the Central

Pacific for the Pacific promoters, laid down the tracks at an average cost of $100,000 a mile whereas the physical value of the property, put at its most liberal figure, could not total more than half that sum. One may seriously question whether individual enterprise, heavily assisted as it was by government, was entitled to a reward of close to $50 million in cash (discounting the paper received at one-half) for the building of the Union Pacific-Central Pacific system.

In 1867, the construction of the two lines was taken up in earnest. Discharged soldiers, Irish immigrants, and Chinese coolies (on the Central Pacific) filled the construction camps and worked in a veritable frenzy to complete the task. Marauding Indians, the parching heat of the deserts, the rigors of mountain winter, the absence of creature comforts of the most elementary character—none of these was permitted to interfere in the task of spanning the continent. To spur the builders on, the government had turned the construction of the railroad into a contest between the Union Pacific and the Central Pacific by holding out promises of government bonds and government land for each mile of track laid down. The Central Pacific could penetrate as far east as it might beyond the borders of California; the Union Pacific, too, could go as far west as its resources would permit. Throughout the winter of 1868 men toiled in the mountains, in one day laying down as much as eight miles of track. That winter saw 20,000 men engaged in railroad building. By the spring of 1869 both gangs were in western Utah; on May 10 of that year, their work was finished when locomotive head touched locomotive head at Promontory Point, five miles east of Ogden, Utah, and the last spike—this one of gold—was driven into the ties.

The Union Pacific was built: in the light of its heritage it is no wonder that for the next twenty-five years its history should have been unhappy. During the seventies and eighties the dark figure of Jay Gould moved in and out of its affairs, at one time controlling the road, at another time collecting together the component parts of a new system that would entirely encircle it. In 1880, so effectively had Gould trapped the Union Pacific, it was compelled to buy from him at high prices the competing Kansas Pacific and Denver Pacific. Gould bought the Missouri Pacific, the Texas and Pacific, the St. Louis, Iron Mountain and Southern, and the Wabash. He built additions and branches, he engaged in ruinous rate wars with his competitors, he paid out unearned dividends and almost threw into bankruptcy the profitable Chicago, Burlington and Quincy, and by a series of leases and stock transfers, he got rid of his holdings, enriched himself at the expense of the trusting investors who believed in his star— and yet managed to retain control!

It was railroading of this character which turned the Far West into a cockpit in the period following the completion of the Union Pacific. Not only had the original lines been left with great burdens of debt, but new lines, very often manipulated as Gould had used his properties, had come in to aggravate the situation. When the Union Pacific failed in 1893, it was apparent to the informed that failure had not been due to the original optimism which had prompted the building of the railroad far in advance of civilization into the desert and mountains. Rather, collapse was due to the following: its management had been inefficient and extravagant and it had overexpanded, particularly in the construction of branch lines; it had destroyed its credit through its failure to pay the interest or amortize the principal of the mortgage bonds lent by the government; it had been forced to engage in rate wars with the new and competing lines that had come into the Far West. When it went into the hands of the courts, in 1893, the Union Pacific was trying to operate 8000 miles of railroad. It required the abilities of Harriman to rehabilitate this railroad and to make it a paying property.

Similarly, it took the equally magic touch of James J. Hill to give permanent success to the other great government-aided transpacific railroad, the Northern Pacific. Of the early history of this road it is only necessary to say that it was chartered by Congress in 1864; given huge land grants but lent no bonds; financed by Jay Cooke until he and the road both went into bankruptcy in 1873; rehabilitated for a time by Henry Villard, aided by German money; and again in trouble in 1893. From this second collapse it was rescued by Hill.

Of all the individuals who figured in the country's railroad history it was James J. Hill who possessed the authentic mark of greatness. Already on the verge of middle age, a man of slender fortune and known locally only as a spinner of dreams, Hill still looked to the future for the opportunity to prove that the Northwest had in it the potentialities of a great empire. In 1878, Hill, grasping his chance, entered railroading. In association with the Canadians Lord Strathcona and Lord Mount Stephen, he bought up a short Minnesota line which started from St. Paul and ended in the northern prairies. Carefully these men began to build north and west without governmental aid, and by 1890 their system, named the Great Northern, had 2775 miles of railroad running across Minnesota, North Dakota, and Montana. In 1893, the Pacific coast was touched. Hill knew that his railroad was not worth one penny more than the Northwest itself; that the prosperity of both was indissolubly joined. The settlers of the Northwest, therefore, had his real concern and he followed their progress with the interest of an enlightened feudal lord. He helped in the building of communities; he guided agricultural projects, bred blooded cattle, taught crop rotation and fertilization; he opened banks and made possible the erection of churches and schools. But ever with an eye open for business Hill was among the first to sense the importance of Far Eastern markets for the products of the new American industrialism. He built steamers and made one unbroken bridge of the distance from the Mississippi to Japan and China, and soon Minnesota flour and Ohio nails, shipped by way of the Great Northern, were being landed in Hong Kong, and Mississippi cotton and Pennsylvania rails were reaching Yokohama. On the other hand, Iowa barns were being built from the timber of the forest lands of the Washington and Oregon country which the Great Northern tapped.

During the first decade of the twentieth century Hill continued building, extending the feeders of his railroad into the Canadian prairie provinces and to the Canadian Pacific coast at Vancouver. To strengthen his terminal facilities in Washington, Oregon, and at Chicago, Hill bought out the Northern Pacific and operated the two roads under joint control. To join his possessions (for the Northwest was peculiarly his handiwork) with the older industrial centers of the east and south, Hill added the Chicago, Burlington and Quincy to his lines. Hill's death, during World War I, came after his work had been completed: the states of Minnesota, North Dakota, Washington, and Oregon were supporting great agricultural populations; the lands of the Northwest (and this includes the Canadian prairie provinces), instead of being the howling wilderness of the eighties, were now an integral part of America, linked by transportation lines to East, South, West, and North; and the Hill railroads were significant and successful properties.

Harriman was the last of the great American railroad builders. He had become a railroad power as a result of his successful operation of the Illinois Central, but so little was his reputation known that Jacob H. Schiff of Kuhn, Loeb and Company had not yet heard of him when he appeared in New York, after the disaster of 1893, with a proposal for refinancing the Union Pacific. Schiff in a short time came to be impressed with the insignificant-looking little man and between them, toward the end of the nineteenth century, they laid plans for the upbuilding of America's first transpacific, and strategically most important, railroad. With the aid of Schiff, Harriman spun his schemes for purchasing the Southern Pacific and for linking the Union Pacific with the Illinois Central to give the main line outlets into Chicago, St. Louis, San Francisco, and Los Angeles. Thwarted by the Supreme Court in his efforts to reach into the Northwest, when the Northern Securities Company, set up by Hill and himself, was ordered dissolved, Harriman turned his attention eastward. He bought the Baltimore and Ohio, he bought into the Reading system, he acquired the Central of Georgia Railway. He for the moment realized the dream of every great railroad builder, that of an Atlantic-Pacific railroad. His lines had terminals in New York as well as in California and Oregon. Besides, the Illinois Central, with its 5000 miles of track, was reaching into Chicago,

St. Louis, New Orleans, Atlanta, Savannah, and Sioux City, Iowa. But the system could not hold together for long. The Union Pacific was ordered severed, under the Antitrust law, from the Southern Pacific by the Attorney-General's office; the control of the Baltimore and Ohio was relinquished in a special stock dividend to the Union Pacific's shareholders; and not long after Harriman's death (in 1909) the Union Pacific was again where Harriman had found it when he stepped into its destinies in 1898. But instead of a bankrupt and inefficiently operated railroad, he left it rich and secure.

Railroad building did not pass the South by in the decades immediately after the Civil War. By 1874, a line was running from Richmond to Atlanta and branches were reaching into South Carolina. Under the leadership of the Pennsylvania Railroad the old South was soon seeing a system develop with feeders in eastern Tennessee, Virginia, and Georgia. Holding companies and consolidations played their roles during the eighties and nineties with the customary accompaniments of overexpansion, failure, and reorganization. In 1893, the collapse of the Richmond Terminal Company, the largest of these consolidations, brought the ubiquitous Morgan on the scene. In 1894, he created the Southern Railway Company and by the usual devices of slashing obligations, wiping out stock issues, and placing levies on stockholders, Morgan was able to breathe life into the South's railroad system. Ten years were spent in laying down new tracks and building into more profitable territories. The Southern Railway Company was soon running its trains not only to Ohio River points and cities on the Atlantic and Gulf coasts, but into St. Louis on the west, Florida on the south, and Ohio and Illinois on the north. Southern cotton, naval stores, fruits, and manufactured iron goods, now were reaching the outlets of the Gulf, the Great Lakes, and the Atlantic seaboard, while the Southern Railway's traffic arrangements with the Pennsylvania and the Baltimore and Ohio brought the South into closer relationship with the metropolises of New York and Philadelphia. Even after the Central of Georgia Railway was sold to Harriman to be combined with his Illinois Central, the Southern Railway Company was operating 9000 miles of line in the first decade of the twentieth century.

Thus the South became again an integral part of the American life—not because politicians had grown more tolerant but because northern financiers had joined South and North together with bands of steel. Magazines and books published in New York and Philadelphia now were to be found on southern tables as quickly as they were on those of the Middle West; the clothes and house furnishings of New York, Chicago, and Cleveland adorned the persons and the homes of the residents of Atlanta, Shreveport, and Mobile as well as those of Providence, Buffalo, Salt Lake City, and Duluth. America became a nation with the standardization of taste and the ordinary round of daily living. The railroads, more than any other single factor, had brought about this result.

FINANCING THE RAILROADS

It is important to understand that individual initiative and enterprise were not solely responsible for the building of America's great railroad net. Had it not been for the generosity of the federal, state, and local governments and the important aid rendered by foreign capital, the American rails could scarcely have reached their high degree of development.

The United States government was particularly interested. The first federal grant in aid of railroad construction came in 1850 when Congress gave the states of Illinois, Alabama, and Mississippi almost four million acres of the public land to be held in trust toward the completion of the Illinois Central Railroad. From 1850 to 1871, Congress made eighty such grants to the states in the Mississippi Valley. During the decade of the sixties, Congress chartered four transpacific railroads and made them grants of land directly. These were the Union Pacific, the Northern Pacific, the Atlantic and Pacific, and the Texas and Pacific. In addition, the Central Pacific, though a California corporation, received sections of land on the same terms as the Union Pacific. During the two decades of the fifties and sixties there passed, as a result of this Congressional policy, a total of 158,293,000 acres into the hands of western railroad promoters, an area almost equaling that of the New England states, New York, and Pennsylvania combined. Of course not all the railroads were completed; many failed to fulfil their terms of the contract because of delays in construction. Mrs. Laut, after a careful examination, estimates that only twenty-seven railroads earned their land grants and these were able to certify and patent 115,832,000 acres. In addition to federal land grants, the individual states gave from their public lands to hasten railroad construction. Texas alone made awards totaling 32,000,000 acres; the states of the Mississippi Valley gave away 20,000,000 acres. The total acreage thus actually distributed reached the great figure of 167,832,000 acres or 262,238 square miles, a domain approximately the size of Texas. To place a value on this land would of course be impossible; some of it had no market, some on the other hand was rich mineral and timber land. Even estimated at the nominal price of $2 an acre, the public lands donated to encourage railroad building were worth $335 million.

The actual money grants made to the railroad builders were even greater; in fact a conservative estimate (made by Professor Ripley) has placed the amount thus received from all public sources at $707,100,000. By 1870, when this form of aid had largely ceased, public financing had contributed at least two-fifths of the costs incurred in the construction of the 50,000 miles of line then in operation. If the value of the land cessions is added, it can be seen that three-fifths of the cost of laying down the rail net had been borne by public authority.[1]

State experiences with the roads were very unhappy. Before the Civil War a number of the southern and western states had tried the construction of railroads themselves, on the score that they were internal improvements, and had ended by repudiating their debts. In the fifties there had appeared the policy of making loans to railroad builders, through the issuance of state securities. Missouri, the first of the western states to lend public assistance, amassed a total of such obligations of $25 million, fully $19 million of which was irretrievably lost. Minnesota spent $5 million in this way and never got much of it back. The history of these misfortunes was repeated in the annals of almost all the western and middle-western states during the decades of the fifties, sixties, and seventies, with the result that of the estimated $228 million lent by the states for railroad construction very little ever was returned. Only Texas appears to have handled its problem with intelligence.

The railroad craze touched every political subdivision from populous counties and great cities down to the smallest villages. Not merely in the railroad-hungry West, whose very existence depended upon transportation, but in the Ohio Valley, Massachusetts, and New York, local officials vied with one another to see who could hold out the richest inducements to the railroad promoters and builders. Stupidity, pride, cupidity, all spurred the local officialdom on: municipalities even had their agents in the financial centers of the East, besieging the railroad men to take their fill out of the public coffers! Ripley has estimated that loans from local governments to the railroads reached the staggering total of $300 million. Local authorities issued bonds, bought stock, hawked tax certificates, made grants of publicly owned sites, and sold county lands to permit them to buy railroad securities. Apparently, there was no need to see that the railroad was ever begun, let alone to await its completion, before public aid was granted. And many a rural line, which was to make some little four-corners a metropolis, never got beyond the fascinating blueprints of the promoters.

The day of reckoning came swiftly. The decade of the seventies saw many of these public issues maturing with the local treasuries empty. The railroads either had never been built, or when completed had not brought the promised plenty. Repudiation was tried but unfortunately municipal corporations were not invested with those attributes of sovereignty which

[1] Toward the end of the century the federal government, by threatening foreclosure proceedings, was able to get back from the nationally chartered railroads the $64 million it had advanced (principally to the Union Pacific and the Central Pacific). But it was necessary to scale down the amount of the long overdue interest very considerably.

allowed the states to accumulate debts and then refuse to pay them. The Supreme Court, in 1872, found the counties, townships, cities, towns, and villages liable for all the debts they had ever contracted to foster railroad building, and the payment of the $300 million was begun. It is interesting to note that the chapter has not been completely closed; many an obscure hamlet is still wrestling with the burdens so cheerfully assumed by its town councils in the fifties, sixties, and seventies. The Granger constitutions and laws stopped these public loans, though probably the Supreme Court decision dampened all local enthusiasm for railroads forever.

To finish the railroads so lightly begun, to repair the damages committed by the early inexperienced and often dishonest builders, and to supply the working funds needed for operation, additional stores of capital were required; and these Europe supplied. The first local lines had been financed by stock issues which were held locally; even the Union Pacific promoters thought they might underwrite their project through stock sales. But domestic capital was not sufficient, with the result that bonds came to be the chief reliance of the financiers of the railroads, and these bond issues were for the most part sold in England, Germany, and Holland. European confidence in American railroad securities was at times rudely shaken: the panic of 1873 hit hard German investors in American rails; Villard's lack of success with the Northern Pacific involved Dutch and German security holders; the English paid the piper for the Baltimore and Ohio and Erie mismanagements; the panic of 1893 was to an extent occasioned by the fright of European investors who had begun to dump their American rail securities for what prices they would bring. In the nineties, however, encouraged by the skilful management of the House of Morgan and that of Kuhn, Loeb and Company, European investors again returned to the American rail market. Of the $3,330,000,000 worth of American securities held abroad at the end of the nineteenth century, the greater part was made up of railroad stocks and bonds. In England, the total held was $2,500,000,000; in Holland $240,000,000; in Germany, $200,000,000; in Switzerland, $75,000,000; in France $50,000,000.

American capital became more plentiful following the Spanish-American War, with the result that American securities, in increasing amounts, returned home. The upshot was that by 1905 American rails were, to a very considerable extent, domestically owned. The process was completed during World War I, when European-owned securities were repatriated in order to finance Allied military purchases in the United States. In 1900, the capitalization of the American railroads was put, by the Interstate Commerce Commission, at $11,490,000,000, of which half was represented by the stocks outstanding and half by the bonded indebtedness.

· 9 ·

The New Agriculture

THE CHARACTERISTICS OF THE NEW AGRICULTURE

AMERICAN agriculture, in the period following the Civil War, underwent a complete transformation. It not only increased in size but changed its characteristics, and from the self-sufficiency of a pioneer economy it became commercial. In many regions, the American farming community before the Civil War—like all those from the beginning of time—had been a complete microcosm in itself. Food, wearing apparel, all the essentials for its self-perpetuation, the agricultural community had produced itself or by the simple agency of barter had obtained at first hand. The local blacksmith shod the horses and made the nails, the local tanner cured the leather for footgear and harnesses, the local butcher slaughtered the animals for the farmer's table. Lumber was obtained from the wood lot, vegetables were grown in the kitchen garden, bread for the table came from the wheat field, the corn needed for the fattening of the barn animals was homegrown, wool from the backs of the sheep made the homespun articles of clothing, butter was churned in the home dairy. The simple primitive tools—the plow, the sickle, the cradle, and the flail—were heritages from a past whose origins were so remote that changing their forms would have necessitated as complete a revolution in attitude as brought on, let us say, the Protestant Reformation.

Yet the narrow confines of this little world were split asunder in less than fifty years. And though his fields might ever be seas of waving wheat and his barns might be choked with corn and hay, the American farmer of the latter half of the nineteenth century, so completely had he become a part of the capitalistic world, might often be plunged to the very brink of ruin, if not, in fact, of starvation. The farmer was no longer master of his own destiny. He plowed his acres, harvested his crops, and fattened his stock—but no longer for himself alone. He fed distant New York and Philadelphia as well as Manchester, Trieste, and Milan overseas. He had become a producer of foodstuffs, of wheat, or cattle, or pork, just as his fellow Americans had become producers of hats or of cotton cloth or of cheap tin pans. He had become, in short, a man of business, selling what he made and buying what he, his womenfolk, and his children needed.

What had caused this astounding upheaval in American agricultural economy? Merely this: the factory system had brought together in great urban centers large units of population which had to be supported; and it became incumbent upon the farmers of the world to produce the surpluses necessary for their physical maintenance. If isolated events may be singled out as being the prime factors in causing revolutions (and indeed sometimes they may), then the repeal of the corn laws in England in 1846 and the passage of the Homestead Act in 1862 and the chartering of the transpacific railways transformed American agriculture. By the first measure, the middle-class masters of the English people definitely abandoned their domestic agriculture and converted the English nation into an industrial economy. England thenceforth, said Peel, Cobden, and Bright, was going to make the clothes, the tableware, and the house-furnishings of a whole world—and let who would, as long as it could be done cheaply, feed the English factory hands, sailors, navvies, and countinghouse clerks. The Homestead Act of 1862 and the building of the western trunk systems threw open the American public lands and the United States became one of the great granaries of the world. The Confederate states counted on cotton to win their war for them; but it was northern and western wheat which kept England neutral and closed the Civil War triumphantly. The wheat of the western prairies and plains beat the South to its knees and, ironically enough, served the additional purpose of strengthening the hands of the new American industrialists. For while the manufacturers slowly laid their plans for converting America into an industrial nation, behind the bulwarks of the protective tariff system also erected during the Civil War, they used the farm surpluses of wheat and corn (which took the place of cotton) to pay for American adverse balances of trade in the international market.[1]

The American farmers, then, poured into the West to raise the surplus foodstuffs necessary to feed England and the industrial centers of our own East in order to pay the interest on English capital in our railroads, and for English machinery, for Brazilian coffee, East Indian tea, and British dyestuffs. And because what the farmer produced he sold, he became a member of a great capitalistic economy. In every particular but

[1] American exports of wheat and wheat flour increased from 17,000,000 bushels in 1860 to 62,000,000 bushels in 1862; in 1863, the export of these products was 58,000,000 bushels. Almost the entire surplus of wheat and wheat flour went to the United Kingdom. Schmidt points out that in 1859 the United Kingdom depended upon this country for but 11.2 per cent of its wheat imports; by 1862, the American proportion had become 43.5 per cent; by 1863, 38.4 per cent. On the other hand, the United Kingdom, in 1860, imported 2,580,700 bales of cotton from the United States, which represented 76.6 per cent of its total cotton imports. In effect, the Civil War was a race between cotton and wheat, and wheat won. See L. B. Schmidt's article called "Wheat vs. Cotton," included in L. B. Schmidt and E. D. Ross, *Readings in the Economic History of American Agriculture*.

one, he was exactly like his brother or his uncle or his cousin who had taken himself off to the big city to set himself up as a manufacturer of iron rails, woolen goods, nails, or shirts or shoes. It was the one exception that made all the difference between middle-class American agriculture and middle-class American industry. The American farmer could not control the price of his wares to any extent while the manufacturer could to a greater or less degree. The manufacturer was able to influence the resale price of his commodity to the ultimate consumer by the aid of some or all of the following devices: he had the protective tariff which assured him supremacy in the domestic market; he could create trade agreements or even monopolies for checking output or fixing prices; he might control the distributors through tying contracts; by large expenditures for advertising he might create a seemingly distinctive product for which people would be willing to pay more. But the American farmer produced blindly in a world market. He grew staples because they were the cheapest thing to grow, and he grew them in competition with farmers, situated like himself, in Russia, India, Argentina, Australia, and Canada. Once having grown his wheat or barley or corn he waited for Liverpool, Chicago, and Minneapolis to tell him what his product was worth. If nature smiled on the wheat fields the world over, the American farmer was ruined. If war closed the Russian ports, drought parched the Argentine fields, and locusts devastated the Australian crops, he had money in his pockets and paid his mortgage interest and his wife had a new sewing machine. The American farmer could not hold his wheat or cotton against a rise in price, he could not combine with other farmers the world over for the artificial creation of a price, as did the sugar refiners, the steel manufacturers, and the railroads in his own country. He was a poor man and there were so many small farmers! During the eighties and the nineties, then, farm commodity prices tumbled and the farmer suffered cruelly while the results of his labor doubled and tripled and in some cases quadrupled the American production of foodstuffs and fibers.

It has been said above that increased demand for the products of the farm, our international position as a debtor nation, the opening of the public lands, and the building of the railways were the chief factors in the metamorphosis of American agriculture following 1860. There were other contributory causes, among which may be cited the following: the increase of immigration into the country, which furnished a large part of the labor supply needed for the opening of the new farms; the invention and improvement of farm machinery, which permitted the maintenance of an agricultural economy on an individualistic basis and at the same time allowed for the single-cropping of large areas; the improvement of milling processes, which made possible the milling of fine white flour from hard spring wheat (this opened up Minnesota and Dakota to the wheat farmer); the aid of science and research, which helped solve some of agriculture's vexing problems of production.

In the forty years 1860 to 1900, the size of the American farm domain more than doubled. In 1860, 407,000,000 acres were in the possession of American farmers; by 1900, their holdings had been increased to 841,000,000 acres. Also, the acreage under crops increased not only absolutely but proportionately as well. In 1860, 163,000,000 acres, representing 40.1 per cent of the total, were improved land; in 1900, the size of the tilled area had grown to 414,700,000 acres, or 49.3 per cent. In 1860, the value of the farm property of the country, in land, buildings, implements, and live stock, was little less than $8 billion; by 1900, it was a little over $20 billion. The average size of the American farm in 1900 was 146.6 acres. The production of the great staples, corn, wheat, oats, cotton, sugar, and tobacco, multiplied many times. The first three of these were produced mainly in the West; the last three, in the South. Wheat and cotton will be discussed at some length.

WHEAT

In a sense, the history of American agriculture may be epitomized in the single word "wheat." Wheat is the frontier staple of all new lands: it stores and transports well and lends itself to extensive cultivation where land is cheap, credit hard to obtain, labor scarce or too expensive for the modest purse of the individual farmer. With machinery a single farming family has no difficulty in planting and harvesting from 100 to 200 acres of the crop. Because wheat has followed the frontier, its crop yield per acre (about 12 bushels) has varied but slightly. The wheat farmer must either sell out and move on when the capital invested in land becomes too great to make wheat planting profitable, or give up wheat. Thus the center of wheat production in the United States, in the fifty years covered by the period 1850 to 1900, moved 99 miles north and 680 miles west. In 1849, the center of American wheat growing was 57 miles northeast of Columbus, Ohio; in 1899, it was 70 miles west of Des Moines, Iowa. The figures on the next page show how the principal areas of wheat growing changed within short intervals.

Irrigation has taken wheat to its last stand, to the desert and the mountain valleys: here, for a time, the frontier farmer can grow crops profitably with his costly methods of production. Meanwhile Minnesota and most of Iowa have turned to diversified farming, California and the Palouse country of Oregon and Washington are growing fruits, the Middle West has become the great corn belt of the nation, and the Genesee Valley of

New York—America's wheat country of an earlier day—has long since forgotten wheat and is producing apples, peaches, potatoes, dairy products, and wine.

For a half-dozen years at the end of the seventies, the American wheat crop, so rapidly did it expand, practically dominated the world. The unfortunate crop failures in Europe after 1875 and the Russo-Turkish War of 1877 to 1878, which closed the Russian ports, made for American supremacy. Prices were comparatively good; and the wheat acreage grew by leaps and bounds. The annual average acreage for the ten years 1866 to 1875 was 20,470,000 acres; for the next ten years the annual average was 34,433,000 acres. With the eighties the situation changed. India, Russia, and Australia entered in earnest the wheat markets of the world, while

LEADING WHEAT PRODUCING STATES, 1859–1929

(Figures in thousands of bushels)

1859		1869		1879	
Illinois	23,837	Illinois	30,128	Illinois	51,110
Indiana	16,848	Iowa	29,435	Indiana	47,284
Wisconsin	15,657	Ohio	27,882	Ohio	46,014
Ohio	15,119	Indiana	27,747	Michigan	35,532
Virginia	13,130	Wisconsin	25,606	Minnesota	34,601
Pennsylvania	13,042	Pennsylvania	19,672	Iowa	31,154
New York	8,681	Minnesota	18,866	California	29,017
Iowa	8,449	California	16,676	Missouri	24,966
Michigan	8,336	Michigan	16,265	Wisconsin	24,884
Kentucky	7,394	Missouri	14,315	Pennsylvania	19,462
Other States	42,611	Other States	61,153	Other States	105,159
Total	173,104	Total	287,745	Total	459,483

1889		1899		1929	
Minnesota	52,300	Minnesota	95,278	Kansas	138,060
California	40,869	North Dakota	59,884	North Dakota	93,396
Illinois	37,389	Ohio	50,376	Nebraska	56,555
Indiana	37,318	South Dakota	41,889	Washington	44,910
Ohio	35,559	Kansas	38,778	Oklahoma	44,478
Kansas	30,399	California	36,534	Montana	40,098
Missouri	30,113	Indiana	34,986	Texas	37,800
North Dakota	26,403	Nebraska	24,924	Illinois	36,537
Michigan	24,771	Missouri	23,072	Ohio	33,770
Pennsylvania	21,595	Iowa	22,769	South Dakota	30,247
Other States	131,657	Other States	226,940	Other States	250,657
Total	468,373	Total	658,534	Total	806,508

tariff walls against American wheat were raised by France, Germany, Italy, and Spain. So great did the world surplus become that American average farm prices for the staple dropped like rockets. The following figures tell in a word what befell the American wheat grower: average annual price for 1866 to 1875, 105.3 cents per bushel; [2] average annual price for 1876 to 1885, 92 cents per bushel; average annual price for 1886 to 1895, 67.3 cents per bushel; average price, 1896, 71.7 cents per bushel; average price, 1900, 62 cents per bushel. In short, between 1870 and 1900 the yield of wheat was two and one-half times as great in the later year as in the earlier; yet the total value of the crop was not one-half again as large in 1900 as it had been in 1870. And the exportable surplus grew in the period from 20.7 per cent of the annual crop over 1866 to 1875 to 36.6 per cent in 1900. During the decade of the fifties the average annual crop of wheat for the whole world was 1,198,000,000 bushels, of which American production accounted for 137,000,000 bushels (11.4 per cent). By the year 1900 the world's wheat crop was totaling 2,610,000,000 bushels, of which 602,708,000 bushels were produced in the United States (23 per cent).

COTTON

The price of cotton at the close of the Civil War was high and cotton was easy to grow; in cotton lay the broken South's salvation, but the difficulties that confronted the returning Confederate soldier were indeed great. His once steady labor supply was now as volatile as a free gas. The rumors that flew up and down the southern cotton belt that the whites were to be displaced wholesale and their lands turned over to the emancipated Negroes; the ability, after 1866, of the free Negro to migrate into the Southwest to take up a homestead for himself; the pauperization that the blacks underwent at the hands of the Freedmen's Bureau and the northern philanthropists during the whole decade of the sixties; the greater attractions that the cities had for them; the loose talk of an hegira to Liberia where the black republic awaited the coming of American Negroes; the Negro's refusal to return to the gang system of labor that was at the basis of the antebellum plantation system—all these factors made the southern labor supply uncertain and hard to control. In addition, there was no capital, little credit, no hope of attracting the cheap white labor that was flooding the North and West, and, into the bargain, the threat of competition in the cotton markets of the world at the hands of India, Egypt, and Brazil.

To overcome these obstacles a drastic step was necessary: the plantation had to go. In the whole cotton belt, up and down the Atlantic coast from North Carolina to Georgia and across the Gulf lands through Alabama,

[2] The first figure is really in greenbacks; the actual value was about 86 cents.

Mississippi, Arkansas, Louisiana, and Texas, the old plantations were dismembered. The following figures show how the average size of southern farms fell in forty years: South Atlantic states, average size of farm in 1860, 352.8 acres; in 1900, 108.4 acres. South Central states, 1860, 321.3 acres; 1900, 155.4 acres. The prewar plantation system was abandoned and the southern farmer grew cotton and some other staples, buying all his necessities from the local merchant, who had become the southern planter's banker.[3] The country merchant, because he was willing to stake the planter to seed, tools, food, and clothing during the period that the crop was growing, became the keystone of the situation: he it was who revived the South where there was no credit and where lands had no value—but he also kept the southern farmer in bondage, for he called for cotton plantings and exacted a crop lien, or mortgage, with which to bind the planter. The cotton crop then, before it was yet in the ground, was mortgaged and these crop liens financed the planter. Says Hammond, the first trained economic observer of the South's dilemma: "Escape from this vicious circle proved impossible for most of the Negro croppers and some of the white ones, and the cropping system and the system of crop liens thus worked conjointly in causing overproduction of cotton and agricultural depression in the South."

The second element in the breakup of the plantation system was the need for securing the labor supply. The emancipated Negro or the landless white, as a rule, preferred not to work for wages, and he had no money with which to buy land and become a farmer in his own right. The inevitable solution was tenancy, and because of the lack of capital all around, share tenancy, or sharecropping as it came to be known, had to be the outcome. By 1880, share tenancy had gripped the South. In that year, in Georgia for example, only a little more than half of the farms were operated by their owners, while one-third were tilled by share tenants and only one-sixth by cash tenants. By 1900, in the same state, only two-fifths of the farm operators were owners, while one-fourth were cash tenants and one-third were share tenants. By 1910, the sharecroppers exceeded the owners, the proportions for the different systems being as follows: farms operated by owners, one-third; farms operated by cash tenants, three-tenths; farms operated by sharecroppers, three-eighths. Under sharecropping, the landlord supplied the land, the cabin, the mule, the tools, the seed, and the food needed for the sustenance of the renter and his family, and got but one-half the money from the sale of the crop.

[3] This is true, of course, only in a general sense. In many cases, the planter became a merchant, while numerous merchants found themselves in the possession of agricultural land through mortgage foreclosure. In both cases, the land was tilled as an adjunct to the conduct of the mercantile business. It was this very group of merchants, assisted by the southern physicians, dentists, and lawyers that, through the accumulation of small surpluses, was able to reintroduce industry into the South in the late decades of the nineteenth century.

Thus the cotton plantings grew, and the areas under cotton spread west and north as well, into western Texas and Oklahoma and into new sections of the Carolinas, Georgia, Arkansas, and Tennessee. During 1866 to 1875, the annual area (average) under cotton was 8,810,000 acres; by 1900, cotton was being grown on 24,933,000 acres. The crop of 1860 was equaled by that of 1878; the crop of 1879 surpassed it; the crop of 1899 more than doubled it. In 1859, the southern states grew 4,300,000 bales, and of this yield more than half was picked in Mississippi, Alabama, and Louisiana. In 1899, the total crop was 9,400,000 bales; but now Texas had become the leading cotton-growing state and Mississippi was second, with Georgia third, Alabama fourth, and South Carolina fifth. In 1919, the total crop was 11,300,000 bales; of this Texas alone was producing more than one-fourth, while Georgia and South Carolina had pushed Mississippi into fourth place. The opening of new areas in Georgia, North Carolina, and South Carolina was due largely to the extensive use of commercial fertilizers. The following table indicates the advance of cotton west and north in the seventy years from 1859 to 1929.

PRODUCTION OF COTTON IN LEADING COTTON-GROWING STATES, 1859–1929

(Figures in bales—one bale equals 500 pounds)

	1859	1879	1899	1919	1929
Mississippi	962,000	963,000	1,286,000	957,000	1,915,000
Alabama	791,000	699,000	1,093,000	718,000	1,335,000
Louisiana	622,000	508,000	699,000	306,000	810,000
Georgia	561,000	814,000	1,232,000	1,681,000	1,345,000
Texas	345,000	805,000	2,584,000	2,971,000	3,950,000
Arkansas	293,000	608,000	705,000	869,000	1,490,000
Tennessee	237,000	330,000	235,000	306,000	515,000
South Carolina	282,000	522,000	843,000	1,476,000	845,000
North Carolina	116,000	389,000	433,000	858,000	735,000
Oklahoma	......	......	227,000	1,006,000	1,200,000
Others	100,000	117,000	107,000	228,000	779,000
United States	4,309,000	5,755,000	9,434,000	11,376,000	14,919,000

As the years rolled on the proportion of the country's cotton crop that was exported dropped. In 1860, 76.5 per cent of the total yield was sent out of the country; in 1878, the proportion was at 71.2 per cent; in 1890, it was at 68 per cent; in 1900, it was at 66.3 per cent. In 1860, England was getting more than five-sixths of all its cotton from the United States; forty years later, she was getting considerably less than three-fourths from the southern cotton fields. Less and less cotton was entering into America's international payments, and by the turn of the century cotton had been definitely supplanted by grain and meat. By 1900, 35 per cent (in value) of America's farm products sent abroad was represented by cotton as against the 25 per cent which stood for grain and grain products and another 25 per cent which stood for meat and meat products. In 1900, but 25 per cent of the total exports of the country, in dollars, was made up of cotton, a proportion but half as great as that of 1860.

The domestic consumption of cotton was becoming more significant with every decade. In 1860, the United States utilized but one-third as much cotton as did England; in 1880, the ratio was two to three; in 1900, our domestic mills were using as much raw cotton as were those of England. In 1860, of the 5,200,000 spindles in the country, only some 300,000 were to be found in the South; in short, southern cotton was being spun into yarn and woven into cloth in the mills of Massachusetts, Rhode Island, New Hampshire, and Connecticut. Twenty years later, so slowly did the South turn to local fabrication, the ratio of southern to northern spindles was even less. But by 1900, as a result of the slow accumulation of local capital surpluses, the number of southern spindles had greatly increased; and by 1915 there were 12,711,000 spindles in southern mills as against 19,396,000 in the mills of the North. In the same year close to 60 per cent of the domestically consumed cotton was being used in the southern states; and this proportion has been increasing steadily in recent years.

Another outstanding postbellum activity in the South was the utilization of the cotton seed for the manufacture of cottonseed oil, oil cake, and hulls. From 1867 to the end of the century some three hundred cottonseed mills were erected throughout the South, but principally in Texas and Tennessee. The oil derived from the pressed seed was used in the making of substitutes for olive oil, oleomargarine and lard, and for soap. Oil cake was used as a fertilizer and as feed for cattle; the hulls were used for cattle feed. At the end of the century the annual production of these cottonseed mills was worth from $50 million to $60 million and one-half of the product was being exported abroad.

THE AMERICAN FARM SURPLUSES

American farm products, in very large degree, sustained Europe in the years following the sixties and helped hasten the processes of the industrial revolution, in England particularly. In that country, so unprofitable had domestic agriculture become, the number of agricultural laborers decreased from 996,000 in 1871 to 595,000 in 1901. Not without cause was an Austrian observer able to say that the American agricultural surpluses constituted the greatest economic event of the nineteenth century, comparable only to the exportation of American gold to Europe three hundred years before. By the end of the century American farm exports reached the impressive value of $663,500,000 (annual average, 1894–98). These represented seven-tenths of the total American exports and almost twice the value of the imported food products (coffee, tea, sugar, etc.). The significance of the country's agricultural exports can be grasped only in the light of the international payments situation. Our agricultural exports almost paid for the total American imports and their entrance into the world markets gave the United States a favorable balance of trade as far as visible items were concerned. Note these figures for American foreign trade (annual average, 1894–98): value of total imports, $709,400,000; value of agricultural imports, $368,700,000; value of total exports, $953,600,000; value of agricultural exports, $663,500,000.

Of the farm exports of the period, cotton made up but 36 per cent of the total value and, except for comparatively slight contributions on the part of tobacco and cottonseed products, foodstuffs constituted the remainder. The greatest era of American farm surpluses was to be found in the years immediately preceding and in those following the opening of the twentieth century. The exportation of wheat and wheat flour was 91,000,000 bushels in 1873; thirty years later the exportation of these was two and one-half times as great. In 1900, the United States wheat growers were exporting two-fifths of their total crop. By 1904, the exportable surplus was only 8 per cent and the average for the years 1904 to 1913 was but 15 per cent. The same story was to be told in the case of live cattle, beef products, butter, and cheese. Before the twentieth century was far on its way, Canada, Argentina, and Australia had taken upon themselves the task of feeding the world while ocean-going ships were carrying the finished products of the new American industrialism to Bangkok, Shanghai, Rio de Janeiro, and Danzig, and American salesmen were competing on terms of equality with the salesmen of Germany and England in Africa, Asia, and South America. By the end of the first decade of the twentieth century, American farm surpluses constituted but a little more than half of the value of all the country's exports.

By the turn of the century, then, American agriculture had served its chief purpose; its surpluses had permitted the building up of a great domestic industrial economy. As manufactured articles (and later credit) began to assume first place in the American export trade our international status, too, changed. As an agrarian nation we might justly close our eyes and ears to the outside world; as an exporter of surplus manufactured goods and capital it was imperative that we watch closely every land, no matter how obscure, lest political and financial disturbances jeopardize the interests of our citizens. It was no mere coincidence that with our growth as a manufacturing and capitalistic people our statesmen should adopt a vigorous foreign policy.

SCIENCE ROUTS THE OLD-FASHIONED FARMER

Well into the first half of the nineteenth century the processes of American farming were as elementary as those under the most primitive economy. The plows used were heavy and clumsy, the moldboards being of either wood or a hard, brittle iron; the seed was sown by hand and very often harrowed into the ground with bushes; the grain was cut with sickles or a cradle and was threshed on the barn floor with flails; winnowing was accomplished through the use of a sheet which was tossed up and down until the wind had removed the chaff. What was true of planting and harvesting the wheat was equally true in the case of every other farm operation: from time immemorial, husbandry was associated with the wooden plow, the scythe, the sickle, and the plodding ox team and springless wagon. Before the nineteenth century was over all this had been changed and machinery had come to lighten the way of the farmer.

The first of the farming implements to hasten the revolution in agricultural processes was the perfected plow. In the fifties the Deere plow with its steel moldboard made its appearance on the midwestern prairies. In 1870, the Oliver plow, fabricated of chilled steel, was being manufactured. Inventions now followed fast on the heels of one another, with the result that there was quickly evolved the gang plow of modern times, with which there were combined the seeder and the harrow. Some slight notion of how all this facilitated the rapid exploitation of the virgin soils of the West and made the United States for at least three decades the granary of the world may be gained from the fact that it took 2.2 minutes in 1900 to prepare the soil for a bushel of wheat as compared with the 32.8 minutes of 1830. The reaper played as significant a role in the development of the new agriculture. The first successful reaper of modern times was patented by Obed Hussey in 1833; the very next year the McCormick reaper made its appearance. Cyrus H. McCormick left the Shenandoah Valley of his birth and took his new machine west, first opening his factory in Cincinnati and then in 1847 in Chicago. In a short time McCormick's agents filled the Middle West, and soon the work of the prairie farms was being lightened by these machines that cut the grain and raked off the straw at the same time. Binding was still a hand process, but it was not long before the McCormick machine was accomplishing the job of binding, too, with the use of wire. In 1879, appeared the Deering binder, which bound the sheaves of grain with twine. There now followed the modern threshing machine, propelled by horsepower, steam, or gasoline, and finally the great grain combine which united the processes of harvesting and threshing so that the grain was ready for the mill before it was off the grain field. In the short-lived so-called bonanza farms of the new Northwest, in the eighties and the nineties, where it was not uncommon for four to six thousand acres to be planted under a single staple, the operations were almost entirely conducted by machinery. One of these farms included in its inventory 67 plows (of which 11 were gang plows), 64 harrows, 32 seeders, 6 mowers, 34 self-binding harvesters, 7 steam engines and threshers, 50 wagons, and 125 head of farm animals.

The saving in human labor through the perfection of all these devices was, of course, well-nigh incalculable. It was said, in 1900, that the amount of human labor needed to produce a bushel of grain from beginning to end was 10 minutes as compared with the 183 minutes of 1830. In the cost of production in 1900 as compared with that in 1830, there was saved in labor-power cost in a single year $523 million in growing the corn crop, $79 million in growing the wheat crop, $52 million in growing the oat crop, as well as other large sums for the other grains. There was no question that the manufacture and consumption of agricultural machinery had increased enormously. In 1859, for example, the value of the products turned out by the farming implements factories was $8 million; by 1899, the value was greater than $100 million. There was no reason why the manufacture and distribution of farm machinery should not fall under the same influences that were shaping the new American industrialism generally. Trade wars, secret agreements, and combines were common, the inevitable outcome making its appearance here as it did in steel, sugar, tin plate, and tobacco. In 1879, there were one hundred fairly large manufacturers of harvesting machines; by 1900, their number had been reduced to fourteen. In 1902, with the aid of House of Morgan, the McCormick interests organized the International Harvester Company; and by the next year, through further consolidations, a monopoly had been created. Similar monopolies were dominating the manufacture of springtooth harrows and grain drills. Already in 1900 some 12 per cent of the total agricultural machinery production was being sent abroad and by 1945 the proportion had grown to nearly 39 per cent.

Federal aid contributed its share toward the metamorphosis that was taking place. The land-grant agricultural colleges were made possible by the passage of the Morrill Act of 1862 and the supplementary measure of 1890. The first turned over to the states large tracts of the public land, the funds from whose sale were to be used for the endowment of institutions of learning, while the second provided for federal money contributions. At the end of the century there were more than sixty colleges teaching agriculture and the mechanical arts and at least one of these was to be found in every state and territory of the Union. In addition, through funds provided by the Act of 1890, there were being operated separate institutions for Negroes in the states of Alabama, Delaware, Florida, Mississippi, North Carolina, South Carolina, and Virginia. Not only were young men and women given formal instruction in the science of agriculture but the college programs also included short-term courses for practical farmers, extension services, and demonstrations.

The second governmental device to make its appearance was the agricultural experiment station, the first to be supported from public funds being that of Connecticut (1875). In 1887, the federal Hatch Act provided for the establishment of an experiment station in every state where there was functioning a land-grant college. Finally, the Federal Department of Agriculture made its appearance, to become the keystone of the whole public agricultural system. In 1862, the then Bureau of Agriculture was raised to the rank of a Department, under the supervision of a commissioner. In 1889, the Department chief was invested with the title of Secretary, and Jeremiah Rusk of Wisconsin was the first appointee to take his place in the Presidential Cabinet. The Department's work expanded greatly in the next few years and soon it was working through a group of great bureaus, the most prominent of which were the Bureau of Animal Husbandry, the Bureau of Plant Industry, the Bureau of Biological Survey, the Bureau of Entomology, and the Weather Bureau. The Bureau of Animal Husbandry, for example, discovered the tick that carried the cattle fever; the Bureau of Entomology did yeomen service in fighting the locust, the corn borer, and the cotton boll weevil; the Bureau of Plant Industry was responsible for the introduction of more than 30,000 new varieties of plants into the United States. The greatest single feat of all was the mapping of the natural agricultural belts of the country by the Bureau of Biological Survey, for the purpose of helping the American farmer break down the evil of single cropping.

The government, too, set its hand to the reclamation of the desert areas of the Far West. In 1894, the Carey Act was passed for the purpose of encouraging the launching of state projects in the arid regions; but this not proving a success, the federal government, in 1902, undertook the task itself. By building great concrete diverting dams with sluices and headworks, providing reservoirs for storage, and laying out a complete system of canals and ditches, the federal government made possible the reclamation of more than two million acres of desert waste. Here, in Arizona, Colorado, California, and Utah, in the first decade of the twentieth century, grains and fruits were already growing.

All these efforts were not to leave the agriculture of the nineteenth century unmarked. Increasingly the older areas of the country, stimulated and inspired by the friendly interest of governmental agencies, turned their backs on the single cropping of their fathers and by crop rotation, the cultivation of clover, careful tillage, and the use of manure and artificial fertilizers, restored the soil's fertility and made possible the production of paying crops. Indeed, economic necessity, as much as education, was at the root of the matter for the increasing value of farm land made it imperative that more valuable crops be planted. The exhaustion of the free lands had struck a deathblow at the frontier farming of the seventies, eighties, and nineties, and single cropping, because it was so wasteful of the soil and so uncertain in its returns, was destined to go sooner or later.

THE FARMERS' DILEMMA

For nearly the whole thirty years of the seventies, eighties, and nineties, American agriculture, though it extended its horizons almost boundlessly, was in reality being operated at a small profit to the farmer or none at all. The only thing that sustained the individual farmer was the constant appreciation of his land values. The West was a magnet whose force the farmers of the East and the Old World could not shake off; and they and their sons kept on streaming into the newer territory to seek out the few remaining homesteads and to become renters if need be when quarter sections should no longer be available. Having accumulated a little capital, these newer settlers sought to buy farms of their own. The result was that in twenty years, in Nebraska for example, such competition on the part of buyers ran the price up from $7 or $8 an acre to $25 or $30. And it must be remembered that the crop of the early nineties was worth much less than the crop of the early seventies! The farmer's capital, then, was his land and improvements and only because these were steadily mounting in value could he keep his head above water. The high value of his land permitted him to convert his floating debts into mortgages with the result that the mortgage indebtedness was becoming heavier every year. In the corn belt, in the nineties, it was nothing unusual for the mortgage burden to average well over one-third of the total capital value of the farm plant. This situation, in short, strikingly reveals the dilemma that was at the basis of the whole agricultural problem. Prices were falling and credit was tight, there was world overproduction and a stringency in the world's gold supply, yet a larger and larger share of the farmer's crops (because of his indebtedness and the increased valuation of his land) went for the payment of interest charges and taxes.

To the farmer his enemies were the railroads with their high rates for carriage and their discriminations in favor of the large shippers; the manufacturers who were able to maintain high prices because their wares were protected by the tariff; the bankers and moneylenders because they refused to lend the farmer money on his crop and because they charged high interest rates on mortgages; the governmental officials because the greater burden of taxation was placed on realty values and not on income or personalty. Curb the railroads, check the monopolies, change the system of taxation, make credit easier, erect government elevators and issue warehouse receipts so that grain could be kept out of the market when there was a surplus and yet furnish the farmer with ready cash, and inflate the currency—this was the economic program of the American farmers in the eighties and nineties. It was a sound analysis of a grievous state of affairs. Unfortunately, in its major essentials, the program could never work because the factors that affected farm prices were international in their operation and not national. Let us analyze in detail the farmer's complaints.

The farmer's burden of debt was mounting alarmingly. By 1900, 31 per cent of the farms of the country were carrying mortgages; in the North Central states—the seat of the new agriculture—debts encumbered more than two-fifths of the farms. The census of the year revealed that 45 per cent of the Wisconsin farmers paid annual interest charges on mortgages; in Michigan the ratio was 48 per cent; in Minnesota it was 45 per cent; in Iowa it was 53 per cent; in Nebraska it was 45 per cent. In almost every case the accumulated mortgages covered from one-fifth to one-third of the capital valuation of farm properties. Many New England moneylenders despoiled the Western homesteader. Boston alone had fifty busy agencies in the wheat and corn lands west of the Mississippi battening on agrarian distress. While rates of interest were fixed by law, and averaged from 7 to 10 per cent, bonuses, service charges, and the rest brought the annual interest cost very often to from 15 to 40 per cent. To pay growing interest charges on land, machinery, and improvements with a crop whose monetary value was ever depreciating was one of those little ironies whose point statesmen, industrialists, and eastern molders of public opinion could not quite see. Senator Peffer of Kansas, writing in the following vein, tickled the risibilities of many an academic economist of the nineties: "The influence of money as a power must be neutralized in some way and there is only one way to do it: remove from money its interest-bearing function to the extent, at least, of bringing the value of money as a profit-bearing investment to the same level with land and labor." But only Kansans could really appreciate the grim humor of a state of affairs that led, in the single year 1890, to the forced sale of 5300 of their farms in mortgage foreclosure proceedings. Money was hard to obtain, and the only credit relief possible lay in the extension of already burdensome farm mortgages at usurious interest rates. Is it to be wondered at that the whole agrarian program of the revolting West turned about a single center and that this was "cheap" money?

The tax load rested on the shoulders of the farmer. Henry George had taught his lesson well: western farmers cried out that the land tax was the only form of public levy that could not be shifted and that in their case assessed valuations were many times higher than in that of favored corporations, particularly the railroads. Not only were the tariff duties shifted back to them, as the ultimate consumers, but in mounting local tax bills the farmers saw themselves paying for disastrous railroad programs, public improvements, and the swelling salary rolls of an inefficient if not corrupt officialdom. That the Supreme Court was quick to find the income tax law of 1894 unconstitutional was a bitter pill for the farming West to swallow.

With land becoming scarce, available farms became fewer in number and tenancy increased. In 1880 (the first census to record the information), 25.8 per cent of the American farms were cultivated by renters; in 1890, the proportion had grown to 28.4 per cent; in 1900, the proportion was 35.3 per cent; in 1910, 37.0 per cent (a proportion which rose steadily until 1930, when it reached 42.4 per cent, and then declined to the 31.7 recorded in 1945) of the nation's farm operators were tenants who raised the produce to feed the nation, paying for the privilege in money or shares, to absentee landlords who quite frequently lived in Boston, Pittsburgh, and far-away Scotland. Farm tenancy was not peculiarly a southern institution: the Negroes of the South Atlantic and South Central states had, indeed, become a landless class, their economic status no whit better than under the forced labor of the slave system of earlier days; but so had, too, more than a quarter of a million free white farm tenants of the North and West and an equal number in the South.

The farmer became the bitter foe of the middleman and the manufacturer because of the high and often monopoly prices he had to pay for the wares he bought. He was at the mercy of the local grain dealers and drovers; he was cheated by many owners of the district elevators; he was a pawn in the operations of the brokers and speculators in the grain and meat markets of Chicago, Minneapolis, and Kansas City.

After the first enthusiasm for railroad building had spent itself, the farmers of the West began to regard the railroad managers as their arch foes. High rates, pooling devices, rebates, discriminations between long and short hauls, incivility, bribery, dishonesty—these were some of the practices whose weight the farmers of the nation began to feel with the result that demands for railroad regulations and rate fixing arose from the West.

It is a little difficult for us today, living in the continuously contracting world of the twentieth century, to sound the depths of drudgery, loneliness, and futility in which the average American farming family of the seventies and eighties lived. Fifty years ago in rural America there were no macadam roads, no telephones, no radios, no movies, no automobiles, no consolidated schools, no rural free delivery, no popular magazines, no household appliances for washing and cleaning and lighting—nothing, in fact, to bring the great outside world to the doorstep of the farmer. The life was bleak, unadorned, of continuous toil for father, mother, and even small children. How can one marvel that occasional waves of fanaticism swept this dreary country, that it became H. L. Mencken's "Bible Belt," that all sorts of cranks and zealots found no difficulty in obtaining followings, and that the silver-tongued William Jennings Bryan became its great crusader?

How western farmers, joined by allies from the South, organized and entered politics with high hopes of having their grievances redressed, and what they accomplished, will be told in some detail in subsequent chapters.

> Section IV
> THE PROCESSES
> OF INDUSTRIALIZATION

· 10 ·

The New Industrialism

WHAT MADE THE NEW INDUSTRIALISM POSSIBLE

FROM the middle of the nineteenth century onward, it may be said that the American life was moving in a new tempo. The domestic economy that had characterized the first half of the industrial revolution was drawing to its close: the time when industry had been to a large extent the enterprise of the artisan and his family, when the relationship between the factory owner and his help was paternalistic, when the workshop was small and the market was a local one, when the form of ownership was individual or through a small group of partners—that day was done. In a brief fifty years industry in America, and the whole aspect of the American life as well, were to be changed beyond recognition. Out of the provincialism of the Concord of Emerson and Thoreau, where the whole life of man was spun out in a narrow, intimate, personal series of relationships, there was to appear Pittsburgh: great, noisy, smoky city, with its showy millionaires, its hordes of unskilled laborers, its great extremes of wealth and poverty. Pittsburgh, fifty years after Concord, typified the new America: the ore for its blast furnaces came from Lake Superior, one thousand miles away; its coal was dug in many distant mines and near at hand in the Pennsylvania area; its toiling masses came from the villages of Transylvania, Sicily, the Baltic coast, and the sunny lands of the eastern Mediterranean; and the rails, the tin plate, the iron hoops, the nails, wire, and bridge parts that Pittsburgh made—in addition to supplying the domestic market, these went to China, Japan, Java, the Argentine plains, and the mountain valleys of Bolivia and Peru. By 1900, American industry was international, corporate, impersonal, standardized, everything, in short, that it had not been fifty years before. How had all this come about?

The following factors had contributed toward the evolution of the new American industrialism in the years following 1850: The triumphant Republican party, from 1861 on, had created a climate in which industrial capitalism could flourish. Through tariff, railway, banking, and immigration legislation it untied the hands of industrialists and their banking allies and permitted unexampled expansion in new areas of enterprise. The great growth of the American population and the vastness of the continental area made for a domestic market unhampered by conflicting currencies, trade regulations and barriers, and the demands of local tastes and customs. The protective tariff erected walls against the competition of the cheaper-made British wares. Immigration contributed the needed labor supply. The development of the railroads opened natural resources and permitted the reaching of distant domestic markets. The abundance of natural riches to be found in the American coal mines, iron and copper deposits, oil fields, and forests made the United States independent of the rest of the world as far as raw materials were concerned. Because agriculture was on a capitalistic basis and the farmers of the country grew staples mainly, they had to buy their foodstuffs, clothing, and all the other necessities of life. America's adverse balance of trade made the employment of foreign capital imperative. British, Dutch, and German capital helped build the railroads, and the savings of the *petite bourgeoisie* of Europe were to be found in American cattle ranches and textile mills. The American government gave a helping hand. The federal acts that chartered the transcontinental railroads called for the use of American-made rails; the laws that authorized the building of the new Navy required the use of American-made steel; the specifications for the first American battleships demanded American-made armor plate. The ingenuity of American inventors helped in the invention of new devices and the perfection of processes brought over from England, France, and Germany. The needs of the northern military establishment during the Civil War speeded along the processes of mechanization. Clothing, boots and shoes, and leather goods, in particular, because they had to be turned out in huge quantities, came to be manufactured in large factories and in standardized patterns. The absence of hampering traditions, such as existed in England and France, encouraged experimentation in management and the use of new machines. American enterprise showed a willingness to scrap obsolescent plants and abandon factories not strategically located. Also, the continual introduction of new blood into American industry eliminated any sentimental attachment to past methods. In England and on the Continent, industry, after all, had evolved in an unbroken sequence from the remote Middle Ages; in the new America there were no past and no accepted patterns that had been handed on from father to son. In America there were no social castes and no traditional pauperism. And the Protestant tradition of working and saving started off many a lad from humble origins on a successful career. All this fostered middle-class attitudes—and higher standards of living. A new type of salesman made his appearance, who sold not commodities necessarily but the belief in American prosperity, a vision of American greatness, a creed of optimism, growth, democratic wealth. Carnegie was the archetype, he was the American booster par excellence, and he was to find worthy successors in Schwab and Ford. And government kept aloof: the prevailing economic doctrine of laissez-faire had governmental approval and blessing.

As a result of the play and interplay of all these forces the Americans of the generation following the Civil War lived in a new world. It was to be, in the beginning, an age of Steel, of Electricity, of Corporations; it was to become, later, as well, an age of Mechanization, Mass Production, Standardization. It was to be a civilization of cities, of great fortunes and humble living, and of individual striving and yet of world interdependence. We grew wheat to feed the wharf laborers of Salonika; Malays under Dutch masters toiled in tin mines to keep the wheels of a Pittsburgh tin-plate mill going; Japanese railroad cars ran on steel rails made possible through the efforts of Finns collecting iron ore in Minnesota, Negroes mining coal in West Virginia, Slavs and Bohemians working in the furnaces of Joliet, Cleveland, Youngstown, and Duquesne, all under the general supervision of a little Scotchman, at Pittsburgh, whose assistants had started out in life as bookkeepers, puddlers, and small salesmen in hardware stores. The world had become smaller, too: distances were bridged and space almost eliminated by speedy steamship lines, transoceanic cables, the telephone, and the telegraph. Capital was collected in great aggregations; labor was mobilized; industrial armies engaged in cruel conflict. And finally, as the nineteenth century closed, American industrialists began to match their wits against those of England, Germany, and France as they, too, scoured the world for raw materials and sought to develop markets for their finished goods.

HOW AMERICAN INDUSTRY GREW

From 1850 to 1900, while the population of the country tripled and the production of agriculture showed a similar increase, the amount of capital invested in American manufactures increased nineteenfold, the value of the products increased twelvefold, the value added by manufacture increased thirteenfold, and the industrial population increased fivefold. By 1890, for the first time, the value of the country's manufactured goods was already greater than that of its agricultural products; in another ten years, manufactured products were worth twice as much as those of the farm, the orchard, and the dairy. The following table presents these significant figures for the fifty years in question.

GROWTH OF MANUFACTURES IN THE UNITED STATES, 1849–99 *

(In thousands)

Year	No. of Establishments	Wage Earners	Amount of Capital Invested	Value of Products	Value Added by Manufacture
1849	123	957	$ 533,000	$ 1,019,000	$ 464,000
1859	140	1,311	1,009,000	1,886,000	854,000
1869	252	2,054	2,118,000	3,386,000	1,395,000
1879	254	2,733	2,790,000	5,370,000	1,973,000
1889	355	4,252	....	9,372,000	4,210,000
1899	512	5,306	9,835,000	13,014,000	5,656,000

* Including all factories, hand and neighborhood establishments.

In 1880, there were twelve industries whose products were each worth more than $100 million. Flour and gristmill products led the list with a total value of $300 million; scarcely behind came slaughtering and meat packing; then followed the iron and steel industry; after these, in order, were to be found woolen manufactures, lumbering, foundry and machine-shop products, cotton goods, men's clothing, boots and shoes, sugar and molasses, tanned leather, malt liquors. In 1900, just twenty years later, there were sixteen industries in the country whose products were worth more than $200 million each. Iron and steel this time headed the list with a total value of $800 million (an increase of 170 per cent); slaughtering and meat packing came second with a total value of a little less than $800 million (also an increase of 170 per cent); foundry and machine-shop products were third with a total value of $645 million; lumbering was fourth with a total value of $570 million; and flour and gristmill products had slipped from first to fifth place with a total value of $560 million. The woolen manufactures and boots and shoes industries had not shown important increases, but men's clothing, tanned leather, malt liquors, and cotton goods had. New important industries to appear on this list for 1900 were: printing, the manufacture of cars and the work of railroad shops, and the building trades.

In 1900, each of the four following states had manufacturing industries whose combined products were worth more than $1 billion: New York, Pennsylvania, Illinois, and Massachusetts. Ohio and New Jersey were a considerable way behind these leaders, though each showed products worth more than $500 million. The significance of these great industrial states may be appreciated from the fact that the whole South, despite the great progress it had made in manufacturing in the eighties and nineties, produced articles whose total value was but $1 billion. It is interesting to note that there was a decided movement of industry westward, as of population and agriculture. In general, the manufacturing industries were establishing themselves in those areas where the labor supply, raw materials, capital, and consuming markets were easily reached. In 1850, the center of manufactures was in central Pennsylvania, forty-one miles northwest of Harrisburg; in 1900, it was in central Ohio, in the neighborhood of Mansfield. Great industries had changed their principal seats of activity in a short space of time. Meat packing, for example, had moved from Cincinnati to Chicago, Kansas City, and St. Joseph; flour milling had moved from Rochester to Minneapolis; iron making no longer centered entirely on the banks of the Allegheny in Pennsylvania and in the Mahoning Valley in Ohio, but large plants also were to be found in Birmingham, Joliet, and Cleveland.

Nothing more graphically indicated the changed aspects of the American life than the records of the Patent Office at Washington. During the decade of the fifties, the Washington authorities granted 25,200 patents on original or improved devices; during the nineties the total had soared to 221,500. Whole industries were revolutionized by extensive changes in machinery and new ones were entirely created. The common use of steel was made possible as the result of American inventions and improvements; the same was true of electric lighting and photography. Railroading was made safer and more comfortable, the textile industry was completely transformed and so was agriculture, as we have seen. It is hard to believe that the sixties and the seventies knew little or nothing at all of the use of the telephone, the bicycle, the trolley car, the arc lamp, the camera, the typewriter, the fountain pen, the phonograph, the cash register, the linotype machine, glucose, oleomargarine, the incandescent lamp, the chemical fire extinguisher. Yet the fact is, all these made their general appearance during the decades from 1880 to 1900. The numerous inventions cited (and many others) made for greater comfort, safety, and variety in the daily life. But one must not lose sight of the chief accomplishment of American inventive skill: all this increased the productivity of labor.

Not the least among the factors making for American supremacy was the lavish endowment of those natural resources needed for industrial enterprise. Not only were there coal, iron, and limestone deposits in great profusion, but the country's petroleum, copper, aluminum, lead, zinc, and silver resources were well-nigh incalculable. The fact is, in the production of the minerals mentioned, the United States led the world at the turn of the century. In 1880, the total value of the country's minerals was put at $369 million; by 1900, their worth was $1 billion; another twenty years later, the figure had risen to almost $7 billion. The following table shows the increase in production among the more important minerals in the space of twenty years; figures for 1947, too, are given.

MINERAL PRODUCTION, 1880, 1900, 1947

	1880	1900	1947
Coal, long tons	63,000,000	263,000,000	635,713,000
Pig, iron, long tons	3,375,000	13,789,000	70,843,000
Copper, pounds	60,000,000	606,000,000	1,742,000,000
Gold, fine ounces	1,741,000	3,829,000	2,090,000
Silver, fine ounces	30,000,000	57,000,000	75,698,000
Petroleum, barrels	26,000,000	63,000,000	1,856,100,000

STEEL

Just as, in a sense, the story of America from 1825 to 1865 can be told almost entirely in terms of cotton and wheat, so its history from 1865 to 1900 can be written in terms of coal, iron, and steel. By the end of the nineteenth century, the United States led the world in the production and manufacture of these articles. Only the richness of the country's natural resources made this possible.

There are one-half million square miles of bituminous coal lands in the United States; coal is to be found in thirty states, but the veins are particularly rich in the Appalachian region (from northwest Pennsylvania into Alabama), in the central area of Indiana, Illinois, Iowa, and Missouri, and in the northwest of North Dakota and in Montana. Up to 1860, bituminous coal was of no significance in American industry for the coal then known was obtained almost entirely from the anthracite mines in eastern Pennsylvania. In 1860, but 14,600,000 tons of coal were mined in the United States; by 1890, the total of coal production was 269,600,000 tons; by 1947, it was 676,000,000 short tons. The opening of the great coal deposits of western Pennsylvania ushered in the modern era of iron and steel making, for from this easily accessible coal, coke could be made in great quantities and the necessary fuel supply was assured. Up to 1875 anthracite and coke production continued on equal terms; at the beginning of the last quarter of the century coke pulled ahead and this victory marked the definite emergence of Pittsburgh. The terrain of the Pittsburgh area is irregular and cut up by sharp valleys through which run a series of swift streams. The natural routes of transportation follow these watercourses. Forty miles up the Monongahela is Connellsville, the center of the greatest coke ovens in the world; in the hills are great limestone deposits (essential to the making of steel); iron beds are to be found in close proximity, too. Pittsburgh, at the confluence of two great rivers, down which could float naturally the barges of coke, limestone, and iron, was destined to greatness. By the early eighties, the center of the country's iron and steel production was in the Pittsburgh area.

The discovery of the great ore deposits of the Lake Superior country, though almost a thousand miles away, only strengthened Pittsburgh's position, for there was a complete water route from the upper lake region to the lower end of Lake Erie. At the western end of Lake Superior, spreading to the north and south in a vast area, lie ranges of hills made up of solid masses of iron ore. The seams are so soft and so near the surface (or were, at any rate until the end of World War II) that the ore can be scooped up with steam shovels. Human labor is practically unnecessary. The shovels drop the ore into waiting freight cars; these are run to the lake harbors of Duluth, Superior, Ashland, and Marquette where mechanical contrivances empty the cars into the waiting ore ships. The first iron range to be worked extensively was in the Vermilion Lake district; other famous ranges were the Marquette, Gogebic, and Menominee. By 1890, some 9,000,000 tons of ore were being sent through the "Soo" Canal to the waiting furnaces of Pittsburgh, Cleveland, and Buffalo. But the greatest range of all was opened in 1892, the so-called Mesabi, lying deep in St. Louis County, Minnesota. It had been developed by the Merritts after heartbreaking setbacks, and in 1893, when they were prepared to reap the rewards of their vision and toil, the panic wiped them out. J. D. Rockefeller, already the king of the lake ore ships, stepped in and acquired the range. By the end of the decade the Mesabi was sending 13,000,000 tons of ore down from the Great Lakes. The Mesabi was furnishing one-third of all the iron ore mined in the United States, one-sixth of the world's supply, one-half of the total raw materials required by the steelmasters of Pittsburgh, Joliet, Youngstown, and Wheeling.

Coal or coke, iron, and limestone are the necessary elements in the making of steel. In 1870, steel was still a rarity; it was used only for fine tools and cutlery, and the steel of our modern industrial life was still unknown. The general use of steel waited on the perfection of a process for the refining of the molten pig iron to free it from the impurities of carbon, sulphur, and phosphorus. In the fifties, two men hit on the method. One was the Englishman Bessemer and the other was the American William Kelly. Because Bessemer pushed the development of this method further than Kelly and made its practical application possible, his is the name generally associated with the opening of the possibilities of steel. In 1864, the first American Bessemer plant was in operation; in 1873, 157,000 tons of steel had been manufactured; twenty years later the output of Bessemer ingots alone was 4,660,000 tons. In the sixties, another (and superior) process for the oxidizing of the iron's impurities was invented, the combined work of the Siemens Brothers, who were Germans, and a Frenchman named Martin. This method, generally known as the open-hearth process, was particularly suitable for ore with a high phosphorus content (in other words, the lower-grade ores). By the end of the century, open-hearth steel had forged ahead of Bessemer steel. Other improvements followed fast. The result in the United States was that whereas in 1860 a little less than 1,000,000 tons of pig iron was made, by 1880 the production of iron and steel totaled 6,486,000 tons and in 1900, 29,507,000 tons. At the turn of the century, 220,000 workers were manning the blast furnaces and the value of the products was $804 million. Steel had definitely taken the place of iron. Whereas in 1880 less than one-third of the pig iron was converted into steel, by 1900 the proportion was four-fifths. And the United States as a steelmaker led the world by 1900, its output almost doubling Great Britain's.

At the end of the century, two-thirds of the country's pig iron was being made in the Pittsburgh area. (The other producing regions were Illinois, Chattanooga-Birmingham, and Colorado.) And Andrew Carnegie was the uncrowned king of Pittsburgh. This Scotch immigrant had gone into the iron business in 1864 and had become a millionaire before the era of steel. A visit to Europe in the early seventies opened his eyes to the possibilities of steel, and he returned to Pittsburgh to enter upon its manufacture. Carnegie saw that the needs of the railroads were boundless: he effected an understanding, therefore, with Thomson and Scott of the Pennsylvania system and began turning out rails in great quantities. In 1879, Carnegie organized his first large company at a capitalization of $5 million, having started a decade earlier with a capitalization of $700,000. In 1882, he made certain of the permanency of his coke supply by buying out and taking into his business H. C. Frick, who in the seventies had gained control of most of the coke ovens of Connellsville. Carnegie and Frick made an extraordinary team. The former was the imaginative master of industry, the prophet of democracy, the friend of Gladstone and Morley, the philanthropist, builder of libraries, and creator of hero funds. Controlling his company through majority-stock ownership, he could use his profits for plant expansion and in a ruthless (and sometimes unfair) warfare against his competitors. He made his subordinates junior partners, thus holding their loyalty; he pushed steel prices down, thus expanding the market for steel products; and he took advantage of rebates, pools, and tariffs. But he built the steel industry—and in the process industrialized America. Frick was the hard-headed man of affairs who filled Pittsburgh with tens of thousands of imported laborers from every obscure hamlet of Eastern and Southern Europe, who fought trade unionism, and who hired Pinkertons to break the terrible Homestead strike of 1892. Between them they created a great vertical combine of coal fields, coke ovens, limestone deposits, iron mines, ore ships, and railroads. In 1892, when the Carnegie Steel Company, Limited, was formed, at a capitalization of $25 million, the Carnegie group of Pittsburgh magnates controlled all the needed sources of supply; and it was soon making one-fourth of all the unfinished or crude Bessemer steel being turned out in the country. These men had the touch of Midas. In the twenty-five years, 1875 to 1900, the Carnegie Company made profits aggregating $133 million; in 1900 alone the profits of the company were $40 million. (A large part of these, of course, were plowed back into new plant.) At the turn of the century it became a New Jersey corporation with a capitalization of $160 million.

Other great groups followed in Carnegie's footsteps. The Illinois Steel Company, formed at Chicago in 1889, was originally capitalized at $25 million; two years later its capitalization was doubled. It possessed plants in Chicago, Milwaukee, and Joliet; it had thousands of acres of coal lands in Pennsylvania and West Virginia; it owned iron lands in Wisconsin, forests in Michigan, and stone quarries in Indiana. The Colorado Fuel and Iron Company (a Rockefeller organization) began operating in 1880; twelve years later it was capitalized at $13 million. Its possessions were imperial, the catalogue including 69,000 acres of proved coal lands, 15 developed mines, 800 coke ovens, 2 blast furnaces, as well as steel works, rolling mills, iron mines, and foundries. In the South there was the gigantic Tennessee Coal, Iron and Railway Company, organized in 1881. Ten years later this corporation was the largest single possessor of coal and ore lands and iron plants in the country, with 400,000 acres of coal and iron and seventeen large furnaces.

These organizations made the pig iron and the unfinished or crude steel, that is to say, the ingots, bars, plates, and rails. In the nineties there emerged the great companies making finished steel products, such as nails, barbed wire, tin plate, tubing, sheet metal, hoops. Morgan and Judge W. H. Moore of Chicago were their guiding geniuses. Heretofore, the financing of the steel industry had been a local enterprise or largely a personal one (as in the case of the Carnegie Company and Rockefeller holdings). But when Morgan and Moore, in 1898, appeared on the scene, steel was translated from the plane of industry to the more rarefied one of finance capitalism. The National Tube Company and the American Bridge Company were promoted by the House of Morgan; the Moore companies were the American Tin Plate Company, the American Steel Hoop Company, and the American Sheet Metal Company. In 1898, too, Morgan had financed an organization making unfinished steel, that is to say, the Federal Steel Company, built up largely about the Illinois Steel Company, mentioned above. This corporation was capitalized at $200 million and was headed by Elbert H. Gary, an Illinois attorney. The very next year, Moore had also promoted the organization of the National Steel Company, also a manufacturer of unfinished steel.

Thus, as the decade and the century ended there were four outstanding personalities in the iron and steel industry: the leading one was Carnegie, who made steel and had been America's first builder of a vertical integration; the second was Rockefeller, who with his untold surpluses had acquired separate units of strategic importance, that is to say, iron mines, coal lands, railways, and ore ships; the third and fourth were Morgan and Moore, financiers, promoters, capitalists, who had welded together great companies not chiefly because economies would necessarily arise from large-scale production, though this was urged in their defense, but because new and larger capitalizations offered quick returns from stock sales. To Morgan and Moore looked John W. Gates, D. G. Reid, W. B. Leeds, and other lesser steelmasters for their inspiration.

Carnegie was preparing to give up active control of his properties and had already listened to offers for them when he learned that the companies making finished steel were quietly laying their plans to go into heavy steel manufacturing. Gates, of American Steel and Wire for example, to free himself from the domination of Carnegie, was buying up coal and iron lands and dickering for ore ships. Carnegie moved quickly. He publicly opened negotiations with George Gould for the construction of a new Pittsburgh-to-Atlantic-seaboard railway; he announced his acquisition of additional ore ships through the purchase of the Pittsburgh Steamboat and Steamship Company; he bought a large tract at Conneaut, a lake port at the eastern end of Lake Erie; and he at once began erecting a plant for the manufacture of finished steel. Carnegie was going to make himself independent of the Rockefeller and Morgan groups entirely, not only by controlling his raw materials, but by freeing himself from any possible dependence on Morgan railroads and Rockefeller ships. Into the bargain, he would enter the peculiar domain of Gates, Reid, Leeds, and the rest.

Whether Carnegie meant all he threatened is hard to say, but the celerity with which the old man moved threw the finished-steel men into a panic. Their overcapitalized companies were in danger and their easily made fortunes in jeopardy in the face of such competition. Peace in steel was now the new watchword and a new and larger organization with the Carnegie Company and all the others combined in it offered the only solution. Why not buy out Carnegie and form a real monopoly in steel, uniting raw materials, transportation, steel works, and finished-steel plants? In January, 1901, Carnegie had thrown down the gage; in April of the same year, Morgan had launched the United States Steel Corporation. Carnegie was bought out at his own price, getting close to $250 million for his personal holdings. Rockefeller was bought out at his price (which was close to $90 million), for his fleet of one hundred ore ships and his great ore deposits were vital to success. The Federal Steel Company (of which Elbert H. Gary was president), the American Steel and Wire Company (of which John W. Gates was the head), the American Tin Plate Company (headed by D. G. Reid and W. B. Leeds), the National Steel Company (the Moore organization), and six others pooled their resources to form the first billion-dollar corporation in the country. At the end of its first year, in April, 1902, the United States Steel Corporation published the following as its capitalization:

Gold bonds (largely held by Carnegie)	$366,097,697
Preferred stock	510,281,100
Common stock (par value, $100 per share)	508,302,500
	$1,384,681,297

What had the United States Steel Corporation been worth in 1901? Wall Street opinion, in that year, based on the common stock at 50 and the preferred at par, placed the corporation's value at $764 million; the Industrial Commission's figure was $559 million; the Bureau of Corporations (perhaps the most reliable authority) later estimated that the total value of tangible property was $676 million. It was generally agreed, however, that the estimated replacement value of the plants and properties (a large number of which were run down and in time were abandoned) was in the neighborhood of $500 million. In other words, there was close to 50 per cent of water in the Company's stock, not to speak of the indebtedness of $366 million in first mortgage bonds. This burden the country's steel users, which meant the whole American nation, had to carry because a group of Chicago and New York millionaires had tried to question the supremacy of a group of Pittsburgh millionaires in the realm of steel!

ECONOMIC LAISSEZ-FAIRE AND THE SUPREME COURT

It was inevitable, as the United States grew to industrial might, that its captains of industry should develop a philosophy of conduct. After all, the rulers of the rails, steel, oil, and public utilities were no pariahs who performed their works at night or behind closed doors. They were respected members of society, pillars of the American churches, philanthropists: they sat at the council tables of the nation, represented the American people at foreign courts, were called upon for advice in matters of great national concern. How was recognition thus achieved?

For forty years, that is to say, from the close of the Civil War well into the first decade of the twentieth century, the philosophy of individualism or laissez-faire justified men's actions in the sphere of politics and industry. The state's role, ran this doctrine, was to be one of passivity; it was to protect life, liberty, and property, but that was all. Government was to observe a policy of hands-off, while the individual was to go his way unmolested about his own affairs. The individual's enterprise, his initiative, his imagination, the responsibilities he was voluntarily willing to assume as employer and entrepreneur—these were the guides to conduct and not a closely written set of rules. Indeed, governmental interference or paternalism must inevitably lead to the hampering of the individual's activities, stultification, and the undermining of progress. Such were the precepts which English and American classical economists had been expounding for half a century.

The industrialists themselves were not inarticulate. Andrew Carnegie, in a series of books, hymned a democracy where opportunity was open for all, though great accomplishments were, of course, effected by great leaders. Said he, in a characteristic passage: "It is the leaders who do the new things that count, and all these have been individualistic to a degree beyond ordinary men, and worked in perfect freedom." Finally, a legal doctrine came to be the capstone of the whole structure. When Justice Holmes, in 1905, protested that "the Fourteenth Amendment does not enact Mr. Herbert Spencer's *Social Statics*," he was not describing an attitude then in process of formation. The fact is, from the middle of the eighties, Spencer's philosophy of individualism had been the very basis of American legal doctrine. The place of the Supreme Court, in helping in the creation of the new industrialism, thus takes on a significance that has been only too often overlooked.

To a very large extent, the decisions of the Supreme Court that underwrote the individualistic philosophy of industrialism revolved about the interpretation of the Fourteenth Amendment. The Fourteenth Amendment was proclaimed in July, 1868; it was, as we have noted, presumably designed to protect the liberties of the newly emancipated Negroes and to place certain disabilities on the former Confederate states and soldiers. But from 1886 on, so complete a transformation had been wrought in it through interpretation, the amendment had become a weapon in the hands of the judiciary, to be wielded in the defense of property as against human rights. Its first section is of the greatest import. It reads:

> All persons born or naturalized in the United States, and subject to the jurisdiction thereof, are citizens of the United States and of the states wherein they reside. No state shall make or enforce any law which shall abridge the *privileges or immunities* of citizens of the United States; nor shall any state deprive any *person* of life, liberty or property without *due process of law;* nor deny any *person* within its jurisdiction the *equal protection of the laws.*[1]

The first time the Supreme Court was called upon to interpret this section was in the Slaughterhouse cases in 1872.[2] The Carpetbag government of Louisiana had granted a monopoly of the slaughterhouse business, in certain parishes of New Orleans, to a single corporation, thus driving fully one thousand persons out of this form of enterprise. The petitioners claimed a violation of the Fourteenth Amendment, on the score that the

[1] Italics ours.
[2] 16 Wallace 36.

monopoly hampered their "privileges and immunities." But the majority opinion of the Court refused to grant the relevance of the contention. The Fourteenth Amendment had been written to protect the civil rights of the former slaves; there was nothing in it, therefore, to warrant the assumption that states might not interfere with the activities of corporations in the furtherance of their police power.

Again, in 1876, the Court denied its jurisdiction, when the Fourteenth Amendment was invoked. This was in the so-called Granger cases, growing out of laws passed by western states for the purpose of regulating the rates of grain elevators and railroads.[3] The majority opinion did not deny that property had its rights; indeed, property was entitled to a reasonable return on its investment. But, said the Court, this question belonged in the province of the legislative branch of government. For:

> In countries where the common law prevails it has been customary from time immemorial for the legislature to declare what shall be a reasonable compensation. . . . We know that this is a power which may be abused, but that is no argument against its existence. For protection against abuses by legislatures, the people must resort to the polls, not to the courts.

While the industrial East protested against these decisions and some prophesied the destruction of private property as a result of the socializing legislation of the western states, lawyers accepted the Court's limits placed upon the Fourteenth Amendment. To most Americans it seemed an historic incident in the emancipation of the Negro; and from 1872 to 1888 but seventy cases were decided under the Amendment. Nevertheless, in the brief space of the succeeding decade, the leveling doctrine of the Court was to be discarded and before the century was over, the Court was to rule (basing its findings on the meanings it was to give to "due process" and "equal protection of the laws"): 1. that a corporation is a "person" within the meaning of the Fourteenth Amendment; 2. that corporations are entitled to a reasonable return on capital invested; 3. that judicial review may be employed for the purposes of determining reasonableness.

It was in 1886 that the Supreme Court, accepting the wider definition of "person" as including corporations, invoked the "due process" clause of the Fourteenth Amendment. Roscoe Conkling, freshly retired from the Senate, appeared before the Court in 1882 to contest the right of San Mateo County in California to levy a corporation tax on the Southern Pacific Railroad. It was Conkling's argument that brought about the significant reversal in the Court's attitude. Conkling's story ran: The Joint Committee of Fifteen, which had written the Fourteenth Amendment, and of which he had been a member, had set out to labor not only in the interests of the Negro's civil rights; it was seeking to protect property rights, as well, against the encroachments of state legislatures. It had therefore

[3] The most important of these decisions was Munn v. Illinois, 94 U.S. 113.

advisedly written the word "person" into the Amendment because it meant more than "citizen"; it meant "person" in its ordinary juristic meaning of corporation, too. In short, corporations, as well as Negroes, were to be protected in their rights to life, liberty, and property against state legislation. And Conkling referred to the journal of the Committee, which he then held in his hand.

The Court, when it handed down its decision in the San Mateo case, in 1885, took no cognizance of Conkling's arguments, deciding the matter on other points of law. But in the very next year, in a similar case,[4] the Court in an *obiter dictum* accepted Conkling's wider definition of the word "person." And in two cases decided in 1888 and 1889 the interpretation was formally incorporated into the decisions.[5]

The second step came in the Minnesota Rate case, when the Chicago, Milwaukee and St. Paul Railroad petitioned the Supreme Court to restrain the Minnesota State Railway Commission, as an agency of the legislature, from depriving it of its property through the fixing of confiscatory rates.[6] This the Court did; the law was held unconstitutional and the majority opinion declared: "This power to regulate is not the power to destroy, and limitation is not the equivalent of confiscation." Also, passing upon the reasonableness of a rate was "eminently a question for judicial investigation, requiring due process of law for its determination." Finally, in 1898, in Smyth v. Ames, the doctrine of judicial primacy was enunciated in its full splendor.[7] The Court held, in passing on a Nebraska statute which sought to fix maximum rates to be charged by railroad companies within the state, that all the three principles outlined above were definitely accepted by it: 1. the personality of corporations; 2. the necessity for reasonableness of rates; 3. the function of judicial review in passing on rate-fixings, that is to say, the earnings to be allowed the railroads.[8]

---

[4] Santa Clara County v. Southern Pacific R.R., 118 U.S. 394 (1886).

[5] Pembina Mining Co. v. Pennsylvania 125, U.S. 181 (1888). Minneapolis and St. Louis R.R. Co. v. Beckwith, 129 U.S. 26 (1889). It is true that the "due process" clause of the Fourteenth Amendment made its first appearance in a judicial decision in 1886. But it must not be assumed that "due process" was without background in our judicial history. Some of the early judges, e. g., Kent, Story, Chase and others, had intimated that statutes against natural and inalienable rights would be held void, apart from express constitutional provisions, and such dicta began to increase after the middle of the century. Thomas M. Cooley, in his *Constitutional Limitations* (1868), systematized these early "natural law" cases under a broad doctrine of implied constitutional limitations. See William Seagle, "Thomas M. Cooley," in the *Encyclopaedia of the Social Sciences,* Vol. IV (1931).

[6] 134 U.S. 418 (1890).

[7] 169 U.S. 466 (1898).

[8] The Smyth v. Ames decision was to be one of the landmarks in the history of American constitutional law. In addition to enunciating the tripartite doctrine above indicated it laid down the rule that legislatures and commissions, in arriving at the rate base for the fixing of reasonable rates, were to take cognizance of the factor of "reproduction cost new." The Court declared that the basis for the calculation of rates

THE NEW INDUSTRIALISM

In contrast with the earlier period, it is interesting to see that so completely was the Fourteenth Amendment regarded as a bulwark against oppressive state legislation, particularly as it affected the rights of property, that between 1888 and 1918 the Amendment was invoked in 790 cases brought before the Supreme Court.

It should be noted, at this point, that nowhere has the Court ventured to define "due process." Nor has it made any effort to indicate where interference by the states, in the interests of the health, safety, morals, and general well-being of their inhabitants, must end and where confiscation of property under the Fourteenth Amendment begins. The states have sought to defend their right to the passage of welfare and regulatory legislation under the police power.[9] But the federal courts consistently resisted —at any rate, this was true until 1936—the wide extension of this power and only the pressure of public opinion compelled the acceptance of the more humane point of view advanced by the states. Thus, in Lochner v. New York,[10] the Supreme Court held New York's 10-hour law for bakers to be unconstitutional on the ground that it arbitrarily interfered with labor's rights of contract. But in 1908, the Supreme Court placed the stamp of its approval on an Oregon 10-hour law for women; and in 1917, the Court upheld the constitutionality of an Oregon law that established the 10-hour law for all persons working in factories.

Thus, in general, the Court moved to check state interference with the rights of private property. It is important to recall that the outstanding decisions handed down all came in the decade of the nineties and that, for the most part, these were aimed at Populist state legislatures whose farmer constituencies had demanded relief from the high-handed deportment of the railroad managers. In another group of decisions, also written in the same decade, the Supreme Court denied the right of the newly established Interstate Commerce Commission to assume the rate-fixing power.[11]

In the single year 1895 three additional decisions were rendered, all of which had important economic implications. In U. S. v. E. C. Knight Company, the so-called Sugar Trust case, the Court held that a monopoly in the manufacture of sugar was not commerce, in the meaning of the

---

was to be "the fair value of the property." What were the factors entering into fair value? These, said the Court: 1. the original cost of construction; 2. the amounts expended in permanent improvements; 3. the amount and market value of the outstanding stocks and bonds; 4. the reproduction cost new; 5. the probable earning capacity of the property under the rate fixed; 6. the sum required to meet operation expenses.

[9] The police power was defined by Chief Justice Shaw of Massachusetts as "the power vested in the legislature by the Constitution to make, ordain, and establish all manner of wholesome and reasonable laws, statutes and ordinances, either with penalties or without, not repugnant to the Constitution, as they shall judge to be for the good and welfare of the Commonwealth and the subjects thereof."

[10] 198 U.S. 45 (1905).
[11] See below, page 236.

Constitution.[12] In view of the fact that the Sherman Antitrust Law was based on the commerce clause, the prosecution of monopoly was seriously hampered for a considerable length of time. In the Debs case, the Court unanimously upheld a verdict of the circuit court which had found Eugene V. Debs guilty of contempt for violating an injunction sued out under the Sherman Antitrust Law.[13] While the Supreme Court itself ruled against Debs on other grounds, the lower court had sanctioned the use of the injunction in labor disputes, and the swiftness with which the weapon was employed to strike down Debs put organized labor in no easy frame of mind.

Thus farmer and labor were antagonized. But the decision in the Income Tax case provoked such outspoken censure of the Court, among the lower middle classes generally, that the Democratic party platform of 1896 adopted the same bitter tone. It will be recalled that the Tariff Act of 1894 carried an income-tax provision placing a tax on incomes in excess of $4000. Despite the fact that the Supreme Court had declared the Civil War income taxes constitutional, the new income tax law was contested at once. The array of opposing counsel was a brilliant one, Joseph H. Choate, Benjamin H. Bristow, William D. Guthrie, and Senator G. F. Edmunds appearing for the appellants in the case of Pollock v. Farmers' Loan and Trust Company.[14]

The argument of Choate, in particular, was convincing to the Court, for it ruled, following the lines of his brief: 1. that a tax on income from land was a direct tax and therefore was to be apportioned among the states on the basis of population; 2. that a tax on income from municipal bonds was unconstitutional because the federal government had no power to tax the agencies of states. But because only eight justices were sitting, and because they divided four to four on the question, no decision was reached on the legality of a tax applied to incomes derived from other forms of personalty. A reargument was ordered and this time the full bench sat. On May 20, 1895, by a vote of five to four, the court held that a tax on income from salaries, stocks and bonds, etc., was a direct tax and therefore that it, too, required apportionment.[15] Thus, the whole income-tax law was invalid.

[12] 156 U.S. 1.
[13] 158 U. S. 564.
[14] 157 U.S. 429.
[15] 158 U. S. 601.

· 11 ·

Money and Trade

THE RESUMPTION OF SPECIE PAYMENTS

THE Civil War was financed by greenback issues, taxation and borrowings: out of this last policy arose the heated wranglings of forty years. The high Civil War tariff acts were presumably fiscal devices, but they brought in only some $305,360,000 in revenues. The internal revenues gave the government $291,760,000. The income tax of 1861 to 1865 netted $55,085,000. In brief, total taxation accounted for two-thirds of a billion dollars. But the total produced by loans was four times as great, for during the war the Treasury issued long-term and short-term notes to the value of $2,142,000,000. In addition, on three separate occasions—by acts in February, 1862, July, 1862, and March, 1863—Congress authorized the issuance of $450,000,000 in legal tender or greenbacks. Finally, during the Civil War, there was struck off $50,000,000 in fractional currency. These borrowings—for using the printing presses is a form of borrowing—thus totaled more than two and one-half billions of dollars.[1] At the end of 1861, too, the government suspended specie payments, so that the nation was on a paper basis. And up to the beginning of the year 1864 (by the direction of Secretary of the Treasury Chase) holders of greenbacks of the first two issues could convert their paper into 6 per cent government gold bonds. The later significance of this Act lay in this: the greenbacks had depreciated badly as confidence in the government had waned so that the average value, in gold, of a greenback dollar in 1864 was 64 cents; in fact, its low was 39 cents. Yet greenbacks could buy gold bonds. The inflationists of the eighties and nineties were not far from wrong when they contended that the Civil War had been financed with a 50-cent dollar and was being paid back with a 100-cent dollar.

Funding the war debt was a continual concern of the government. Funding measures were enacted in 1865, 1870, 1871, 1873, 1875, 1879, and by this last year the debt was cut down to $2,349,600,000 of which $346,681,000 was in greenbacks. It is important to trace the history of the greenbacks in greater detail, for around them is to be found revolving the initial phase of the currency dispute.

[1] On September 1, 1865, the net public debt stood at $2,758,000,000.

The first point at issue was the mode of redemption of the war bonds. Some of them had called for payment of principal and interest in gold, some specified coin, while some said nothing of the kind of money in which they were to be redeemed. However, in 1869, an act was passed promising that these bonds would be paid back in coin. The Middle West had protested, insisting upon redemption in paper, and a demand to this effect had been incorporated in the Democratic platform of 1868. But to no avail; and thus, the first skirmish was lost by the inflationists. The second matter to be cleared up was this: Were these legal tenders or greenbacks constitutional? In 1870, the Supreme Court ruled the three legal tender laws of 1862 and 1863 unconstitutional.[2] The very next year the Court, with slightly different make-up, reversed itself and found that the greenbacks could be presented to satisfy any debt contracted before or after the legal tender acts had been passed.[3] The third question was: How many greenbacks should there be? The inflationists wanted as many as possible; the contractionists none at all, if this could be accomplished. The inflationists were the debtors generally and the farmers in particular, who sought more money to maintain high crop prices and to make their debt burden as light as possible. The contractionists (they called themselves "sound" money men) were usually the bondholders who had paid for their bonds in paper and hoped to see their holdings appreciate with the contraction of the currency. After considerable juggling Congress finally, in 1878, determined that the amount of greenbacks then outstanding, $346,681,000, should remain a permanent part of the country's currency system.

Meanwhile, the value of the greenbacks, in terms of gold, remained uncertain. In 1862, the average value of a paper dollar had been 90 cents in gold; in 1863, the average value had been 72.9 cents; in 1864, 64 cents; in 1865, 49.5 cents; in 1866, 71.2 cents; in 1869, 72.7 cents. During the early seventies, the greenbacks had begun to climb in value, the action of the Supreme Court and the definite indication that Congress was not committed to limitless expansion having given the "sound" money interests heart. In 1870, the average value of the greenback was 81.1 cents; in 1875, it was 88.4 cents. And then, with resumption of specie payments assured, it was only a matter of time when the paper dollar would be worth 100 cents in gold. In January, 1875, a lame-duck Republican Congress passed the Resumption Act, which called for the resumption of specie payments on January 1, 1879, and further provided: 1. that the volume of greenbacks be reduced to $300 million (subsequently modified, as stated above); 2. that the paper fractional currency be withdrawn to be replaced by gold coin; 3. that to resume specie payments the Treasury use the surplus specie in its possession, or, if need be, sell bonds for coin. Thanks to the subsidence

[2] Hepburn v. Griswold, 8 Wallace 603.
[3] Knox v. Lee, 12 Wallace 457.

of the depression (which had begun in 1873), to good crops, and to a favorable balance of trade, the Secretary of the Treasury had no difficulty in carrying into effect the mandates of the law.

THE NATIONAL BANKING SYSTEM

In the national banking scheme, inaugurated during the Civil War, we find, almost entirely, the heart of the country's agricultural dilemma. The National Bank Act of 1863 (amended in 1864) provided the following: 1. A banking association, by depositing federal bonds with the government, might emit circulating notes to the value of 90 per cent of the bonds so deposited. 2. Such notes were legal tender for all government dues except import duties, and might be used by the government for all its transactions except payment of principal and interest of the national debt. 3. The amount of notes thus emitted was, in the beginning, limited to $300 million. 4. National banks might not lend money on mortgages. 5. The banks were to be taxed by the national government. 6. A bureau of currency in the Treasury Department was set up for the supervision of the system. Proponents of the plan, when it was first debated in Congress, argued that the national banks, thus being founded on the basis of federal bonds, would absorb a large portion of the war issues; that they would be useful as governmental depositories; and that they would make for order out of the chaos then reigning in the banking system. It was estimated, in 1862, that there were about 1600 state banks of which 1500 were issuing circulating notes. Says D. R. Dewey, describing the situation:

> They were established under the laws of twenty-nine different states; they were granted different privileges, subjected to different restrictions and their circulation was based on a great variety of securities of different qualities and quantities. There were state banks with branches, independent banks, free banks, banks organized under a general law, and banks with special charters.

On January 1, 1862, these banks possessed an aggregate capital of $420,000,000 and had in circulation $184,000,000 in notes. Of these notes, A. B. Hepburn says: "It was estimated that there were 7000 kinds and denominations of notes and fully 4000 spurious and altered varieties were reported." To give the national banks a securer footing an act in 1865 taxed the state bank notes out of existence by levying a federal 10 per cent tax on them. Thus encouraged, the national banks increased from 1295 in 1865 to 3689 in 1896; their capitalization and surplus increased from $380,000,000 in the earlier year to $983,000,000; their deposits from $398,000,000 in 1865 to $1,668,000,000 in 1896; and their loans from $362,000,000 to $1,972,000,000.

In one important particular, the banks thus created fell down lamentably. Rather than easing credit, their dependence on federal bonds for note emissions made for credit stringency. As the years went on, particularly during the eighties and nineties, the shrinkage in national bank notes became more and more marked. In 1865, there was a total of $171,300,000 in bank notes in circulation; in 1870, $291,800,000; in 1880, $344,500,000; in 1885, $318,600,000; in 1890, $186,000,000. Contraction was due to the following: 1. Government refunding programs made for the withdrawal of federal bonds. 2. There was great competition for bonds, from trustees and estates, for investment purposes. 3. The bonds advanced to high premiums so that the banks could not afford to buy them. The fact is, the system had an inverse elasticity: in times of stringency when credit was tight, bonds rose in value and the banks sold, thus narrowing their credit base. In times of boom, banks could buy bonds at lower prices, thus making it possible for them to expand credit. A sound banking system worked the other way around.

There was another great difficulty. The banking law required a minimum capitalization of $50,000 for banks established in places under 6000 population. The result was that rural communities were poorly served under the system, the natural tendency for the banker being to gravitate toward the industrial communities where his money could be expected to move faster. Then, too, under the banking law, the older banks had received first the privilege of note emission, and these banks were to be found for the most part in the industrial districts. More than two-thirds of the national banks and more than three-fourths of the total capitalization were to be found in the states north of the Potomac and Ohio and east of the Mississippi. And how badly the rural communities needed credit facilities—which the national banks did not supply—may be noted from the fact that one-half the state banks in Kansas, Nebraska, and Missouri, and more than three-fourths of the state banks in North Dakota, were capitalized at less than $20,000 each.

Still a third difficulty lay in the nature of the reserve system set up. Country banks were to keep their reserves in reserve cities; these in turn were to use the banks of central reserve cities of which there were three by the eighties, New York, Chicago, and St. Louis. Notably in New York, banks lent out these reserves on call and they were used to finance brokers' loans and therefore security speculation. At the first sign of trouble the country banks withdrew their reserves—and brokerage houses at once encountered storms. This happened in 1873, 1893, and 1907. The Federal Reserve Act of 1913 sought to rectify this situation.

From the point of view of the agricultural communities, these objections were of a very serious nature. The farmer, like most enterprisers, must work with credit; but rural credits are conditioned by somewhat peculiar circumstances. They generally must be longer than the commercial 60-day or 90-day loans. The farmer needs advances for living expenses, tools, seed, fertilizer, labor and marketing operations, and he cannot repay his loans until his crop is successfully sold. The lender must be willing to become a partner in a more or less hazardous enterprise: take the risk that the crop will be successful; be willing to gamble that surpluses will not be too heavy; and hope that the farmer can afford to wait to move his crop until the price appears most favorable.

The national banks were not created to work hand in hand with the agricultural interest; in fact, their inadequacy was at the bottom of agricultural currency agitation. We have seen already that the dependence of the national banks upon bonds made for an inelastic and in fact contracting currency. The rural areas were hardest hit, as the currency contracted, because farmers used cash for their medium of exchange and not bank paper. And the elimination of state bank notes, by the law of 1865, wiped out those small banks that were willing to operate in the rural districts. The high capital requirements for national banks kept them out of the farming districts. The fact that the older banks received first the privileges of note emission led to sectional discrimination because the newer banks were in the South and West. We may note the following additional complaints which were raised: 1. The interest rates were high, for many banks required a minimum balance on deposit before they would make loans, and many deducted the interest first. Service charges, too, were not uncommon. 2. The concentration of the credit facilities in the hands of a few men gave them great political power, which they were not slow in using. 3. The banker obtained a double profit, drawing interest from the bonds he deposited with the Treasury and getting interest on the money he lent with the bank notes the government permitted him to issue. 4. Finally, the national banks could not lend on mortgages.

The inadequacy of rural long-term credit facilities was as great an evil. Money for investment, that is to say, for the purchase of real estate, improvements, heavy machinery, and stock, had to come either from local lenders or from outside capitalists. Insurance companies, mortgage companies, and private investors came forward to offer funds for farm mortgages in those districts where there were no local capitalists. Rentiers of the East, with the contraction of government bond issues, found a favorite field for investment in this form of paper. They were an excellent risk, in view of the fact that the existence of a large landless group made for high farm prices. But the farmer paid heavily. Interest rates were high; the mortgages were usually for short terms and the employment of a system of agents for negotiating them made for high service charges; no amortization was provided; and the farmer, tempted by rising land values, generally borrowed more and more.

What did statesmen do about this deplorable state of affairs? Really nothing for nearly sixty years. The National Bank Act of 1863 was substantially amended first in 1900 when the Currency Act of that year, in addition to making gold the single standard, permitted the banks to issue notes to the full par value of the bonds deposited (instead of the 90 per cent heretofore allowed) and reduced the capitalization requirement for towns of less than 3000 population to $25,000 instead of the former $50,000. But real reform, as far as short-term credits were concerned, did not come until the enactment of the Federal Reserve Act of 1913 and the Agricultural Credits Act of 1923; and as for long-term credits, not until the Federal Farm-Loan Act of 1916.

SILVER

The whole silver debate is significant for but one reason: with the failure of the agitation for an expanded paper currency, silver became the chief reliance of the inflationists in their quest for more or cheaper money and hence easier credit. To understand the silver controversy, and more particularly the crisis that was reached in 1896, it is imperative that the events of the twenty years 1873 to 1893 be unraveled with some care.

In 1873, after having debated the question in desultory fashion for two years, Congress enacted a law entitled: "An Act revising and amending the laws relating to the mints and the assay offices and the coinage of the United States." Hidden away in the verbiage of a long and involved piece of legislation was a clause which, in effect, permitted the suspension of the minting of silver, for it omitted the silver dollar from the list of coins. By the laws of 1834 and 1837, the United States had been continued on the double standard: possessors of gold or silver could have their bullion minted into coin at Treasury offices at a ratio which was changed from time to time, being finally fixed at 16 to 1. But for twenty years preceding 1873 silver had been out of commercial use in the United States. In 1870, the market value of silver was in the ratio of 15.57 to 1; in 1873, 15.92 to 1. In other words, in 1873, the silver dollar was worth $1.02, and hence was not being minted. But about that time, that is to say, in the middle seventies, the silver production of the world began to increase with the discovery of new lodes in Colorado, Nevada, and later Utah. Silver was no longer at a premium but was worth less than gold. In 1874, the ratio fell to 16.7 to 1; in 1878, it was at 17.94 to 1; in 1879, at 18.39 to 1. Then it became profitable to mint silver dollars; but when the possessors of silver bullion took their stock to Treasury offices, they found that the law of 1873 had demonetized silver. Thus arose that outcry of the "crime of 1873." To Silverites, the Act had been born in iniquity and sin; it had been a conspiracy concocted by the American money powers in conjunction with British financiers: their purpose was to force the single gold standard on the world for the benefit of creditors and in the interest of a dearer dollar. This charge of a "conspiracy" we may dismiss, for there is no evidence in the Congressional debates of any intent other than a recognition on the part of Congress that the silver dollar, up to that time, was no longer being minted. Yet the subject became a favorite theme of silver orators, and the force of the charge increasingly was calculated to arouse agrarian audiences when it became plain that in the unlimited coinage of silver there was the only avenue of escape from dear money and tight credit.

Plausibility was given to this talk of an international conspiracy when the rest of the world began to abandon silver. Germany, in 1871, had gone on a gold basis; the Scandinavian countries, Spain, and Holland, by 1875, had adopted the gold standard; in 1873, the Latin Monetary Union (France, Switzerland, Belgium, Italy, and Greece), after having used silver freely for almost half a century, moved to limit the coinage of the lesser metal. The Silverites of the United States were becoming increasingly isolated, but in the free coinage of silver they could see their only salvation.

During the later seventies, the eighties, and the early nineties, almost every Congress was to see presented a bill calling for the unlimited coinage of silver, first at the ratio of 16 to 1, and then, as silver dropped in value, at any ratio—17 to 1, 18 to 1, even 20 to 1. Richard P. Bland of Missouri, "Silver Dick" to his contemporaries, pressed the issue in every Congress in which he sat, that is to say, from 1873 to 1899. Bland's bill in 1877 started out as a free silver bill; he, too, tried to make a House bill in 1889 a free silver bill. The Senate, in 1890, passed a free coinage bill by a vote of 42 to 25; this was the measure that was metamorphosed into the Sherman Act of 1890 as a result of the work of the conference committee. In 1892, a free coinage bill passed the Senate by a vote of 29 to 25. Two years later a bill, which passed both houses, called for the coinage into money of the silver bullion stock then in the Treasury. Cleveland vetoed the measure and the House was unable to muster the votes necessary to override the veto. The silver legislation which was written called for but limited coinage; it can be seen, however, that unlimited coinage was ever the goal for which the Silverites strove.

The first silver law to be written was the Bland-Allison Act of 1878. Bland's bill, after Allison of Iowa persuaded the Senate to amend it, provided that the Treasury was to buy from $2 million to $4 million in silver bullion monthly, at the market price, for coinage into dollars. On the deposit of silver dollars, the Treasury was authorized to issue silver certificates in denominations of not less than $10, and therefore not having legal-tender value. (In 1886, a Congressional enactment provided for silver certificates of smaller denominations.) The measure was carried by a sectional vote which disregarded party lines. In the House but six votes were cast against the original Bland bill by Congressmen from districts south and west of Pennsylvania, and it received but nine votes from Congressmen from the Middle Atlantic and New England states. On the final Bland-Allison Act the sectional division in both houses was scarcely less sharp. That the silver "heresy" was popular enough in these early days of the debate may be seen from the fact that the following notables gave it their votes: Cannon of Illinois (later Speaker of the House), Carlisle of Kentucky (later Secretary of the Treasury under Cleveland), Foster of Ohio (later to occupy the same post under Harrison), and McKinley of Ohio (to be the Republican gold-standard-champion in 1896). It should be noted that Hayes vetoed this bill but both houses overrode the veto. During the twelve years (1878–90) that the law was in operation the Treasury coined $378,166,000 in silver dollars.

Official Washington was hostile toward the law. Sherman, Hayes's Secretary of the Treasury, inveighed ceaselessly against it; so did Cleveland's Secretary of the Treasury Manning, who in 1885 asked Congress for the law's suspension. To Cleveland, the coinage of silver and the presence of the silver certificates were largely responsible for the Treasury's inability to maintain an adequate gold reserve. But the country, and the agrarian interest particularly, saw no evil in the metal and clamored for more to dissipate the heavy clouds of economic depression that hung over the farming country during the late seventies, the late eighties, and the early nineties.

The Silverites won a further concession with the passage of the Sherman Silver Purchase Act of 1890. This bill, introduced first in the Senate, started out by being a free-silver measure. The Republican administration saw that ground would have to be yielded to the western Congressmen, for the passage of the McKinley tariff bill depended upon their support. But largely through the instrumentality of Senator Sherman in the conference committee, unlimited coinage was staved off, in principle at least, by the writing of a more liberal purchase law. Western Republicans accepted the compromise and passed the McKinley Tariff Act. This Silver Act of 1890 (though silver by that year had fallen to a ratio in the market of 19.77 to 1) authorized the Treasury to purchase monthly 4,500,000 ounces of silver bullion for coinage into dollars. Unlike the Act of 1878, the new bill called for the issuance of Treasury certificates which were to be full legal tender. Thus, the new law actually provided for more silver coinage and placed gold and silver on a parity because the Treasury certificates, in view of the fact that they were full legal tender, could be redeemed in either gold or silver (at the discretion of the Treasury). Sherman put the purchase in terms of bullion instead of the dollars of the Bland Act, for he saw that the dollar additions to the Treasury would grow less if silver prices continued to fall. (A silver dollar was worth 60 cents in 1893.) The fact is, prices did decline, but this did not prevent the Treasury from purchasing 168,674,682

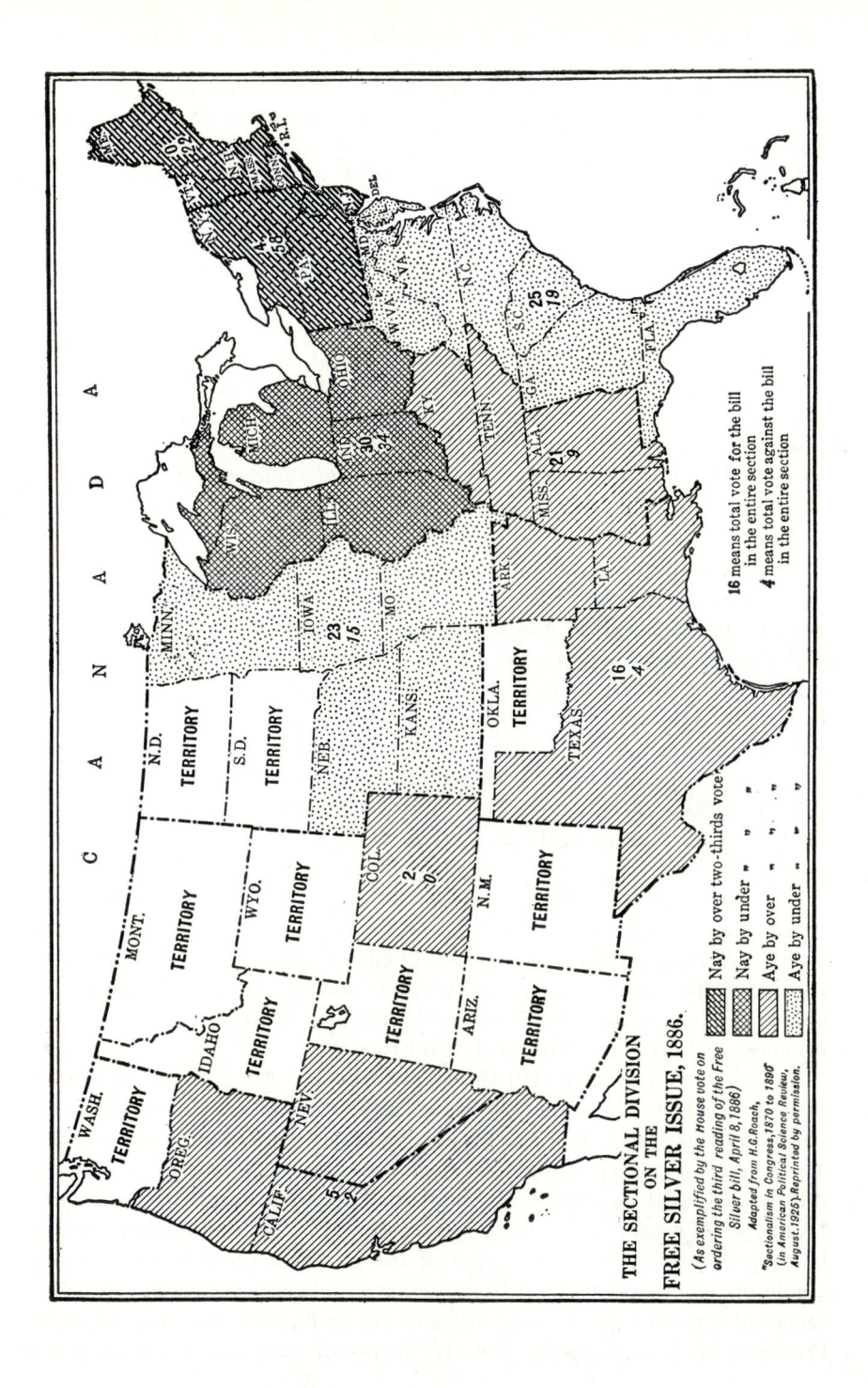

THE SECTIONAL DIVISION ON THE FREE SILVER ISSUE, 1886.

(As exemplified by the House vote on ordering the third reading of the Free Silver bill, April 8, 1886.)

Adapted from H.G. Roach, "Sectionalism in Congress, 1870 to 1890" (in American Political Science Review, August, 1925). Reprinted by permission.

16 means total vote for the bill in the entire section
4 means total vote against the bill in the entire section

Nay by over two-thirds vote
Nay by under " " "
Aye by over " " "
Aye by under " " "

ounces of fine silver in the three years under the law's operation. And this, be it noted, was practically the full output of the American mines for those years.

Cleveland was a "sound" money man and the Sherman Law he regarded with particular abhorrence. To him, the financial difficulties of the country, and of the Treasury particularly, were in large part ascribable to the debased silver currency which was driving gold out of circulation. The depression of 1893 held the country in its grip and made the situation only the more pressing. In that single year 158 national banks had gone under, as well as some 450 other banking institutions; 74 railroad corporations, operating more than 30,000 miles of track, had passed into receivers' hands; more than 15,000 commercial failures, involving liabilities of $346 million were to be recorded before the year had run its course. Coal and iron production dropped; droughts burned up the corn and wheat crops; unemployment was widespread and strikes and industrial unrest were phenomena of the period.

To Cleveland there was but a single reason for all this: it was silver. The world, he argued, feared the inability of the United States to maintain a gold standard, and was draining off our precious metal. The fact is, the depression had begun to spread over the western world in 1890 with the collapse of the British house of Baring Brothers, as a result of its unfortunate Argentine investments. British holders of American securities had begun to sell their bonds, and the outflow of gold from America was due largely to this reason. Again, there had been overexpansion in American rails (due to the importation of British capital) and the boom had collapsed when the railroads could not meet their carrying charges. It was natural, in times of panic, that hoarding should take place and gold had gone into hiding because it was the more precious metal. Finally, Congress itself had added to the difficulties by disposing of the Treasury surplus in liberal pension grants and through a high protective tariff which cut down revenues from customs. Thus, the situation was complex; and whether the Treasury purchases of silver played a stellar role in hastening or prolonging the general economic collapse, one finds it difficult to say.

But Cleveland insisted that the Silver Purchase Act of 1890 must be repealed to rescue the Treasury from jeopardy, and he called the newly elected Democratic Congress into session, in August, 1893, for that purpose. The western Congressmen were recalcitrant and it appeared, at first, that they would resist the President. Bland, on August 12, and Bryan, on August 16, made telling addresses in the lower house, that of Bryan's, in particular, being a consummate presentation of the agrarian point of view on the whole currency and credit situation. But the House voted for repeal, on sectional lines of course, with enough eastern Republicans rallying to the President to overcome the negative votes of southern Democrats and western Populists. The final vote in the House was 239 for repeal and 108 against. But in the Senate the contest was a bitter one. The debate continued through August, September, and October, and it was only when the President had called upon his last line of reserve, that is to say, the federal patronage, that the Senate yielded. Repeal was carried by a vote of 43 to 32. Including pairs, 22 Democrats and 26 Republicans voted for repeal while 22 Democrats, 12 Republicans and 3 Populists voted against.

Cleveland, thus, triumphed over the recalcitrants of his own party, but it was a bitter victory and it was soon seen that his leadership over the Democracy was gone forever. The stinging rebuke that was administered him by his party's convention in 1896 was regarded by the westerners as being a fit return for his desertion of the common man in the struggle between the people and predatory wealth. From 1893 to 1896, with the spread of Populism over the West and the surrender of the southern Democracy to the free silver cause, it became increasingly apparent that the Presidential year 1896 would witness the closing act of this great drama.

Cleveland's troubles were not over with the repeal of the Silver Purchase Act. The Treasury was still vulnerable because the gold reserve being maintained to safeguard the greenbacks was constantly being eaten into by the presentation of Treasury (silver) certificates and legal tenders (greenbacks) for gold coin. (At least, this was Cleveland's explanation. The use of gold for export account, through the continued sale of American securities by foreign shareholders, was as much at the heart of the difficulty.) In 1891, this gold reserve had stood at $300 million; in April of 1893, it had fallen below $100 million; in November, it was at $59 million. The Treasury regarded $100 million as the minimum amount required for safety, with the result that Secretary of the Treasury Carlisle, with Cleveland's consent, sought to build up the surplus through the sale of bonds for gold. Four such operations were embarked upon. The first took place in January, 1894, when Carlisle placed a loan of $50 million (at 5 per cent for 10 years) with New York bankers. The second took place in November and was for an additional $50 million. It was also sold to a private syndicate. But relief to the reserve was only temporary, for the wise bankers got their gold largely from the Treasury itself through the presentation of legal tenders or certificates for redemption.

In February, 1895, the gold reserve was again below the safety point, being at $41 million. The third loan which was floated broke another storm about Cleveland's head. Disdaining a recourse to the public, Cleveland again dispatched Carlisle to Wall Street, in February, 1895, to place another issue with a banking syndicate headed by Belmont and Morgan. The bankers were to promise not to get their gold from the Treasury itself; they were, too, to raise half of it abroad. Wall Street was to furnish 3,500,000 ounces of gold for which it was to receive United States bonds at 4 per cent for 30 years. In effect, the bonds were sold to the syndicate for 104½ at a time when existing United States 4's were bringing 111 on the open market. The bankers drove a sharp bargain, for they immediately found quick purchasers for the bonds at prices that averaged around 118. It was calculated by contemporary observers that the Belmont-Morgan group cleared close to $7 million in profits for handling a loan of $60 million. Nothing more clearly proved to western and southern men how closely government and the financial interest were bound together than this episode. Even the habitually courteous Bryan poured out the vials of his wrath on Cleveland's head.

But again failure. In December, 1895, the gold reserve had sunk to $79 million. Cleveland, this time, went to Congress and asked for the retirement of those legal tenders which were causing all the trouble, due to the fact that they were able to drain off the Treasury reserve each time the bond sales had built it up. Congress refused, however, and again Cleveland resorted to a bond issue (January, 1896). This time public subscriptions were called for, the books remaining open for a month. In that time 4600 bids were received, ranging from 110⅝ to 120 for the offered United States 4's—30 years. (The loan in this case was for $100 million.) The offering was oversubscribed by $400 million, and the price obtained averaged 111. It is interesting to record that J. P. Morgan and Company took $62 million of this issue for 110$7/10$. The futility of these operations may be noted from the fact that fully $40 million in the gold the Treasury sought came from the Treasury itself by the presentation of legal tenders for redemption. Gold came out of its hiding the very next year, but not soon enough to end Cleveland's troubles. Whether McKinley's election did it or the increased output of gold the world over (together with improved methods in its refining), it would be exceedingly difficult to say. New gold sources were opened in the Yukon Valley and on the Rand in South Africa, and the world's production of the metal in 1896 doubled that of 1884. But then, McKinley's election, with its promises of new high tariffs and the end of the silver threat to bondholders in the East and England, might have done just as much to free the Treasury from the nightmare of that endless chain made up of legal tenders, gold borrowings, governmental payments in paper, more legal tenders, more gold borrowings.

FOREIGN TRADE

Except for a brief interval in the forties, the United States had an unfavorable trade balance, on commodity account alone, until the decade of the seventies. In 1874, the balance definitely turned and from then on, with but two or three exceptions, every year following showed that the country exported more goods than it imported. But an important distinction must be made: the balance of trade was favorable with respect to visible items only, that is to say, exports and imports of merchandise and specie. If invisible items are taken into consideration, namely, freight payments, interest on foreign capital invested in this country, tourists' expenditures, and immigrants' remittances, then the balance of international payments was in reality unfavorable to the United States for the whole period down to the outbreak of World War I. In other words, these invisible items really absorbed the whole favorable visible trade balance. And the differences that we owed foreigners they continued to reinvest in this country, building our railroads, financing mortgage companies, and buying huge acreage in western and southern lands. The presence of foreign capital in this country, up to the outbreak of the first World War, is really not understandable unless we appreciate that the invisible items in the foreign trade actually kept us debtors and that the adverse balances were retained in this country in the shape of purchases of American securities and land. By 1914, Europeans owned probably $7,000,000,000 in American bonds and stocks, factories and farms, collected as a result of the accumulation of these adverse trade balances.

Beginning with the decade of the seventies, America's foreign trade was in excess of $1,000,000,000 annually; by the time the turn of the century was reached, the value of our foreign trade totaled almost $2,000,000,000. The fact is, the yearly average for the period 1896 to 1900 showed a trade of $1,898,800,000, of which exports represented $1,157,000,000 and imports $741,519,000, or a favorable balance of $415,799,000. If we consider all the visible items together, namely, the exports and imports of merchandise and specie, for the half-century 1851 to 1900, we find this result:

Total exports	$32,740,180,000
Total imports	28,348,837,000
Balance in favor of U. S.	$ 4,391,343,000

However, on the transactions of the fifty years the United States did not actually accumulate a favorable balance of more than $4,000,000,000. Indeed, we might almost say the reverse was the case, because, after the seventies, every year saw American funds moving overseas in such invisible payments as we have noted. In fact, in the two decades from 1874 to 1895, the item of interest payments on foreign capital, alone, amounted to a debit of close to $2,000,000,000.

At the turn of the century, in 1900, there was something like $3,330,000,000 in American securities that foreign investors held. We have seen above to what extent British, Dutch, and German capitalists owned bonds in American rails. Up to the end of the century these foreign rentiers had large holdings in American lands, and the cattle boom of the eighties, too, was stimulated by English and Scottish investments in western ranches.

The tribute to these absentee landlords in the West and the South was a cause of much concern to the Populists and a demand for the termination of foreign land ownership was one of the chief planks of the Populist platform of 1892. Six years before, a House report had presented a tabulation of land holdings by foreigners, in which it was indicated that over 30,000,000 acres in the South and West belonged to English, Scottish, German, Dutch, and Danish capitalists. The alarm that this occasioned may be seen in the following sentence from the House report: "It may happen that the nation which failed to conquer us with its arms may yet prevail with its treasure."

We have noted, in the discussion of agriculture above, how the products of the American farms entered largely into the American export trade in the post-Civil War era and permitted the importation of European capital to build our railroads. However, the exports of manufactured goods and minerals gradually took on significance so that, by 1900, the role of agriculture was becoming less prominent in the balancing of international payments. The following percentages show the growing importance of manufactured goods and minerals in the American foreign trade.

Domestic Exports, by Groups, 1870–1900

(In terms of per cents of total)

Year	Total	Agricultural Products	Manufactured Goods	Minerals	Products of Forests
1870	100.0	79.3	15.0	1.1	3.3
1880	100.0	83.3	12.5	0.7	2.1
1890	100.0	74.5	17.9	2.6	3.5
1900	100.0	60.9	31.6	2.8	3.8

The chief items that entered into the American export trade, to the turn of the century, were grains, cotton, meat and meat products. But iron and steel, refined oil, copper, leather and leather goods, oil-cake, agricultural implements, and chemicals and drugs were slowly forging to the front. In 1880, to take but one example, the value of the country's iron and steel exports (including machinery) was less than $15,000,000; in 1900, the total for iron, steel, and machinery was $121,900,000.

During the period, Europe was our best customer. European peoples took our surplus foodstuffs, cotton, meat products, beef cattle, tobacco, vegetable oils, petroleum, lumber, and copper. The percentages on the next page show that during 1870 to 1900, our markets remained comparatively the same.

What did we buy? Largely foodstuffs and raw materials for use in manufacturing, such as sugar, coffee, chemicals and drugs, crude rubber, wool, hides, raw silk, fibers, tin. In 1850, more than 70 per cent of our imports

Domestic Exports for 1870 and 1900

	1870	1900
Proportion of Exports taken by Europe	79.0%	74.6%
" " " " " North America	13.0	13.5
" " " " " South America	4.0	2.8
" " " " " Asiatic Countries	2.0	4.7

consisted of manufactured goods. In 1870, manufactured goods made up 39.8 per cent of all our imports, and in 1900 but 23.9 per cent of the total. Our protective tariff system was shutting out the finished manufactured goods of the rest of the world.

Because we were not seriously scouring the civilized world for markets for our finished goods until well into the twentieth century, governmental interest in our foreign trade was slight. In 1884, an enactment of Congress provided for the appointment of a Central and South American Commission to visit Latin America in the interests of trade, but nothing came of the venture. That the government made no real efforts to collect information concerning our nearest neighbors, that is to say, with regard to their habits, tastes, and national peculiarities, for the enlightenment of businessmen, was certainly a serious reproach. America was represented abroad by a corps of consular agents of whom the kindest thing that might be said was that the best of them were men of letters (like William Dean Howells) though the generality were obscure political hacks. Up to 1906, the American consular service was operating under a code of laws written in 1856. How insecure tenure of office was may be seen from the fact that President McKinley, when foreign trade in manufactured goods was becoming important, removed 238 members of the consular service out of a total of 272. But businessmen interested in foreign markets made their voices felt at Washington with the result that reform was finally encompassed. The Department of Commerce was established in 1903; the Bureau of Foreign and Domestic Commerce was created in 1912; the consular service code was completely revised in 1906; trade commissioners were appointed beginning with 1905; and commercial attachés, to the diplomatic corps, made their appearance in 1914. Later, we shall have occasion to note how Herbert Hoover transformed the Department of Commerce, and made every American representative abroad an active salesman for American manufactured goods.

THE DECLINE OF THE MERCHANT MARINE

The Civil War broke the planter aristocracy of the South; that, too, it should drive the American flag from the high seas was one of the curious results of that titanic struggle. Up to the sixties, American shipping was second only to Great Britain in tonnage and carrying trade; indeed, before war broke out, there were strong indications pointing to ultimate American supremacy in the role of the world's maritime power. Hugh McCulloch, viewing those earlier times, could say truthfully: "The best ships in the world were then built in the United States, chiefly in New England, and our shipyards not only supplied the home demand but to a considerable extent the foreign demand also."

But the war, the policies that rose out of it, and governmental indifference seriously struck at the prestige of New York, Boston, and Philadelphia as maritime centers and grew grass in the streets of the once glamorous Salem, Marblehead, and Nantucket. The following figures tell the story succinctly enough. In 1860, the tonnage of American vessels engaged in the foreign trade was 2,500,000 gross tons; in 1870, it was 1,500,000 gross tons; in 1900, it was 817,000 gross tons. In 1860, American vessels carried 66.5 per cent of the value of all the goods entering into the American foreign trade; in 1870, the proportion was 35.6 per cent; in 1900, it was 9.3 per cent.

What were the reasons contributing to the decline of the American merchant marine in the years following the Civil War? These may be noted: 1. Congress' refusal, during the Civil War, to permit American shipowners to enroll under a foreign registry. The Confederate commerce destroyers were thus able to take an enormous toll. 2. The shift to iron and steel gave Great Britain the advantage. The American tariff laws put heavy duties on the import of the materials that went into the fabrication of the new ships and in view of the fact that we did not begin to make steel seriously until the eighties, English shipyards could turn out boats at much lower construction costs. 3. An obsolete statute, not repealed until 1914, prevented American shipowners from buying foreign-made ships for American registry. 4. Under the protective tariffs, there were more profitable fields of investment for capital in the country, particularly in manufacturing. 5. Congress' neglect to remove the war-revenue taxes on shipping until 1868, its refusal to grant mail subventions to encourage shipbuilding, and its failure to appreciate that new naval construction would set the pace for private shipbuilding, were other contributory factors. 6. Finally, as opposed to our coolness toward ship subsidies, foreign powers, by liberal money grants, did everything they could to encourage the activities of their native shipbuilders.[4]

Ship subsidies were not unknown to American policy in the period before the Civil War. Between 1845 and 1858, for example, grants to ship-

---

[4] These observations apply, of course, only to the decline of the merchant marine engaged in the foreign trade. It should be noted that America possessed a great fleet of ships in the coastwise trade, made possible by an old statute of 1817, which denied ships of foreign registry the right to enter into our domestic commerce.

owners, through mail contracts, were a common occurrence. A feeble effort at the renewal of the program was made after the war, but in 1875 the last mail contract expired and was not renewed. In 1891, with the passage of the Ocean Mail Act, it appeared that the earlier aggressive program of governmental aid to American shipowners was going to be resumed. The measure provided for the payment of mail subventions to vessels that were built, owned, officered, and at least partly manned by American citizens. But the results of the law were disappointing: proponents of ship subsidies argued that the payment for mail services was not enough. The fact is, the Act did not aid the development of new lines, and such contracts as were awarded were given to ships already in the service. Up to 1898, no American lines had contracted to carry the mails on the Pacific; of the eleven contracts entered into in 1891 only six were still in force in 1913, and on these the lines were receiving $980,000 yearly for the carriage of mail as against $3 million paid out to other lines not under contract.

A few shipping companies did make their appearance, but they were of slight significance in the light of the competition offered by the crack British, German, and Dutch boats engaged in the transatlantic and South American trades. In the early seventies the Pennsylvania Railroad launched its subsidiary, the American Steamship Company, in the transatlantic run and for twenty-five years this company operated four iron ships across the ocean. The Red D line also appeared, to ply three iron steamers between New York and Venezuela; the Ward line, beginning with 1877, began to conduct a regular service to Cuba and Mexico. Encouraged by the act of 1891, the International Navigation Company was chartered and it entered four large steamers in the run between New York and Southampton. But governmental assistance did not amount to much, for the total mail contracts received by the company came to but $647,000 in 1900. It is interesting to note that even the magic hand of Morgan failed when it came to American shipping. In 1902, he used the International Navigation Company as a basis for his reorganized and expanded International Mercantile Marine Company, but the new combine never made money.

Meanwhile, the subject of ship subsidies, in the way of direct grants to American shipbuilders, failed to receive any serious attention from the American Congress. A world war was necessary to revive the early dreams of American sea power.

· 12 ·

The Organized Workers

GENERAL CHARACTERISTICS

THE new American industrialism marched unerringly to its predestined goals: to greatness, concentration, and international power. The lines of its destiny were clearly indicated; and the confidence with which men like Carnegie, Frick, Gates, Armour, and Rockefeller carried themselves proved that they knew what they wanted and how best attainment of their purposes was to be achieved. But if all was sureness in the case of the industrialists, exactly the contrary was true in the case of the workingmen. In fact, it would not be difficult to draw up a table of antitheses to show that organized labor lacked all those qualities for outstanding success which capital and management possessed. From the conclusion of the Civil War until close to the end of the nineteenth century the annals of organized labor formed a record of uncertainty, failing leadership, and confusion of method. There was no plan or steady evolution. Leaders of labor went into politics and then shunned it; championed a form of Christian Socialism and then lost all hope for the creation of a producers' commonwealth; sought to organize all forms of labor into a single confederation and then relinquished their interest in the unskilled, the casuals, the farm laborers, and the Negroes. The American Federation of Labor, which emerged in the early eighties, was based on a knowledge of organized labor's limitations rather than its power. What America, at the dawn of the new century, saw was not an army of workingmen claiming an equal voice in the solution of the new industrial problems, but a small and select group of skilled workers guided entirely by a job philosophy.

TRADE UNIONISM IN THE SIXTIES AND SEVENTIES

Trade unionism, before the Civil War, had largely been of a parochial nature, being subject to the same limitations which restricted the boundaries of industry. But as natural barriers began to give and as machinery began to make inroads into the handicrafts, it became apparent that labor's control of the job was growing less certain. Hence, beginning with the sixties, labor leaders began to preach the unity of labor and the need for a closer supervision over entry into the trades. The Civil War, with its drain upon man power, placed the labor world in a strategic position so that organization grew by leaps and bounds. Too, the lag between wages and the mounting cost of living during the war furnished an economic spur. The result was the appearance, beginning with the sixties, of national unions in increasing numbers. In 1869, the number of trade unionists had grown to 170,000; three years later the total was probably 300,000. In 1872, there were in existence some thirty-two national unions, of which the most powerful were those of the bricklayers, the typesetters, the shoemakers (Knights of St. Crispin), the iron molders, the miners, and the locomotive engineers.

From national unionism to confederation was a natural step. In 1866, therefore, there appeared the National Labor Union, to which rallied the trade unionists and a miscellaneous collection of reformers. At the first meeting, resolutions were passed in favor of trade unionism, the 8-hour day, and independent political action. In the beginning, the National Labor Union, led in its earlier years by W. H. Sylvis, who tried to find the key to the new problems of industrialization in a commonwealth based on producers' co-operatives, attracted a large number of trade unionists. At the 1868 convention, for example, the delegates represented some 600,000 organized workingmen. But while the nucleus of the confederation consisted of workers' organizations and most of the leadership was drawn from the ranks of labor, the leading characteristic of this first national labor body was not industrial solidarity but social reform. The strike, as a weapon, was minimized and much greater importance was attached to the passage of currency legislation, the stimulation of co-operative societies, and the formation of a third party which could seek support from workingmen as well as farmers and monetary reformers.

It was but a matter of time, therefore, when the role of the labor groups was to dwindle and disappear altogether. To the gathering of 1871, for example, not a single national trade union sent delegates. In the next year, when the National Labor Union went into politics to form the National Labor Reform party, labor was entirely unrepresented and the decision was taken by a body of social reformers and delegates from local political clubs. The poor showing made by this group in the Presidential election of 1872 and the greater successes that labor met with in local strikes in the same year, presaged the doom of the organization. Its congresses met no more after 1872. The National Labor Union, nevertheless, had a certain significance in the history of American labor. It was a direct forerunner of the Knights of Labor and the American Federation of Labor and proved that a national confederation of workingmen was not impossible. Its short life indicated that spokesmen for labor had not yet cleared up in their own minds what was to be the proper place of the worker in the new industrial world. They looked to legislation, currency and land reform, and self-help through producers' co-operatives to redress the unequal balance between the workers and the employers. The Union made no efforts to perfect a lasting organization, through the maintenance of general offices and the assessment of individual members. It was in reality only a loose federation of autonomous groups, and when these withdrew their support collapse was inevitable. The successors of the National Labor Union were to profit by these errors.

THE KNIGHTS OF LABOR

For the next fifteen years the Noble Order of the Knights of Labor dominated the labor world. Beginning in 1869, at Philadelphia, as a secret society made up of a handful of garment cutters of whom the leader was Uriah S. Stephens, the Order grew by leaps and bounds until by the end of 1873 it could boast of eighty local assemblies. In that year the Order moved toward centralization with the formation of a central body to which was given the name of Assembly Number One. Finally, in 1878, the General Assembly made its appearance. Several influences lay back of the growth of the organization. With its ritual and its secrecy, it was part of that larger movement of American fraternalism which has always played such a significant part in the American social life. It was not unfamiliar with the activities of Marx's First International, and from this body it borrowed the technique of centralized control and common action. Its presence attracted the trade unionists of the seventies whose unions were being disbanded as a result of the warfare waged upon them by the employers. The decade of the seventies marked the low-water mark in trade-union history. The number of national unions declined from thirty at the beginning of the decade to a bare half-dozen at its end, and from a membership of half a million to less than fifty thousand by 1878. Nothing indicated more clearly the weakened condition of labor in the seventies than the unsuccessful termination of the railroad strikes of 1877. These had broken out as a result of a series of wage reductions and the use of the blacklist against trade unionists. Baltimore, Pittsburgh, Toledo, Chicago, St. Louis, and San Francisco were the scenes of wild disorders as what took on the characteristics of a general strike swept the country. Federal troops appeared in Baltimore; Pennsylvania militia fired on mobs in Pittsburgh as strikers destroyed railroad property to the value of $5 million; other cities reported similar occurrences. The strikes failed in every case and employers took heavy reprisals, not only blacklisting strikers but using the courts to evoke the conspiracy laws against the unions. The secrecy of the Knights looked like a well-sheltered haven for those trade unionists who had suffered in the industrial conflicts.

What were the chief characteristics of the Knights of Labor? The following may be cited: In the first place it stood for one big unionism as opposed to the craft distinctions of the older trade unions. All members of the working-class were invited to join—women with men, Negroes with whites, the unskilled with the skilled. Workers were grouped together in local assemblies, on the basis of residence usually, and not occupation or craft. These local assemblies sent delegates to their district assemblies which in turn were represented in the General Assembly, the governing body of the organization. In the second place, the Knights refused to enter the political arena as an acknowledged labor party. Furthermore, their program contained many of the social and humanitarian reforms advocated by the earlier National Labor Union. Finally, its leadership frowned on industrial warfare and believed that the solution to industrial misunderstanding lay not in strikes but in arbitration and the establishment of producers' co-operatives.

The preamble of the Order's constitution and its declaration of principles indicate how sentiment and sense were inextricably intertwined in the purposes of the group. Thus, the preamble read:

The alarming development and aggressiveness of great capitalists and corporations, unless checked, will inevitably lead to the pauperization and hopeless degradation of the toiling masses. It is imperative, if we desire to enjoy the full blessings of life, that a check be placed upon unjust accumulation and the power for evil of aggregated wealth. This much-desired object can be accomplished only by the united efforts of those who obey the divine injunction: "In the sweat of thy face thou shalt eat bread."

The following were to be its aims:

To make industrial worth, not wealth, the true standard of individual and national greatness.
To secure for the workers the full enjoyment of the wealth they create; sufficient leisure in which to develop their intellectual, moral, and social faculties. . . .

The Order dedicated itself to a political program of which the following were the outstanding demands: the establishment of bureaus of labor statistics; the reservation of public lands for settlers only; the abrogation of all laws that did not bear equally on capital and labor; the passage of safety and public health codes; the recognition of trade unions by law by allowing them the privileges of incorporation; weekly-pay laws and mechanic's-lien laws; the abolition of the contract system on public works; the passage of laws requiring arbitration in industrial disputes; the abolition of child labor; the prohibition of convict labor; income taxes; abolition of national banks; issuance of legal tenders by the federal government; prohibition of contract foreign labor; establishment of postal savings banks; government ownership of railroads and telegraphs. And these were the chief tenets in the industrial program of the Knights: the creation of producers' and consumers' co-operatives; equal pay for equal work for both sexes; the 8-hour day; arbitration in industrial disputes.

The great expansion of the Knights of Labor followed the establishment of the General Assembly (1878), the dropping of secrecy (1879) and the election of Terence V. Powderly as the Grand Master Workman (1879). As a result, the membership increased from 9287 at the end of 1878 to 51,914 at the end of 1883. Interestingly enough, however, the Order's idealism, that is to say, its devotion to industrial brotherhood, education, and the co-operative principle, while attractive to the reformers, was not such a source of strength as its proved ability to win strikes. The early eighties began to witness a series of triumphs that resulted in making the Knights one of the most powerful groups in the land and its spokesman, Powderly, a molder of opinion whose utterances were as eagerly followed as were those of a Blaine or a Cleveland.

Hard times, appearing in 1884, were inevitably productive of labor unrest. Fresh recruits swelled the ranks of the Knights and their demands for immediate action forced the leadership to countenance the use of the weapons of industrial warfare, that is to say, the strike and the boycott. In 1885, a strike on the Gould-owned Wabash railway system was successfully handled by the Knights and resulted in a stay of wage reductions. A second strike on the same system was quickly ended when Jay Gould treated with the leadership directly and gave his personal word that labor activities would not be employed as an excuse for the discharging of employees. This open recognition of the Knights of Labor by one of the largest employers of labor in the country had sensational results. The membership swelled until it reached 700,000 in 1886, Powderly's advice was eagerly sought after by politicians, and the Knights met with a great success when their insistence forced Congress to pass a law raising bars against the admission of contract-labor immigrants.

The year 1886, to alarmed industrialists and politicians, showed all the signs of a general labor uprising. The nation was swept by sympathetic strikes; employers were not slow to retaliate with the lockout and the blacklist; there were widespread disorders followed by the destruction of property. Particularly ominous was the growing participation of the unskilled workers in these manifestations, not the least important being the Negroes. From 989 local assemblies with a membership of 104,066 persons in July, 1885, the Knights could boast of 5892 local assemblies with a membership of 702,924 persons in July, 1886. Of these no less than 60,000 were Negroes. In New York City there were 60,809 Knights, in Philadelphia 51,557 and in Boston 81,191.

The May Day strikes of 1886, called by the Federation of Organized Trades and Labor Unions (discussed below) to force the general adoption of the 8-hour day, were supported by the rank and file of the Knights. It was generally estimated that some 340,000 workers took part in these demonstrations, of whom fully one-half were able to report victories. And then there took place one of those unhappy events, so horrifying in its results that the revulsion of feeling which followed checked abruptly labor's onward march and turned victory into a rout. The unforeseen incident was the explosion of a bomb in Haymarket Square, Chicago, on May 3, which resulted in the killing of a policeman, the fatal wounding of seven others and the injury of at least fifty more.

While earlier industrial disputes and the May Day strikes of Chicago had been called by the regular labor organizations, the participation in them of the Chicago section of the Black (or Anarchists') International had made the Windy City the scene of particularly violent outbreaks. There were not more than 2000 organized anarchists in Chicago at the time; while at least 80,000 workers were participating in the strikes centering around the city's reaper works, stockyards, steel plants, and railroad shops. A row between strikers and strikebreakers on May 3 had resulted in police interference and the firing on rioters in which four persons were killed. The next day a protest meeting assembled in Haymarket Square; the program of speeches had almost come to a successful termination and the gathering was in process of dispersing when, for some unknown reason, a cordon of police descended on the few remaining participants. A bomb was thrown into the ranks of the policemen; the police retaliated by firing into the crowd. Supported by an aroused public opinion the Chicago law officers rounded up eight of the leaders of the Black International (all but one of whom were foreign-born) and brought them to trial for the murder of the police officers. The presiding judge ruled that it was not necessary to prove the presence on the spot of the accused or their direct participation in the outrage; it was enough that their counsels had fomented disorders and had encouraged the use of violence. On the strength of such a charge the jury found all eight anarchists guilty, ordering the death sentence for seven and imprisonment for the eighth. With the Illinois Supreme Court affirming the verdict, the State of Illinois took its toll on November 11, 1887, when it hanged four of the convicted men. One had escaped the extreme penalty by committing suicide while the sentences of two others had been commuted to life imprisonment. In 1893 the Democratic governor of Illinois, J. P. Altgeld, braved the fury of mob hysteria, when he issued an order pardoning the three remaining anarchists.

The unsuccessful termination of many of the May Day strikes, and particularly the unfortunate Haymarket Square affair, led to the crumbling of the power of the Knights of Labor. More fundamental causes for the collapse of the Order were the following: 1. The failure of most of the producers' co-operatives in which the Knights had engaged. At the height of their activities, they were running, through local assemblies, some two hundred enterprises, largely made up of mines, cooperage works, and shoe factories. The General Assembly tried to guide the movement through propaganda and preaching the use of the Order's label. But mismanagement and unfair competition were too difficult to cope with and by 1888 the co-operative movement was finished. 2. The leadership devoted too much of its attention to the perfection of its social reform program and not enough to the realities of trade-union organization. Strikes were called, for example, without adequate preparation or the building up of financial reserves. Too much reliance was placed on the sentiment of industrial brotherhood and the hope that sympathetic strikes would force employers' concessions in all disputes, no matter how local or trivial. 3. There was too much preoccupation with the furtherance of the Order's political program. 4. Overcentralization of power led to jealousies and internal dissensions. 5. The desire to organize the unskilled, benevolent as was its intention, had in it elements of great weakness: the unskilled were easily replaceable in times of strike, while their great mobility made the possibility of building up a permanent labor organization with them as a base a difficult achievement. 6. The skilled crafts quickly tired of pulling the chestnuts out of the fire for the unskilled. This, perhaps, was the most significant cause for the disintegration of the Knights of Labor and its replacement by the American Federation of Labor. The crafts bore the brunt of retaliatory measures when labor disputes ended in disaster. An unskilled worker could move on to another lumber camp or steel mill. The skilled worker ran the risk of finding his name on a blacklist and all doors shut in his face when he went to look for other employment. The crafts that refused to affiliate with the Knights kept up an unending warfare during the eighties against one big unionism, and in this they came to be joined by the crafts in the Order itself, which insisted upon the right to form national trade assemblies (on craft lines). When the great organization began to slip, the crafts quickly got together, being perfectly willing to forget industrial brotherhood, equalitarianism, and the raising of the status of the unskilled, and effected a union for their own advantage. 7. Finally, industry perfected a series of weapons that made it invincible. By the use of the lockout, the blacklist, the refusal to arbitrate, and the employ of the "ironclad oath" (comparable to the later "yellow-dog contract"), employers were able to fight back successfully.

The result of all this was that from a membership of 700,000 in 1886 the Knights' strength dwindled to 100,000 in 1890. Its power in the big cities vanished as the skilled workers turned again to the more cautious but more successful trade unions. In the nineties the Knights' membership was to be found for the most part in small American communities where its activities partook of the characteristics of a friendly society. It joined with the Farmers' Alliances in forming the People's party in 1892 and in 1893 it definitely lost its labor stamp when a farmer-editor of Iowa replaced Powderly in the office of Grand Master Workman.

CRAFT UNIONISM

It is not to be understood that the Knights of Labor, even at the height of its power, attracted the support of all bodies of workers. Craft unionism was still alive and it slowly grew, under the careful tending of a small group of leaders who had been brought up on the European doctrine of the class struggle and who were watching the slow but sure successes of the English trade-union movement. That is to say, the new spokesmen for labor—Adolph Strasser, P. J. McGuire, and Samuel Gompers—had none of the illusions of the leaders of the National Labor Union and the Knights concerning the effectiveness of political programs and currency reform; nor did they place very much faith in the rosy dream of a producers' commonwealth. Theirs was the hard-bitten, realistic philosophy of job consciousness. What they sought, in effect, was the recognition of labor's monopoly of the job just as capital possessed a monopoly of business enterprise. Labor was to strive for the right to decent pay and a shorter working day; its medium of expression was to be the closely knit craft union; its weapons were to be collective bargaining and the strike. While in a sense, therefore, the new unionism stemmed from the Marxian philosophy of the class struggle in that it accepted the doctrine of a deep gulf between capital and labor, it stopped short of the socialist program of political action and government ownership of the means of production and distribution.

The realism of these new leaders was displayed in the rebuilding of the International Cigar Makers Union, which had been crushed in the strikes of 1877. Strasser and Gompers set for themselves these objectives: to establish a national union [1] with full authority over the locals; to create a union fund, on the basis of regular membership dues; and to devise a benefit-system that could take care of cases of illness, superannuation, and death (this last, in particular, was borrowed from the English trade-union movement). By 1879, the new union had risen out of the ashes of the old and was meeting with such success that other craft groups made haste to follow its example.

In 1881, representatives from a number of the crafts met at Pittsburgh and formed the Federation of Organized Trades and Labor Unions of the United States and Canada. This body marks the first appearance of the American Federation of Labor (the name was changed in 1886) on the American scene. The constitution provided for restriction of membership to "trades and labor unions," fixed representation in the federation on the

[1] These national unions called themselves "internationals" in view of the fact that almost all of them had locals in the Canadian cities.

basis of membership, and provided for a permanent revenue through the imposition of a per capita tax of three cents. The program of demands included: legal incorporation of trade unions (to free them from attacks under the state conspiracy laws); compulsory education for children; prohibition of the labor of children under fourteen years of age; uniform apprenticeship laws; the enactment of a national 8-hour-day law; a protective tariff; an anticontract immigration law; and the establishment of a national bureau of labor statistics. Membership of affiliated national unions, city councils, and local trade unions totaled not more than 50,000 in 1884. By 1886, however, the number of trade unionists under the aegis of the Federation numbered 140,000.

In the beginning, the new Federation worked in harmony with the Knights of Labor, but the truce, for such it was, was only of short duration. By 1883, the hostility between the two groups had come to the surface and by 1886 it had turned into a struggle for supremacy. When, in 1886, a group of national trade unions refused to join the Knights but went over to the Federation, the success of the new grouping became definitely assured. At the 1886 convention, at which there were in attendance representatives from twelve national trade unions, the new name of American Federation of Labor was adopted and Samuel Gompers was elected president. The little New York cigar maker, born in England and of Jewish parentage, was to guide the destinies of the Federation from that year until he died in 1924.[2]

Between the middle eighties and the end of the century, the American Federation of Labor moved definitely ahead to a greater position of security and power. The elimination of the Knights of Labor from the national sphere left it in undisputed possession of the field as the only confederation of national and international trade unions. The depression of 1893, instead of ending in the usual debacle of trade unionism, found the national bodies for the most part unimpaired in strength. And in 1894 the American Federation of Labor definitely parted with socialist doctrine and the agitation of political reform, when its convention repudiated a program of political demands which the previous convention had endorsed.[3] A socialist minority continued to exist in the American Federation of Labor; but during his life, Samuel Gompers succeeded in thwarting every effort that this group made to force the Federation into becoming a political party. The Federation proved its strength in the following four ways: 1. It success-

[2] Gompers failed of re-election but once, in the year 1895.
[3] This platform is of value as showing the political interests of the labor world of the nineties. The planks included: compulsory education; the adoption of the initiative and referendum; an 8-hour day established by law; government inspection of mines and factories; the abolition of sweating; employers'-liability laws; abolition of the contract system on public works; municipal ownership of public utilities; nationalization of telegraphs, telephones, railroads, and mines; and "the collective ownership by the people of all the means of production and distribution."

fully led a number of crafts in the gaining of the 8-hour day. 2. One of its affiliated national unions, the stove molders, in 1891 succeeded in writing a trade agreement with the manufacturers by which the union was recognized as the representative of the workers, and machinery was set up in the industry for the settlement of disputes. 3. National unions began to occupy themselves with benefit schemes and created funds to cope with the problems of sickness, unemployment, and death. 4. Recognition was obtained from the world of capital with the creation of the National Civic Federation (in 1901), in which representatives from both capital and labor sat for the purpose of discussing problems common to both. The National Civic Federation accepted collective bargaining and trade agreements as being essential to industrial peace.

In 1890, unions affiliated with the American Federation of Labor, and paying the per capita tax for the support of the central organization, had a membership of 190,000; in 1900, the membership was 550,000; in 1905, it was 1,570,500; by 1914, membership had reached 2,000,000. By the turn of the century, practically every important labor organization in the country, with the exception of the four railroad brotherhoods, was affiliated.

We may, at this point, sum up the salient characteristics of the American Federation of Labor, as they appeared to Americans in the early nineteen hundreds. The Federation was a union of great national bodies. The membership had no direct contact with the Federation but worked in its own locals, city centrals, and state federations. It was a decentralized organization, for the individual crafts reserved to themselves the complete rights of autonomy. It was founded on the principle of craft unionism and evinced no interest in the unskilled or the more humble members of the laboring population. It did not try to organize the Negro. As contrasted with the idealism of the Knights of Labor, the Federation was made up of opportunistic, job-conscious workers, who fought stubbornly to have recognized their monopoly in their jobs and whose primary concerns were better pay and a shorter working day. The Federation regarded the strike as the worker's chief weapon and the trade agreement, by which collective bargaining was to be accepted, as the goal of unionism. The Federation was nonsocialistic and took part in political campaigns only to reward its friends and punish its enemies. Resolutely, the Federation leaders stood against the creation of an independent labor party.

VIOLENCE

While, by 1900, a small group of enlightened employers was willing to recognize trade agreements and labor's monopoly of the job, it must be understood that this was not the sentiment of industry, by and large, and that what small gains the workers made were won with much travail. The two decades preceding the end of the century, particularly, were marked by a vicious industrial warfare. Industry fought the workers with an armory of weapons that ranged from the blacklist, the ironclad oath, and armed thugs to slow starvation and ingeniously contrived legal obstructions.[4] In most cases, industry was victorious. Due to a dearth of labor, the *real* wages of American workers had steadily increased in the decades following the Civil War so that by 1900 real wages were 100 per cent higher than they had been in 1850. But there was a slowing down of the rate of growth after 1896 and *real* wages stopped advancing altogether from 1900 to 1914. This fact helps to account for some of the turbulence in the American industrial scene.

From 1881 to 1900, according to figures collected by the federal Bureau of Labor, a total of 23,798 strikes occurred in which were involved 127,442 establishments and 6,610,000 workers. The total direct loss suffered by employers and workers was $450,000,000 and the number of days lost was 149,000,000. In terms of annual averages the figures were: 1190 strikes a year in 6372 establishments, involving 330,500 workers with an accompanying loss of 7,450,000 days and $22,500,000 in wages and property damage. In 1886, when strikes were particularly numerous, the total number of workers out was 610,024 and the monetary losses suffered reached the great total of $33,580,000. In the twenty years, only 35 per cent of the strikers were completely successful, while 17 per cent had to accept compromises and 48 per cent acknowledged defeat and either went back to work on the old conditions or stoically set out to hunt for new jobs. The larger part of the strikes were fought over wages and hours of work. The percentage of strikes involving one or both of these causes was 58.

The Homestead strike of 1892 and the Pullman strike of 1894 may be cited as examples of how bitterly the employers fought back when labor resorted to strikes to accomplish its ends. On June 30, 1892, at the Homestead (Pa.) plant, one of the units of the Carnegie Steel Company, a strike was called by the Amalgamated Association of Iron and Steel Workers. This national union was perhaps the most powerful one of its day: it could boast of 24,000 members, a satisfactory money reserve, a well-disciplined membership, and a history of earlier successful contests with employers. In 1889, it had written a 3-year wage scale with the Carnegie Company officials and it was over the failure to agree on a new wage scale that the two sides, presumably, came to blows. Carnegie and Frick insisted that the introduction of labor-saving machinery warranted a re-examination of wage rates for many processes. There are evidences

---

[4] As has been said, the "ironclad oath" was the counterpart of the modern "yellow-dog" contract. Ely defined the ironclad oath, in 1886, as follows: "The ironclad oath is an agreement to do or not to do certain things as a condition of employment; generally not to join a labor organization."

to indicate, however, that Frick, at any rate, had decided not to submit any longer to the dictation of the union and was willing to see a contest take place as a test of strength between the two.[5] Meanwhile Carnegie went to his estate in Scotland and left Frick in charge of the negotiations.

Frick hired three hundred Pinkerton detectives to guard the Homestead mills and these men were pulled up the river in two barges. The strikers, incensed at the interjection of an outside armed force into an industrial dispute, opened fire on the boats and in the battle that followed ten persons were killed. The Pinkertons surrendered and were permitted to entrain for Pittsburgh. But this first reversal merely intensified the determination of the management. The state was called upon to protect the Carnegie Company properties and responded with the dispatching of the entire state National Guard, 8000 strong, to Homestead. At first general sympathy was with the strikers, but when Alexander Berkman, the anarchist, made an attempt on Frick's life in July, the public was alienated. The strike resolved itself, then, into a war of attrition and the men's resources failed first. On November 20, the strike was called off. Fewer than 1000 of the old 5000 Carnegie Company employees were taken back and then only on condition that they surrender their trade-union membership. Other steel companies, in the Pittsburgh area, refused to deal with the union with the result that the Amalgamated was smashed.

The Pullman strike broke out in the Chicago area on May 11, 1894, over an attempt on the part of the management of the Pullman Parlor Car Company to reduce wages (without, however, lowering the rents on the homes in the company's model town in which the men lived). In March of the same year some 2500 men had joined the American Railway Union, an industrial union which had been created in 1893 by Eugene V. Debs, a former railway fireman. The Pullman Company shut down its plant and did not open it for three months. The American Railway Union offered its offices as mediator, but these the company rejected. On June 21, therefore, the union voted not to handle Pullman cars attached to the trains on which its members worked and in a few days this boycott had spread over the middle western and far western states. Five days later, when the railroad managers indicated their intention not to detach Pullman cars, a sympathetic railroad strike was declared. Pitted against the American Railway Union was now the General Managers' Association, made up of representatives from twenty-four roads centering in Chicago.

Lawlessness took a heavy toll in Chicago. Railroad property was destroyed and fired and business, generally, was impeded. Suddenly federal authority descended on the scene. On the score that the carriage of the mails was being obstructed, Olney, Cleveland's Attorney-General,

---

[5] See, for example, Carroll D. Wright, United States Commissioner of Labor, in *The Quarterly Journal of Economics*, Vol. VII (July, 1893).

directed the federal law officers of Chicago to obtain an injunction against the American Railway Union. As a result of Olney's opinion that the union could be proceeded against under the Sherman Antitrust Law, a court decree was issued ordering the officials of the union to desist from obstructing the carriage of the mails or from injuring the property of the railroads or from "compelling by threats, intimidation or persuasion, force or violence, any of the employees of any of the said railways to refuse to perform any of their duties as employees." Similar injunctions were asked for and obtained in many other centers of the Middle West where the strike was raging. To enforce the terms of the injunction, the federal law officers at Chicago requested Cleveland to send federal troops, although the United States marshal had been permitted to enroll 5000 deputies. Without consulting Governor Altgeld, Cleveland at once complied and on July 4, 1894, 2000 United States soldiers were pitching their tents in Chicago. They were not withdrawn until July 20, but by that time the strike had been broken, and the men compelled to return to work on the terms of the railway companies.

Meanwhile, on July 17, Debs and the other strike leaders had been cited for contempt for their persistence in carrying on the strike, and on their refusal to give bail were sent to jail. On December 14, the federal circuit court found the prisoners guilty of the contempt charge and Debs was sentenced to prison for six months. The presiding judge, in his decision, indicated that capital had now at hand a powerful weapon against labor, for the opinion cited the Sherman Law and approved its use against trade unions where it could be shown that they were engaged in "a conspiracy to hinder and obstruct interstate commerce." On May 27, 1895, the United States Supreme Court sustained the Debs sentence.[6]

Of course employers had learned long before the nineties that the workers could be fought in the courts. In the sixties, for example, trade unions had been successfully prosecuted under the conspiracy laws, and many union officials had gone to jail because of their issuance of calls to strike. This had led to a counter agitation for the enactment of legislation to legalize trade unions as corporations and a demand for such laws is to be found in the platform of the Knights of Labor. In the seventies a number of industrial states passed acts permitting labor unions to incorporate. Nevertheless, prosecutions on the basis of conspiracy continued into the nineties, when lawyers dropped the method for the more expeditious one of injunction suits. Injunctions could be obtained under both the federal and the state laws, and inasmuch as they involved equity proceedings jury trials were not necessary. The trade unions were further hampered in their fields of action when, in the nineties, the labor boycott also fell under court ban. On the other hand, the courts raised no

[6] See above, page 170.

objections to the use, by employers, of both the blacklist and the ironclad oath. Legal obstacles such as these were formidable, and for the next thirty years the American Federation of Labor applied itself seriously to the problem of protecting labor's right to strike. We shall have occasion to see that labor's requests for relief were without success until the nineteen thirties.

· 13 ·

American Life, Letters, and Art 1865–1900

CHARACTERISTICS OF THE SOCIAL SCENE

It was a new America that the close of the Civil War ushered in. The conflict between the sections not only had destroyed the political power of the planter aristocracy but had leveled, as well, a series of other institutions: the true balance the generation of the forties and fifties had created between the industrial and agricultural economies; the flourishing regionalism of the South and New England; the universal acceptance of a set of cultural standards—of moderation, the golden mean, individual independence—so finely wrought by the Concord of Emerson and Thoreau. Across the broken dikes now rushed all those forces unleashed by the termination of a successful war. The Civil War Congresses, as we have seen, had worked successfully to make sure of the final results of victory: they had passed, while the two armies were locked in a death struggle, protective tariff measures, a homestead law, a national banking law, a law providing for the construction, with governmental aid, of the first transcontinental railroad. Thus had been cleared the way for the exploiter of natural resources, the financial promoter, the cattle baron, and the manufacturers of iron, steel, and textiles. The upper middle class—of the market place, the countinghouse, and the mill and factory—was now in the ascendant, and its Gargantuan appetites, its will-to-power, its ever-unappeased hunt for profits set the tone for the American civilization for fully half a century.

Nothing revealed more completely the heedless, rushing anarchy of this Gilded Age of the seventies, eighties, and early nineties than its architecture and its interior decoration. The nation's industrial development had made everything cheaper; power to buy far outran the development of an ability to choose. Here was a bad taste, boldly displayed for the outside world to see and for one's friends and sycophants to admire, truly regnant. Houses were copied from the Italian, the English, the Swiss, the Persian, the French. It was the age of the jig-saw, the cupola, the mansard roof with its dormer windows, an orgy of decoration in which every architectural element was made to look like something else. As Parrington says of it:

> Flamboyant lines and meaningless detail destroyed the structural unity of the whole; tawdry decoration supplanted beauty of materials and a fine balance of masses. A stuffy and fussy riot of fancy, restrained by no feeling for structural lines, supplied the lack of creative imagination, and architecture sank to the level of the jerry-builder.

The interiors were pitched in the same noisy key: rooms were loaded down with massive furniture of black walnut or golden oak, the tables had jig-sawed skirts, the sideboards were rarely complete without their complements of irregularly ordered shelves topped by pointed arches. On open shelves—on the walls, in whatnots, surmounting moldings—were statuettes, bronzes, shells and vases, and china and porcelain from every corner of the earth. Even the human figure seemed to take on the prevailing grossness. People overate and overdressed. Men affected long-skirted coats of black broadcloth, wore polished, heavy top boots, permitted their faces to become covered with hair. The women were encased in series of enfolding garments that concealed the natural contours of their bodies and left no parts revealed but face and hands.

The wealth of the new urban bourgeoisie was everywhere visible—so was the wretched poverty of the new urban masses. The industrial processes filled the great cities of the country with a slum-dwelling population, the meanness of whose lives one has difficulty in recording dispassionately. Huddled in foul rookeries, exploited by sweatshop proprietors, denied the simplest protections by government against cheating enterprisers and indifferent public service corporations, America's workingmen, made up of European peasants and sons and daughters from its own countryside, went through a cycle whose days were a drab record of squalor and poverty. The city's poor lived in tenements that were cheerless, cold, closed to the sun and air, often without running water, and that could not offer the bare elements of a decent private life. For blocks and blocks in the slum areas, covering every inch of building lot, without breathing space or open area to afford some relief against the close confinement of the interiors, towered those ugly structures—monuments to the rapacity of the ground landlords of America's cities. In the nineties, according to an estimate made by the federal Commissioner of Labor, fully one-tenth of the population of the sixteen largest cities in the country lived in these slums. How often death stalked in those teeming streets may be seen from the fact that as late as 1888, in a group of blocks on New York City's East Side, the death rate for children under five years was 139.83 [1] per 1000. Contagious diseases—typhoid fever, scarlet fever, smallpox, diphtheria—

---

[1] The death rate for the same age group in the whole city was around 85 per 1000; today, it is 7.6.

took a terrible toll. The dread white plague, tuberculosis, scarcely left a slum home untouched. It was not until the development of rapid-transit facilities—in the next century—that the meaner congested areas slowly began to melt away, as workers found it possible to travel quickly to the peripheries of the cities to make their homes.

Reviewing this scene, one is tantalized by the question: How could it endure so long? Charles and Mary Beard have hazarded the conjecture that the urban masses found their lot supportable only because of the ministrations of certain agencies, notably, the municipal party machines, the Catholic Church, the corner saloon, and cheap commercial amusements. Yet one must not lose sight of the fact that the workers were not constantly complacent under its privations. The history of the seventies, eighties, and nineties is filled with a record of industrial conflict whose violence sprang only too often from a frenzy born of despair. Nevertheless, the tale is one of acceptance of the prevailing order of things: this was not, however, a compliance lulled by soporifics but rather one fed by hope. In free, democratic America where there existed no system of social castes and no government to frown on exploitation, where (as the school texts taught) every native-born lad, however humble his birth, could aspire to the Presidency, where Cornelius Vanderbilt had been a ferryman, Daniel Drew a drover, and James J. Hill a bankrupt dreamer well into middle life—in such a land, every worker could aspire to the middle class and to comfort, security, and perhaps power. If not for himself, certainly for his children.

For America in this period, despite the great extremes of wealth and poverty as expressed by the lives of the new industrial masters and the slum-dwellers, was still the land of the *petite bourgeoisie*. Millions of American families lived in thousands of towns and small cities up and down the land, where they spent their days in a quiet round of pleasant activities. The heads of families were the small merchants, physicians, and lawyers, plant superintendents and skilled factory craftsmen for whom Bryan pleaded so eloquently in 1896. Their houses were ample and comfortable and were more often than not set in large front yards; by the seventies, they were already enjoying the conveniences of bathrooms, central heating, and plumbing; pianos, pictures, and books everywhere spoke of cultural yearnings. The community life of America's villages still had about it much of the neighborliness of the Middle Period. These were the people who supported America's great evangelical churches and small denominational colleges, who regularly went to the polls to express their abiding faith in American democracy, who joined the Women's Christian Temperance Union and the Anti-Saloon League. Nor did this American *petite bourgeoisie* want for its diversions: it was learning to play lawn tennis and to ride bicycles; it went on frequent picnics and on railroad and trolley excursions; it had its local opera houses, which were frequently visited by touring theatrical companies; it thronged the lyceums of the seventies and the Chautauqua assemblies of the eighties and nineties. Its men had their fraternal lodges and mechanics' halls, its women their clubs where they studied Shakespeare, Browning, and the civilizations of Greece and Rome, its young people their singing societies. The great world of Europe and the Far East (save through the agency of the foreign missions) rarely knocked on the doors of this America of the Valley of Democracy, and in it reigned peace and contentment.

There is one characteristic of the age one meets with everywhere: this was the growing stature of its womenfolk. The women of America were becoming released from the drudgery of the kitchen, leisure time afforded them an opportunity to cultivate polite letters and the arts, the bolder among them were beginning to seek out educational opportunities and even to demand political equality. As we shall see, women's colleges and coeducational institutions appeared in increasing numbers in the three decades following the Civil War. The movement for woman suffrage was ably led by Mrs. Elizabeth Cady Stanton and Miss Susan B. Anthony; it began to meet with successes in the states and it was apparent, by the time the nineteenth century closed, that the universal recognition of the sex in the political sphere could not be denied for long.

SOME ASPECTS OF AMERICAN SOCIETY

Public education advanced mightily in the period we are examining. Spurred on by the demands of workingmen's organizations and unable to shut their eyes to the great progress being made in elementary education abroad, America's state and municipal authorities passed compulsory school attendance laws, built new schoolhouses, and radically revised curriculums. The first compulsory attendance law had not been passed until 1854, by Massachusetts; but by 1900 nearly all of the states and territories in the North and West had such legislation on their statute books. The results were that the number of pupils receiving instruction in public schools increased from 6,900,000 in 1870 to 15,500,000 in 1900 and that the proportion of children of school age enrolled grew from 57 per cent in the earlier year to 72 per cent in the later year.

Courses of study, too, were undergoing radical adjustments in the light of the lessons of the new child psychology, American educators were learning from Europe and their growing awareness of the changed social and industrial America in which they were moving. As early as 1895 John Dewey's insistence that the school was "life, not a preparation for life" was already receiving wide attention. What was even more amazing was the development of the public high school and the recognition by the state of its responsibilities for vocational education. In 1865, there had been not more than 200 such institutions in the country; by 1900, their numbers had increased to 6000 and their student body was more than 500,000. A large number of these higher schools, too, were not regarding themselves as merely preparatory institutions for the colleges but were teaching their adolescent pupils manual crafts, domestic arts, and commercial subjects.

Popular education for adults became effectively organized. In the seventies, there had flourished the lyceums and lecture platforms, managed largely by James Redpath and J. B. Pond, and as a result of the activities of these energetic persons adult America was given the opportunity to hear the didactic discourses of Charles Bradlaugh, Henry Ward Beecher, and Theodore Tilton; the scientific lectures of Louis Agassiz; and the humorous addresses of Mark Twain, Artemus Ward, and Josh Billings. By the eighties, the lecture platform, as a mode of instruction, was supplanted by the formal programs of the Chautauqua. The Chautauqua Literary and Scientific Circle was first organized in 1873 in the little New York town from which it took its name, combining summer recreation and a plan for adult education. Starting out as a summer assembly devoted especially to Sunday-school teaching methods, it quickly developed an elaborate curriculum of home study and reading, and its texts and study courses were soon to be found in a great many of America's middle-class homes. The idea was at once copied and before the end of the first decade of the twentieth century hundreds of small communities saw each summer the familiar pitched tent of their own local, or an itinerant, Chautauqua assembly, where for a week or ten days America gathered to hear concerts, listen to lectures on foreign missions and addresses on political, literary, and scientific subjects by celebrities of the day.[2]

The churches, particularly those of the evangelical sects, played a prominent role in the life of post-Civil War America. By 1870, for example, there were more than 70,000 separate church organizations in the country, with the Methodists and Baptists leading, the Presbyterians third, and the Catholics fourth. Church attendance was a common middle-class practice, and most Americans looked to the clergy for guidance in intellectual, scientific, and social problems. It was not strange, in an age when religious devoutness was the rule rather than the exception, that two clergymen,

[2] The brown-topped tents of the itinerant Chautauquas flourished for some two decades, and then they too disappeared into the past, along with the other evidences of pioneer America. In an age of good roads and the cheap car, small-town America no longer found it necessary to wait for the coming of its amusements; it sought them out for itself. By 1930, there were few traveling Chautauquas left.

Henry Ward Beecher and Phillips Brooks, should be numbered among the country's great national leaders.

The flame of evangelism was kept brightly burning, during those decades, by a number of activities, of which the following more important may be enumerated: 1. The revivalism of Dwight L. Moody and his singing partner, Ira D. Sankey, marched through all the great cities of the land; here was expounded a gospel not far removed from the oldest forms of English dissenting Protestantism. 2. The Young Men's Christian Association movement, modeled after similar organizations existing in England, was brought to America in the fifties, for the chief purpose of serving the young men who were flocking to the cities. While the society's original concern was over the salvation of their souls, it was not unmindful of the fruitful work that could be done in other directions. The Y.M.C.A. branches thus busied themselves with athletic, educational, and social programs, opened employment agencies and sought to serve their members in other ways. By the end of the century there were fully one-fourth of a million young men enrolled as paying members in the various branches throughout the country. The Young Women's Christian Association also made its appearance; but probably because it was less interested in religious problems and more in social and industrial questions of the day, its branches did not multiply so rapidly as did those of the Y.M.C.A. 3. The Salvation Army sought to bring evangelism into the homes of the poor, by maintaining its mission stations in the slum areas of the great cities. By the nineties, it became apparent to the organization's commanders that preaching the gospel was not quite enough; that the crying need among the urban poor was for social services. The result was that the Army's funds were poured increasingly into the maintenance of lodging houses, food depots, rescue homes, and employment agencies.

Two other phases of the country's religious life might well be mentioned, that is to say, the expansion of the Catholic Church and the appearance of Christian Science. The Catholic Church grew from 30,000 communicants in 1789 to 9,000,000 in 1900 (its amazing development being due largely to the accretions first of German and then of Irish and Italian immigrants), and by the end of the century Catholic churches, parochial schools, convents, and orphanages were familiar sights in all of America's large cities. St. Patrick's Cathedral, the first of the Church's great edifices, was begun in New York City in 1858 and finished twenty years later. The Christian Science movement owed its inspiration to the teachings of Mary Baker Eddy, whose *Science and Health* was published in 1875 and who organized the first Christian Science Association, at Lynn, Massachusetts, in 1876. When Mrs. Eddy died in 1910, there were 1000 churches in the country, whose communicants were variously estimated at from 300,000 to 1,000,000. The central teaching of the new creed was healing by faith, not a new religious practice, of course; what was extraordinary about the spread of this cult was that it found its adherents not among the poor but among those middle classes who were becoming increasingly familiar with the advances of science in our modern life.

Whether from a sense of overconfidence in their own strength or timidity it is hard to say, but it is interesting to note that it was not until the nineties that the churches began to pay some attention to the new social and industrial forces that were so strangely shaping America. As the historian Allan Nevins points out, while the cities were beginning to teem with millions of newly arrived Americans and the nation was rapidly becoming industrialized, the country's churches still "clung in the main to the aims of a rural age." When, before the new century opened, the theological seminaries did begin to examine social and industrial problems and preach the need for social services, carried on by churchmen, it was, in fact, too late. The drift away from the churches had already begun; and leadership in philanthropy had been captured by lay groups. The first of these were the social settlements; the second were the organized charity societies.

The social settlements, in America, grew out of university extension experiments that the Christian Socialists had been carrying on in England at Oxford University. Robert A. Woods, freshly returned from a residence in Toynbee Hall, London, had founded Andover House in Boston and had published *English Social Movements.* Woods's accomplishments and preachments had attracted the attention of Jane Addams, whose Hull House, opened in Chicago in 1889, at once embodied all that was finest in the settlement-house idea. The settlement house was defined in the nineties as "a colony of members of the upper classes, formed in a poor neighborhood, with the double purpose of getting to know the local conditions of life from personal observation and of helping where help is needed." If the movement's motto "Elevation by contact" carried a note of condescension and if Miss Addams' hope for it that it would make "the entire social organism democratic" fell far short of realization, there is no denying that the early residents of these houses accomplished much. They organized clubs and classes for the submerged tenth, operated day nurseries and diet kitchens, encouraged talent in the arts in a time when the public schools were concerning themselves only with the great common average, and agitated ceaselessly for new factory and public welfare codes. Some of them kept abreast of the times: Hull House became one of the greatest forums in the land for the free discussion of social, economic, and international questions; Henry Street Settlement (New York) perfected later a visiting nurse service.

Organized philanthropy, by the nineties, was fairly common in the country's larger cities. The first charity organization society, following English example, made its appearance in Buffalo in 1877. By 1893, there were almost one hundred such organizations in America. Heretofore, aid for the needy had come through public relief, the individual benevolences of charitably inclined persons, or the small efforts of ladies' clubs, church groups, and the like. It was the intention of these charity organization societies to institutionalize philanthropy, abolish public outdoor relief, and check mendicancy. Thus, the charity organization societies, with the larger funds at their disposal, were able to maintain elaborate filing systems under which all dependent persons were catalogued; they hired staffs and trained them in the arts of investigation to be able to separate the "worthy and upright poor" from the "willing paupers" and "voluntary dependents;" they co-operated with the police in a war on professional beggars and on unworthy causes.

The growth of the popular newspaper was another sign of the times. All the great leaders of the American press of the Middle Period were to pass from the scene before the seventies were over: Raymond died in 1869, Greeley and Bennett in 1872, Bowles in 1877, and Bryant in 1878. While Godkin of the *Nation* and the *New York Evening Post* and Dana of the *Sun* still were to keep the tradition of an individual, conservative journalism alive until the close of the century, they were to be eclipsed, in the eighties and nineties, by two men who more closely read the minds and hearts of the people of this new industrial America. First Joseph Pulitzer and then William Randolph Hearst appeared on the journalistic scene to amuse, startle, and champion the country's urban masses. Joseph Pulitzer in 1883, when he entered New York by buying the *World* from Jay Gould, had already achieved repute in St. Louis as proprietor of the *Post-Dispatch*. A penniless immigrant lad of Hungarian-Jewish parentage, he had landed in Boston in 1864; nineteen years later at the age of thirty-six he was in possession of the $346,000 Gould had set as the price for the moribund *World*. Within two years, Pulitzer metamorphosed the *World* into an aggressive, flamboyant journal, ran its circulation from 16,000 up to 116,000, brightened its pages with pictures and special features, and set forth before its readers a daily dish made up of local scandals, crimes of passion, pretty romances and the like. The news reporting, however, was of a high standard; the editorial columns were ever ready to take up arms against local corruption and to fight injustices everywhere.

The successes of Pulitzer attracted a formidable rival to the scene. William Randolph Hearst, son of a fabulously wealthy California pioneer, in 1895 came east and acquired the *New York Journal*. By the end of his first year, largely by surpassing Pulitzer at his own game, Hearst ran the circulation of his paper up to 400,000. Hearst, too, assumed the role of tribune of the people; but, more particularly, he filled his pages with

210   PROCESSES OF INDUSTRIALIZATION

feature writers and artists, first introducing to the American public such well-known newspaper figures as Homer Davenport, Frederick Opper, Winifred Black, Bruno Lessing, and Alan Dale. In the campaign of 1896, Hearst was the only New York editor to support Bryan. Following the destruction of the *U.S.S. Maine,* both the *World* and *Journal* bent every energy to involve the United States in the conflict with Spain. At the height of the war, each paper had a daily circulation in excess of 1,000,000. But before long, Pulitzer was compelled to give up the unequal race and to leave the field of yellow journalism exclusively to Hearst. The pages of the *World* assumed a more conservative aspect and its news columns more and more devoted their attention to national and international concerns. Even Hearst, however, was to meet his master when the tabloids came on the scene in the nineteen twenties.[3]

THE INTELLECTUAL LIFE

It has become a literary fashion, in recent years, to insist that the three decades following the close of the Civil War were everywhere characterized by a materialism and an acquiescence in its works that cannot but mark the period as among the least satisfactory in the history of the American people. That this was outwardly true, there are ample evidences to indicate. The new plutocracy of this Gilded Age, without standards of conduct or any sympathy with the traditions of the past, did succeed in perverting tastes and debauching the political life to a remarkable degree. But the life of the spirit and the creative arts flourished mightily.

The intellectual and artistic life of this so-called Gilded Age was among the richest that our American civilization has yet seen. Too long have conservative commentators on the one hand and hostile critics on the other preoccupied themselves with the activities of the second-rate thinkers and artists. The praise by the one camp and the condemnation by the other of William Dean Howells, Thomas Bailey Aldrich, and John Hay in letters, W. M. Hunt, Charles F. McKim, and Stanford White in architecture, and John Singer Sargent and Abbott H. Thayer in painting have only succeeded in diverting attention from the lives and achievements of those other people whose contributions in their various realms were of the first order. It is hard to find an age in American annals of which Americans could be more justly proud: of the work of Gilman and Eliot in education; Henry George and Thorstein Veblen in economics; Charles S. Peirce and William James in philosophy; Walt Whitman, Henry James, Mark Twain, Emily Dickinson in letters; John A. Roebling, H. H. Richardson, Louis H. Sullivan in architecture; Thomas Eakins, Winslow Homer, Albert P.

[3] In 1931, the Pulitzer properties in New York were sold to the Scripps-Howard chain and the morning *World* suspended publication.

Ryder in painting; Willard Gibbs, Lewis H. Morgan, Simon Newcomb in the sciences. It is true that for the most part these labored in obscurity: they did not receive the just recognition that the Periclean, Renaissance, Elizabethan ages, and our own Middle Period, accorded their thinkers and artists. To this extent, perhaps, they were not the children of their age. But on the other hand, it is important to recall that they were wholly authentic contrivers and artists: they worked with the materials at hand; they recorded the reactions the life about them had on their thoughts and dreams; the America in which they moved they expressed in stone and steel, poetry and novels, economic tracts, and educational plans. The outer crust of this Gilded Age may have been cruel and hard, vulgar and debased, but underneath were cool springs to sustain the genius of an Emily Dickinson, an Albert Ryder, and a Louis Sullivan. Let us examine the too-often unacclaimed accomplishments, in the various fields of education, science, thought, letters, and art, of those three decades following the Civil War, over which the shadows of the new industrialism hung so heavily.

Higher education was revolutionized, and by the time the twentieth century opened learning had shaken off the fetters of the old classical faculties and was ranging freely in the physical, natural and social sciences, the arts and the humanities. The first influence to be noted is the emergence of a new school of university presidents: Andrew D. White at Cornell (1867); F. A. Barnard at Columbia (1864); Charles W. Eliot at Harvard (1869); Noah Porter at Yale (1871); James B. Angell at Michigan (1871); Daniel Coit Gilman at Johns Hopkins (1876). Of these the most famous were Gilman and Eliot. Gilman built at Johns Hopkins the first great graduate faculty of America where the tradition of learning was cultivated with unexampled zeal; Eliot created a rounded university whose college and medical and law schools quickly took their place among the first institutions of learning in the world. Aided by the generous land grants provided for in the Morrill Act of 1862, the states were able to create universities of their own. The University of Wisconsin's scope was greatly extended (1866); the Universities of Illinois (1867) and California (1868) were founded; New York State contributed its subsidy to help the establishment of Cornell (1868); Massachusetts did similarly in the case of the Massachusetts Institute of Technology (1865). By the turn of the century, all but some ten of the commonwealths could boast of systems of public education reaching from the kindergarten to the great university with its graduate professional schools.

A third influence of great importance came from philanthrophy. The benefactions of Johns Hopkins, Ezra Cornell, Leland Stanford, John D. Rockefeller (who revived the faltering University of Chicago in 1892), furnished endowments from which great institutions sprang up. The education of women was given serious attention for the first time, and Vassar made its appearance in 1865, Wellesley in 1875, Smith in 1875, Bryn Mawr in 1885, Barnard (as a college in Columbia University) in 1889, and Radcliffe (attached to Harvard University) in 1894. Coeducation was encouraged at Cornell and all the western universities. Professional education received the fostering care both of university administrators and of philanthropists with the result that before the century was over almost all the large centers of learning were training doctors, lawyers, engineers, chemists, and architects. Among the earlier of the specialized institutions may be enumerated the Columbia School of Mines (1864), the Massachusetts Institute of Technology (1865), Stevens Institute (1871), the Johns Hopkins Medical School (1893).

Nor is there to be overlooked the appearance of learned societies, which met at least once a year for discussion, printed journals, published erudite treatises and performed wonders in maintaining scholarship at a high level among the university teachers of the land. The first such society to make its appearance was the American Historical Association in 1884. The American Economic Association was founded in 1885; the American Anthropological Association in 1902; the American Political Science Association in 1904; the American Sociological Society in 1905. By the nineteen twenties there were in all some fifty of such learned groups, and under their stimulus American scholarship came to rank equally with that of German, British, and French savants.

Science was cultivated assiduously by the America of the period. Darwinism reached the American shore in the seventies and before long was to color profoundly biological and theological thinking. The efforts of John Fiske, a Harvard scholar, and Robert G. Ingersoll, a popular lecturer, shook the faith of countless Americans in revealed religion and made them follow with more than curious attention the new truths in biology, geology, and anthropology which scientific workers, following the trail the great Englishman had blazed, kept constantly disclosing. For those who craved a complete system, founded on the evolutionary doctrine, the teachings of Herbert Spencer were ready at hand. Spencer, in fact, was a far greater prophet in America than in his own land and his synthetic philosophy (which attempted to prove that the social sciences as well as the natural all conformed to the same laws of progress) was sympathetically received. Nor were original contributions by American scientists wanting. Benjamin Peirce worked in mathematics, Lewis H. Morgan in anthropology, Simon Newcomb in astronomy, Willard Gibbs and Joseph Henry in physics, John William Draper in chemistry. The *Popular Science Monthly,* edited by E. L. Youmans, opened its pages to the new winds of doctrine blowing across the late nineteenth century world and made the intelligent American layman familiar with the achievements of the quiet students of the book and the workers behind laboratory tables.

In the field of thought, America was not without its giants. Josiah Royce, in his *Religious Aspects of Philosophy* and especially in *The World and the Individual,* was responsible for the most complete expression of metaphysical idealism penned in America. Royce's defense of human immortality, done with a dazzling display of learning, was as a rock for those churchly creeds so sorely beset by the new sciences: but even this fortress began to crumble under the attacks of the pragmatists and other anti-intellectualists. Royce's work was filled with the echoes of an earlier, simpler day; it had little to offer the modern America of ever-growing complexity and ceaseless change. Charles S. Peirce, the son of the mathematician Benjamin Peirce, bore the authentic marks of the great thinker. While Peirce lacked the patience to indite a systematic philosophic treatise (for his interests were as wide as the physical sciences themselves and he was equally at home in astronomy, geodesy, and physics), he gave expression in his occasional papers, nevertheless, to many of the ideas at the bottom of American philosophical thought today. His "How to Make Our Ideas Clear," published as early as 1878, was the initial formulation of that pragmatic principle which held that the meaning of any concept was to be found "in all the conceivable experimental phenomena which the affirmation or denial of a concept could imply."

William James, more completely than any other American of his day, breasted the full current of the modern life. Youthful, acquisitive America was on the march: what use had it for first principles or suspended judgments? In Peirce's pragmatism James found a philosophical approach that exactly suited his own sanguine nature and the land whose temper he was able to read so well. James seized upon pragmatism and developed it: in his hands, ideas were compelled to submit to empirical tests; practical results were the things that mattered to the individual; the future, not the past, was to judge the validity of our aspirations. And because he phrased so glowingly the American credo, unbounded faith in democracy, belief in the will, the superiority of the life of action, the significance of the concrete, James received the wide acclaim of his contemporaries and was honored as few living philosophers are by their fellow men. Whether James's metaphysics will withstand the more severe tests of time, we have no way of knowing; but his contributions to psychology were of the first order, and despite the great distance other workers after him have traveled, his *Principles of Psychology* still stands as a landmark.

While William G. Sumner propounded an elaborate defense of the prevailing economic laissez-faire doctrines, there were not wanting critics to submit the new industrial processes to searching examination. Chief among the voices raised in dissent were Henry George, Henry Adams, and Thorstein Veblen. Henry George's *Progress and Poverty* made a profound impression on Europe as well as America. Moved by the inequalities of wealth already apparent, Henry George proposed that the unearned increments in land values be confiscated for the benefit of the whole polity. His device of "the single tax," held George, would adjust those economic disparities from which modern society suffered. Thus he said:

> We hold that to tax labor or its products is to discourage industry. We hold that to tax land values to their full amount will render it impossible for any man to exact from others a price for the privilege of using those bounties of nature in which all living men have an equal right of use; that it will compel every individual controlling natural opportunities to utilize them by employment of labor or abandon them to others; that it will thus provide opportunities of work for all men and secure to each the full reward of his labor; and that as a result involuntary poverty will be abolished, and the greed, intemperance and vice that spring from poverty and the dread of poverty will be swept away.

Henry Adams was less sure of which way salvation lay, and his flight to the Middle Ages, personal escape though it was, nevertheless embodied the profound dissatisfaction of a powerful mind that had carefully weighed its age and found it wanting. *The Education of Henry Adams* was written from the author's despair: the world was controlled by mechanical power, it was futile for the individual to rebel. Thus he wrote:

> Modern politics is, at bottom, a struggle not of men but of forces. The men become every year more and more creatures of force, massed about central powerhouses. The conflict is no longer between the men, but between the motors that drive the men, and the men tend to succumb to their own motive forces. This is a moral that man strongly objects to admit, especially in medieval pursuits like politics and poetry, nor is it worth while for a teacher to insist upon it.[4]

So Adams fled and his *Mont-Saint-Michel and Chartres* depicts the "naïve, credulous world" of the eleventh, twelfth, and thirteenth centuries in which he found refuge. The confusion and multiplicity of the nineteenth century were too much for him: in the cathedral of Chartres, the adoration of the Virgin, the scholasticism of Thomas Aquinas, civilization had once, and only once, reached perfection: so spoke the great-grandson of that characteristic product of Puritan Massachusetts, John Adams.

Thorstein Veblen neither hoped with George nor despaired with Adams: he set himself the task of subjecting the ways of the new industrial masters to a pitiless examination, and in a series of books led off by *The Theory of the Leisure Class* he turned a mordant wit on a society which permitted its every institution to accept the standards of those who hunted only for profits. To Veblen, business enterprise, interested entirely in the production

[4] Reprinted by permission of the publishers, Houghton Mifflin Co.

of money values, was ever seeking to pervert the legitimate achievements of the artisan and the technician. In the words of Max Lerner writing in the *New Freeman:*

> Veblen took as his theme the unproductiveness and inutility which become the ideals of a leisure class, and their psychological effects upon the whole of society. He showed how, in such a society, prestige depends upon the flaunting of superfluous wealth through "conspicuous consumption" and "conspicuous waste" and through the "vicarious consumption" and "vicarious leisure" of the lady of the house and the corps of servants. He showed how the pecuniary values that dominated such a social structure informed every phase of life—religion, art, government, education; and in the tracing of the ramifications of leisure-class ideals through the whole of bourgeois culture he fulfilled the subtitle of the book—"An Economic Study of Institutions."

Other protestants were Wendell Phillips of Boston, who, after the Abolitionist fight was won, turned his shafts against industrial exploiters; George William Curtis of New York, civil service reformer; and Henry D. Lloyd of Chicago, whose *Wealth Against Commonwealth* was the first searching examination of the havoc being wrought by monopoly practices, those of the Standard Oil Company in particular.

LETTERS, ART, AND ARCHITECTURE

In letters, the America of the Gilded Age was not without its master spirits: Walt Whitman, Mark Twain, Henry James, and Emily Dickinson are names worthy of a place in any select literary roll. Walt Whitman's *Leaves of Grass* was first published in 1855 and a variety of editions appeared during the next three decades, each successive one containing changes in old poems and additions of new ones. Walt Whitman was as large as the continent and the people whose glories he sang. He was more American than Franklin, more so even than Emerson; he was gusty, sensual, he thrilled with the flow of life. Every part of the American scene he hugged to his bosom: the broad prairies, crowded Manhattan, the soldiers, farmers, mechanics, and miners of everyday United States. Whitman always had an extraordinary faith in the processes of democracy, and though in his *Democratic Vistas* he was moved to protest against the excesses being practiced by the postwar political and industrial leaders, he never surrendered his hopes for the American people.

Mark Twain was cut from the same cloth. He was a child of the frontier; like Whitman he embodied the spirit of pioneering America. He had been reared in Missouri, had known the turbulent, colorful life of the Mississippi, the silver camps of the Rockies, and bizarre San Francisco. He had come east, when still a youth, and out of his memories had recorded for all time the tale of that eventful epoch when America was on the make. His *Innocents Abroad, Roughing It, The Gilded Age, Tom Sawyer, Life on the*

Mississippi, Huckleberry Finn, all reveal that mixture of Gargantuan coarseness and fine idealism which made the frontier period so distinctively a part of our native heritage. Even his ventures into other ages—*The Prince and the Pauper, A Connecticut Yankee in King Arthur's Court*—were neither flights from reality, of the kind Henry Adams indulged in, nor admissions of inferiority, but an expression of confidence in the superiorities of democracy. It is true that in later life this robust, hearty humorist turned satirist and produced those dark tracts, *The Mysterious Stranger* and *What Is Man?* It has been maintained that these secret writings recorded Mark Twain's mature reactions to the middle-class timidities and compromises of Aldrich, Howells, and his wife: that he indulged in these savage strokes to express his contempt for the confining respectability of the Hartford of the nineties in which he was compelled to move. This is hardly the whole truth. Mark Twain was a child of his age. Had he not said, "Here I am, one of the wealthiest grandees in America—one of the Vanderbilt gang in fact"? Mark Twain was of the same generation as the great railroad builders and steel masters and probably as little inclined to introspective searchings as they. It is more probable that his pessimism came, as Parrington suggests, with old age. Whatever the explanation of his later life, there can be no question that the creative artist was fulfilled in *Life on the Mississippi, Tom Sawyer,* and *Huckleberry Finn.*

Henry James fled from America when a young man, and from the seventies on continued to make England his home. He pursued a wistful ideal, a rainbow's end that really did not exist, for mid-Victorian England, instead of being that cultured, gentle clime he made it out to be, was shot through with middle-class notions fully as much as was his native New York. To try to explain physical escapes such as these in terms of revulsion from environment is futile; for others, too, before and after James, had fled and were to continue to do so: Heine from Germany, Shelley and Byron from England, Turgenev from Russia, Gauguin from France. Rather we may put it down to an expression of that romantic temperament which looks upon every other time and place as being happier than its own. James might have made a similar compromise with living in America had he tried. In any case, the novels he produced in self-imposed exile were the works of an American, whose birth, training, influences, and interests are unmistakably revealed, and as such they rightfully belong in any American record of artistic achievement. His *Roderick Hudson, Daisy Miller, Portrait of a Lady, The Bostonians* show unmistakable signs of a first-rate ability growing in power; his later works—*The Wings of the Dove, The Ambassadors,* and *The Golden Bowl*—entitle him to a place among the great novelists of modern times.

Emily Dickinson was unknown to her generation; yet she stands out as the greatest poet of her own day and one of the authentic geniuses of the nineteenth century. Born in 1830 at Amherst, Massachusetts, she lived and died in this little New England town, and during her whole fifty-six years rarely sought to make the acquaintance of the strange, new world that was eddying around her sheltered garden. It was not until the nineties that her hidden poems were printed in part; not until the nineteen twenties, with the publication of her collected poems and letters, that her full stature stood revealed. It was then seen that the timid New England recluse, who had been indulgently regarded as "queer" by such mighty ones as Colonel T. W. Higginson, was a great lyrical poet, whose boldness of imagery, curious fancies, and experiments with meters and words put her in the company of William Blake.

Even the second rank, among American men of letters, was thronged with worthy figures. One may mention Hamlin Garland, whose *Main-Travelled Roads* and *Prairie Folks* depicted with bitter fidelity the hardships of the farming families of the Middle Border; Ambrose Bierce, whose short stories of the Civil War and the frontier were tales of unrelieved horror, because he hated mankind so fiercely; Stephen Crane, to whom life was cruel and who died while still young, but whose *Red Badge of Courage* nevertheless remains as the best novel of the Civil War; Frank Norris, who wrote naturalistic novels with an epic sweep in *The Octopus, McTeague,* and *Vandover and the Brute.* The works of these writers, today, loom much larger in the American literary tradition than the pleasant, proper creations of William Dean Howells and Thomas Bailey Aldrich.

In painting, there was a high quality in the work produced; in fact, the canvases of Eakins, Homer, and Ryder merit our calling the age the most significant one in American painting. These men labored obscurely, and it fell to the lot of lesser ones to receive the plaudits and fat commissions of the art patrons of the day. Thomas Eakins was born in Philadelphia in 1844, and there he continued to stay until his death in 1906. He dipped his brush deeply into the America of the day and took for subjects the life about him: boating scenes on the Delaware River, prize fighters in the ring, surgeons at work in their operating rooms, portraits of churchmen, scientists, actresses, the elect of his native city. Suzanne La Follette says of him: "He was too much interested in penetrating to the reality of the objects he painted to seek refinement of tone or beauty of color.... He modeled strongly in light and shadow, and his color, like his form, is simply that of the objects he saw before him, stated with the same literal honesty."

Winslow Homer, too, sought out American life for his canvases, but he went to the sea and to the forest. He had been born in Boston in 1836, had been through the Civil War as a war correspondent and illustrator, and when he was in middle life settled down to a recluse's existence on the Maine coast. Here he painted those memorable pictures of surging waters and stormy skies, of fishermen and Yankee mariners, of sturdy sons of the soil who trapped wild animals, shot the rapids of the swift Maine streams, and plowed the stubborn earth of New England. Tropical lands, too, attracted him, and with the bold, sure strokes of the great water colorist, he was able to catch on paper the poetry of southern seas and palms, white houses shining in the sun, and strong, swimming black bodies.

Albert P. Ryder was born at New Bedford, Massachusetts, in 1848. He was the romantic and the mystic among the group of great painters: Chaucer, Wagner, the New Testament, as well as the sea and sky of his native country furnished the themes for his palette. His small canvases are harmonies of subdued color; his vaguely suggested figures of men, kine, and boats are projected against a natural grandeur, which, one feels, must have always moved Ryder deeply. It was not strange that such a man, poet and dreamer that he was, should be deeply religious, and his *The Resurrection* and *The Wayside Cross* are among his best works.

Besides these, there were other painters of outstanding merit. Ralph Blakelock, like Ryder, was a man of real imaginative gifts, though he was much more limited both in interests and in technical skill. He, too, was a painter of nature, and great forest interiors, often filled with reminiscent Indian figures, appear frequently on his canvases. George Inness, Alexander H. Wyant, and Homer D. Martin continued the romantic tradition of the Hudson River School of the Middle Period. Inness' pictures record the smiling country of the New Jersey meadows: of pleasant landscapes, noble prospects, sky and forest combined in a single composition. Wyant was an Ohioan and he painted the scenes of his native countryside. Martin was a New Yorker who went to the Westchester hills and the Adirondacks for his subjects; and though he was always in ill health and desperately poor he was able to create landscapes of strength and poetic quality.

One may mention, too, John La Farge, who was an artist of many gifts and who painted flower pieces, decorated church interiors, and worked in glass; John Singer Sargent, whose later life (probably because he became the smart painter of the fashionable and rich) never fulfilled the real promise of his youth; John H. Twachtman, J. Alden Weir, and Childe Hassam, who returned from the studios of the great French Impressionists to paint like Monet, Renoir, Sisley, and Pissarro; Frank Duveneck and William Merritt Chase, who studied at Munich and who came to paint portraits like old masters. The productions of the sculptors might be mentioned briefly. Among the outstanding figures of the period were Augustus Saint-Gaudens (remembered for his statues of Farragut in New York's Madison Square and his Lincoln in Lincoln Park, Chicago); Daniel Chester French (who did the seated Lincoln of the Lincoln Memorial at Washington) and George Grey Barnard, who was profoundly influenced by Rodin.

In the decades following the Civil War, too, the great public art collections of the country began to make their appearance. The Corcoran Art Gallery was opened at Washington in 1869; the Museum of Fine Arts made its appearance in Boston in 1876; the Metropolitan Museum of Art was opened in New York in 1879. Private taste, however, was not yet high and it was not until the twentieth century that there emerged private collectors who were able to gather together under their own roofs great arrays of authentic masterpieces of earlier, modern, and contemporary masters.

We have already spoken of the excesses indulged in, during the Gilded Age, by American architects, who on the one hand raised French chateaus for the supremely wealthy; Gothic, Swiss and Persian villas (frequently the styles jumbled together) for the middle class; and dumbbell tenements for the masses. It would be a mistake to believe, however, that real architects did not exist. On the contrary, the works of H. H. Richardson and Louis H. Sullivan were as important in their spheres as were those of the great novelists, poets, and painters in their own. Richardson, leaning heavily on the Romanesque, was able to construct noble buildings of stone, which, with their correctly proportioned masses and their sparing use of decoration, were in pleasing contrast to the simpering prettiness of the houses of the wealthy and the unabashed ugliness of the public buildings.[5] Richardson was permitted to spread his work over the country with a generous hand, and his Trinity Church in Boston, his Pittsburgh Court House, his New England public libraries and railroad stations, prove that public taste was not entirely debased. Sullivan was the herald of the new day: he saw the revolutionary possibilities of steel in construction, and it was his vision that, after three decades, brought about the era of the modern skyscraper in which, according to his precept, "form follows function." In his *Autobiography of an Idea* he wrote "that masonry construction was a thing of the past ... that the old ideas of superimposition must give way before a sense of vertical continuity." And Sullivan's Guaranty Building in Buffalo, with its fine, simple shaft and unhackneyed use of ornament, was a promise of what American architecture was to perform after it had shaken off the influence of the neoclassicism of McKim, Mead, White and their school.

Another outstanding architectural achievement of the age was the building of the Brooklyn Bridge, designed by John Roebling and completed by his son Washington. The bridge was opened in 1884 and (says Lewis Mumford) "was a testimony to the swift progress of physical science. The strong

---

[5] Mullett's War, State and Navy Building in Washington and his Federal Building in New York are notorious examples of this style that presumably derived from the Renaissance.

lines of the bridge and the beautiful curve described by its suspended cables were derived from an elegant formula in mathematical physics—the elastic curve."

It was amazing that the world of architecture could put these wholly American triumphs behind it when it came to design the buildings of the World's Columbian Exposition at Chicago (1893); it did, nevertheless, and the White City then erected, true though it was in its Grecian and Roman forms, had as little to do with late nineteenth century America as the temples to Venus and Jupiter which these architects so coolly copied. From that achievement sprang the arid architecture of the next twenty years which insisted upon treating libraries, railroad stations, and public buildings generally like so many imperial monuments.

America's musical tastes were highly developed during the period. The new immigrants brought their love for music with them to their adopted land; the new philanthropists built concert halls and furnished the funds to endow musical organizations; the new bourgeoisie supported musical performances with its patronage. European artists and conductors flocked to our shores with the result that our concert stages, symphony orchestras, and opera were as splendid as those of the Old World. In 1866, the Philharmonic Society of New York acquired its first permanent conductor and in 1877 Theodore Thomas took up the baton and introduced the East to Wagner and Brahms. The very next year Leopold Damrosch organized the New York Symphony Society; the Boston Orchestra made its appearance in 1881; the Chicago Orchestra in 1891; the Cincinnati Orchestra in 1895; the Pittsburgh Orchestra in 1896; while the celebrated Philadelphia Orchestra began its long history of service in the cause of good music in 1900. In the late eighteen nineties, American concert-goers were regularly enjoying the works of Wagner, Brahms, Tschaikowsky, César Franck, and Richard Strauss. The opera, too, was cultivated and the splendid Metropolitan Opera House was opened in New York in 1883 to play not only the musical dramas of the popular Italian and French composers but the works of Wagner as well. Americans themselves, it seemed, had not yet learned to work profoundly in music as an art form: their compositions, for the most part, were plainly derivative, and while some of the work was pleasing none of it could be considered as important in an age that had produced the European giants. The better known of these American composers were E. A. MacDowell, John K. Paine, G. W. Chadwick, Horatio Parker, and Arthur Foote. Time has been less cruel to MacDowell's smaller lyric compositions than it has been to the more pretentious operas, symphonies, and oratorios that were being written in America then.

Except for the comparatively unimportant plays of Bronson Howard and James A. Herne, the drama had not yet come of age. Howard's outstanding work was *Shenandoah*, a play of the Civil War. Herne's plays

Fuermann
Guaranty Building, Buffalo, 1894–95

Ewing Galloway, N.Y.
The Court of Honor at the World's Columbian Exposition
Chicago, 1893

FUNCTION AND FAÇADE IN AMERICAN ARCHITECTURE

were filled with a group of kindly, sentimental Down East rustics, his *Shore Acres* (1892) being the best example of this type of dramatic production. The theater, however, thrived and there was not a community in the land, no matter how small, that did not boast of its opera house to which came regularly traveling companies to present Shakespeare, *Uncle Tom's Cabin*, the thrillers, and the so-called English society plays of the period. In New York the stage was dominated by two outstanding personalities. The first was Augustin Daly, who flourished during the seventies and eighties; the second was Charles Frohman, who from the time he first presented *Shenandoah* (1889) to his drowning (on the *Lusitania*) in 1915 was the country's leading theatrical producer. Frohman brought the prevailing industrial technique into the theater: he acquired playhouses in America and Europe, subsidized dramatists, trained stars, and kept a round of traveling companies circulating over the land. He introduced the best of the current European plays to the American stage, and that the native theater-going public learned of the works of Barrie, Sutro, Pinero, Jones, Guitry, Rostand, Haddon Chambers, and others was due to his enterprise.

> Section V
> AGRARIAN DISCONTENT

· 14 ·

Curbing the Railroads: The Interstate Commerce Act of 1887

THE SPRINGS OF WESTERN UNREST

WESTERN discontent, once it became articulate and mobilized, moved on many wings. The bankers, whom the West blamed for deflation and tight credit facilities, were the principal enemy. But there were other oppressors: the tariff-protected large industrialists who by monopolistic devices were able to charge extortionate prices for the necessities of life; the commission men and brokers who controlled the prices of farm produce; the railroad managers who by combinations and secret agreements fixed rates, bribed public officials, and evolved the pernicious system of discriminations between the large shipper and the small. Against these enemies the West sought relief in governmental action: Greenbackism, free silver, the whole Populist program, government regulation of railroads and monopolies—these are all phases of the same discontent.

It was because of this situation that laissez-faire in America had to give way. The West was unsuccessful in its attack on currency and credit abuses. It was unsuccessful in trying to break the monopolistic hold that tariff-protected industries had on the domestic market. But it did gain an outstanding victory in its fight on the railroads and by so doing the first encounter in a long—and not yet finished—engagement was won. The same western discontent which had clamored for greenbacks and free silver and for the curbing of industrial monopoly was responsible for the writing of the first piece of federal legislation of any broad economic significance. The same western states which experimented with railroad legislation in the seventies were the first American commonwealths to begin the writing on their statute books, thirty years later, of those social laws which opened the way for the New Deal in the federal sector in the nineteen thirties. The significance of the Interstate Commerce Act lies in this fact: it was the initial evidence of a conscious drive toward the regulation of industrial capitalism in the interests of society at large. And by the passage of this law, in 1887, the federal government entered upon a career of social legislation whose ramifications were eventually to reach into every field of private endeavor. The passage of the Interstate Commerce Act indicated that the twilight of individualism in the United States had set in, though it was to turn out to be a long twilight indeed.

RAILROAD ABUSES

The following were the outstanding reasons for the appearance of western clamor against the American railroads:

Railroad management in the seventies and the eighties was often arrogant, brutal, and dishonest. The operation of the roads was more frequently than not in the hands of subordinates, while the policies of the roads, with a complete disregard for local conditions, were determined from distant offices. The Northern Pacific Railroad, which began at Lake Superior, was presided over by a gentleman resident in Vermont who had never been in the Northwest and apparently never thought of going. The affairs of almost all the western railroads were conducted from offices in New York, Philadelphia, and Boston. It was general knowledge in the West of the seventies that more than fifty railroads in Texas, Louisiana, Alabama, Arkansas, Kansas, Nebraska, and Iowa were managed from eastern cities. It was no wonder that contracts were disregarded, dishonest agents could not be controlled, and that legitimate claims could be satisfied only with the greatest difficulty. For one Hill in American railroading there were a hundred Goulds.

By the seventies, the American public had learned the lengths of which railroad financing was capable. Not only had states and municipalities been loaded with burdens of debt incurred in ill-starred railroad enterprises, but the number of duped individuals reached a mighty host. The credulous western farmer, anxious for a market for his produce, had been a ready victim. He had bought shares in the projected railroads, paying for his hopes in land, labor, and even farm mortgages. Sometimes the railroads were never built; more frequently, when they were actually laid down and in operation, the investors saw their legitimate profits being diverted into the pockets of the promoters. The customary device was stock-watering. Vanderbilt's increase of the capitalization of the New York Central by almost 100 per cent, at a single stroke, has already been mentioned. The wretched history of Erie financing, too, was no isolated phenomenon. In the eighties, testified a railroad expert before the Cullom Committee (the

Congressional body which finally wrote the Interstate Commerce Act), fully one-third of the rail capitalization of the country was water. If the investor was being cheated, the shipper was no less the victim. Increased capital values demanded a greater earning power that could be realized through but two devices—higher rates and discriminations in favor of the larger shipper. Indeed, these two phases of railroad history set off the train of events that led to government regulation.[1]

The railroads had contributed their share in the corruption of the public life. Complicity between the railroads and federal officialdom was merely suspected: how then to account for the lavish land grants, the wasteful construction of the transpacific railroads and the refusal of the Union Pacific and the Central Pacific to fund the governmental loans? But venality in the state capitals was not even disguised. Not only did the railroads maintain lobbies at all the legislatures, but by favors, threats, and bribes they played a real part in the shaping of legislation. Judges, juries, and state officials were recipients of the largesse of the railroads; the pass was the least of the common evils indulged in. In Missouri, for example, it was frankly admitted by all involved that the Missouri Pacific had paid the state legislators several hundred thousands of dollars to release the railroad from the mortgage which the state held. The Cullom Committee found that all of the subsidized railroads used money to influence legislation. Not only did legislators condone illegal stock issues and wink at extortionate practices: they gave their sanction to an unequal distribution of the tax burden. In Iowa, for example, the railroads, owning one-fourth of the assessable property in the state, paid less than one-twentieth of the taxes. Other western states saw the same discrimination practiced.

The processes of consolidation, effected throughout the seventies, with their threats of monopoly, furnished additional reasons for discontent. The appearance of the railroad pool, particularly because it could be quietly manipulated, stirred western men to anger. As long as railroads competed for traffic, the shipper who was fortunate enough to find two roads at his service was in a position to benefit by playing off one agent against the other. When, however, railroad executives reached agreements for the stabilization of rates and the division of traffic even the slight protection offered by competition was broken down. The first pooling arrangement was established in 1870 by the railroads serving the district between Omaha and Chicago. Five years later a similar pool controlled the southern area; before the decade was over all the trunk lines leaving Chicago for

[1] A British investment banker warned his countrymen that American rail executives were employing the following devices to inflate the capitalization of the railroads: the fraudulent issuance of bonds and stocks; paying too much for construction; purchasing properties at excessive prices; buying up unnecessary competing lines; selling securities at a discount; declaring stock dividends. See S. F. Van Oss, *American Railroads as Investments* (1893).

the East were either dividing the traffic or pooling the net earnings collected from transportation. With what thoroughness these rail executives moved may be seen from the fact that the committee which controlled the destinies of the Chicago–New York lines had the power to apportion the total competitive traffic, fix the rates, and formulate the rules for the carriage of the joint traffic shared by all the roads. By 1887, every railroad in a competitive field was a member of some pooling arrangement.

The deportment of the land-grant railroads was particularly offensive. They refused to patent the lands granted them along the right of way, with the result that they were able to avoid state and local taxation and at the same time keep prospective settlers away, for the homesteader was unable to tell which was government land and which railroad. A practice that rankled even deeper was the policy of holding out the indemnity lands. By the charters of the Union Pacific, Central Pacific, and Northern Pacific, the railroad officials were permitted to choose sections of land from an area lying from ten to twenty miles on each side of the track, as indemnification in the event that the land granted them along the right of way was already pre-empted. Between 1872 and 1887, with the approval of the General Land Office, these indemnity lands were closed to settlers while, interestingly enough, the railroads sold their timber rights to favored lumbering companies. For fifteen years then, the homesteader, very often, could get no closer to a railroad than ten or twenty miles. It was not until 1887, through an order of Grover Cleveland, that these lands were thrown open for general settlement. The size of the evil may be gauged from the fact that almost twenty million acres were involved.

Such were the methods of railroad policy and administration that aroused popular ill will, particularly in the West. Railroad abuses ran the gamut from pettiness to actual misrepresentation and fraud. It was only natural that these engendered a resentment whose intensity did not spend its force for years.

It was on a more fundamental set of abuses, however, that the antagonism of the shipper, particularly in the West, was fed. Up to 1875, the chief complaint against the railroads centered in the high rates being charged. There is no question that the price which the western farmer received for his wheat or corn was eaten up, quite often, almost completely by the transportation charges. Tales of sending corn to the eastern markets and receiving just enough to cover the freight charges occur in the literature of the period with monotonous regularity. The railroads were responsible for this state of affairs: they charged what the traffic would bear, particularly if water competition was absent; nor had the time yet come when the railroad manager regarded the perfection of railroad economies as his chief function, instead of the wresting of business away from his competitor.

It was not until the railroad industry was stabilized that rates began to fall. In the early seventies, the change was already perceptible; by 1875, it was an assured fact. By that time railroad consolidation and the formation of traffic associations had placed railroading on a business basis with the result that radical reforms at once were introduced. The steel rail began to replace the iron one and it thus became possible to build heavier cars and handle bigger loads. The general acceptance of the standard gauge permitted easier routing of through shipments. Freight cars were being used both ways instead of returning empty. The rate wars among the trunk lines had a permanent effect in the depressing of carrying charges. The results were magical. In 1869, it had cost 35.1 cents to ship a bushel of wheat from Chicago to New York; in 1874, it cost 28.7 cents; after 1875, the price averaged between 17 and 18 cents.

As a result of all this, the charge of rate extortions gradually receded into the background and the more serious one of discrimination took its place. Discrimination partook of two forms: discrimination between places and discrimination between persons. It became a common railroad practice to exact a higher rate between intermediate points, where no competition existed, than was charged between large termini where a number of roads might be expected to vie for the traffic. In other words, a railroad very often got much more, proportionately and even literally, for a short haul than it received for a long haul. How much opportunity there was for this sort of discrimination can be seen from the fact that in 1887 there were some 30,000 communities in the United States served by but a single railroad, while not more than 2700 points could boast of two or more lines entering them. Western men repeatedly told tales of sending their produce by long and roundabout journeys so that they might benefit from the competitive rates of the long haul.

If this was objectionable the practice of discriminating between shippers was even more reprehensible. It was an ordinary thing for large shippers to get from the railroads preferential rates or rebates (as they were called), which would enable them to undersell their rivals. Western farmers suffered from this type of practice acutely: the owners of the bonanza farms of the West, for example, received large reductions from the regular charges; railroads also made it a general habit to favor grain commission men with special rates while farmers' co-operative societies were denied the same privileges.

It was the cry that discrimination (in the form of rebating) was strengthening the hand of monopoly that banded East and West together and assembled the force which in 1887 was able to sound the death knell of unregulated railroad management. For if the agricultural West came to look upon the monopolists of the distant East as ogres at whose door might be placed all the ills to which they had fallen heir, the small merchants and manufacturers of the East were able to view the processes at first hand.

Local investigations as far back as the seventies had shown that large shippers were receiving rebates on freight charges. A New York legislative committee investigation of 1879 had revealed the fact that the New York Central had in a single year made 6000 special contracts for granting rebates. The same inquiry had brought to light, for the first time, the devious methods evolved by the directors of the Standard Oil Company to give them control of the oil industry of the country. Then an aroused nation had read how in a short eighteen months' time the Standard Oil Company as the price for its patronage had received back from the railroads the sum of $10 million, based not only on their own shipments but on the shipments of competitors as well. When the Cullom Committee moved around the country taking testimony in 1885, it was met by oil and coal men, packers and merchants, and grain dealers from all sections of the country, all of whom testified to the same effect: the railroads were checking free competition, building up monopolies, throttling the life of trade. When Swift, the Chicago packer, and the respected New York Board of Trade voiced their grievances publicly, then the time for action had come indeed.

STATE REGULATION AND THE SUPREME COURT

The first state law for the general regulation of the railroads was enacted in Massachusetts in 1869. By this measure there was set up a board of commissioners with powers to investigate railroad methods, to listen to complaints, and to report all discriminatory acts to the legislature or to the state attorney-general. In reality, the commission's powers were only supervisory: its chief weapon was the creation of an articulate public opinion. But it met with considerable success, largely because C. F. Adams, Jr., guided its functions in its formative years. The example of Massachusetts was followed generally in the East, and in New York and the remaining New England states similar commissions were soon at work.

The western states required stronger fare before they could be satisfied; and with the entry of the western farmer into politics the first mandatory railroad laws were placed on American statute books. These agrarian parties, in the early seventies, had grown out of a farmer organization called the Patrons of Husbandry, but more popularly known as the Grange. The Grange had been founded in 1868 and its original scheme, patterned after the always fascinating secret societies, had planned for the development of a social and cultural movement with a ritual, lodges, and the rest. By 1874, the order had 15,000 local branches and a membership of one and one-half million farmers. The founders of the society, from the beginning, made the extortionate practices of the large manufacturers and the monopolists the chief points of their attack and urged the establishment of farmers' cooperatives for the purposes both of manufacture and of distribution. The fact is, during the brief history of this first farmers' movement, a number of such enterprises were launched and state Granges were soon operating harvester works, plow factories, grain elevators, packing plants, insurance companies, and even banks. Co-operative retail stores were particularly numerous. Unfortunately, this early effort at agricultural co-operation was short-lived. The manufacturing companies were involved in costly patent suits; private elevators drove the Grange elevators out of business through unions with the railroads; the retail stores failed because of the inexperience of their managers and the essentially individualistic character of the communities they tried to serve. The Rochdale plan of co-operation was still generally unfamiliar to Americans, and profits were distributed not on the basis of purchase but on that of stock ownership.

Though the Granges themselves were ostensibly nonpolitical in character it was hard to keep the western farmers, once they had got together under a common roof, from effecting political organizations. In 1873 and 1874, in eleven western states, farmers' parties named state and local tickets and triumphantly returned large blocs to the legislatures: these were the law-makers who were the first to move effectively against the railroads. In Illinois, a series of laws was passed which provided the following: the establishment of a commission with the power to prepare schedules of maximum rates; a declaration that discrimination between persons and places was illegal; a further declaration that the state railroad commission's rulings were to be regarded as prima facie evidence of reasonableness. Iowa sought to check railroad abuses entirely by statute without troubling to set up the intermediary of a commission: in 1874, an elaborate code was enacted in which rates were fixed for all the railroads operating in the state. In the same year both Wisconsin and Minnesota, under the spur of farmer majorities in the state legislatures, passed similar measures. In the newly written constitutions of Missouri, Nebraska, and California and many of the southern states, in the decade of the seventies, pronouncements were made against the pass evil, the short-haul abuse, pooling, and similar railroad practices.

A variety of reasons made these so-called Granger laws of the western states short-lived. The Minnesota law was repealed in 1875; the Iowa law remained but one year on the statute books; the Wisconsin law was in operation for only two years; the injunctions of the southern constitutions upon the state legislatures were never really obeyed. The Granger laws failed for the following reasons: 1. There was a complete lack of technical skill on the part of the persons invested with the problem of regulating the roads. 2. The hostility and the ingenuity of the railroad managers were more than enough to offset the untutored zeal of the farmer-commissioners. 3. The financial depression of the seventies checked railroad construction and made the West apprehensive lest its drastic action put a stop to new building altogether. 4. The rate wars of the late seventies resulted in a permanent lowering of freight charges. 5. The decline of the Grange and the agrarian parties that stemmed from it removed the pressure of public opinion from the lawmaking bodies. By 1880, the Patrons of Husbandry had largely run its course, better prices for farm products, lower freight rates, and the failure of many of the co-operatives contributing to the general result.

In 1876, the Supreme Court invested the Granger laws with the authority of its lofty sanction; ten years later, the whole basis of state action was cut away—and by the Supreme Court, too. In 1876 the Supreme Court, in reviewing a number of cases rising out of the Illinois, Iowa, Minnesota, and Wisconsin railroad acts (the so-called Granger cases), laid down the following principles of state action: A state might regulate a business of a public nature, particularly one in which there were to be found the elements of monopoly. The power to regulate had not been contracted away unless the legislature had specifically so declared. Powers of regulation rested with the legislature and not the judiciary. The courts could not pass in review the exercise of the regulatory power by the legislature. In other words, the courts were not competent to review the question of the reasonableness of rates fixed by the legislatures or their agencies. If there were legislative abuses, said Chief Justice Waite in writing the decision in Munn v. Illinois, then the polls were the refuge of the people, and not the courts.[2] Finally the highest authority in the land ruled that until Congress might see fit to act, the states had the power to regulate interstate commerce in so far as the welfare of their own particular citizens was concerned.

The illusory hope of the last dictum, which held out every promise of a system of state codes without the necessity for resorting to Congressional action, was dashed by the Wabash decision of 1886. In the case of the Wabash, St. Louis and Pacific Railroad Company v. Illinois,[3] which had been decided by the Illinois courts along the lines of the Granger cases, the Supreme Court reversed the principle of the 1876 decisions and once and for all declared that the states had no right to regulate interstate commerce or to interfere with traffic moving across their borders. Their jurisdiction extended solely and exclusively over intrastate commerce; relief could come only through Congress in legislation of a national character. The Wabash decision swept away nine-tenths of the state railroad-rate laws: Congress had to act to check the rising tide of national discontent.

THE EVOLUTION OF FEDERAL CONTROL

From 1867 on, a steady stream of bills and resolutions concerned with the rail power and its abuses poured into the Congressional hopper. In

[2] 94 U.S. 113.
[3] 118 U.S. 557.

A MEETING OF THE GRANGERS
Near Winchester, Scott County, Illinois

From *Frank Leslie's Illustrated Newspaper*

the Fortieth Congress, three resolutions were introduced; in the Forty-second Congress, the total had grown to sixteen; in the Forty-fourth Congress, nine railroad measures were before the House and Senate; in the Forty-seventh Congress, twenty-seven were recorded on the journals of both houses. Washington took official cognizance of western mutterings as early as 1872, when President Grant suggested to Congress the appointment of a committee to consider "various enterprises for the more certain and cheaper transportation of the constantly increasing western and southwestern products to the Atlantic seaboard." The Senate committee that resulted (the so-called Windom Committee), after holding hearings in the East, at Washington, and in the Mississippi Valley, filed in 1874 a report that displayed a complete failure to recognize the essential characteristics of the railroad problem. Not regulation but competition, not governmental action but laissez-faire economics was the answer, said the committeemen. To encourage further competition the committee recommended the following: the improvement of the natural waterways of the country; the construction of a double-track freight railway running from the Mississippi to the Atlantic seaboard; publicity for rates; prohibition of discrimination against lake or river ports; the establishment of a bureau of internal commerce to collect information concerning railroad practices.

The West's reply came in no uncertain terms: only governmental regulation was acceptable. In 1874, therefore, prodded by the insistent clamor of western legislatures and farmer organizations, the House passed a measure that incorporated the demands of the West. The McCrary bill, introduced by an Iowa representative, called for the creation of a federal commission with the powers of fixing maximum rates, summoning witnesses, investigating complaints, and preparing charges against the carriers. Too, the commission's schedules of rates were to be considered prima facie evidence of reasonableness by the courts. The vote, after a stormy debate in which the opposition expressed again and again its faith in unhampered individualistic activity, was 121 yeas to 116 nays. The sectional character of the measure and the alignment of East against West is unmistakably indicated in the final vote.

VOTE IN HOUSE ON McCRARY BILL, 1874

	Yeas	Nays
New England States	7	13
Middle Atlantic States	17	35
North Central States	64	26
South Atlantic States	12	17
South Central States	17	23
Far Western States	4	2
Totals	121	116

The Senate refused to consider the McCrary bill and the debate continued. By 1878, the real objections to railroad practices had crystallized; discrimination was the heart of the problem. In that year Reagan of Texas presented to the House a bill which incorporated the following: discriminatory rates were to be forbidden; so were the grantings of rebates and drawbacks; so was the creation of pools for the distribution of freights or earnings. All freight schedules were to be posted conspicuously and a five-day notice of contemplated rate changes was to be required. Included in the bill was a drastic long- and short-haul clause which was equivalent to the fixing of a pro rata charge. In December, the House passed this bill by a vote of 139 yeas to 104 nays. Again, an examination of the sectional voting on the measure throws light on the economic conflicts that divided the country. It will be seen that by 1878 the South had definitely joined the West against the East.

Vote in House on Reagan Bill, 1878

	Yeas	Nays
New England States	2	21
Middle Atlantic States	29	27
North Central States	54	31
South Atlantic States	18	12
South Central States	32	10
Far Western States	4	3
Totals	139	104

In this case, too, the Senate took no action. But it had become increasingly apparent that Congress must sooner or later bow before the popular storm, for the petitions that kept on pouring into the House and Senate were no longer confined to the frontier but were coming from the boards of trade of metropolises, eastern legislatures, and from citizens of Maine, New Hampshire, New Jersey, Pennsylvania, and Massachusetts. Reagan reintroduced his bill in 1880; in 1881 to 1883, the railroad question appeared to have been the chief Congressional concern, for twenty-seven measures were put before that Congress; in 1885, the House passed the Reagan bill for a second time. Finally the Senate stirred into life and before the close of the Forty-eighth Congress it had accepted a resolution, introduced by Cullom of Illinois, for the holding of a Senate committee investigation.

The inquiry that the Cullom Committee conducted was conclusive. It conducted hearings during the latter part of 1885 in the principal cities of the country; it listened to railroad presidents, state commissioners, economists, professors, farmers, merchants, manufacturers, packers, and millers; it collected two thousand pages of testimony made up of apologies on the part of the rail executives and bitter complaints on the part of all other economic forces of the nation. So universal was the insistence for regulation that the Cullom Committee, composed entirely of conservative gentlemen, found it necessary to report: "It is the deliberate judgment of the Committee that upon no public question are the people so nearly unanimous as upon the proposition that Congress should undertake in some way the regulation of interstate commerce."

A whole year of legislative debate was necessary before the Interstate Commerce Act was finally to emerge. In January, 1887, Senate and House accepted a compromise measure written in Conference Committee, and with the Presidential signature affixed (not without considerable hesitation on the part of Cleveland, who was bothered by fine points of constitutional law) the Interstate Commerce Act was formally inscribed on the nation's statute books on February 4. A revolution had taken place in the relations between government and industry: for the first time since the inauguration of the new industrialism the federal government had been compelled to move against the defenses of the laissez-faire doctrine. The citadel of individualism had not proved invulnerable after all, and it became apparent that the same government which had given so freely of its bounty—in land grants to railroads and bond issues—could also be compelled to take away.

The first three sections of the Interstate Commerce Act were largely based on the English law of 1854. They provided that all charges made by carriers should be "reasonable and just;" that special rates, rebates, and drawbacks were illegal; and that discriminations between persons, places, and commodities were to be proceeded against. Section 4 of the act embodied the chief remedy sought by the West. It made it unlawful for a carrier to charge more for transportation or carriage for a short haul than for a long haul, when the conditions were substantially the same, when the same line was doing the hauling and when the shorter distance was included in the longer. Section 5 made pooling operations illegal. Section 6 made it incumbent upon the railroads to file schedules of rates with a commission that was to be set up, and to give ten days' notice of all advances in rates. The following relief was provided in the event of discrimination: aggrieved shippers might sue for full damages with costs; shippers might file their complaints with the Commission or commence suit themselves; carriers found guilty of committing violations were to be subject to a fine not greater than $5000 for each offense. Sections 11 to 21 provided for the establishment of the Interstate Commerce Commission and outlined its powers. It was to be made up of five members to be appointed by the President with the advice and consent of the Senate. The Commission was to have the authority to inquire into the management of interstate carriers, summon witnesses, compel the production of papers, and invoke the aid of the federal courts. The Commission was to have the power of making reports containing the findings of fact upon which its conclusions were based, "which findings shall thereafter in all judicial proceedings be deemed prima facie evidence as to each and every fact found." Finally the Commission was to have the right to require the carriers to file annual reports and to install a uniform system of accounts devised by itself.

THE FRUSTRATION OF THE INTERSTATE COMMERCE COMMISSION

The federal government had definitely indicated its interest in the operations of a business invested with a public character; a law was on the statute books; popular demand for the measure had plainly revealed that public opinion was universal in its cry for relief; yet twenty years were to go by before the railroad situation was really in hand and the Interstate Commerce Commission was a functioning organization.

President Cleveland, who named the first Commission, went to the bar and the bench for his appointees. Despite the fact that the agitation for regulation had come out of the West but one commissioner, the tariff-reformer Morrison of Illinois, could be said to represent the western elements in the Democratic party. The others were conservative gentlemen, none of whom was likely to create too much alarm in the breasts of railroad managers and directors.

For three short years the carriers appeared to show a willingness to conform with the outward requirements of the law. They continued the reduction of local rates, they simplified their schedules, they announced the disbanding of pools, they filed their statistical returns with the Commission. But it soon became evident that traffic associations and "gentlemen's agreements" could control rates as well as the old formally established pools, and that accounting devices could conceal rebates and discriminations to large shippers. In 1890, the opposition to the Interstate Commerce Commission was out in the open. Before the decade of the nineties was over, the railroads, with the support of the courts, had tied the hands of the Commission so completely that from a regulatory body with judicial functions it had been converted into an agency for the collection and publication of statistics. In its annual report for 1898 the Commission recorded its own failure.

The frustration of the Commission was encompassed in the following ways: 1. Witnesses refused to testify, particularly when questions of rebating were involved. Not before 1896 did the Supreme Court finally decide that witnesses could be summoned and compelled to give material evidence. 2. The carriers denied that the Commission was invested with judicial powers. Not until 1894 did a Supreme Court decision finally find for the Commission. 3. So slowly did the machinery of the Commission function that it did not take long for interested persons to see that relief in the case of the individual shipper was well-nigh impossible. Decisions were appealed to the federal courts; cases went back, then, to the Commission for the filing of a new order. The processes of appeal usually averaged four years. The upshot was that by 1900 only nineteen petitions for relief against discriminations had been filed. 4. The Commission fell into popular disrepute as a result of the long list of reversals that its decisions met with at the hands of the Supreme Court. While the Commission was not entirely to blame, it was hard to convince the average person that its work was in any way effective when, in the years 1887 to 1905, out of sixteen decisions appealed from the Commission, the Supreme Court ruled for the railroads in the case of fifteen.

In 1897, the Supreme Court sent the whole house of cards toppling to the ground when it ruled, in the Maximum Freight Rate case,[4] that the Commission had no authority to set a maximum rate. The Commission had never claimed the rate-making power; it had, however, repeatedly said that it might prescribe a modification of rates if discrimination had been established. This the Court denied. In its decision it declared that the power to fix rates was a legislative and not an administrative or judicial function; that Congress had not transferred this power to the Interstate Commerce Commission; and that the Commission had not been given the power of prescribing rates and therefore could not seek aid from the courts to compel carriers to accept its schedules. In other words, the Court put the Commission's dilemma in this way: by its investigations it might find that the schedules of a certain railroad had been unreasonable in the past; it could not, however say what the railroad's rates ought to be in order to make them reasonable. What was left for the Commission? The Court declared that the Commission's functions consisted of the following: it had the duty of collecting railroad statistics; it had the right to demand the publication of rates by the companies; it could concern itself with seeing that the carriers did not indulge in rebating and did not discriminate between the long hauls and the short hauls.

The very same year the Supreme Court declared that the Commission was not empowered to render arbitrary judgment in the case of long and short hauls unless it had considered every conditioning factor in the situation. This decision at once destroyed the effectiveness of the most important section of the Interstate Commerce law. In the Alabama Midland case [5] the Court ruled that the "substantially similar circumstances" of the fourth section were to be literally interpreted: Were the conditions of competition the same? By water? By rail? Were the two places affording the same kind of market outlets? Unless the Commission could prove these and other

[4] 167 U.S. 479.
[5] 168 U.S. 144.

CURBING THE RAILROADS 237

factors to be exactly similar then it had no right to declare a rate unreasonable even if it was on a shorter haul.

So low did the Commission fall in the popular estimation, as a result of its inability to enforce its decrees on the carriers, that the number of complaints formally filed with it steadily dwindled. In 1892, the formal complaints numbered 39; in 1900, they numbered 19. Not until 1906, as a result of the campaign that Theodore Roosevelt waged in the interest of railroad regulation, did Congress finally act. In that year the Interstate Commerce Commission, after twenty years of existence, began once more to take on the semblance of life, when the Hepburn Act gave it the right to reduce rates when complaints had shown them to be unreasonable or discriminatory. In 1910, by the elimination of the "substantially similar circumstances" of the fourth section, the long- and short-haul clause again came to mean something. And in 1913 the Interstate Commerce Commission was given the right to make a physical valuation of railroad properties as the first step toward arriving at a scientific basis of rate-making. We shall have occasion to examine, below, the forces that compelled these radical amendments of the original Interstate Commerce Act.

· 15 ·

The Sherman Antitrust Law

THE PROCESSES OF CONCENTRATION

It was in the natural order of events that the units of business enterprise in post-Civil War America, under the stimulus of the many forces that were so favorable to private activity, should increase in size. Magnitude in itself was no evil, for the economies possible under large-scale operations were known to everybody. Thus, a good deal of the effectiveness of American industry arose from the plowing back of profits into plant expansion and integration. To enterprisers of this kind, cutthroat competition often stood for economic waste and not progress. Concentration, therefore, frequently led to efforts to curb competition; for short periods and in some industries monopoly devices and practices resulted. Of course, there were exceptions. Carnegie for example, though he did obtain rebates from railroads, did not carry on unfair warfare against competitors. The greatness of his company was built up on the fact that he made steel more cheaply because he controlled all the processes he needed, from mines up to rolling mills. Henry Ford, later, was to emulate Carnegie's example. But for one Carnegie Steel Company there were literally dozens of large corporate groups which obtained strangle holds on their markets not because they made particularly significant contributions to business enterprise but because they had killed off competition. And without an umpire to see that rules were observed in the conduct of business, competition was easy enough to restrain.

The processes of attaining monopoly had gone through a variety of stages. There had been evolved, in the beginning, the pool, first to attract public attention in the case of the railroads. The pool was an informal device by which a group of individuals engaged in manufacturing or handling a competitive product pledged themselves to maintain prices or divide markets. Because pools were not enforceable under the common law, their only strength lay in the fact that self-interest demanded that pledges thus made be kept. But because these agreements were quickly broken, the pool was soon supplanted by another agency. This was the "trust," which first made its appearance in 1879 with the organization of the Standard Oil Trust. The participants in the trust, whether individuals or corporations, did not surrender their identities; nor did the "trust" own all the component elements figuring in the combination. The usual method was the creation of a small board of trustees to whom were assigned the stocks of the cooperating members, together with the power of voting them. The trustees then proceeded to evaluate the properties making up the combination and issued "trust certificates" on the basis of which profits were divided. Thus the Standard Oil Trust agreement, as revised in 1882, was ruled over by nine individuals, among whom the leading figures were John D. Rockefeller, William Rockefeller, H. M. Flagler, and John Archbold. These nine men voted the stock of the forty companies that were party to the agreement and that, together, represented 90 per cent of the oil-refining business of the country as well as 90 per cent of the pipe lines.

Between 1879 and 1896, this being the period when the trust proper flourished, some ten or twelve of these large combinations made their appearance. The more important were: American Cottonseed Oil Trust (1884), National Linseed Oil Trust (1885), National Lead Trust (1887), Distillers' and Cattle Feeders' Trust (the Whiskey Trust, 1887), Sugar Refineries Company (1887), National Cordage Association (1887). The trust phase in the combination movement was short-lived because the trusts were so vulnerable. In view of the fact that the trustee agreements were matters of record, the trusts could be moved against by the courts under the common law. Thus, Louisiana started a prosecution of the Cottonseed Oil Trust in 1887; the attorney-general of New York began a dissolution suit against the Sugar Trust two years later; and the attorney-general of Ohio began similar proceedings against the Standard Oil Trust in 1890. In 1890, the New York Court of Appeals ordered the revocation of the charter of the particular member of the Sugar Trust against which the action had been filed and in 1892 Ohio's Supreme Court handed down a similar decision in the case of the Standard Oil Company of Ohio. Thus condemned by courts of high standing, the trusts accepted the inevitable and began to dissolve, but not to disappear.

The trust was supplanted by the holding company or consolidation, which actually became the possessor of the physical plants of the subsidiaries making it up. The holding company either bought outright all the properties of the separate organizations (as did the United States Steel Corporation, for example) or acquired control of each company through purchase of a majority of the stock. In the latter case, consolidation was effected through the election of common directors who sat on the boards of all the participating companies. Of course the holding company was designed to perform exactly the functions of the supplanted trust. But what gave the holding company or consolidation a better chance in the struggle with the state law officers was the fact that New Jersey in 1889 amended her corporation law to permit the chartering of exactly such devices. In 1896, the New Jersey law was further liberalized to allow any corporation to purchase the shares or bonds of any other corporation whether chartered in New Jersey or in any other state. Other states to follow in the footsteps of New Jersey were Delaware, West Virginia, Maine, South Dakota and, later, Nevada and Florida. New Jersey was favored by most of the larger consolidations because of its proximity to New York City, and here were chartered the American Sugar Refining Company in 1891 (really the former Sugar Refineries Company) and the Standard Oil Company of New Jersey in 1899 (out of the older local company of the same name).

The vindication of the sugar holding company in 1895 in the Knight decision [1] showed plainly enough that such devices had little to fear from federal prosecution under the Sherman Antitrust Law, with the result that between 1897 and 1903 there was a veritable mass movement towards the creation of such groups. The census enumeration of 1900 found 185 industrial combinations whose total capitalization of $3 billion represented one-third of all the capital invested in manufacturing activities in the country.

It may be noted at this point that the earlier efforts at attaining monopoly through holding companies or consolidations practically ceased about 1904. One reason was, the process was almost completed as far as the basic industries of the nation were concerned. Again, the investing public began to show a decline in confidence, in view, particularly, of the lack of success of some of the more spectacularly promoted consolidations. Seager and Gulick report that in October, 1903, the securities of one hundred of the principal combinations showed a shrinkage of 47 per cent from the high prices of 1899 and 1900. Finally, the energy displayed by the federal Department of Justice, beginning with 1903, in seeking to obtain a more rigorous enforcement of the Sherman Antitrust Law, cooled the ardor of the promoters. In the two and a half decades which followed 1904 other consolidations, of course, were to make their appearance, for the most part in the newer industries. But their chief concern was not to be the creation of monopoly pure and simple (though monopoly might exist incidentally through ownership of basic patents, as in the case of the Radio Corporation of America) as much as the perfection of economies arising out of large-scale operations. Certainly this does not mean that free competition was again triumphant after 1904: competition came to be controlled by other means.

As in the case of railroad regulation, a popular demand arose for the formulation of a governmental program aimed at monopoly. Beginning with the late eighties, the activities of these large industrial combinations became subjects of general attention and concern, and statesmen were

[1] See below, page 250.

called upon to devise plans for curbing the new menace. The popular magazines were filled with alarming tales of plots and stratagems that were designed to strangle competition, ruin the producers of raw materials, and levy exorbitant prices on the unprotected consumers—all for the purpose of the enrichment of the few. The new sensational press, using the cartoon with telling effect, made the names of a small group of individuals household synonyms for all that was selfish and depraved. Indeed, there was not a little justification for this, for the conduct of some of these earlier trust promoters and organizers could not have been better designed to arouse hostility.

Thus, public insistence goaded lawmakers into action. Western and southern states, controlled by farmer legislators, passed antitrust laws that were more hopeful than effective. Other states held investigations. In 1888, for example, the New York State senate created a commission for the purpose of investigating the trusts flourishing in the state. Out of the hearings arose the prosecution, the same year, of one of the members of the Sugar Trust with the eventual revocation of the company's charter. In 1888, too, the House Committee on Manufactures undertook an inquiry into some of the outstanding monopolies. It looked into the operations of the Standard Oil Trust, the Sugar Refineries Company, the Cottonseed Oil Trust, the Whiskey Trust, and the Beef Trust; it summoned witnesses and examined books; and it met with failing memories and an ignorance of essential detail which did credit to the highly skilled lawyers who had coached their clients. The upshot was the collection of a mass of interesting data and the presentation of a number of bills in Congress that died in committees. Be it said, legislators themselves were hardly in agreement. Should legislation check all consolidations? When did a trust lose its beneficent qualities and begin to assume threatening proportions? What rule of thumb could be created for measuring degrees of good and evil, and how were the bad trusts to be banned forever? These were indeed vexing questions to which no answers could be found despite the brave fronts assumed by statesmen when discussing the "trust problem." So, Senator Sherman could say in 1890:

> They had monopolies and mortmains of old, but never before such giants as in our day. You must heed their appeal [of the American people] or be ready for the socialist, the communist, the nihilist. Society is now disturbed by forces never felt before. Congress alone can deal with the trusts, and if we are unwilling or unable there will soon be a trust for every production and a master to fix the price for every necessity of life.

THE STANDARD OIL COMPANY

Of the trusts or consolidations, which Americans spoke of in the eighties or nineties, none was calculated to arouse more alarms or point more morals than the Standard Oil Trust. Here, better than anywhere else, was an example of the effects of concentration in a great industry. The Standard Oil Company had entered a highly competitive field and in a comparatively short time it was able to dominate oil. How was it done? Hostile commentators, Henry D. Lloyd the first among them, saw a black record of unfair trade methods, of railroad rebating, of bribery and blackmail, of an alliance between business and politics by which legislators, officials, and judges found it convenient to shut their eyes to or to condone practices that manifestly violated the law. On the other side it was argued that Standard Oil had brought order into a highly chaotic industry and through its competent management had succeeded in introducing efficiencies, lowering prices, and creating a great industry. There could be no doubt, however, that Standard's methods were ruthless and illegal and that none of them would be countenanced today.

The discovery of oil in western Pennsylvania in the late fifties turned the attention of ingenious minds to a new means of attaining wealth. It was soon found that the petroleum obtained from the wells could yield an excellent illuminant, which was better and cheaper than the whale oil heretofore used. There were important by-products, too—those of paraffin, naphtha, vaseline, and lubricating oils, for which commercial markets soon were developed. There was money not only in the production of oil but in its refining and transporting, and each of the three branches of the industry quickly collected its hosts of entrepreneurs and exploiters. The oil was produced for the most part in Venango County, Pennsylvania. Beginning with the early sixties, pipes were laid down for the conveying of the crude oil from the wells to the railroads. The pipes were used for the short journeys, the railroads for the longer hauls. Refineries sprang up not only in the well region but near the chief marketing centers, particularly at Pittsburgh, Philadelphia, Cleveland, New York, Brooklyn, Baltimore, and Boston. Because each of the processes involved (except railroading, of course) was comparatively simple and the units of capital required were not necessarily very large, competition had free rein and the prices of crude and refined oil fluctuated wildly. The entry of John D. Rockefeller on the scene, in the early sixties, resolved order out of the prevailing chaos.

Rockefeller had been born in 1839 at Richford, New York, and at the age of nineteen was already engaged in business for himself in the city of Cleveland. At the age of twenty-three, that is to say in 1862, Rockefeller quit the produce commission business and went into oil, a natural enough procedure, for Cleveland was already at that early date one of the great oil-refining centers of the country. Rockefeller was perhaps a little more successful than other refiners—undoubtedly he was keener in making rebating arrangements with the railroads (though it was a common enough practice)—for in 1870 there was chartered the Standard Oil Company of

Ohio with a capitalization of $1 million. The competitive character of the business may be seen from the fact that in Cleveland alone, in 1870, there were at least twenty-six companies refining oil.

Entering the oil district and spreading out fan-like into the large refining centers were the three great rail systems of the Pennsylvania, the New York Central, and the Erie. Serving the same territories as they did, it was inevitable that a fierce competition should ensue among them, which led to rebates to large shippers and very often to rates so low that carrying oil was unprofitable for the roads. Agreements among the roads had been made only to be broken: the roads would be glad to pay for the hire of some person or group that could assure all of them a fair share of the carriage of oil with reasonable profits. Thus the stage was set for the entry of the South Improvement Company, a Pennsylvania corporation with an ambiguously worded charter, formed in 1870. The South Improvement Company's shares were owned by oil refiners in Cleveland, Pittsburgh, and Philadelphia. The largest individual block of stock was held by John D. Rockefeller and his brother.

Early in 1872, the South Improvement Company's directors divulged their purposes to the managers of the three railroads. They would act as an "evener" among the lines, that is to say, apportion the oil traffic among them, for the following considerations: the South Improvement Company was to get preferential rates or rebates on its own shipments; the South Improvement Company was to receive daily duplicates of the waybills of shipments made by competing refineries; on all oil shipped by other refineries the South Improvement Company was to receive a "drawback" or a portion of the freight rates paid, averaging 50 per cent of the rates for the carriage of crude oil and 25 per cent of the rates for the carriage of refined oil; the railroads were to agree to raise or depress rates on the request of the South Improvement Company. The Erie, the Pennsylvania, and the New York Central all signed such agreements. The South Improvement Company, be it said, never actually functioned. The terms of the agreement were bruited about and indignation was so intense that the railroads were forced to repudiate their contracts; too, the Pennsylvania legislature the same month (March, 1872) withdrew the charter of the organization.

Yet the purpose of the company had been admirably achieved nonetheless. The Standard Oil Company, as well as the other members of the plot in Philadelphia and Pittsburgh, had forced their local competitors to sell out under threat of bankruptcy. In such negotiations, the agreement of the South Improvement Company with the railroads was hinted at, if not actually shown. The result was that Standard Oil, in 1872, acquired the properties of twenty of the twenty-six refineries in Cleveland and was controlling one-fifth of the refining capacity of the country. Two years later, the Standard was owning great plants in Philadelphia, Pittsburgh, New York, and Brooklyn. In 1875, the Standard was capitalized at $3,500,000; three years later it had possession of 90 per cent of all the refineries in the land. But we must look again at transportation, for in its control of the carriage of oil, rather than of its production or refining, is to be found the secret of the Standard Oil monopoly.

Early in the seventies, the Standard began to buy into the local pipe lines that fed the railroads; by 1874, it had possession of the largest of these companies. The Pennsylvania Railroad, realizing that the pipe lines were the key to the situation, sought to stave off monopoly by setting up a competitor, the Empire Transportation Company. Against this, the Standard waged war with all the weapons in its possession and with such success that in 1877 the Pennsylvania capitulated and sold out to the Rockefellers. The same year, so firmly was the Standard intrenched in the field, it individually assumed the chief role that had been designed for the South Improvement Company. It became the "evener" for all the leading railroads in the oil regions and with the rebates it thus secured was able to compel the capitulation of the few great independents who still held out.

Danger still threatened in one other quarter, that is to say, from the owners of the oil wells. These sought to keep clear of the Standard net by piping their own oil, and in 1879, for this purpose, there was organized the Tidewater Pipe Company. Against this the Standard aligned all its forces, using, too, the rails in alliance with it, so that in 1881 the Tidewater gave up the unequal struggle and became a Standard subsidiary. Early in the eighties, the Standard took the final step necessary to make its possession of the field secure. It cut off its dependence upon the rails for long hauls by building pipe-line trunks from the wells to its refineries in Cleveland, Buffalo, Pittsburgh, Philadelphia, and even into New York Harbor. From this time on Standard's history was merely a matter of expansion through the opening of new refineries and the extension of its pipe-line systems. The Standard Oil Trust, as we have seen, was organized in 1879 and reorganized in 1882. In 1899, the Standard followed in the footsteps of the other great consolidations when it took out a New Jersey charter for its subsidiary, the Standard Oil Company of New Jersey. The old New Jersey company had been capitalized at $10 million; the new one, which was the holding company for all of the Standard subsidiaries, was capitalized at $110 million. A brief thirty years before, Rockefeller had launched the first Standard Oil Company in Ohio at a capitalization of $1 million.

The nature and the development of the Standard Oil monopoly will help explain the dread with which its activities were regarded by producers of oil and consumers of oil products alike. The Standard did not trouble to control the wells. Here ruinous competition was permitted to take its course, so that the Standard was able to dictate the price at which it would buy on the basis of the supply then on the market. In 1895, the oil exchanges were discontinued, the Standard price being accepted as the market price. By 1904, the newly established federal Bureau of Corporations' investigation divulged, the Standard was taking 84.2 per cent of all the crude oil being produced in the country. The Standard controlled 40,000 miles of pipe lines as against 550 miles owned by its only rival. Competition with the Standard was impossible because independent refiners were compelled to pay Standard prices for piping the oil. Standard produced, in its great group of refineries scattered all over the country, 90 per cent of the country's refined oil.

The Standard was making its monopoly secure, according to the Bureau of Corporations, in the following ways: It was still negotiating secret rebates from railroads, this despite the injunction against the practice in the Interstate Commerce Act of 1887. It had different sets of prices for different sections of the country, charging whatever it pleased where there was no competition and ruining competitors in other places by price wars. It sold its wares abroad for lower prices than it charged at home. It kept informed as to the activities of competitors by a well-designed system of espionage, having in its pay railroad employees and dishonest officials of competing plants. Despite its vaunted claims of economies and the effective use of by-products, the margin between cost price and sales price mounted. Thus, in 1898, this margin was 5.3 cents; in 1903, it was 7.1 cents. Its profits were so extraordinary that the contemplation of them dizzied the imagination. During the twenty-four years 1882 to 1906, for example, the Standard Oil Company declared profits of more than $500 million, or an average of something like $22 million a year. Of course, a good part of this went back into plant, helping to account for the extraordinary growth of the company. Of the great store of wealth that represented the accumulated properties and distributed earnings of the Standard Oil Company, John D. Rockefeller held title to more than one-fourth.

As a result of the Bureau of Corporations' disclosures in 1906, the federal prosecution of the Standard Oil Company of New Jersey was commenced. The case was fought for five years and finally the Supreme Court, in a unanimous decision handed down on May 15, 1911, found that the Standard Oil was violating the Sherman Antitrust Law and ordered a dissolution into its many component corporations. But the same group of persons who had managed the destinies of the New Jersey holding company continued to hold the reins over the separate units. For a while, at any rate, for by the nineteen twenties some of the Standard Oil companies were in active competition with one another.

Against the ingenuity, the towering ambition, and the fierce hunt for profits which went into the making of such monopolies as Standard Oil the statesmen of the nation sought to match their wits when, in 1890, they sat down to write the Sherman Antitrust Law. Time was soon to disclose how ineffectual that measure was.

THE COMMON LAW AND STATE ACTION

It was known, of course, to lawyers that in the common law, through the centuries, there had been formulated a set of rules applying to restraints of trade. Under the common law, agreements or contracts designed to restrain trade were void and unenforceable; though the courts had come to look with tolerance upon restraints which were calculated to protect "the legitimate interests" of the parties involved and which were "not specifically injurious to the public." [2] It may be noted however that contracts incorporating restraints of trade, when brought into court, were merely held invalid; the makers could not be indicted nor could victims enlist the aid of the law officers on the ground that injuries had been suffered. There was another difficulty: the federal government as such had no common law, with the result that restraints committed in interstate and international commerce could not be passed upon by federal courts.

In order to overcome these various deficiencies, the state legislatures and Congress were called upon for the enactment of new legislation. From 1889 to 1893 a group of states, almost entirely in the South and West and hence under Populist influences, passed measures designed to outlaw restraints of trade or monopolies, specifying what were illegal practices, and also placing penalties on the participants in such agreements. In these statutes the following illegal practices, usually, were specified: price fixing; the prevention of competition in manufacturing or selling; agreeing to restrict the output of products; the bribing of employees of competitors; the making of contracts with distributors by which they were compelled to agree not to handle the products of competing manufacturers, etc. The first such antitrust law was passed in Kansas in 1889; fifteen other states and territories joined Kansas in the next four years. In time, all states carried such legislation on their statute books.

However well-meaning the state laws were, it soon became apparent that they could not cope with monopolies engaged in interstate commerce: this was the peculiar field of action of the federal authorities alone.

THE WRITING OF THE SHERMAN ANTITRUST LAW

In January, 1888, the first Congressional resolution calling attention to the problem of trusts and combinations was introduced in the House.

[2] A Michigan decision handed down in 1873.

Others followed fast on its heels. The House bills and resolutions sought to define trusts, to check the operations of trusts, to punish persons engaged in making trusts, to prevent trusts, and to investigate certain of the larger monopolies. Reagan of Texas, who had been so prominently identified with railroad legislation, introduced a bill in the Senate on the trust problem, in August, 1888. Meanwhile, both parties in their Presidential platforms had made explicit declarations against monopoly and pledged their support to Congressional legislation for relief. Congress, however, did not act until December, 1889. In that month Senator Sherman introduced an antitrust measure, which was sent to the Senate Committee on Finance. The Committee reported out Sherman's bill, but the first debate on it, in February, indicated a general belief in its unconstitutionality. The bill was then recommitted and a substitute was written by the Committee members. The ensuing discussion, late in March, showed unanimous agreement among the Senators on the necessity for regulation, though there was no clear understanding manifested as to how regulation was to be achieved. A motion was again carried for recommitting, this time the Finance Committee substitute and all the other measures being sent to the Committee on Judiciary.[3] Between March 27 and April 2, 1890, the Judiciary Committee wrote the Sherman Antitrust Law as it was finally enacted.

The Sherman Law was devised neither by Sherman, after whom it was named, nor by Senator Hoar, who claimed authorship, but by the Judiciary Committee. Edmunds of Vermont, its chairman, wrote most of the Act, being responsible for Sections 1, 2, 3, 5, and 6. Senator George of Mississippi wrote Section 4; Senator Hoar of Massachusetts wrote Section 7; while Senator Ingalls of Kansas wrote Section 8. The Senate debated the bill on April 8, voted down all amendments and passed it as it stood by a vote of 52 yeas and 1 nay. The bill met with some difficulty in the House, which insisted upon adopting an amendment, introduced by Bland, designed to outlaw every contract whose purpose was to prevent competition in goods entering into interstate commerce. Upon the Senate's refusal, however, to accept the amendment, the House finally yielded and on June 20 the Senate Judiciary Committee bill was passed in its original form without a dissenting vote. President Harrison signed the measure on July 2, 1890, and the bill became law.

The eight sections of the Sherman Antitrust Law contained the following provisions: 1. "Every contract, combination in the form of trust or other-

[3] Among the measures sent to the Committee on Judiciary was a proviso introduced by Senator Sherman excluding labor and farmers' organizations from the terms of the Act. Sherman's proviso was not included in the final draft of the act, largely because the Senators felt that it was unnecessary. Yet as soon as the Antitrust Law was on the statute books, it was invoked against labor, and with great success. The Debs case, for example, has already been commented on above.

wise, or conspiracy, in restraint of trade or commerce among the several states, or with foreign nations, is... illegal." 2. Persons monopolizing or combining or conspiring to monopolize any part of the trade or commerce among the several states, or with foreign nations, shall be deemed guilty of a misdemeanor and punished by fine or imprisonment. 3. Every contract in the form of a trust or otherwise, or conspiracy in restraint of trade or commerce among territories and states or territories and foreign nations is illegal. 4. The federal circuit courts are invested with jurisdiction, the federal district attorneys are empowered to institute proceedings in equity to restrain violations. 5. The court may include other persons than those specifically enjoined under authority of Section 4. 6. Any property owned under a contract involved in a conspiracy in restraint of trade may be seized and condemned by the federal authorities. 7. A person injured by a company in restraint of trade may sue in the federal courts for three times the damage sustained by him, together with costs and attorneys' fees. 8. The word "person" shall be construed to include "corporations."

THE ENFORCEMENT OF THE LAW

It is hard to do other than assume the good faith of the Congress that wrote the Sherman Antitrust Law. Popular sentiment was so hostile toward the activities of the trusts, or monopolies, and demands for relief were so widespread that Senators and Representatives, if they valued their political futures, were compelled to give ear to the complaints of their constituencies. If the law was not worded specifically enough it remained to be seen what inadequacies the courts would point out. In other words, responsibility for the Sherman Law's enforcement rested squarely with the federal law officers and, in the final analysis, upon the zeal the Presidents would display in directing the work of their subordinates.

One cannot avoid the conclusion that the Presidents from Harrison through McKinley were strangely remiss. An examination of the Presidential messages reveals that Harrison did not mention the Sherman Law once, nor did the annual reports of his Attorney-General. Cleveland did not bring up the subject until his final message to Congress in December, 1896. Cleveland's first Attorney-General, Olney, made some passing comments on the law, but it remained for his successor, Judson Harmon, to give it more than casual attention. In a letter sent to Congress in February, 1896, Harmon outlined a series of amendments that, he hoped, would make the law more effective. Nothing came of the suggestions. Cleveland's attitude is to be noted particularly. In the message to Congress spoken of, Cleveland expressed himself as being skeptical of the effectiveness of the Sherman Law and insisted that in his belief only the states could cope with the problems presented by trusts and monopolies. McKinley, like Cleveland, was silent for the greater part of his administration, despite the fact that the period of his Presidency coincided with the greatest era of trust or holding-company expansion. McKinley's message to Congress, in December, 1899, was a request that the terms of the Sherman Law be extended in view of the failure of the states to cope with the situation. In his message of December, 1900, he repeated the same wish.

What was the record of the federal law officers? In the first eleven years that the law was on the statute books, that is to say, during the Harrison, Cleveland, and McKinley administrations, a total of 40 cases was passed on by the courts. Of these, but 18 were brought by federal district attorneys; another 18 were brought by private individuals; while 4 were defended by private parties being sued for damages. Of the 18 brought by private parties, only 2 were successful; while of the 4 damage suits, the courts vindicated the defendants in 3 of the actions. With regard to the 18 cases prosecuted by the United States, it is interesting to note that 10 were successful while 8 were not. The failure of the Sherman Antitrust Law is demonstrated by the nature of the defendants haled before the federal courts by the Department of Justice. Against the Sugar Trust, the Whiskey Trust, and the Cash Register Trust—the only large monopolies attacked—the Department of Justice could meet with no success, largely because of the inexpert tactics of the prosecuting attorneys. But on 4 labor unions, 3 local associations of coal operators or dealers, 2 railroad associations, and 1 cast-iron pipe pool, the federal district attorneys descended with vigor and success. Against this record of timidity, there are to be placed the prosecutions in the seven and a half years of Theodore Roosevelt's administrations when the Department of Justice obtained 18 bills in equity, 25 indictments, and 1 forfeiture proceeding.

As a final commentary on the period that ended with the death of McKinley, the record of the twenty-one months, December, 1899, to September, 1901, may be of interest. On December 5, 1899, McKinley addressed Congress for the first time on the subject of trusts and monopolies. Said the message: "Combinations of capital organized into trusts to control the conditions of trade among our citizens, to stifle competition, limit production, and determine the prices of products used and consumed by the people, are justly provoking public discussion and should early claim the attention of Congress." The day before, the Supreme Court had handed down a clear-cut decision, in the Addyston Pipe Case,[4] which, one might have supposed, would have given McKinley's Department of Justice heart to continue the great struggle. The President looked with disapproval on the deportment of the trusts; the Supreme Court had moved against one of them, even if it was only a small pool. Yet, with everybody in agreement, McKinley's Department of Justice in the twenty-one months

[4] See below, page 251.

between the President's Congressional message and his death, did not initiate a single prosecution under the Sherman Law!

The conduct of the Supreme Court was less equivocal. In 1895, that tribunal was called upon to pass for the first time on the legality of the Sherman Law in the case of U. S. v. E. C. Knight Company.[5] The American Sugar Refining Company, a New Jersey corporation, in the course of its building up a monopoly of refined sugar, had purchased all the stock of the E. C. Knight Company, as well as the properties of three other Philadelphia sugar refining companies. Evidence was submitted to show that the Sugar Trust had already obtained control of more than 95 per cent of the production of refined sugar in the country. But the heart of the Attorney-General's case did not rest in the practices of the consolidation; he contented himself with arguing that the *purchase* of the four Philadelphia companies was enough to indicate that an illegal restraint on interstate commerce existed. On the basis of such a presentation the majority opinion of the Court was compelled to declare that the Sherman Law had not been violated. On the major point at issue, Chief Justice Fuller wrote: "The contracts and acts of the defendants related exclusively to the acquisition of the Philadelphia refineries and the business of sugar refining in Pennsylvania, and bore no direct relation to commerce between the States or with foreign nations." Harlan, in a dissenting opinion, strove manfully to point out the bearing of the law in the case of the Sugar Trust, but in view of the fact that the Attorney-General did not prove conspiracy or a monopoly functioning to restrain trade among the states, the dissent had to limit itself to generalities.

However, in two decisions handed down in 1897 and 1898, the Supreme Court ruled not only that the Sherman Law applied to railroads but also that both "reasonable" and "unreasonable" contracts in restraint of trade were illegal. In the Trans-Missouri Freight Association case (1897)[6] the Court in its majority opinion made the significant declaration that "the language of the Act included every contract, combination in the form of trust or otherwise, or conspiracy in restraint of trade or commerce...." Further the Court said:

In other words, we are asked to read into the Act by way of judicial legislation an exception that is not placed there by the lawmaking branch of the government, and this is to be done upon the theory that the impolicy of such legislation is so clear that it cannot be supposed Congress intended the natural import of the language it used. This we cannot and ought not to do.... It may be that the policy evidenced by the passage of the Act itself will, if carried out, result in disaster to the roads.... Whether that will be the result or not we do not know and cannot predict. These considerations are, however, not for us. If the Act

[5] 156 U.S. 1.
[6] 166 U.S. 290.

ought to read as contended for by the defendants, Congress is the body to amend it, and not this Court by a process of judicial legislation wholly unjustifiable.

The decision was a five-to-four one, and the minority filed a vigorous dissent.[7] In 1898, in the Joint Traffic Association case,[8] the Court boldly defended the stand taken in the Trans-Missouri decision, but it denied that most business contracts in one way or another restrained trade. In the Addyston Pipe Company case (1899),[9] which involved a pool of all the cast-iron pipe manufacturers in the country created for the purpose of division of territory and hence the elimination of competition, the Court ruled that the pool agreement was concerned with the buying and selling of pipe across state lines and therefore was interstate commerce. The decision against the pool was a unanimous one; it plainly indicated a desire on the part of the Supreme Court to aid the government in the formulation of a positive program in the interest of better business methods.

Thus, by 1899, the Knight decision was, to all intents and purposes, reversed and the Department of Justice had a clear mandate to proceed against contracts or conspiracies in restraint of trade, whether it was proved that they were "reasonable" or "unreasonable." We have seen how the law officers failed to seize the opportunity and permitted the Sherman Law to lapse into desuetude. In 1903, at the insistence of Roosevelt, the federal authorities were furnished with a weapon necessary to the preparation of proper cases against monopolies, that is to say, through the creation of the Bureau of Corporations. The history of the trust prosecutions of the ten years that followed showed that the Sherman Antitrust Law could be invoked to obtain favorable verdicts against corporations operating in restraint of trade. Whether the dissolution orders which were handed down were really effective, or, indeed, whether monopolies could not be handled more successfully by rigorous governmental supervision, were questions that were not often asked. Government and the public, apparently, came to be satisfied with the physical break-up of large consolidations. At times, it almost appeared that the size of the trusts, alone, had been the factor that had occasioned so much alarm in the three decades from 1880 to 1910.

[7] In 1911, White, who had been one of the dissenters in 1897, as Chief Justice of the Court converted the earlier minority opinion into the opinion of the majority. In the later year, in the Standard Oil and American Tobacco cases, the Court differentiated between reasonable and unreasonable contracts or conspiracies and declared the Court's right to the exercise of its judgment in each individual case.
[8] 171 U.S. 505.
[9] 175 U.S. 211.

· 16 ·

The Agrarian Revolt: Greenbackism, Populism, the Election of 1896

WHAT POPULISM IMPLIED

WE shall understand the Greenback movement and Populism if we see them almost entirely as the political phases of the agrarian discontent of the late seventies, late eighties, and early nineties. While the Greenback party received its original impulse from a labor group, and while labor representatives and a small band of Chicago radicals figured in the early councils of the People's party, both movements were inspired by the grievances of the farmers of the nation; too, their political captains were from the very beginning the spokesmen of the agricultural interests of the West and South. In short, both Greenbackism and Populism were essentially the expressions of revolt of a propertied interest. It was inevitable, therefore, that Populism should yield to the blandishments of Bryan (discussed below) and his simplified program of relief rather than follow the sterner admonitions of the spokesmen of labor, who had their misgivings about free silver as the cure-all for a complicated economic disorder. But the threat of the Greenback party and more particularly that of Populism were none the less real. Granted that the programs advanced did not strike at the whole system of industrial capitalistic domination as did the revisionist socialism of the labor radicals; nevertheless, the success of Populism would have marked a revolution in political institutions almost as unsettling, as far as the future of industrialism in America was concerned.

The Populists sought a reorientation of government in the interests of agriculture that would have implied: the end of laissez-faire and protective tariffs; governmental ownership of railroads and telegraphs; stringent governmental control of the nation's natural resources; and certainly the operation of the financial system for the greater benefit of the farming class. A real Populist victory would have meant the wiping out of the gains the industrialists and money interests had obtained by the destruction of the Southern aristocracy in the Civil War. Populism was not radicalism, certainly, in our contemporary sense; nevertheless it was a revolt against the industrial masters of the nation. It has another significance too often overlooked. Populism represented the last united stand of the country's agricultural interest; it was the final attempt made by the farmers of the land to beat back an industrial civilization whose forces had all but vanquished them already. The farmers of the West and South put forth their mightiest efforts—but they lost, and with the defeat of Populism went the submergence of the American agrarian order. From 1896 on, there was none to stand in the way of the steady forward march of American industrial enterprise. That agrarianism which had so closely contested control of the country with the men of the towns and the cities—the agrarianism of Jefferson, Jackson, and Calhoun—and which had had its triumphs in 1800, 1828, and in the fifties, had run its course and was now done. The comparative well-being of the farmers during 1900 to 1919 was merely one of those brief rallies by which moribund men and institutions often deceive their sympathetic friends: the wretched tale of the decade of the nineteen twenties proved how complete the collapse of agriculture really was. And in the nineteen thirties only an elaborate program of government subsidy was able to maintain the nation's producers of agricultural staples. Because Populism, therefore, represents the final great political effort of the American farmers, its story is one of unusual importance in the history of the United States.

THE GREENBACK MOVEMENT

The federal government's financial policy in the late sixties, particularly the limitation on the volume of greenback circulation and the guarantee of the payment of the war bonds in coin (by the Act of March, 1869), accounted for the appearance of Greenbackism in politics. Mention has already been made of the "Ohio Idea" (for the redemption of the war bonds in paper), which got into the Democratic party platform of 1868. But the espousal of Greenbackism by the Democratic party and the fact that the Democratic host saw nothing strange in choosing for its standard-bearer in 1868 Governor Seymour, who was a "hard" money man, scarcely pleased the radicals. Consequently, the National Labor Union decided to organize an independent party with a program calling for the abolition of the national banks, "a true national currency," and repudiation of the government's funding program.[1] Taking the name of National Labor Reform party, this group in 1872 tendered its nomination for the Presidency to Supreme Court Justice David Davis of Illinois. Davis refused the honor, though he expressed himself as being in sympathy with the movement, with the result that Charles O'Conor, a New York lawyer, headed the ticket in the Presidential election. O'Conor received fewer than 30,000

---

[1] See above, page 189.

votes, and the laborites, disheartened by their inability to shake the public out of its indifference, turned to other interests.

Greenbackism, however, was too real an issue to be dropped. In November, 1874, another group, this time made up largely of agrarians, met at Indianapolis to create another national independent party. A second meeting was assembled in March, 1875, and a third met in May, 1876, to promulgate a platform and nominate candidates for the forthcoming elections. Calling itself the Independent National party, the convention named as its standard-bearers the philanthropist Peter Cooper of New York and S. F. Cary of Ohio (the original begetter of the "Ohio Idea"). The platform was almost entirely concerned with financial matters. It called for the repeal of the Specie Resumption Act of 1875; demanded that the government issue legal tender notes which could be converted on demand into bonds bearing a low rate of interest; insisted that the national bank notes be suppressed; and proposed that the government be stopped from issuing gold bonds for sale in foreign markets. But the excitement of the Democratic-Republican canvass and the ineffectiveness of the Greenback nominee produced disappointing results. Cooper polled only 81,700 votes: their distribution showed that the Greenback sentiment prevailed largely in Illinois, Indiana, Iowa, Kansas, Michigan, and Missouri.

The hard-fought strikes of 1877 and the continued economic depression gave these dissentients heart to continue the uphill struggle, with the result that a meeting in 1878, held at Toledo, attracted some eight hundred delegates. At this gathering the National Labor Reform party was formally absorbed and the new name "Greenback Labor" was adopted. The platform divided its concern between labor and financial demands, though the latter received the larger share of attention. The financial planks were: the national bank notes were to be suppressed; the circulating medium was to be a government issue exclusively and was to be full legal tender for all debts and taxes; government bonds were to be paid in legal tender; the coinage of silver was to be placed on a parity with that of gold; there was to be an adequate supply of money; government bonds were to be taxed; an income tax was called for; public lands were to be reserved for actual settlers. In the Congressional and state elections of that year Greenback candidates polled fully 1,000,000 votes. In California, Georgia, Illinois, Indiana, Maine, Ohio, New York, Pennsylvania, and throughout the Middle West farmers and workingmen flocked to the polls to vote the Greenback ticket. In rock-ribbed, conservative Maine, the Greenback candidate for Governor received 41,400 votes as against the successful Republican candidate's total of 56,500. In all, fourteen Greenback candidates were sent to Congress, and they joined with the Democratic majority to stop the further contraction in the volume of greenbacks.

In 1880, the Greenback strength was manifested by the assemblage of eight hundred delegates at its Chicago convention: except for some Socialist Labor party onlookers, the gathering was largely agrarian in its make-up. General J. B. Weaver, who was nominated for the Presidency, despite a spirited campaign polled only 308,500 votes, almost 200,000 of which were cast in the upper Mississippi Valley with 60,000 coming from the southern states. The workingmen had turned to the Knights of Labor in the interim, and their defection accounted for the slight support received by the ticket.

By 1884, interest had largely waned. General Benjamin F. Butler, who had been elected governor of Massachusetts by the Greenbackers and Democrats in 1882, accepted the nomination of the Antimonopoly party and, when he could not obtain the Democratic nomination, consented, too, to carry the Greenback banner. He received but 175,400 votes. In 1888, Greenbackism again had to accept a secondary role. Labor once more made a temporary appearance in politics with the formation of the Union Labor party, and with this group the Greenbackers combined. The Union Labor party went to the ranks of labor for its candidate and nominated A. J. Streeter of Illinois for the Presidency. Its platform was much wider in scope than the customary program of the Greenback demands; in fact, it was the immediate precursor of the Populist manifestoes. It opposed land monopoly, the importation of contract labor and the reopening of free Chinese immigration; it advocated government ownership of railroads and telegraphs, called for a graduated income tax, and promised direct election of United States Senators and woman suffrage. But labor could not be aroused; the Union Labor party drew its strength largely from the Greenback country. Streeter polled 144,800 votes, about two-thirds of which came from the West and Northwest and one-third from the South and Southwest. The vote in the industrial states was negligible. The Greenback agitation disappeared from the political scene with this rather sorry failure, though some of its leaders were to crop up again in the Populist camp.

POPULISM

Though the efforts of the third-party politicians to get the farmers to the polls met with small success, interest in agrarian, and particularly financial, reform grew more and more intense with each passing year. The Grange had collapsed by the early eighties, but before the same decade was over there had emerged, in its place, a group of powerful farmers' organizations in the South and West. The Agricultural Wheel appeared in Arkansas; the Texas State Alliance was formed in the Southwest; the Farmers' Union sprang up in Louisiana. In the South and Southwest, these farmers' organizations soon fused their energies under the banner of the

National Farmers' Alliance and Industrial Union (known popularly as the Southern Alliance) and by 1890 they were claiming a membership of three million persons. In the Northwest, the National Farmers' Alliance (known as the Northwestern Alliance) came into being with a fighting program which pledged its membership to combat "the encroachments of concentrated capital and the tyranny of monopoly; ... to oppose, in our respective political parties, the election of any candidate to office ... who is not thoroughly in sympathy with the farmers' interests."

In St. Louis, in December, 1889, the Southern Alliance met in annual convention. There gathered in this city, at the same time, representatives from the Northwestern Alliance, the National Colored Farmers' Alliance, the Farmers' Mutual Benefit Association, as well as delegates from the Knights of Labor. These organizations assembled to transact their business as farmers' mutual organizations.[2] There was some talk, it is true, of amalgamating the Southern and Northwestern Alliances, but nothing came of the suggestion because the Southern Alliance refused to surrender the ritual and paraphernalia it was operating under as a secret society, and it declined to admit Negro farmers on terms of equality. However, a set of resolutions was adopted by the Southern Alliance in which the Northwestern Alliance concurred. These called for: the free coinage of silver; the abolition of national banks; plenty of money; government ownership of railroads and telegraph; ownership of lands by Americans only; prohibition of trading in grain futures; the limitation of the revenues of states and nation to legitimate expenses (a veiled attack on the tariff). A separate resolution, passed by the Southern Alliance only, advocated the adoption of the famous subtreasury plan which hinted, in effect, at government subsidy for agriculture.

The subtreasury plan was the work of C. W. Macune, the editor of the *National Economist,* the leading Alliance paper. It was a scheme for financing agricultural marketing and for extending short-term rural credits with government funds. Under it, the federal government was to establish in every county that offered for sale each year more than one-half million dollars' worth of farm products, a subtreasury office and a warehouse or elevator. To this warehouse, the farmer might bring his "nonperishable" products—grain, tobacco, cotton, sugar, or wool—and for them obtain a certificate of deposit. Upon presentation of his certificate to the subtreasury office, the farmer would then be entitled to a loan in legal tender notes up to 80 per cent of the market price of the products stored. The certificates of deposit were negotiable and anybody holding them might receive a loan in

---

[2] By the end of the eighties, the Knights of Labor was to find its chief strength not in the great industrial centers but in the smaller communities of the country. Hence its interest in agrarian matters. The Knights participated in all those early discussions that finally ended with the formal creation of the People's party.

legal tenders, or the merchandise stored in the warehouses. Finally, all products were to be removed within a year; if not, the custodians were to sell them at public auction.

This plan was deemed by many a sound and plausible device for using government for the aid of agriculture just as government was being employed to help banks, railroads, and even private business enterprise. The plan, too, was founded on a system of commodity credit as against specie credit. It was largely designed, as well, to furnish the sorely needed easy credit for farm marketing operations. That it saddled the government with the business of marketing farm surpluses was the chief weakness of the program. It is interesting to note that a somewhat similar scheme of price support for farm commodities was the basis of the New Deal's agricultural program of the nineteen thirties.

Thus the subtreasury plan as an economic device was intended to set up a commodity basis for credit; to remove the dependence upon gold for the fixing of prices; to free the farmers from having to rely on the banks for their short-term credit needs; to make possible the marketing of the crops over the year and thus prevent glut; and to use the governmental Treasury surpluses for farm credit.

It will be observed that this first farmers' platform did not advocate concerted political action. Nevertheless, in 1890, the farmers were at the polls. In Kansas, they were enrolled definitely under the standard of what was called the People's party. In Nebraska, the farmers' party bore the name of People's Independent party. In South Dakota, the rubric employed was the Independent party. In these very states, the fires of revolt were first lighted by the aroused farmers. During the decade after 1887, the Great Plains were parched by drought and swept by hot dry winds that robbed the soil of the little moisture it had. A few bare figures reveal the tragedy that engulfed the farmers on the plains in those dark days: In 1885, the Kansas corn crop totaled 158,390,000 bushels; in 1887, the total was 76,547,000 bushels; in 1890, it was 55,269,000 bushels. One finds little cause for wonder that the farmers organized. The People's party was formally launched in Kansas in June, 1890.

One must go back to medieval Europe, on the eve of the First Crusade, for an emotional situation comparable to that in which Kansans moved. Every conceivable gathering place—the schoolhouses, the churches, the rural town halls, open squares, and meadows—was regularly thronged with great crowds which came to listen, sing, shout, and cheer on the local leaders who had sprung up almost miraculously. Mary E. Lease, Anna L. Diggs, S. N. Wood, Jerry Simpson, W. A. Peffer—these were the local prophets whose fame gradually began to seep out of Kansas into the East, to fill the breasts of the urban middle classes with wonder, and at times alarm. Mrs. Lease's famous utterance: "What you farmers need to do is raise less corn and more Hell!" seemed a portent. For though we may describe the ferment that was Kansas in terms of revivalism, and though we may smile at Jerry Simpson who was reputed to go sockless and at the recollection of the incredible whiskers of Peffer, we must appreciate how modern the vocabulary that Kansas employed really was. Kansas talked of the railroads, the trusts, national banks, mortgages, usury, credit. There was money scarcity, interest rates were high, taxes were exorbitant, prices were low, the railroads, the middlemen, the protected interests were parasitically living off the farmer! In 1890, Kansas marched to the polls and elected five Populist Congressmen, a majority in the lower house of the state legislature, and retired United States Senator J. J. Ingalls to a long-merited obscurity. Editor Peffer with his whiskers, his broad-brimmed hat, and his heavy boots, went to Washington to sit in the Senate with Hill of New York, Quay of Pennsylvania, and Hoar of Massachusetts.

Everywhere, in the South and West, candidates under pledge to the Alliances were sent to Congress and the local legislatures. In South Carolina, farmers' representatives swept the state, electing Tillman governor and sending a Senator and a majority of the state's Congressmen to Washington. In Georgia, the Farmers' Alliance chose the governor, elected a majority of the members of the state legislature and won six out of the state's ten Congressional districts. In Virginia, North Carolina, Mississippi, Kentucky, and Missouri, at least twenty-five of the Congressmen elected on the Democratic tickets were definitely pledged to Alliance policies. In South Dakota the Independent Party sent the Rev. J. H. Kyle to the United States Senate. In the West, in all, eight Congressmen were elected who called themselves Populists or Independents.

The second significant convention of the Farmers' Alliance was held at Ocala, Florida, in December, 1890. It was principally a gathering of Southern Alliance men, but there came here, too, representatives from the Colored Alliance, the Farmers' Mutual Benefit Association, the Citizens' Alliance, and the Knights of Labor. The laborites advocated the creation of a new national third party; but the Southern Alliance men were reluctant. They had captured the southern Democracy in at least two states, were powerful in party councils in several others, and the Negro presented a problem they did not wish to cope with just yet. This meeting, then, adopted another platform almost in every particular resembling the earlier St. Louis document. It called for the free coinage of silver; the abolition of the national banks; plenty of money; ownership of land by Americans only; prohibition of trading in grain futures; the limitation of the revenues of the states and nation to legitimate expenses. These changes from the earlier platform are to be noted: 1. The subtreasury plan was written into the main platform and its operation was extended to include loans or mortgages on real estate. (In other words, the farmers were now looking to the government for long-term loans as well as short-term credits.); 2. Tariff revision was demanded; 3. Government control of railroads and telegraph was substituted for government ownership.

It was at a third meeting, held in May, 1891, in Cincinnati, that the farmers definitely decided to form a national party. This convention was made up largely of men from the Northwestern Alliance; of the fourteen hundred delegates present, Kansas, Nebraska, Ohio, Illinois, and Missouri furnished three-fourths. It is to be noted that the southern men still hesitated to take the final step, and for this reason southern representation at the Cincinnati meeting was slight. A resolution was passed stating that the "time has come for the crystallization of the political reform forces of our country, and the foundation of what should be known as the People's party of the United States of America." The platform adopted resembled in almost every particular the economic demands embodied in the Ocala program, with some additions designed to catch labor and liberal votes. These were an 8-hour day, universal suffrage, and the election of the President, Vice-President, and Senators by direct vote.

It is significant to point out how aware these western and southern farmers were of the economic forces that oppressed them. Thus, in July, 1891, the *National Economist* (which was to become the organ of the new movement) said:

> In every campaign since 1872 the tariff has been the leading issue to the exclusion of all others. During the past twenty years the people have grown poorer —their burden of indebtedness has grown larger.... In Kansas last fall [1890] the Republicans started out on a campaign of tariff and bloody shirt. As a result the people refused to attend their meetings and flocked by the thousands to listen to Alliance and Independent speakers discuss the living questions of financial and other reforms.... Suppose a strong third party should take the field ... and suppose they should ignore entirely the question of the tariff and discuss finance, land, transportation, and other live questions.... The Alliance believes in and demands a reduction of the tariff on the necessities ... but it will not, neither can it, be driven to consider that question as more than subordinate to a number of others.... The Alliance is determined to have finance, land, and transportation discussed and settled in preference to all other economic questions.

This certainly was not political immaturity but a wisdom that might well have given the East cause for reflection.

The fourth meeting of the embattled farmers saw the formal launching of the People's party. At St. Louis, on February 22, 1892, there met some 860 persons, delegates from every agricultural order in the country, as well as representatives from several labor and trade union groups, and a number of spokesmen for the western intellectuals. There were here at St. Louis all the leaders of the farmers of the West and South: Senator Peffer of Kansas, Senator Kyle of South Dakota, Jerry Simpson of Kansas,

General J. B. Weaver of Iowa, H. E. Taubeneck of Illinois, Ignatius Donnelly of Minnesota, Robert Schilling of Wisconsin, Thomas E. Watson of Georgia, and the "big five" of the Southern Alliance—Polk, Macune, Livingston, Tillman, and Terrill. For the Southern Alliance had yielded to persuasion and was now committed to the cause.

Ignatius Donnelly, that curious product of the American frontier of the Northwest, wrote the preamble to a platform that fired the imagination of the South and West. It had that combination of flamboyancy and sense which exactly hit off the temper of the times, for the farmers of the nation were embarking on an economic crusade. The opening paragraphs of Donnelly's preamble read:

> The conditions which surround us best justify our co-operation. We meet in the midst of a nation brought to the verge of moral, political, and material ruin. Corruption dominates the ballot box, the legislature, the Congress, and touches even the ermine of the bench. The people are demoralized; most of the states have been compelled to isolate the voters at the polling places to prevent universal intimidation or bribery. The newspapers are largely subsidized and muzzled; public opinion silenced; business prostrated; our homes covered with mortgages; labor impoverished; and the land concentrating in the hands of the capitalists. The urban workmen are denied the right of organization for self-protection; imported pauperized labor beats down their wages; a hireling standing army, unrecognized by our laws, is established to shoot them down, and they are rapidly degenerating into European conditions. The fruits of the toil of millions are boldly stolen to build up colossal fortunes for a few, unprecedented in the history of mankind; and the possessors of these, in turn, despise the government, and endanger liberty. From the same prolific womb of governmental injustice, we breed the two great classes of tramps and millionaires.
>
> The national power to create money is appropriated to enrich bondholders; a vast public debt, payable in legal tender currency, has been funded into gold-bearing bonds, thereby adding millions to the burdens of the people. Silver, which has been accepted as coin since the dawn of history, has been demonetized to add to the purchasing power of gold by decreasing the value of all forms of property as well as human labor; and the supply of currency is purposely abridged to fatten usurers, bankrupt enterprise, and enslave industry. A vast conspiracy against mankind has been organized on two continents; and it is rapidly taking possession of the world. If not met and overthrown at once, it forebodes terrible social convulsions, the destruction of civilization, or the establishment of an absolute despotism.

The planks of the platform that the assembled delegates adopted resembled the earlier Southern Alliance documents in every significant particular. The following changes are to be noted: government ownership of railroads and telegraph was again demanded; postal banks were to be established; the plank calling for the abolition of the national banks was dropped. A call was sent out for the meeting of a nominating convention to be held at Omaha on July 2, 1892.

On July fourth, at Omaha, the new People's party broadcast its program to the world. The Omaha platform, the first formal Populist document, reads like a brief text in agricultural economics. Its chief planks were three: financial reform, government ownership of railroads and telegraph, and the elimination of corporate and foreign ownership in land. The financial was the first and the most comprehensive. It will be noted how completely it covers the outstanding grievances of the agrarian interests.

We demand—
First, Finance. A national currency, safe, sound and flexible, issued by the general government only; a full legal tender for all debts, public and private, and that, without the use of banking corporations; a just, equitable, and efficient means of distribution direct to the people, at a tax not to exceed two per cent per annum, to be provided as set forth in the subtreasury plan of the Farmers' Alliance, or a better system; also, by payments in discharge of its obligations for public improvements.
(a) We demand free and unlimited coinage of silver and gold at the present legal ratio of 16 to 1.
(b) We demand that the amount of circulating medium be speedily increased to not less than $50 per capita.
(c) We demand a graduated income tax.
(d) We believe that the money of the country should be kept as much as possible in the hands of the people, and hence we demand that all state and national revenues shall be limited to the necessary expenses of the government economically and honestly administered.
(e) We demand that postal savings banks be established by the government for the safe deposit of the earnings of the people and to facilitate exchange.
Second, Transportation. Transportation being a means of exchange and a public necessity, the government should own and operate the railroads in the interests of the people.
(a) The telegraph and the telephone, like the post-office system, being a necessity for the transmission of news, should be owned and operated by the government in the interest of the people.
Third, Land. The land, including all natural sources of wealth, is the heritage of the people, and should not be monopolized for speculative purposes, and alien ownership of land should be prohibited. All land now held by railroads and other corporations in excess of their actual needs, and all lands now owned by aliens, should be reclaimed by the government and held for actual settlers only.

Free silver was thus but one, and a minor one, too, of the proposed solutions of the Populist platform-makers for the obsolete credit system then in operation. It is important, also, to note that the free-silver formula had not yet gripped the rank and file in the Populist army. Writing in 1896, before Bryan had worked his magic on the Populist host, F. L. McVey,[3] who was not a friendly observer, declared that "even in the silver states the leaders of this movement were not able to control the Populist party. The presence of the silver faction had obscured the real purpose of the party...."

[3] In American Economic Association, *Economic Studies,* Vol. 1., No. 3 (1896).

Thus on the standard of the new farmers' party were inscribed three economic demands: namely, financial relief, government ownership of railroads, and land reform. An additional set of resolutions, not written as such into the main platform, sought to enlist the support of a wider following. These planks included: pensions for war veterans; the restriction of undesirable immigration; the rigid enforcement of the 8-hour law for governmental employees; the abolition of private detective agencies (this had reference to the use that had been made of the Pinkertons in the Homestead strike); a Constitutional amendment providing for a single term for the President and for popular election of Senators; and recommendation to the states that they adopt the initiative and referendum and the Australian ballot.

Upon the refusal of Judge Walter Q. Gresham to accept the Populist nomination for the Presidency, General Weaver was named as the head of the ticket with General James G. Field of Virginia (a Confederate soldier) as his running mate. The results of the election of 1892 were phenomenal, when it is considered that this was the first national appearance of the People's party. Weaver polled 1,041,600 votes and received 22 votes in the electoral college. The Populists carried Colorado, Idaho, Kansas, and Nevada, and elected single electors in the states of North Dakota and Oregon. In the South, the Populists openly split with the reigning white man's party, that is to say, the Democracy. In the state of Louisiana, there was fusion between the Populists and the Republicans; in Georgia and Alabama, the Populists would have won had the election been confined to the whites. In these two states, the Bourbon Democracy marched the Negroes to the polls to vote for Democratic electors and the Democratic state tickets. In South Carolina, while the Tillman machine ostensibly functioned under the standard of the Democratic party, it was Populist in spirit and openly condemned Cleveland, speaking of his candidacy "as a prostitution of the principles of Democracy, as a repudiation of the demands of the Farmers' Alliance, which embody the true principles of Democracy, and a surrender of the rights of the people to the financial kings of the country." In Kansas, the Populists elected their whole state ticket, as well as 25 state senators and 58 representatives to the lower house of the legislature. A total of 10 Congressmen, 5 Senators, 50 state officials, and 1500 county officers and state legislators was the Populist harvest in the Presidential year 1892.

The off-year elections of 1894 repeated this triumph. Cleveland was definitely repudiated by the Democracy of the South; the continued agrarian distress only strengthened the faith of the western farmers; hard times and labor unrest—these had their political repercussions in the heavy votes Populist candidates received in the industrial districts. In South Carolina, for example, a Tillman Democrat was elected governor of the state and Tillman himself was sent to the Senate to drive another thorn into the side of the long-suffering Cleveland. A fusion of Populists and Republicans in North Carolina resulted in the election of an anti-Democratic legislature and the choice of one Populist and one Republican for the posts of United States Senators. In Texas, a Republican-Populist fusion elected two Congressmen. In Alabama, a similar alliance resulted in the election of a Populist Congressman. In all, the Populist vote totaled 1,471,600, which was a gain of 42 per cent over that of 1892. The total of elected Populist Congressmen, that is to say, of those who accepted that designation, was seven. Six Populist Senators were elected: one each came from Kansas, Nebraska, North Carolina and South Dakota, and Nevada sent two. Henry Demarest Lloyd, one of the wisest men of his generation, was so impressed by the soundness of the Populist program that he consented to run for Congress, on the Populist ticket, in one of the Chicago districts. Lloyd proclaimed the movement as "one of those pacific revolutions which this free government was created to encourage, and make as frequent as possible." And he adopted as the slogan for his campaign the following: "People's transportation ... people's money ... people's land ... people's wealth ... and people's co-operation."

The East, on the other hand, regarded the Populist uprising with mingled emotions, in which amusement struggled with something very akin to dread. The Populist leaders were savagely caricatured; unpleasant sobriquets were fastened on them (Jerry Simpson, for example, was the "Sockless Socrates of Kansas"); they were called socialists, communists, and anarchists. McVey, in the article spoken of, tried to show the scholarly world that there was not a ha'penny-worth of difference between the Populist program and the creed of Marxian socialists. On the heads of Kansans descended a large part of the obloquy and the *New York Evening Post* gave respectable businessmen of the North and East something to shake their heads approvingly over when it said: "We don't want any more states until we can civilize Kansas."

Meanwhile, the Populist leaders confidently laid their plans for the Presidential year 1896. State committees and local clubs were organized; lecturers went up and down the land; and, as a final preparation for the victory that was within arm's reach, the Populist National Committee fixed the date of the party's nominating convention to follow those of the Republicans and Democrats. They were sure that the "gold bugs" would win the day on the floors of the conventions of the two older parties. Inevitably, therefore, the malcontents and the rebels, the Silverites, the land reformers, the friends of labor, would flock to the banner of the People's party to repeat the victory of the young Republican party in the election of 1860. The sanguine already could read the early histories of the two political movements in parallel columns.

THE BATTLE OF 1896: THE GATHERING FORCES

Thanks to the thoroughness with which Mark Hanna, the Cleveland capitalist, had done his work, the Republican delegates, when they assembled in convention at St. Louis on June 16, 1896, found their platform and candidate already prepared for them. The Republican party was going to carry aloft the banner of the gold standard; and its proposed nominee was openly committed to the cause of "sound" money. On the acceptance of the money plank itself, Hanna was to meet with considerable opposition. The Republican party pledge, when it finally emerged from the convention's resolutions committee, read as follows:

The Republican party is unreservedly for sound money. It caused the enactment of a law providing for the resumption of specie payments in 1879. Since then, every dollar has been as good as gold. We are unalterably opposed to every measure calculated to debase our currency or impair the credit of our country. We are therefore opposed to the free coinage of silver, except by international agreement with the leading commercial nations of the earth, which agreement we pledge ourselves to promote; and until such agreement can be obtained, the existing *gold* [4] standard must be maintained. All of our silver and paper currency must be maintained at parity with gold, and we favor all measures designed to maintain inviolably the obligations of the United States, and all our money, whether coin or gold, at the present standard, the standard of the most enlightened nations of the earth.

In addition, the Republican platform pledged the party to the protective tariff and reciprocity; pensions for Civil War veterans; the employment of our good offices in Cuba "to restore peace and give independence to the island"; "a firm, vigorous, and dignified" foreign policy; American control of the Hawaiian Islands; the purchase of the Danish West Indies; enlargement of the Navy; a literacy test for immigrants; a national board of arbitration to settle labor disputes in interstate commerce. Silver Republicans made an effort to change the money plank, and when they were unsuccessful thirty-four western delegates, headed by Senator Teller of Colorado, withdrew from the convention.

For its standard-bearer, the Republican convention, on the first ballot, nominated Hanna's friend and protégé, Governor William McKinley of Ohio. Garret A. Hobart of New Jersey was named for the Vice-Presidency; Hanna himself was selected chairman of the Republican National Committee.

Hanna and McKinley make a curious constellation in America's political annals. They were joined, apparently, by mutual feelings of sympathy, understanding, and admiration. It almost seemed that their characters complemented each other: the politician was simple-mannered and amiable; the businessman was arrogant, self-possessed, and a firm believer

[4] Italicized in the text of the platform.

in his own destiny. Hanna's adult life had been exactly like that of hundreds of captains of industry in whose company he moved. He had started out as a dealer in coal and iron; and he had ended by owning iron and coal mines, railroads, a shipbuilding company, a newspaper, a bank, a street traction company, and an opera house. He had, finally, become the director of the destinies of the Republican party in Ohio. In his person there was exemplified that union between politics and industrial capitalism that had become the prevailing characteristic of American public life.

Ever interested in rising young politicians, Hanna had been early attracted to William McKinley: here was real Presidential timber. There could be no question of McKinley's "availability" as a candidate. Born in Ohio, of Scotch-Irish stock, of middle-class antecedents, a devout Methodist, a loyal husband whose wife was a chronic invalid, impeccable in person, a good neighbor, with simple tastes and no pretensions to learning or profundity: William McKinley was indeed the typical American citizen. He had served in the Civil War as a staff officer and had been mustered out a major. He had studied law, and like Cleveland had held a series of petty local offices. In 1876, he had been elected to Congress, where he had sat continuously, except for two years, until 1890. In 1880, he had been appointed to the House Ways and Means Committee, and from that time, he had made the tariff the field of his particular interest. As chairman of the Ways and Means Committee, he had become associated with the Tariff Act of 1890, and the writing of that measure by his committee had broadcast his name up and down the land as the friend of protectionism. In that same year, too, he had gone down to defeat in his contest for re-election to Congress. But Hanna had stood by his friend; the result was that McKinley was elected governor of Ohio in 1891 and again in 1893. The gubernatorial career of McKinley was not entirely a happy one. He had indorsed the notes of an acquaintance who had failed him, and was confronted by ruin when Hanna made up a purse large enough to pay off all of McKinley's debts. Ill-natured persons regarded it as a strange coincidence that the governor should steadfastly oppose all legislative attempts at the regulation of public utilities corporations, particularly in view of the fact that Hanna was one of the outstanding magnates in this field in the state.

This affair was not nearly so unsettling as McKinley's flirtation with the free-silver cause. Coming from Ohio, the original home of the money controversy, McKinley had been compelled to make a choice, and being a young politician, had chosen inflation. He had, therefore, voted for the Bland-Allison Act in 1878 and had again voted with the majority to override the Presidential veto. In the Congress of 1890 he had been one of the champions of the original free-silver bill; and from time to time, he had made a number of public statements that had definitely identified him with the silver "heresy." But from 1890 on, he had become more circumspect, first turning international bimetallist and then accepting wholeheartedly Hanna's prescription of the gold standard as the cure for the nation's monetary ills. McKinley was fifty-three years old when chosen as the candidate of the Republican party.

On the eve of the assembling of the Democratic convention, all was uncertainty and disorder. The party was not only leaderless, but divided by bitter strife. In state convention after convention, Democrats had turned against Cleveland, and despite the power of the Presidential patronage had passed resolutions favoring the free and unlimited coinage of silver. Thirty states in all had joined to swell the list; but one state, Florida, had not committed herself on the money issue; and in only fourteen (all but three of which were eastern states) had Cleveland received vindication at the hands of his own party. As the throngs began pouring into Chicago, preparatory to the opening of the proceedings on July 7, it was apparent that the silver men would leave no stone unturned in their efforts to convert the Democracy into a free-silver party. The fact is, they met with two early successes, which showed at once they were the masters of the situation. They picked their own temporary chairman, disregarding the candidate chosen by the Democratic National Committee; and they voted to unseat the Nebraska gold delegation and give their places to the challenging silver men. Former Congressman William Jennings Bryan was among the latter.

The final triumph of the silver faction came in the writing of the party platform in the resolutions committee. The majority report met the currency issue foursquare. The money plank read:

We are unalterably opposed to monometallism, which has locked fast the prosperity of an industrial people in the paralysis of hard times. Gold monometallism is a British policy, and its adoption has brought other nations into financial servitude to London.... We demand the free and unlimited coinage of both silver and gold at the present legal ratio of sixteen to one without waiting for the aid or consent of any other nation.

This declaration came first on the platform; on it the Democracy was prepared to stand or fall. Repudiation of Cleveland went further. Other planks pledged the party to opposition to the further issuance of interest-bearing bonds in times of peace and to the emission of bank notes by the national banks. The Democratic party renewed its loyalty to tariffs for revenue only. It attacked the Supreme Court for its decision against the income tax law and hinted at a reconstitution of the Court in the event of victory. It called for the enlargement of the powers of the Interstate Commerce Commission. It flayed the President, by indirection, for sending troops to Chicago and it inveighed against "government by injunction."

It opposed life tenure in the public service; it favored pensions for Civil War veterans; it extended the sympathy of the Democracy to the Cuban people "in their heroic struggle for liberty and independence."

The minority of the committee on resolutions submitted a report, too. Its resolutions were but two in number: the first condemned the adoption of bimetallism by the United States alone; the second praised the work of the Cleveland administration. Six men participated in the debate on the majority and minority reports of the committee on resolutions. The international bimetallists and foes of free silver were represented by Hill of New York, Vilas of Wisconsin, and Russell of Massachusetts; the Silverites by Tillman of South Carolina, Jones of Arkansas, and Bryan of Nebraska. On the night of July 9, the young Bryan rose to close the debate on the party's proposed platform: before he had finished, the assembled host knew that the Democracy had at last found its leader.

Was there any wonder that words such as these thrilled the listening men and women and were echoed up and down the land?

> We say to you that you have made the definition of a businessman too limited in its application. The man who is employed for wages is as much a businessman as his employer. The attorney in a country town is as much a businessman as the corporation counsel in a great metropolis. The merchant at the crossroads store is as much a businessman as the merchant of New York. The farmer who goes forth in the morning and toils all day—who begins in the spring and toils all summer—and who, by the application of brain and muscle to the natural resources of the country, creates wealth, is as much a businessman as the man who goes upon the board of trade and bets upon the price of wheat.

And again:

> You come to us and tell us that the great cities are in favor of the gold standard. We reply that the great cities rest upon our broad and fertile prairies. Burn down your cities and leave our farms, and your cities will spring up again as if by magic; but destroy our farms, and the grass will grow in the streets of every city in the country.

And finally, that stirring peroration:

> Therefore, we care not upon what lines the battle is fought.... If they dare to come out into the open field and defend the gold standard as a good thing, we will fight them to the uttermost. Having behind us the producing masses of this nation and the world, the laboring interests, and the toilers everywhere, we will answer their demand for a gold standard by saying to them: You shall not press down upon the brow of labor this crown of thorns—you shall not crucify mankind upon a cross of gold!

The results of the proceedings, thenceforth, were in little doubt. The minority resolutions were defeated; the platform was adopted; and on the fifth ballot Bryan was acclaimed as the choice of the Democratic party. The convention made a slight gesture of conciliation toward the East by nominating for the Vice-Presidency Arthur M. Sewall of Maine, a banker and shipbuilder but a free-silver advocate nevertheless.

Bryan was but thirty-six when he was called upon to carry the Democratic standard. He had been born in Salem, Illinois, had been graduated from a local college, and had studied law at Chicago. He had practiced for four years in an Illinois village, had married, and then, in 1887, had moved to Lincoln, Nebraska. Politics soon engaged his attention: first because he was a ready speaker, and second because the emoluments of the law were too slender to support a growing family. Entering the political lists in 1890 to contest a strong Republican Congressional district, he gathered sufficient farmer support to be successful and went to Washington for two terms. He was at once placed on the important Ways and Means Committee, and as a result of careful study was able to make a forceful antiprotectionist speech. He added further to his reputation by the excellent address he delivered in 1893 against the repeal of the Sherman Silver Purchase Act.

The hostility that the young Congressman had displayed toward his party chief's financial program made administration support, for his re-election, unlikely. He did succeed in getting his party's nomination to the United States Senate, but the Nebraska legislature that was elected had a Republican majority and Bryan was retired to private life. But not to the law; and not to obscurity. In September, 1894, at the modest salary of $30 a week, Bryan became the chief editorial writer of the *Omaha World-Herald,* a free-silver organ. Throughout 1895 and the first half of 1896, the tall, black-haired, charming, and magnetic Bryan was up and down the Mississippi country and in and out of the deep South. He spoke at Democratic clubs, before state conventions, at county fairs, in schoolhouses, to lodges and farmers' gatherings. He renewed old acquaintances, sought out Congressional associates and made himself known to the delegates to the coming national convention. Agricultural distress was his theme in general; of the virtues of free silver, he spoke in particular. When the Democracy assembled in July, 1896, he was widely known and his Presidential aspirations were no secret.

This was the Bryan who went in August to New York City—"the enemy's country"—to receive the formal notification of his nomination; Abraham Lincoln, in the year of Bryan's birth, had made a similar journey.

When the People's party assembled at St. Louis on July 22, there was nothing left for it but to indorse the Bryan candidacy and accept the free-silver issue as the paramount one of the forthcoming contest. It is true that the Populist platform echoed, to an extent, the earlier Omaha declaration of 1892. It was divided, again, into three major sections: namely, finance, transportation, and land. Supplemental resolutions advocated the adoption of the initiative and referendum; the popular election of Senators;

the employment of idle labor on public works in times of depression; the halting of "government by injunction"; pensions for disabled soldiers; the recognition of Cuban independence. But the subtreasury plan, the very heart of the Populist agitation for governmental aid to agriculture, was dropped.

The threatened submergence of what had promised, only a year before, to be a significant political movement caused uneasiness among many of the delegates. A group of the irreconcilables made an effort at the preservation of independence by insisting that balloting for the Vice-Presidential nominee take place first. Bryan they would take if necessary; but Sewall, the banker and employer of labor, was too much. A crumb of comfort was thrown to the radicals in the naming of Tom Watson of Georgia for the Vice-Presidency.

That Populism had drained the poisoned cup was plain to a number of farsighted individuals. The leaders of radicalism saw in the espousal of the free-silver doctrine the beginning of the end. Thus, Henry Demarest Lloyd, who had labored hard to prevent the endorsement of Bryan, wrote in October, 1896:

> The People's party convention at St. Louis was the most discouraging experience of my life. It was not so much that the leaders tricked and bulldozed and betrayed, but that the people submitted. The craze for success "this time" had full possession of them. . . . The free-silver movement is a fake. Free silver is the cowbird of the reform movement. It waited until the nest had been built by the sacrifices and labors of others, and then it laid its eggs in it, pushing out the others which lie smashed on the ground.

In some of the southern states, the irreconcilables refused to surrender and set up independent tickets under the Populist insignia. In twenty-six states, however, Populists and Democrats combined, dividing the Presidential electors between them. Other groups to participate in the election were the Prohibitionists, the Socialist Labor party, the National Silver party, and the National Democratic party. The National Silver party, meeting at St. Louis on July 22, endorsed the Bryan and Sewall candidacies. The National Democratic party, made up of gold men and Cleveland followers, met in convention at Indianapolis on September 2 and nominated its own candidates. The Silver Republicans did not secede but Senator Teller, their leader, issued an address in which he advised them to support the Bryan electors.

THE BATTLE OF 1896: THE CAMPAIGN

Never had there been such a three months in American political annals as August, September, and October, 1896. Everything seemed to be pitched in a high key of emotionalism. People used hot, angry phrases in their speech; newspaper artists made vicious drawings which were meant to hurt; slander, contumely, and vituperation were frequently on men's tongues as customary amenities were forgotten. Theodore Roosevelt was reported as saying that the silver men might well "be stood up against the wall and shot." The otherwise imperturbable John Hay, writing to Henry Adams in London, could say of Bryan: "The Boy Orator makes only one speech—but he makes it twice a day. There is no fun in it. He simply reiterates the unquestionable truths that every man who has a clean shirt is a thief and should be hanged, and there is no goodness or wisdom except among the illiterates and criminal classes..." Henry Watterson in his *Louisville Courier-Journal* declared: "Mr. William Bryan has come to Kentucky and Kentuckians have taken his measure. He is a Boy Orator. He is a dishonest dodger. He is a daring adventurer. He is a political faker."

What had occasioned this alarm? In unerring flight, Bryan's shaft had struck at the heart of a democracy's strength—and its weakness. By simplifying a complex series of causes, by dramatizing a conflict into the age-old struggle between the powers of good and evil, by personalizing the enemy so that he could be seen, felt, and reviled—by such methods Bryan aroused a whole people and made every man and woman in the nation a bitter partisan.

To call the campaign of 1896 a process in mass education, as has so often been done, is palpably an absurdity. Homer Davenport's cartoon of Hanna, as a gross figure covered with dollar signs, had nothing to do with education. The ingenious little tract, which the Democrats circulated in extraordinary quantities, called *Coin's Financial School*, with its crude woodcuts of bloated plutocrats and starved sons of toil, and its pat arguments: this could be called education only by the most generous definition. Hanna's special train of aging Civil War heroes who toured the Middle West in a cloud of patriotic oratory—there was no education here. Everything that was done in the campaign was calculated to awaken passions, evoke fear, mobilize popular sentiment.

Bryan's deeds were cast in an heroic mold. Beginning in August and continuing until the last hours of the canvass, he carried on a brilliant, tireless, and aggressive campaign. He made some 600 speeches, he visited 29 states, he traveled in all some 18,000 miles. Under the stresses and strains of an effort that would have broken down three men, he was ever affable and courteous. Hanna's talents lay in another direction: he was the skilled organizer, the staff commander, the master of strategy. He established two headquarters, one at New York and one at Chicago, and he busied himself enlisting the support of every mighty industrial and financial group in the nation. Hanna declared later that he received, and nearly spent, three and a half million dollars for the expenses of the

POPULISM IN 1892

Weaver, the Populist candidate, received 22 electoral votes indicated by ④

Size of Populist vote by per cent of total

- 67-50
- 43-35
- 23-14
- 11-5
- Less than 5
- Territories

THE POPULISTIC DEMOCRACY IN 1896

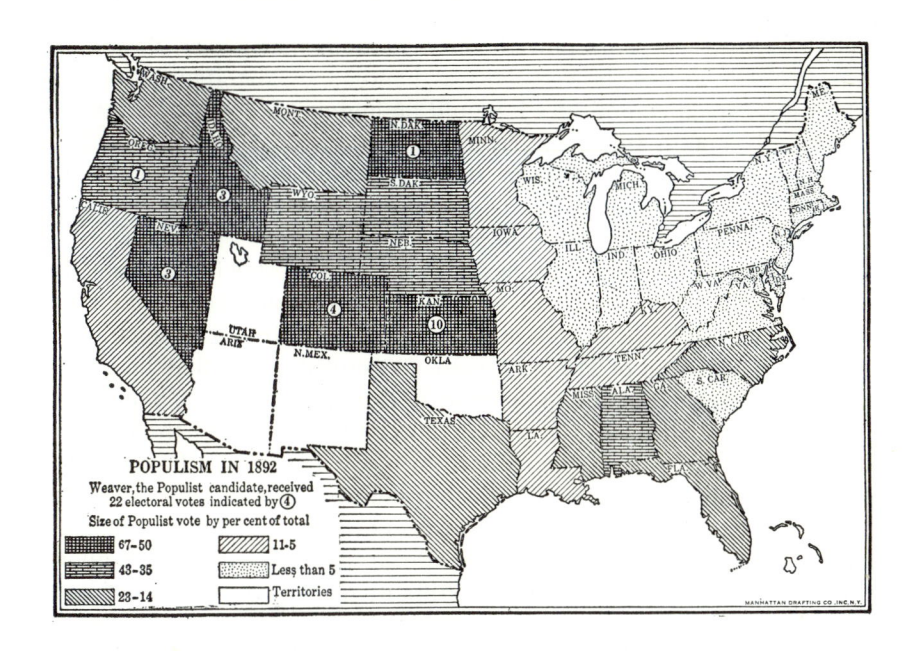

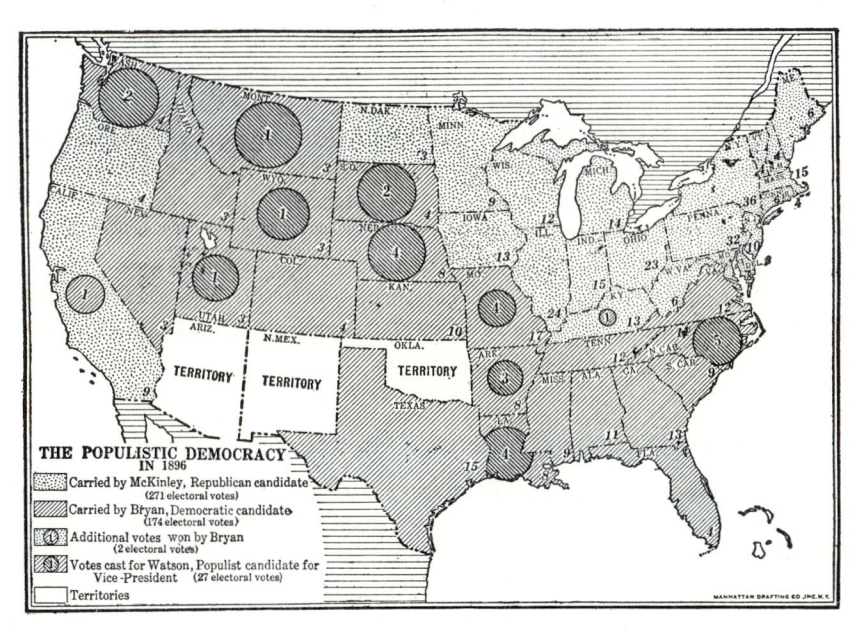

- Carried by McKinley, Republican candidate (271 electoral votes)
- Carried by Bryan, Democratic candidate (174 electoral votes)
- Additional votes won by Bryan (2 electoral votes)
- Votes cast for Watson, Populist candidate for Vice-President (27 electoral votes)
- Territories

POPULISM IN 1892 AND 1896

campaign. But these were only the contributions that passed through the national headquarters; how much was handled by the Republican state and Congressional committees it would be impossible to say. In any case, Hanna had enough funds to pay for the services of 1400 speakers; to subsidize country newspapers; to issue tons of leaflets; to hire bands; and to buy bunting, posters, brassards, and buttons for all the clubs, political hangers-on, and small boys of the nation.

Hanna had two other weapons in his armory. McKinley, instead of swinging around the circle, stayed at home and contented himself with delivering carefully prepared little addresses to visiting delegations of admirers. It was one of Hanna's great accomplishments that he did not expose his party's candidate to the gibes of hostile audiences. To diplomacy there was added terror. In the closing days of the campaign, the word was broadcast that Bryan's election would bring swift disaster. Farmers were informed that mortgages would not be renewed; workingmen were told that factory gates would be shut in the event of Bryan's election; businessmen, in placing orders for goods, made acceptance contingent upon a McKinley victory. These factors undoubtedly must have helped determine the final result.

The victory fell to Hanna and McKinley, and McKinley's majority in the electoral college was a decided one. He received 271 votes to Bryan's 176. Almost 14,000,000 popular votes were cast, fully 2,000,000 more than in 1892. McKinley received 7,107,000 votes; Bryan, 6,533,000. In Indiana, McKinley won by 18,000; in Ohio, by 48,500. In Kentucky, Delaware, West Virginia, North Dakota, and Oregon, McKinley's pluralities were even smaller. Bryan could not carry a single industrial commonwealth. In addition to the eleven states in the Solid South, he won the border state of Missouri, and the western states of Colorado, Idaho, Kansas, Montana, Nebraska, Nevada, South Dakota, Utah, Washington, and Wyoming. Also, he obtained single electoral votes in California and Kentucky. Nothing can reveal more plainly the sectional and economic lines upon which the battle of 1896 was fought.

AFTERMATH OF THE FREE-SILVER CONTROVERSY

The dire prophecies of the silver orators never came to pass. Somehow, the curtain of gloom which hung over the land lifted and before even the year 1896 was entirely over there were hints of a returning prosperity. We may indicate briefly some of the forces through whose operations the American farmer was converted from a flaming revolutionary into a staid husbandman.

There was a rise in the price of agricultural staples, due to the failure of the India wheat crop of 1896 and the shortness of the European wheat crop of 1897. Large-scale production in industry made possible the entry of more manufactured articles into the nation's foreign trade. Thus the strain upon gold, for the balancing of international payments, was relieved. The world's production of gold grew greatly. The opening of new mines in the Klondike and on the Rand (South Africa) and the invention of the cyanide process for extracting gold from low-content ores resulted in an extraordinary increase in the world's gold supply. In 1883, the world's gold production had been $95,400,000; by 1899, it was $306,700,000. The volume of money in circulation also grew. The banks were aided by the emission of new bond issues to finance the Spanish-American War and by the liberalization of the National Bank Act. Increases in immigration expanded the domestic population greatly, making for more mouths to feed. The acquisition of new territories, as a result of the war soon to come, created more markets for American manufactured goods and capital, thus aiding in the industrial revival.

The Currency Act of March 14, 1900, definitely ended all fears of further silver and other "cheap" money scares. The new law put the currency of the country on a gold standard; established a Treasury reserve fund of $150,000,000; and provided for the maintenance of this reserve by the sale of short-term bonds. The national banks were given the right to issue notes up to the par value of bonds deposited with the Treasury, instead of 90 per cent as was the case before. Finally, a concession was made to the rural districts in the further amendment of the National Bank Act to permit the organization of national banks, with a minimum capital of $25,000, in towns of 3000 or less.

Part Two

THE EMERGENCE OF IMPERIAL AMERICA

Section VI

EXPANSION OVERSEAS

· 17 ·

Republicanism Triumphant

THE McKINLEY ADMINISTRATION

NEVER was a Presidential administration ushered in more auspiciously than was McKinley's in March, 1897. Business was content, knowing that its interests would be safeguarded for at least four years; the farmers had suddenly dropped their zeal for politics and were back at their plows and threshers; the politicians looked forward to a long period of plenty. The Republican triumph could not have been more complete. For the first time in twenty years (except for the two years 1889 to 1891) the Republican party controlled all the branches of government, although in the Senate its majority was too slender to permit the passage of conservative financial legislation at once.

The Presidential appointments filled no breasts with alarm. The Cabinet was composed of elderly men, all but one being more than sixty years old. Senator John Sherman of Ohio, then seventy-four years old and a veteran in legislative matters, was given the State Department portfolio. It was commonly admitted, and none of the principals denied it, that Sherman had been "kicked upstairs" into the Cabinet to create a vacancy in the Senate for Mark Hanna to fill by gubernatorial appointment.[1] It was no secret that Sherman was ill-fitted, physically, to handle the arduous details of his office and it soon became apparent that even on matters of policy the decision lay with W. R. Day, his first assistant. In April, 1898, Sherman surrendered an honor that was only nominal and Day became Secretary of State in name as well as in fact.

Not many commentators took objection when the new President, in his inaugural address, declared that he regarded his election as a mandate for immediate tariff legislation. The President's phrasing took a peculiar turn: he was pleased to consider tariff reform as a revenue device through which the Treasury deficits of the last four years would be converted into

[1] In 1897, Hanna was formally elected by Ohioans for the short and long terms and he sat in the Senate until his death in 1904.

surpluses. The claim was plausible enough, on the surface, for the Treasury deficits of the Cleveland administration had indeed been serious. In 1893 to 1894, the deficit had been $68,800,000; in 1894 to 1895, $42,800,000; in 1895 to 1896, $25,200,000; and in 1896 to 1897, $18,000,000. That under the beneficent operations of the Dingley tariff the deficit during 1897 to 1898 would be $38,000,000, the President of course could not foresee.

Other factors made the primacy of the tariff question inevitable. The Republicans had pledged themselves to renew, by reciprocity treaties, their earlier efforts for the encouragement of foreign trade. Tariff revision had been promised to the business interests of the country. There was small likelihood of the enactment of currency legislation, in view of the make-up of the Senate. Steps already taken pointed to the early and successful passage of tariff legislation. The House, in the Fifty-fourth Congress of 1895 to 1897, was Republican, and Reed, the Speaker, and Nelson Dingley (also of Maine), the Chairman of the Ways and Means Committee, had spent much of their time whipping into shape a protective tariff bill that would be acceptable to party leaders and large business groups. In short, when McKinley spoke to the nation, it appeared to him that the new tariff law was all but ready for the Presidential signature. Congress was therefore called in special session on March 15, 1897.

After rather more than the usual amount of trading and log-rolling, the Dingley Act was passed in July by what was practically a strict party vote. Various concessions were made to western interests, the wool, hides, and lead schedules particularly being higher than ever before. Despite the President's original views to the contrary, as expressed in his inaugural, the Tariff Act of 1897 was concerned not with revenue but with protection. The fact is, in the first year of its operation, the duties collected on imports totaled but $149,500,000 as against the $176,500,000 collected under the Wilson Act during 1896 to 1897. The average of duties was between $49\frac{7}{8}$ per cent and 52 per cent ad valorem as against an average of $49\frac{1}{2}$ per cent in the act of 1890 and an average of 40 per cent to $41\frac{3}{4}$ per cent in the act of 1894. The chief features of the new law were the following: the reimposition of duties on wool and hides; higher duties on silks, linens, and chinaware; the restoration of the duties of 1890 on metals; a sugar schedule that was eminently satisfactory to the refiners; and an attempt at the fostering of reciprocity treaties for the purpose of stimulating American foreign trade. It is important to examine some of the schedules in greater detail.

The wool schedule was the heart of the new law. As a result of demands of Middle West woolgrowers, the high rates on combing and clothing wools, in the act of 1890, were restored; on carpet wool, the new rate was higher than any ever fixed before. Senators from Ohio, Michigan, and Pennsylvania clamored for protection for clothing and combing wools, in effect, against the competition of the cheaper lands of Wyoming, Montana, and Idaho; the Senators from the latter states, as an offset, asked for and obtained the higher rates on the carpet wools. And to compensate the woolen manufacturers, the rates on woolens were raised to duties averaging 55 per cent, being higher even than those in the schedule of 1890. The purchaser of clothing was thus compelled to suffer doubly: for the avarice of the woolgrowers, and again for the injured feelings of the woolen manufacturers.

The buyer of shoes paid, too, to appease the Far-Western Senators. For the first time since 1872, hides were taken from the free list and a duty of 15 per cent imposed. The metal schedules were unchanged, except in those cases where the Far-Western Senators brought pressure to bear to compel protection for local industries. Thus, the lead and lead ore duties of 1890 were restored. However, the rates of 1894 continued to operate in most cases. Pig iron was taxed at $4.00 a ton; iron ore at $0.40 a ton; steel rails at $7.84 a ton; coal at $0.67 a ton. Copper was on the free list; while duties on tin plate were but of a nominal character. But on finished steel products, there was a return to the duties of 1890. One may note that the iron and steel industry, the peculiar concern of earlier tariff makers, was no longer interested in protection and had made such giant strides since the eighties that already American steel masters were competing in world markets with those of Great Britain. Indeed, American steel rails, despite higher wage costs, were being sold on the London market in active competition with English rails.

The sugar schedule attracted the greatest public notice. The acts of 1890 and 1894 had paid particular attention to sugar; nay, their solicitude for the Sugar Trust and the "differentials" that had been granted to the refiners of sugar had been among the minor scandals of the nineties. The interests of sugar had been defended brazenly in the Senate, and that Senators had made private gains out of sugar speculation was everywhere regarded as a happy coincidence. The Act of 1894 had placed an ad valorem duty of 40 per cent on raw sugar; the Act of 1897 came to the matter more circumspectly, though the tax on the consumer ended by being very much the same. The duty on raw sugar was now 1.65 cents per pound for the usual grade (testing 95 per cent); on sugar testing 100 per cent, the duty was 1.83 cents a pound; on refined sugar, the duty was 1.95 cents a pound. There was thus a "differential," as it was called, of one-eighth of a cent a pound over and above raw sugar testing 100 per cent. To protect further the sugar industry from foreign competition, particularly the German beet sugar growers, the Secretary of the Treasury was ordered to place an additional duty on all imported sugar receiving the assistance of government bounties. It is to be noted that the sugar schedule was written in the interests of the Louisiana cane growers, the western beet growers, and, more particularly, the Sugar Trust or the American Sugar Refining Company, which controlled almost entirely the nation's business of sugar refining. The American sugar growers of Cuba and Hawaii were not provided for, it is true. But in a comparatively short while their troubles were over, for Hawaii was annexed in 1898 and Cuba received a preferential tariff rate as a result of the commercial treaty of 1903.

The tariff law of 1897, finally, gave particular attention to foreign trade and included three separate devices for the purpose of encouraging reciprocity: 1. The penalty sections of the new Act were somewhat comparable to those in the 1890 law. Tea, coffee, tonka beans, and vanilla beans were put on the free list: the President might suspend the free admission of these articles if the exporting countries in any way discriminated against American goods. Under this clause, treaties were written with Brazil, the Dominican Republic, Salvador, Nicaragua, Honduras, Guatemala, Spain (for Cuba and Puerto Rico), and Great Britain (for her island possessions in the West Indies). In these treaties American wares were treated very handsomely. Thus Brazil, in order to insure the free admission of her coffee here, placed American wheat, flour, pork, agricultural and mining machinery, coal, and railway materials, on her free list. To show that Washington meant business, penal duties were actually applied against Haiti, Venezuela, and Colombia. 2. The President was authorized, in return for concessions, to reduce by a definite amount duties on certain enumerated articles, namely, argols, brandies, wines, pictures, and statuary. Presidential proclamation was enough to announce the completion of the agreements, and during 1898 to 1908 a number of such were made: with France in 1898 and 1908, with Germany in 1900 and 1907, with Italy and Portugal in 1900, with Switzerland in 1906, with Spain in 1906, with Bulgaria in 1906, and with the Netherlands in 1908. 3. The President might make treaties (with the advice and consent of the Senate) looking toward reductions, up to 20 per cent, on all articles. Some eleven such treaties were negotiated by a special commissioner, but the Senate rejected them all. In conclusion, it may be said that these elaborate efforts to increase the American foreign trade by what Washington was pleased to call "reciprocity" effected very little, and our South American trade, which was the chief concern of statesmen, continued to be of small importance until after World War I.

Except for the sugar duties, the new tariff law elicited little public comment. The trust problem was a more pressing national concern; silver still loomed large in the minds of men; and soon, the clamor of the popular press over Cuba was to relegate every other public interest into the background. By the turn of the century American horizons had widened so markedly that President McKinley could declare, in his speech at Buffalo on September 5, 1901:

A system which provides a mutual exchange of commodities is manifestly essential to the continued healthful growth of our export trade. We must not repose in fancied security that we can forever sell everything and buy little or nothing.... Reciprocity is the natural growth of our wonderful industrial development under the domestic policy now firmly established. What we produce beyond our domestic consumption must have a vent abroad. The excess must be relieved through a foreign outlet and we should sell everything we can, and buy wherever the buying will enlarge our sales and productions, and thereby make a greater demand for home labor.

The period of exclusiveness is past. The expansion of our trade and commerce is the pressing problem.... Reciprocity treaties are in harmony with the spirit of the times; measures of retaliation are not. If, perchance, some of our tariffs are no longer needed for revenue, or to encourage and protect our industries at home, why should they not be employed to expand and promote our market abroad?

Between 1897 and 1901 many crowded events were to occur to make the complacent reception of such a remark possible. McKinley, who had been elected on a domestic issue of widest significance, one, indeed, that had threatened the stability of the new American industrial order, was destined to become a war President; and the United States, at the end of the century, was to emerge one of the great powers of the world with colonial possessions, an expanding foreign trade, and new problems. We must turn our attention to the island of Cuba, American concern over which brought all this about.

POLITICAL AND ECONOMIC INTERESTS IN CUBA

Cuba did not suddenly burst upon our eyes in the nineties: its proximity had been a cause for concern to American Presidents and Secretaries of State, on and off, since the beginning of the nineteenth century; while its opportunities for trade and capital exploitation had been appreciated by enterprising Americans, and, to a small extent, taken advantage of. The besetting fear of American statesmen was this: suppose Spain should lose Cuba and some mightier power, Great Britain, for example, should take possession of the island to dominate the Caribbean and menace the adjacent American shore? The maintenance of Spanish sovereignty, therefore, was the keynote of early American Cuban policy. Then, in the fifties, the emphasis changed, and acquisition of the island by purchase had the support of our State Department. President Buchanan, particularly, was the champion of such a policy, and Congress was considering the project with favor when the domestic situation diverted attention to more important matters. The outbreak of insurrection in the island, in 1868, brought another change in the American attitude.

The Ten-Years' War, from 1868 to 1878, kept the island in constant turmoil. Prosecution of the war cost Spain the lives of 80,000 soldiers and the expenditure of upwards of half a billion dollars. Diplomatic relations between the United States and Spain were often strained, the affair of the *Virginius* in 1873 (as we have seen) in particular threatening the peace. Finally, in 1878, after a war of attrition, hostilities were terminated, Spain promising a political amnesty, emancipation of the Negro slaves who had fought in the insurrection, and the carrying out of various governmental reforms. The leaders of the insurgents went into exile; some became American citizens and took up residence in the United States to continue agitation for Cuban independence.

American economic interests in Cuba in the seventies, eighties, and nineties made our concern over political stability of greater moment than the matter of sovereignty.[2] By the middle of the nineteenth century, American trade with Cuba was already more significant than the Cuban-Spanish commerce. Jenks records the fact, for example, that more than half of the vessels entering Cuban ports during the five years 1851 to 1855 flew the American flag. Up to the sixties, coffee was the chief agricultural staple of the island; then the change was made to sugar and tobacco, with the former the more important. Sugar planting was possible on a great scale because lands were cheap and still unexploited, because slavery furnished the needed labor supply, and because Great Britain and the United States provided the necessary market for the raw sugar. However, after the Civil War, with the development of the beet sugar industry in Central Europe, the United States became the chief market for Cuban sugar. Sugar figured so large in our foreign trade that in the eighties the sugar duty annually brought $50 million into the American Treasury. On the other hand, Cuban interests purchased from us flour, lard, lumber, furniture, and particularly implements and machinery for grinding the cane. By the late eighties, the freighters of six American lines were making regular calls at the ports of the island. American merchants at New York and Boston financed the Cuban sugar planters, playing the same role that the pre-Civil War cotton factors had done in the planting of southern cotton. These merchants financed the crop, extended credit for the purchase of provisions and machinery, and took up the raw sugar when it reached New York and Boston. So profitable was this trade that the most prominent American sugar factor, Moses Taylor of New York, left an estate of $40 million when he died in 1882. Taylor became the president of the City Bank in 1855; it is perhaps, therefore, more than a coincidence that the National City Bank in the nineteen twenties should have become the most important single element in Cuban sugar.

A series of economic events brought the Cuban situation once more to a head in the nineties and made the second revolution of 1895 inevitable. The Cuban labor supply underwent a transformation as a result of the

[2] We are indebted to Leland K. Jenks's *Our Cuban Colony* for most of these facts on American economic interests in Cuba.

emancipation of the slaves; the growing importance of the European beet industry caused a general depression in price and made Cuban sugar dependent upon a world price fixed at Hamburg; the large-scale capital investments necessary to make the industry keep up with the trend of the times gave it all the usual aspects of a vested interest. Finally, in the early nineties, there appeared on the scene the American Sugar Refining Company to tighten its monopoly grip on the American market and control fully 90 per cent of the refined sugar being consumed in the United States. These developments touched and left their influence on every aspect of Cuban life. The Cuban population was tied up, more so than ever before, with the destinies of sugar. The planters depended upon the good wishes of the American Sugar Trust, which had become their chief outlet. Importation of American capital became a necessity as a result of the mechanization of the industry. The slightest jar would dislocate these delicate relationships and bring misery to the millions in the Cuban population and ruin to the planters. Disaster came in 1894 with the enactment of the American tariff law of that year, which put a duty of 40 per cent on raw sugar and thus abrogated the reciprocity treaties of 1890. The injurious effects on Cuban industry at once made themselves felt. Edwin F. Atkins, the leading American planter, described, tersely enough, the sequence of economic events that led to the outbreak of hostilities in 1895. Said he:

> By this Act, the reciprocity treaties were abrogated, Cuban raw sugar was taken off the free list and Spain retaliated by returning to her old discrimination against the United States imports into Cuba; the cost of living in Cuba advanced and the price of sugar dropped, credit became impaired, the estates upon finishing their crop in 1895 discharged their hands, and unrest flamed out into insurrection that ended in the Spanish-American War.

The first important American economic interest on the island had been in the business of the sugar factors, of whom Moses Taylor was the chief example. In the eighties, Taylor's place had been taken by the Boston firm of E. Atkins and Company, which, as a result of the havoc wrought by the Ten Years' War, was able to pick up estates at nominal prices. The Atkins family bought its first estate in 1883; in the nineties, its principal plantation in southeast Cuba comprised more than 12,000 acres. By 1896, the American sugar interests were worth in the neighborhood of $30 million and American sugar growers, on the island, were turning out more than 10 per cent of the total production. The Sugar Trust, as such, did not invest in Cuban lands until 1898. However, the Atkins refinery was one of the original members of the combination; H. O. Havemeyer, too, had personal holdings on the island.

Another important American interest, beginning with the eighties, was in Cuban mines: iron ore, largely, but manganese and nickel ore, too. In 1893, the Pennsylvania Steel Company and the Bethlehem Iron Works acquired large ore deposits near Santiago; in the nineties, the Lake Superior Consolidated Iron Mines (a Rockefeller company) bought into Cuban mines. By 1898, Cuban shipments of iron ore to this country reached the large total of 400,000 tons. These mining activities were more exclusively American than any other economic enterprise on the island, and in 1896 were believed to be worth in the neighborhood of $15 million. In addition to American sugar and iron properties, other investments, including tobacco, were valued at $5 million. Thus, American direct investments were in the neighborhood of $50 million when the American people began to regard with interest the events transpiring in the "Pearl of the Antilles."

Our trade with Cuba had reached significant proportions, particularly under the operations of the Tariff Act of 1890. In 1860, the American-Cuban commerce was valued at $44 million; in 1890, it was valued at $67 million; in 1893, at $103 million. In 1895, the trade had dropped to $65 million. The importance of our commercial intercourse with Cuba will be quickly grasped in the light of the following figures: imports from Cuba in 1890 represented 31 per cent of our total Latin-American imports; exports to Cuba, in the same year, represented 20 per cent of our total Latin-American exports.

It must be appreciated, nevertheless, that the chief economic stake in Cuba was not American by any means. We did not own Cuba in any sense of the term. The railroads were controlled by British capital; banking facilities were largely in the possession of British, German, and French nationals. In other words, relatively speaking, our Cuban business interests were small. In the second place, despite the rather easy assumption of some writers, economic matters had little to do with the outbreak of hostilities between Spain and the United States. American businessmen did next to nothing to encourage the independence movement and regarded the establishment of a Cuban republic with considerable misgiving.

The American Cuban policy during the Cleveland administration was in large part shaped upon the advice of Americans in Cuba. Of these, the most important was the previously mentioned Edwin F. Atkins, who had the ear of Olney, Cleveland's Secretary of State. The upshot was, a steadfast refusal, on the part of Cleveland, to recognize the belligerency of the insurgents. On June 12, 1895, Cleveland proclaimed Cuban insurgency and warned all persons in the United States against violating American neutrality laws by intercourse with the rebels. Gun-running was declared illegal and the coast guard succeeded in stopping all but two or three ships engaged in bringing aid to the revolutionists. Congressional interference Cleveland refused to countenance, and a concurrent resolution, passed by Congress in April, 1896, recognizing the existence of a state of war on the island, met with a stony silence on the part of the President. Of the rectitude of Cleveland's course there can be no question. The revolutionists had established no government, possessed none of the important towns, had no fixed sources of revenue, and did not have the support of the conservative elements in the population: they had not, in short, established any claims to recognition as belligerents. However, the American government looked with favor on autonomy for Cuba, and Olney addressed Spain on the matter in April, 1896; middle-class Cubans wanted autonomy in preference to independence; so did American business interests. Autonomy would have come in time—had it not been for the stupidity of the Weyler administration in Cuba, the meddling of the American popular press, and the desire for war by certain American politicians.

The so-called Cuban War of Independence broke out on the island on February 24, 1895. The leaders of the insurgents were Máximo Gómez and Antonio Maceo, both of whom had figured in the earlier Ten-Years' War. In April, Spain made a determined effort to put down the insurrection by dispatching her greatest soldier, Martínez Campos, with a large army, to the island. Campos had the support of the Spanish government with men and money; in time the Spanish expeditionary force numbered 200,000 men. He found it difficult, however, to cope with the guerrilla tactics of the insurgent units. The revolutionists were wise enough not to risk their fortunes in battle but took to the hills and brush and devastated the countryside. They relied upon an economic breakdown to force the hand of Spain—and perhaps involve the United States. Thus, Gómez issued orders against the grinding of sugar cane; his men levied assessments on the sugar estates; and in November, 1895, a proclamation was made public calling for the destruction of plantation buildings and railroad connections and the shooting of all plantation laborers who persisted in working in the fields.

In January, 1896, Campos was recalled to Spain and General Valeriano Weyler succeeded him as Governor of Cuba and Captain-General of the Spanish army. Weyler met terror with terror. His devices were two: he built a series of blockhouses, joined together by wire entanglements, across the island in the hope of corralling the insurgent forces in a gradually restricted area; and he took measures to stop the rebels from living off the countryside by ordering the concentration of the island's population into camps under the surveillance of troops. This was the famous "reconcentration" system. In time, there were some 400,000 of these unfortunates herded into the camps, a considerable number of whom, because of Spanish indifference, ignorance, and, incidentally, lack of funds, fell prey to the ravages of hunger and disease.

That general indignation should be excited was not unnatural. American sympathies were played upon assiduously by the newly developed popular press of New York City. The rivalry between Pulitzer of the

World and Hearst of the *Journal,* for circulation and prestige, led these enterprising newspaper proprietors to expend great sums of money. They overran the island with a veritable host of correspondents, special writers, artists, and photographers—who, because of their ignorance of Spanish, were easily imposed upon by sympathizers of the revolution and who, too, quite often stooped to fabrication to heighten the sensationalism of their reports. These, then, were volunteer friends who did good work, it is true, in arousing the interest and playing upon the heartstrings of the American public. But the Cubans had other and more powerful resources in the United States. There was a large native-born Cuban population, of American citizenship, residing in the country, in Florida, New York, and New Orleans for the most part. These organized themselves into committees or "juntas" for the purpose of furthering the revolution with money and guns. The Cuban junta in New York was naturally the most important of these, and it had the good fortune to be headed by an estimable gentleman, one Tomás Estrada Palma, who was to become the first president of the Cuban Republic. The junta engaged in propaganda, visited Congressmen and Senators, enlisted volunteers, bought munitions, and fitted out filibustering expeditions. It collected funds, too, for the revolutionists and sold a bond issue which fell into the hands of speculators. In April, 1898, when American intervention seemed highly probable, the Cuban "Bonds of the Revolution" (as they were called) were selling at 40. Later these bonds were recognized by the Cuban Republic and a total of $2,196,000 of them was funded (as well as accrued interest at 6 per cent). However, the insurgents lived largely off the countryside and got much of their revenues by levying assessments on the planters.

The Spanish Conservative ministry, which was supporting Weyler, fell in October, 1897, and the Liberal ministry that succeeded, fearing for the dynasty and being uncertain of the intentions of the new American President, recalled the Captain-General whom Americans had learned to call "The Butcher." General Ramón Blanco was sent to the island in November, 1897, and the American minister at Madrid was assured that autonomy would be granted as soon as the insurrection was in hand. Blanco was ordered, too, to modify the "reconcentration" decrees. The new government showed its good faith by proving that not a single American citizen was under arrest or in jail.

EVENTS LEADING UP TO THE WAR WITH SPAIN

The inhabitants of Havana were Spanish loyalists and opposed to autonomy. The encounters between autonomists and antiautonomists, which broke out in the capital city, made our consul-general fear for the safety of American citizens and property, and at his request Washington consented to the dispatching of an American man-of-war to Cuban waters. Pains were taken to assure Spain of the friendly nature of the visit; and that country prepared to return the courtesy by sending a Spanish cruiser to New York harbor. Late in January, 1898, the *U.S.S. Maine* steamed into Havana and its officers and crew were received by the Blanco government as the official guests of the Spanish nation. On the evening of February 15, the *Maine* was destroyed by an explosion which resulted in the death of 2 officers and 258 members of the crew. Every effort was made to hold American public opinion in leash. A naval court of inquiry was at once convened and investigations were carried on, on the spot, while the country waited breathlessly. Had the explosion been external or internal? If external, had a mine been set off by agents of the Spanish government, by Spanish loyalists, or by Cuban insurgents who sought, in this way, to embroil the United States? Only the first question was answered, and the findings of the investigations were emphatic.

On March 28, the President submitted the naval court's report to Congress. It ran in part: "In the opinion of the court the *Maine* was destroyed by the explosion of a submarine mine which caused the partial explosion of two or more of the forward magazines. The court has been unable to obtain evidence fixing the responsibility for the destruction of the *Maine* upon any person or persons." To the American public, however, there was no hesitancy about fixing responsibility. "Remember the *Maine*" became a popular watch-cry that spelled the ultimate doom of Spanish empire. On March 9, before even the court of inquiry had reported, Congress had appropriated $50 million for the "national defense" and placed the fund in the hands of the President to be used at his discretion.

Another event had meanwhile occurred to inflame public opinion. On February 9, Hearst's *New York Journal* displayed prominently a letter that had been written by Dupuy de Lôme, the Spanish minister at Washington, to a friend in Cuba in which certain tactless observations had been made on McKinley's deportment and on his message to Congress in December, 1897. In one passage De Lôme had declared: "Besides the natural and inevitable coarseness with which it repeated all that press and public opinion in Spain have said of Weyler, it shows once more that McKinley is weak and a caterer to the rabble, and, moreover, a cheap politician who wishes to leave a door open to himself and to stand well with the jingoes of his party." [3]

The letter, of course, was in flagrant violation of good taste; it was, too, an unjust observation in that McKinley was no warmonger. It is to be noted, on the other hand, that the letter had been privately written and the *Journal* had connived at theft in accepting it and making it public. De

[3] The translation is H. T. Peck's. The objectionable phrase was *"debil y populachero y ademas un politicastro."*

Lôme quickly cabled his resignation; Spain disclaimed all responsibility for its minister's comments, and on March 3 the State Department announced that the incident was closed. The damage had been done, nonetheless, and it was irreparable.

The American war party numbered not only sensational journalists and nondescript politicians, who were seeking to strengthen their holds on indifferent constituencies, but, as well, a group of men whose social positions, wealth, and culture assured them of a hearing among the respectable members of their communities. Theodore Roosevelt, John Hay, Henry Cabot Lodge, and Whitelaw Reid were for war. Roosevelt in the Navy Department, Hay as ambassador at London, Reid as proprietor of the eminently respectable *New York Tribune,* and Lodge in the Senate, occupied places of great influence, and their correspondence and private remarks could not but contribute mightily to the engendering of the war spirit. These were mischief-makers who could do great harm—more, by far, than the buzzings of the Republican politicians who kept urging on the President a war declaration in order to strengthen their party's hold upon the country.

The threat of war aroused a variety of emotions: a hope for adventure, cupidity, the stirrings of real patriotic feeling. There were all sorts of restless and turbulent spirits in the country who looked forward to a war with Spain to justify their cravings for excitement. There was, again, the shabby hope for gain that certain jingoes did not have even the sense to conceal. Thus Senator Thurston of Nebraska, on March 25, 1898, said: "War with Spain would increase the business and the earnings of every American railroad, it would increase the output of every American factory, it would stimulate every branch of industry and domestic commerce...." An awakening nationalism, a vision of a greater America, a feeling that America's place was rightly beside Great Britain at the council-tables of the world—this was another war strain pitched in a loftier key. Thus Theodore Roosevelt, before the Naval War College at Newport, R. I., on June 2, 1897: "Cowardice in a race, as in an individual, is the unpardonable sin, and a wilful failure to prepare for danger may in its effects be as bad as cowardice.... As yet no nation can hold its place in the world or can do any work really worth doing unless it stands ready to guard its rights with an armed hand."

Against such forces, and in the face of a public sentiment which was fast becoming overwhelming, the President's position was an unhappy one. He did all in his power to prevent the embarrassment of the Spanish government: he knew that the Liberal cabinet must move slowly lest it antagonize Spanish public opinion by a hasty surrender and thus bring on the fall of the dynasty. In his wish for peace, McKinley had the backing of the greater part of his party and of American business leaders as well. The antiwar group included the whole Cabinet (excepting Secretary of War Alger), the Vice-President, Speaker Reed, and Senators Hanna, Allison, Aldrich, Fairbanks, Hale, Platt (Conn.), and Spooner. Wall Street was opposed to war; so, too, were the American sugar planters in Cuba as well as the Sugar Trust. Up to the eve of the Presidential message to Congress, McKinley's attitude (as reflected in the State Department's communications to Minister S. L. Woodford at Madrid) was conciliatory. On March 27, Woodford was asked to report to the Spanish cabinet that the United States did not seek the acquisition of Cuba; immediate peace was our sole objective. The President therefore urged the establishment of an armistice on the island until October 1 and the immediate revocation of the "reconcentration" order.

The Spanish government did not see fit to reply until March 31. The Spanish memorandum declared: 1. Spain was prepared to submit to arbitration the differences arising over the sinking of the *Maine;* 2. the "reconcentration" order, as it applied to the Cuban western provinces, had already been revoked; 3. American relief work was to be permitted; 4. the Spanish government was intending to take up with the Cuban parliament, called to meet May 4, plans for pacification; 5. an armistice would be granted only if the insurgents asked for it. This last was the heart of the matter, and on the question of an armistice the Spanish government was not prepared to yield. Woodford knew the difficulties confronting the ministry: that an unconditional surrender to the American demands would be received with popular indignation. Thus our minister wrote to Day on April 3:

> The Spanish minister for foreign affairs assures me that Spain will go as far and as fast as she can.... I know that the queen and the present ministry sincerely desire peace and that the Spanish people desire peace, and if you can still give me time and reasonable liberty of action ... I am sure that before next October I will get peace in Cuba, with justice to Cuba and protection to our great American interests.

Woodford did not give up hope, knowing that the Pope, also, was interesting himself in the Cuban situation, and had made representations to the Spanish queen. Meanwhile on April 7, Sir Julian Pauncefote, the British ambassador and the dean of the diplomatic corps at Washington, on behalf of himself and his German, French, Russian, Italian, and Austro-Hungarian colleagues, read a memorandum to the President in which they, as the representatives of the European powers, appealed for peace. On April 9, Woodford was able to cable the glad tidings to Day: an armistice had been granted to take place at once. The next day, which was Sunday, Woodford telegraphed to the President himself. His message is of the utmost significance in the light of subsequent events. Woodford said:

In view of action of Spanish government as cabled Saturday April 9 I hope you can secure full authority from Congress to do whatever you shall deem necessary to secure immediate and permanent peace in Cuba *by negotiations,* including the full power to employ the Army and Navy, according to your own judgment, to aid and enforce your action. If this be secured I believe you will get final settlement before August 1st on one of the following bases: either such autonomy as the insurgents may agree to accept, or recognition by Spain of the independence of the island, or cession of the island to the United States. I hope that nothing will now be done to humiliate Spain, as I am satisfied that the present government is going, and is loyally ready to go, as fast and as far as it can. *With your power of action sufficiently free you will win the fight on your own lines. . . .*[4]

But the President had given in to the war party. The very next day, April 11, McKinley went to Congress to place the facts before the people's representatives. In reciting his efforts on behalf of Cuba, McKinley, however, made only passing mention of the Woodford cable of the day before; in short, he said nothing of what was in effect Spain's complete surrender.

Why did the President appeal to Congress, knowing as he did that such a move meant war? One may hazard the following conjectures: 1. He had no faith in the sincerity of the Spanish government, which had procrastinated and had broken earlier promises. 2. He could not believe in the ability of the government to carry out its whole program in the face of a hostile Spanish public opinion, which had not been adequately prepared for such a *démarche.* 3. He had no assurances of the permanence of the Liberal ministry. If it should fall and be followed by a Conservative government, the whole tedious affair would have to be reopened. 4. He was tired of fighting the American jingoes, the sensational press, and his fellow Republicans. He knew the slurs that Roosevelt had cast on his strength of character. He knew that war would be popular, short, and would probably redound to his everlasting fame. He was a resourceful politician—none among his contemporaries was his superior—and he saw, no doubt, the political advantages of a war as clearly as did the most obscure hack. War would take the minds of men from more vexing domestic concerns, particularly the currency question. War would make him, McKinley, the undisputed leader of his party and of the nation. War would assure the election of a Republican Congress in 1898 and would make his own re-election in 1900 inevitable.

In his message to Congress on April 11, McKinley reported that he had exhausted every resource calculated to relieve the situation in Cuba. He stood ready, he said, to carry out the obligations imposed upon him by the Constitution and asked that he be given power by Congress to "take measures to secure a full and final termination of hostilities between the government of Spain and the people of Cuba . . . and to use the military and naval

[4] Italics ours.

forces of the United States as may be necessary for these purposes...."
The Woodford cable was not submitted to Congress; the President merely reported the incident in these words: "Yesterday, and since the preparation of the foregoing message, official information was received by me that the latest decree of the queen regent of Spain directs General Blanco, in order to prepare and facilitate peace, to proclaim a suspension of hostilities, the duration and details of which have not yet been communicated to me."

The houses of Congress could not agree on the wording of the war resolution until April 19. The House's resolution, as it was passed, simply empowered the President to intervene. But the Senate was more wary. What was to be the situation of the so-called Cuban Republic? What exactly was to be the American position with regard to the guarantee of independence? The antiannexationists won and the war resolution, as finally written and passed, made the most unequivocal promises of American disinterestedness. The war resolution contained four clauses as follows: 1. The people of Cuba were, and of right ought to be, free and independent. 2. The President was authorized to demand that Spain surrender her sovereignty and withdraw from Cuba. 3. The President was empowered to use the naval and military establishments to carry out these demands. 4. The United States disclaimed any intention of assuming sovereignty over Cuba and pledged herself to leave the island in control of the Cuban people with the successful termination of pacification. (This last clause was added at the insistence of Senator Teller of Colorado.) The final vote, for intervention, in the House was 311 yeas against 6 nays; in the Senate, 42 yeas against 35 nays.[5] On April 20, the President signed the resolution. This meant war; and Congress formally said so five days later.

[5] The large antiwar vote in the Senate was due to the fact that the war resolution did not specifically recognize the existence of the Cuban Republic.

· 18 ·

A Short and Glorious War

WAR PREPARATIONS

BY 1898 the new Navy, which zealous Secretaries had been quietly building up since the eighties, was ready for its supreme test. The whole establishment was on a war footing. A Naval War Board was sitting at Washington working out plans for offense and defense; the fleet was distributed in both oceans ready to meet attack from any unexpected quarter; practice in gunnery had given officers and crews a high degree of confidence in their abilities. The Navy looked forward to the outbreak of hostilities as an opportunity in which its mettle could be tried and its worth demonstrated not only to the American people but to Europe, too. By 1898, the chief strength of the American naval force consisted of seven armored battleships and a large number of protected cruisers as well as the customary auxiliary craft. Against this force, Spain had but one first-class battleship and five armored cruisers. It had not nearly so many protected cruisers and torpedo boats, but it did have a group of torpedo-boat destroyers, which were unknown to the American fleet.

The American armored ships, except for the *Oregon*, were concentrated in the Atlantic. The Main Fleet, commanded by Rear-Admiral W. T. Sampson, lay off Key West, while the Flying Squadron, commanded by Commodore W. S. Schley, was stationed at Hampton Roads. To allay the fears of the northern cities, an imposing, though quite ineffectual, array of auxiliary ships was collected in northern waters and given the name of the Northern Patrol Squadron. On March 19, the *Oregon*, then on the Pacific coast, was ordered to proceed around Cape Horn to join the Atlantic fleet at Key West, and that valiant ship steamed 14,000 miles to reach its destination. It arrived at Key West in excellent fighting trim on May 26. Finally, the Asiatic Squadron, under the command of Commodore George Dewey, was cruising in Chinese waters awaiting further commands.

The Navy Department was not content with this force, and beginning in January, 1898, started to augment its fleet. The Congressional appropriation of March 9 gave it $30 million, and most of this money was expended in the purchase of additional ships. Two protected cruisers, being built for Brazil in English yards, were acquired, as well as one gunboat and two torpedo boats. In addition, the Navy bought 97 merchantmen which it fitted up as auxiliary ships, and it took over the 4 ocean-going steamers that the International Navigation Company was operating in the transatlantic passenger trade. Also, the seagoing personnel was increased from 1232 officers and 11,750 men to 2088 officers and 24,123 men. During the months of February, March, and April, the Navy offices fairly hummed. Not a little of this activity was inspired by the enthusiasm of the young Assistant Secretary, Theodore Roosevelt, who scoured the harbors for available ships, bought munitions and supplies, ordered gunnery practice, and kept officers and men in a high fever of expectation. J. D. Long, his chief, regarded this human dynamo with some misgivings and left the Department in Roosevelt's charge only on rare occasions. On February 25, Long rushed back to his Washington desk hurriedly, giving in his journal his reason as follows: "I return to the office, both because I feel so much better and because I find that Roosevelt, in his precipitate way, has come very near causing more of an explosion than happened to the *Maine*." Roosevelt had merely taken it upon himself to petition Congress for immediate legislation by which the Navy could enlist an unlimited number of seamen! Nor was this the only significant piece of work Roosevelt had accomplished that afternoon (though Long omitted mention of it in his published journal.) The Assistant Secretary had sent a telegram in his own name to Commodore Dewey. It read:

Secret and confidential. Order the squadron, except *Monocacy*, to Hong Kong. Keep full of coal. In the event of declaration of war [against Spain] your duty will be to see that the Spanish squadron does not leave the Asiatic coast, and then offensive operations in Philippine Islands. Keep *Olympia* until further orders.

That the war opened so auspiciously for our arms was due to this major stroke of strategy. On the other hand, the Army was never ready for war, even in the midst of hostilities. It had no War College for the training of its senior officers, no General Staff to map out the strategy of campaigns, no reserve and, indeed, no trained fighting force. The regular Army, which consisted of 28,000 men, was distributed largely among the far western posts where it had fought Indians, when it had done any fighting at all. With no machinery at all, and headed by an incompetent Cabinet member who regarded his office largely as a patronage agency, the Army was called upon to double its regular force in a few weeks and to clothe, train, and mobilize 200,000 volunteers. Secretary Alger had been the outstanding jingo in the Cabinet, if not in the whole country; at every Cabinet meeting he had given assurance of the readiness of the Army; yet as late as May 26 he was compelled to confess that he needed another two or three weeks before he was prepared to send out his Cuban expeditionary force. It was no wonder that these men went into Cuba, to enter upon a tropical campaign, outfitted in heavy blue winter uniforms, without real hospital equipment or the assistance of a sanitary corps, and without any proper provision being made for a food regimen that would protect against dysentery, scurvy, and the like. The real victims of the war were not the few hundreds felled by Spanish bullets but the thousands of men who succumbed to yellow fever, malaria, typhoid, and intestinal disorders. Fully 20,000 soldiers were treated for disease at the single hospital camp located at Montauk Point, Long Island.

Congress was not niggardly in making war appropriations. In addition to the $50 million voted in March, it authorized in June the floating of a bond issue of $200 million. And on July 1 a new revenue act began to impose higher internal duties on beer and tobacco as well as stamp taxes on checks, drafts, telegraphic messages, railway tickets, and a whole variety of commercial and legal documents.

ATTITUDE OF THE EUROPEAN POWERS

On the eve of war (and for many years later) it was commonly believed by Americans that Germany had sought to organize a European concert against the United States in the interests of Spain. The German press was openly unfriendly; the rumors of German activities in seeking to prevent hostilities were regarded as fact and as evidence of a plot to frustrate the United States in bringing Spain to book. Indeed, the presence of a powerful German fleet in Manila waters, in June, only strengthened these convictions. It is true that the Kaiser and his staff were apprehensive lest a Spanish defeat should jeopardize the whole monarchical principle throughout Europe; too, an American victory might interfere with Germany's plans for the acquisition of portions of the Spanish empire in the Pacific. With war imminent, the Kaiser had sounded out the chancelleries of Europe on the question of intervention. He had, as well, interested the Pope in Spain's predicament with the result that Archbishop Ireland had been ordered to Washington to work in the cause of peace. Austria-Hungary, France, and Italy received the German advices with interest; but when none of these powers showed a willingness to organize and head a European demonstration against the United States, Germany dropped the matter.

Unfortunately for Germany, however, Great Britain's foreign policy was not conditioned by the European situation. Great Britain could, therefore, be friendly to the United States, and the conduct of her press and her officialdom was everything that the Anglophile John Hay, America's ambassador at London, might have desired. The British Foreign Office was so cool to unofficial feelers in the matter of a European demonstration that it was never formally approached. The colonial secretary,

Joseph Chamberlain, in a public address on May 13, 1898, actually suggested the creation of an Anglo-American alliance. The prime minister, Lord Salisbury, was no less friendly. Finally, in the conduct of the peace negotiations, Great Britain stood by the United States in the matter of the Philippines. Thus, it was this open and friendly assistance, as opposed to the Kaiser's tortuous diplomacy, that made American public opinion and American public men pro-English in temper. The British were more farsighted than the Germans and probably were preparing against that day when America might be called upon to remember the good will that Great Britain had shown in 1898.

THE CONDUCT OF THE WAR

The short war between the United States and Spain consisted of the following five operations: 1. the defeat of the Spanish fleet at Manila; 2. the blockade of Cuba; 3. the hunt for the main Spanish fleet (commanded by Admiral Cervera); 4. the land and sea battles of Santiago; 5. the invasion of Puerto Rico.

The first blow was struck at the Philippines because here, it was believed, could be gained that quick and decisive victory which would break the heart of the Spaniards and unify American public opinion. On April 23 Dewey quitted the harbor of Hong Kong; four days later his squadron of six ships was heading southward toward Luzon, and particularly Manila Bay, where the Spanish fleet had arrived. Arriving at the entering channel in the late hours of April 30, Dewey boldly steamed through the narrow opening of the harbor to confront the Spanish fleet lying in a deep crescent off Cavite Point, ten miles south of the city proper. The Spanish fleet consisted of two cruisers, five gunboats, and a number of smaller craft. Dewey's fleet of six ships, led by the flagship *Olympia* and steaming in a line a mile long, waited until it had approached within 5000 yards of the enemy. At five A. M. the order to fire was given. Five times the American fleet moved past the anchored Spanish ships, three times to the westward and twice to the eastward, keeping up a deadly fire at ranges varying from 5000 to 2000 yards. At 7:35 A. M. the squadron stood out into the bay for breakfast and to take stock of munitions. At 11:16 A. M. the American ships returned to the work of destruction; at shortly past noon the battle was over. The toll taken was a deadly one: 10 Spanish ships had been destroyed, 3 shore batteries had been silenced, and 381 Spanish seamen were dead or wounded. The total American casualties consisted of 7 wounded men; not a single ship had been damaged.

For two months Dewey looked expectantly eastward for the arriving military reinforcements that Washington had promised. Without them, it was plain to him, the city of Manila could not be invested. Dewey's position soon became increasingly embarrassing as foreign men-of-war began to gather in Manila Bay to protect the interests of their nationals and to observe the carrying out of the American blockade. By the middle of June there had assembled in Manila waters three British warships, one French cruiser, one Japanese, and five German ships. The news of the arrival of the German admiral, von Diedrichs, was made much of by the American press, and the rumors of his warlike plans (largely inspired by British dispatches) gave the sensation-mongers much to vociferate about. Von Diedrichs was boldly flouting Dewey's blockade; he was running provisions into Manila; he showed real hostility toward Dewey, and only the refusal of the British commander to side with him prevented open hostilities. So the stories ran. Apparently a number of misunderstandings did take place between the two admirals, largely revolving about Dewey's interpretations of the rules of neutrality. Germany's interest in the ultimate disposition of the Philippines had led to the dispatching of von Diedrichs to the islands; but there is no evidence that he received orders to harass Dewey, let alone engage him in combat.[1]

Dewey's position became more comfortable with the arrival of 2500 American troops at Manila on June 30. By July 25, the American army before Manila, under the command of General Wesley Merritt, numbered 10,700 men. The American troops were supported by Filipino insurgents led by Emilio Aguinaldo and before the assault of these forces the Spanish garrison at Manila surrendered on August 13, one day after the peace protocol had been signed.

In the West Indies theater of war, the American fleet at once made its superiority felt. A blockade was thrown about the island of Cuba, and so effectively did the squadrons under Sampson and Schley do their work that, except for Cervera's fleet, not a single Spanish ship was able to get to a Cuban port. The completeness of the blockade would have starved the Spanish soldiery into submission, anyway, even if the American Navy had not performed its work with such telling dispatch.

But where was Cervera? On April 29, the Spanish admiral, commanding a fleet of four armored cruisers and three destroyers, departed from the Cape Verde Islands for some unknown destination to the westward. Was his objective New York, the Jersey coast, Washington itself? As three long weeks went by and the search for Cervera's fleet continued without result, the whole Atlantic coast fell into a panic. Finally, information was received that Cervera had put in to Santiago harbor, on the southeast coast of Cuba, on May 19. On May 28, Schley's Flying Squadron reached the waters off Santiago, to find Cervera still lying under the guns

---

[1] See L. B. Shippee, "Germany and the Spanish-American War," *American Historical Review*, Vol. XXX (July, 1925), for new light thrown on this incident, as a result of the opening of the German archives after World War I.

of the shore batteries. On June 1, Admiral Sampson arrived with the rest of the Atlantic fleet and Cervera's last opportunity for flight had vanished. An early effort was made to seal up Cervera in the narrow Santiago harbor when, on the night of June 3, Lieutenant Hobson took the collier *Merrimac* to the mouth of the channel and endeavored to sink her. He was discovered by the Spaniards before he had effected his purpose, so that the enemy's fire shot his steering gear away. When the *Merrimac* finally went down she was too far in the harbor to bottle up the Spanish fleet. The upshot was, the American fleet sat down to starve out the Spaniard and to await the coming of the American Expeditionary Force, when a combined attack on land and sea might have a better chance of forcing the capitulation of Santiago's forts.

Finally, on June 14, and under the command of General W. R. Shafter, the American army, 16,887 strong, put out from Tampa. None of the officers had had any experience in handling a large body of men, with the result that the force did not reach its destination until June 22 and was not finally disembarked until June 26. Four days later the movement on the city was ordered. The American army was divided into three units: the First Division, headed by Brigadier General J. F. Kent, moved on San Juan Hill; the Second Division, under Brigadier General H. W. Lawton, first took the village of Siboney and then moved on El Caney, lying to the right of San Juan Hill; the (dismounted) Cavalry Division, under Major General J. Wheeler, took Las Guásimas, on the road to San Juan, and then moved to assault Kettle Hill and later San Juan. It was to Wheeler's division that there was attached the famous First Volunteer Cavalry Regiment, headed by Colonel Leonard Wood and Lieutenant Colonel Theodore Roosevelt, erstwhile Assistant Secretary of the Navy. Roosevelt had been largely instrumental in recruiting the regiment in the southwest ranch country and most of its men were cowboys from the plains. Hence its popular nickname of the "Rough Riders."

The contests over El Caney and San Juan Hill were stubborn. Lawton lost 440 in killed and wounded out of his 3500 men before the fortified village of El Caney was his. The assault on San Juan Hill was equally desperate: the American troops had to proceed across broken country and through a rough scrub in the face of a withering fire delivered by a concealed enemy. A heavy toll was taken among both officers and men, one brigade losing four commanders in succession before the operation was completed. Finally, after twelve hours of fighting, the night of July 1 saw American troops in control of San Juan Hill, Kettle Hill, and El Caney —in other words, all the heights commanding the northern and eastern sides of Santiago. The total American casualties in the three movements had been 112 officers and 1460 men in killed, wounded, and missing.

There was now nothing for Cervera to do but make a run for it. On

July 3, in broad daylight, the Spanish fleet steamed out of Santiago harbor and streaked off to the westward. Admiral Sampson had given explicit directions to his captains in preparation for such an eventuality, but he had expected the movement in the dead of night. On the morning of July 3, therefore, he had had himself taken ashore to discuss with General Shafter the further strategy of the common campaign. Nominally, Schley was in command of the battle fleet when the American squadron took up the pursuit of the fleeing Spanish ships; actually, it was to be a "captains' fight." At 9:35 A. M., with the *Maria Teresa* in the lead, the Spanish fleet had been discovered. At 10:15, the *Maria Teresa*, wholly in flames, was beached six miles west of Santiago; at 10:20 the *Oquendo* blew up; at 11:05 the *Vizcaya* found haven on the shore, fifteen miles west of Santiago; at 1:15 P.M. the last Spanish cruiser, the *Cristóbal Colón*, struck her colors and sought refuge close to shore some fifty miles west of Santiago. In addition, two smaller Spanish craft were destroyed. Thus, in a running fight of less than four hours the glory of the Spanish Navy had been annihilated and proud Spain saw herself reduced to a second-rate power. But one American sailor had been killed; the wounded totaled a handful. Against this extraordinary record there were to be placed the Spanish losses of 323 killed, 151 wounded, and 1750 prisoners.

The destruction of Cervera's fleet was the beginning of the end, and on July 17 Santiago's garrison surrendered. Miles, Commander-in-chief of the Army, was before the gates of Santiago to watch the surrender of the Spanish governor in person. He then proceeded to Puerto Rico and before the end of July he was commanding an army of some 17,000 officers and men. Only by the wildest stretch of the imagination could this be called a campaign. Everywhere the invading American troops were received with expressions of joy by the native Puerto Ricans, with the result that in two weeks Miles had in his possession the whole southern and western portions of the island. However, the signing of the peace protocol ended hostilities before Miles had entirely pacified it. The total American losses consisted of 3 killed and 40 wounded.

THE PEACE OF PARIS

On July 26, Spain, through the French ambassador at Washington, sued for peace. Four days later President McKinley outlined the terms under which the United States was prepared to suspend hostilities, and on August 12 the peace protocol was signed. War was over after 113 days of fighting. The peace protocol set out the five following demands: 1. Spain was to relinquish all claim of sovereignty over Cuba; 2. Puerto Rico was to be ceded to the United States; 3. an island in the Ladrones group in the Pacific, to be selected by the United States, was to be yielded up, too; 4. Spain was to evacuate at once the islands of Cuba and Puerto Rico, and its other insular possessions in the West Indies; 5. the United States was to occupy the "city, bay, and harbor of Manila pending the conclusion of a treaty of peace which should determine the control, disposition, and government of the Philippines."

On October 1, at Paris, the Peace Commission formally opened its proceedings. The American delegation was made up of W. R. Day, who surrendered the Secretaryship of State to head the Commission, Whitelaw Reid, proprietor of the *New York Tribune,* and Senators C. K. Davis (Minn.), W. P. Frye (Me.), and George Gray (Del.). There soon developed two points of conflict between the American and Spanish Commissioners: the first related to Cuba, the second to the Philippines. What was to happen to the Cuban debt? Spain had spent considerable sums of money on public works, while the costs of putting down the last two insurrections had been heavy. Spain advanced the claim that assumption of the debt should go with sovereignty and tried to induce the American Commission to accept Cuba on such a basis. But the Americans were firm on the question of nonresponsibility of the debt and on the issue of Cuban independence. Spain was compelled to yield.

The disposition of the Philippines constituted another and more serious matter. A swift blow had been struck at the Philippines, and this was fair enough in war, but the sovereignty of the islands in the Pacific had never entered into any of the discussions that had preceded the outbreak of hostilities. Further, American claim to the islands, or any part of them, was somewhat weakened by the fact that Manila had not capitulated until August 13. The fact is, the terms of the peace protocol bearing on the Philippines had been left purposely vague, for neither the President nor his advisers had quite made up their minds on the vexing problem. As late as September 16, in instructing the Peace Commissioners, the President had told them that the United States could not accept anything less than the cession of the island of Luzon. The middle of October had now come and the American Peace Commissioners were perplexed. They had inquired diligently into the history, possibilities, and desirability of the islands and had even conducted hearings. The Commissioners had made up their minds, but there was disagreement among them. On October 25 the President was appealed to for explicit instructions: Davis, Frye, and Reid were in favor of claiming the whole archipelago; Day was willing to ask for but a portion of the group; Gray was opposed to any cession. Gray's position, of course, stood best the test of logic. Extraterritorial possessions struck at the time-honored continental policy of the country; besides, the war had been fought to free Cuba.

By October 26 the President had apparently made up his mind, for Day was told on that day that the whole archipelago must be asked for.

Two days later Secretary of State Hay cabled Day that a unanimous Cabinet supported the President. There were some misgivings at Paris: Was not Spain entitled to an indemnity, in view of the fact that the islands had never really been seized? Offer $10 million to $20 million, came back the instructions from Washington. Day offered $20 million; the Spaniards submitted all sorts of counterproposals; finally, after a month of bickering, on November 21 the ultimatum was submitted. The United States wanted all the islands and would pay $20 million for them. The Spanish Commissioners bowed to the inevitable, and on December 10 the treaty was signed. Its leading provisions were the following: Spain relinquished all claim to sovereignty over Cuba; Spain ceded to the United States Puerto Rico and the other Spanish insular possessions in the West Indies, the island of Guam in the Ladrones, and the Philippines; for the Philippines Spain was to receive $20 million; the United States agreed to admit Spanish ships and merchandise to the Pacific islands, on equal terms with American ships and cargoes, for ten years; each country was to assume the claims of its own nationals against the other country; the United States was to pay for the repatriation of all Spanish prisoners taken when Manila fell.

The motives that lay back of the American demand for the Philippines are hard to disentangle. McKinley sought to voice an explanation some time later but the ingenuousness of his statement, while it may have been satisfying to his audience in 1899, is not quite enough for us today. To a group of Methodist ministers McKinley put his perplexities in this way: The United States could not give the islands back to Spain, for "that would be cowardly and dishonorable." The United States could not turn them over to France or Germany, for "that would be bad business and discreditable." The United States could not leave the islanders to themselves, for they were unprepared for self-government. Was not the conclusion irrefragable? Hence, "there was nothing left for us to do but to take them all, and to educate the Filipinos, and to uplift and civilize and Christianize them, and by God's grace do the very best we could by them as our fellowmen for whom Christ also died." Overnight, the "white man's burden" had become part of the American political ideology.

There is no question that a well-organized sentiment for annexation had developed by the middle of October. From the Middle Atlantic, North Central, and Far Western states, the urban centers particularly, there arose a demand for empire. Owning the Philippine Islands would add to America's prestige; it would be good for business, for through Manila we should hold the key to the Chinese trade. So said Mahan, Reid, Roosevelt, Lodge, and John Hay—in short, all those public men who had been following with such keen interest the British imperial adventure and who believed that the United States could do no better than imitate England.

Nor are we to disregard the obscure and hidden currents of international

A TRIFLE EMBARRASSED

Uncle Sam:—Gosh! I wish they wouldn't come quite so many in a bunch; but if I've got to take them; I guess I can do as well by them as I've done by the others!

© 1898, by Keppler and Schwartzmann, from Puck, 1898

politics and intrigue. Germany was watching the drama in the Far Eastern theater; Great Britain was watching Germany. Germany had made no effort to conceal the fact that it saw in the disintegration of the Spanish Empire an opportunity for the acquisition of Pacific possessions—which it sorely lacked. Germany broached the idea of the common control of the Philippines to Russia and France, but meeting with no encouragement began to weave schemes for a division of the spoils. White, at Berlin, was told of Germany's need for coaling stations in the Pacific, preferably in the Philippines, and he listened sympathetically. But as early as July the English Foreign Office had whispered to Hay, at London, that Great Britain would not be averse to American retention of the islands. Great Britain was prepared to back up America! Germany's interest was dictated by the hope that all the powers could be induced to partition among themselves the Spanish lands overseas; this failing, to get strategic points elsewhere. Great Britain, on the other hand, wanted to see Germany frustrated and was prepared to support the United States in the acquisition of an empire as long as Germany would be balked. With British encouragement, therefore, we launched on our first adventure in colonialism.

Opposition to the acquisition of the Philippines was not lacking. Throughout the whole month of January, 1899, the Senate debated the treaty. The genius of the American Constitution was opposed to foreign possessions; this was a government that derived its powers from the consent of the governed; there was danger in our being entangled in alliances with European powers. So ran one side of the debate. On the other: the destiny that was rightfully ours beckoned us to expansion and power; it was our duty to civilize and Christianize the heathen. Democrats, opposed to the treaty, found unexpected support in New England Senators. But late in January, Bryan appeared at Washington to urge upon Democratic Senators that the issue was too momentous to be decided in this fashion. He counseled his followers to vote for ratification and leave final disposition of the question of the Philippines to the determination of the electorate in the Presidential campaign of 1900. In short, the issue of imperialism would be the ground on which McKinley's re-election would be fought. The outbreak, on February 4, of hostilities between American soldiers and Filipinos probably helped a number of doubtful Senators make up their minds. The upshot was that when the vote was taken in the Senate on February 6 it was seen that ratification had been gained by but one vote more than the necessary two-thirds required by the Constitution. The vote stood: for the treaty, 57; against, 27. The party line-up was as follows: yeas—40 Republicans, 10 Democrats, 3 Populists, 2 Silverites, 2 Independents; nays—22 Democrats, 3 Republicans, 2 Populists.

The results of this one-hundred-days' war may be summed up at this point: The United States emerged a world power with island possessions in the Caribbean and the Pacific. Our Navy had been tested in battle and had emerged with colors flying. We had earned the regard of Englishmen, and the European powers began to consider the potentialities of America, as they spun their fine webs of intrigue. We spent $200 million in the prosecution of the conflict and the issue of war bonds strengthened the position of the national banks. War needs had brought boom times to factories, and the whole industrial process suddenly entered upon a period of prosperity. The toll of young life that the war had taken was not so heavy, all things considered. The total deaths from all causes were 2926; the total wounded were 1645. Those who died from disease made up nine-tenths of the fatalities. The blunderings and stupidities of the Army brought about salutary reforms in the nation's military establishment. As a result of the activities of Elihu Root (who became Secretary of War in 1899), in time a number of changes for the better were effected, the most important being the establishment of the General Staff (1903) and the creation of the Army War College (1907).

THE ELECTION OF 1900

Republicanism was triumphant. A war had been successfully waged; we had gained great colonial possessions as a result; times were better; and individual initiative in industry had the blessing of the government. Well might McKinley claim popular approval when he made a speaking tour in the general interests of Republican Congressional candidates. The result was the election of another Republican Congress in the fall of 1898. When the Fifty-fifth Congress assembled in the next year it was seen that the Republican majority in the House continued to be a substantial one, though it had been cut into. The Populists suffered more severely than any other group, their representation being reduced from twenty-six Congressmen to seven. More important than the control of the lower house was the victory attained in the Senate. The independent Senators, who had held the balance of power during 1897 to 1899 and had prevented the passage of currency legislation, had been routed, and there was now a clear majority ready to do the administration's bidding. The Presidential message of December 5, 1899, called for a "continuance of the gold standard;" the result was the passage of the Currency Act of March, 1900, which once and for all (at any rate until 1933) made gold the single standard of the nation's currency. Another political event of outstanding importance in 1898 was the election of the Spanish-American War's only military hero, Theodore Roosevelt, to be governor of New York State.

In the face of such triumphs there could be little doubt of McKinley's renomination by the Republican host when it assembled in convention at

Philadelphia in June, 1900. The platform, too, thanks to Hanna's adroit management, was completely prepared and awaited the approval of the docile delegates. About the choice of a Vice-Presidential candidate there was, however, some uncertainty: Hanna favored Cornelius N. Bliss of New York, who had been his right-hand man in 1896, and who had sat in McKinley's Cabinet as Secretary of the Interior. Senator Thomas C. Platt of New York (the Empire State's "boss") supported Governor Roosevelt in order to get him out of New York politics. Although Roosevelt said he did not want the nomination there uprose a popular clamor for him among the western delegates. He was a war hero, he would strengthen the ticket in the West, he was as good a campaigner as Bryan. All bowed to the inevitable and both McKinley and Roosevelt were unanimously nominated by the Republican convention. The platform pointed with pride to McKinley's achievements and to the nation's prosperity. It pledged the Republican party to the gold standard and the protective tariff, contained an ambiguously worded trust plank, called for the restriction of immigration and the protection of the nation's workingmen against contract and convict labor, and approved of governmental encouragement of a merchant marine. The country was justified in annexing Hawaii; we would get out of Cuba as soon as pacification was completed; the Philippines were rightfully ours.

Peace reigned, too, over the deliberations of the Democratic convention when it met at Kansas City on July 4. There was no question of Bryan's ascendancy, and even his once bitter foe, former Senator Hill of New York, was present to second the nomination. Bryan was unanimously chosen and Adlai E. Stevenson of Illinois was named for the Vice-Presidency. The Democratic platform reflected the interests of the party's candidate. Imperialism was named the "paramount" issue of the campaign and Republican policies in Puerto Rico, Cuba, and the Philippines were denounced. Said the platform: "We assert that no nation can long endure half republic and half empire and we warn the American people that imperialism abroad will lead quickly and inevitably to despotism at home." With regard to the Philippines, therefore, the Democrats favored the establishment of a stable form of government, independence, and protection from outside interference. Other planks included: a promise to carry on unceasing warfare against monopoly; a condemnation of the Tariff Act of 1897 as "a trust-breeding measure;" a pledge to enlarge the scope of the Interstate Commerce Act; a free silver declaration; a demand for the direct election of Senators; an attack on government by injunction; a pledge to construct the Nicaraguan Canal.

A large group of minor parties participated in the election of 1900. The Social Democratic party, appearing for the first time in a national election, named Eugene V. Debs for the Presidency. While the Populist party endorsed Bryan, the Middle-of-the-Road faction, which had so disapproved of the wisdom of fusion in 1896, this time asserted its independence and named its own candidates, selecting Wharton Barker of Pennsylvania for the Presidency and Ignatius Donnelly for the Vice-Presidency. The United Christian party, the Socialist Labor party, and the National Prohibition party also nominated standard-bearers. The Silver Republican party and the Anti-Imperialist League endorsed Bryan.

Bryan repeated the feats of his 1896 campaign, but the issue was never in doubt. Theodore Roosevelt and Mark Hanna invaded the erstwhile silver country, and the easy platform manners and good humor of both did much to destroy Bryan's warnings of continued government by the interests. After all, prosperity had come and the prices of agricultural staples had been steadily mounting. The "paramount" issue of imperialism was too remote to inflame the American mind, and the average American, brought up in the school of evangelical Christianity, was prepared to take up gladly the white man's burden with regard to his little brown brother in the distant Philippines. Hanna's machine, too, worked smoothly so that the Republican campaign did not want for funds. Hanna's assessments on the corporations were met without question, and even his return of unexpended moneys to contributors was accepted without too much surprise.

Bryan carried but four states outside of the Solid South, and these were the mining states of Colorado, Idaho, Montana, and Nevada. Even his own Nebraska voted for McKinley. McKinley's total popular vote was 7,220,000 against Bryan's 6,359,000. Debs received 94,800 votes and Barker, the Populist, 50,600. In the electoral college, McKinley's total was 292, Bryan's 155. A Republican Congress was again elected. There was no question of the significance of the victory: the free silver heresy had been routed; Populism, with its threat of governmental meddling in industry, banking, and transportation, had been effectively disposed of; the Democratic opposition was discredited. The country had complacently accepted the union of Republicanism and industrial capitalism and had refused to take too seriously all the talk of monopoly, protective tariff, and exploitation of labor and agriculture in the interests of the few.

The new era of good feeling that Republican orators hailed was suddenly disturbed by a shocking event. President McKinley had gone to Buffalo early in September to attend the Pan-American Exposition, and there, on September 5, he had spoken on tariff reciprocity as a means of uniting the United States with Latin America in greater bonds of friendship. The next day the sad news was flashed up and down the country and around the world: America's war President had been shot down by a demented anarchist. Eight days later McKinley was dead and the turbulent, volatile, and frank-spoken Roosevelt was President of the United States.

· 19 ·

A World Theater

IMPERIALISM IN THE UNITED STATES BEFORE WORLD WAR I

It is not unusual for commentators to state that the declaration of war against Spain in 1898 signalized the launching of the United States upon an imperialistic career. To them it is difficult to account for a conflict in which neither national honor nor the protection of American interests in Cuba was involved. To many, the Spanish-American War was in reality a pretext for the acquisition of territory and the extension of America's sphere of influence into the Pacific. With 1898, the American people joined the company of the European powers who were scrambling to divide Africa, the Levant, and the Far East among themselves. The series of events that occurred in the spring and summer of 1898 presented a chain of evidence that must have convinced many. On March 6, Germany had wrested from China a long-term lease on Kiaochow Bay; on March 27, Russia had occupied Port Arthur; on May 27, France had taken Kwangchow; on July 1, Great Britain was settled in Weihaiwei and at Mirs Bay. And on April 19, the American Congress had declared war on Spain! Imperialism was in the air in the last quarter of the nineteenth century; China and the islands of the Pacific were being partitioned among the mighty. What was more natural than the wish on the part of the United States, now grown to greatness, to participate in the division before all the spoils had disappeared?

Certainly, it is not to be denied that the United States had its share of public men who had learned to employ the exalted jargon of the Rudyard Kiplings, Joseph Chamberlains, William II's, and Théophile Delcassés: the whole vocabulary of white man's burden, place in the sun, and the rest. The writings, the speeches, the correspondence, and the table talk of Captain Alfred T. Mahan, Theodore Roosevelt, John Hay, Henry Cabot Lodge, and Whitelaw Reid were thus flavored. But how much did all this have to do with imperialism? Really, very little. A close examination of the situation compels the conclusion that the United States did not adopt a policy of imperialism (in its modern sense) at this time at all. These three circumstances are to be noted: 1. European extraterritorial expansion was forced by a number of factors none of which existed in the United States at the end of the nineteenth century; 2. our so-called imperialists were not expressing a conscious American need but were only imitating a set of ideas they had acquired from the English; 3. American sentiment, as expressed in the press and in Congress, was opposed to expansion and raised all manner of obstacles to American imitation of European foreign policy.

Beginning with the second half of the nineteenth century, the powers of Europe turned their attention to the backward regions of the earth, largely because of the following reasons: They demanded new outlets for capital investments. They required a large variety of raw materials most of which they themselves did not possess. They needed markets for their surplus manufactured goods. The pressure of their own surplus populations forced them to concern themselves with programs of settlement and emigration. The comparatively limited opportunities at home for individual advancement spurred the younger and impecunious sons of the middle class to seek their fortunes in every obscure corner of the earth. For these reasons the imperialism of the late nineteenth century differed materially from the overseas expansion of the sixteenth, seventeenth, eighteenth, and early nineteenth centuries; territorial expansion, in its larger outlines, centered in the notions of permanent settlement and of trade pure and simple, with the mother country as the chief beneficiary; imperialism, however, was based, primarily, on the exploitation of native resources and populations. At its core was the need for finding outlets for home savings in enterprises overseas.

It is to be noted that in the eighties and nineties, indeed up to the outbreak of World War I, the American capitalistic economy was troubled by none of the difficulties that compelled Europeans to turn to an imperialistic policy. America was a debtor nation and American capital surpluses were so slight that we had, by the turn of the century, but half a billion dollars invested abroad (two-thirds of which was in Canada and Mexico) as against the three-and-one-third billions that foreigners owned in American securities and properties. Further, of raw materials—of foodstuffs, cotton, minerals, vegetable oils—the North American continent had a fabulous store. The manufactured goods we produced we consumed almost entirely at home, and our industrial life was not yet confronted by the problem of disposing of surpluses. That America was the golden land of opportunity and that fame and fortune were the quickly gained prizes of all those possessing enterprise and imagination, the careers of her industrialists adequately demonstrated. And as for the pressure of population, it is enough to recall that the growing needs of American industry required the continuous importation of foreign skilled and unskilled labor for another twenty years. It must be apparent that as far as motives were concerned, American expansion into backward regions had none of those aspects of necessity that were to be found in the European movement overseas.

In brief, it may be said that while European imperialism was coming to flower in the crowded years of 1900 to 1914, the United States was in reality engaged in territorial expansion simply. Roosevelt and his friends thought we were following in the footsteps of the England of the twentieth century; before we were finished, however, it was to be seen that it was the England of the eighteenth century that was our model. In the nineteen twenties, Americans began to perceive that our overseas adventures had cost us a pretty penny, and that there was not the slightest prospect that any return could ever be realized on the huge sums expended. When, in the nineteen thirties, certain Americans demanded the immediate independence of the Philippines they were not prompted by the sentimental liberalism of twenty years earlier but by a hard-headed understanding of the facts. Keeping the Philippines—and Puerto Rico, too—simply had not paid out economically.

THE UNITED STATES IN THE PHILIPPINES

The Philippine Islands are an archipelago in the North Pacific, three days' steaming from South China, and seven from Shanghai; Manila, the capital, is 6221 miles from San Francisco. There are 3141 islands in the group with a land area of 114,400 square miles. However, nine-tenths of the land area is to be found in 11 of the islands, of which Luzon and Mindanao are the largest. The total native population is said to consist of 43 different ethnological groups speaking 87 different languages or dialects. In 1903, the islands had a population of 7,635,426; in 1918 (census), 10,314,310, of whom nine-tenths were Christian. The census of 1939 counted 16,382,000 and, in 1947, the population was estimated at 18,500,-000, 1,490,000 of whom lived in cities of more than 50,000 people. In 1939 to 1940, there were 166,631 foreigners recorded: 117,487 Chinese, 29,057 Japanese, 11,378 Europeans, and 8709 Americans, exclusive of military personnel.

Filipinos under the lead of Aguinaldo, made common cause with the Americans against the Spaniards and had succeeded in subduing the island of Luzon before the appearance of General Merritt's force on the scene. The natives began to entertain doubts concerning the American intentions upon Merritt's refusal to permit the insurgents to enter Manila when that city capitulated on August 13, 1898; and doubts gave way to certainty when the conditions of the peace treaty were announced. The upshot was the outbreak of hostilities between Filipinos and Americans in February, 1899. For the next three years an American army, 60,000 strong, was engaged in the business of pacifying the islands. The resistance of the insurgents was stubborn; American troops, not wisely led, were permitted to fall back on the devices of guerrilla warfare, so that the American public was horrified to hear tales of fire and looting, the killing of prisoners, the administering of the "water cure," and even the erection of concentration camps. Despite the capture of Aguinaldo on March 23, 1901, another year was necessary before Washington could announce the termination of the insurrection. It had cost us $175 million and the lives of 4300 men to convince the Filipinos that we meant to rule the islands for their own good.

In January, 1899, President McKinley announced his Philippine policy. Said he: "The Philippines are ours, not to exploit but to develop, to civilize, to educate, to train in the science of self-government. This is the path of duty which we must follow or be recreant to a mighty trust committed to us." The result was the dispatching of two commissions to the islands: the first, headed by President Shurman of Cornell, for the purpose of investigation (January, 1899); and the second, headed by Judge William Howard Taft, for the purpose of erecting a civil government (April, 1900). On June 21, 1901, as a result of Congressional authorization, McKinley appointed Taft the first civil governor of the islands and civil officials replaced the military in all but a few of the provinces. Congress, on July 1, 1902, passed an Organic Act, constituting the archipelago an "unorganized" territory and making its inhabitants citizens of the Philippine Islands, and as such entitled to the protection of the United States. Under the Taft rule, Americanization was vigorously pushed. The original Taft Commission, enlarged by the addition of three Filipino members, was retained in the islands as a legislative and executive body, and measures were enacted to prepare the Filipinos for the self-government promised by American policy. Particularly commendable was Taft's preoccupation with the extinguishing of the friar land titles. The Catholic orders held some 400,000 acres of the choicest land in the archipelago, and these Taft was able to acquire from Rome in December, 1903, through the payment of $7,239,-000. Taft surrendered his post in the same month to enter Roosevelt's Cabinet as Secretary of War.

On October 16, 1907, after a census had determined the bases of choice and elections had taken place, the first Philippine assembly was opened. Some eighty members took their seats, of whom the majority belonged to the Nationalista party. The Commission, spoken of above, continued to act as an upper chamber. By 1913, the Republican administrations had expanded the Commission to nine members and had given places on it to four Filipinos. Only one of these, however, held a portfolio. Four governors-general followed Taft in comparatively quick succession in the years 1903 to 1913. W. Cameron Forbes, governor-general during Taft's administration, built schools, stabilized finances, separated church and state, and expended large sums in public works. It was an enlightened colonial policy—without, however, progressing very far in the direction of that home rule which Roosevelt and Taft and their Secretaries of War had regularly been promising.

The victory of the Democrats in 1912 was hailed with rejoicings in the islands. Since 1900 Democratic platforms and leaders had been speaking of immediate or early independence, the 1912 declaration, particularly, being unequivocal. Wilson's governor-general, Francis Burton Harrison, though new to colonial rule and indeed the Orient, apparently had definite notions as to how autonomy and the day of independence were best to be advanced. The Civil Service was quickly Filipinized, and from 2623 American officials in 1913 the number was reduced to 614 in 1921. Upon Harrison's recommendation, Filipinos were given a majority of the seats in the appointive Commission. The Philippine government was permitted to embark upon a number of significant commercial enterprises, the outstanding ones being the purchase of the Manila Railroad and the organization of the Philippine National Bank, the National Coal Company, and the National Development Company (a general promotion corporation). Railroads were built, wireless stations erected, and rural credit societies were established to aid native agriculture.

On August 29, 1916, Congress passed the Jones Act, which continued to be the frame of government for the islands until 1934. An organized effort was made to compel the naming of a day for recognition of Philippine independence, but this was stubbornly contested and in the end the opponents won. The preamble of the Jones Act declared the United States to be committed to Philippine independence as soon as a "stable government" could be established. All the inhabitants of the islands who had been Spanish subjects on April 11, 1899, and the descendants of these, were recognized as citizens of the Philippines. In addition to a bill of rights, the act provided for male suffrage for all those who could read and write Spanish, English, or a native dialect. In place of the appointive commission there was set up an elective senate, with the result that the natives were to control both houses of the legislature. Of the six executive departments but one, that of instruction and health, was to be filled by an American, who was to carry the title of vice-governor. He, like the governor-general, was to be appointed by the President with the advice and consent of the American Senate. The veto power was vested in the governor-general, with a final veto in the hands of the President of the United States when legislation was adversely passed upon. Governor-General Harrison, interpreting the Jones Act in the spirit of its preamble, tried to make the government truly parliamentary by establishing a liaison officer between the legislative and executive departments and, in 1917, by setting up the extralegal Council of State, made up of the six members of the cabinet, the president of the senate, and the speaker of the house. This Council created the native policies under which the islands were governed for the four years up to 1921.

In his message to Congress on December 7, 1920, President Wilson asked for independence for the islands on the ground that the condition set by the Jones Act preamble, that is to say, "stable government," had been fulfilled. But the Republicans were at the helm and they proceeded at once to turn from the, to them, dangerous course upon which Wilson and Harrison had embarked. President Harding dispatched a third commission to the islands, the so-called Wood-Forbes Commission, made up entirely of Army men except for Forbes himself. On October 8, 1921, the Commission reported a general sentiment among the Christian Filipinos for independence but insisted that the natives had not yet had time to "absorb and thoroughly master the powers already in their hands." Filipinization of the government services had been too hasty; immediate independence was out of the question, and the United States ought not to be left in a position of responsibility without authority. General Leonard Wood stayed on in the islands as Harding's governor-general. For two years the Filipino leaders gave him a measure of co-operation, but as his policies took shape passive acceptance was followed by active opposition. Wood undid most of Harrison's work. He took the Philippine government out of business and transferred most of the commercial enterprises to private capitalists. He assumed active control over the government by abolishing the Council of State. He denied ministerial responsibility to the local legislature by supervising the executive departments himself. He chose as his advisers a group of military assistants, whom the natives dubbed "Wood's Khaki Cabinet." In 1923, the Filipino cabinet resigned, and for the next four years legislature and executive were openly hostile.

President Coolidge gave the Wood program his support, but he could not shut his ears to the rumblings of discontent nor entirely disregard the action of the Philippine senate in unanimously voting for a plebiscite on independence (November 6, 1925). Also, the Filipinos were conducting a skilful propaganda in the United States and were gaining a growing body of American sympathizers. In May, 1926, therefore, Coolidge sent another mission to the islands, headed by Carmi A. Thompson. Thompson filed his report on December 4, 1926, and recommended that independence be postponed. He suggested the creation of a new colonial department to supervise the administration of the American possessions; that steps be taken to re-establish co-operation between the legislative and executive branches; that the governor-general's military advisers be replaced by civilians; that the Jones Act be neither amended nor repealed; that the policy of home rule be enlarged; that the Philippine government continue liquidating its business enterprises; and that the land laws, against large holdings, be amended in order to attract corporations into the development of coffee and rubber. Thompson's findings were a veiled criticism of Wood's governorship, but the Coolidge administration was spared further embarrassment when the general died August 7, 1927, after a short illness. Henry L. Stimson accepted the post of governor-general in December, and though he announced his intention of continuing his predecessor's policies it at once became evident that conciliation was to be his guide. The cabinet he appointed had the consent of the majority leaders of the legislature; the Council of State was re-established; and cabinet members were again made responsible to both legislative houses as had been the case under Harrison. In March, 1929, Stimson resigned to take the post of Secretary of State in President Hoover's Cabinet, and he was succeeded by Dwight F. Davis, former Secretary of War.

Heretofore, American opposition to continued stay in the islands had been on sentimental and liberal grounds: by 1929, however, it became apparent that there was a well-organized opinion, based on economic considerations, for their release. American economic conquest of the Philippines had not been pushed very far and American interests in the islands were small. The assessed value of all taxable property in the islands for 1927 was but $832 million. Despite the large exportations of American capital in the years following World War I there was not more than $160 million of American money invested in the Philippines by 1930. More than three-fourths of this was to be found in government securities, municipals, rails, and public utilities. By 1939 to 1940, however, Americans had some $200 million invested in the Philippines, with mining properties, public utilities, and sugar production accounting for the largest amounts.

There had been governmental encouragement of trade through the lowering of tariff barriers, but our commercial relations with the Philippines became significant only in the late nineteen thirties, when world trade as a whole diminished. The Tariff Act of 1902 permitted Philippine products to enter the United States at a reduction of 25 per cent from the rates of the Dingley Tariff. The Tariff Act of 1909 established free trade between the islands and the mainland, except that duty-free sugar exports were limited to 300,000 tons. There was a somewhat similar restriction on tobacco exports to the United States. The Tariff Act of 1913 provided for free trade without restrictions of any sort, and the policy was continued in the 1922 and 1930 tariff.

The United States–Philippine trade was valued at $203,300,000 for 1929 to 1930, of which imports from the United States came to $89,900,000 and exports to the United States to $113,500,000 (corresponding figures for 1940, $89,600,000 and $93,300,000). This was a per capita trade of $17.00 for each Filipino. On the other hand, the United States–Hawaiian trade had been worth $194,770,000 in 1928, or a per capita trade of $584.40

for each Hawaiian. Even Puerto Rico was more valuable to the United States, for the per capita trade for each Puerto Rican was $107.00 in 1928 to 1929.

What were we importing from the Philippines? Largely, sugar; and to a less extent, cocoanut oil, copra, cigars and abacá (Manila hemp). During the late nineteen thirties, gold and chrome ore came to be significant items in our trade with the Philippines. More important politically was the fact that in the period 1920 to 1934, Philippine sugar production increased until it was supplying 19 per cent of our requirements. Here was where the shoe pinched. Philippine sugar, produced for the most part by non-American capital, was entering the United States duty-free, to compete with the American-raised sugar of Cuba, Puerto Rico, the Hawaiian Islands, Louisiana, and the American beet-growing states. Thus, the United States took $51,900,000 worth of Philippine sugar in 1929 to 1930 and about $41,000,000 worth in 1940 (since World War II, copra and cocoanut oil products have been the chief factor in the islands' economic revival through trade). Similarly, Philippine cocoanut oil was competing seriously in American markets with the products of our own dairying industry. It was not strange, therefore, that in October, 1929, when the Senate was discussing the sugar schedule of the Smoot tariff bill, Senator King of Utah (the leading beet-growing state) and Senator Broussard of Louisiana (the leading cane-growing state) should introduce amendments calling for the immediate independence of the Philippines. The King measure was voted down, but the poll showed 36 yeas against 45 nays. American proponents of independence were not disheartened by this initial setback, and during 1930 and 1931 they continued to press for the release of the islands. This agitation was regarded with disapproval by Washington; the lines of the impending struggle were clearly drawn in October, 1931, when President Hoover, after a short visit to the islands by his Secretary of War, declared that "economic independence of the Philippines must be attained before political independence can be successful." And, according to the President: "Independence tomorrow without assured economic stability would result in the collapse of Philippine government revenues and the collapse of all economic life in the islands." The New Deal was more sanguine; and, as will be pointed out, not only promised independence but gave it to the Filipinos as soon as World War II was over.

In another respect, the Philippines were disappointing. It was generally held, in 1898, that the Philippines would serve as a center for the tapping of the Chinese trade. Thus Whitelaw Reid, in urging annexation, wrote:

To extend now the authority of the United States over the great Philippine archipelago is to fence in the China Sea and secure an almost equally commanding position on the other sea of the Pacific—doubling our control of it and of the fabulous trade the twentieth century will see it bear.... The trade in the Philippines will be but a drop in the bucket compared to that of China, for which they give us an unapproachable foothold.

The prophecy simply was not fulfilled, for the regular Pacific steamship lanes passed outside the islands and great re-export depots were never established. In 1895, the Philippine-China trade was valued in the neighborhood of 20,000,000 pesos; in 1926, it was valued at 19,600,000 pesos. American businessmen employed the ports of Hong Kong, Shanghai, and Singapore as distribution centers for the Chinese and British Malayan trade.

Finally, as far as security was concerned, it was commonly recognized that the islands constituted a danger rather than otherwise, in the event of a Pacific war. The concentration of an American fleet in Philippine waters could protect neither the Hawaiian Islands nor our California coast, and its great distance from the American shores would make it vulnerable to attack from easily supported enemy fleets whose bases happen to be in Asiatic waters. Indeed, so it turned out to be in World War II.

American rule over the islands was distinguished for its humanity in a portion of the earth where the white man's burden was lightly held. When the United States occupied the islands, the proportion of illiteracy was 85 per cent; in 1939, census figures showed that reduced to 51.2 per cent. The public-school system was reaching more than half the school-age population, 1,944,569 children in 1939; in that year there were 6894 students with collegiate standing in the University of the Philippines and 1080 training for the professions, while 83,692 persons were enrolled in 1498 projects for adult education. Deaths from cholera and smallpox were practically eliminated; order was maintained and justice honestly dispensed; the native population was given employment in large public-works programs; small agricultural holdings were encouraged, and a public land policy made homestead grants and restricted the maximum acreage of corporations. In an imperialistic economy where exploitation of native populations was the rule, the Filipino peoples were singularly free.

THE UNITED STATES IN PUERTO RICO

Puerto Rico, smallest and easternmost island of the Great Antilles, in the West Indies, has an area of 3670 square miles. In 1940, its population was 1,869,225 an increase of more than 21.1 per cent over the previous decade; the island's estimated population for 1948 was approximately 2,200,000. The population is preponderantly rural, 69.7 per cent being engaged in agriculture.

For eighteen months, American military authorities governed the island. Congress, on April 12, 1900, by virtue of the passage of the Foraker Act, authorized the establishment of a civil government and this was done May 1. Puerto Rico was given the status of an "unorganized" territory and its inhabitants were made citizens of Puerto Rico. Government was vested in an elective house of delegates and an executive council of eleven. These councilors, together with the governor-general, were appointed by the President with the advice and consent of the American Senate. American control was maintained through the fact that six of the eleven councilors (who at the same time headed the executive departments) were always Americans. Up to 1917 the local legislative assembly was the scene, frequently, of turbulent debate because of the dominance of Americans in political affairs, and the lower house sought to frustrate executive policy by refusing to pass appropriation bills. In 1909, the United States Congress was forced to take cognizance of these dilatory tactics when it amended the island's organic law to provide the carrying-over of the previous year's appropriation bills in the event of the lower house's refusal to enact new legislation. Another source of discontent was the anomalous citizenship accorded to the islanders.

In 1917, the Wilson administration, by the passage of the Jones Act, applied itself to the resolution of both these difficulties. The new organic law made Puerto Ricans citizens of the United States, and a bill of rights gave them almost all those civil prerogatives enjoyed by Americans under the Constitution (except the right to demand a trial by jury). Both houses of the legislature were made elective and given complete legislative powers, subject to Presidential veto. Of the six executive departmental heads but two were to be appointed by the President with the approval of the American Senate. The President, too, appointed the governor, the auditor, and the insular supreme court. While this was a more satisfactory status than the previous one, it still was not home rule, in view of the President's right to the veto power and his control over appointments. In 1928, the Puerto Rican legislature petitioned President Coolidge for the grant of full autonomy (not statehood). Coolidge's reply was tart. He reviewed the history of the island under American dominion, pointed out the benefits that had accrued to the islanders, and ended by saying that "it certainly is not unreasonable to ask that those who speak for Puerto Rico limit their petitions to those things which may be granted without denial of such hope." With the exception of the appointment in 1946 of an islander as governor by President Truman, the hopes of Puerto Ricans for a larger measure of self-rule were not farther advanced during the nineteen thirties and forties until August, 1947, when the Butler-Crawford Act gave the island the right to elect its governor, who was to appoint his own councilors. The President of the United States retained the right to appoint the auditor, the justices of the insular supreme court, and the federal co-ordinator of civilian activities for Puerto Rico.

American statesmen have shown small disposition to understand the fundamental difficulties which confront the Puerto Rican population. It is true that, superficially, extraordinary progress has been made under American rule. The death rate has been more than cut in half, great public works have been built, the benefits of public and compulsory education have been extended so that more than half the school-age population is being reached, albeit on a part-time basis. In 1946, there were 364,944 children enrolled in the public schools and the $28,869,054 spent on education was about 21.5 per cent of the island's budget. Puerto Rico has grown rich and its trade has multiplied since the coming of the Americans. Thus, in 1901, the assessed valuation of property on the island was $96,400,000; by 1940, it was $311,800,000, and it rose to more than $376,000,000 by 1946.

Yet in reality, Puerto Rico is a land of peons. In 1928, there were fewer farms than in 1896; the number of agricultural laborers and tenants has steadily increased (four out of every five persons living in the country are landless); the growing acreage in sugar cane has cut heavily into the amount of land under food crops and coffee. Out of the island's total area of 2,000,000 acres, one-third, it is estimated, is in the hands of fewer than 500 owners. By the extension of the American tariff to include the island—in March, 1902—the islanders have been compelled to buy their necessities, and they import almost all their foodstuffs, at American prices. Nothing more completely revealed the unhappy condition of the people than the year 1930, when Governor Theodore Roosevelt was compelled to appeal to Congress and private philanthropy to relieve the great distress caused by stoppage of work (and, to a lesser extent, by the hurricane of 1928). In the winter of 1930, 60 per cent of Puerto Rico's population was unemployed and a large part of it was starving. Puerto Ricans grew only staples, and staples in 1930 were a glut in the world market.

During the nineteen thirties, efforts were made to meet some of these problems. Thus, the New Deal attempted to further rural rehabilitation through a Puerto Rico Reconstruction Administration; and the Agricultural Adjustment Administration made the payment of sugar and tobacco benefits contingent on the planting of some food crops. Drawbacks of federal taxes on Puerto Rican rum help pay for some island services. The insular legislature has tried to foster industrialization through blanket tax exemptions and the activities of the Puerto Rico Development Company, while it attacked concentration of land ownership by enforcement of a United States law of 1900 forbidding corporations to hold more than 500 acres. Education, and the legalization of birth control information, are expected to check the rapid rate of population increase. Emigration to the mainland, New York City particularly, has, as yet, created problems both for individuals and the community rather than afforded real relief from the pressure on Puerto Rican living standards.

In 1941, a WPA survey found the average income per family, in cash and in kind, to be $341 a year, about $11 less than the cost of food alone. In 1946, weekly earnings in the sugar fields, where collective bargaining of a sort raised wages above those in other agricultural occupations, averaged $5.07 a week (plus a federal subsidy of 23 cents for 8 hours' work). Sugar accounted for 62.8 per cent of the island's exports in 1947, with needlework, tobacco, rum, and fruits next in order. Coffee, pre-eminently the crop of the small farmer, had disappeared from the export list, partly because of the concentration of land ownership, partly because of hurricane damage and South American competition. American manufacturers found a paradise of cheap labor in Puerto Rico, with the result that exports of manufactured goods have increased. In 1922, the export of cigars and tobacco was valued at $6,270,000; in 1946, at $21,373,775. In 1922, the export of wearing apparel was valued at $3,790,000; in 1946, at $10,068,797. With the repeal of the Eighteenth Amendment, rum became an important export, valued at $12,487,000 in 1946.

In the late nineteen forties, as in 1928, a large part of the island's wealth was owned abroad, chiefly in the United States. Foreign investments were heaviest in sugar (land and mills valued at $68,964,942), rum, banking ($130,269,356 in assets), and insular and municipal securities ($33,988,317). Although insular government agencies such as the Water Resources Authority took over some mainland investments in utilities, the bonds which provided capital for these projects (in the amount of some $27,000,000 above the $33,988,317 in insular and municipal securities) were largely mainland-owned.

In the light of this situation, the demands of native Puerto Ricans are understandable. They seek autonomy: to provide homesteads for the peasantry; to free the island economy from the restrictions of the American tariff and from complete dependence on the production of even subsidized staples, which suffered so severely from the fluctuations of world markets during the twenties and thirties; to cope with absentee landlordism; to check the proletarianization of the island, a process which has divided its population into bosses and peons; and, finally, to allow the development of a significant cultural life, for the Puerto Ricans are Latins at heart (72.2 per cent of the population spoke no English in 1940) and the Anglo-Saxon learning of the upper classes is only a thin veneer.

THE CONSTITUTION AND OUR ISLAND DEPENDENCIES

In the early years of American possession of Puerto Rico and the Philippines, the United States Supreme Court was called upon to determine the constitutional status of these dependencies. The first questions arose out of the operation of the American tariff. In 1901, in the case of De Lima v. Bidwell [1] the Court ruled that Puerto Rico had become American territory and that Puerto Rican products could enter the mainland duty-free. This case had been concerned with the imposition of duties before the passage of the Organic Act for the island in 1900. But the Foraker Act changed matters, held the Supreme Court in Downes v. Bidwell.[2] Under this law, Congress had extended the Dingley Tariff to Puerto Rican products, reducing the rates, however, to 15 per cent of the duties imposed in the original schedules. This act the Supreme Court proceeded to declare constitutional. Justice Brown, who wrote the majority opinion, ruled that while Puerto Rico had become a territory of the United States by the treaty of cession and was subject to the jurisdiction of the United States, it was nevertheless not to be regarded as being incorporated into the country. Hence, the Constitution was not to be considered as being applicable, in every particular, to all lands over which American sovereignty held sway. While it is true, said the Court, that Congress by the Constitution was prohibited from the exercise of certain legislative powers, it was to be understood that many of these prohibitions held only in the case of the United States and did not apply to other territory "subject to the jurisdiction thereof." The majority opinion was concurred in by four other justices but they advanced different reasons for agreeing with Mr. Justice Brown that the "Constitution did not follow the flag."

In decisions that followed, the Court denied the extension of the Constitution's Bill of Rights to the dependencies. In these cases the Court drew a distinction between the "fundamental" and the "formal" provisions of the Constitution: the first group the Congress and the federal authorities might not abridge; the second could be disregarded as far as the insular possessions were concerned. Thus in Hawaii v. Mankichi [3] the Court declared that indictments by grand juries were not necessary and that a felon might be found guilty even if the petit jury's decision had not been reached by an unanimous vote. And in Balzac v. People of Puerto Rico [4] the Court ruled that the Jones Act of 1917, though it had invested Puerto Ricans with American citizenship, still had not incorporated the island into the United States. Hence the plaintiff in error, who, without a jury trial, had been sent to jail for committing criminal libel, could not demand a new hearing on the basis of violation of his constitutional rights.

In other words, the American executive and Congress might go as far as they pleased in Americanizing our subject peoples—they might compel

[1] 182 U.S. 1.
[2] 182 U.S. 244.
[3] 190 U.S. 197 (1903).
[4] 258 U.S. 298 (1922).

Filipinos and Puerto Ricans to speak the English language and conform to the way of life of our industrial civilization—but they were not in duty bound to extend to the islanders the constitutional guarantees which Americans of the mainland enjoyed.[5]

These Insular Cases, as they have been called, may be said to have established the following principles as underlying American colonial policy: The United States possesses the power to acquire new territory. The United States has authority to provide the governments and administer such possessions. The power of governing new territory is vested exclusively in Congress, which is subject, practically, to no limitations. Except for what may be called the "fundamental" provisions of the Constitution, neither the Constitution nor the general statutes of the country are extended to the new territories by the simple fact of acquisition. The Constitution and the statutes apply only as a result of specific Congressional enactment.

THE UNITED STATES IN CUBA

By the Treaty of Paris, which terminated the Spanish-American War, the United States had pledged itself to pacify Cuba and protect private property. The result was American military occupation of the island up to May 20, 1902. General Leonard Wood, invested with dictatorial powers, ruled the island and laid the groundwork for a stable government. Church and state were separated, heroic sanitation programs (under Major Gorgas) were started, a school system was inaugurated, Havana was converted into a modern city, and the public finances were put on a sound basis.

But how long could we in decency stay in Cuba? On the one hand there was the Teller resolution, passed at the time of the declaration of war with Spain, which was an unequivocal pledge of withdrawal upon the completion of the island's pacification; on the other, there was our economic stake in the Cuban sugar and ore lands and hence our interest in political stability. While a Cuban constitutional convention, beginning with November 5, 1900, sat in deliberation, Americans, Elihu Root the chief among them, were giving earnest thought to the question of the future of American-Cuban relations. Early in 1901, the key to the puzzle was found and Congress was asked to pass the so-called Platt Amendment, made up of

[5] Interestingly enough, in Rasmussen v. United States (197 U. S. 516 [1905]), the Supreme Court declared that Alaska belonged in another category. Alaska, said the Court, was incorporated into the United States and therefore its inhabitants might claim the customary constitutional guarantees for procedural and substantive rights. The reason advanced was that incorporation had been specifically promised in the treaty of acquisition. Of course, in Alaska, the government was not confronted by the problem of a long-established alien people, so that the Court's rationalizations are not hard to explain.

eight sections, that had been added to the military appropriations bill for 1901 to 1902. The bill was signed by McKinley on March 2, 1901. It called upon the Cuban constitutional convention to incorporate the Platt Amendment into the new constitution. Thus confronted by what was tantamount to an ultimatum, and under pain of continued American occupation, the convention could not but comply, and on June 12 (by a vote of 17 to 11) tacked the Platt Amendment on to the new Cuban fundamental law. In 1903, the Amendment was written into a permanent treaty between the two countries. The following were the eight provisions of the Platt Amendment: [6]

1. The Cuban government was not to make any treaties with foreign powers which might impair Cuban independence; nor was it to permit any foreign powers to alienate Cuban territory.

2. The Cuban government was not to assume any public debts for which the ordinary revenues might be inadequate.

3. "That the government of Cuba consents that the United States may exercise the right to intervene for the preservation of Cuban independence, the maintenance of a government adequate for the protection of life, property and individual liberty, and for discharging the obligations with respect to Cuba imposed by the Treaty of Paris on the United States, now to be assumed and undertaken by the government of Cuba."

4. All the acts of the United States in Cuba during the military occupation were to be ratified and held valid.

5. The Cuban government was to continue the American sanitation program.

6. The Isle of Pines did not belong to Cuba and its disposition was to be the subject of further discussion.[7]

7. The United States was to have the right to lease or buy from Cuba such lands as might be deemed necessary for coaling and naval stations.[8]

8. These sections were to be embodied in a permanent treaty with the United States.

In explanation of Section 3, which was the heart of the amendment, Root assured the Cubans that the instrument would be regarded only as an extension of the Monroe Doctrine. We would intervene only when Cuban independence appeared threatened as a result of internal anarchy or foreign attack. In 1906, the United States did intervene—upon entirely justifiable grounds; in 1912 and 1917, the reasons for American intervention were nothing short of frivolous. In 1920, there took place a fourth intervention, the consequences of which we shall note presently.

Commercial relations between the two nations still remained to be settled, a consummation less easily accomplished than the political un-

---

[6] Abridged in paraphrase except for Section 3, which is quoted in full.

[7] In March, 1925, the American Senate finally ratified a treaty for the cession of the Isle of Pines to Cuba.

[8] Cuba leased to the United States, for $2000 per year, naval stations at Guantánamo Bay and Bahía Honda. After 1913 the latter was abandoned, but as a result of subsequent arrangements the naval reservation at Guantánamo Bay was extended.

derstanding. During the fall of 1901 and the whole of 1902 and 1903 the Roosevelt administration bent all its energies toward the acceptance, by Congress, first, of an amendment to the Dingley Tariff Act, and then of a reciprocity agreement by which Cuban sugar would be admitted at reduced rates. Roosevelt championed the plan in the grand language of statesmanship. Said he: "Cuba is an independent republic but a republic which has assumed certain special obligations as regards her international position in compliance with our request. I ask for special concessions in return." The cynical were quick to point out that the Sugar Trust could be the only beneficiary of such an arrangement; while Congressional representatives from a dozen beet-sugar states steadily opposed the granting of reductions from the Dingley Tariff rates. On December 11, 1902, Col. Tasker H. Bliss, as Roosevelt's special commissioner, negotiated a reciprocity treaty with the island by which Cuban products were granted a reduction of 20 per cent from the original duties while American products were to be accorded preferential duties ranging from 20 to 40 per cent off. It was not until December 17, 1903, that Congress gave way and approved the reciprocity treaty. By that time the Havemeyer sugar interests had bought into the leading beet-sugar companies and opposition from the western states was stilled. That the situation of the American consumer remained unchanged—in view of the fact that the price of sugar was based on the cost of production plus the whole duty—was apparently nobody's concern.[9]

In October, 1906, the first American intervention under the Platt Amendment took place. The Cuban elections of the summer of 1906, resulting in the triumph of President Estrada Palma, had brought charges of fraud, and Estrada Palma had resigned after dissolving the Cuban legislature. Roosevelt hesitated for some time before yielding to the American consul-general's demands for intervention and consented only after surveys made on the spot by Secretary of War Taft and Assistant Secretary of State Bacon convinced him that anarchy threatened. In October, Secretary Taft sent an American military force which remained on the island until 1909 while an American civilian governor performed the executive functions of government. In 1912, President Taft dispatched American marines to Cuba when stories of race riots reached Washington. Despite the fact that the disorders had gained headway in but one province and were under control before the first month was over, the American State Department adopted a bellicose attitude and maintained marines for some time. In February, 1917, President Wilson ordered the third intervention. Marines were rushed to the island when members of the Liberal party, charging that President Menocal's re-election had been encompassed by fraud,

[9] The 20 per cent preferential treatment for Cuban sugar has continued in all the tariffs since written.

revolted, and took possession of a number of towns. Secretary of State Lansing warned the rebels that the United States would recognize no government based on revolution. The result was American occupation of Santiago and the holding of new elections under the supervision of American marines. Menocal was returned to office as a result of the refusal by the Liberals to participate in the new balloting. Cuba's entry into World War I, on the side of the Allies, furnished an excellent pretext for the continued stay of the American military so that the last of our troops did not quit the island until January, 1922.

American economic penetration, up to 1914, slowly made further advances into the Cuban life. During 1907 and 1909, American companies acquired possession of the Cuban iron reserves. In the same period, the American Tobacco Company bought up great holdings in Cuban lands. But it was in sugar that the American influence came to be largely felt. Aided by the preferential duties of the American tariffs and the growing interest of the Havemeyers in Cuba, the sugar harvests grew by leaps and bounds. In 1914, Cuba was producing 14 per cent of the world's supply of sugar and furnishing almost all of the United States' foreign sugar imports. In the same year, 35 per cent of the Cuban crop was being milled in sugar centrals owned by American capital. The ten years 1914 to 1924 were to see the Cuban economy converted into a complete dependence upon that single crop as well as the forging of the gold chains that were to make Cuba in reality an American protectorate. According to Professor Jenks, in the years 1914 to 1924 American capital investments rose from $200,000,000 to an estimated value of $1,200,000,000, with three-fourths of the sugar industry in the hands of American corporations.

Sugar boomed during the years of the first World War and an orgy of speculation took place. In May, 1920, sugar was selling at 22½ cents a pound on the New York market. By October the collapse had set in, and in December sugar was selling at 3¾ cents. The danger of political revolt and the serious jeopardy in which American economic interests were placed led to the fourth American intervention. In November, 1920, President Wilson dispatched General Enoch H. Crowder to Cuba, ostensibly to confer with President Menocal on political and financial conditions, but in fact to take control of the government. While Crowder held the reins of political power, American financial groups extended their sway over the island. The National City Bank of New York and the Royal Bank of Canada, because of the large quantity of sugar paper they carried, replaced the Banco Nacional and the Banco Español as the outstanding financial institutions while the House of Morgan floated in the United States in 1922 the bonds of an external loan of $50 million. When in January, 1923, Crowder was accorded an official recognition through his appointment as the first American ambassador to Cuba and the pressure from Washington was relaxed, it was seen that American domination was complete. But the next decade saw a reversal of these policies and under the New Deal Cuban independence and sovereignty were assured.

SECRETARY HAY AND CHINA

With new responsibilities in the Philippines and Samoa, and with an expanding Far Eastern trade, what was more natural than that the United States should begin to regard herself as a Pacific power? Events in China, particularly, began to attract the attention of statesmen, shipowners, and merchants, and as reports reached our shores, in the middle nineties, of the strange developments in that distant land interest gave way to anxiety. Americans, of course, were no strangers to the peoples of the Far East. We had followed hard on the heels of the British into China in the forties, and the treaty written by Caleb Cushing in 1844 had opened to Yankee merchant ships the ports of the China Sea. An intrepid American sailor, Commodore Perry, in 1853, had been the means by which the barred gates of Japan had been thrown open to the traders of the Western world. Since then our contacts with both nations had been cordial. Our policy had been the maintenance of equal opportunities for purposes of trade to the merchants of all countries and our diplomacy for fifty years adopted every possible expedient to guarantee that result. We had never, however, entered into alliances with foreign powers.

But apparently European policy was taking a new tack in the last decade of the nineteenth century. First Japan had humiliated China in the war of 1895, obtaining the island of Formosa and the recognition of Japanese sovereignty over Korea. And then the European powers, seeing how vulnerable the Chinese were, had begun, themselves, to establish footholds in the empire. The Europeans were no longer interested in trade pure and simple. They were carving up China among themselves, through so-called spheres of influence, for purposes of capitalistic exploitation and to render secure the money their nationals were beginning to put into governmental loans, railroads, mines, harbors, and the like. A sphere of influence meant, in effect, that the particular power was to have monopoly rights in the placing of public loans and in the development of natural resources, such rights to be respected by China and the other Europeans. The latter was assured by the writing of agreements among the European nations.

Secretary of State Hay felt that the status of American trade with China would be seriously jeopardized by these maneuvers. It is to be noted that his chief interest was not capitalistic exploitation but merely a fear that the Europeans, in their spheres of influence, would attempt to check the goings and comings of American ships. We had insisted upon the Philippines to make things easier for American commerce in the Far East; shutting the Chinese treaty ports and closing their hinterlands to our merchants would really rob us of the fruits of victory. Hence, on September 6, 1899, Hay sent a circular note to the American ambassadors at London, Berlin, and St. Petersburg which they were to read to the chanceleries to which they were attached. Hay's note embodied three propositions: 1. that the powers claiming spheres of influence in China should commit themselves to keeping the treaty ports open and not interfering with any "vested interests" already in their spheres; 2. that the powers allow the application of the Chinese treaty tariff to the ports under their control without discrimination against other nationals; 3. that the powers would not levy higher harbor charges on vessels of other nationals calling at their ports, or fix higher railroad rates.

This Open-Door note of Hay was designed, first, to protect the integrity of China against the exercise of actual territorial control by foreigners in the spheres of influence. In the second place, it was intended to assure equal commercial rights for all nationals. Hay did not speak of equal rights for capitalistic enterprise. Apparently he did not see that the capitalists had taken first place away from the merchants and that Europeans were battling over the Chinese spoils not because of trade but because of the valuable financial, railroad, and mining concessions to be obtained. We shall have occasion to see how American diplomacy again and again turned its attention to China on behalf of the capitalists whose interests Hay had overlooked.

The European powers quickly acceded to Hay's demands. Great Britain agreed first on November 30, and was followed by Germany, France, and Russia. Japan and Italy, when approached later, also accepted the terms of the Hay Open–Door note. On March 20, 1900, Hay made a public announcement in which he expressed himself as satisfied with the results of his intervention. The guarantees of the powers, he said, were "final and definitive" that the Open Door to China would be maintained and Chinese sovereignty in the spheres of influence respected.

A few months later Hay was again intervening in Chinese affairs. As a result of the weaknesses displayed by the ruling dynasty, the concessions granted to the foreign powers, and the progress being made by Western ideas and habits, China became the scene of internal discord. Chinese patriots, banded into a society known to the Europeans as the Boxers, began in 1898 to threaten the safety of foreigners resident in the empire. Sporadic riots turned into an organized rebellion and early in 1900 a Chinese army was marching on Peking. The major European nations, Japan, and the United States took alarm, and in June, 1900, orders were given to the commanders of foreign warships stationed in Chinese waters to send a relief expedition to raise the siege of Peking. In this demonstration the

United States participated. Hay took advantage of this new crisis to affirm again the American policy with regard to China. In a circular note sent to the powers on July 3, Hay called upon them to unite to preserve peace in China, assure her territorial and administrative integrity, and "safeguard for the world the principle of equal and impartial trade with all parts of the Chinese Empire."

The international force took Tientsin, eighty miles from Peking, on July 13 and entered the quarters of the foreign legations in Peking on August 14. The imperial city itself was broken into and looted by the foreign soldiery. In September, 1901, the Chinese government accepted the terms of the protocol drawn up by the foreign powers. Under this, China was compelled to pay an indemnity of $333,000,000 in thirty-nine annual instalments and to set up an exclusive reservation for the legations at Peking. The American share of the indemnity was fixed at $24,440,700. After meeting claims of American citizens for losses suffered in the uprising (totaling $12,479,600) the Department of State declared in 1907 that the balance of the indemnity would be renounced. The understanding reached between the two governments was that the remaining $12,000,000 would be employed for the creation of an educational fund to provide scholarships for Chinese students desiring to study in the United States.

Section VII
THEODORE ROOSEVELT
AND REFORM

· 20 ·

Theodore Roosevelt and William Howard Taft

THE FIRST ROOSEVELT ADMINISTRATION

THEODORE ROOSEVELT was not quite forty-three years of age when he took the Presidential oath of office on September 14, 1901. A native New Yorker, a graduate of Harvard, possessing impeccable social antecedents, and with no real necessity for concern over the sources of a livelihood, the young Roosevelt had singled out politics as his chosen career. When but eighteen months out of college he had been elected to the New York Assembly, and he had held his seat for three terms. In the campaign of 1884, after joining the ranks of the Republican Mugwumps in the preconvention fight on Blaine, he had loyally supported the "Plumed Knight" when the Republicans picked him as their standard-bearer. The years 1884 to 1886 he had spent on a Dakota ranch he owned, where he rode the range, made many western acquaintances, and busied himself with a form of literary historical work then popular with public men. In 1886, he had presented himself as the Republican candidate for the New York City mayoralty and engaged in a hot three-cornered fight against Abram S. Hewitt, Democrat, and Henry George, the single tax advocate. Hewitt won and Roosevelt took advantage of the following period of idleness to visit London and meet in person the celebrated folk with whom he had been carrying on a correspondence.

In 1889, Roosevelt was again in the public eye. In that year President Harrison asked him to become a member of the United States Civil Service Commission, and with this body he was associated for the next six years, for the greater part as its chairman. From 1895 to 1897, he was head of the police board of New York City; from 1897 to the outbreak of the Spanish–American War, he was Assistant Secretary of the Navy; in November, 1898, he was elected governor of New York State, in recognition of his war services; and from his native state he was called to become the Vice-President on March 4, 1901.

Never before was there a figure in American public life, except perhaps Thomas Jefferson or Andrew Jackson, who knew so well how to attach to himself the devotion of other men. His interests were wide, he appeared to read everything, he knew how to attract and sustain a lively public interest in everything he did. From 1888 until he died in 1919 it may be said that not for a single instant was he a private person. Whether because he had a sixth sense or because he had a positive genius for reading the minds of the populace, he knew how to express—and to capitalize to his own advantage—the sentiments, wishes, and yearnings of most Americans. When sport was becoming popular, he was the amateur sportsman par excellence. When great wealth was in ill-repute, he was the first politician to lecture it sternly. When political reform had become a popular cry, lo! Theodore Roosevelt was in the van of the procession, proudly carrying aloft the standard that men like La Follette, Bryan, and other westerners had been bearing patiently for years. (But with a difference, for he sensed that Big Business had come to stay. What was needed was not its fragmentation but its control through the central government. To this extent Franklin D. Roosevelt's New Deal was built on the New Nationalism of Theodore Roosevelt and not the New Freedom of Woodrow Wilson.) He coined fighting and derogatory phrases: "malefactors of great wealth," "undesirable citizen," "the square deal," "speak softly and carry the big stick," "malevolent mummifaction." He adopted a vigorous foreign program; he advanced the United States to a position of prominence among the nations of the world; and he launched us on a naval race with Great Britain and Germany.

The three and a half years of his first administration Roosevelt spent chiefly in cautiously feeling his way. His concerns were two: to win over the confidence and support of the Republican party machine and to entrench himself safely in the popular regard. He therefore retained the McKinley Cabinet and kept on terms of friendship with the Old Guard rulers of the Republican party in both branches of Congress. Toward Hanna particularly the President was conciliatory. So powerful did the Ohio Senator remain not only within the councils of the party but also with spokesmen for capital and labor alike that it was not until he died early in 1904 that the country was finally certain that Roosevelt was the head of the Republican host in fact as well as in name.

Popular regard was an easier thing for Roosevelt to attain. His first administration was associated with a series of enterprises that quickly made him the cynosure of all eyes and the idol of the middle-class social reformer. His first Congressional message, delivered on December 3, 1901, was an elaborate text in public affairs, containing in all some thirty thousand words. He called for a greater measure of regulation for corporations and trusts; the extension of the powers of the Interstate Commerce Commission; an immigration policy; more reciprocity treaties; the governmental encouragement of a merchant marine; the conservation of natural resources and a program of irrigation works; the construction of an Isthmian canal; a bigger navy and a better army; justice to the Civil War veterans; the reform of the consular service and the extension of the Civil Service; a colonial policy in the territories. And he spoke of Cuba, the Monroe Doctrine, China, the American Indians, the Library of Congress, and the federal census. In February, 1903, Congress at his request passed the Elkins Act, for the purpose of helping in the rehabilitation of the Interstate Commerce Commission. In the same month, Congress established the new Department of Commerce and Labor and also provided for the creation of a Bureau of Corporations with power to investigate the affairs of large business aggregations.

Roosevelt's popularity began to increase rapidly in 1902 when in a series of public addresses in New England and the West he outlined his program for government regulation of industry. He favored publicity of corporate business; the checking of overcapitalization; the protection of the investing public. The Sherman Antitrust Law would be enforced vigorously, and "when a suit is undertaken it will not be compromised except upon the basis that the government wins." In line with this policy he had ordered his Attorney-General to move against the Northern Securities Company, a holding company organized by James J. Hill and backed by the House of Morgan for the purpose of acquiring control of the Northern Pacific Railroad, the Great Northern Railroad, and the Chicago, Burlington and Quincy. The federal lower courts found for the government and on March 14, 1904, the Supreme Court sustained this decision and ordered the corporation's dissolution.[1] Though the verdict of the Court was by a five to four vote, and though the results of the litigation soon proved of no significance, the decision was a great political triumph. It encouraged the federal law authorities to continue their suits for the dissolution of the great trusts—and it heightened the favor the President had been finding in the eyes of the man in the street.

Roosevelt further attracted popular applause as a result of his successful interference in the anthracite strike of 1902. In 1897, the United Mine Workers had gained a great victory in the bituminous central competitive field and were therefore heartened to push their activities into the anthracite coal districts. Unionization went on quickly with the result that a bid was made for general union recognition with the calling out of a general strike in 1900. One hundred thousand miners responded to the strike call. The operators were obdurate, however, and matters were taking

[1] 193 U.S. 197.

on an ugly temper when Hanna, fearing the effects on McKinley's campaign for re-election, stepped in. As a result of his intervention, a truce was patched up which did not, however, yield completely to the miners' demands.

In May, 1902, the miners again struck, this time demanding union recognition, a 9-hour day, and a wage increase of 20 per cent. The strikers were excellently disciplined under the leadership of John Mitchell; and, aided by a strike fund which other miners collected for them, 150,000 men held their ranks firm for five months. On October 3, President Roosevelt intervened, in the public interest. He summoned the leaders of both sides to Washington and urged upon them the necessity for conciliating their differences before the coming winter brought widespread suffering. The operators declined an offer of mediation and demanded federal military intervention and the prosecution of the United Mine Workers under the Sherman Law.

Roosevelt moved with characteristic energy. He announced his intention to appoint a commission to investigate the dispute, and let hints drop that he would employ United States troops to seize and work the mines. Morgan now appeared to join his counsels to Roosevelt's thinly veiled threats, with the result that the coal operators humbly petitioned President Roosevelt, on October 13, to appoint his commission to investigate and mediate. The men returned to work, and six months later the Presidential commission announced its award: the men were to get a 10 per cent increase in wages and a 9-hour day. Arbitration machinery was set up though formal recognition was not accorded to the union.[2]

As a result of these triumphs, and with additional laurels won in obtaining the Panama Canal Zone for the United States late in 1903,[3] little doubt could remain in the minds of the Republican party managers as to the completeness with which Roosevelt had captured the popular fancy. Hanna's death totally routed the machine politicians. When, therefore, the Republican nominating convention met at Chicago on June 21, 1904, they adopted the usual colorless platform and named Roosevelt by acclamation with Senator Charles W. Fairbanks of Indiana as his running mate. The Democrats met at St. Louis on July 6 and despite the presence of the magnetic Bryan and the strongly worded platform planks with regard to tariffs and trusts, the delegates showed an inclination to place behind them the earlier Democratic intransigency. Thus the demand for an income tax law and the free-silver plank were dropped and the nomination was given to the eminently respectable Alton B. Parker, chief justice of the New York State Court of Appeals. Parker insisted that he could run only

[2] The anthracite miners struck again in 1912 and in 1916. In 1916, they finally won the 8-hour day, the check-off, and union recognition.
[3] See below, page 370.

if it were understood that the gold standard was "irrevocably fixed" and that he therefore would have nothing to do with the silver "heresy"; and to this the Democratic convention acceded, even Bryan pledging his support.

The campaign was without incident and resulted in the triumphant re-election of Roosevelt, with the greatest popular and electoral majorities given to a candidate up to that time. Roosevelt received 7,628,834 popular votes against Parker's 5,084,491; and 336 electoral votes against Parker's 140. Parker carried but 1167 counties in the country, and of these only 85 were outside the Solid South; too, Parker lost Missouri and one vote in Maryland. The Socialists polled 402,283 votes for their candidate, Eugene V. Debs; and the Populists gave their candidate Thomas E. Watson 117,183 votes. The Congressional elections ended even more disastrously for the Democrats. The make-up of the new Congress was to be as follows: in the Senate, 57 Republicans and 32 Democrats; in the House, 249 Republicans and 137 Democrats. So pleased was Roosevelt over his personal victory that on the night of the election he made a public announcement in which he said that "under no circumstances will I be a candidate for or accept another nomination."

THE SECOND ROOSEVELT ADMINISTRATION

The Roosevelt doctrines were enunciated with great vigor in the four years of the second administration, though the President continued in harmony with the party chieftains. The high protectionist Aldrich of Rhode Island remained the recognized leader of the Senate; Cannon of Illinois lorded it over the House. Allison, Spooner, Hale, Lodge, Penrose, and Republican stalwarts of the same class remained in possession of the Presidential ear and Roosevelt had only an ill-concealed contempt for the more progressive members of his own party like La Follette in the Senate and Poindexter in the House. It is, in fact, hard to reconcile Roosevelt's associates with the disturbing character of his public pronouncements. As his term neared its end his assaults on "the malefactors of great wealth," the conservative judiciary, and the unrepresentative character of party government became more outspoken. He advocated income and inheritance taxes, gave his approval to the creation of methods for the popular control of the party machinery and issued a portentous warning to those members of the judiciary "who have lagged behind in their understanding of those great and vital changes in the body politic, whose minds have never been opened to the new applications of the old principles made necessary by the new conditions." Presidential messages, speeches, interviews, and inspired articles poured out in an unending flood.

Yet achievement was remarkably small, when reckoned in terms of the promises publicly made. Roosevelt's two Congresses, despite great Republican majorities in both of them, failed to pass bills calling for the following:

the rehabilitation of the merchant marine, currency and banking reform, the national regulation of insurance companies, the federal control of child labor, copyright reform, the lifting of the Philippine tariff restrictions, the limitation of the powers of the federal courts in injunction proceedings.

The following were the chief measures enacted by Congress: the Hepburn Act of 1906, which further extended the powers of the Interstate Commerce Act, but which stopped short of real accomplishment, as La Follette justly insisted, by failing to vest in the Commission the right to fix the valuations of the railroads; the Meat Inspection Act and the Pure Food Act, both of 1906, aimed at stopping the shipment in interstate commerce of adulterated meats, other foods, and drugs; the Employers' Liability Act of 1906, affecting common carriers and relating to injuries to employees, which, however, the Supreme Court declared unconstitutional (another law was enacted in 1908); a law, passed in 1908, limiting the hours of trainmen and telegraph operators, working on interstate railroads; and finally an act, passed in 1907, prohibiting contributions to political campaign funds by industrial corporations.

The President continued to give the Department of Justice his support, and a number of important prosecutions against trusts were undertaken. It is to be noted, however, that Taft's Attorney-General inaugurated twice as many suits under the Sherman Law, in four years, as did Roosevelt's in seven and a half years. Closer to the heart of Roosevelt than any of these programs was his campaign on behalf of the conservation of the country's natural resources. It may be said that this was his greatest contribution to domestic policy. The subject is treated at length in the following chapter.

One untoward event darkened, for a brief time, the pleasant skies under which Roosevelt reigned. This was the financial panic which struck the country in the fall of 1907. For a time business was deranged, unemployment was severe, and wages fell. A number of railroads went into receivers' hands and thirteen banking institutions in New York City, the seat of the panic, closed their doors. Roosevelt worked hard to restore the shaken confidence of industrialists, even going so far as to give his approval to the United States Steel Corporation's acquisition of the Tennessee Coal and Iron Company when Wall Street assured him that only by this measure could a major disaster be averted. By the middle of January, 1908, the flurry had passed on and the skies were again serene—at least, as far as Wall Street was concerned.

The Republicans could therefore contemplate the coming Presidential election of 1908 with confidence, particularly in view of Roosevelt's announcement that he would not be a candidate for renomination. There was no question that anyone the Republicans would choose would be eminently satisfactory to the business interests, whether it was to be Root or Hughes of New York or Taft of Ohio. Roosevelt finally decided on

Taft (then his Secretary of War) as his successor and by using the patronage to win over the southern delegates made Taft's choice inevitable. The Republicans assembled at Chicago on June 16, 1908, with Henry Cabot Lodge presiding as permanent chairman. The opposition of a handful of western delegates was crushed relentlessly. A minority report on the platform submitted by the resolutions committee (this minority report was fathered by La Follette) proposed the following reforms, among others: a physical valuation of the railway properties as the basis for governmental rate making; a revision of the tariff on the basis of the difference in costs of production at home and abroad; a permanent tariff commission; popular election of Senators; publicity for campaign contributions and expenditures. The minority report, after being stigmatized as a "socialistic and Democratic" document, received but twenty-eight votes.

The Republican platform, as adopted, praised the Roosevelt administrations and pledged the Republican nominee to a continuance of the Roosevelt policies. Tariff revision was promised, as was, also, the strengthening of the Sherman Law and the Interstate Commerce Act. An injunction plank was included but was so ambiguously worded as to be practically meaningless; currency reform was spoken of, without a specific program, however. Taft was nominated on the first ballot and James S. Sherman, a New York Congressman, was named for the Vice-Presidency.

Democracy's host met at Denver, July 7, with Bryan once again dominating the proceedings. The platform, as adopted, indicated that the Democratic party could scarcely be called socialistic, despite the charges of Republican orators. The plank on trusts, the work of Bryan, had the merit of explicitness. Other planks called for the removal of duties on "trust-made" goods, the passage of an income tax, and the prohibition of the use of the injunction in labor disputes. Bryan was nominated on the first ballot and John W. Kern of Indiana was named to run with him.

The campaign that followed was not much unlike the campaign of 1904, the only important development being the support given to Bryan's candidacy by Samuel Gompers, the president of the American Federation of Labor. Taft received a popular vote of 7,677,788 against Bryan's vote of 6,407,982. Debs, the Socialist party candidate, received 420,890 votes and Watson, the Populist, received 29,146 votes. Bryan got 1,323,000 more votes than Parker had received in 1904, though he did not equal his own 1896 vote. The electoral vote was 321 for Taft and 162 for Bryan with the Democratic candidate carrying the Solid South, all the border states (except Maryland) and the three western states of Colorado, Nebraska, and Nevada. To the lower house of the Sixty-first Congress there were elected 219 Republicans and 172 Democrats. The new Senate's composition was to be 32 Democrats and 60 Republicans. Theodore Roosevelt, having seen his friend and successor inducted into office, took his departure immediately from the American shore to hunt big game in Africa and to make a triumphal tour of the European capitals. But the shadow of Roosevelt filled the White House and his name was more frequently on men's lips than that of the new President.

THE PRESIDENCY OF WILLIAM HOWARD TAFT

William Howard Taft was fifty-two years old when he took the Presidential oath. A native of Ohio, he had attended Yale College and had studied law at Cincinnati. A year after his graduation he was launched on a public career and until his election to the Presidency he continued an officeholder, being elected to but one post and appointed to eight. In his career in politics Taft had been befriended by two men, his elder half-brother, Charles P. Taft, who had helped financially, and his chief, Theodore Roosevelt, who had advised, encouraged and finally had bestowed the Presidential succession on him. Taft was grateful and never missed an opportunity to show and voice his appreciation to his two mentors. At any other time, Taft would have made a thoroughly acceptable chief executive, for he had all the personal qualities that make for success. He was extraordinarily good-natured, placid in temperament, slow to awaken to suspicion, more than willing to let others work for him. He was fond of travel and speechmaking, had a positive gift for extemporaneous address, and liked to show himself to the public, appearing times innumerable at conventions, dinners, cornerstone layings, and the dedication of public monuments. His idea of the Presidency was quite simple: one partitioned the executive functions among a trusted group of advisers, respected the legislative prerogatives of Congress, maintained harmony in the party by a judicious employment of the federal patronage, and placed one's faith in the genius of the Republican party. But it was his unhappy lot to reap the whirlwind his predecessor had sown, and his administration, despite its solid achievement, was destined to end in disaster with public confidence gone and the Republican party disrupted by factional quarrels. Theodore Roosevelt made Taft President and Theodore Roosevelt's unredeemed promises of a new day made the Ohioan's administration a nightmare.

Taft's Cabinet was not particularly distinguished. The State office he gave to the capable Philander C. Knox, the Attorney-General of Roosevelt's administration, but the strongest person in the Cabinet was George W. Wickersham of New York, who was appointed Attorney-General. Taft refused to name William Loeb, Jr., Roosevelt's private secretary, to his Cabinet or retain James R. Garfield in the Department of Interior, and this action caused the first rift between the two men.

Taft ran into trouble with the very opening of his administration. Since 1905 the demand for tariff reform had been insistent, and the Republican platform of 1908 had pledged the party to revision, promising as the basis of a new tariff the imposition of duties that would equalize foreign costs of production with American. The American people understood revision to mean revision downward, and Taft had definitely pledged himself, in his campaign addresses, to such a program. Americans therefore confidently looked forward to the presentation of a bill with lower schedules. The House Ways and Means Committee (headed by Sereno E. Payne) had been conducting hearings during the winter, and when the Sixty-first Congress met in special session on March 15, 1909, the new bill was ready. It did call for an expanded free list and for sizable reductions. Coal, iron ore, hides, flax, and wood pulp were to be admitted free; there were to be reduced duties on iron, steel, lumber, chemicals, and refined sugar; what increased duties were imposed were justified on the principle of the equalization of costs. The House measure, too, provided for free trade between the United States and the Philippines and imposed a progressive tax on inheritances. The Republican machine in the House functioned almost noiselessly and the tariff bill was passed April 9 by a strict party vote.

The country's first intimation that reaction was in the saddle came with the presentation of the Senate's tariff bill. Prepared in a conservative Finance Committee and put together particularly by high-protectionists, the Aldrich bill frankly disregarded party pledges and the elaborate testimony gathered by the House and worked in the interests of protection undisguised. Iron ore and flax were restored to the dutiable list, increased rates were placed on iron and steel goods, the duties on agricultural products were maintained at their old levels, the inheritance tax was dropped. In all, the Aldrich bill reported some six hundred increases over the House schedules.

Then there took place one of the most memorable tariff debates in American legislative annals. For eleven weeks western Senators stormed against the Finance Committee bill and so fierce was their attack that even the usually silent Aldrich was moved to a heated rejoinder. Led by La Follette of Wisconsin, the group of Republican dissidents, who came to be known as "the insurgents," stripped the tariff bill bare of all its lofty pretense. Taft, in a too tardy effort to check the disintegration of his party, prevailed upon the Finance Committee to put hides on the free list, to add a small tax on the net earnings of corporations, and to prepare for submission to the states an income-tax amendment to the Constitution. But the insurgent Senators were unappeased and all of them voted with the Democrats against the bill, on July 8. The bill went into conference committee and emerged largely as the Senate had written it. In its final form it was passed by the House by a vote of 195 to 183 with 20 Republicans voting in the negative, and in the Senate by a vote of 47 to 31 with 7 insurgent Republicans voting with the Democratic minority. Taft signed the bill August 5 and regarded it as a great victory for himself, even going so far as to laud its provisions in a series of speeches in the following weeks. But the Payne-Aldrich Tariff Act was really the first event that contributed toward Taft's downfall.

The new Act marked no serious departure from the high protective principle written into the Dingley Act of 1897; it continued to show the same indifference toward American foreign trade. Duties were lowered on commodities where there was no competition or where American products dominated the world market. Thus, on coal, iron ore, lumber, and fabricated iron and steel the rates were lowered, though, as Taussig says, if the principle of equalization of costs had been applied these duties would have been entirely eliminated. Raw hides, wood-pulp, and oil were put on the free list and a concession was made to the farmers in the lowering of the duties on harnesses, lumber, and window glass. The indefensible wool schedule (the so-called Schedule K), on which popular indignation was largely centered, was practically untouched, for only three of its seventy-eight items were changed. The sugar rates, too, were permitted to stand except for the lowering of the differential on refined sugar from $12\frac{1}{2}$ cents to $7\frac{1}{2}$ cents per 100 pounds. The Act permitted the importation, duty-free, of 300,000 tons of Philippine sugar, continued to allow the free importation of Hawaiian and Puerto Rican sugar, and maintained the 20 per cent reduction on Cuban sugar. The upshot was that the domestic cost of production plus the Cuban sugar duty fixed the price for the American consumer and therefore the real gainer was the Sugar Trust, which was by now heavily interested in the American beet-growing industry. Thus the sugar rates, originally contrived as a revenue-producing device, had been turned into a protective schedule to enrich a monopoly.

The 1909 Act contained the following new administrative changes: It set up the principle of maximum-minimum rates common to European tariffs. The rates of the Act were to be regarded as the minimum rates and the President was empowered to impose a higher set of duties (based on an increased valuation of 25 per cent on the imported articles) on the commodities of countries discriminating against American products. But on April 1, 1910, Taft announced that no discrimination was being employed by any nation, with the result that only the minimum rates applied. A Tariff Board was created. Taft had had high hopes for this Board and expected it would employ its time in studying American production costs with the end in view of preparing a scientific set of schedules. But the Board was used largely to determine whether foreign discrimination existed, in accordance with the requirements of the maximum-minimum provision; it did prepare three reports, however. The Democratic House withdrew the Board's appropriation in December, 1912, and it thus passed silently from the scene. The reciprocity provisions of the Act of 1897 were dropped and the President was empowered to terminate the few inconsequential agreements which had been made under them. An excise tax of 1 per cent on the net incomes of business corporations was imposed. In the first year of its operation it produced but $20,950,000, so it could not have been regarded as being particularly oppressive.

There had been an early hint of the trouble that lay in store for Taft in the organization of the House, as soon as the special session opened on March 15, 1909. Twelve insurgent Republicans had broken from the party caucus and had refused to vote for the re-election of the Speaker, Joseph G. Cannon of Illinois, who had been presiding since 1903. The position of the Speaker of the House, under Cannon, had become one of extraordinary importance. He appointed all the House committees and named their chairmen; through the Rules Committee (which he shared with but two other colleagues), he prescribed the procedure of the House and controlled its debate; he had the exclusive right to recognize private members from the floor; and he could slow up the legislative process unduly by objecting to a request for "unanimous consent."

The insurgent Republicans moved to unhorse Cannon when on March 19, 1910, one of their number (Norris of Nebraska) introduced a resolution to provide for the election of the Rules Committee by the House and to exclude the Speaker from its membership. When Cannon ruled the motion out of order, he was defeated on an appeal from the chair. Another resolution, to declare the office of Speaker vacant, was lost because Tammany Democrats came to Cannon's rescue. But the insurgent program was pushed to a successful issue with the result that the Rules Committee membership was increased to seven and its election by the House was provided for. When the Democrats organized the House, in 1911, they went even further and deprived the Speaker of the right to appointment of the other standing committees of the House. This power was vested in the Ways and Means Committee, subject to approval of the membership at large.

Robert La Follette was the leader of the insurgent Republicans in the Senate. Graduated from the University of Wisconsin in 1876, he had gone to Congress for two terms beginning with 1885. In the nineties, he had turned his attention to the local political situation in his native Wisconsin and had done yeoman work in rousing the citizens of the state to the vicious union that existed between the Republican machine and the railroad corporations. After two unsuccessful efforts he captured the governorship and occupied that office for six years. Under La Follette's wise rule the United States was given a lesson in the successful functioning of a democracy. The overweening power of the railroads was broken, a system of complete rate regulation was introduced, the direct primaries were installed to place control over the political machinery in the hands of the party membership, and an inheritance tax law, an antilobby law, and the beginnings of an enlightened labor code were enacted. La Follette, therefore, was already a national figure when he took his seat in the United States Senate in January, 1906.

La Follette fought his fight against standpattism in politics and business, alone, during the years 1906 to 1909, for Roosevelt so filled the public eye that all other individuals were dwarfed into insignificance. But with Taft's advent, insurgency had its opportunity. The revolters against the Aldrich bill were joined by new recruits, and they waged unending war on the administration and its Old Guard defenders. They attacked the Republican railroad bill, the postal savings bill, and the Canadian reciprocity proposal, and by their insistence forced salutary changes in many measures. They made capital of the Alaskan coal lands scandal and succeeded in driving Secretary of the Interior Ballinger out of the Cabinet.[4] They embarrassed the President by supporting the Democratic House of 1911 to 1913 in the passage of a series of tariff revision bills; these Taft vetoed— to his further loss of prestige. The insurgents contributed mightily toward the Republican loss of the House in the election of 1910, and they formed the nucleus of that Progressive movement which Roosevelt was to lead in 1912.

In the elections of 1910 Republican insurgency triumphed in Wisconsin, Michigan, and Indiana, and in every Republican state west of the Mississippi, with the exception of Colorado, Utah, Wyoming, and Montana; and there was sent to Congress a group of legislators pledged to a "scientific revision of the tariff," to "a more direct control of legislative procedure" and to "a more careful supervision of corporate power." In the northern and middle-western states the Democrats made heavy gains so that the Sixty-second Congress of 1911 to 1913 had a Democratic majority in the House. The political line-up was as follows: in the House, 229 Democrats, 161 Republicans, 1 Socialist; in the Senate, 51 Republicans, 41 Democrats. Democratic governors were elected in Massachusetts, Connecticut, New York, Ohio, and New Jersey. In the last-named state, the new executive was an erstwhile college president, Woodrow Wilson. The Democrats organized the House, electing Champ Clark of Missouri to the Speaker's chair and choosing Oscar W. Underwood of Alabama to head the Ways and Means Committee.

Taft made one successful stand against legislative opposition, when he forced the passage of an act providing for tariff reciprocity with Canada. American manufacturers were distinctly favored by the arrangement and their advocacy of the measure led eastern legislators to support it, regardless of party. The agricultural West resented the inclusion in a free list of farming commodities, but despite this opposition the bill was passed by both houses in July, 1911. Taft was destined to see his one serious effort at

[4] See below, page 351.

leadership end in failure, for Canadian resistance was so great that the government was compelled to submit the question to a general election. The Liberal ministry, which had been party to the agreement, went down to defeat, and this, of course, ended tariff reciprocity with Canada until the nineteen thirties. Except for the creation of the parcel post system in 1912, the antagonism between Taft and Congress resulted in legislative stultification.

The insurgents, emboldened by their success, looked forward to the capture of the Republican party, and on January 21, 1911, they organized, with this end in view, the National Progressive Republican League. Their declaration of principles said, among other things:

> Under existing conditions legislation in the public interest has been baffled and defeated. This is evidenced by the long struggle to secure laws but partially effective for the control of railway rates and services, the revision of the tariff in the interests of the producer and consumer, statutes dealing with trusts and combinations, ... wise, comprehensive and impartial reconstruction of banking and monetary laws, the conservation of coal, oil, gas, timber, water powers, and other natural resources belonging to the public, and the enactment of all legislation solely for the common good.

To hasten the realization of popular government the insurgents advanced a program whose major tenets were: the direct election of United States Senators; direct primaries; Presidential primaries and the direct election of delegates to the nominating conventions; the initiative, referendum, and recall; the passage of corrupt-practices acts.

This manifesto was, really, in the nature of a trial balloon. How would Theodore Roosevelt take it? Theodore Roosevelt had returned from his African and European triumphs in June, 1910, and for a number of weeks his silence had perplexed standpatters and insurgents alike. To Taft he was polite but cool. He gave his approval to the Payne-Aldrich Tariff, was noncommittal about the Pinchot-Ballinger row (described below), and busied himself trying to elect his friend Henry L. Stimson governor of New York. All this did not appear too threatening to Taft's hopes for his party's renomination. But, on the other hand, Roosevelt had delivered an address at Osawatomie, Kansas, on August 31, 1910, in which he had voiced his creed of the New Nationalism. He had attacked large aggregations of capital with his old vigor; had called for greater governmental participation in the economic and social life of the nation; and had enunciated an elaborate program of reforms. He had said, then:

> I stand for the square deal. But when I say I am for the square deal I mean not merely that I stand for fair play under the present rules of the game but that I stand for having those rules changed so as to work for a more substantial equality of opportunity and of reward for equally good service.

And these were some of the measures he championed, to make the square deal a possibility: publicity of corporate affairs; prohibition of the use of corporate funds for political purposes; governmental control over the capitalization of corporations; governmental supervision of corporations controlling the necessities of life; an expert tariff commission and a revision of the tariff; income and inheritance taxes; conservation; publication of campaign contributions before the day of election; workmen's-compensation acts; state and national laws to regulate child labor; labor codes; and the direct primary. In subsequent addresses, and in his writings for *The Outlook,* he had placed his stamp of approval on the La Follette program of direct government, that is to say, the initiative, referendum and recall.

The insurgents, in the light of these pronouncements, called upon Roosevelt to join the Progressive Republican League. Roosevelt refused. He was not unfriendly toward the insurgents, however, for in the spring of 1911 he sent an emissary to their leaders to suggest that it was their duty to put the name of La Follette in nomination at the Republican convention. In the summer of 1911 the La Follette campaign was launched, and by the winter it had made rapid headway—so rapid and so successful, in fact, that Roosevelt became convinced that the opposition stood a fair chance of defeating Taft for the nomination. La Follette had done his work well: the American people were ready to follow the banner of reform. Roosevelt, apparently, awaited the call. It came on February 10, 1912, when seven Republican governors and seventy other Republican leaders from twenty-four states met at Chicago and issued a statement calling upon all Progressive Republicans to support Roosevelt. But would Roosevelt take the nomination if it were proffered? On February 24, Roosevelt crossed the Rubicon: he would, he said, accept the Republican designation. In other words, he would approve a contest for delegates against his one-time friend and protégé William Howard Taft. Thus were the lines drawn for the contest for the Republican nomination of 1912.

· 21 ·

Rooseveltian Policies at Home

THE TRUST PROBLEM

WHILE Theodore Roosevelt boldly attacked great aggregations of capital in his Presidential messages and speeches, and while his and Taft's Attorneys-General filed a large number of suits under the Sherman Antitrust Law, it may be said that the results scarcely measured up either to all the executive threats made or, indeed, to the activity displayed. Trust-busting—which is what Roosevelt's campaign was popularly called—was regarded with favor, but the trusts, apparently, were a hardy growth, for they survived both vilification and legal attack.

At the close of the Taft administration, following twenty-two years of experience with federal prosecutions, the results stood somewhat as follows: In the first place, the Sherman Antitrust Law was being enforced, apparently, to the best of the Department of Justice's ability. Further, the Supreme Court was insisting that not all combinations in restraint of trade were illegal, that some combinations were reasonable and some unreasonable, and that it was the business of the Supreme Court to separate the sheep from the goats. Again, a number of dissolutions of outstanding trusts had been ordered by the courts, but it was apparent to the discerning that competition was no freer and that the same personalities continued to dominate the industries over which they had formerly held sway. Finally, neither Roosevelt nor Taft succeeded in obtaining from Congress remedial legislation to cover the inadequacies of the Sherman Law.

In his Congressional message of December, 1907, Roosevelt was still repeating the same proposals, substantially, that he had laid before Congress in his exhaustive message of December, 1901. Thus, the 1907 program included, among others, the following: the federal incorporation or licensing of businesses engaged in interstate commerce; full publicity of accounts; protection accorded to the investing public; and the outlawing of certain corporate practices. Said the message, on this last point:

> At least the Antitrust Act should be supplemented by specific prohibitions of the methods which experience has shown have been of most service in enabling monopolistic combinations to crush out competition. The real owners of a corporation should be compelled to do business in their own name. The right to hold

stock in other corporations should be denied to interstate corporations unless approved by government and a prerequisite to approval should be the listing with the government of all owners and stockholders.

Taft's recommendations to Congress were much more specific. At one time or another, he called for the passage of a voluntary federal incorporation law, for legislation to put an end to stock-watering and the creation of holding companies, and for the erection of a body, comparable to the Interstate Commerce Commission, to supervise the granting of federal charters. He also thought it desirable that Congress should pass legislation enumerating certain specified unfair practices as being in restraint of trade. It is important to note that Taft's messages had a considerable influence on the character of the antitrust legislation written in the first Wilson administration.

Congress took small notice of these requests for the strengthening of the Sherman Law. But two acts of any importance were passed in the Roosevelt and Taft administrations, and both of these came in 1903. The first concerned itself with procedure and was designed to hasten court action, by requiring the federal circuit courts to give precedence to cases in equity rising out of the Sherman Law (and the Interstate Commerce Act). The second, in response to Roosevelt's suggestion, established a Bureau of Corporations in the newly created Department of Commerce and Labor; and to this agency was given the power of making investigations into the affairs of corporations engaged in interstate commerce. The first chief of this bureau was James R. Garfield, later Roosevelt's Secretary of the Interior, and under him a series of vigorous inquiries was conducted. The reports published on the Standard Oil Company and the American Tobacco Company were of material assistance to the Department of Justice in the suits filed against these corporations. During the six years 1903 to 1909 but one bill, applying to trusts, ever got out of the Congressional committees, and this measure died in the Senate.

How vigorously were prosecutions of trusts pushed? During the seven and a half years of the Roosevelt administration, Knox and Bonaparte in the Department of Justice brought 18 bills in equity, obtained 25 indictments, and participated in one forfeiture proceeding. Actions were filed against outstanding corporate groups, the more notable being the so-called Oil, Tobacco, Powder, and Beef Trusts. Too, proceedings were started against a number of important railroad combinations, including the Northern Securities Company, the Reading Company, the Union Pacific Railroad Company, and the New York, New Haven and Hartford Railroad Company. The record of the Taft administration exceeded this. A total of 43 proceedings had been the fruits of Roosevelt's labors; Taft's Attorney-General Wickersham was responsible for 90 suits. These were of the following types: 46 bills in equity, 43 indictments and 1 contempt proceeding. And these were some of the combinations moved against: the United States Steel Corporation, the American Sugar Refining Company, the United Shoe Machinery Company, the International Harvester Company, the National Cash Register Company, the Corn Products Refining Company, and the General Electric Company.

Up to 1911, the Supreme Court continued to be guided by the principles enunciated in the Trans-Missouri decision of 1897 [1] and either condemned their activities or ordered the dissolution of a number of prominent corporations where contracts or combinations in restraint of trade were proved. Mention has already been made of the Northern Securities case of 1904.[2] Another outstanding suit was that filed against the Beef Trust, made up principally of Swift and Company, Armour and Company, and Nelson Morris and Company. These packers, in company with several others, had formed in 1902 the National Packing Company for the purpose of buying up a number of independents in the Middle West. The federal law officers appealed, successfully, for an injunction restraining the members of the Beef Trust from indulging in certain practices calculated to check competition in the slaughtering and meat-packing business, and on January 30, 1905, the United States Supreme Court concurred in the findings of the lower court.[3] The decree enjoined the packers from using the following methods to strangle competition: agreements among themselves not to bid against each other; the fixing of prices offered livestock dealers and the fixing of the resale price of dressed beef; the maintenance of a blacklist; fixing of excessive charges for cartage; obtaining rebates from railroads. The National Packing Company was not dissolved, and after the lapse of a short interval its members continued with their old methods, even successfully fighting off criminal prosecution on the score that they had obtained immunity when they divulged their trade practices to the federal Bureau of Corporations. Despite popular clamor against the packers, the courts refused to entertain any further suits against them. Thus, in 1910 a dissolution proceeding brought against the National Packing Company was dropped and criminal indictments were quashed or the defendants were released. Ten years later, as we shall see, federal action against the packers met with more success.

In 1911, however, in the Standard Oil and American Tobacco cases, the Supreme Court abandoned the position it had taken in 1897 when it had declared that all combinations in restraint of trade, whether reasonable or unreasonable, were illegal. The new decisions laid down the "rule of reason," that is to say, declared that combinations only in unreasonable restraint of trade could be enjoined or ordered dissolved. In November,

[1] See above, page 250.
[2] See above, page 328.
[3] 196 U.S. 375.

1906, the government had brought suit against the Standard Oil Company of New Jersey, seventy subsidiaries and seven individuals, on the ground of violation of the Sherman Law. In 1909, the federal circuit court held that the combination was a monopoly and its acts were in restraint of trade, and ordered the dissolution of the holding company. The Supreme Court heard the defendants' appeals during 1910 and 1911; on May 15, 1911,[4] it handed down its decision. The decree of the circuit court was affirmed and the holding company, the Standard Oil Company of New Jersey, was ordered to be dissolved into its component parts. More important than this action, however, was the dictum enunciated by the court. In an opinion written by Chief Justice White in which the whole bench, with the exception of Justice Harlan,[5] concurred, the dissent of the minority in the Trans-Missouri case now became the majority opinion of the Court. After elaborately examining Sections 1 and 2 of the Sherman Law, bearing on restraint of trade and combinations and conspiracies for purposes of monopoly, the Chief Justice declared:

> The statute, under this view, evidenced the intent not to restrain the right to make and enforce contracts, whether resulting from combinations or otherwise, which did not unduly restrain interstate and foreign commerce, but to protect the commerce from being restrained by methods, whether new or old, which would constitute an interference that is an undue restraint.

In other words, concluded White, because Sections 1 and 2 were so sweeping, to apply them "necessarily called for the exercise of judgment"; and "this required that some standard should be resorted to for the purpose of determining whether the prohibitions contained in the statute had or had not in any given case been violated." Such a standard was the "rule of reason," and the only agency that might measure out its magical quantities was, of course, the Supreme Court.

A similar finding was enunciated in the case of the American Tobacco Company on May 29, 1911.[6] This suit had been brought in July, 1907, against the holding company the American Tobacco Company of New Jersey, 67 American subsidiaries, 2 English subsidiaries and 29 individuals. The circuit court, in November, 1908, had found the combination illegal and had ordered its dissolution. By a similar unanimous decision, with Harlan dissenting, however, against the "rule of reason" dictum, the Supreme Court affirmed the verdict of the lower court on the basis of the "rule of reason." As a result of the Court's action, these great holding companies were disbanded and competition was again, presumably, untrammeled. Of course, nothing of the sort occurred immediately, for the

[4] 221 U.S. 1.
[5] Harlan dissented only against the "rule of reason" dictum, concurring in the order of dissolution.
[6] 221 U.S. 106.

same persons who had dominated the activities of the trusts were in control of the smaller companies; the holding company, as a device, was merely supplanted by the earlier "community of interest" arrangement. Americans were not to be blamed for refusing to excite themselves over what President Taft hailed as a great legal victory.

THE MONEY POWER

While there began to evince itself, as the first decade of the new century was closing, a distinct lessening of public interest in the affairs of industrial corporations, concern over the great power of a handful of banking groups became more apparent. More and more there was talk of the Money Power and popular magazines and rural Congressmen began to insist that the real enemy was not the industrial monopolist but the banker, and particularly, five or six individual bankers. These were the secret masters in the United States. Finally, in 1912, a Congressional investigating committee, headed by a southern Representative, called these mighty ones to the stand, where, despite the aggressive examination conducted by Samuel Untermyer of New York, they turned out to be very mild—and absent-minded—witnesses.

The reputed ruler of the empire of finance was J. Pierpont Morgan, head of the New York firm of J. P. Morgan and Company. The Morgan house had originated in 1837, when the London bankers, George Peabody and Company, began to float American securities. In 1864, Junius S. Morgan supplanted Peabody, and in the same year his son J. P. Morgan (who arrived in New York in 1857) formed an American branch. In 1871, the younger Morgan entered into a partnership with the Philadelphia Drexels, and this new banking house began to play a significant role in the refunding of the Civil War loans. When Jay Cooke failed in 1873, the Drexel-Morgan group became the outstanding American bankers and, largely supported by their powerful London connections, succeeded in rehabilitating many of America's important railway companies. In 1885, Morgan sold $25 million worth of W. H. Vanderbilt's New York Central stock in the London money market; in 1887, he refinanced the Baltimore and Ohio; in 1888, he handled the Chesapeake and Ohio's financial program; in 1893, he formed the Southern Railway Company. The Erie, the Reading, the Hocking Valley, and the Northern Pacific were also to have the assistance of Morgan's magic hand.

In the nineties, Morgan turned to steel, and his successful financing of the Federal Steel Company, the National Tube Company, and the American Bridge Company made it inevitable that his house should be the promoter of the country's first billion-dollar corporation, the United States Steel Corporation, launched in 1901. In the early nineteen hundreds,

Morgan's firm also advanced its influence into the concerns of the following American industrial corporations: the International Mercantile Marine Company, the International Harvester Company, the General Electric Company, the American Telephone and Telegraph Company, the Western Union Telegraph Company, the Interborough Rapid Transit Company (operators of New York City's first subway), the Hudson and Manhattan Company (builders of the railway tubes under the Hudson River), and the great Equitable Life Assurance Society. Morgan partners sat on the boards of all these companies and helped in the guidance of their financial operations. In 1899, Morgan participated in an international syndicate, marking the first appearance on equal terms of American bankers in the company of the European moneylenders. In 1899, J. P. Morgan and Company, in association with J. S. Morgan and Company of London, the Deutsche Bank, and the Dresdener Bank, issued a Mexican refunding loan of $113,500,000, and bonds were sold simultaneously in the Berlin, London, and New York markets. This beginning was soon followed by others, and in 1904 Speyer and Company floated a Cuban loan and Kuhn, Loeb and Company, aided by British bankers, floated a Japanese loan on the New York and London markets. While Europe was still the world's banker and continued so until 1914, these performances indicated that American capital was to be reckoned with in the international money market.

The National City Bank of New York followed not very far behind the House of Morgan, largely because the Rockefeller wealth supported it. In fact, as a banking institution, it was the most powerful one in the country. Headed by James Stillman and supported personally by William Rockefeller, the National City Bank, by the early nineteen hundreds, was figuring in the destinies of the New York, New Haven and Hartford Railroad Company, the Amalgamated Copper Company, the Consolidated Gas Company of New York, the Mutual Life Insurance Company, and some fifty lesser banking houses.

A third great banking power was the First National Bank of New York, whose presiding genius was George F. Baker. A fourth was the investing house of Kuhn, Loeb and Company, headed by Jacob H. Schiff, a German Jew. Schiff was second only to Morgan in acting as the financier of great American railway systems and his union with Harriman had made possible the reorganization of the Union Pacific. Other banking groups of importance, in the early nineteen hundreds, were Lee, Higginson and Company and Kidder, Peabody and Company, both of Boston and New York.

Upon these, by authorization of the House of Representatives, the so-called Pujo investigating committee [7] descended in May, 1912. It set itself the task of inquiring into: 1. the operations of clearing house associations;

[7] Really a subcommittee of the House's Committee on Banking and Currency.

2. the business of the New York Stock Exchange; 3. the concentration of control of money and credit. The existence of the Money Power was what troubled the inquisitors, and their report was therefore concerned largely with the last of the three indicated purposes. The committee found what it considered a truly dangerous state of affairs. The combined resources of J. P. Morgan and Company, the National City Bank, and the First National Bank totaled $632,000,000. If to the resources of these were added those of their affiliated New York banks and the Equitable Life, then the total was really $2,104,000,000. The partners of the 3 banking groups held 341 directorships in 112 corporations whose combined capitalization was $22,250,000,000. In addition, not only were the activities and interests of the bankers interrelated but by the device of interlocking directorates everything was concentrated in the hands of the same few persons.

Thus, the Pujo committee reported that the concentration of credit and money did exist and that this had been brought about by the following methods: mergers of competitive banks and trust companies; purchase of stock in competitive banks; interlocking directorates; the extension of banking influence into insurance companies, railway companies, and public utilities; syndicate financing of security issues. This conclusion was therefore inevitable:

> Your committee is satisfied from the proofs submitted ... that there is an established and well-defined identity and community of interest between a few leaders of finance, created and held together through joint stock ownership, interlocking directorates, partnership, and joint-account transactions, and other forms of domination over banks, trust companies, railroads, and public service and industrial corporations, which has resulted in great and rapidly growing concentration of the control of money and credit in the hands of these few men.

The report was released to the public on February 28, 1913, four days before the inauguration of the new Democratic President, Woodrow Wilson. How the New Jersey schoolmaster was going to cope with this new monster was a question frequently raised in the early days of that year.

RAILROAD LEGISLATION

We have seen, above, how the Interstate Commerce Commission, by 1900, had been reduced to the minor role of a fact-finding agency. By a series of Supreme Court decisions, the Commission had been shorn of the power of passing upon the reasonableness of rates and of enforcing the long- and short-haul clause. By the early nineteen hundreds it became evident that unless these and other limitations were removed the doctrine of government regulation of railways would soon take its place among other discarded legislative lumber. However, in the ten years 1903 to 1913, as a result of the activities of Roosevelt and Taft and the continuous and relentless prodding by La Follette in the Senate, legal and administrative inadequacies were overcome and the principle of federal control over carriers engaged in interstate commerce became a permanent fixture of American public law.

The first measure for the effective amendment of the Interstate Commerce Act came in 1903 with the passage of the Elkins Act. This contained the following provisions: Railroads were forbidden to deviate in any way from their published schedules of rates. Not only were the railway companies liable to punishment, in cases of rebating, but railway officials, their agents and favored shippers were also to be visited with punishment. The penalty of imprisonment was removed, making conviction easier. Variations from the published tariffs were to be considered *prima facie* evidence of violation. Injunction proceedings could be inaugurated to restrain carriers from violating the law.

On June 29, 1906, despite terrific pressure brought to bear by a powerful railroad lobby, Congress finally yielded to an aroused public opinion and passed the Hepburn Act. The provisions of this new amendment to the Interstate Commerce Act were as follows: The membership of the Commission was raised from five to seven. The law was amplified in scope to include the operations of express companies, sleeping-car companies, pipe lines, bridges, ferries, and terminal facilities. Part-rail and part-water transportation was included. The Commission was given the power to reduce a rate found to be unreasonable, where complaints of discrimination were filed by shippers. The so-called "midnight tariffs," under which special shippers were favored, were declared illegal. The Commission was authorized to standardize accounting procedure. Passes were abolished. The penalty of imprisonment was restored. The Commission was freed from judicial interference with the declaration that the burden of proof, in a contest with the Commission, rested with the carrier and not the Commission. However, a concession was made to the carriers in the provision that new orders and schedules were suspended pending judicial review. Carriers were forbidden to engage in the transport of commodities they themselves produced, unless such products were needed for railroad operation, an exception being made in the case of timber. (This was the so-called commodity clause and was designed to force the railroads out of other businesses, particularly mining.)

This was a long step toward the attainment of government regulation. It is to be noted, however, that judicial interference was not yet completely checked and that the rate-making power vested in the Commission was but a negative one. In other words, as La Follette was quick to point out, the Commission could determine only whether a rate was "relatively reasonable" and not "reasonable per se." La Follette insisted that rate making could never be effective until the Commission had been vested with the function of evaluating the railroad properties and fixing a rate on the basis of a fair return for the true investment.

Results were quickly apparent. Within two years after the passage of the Hepburn Act some 9000 appeals by shippers were filed with the Commission. Of these, 1500 were formal complaints. This situation, as an indication of public confidence, may be contrasted with the fact that but 878 formal complaints had been filed in the nineteen years 1887 to 1906. The Commission applied itself assiduously to the standardization of schedules, and by 1911 had cut in half some 194,000 of the rates existing in 1906. Too, the Supreme Court, during the years 1909 to 1913, repeatedly moved to strengthen the hands of the Commission. In 1909, the Court upheld the constitutionality of the antirebating and commodity clauses. In 1910, the Court recognized Congress' right to lay down the general principles under which the Commission was to operate, when the Court ruled that it could not pass on the legality of a Commission order merely because such action was unwise or inexpedient. Carriers could expect relief from the courts only if they proved confiscation "beyond any just or reasonable doubt." In a 1913 decision the Court once and for all declared that it concurred in the Commission's right not only to regulate rates but to intervene in the internal administration of railway companies.

Not that the victory was as clean-cut as all this might indicate. While the commodity clause of the 1906 act was upheld, the Court really rendered it ineffective by declaring that its provisions would be satisfied if railroad companies merely transferred their stock in coal mines to separately organized coal companies.[8] And while the government might bring rebating suits, claims for excessive damages would not be countenanced. Thus, the higher courts set aside as confiscatory Judge Kenesaw Mountain Landis' decision of 1907, against the Standard Oil Company of Indiana, in which he found the defendant guilty of accepting rebates in 1462 different instances and fined the company $29,240,000. When the retrial was held, the indictments were dismissed by another judge.

On June 18, 1910, Congress further amended the Interstate Commerce Act with the passage of the Mann-Elkins Act. This had started out as a Presidential measure but had been immeasurably strengthened at the insistence of the Republican insurgents. The leading provisions of this new law were: The Commission's jurisdiction was extended to include telephone, telegraph, cable, and wireless companies. The Commission was given the right to move against a carrier without waiting for the federal law officers. The Commission could suspend a new schedule while it

[8] But in 1920, in U. S. v. Reading Company (253 U.S. 26) the Court ruled that a holding company possessing the stock of railroads and coal companies was acting in violation of the antitrust laws as well as of the commodity clause. Thus the commodity clause was revived.

examined into its reasonableness. The long- and short-haul clause was rendered once more effective through the elimination from the 1887 law of the troublesome clause "under substantially similar circumstances and conditions." [9] Appeals from the Commission's rulings were expedited through the creation of a new court. Five circuit court judges were to be assigned by the Supreme Court to constitute this new Commerce Court, which was to sit at Washington. Appeals from the Commerce Court were to be carried directly to the Supreme Court. In 1912, however, Congress abolished this court as the result of a scandal involving one of its judges.

Finally, in 1913, the insurgents attained the end for which they had been pressing since that day, seven years before, when La Follette had begun his singlehanded fight in the Senate. On March 1, 1913, President Taft signed an Act giving to the Interstate Commerce Commission the right to make a study of the physical valuation of the railroads for the purpose of providing, ultimately, a scientific basis for rate making. This Physical Valuation Act required the Commission to report the value of all property owned by every common carrier subject to its jurisdiction. The Commission was to prepare three sets of valuations, namely, the original cost to date, the cost of reproduction new, and the cost of reproduction less depreciation. Such valuations, when completed, were to be accepted as prima facie evidence of the worth of the property in all proceedings under the Interstate Commerce Act. The Commission set to work at once and by 1921 had completed its field surveys.

CONSERVATION

The domestic policy of Theodore Roosevelt that was pushed with greatest energy was his conservation program. The squandering of the nation's natural resources had gone merrily on since the day when the Homestead Act had thrown the public lands open to entry, and forests had been stripped, oil, coal, and natural gas recklessly wasted, and public waterpower sites converted to private use by enterprisers, who were supported in their quick hunt for profits by an indifferent government. A feeble effort at halting the spoliation had been made in 1891 when Congress had granted to the President the power to withhold timber lands from entry, but Cleveland had been the only executive to exercise the right with any zeal. True, a Forestry Bureau had been created in the Department of Agriculture, and the Geological Survey of the Interior Department, under the initial stimulus of J. W. Powell, had competently applied itself to surveying and cataloguing the great natural resources the country possessed; but aside from this, progress was slight.

It remained for the Roosevelt administration to arouse public opinion

[9] See above, page 236.

to the need for governmental action and the creation of an enlightened conservation program. None contributed more to this awakening than Gifford Pinchot, director of the United States Forestry Service. The unmasking of wholesale land frauds, the unseemly squabbling over water sites among private irrigation companies in the West, and the promptings of Pinchot caused Roosevelt in December, 1906, to close 64,000,000 acres of the public lands and then, in March, 1907, to establish an Inland Waterways Commission for purposes of investigation. The Commission wisely looked into the whole problem of the natural resources and advised the President to call a conference of governors for the creation of a nation-wide program.

Out of this suggestion grew the White House Conference of May 13, 1908, which was attended by the governors of twenty-four states, Cabinet members, Supreme Court judges, Congressmen and Senators, the heads of the federal scientific bureaus, and other interested persons. The conference submitted a series of important resolutions, which recommended the protection of the source waters of navigable streams, the adoption of effective means for checking forest fires, the regulation of timber cutting on public and private lands, the granting of separate titles to the surface of public lands and the subsurface minerals, and the retention by the government of title to all public lands in which there were phosphate rock, coal, oil, or natural gas.

To press further the enlightenment of the public, Roosevelt appointed the National Conservation Commission headed by Pinchot, which in its first report (January, 1909) issued a complete inventory of the nation's natural resources. Hard on the heels of this body there appeared forty-one state conservation commissions and at least fifty conservation committees representing private national organizations. Under order from the President, Secretary of the Interior Garfield withdrew from entry not only 148,000,000 acres of forest lands but, as well, 80,000,000 acres of coal lands, 1,500,000 acres of waterpower sites, and 4,700,000 acres of phosphate lands. Roosevelt called upon Congress, without success, however, to enact legislation for the retention by the government of the fee of all the coal, oil, and gas lands still unalienated, and the establishment of a system of leaseholds only. It was not until 1920 that this policy was underwritten by Congress, with specific application to coal, petroleum, natural gas, oil shale, phosphorus, and sodium salt lands. By that time there remained in the possession of the government but 29,883,000 acres of coal lands and 5,000,000 acres of petroleum lands.

Another part of the conservation program was the reclamation of the arid and semiarid regions of the Far West. In 1894 the Carey Act had permitted the government to patent arid lands in the names of the states, on condition that they inaugurate irrigation projects. These had been pushed but tardily with the result that the Newlands Act of 1902 authorized the federal government to build its own irrigation works. The first such plant was ready for use in 1905. By 1940 to 1941, $250 million had been spent in construction work alone and there had been made available for tillage almost 2,369,820 acres. All this activity was not an unmixed blessing, for by the addition of these new acres, and with the help of the dry farming, which had also been developed in the once-arid regions of the Far West, there was to be found one of the reasons for overproduction of agricultural staples, and hence agricultural distress, in the nineteen twenties.

The Roosevelt conservation policy was continued by President Taft, who succeeded in obtaining the Congressional authorization for those land withdrawals which had been denied his predecessor. In 1910, Taft laid before Congress a program which called for the enactment of nine bills, the most important providing for the separation of subsurface from surface titles and the withdrawal of waterpower sites and many mineral lands. These were passed. The doubtful legality—at any rate, Taft's Secretary of the Interior considered it so—of Roosevelt's orders in closing valuable public lands without Congressional consent precipitated a bitter controversy which alienated many of Roosevelt's liberal friends from the Taft administration.

In the summer of 1909, Pinchot divulged that Secretary of the Interior Ballinger had restored to private operations a number of important waterpower sites in Montana and Wyoming; and he proceeded to charge him with the betrayal of the conservation program. Fuel was added to the flames when L. R. Glavis, an official in the Public Land Office, accused Ballinger of having unnecessarily hastened the patenting of Alaskan coal lands owned by the Guggenheim-Morgan interests. Taft agreed to the immediate dismissal of Glavis and then removed Pinchot from the Forestry Service in January, 1910, when the latter took his complaints to Congress, instead of reporting to his superiors. A Congressional committee, by a majority vote, exonerated Ballinger, but the hostility toward the Cabinet officer was so great that in March, 1911, Taft accepted his resignation. Political expediency demanded the maneuver, for Roosevelt's coolness toward Taft, in part, was attributed to the ex-President's acceptance of Pinchot's and Garfield's interpretations of Taft's conduct. After the lapse of forty years, one is compelled to conclude that Taft, in this instance, was a cruelly maligned man who tried to move with circumspection because his legal training convinced him that Roosevelt had more enthusiasm than statutory right on his side in his land withdrawals. Besides, it should be remembered that Ballinger had been an original Roosevelt appointee, having been in charge of the General Land Office before his promotion by Taft. There is no question that Roosevelt was quick to make political capital out of a situation for which Taft was not responsible.

· 22 ·

The Triumph of Reform

FACTORS INFLUENCING THE REFORM MOVEMENT

It was to be expected that the economic individualism, so characteristic of the last quarter of the nineteenth century, would not be permitted to reign, unmolested, forever. There had been early stirrings of revolt against the laissez-faire doctrine, as we have seen, in the West, and out of these demands for government interference there had appeared the Interstate Commerce Act, the Sherman Antitrust Law, the Populist movement, and the free-silver agitation. The total accomplishments of the western dissidents, however, had been slight. But the first fifteen years of the twentieth century were to see appearing a new and ever growing protest which, before it had run its course, was to sweep the whole country and was to effect a profound transformation in popular attitudes both toward government itself and toward the relations of government and business. The movement for reform was general; but never did there actually appear a united sentiment to support an integrated program. Said the protestants: there was need for greater intelligence, more devotion, more honesty in government; there was need for the acceptance, by industry, of a greater responsibility toward the workers and the victims of the industrial process. There made their appearance, therefore, reformers who singled out various evils for attack: there were the conservationists, the settlement house workers, the suffragists, the advocates of direct as opposed to machine government, the budget experts, the municipal reformers, the commission-government supporters, the advocates of workmen's-compensation laws, mothers' assistance, and liberal factory codes. More often than not, one was to find a small coterie of earnest persons agitating for the acceptance of but one principle, or at most a related group of them. And the reformers, very often, expressed not the slightest interest in one another's programs. In other words, the period saw no organized or disciplined movement, led by recognized chiefs, who had designed a plan of attack and who were prepared to advance from the capture of one outpost on to the next. What there was, really, was something akin to a mass movement, as though a great horde of people had suddenly become inspired by the same objectives and had simultaneously hit upon the idea of taking to the road. In-

352

deed, it might be said that American democracy was on the march in the first decade and a half of the new century.

The forces that had unleashed this curious movement were diverse, some being native and some foreign in origin. First, perhaps, was the influence of the Populist agitation which, though defeated in 1896 in the national arena, was to have a profound and lasting effect in the states. The second influence was the appearance of reform governors, of whom Robert La Follette in Wisconsin was at once typical and the best known. These men fought, often singlehanded, to break down the insidious alliance between business and machine politics, to compel reluctant legislators to give the electorate a measure of direct government, and to obtain enlightened factory codes. The third influence was a growing familiarity with the doctrines of socialism and with the progress that state socialism was making in European countries and in the Antipodes. The American socialist press, which was remarkably active and intelligent (because it had the whole of European radicalism from which to draw), had a much greater effect than the support given to its political program showed. While Americans might not be prepared to vote for socialist candidates, they were quite ready to believe many of the things these persons had to say of the deplorable state of affairs existing in government and business. The fourth influence was the appearance of the "muckrakers" in the new popular magazines. The fifth influence was the work of the political and social thinkers. These last two we may notice a little more fully.

The muckrakers were given their name by Theodore Roosevelt in 1906, and he used the term invidiously. The time had come for a halt to be called on the mere collection of noxious facts about business and government; let us, said the President, turn our attention to constructive work. But there was no denying that public enlightenment could not have advanced very far had it not been for the sensational tales of the young magazine writers, who displayed a diligence in tracking down scandals which was nothing less than astonishing. Encouraged by the editors of a group of popular and highly successful magazines, staff contributors and free-lance writers scoured the land to collect examples of existing corruption. They went into the cities and wrote stories of franchise sales, the fraudulent letting of contracts, payroll padding, the alliance of the police with vice, of foul slum dwellings, and the sufferings of the poor. They visited state capitols and returned with tales of the insidious and pervasive influence of lobbyists, the bribing of legislators, franchise-grabbing, and the workings of the "invisible government" of machine politics. They looked into the conduct of business enterprise and exposed worthless stock schemes, dishonest insurance companies, and the crooked practices of monopolies.

A group of notable exposés appeared as a result. First in the list stood

Ida M. Tarbell's *History of the Standard Oil Company* which *McClure's* began printing in 1903. Lincoln Steffens' *Shame of the Cities*, an exposure of municipal corruption in six metropolises, was printed in *McClure's* in 1904. Ray Stannard Baker, for the same magazine, wrote *Railroads on Trial* in 1905 and 1906. *Everybody's* printed Thomas W. Lawson's *Frenzied Finance* in 1905. Charles E. Russell, for the same magazine, wrote a series of articles on the Beef Trust in 1905. Judge Ben B. Lindsey, in 1909, wrote for *Everybody's* a group of articles on criminal law and juvenile delinquency. Samuel Hopkins Adams, in 1905, began the publication of a number of articles in *Collier's* concerning patent medicines and how newspapers were being muzzled by the heavy advertising revenues derived from proprietary medicine manufacturers. David Graham Phillips, in the *Cosmopolitan*, in 1906, wrote a caustic series on the business affiliations of United States Senators.

A number of novelists swelled the ranks of the pamphleteers and employed as their themes the evil influences being exerted by Big Business in the American life. The most important of these works, as a document of social injustice, was Upton Sinclair's *Jungle* (1906), which concerned itself with the Chicago stockyards. Frank Norris' *Octopus* (1901) had as its subject the struggles of the farmers against the domination of the Southern Pacific Railroad, and his *The Pit* (1902) told of the operations of traders on the wheat exchange. The novelist Winston Churchill in his *Coniston* (1906) depicted the political processes in a New England state, while David Graham Phillips wrote a number of novels of the new plutocracy. To the exposures of the muckrakers might be traced certain definite reforms: the life insurance investigations in New York State, the passage of the Pure Food and Drugs Act and the Meat Inspection Act by Congress, the purging by newspapers of their advertising columns, more vigorous control over the listing of securities by the stock exchanges, the formation of various social work organizations.

The political and social thinkers did their share in the organization of American public opinion. In his *Promise of American Life* (1909) and *Progressive Democracy* (1914) Herbert Croly called for the formulation of a social program and the creation of a government that would be responsive to democracy's needs. He was not committed to any particular economic or political doctrines, but preached the ideas of a more alert leadership and a larger social and industrial outlook by government. Walter Lippmann's *A Preface to Politics* (1913) and *Drift and Mastery* (1914) were widely read. Deeply influenced by H. G. Wells, Bernard Shaw, and Graham Wallas, this young New York writer made a brilliant appeal for a change of motives in a world dominated by the hunt for profits and ruled over by a routinized officialdom. To humanize politics, Lippmann pointed out, it was first necessary to understand the needs and aspirations of men; only then might society begin its preoccupation with governmental forms. Walter Weyl, in his *The New Democracy* (1912), after attacking the plutocracy in business and government, outlined a complete program for political reform. Jane Addams contributed to the swelling chorus her *Newer Ideals of Peace* (1907), *The Spirit of Youth and the City Streets* (1909), and *A New Conscience and an Ancient Evil* (1912). All these were enthusiasts, all these were sure that the new day could be hastened without the need for stirring up the class hatreds that were so much part of the creeds of the socialists and syndicalists.

Working in other vineyards, and quite as effectively, were the writers on sociological jurisprudence, notably Ernst Freund and Roscoe Pound. As early as 1904 Freund began to insist that the law must place social interests before the rights of property; and he greatly extended the doctrine of the police power of the state. It was the purpose of the state, he said, "to promote the public welfare, and its characteristic methods are those of restraint and compulsion." Hence, in the interest of public welfare, it was the state's business, on the basis of its police power, to protect the safety, health, morals, and even the dependents of its citizens. Pound extended the philosophy of Pragmatism into the law: the law was to shape itself ceaselessly to changing human conditions; it was to surrender its slavish obedience to first principles and try to arrive at justice on the basis of the facts of the case and not through the application of hoary legal maxims. A new kind of legal brief, as a result of these teachings, made its appearance, which not only cited legal precedents and decisions, but also presented statistical and sociological exhibits to prove that social and economic legislation was justifiable to protect health, safety, and morals. Examples of this type of argument were Louis D. Brandeis' brief before the United States Supreme Court, in support of the Oregon 10-hour law for women (1908), and Felix Frankfurter's brief in behalf of the Oregon 10-hour law for men (1917).

POLITICAL REFORM

We may now examine at some length the actual accomplishments of the various groups of reformers and see to what extent their programs met with success. As one might expect, the influence of La Follette was instrumental in causing Wisconsin to lead the way. Here, the direct primary was established, a corrupt practices Act was passed, separate ballots for national, state, and local elections were decreed. The political machine was smashed, said the reformers, and one of the chief of them, Frederic C. Howe, thus hailed the new day in Wisconsin in this lyrical passage:

> These laws form the machinery of popular representative government. They insure responsibility and responsiveness. They abolish all intermediaries between

principal and agent. Candidates make pledges only to the people who elect them. Through them the power of the boss, of the machine, and of wealth are reduced to a minimum.

Wisconsin passed its direct primary law in 1903, and other states were quick to follow her example; at the close of 1915, primaries for state elections were to be found in thirty-seven jurisdictions and were usually accompanied by corrupt-practices acts. Beginning with 1910, Oregon extended the primary to make provision for the instruction of delegates to the Presidential nominating conventions; by 1912 thirteen states were employing this device.

In 1913, the Seventeenth Amendment for the popular election of United States Senators, having been ratified by the required number of states, was proclaimed. In 1904, Oregon had created, in effect, the popular election of Senators by holding its legislators morally responsible for the naming of Senators chosen in elections by the people, and by 1912, twenty-nine commonwealths were employing a similar system. The United States Senate had finally yielded to the popular clamor and in 1911 had adopted a resolution for the constitutional amendment; the House had passed it in 1912; ratification was secured in one year.

Oregon was the first state, in 1902, to adopt the thoroughgoing use of the initiative and referendum, though South Dakota (1897) and Utah (1900) had accepted this form of direct legislation for ordinary measures only. Before the Progressive movement had spent itself some twenty states adopted the reform. In its plainest form, this device of the reformers meant that a small portion of the electorate (usually 5 per cent) might initiate measures, while a majority of those voting could enact them. In the first years of their existence, the initiative and referendum were employed with great zeal. Thus in Oregon, in six biennial elections (1904 to 1916), the voters were asked to pass upon forty-one constitutional amendments and sixty-two statutes.

The recall of elective officials was first adopted in Los Angeles in 1903 and in Seattle in 1906. Oregon, in 1908, extended the device to include all elective officials. In the next six years, ten other states followed Oregon's example. The recall of judges was solemnly discussed by wearers of the robe, political officials, and laymen, and Congress, in 1911, was thrown into a great panic over this new "heresy" when Arizona, asking for admission into the Union, submitted a frame of government that included the recall of judges. On the recommendation of President Taft, Arizona was granted admission only after she had promised to expunge the undesirable provision from her constitution. The very next year, the legislators of the sovereign state of Arizona wrote it in again. In all, eight jurisdictions permitted the recall of judges, and one, Colorado, in 1912 adopted a constitutional amendment providing for the recall of judicial decisions.

THE TRIUMPH OF REFORM

The agitation for the granting of the suffrage to women was taken up with enthusiasm by the reformers. The territory of Wyoming had been permitting women to vote since 1869; the franchise had been granted to women in school elections in Michigan and Minnesota in 1875. Full suffrage had been accorded to women in three other western states before the turn of the century; between 1910 and 1918, eleven other commonwealths joined the roll. But Congress had steadfastly refused to adopt a resolution for the submission of a constitutional amendment to the states and in 1918 defeated for the thirteenth time such a proposal. Finally, in 1919, the resolution was carried and by March, 1920, thirty-five states had ratified it. The Nineteenth Amendment was proclaimed on August 26, 1920.

The reformers sought to attack privilege in the states by passing anti-lobbying laws, laws regulating the granting of franchises, and laws creating public utilities commissions to regulate the practices of transportation, electric, gas, and water companies. The number of state elective officials was reduced, the executive budget was created, and the Civil Service was extended. To purify governmental processes in the cities, the following reforms were adopted in many places: home rule for cities; new charters providing for the centralization of responsibility in the hands of a small elective commission; the city manager plan; executive budgets; public letting of contracts; central purchasing of supplies; standardization of salaries; training schools for firemen, policemen, and teachers; city planning; and municipal ownership of subways, water supply systems, and gas and electrical plants. By 1931, the city manager plan existed in some four hundred cities, among which were to be numbered Cincinnati, Kansas City, Indianapolis, Rochester, and Dayton.

What had all this tinkering with the governmental machine achieved? Did it make the electorate more alert, reduce the power of the bosses, achieve greater honesty in government, eliminate the influence of privilege from the councils of the land? Did the doubling of the electorate, by the grant of the suffrage to women, purify politics? One cannot give a categorical reply. The United States is a democracy and consistently honest and efficient government is dependent, as the reformers sadly learned, upon the willingness of the people to maintain a high level of interest in public affairs. In the final analysis, public opinion is the real ruler, and this, only too often, is capricious and easily diverted; it falls readily under the influence of propaganda and is, too, not profoundly interested in statecraft. Direct primaries and corrupt-practices acts have not eliminated the boss and the power of money in elections (more money is merely being spent in primary contests!); the threat of direct government by the initiative and referendum has not destroyed the legislatures; the popular election of Senators did not fill Congress' upper chamber with the people's choices; the executive budget and the efficiency movement in local government have not checked waste and graft. And as for woman suffrage, though the grant of the ballot to the sex was eminently just, women as women accounted for no distinct change in the complexion of the political life. They accepted party loyalties as blindly as the men, voted with the machine as consistently, and, too, showed that they were not beyond fraud and corruption while in office.

Yet there have been gains of a real sort. The executive budget is a work program and allows for intelligent scrutiny; the short ballot does contribute a measure of centralization so that the executive can be called to account; the initiative and referendum help, even if only slightly, in the education of the electorate; city government, though it is still controlled by the politicians and is extravagantly administered, more and more is performing larger social services for our urban populations. More than anything else, a principle has been accepted that is helping in the resolution of many perplexing social and economic difficulties. Under its operations, state legislatures are expected to work consistently in the public interest, regardless of the exalted ideas of property written into the Fourteenth Amendment by the Supreme Court. And, largely as a result of the reform movement, the forty-eight states have been turned into so many social laboratories where continuous experimentation has been going on in the formulation of new social and economic codes. Constitutions are no longer regarded with awe; the doctrine of the police power in the interests of health, safety, and morals has been accepted; and the first faltering steps of pioneer states are quickly followed by almost all the others. This has been the history of mothers'-assistance acts, workmen's-compensation laws, school-attendance laws, and even old-age pension legislation. In other words, while the political side of the reformers' programs did not meet with overwhelming success and party and boss rule is as firmly entrenched as ever, the agitation did produce a heightening of sensitivity on the part of legislators and an acceptance by them of the rule that it was their function to labor for the common weal.

SOCIAL AND ECONOMIC LEGISLATION

Not in the federal Congress, therefore, but in the state legislatures was there to be found a preoccupation with social and economic problems. During the years immediately following 1900 there began to appear on state statute books laws establishing workmen's-compensation systems to cover cases of industrial accident; laws raising the ages of entry of children into industry; laws fixing hours of work for children, women, and even men; minimum-wage laws for women; safety and health codes; mothers'-assistance acts to furnish public aid to dependent children; and old-age pension laws. Significant as they were, it is not to be understood that these new statutes furnished the solution to all the prevailing forms of economic insecurity. But they indicated that through the agency of the states a means existed for the handling of these problems and that the laborious and uncertain method of federal constitutional amendment was not necessary.

Workmen's-compensation laws were devised to overthrow those barbarous precepts of the common law that had placed the burden of proof squarely on the shoulders of the injured employee. Under the common law a worker injured in an industrial accident was entitled to damages in a court of law only if he could prove: that the employer had not used reasonable care for the protection of his employees; that the accident had not taken place as a result of the negligence of a "fellow-servant"; that there had not been "contributory negligence" on his own part; that the risk assumed was an extraordinary one. This legal mumbo-jumbo the reformers impatiently brushed aside. Workers injured in industrial activities were in need of quick relief for the protection of themselves and their families, and the only way such relief could be obtained was through the creation of funds from which the injured worker might be recompensed.

The principle of workmen's compensation, therefore, demanded the payment of benefits in the event of permanent disability or death, for medical treatment, and as compensation in cases of temporary disability while the worker was under care. To protect the worker in his rights, the system invariably called for participation in an insurance fund by the employer. In 1906, Congress had passed the Employers' Liability Act making railways liable for damages despite the existence of contributory negligence or the fault of a fellow employee. The Supreme Court declared the law unconstitutional on the ground that it did not directly specify that only railroad men engaged in interstate commerce were affected. In 1908, Congress enacted a second measure incorporating the required changes. The first state workmen's-compensation law was that of Maryland in 1902; the first law of wholesale application was New York's in 1910, and though this was declared unconstitutional, a constitutional amendment made a strong law possible in 1914. By 1920, there were laws on the statute books of all the states and territories except five and one of these adopted a compensation law in 1929. Civil employees of the federal government were also protected, and in 1927 a federal act extended the benefits of compensation to longshoremen and harbor workers. In 1917, the United States Supreme Court affirmed the constitutionality of these state codes. By 1943, every state but Mississippi had a workmen's-compensation law and by 1948, thirty-nine states included at least certain occupational diseases among compensable injuries.

The protection of children and women in industry gained new impetus as a result of the reform movement. Even before the Civil War, states had applied themselves to the limitation of the hours of children in factories, but the absence of governmental machinery made these laws dead letters. In 1903, however, new legislation began to make its appearance, accompanied by the creation of state departments of labor or industrial boards, so that enforcement was assured. By 1930, thirty-seven states had established the 8-hour day and the 48-hour week for children in factories; five states had a maximum 10-hour day and 54-hour week; only two were allowing a 60-hour week. Too, as a result of the work of the National Child Labor Committee (organized in 1904) and the Children's Bureau of the Department of Labor (set up by Congress in 1912) a persistent agitation was carried on against child labor. By 1930, as a result of state action, forty-one states were forbidding certain types of work for children under fourteen years; five states were forbidding certain types of work for children under fifteen years; and two fixed the minimum age for entrance into industry at sixteen years. School-attendance laws similarly were strengthened. In fifteen states, the completion of the eighth grade was required if the child was fourteen years or under; in five states, the completion of the eighth grade was required if the child was under sixteen years; and in fourteen states school attendance was compulsory until the attainment of either the seventeenth or the eighteenth birthday.

Impatient at the tardy efforts of southern states to safeguard children against industrial exploitation, reformers worked unceasingly for a federal child-labor law or constitutional amendment. The first resolution for a constitutional amendment to make its appearance was championed by Senator Albert J. Beveridge in 1906 and called for the denial of carriage in interstate commerce to products of a factory or mine in which children under fourteen years were employed. In 1916, at the intervention of President Wilson, Congress passed the Keating-Owen bill which forbade the shipment in interstate commerce of the products of any factory, shop, or cannery where children under fourteen years were working; of products of the mines where children under sixteen years were working; and of the products of any of these establishments where children under sixteen years worked more than eight hours a day or at night work. The constitutionality of the law was contested in North Carolina, and in 1918 the United States Supreme Court denied the validity of the statute on the ground that the law interfered with the power reserved to the states under the Tenth Amendment. Another effort at federal action was made in 1919 when Congress passed an act placing a high tax on the profits of factories in which children under fourteen years labored. But again the judicial lightning struck, the Supreme Court ruling this time, in 1922, that Congress was using its tax power illegally, that is to say, to punish and not to raise revenue. A unanimous bench therefore declared the law unconstitutional.

Finally, another attempt was made at constitutional amendment when, in 1924, Congress adopted a resolution for submission to the states. Section 1 of the proposed amendment read: "Congress shall have the power to limit, regulate, and prohibit the labor of persons under eighteen years of age."

Despite a nation-wide agitation to which the American Federation of Labor lent its support, the amendment quickly went down to defeat. By January, 1925, it was apparent that it had been lost inasmuch as, by that time, thirteen state legislatures had already turned their thumbs down. The amendment was never ratified but its intention was achieved indirectly in 1938 through the passage of the Fair Labor Standards Act.

Laws were devised, too, for the protection of women in industry. The movement to fix controls over the hours of women had a long history, and it was not until the early nineteen hundreds that the principle was accepted by legislatures. The Supreme Court in 1908 gave its consent to the process when it passed favorably on an Oregon 10-hour law for women.[1] The result was that by 1930 all except five states were carrying on their statute books acts fixing limitations on the number of hours women might work. In the majority of the states, the maximum day was set at 9 hours; in sixteen states, night work was forbidden; and in a number of jurisdictions codes were prepared listing dangerous occupations from which women were to be barred. Six states went even further than the enactment of statutory prohibitions by placing in the hands of industrial commissions general powers to draw up regulations for the employ of women, such rules to be dependent upon the conditions existing in particular industries.

The first minimum-wage law in the United States was passed in Massachusetts in 1912 and set up a commission to establish minimum-wage schedules for women and children. The commission, however, was not given mandatory powers, but had to depend upon publicity and the aid of public opinion for the acceptance of its decrees. In 1913, eight other states passed similar laws, except that in their cases either statutory minimums were set up or wage boards were given mandatory powers. By 1923, six more states and the District of Columbia had joined the roll. In 1923, however, the United States Supreme Court, in reviewing the District of Columbia law, found the principle of minimum-wage regulation for women unconstitutional on the ground of impairment of the freedom of contract.[2] It is interesting to note that Chief Justice Taft and Justice Holmes delivered vigorous dissents. In Kansas (1925) the state supreme court handed down a similar decision, based on the Supreme Court precedent. In the other jurisdictions state wage boards continued to exercise their functions, hoping for and very often receiving the co-operation of employers. In California, Oregon, and Wisconsin the boards were particularly energetic. The Adkins decision of 1923 did not, however, interfere with the functioning of the minimum-wage laws so far as children were concerned.

Attempts at state regulation of hours for men met with judicial resistance, but by 1917 this principle, too, had received the sanction of the Supreme

[1] Muller v. Oregon, 208 U.S. 412.
[2] Adkins v. Children's Hospital, 261 U.S. 525.

Court. In 1898, the highest court of the land had accepted a Utah law fixing the 8-hour day for men working in mines and smelters.[3] But in 1905, in the Lochner v. New York decision the Court refused to countenance a New York statute fixing the working day for bakers at ten hours.[4] The majority opinion, in support of this stand, said: "We think the limit of the police power has been reached and passed in this case. There is, in our judgment, no reasonable foundation for holding this to be necessary or appropriate as a health law...." That the whole bench did not agree, however, many be seen from the fact that four of the nine judges dissented. In twelve years the court accepted the opinion of the minority, for in 1917, in reviewing an Oregon law fixing 10 hours as the legal maximum for all factory employees, the Court approved the statute as a justifiable exercise of the police power.[5] In the same year, the Supreme Court gave its approval to the Adamson Law, a federal statute establishing the 8-hour day on interstate railroads.[6] By the end of 1930, the 8-hour day was in force on federal public-works construction as well as in thirty jurisdictions, while in many states there were to be found statutes limiting the hours of labor for men working in mines and smelters, on railroads and street railways, in electric plants, plaster and cement mills, and the like.

Even more significant than this legislation was the acceptance of public responsibility for the dependency of children and the aged. The Elizabethan Poor Law was firmly fixed in the American common law, but this code was interpreted to mean merely that the states were responsible for the care of the indigent in almshouses or by the indiscriminate grant of outdoor relief through county agencies. It was not until 1911 that American commonwealths accepted the notion that the interests of society could best be served if dependent children were kept in their own homes. The result was the writing of mothers'-assistance acts on the basis of which public agencies granted regular relief (or pensions) to mothers with dependent children. The first such statute was passed by the Missouri legislature to apply to Jackson County (in which Kansas City is located); the first state-wide law was enacted in Illinois in the same year. In 1912, Colorado adopted a similar law by popular referendum. In 1913, eighteen states enacted mothers'-assistance laws; and by the end of 1930 such codes were operating in the District of Columbia, Alaska, Hawaii, and all the states of the Union except four.

In many of the jurisdictions these acts covered not only widows with dependent children, but all cases where child dependency was to be found, whether the father was dead, divorced, physically or mentally incapacitated, in prison, or had deserted his family. The maximum ages of children

[3] Holden v. Hardy (169 U.S. 366).
[4] Lochner v. New York (198 U.S. 45).
[5] Bunting v. Oregon (243 U.S. 426).
[6] Wilson v. New (243 U.S. 332).

eligible for aid ran from fourteen to seventeen years. In some states, the size of grants was fixed by statute; in others, public boards were permitted to employ their discretion in the granting of allotments. It was estimated by the federal Children's Bureau that at any one time at least 200,000 dependent children were receiving aid in their own homes.

Not until 1914 was the same principle extended to apply to the care of the indigent aged in their own homes. The first state establishing an old-age pension system was Arizona (1914), but the state supreme court found this statute to be unconstitutional. In 1915, the Alaska legislature enacted a statute calling for the payment of old-age pensions by the territory. In 1923, Montana, Nevada, and Pennsylvania followed. In this last state, however, the Supreme Court declared the law unconstitutional in 1925. The movement for old-age pensions took on impetus in the late nineteen twenties, largely in consequence of the intelligent propaganda conducted by the American Association for Old Age Security. The result was the writing of laws in thirteen states between 1927 and 1931. In a number of these, the laws were made mandatory and required that the local authorities grant pensions to aged persons possessing the following qualifications: American citizenship, a comparatively long term of residence in the state (generally ten to fifteen years), and the absence of other means of support. The pensionable age was sixty-five years in some states and seventy years in others, and the maximum pension was usually $30 a month. The reader is to observe that these measures, in providing for the payment of pensions to aged persons by the public authorities, differ radically from the social insurance codes of European countries which call for the building up of funds on the basis of contributions from the state, employers, and employees. Such statutes did not appear until the New Deal was installed.

SOCIALISM IN THE UNITED STATES

The success of the reform movement of the nineteen hundreds was in no slight measure due to the spread of socialism, whose doctrines gained a wide audience and in time came to be supported at the polls by a sizable group of voters. Socialism has had a long history in the United States, though it did not become politically significant until the period we have been examining.

Marx's *Revolution and Counter Revolution,* written after the failure of the 1848 uprisings in several European countries, was first published serially in Greeley's *New York Tribune.* Also, Marxian socialism was brought into the United States by the German immigrants of the fifties, and the American labor movement participated in the work of Marx's First International, which was organized in 1864. Five years later, the National Labor Union elected a delegate to the First International; in 1872, the office of Marx's organization was transferred to New York in an effort to revivify what was already a moribund affair. But in 1876 an independent socialist group was launched in the United States when the Socialist Labor party held its first convention at Philadelphia. For fifteen years this body led an obscure and precarious existence. Its efforts to win over labor support met with small success and its future would have been that of other dissident minorities had not two significant events breathed new life into it. These were the publication of Edward Bellamy's *Looking Backward* in 1887 and the appearance of Daniel De Leon on the scene.

Bellamy's book, with its enticing picture of a socialist commonwealth, reached a wide public, and at least 500,000 copies were sold. Clubs sprang up to spread the new faith; an interest in socialism was renewed; and for the first time an American audience gave ear to socialistic doctrine. De Leon contributed the needed militancy to give the movement continued life.

De Leon was a son of a Dutch Colonial official who came to New York to study and who for a time lectured at Columbia University. In the late eighties he threw himself into the class struggle and by 1890 had converted the Socialist Labor party into a personal organ. His first efforts were directed toward the capture of the Knights of Labor and the American Federation of Labor, and his defeat in both these attempts only served to heighten his intransigency. The American labor movement would never get anywhere, he maintained, unless it surrendered its opportunistic philosophy and adopted the revolutionary creed of the European trade unionists. For the Gompers brand of "pure and simple" trade unionism, he had the utmost contempt. Thus he wrote in 1894, after Debs's failure in the railway strike:

> The union of the workers that expects to be successful must recognize:
> 1. The impossibility of obtaining a decent living while capitalism exists; the certainty of worse and worse conditions; the necessity of the abolition of the wage and capitalist system, and their substitution by the socialist or co-operative commonwealth, whereby the instruments of production shall be made the property of the whole people.
> 2. The necessity of conquering the public powers at the ballot box by the vote of the working class, cast independently.

De Leon pressed his fight along two fronts, the political and the economic. The Socialist Labor party nominated a Presidential ticket in 1892 and its candidates appeared on the ballots of six states. The total vote cast in 1892 was 21,500; in 1896, 40,000; and in the Congressional elections of 1898, 82,000. In 1895, to further revolutionary trade unionism, De Leon organized the Socialist Trade and Labor Alliance, which soon attained a membership of 15,000. Its chief strength lay in New York's East Side, in the so-called United Hebrew Trades. But De Leon's vitriolic tongue and his refusal to compromise with trade unionism were estranging those socialists who hoped to attain the people's commonwealth by the ballot and who were influenced by the milder tactics of the British Fabians and the German Social Democratic party. The result was that in 1899 the two factions fell out and the anti-Leonites joined the newly organized Social Democratic party.

The guiding forces directing the Social Democratic party were Victor L. Berger of Milwaukee and Eugene V. Debs, the latter having been converted to socialism while serving his jail sentence. To join their ranks came Morris Hillquit and the other anti-Leonites, and the result was the creation of the Socialist party of America (1901) with a program of immediate demands and a policy of friendliness toward trade unionism. The Social Democrats, in 1900, nominated Debs for the Presidency and polled 96,800 votes. While they advocated public ownership of the means of production and distribution, consonant with socialist doctrine, they also presented a long list of immediate demands, which included: the extension of the franchise to women; public ownership of all industries controlled by monopolies; public ownership of railroads, telegraphs, and public utilities; public ownership of mines; reduction of the hours of labor; the inauguration of a system of public works to alleviate unemployment; release of inventions for the free use of the public; national labor-legislation codes; social-insurance codes; equal civil and political rights for men and women; the initiative, referendum, proportional representation, and the recall; the abolition of war.

In the next twelve years the Socialists grew in numbers and their program in prestige. The indoctrination of trade union ranks was carried on with such success that in 1912 Max S. Hayes, a socialist, received one-third of the total vote cast for the presidency of the American Federation of Labor. The party platform became more pointed, and its immediate demands threw a sharp light on the prevailing economic inequalities. Thus, the 1908 platform had this to say of the class struggle:

> The struggle between wage-workers and capitalists grows ever fiercer and has now become the only vital issue before the American people. The wage-working class, therefore, has the most direct interest in abolishing the capitalist system.

And these were the immediate demands:

I. (General) Government relief for unemployment, the collective ownership of railroads, the organization of industry, on a national scale, the extension of public control over mines and oil wells, absolute freedom of the press and speech.

II. (Industrial) A shorter working day, abolition of child labor, compulsory insurance against unemployment, illness, accident, invalidism, old age, and death.

III. (Political) Inheritance and income taxes, equal suffrage, initiative, referendum, proportional representation, recall, abolition of the Senate, abolition of the Supreme Court's right to pass on the constitutionality of legislation, election of all judges for short terms.

In 1904, the Socialists once more nominated Debs and he polled 402,400 votes; in 1908, Debs, again the standard-bearer, got 420,820 votes; in 1912, he received 897,011 votes. In 1910, the Socialists of Milwaukee elected Emil Seidel mayor and sent Berger to Washington as the first Socialist Congressman. By 1912, Socialist councilmen and other local officials were no longer rarities in the municipalities of the country's industrial regions.

The Socialist press was extensive and well edited because of the large numbers of intellectuals who carried the cards of the party. In 1912, when the Socialist movement was at the height of its power in America, it could boast of 5 English dailies, 8 foreign language dailies, 262 English weeklies, 36 foreign language weeklies, 10 English monthlies, and 2 foreign language monthlies. The *Appeal to Reason,* a Socialist English weekly, was published from Girard, Kansas, and reached a circulation of 500,000, most of it in rural and small urban centers. The *New York Call* (daily) was founded in 1908; the *International Socialist Review* (monthly) began publishing in 1900; the *Masses* (literary monthly) made its appearance in 1911. Before the outbreak of World War I, socialism appeared to be occupying a firm place in the American party system and its adherents looked to the future with confidence.

· 23 ·

Rooseveltian Policies Abroad

ROOSEVELT IN VENEZUELA AND PANAMA

THEODORE ROOSEVELT came to the Presidency with certain notions already firmly fixed in his mind: he was a nationalist, an annexationist, an imperialist, a big-navy advocate. Familiar with modern European affairs as few Americans of the day were, he made it his business to imitate the example of ruling European statesmen. He rattled the saber, he seized territory and made explanations later, he entered on secret alliances, and he clamored for bigger and better naval armaments. When he left the White House, these two precepts had been made permanent fixtures of American foreign policy: that the United States, with economic interests in Africa and Asia, was an international power whose spokesmen were entitled to an equal place at the council tables of the world; that the United States was sovereign in the Western Hemisphere and that Europe might look to us to see that peace was maintained and financial obligations to foreigners were discharged by Latin-American peoples. We shall see how these policies were developed as a result of American activities in the Caribbean and in the Far East, and in the dealings with European nations.

Roosevelt's intervention on behalf of Venezuela, in 1902, gave no hint of the radical transformation the Monroe Doctrine was to undergo later at his hands. In 1902, largely at the prompting of Great Britain, the British, Germans, and Italians decided to engage in a demonstration against Venezuela because of the failure of that South American country to meet her debt services and to satisfy the claims of foreign nationals arising out of losses suffered from civil war. In December, 1902, after the British Foreign Office had sent three ultimatums to the Venezuelan dictator Castro, Great Britain, Germany, and Italy withdrew their legations from Venezuela, seized a number of that country's gunboats and threw a formal blockade around five Venezuelan ports and the mouths of the Orinoco River. On December 17, at the urging of our State Department and after Castro had expressed a willingness to submit the European claims to a mediator, the European allies consented to arbitrate. The blockade was lifted in February, 1903, a mixed commission was set up by The Hague

Tribunal to pass on the foreign claims against Venezuela, and the flurry blew over. Roosevelt, contemporaries saw, studiously observed the requirements of accepted American policy: he had recognized the justice of the claims of the European allies that the property and persons of their nationals were entitled to protection; he had warned them that the seizure of territory would be considered a violation of the Monroe Doctrine; he had regretted the necessity for the blockade but could see no warrant for interfering to relieve the pressure. Finally, he had merely passed on Castro's request for arbitration and then had employed his good offices to hasten the speedy termination of the dispute.

Roosevelt's leadership was much more important in bringing the whole Isthmian canal debate to a quick conclusion. There can be no doubt, too, that Panama's freedom and the construction of the Panama Canal were his handiwork. By the turn of the century it was generally recognized in the United States that our interests required that a passageway across the isthmus, either through Panama or through Nicaragua, be cut. But there were three matters that tended to tie American hands. Those were: 1. The Clayton-Bulwer Treaty with Great Britain of 1850; 2. The concession for the building of a canal held originally by a French company; 3. The treaty of 1846 between the United States and New Granada (later Colombia).

The Clayton-Bulwer Treaty provided that any Isthmian canal constructed by either the United States or Great Britain would be jointly controlled, would never be fortified, and would be neutralized for the service of all nations. It has been noted how Secretaries Blaine and Frelinghuysen entered into unsuccessful negotiations with Great Britain for the purpose of obtaining the recognition of American primacy. There the matter rested until 1899 when Hay, assured by increasing British friendliness that this time the American claims to a leading interest would be crowned with success, reopened the conversations with Pauncefote, the British ambassador at Washington. In February, 1900, a treaty was drawn up by the two diplomatists that called for the American construction of a neutralized canal, having somewhat the status of the Suez Canal. But the Senate wanted a distinct break made with the Clayton-Bulwer convention, and it therefore rewrote the treaty in a number of important particulars, the most significant one being the rejection of the neutrality provision. Great Britain rejected the first Hay-Pauncefote Treaty, in its amended form, and negotiations were again renewed in April, 1901. On December 16, 1901, the American Senate gave its approval to the new treaty, and on February 21, 1902, ratifications between the two nations were formally exchanged. The new Hay-Pauncefote Treaty provided for the following: the Clayton-Bulwer convention was abrogated; fortification was to be permitted; the United States was to construct and control the canal; its neutrality was to be maintained, but under the supervision of the United States, which was to guarantee its use to all nations on equal terms. Thus, the first obstacle was removed.

But serious efforts had already been made to build a canal, and a French company had expended a huge sum in starting digging operations. Where was the United States to build? In 1895 and in 1897, American commissions had recommended the Nicaraguan route. In 1901, the Walker Commission, after carefully going into the respective merits of a Panama canal as against a Nicaraguan canal, had decided upon the latter, too. One of the difficulties in the way of construction at Panama was the New Panama Canal Company which had taken over the properties of the earlier bankrupt De Lesseps company, had had its concession extended to 1904, and had placed a value of $109,141,000 on its property and rights. In line with the Walker Commission recommendations on January 9, 1902, the lower house, by a vote of 308 to 2, passed a measure ordering construction at Nicaragua. Things began to move quickly at Washington in the following days. The New Panama Canal Company (now controlled by American promoters) reduced its price to $40,000,000 and redoubled its efforts, at Washington, in an attempt to convince Senators of the superiority of the Panama route; President Roosevelt himself, though once partial to Nicaragua, brought pressure to bear in favor of Panama; the Walker Commission changed its mind overnight and submitted a new report favoring Panama. The result was the passage in June of the substitute Spooner bill, in the Senate, calling for the purchase of the New Panama Canal Company's rights for $40,000,000, the acquisition from Colombia of perpetual control over a canal zone, and the immediate start of construction. Should the President fail in negotiations either with the French company or with Colombia he was authorized to build the canal through Nicaragua. On June 28, 1902, by a vote of 260 to 8, the House accepted the Spooner bill and the President signed it. Thus the second obstacle was removed.

There was still the old treaty with Colombia under which the United States had committed itself to protecting the neutrality of Panama; to guaranteeing the sovereignty of Colombia over the Panama Isthmus; to preserving, with the consent of Colombian authorities, the freedom of transit; and, incidentally, to refraining from interference with the movement of Colombian troops in the event of internal disorders. In order to extinguish Colombian sovereignty in the proposed canal zone an additional treaty was necessary and negotiations were begun in March, 1902. The resulting Hay-Herran convention was signed in January, 1903, and ratified by the American Senate in March. Under its terms the United States was to get a lease over the Canal Zone for ninety-nine years with an option of renewal; for this, the United States was to pay $10,000,000 in cash and an annual rental of $250,000 in gold, beginning nine years after the exchange of ratifications. But the Colombian Senate was in no haste to ratify. It refused to meet until the summer was well under way; it refused to yield to the State Department's none too veiled threats; and when it learned that Hay would not tolerate Colombian negotiations with the New Panama Canal Company for the purpose of obtaining compensation for allowing the transfer of the concession, it turned around and rejected the treaty (August 12). On October 31, the Colombian Senate adjourned, as though to indicate its complete loss of interest in the affair.

By that time, apparently, Roosevelt, too, had made up his mind. In drawing up his message to Congress, this tentative proposal was included:

> Either we should drop the Panama Canal project and immediately begin work on the Nicaraguan Canal, or else we should purchase all the right of the French company and without any further parley with Colombia enter upon the completion of the canal which the French company has begun. I feel that the latter course is the one demanded by the interests of this nation.

Happily Roosevelt never found it necessary to ask Congress for its consent, for the province of Panama revolted on November 3, 1903, the United States recognized the new Republic of Panama on November 6, and on November 18 a treaty was prepared which was even more favorable in its terms than the discarded Hay-Herran convention. When Congress met in December it was confronted by a *fait accompli.* These amazing events had unwound themselves somewhat in this fashion: Developments in the United States, during the late summer of 1903, were being closely followed by three interesting persons, namely, W. N. Cromwell of New York, the attorney for the New Panama Canal Company; Philippe Bunau-Varilla, one-time chief engineer of the company; and Dr. Manuel Amador, Panama patriot and acknowledged chief of those Panamanians who resented Colombia's rejection of the Hay-Herran treaty and who were looking for American support for a revolution. Bunau-Varilla learned that American gunboats were on their way to the isthmus and the waiting patriots in Panama were so informed. Were the gunboats ordered because the United States believed a revolt in Panama impended and that this would interfere with that "free and uninterrupted transit" across the isthmus, which we had pledged ourselves to maintain? Or were the gunboats sent to encourage, by their presence, the timid would-be revolters? All the principals have kept discreetly silent on what will always remain an interesting historical mystery.

The revolt broke out at last on November 3 and neither were shots fired nor was blood spilled, for Colombian troops were prevented from crossing the isthmus by the commander of the *U.S.S. Nashville.* Within a week, there were seven United States warships in Panama waters, and on November 18, in the Hay–Bunau-Varilla Treaty, the United States formally recognized Panama. The other terms of the treaty were as follows: the United States was granted, in perpetuity, the use of a Canal Zone ten miles wide; the

Republic of Panama transferred to the United States the properties of the New Panama Canal Company and the Panama Railroad Company; the United States was to pay Panama $10,000,000 in gold and an annuity of $250,000; the United States guaranteed the neutrality of the Canal and in return was accorded permission to fortify it.

There were still some important questions to be settled before the building of the canal could be undertaken in earnest. In June, 1906, Congress accepted the Isthmian Canal Commission's recommendations and authorized the use of locks as against a sea-level canal; the actual task of construction was placed in the hands of the United States Army's corps of engineers; and in 1908, Colonel G. W. Goethals superseded the Canal Commission, taking over not only complete control of operations but the civil, military, and sanitary supervision of the Canal Zone as well. Thanks to the splendid work of Doctor W. E. Gorgas the isthmus was made a fit place to live in, and by 1907 the preliminary preparations were over and the dirt was really flying. The first ocean steamer passed through the completed Panama Canal on August 15, 1914. The Canal cost us $275,000,000 to build and another $113,000,000 to equip with military and naval defenses.

In 1912, anticipating the early opening of the Canal, Congress turned its attention to the question of toll charges. Despite the fact that the Hay-Pauncefote Treaty called for equality of treatment for the ships of all nations, Congress insisted upon regarding vessels engaged in the American coastwise trade as belonging in a separate category and passed an exemption act allowing these free passage through the Canal. But the protests of Great Britain (and of American railroad interests, too) could not go unheeded, and President Wilson asked Congress to repeal the tolls act. In June, 1914, Congress yielded and the same toll charges were ordered to apply to coastwise and oceanic vessels equally.

American Secretaries of State were not unmindful of the ill will the cavalier treatment of Colombia had stirred up among Latin-American peoples, and Secretaries Root and Knox made a number of efforts to conciliate Colombia. In 1913, when Knox was informed that Colombia would accept nothing less than the submission of the whole subject to international arbitration, he washed his hands of the matter. Wilson's Secretary of State, William Jennings Bryan, willingly resumed the conversations, and in 1914 a treaty negotiated by him was placed before the Senate. It expressed "sincere regret that anything should have occurred to interrupt or mar the relations of cordial friendship" between the two nations, called for the payment of $25,000,000 in cash to Colombia and gave Colombia preferential rights in the use of the Canal. Colombia, in turn, recognized the independence of Panama. Roosevelt's friends in the Senate rallied to the Colonel's defense, and the treaty failed of ratification. In April, 1921, however, after the partisan fires had died down, and with Roosevelt dead, the Harding administration negotiated a somewhat similar treaty, which this time the Senate accepted, even Roosevelt's lifelong friend Senator Lodge casting his vote for it. Bryan's "sincere regret" clause was deleted and for it was substituted the more circumspect: "to remove all misunderstandings growing out of the political events in Panama in November, 1903." Colombia was to receive the earlier proffered $25,000,000, this time in five annual installments. The treaty was proclaimed in March, 1922.

Interoceanic canals were not yet a closed chapter in American history, for in 1912 and again in 1914 our statesmen once more turned their attention to the possibilities of a Nicaraguan canal. In the latter year Bryan negotiated the Bryan-Chamorro Treaty which gave us the right to build and operate a canal across Nicaragua. The Senate ratified this convention in February, 1916. In 1929, Congress authorized the survey to be made, and in 1931 the Army engineers reported favorably on the project. But nothing was done in the next two decades, despite the fact that the Panama Canal alone was inadequate for all the traffic seeking to pass through.

THE ROOSEVELT COROLLARY OF THE MONROE DOCTRINE

Roosevelt's interest in the Caribbean was not to end with Venezuela and Panama, and in 1904 to 1905 he was to lead American foreign policy into strange paths. The Dominican Republic was the first of the lesser Caribbean countries to attract his attention. Its history had been typical of that of so many of the Latin-American nations: venal politicians had contended for its control for the single purpose of looting its treasury to line their own pockets and to obtain funds with which to hold the loyalty of their ragged followers. Between 1899 and 1905, there had been a series of insurrections while the public debt mounted alarmingly. In 1904, the Dominican Republic's debt stood at $32,280,000, two-thirds of which was owed to European nationals. The insistence of Dominican officials that a large part of this debt had never actually been contracted, their inability to meet the services on it, and their helplessness in the face of the pressure which European countries were increasingly applying to compel payments brought on a crisis in the winter of 1904.

With his eyes on the Dominican situation, Roosevelt made a bold announcement in his Congressional message of December 2, 1904. Said he:

> If a nation shows that it knows how to act with reasonable efficiency and decency in social and political matters, if it keeps order and pays its obligations, it need fear no interference from the United States. Chronic wrongdoing, or an impotence which results in a general loosening of the ties of civilized society may in America, as elsewhere, ultimately require intervention by some civilized nation, and in the Western Hemisphere the adherence of the United States to the

Monroe Doctrine may force the United States, however reluctantly, in flagrant cases of such wrongdoing or impotence, to the exercise of an international police power.

This statement, which has come to be called the "Roosevelt corollary" of the Monroe Doctrine, was a declaration of the first importance. It, in effect, accepted Lord Salisbury's challenge of 1895 by agreeing that American supremacy in the Western Hemisphere was conditioned upon our assumption of responsibility for the maintenance of the peace and the payment of debts by Latin-American peoples. The doctrine was a disquieting one: not to Europeans, who were perfectly willing to see the United States collect their questionable debts for them, but to Latin Americans, who saw hanging over them the threat of American intervention to preserve order and compel the meeting of financial obligations.

The doctrine had another implication. Roosevelt, having obtained the Panama Canal site, was concerned about European intervention in the Caribbean and therefore the presence of potentially hostile powers in an area from which American security could be threatened. To this extent, his interest in the region was a military rather than a financial one.

Santo Domingo read the handwriting on the wall, and on December 30, 1904, asked our State Department to assume control over the Dominican revenues. In the middle of February, 1905, an agreement was entered into under which an American collector was to administer the Dominican custom houses and the United States, after turning over 45 per cent of the revenues to the Dominican Republic, was to apportion the balance among the country's various creditors. Roosevelt's special message to the Senate, sent on February 15 and transmitting the above agreement, contained this significant paragraph:

> Under the accepted law of nations foreign governments are within their right, if they choose to exercise it, when they actively intervene in support of the contractual claims of their subjects.... In view of the dilemma in which the government of the United States is thus placed, it must either adhere to its usual attitude of nonintervention in such cases—an attitude proper under normal conditions, but one which in this particular kind of case results to the disadvantage of its citizens in comparison with those of other states—or else it must, in order to be consistent in its policy, actively intervene to protect the contracts and concessions of its citizens engaged in agriculture, commerce, and transportation in competition with the subjects and citizens of other states. This course would render the United States the insurer of all the speculative risks of its citizens in the public securities and franchises of Santo Domingo.

These implications were unacceptable to the Senate, and it rejected the protocol. Meanwhile, however, American warships were patrolling Dominican waters and United States marines were on the streets of the capital city of Santo Domingo. A way out of the difficulty was found when Santo

Domingo appointed an unofficial American collector (recommended by Roosevelt) and the balance of the revenues over and above the amounts required for domestic purposes were impounded in a New York bank. Finally, in February, 1907, the Senate ratified the protocol, in revised form, and the surplus revenues were now available for distribution among the country's creditors. As a result of the administration of the American collector, customs receipts had doubled, a surplus had been built up and foreign creditors had expressed a willingness to scale down their claims to $17,000,000 in place of the $32,280,000 they held paper for. On July 31, 1907, the American administration quit the country. But so successful had the procedure been that succeeding American Presidents for the next two decades were to follow Roosevelt's example, until, by the nineteen twenties, the Caribbean was to have all the aspects of an American lake.[1]

In 1906, Roosevelt offered his services as peacemaker to bring to an end a war involving most of the Central American countries. In 1907, he was again on the scene when a renewal of hostilities threatened the general peace. As a result of this intervention there was held in November, 1907, a Central American peace conference at Washington, which adopted a number of important conventions. The chief of these called for the establishment of a Central American court of justice, and though the court went out of existence in 1918, peace continued to reign in Central America, at any rate as far as international disputes were concerned.

ROOSEVELT AND THE FAR EAST

Roosevelt was not extending the American influence in the Western Hemisphere only. He followed the development of international politics with interest and exercised himself, in a number of instances, to strengthen the position of the United States in world affairs. The happiest of these interpositions led to the termination of the sanguinary Russo-Japanese War, which had broken out in February, 1904. In offering his services as mediator to the combatants, in the summer of 1905, Roosevelt was not moved by disinterested motives entirely. The United States, because of the Philippines, was a Pacific power and a too powerful Japan might threaten our position and, indeed, place in jeopardy that whole Far Eastern policy that Hay had labored so painstakingly to create. These arguments Roosevelt advanced to the Russians when he urged a termination of hostilities. And the Japanese, though flushed with victory, were glad to accede to Roosevelt's proposals, for they were close to exhaustion themselves. We know now that Japan, a number of times, invited Roosevelt's mediation before Russia was ready to call quits. In June, 1905,

---

[1] It was not until 1930 that the Roosevelt corollary of the Monroe Doctrine was repudiated by the State Department. See below, page 491.

Russia formally requested Roosevelt to intervene, and on August 9, the peace conferees opened their proceedings at Portsmouth, New Hampshire.

Roosevelt watched the developments closely from his summer seat at Oyster Bay with the result that he was able to step in when a crisis appeared over the disposition of Sakhalin Island. The sessions from then on continued without friction so that the Peace of Portsmouth was signed on September 5. By the treaty Russia surrendered the Liaotung peninsula (including Port Arthur) to Japan, recognized Japanese interests in Korea, agreed to evacuate Manchuria (as did also Japan), and ceded the southern half of Sakhalin Island to Japan and her interests in the South Manchuria Railway. Japan consented to relinquish her claim to an indemnity of $600 million. The balance of power in the Pacific thus was preserved and the national honor of both combatants emerged unimpaired.

But Roosevelt was not content with this personal triumph. Impressed by the military and naval strength of the Japanese, he entered into a secret agreement with the Japanese government which committed the United States to a recognition of Japanese interests in the Far East. The document was never submitted to the Senate; but it meant that an alliance existed, certainly as long as Roosevelt remained President. On July 29, 1905, an American agent (whose name is unknown) reached an understanding with the Japanese Prime Minister along the following lines: Japan recognized American sovereignty over the Philippines. The United States became party to the Anglo-Japanese alliance (of 1902, strengthened August 12, 1905) as far as the maintenance of the peace in the Far East was concerned. On this point, the American negotiator assured the Japanese:

... that he felt sure that without any agreement at all the people of the United States were so fully in accord with the policy of Japan and Great Britain in the maintenance of peace in the Far East that, whatever occasion arose, appropriate action of the government of the United States, in conjunction with Japan and Great Britain for such a purpose, could be counted on by them quite as confidently as if the United States were under treaty obligations.

The United States recognized Japanese sovereignty over Korea.[2]

Despite these valiant efforts to enlist Japanese friendship, it cannot be said that Roosevelt was entirely successful. For one reason, the Japanese showed irritation over the part the American President had played in persuading their peace commissioners to relinquish their claims to a war indemnity from Russia. In the second place, anti-Japanese agitation in America, particularly in California, was regarded as being distinctly unfriendly. California Congressmen, in 1906, sought the passage of national legislation to exclude Japanese immigrants from the country and delivered themselves of a number of patriotic sentiments which could not be con-

[2] This secret document was made public by Tyler Dennett in *Current History* for October, 1924.

strued as being complimentary to the Japanese people. In October, 1906, the insult direct was given when the San Francisco School Board adopted a resolution requiring all Japanese pupils to attend a separate Oriental school. Roosevelt's swift action averted a real unpleasantness, for the Japanese government had filed a formal protest. The President sent his Secretary of the Navy to San Francisco, where he found that the Japanese menace in the schools consisted not of 1000 pupils, as was commonly supposed, but altogether of 93 youngsters who were divided among 23 school buildings. To avoid further ridicule, the local school board withdrew its edict.

During 1907 and 1908 Roosevelt labored with the Japanese government to prevent a crisis over the immigration question. As a result of prolonged communications conducted by Secretary Root an informal understanding was reached which came to be known as the "Gentlemen's Agreement." Under it, Japan was to refuse to grant passports to laborers seeking to make their homes in the United States, while the United States was to be recognized in its right to deny admission to all those who did not hold these visas. The Immigration Act of 1907 extended the "Gentlemen's Agreement" to apply to Japanese immigrants coming from the American Pacific dependencies by way of Canada and Mexico.

California was, however, a sovereign state and could claim with entire justice that the settlement of its internal problems was its own concern. During the next decade the California legislature moved to restrict the activities of Japanese residents within its boundaries. In 1913, a law was passed denying to aliens ineligible to citizenship the right to acquire agricultural lands or to take up leaseholds for more than three years. To check the transfer of such lands to native-born children, who were citizens of the United States, California in 1920 denied aliens ineligible to citizenship the power to act as guardians for minors possessing agricultural properties. Nor did California stand alone, for her example was followed by Washington, Arizona, New Mexico, Texas, Louisiana, and Delaware. Finally, in 1924, western agitation having been successful, there was incorporated in the Immigration Act of that year a clause designed to exclude entirely immigration from Oriental lands. (It is interesting to observe that an exception was made in the case of the Chinese during World War II—because China was our ally. The Chinese Exclusion Acts were repealed in 1943 and Chinese immigration was put on a quota. However, only 100 Chinese were to be admitted annually.)

ROOSEVELT AND EUROPE

In his relations with European nations Theodore Roosevelt was just as busy. A hint dropped by him hastened the settlement of the long-outstanding Alaskan boundary dispute; he played a role of considerable importance in the Algeciras Conference of 1906; through his State Department he figured in the life of the second Hague Conference and also in the writing of a number of arbitration treaties with the leading nations of the world.[3]

The Anglo-American joint commission of 1898 had tried to settle the Alaskan boundary difficulty between the United States and Canada but had got nowhere because of the United States' refusal to accede to Canada's demands for additional water outlets. The subject had been reopened by Hay in 1902 with the proposal that the difficulty be submitted to a joint commission of "six impartial jurists," to which the British had replied with the suggestion of arbitration by an international tribunal. In January, 1903, Hay had his way and a convention was signed setting up a mixed commission on which were to sit three Americans, two Canadians, and a British representative. The commission met and soon was in difficulties. Roosevelt was determined that the boundary be laid down once and for all, and in the summer of 1903 he wrote a letter to Justice O. W. Holmes, then in London, which, he hinted, was really for British eyes. In this missive he declared that unless the commission came to a speedy decision he would ask Congress for the right "to run the line as we claim it, by our own people, without any further regard to the attitude of England or Canada." The upshot was that the British Commissioner Lord Alverstone was instructed to vote against his Canadian colleagues and on October 20 a decision was promulgated which satisfied in every particular the American claims.

As Roosevelt intervened in the Russo-Japanese War to avert a dislocation of the balance of power in the Far East, so he took a hand in the Moroccan crisis of the same year to prevent the disordering of European relationships. France had established a sphere of influence over the sultanate of Morocco; England had given the act its sanction; then had appeared the Kaiser to protest over France's and England's failure to consult Germany in the disposal of the little that still remained of free Africa. The Kaiser had every reason to claim justice on his side, but the characteristic intemperance of his speech made him appear the aggressor in espousing a policy which, superficially at any rate, threatened to embroil Europe in international conflict. It was this threat to the peace of the world, so Roosevelt told his friends, that prompted him to interfere in European politics in disregard of America's traditional policy of isolation.

At the behest of the Kaiser, Roosevelt brought pressure to bear on the French, and on June 23 France consented to the calling of a conference to discuss the Moroccan question. This congress assembled on January 16, 1906, at Algeciras, Spain, the United States being represented by Henry White, our ambassador to Italy, and S. R. Gummere, American consul-general at Morocco. The convention that resulted recognized Morocco's

[3] The peace movement is discussed in detail below. See page 412.

territorial integrity, guaranteed the Open Door to the merchants and investors of all nations, stabilized Moroccan finances by setting up an international bank, and created a native police force under the joint supervision of France and Spain. The American Senate regarded the whole proceedings coldly, and it ratified the convention late in December, 1906, only after adopting a reservation which declared that our participation in the Algeciras Conference did not signify a relinquishment of America's long-accepted policy of aloofness so far as European affairs were concerned. The Algeciras Conference established exactly nothing: there were to be other Moroccan crises and more saber-rattling. Whether it was his intention or not, Roosevelt as President of the United States had made the American people party to a European dispute whose only result was the cementing of the newly created Anglo-French Alliance.

DOLLAR DIPLOMACY

It was Taft's unfortunate lot to reap the whirlwind Roosevelt had sown. Taft and his official advisers applied themselves earnestly to the continuance of the Roosevelt policies, and in foreign as well as domestic concerns the line of conduct was unbroken. But Roosevelt possessed a magic hand; he could surround everything he did with a rose-colored illusion; and not a little of this happy state was created by the torrent of words he always was able to pour forth in explanation and justification of what he happened to be doing. Taft, unfortunately, was a more prosaic individual: he labored honestly but without much imagination or effort at rationalization. The result was soon apparent, and in almost everything he did Taft met with a hostility that was vindictive and ill-natured. What was true of domestic problems was equally true of foreign relations. Roosevelt's course in Asia, Europe, and the Caribbean (so it was said) was dictated by the loftiest motives of patriotism; Taft's policy in the Caribbean and in China was low and materialistic. Contemporaries sneeringly called it "dollar diplomacy." They rarely stopped to think that Taft's intervention in Honduras and Nicaragua was in direct line with Roosevelt's interpretation of the Monroe Doctrine, and that what Taft was doing in Central America Roosevelt had already done in Santo Domingo. And if Taft meddled in Chinese affairs, he was merely applying a touch of realism to a situation which Hay had sadly beclouded with his talk of the Open Door and respect for Chinese sovereignty.

In 1909, Philander C. Knox, Taft's Secretary of State, broke off relations with Nicaragua because the local dictator had permitted the execution of two Americans. The unsettled state of affairs in this turbulent land, and in Honduras to the north, led Knox in 1911 to attempt to follow the policy pursued in Santo Domingo, by Roosevelt. Knox wrote conventions with

Honduras and Nicaragua which provided the following: in an effort to rehabilitate the local finances, new Honduran and Nicaraguan loans were to be placed with private American bankers; the customs were to be pledged as security; an American receiver of customs was to be appointed in each country. But the Senate refused to ratify these conventions.

A protectorate was effected notwithstanding, for in August, 1912, at the behest of the new Nicaraguan president, American marines were rushed to Managua, the country's capital, and to Bluefields, its chief port on the east coast. Before the disorders were in hand there were 2350 American bluejackets and marines in Nicaragua. While the country's fiscal affairs were turned over to an American collector, the Nicaraguan national bank was controlled by New York financiers and the Nicaraguan government was put on a monthly allowance doled out to it by a high commission made up of one Nicaraguan and two Americans. Not until 1925, as we shall see, did the last of the marines quit the country, and then their withdrawal was only for a short period. Before another year had run its course, an American expeditionary force again walked the streets of Managua and there it stayed until the early nineteen thirties. Following the successful intervention of 1912 Knox sought to put American interests in Nicaragua on a more substantial basis by negotiating a treaty giving us the right of way for an interoceanic canal as well as a naval base on the Gulf of Fonseca and long-term leases over the Great Corn and Little Corn Islands (in the Caribbean). The Senate refused to consider this convention and it fell to the following Wilson administration to gain the ratification of a similar pact in 1916.

Knox's labors were crowned with a more substantial success in China. Reference has already been made to Hay's failure to regard China as more than a market for American-made wares and his belief that the acceptance of the Open-Door policy by the powers extended equal commercial opportunities to American nationals. Not until the first decade of the new century were Americans really to appreciate the nature of the prizes that were interesting British, French, Belgian, Russian, and Japanese entrepreneurs in the Celestial Empire. Then, when American bankers, with surplus capital to invest, turned their eyes Chinaward, they found Europeans in complete possession of the field. By the turn of the century, foreign capitalists held contracts for the construction of some 6420 miles of railway in China; between 1898 and 1923 the bankers of Europe and Japan were to lend the Chinese government £61,217,607 to finance railway projects. Diplomacy went hand in hand with business, for the bankers secured their loans not only by taking mortgages on the railroads but by receiving first liens on provincial and opium revenues and on special salt taxes. As a result of the treaties creating the spheres of influence, the European powers could maintain representatives on the spot to see that the pledged taxes were being applied to railway debt services. Americans were to share in none of these lucrative schemes until Taft's intercession in 1909, and then they were admitted only as partners in a four-power consortium created to float an issue of £6,000,000 for the construction of the Hukuang Railways. In 1923, there were forty-two such foreign railway loans recorded, distributed among foreign banking groups in the following fashion: British, 15; Japanese, 12; Belgian, 6; Anglo-German, 4; Franco-Belgian, 2; Anglo-French, 1; Franco-Russian, 1; four-power consortium, 1.

The difficulties standing in the way of American participation in Chinese financing projects were demonstrated by E. H. Harriman's failure in 1907 to obtain a concession for the construction of a Manchurian railroad. In 1909, however, Wall Street reached the ear of Washington, and both Taft and Knox made official representations on behalf of American bankers. J. P. Morgan and Company, Kuhn, Loeb and Company, the First National Bank, and the National City Bank sought to participate, along with British, French, and German capitalists, in the financing of the Hukuang lines in the Yangtse valley. Taft, in fact, cabled the Chinese government himself, saying: "I have an intense personal interest in making the use of American capital in the development of China an instrument for the promotion of the welfare of China...." And Knox wrote that "the government of the United States regards full and frank co-operation as best calculated to maintain the Open Door and the integrity of China ... and that the formation of a powerful American, British, French, and German financial group would further that end."

In May, 1910, the Americans were admitted into the consortium and the loan was floated. In 1912, American bankers were invited to become parties to an even more pretentious undertaking, this one being the floating of a currency loan of £25,000,000 for the new Chinese Republic. Taft gave this second enterprise his blessing, too. In 1913, however, Wilson threw cold water on the scheme, and when he refused to give the loan the formal encouragement of the American government our bankers found it necessary to withdraw. One may idly speculate what would have been the history of the struggle for power in China after World War II if Harriman's dreams had been realized.

NAVALISM

Under the administrations of Roosevelt and Taft the American Navy grew in size and power so that on the eve of World War I American naval enthusiasts could boast that we were the possessors of a fleet that was second only to Great Britain's. Roosevelt made the expansion of the Navy one of his leading domestic concerns and steadily urged Congress on to greater and greater efforts: in 1907, for example, he seized upon the failure of the second Hague Conference to limit armaments to call for the building of four first-class battleships. Happily Congress refused to deviate from its policy of two battleships a year; otherwise the world would have then witnessed a race for naval supremacy between the United States and Great Britain. Some notion of the role navalism was beginning to play in American affairs may be gained from the totals expended annually for the maintenance of the naval establishment as compared with the government's total ordinary expenditures.

ORDINARY AND NAVAL EXPENDITURES, 1890-1914

Fiscal Year Ending	Total Ordinary Expenditures	Total Naval Expenditures	Naval Expenditures Per Cent of Total
1890	$318,041,000	$ 22,006,000	7.0 per cent
1900	520,861,000	55,953,000	10.8 "
1909	693,744,000	115,546,000	16.7 "
1913	724,512,000	133,263,000	18.4 "
1914	735,081,000	139,682,000	19.0 "

Beginning with 1903, the Navy Department began to lay down two capital ships a year, each at a cost of $5,382,000. In 1907, the era of the dreadnought had its inception with the building of two ships of 20,000 tons, carrying ten twelve-inch guns and costing $8,225,000 each. In 1913, the Navy proudly announced that a first-class battleship was now costing the American people $14,000,000.

On November 1, 1909, the Secretary of the Navy reported to Congress that our warship tonnage was 682,785 as compared with Great Britain's strength of 1,758,350 tons and Germany's strength of 609,700. That Washington was watching the naval race going on in Europe with close attention is apparent from the Navy Department's reports for the years 1909 to 1913. Secretary of the Navy Meyer filled the pages of his annual statement with comparative tables, showing how powerful other nations' fleets were, how great their naval estimates were annually, and the like. And Congress was regularly being warned that others would outdistance us unless more ships were built. But Meyer's own figures belied his dark prophecies. Thus the 1911 report presented the following naval estimates for 1911 to 1912: Great Britain, $216,036,101; United States, $129,248,000; Germany, $107,232,000; France, $80,371,000; Japan, $42,944,000.

In June, 1914, the following was the strength of the American naval establishment (ships already afloat and in process of construction).

AMERICAN NAVAL ESTABLISHMENT IN 1914

First-line battleships (under 10 years old)	17
Second-line battleships	25
Armored cruisers	10
Protected cruisers	24
Monitors	9
Destroyers	68
Torpedo boats	19
Submarines	58

Both Roosevelt and Taft were keenly sensible to the necessity for winning over popular approval to their great naval building programs and each applied himself to devising a series of spectacles for the education, amusement, and delectation of the American public. In December, 1907, Roosevelt sent a fleet of 16 battleships, manned by a personnel of 12,000, on a triumphal cruise around the world. With the flagship *Connecticut* in the van, the fleet steamed proudly out of Hampton Roads and without a single mishap made its way through the Straits of Magellan. A stop was made at San Francisco, admirals were changed, and the ships took their way across the Pacific. The battleships put in at Australia, New Zealand, the Philippines, China, and Japan, where the American bluejackets were cordially received and lavishly entertained. Newspapers made much of the greater respect being shown America by Japan as a result of this display of our strength. (It will be recalled that Japanese-American relations were delicate at this time in view of the California exclusion policies.) The final leg of the journey took the fleet through the Suez Canal and across the Atlantic. It arrived home in February, 1909, after an absence of close to sixteen months. From then on, Theodore Roosevelt was associated in the American mind with the development of the country's navy, and not long after his death national and local statesmen began to call each year upon their fellow citizens to honor the birthday of Roosevelt (October 27) as Navy Day.

President Taft, on his part, prepared a naval pageant that was equally thrilling. On November 1, 1911, at his order, there took place the mobilizations of the Atlantic fleet at New York City and the Pacific fleet at San Diego, California. Under the eyes of the Presidential party and the local officialdom America's mighty war array assembled in the Hudson River. In all, there were 98 war vessels, of which 4 were dreadnoughts, 20 were battleships, 2 were armored cruisers, 2 were protected cruisers and the rest were lesser craft. The Pacific fleet mobilization was made up of 26 vessels. Naturally the doings of the Navy and the speeches public officials made at the various dinners and entertainments that followed the mobilizations filled the press for days. So successful was this event that it was repeated on October 14, 1912, when 123 ships belonging to the Atlantic fleet again assembled in the Hudson. This time there were 6 dreadnoughts and 25 battleships to lead off the line.

There were not many voices lifted to question Taft's statement that a powerful navy was a form of national insurance against unforeseen danger. All this was a further sign of our arrival at man's estate in the company of nations. The mobilizations of the fleets showed that America was in fit condition to fight anyone at the drop of the hat.

Section VIII
WOODROW WILSON AND WORLD WAR I

· 24 ·

The New Freedom

THE ELECTION OF 1912

By February, 1912, it was definitely known that Roosevelt's "hat was in the ring": he meant to contest with Taft for the Republican Presidential nomination. Despite Taft's control of the party machinery, it was soon apparent how very effective was Roosevelt's preconvention campaign. He carried the preferential primaries of Illinois, California, New Jersey, Nebraska, Maryland, and Oregon; he gained the support of Massachusetts' eight delegates at large; he was victorious in the state conventions of Pennsylvania, South Dakota, and Ohio. Taft, on the other hand, could claim only the hand-picked delegations of the southern states, the district delegates of Massachusetts and the boss-dominated votes of New York and Connecticut. In Indiana, Michigan, and Washington the issue was in doubt and both factions named contesting delegations.

The Republican National Committee, headed by Taft's Postmaster-General, made short work of the Roosevelt boom. For a week before the delegates assembled for the Republican convention, the Taft managers listened solemnly to the claims of the warring delegations—and then proceeded to seat almost all of the Taft adherents. Roosevelt had lost before the official proceedings had even opened. From June 20 to June 22, the steamroller smoothly did its work. Taft was renominated on the first ballot; so was Vice-President Sherman; a minority report of the resolutions committee was tabled; and a conservative platform was adopted.

There was no doubt in the minds of Roosevelt and his friends that the whole history of the convention had been tainted with fraud, and as the Roosevelt delegates withdrew to lay their plans for a gathering of their own they issued a bitingly denunciatory statement. It closed as follows:

Any man nominated by the convention as now constituted would merely be the beneficiary of this successful fraud; it would be deeply discreditable to any man to accept the convention's nomination under these circumstances; and any man thus accepting it would have no claim to the support of any Republican on

384

party grounds and would have forfeited the right to ask the support of any honest man of any party on moral grounds.

Bryan, who had been an interested spectator of the internecine contest that had rent the Republican ranks, hurried off to Baltimore to prepare his party for the victory that was at last to perch on its banners. The Democracy, assembling on June 25, was confronted by two powerfully backed contenders for its nomination. The first of these was Champ Clark of Missouri, Speaker of the House in the Sixty-second Congress; the second was Woodrow Wilson, elected governor of New Jersey in 1910. But neither had the support of the two-thirds vote necessary for a choice. Bryan had not entered the preliminary contests and his name was not put in nomination. But that he hoped that out of a possible deadlock, with each of the two determined antagonists refusing to yield, he would again be chosen as his party's nominee did not go unsuspected. He bestowed his smiles now on one aspirant, now on the other; and he assured the friends of Clark and Wilson that each was eminently fitted to lead the Democratic host.

The voting began June 28 and lasted at intervals until July 2. On the opening ballot Clark led, and on the tenth ballot his lead was measurably increased when New York's delegation, headed by "Boss" Murphy of Tammany Hall, threw its support to him. But this very act doomed the Clark candidacy, for after the fourteenth ballot Bryan announced that he could no longer vote with the Nebraska delegates for the Missourian. Bryan voted for Wilson—and Clark's support slowly began to crumble. On the forty-sixth ballot, Woodrow Wilson was named for the Presidency. Governor Thomas R. Marshall of Indiana was nominated as his running mate.

The platform was a Bryan document. It attacked the high protectionism of the Republican party and attributed the plight of agriculture and labor to the Payne-Aldrich Act's schedules. It asked for the application of the Sherman Law's criminal provisions against trust officials and promised additional legislation to prevent holding companies, interlocking directorates, stock-watering, price discrimination, and "the control by any one corporation of so large a proportion of any industry as to make it a menace to competitive conditions." The platform favored railroad valuation as a basis for rate-fixing; called for the reform of the country's banking laws; hoped something could be done for the farmers in the way of easing rural credits; and advocated anti-injunction laws, Presidential primaries, a single term for the President, and conservation measures. The Republican administration of the Philippines was condemned and the platform pledged the Democratic candidates to a recognition of Philippine independence "as soon as a stable government can be established."

On August 5, there gathered at Chicago two thousand men and women from forty states in the Union to form the Progressive party. Here were assembled Republican leaders who were honestly sick of their boss-ridden party, certain rich men who had fallen under the influence of Roosevelt's persuasive tongue, social workers who had labored in the slums of the great cities and knew the wretched lot of the poor, and a miscellany of reformers and cranks with plans, proposals, and schemes enough to daunt the hardiest. "There was room on that platform," said one of the young workers in the cause, much later, "for anyone who had seen Peter Pan and believed in fairies." Nobody was turned away, all were made welcome, everybody joined in singing "Onward, Christian Soldiers," and in cheering the hero of the day to the echo.

Roosevelt was named by acclamation; Hiram W. Johnson, California's reform governor, was nominated for the Vice-Presidency; Roosevelt delivered a long and solemnly worded address as befitted the occasion (he called it his "confession of faith"); a platform was adopted which was labeled "A Contract with the People"; and on August 7 the convention adjourned and the delegates trooped home to await the blessed day when victory would be theirs.

The Progressive platform had something in it for almost everyone. It promised support for the direct primary, Presidential preferential primaries, the popular election of United States Senators, the short ballot, the initiative, referendum and recall, easy amendment of the Constitution, equal suffrage for men and women, antilobbying legislation, and the recall of judicial decisions. To labor the Progressive party offered anti-injunction laws and trials by jury in cases of contempt arising out of injunction suits. The welfare code championed was very full and included safety and health laws, the prohibition of child labor, a minimum wage for women, an 8-hour day for women and children and the abolition of night work, abolition of the convict contract labor system, workmen's compensation, continuation schools, and the establishment of a Department of Labor in the Cabinet. There was a straight-forward pledge to enact social-insurance laws to protect the workers against sickness, unemployment, and old age.

Domestic problems were treated in the same frank fashion. Large corporations were considered inevitable, and the Progressives did not propose to break them up. They advocated, however, rigorous federal supervision, by a trade commission, of all business entering into interstate commerce. Other planks promised government retention of all natural resources except agricultural lands, a protective tariff to "equalize conditions of competition between the United States and foreign countries," the physical valuation of railroads, a graduated inheritance tax, currency reform, rural credits, and the ownership by the government of the Alaskan railroads. Here, in short, was a program of large-scale government inter-

ELECTION CIRCUS, 1912

vention which presaged the promises and achievements of the New Deal of twenty years later.

The Socialists met at Indianapolis, May 12–18, and adopted a platform which called upon the workers to organize politically and economically so that they might "resist successfully the capitalist class, break the fetters of wage slavery, and fit themselves for the future society which is to displace the capitalist system." Eugene V. Debs was once again nominated for the Presidency and Mayor Emil Seidel of Milwaukee was named for the Vice-Presidency.

The canvass following the nominations resolved itself into a contest between Roosevelt and Wilson. Taft, as early as July, privately conceded his defeat and did not unduly exert himself. Roosevelt and Wilson, on the other hand, displayed the greatest energy as they sought to place their opinions before the electorate in person. The differences between the two may be summed up succinctly as follows: Roosevelt was for a strongly organized central government which was to act as the reforming agency. Wilson placed his faith in the states. In short, neither denied the necessity for political and social change, but they disagreed on the method to be employed. Roosevelt regarded the process of concentration and corporate activity in business as being inevitable, but he advocated the strictest governmental supervision to protect the consumer and to give the smaller producer opportunities for enterprise. Wilson was not opposed to Big Business but only to those trusts that had unfairly attained their monopoly control; these latter he would smash. Roosevelt called his creed the "New Nationalism"; Wilson called his the "New Freedom." William Allen White, though he admired both men, was to say later of their efforts: "Between the New Nationalism and the New Freedom was that fantastic imaginary gulf that always has existed between tweedledum and tweedledee." But White really was wrong: for the New Nationalism put the federal government at the heart of affairs and made it assume responsibility for welfare.

Woodrow Wilson was listened to with great attention; yet it is to be doubted whether the so-called independent voters came to his aid at the polls. If anything, they voted for Debs, for the Socialist vote increased from 420,000 in 1908 to 987,000 in 1912. In fact, a close examination of the ballots cast indicates that Wilson was supported by a straight-party vote while the Republicans divided their allegiance between Taft and Roosevelt. Only because of this schism was Wilson elected President. His total popular vote was 6,286,000; Roosevelt's was 4,126,000; Taft's was 3,484,000. Wilson carried by a majority vote only 14 of the 16 states that had gone for Bryan in the previous election. When the analysis is pursued further into the counties, it becomes plainly apparent that Wilson was a minority President. Of the 2975 counties in the United States in 1912, Wilson received a plurality in 2196; Taft obtained a plurality in 281; and Roosevelt obtained a plurality in 490. But Wilson carried only 1431 counties by a majority vote and of these 1018 were in fifteen southern and border states. The electoral vote, which made Wilson President, was as follows: Taft, 8 (Vermont and Utah); Roosevelt, 88 (Pennsylvania, Michigan, Minnesota, South Dakota, Washington and 11 of California's 13 votes); Wilson, 435 (the other 40 states). The Democrats, too, were victorious in the Congressional and Senatorial elections for the first time since 1892.

WOODROW WILSON, PRESIDENT

The man who moved into the White House on March 4, 1913, was a rare phenomenon in American public life. He was a northerner of southern birth; he had not been trained in the hurly-burly of ward politics but was a product of academic groves; statecraft, except for a brief two-years' experience as the governor of New Jersey, he had learned from books. English political thinkers and statesmen rather than American were his mentors and models: Edmund Burke, Walter Bagehot, John Bright, and W. E. Gladstone, and not Jefferson and Lincoln. Wilson prided himself on his intellect, but it is amazing to note what little intellectual curiosity he really possessed. He knew next to nothing of the arts; his tastes in literature were conventional; contemporary movements in social thought he simply let pass by without an interrogation. He was an orator rather than a thinker, a preacher rather than a philosopher. What influences had conditioned him one may only guess. Was it his Presbyterian ancestry? his pedagogical training in the classroom, where too often, sweeping statements go unchallenged? his drinking deep at the fount of English nineteenth century Liberalism? J. M. Keynes, in discussing Wilson's role at the Peace Conference, put his finger on a fundamental weakness:

He [Wilson] had no plan, no scheme, no constructive ideas whatever for clothing with the flesh of life the commandments which he had thundered from the White House. He could have preached a sermon on any of them or have addressed a stately prayer to the Almighty for their fulfilment; but he could not frame their concrete application to the actual state of Europe.

Woodrow Wilson was born on December 28, 1856, at Staunton, Virginia. His paternal grandparents were born in the north of Ireland; his mother was born in Scotland. His boyhood was spent in the South, from which he came north in 1875 to enter Princeton College. Upon graduation, he studied law; and he was admitted to the bar in 1882. But he had small taste for the courts and the same year saw him matriculating in the graduate school of Johns Hopkins. Here he studied political science and jurisprudence and here, in 1885, he wrote his first and best book, *Congressional Government*. Then followed seventeen years of teaching and a good deal of writing on politics and American history. In 1902, he became the president of Princeton University, and here he labored successfully in the interests of a number of academic reforms. His stay at Princeton was becoming increasingly difficult, however, because of disagreements with his board of trustees, and when, in 1910, the Democratic leaders of New Jersey asked him to contest the gubernatorial election, he saw a way out of his difficulties. Wilson resigned from Princeton, stood for the election, and won it by a majority of some 50,000 votes.

As governor, Wilson made an admirable record, championing a workmen's-compensation act, a direct primary law, ballot reform, a corrupt-practices act, the creation of a public-utilities commission, the equalization of taxes. Following the Presidential election, he finished out his gubernatorial term and was instrumental in having enacted a group of laws designed to regulate the many trusts and holding companies which had settled in New Jersey because they had met here with such slight governmental interference.

It became immediately apparent that Woodrow Wilson, as President, meant to lead his party. But it was a party leadership not frequently met with in American politics. His conception of leadership was English rather than American: he regarded himself as something of a triumphantly elected prime minister to whom fealty by the rank and file was to be taken as a matter of course. He was, therefore, completely disdainful of the bread and butter of politics. Patronage meant nothing to him; he did not interest himself in the state machines. Such appointments as he bothered himself over, he made on the basis of personal choice; the rest he let, for the most part, his secretary Joseph P. Tumulty take care of. All this enraged the machine leaders; nevertheless, they followed Wilson's lead, enacting his legislative program, letting him have his way in foreign affairs, standing for his personal appointments. Their reluctance was undisguised, yet they accepted the President at his own valuation.

Wilson's Cabinet was made up, to a large extent, of unknown persons. Bryan was given the State portfolio; the Treasury office went to William G. McAdoo of Georgia and New York; the Navy Department was headed by Josephus Daniels, a North Carolina editor and an original Wilson man; the Post Office fell to Albert S. Burleson of Texas. Wilson's diplomatic appointments were not prompted by political expediency, with the result that many of the posts came to be filled by men who had minor reputations as men of letters. Walter H. Page, who went to London, was the chief example of this type. Wilson filled three vacancies on the Supreme Court bench, as follows: James C. McReynolds, named in 1914; Louis D. Brandeis, named in 1916; and John H. Clarke, also named in 1916. The first of these was conservative in his tendencies; Brandeis and Clarke were outstanding liberals.

Both houses of Congress were organized by Democratic steering committees, which made the committee assignments. Thus the long sway of the Speaker of the House was broken, and under Democratic rule he once more assumed his rightful and only function as chairman over the lower house's proceedings. In 1914, because the Republican party was still divided, the Democrats succeeded in capturing Congress again, though their majority in the lower house was considerably reduced. The Progressive party's Congressional candidates polled but 1,746,000 votes as against the 4,126,000 of the two years previous. It was already plain that Roosevelt's schismatic group was moribund.

THE TARIFF ACT OF 1913

In his first inaugural President Wilson had pledged his administration to the support of three major domestic policies, namely: tariff revision, banking and currency reform, and additional trust legislation. Thanks to his capable leadership these programs were successfully achieved in less than a year and a half and represented a body of work of the highest order.

The tariff received the President's first attention. Accepting his election as a clear mandate for revision downward, Wilson summoned the newly elected Sixty-third Congress in special session on April 7, 1913, and, in person, called upon Congress to enact a law that would re-establish "effective competition" between American and foreign manufacturers. The House Ways and Means Committee, led by Underwood of Alabama, had been at work on a bill since the previous December; this measure was at once placed before the lower chamber and adopted after only perfunctory discussion on May 8. The vote was 281 for and 139 against, with party lines being almost strictly adhered to. The Senate scrutinized the House's bill with greater care; and it began to appear as though the upper house would repeat the performances of 1890, 1894, and 1909 when Senators rewrote the lower house's bills in the interest of higher protection. But the President turned a stern face against tariff-tinkering and issued a public warning to the lobbyists who were beginning to flock to Washington. The result was that the Democratic caucus held the rank and file in line and the trading of votes for local advantages was stopped before it could begin. On September 9, the Senate passed the tariff bill by a vote of 44 to 37 with the insurgent Republicans La Follette and Poindexter voting for the measure and the two Louisiana Senators voting in opposition. The conference report was quickly adopted by both houses, and with the President's signature on October 3 the Underwood Tariff Act of 1913 became law.

The new tariff was not, of course, solely for revenue. Its fourteen schedules showed 958 reductions, 86 increases (for the most part covering chemicals), and 307 items that were left unchanged. The average rate of duty under the Act of 1909 was 36.86 per cent; under the 1913 Act it was

26.67 per cent. The reductions covered largely those commodities on which protection had already served its purpose or where American goods dominated the world markets. Yet the Act itself was of the first importance. It marked, for one, a definite parting with the protective principle as Republican legislators had understood it since the Civil War. That is to say, it aimed at moderate protection and not at the choking off of all foreign competition. In the second place, it was an honest bill, for it was based throughout on easily understood ad valorem duties in place of the specific rates, with their hidden devices and "jokers," which had become the hallmark of Republican tariff acts. In the third place, its free list, particularly of daily necessities and of articles in common use by farmers, was very large. In the fourth place, it was the first tariff act to incorporate an income tax as a revenue-raising expedient.

The greatest Democratic triumphs were gained in the rewriting of the wool and sugar schedules, which had become the bulwarks of Republican tariffs. Wool and sugar were both put on the free list; in the case of wool, there was to be immediate application; in the case of sugar, the new schedule's operations were postponed until May 1, 1916, to allow the income-tax law sufficient time in which to obtain the required revenues.[1] As a result of free wool, the compensating specific duties allowed the woolen manufacturers were swept away while the ad valorem duties were also submitted to drastic cuts (from an average of 50 per cent to an average of 35 per cent). The iron and steel schedule was also reduced. Iron ore, pig iron, scrap iron, Bessemer steel ingots, as well as the needed spiegeleisen and ferromanganese, were put on the free list. So were barbed wire (an agricultural necessity) and steel rails. For the most part, these represented heavy or unfinished steel products which American manufacturers could already sell cheaper in European markets than did the native producers. On fabricated steel goods there were moderate ad valorem duties, for example, 5 per cent on bar iron, 15 per cent on tin plate, 20 per cent on steel tubes.

The free list further included agricultural implements, hides, leather, boots and shoes, cement, flax, hemp and hemp tow, soda ash and nitrate of soda, coal, wood, timber, and wood pulp. These were articles used by the farmers of the land and were designed to lower their costs of production. The free list of foodstuffs was imposing. It included buckwheat and buckwheat flour, corn, wheat and wheat flour, rye and rye flour, eggs, meat, milk and cream, cattle and sheep, and salt. The rates on barley and rice were cut in half and that on oats was reduced by three-fourths. These

[1] The act provided that foreign sugar was to carry a duty of 1.25 cents a pound and Cuban sugar 1 cent a pound up to May 1, 1916; thenceforth all sugar was to be admitted free. But on April 22, 1916, Congress voted to retain the sugar duties as they stood in the Act.

reductions were designed to help materially in the lowering of prices for consumers who could be reached by the foodstuffs of Canada, Argentina, Australia, and New Zealand.

The administrative features of the act were many. There was an anti-dumping section written into the law; the Secretary of the Treasury was authorized to penalize bounty-supported imports by additional duties; the maximum and minimum duties of the 1909 Act were eliminated; the President was empowered to negotiate reciprocity trade agreements, acceptance being dependent upon the consent of both houses; the Tariff Board, which Congress had permitted to die in 1912, was not recreated. In addition, the Cuban reciprocity agreement was renewed and absolute free trade with the Philippine Islands was established.

It was believed that the reduction in duties, because of the new tariff, would result in a loss of revenue variously estimated as running from $38 million to $57 million. To make up this deficit, the Democratic lawmakers turned to the personal income tax whose use had been authorized by the ratification of the Sixteenth Amendment. It will be recalled that this Constitutional amendment had been submitted to the states in 1909. On February 25, 1913, Secretary of State Knox, having been informed that three-fourths of the states had ratified, proclaimed the new Constitutional provision. Incorporated, therefore, in the Tariff Act of 1913 were the following income taxes: an annual levy of 1 per cent was placed on all net incomes in excess of $3000; for married men a further exemption of $1000 was allowed; above $20,000, incomes were to be submitted to a graduated surtax starting at an additional 1 per cent and going to 6 per cent on incomes in excess of $500,000. The corporation tax of 1 per cent on net incomes in excess of $5000 was retained. The result was that the government was able to balance its budget for the fiscal year 1913 to 1914, and only when World War I began to cut seriously into customs revenue was it confronted by a deficit.

The dislocation of trade arising out of the war and the growing feeling that Congress was in need of expert assistance in the scrutinizing of tariff schedules led to a demand for the establishment of a tariff commission. Though both parties regarded the matter coldly Wilson himself became converted; the upshot was the yielding of Congress and the creation of the Tariff Commission by the act of September 8, 1916. The functions of the Commission were to be those of investigation purely: it was to study the administrative, fiscal, and industrial effects of the rates, look into the relations subsisting between the duties on raw materials and those on finished goods, weigh the respective advantages of ad valorem and specific duties, examine the effects of the tariff laws on foreign trade, and place itself at the service of the President and the Congress. The Commission was organized early in 1917 and began to function immediately thereafter under the chairmanship of Professor F. W. Taussig of Harvard. During 1917 to 1921 the Commission devoted itself with zeal to these modest purposes, and when the Republican House began to consider its tariff bill in 1921 the Commission was in a position to help rewrite the administrative sections and to furnish data for the new rates.

THE FEDERAL RESERVE SYSTEM

We have seen in an earlier chapter how serious the limitations of the national banking system were. By the first decade of the twentieth century, it was more or less generally recognized by legislators, bankers, and businessmen that there were two major evils inherent in it, namely: that it furnished the country with an inelastic currency and that the reserves it provided for were only fictitious in character and so widely scattered as to be of small use in times of stress. The panic of 1907, particularly, had brought its lesson home to those concerned over the situation. In 1908, Congress had tried to cope with the problem by the enactment of legislation, but it was understood in all quarters that the Aldrich-Vreeland Act of 1908 could be regarded as but an emergency measure.

The Aldrich-Vreeland Act permitted national banks to issue bank notes on the basis of the following other securities, in addition to federal bonds: through the deposit with the Treasury of approved state, county, or municipal bonds; through the deposit of commercial paper with voluntarily constituted "National Currency Associations" (which were very much like clearing house organizations). Such bank note issues were, however, to be limited in amount and subject to heavy taxation. It is to be noted that no issues were emitted under this statute until 1914, when the outbreak of the war led to the draining off of our gold reserves by European nations. Then these emergency issues made their appearance and a total of $386 million was added to the nation's currency by this expedient. All these bank notes were retired by June 30, 1915.

More important was the provision in the act for the creation of a National Monetary Commission, made up of Senators and Congressmen. This Commission, under the chairmanship of Senator Aldrich, was constituted in 1908, and for four years it conducted its inquiries. It made elaborate examinations into the banking and currency systems of European nations, collected an imposing library and finally, in 1912, submitted to Congress a report of some forty-odd volumes and a bill proposing a complete change in the American banking law. This Aldrich bill of 1912 never received the formal attention of Congress; but its provisions were widely known, and they helped in the shaping of the Federal Reserve Act of the following year.

Early in the special session of the Sixty-third Congress, Wilson put in an appearance a second time, on this occasion to urge the passage of banking and currency legislation. He asked for a measure that would embody the following four desiderata: 1. an elastic currency to be based on commercial paper rather than on the bonded indebtedness of the country; 2. the mobilization of bank reserves; 3. public control of the banking system; 4. decentralization rather than centralization. Over elasticity and mobilization of reserves there was no dispute; about government control and decentralization all the controversy centered.

On June 26, 1913, Carter Glass, chairman of the House Committee on Banking and Currency, introduced a banking bill. The House passed the Glass bill on September 17 substantially as it had been presented, with 24 Republicans and 14 Progressives voting with 248 Democrats in the affirmative. The original Glass measure provided for at least twelve reserve banks, placed only an unimportant emphasis on central control, and made bank notes the money of the country. The Senate was less compliant and insisted upon the creation of a smaller number of regional banks, greater governmental participation, and the use of Treasury notes as the circulating medium instead of bank notes. On December 19, the Senate passed its amended bill by a strict party vote with but three Republicans joining the Democratic majority. The conference committee quickly came to terms, and its report was adopted by the House December 22, and by the Senate on the next day. The same evening President Wilson signed the bill and the Federal Reserve Act was law.

The outstanding characteristics of the Federal Reserve System, as embodied in the conference report, were the following: There were to be regional banks as against a central bank. There was to be an elastic currency based on commercial (and agricultural) paper. There was provided the mobilization of reserves in the regional reserve banks which made them, as Glass said, "instead of private banks in the money centers, custodians of the reserve funds of the nation." Government money, in place of the bank notes of the former national banking system, was to be the basis of the country's currency. That is to say, the reserve bank notes were to have behind them the full guaranty of the United States government. Governmental control of the Federal Reserve System was provided.

We may now enter into a more detailed examination of the Act:

The country was to be divided into not less than eight and not more than twelve districts, in each of which a federal reserve bank was to be established.[2] The whole system was to be under the control of a Federal Reserve Board of seven members. Two of these were to be the Secretary of the Treasury and the Comptroller of the Currency, and the other five

[2] The twelve cities finally decided upon as the seats for these regional banks were as follows: Boston, New York, Philadelphia, Cleveland, Richmond, Atlanta, Dallas, Chicago, St. Louis, Minneapolis, Kansas City, San Francisco.

were to be appointed for 10-year terms by the President with the consent of the Senate. (A sixth member was added in 1922.) One of these members was to be designated the governor of the Federal Reserve Board.

The stock of the federal reserve banks was to be owned by the "member banks," and all national banks were required to become members, while state banks and trust companies might join. To become a member, a bank had to subscribe to the capital stock of the federal reserve bank in its district an amount equal to 6 per cent of its own capital and surplus, one-half of which was to be paid in.

Each federal reserve bank was to be governed by a board of nine directors, six of whom were elected by the member banks and three of whom were appointed by the Federal Reserve Board.

The federal reserve banks were to be bankers' banks. They were to rediscount the commercial and agricultural paper of member banks, buy and sell bills of exchange, and grant loans to member banks upon governmental securities as collateral. The rediscount period for commercial paper was to be three months; for agricultural paper, six months. The privilege of rediscounts did not apply to notes and bills of exchange issued "for the purpose of carrying on trading in stocks, bonds or other investment securities, except bonds and notes of the United States." This rediscounting of commercial and agricultural paper was to be the chief means for furnishing the needed elasticity. When a member bank wanted to expand its deposit credits to its customers, it could take part of its bills and notes to the federal reserve bank in its district for rediscount. The Federal Reserve Board might require reserve banks to rediscount commercial paper for each other.

The currency for the whole system was to be founded largely upon this rediscounted paper. The federal reserve banks could issue notes to any amount, based on the bills they had taken up from their member banks, the only limitation on this function being that a 40 per cent reserve was to be kept in gold. The United States 2-per-cent bonds, which had served as the basis of the national bank circulation, were to be retired at the rate of $25 million annually. A check was placed on possible inflation by requiring that no federal reserve bank should pay out the notes of another reserve bank; instead, they must be returned to the issuing bank for retirement.

The federal reserve banks were to hold the reserves of the member banks. Bank reserves were to consist of money in the vaults of the banks and deposit credits with the federal reserve bank. Member banks located in cities in which the central federal reserve banks were established were to maintain reserves totaling 18 per cent of their demand liabilities. The proportions were smaller for banks located in other cities and in rural areas. The federal reserve banks themselves were to carry reserves of 35 per cent against deposits.

In addition, the federal reserve banks might act as governmental depositories, buy and sell gold coin and bullion, and buy and sell bills of exchange arising out of foreign and domestic trade.

The Federal Reserve System, in a short time, gained the support of the banking institutions of the land. In 1915, there were some 25,000 banks in the country, of which 7615 belonged to the system. The total resources of all banks was $22,246,100,000, of which the resources of the member banks totaled $11,887,000,000, or about half. By the end of 1928, out of the 24,806 banks in the country, 8837 belonged to the system. However, out of the total resources of all the banks of $60,178,900,000, the resources of the member banks were $48,936,646,000 or more than four-fifths. In other words, almost all the financial resources of the nation were concentrated under the Federal Reserve System less than fifteen years after its establishment. The Federal Reserve System, too, increased the money stock in the country as well as the money in circulation. We may gain some slight notion of the elasticity of reserve banking in the country by comparing the following figures of federal reserve notes in circulation: on June 30, 1918, $1,847,580,000; on June 30, 1920, $3,405,877,000; on June 30, 1928, $2,002,811,000.

TRUST LEGISLATION

On January 20, 1914, President Wilson once again appeared before Congress, this time to ask for the vindication of his campaign pledges concerning the trusts, and more particularly for legislation to establish that new industrial order whose coming he had foretold in his various addresses. The keystone of the President's trust program was the proposition that "private monopoly is indefensible and intolerable." The Presidential mandate was carried out with alacrity, and there were soon placed before Congress a number of administration bills, out of which there finally emerged the Federal Trade Commission Act (signed September 26, 1914) and the Clayton Antitrust Act (signed October 15, 1914).

The Federal Trade Commission Act abolished the Bureau of Corporations and set up in its place a bipartisan commission of five members to be appointed by the President with the advice and consent of the Senate for 7-year terms. The Commission was to have investigative and regulatory powers. The investigative powers were these: It could examine into the activities of corporations engaged in interstate commerce and require from them both annual and special reports. On its own volition, or at the request of the Department of Justice, it might inquire into the carrying out of court decrees relating to industrial corporations. At the direction of the President or either house of Congress, it was to examine into the alleged violations of antitrust laws. Upon the request of the court, and as a master in chancery, it was to examine and report an appropriate form of decree in equity proceedings brought under the antitrust laws by the Department of Justice. It might make public such of its reports as it deemed necessary for the public interest. It was to investigate trade relations with foreign countries. The Commission's regulatory or legal powers were to be of the following nature: 1. Under Section 5, the law declared that "unfair methods of competition in commerce" were illegal. The Commission, therefore, was directed to issue "cease and desist" orders, when complaints filed with it were proved to be true, to prevent persons, partnerships, or corporations, except banks and common carriers, from using unfair methods of competition. 2. Persons visited with such orders might obtain reviews of these in the federal circuit court of appeals. 3. The findings of the Commission as to facts were to be held to be conclusive. 4. The judgment and decree of the court was to be final, except that appeal might be taken to the Supreme Court. It is to be observed that criminal or civil penalties for violations of the Commission's orders were not incorporated in the Act; it was the intention of Congress to purge business of dishonest practices in the interest of "effective competition," and the Trade Commission was to be employed as the agency for establishing the alleged facts. Once unlawful restraints of trade or monopolies were complained of and proved by the Commission, there existed the Sherman Law and the newly enacted Clayton Law as weapons in the hands of the federal law officers.

The Clayton Act was an amendment to the Sherman Law and contained, principally, three distinct sets of provisions, namely: it prohibited certain corporate practices; it prescribed certain remedies for relief; it made exceptions in the case of labor to protect it from suit under the antitrust laws. The prohibitions were these: Price discriminations were declared illegal "where the effect of such discrimination may be to substantially lessen competition or to tend to create a monopoly." Exclusive selling or leasing contracts (so-called "tying" contracts which put the purchaser or dealer under promise not to handle the wares of a competing manufacturer) were also declared illegal. Intercorporate stock holdings were banned. Interlocking directorates in industrial corporations, capitalized at $1 million or over, which were or had been competitors, were made illegal. The remedies allowed were these: Individual suits for threefold damages might be brought in cases where discrimination and "tying" contracts were proved to exist. Final judgments or decrees in government suits were made prima facie evidence of wrongdoing for private actions for damages. Individual directors, officers, and agents of corporations violating the penal provisions of antitrust laws could be held responsible. Individuals might bring suits for injunctive relief. Injured parties might appeal to the Federal Trade Commission for orders calling on violators to desist from the illegal practices enumerated. It is to be noted that criminal penalties were eliminated from this Act as they were from the earlier Federal Trade Commission Act.

The labor provisions of the Act were to be found in Sections 6 and 20. Section 6, particularly, was regarded by trade union officials as labor's Magna Carta and was hailed by the oversanguine as the final victory in the workingman's long battle for legal recognition. Section 6 declared that:

> The labor of a human being is not a commodity or article of commerce; nothing contained in the antitrust laws shall be construed to forbid the existence and operation of labor, agricultural and horticultural organizations ... nor shall such organizations or the members thereof be held or construed to be illegal combinations or conspiracies in restraint of trade under the antitrust laws.

Section 20 sought to protect workers from the injunction evil. It prohibited the use of the injunction in a labor dispute unless it was deemed necessary by the court to prevent irreparable injury to property rights; it prescribed trials by jury in contempt cases, unless the contempt was committed in the presence of the court; and it declared that strikes, picketing, peaceable assembly, boycotts, and the collection of strike benefits were not in violation of any federal law. Unfortunately, as we shall see below, the federal courts, in less than a decade, found a way of reducing both Section 6 and Section 20 of the Clayton Act to impotence.

The spirit which prompted the passage of these measures was not the punitive one of 1890, but was more in keeping with the attitude of the enlightened times ushered in by the New Freedom. The preservation of competition was the important consideration. How better could this precious thing be safeguarded than by setting up a governmental agency to weigh carefully all charges of unfair methods and to proceed with dispatch against their practitioners before the damage had become irreparable? In other words, the Federal Trade Commission, aided by the Clayton Act, would nip promising monopolies in the bud before they could grow to the luxuriance of the earlier days.

In one instance, the disciples of the New Freedom were willing to make an exception as far as the assuring of "effective competition" was concerned. This instance was foreign trade. In preparation against the day when the manufacturers and merchants of Europe would be in a position to claim their former leadership in the markets of the world, Congress was urged to permit American corporations to combine for the exploitation of foreign markets. Out of this agitation grew the Webb-Pomerene Act of 1918. The House passed a bill along these lines in September, 1916, but the Senate delayed until the spring of 1918. Finally it approved, and on April 10, 1918, President Wilson signed the act. The Webb-Pomerene Law gave sanction to the creation of export associations, made up of producers of the same articles, who were interested in developing commercial relations outside of the United States. Such associations were to be exempted from the restraints laid down in the Sherman Law and from the section of the Clayton Act which made interlocking directorates illegal.

Under the Wilson administration the Federal Trade Commission was a vigilant and intelligent agency, and it did yeoman work in applying itself to the problems in hand, even if its task, before long, began to resemble the Herculean one of cleaning out the Augean stables. In the six years from March 16, 1915, to June 30, 1921, it received 2416 "applications for complaints," served 788 "formal complaints," and issued 379 "cease and desist" orders (against specified unfair practices). Its annual report for the year ending June 30, 1920, carried a list, two pages in length, of the competitive methods against which "cease and desist" orders had been issued by the Commission. The more important of these were:

Misbranding of fabrics and other commodities; adulteration of goods; bribery of buyers or other employees of customers; payment of bonuses by manufacturers to salesmen of jobbers and retailers to push their goods; procuring business or trade secrets of competitors by espionage or bribery; making false or disparaging statements about the wares of competitors; the use of false or misleading advertising; threats to the trade of suits for patent infringements; false claims to patents; trade boycotts; the sale of "knockers;" misrepresentation in the sale of the stock of corporations; harassing competitors by requesting estimates on goods; all schemes for compelling retailers and wholesalers to maintain resale prices; combination of competitors to enhance prices, maintain prices, bring about substantial uniformity in prices, or combinations to divide territory or business.

The Wilson administrations had a much less imposing record of suits under the Sherman Law than the Taft administration. During Wilson's first term in office, 13 bills in equity and 21 indictments were filed (as compared with Taft's total of 90); in the second term, 28 bills in equity were filed and 30 indictments from federal grand juries were obtained. This decline in the number of dissolution suits may be attributed to a variety of factors; namely, the continued use of the "rule of reason" by the Supreme Court; the acceptance by a large number of combinations of consent decrees; the fact that the outstanding trusts had already been moved against by the Roosevelt and Taft federal law officers; the Wilsonian faith in the efficacy of the Federal Trade Commission's work to check monopoly practices before they had gained too great headway; the entry of the United States into World War I and the mobilization of industry that was necessary for victory.

The Supreme Court continued to examine critically governmental actions under the Sherman Law. Thus, it refused to order the dissolution of the United Shoe Machinery Company as a monopoly, when it concurred in the action of the district court in dismissing the government's bill (May 20, 1918).[3] And on March 1, 1920, the Supreme Court found in favor of the United States Steel Corporation.[4] This suit had been begun by Attorney-General Wickersham in 1911 and was based upon the Corporation's acquisition of the Tennessee Coal and Iron Company in 1907, the fact that a number of the Corporation's subsidiaries had had monopoly control over their markets before their entry into the combination, and that under Judge Gary's direction the United States Steel Corporation had reached understandings with other steel manufacturers for the fixing of prices and the division of markets. The case dragged on for almost a decade. On June 3, 1915, four judges in the district court of New Jersey decided to dismiss the government's bill and refused to order the dissolution of the Corporation. The government appealed and the case was argued before the Supreme Court on a number of occasions. Finally, in 1920, with but seven justices participating, the bill was dismissed by a vote of four to three.

The majority opinion held that the United States Steel Corporation was not a monopoly in that it did not control the manufacture of steel in the country; that even if it had once joined with competitors in fixing prices, it had abandoned the practice later; that its ways of doing business were "genuine, direct and vigorous," and that it did not indulge in unfair methods of competition; that Theodore Roosevelt himself had given consent to the Tennessee Coal and Iron Company purchase; and that its size alone was no reason for penalizing the Corporation.

This does not mean that Wilson's Department of Justice did not meet with substantial success in its proceedings against combinations. The International Harvester Company, in 1918, came to an agreement with the Department of Justice under which the company accepted the dissolution decree of a lower court. In 1919, the Corn Products Refining Company came to terms with the government, too, and accepted a similar dissolution decree. On February 27, 1920, the "Big Five" among the meat packers (Swift and Company, Armour and Company, Morris and Company, Wilson and Company, Cudahy Packing Company) consented to a decree that enjoined them from continuing a number of practices that had come to the unfriendly attention of the Federal Trade Commission. This particular consent decree was a sweeping one. Under it the packers pledged themselves to refrain: from maintaining any contract or monopoly in restraint of trade; from owning stockyards, stockyard terminal railways, or market newspapers; from using their distributive systems to handle fish, vegetables, fruits, confectionery, soft drinks, and groceries generally; from

[3] 247 U.S. 32.
[4] 251 U.S. 417.

engaging in the manufacture, jobbing or selling of any of these commodities; from operating retail meat markets and from dealing in milk and cream; from employing any illegal trade practices.

AGRARIAN LEGISLATION

We have had occasion to see how much the troubles of the farmers grew out of their inability to obtain easily and at reasonable interest rates credit facilities for long-term and short-term operations. The plight of the West and South had led to the agrarian revolt of the eighties and the nineties and had produced the programs of the Populists and the free-silver advocates. The Wilson administration attempted to apply itself seriously to the problems that had sprung up from the country's inadequate and obsolete private banking system. The result was twofold: in the Federal Reserve Act of 1913 special provisions were made for the handling of agricultural short-term paper; while through the Federal Farm Loan Act of 1916 a real step forward was taken in resolving the long-term credit difficulties of the farmers.

The Federal Reserve Act sought to offer credit relief to the agricultural interest in three ways: 1. It permitted national banks to lend money on farm mortgages. Such loans were to run for five years and were not to be in excess of 50 per cent of the value of the property offered as security. 2. It was hoped that the Act's provisions for elastic note issue would benefit the farmer. 3. The Act set the rediscount period for agricultural paper at six months while commercial paper was allowed only three months. Before long it became apparent that none of these expectations was being fulfilled with a large degree of success. In 1915, for example, the national banks were lending less than one-twentieth as much as the state banks on long-term paper. But the long-term credit problem was solved when the Federal Farm Loan Act in 1916 set up a new machinery for the handling of farm mortgages. As far as short-term credits were concerned, relief did not come until 1923, when Congress, with government funds, established the federal intermediate credit banks for the purpose of rediscounting the agricultural paper of banks and for extending credit direct to agricultural co-operatives.

The Federal Farm Loan Act was written in 1916 after having been considered for two years by Congress. On May 4, 1916, the Senate accepted a Congressional joint committee bill by a vote of 57 to 7; on May 15, the House followed suit, its vote being 295 to 10. President Wilson approved the Act July 17, 1916. The purpose of the act, ran its preamble, was "to provide capital for agricultural development, to create standard forms of investment based upon farm mortgage, and to equalize rates of interest upon farm loans."

The Act set up a Federal Farm Loan System similar to the Federal Reserve System. Its destinies were to be guided by a board, composed of the Secretary of the Treasury and four members appointed by the President. Under this board were to operate twelve federal land banks in as many districts. Each of these banks was to have an initial capital of $750,000, to which any person might subscribe, though it was stipulated that the government was to supply the difference between private subscriptions and the required initial capital. In the beginning the government took most of the stock, but by December 31, 1925, it had been able to reduce its holdings from $8,892,130 to $1,331,930, and by June 30, 1930, to $292,500. Operating under these land banks were to be co-operative farm loan associations, made up entirely of farmers desirous of borrowing money on farm mortgages. Each borrower bought stock in his local association, taking $5 worth of stock for each $100 he wished to borrow. Each farmer could borrow up to 50 per cent of the value of his land and 20 per cent of the value of his permanent improvements.

After a request for a loan was approved and a mortgage received, the land bank was called upon to furnish the funds. The land banks were to obtain their capital from the issuance of farm-loan bonds, which were to be secured by the farm mortgages and which were to be tax-exempt. In short, the entire scheme was neatly dovetailed. As Miss Eliot says: "The whole system stands behind the bonds, which thus have the mortgage security, the farm loan association, the issuing land bank and the other eleven land banks to insure their redemption."

These were the advantages to the farmers: The plan insured easy loans at interest rates running from 5 to 6 per cent. Provision was made for amortization of mortgages so that the standard loan period ran for 33 years and at the end of that time interest and principal were entirely paid. The size of the mortgage was comparatively high. Thus, the average loan increased from $2130 in 1917 to $3685 in 1930. The co-operative farm-loan associations made profits which were distributed among the participating members. By the end of 1925, the system had made net earnings of $34,964,000 and had distributed $14,590,000 in dividends. On June 30, 1930, there were operating 4659 farm-loan associations; 506,358 loans had been closed from the organization of the system to that date; a total of $1,631,420,000 had been lent in the same period; and the land banks had outstanding $1,192,719,000 lent on mortgage. The Act also authorized the establishment of privately created joint-stock land banks which could deal directly with borrowers. These banks were to finance themselves by the sale of bonds (secured by farm mortgage), and such bonds, like the land-bank bonds, were to be tax-exempt. On June 30, 1930, there were in existence forty-eight such banks, and they had lent a total of $891,000,000 from the time of organization to that date.

OTHER LEGISLATION

The above were the outstanding accomplishments, in the field of domestic legislation, of the two Wilson administrations. There were, too, other measures enacted, of equal importance in their own realms. On March 4, 1915, President Wilson signed the La Follette Seamen's bill. This was a charter of liberties for America's seamen and freed the men in the forecastle from the tyranny of the bridge. The Act of September 7, 1916, set up a United States Shipping Board, devised to encourage and create a naval auxiliary and to foster the development of an American merchant marine. We shall have occasion to see how through the agency of this Board the United States was able to mobilize a great fleet of merchant ships during World War I and, in the years following, to make America once more a significant factor in the world's carrying trade. On May 9, 1913, the Secretary of State proclaimed the ratification of the Seventeenth Amendment (for popular election of United States Senators). In September, 1916, the Keating-Owen Child Labor Act, to prevent the entry into interstate commerce of the products of child labor, was passed. In the same year, the Adamson Law, establishing the 8-hour day on interstate railways, was enacted. In December, 1917, both houses of Congress adopted a resolution for the submission of the Eighteenth Amendment (Prohibition) to the states. On January 29, 1919, the Secretary of State proclaimed its ratification. In 1919, both houses voted to submit the Nineteenth Amendment (Woman Suffrage) to the states and in August, 1920, the thirty-sixth state having ratified, the amendment was proclaimed by the State Department.

· 25 ·

Foreign Affairs in the Wilson Administrations

WOODROW WILSON AND MEXICO

For more than forty years, after the downfall of the Mexican Empire in 1867, the relations between the United States and Mexico had been on an amicable footing. Diplomatic interchanges had largely been of a routine nature: for the policing of the frontier, for commercial intercourse, for the extradition of felons and the like. The rule of Porfirio Díaz, nominally as president, actually as dictator, had started in 1877, and except for four years had continued unbroken until 1911. Under him, popular government had become a farce, nepotism was in the saddle, the officialdom was venal and worked hand in glove with foreign concessionaires, while the humble Mexican peon possessed the status of a landed serf. Though the economy of the country was almost entirely agricultural, fully 85 per cent of its population was landless.

Mexico had become the happy hunting ground of American, British, French, and German nationals who had surplus capital to invest. Under the beneficent eye of the Díaz regime, railroads had been built, silver, copper, and lead mines worked, petroleum wells opened, rubber plantations started, and great stock-raising ranches established. The American-Mexican trade had boomed as a result, and by 1910 was worth $117 million annually. And American capital investments had grown from $185 million in 1900 to $1 billion a short decade later. By 1910, from 40,000 to 75,000 American citizens lived in Mexico.

There was, however, only an outer semblance of peace and prosperity. Aspirants to the presidential succession—and the dictatorship—schemed and plotted, waiting for the day when senility should overcome Díaz; there was a small group of sincere democrats who looked forward to the time when the Mexican peon might be raised from his debased estate. The blow suddenly fell in the spring of 1911 as hostile forces, following the banner of Francisco Madero, Jr., began to converge on the capital. The octogenarian Díaz saw his trusted military supporters deserting him and, accepting the inevitable, signed his own abdication on May 25. Twelve days later Madero entered Mexico City in triumph. For a half-year Madero struggled to assert his supremacy. Then the situation got out of hand, and the next year and a half was to see a contest for power between the Madero forces and bands of revolutionaries.

The attitude of the American government was a hostile one. During 1912, troops were massed on the border, warships were sent to the Atlantic and Pacific coasts of Mexico to take home such American nationals as wished to leave, and sharp notes were dispatched to the Madero government warning it that it would be held accountable for loss of American lives and destruction of property. The unfortunate Madero was rendered miserable by our embassy's threatening attitude on the one hand, and by the guerrilla tactics of the insurgent forces in the northern states on the other. Finally, on February 18, 1913, his short-lived career as Mexico's savior ended, for on that day he was arrested; on February 23, he was shot in cold blood. Victoriano Huerta, who was commonly held responsible for Madero's death, installed himself as provisional president, and proceeded to promise the diplomatic corps at Mexico City the restoration of peace and the protection of foreign concessionaires and interests. This was the situation as Woodrow Wilson was preparing to take the oath of office.

President Wilson's policy was quickly enunciated on March 11, 1913. He would have nothing to do with Huerta or with any governments based on military seizure; he was interested in seeing a truly democratic government established in Mexico, and to the consummation of this he would render every assistance; he would not, however, send an armed force into Mexico for the protection of American capitalistic interests. Wilson, therefore, refused to accord recognition to Huerta, in which action he was followed by Latin-American countries; not so, however, the European powers and Japan, which, by the middle of 1913, recognized Huerta's de facto government. On October 27, 1913, in a speech delivered at Mobile, Alabama, Wilson warned Americans, with financial interests in Mexico, as well as the European chancelleries that he expected that his leadership in Latin-American affairs would be accepted. He adverted to the hold which foreign economic groups had obtained over Latin-American peoples. He expressed the hope that this hold would soon be broken. Of his own attitude toward intervention to protect American property, he left no room for doubt when he said: "It is a very perilous thing to determine the foreign policy of a nation in the terms of material interest. It not only is unfair to those with whom you are dealing, but it is degrading as regards your own actions."

Europe bowed before Wilson's defiance, and toward the end of the same year the British ambassador at Mexico City announced to Huerta that he could no longer look for support to England. On December 3, 1913, Wilson repeated that he would not deviate from his policy of "watchful waiting," but he encouraged insurrection against Huerta by lifting the embargo against the exportation of arms and military supplies to Mexico. Wilson was willing to wait for Huerta's downfall, but he waited impatiently. In April, 1914, because of Huerta's refusal to salute the American flag following the unnecessary arrest of a number of American bluejackets, Wilson ordered a blockade of the Mexican harbors. And on April 21, to prevent the landing of a cargo of munitions for Huerta, he gave the order for the seizure of the port of Vera Cruz. Eighteen American marines were killed before the operation was completed. American troops did not evacuate the city until November 23.

This was the beginning of the end for Huerta. Before the summer was over, he had fled from the capital, and on August 20, 1914, the victorious forces of Venustiano Carranza entered Mexico City. There followed another year of turmoil as Carranza, Villa, and Obregón first sought to consolidate the results of their successful revolt and then proceeded to war against one another. The rival leaders having failed to settle their differences amicably, Wilson enlisted the support of the other Latin-American peoples, and the result was a decision to recognize Carranza as president of a de facto government, October 19, 1915. European governments followed Wilson's lead; the hand of Carranza was further strengthened by the decision of the State Department to allow him to import arms and supplies freely.

This decision was not accepted by all parties. Francisco Villa, incensed at the favors bestowed on his successful rival, resorted to reprisals, and on January 10, 1916, took eighteen Americans from a train near Santa Ysabel, in the north, and shot them. On March 9, Villistas crossed the border into New Mexico and raided the town of Columbus, killing seventeen American citizens. The American interventionists, who had been regarding Wilson's "watchful waiting" policy with disdain, were now whipped into a frenzy. Republican statesmen pointed to McKinley's patriotic action in cleaning out the Cuban nuisance and demanded that Wilson send an army of half a million men into Mexico. The impending Presidential campaign threatened to make of Mexico a major issue, with the result that some action was required. Therefore, on March 15, Wilson ordered Brigadier General John J. Pershing to lead a "punitive expedition" of 6000 men into Mexico to capture Villa. Another 6000 men were sent to join the party, while in June Wilson called upon all the state militias of the nation to mass on the border. Pershing stayed in Mexico nine months and came out in February, 1917 without having succeeded in his mission.

On January 2, 1917, diplomatic relations between the two nations were resumed and Ambassador Fletcher took up his duties in March at Mexico City.

A Mexican constitutional convention met in February, 1917, and completed its labors before April was over. The Mexican Constitution that was promulgated on May 1 was a radical document in a number of ways. (Be it said that its radical character was due not to Carranza but to the followers of Obregón, who were anticlerical and prolabor.) The 8-hour day, protection of women and children in industry, and social insurance regulations were promised; church edifices were to become national property; schools and eleemosynary institutions were to be secularized; the soil and subsoil of Mexico were declared to belong to the Mexican people. The last was incorporated in the famous Article xxvii of the new constitution. Specifically, it stated that the ownership of the land and waters of Mexico had always resided in the Mexican nation; that, by ancient Spanish law, the possession of the subsoil deposits belonged to the state; and that these were inalienable and could not be lost by prescription. Only Mexican citizens and Mexican companies might acquire ownership in land or receive concessions for the development of mines, waterways and waterpower sites, and petroleum and gas deposits. All companies chartered in Mexico were to accept automatically the supremacy of Mexican law. Within a zone of 100 kilometers of the frontier and 50 kilometers of the coast, all foreign ownership of land and water rights was banned. However, the provisions of the article were not to be retroactive in character. To the Mexican people, the constitution promised the division of the large estates and the development, with governmental assistance, of small landed holdings.

It was inevitable that American corporations, particularly those possessing mineral and oil lands, should take alarm. With the conclusion of World War I, the clamor of the American interventionists redoubled its fury. A powerful propaganda was conducted by the oil interests through the agency of the Association for the Protection of American Rights in Mexico; a Senate subcommittee poured oil on the flames when, in September, 1919, it issued a report that incorporated a vicious attack on the Carranza government and all its works. When a number of Wilson's Cabinet officers, specifically Secretary of State Lansing, Secretary of the Interior Lane, and Attorney-General Palmer, gave ready ear to the indignant charges of the interventionists, it was not hard to see that the United States was on the brink of another war. The *casus belli* was furnished in the seizure of the American consular agent, one Jenkins, at Puebla; Lansing issued a stern warning to Mexico City; and the war party in the American Senate at once passed a resolution approving "the action of the Department of State in reference to the pending controversy" and demanding the ending of diplomatic relations. Woodrow Wilson lay ill in the White House: it was plain that the threatening gesture of Lansing had been concealed from him. Somehow, he was apprised of the latest developments in the Mexican crisis and his appearance on the scene silenced his State Department and subdued the Senate warmongers. The Mexican government promised its assistance, Jenkins was released, and the war clouds blew over.

The year 1920 witnessed further disorders as the Mexican presidential election approached. Carranza sought to disregard the strong claims of Alvaro Obregón to the presidency and attempted to pick his own successor. Obregón took to the field, was joined by other military leaders, and by April was so successful that the whole west and north were up in arms. On May 7, after Vera Cruz had capitulated to the insurgents, Carranza gave up all hope and fled. His flight was impeded at almost every step, and on May 21, he surrendered, only to be shot to death while he lay asleep. Three days later the Mexican Congress declared the presidential chair vacant and chose Adolfo de la Huerta, a follower of Obregón, provisional president. In the regular election of the following September, Obregón was named president of the republic in the face of only a nominal opposition. The new government was at once recognized by Japan, Brazil, Holland, and Germany; Obregón sought to conciliate American public opinion and to gain Wilson's support by openly expressing his friendship for the United States. But Wilson was an ill and broken man and had no heart for the formulation of a new Mexican policy. He let the next six months slip by without making a decision on the question of Mexican recognition: to his successor he bequeathed the vexing problem, as he himself had inherited it eight years before from his predecessor. In another eight years American-Mexican relations were to be established on a sound and permanent basis.

What had Wilson accomplished? He had respected the nationalistic aspirations of the Mexican people and had looked forward to the time when democratic institutions would rule the land. He had courageously held American interventionists in leash and had refused to countenance armed interference despite the presentation of a number of plausible pretexts. He had refused to make an issue of the 1917 constitution, and oil played no role in his foreign policy. But he had committed a number of grievous sins of omission. He had taken it for granted that Mexicans were as fully conscious of his lofty and disinterested motives as he himself was. He had made no effort to display positive signs of his friendship; for example, no American ambassador directed the Mexico City embassy between 1913 and 1917. Mexican public opinion, during 1913 to 1921, was puzzled about Wilson and suspicious of American intentions. Yet without Wilson's groundwork, the later triumph of Coolidge in Mexico would not have been possible.

WOODROW WILSON AND THE CARIBBEAN

If President Wilson pursued a wholly honorable course in the case of Mexico, his actions with respect to the smaller Caribbean countries were less able to stand close scrutiny. One may dismiss, at once, the notion that economic imperialism had anything to do with Wilson's meddling in the Caribbean. His Mobile speech had plainly indicated his contempt for the dollar diplomacy of those nations who could regard with equanimity the use of government as a cat's-paw to pull out of the fire the unsuccessful ventures of private concessionaires. Besides, our financial and commercial stake in the Caribbean countries in whose domestic affairs we interfered was of next to no value. To this extent, Wilson deviated little from the Rooseveltian philosophy or policy.

The American fiscal protectorate established over the Dominican Republic by Theodore Roosevelt was continued by Wilson. In 1916, following an insurrection, and the refusal of the new presidential incumbent to observe the terms of the convention of 1907, marines were landed, and on December 29, an American naval administration was set up on the island. The local parliament was suspended and the affairs of the country were turned over to officers from the American warships. The next five years witnessed a period of sizable achievement, as far as external accomplishments went. Education was promoted, roads were built, a native constabulary was established, and finances were put on a sound footing. Before the occupation, internal revenue receipts were $700,000 annually with 15 per cent charged against the cost of collection; in 1920, revenues totaled $4,500,000 and the collection cost was only 5 per cent. If there came to the ears of Americans occasional tales of a rigorous press censorship, the stern justice meted out by naval courts, and even the employment of water torture, the administration apparently heard nothing, and the American military occupation continued.

The tale was largely the same in Haiti. In 1914, the inability of the Haitian government to meet its debt services led the American State Department to propose a convention similar to the one made with Haiti's sister republic; in other words, the establishment of a fiscal protectorate. When the overture was rejected the matter was dropped. But late in July, 1915, local disorders caused American marines to be rushed to the scene; in another month, martial law had been proclaimed by an American admiral; and before September was over a treaty had been signed with the Haitian administration which put Americans in control of affairs, largely on the same basis as in the Dominican Republic. The treaty was proclaimed May 3, 1916, was to run for ten years, and was subject to renewal. The marines stayed on throughout Wilson's administrations.

Another American protectorate had been set up in Nicaragua in 1912 and was continued through the nineteen twenties. The Bryan-Chamorro Treaty, mentioned above, which was ratified in 1916, gave to the United States the right of way for an inter-oceanic canal; turned over to us, on a 99-year lease, Great Corn and Little Corn Islands; and permitted our Navy Department to set up a naval base on the Gulf of Fonseca. For these privileges, the United States paid Nicaragua $3 million in gold. The protests of Costa Rica and Salvador, which insisted that the treaty violated their territorial rights, were given slight attention. Though the complaint was presented to the Central American Court of Justice and though that tribunal found against Nicaragua, the United States coolly disregarded the decision. Not only were marines maintained in Nicaragua to protect, presumably, our right of way for the canal, but American officers directly intervened in local elections. As a result of American support, the local conservative government found no difficulty in maintaining itself in office.

In 1917, after more than fifteen years of negotiations, the United States was finally able to acquire the Virgin Islands, in the West Indies, from Denmark. In 1901, the United States had completed a treaty with Denmark for the acquisition of the islands, the purchase price being fixed at $5 million. The American Senate had ratified the treaty in 1902, but the Danish upper chamber had rejected the convention, primarily, it was believed, as a result of pressure brought to bear by Germany. In 1917, with Germany engaged in a life-and-death struggle, Minister Egan at Copenhagen was able to push matters to a successful conclusion. We paid Denmark $25 million. For that large sum we got three islands with a total area of 132 square miles and a population of 26,000, of whom 90 per cent were Negroes. The administration of the islands was placed in the hands of a governor, to be chosen by the President of the United States. From 1917 to 1930, all the governors came from the United States Navy; in February, 1931, Washington set up a civil government at St. Thomas (the capital), and Paul M. Pearson was appointed the first civilian governor. In the short period we had owned the group, the Virgin Islands had fallen into a decline. Prohibition crippled the native rum-making industry, while the growing use of oil for fuel ended the importance of the islands as a Caribbean coaling station. By 1931, the population had dwindled to 22,000. To President Hoover, who made a brief visit to St. Thomas in March, 1931, the Virgin Islands were "an effective poorhouse," 90 per cent of whose population was dependent upon the patrimony of the United States. There was small likelihood of their abandonment, however, in view of our Isthmian policy, which regarded them as necessary for the naval defense of the Panama Canal and the proposed Nicaraguan Canal.

THE PEACE MOVEMENT

While our naval establishment grew and the American Army was modernized, while American marines walked the streets of Port-au-Prince and Managua, there were citizens among us who labored indefatigably in the cause of international peace. The fifteen years immediately preceding the outbreak of World War I saw the peace movement take on impressive proportions. Contributions from American philanthropists furnished the funds needed for publicity, research, publication, the meeting of conferences, institutes, and round tables, and the exchange of professors between the United States and the other nations of the world. So, in 1910, Edwin Ginn, a Boston textbook publisher, set aside a fund of $1 million for the endowment of the World Peace Foundation. Even more splendid were Andrew Carnegie's efforts. In 1911, with a grant of $10 million, he created the Carnegie Endowment for International Peace; and in addition, he set himself the task of signalizing the labors of men in the peace cause by the erection of a group of magnificent public buildings. It was Carnegie who built the Peace Palace at The Hague, the Pan-American Union's building at Washington, and the headquarters of the short-lived Central American Court in Costa Rica.

Statesmen were not unmindful of these activities and hastened to make their contributions. At the call of the Czar of Russia, two great peace assemblies met at The Hague, the first in 1899 and the second in 1907. Though the first Peace Conference was ostensibly called in the interest of disarmament, the proposal had the support of none of the great military or naval powers and no agreement was reached. But three accomplishments did emerge, as follows: a compact was signed permitting neutral powers to tender their good offices to prevent hostilities or to bring hostilities to a close after they had already commenced; a second compact permitted a nation involved in an international dispute to call for the creation of a commission of inquiry, without, by this act, prejudicing its case; a third provided for the creation of a Permanent Court of Arbitration at The Hague where nations, after agreeing on the facts in dispute, might submit their controversies. The second Peace Conference of 1907 was unable to contribute anything further to this comparatively slight body of achievement. However, it did set up an international prize court, and it also made provision for the holding of a special naval conference in 1908 at London which was to draw a new code for regulating naval warfare.

In 1904, the American State Department negotiated with France, Great Britain, Germany, Portugal, and Switzerland a series of conventions calling for submission to the Hague Court of all international disagreements except those involving "the vital interests, the independence, or the honor" of the high contracting parties. In keeping with one of the understandings of the first Hague Conference, these treaties contained a clause requiring the parties to a controversy to "conclude a special agreement defining clearly the matter in dispute," before placing their case before the Hague Court. The Senate was hostile, balking particularly at the word "agreement," and amended the conventions by substituting the word "treaty" for "agreement." The thought was, of course, to force the participation of the Senate in such proceedings. But President Roosevelt regarded the amendment as destroying the usefulness of the conventions and refused to announce their ratification. In 1908, Root, then Secretary of State, accepted the Senate's point of view and transmitted the conventions in their amended form to the other contracting parties. Ratifications were exchanged between 1908 and 1910.

In 1911, Secretary of State Knox sought to extend the subjects for arbitration to include all justiciable questions and entered into negotiations with France and Great Britain. Treaties with these powers were signed, but again the Senate evinced a marked hostility. The treaties were never approved, and the Taft administration let the matter drop.

It remained for Secretary of State Bryan to evolve a working formula for the settlement of international disputes. In 1913 and 1914, he entered into an elaborate correspondence, with all those powers that had diplomatic representation at Washington, for the purpose of writing a new series of arbitration treaties. Bryan's proposed treaties were based on the assumption that cooler counsels would prevail, when war threatened, if disputants were compelled, by agreement, to wait for the lapse of a stipulated interval. Thus, most of the treaties he wrote provided for the submission by the contracting parties of "all questions of whatever character and nature in dispute between them" to international commissions of inquiry for investigation and report. While these commissions of inquiry sat, the disputants were to refrain from war or the increase of their armaments. Bryan met with an immediate and cordial response, and on June 15, 1914, while the European skies were still untroubled, he could report the signing of fifteen such treaties. In August, the Senate ratified all these without raising a single serious question. Despite the outbreak of war and the mortal blow thus rendered to the high hopes of the peace advocates, Bryan continued his efforts, and before the fall was over he could report treaties with thirty powers, among which were Great Britain, France, Spain, China, Sweden, and Russia. Only Austria, Germany, Mexico, Turkey, and Japan did not see fit to participate.

Bryan and the other peace advocates were much too sanguine, and before the summer of 1914 was over the temple of peace had been shattered. On June 28, 1914, at Sarajevo, the capital of the Austrian province of Bosnia, two revolver shots were fired by a young Bosnian patriot. The first bullet mortally wounded Archduke Franz Ferdinand, heir to the Austro-

Hungarian throne. The second killed his wife. Americans read the account of the double tragedy with indignation, and it was generally hoped that the assassin would swiftly meet his deserts. In the month that went by before Austria acted, Americans, not familiar with European international politics, had a chance to let the memory of the unfortunate occurrence slip from their minds. Certainly, there were a few individuals among us who sensed that the whole of Europe was nearing the brink of a precipice; but for the great majority of Americans all was serene. It was small wonder that the events of July 23 to August 5 shocked the average American citizen. It seemed that the whole of Europe was unaccountably plunged in a deadly war of destruction. Within two crowded weeks, Austria had declared war on Serbia; Germany had declared war on Russia and France; Belgium had been overrun by the German armies; Great Britain, in defense of Belgian neutrality, had taken up arms against Germany. Such were the events the screaming headlines placed before the eyes of their American readers. Many believed that Germany and her ally were the only aggressor nations; indeed, long after the war's close, and despite the serious doubts cast by many scholars on the thesis of exclusive German guilt, there were many Americans who continued to hold honestly to this conviction.

AMERICAN NEUTRALITY: THE BRITISH BLOCKADE

American neutrality was proclaimed August 4, 1914; two weeks later Wilson called upon his countrymen to remain "impartial in thought as well as in action." In the quarrels of Europe he had no desire to intervene; America's function was to hold herself in readiness "to do what is honest and disinterested and truly serviceable for the peace of the world." The President's stand was widely applauded, and even Theodore Roosevelt, writing in the columns of the *Outlook* the next month, congratulated the United States upon its happy detachment from the European scene.

Isolation, however, was impossible. Every day events were transpiring that were bringing us nearer and nearer to the holocaust overseas. On the one hand, American neutrality was being sorely tried by the British, whose rewriting in their own interest of maritime law gravely abridged American freedom of the seas; and, on the other hand, the declaration by Germany of unrestricted submarine warfare, with its threat to American lives as well as of shipping, was even a greater menace. Legally, there was little to choose as between our grievances against Great Britain and those against Germany. Thus, Wilson's Attorney-General Gregory, writing in 1925, declared:

> Up to the time that Germany began its atrocious submarine warfare culminating in the *Lusitania* we had far less cause for complaint against her than we had against Great Britain; the latter had repeatedly seized on the high seas our vessels

bound for neutral ports; it had appropriated these vessels and their cargoes; it had opened our mail and prevented its delivery; it had ignored our protests and in some instances had for weeks and months even failed to acknowledge their receipt. These were substantially the same acts that brought on the War of 1812.

It is necessary to review at some length those methods adopted by the warring nations that both threatened our national security and hampered our normal intercourse with other nations.

As soon as war broke out, the American State Department inquired if it was the intention of the belligerents to observe the terms of the Declaration of London of 1909, which was, in effect, a codification of the existing rules regulating the sea rights of belligerents and neutrals in time of war. The Declaration had been signed by the principal powers and to this degree it was morally binding. But ratifications had not been exchanged, and the British House of Lords had definitely refused to pass a bill embodying many of the Declaration's provisions. In answer to the State Department's question, the Central Powers wrote they were willing to rule themselves by the Declaration; France and Russia also gave their assent, contingent, however, upon Great Britain's acceptance. But Great Britain, in its reply, so seriously modified the terms of the Declaration that Washington was compelled to rejoin:

> ... the United States feels obliged to withdraw its suggestion that the Declaration of London be adopted as a temporary code of naval warfare to be observed by belligerents and neutrals during the present war; ... therefore this government will insist that the rights and duties of the United States and its citizens ... be defined by the existing rules of international law ... irrespective of the provisions of the Declaration of London.

The Declaration of London had laid down the following definitions of a blockade: a blockade was not to extend beyond the ports of the enemy; it could not subject to capture ships destined for nonblockaded ports; it could not prevent access to neutral ports; it must be effective; it must be applied impartially; it must be established through a formal order. The Declaration had denied the theory of continuous voyage. Finally, this document had drawn up a rigid list of articles that were to be regarded respectively as absolute contraband, conditional contraband, and noncontraband. Under absolute contraband were classified such articles as were immediately necessary to the maintenance of the armed forces of the enemy; under conditional contraband were listed those articles that might be used equally for "warlike or peaceful purposes," but that could be proved to be destined for the use of the enemy government or its armed forces; on the free list, or as noncontraband, were included those articles that were needed for the maintenance of the life and industrial activities of the civilian populations.

We may now examine those measures Great Britain took to embarrass

American activities on the high seas, not only in contravention of the Declaration of London but, generally, in disregard of almost all the existing rules of sea law.

Great Britain set up what was, in reality, an illegal blockade. On March 11, 1915, the British declared that all German ports were blockaded and that every merchant vessel destined for or coming from a German port was liable to seizure. But Great Britain could not maintain the blockade effectively because the threat of submarine torpedoing prevented the continuous patrolling, by British ships, of German North Sea ports. What Great Britain did was to patrol the English Channel and the extreme north edge of the North Sea between Scotland and Norway and to stop all vessels trying to enter, whether they were bound for the Netherlands, Norway, Sweden, Denmark, or Germany. Further, on the alleged ground that the North Sea was filled with floating mines, Great Britain by Orders in Council issued in May, 1916, and January, 1917, extended the war area so as to prevent the conduct of all sea-borne commerce with Northern Europe. Against such measures, our State Department was quick to protest. Thus, in its note of March 30, 1915, it made these two points: first, that the blockade "embraces many neutral ports and coasts, bars access to them, and subjects all neutral ships seeking to approach them to the same suspicion that would attach to them were they bound for the ports of the enemies of Great Britain, and to unusual risks and penalties"; second, that the British blockade was discriminating between neutrals in view of the fact that it could not check the Scandinavian and Danish trade with German Baltic ports, while it could interfere with the American North Sea commerce.

The British revived the doctrine of the continuous voyage, quoting its American use in the Civil War. This doctrine held that "goods which could be proved to be ultimately intended for an enemy country were not exempted from seizure on the ground that they were first to be discharged in an intervening neutral port." A number of expedients were devised to make the continuous voyage rule effective, of which the following were the most important: A "black list" of Dutch, Scandinavian, and Danish neutrals, who were suspected of dealing with the enemy, was drawn up and all cargoes bound for these neutrals were seized. Agreements were made with neutral shippers, carriers, and consignees that goods they handled would not be reshipped to the enemy. In other words, neutrals had to submit to licensing. Supplies destined for neutral European countries were rationed on the basis of their normal needs. That is to say, the neutral North Sea countries could not receive, for example, more fats, cotton, rubber and ores than they had been using before the war broke out. Bunker coal was denied all ships not on a "white list."

The British took it upon themselves to draw up their own lists of contraband. By the Orders in Council of August 20 and October 22, 1914, the lists of contraband and noncontraband in the Declaration of London were rejected; in March, 1915, continuous voyage was applied both to absolute and to conditional contraband; in April, 1916, finally, the distinction between absolute and conditional contraband was completely wiped out. The prohibited articles were regularly being added to, so that, in time, practically all commodities that Germany normally imported were placed on these interdicted lists. For example, iron, copper, lead, rubber, sulphur, and glycerine were first made conditional contraband and then absolute contraband. Food was declared contraband of war in January, 1915. In August, 1915, cotton was declared contraband. In all some 15 proclamations were issued, naming 230 items liable to seizure.

The right of search was extended by Great Britain. Claiming that stoppage and search on the high seas were fraught with danger because of the submarine threat, Great Britain took to compelling neutral ships to put into British ports for search. Here ships and cargoes were detained, on suspicion only, often for months on end, as shipping costs mounted and cargoes became liable to deterioration.

The British opened American mail pouches and confiscated packages addressed to neutral countries, on the score that they were destined for the enemy. They even tampered with mails from European neutral countries addressed to us.

The British refused to license German exports needed for American industry and even the safeguarding of American health. The British held up the shipment of drugs, sugar beet seeds, and dyestuffs to the United States, devoting months to an elaborate examination of the American contention that such articles were absolutely required here. Particularly objectionable was British action in handling the American complaint that German machine knitting needles were prevented from getting to American manufacturers. A note to this effect was sent on May 29, 1916. The British did not see fit to reply until September 18; then they said there was no need for Americans to import these articles from Germany, they themselves could fill the American demand. On November 25, the American State Department declared there seemed to be no possibility of British manufacturers supplying American needs; on December 4, Secretary of State Lansing wrote to Ambassador Page that the British style of knitting needles could not fit American machines anyway. Meanwhile, the State Department had learned that these very needles, which were being denied to American manufacturers, were being freely imported into England. At this point, Lansing wired tartly to Page: "... unless prompt favorable action is taken on Keegan application, Department will find it difficult to avoid the conclusion that this is a discrimination favoring English at the expense of American commerce under the guise of a war measure."

When the British Foreign Office was confronted with these facts, it agreed on February 15, 1917, to issue permits allowing American importation of the German needles. Almost nine months therefore elapsed before satisfaction could be obtained.

Legally, the American right to the freedom of the seas was set forth with a cogency and logic which reflected great credit on the note writers in our State Department. But, while protests against the British blockading system were numerous, no pressure was brought to bear. Thus, on October 21, 1915, a fully documented note was filed setting forth all the American complaints in careful detail. Great Britain was told that its blockade "cannot be recognized as a legal blockade by the United States"; that it was "ineffective, illegal, and indefensible"; and that the United States expected Great Britain to be governed "not by a policy of expediency but by those established rules of international conduct upon which Great Britain in the past has held the United States to account when the latter nation was a belligerent engaged in a struggle for national existence." But Great Britain did not reply until April 24, 1916. Then a note came to Washington which refused to yield a single point in the whole elaborate American bill of particulars. We were in the midst of our controversy with Germany over the sinking of the *Sussex;* and England was permitted to go on its way unchecked.

The reasons why the issue was not pressed with great vigor were various. The following may be indicated: First, the American ambassador at St. James's, Walter Hines Page, was an Anglophile and he did much, by his private representations to Sir Edward Grey, to remove the sting from most of the American contentions. Second, Colonel House, President Wilson's closest adviser, assured the British ambassador at Washington that the American notes were largely for home consumption. Third, by the middle of 1915, Secretary of State Lansing had become convinced that the Allies were fighting the battle of democracy against Germany. Fourth, late in 1915 and throughout 1916 American trade increasingly was directed into Allied channels. Any attempt to bring Great Britain to book would have met with a storm of protests which might have overwhelmed Wilson in the impending Presidential election. House was frank enough to tell von Bernstorff, the German ambassador at Washington, in May, 1916, that "Wilson no longer had the power to compel England to adhere to the principles of international law."

The upshot was that by the fall of 1916, in the words of Kenworthy and Young, "America had been brought into a benevolent neutrality towards the British blockade that was comparable to that of Portugal at the outbreak of the war, and was more than half-way towards belligerency."

AMERICAN NEUTRALITY: SUBMARINE WARFARE

To retaliate against the British blockade and the placing of food on the contraband list, Germany, on February 4, 1915, issued a proclamation declaring that the waters surrounding Great Britain and Ireland, and including the whole English Channel, constituted a war zone in which all enemy merchant vessels would be destroyed at sight beginning February 18. Neutral vessels entering the zone did so at their own risk. This was the opening of Germany's campaign of submarine warfare.

On February 15 the American government filed a vigorous protest against the German "war-zone proclamation": the German government was told in terms whose solemnity far surpassed any warnings directed to Great Britain that it would be held to "a strict accountability" in the event of the torpedoing of American merchantmen. It was plain that both the State Department and large numbers of Americans refused to regard both blockades as at all comparable: the Germans, through the submarine, menaced directly human lives as well as shipping; the British, only our foreign trade. Events rapidly approached a crisis. On March 28, the British ship *Falaba* was torpedoed in the Irish Sea and an American citizen lost his life. On May 1, the American ship *Gulflight* was torpedoed off the Scilly Islands and two American lives were lost. On May 7, the *Lusitania,* the British Cunard line's crack ship in the North Atlantic passenger trade, was struck by two torpedoes when off the Irish coast and sank in eighteen minutes. More than 1100 passengers and crew went down with the ship, among them 124 American men, women, and children.

The *Lusitania* disaster presaged war: indeed, almost the whole American diplomatic corps in Europe prepared for a war declaration. But President Wilson refused to give heed to the clamor of the war party in America, though in the note he wrote on May 13 he once again issued a solemn warning to Germany. To the German complaint of necessity, he turned a deaf ear.

> This Government [he said] has already taken occasion to inform the Imperial German Government that it cannot admit the adoption of such measures or such a warning of danger to operate as in any degree an abbreviation of the rights of American masters or of American citizens bound on lawful errands as passengers on merchant ships of belligerent nationality; and that it must hold the Imperial German Government to a strict accountability for any infringement of those rights, intentional or incidental.

Wilson's note (which was reluctantly signed by Bryan) made the following points against the use of the submarine: the submarine could not exercise the right of visit and search; it could not take prizes; it could not provide for the crews of destroyed ships; it could not give proper warning to ships before opening fire on them. The note ended by calling on the German government to prevent "the recurrence of anything so obviously subversive of the principles of warfare...."

A second American note followed the first, and a third the second, as Germany refused to give the assurances Wilson sought. On June 7, two days before the second note was dispatched, Bryan resigned. He had, from the beginning, feared that Wilson's firmness might bring on hostilities; with many western and some southern Senators he agreed that Germany had the right to prevent contraband from getting to the Allies, that the carrying of explosives by passenger ships was a wanton act, and that American citizens ought to be warned against traveling on the ships of belligerents.

The third note of July 21 had all the characteristics of an ultimatum. Lansing (who had become Secretary of State on June 23) asked the German government to disavow the sinking of the *Lusitania* and to pay reparation for the lives of the Americans that had been lost. The German offer of safe conducts through the war zone to a certain number of neutral vessels was rejected; and the German Imperial Government was warned that a repetition of acts in contravention of our rights on the high seas would be regarded "as deliberately unfriendly." On August 17, the British steamer *Arabic* outward bound from Liverpool to New York was sunk without warning, with the loss of two American lives. This brought matters to a head and on September 1, von Bernstorff informed Lansing of the abandonment of unrestricted submarine warfare against passenger ships. The pledge was simply worded, as follows: "Liners will not be sunk by our submarines without warning and without safety of the lives of non-combatants, provided that the liners do not try to escape or offer resistance."

The whole diplomatic controversy was not without its repercussions in Congress. Many Senators and Congressmen agreed that the British practice of arming merchantmen justified German submarines in releasing their torpedoes without any warning: it was appreciated that the frailty of the U-boats exposed them to quick destruction if they emerged to challenge ships on the high seas. The State Department conceded the reasonableness of the claim when it sought to open negotiations with the ambassadors of the Allies for a quid pro quo exchange between the belligerents: the Allies to stop arming merchant vessels, German submarines to give warning of attack. Accepting the soundness of the same principle, Representative McLemore and Senator Gore introduced in both houses of Congress resolutions whose purpose was to warn American citizens to refrain from traveling on armed merchantmen. The Gore resolution had the strong support of Senator Stone, Chairman of the Committee on Foreign Affairs, and for the first time it appeared as if the Wilson leadership might be successfully contested. But after a hard-fought struggle, Wilson won, and in February, 1916, the McLemore resolution was defeated while the Gore resolution was never submitted to a vote. The President still had his hands untied.

In May, 1916, Germany met her second diplomatic defeat as the result of American pressure, and this time the effectiveness of the submarine was almost completely destroyed. This second German *démarche* followed the torpedoing, on March 24, 1916, of the French Channel steamer *Sussex*, which, it was quickly established, was unarmed and was attacked without warning. Though the ship did not sink, some eighty passengers were killed or injured, of whom three were Americans. On April 19, Wilson resorted to the unusual procedure of summoning both houses of Congress in joint session and reading to them his ultimatum to Germany. Lansing and House had advised the severance of relations with Germany; and it is not unlikely that Wilson heeded them, for this action, and the subsequent instructions to American diplomatic representatives in Europe, indicated a preparation for war. The Wilson note, after declaring that submarine attacks on shipping were "utterly incompatible with the principles of humanity, the long-established and incontrovertible rights of neutrals, and the sacred immunities of non-combatants," closed with this ominous statement:

> Unless the Imperial Government should now immediately declare and effect an abandonment of its present methods of submarine warfare against passenger and freight-carrying vessels, the Government of the United States can have no choice but to sever diplomatic relations with the German Empire altogether. This action the Government of the United States contemplates with the greatest reluctance but feels constrained to take in behalf of humanity and the rights of neutral nations.

On April 25, Page (at London) was asked to ascertain what nation Great Britain wished chosen to handle the British interests in Berlin; on April 28, Gerard (at Berlin) was told Spain had been decided on as the American spokesman at the German capital. This was, in the language of diplomacy, an unmistakable hint that the breaking off of relations with Germany was contemplated. On May 4, the German government capitulated. In its note of that date, it acceded to the American demand and promised that:

> In accordance with the general principles of visit and search and destruction of merchant vessels recognized by international law, such vessels, both within and without the area declared as naval war zone, shall not be sunk without warning and without saving human lives, unless these ships attempt to escape or offer resistance.

The German government did not shut off all avenues of escape, however. It called upon the United States to demand a similar observance of the dictates of humanity, on the part of Great Britain; a failure on the part of the United States to effect such ends, said the German Foreign Office, would produce a new situation "in which it must reserve to itself complete liberty of decision." This last reservation the State Department rejected in a second note; but here the matter ended, and the threat of war was laid at rest for another nine months.

· 26 ·

The United States Enters World War I

INTERLUDE: THE ELECTION OF 1916

NEVER had a President in American history met with more signal triumphs than had fallen to Wilson's lot in the three years 1913 to 1916: he had been responsible for the most significant body of domestic legislation in a generation; he had acted with restraint, when sorely tried, in the case of Mexico; he had compelled the proud Imperial German Government to bend the knee. It was no wonder that Republican chieftains, laying their plans for the Presidential election of 1916, regarded their chances in that contest with considerable misgiving.

The Republican convention met at Chicago on June 7, with the conservatives in control. With the Progressives, who were also meeting in Chicago, no common basis for action could be discovered with the result that both groups continued to go their separate ways. On the third ballot, Supreme Court Justice Hughes was nominated; Fairbanks of Indiana was named his running mate. The Republican platform was as uninspiring as had been the convention proceedings. It devoted great attention to foreign affairs; charged Wilson with having been criminally neglectful of American interests in Mexico and elsewhere; pledged itself to restore order in the turbulent land to the south; made much of the need for military and naval preparedness; gave its approval to the Monroe Doctrine; and attacked the Underwood Tariff Act and the Democratic merchant marine program.

The Progressives nominated Roosevelt again and chose John M. Parker of Louisiana as his running mate. Their platform was an echo of the 1912 document (now very much outmoded because of the successful Democratic legislation); and they joined with the Republicans in attacking Wilson's foreign policy and in demanding military and naval preparedness. The Progressives, despite their high hopes of four years earlier, were doomed to a quick death—at the hands of their own champion. Roosevelt, writing to the Progressive National Committee, declined the nomination, on the score that the defeat of Wilson transcended all other considerations, and he informed his followers that Hughes was worthy of the support of all "progressive-minded and patriotic men." Thus abandoned, most Progressives gave up the struggle, except for the valiant Vice-Presidential candidate who insisted upon making the canvass alone.

The Democratic convention, meeting at St. Louis on June 14, was a personal triumph for its leader. Wilson was nominated by acclamation and Marshall was again chosen for second place on the ticket. The platform pointed with pride to the achievements of the two Democratic Congresses, acclaimed the Wilson policy of nonintervention in Mexico, and praised Wilson's handling of the many European problems that had confronted him. The Socialists held no convention but named their candidates, Allan L. Benson of New York and George R. Kirkpatrick of New Jersey, and adopted their platform on the basis of a mail referendum.

The conduct of the Republican campaign left much to be desired, and it was apparent that its managers were at a loss for an issue. Wilson was attacked for his vacillating attitude toward Mexico and Germany; for his giving lip service, only, to the cause of preparedness; and for his surrender to railway labor by countenancing the passage of the Adamson 8-Hour Law in September, 1916. On the other hand, German-Americans and Irish-Americans were sedulously wooed by the Republican National Committee. Hughes's greatest error was his refusal to tender the olive branch to the Progressives, his failure to meet Hiram Johnson when in California definitely contributing toward his defeat in that state. In the closing weeks of the campaign, Hughes, goaded by his opponents into saying what policies he would pursue if elected, began to speak of the protective tariff! The Democrats, in their turn, made a definite effort to gain again the support of the old Bryan country, that is to say, the South, border states, and Far West. For these was evolved the sentiment "He kept us out of the War" and it was used with great success, by Bryan particularly. But Wilson had an opportunity to show his patriotism, too, and he did not throw it away. Overtures were made to Wilson by alleged leaders of the Irish in America, who proffered their support. Wilson, no doubt remembering the silence of the unfortunate Blaine in the "Rum, Romanism, and Rebellion" incident, quickly replied: "I neither seek the favor nor fear the displeasure of that small alien element among us which puts loyalty to any foreign power before loyalty to the United States." Further, the Democrats were at great pains to cultivate the labor vote, on the strength of their passage of the Clayton and Adamson Laws, and the farmer vote, on the basis of the important agrarian legislation that had been enacted.

After some uncertainty, due to the closeness of the results in a number of the trans-Mississippi states, it was seen that Wilson had been re-elected.

In the industrial East and Middle West, he had carried only New Hampshire and Ohio. But the whole South had voted for him, as had also the states of Maryland, Kentucky, Missouri, and Oklahoma. He also won every state west of the Mississippi with the exceptions of South Dakota and Oregon. California he gained by 4000 votes; Minnesota he lost by a bare few hundred. The division in the electoral college was 277 for Wilson and 254 for Hughes; the popular vote was Wilson 9,129,600, Hughes 8,538,-200, Benson (the Socialist) 585,000. Not only did Wilson get 3,000,000 more votes than he had received in 1912, but he also captured a majority of the counties in the country, winning 2023 out of 3020. The Democrats again triumphed in the Congressional elections and organized both houses of the Sixty-fifth Congress.

WHY WE FOUGHT: THE BACKGROUND

From the very day of the war's inception a fine web was being prepared for the entanglement of the United States. Its strands were made up of deceit, the natural sympathies of men, awkward blundering, economic interest, and the growth of a nationalistic sentiment. Before the year 1916 had run its course it was plain that the United States was to be involved sooner or later. Germany fought a losing battle for the maintenance of American neutrality almost from the beginning. We must examine in some detail the influences of propaganda, economic interest, and patriotism in bringing the United States into the war.

First in the list of these factors was the subtle, unobtrusive, and remarkably effective British propaganda. It did not depend upon Anglophilism alone, though the British were not unaware of the many true friends they had in this country. In the preceding two decades the English upper classes had labored mightily to create a feeling of good will in the breasts of Americans who mattered—and they had succeeded. By financial, social, literary, and sentimental ties they had bound the "society" of the eastern seaboard, men of letters, editors, international lawyers, occasional diplomats, and professors to their cause, and in these they now found an impressive and, what is more important, highly articulate group of champions. In addition, there was a smoothly geared British publicity machinery which functioned night and day to pump its flow of argument and propaganda into American minds. Sir Gilbert Parker, the Canadian novelist, who was in charge of it, lifted the veil from its secret operations in March, 1918. Said he:

Among other things, we supplied 360 newspapers in the smaller cities of the United States with an English newspaper, which gave a weekly review and comment of the affairs of the war. We established connection with the man of the street through cinema pictures of the army and navy, as well as through interviews, articles, pamphlets, etc.; and by letters in reply to individual American critics, which were printed in the chief newspaper of the state in which they lived, and were copied in newspapers of other and neighboring states. We advised and stimulated many people to write articles; we utilized the friendly services and assistance of confidential friends; we had reports from important Americans constantly, and established association, by personal correspondence, with influential and eminent people of every profession in the United States, beginning with university and college presidents, professors and scientific men, and running through all the ranges of the population. We asked our friends and correspondents to arrange for speeches, debates, and lectures by American citizens, but we did not encourage Britishers to go to America and preach the doctrine of entrance into the war. Besides an immense private correspondence with individuals, we had our documents and literature sent to great numbers of public libraries, Y.M.C.A. societies, universities, colleges, historical societies, clubs, and newspapers.[1]

Other reasons making for the successful presentation of the British side before the American public were the complete control of the cables and, hence, the censorship of all messages that went over them; the comparative ease with which the British were able to decipher the German wireless codes and thus keep in touch with German secret moves in this country; and the readiness with which Americans, their palates trained to a diet of horrors since the inception of the yellow press, were willing to accept the tales of German atrocities.

The French propagandists plucked other strings: they touched on Gallo-American friendship since the Revolution; they pointed to France's cultural contributions to the world, and reminded Americans that Paris was the home of all the fine arts; and they adverted again and again to the Satanism of their foes. The French called them *Boches,* and such the Germans remained until after the war was over.

By contrast, the German propagandists in America were stupid and inept: they even committed the unpardonable sin of being caught red-handed. They bought the *New York Mail,* a daily, and their ownership was quickly established. They spent large sums financing American peace societies, and their hand in them was at once apparent. They busied themselves agitating against the American manufacture of munitions for the Allies, so that when strikes and labor disorders broke out in these factories many Americans believed that these had been fomented by German agents. Certain deeds of violence or sabotage took place, though in some cases these were the work of German sympathizers and not of German governmental agents; plots to destroy munition factories and bridges and to place bombs in ships carrying supplies to England and France were exposed, and it was generally held that Germans had a hand in them. Finally, the case for Germany was irretrievably lost when President Wilson demanded the recall of the Austrian Ambassador Dumba (September, 1915)

[1] From *Harper's Magazine,* March, 1918, by permission.

and of the German attachés von Papen and Boy-Ed (December, 1915). All were linked with plots to damage munition plants working for the Allies.[2]

To sentiment one must add economic interest. As the war progressed, Americans increasingly began to have an economic stake in an Allied victory. The first year of the war seriously disturbed the American economic structure. The closing of important European markets to American staples and the haste with which the English and French threw American securities on the New York money market in order to establish credits for war purchases could not but produce their effects. The New York Stock Exchange was compelled to close its doors on July 31, 1914, and did not open them again for unrestricted trading until April 1, 1915. But by the middle of 1915 the clouds were beginning to lift, and before the year was over the United States was enjoying a period of unprecedented prosperity. Only as 1916 closed did the danger signals once more begin to show in the skies, when it became apparent that the English and French had reached the end, as far as American credits were concerned. American prosperity was occasioned by the following three factors: 1. Americans began to supply Allied needs, particularly munitions, raw materials, and foodstuffs; 2. Americans were reaching into new markets, in various parts of the world, heretofore served by European nationals; 3. Americans were selling to European neutrals who, heretofore, had been buying almost exclusively from Russians, Germans, French, and British. We are concerned here, more particularly, with American aid afforded to the Allies.

In the middle of 1915 the house of J. P. Morgan and Company became the central purchasing agent for the Allies, and by the process the greatest single financial agency in the country was united with the destinies of Great Britain, France, and Russia. Morgan bought not munitions alone but all raw materials and foodstuffs necessary for the conduct of the war and the maintenance of the industrial establishments. Before the summer was over these purchasing agents were spending in America in the neighborhood of $10,000,000 a day. The increase in the American munition trade reveals the size of the economic interest we were beginning to have in the successful outcome of the war (from the Allied point of view). In 1914, the American export of munitions was worth $40,000,000; in 1915, this had grown to $330,000,000; in 1916, to $1,290,000,000. The export trade in explosives alone rose from $6,272,000 in 1914 to $467,082,000 in 1916.

[2] Americans, generally, believed that the Black Tom fire in New York Harbor on July 29, 1916, and the Kingsland (N.J.) fire on January 11, 1917, both at munition plants, were the work of German incendiaries. In October, 1930, however, a Mixed Claims Commission disallowed the claim of the American government for $40 million damages, finding no evidence, in either case, to support the American contention that the explosions had been brought about by German agents. This decision was arrived at unanimously.

Great Britain and France shipped gold to the United States and returned American securities; but this was not enough. To help finance these extraordinary purchases recourse to borrowing was necessary. The first great Anglo-French loan, handled by Morgan, was floated in the United States in October, 1915. It was for $500,000,000, was to run for five years, was sold at 98 and brought 5 per cent. The only security pledged was the word of the two governments. In 1916, four additional loans were raised, totaling $504,500,000. Thus, in a little more than fifteen months, the Allied governments sold $1,000,000,000 worth of their bonds to American investors.[8] By the end of 1916, however, the situation had become almost desperate: it was apparent that the American market was no longer able to absorb British and French government securities. Finally, in November of that year came an ominous message from the Federal Reserve Board: too much, it said, of the liquid funds of American banks, which ought to be available for short-term credits for domestic needs, was being tied up in the treasury bills of the Allied governments. This warning was issued on November 27, 1916. A significant paragraph ran:

> While the loans [sale of treasury notes] may be short in form and severally may be collected at maturity, the object of the borrower must be to attempt to renew them collectively, with the result that the aggregate amount placed here will remain until such time as it may be advantageously converted into a long-term obligation. It would therefore seem as a consequence that liquid funds of our banks, which should be available for short-term credits to our merchants, manufacturers, and farmers, would be exposed to the danger of being absorbed for other purposes to disproportionate degree, especially in view of the fact that many of our banks and trust companies are already carrying substantial amounts of foreign obligations and of acceptances which they are under agreement to renew. The Board deems it its duty, therefore, to caution the member banks that it does not regard it in the interest of the country at this time that they invest in foreign treasury bills of this character.

The British and French governments at once took alarm at this threat to their whole credit structure and ordered Morgan to withhold from sale the thirty-, sixty-, and ninety-day bills that he had already advertised.

On the other hand, it is to be noted that Germany made few purchases in this country (because of the blockade) and that not more than $20,000,000 in German securities were sold here. The contrasting situations are illuminating.

---

[8] For all other loans, following the first, the Allies pledged as securities American railroad and industrial bonds. These operations were either Anglo-French joint loans or separate French and British issues. In addition, the Russians sold $75,000,000 worth of certificates and treasury bonds in 1916; the British sold $250,000,000 worth of gold notes in January, 1917; the French sold $100,000,000 worth of gold notes in April, 1917; and the Italians sold $45,000,000 worth of lire notes in March, 1917. Altogether, therefore, Americans had financed the Allied cause to the extent of $1,500,000,000 before our entry into the war.

It was natural that, as the war dragged on, patriotic Americans should join in insistent demand that the United States arm itself for such emergencies as might arise. It was commonly declared that German national policy, directed by an ambitious war lord and sustained by a proud Junker class, was essentially militaristic and hostile to democratic institutions everywhere; more and more Americans began to believe that the United States was destined to be the next victim of German militarism in the event of an Allied defeat on the European battlefields. Hence, societies sprang up among us to clamor for the largest navy in the world, the increase of the American military establishment to half a million men, the creation of a reserve army, even compulsory military service. Individuals, too, raised their voices to swell the chorus, of whom not the least were Theodore Roosevelt, Henry Cabot Lodge, General Leonard Wood, Representative A. P. Gardner, and Secretary of War Garrison. For a time, Wilson resisted the pressure of the preparedness advocates; before the winter of 1916 to 1917 was over, however, he had yielded. He signed the National Defense Act of June, 1916, for the expansion of the Army; the Army Appropriation Act of August, 1916, which called for the setting up of a Council of National Defense; and a naval act authorizing the expenditure of one-half billion dollars over three years. The United States was being armed; and the creation of a war psychology was not the least of the influences among the factors leading to the declaration of hostilities against Germany.

WHY WE FOUGHT: DIRECT CAUSES

War between the United States and Germany, as we have seen, had threatened in 1916, following the torpedoing of the *Sussex*. Yet, apparently, President Wilson had not entirely given up hope that American participation might be averted and the war brought to a close by a peace of negotiation. In 1916 and early 1917, Wilson made three efforts to assume the part of mediator, the first secret, the second and third public. He failed all three times, and the result of his last unsuccessful attempt was the reopening by the Germans of unrestricted submarine warfare.

In January, 1916, the President dispatched his close friend Colonel Edward M. House to Europe with a formula which, he hoped, would appeal particularly to Allied statesmen. But the Wilson proposal was never submitted formally to the British cabinet and after cooling his heels in London and Paris for nearly six months, House was compelled to return to Washington and report that the war was to go on. On December 18, 1916, the President released a circular telegram to the belligerents, in which he called upon them to announce their war aims. The Germans replied promptly and offered to accept a peace by negotiation; the Allies did not answer for almost a month, and then declared that a peace would be unacceptable unless founded on "equitable compensation and indemnities for damages," the restoration of Belgium and Serbia, the evacuation of Northern France, Russia, and Rumania, and the dismemberment of the Austro-Hungarian monarchy. On January 22, 1917, Wilson appeared before the Senate to make a final plea for the ending of the war. What, said he, were the elements required of a just and lasting peace? It could be achieved only by the willingness of the peoples of the world to band together for its maintenance: Mere agreements may not make peace secure. It will be absolutely necessary that a force be created as a guarantor of the permanency of the settlement so much greater than the force of any nation now engaged or any alliance hitherto formed or projected that no nation, no probable combination of nations, could face or withstand it. And to terminate hostilities, a recognition of the following principles was necessary: 1. "... that it must be a peace without victory"; 2. that the principle of nationalism, even of small peoples, must be recognized; 3. that "every great people now struggling towards a full development of its resources and of its powers should be assured a direct outlet to the great highways of the sea"; 4. that "the paths of the sea must alike in law and in fact be free"; 5. that armaments, both naval and military, be limited; 6. that "entangling alliances" be abandoned.

Wilson's efforts to bring hostilities to a close by, in effect, appealing over the heads of statesmen to "forward-looking men and women everywhere" ended in failure. The Allies made no official rejoinder; the German reply, on January 31, 1917, was to announce that on the next day there would begin again the campaign of unrestricted submarine warfare against all ships, passenger and merchant, neutral and belligerent, entering the war zone thrown around the British Isles, the French coast, and around Italy in the eastern Mediterranean. A single American passenger ship, in each direction, might cross the Atlantic each week if it were plainly marked and carried no contraband. The official German justification for the proclamation was the charge that the American failure to obtain the relaxation of the British illegal blockade released Germany from the promise made after the *Sussex* torpedoing.

On February 3, President Wilson announced to Congress that diplomatic relations between the United States and Germany had been severed. On February 26, to maintain the state of "armed neutrality" upon which he had decided, the President asked Congress to enact legislation for the purpose of arming American merchant vessels. The House promptly passed the Armed Ships Act, appropriating $100 million to purchase guns for American ships; but when the measure was talked to death in the Senate Wilson took matters into his own hands and on March 12 issued a Presidential order authorizing the arming of merchantmen.

A number of events now took place to throw America into the arms of the Allies. The first of these was the release, by the State Department on March 1, of a message sent by Alfred Zimmermann, the German Foreign Secretary, to the German minister in Mexico in which orders were given to enlist Mexican support on the side of Germany. The terms of the Zimmermann letter were damning to the cause of Germany. Mexico was to be offered an alliance with Germany, financial assistance, and restoration of the "lost territory" of Texas, New Mexico, and Arizona! The Mexican President was to be asked, on his own initiative, to invite Japan to abandon the Allies and make common cause with Mexico and Germany against the United States. All this, of course, in the event that the United States should declare war following the proclamation announcing the renewal of the submarine blockade.

The second event to make American participation easier was the outbreak of the first Russian Revolution in March. American liberals, in debating our entry into the war in defense of the principles of democracy, could never refrain from casting an uneasy eye toward Russia. There, in the land of the czars, ruled an absolute and cruel despotism where representative government was denied, economic slavery existed, and subject peoples were exploited by a foreign officialdom. The success of the Russian parliamentary coup d'état miraculously cleared the air. Liberals in the United States breathed easier and one of them (Walter Weyl) could say enthusiastically: "The final impelling reason for this declaration of war was the Russian Revolution which cast the influence of a great nation in favor of true democratization of the war and against merely imperialistic use of victory."

The third event was the overt act that led to the war declaration. On March 16 and 17, three American ships, homeward bound, were attacked without warning by German submarines and sunk. On March 21, President Wilson called the Sixty-fifth Congress to meet in special session on April 2. On the evening of that day, before the joint session, and in the presence of the whole Supreme Court bench, the Cabinet and the diplomatic corps, Wilson asked Congress to recognize the existence of a state of war between the United States and the Imperial German government. The German government had repudiated its pledges to spare unarmed passenger and merchant ships; it had turned its weapons against American ships and had sunk them on sight; it had filled our land with plotters and had even sought to enlist Mexican support against us. But our motives for entry transcended these *casus belli*. Said the President:

Our object now, as then, is to vindicate the principles of peace and justice in the life of the world as against selfish and autocratic power and to set up amongst the really free and self-governed peoples of the world such a concert of purpose and of action as will henceforth insure the observance of those principles. Neutrality is no longer feasible or desirable where the peace of the world is involved and the freedom of its people, and the menace to that peace and freedom lies in the existence of autocratic governments backed by organized force which is controlled wholly by their will, not by the will of their people.

We were entering into battle to fight for "the ultimate peace of the world and for the liberation of its peoples, the German people included: for the right of nations great and small and the privilege of men everywhere to choose their way of life and of obedience. The world must be made safe for democracy."

On April 4, the Senate passed a war resolution by a vote of 82 to 6; two days later, the House did similarly by a vote of 373 to 50. War was declared on Germany, April 6; diplomatic relations with Austria-Hungary were terminated, April 8, and war was declared, December 7. Diplomatic relations were broken with Turkey on April 20, though war was never formally declared against the Porte or Germany's other ally, Bulgaria.

In any recital, no matter how brief, of the reasons why we fought, it would be a grave oversight to disregard the hopes and aspirations of Wilson himself. It is quite probable that he desired to play a role of the first importance in the writing of the peace; there must have been on his part, too, a growing realization, as his efforts at mediation failed, that America (and himself) would have no place at the peace table and in the writing of a permanent peace unless the United States took part in the war as a belligerent. The testimony of Jane Addams, on this point, admits of no conflicting interpretations. She recorded, in this fashion, a conversation with the President, which took place some time before the delivery of the war message: [4]

> The President's mood was stern and far from the scholar's detachment as he told us of recent disclosures of German machinations in Mexico and announced the impossibility of any form of adjudication. He still spoke to us, however, as to fellow pacifists to whom he was forced to confess that war had become inevitable. He used one phrase which I had heard Colonel House use so recently that it still stuck firmly in my memory. The phrase was to the effect that, as head of a nation participating in the War, the President of the United States would have a seat at the peace table, but that if he remained the representative of a neutral country he could at best only "call through a crack in the door." The appeal he made was, in substance, that the foreign policies which we so extravagantly admired could have a chance if he were there to push and to defend them, but not otherwise.

MOBILIZING MEN AND MONEY

War had been declared on April 6, 1917. Before two months were past, it was plain to both allies and enemy that America meant to bend every effort to bring the conflict to a successful and speedy close. We applied ourselves to the task of supplying our allies with the materials they so badly

[4] In her *Peace and Bread in Time of War*. (Reprinted through the permission of The Macmillan Company.)

needed; we lent money with a generous hand; and we immediately began the mobilizing of a great army for service on the Western front. Before the end of May, Congress had passed, and the President had signed, a War Bond bill authorizing the raising of the huge sum of $7 billion, Army and Navy bills providing for the expenditure of $4 billion, and the Selective Service Act whose purpose was to summon, on a conscription basis, the young and physically fit manhood of America to the defense of the nation.

The Selective Service Act, providing for universal conscription, was passed by Congress on May 18, 1917.[5] So smoothly did the machinery of the War Department run that 9,586,508 young men between the ages of 21 and 30 inclusive made their way on June 5 to their local draft boards to register for service. On June 5, 1918, another 1,000,000 men—those who had come of age within the year—were added. A third registration in the fall of 1918 called out all the men between the ages of 18 and 45 inclusive and thus another 13,228,762 persons were enrolled. The total number of registered persons, in continental United States and its dependencies and territories, was 24,234,021. Of these 2,810,296 were inducted into the service. If we count in also the 750,000 men who were members of the Regular Army and the National Guard, we have a grand total of some 3,500,000 Americans who saw service under the colors. Training the inducted men followed hard on the heels of registration. Before 1917 was over there had sprung up 32 cantonments which were housing, feeding, and drilling more than 1,800,000 potential soldiers. Sixteen of these cantonments were designed for the National Army (draft) and were located almost entirely in the northern tier of states; another 16 were for the National Guard (state militias), and these were located in the South, largely because they could be equipped at less cost. The National Army cantonments were cities, no less. Each was designed to take care of the needs of 40,000 men; each cost $8 million to build and equip.

In all, 55 American divisions were organized, each consisting of 1000 officers and 27,000 men. Twenty of these divisions were made up from the Regular Army (the 1st through the 20th); 17 were made up from the National Guard (the 26th through the 42nd); 18 were made up from the National Army (the 76th through the 93rd). Forty-two divisions were transported to the battle area, of which 8 were Regular Army units, 17 National Guard units and 17 National Army units. It must thus be apparent that the war was largely fought by Americans who, before April, 1917, had never smelled smokeless powder, heard the rattle of a machine gun, or witnessed the havoc that could be created by a trench mortar.

The government not only applied itself to the task of equipping and training its citizenry for war, but early gave thought to the problems that

[5] Not without resistance, however. In the Senate, the vote was 65 to 8; in the House, 199 to 178.

at once arose out of the fact that so many of the producers and breadwinners of the nation had left their families to enroll or be inducted into service. On October 6, 1917, the Bureau of War Risk Insurance, of the Treasury Department, which had been created in 1914 to write marine insurance, was authorized to amplify its activities along the following three lines: it was to make provision for the support of the dependent families of the men under arms; it was to evolve a program of compensation grants for soldiers and sailors who should be killed or suffer disabilities arising out of war service; it was to offer to officers and enlisted and drafted men insurance policies against death or total disability. The War Risk Insurance Bureau began to sell to all men in the service insurance policies from $1000 to $10,000, with premiums to be paid by deductions from salary allowances. These policies covered death and total disability and up to October 31, 1918, the number of applications was more than 4,000,000 and the total insurance written was $35,762,000,000. Despite these liberal provisions, and before ten years were over, veterans were agitating for the passage by Congress of a service pension act. And national legislators were not able to deny their claims, as we shall see.

The war was largely financed from borrowings, though the contributions from taxes, both absolutely and proportionately, were greater in this case than they had been in any previous conflict. A total of five popular loans was floated during the period June, 1917 to April, 1919, and these brought in upwards of $21,000,000,000. The total cost of the war to the country, from April 7, 1917, to the completion of demobilization in October, 1919, was $32,832,000,000. In other words, the ratio of borrowings to taxes was roughly two to one. Of the $32,000,000,000 expended for the prosecution of the war, only two-thirds went to meet the costs incurred for the maintenance of our own military and naval establishments; the other one-third consisted of advances made to our allies after our entry. In exact figures, we turned over to some twenty different countries that were associated with us $10,338,000,000, which was used to pay for the purchase of war supplies, for relief credits, and for foodstuffs bought from the United States Grain Corporation.

The first war loan (known as the First Liberty Loan) of $2,000,000,000 was offered in June, 1917. It was to run for thirty years, bear an interest rate of 3½ per cent and, to make it particularly attractive, was to be exempted from all federal, state, and local taxation. The Second Liberty Loan for $3,800,000,000 was offered in November, 1917. The interest rate was raised to 4 per cent but the ready acceptance of its predecessor was instrumental in causing Congress to make these bonds exempt only from the basic income tax. The Third Liberty Loan for $4,200,000,000 at 4¼ per cent was offered in May, 1918. The Fourth Liberty Loan at 4¼ per cent for $6,000,000,000 was offered in October, 1918. The final loan, known as the Victory Loan, and bearing an interest rate of 4¾ per cent, was sold in April, 1919, after the war was over. This offering was for $4,500,000,000.

The Treasury Department, at the same time, was given new sources of revenue to tap. In September, 1916, the basic income tax was raised to 2 per cent; in the War Revenue Act of October, 1917, it was doubled and the graduated surtax was increased to run from 1 to 50 per cent. The income tax on corporation incomes was raised to 6 per cent, and in addition an excess-profits tax was imposed on the business earnings of corporations and individuals. Finally, a whole series of excises was devised to bring revenue from club dues, railroad tickets, theater tickets, Pullman berths, chewing gum, phonograph records, telephone and telegraph messages, and so-called luxury purchases. In the Act of September, 1918, a tax of 12 per cent was placed on all incomes over $4000 while the highest surtax (on incomes in excess of $500,000) was raised to 65 per cent. For the fiscal year ending June, 1918, the income- and excess-profit taxes brought in just a little less than $3,000,000,000.

MOBILIZING INDUSTRY AND LABOR

If every resource was bent to the task of equipping and disciplining a fighting force that could quickly take its place on the combat line beside the battle-weary divisions of France and Great Britain, no less was done in converting American industry into one gigantic war machine. Our soldiers had to be fed, armed, and clothed in war array. We needed ships, tanks, airplanes, motor trucks. Our allies clamored for steel to be manufactured into ordnance, coal to keep their factory fires going, cotton for explosives, and food for their civilian populations. All the claims of a normal activity were placed in the background as the minds and the bodies of men were applied to the satisfaction of these demands. An extraordinary group of agencies made their appearance at Washington, and before the year 1917 was over the whole nation, indeed, was mobilized and laboring in the interests of war. Among the more significant of these agencies we may enumerate the War Industries Board, the Railroad Administration, the Emergency Fleet Corporation, the War Trade Board, the Food Administration, and the Fuel Administration.

The War Industries Board, which was the keystone of the whole wartime arch, grew out of the Council of National Defense, set up in August, 1916. The Council itself was composed of the Secretaries of War, Navy, Interior, Agriculture, Commerce, and Labor. More important, however, was the provision for the creation of an advisory committee which was to co-operate with the Council. When war broke out, an effort was made at control of the manufacture of munitions through a committee of the

Council, but authority was too divided to permit of the smooth functioning of this body. Complete centralization, it was seen, was imperative: in short a dictatorship over industry was actually what was needed. With the creation of the War Industries Board, in July, 1917, the first step was taken toward the achievement of this end. Again a reorganization took place, this time in March, 1918, its purpose being further centralization and a greater war effort. In its final form the War Industries Board emerged as a separate executive agency, directly responsible to the President, with complete powers of life and death over American industry. Its chairman was Bernard M. Baruch and he was the economic dictator of America.

These were the powers of the War Industries Board: It was in complete charge of war purchases not only for all the services of the government but for those of our allies as well. It had the power to reorganize the nation's industrial life by indicating what new sources of supply were to be developed and where conservation of facilities and materials was to take place. It could determine priorities of production and delivery. It could standardize products. It could fix prices. How completely the War Industries Board controlled the industrial processes may be seen from the following partial list of raw materials for which prices were fixed by it: iron and steel products, wool, foreign and domestic hides, aluminum, domestic manganese ores, lumber, sulphuric and nitric acid, copper, hemp, Portland cement.

In December, 1917, with the transportation system of the nation on the verge of a breakdown because of congestion, President Wilson appointed Secretary of the Treasury McAdoo director-general of the newly established Railroad Administration, and for eleven months all the railroads of the country were operated as a single system. A similar control was placed over the inland waterways and the railway express companies with the result that the Railroad Administration had in its charge the destinies of the internal transportation agencies of the nation.

The United States Shipping Board had been created on September 7, 1916, as we have already noted. With the outbreak of hostilities, the Shipping Board was converted into a war bureau. Under the powers vested in it by the Shipping Act, it incorporated the Emergency Fleet Corporation, with a capitalization of $50 million, to "purchase, construct, equip, lease, charter, maintain, and operate merchant ships in the commerce of the United States." William Denman was named the first chairman of the Shipping Board and General G. W. Goethals, the builder of the Panama Canal, was placed at the head of the Emergency Fleet Corporation. As a result of differences that developed between the two over the type of ships to be turned out, their resignations were accepted and another start was made with Edward M. Hurley as chairman of the Board and Charles M.

Schwab as head of the Corporation. Under Schwab the preparation of an American merchant marine went ahead at unprecedented speed. Four great shipyards, with a total of 95 ways, were made ready and an extraordinary program for the construction of steel, wooden, and composite ships was prepared. In all, the Emergency Fleet Corporation contracted for 1692 steel ships with a dead-weight tonnage of 11,605,561 and 518 wooden ships and 18 composite ships. In September, 1918, the Shipping Board had under its jurisdiction more than 10,000,000 tons of shipping, made up of the Emergency Fleet Corporation's ships, ships purchased from Allied and neutral countries, and interned enemy ships which were seized when war was declared on Germany.[6]

To control the American foreign trade, for the purpose of preventing American goods from falling into the hands of the enemy and to assure the obtaining of necessary raw materials entering into our manufactures, the War Trade Board was set up under the chairmanship of Vance C. McCormick. A licensing system was established over exports and imports; a conservation list of commodities, which could not be exported, was prepared; bunkerage was controlled; and particular efforts were made to cripple the enemy's trade throughout the world. This last was effected through the preparation of a black list on which were placed all firms who were suspected of carrying on commercial relations with the enemy. To such companies American exporters were denied the privilege of shipping their wares.

The war agency to touch closest the lives of the American civilian population was the Food Administration, of which Herbert Hoover was placed in charge in May, 1917. With the passage of the Lever Act in August, the Food Administration's powers were augmented to include not only the licensing of food necessities but also the fixing of prices. The Administration, in addition, in order to make conservation effective, preached economy and the use of substitutes and inaugurated a series of "wheatless" and "beefless" days. More important than its popular campaign were the Food Administration's operations in the wheat market. The wheat yield in 1915 had been 1,025,801,000 bushels; in 1916, it had dropped to 636,-318,000; every indication pointed to as small a crop in 1917. Whereas wheat had been selling at $2 a bushel at Chicago in November, 1916, the shortness of the crop forced the price up to $3.45 in May, 1917. On August 8, 1917, Congress, alarmed by the situation, authorized the President to go into the market to buy, transport, and sell wheat and to fix a price which in no case was to be below $2 a bushel. To conduct these operations a Grain Corporation, under the general supervision of the Food Administra-

[6] The German ships represented in all some 500,000 tons. Other ships were purchased or rented from other nations.

tion, was set up. It fixed the price of the 1917 crop at $2.20 and, to stimulate greater plantings for the next year, announced that it would buy the whole 1918 crop at $2.26.

The Grain Corporation operated from September 1, 1917, to May 31, 1920, and financed the 1917, 1918, and 1919 crops. The result was, every patch of ground that could be utilized was put into cultivation. Marginal and submarginal lands were opened up, and farm values soared. The 1917 crop (636,655,000 bushels) was worth $1,278,112,000; the 1919 crop (921,-438,000 bushels) was worth $2,080,056,000.

Deriving his powers from the Lever Act, President Wilson, in August, 1917, created a Fuel Administration and placed in charge of it President Harry A. Garfield of Williams College. The breakdown in the country's transportation facilities, with the resulting fuel shortage, and the unusually severe winter of 1917 to 1918, contributed toward the creation of a crisis to meet which extraordinary measures were necessary. Garfield ordered all manufacturing plants east of the Mississippi to shut down for five days and proclaimed a series of "fuelless" Mondays which lasted until March 25, 1918. The introduction of daylight saving, as a wartime measure, also contributed toward the conservation of coal. As a result of the Administration's activities a large number of submarginal mines were opened up so that the production of bituminous coal increased from 422,704,000 tons in 1914 to 579,386,000 tons in 1918.

Despite the strenuous methods employed by the government to control industry and fix prices with regard to vital raw materials, the cost of living could not be checked from its steady upward climb. However, actual money earnings and real earnings increased, too, so that before the conclusion of the war real wages were higher than they had ever been before in American history. A series of factors contributed to effect this result, of which the more important were: the scarcity of labor because of the operations of the draft; the increasing group-consciousness of the workers, resulting in unionization gains; the turbulence of labor in the lumber camps and metal mines of the Far West, compelling concessions with regard to wage and hour policies; the conciliatory policy of wartime administrations, notably in the case of the railroads; the government's earnest efforts to avert industrial disputes by mediation. The following index figures show the situation during the war years as far as cost of living, actual money earnings of factory workers, and real earnings were concerned. (On the base of 1914 = 100.)

The gains in membership in trade unions affiliated with the American Federation of Labor were significant. In 1913, this membership was 1,996,-004; in 1914, 2,020,671; in 1915, 1,946,347; in 1916, 2,072,702; in 1917, 2,371,-434; in 1918, 2,726,478. That is to say, from 1913 to 1918, there was a gain of 37 per cent.

INDEX NUMBERS, 1914–18

Year	Cost of Living	Actual Money Earnings	Real Earnings
1914	100	100	100
1915	98	106	108
1916	107	133	125
1917	129	149	116
1918	157	192	122

The year 1916 was a particularly turbulent one in labor annals, there occurring in it 3789 strikes and lockouts, which involved 2,275,000 persons. The record for 1917 was worse, if anything. In that year, there were 4450 strikes with 2,349,600 persons participating. But in 1918, due to the erection of machinery for conciliation and the mounting wages on railroads, in shipyards, and in munition plants, a marked reduction in disputes and participants took place. The figures were: 3353 strikes; 1,931,000 strikers. In the Far West, strikes led by the Industrial Workers of the World were accompanied by violence and sabotage, and reprisals visited on the "wobblies" were of the same lawless character. At Bisbee, Arizona, for example, in 1917, a strike called by the I.W.W. in the copper mines was broken by the simple and cruel expedient of carrying off over 1100 strikers and leaving them stranded in the New Mexican desert.

In January, 1918, the President created a Labor Administration (actually, the Secretary of Labor). This Cabinet officer, in turn, set up an advisory council and a War Labor Conference Board, which, as a result of its meetings, formulated the following body of principles as basic to a sound national labor program: the ending of industrial disputes during the period of the war; the recognition of collective bargaining; no discharge of workers for participating in trade-union activities; the maintenance of health and safety factory codes; equal pay for women; the 8-hour day; a living wage for labor, consistent with the maintenance of the worker and his family in health and reasonable comfort; the mobilization of the country's working population under the supervision of the Labor Administration.

The War Labor Conference Board, to realize its first aim, recommended the establishment of a National War Labor Board and on April 8, 1918, this body came into existence by Presidential order. The cochairmen of the Labor Board were former President Taft and Frank P. Walsh. For the purpose of conciliating labor disputes, this agency set up local committees; where these were unsuccessful, it sat itself or it appointed umpires. The work of the Board was supplemented by the activities of the War Labor Policies Board, headed by Felix Frankfurter (set up in May, 1918).

This agency was charged with the function of creating policies affecting wages, hours, and working conditions for labor in war industries.

MOBILIZING OPINION AND MORALE

The government left nothing undone in its efforts to concentrate the nation's energies on the successful prosecution of the war. Even the regimentation of the American mind was provided for. By executive decree, on April 14, 1917, there was created the Committee on Public Information with George Creel, a journalist of the Progressive persuasion, in charge. Then there descended on America, and indeed on the whole world, such a torrent of newsprint and talk as had never been witnessed before. Some 30-odd different pamphlets were printed in many languages, and 75,000,000 copies of these were released on the American public. A half-hundred war conferences were held. There was collected a corps of 75,000 volunteer speakers (known as the Four-Minute Men) who invaded theaters, moving picture houses, churches, and civic and charitable meetings to urge the buying of bonds, a fuller war effort, and the crushing of sedition. The committee furnished the foreign language press of the country the news it was to print and dispatched, every week, a vast amount of boiler plate to 16,000 country newspapers. It maintained missions abroad for the purpose of popularizing America's war aims, and it fitted out reading rooms all over the world. Finally, it published, as a daily, the *Official Bulletin of the United States,* which set the tone for the war news the papers of the United States printed.

The persuasion exercised by Creel's Committee apparently was not enough. Means were devised for visiting with severe penalties the enemies within our midst. The Espionage Act was passed June 15, 1917; the Trading-with-the-Enemy Act was passed October 6, 1917; the Sedition Act was passed May 6, 1918. Section 3 of the last measure covered every conceivable form of dissent, even to derogation of the American governmental processes. Article 4 of the same law gave the Postmaster-General the authority to exclude from the mails any printed or written matter which, in his opinion, was in violation of the Espionage and Sedition Acts. Under the Trading-with-the-Enemy Act, the President was invested with the right of censorship over all communications passing between this country and abroad. He could draw up, too, regulations for the foreign-language press.

These laws were enforced by the Post Office, Department of Justice, and federal district judges with a zeal that was little short of Draconian. In the opinion of Zechariah Chafee, Jr., no judicial proceedings within the history of the English common law were ever so ruthless. Up to June, 1919, federal judges condemned at least 11 persons to prison for 10 years, 6 for

15 years, and 24 for 20 years. Eugene V. Debs, four times candidate for the Presidency on the Socialist ticket, was found guilty of violation of the Espionage Act, after a 4-day trial, and was sentenced to prison for 10 years. In March, 1919, the Supreme Court upheld the verdict.[7] Victor L. Berger, Socialist Congressman, was similarly found guilty and sentenced to a 20-year term. The Post Office, in its turn, denied the use of the mails to the *Masses,* a literary monthly, and to the socialist *Milwaukee Leader,* published by Berger.

Conscientious objectors, that is to say, those persons who refused to bear arms because of religious, political, or rational scruples, received short shrift, as well. In all, there were 3989 such men who registered in the draft but who would not don uniforms. Of these, almost 90 per cent were conscientious objectors on religious grounds, and their cases were disposed of in the following fashion: 1300 were assigned to noncombatant service; 1200 were furloughed to agriculture; 99 were sent to the Friends' Reconstruction Unit in France. The other 450, who refused to obey military orders, for political and rational reasons, were tried by courts-martial and sentenced to federal military prisons. The last conscientious objector was not released until November 23, 1920, which was two years after the signing of the Armistice and fifteen months after England had turned all her political prisoners free.

War was waged, too, against the American property of enemy aliens. By the Trading-with-the-Enemy Act, the President was empowered to appoint an Alien Property Custodian who was to take possession of such property and sell or administer it, as he saw fit. A. Mitchell Palmer was chosen for this post in October, 1917, and before long he was managing some 30,000 trusts worth in the neighborhood of half a billion dollars. When Palmer discovered, or believed he had discovered, that German investments in the United States had been made not for purposes of legitimate business enterprise but in reality to gain possession of important key industries to prevent their utilization by the nation in time of war, then the Alien Property Custodian forgot his judicial trusteeship and assumed the garb of avenger. Valuable units were dispersed or sold at nominal figures to American companies; German trade secrets were revealed to American competitors; patents were confiscated and turned over to American industrialists.

Not the least in America's mighty armory were the inspired utterances of her War President. In luminous sentences, he pictured a new and better world which would be free of autocracies, secret diplomacy, insidious alliances, oppressions, and wrongs of all kinds. Our soldiers and our industrial machinery helped to pound the German Empire into submission;

[7] Debs was released from jail, Dec. 25, 1921, by the order of President Harding, without, however, the restoration of citizenship.

but the resistance of the German people, in considerable measure, gave way before the persuasive eloquence of Woodrow Wilson. In a succession of speeches and messages, in 1917 and 1918, he developed his idea of the just peace that was to close this final war.

In his address at Washington, on June 14, 1917, Wilson called the war a "Peoples' War": it was a "war for freedom and justice and self-government amongst all the nations of the world, a war to make the world safe for the peoples who live upon it and have made it their own, the German people themselves included." In his message to Congress on December 4, 1917, he disclaimed the idea of a vengeful peace: "the cause being just and holy, the settlement must be of like motive and quality." On January 8, 1918, in another message to Congress, he outlined, in his famous Fourteen Points, what was to be the nature of this generous peace. It was to provide:

1. Open covenants of peace, openly arrived at.
2. The freedom of the seas, in peace and war, "except as the seas may be closed in whole or in part by international action."
3. The removal of all economic barriers between all nations.
4. The reduction of national armaments "to the lowest point consistent with domestic safety."
5. An impartial adjustment of colonial claims, in which "the interests of the populations concerned must have equal weight with the equitable claims of the government whose title is to be determined."
6. The evacuation of Russia.
7. The evacuation and restoration of Belgium.
8. The restoration of France and the return to it of Alsace-Lorraine.
9. A readjustment of Italy's frontiers "along clearly recognizable lines of nationality."
10. The recognition of the right to autonomous development of the peoples of Austria-Hungary.
11. A recasting of the Balkan States on ethnic lines with Serbia accorded free access to the sea.
12. Self-determination for the peoples of the Turkish Empire.
13. The establishment of an independent Polish State, with free access to the sea.
14. The formation of a "general association of nations." [8]

In his message to Congress on February 11, 1918, Wilson further clarified the purpose of the war:

There shall be no annexations, no contributions, no punitive damages.... Self-determination is not a mere phrase. It is an imperative principle of action which statesmen will henceforth ignore at their peril. Every territorial settlement involved in this war must be made in the interest and for the benefit of the populations concerned, and not as a part of any mere adjustment or compromise of claims amongst rival States. All well defined national aspirations shall be accorded the utmost satisfaction that can be accorded them without introducing new or perpetuating old elements of discord and antagonism that would be likely in time to break the peace of Europe and consequently of the world.

[8] Abridged from the text, except where quotation marks are used.

And again, on September 27, 1918:

1. The impartial justice meted out must involve no discrimination between those to whom we wish to be just and those to whom we do not wish to be just. . . .
2. No special or separate interest of any single nation or any group of nations can be made the basis of any part of the settlement which is not consistent with the common interest of all.
3. There can be no leagues or alliances or special covenants and understandings within the general and common family of the League of Nations.
4. There can be no special, selfish, economic combinations within the League, and no employment of any form of economic boycott or exclusion, except as the power of economic penalty by exclusion from the markets of the world may be vested in the League of Nations itself as a means of discipline and control.
5. All international agreements and treaties of every kind must be made known in their entirety to the rest of the world. . . .

These addresses moved the world. Their nobility and the complete absence of a spirit of vengefulness in them heartened the German people, in the hour of their defeat, to hope for mercy. With these addresses clearly in mind the German government sued for peace, and when the Armistice was granted, on November 11, 1918, it was upon the understanding that the conference to follow would evolve a peace made up of the essential points outlined by Wilson. As Keynes says of the Wilsonian program, it "had passed on November 5, 1918, beyond the region of idealism and aspiration, and had become part of a solemn contract to which all the Great Powers of the world had put their signature." We shall see below how the President's hopes and dreams for a better world fared at the Peace Conference when it assembled at Versailles in January, 1919.

· 27 ·

The Outcome of the War

ON THE WESTERN FRONT

BEGINNING with June, 1917, and ending with the Armistice, American troops and supplies poured into France in what seemed an endless stream, at first thinly and then in the proportions of a torrent. In the nineteen months of American participation, more than two million men were transported overseas: a half-million were carried across in the first thirteen months, a million and a half in the last six months. The passage across the sea, despite the dread menace of the German submarines, was accomplished with outstanding success; the transports were not sent out singly but in fleets, and each fleet was convoyed by a squadron of American warships. So expert was the handling of these operations that not a single American troopship during the whole nineteen months was lost in the eastward voyage. The commander of convoy operations in the Atlantic was Admiral Albert Gleaves, and to him must go much of the credit for destroying the effectiveness of U-boats.

General John J. Pershing was selected by Secretary of War Baker to become commander-in-chief of the American Expeditionary Force. Pershing sailed to assume his duties at once and was in London on June 9, 1917, and in Paris on June 13, 1917. He maintained his headquarters in Paris for a time and then moved them to Chaumont, lying to the south of Verdun, and within easy reach of that sector of the front which he decided was to be the scene of operations when the American Army was formed. On October 21, 1917, American troops entered the line in the quiet Toul sector, at the extreme southern end of the Western Front. This was the beginning of American participation.

American divisions were engaged in battle for some two hundred days, that is to say, from the middle of April until the end of the contest in November, 1918. In all, they took part in thirteen major operations; however, but two of these were under American command. In the others, the American troops were brigaded with French, British, and Italian armies. While it had been the heart of American military policy that sooner or later an independent American Army should be formed, manned, and directed by Americans and should defend its own portion of the battle front, the

British and French commanders were committed to the view that the Americans could be more useful in the role of reserves and replacements. Yet Pershing was insistent: the maintenance of his soldiers' morale, America's pride in her force, the continued support of the war effort at home—all these were intimately intertwined with the creation of an American Army. In this he had the support of Baker and Wilson, and he was finally triumphant. Foch, the generalissimo of the Allied armies, on August 9, 1918, gave his consent to the formation of the First American Army and the taking over of a section of the line under American command. When American activity on the Western Front was at its height, the American Army held almost a fourth of the whole line, indeed, a greater portion than that defended by the British.

The final German offensive began on March 21 and continued to July 18, 1918, consisting of five different assaults. The successive drives met with considerable success; the British line was broken, and so great was the dislocation of the Allied forces that Pershing had to yield to Foch's request for the diversion of American divisions into the northern and central battle zones. The result was, American troops came into action in the battles of the Aisne (May 27–June 5), Noyon-Montdidier (June 9–15) and Champagne-Marne (July 15–18). In the last of these, some 85,000 American troops took part, and their stand at Château-Thierry prevented the Germans from crossing the Marne and from continuing their march on to Paris. The American troops had shown their mettle under a punishing attack.

Not a single day intervened between the last German offensive and the first Allied counterattack. Beginning on July 18 and not ceasing until the Armistice on November 11 put a cessation to hostilities, the Belgian, British, French, and American armies flung their strength against the German line and pushed it back until it lay beyond the borders of France. Only the Armistice prevented a triumphal march into German territory. There were six of these drives in all, and in each one of them American divisions played a part. The first was the battle of the Aisne-Marne (July 18–August 6), and it flattened out the salient again. A quarter-million American troops fought alongside the French divisions. The second was the British Somme offensive (August 8–November 11); the third was the Oise-Aisne offensive (August 18–November 11); and the fourth was the Ypres-Lys offensive (August 19–November 11). In these three battles another 250,000 Americans advanced against the Hindenburg Line. The fifth and sixth assaults were exclusively the work of the First and Second American armies. The fifth was the battle of St. Mihiel (September 12–16), in which 550,000 American soldiers were engaged; the sixth was the battle of Meuse-Argonne (September 26–November 11) in which the total American effectives, numbering 1,200,000 men, were thrown into the fierce encounter.

On September 16, the first American operation was over with the Americans facing the Germans on the Michel Line (the southern extension of the Hindenburg Line). St. Mihiel had been wiped out, but Pershing's hopes of crossing the German baseline and taking Metz were not realized. The American casualties in the operation totaled 7000 men, while there were captured 16,000 prisoners and 443 enemy guns. The Meuse-Argonne battle was part of the larger movement against the whole German front line, with the British attacking on the Cambrai-St. Quentin sector or the left wing, the Americans on the right, the French in the Champagne or center, and the Belgians and British in Flanders. The American assault, on a front of twenty-four miles, began on September 26 and involved nine divisions (with three in reserve) as against five German divisions. The battle settled down into a fierce struggle between the contending armies with the Americans succeeding, by October 8, in driving the Germans out of the Argonne Forest. The Meuse-Argonne battle lasted forty-seven days, engaged 1,-200,000 American troops and resulted in 120,000 casualties. German prisoners taken totaled 26,000, and captured artillery pieces, 874.

The American Navy's role in the war was less spectacular, though it performed its share with equal competence. Headquarters were maintained at London, with Admiral William S. Sims in charge as commander of the United States naval forces operating in European waters. American naval detachments were maintained at Queenstown, Brest, Gibraltar, in the Mediterranean, and off the Azores, and from these points American men-of-war radiated to carry on warfare against the submarine, to sow mines, to engage in minesweeping, to attack submarine bases, to re-enforce the British blockade, and most important of all, to attend, as convoying ships, the American transport fleet. Before the war was over, there were stationed in European waters some 300 American warships, manned by 75,000 officers and bluejackets.

The American air service moved into action less quickly. In the St. Mihiel and Meuse-Argonne battles, however, the Army was supported by large numbers of American-made planes, mostly of the De Haviland–4 type. In these engagements, American combat aviators brought down 755 enemy planes, while their own losses totaled but 357. The De Haviland was the only plane that had been put into quantity production, and before the end of 1918, 3227 of them had been turned out and 1885 had been sent overseas. An American aeronautical contribution to the war was the manufacture of the 12-cylinder Liberty engine, of which some 5000 were sent to the American Expeditionary Force and 1000 to our allies.

The American casualties were as follows: battle deaths, 48,909; wounded, 237,135; missing in action, 2913; taken prisoner, 4434. In addition, 56,991 died as a result of disease and 6522 died from other causes. The total number of deaths of men under arms, both in American camps at home and in

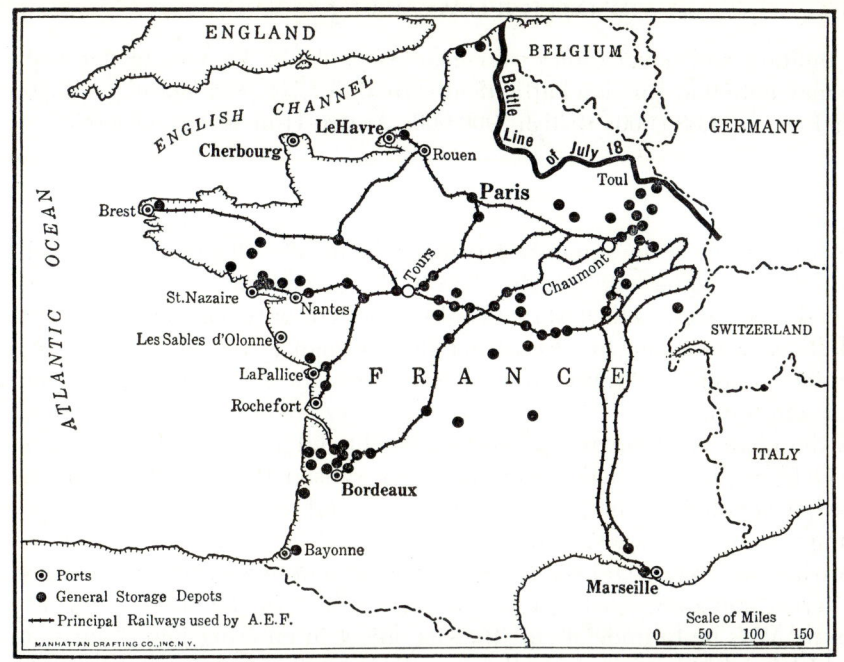

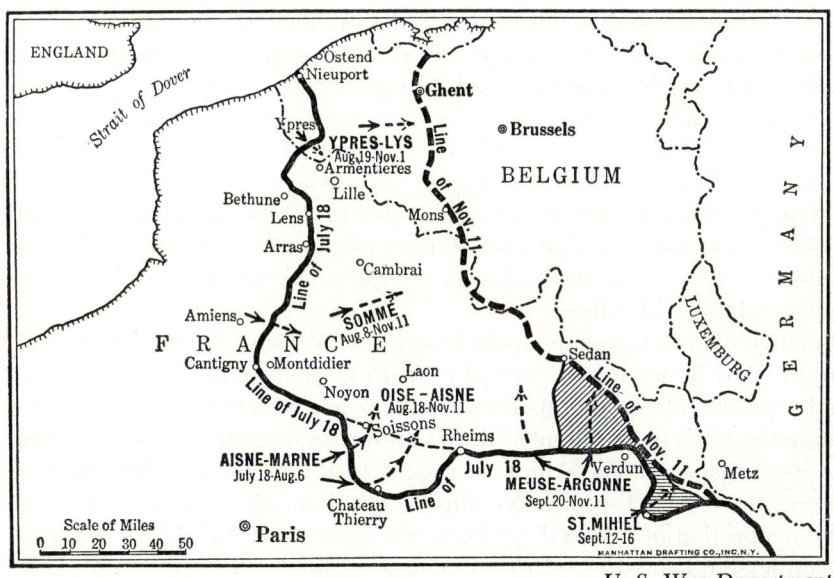

THE AMERICAN ARMY IN FRANCE: WORLD WAR I

the military and naval forces overseas, was 112,422. By way of contrast, one may note that Russian battle deaths totaled 1,700,000; German, 1,600,000; French, 1,385,000; British, 900,000; Austro-Hungarian, 800,000.

ARMISTICE

By the middle of the summer of 1918, as the terrific Allied drive swept all before it, it became increasingly plain to the German high command that the end was in sight. The best that could be hoped for was a merciful peace, and steps were taken to reconstruct the German government along the lines indicated by the Wilson messages and speeches. Socialists were given a voice in the nation's councils, a parliamentary government was installed and the chancellorship was vested in the liberal Prince Max of Baden. On October 5, this government informed Wilson that it agreed to the principles enunciated in the Fourteen Points, and declared it was ready to join in peace negotiations. The President replied October 8 and raised the following questions: Did the German government accept unconditionally the terms laid down in the Fourteen Points and in the subsequent addresses? Was he to understand "that its object in entering into discussion would be only to agree upon the practical details of their application"? Was Germany prepared to evacuate all invaded territory? On October 12, the Germans answered in the affirmative. Two days later, apparently not content, Wilson imposed further conditions: 1. The details of the Armistice were a matter of arrangement for the Allied military chieftains, who were to assure themselves that Germany could not possibly continue the struggle. In other words, Germany had to surrender. 2. Submarine warfare must cease at once. 3. What assurances had he that the new German government was now truly democratic? On October 20, the Germans accepted Points 1 and 2, and with regard to 3 referred the President to their constitution, which made the cabinet responsible to the Reichstag. On October 23, Wilson was satisfied that the German offer had been made sincerely and that it emanated from the German people. He then placed the correspondence before his allies.

On November 5, Germany again heard from Wilson: Marshal Foch had been directed to arrange an armistice with German representatives. The Allied governments were prepared to make peace with the German government on the basis of President Wilson's addresses, except that two reservations were made: 1. The Allies, in regard to the question of freedom of the seas, "reserved to themselves complete freedom." 2. As far as the subject of the restoration of invaded territory was concerned, the Allies declared they understood this to mean that "compensation will be made by Germany for all damage done to the civilian population of the Allies and to their property by the aggression of Germany by land, by sea, and from the air." Meanwhile, late in September, Bulgaria had laid down her arms, and on November 3, Austria had followed suit. On October 27, Ludendorff had resigned; on November 9, the Kaiser abdicated; revolution was on the throne in Kiel, Munich, the Rhine cities, and finally in Berlin. On November 11, at eleven o'clock in the morning, the Armistice terms were accepted by the Germans, and peace once more descended on the world. War-weary peoples looked forward to the formal meetings of the Peace Conference to usher in that new day to which President Wilson had pledged himself in his speeches, and which the Armistice negotiations had specifically confirmed.

THE CONGRESSIONAL ELECTIONS OF 1918

Wilson embarked for Brest, to take part in the proceedings of the Peace Conference, in the first week of December; yet, when he left on his triumphal journey, he went as America's repudiated leader. The dilemma he was in was entirely of his own contriving. Politics had been suspended during the war, Republicans laboring beside Democrats in the common cause. The result was that the contest over the Congressional elections of 1918 proceeded quietly. But Wilson, himself, converted a quiet test of strength into an unusually turbulent partisan canvass. On October 25, with peace already assured as a result of the Armistice negotiations, Wilson broke the eighteen months' calm by issuing an appeal to the American people for the election of a Democratic Congress. The wording of his address left no room for retreat in the event of defeat. A significant sentence read: "If you have approved of my leadership and wish me to continue to be your unembarrassed spokesman in affairs at home and abroad, I earnestly beg that you will express yourself unmistakably to that effect by returning a Democratic majority to both Senate and House of Representatives."

The Republican leaders, for the first time reunited since 1912, rejoined fiercely. Taft, Roosevelt, and Lodge entered the lists: partisanship again was in the saddle. Republicans attacked Wilson's policy of conciliation toward Germany, called for the "unconditional surrender" of the fallen foe, and expressed themselves as distrustful of the proposed League of Nations. When the returns were in, it was apparent that Wilson and the Democracy had been humbled by the electorate. The make-up of the Sixty-sixth Congress was to be as follows: in the Senate, 49 Republicans and 47 Democrats; in the House, 239 Republicans and 194 Democrats. Had Wilson been well advised, he would have taken measures to conciliate the party that was to rule Congress for the rest of his term. But he did not do so, and his slighting of the Senate, when he came to make up his Peace Commission, bore bitter fruit.

THE PEACE CONFERENCE AND THE TREATY OF VERSAILLES

The American Peace Commission consisted of the President, Colonel House, Secretary of State Lansing, General Tasker H. Bliss, and Henry White. The last, who had been ambassador to Italy and France under Roosevelt, was the only Republican in the delegation. The Senate, despite its important role in treaty making, was unrepresented. Accompanying the official American representation was a large party of experts who had been at work since the winter of 1917 to 1918. Wilson arrived in France on Friday, December 13, 1918, and, because the Conference was not ready to meet, and while the Allied leaders temporized to permit the fires of popular enthusiasm to die down, the American President made formal state visits to Paris, London, and Rome. Here, he was met by great outpourings of crowds; everywhere, it was apparent, he was the popular hero. He was cheered, applauded, and blessed; he was hailed as the savior of mankind and the deliverer of the common people from oppression. Yet President Wilson must have known, as he regarded the vast seas of faces that had gathered, in Paris, London, and Rome, to honor him, that the making of a just and lasting peace was to be no easy task. In the first place, there stood the Secret Treaties; in the second place, there was the French desire for revenge; in the third place, there was the difficult question of reparations.

How were the promises embodied in the Secret Treaties, in which England, France, Russia, Italy, Rumania, and Japan had participated, to be reconciled with the noble aspirations set forth in Wilson's addresses? By these treaties, Russia had been promised Constantinople and the Straits; to France had been pledged Alsace-Lorraine, the Saar Valley, and an independent Rhineland; Italy was to get the Trentino, the southern Tyrol, the best ports on the eastern Adriatic, the Dodecanese Islands, and a protectorate over Albania; Great Britain's rewards were to be spheres of influence in Persia and Mesopotamia, a protectorate over Egypt, and the lion's share of the German colonies in Africa and the Pacific. Rumania had been induced to throw in her lot with the Allies with offers of territorial compensation in Transylvania, Bukowina, and the Banat. Japan, for her assistance, was to receive the German colonies in the Northern Pacific and the German interests in the Shantung Peninsula.

It has long been held, by the friends of Wilson, that he was unaware of these designs on German and Austro-Hungarian territory when, in 1918, he publicly released his peace aims to the world. Yet the evidence grows greater that he must have had some knowledge of them both before the Armistice and certainly before the Peace Conference formally opened its sessions. Wilson had either dismissed all the talk of secret understandings among the Allies as a canard; or he had hoped that, backed by the approval of mankind, he could compel Great Britain, France, Italy, and Japan to relinquish their selfish intentions; or he regarded all these preliminary maneuvers as unimportant in the face of the general acceptance of his program for a world league. Whichever conjecture is the true one, the facts remain that he never confronted his allies with the Secret Treaties and that he went to Paris handicapped by their existence.

No less a stumbling block to Wilson's just peace was the French desire for revenge and the destruction of Germany's economic might. In Keynes's phrase, the French leaders wanted a "Carthaginian peace." Germany was to be shorn of her territory outside the European continent; a buffer state was to be created on the Rhine; all hopes for ultimate German restoration to a place of economic power and leadership in world affairs were to be destroyed through seizure of her iron, coal, and transport resources. And as for reparations, it was known that British and French leaders meant to make Germany pay the costs of the war down to the last farthing. Indeed, in the so-called khaki elections of 1918, Lloyd George had been returned triumphantly to power upon his promise to hang the Kaiser and squeeze the Germans "until the pips squeaked."

The first plenary session of the Peace Conference assembled in the Hall of Mirrors of the Palace at Versailles on January 18, 1919; the Versailles Treaty, an extraordinary document containing 440 articles and covering, in the minutest detail, territorial, economic, industrial, and legal matters, was presented to Germany's representatives on May 7; on June 28, Germany signed and the war was formally over, as far as Europe was concerned. It was the Carthaginian peace that France had sought; it gave the British, Italian, Rumanian, and Japanese nations, to a large degree, the territories that had been promised them under the Secret Treaties; and it incorporated Wilson's League of Nations. The American President could solace himself, as he contemplated his handiwork, by the thought that if the peace was not perfect it at least established a permanent machinery in the League of Nations for the eventual redressing of such wrongs as had been committed while war passions were still in the ascendant.

The peace treaty was not written by the Conference; nor was it written by the Council of Ten which began to sit late in January.[1] The essential terms of the Versailles Treaty were the work of Clemenceau for France, Lloyd George for Great Britain, and Wilson for the United States. Wilson was privately closeted with Clemenceau and Lloyd George, away from his fellow commissioners and his great corps of advisers, for long days and weeks on end, where he was submitted to terrific pressure. It must not be supposed that Wilson was entirely unaware of the intentions of the Allied

---

[1] The Council of Ten was made up of two representatives each from the United States, Great Britain, France, Italy, and Japan and met through February and March. Either House or Lansing sat on this Council with Wilson.

statesmen. On three different occasions he openly refused to yield before their more extreme demands and in April, 1919, he went so far as to order the *George Washington,* his transport, to be prepared to take him back to the United States. The result was that he was able to effect salutary compromises. In the case of the Saar Valley, for example, his refusal to countenance outright French possession forced the writing of a new article under which the French were to be permitted to occupy the district up to 1935, when a plebiscite was to be held to determine its final disposition. Again, he refused to give way before Italy's demand for the acquisition of the port of Fiume and went so far as to appeal directly to the Italian people in a statement issued on April 23. The Italian delegation left in a huff, but Wilson gained his point, if only temporarily.[2] In the third instance, he sternly set his face against turning over the German rights in the Shantung Peninsula to Japan. Wilson surrendered to the Japanese only after they had promised that their stay in the Chinese peninsula would be a temporary one. The pledge was kept, for at the Washington Conference of 1921 to 1922 Japan announced that she was prepared to quit Shantung.

With the complex territorial settlements of the Treaty of Versailles we have no concern here, for America emerged from the Conference without the addition of a single inch to her domain. However, certain of the other provisions, notably those relating to reparations and the establishment of the League of Nations, have had direct bearing on American affairs in the decade following the completion of the peace, and at these we may glance briefly.

In Article CCXXXI of the Treaty, Germany was forced to assume the sole guilt for the war's outbreak, and on this basis was compelled to make reparation for the havoc wrought by the war. These losses for which Germany was to pay were not to include the destruction of property merely; to the reparations list were to be added, with the consent of President Wilson, the Belgian war debt and the whole cost of military pensions to be paid out to war veterans and their dependents. The Treaty itself fixed no definite sum but instead set up a Reparations Commission which, by May, 1921, was to receive a total of $5 billion in gold from Germany and at the same time was to set the final amount to be exacted. At the end of April, 1921, Germany was told that she was to pay a total of $33 billion as reparations and that the cost of Belgium's war debt was to constitute a separate payment.

Finally, the League of Nations was made an integral part of the Treaty. This embodied Wilson's faith; this was the instrumentality that was to

---

[2] Fiume was later in the same year captured by the Italian poet D'Annunzio, and in 1924 this seizure was confirmed by a treaty between Mussolini and the Yugoslav government.

secure for mankind that ultimate peace of justice and mercy for which Wilson had led the United States into the war. In submitting the first draft of the covenant to the Peace Conference on January 25, 1919, Wilson had said:

> I can easily conceive that many of these settlements will need subsequent reconsideration, that many of the decisions we make shall need subsequent alteration in some degree.... The settlements may be temporary, but processes must be permanent. The United States regards the project for a League of Nations as the keystone of the whole program. It should be always functioning in watchful attendance upon the interests of the nations.

The constitution of the League (as finally adopted) set up the following agencies:

1. An Assembly, in which all the members of the League were to have equal representation and one vote. The Assembly was to be, almost exclusively, a deliberative body.

2. A Council, which was to have five permanent and four nonpermanent members. The permanent members were to be France, Great Britain, Italy, Japan, and the United States; the nonpermanent members were to be chosen by the Assembly. The Council was to have the powers of drawing up plans for disarmament, of indicating methods to be employed in protecting member states from aggression, of mediating cases involving nations, and of receiving reports from mandatory powers. The decision of the Council was to be unanimous in most matters of which it treated.

3. A permanent Secretariat, which was to be established at Geneva in Switzerland.

4. The Covenant also called for the creation of a Permanent Court of International Justice (more commonly known as the World Court).

To maintain peace and to provide for the adjudication of international disputes, the signers of the Treaties and the members of the League pledged themselves: 1. "to respect and preserve as against external aggression the territorial integrity and existing political independence of all members of the League" (Article x); 2. to recognize it "to be the friendly right of each member of the League to bring to the attention of the Assembly or of the Council any circumstance whatever affecting international relations which threatens to disturb international peace or the good understanding between nations upon which peace depends" (Article xi); 3. to submit to arbitration disputes arising among them, to carry out faithfully awards or decisions made, and to refrain from waging war on a nation complying with such awards or decisions (Article xiii); 4. to submit to the Council such disputes not placed before an arbitral or judicial tribunal (Article xv); 5. to impose economic penalties upon those nations which waged war in disregard of their promises to submit their disputes for arbitration or judicial settlement. The Council, too, might recommend to members of the League the adoption of certain military measures against the aggressor nations (Article xvi).

In addition, the Covenant recognized the validity of the Monroe Doctrine (Article xxi); set up the mandatory system over the former colonies of Germany and her allies, required that the mandatories report annually to the Council, and created a Mandates Commission (Article xxii); provided for the establishment of the International Labor Office; and gave to the League general supervision over slavery and forced labor, and over the traffic in women and children, drugs and arms and munitions (Article xxiii).[3] This was the nature of the peace settlement that President Wilson took back to the United States to submit to the American people.

THE REJECTION OF THE TREATY BY THE SENATE

The President had made a brief visit to the United States in February, to sign the bills of the expiring Sixty-fifth Congress and to explain in person the draft of the League Covenant to the members of the Senate and House Committees on Foreign Affairs. At Washington, despite the pains he took to meet his foes on a friendly footing, he had encountered a deep-seated hostility. Senators were incensed at the slight administered them in the composition of the Peace Commission; western progressives and eastern standpatters alike looked with suspicion upon the coupling of the League of Nations with the Treaty; liberals, who had heard dark tales of the bargaining that was going on over the peace table, refused to swallow Article x with its guarantees of territorial integrity for nations receiving lands to which they were not rightfully entitled. More charitably disposed critics subjected the Covenant to a searching examination and pointed out a number of places where American interests could be better safeguarded. Such persons were Root, Hughes, and Taft, who thought the League Covenant might well recognize the Monroe Doctrine, exclude purely domestic concerns from the sphere of its interests (for example, immigration restriction and tariffs) and permit the members of the League to withdraw at will. To these Wilson gave ear, and the recommendations were incorporated in the final draft of the League constitution.

It was plain, however, that a resolute group in the Senate, which came to be called the "Irreconcilables" and which included on its left wing La Follette, Borah, Johnson, and Poindexter and on its right Brandegee, Knox, Lodge, Moses, Sherman, and McCormick, was determined to have nothing to do with the League or its works. On March 2, when President Wilson was about to re-embark for France, thirty-nine Senators and Senators-elect signed a round robin which declared that the Senate was primarily

[3] The International Labor Office, which was established in Part xiii of the Treaty, was made an autonomous part of the League with its own secretariat, budgets, etc.

interested in making peace and that only after peace was established should the League of Nations become the concern of the negotiators. They threatened to reject any other pact. Wilson accepted the gage of combat, for in a speech made in New York on the night before his departure he said: "When the Treaty comes back, gentlemen on this side will find the Covenant not only in it, but so many threads of the Treaty tied to the Covenant that you cannot dissect the Covenant from the Treaty without destroying the whole vital structure."

Unfortunately, both sides turned out to be right. The League was incorporated in the Treaty—and the Senate did reject the instrument for that reason. The Sixty-sixth Congress had been called in special session in May, 1919; Wilson did not return from France until the first week in July and the Treaty was not formally placed before the Senate until July 10. But copies had been unofficially obtained before that date; the Treaty had been read into the *Congressional Record* and the acrimonious debate had already been begun, when the Presidential message, characterizing the League as the future hope of the world and demanding the Treaty's acceptance without amendment, was received. The enemies of the Treaty and the League did not concentrate their attack. Some objected to the Treaty because it was not severe enough. Some thought it was too harsh. The friends of Ireland condemned the pact for denying the Irish the boon of self-determination when almost every people in Europe had had its nationalistic aspirations recognized. Isolationists, like Borah and Johnson, wanted us to wash our hands of Europe altogether. The foes of the League itself, led by the implacable Lodge, who harassed Wilson as bitterly as the Radical Republicans had harassed President Johnson fifty-odd years before, raised the following specific objections: 1. the United States could not accept the obligations placed upon the members of the League under Article x; 2. the United States ought to reserve to itself the right of withdrawal from the League, after giving due notice; 3. the United States ought to reserve to itself the power to decide what questions came within its domestic jurisdiction; 4. the United States ought to decline to submit for inquiry and arbitration any questions depending upon or arising out of the Monroe Doctrine.

Wilson took his case again to the Senate Committee on Foreign Affairs, but he met with no more success than in his earlier effort in March. He would not accept amendments or reservations, on the score that these would jeopardize the whole work of the Peace Conference. He was adamant, and so were most of the Committee members. The ill feeling which was engendered lost more friends for Wilson than he gained.

While the Senate Committee on Foreign Affairs deliberated and Senators aired their views, the President decided to appeal to the country. On September 4, he set out on a tour of the Middle and Far West, speaking in the more important cities on the way. He had completed the first leg of his journey and was working his way eastward from the Pacific coast when disaster overtook him at Pueblo, Colorado, on September 26. He collapsed as the result of strain and overwork, suffered a paralytic stroke, and for a long time lingered at death's door. Recovery was never complete, and Wilson was never the same man again.

Meanwhile, in September, Lodge, as chairman of the Senate's Foreign Affairs Committee, reported out the Treaty with some 45 amendments to the pact and 4 reservations (those mentioned above) to the League Covenant. The Senate rejected all the amendments; but it did pass, by majority votes, 15 reservations to the Covenant. On November 19, a record vote was taken on the Treaty with reservations and it was defeated by a vote of 41 yeas and 51 nays. An attempt to pass the Treaty without reservations was lost by a vote of 38 yeas to 53 nays. On the same day the special session ended.

Once again the Treaty was considered by the Senate of the Sixty-sixth Congress, this time being the last. It had been reported out on February 10, 1920, with the earlier 15 reservations attached; five weeks of debate had followed; then had come the vote on March 19. For the Treaty with reservations there voted 28 Republicans and 21 Democrats, or 49 in all; against the Treaty there voted 12 Republicans and 23 Democrats, or 35 in all. The necessary two-thirds was lacking and the resolution was lost. The Senate returned the document to the President, stating its inability to ratify. A joint resolution, which simply declared the war with Germany at an end, was passed by both houses, but Wilson vetoed it. A similar resolution was passed in July, 1921, and on the 21st of that month President Harding signed it. The war was over, and America had spurned membership in the League. Later, separate treaties of peace were signed with Germany, Austria, and Hungary, and these the Senate ratified with little delay.

THE COLLAPSE OF WILSONISM

For a year and a half, from September, 1919, to March, 1921, the government of the nation was actually leaderless. Even after recovery, Wilson's physical powers were impaired, and there is no question that for weeks and months he had neither the energy nor the desire for affairs of state. His Cabinet officers wrangled among themselves; a number resigned; Lansing, who tried to carry on, during the illness of his chief, by summoning Cabinet meetings to consider the more important demands placed upon the administration, was peremptorily dismissed on February 13, 1920. There was no administration program for speeding the processes of reconstruction: for easing millions of men again into their peacetime activities; for demobilizing war industries; for conserving the best fruits of the government's great program of wartime regulation; for adjusting the tariff, public finance, labor relations, the needs of agriculture, to the changed and new world in which America lived in 1919 and 1920. Congress passed the Transportation Act, the Merchant Marine Act, and the Federal Water Power Act, all in 1920, but these were the work of the Republican leaders in the Sixty-sixth Congress.

The United States drifted—and, because there were no wiser counsels to prevail, reaction seized the helm. Strikes, of a particularly virulent nature, flared up all over the country, and industry, freed from war-time restrictions, fought back. On the northern Pacific coast, the I.W.W. and the adherents of the "One Big Union" movement attracted followers from the lumber camps, the shipyards, and the docks. There, radical doctrines were met with fire and the sword, and dissent was savagely repressed. A general strike broke out in Seattle, Washington, in February, 1919, and paralyzed the whole life of the community for five days. A strike tied up the steel industry from September, 1919, to January, 1920, and though the public sympathized with the wretched conditions under which the steel workers labored—particularly their poor pay and the 12-hour day—the strikers were defeated. The unrest even touched the municipal firemen and police, and in a number of cities these public servants went on strike. The police strike of Boston, in 1919, attracted especially widespread attention. In all, during 1919, more than four million workers engaged in industrial conflict.

In the war against labor and political agitators, particularly those suspected of communist leanings, the Department of Justice, guided by A. Mitchell Palmer, took the lead. Wholesale arrests were made, some persons held on suspicion had the misfortune to receive brutal treatment, and the Department was not too proud to stoop to the use of *agents provocateurs*. Where it was established that persons believed to have radical leanings were aliens, these were turned over to the Department of Labor for deportation. In December, 1919, 249 foreigners were ordered deported and were taken to Soviet Russia in the ship *Buford*. In many states, criminal syndicalist laws [4] were enforced to clap into jail, for long terms, men and women associated with the I.W.W., the One Big Union agitation, or the Communist party. Even the harmless Socialists were to feel the lash of the reactionary fury. Victor Berger, elected to Congress from a Milwaukee district, was twice denied his seat by his colleagues; five Socialist assemblymen, coming from New York City, were made to surrender their places in the New York Legislature on the ground that Socialists could not loyally enforce the Constitution.

Repression was joined by obscurantism. In the postwar decade, the Ku

[4] See below, page 514.

Klux Klan, which was revived in 1915, grew so rapidly that at the height of its career in 1925 it had from four to five million dues-paying members. To some extent the Klan stemmed from the earlier reconstruction-days society. It grew up in the South; it moved against the Negro; it used secrecy as its chief device; it adopted the same habiliments, ritual, and titles. But in another sense, it was the lineal descendant of the Know-Nothingism of the eighteen fifties. The new Klan was a nativistic movement; its announced slogan was to make the United States safe for white, Protestant, native-born, English-speaking Americans. But not merely was it the foe of Negroes, Catholics, and Jews; it was also up in arms against the advocates of Prohibition repeal, modernism in religion, labor radicals, supporters of easy divorce and birth control, pacifists, and internationalists.

At first the Klan was content to show its strength by displays not unfamiliar to American fraternalism. Mob violence, however, soon followed, and a not inconsiderable number of floggings and even murders in the Black Belt were attributed to its night riders. Beginning with 1922, the Klan's numerical following had become so great, particularly in the South and Middle West, that entry into politics was inevitable. Political demagogues courted the society in Texas, Oklahoma, Louisiana, Kansas, and Indiana, were elected to high office, and proceeded to carry out Klan policies by moving against Catholic parochial schools, school boards using textbooks which set forth the doctrines of evolution, Jewish shopkeepers who violated Sunday-closing ordinances, and the like. In Indiana, the Klan-ridden state administration conducted itself so scandalously that popular hostility compelled a general housecleaning in 1926. From that year on its influence declined, and by 1929 the Klan had sunk into obscurity, to reappear—but not in strength—in a few localities in the Deep South after World War II.

Events such as these heightened the disillusionment which was to be so characteristic of American life in the decade following the end of the war. Wilson had raised men's hopes high and had persuaded millions to believe that a new day was dawning. But the realities of the peace and the terrors of reconstruction saddened and embittered many. There sprang up a contempt for the political processes and for officialdom, and as Americans looked upon the world about them they saw much to sharpen their distaste for statecraft: the corruption of the Harding administration; the open alliance between crime and the police; the frequent wars, particularly during 1918 to 1921, that racked Europe; the continuance of great armaments; the dictatorships in Italy, Hungary, Poland, and Russia; the oppression of subject peoples in the southern Tyrol, Silesia, Rumania, Galicia. The effects were curious. The American electorate did not even trouble to chastise the Republican party for the scandals of 1921 to 1923. Intelligent people listened with indifference to the debate carried on by friends and foes of the League of Nations and the World Court. The literature and thought of the period showed a great preoccupation with personal themes —with religion, morality, aesthetics, psychology—and these, in increasing measure, supplanted the social and economic matters over which men had pondered in the decade before the war.

Woodrow Wilson died in 1924 at the nadir of his reputation. Almost two decades were to go by—with the democratic forces of the world once more fighting for their lives—before men came to realize that his vision had been a sound one. His repute, then, began to grow once more. He had had many shortcomings; his political mistakes were tragic ones; but his belief that world peace and security were impossible without a powerful international organization was demonstrated—unhappily—by the anarchy of the nineteen twenties and thirties. To the forties Woodrow Wilson was one of the major prophets of our times.

Section IX
THE GOLDEN TWENTIES

· 28 ·

Politics in the Nineteen Twenties

THE ELECTION OF HARDING

THE directors of the Republican party, when they foregathered in convention at Chicago on June 8, 1920, had every reason to look forward to the coming Presidential contest with confidence. The result was a spirited preconvention campaign, from which there finally emerged as the favorites General Leonard Wood, Governor Frank O. Lowden of Illinois, and Senator Hiram Johnson of California. Although a quiet boom had been started for Senator Warren Gamaliel Harding of Ohio by his friend National Committeeman Harry M. Daugherty, its strength came from local sources entirely. The convention proceedings were dominated by the conservatives in the party, who wrote a platform which committed the party to a domestic policy reminiscent of the McKinley era in its conservatism. In their arraignment of the foreign policy of the Democratic administrations, the Republicans indicated a return toward isolation. Specifically, they pledged themselves to protect the rights and property of American citizens in Mexico, and declared that the Covenant of the League of Nations failed to promote those agreements among countries that were necessary for the preservation of the peace of the world. Although they refrained from outright condemnation of international co-operation, the vague promise to promote world "justice and peace" was so phrased as to leave upon the minds of the intellectually honest an impression of insincerity.

The balloting for the candidates began on June 11, and on the ninth ballot Harding pulled ahead of Wood, Lowden, and Johnson. On the next roll call the Senator from Ohio was nominated. As his running mate, the convention chose Governor Calvin Coolidge of Massachusetts.

The Democrats met at San Francisco on June 28, with Wilson absent and Bryan hovering only in the background. The leading aspirants for the nomination were William G. McAdoo, late Secretary of the Treasury and the son-in-law of Wilson; Attorney-General A. Mitchell Palmer of Pennsylvania; and Governor James M. Cox of Ohio. The platform was reported out on July 2 and, like the Republican avowal of faith, had nothing of significance to say concerning domestic questions. Clearly the old zeal for reform had run its course. But in relations with the outside world idealism persisted. The Democrats defended the President's Mexican policy, sympathized with Ireland in its aspirations for self-government, and promised independence to the Philippines and territorial status to Puerto Rico. The League of Nations was declared to be "the surest if not the only practical means of maintaining the permanent peace of the world"; the Treaty ought to be ratified immediately "without reservations which would impair its essential integrity"; however, the Democracy was not opposed to "the acceptance of any reservations making clearer or more specific the obligations of the United States to the League of Nations." After forty-four ballots Cox was finally named for the Presidency, and with him was nominated Franklin D. Roosevelt of New York, Assistant Secretary of the Navy.

The Socialists met at New York on May 8 with the right wing completely in control of affairs and Debs was named for the Presidency for the fifth time. A Farmer-Labor ticket also made its appearance, with Parley P. Christensen of Utah named for the Presidency and Max S. Hayes of Ohio for the Vice-Presidency. La Follette would have been a natural choice for this new third-party attempt, but his insistence that the platform be his own and not that of the labor element made him unacceptable to the trade unionists. The Farmer-Labor platform was a right socialist document. It called for government ownership of railroads, mines, and national resources; the lifting of the blockade against Russia; American withdrawal from the Treaty of Versailles; and the enactment of the kind of social codes that had so prominently figured in the Progressive platform of 1912.

The canvass of 1920 was a spiritless affair. At the urging of Wilson, the Democratic National Committee proclaimed the campaign a "solemn referendum" on the question of American entrance into the League and Cox devoted a greater part of his attention to the Treaty and the Covenant. The Democratic candidate toured the country in a hopeless effort to evoke some enthusiasm for his cause. Harding's campaign, on the other hand, was conducted in the best Republican tradition. He greeted visiting delegations from the front porch of his home at Marion, Ohio, and addressed them in a series of orations which were dignified, conciliatory, and for the most part pointless. On the issue of joining the League of Nations, it was difficult to understand where the Republican candidate stood.

Harding was elected by an overwhelming majority, however. Observers agreed that it was not so much a victory for the platitudes and ambiguities of the Republican candidate as a vote in rejection of everything Wilson had stood for. Harding's popular vote was nearly twice that of his Democratic opponent, while in the electoral college Harding received 404 votes against Cox's 127. The Republican victory in the Congressional elections was equally impressive. Truly the voters seemed to crave that return to "normalcy" which the new President promised.

Warren Gamaliel Harding had been born in Ohio in 1865. In Marion, a community of some 30,000 souls, he had become the proprietor of the daily *Star*, and had collected local items, written editorials, and solicited advertising and job printing. He prospered, and before long was a member of the little local group of select persons who controlled the town banks, public utilities, churches, and philanthropies. He became a follower in Senator Foraker's train, was prominent in state election contests and went to the state senate during 1900 to 1904, becoming its presiding officer as lieutenant-governor during 1904 to 1906. Once he ran for governor, but he was defeated. In 1914, he went to the United States Senate; in 1916, he was chosen permanent chairman of the Republican National Convention. As a Senator, Harding's record was negligible: he made speeches for his constituents to read, and he voted at the direction of the party whips. In the words of William Allen White: "He was a voice through which the Republican organization spoke. In Ohio, it was the Ohio gang; in the country, the Republican National Committee."

President Harding surrounded himself by a Cabinet that both cheered and dismayed the elder statesmen of his party. The State portfolio went to Charles E. Hughes; the Treasury office to Andrew W. Mellon, wealthy banker of Pittsburgh; the Commerce Department to Herbert Hoover, who had been Wilson's Food Administrator and who had later been in charge of American relief work in Europe. The chairman of the Republican National Committee, Will H. Hays of Indiana, was made Postmaster-General. Albert B. Fall of New Mexico, who as a Senator had bitterly fought the Wilson Mexican policy and was openly friendly with the country's large oil interests, was made Secretary of the Interior. Harry M. Daugherty of Ohio, director of the President's preconvention campaign, was placed in charge of the Department of Justice. To the other Cabinet posts men as undistinguished as these last three were appointed.

Harding's conception of the Presidency was a modest one. He was to be a spokesman for policies determined by others; the bearer of olive branches; and the guest of honor at conferences, the laying of cornerstones, and the opening of public buildings. Hughes was the Secretary of State: he was therefore the person to handle foreign affairs. Mellon was Secretary of the Treasury: he could be trusted to evolve public finance policies. Hoover was the Secretary of Commerce: problems that concerned the world of business were to have his thought and planning. Over these mighty ones Harding presided only in name. Further, Harding's ultimate loyalties were not to the traditions of the American government but to his party, not to the American people but to his small coterie of Ohio friends. He remained the Ohio politician to the end, regarding public office as the just reward of his followers and public possessions as the spoils that had fallen to the victors. It is not unjust to measure Harding's stature by the persons with whom he associated himself.

A dreary feature of the Harding administration was a crop of major scandals, those in the Veterans' Bureau and the Departments of the Interior and of Justice being particularly noisome. The Veterans' Bureau affair led straight to its director, Charles R. Forbes, who was found, by a Senate investigating committee, to have been guilty of reckless waste, misconduct, and dishonesty in the handling of construction contracts and the purchase of supplies. In 1925, a federal court declared Forbes, who had been driven out of office early in 1923, to be guilty of taking part in a conspiracy to loot the Veterans' Bureau.

The disgraces involving the Department of Justice directly implicated Attorney-General Daugherty. A Senate investigating committee, headed by Smith Brookhart of Iowa, found a trail of illegal withdrawals of alcohol, of suddenly enriched persons (Daugherty not the least among them), and of criminal neglect of duty. Daugherty was asked to resign later in March, 1924, by President Coolidge on the technical charge of refusing to open his Department affairs to Senator Brookhart and his colleagues. One of Daugherty's friends, Thomas W. Miller, who occupied the post of Alien Property Custodian, was dismissed from office and in 1927 was found guilty of conspiring to defraud the government in the transactions arising from the sale of the assets of the American Metal Company, an alien enemy concern. Daugherty was tried on the same charge but the jury could arrive at no decision; in the case of Miller, the verdict of guilty brought a penalty of eighteen months' imprisonment and a fine of $5000.

The taint of oil besmirched the Departments of the Navy and the Interior. In 1912 and 1915 respectively, Presidents Taft and Wilson had set aside rich and extensive naval oil reserves at Elk Hills, California and Teapot Dome, Wyoming. By an executive order in May, 1921, which Harding signed and which had the approval of Secretary of the Navy Denby, the administration of these naval reserves was transferred from the Navy to the Interior Department and fell into the hands of Albert B. Fall. Fall set to work at once to enrich his friends E. M. Doheny and Harry F. Sinclair. On April 7, 1922, secretly and without troubling to obtain other bids, Fall leased the Teapot Dome Reserve to Sinclair; and on April 25, 1922, by one agreement, and on December 11, 1922, by another, Fall leased the whole Elk Hills Reserve to Doheny. In both leases, the interests of the government were very inadequately protected.

The secrecy attending the leases and the sudden wealth of Fall, who was known to have been in financial straits, led to a Senate committee investigation. Under the able direction of Senator Thomas J. Walsh of

Montana, the unsavory details of the affair were gradually disclosed. It was found that Sinclair had made a number of heavy contributions to the Republican campaign fund, that he had personally befriended Fall and had showered him with gifts; that Doheny had made a "loan" of $100,000 to Fall without security or interest; that Fall had gone to considerable pains to conceal the fact that this large sum of money had been borrowed from the oil magnate, evolving a number of fanciful tales to account for the money in his possession. The final results of the scandal were the following: Denby and Fall resigned their Cabinet offices; government civil suits to recapture the oil reserves were ultimately crowned with success in 1927, when the Supreme Court ordered them returned to the government and branded Sinclair and Fall as being guilty of "fraud, conspiracy, and corruption"; Fall was found guilty, in 1929, of accepting a bribe from Doheny and was sentenced to pay a fine of $100,000 and to serve a year's jail sentence. The major actors in the drama, that is to say, Sinclair and Doheny, were acquitted in a criminal prosecution for conspiracy, although Sinclair was subsequently compelled to serve a short prison term at Washington for being in contempt of the Senate and for hiring private operatives to shadow members of the jury sitting on his case.

Before the details of these crimes became public Harding died, August 2, 1923. Had he lived it is difficult to see how he and his party could have escaped responsibility for them. As it turned out, the new President, Calvin Coolidge, with the friendly aid of the conservative press, so skillfully belittled or ignored the scandals that less onus was placed upon the shoulders of the wrong-doers than upon those who had exposed the whole dirty business.

THE ADMINISTRATIONS OF CALVIN COOLIDGE

Such an unworthy attitude on the part of the press was symptomatic of that conservative trend which had set in with the oncoming of the war and which was in full swing in 1919. In that year, a little known, cautious party servant, Calvin Coolidge by name, had become governor of Massachusetts. It turned out that by a series of fortuitous circumstances he was destined to be the chief beneficiary and darling of reaction. The first circumstance occurred in September, 1919, when the Boston police force, suffering under the weight of low salaries and heavy occupational expenses, sought to ameliorate its condition by organizing. Instead of forming the customary benevolent society, the policemen applied for a trade-union charter to the American Federation of Labor and obtained it. The refusal of the police commissioner to treat with his men and his dismissal of their leaders precipitated a crisis, with the result that on September 9 the greater part of Boston's uniformed force went out on strike. Not a little disorder followed. The very next day the mayor moved to take the situation in hand by calling out on police duty those companies of the Massachusetts militia stationed in the city. By the morning of September 11, order had been restored. It was not until that afternoon that Governor Coolidge, who had refused to intercede with the commissioner and who had rejected the mayor's request for militiamen when the strike threatened, appeared on the scene. He assumed control; poured into Boston militia units from other parts of the state; and sent to President Gompers of the American Federation of Labor a tart telegram in which he declared: "There is no right to strike against the public safety by anybody, anywhere, any time." Friends of "law and order"—really the enemies of labor and liberalism—had found their man. They rushed to hail Coolidge's action as the courageous deed of a cool public servant; he was re-elected governor of Massachusetts by a great plurality; his name was prominently mentioned during the deliberations of the Republican convention of 1920; and he was nominated for the Vice-Presidency almost by acclamation.

And then, in August, 1923, came Harding's death—a second fortunate circumstance for Coolidge. There followed the era of frenzied, speculative prosperity which roughly coincided with the years of his Presidency. This prosperity the respectable magazines, newspapers, and radio commentators —in short, nearly all the formulators of public opinion—taught the country to regard as somehow being, if not exactly his work, certainly in large measure the result of his policy of hands-off as far as business was concerned.

Although the President did suffer a number of rebuffs at the hands of Congress his strength was not seriously impaired. When the Republican convention met at Cleveland on June 10, 1924, Calvin Coolidge, though having held office but ten months, was almost the unanimous choice of his party. On the first ballot he received 1065 votes as against 34 votes for La Follette and 10 votes for Johnson. For the Vice-Presidency, General Charles G. Dawes of Chicago was named after Lowden had refused the nomination. The Republican party platform was frankly a conservative document. It pledged its standard-bearers to a program of rigid governmental economy; championed progressive tax reduction; favored American membership in the World Court; continued to regard with hostility entry into the League of Nations; and promised continued support to the principles of high protectionism.

The Democrats assembled on June 24 at New York and sat almost continuously until July 10. A serious disagreement broke out among the members over a resolution calling for the denunciation of the Ku Klux Klan by name. After a prolonged debate the resolution was lost, the vote standing 541.85 for naming the Klan and 546.15 against naming it. The accepted platform spoke of a scientific tariff and tax reduction; stressed the need for honesty in government; promised farm relief without committing the party to a definite program; declared in favor of a readjustment of railroad rates to give agricultural, coal, and ore shippers lower tariffs; and favored government ownership and operation of a merchant marine and immediate independence for the Philippine Islands. The Democrats spoke of their confidence "in the ideal of world peace, the League of Nations, and the World Court of Justice as together constituting the supreme effort of the statesmanship and religious conviction of our time to organize the world for peace." They, however, recommended that the question of joining the League be submitted to a popular referendum. The platform also supported collective bargaining and the child-labor amendment. As for the Ku Klux Klan, the platform said merely: "We insist at all times upon obedience to the orderly processes of the law and deplore and condemn any effort to arouse religious or racial dissension."

On June 30 the balloting commenced, with McAdoo of California and Governor Alfred E. Smith of New York the leading contestants and, incidentally, the chiefs of those two groups that had struggled so bitterly over the naming of the Klan in the platform. Supporting McAdoo were the rural, dry, evangelical Protestant Democrats of the South and the West; clustering about the standard of Smith were the Democrats of the great city machines, who had many Catholics and Jews in their ranks, who were hostile to the Eighteenth Amendment, and who saw that the Negroes of the North were a great political force to be reckoned with and to be won over to the Democracy, if possible. An impassable gulf separated these two factions. Finally, after other efforts to make possible the withdrawal of the chief contenders had failed, it was announced on July 8 that Smith was prepared to release his candidates if McAdoo was. McAdoo's reply that he would let his followers decide for themselves was regarded as tantamount to acceptance, and on the one hundred and third ballot, John W. Davis of West Virginia and New York was nominated. With him was named Governor Charles W. Bryan of Nebraska, the Commoner's brother.

Despite the conservatism of the candidates and platforms of the two parties, progressivism was by no means dead in 1924. The fact is, insurgent Republicans had held the balance of power in the politically close Sixty-eighth Congress, elected in 1922. The Republicans had been nominally in control, but in the Republican majority in the Senate there were five Republican Senators, headed by La Follette, who were consistently at odds with their party's chiefs; and these formed a bloc which, by combining with the Democrats, was able to frustrate Secretary of the Treasury Mellon's tax plan and other Republican party measures. In the House, the situation was largely the same. There was a strong possibility that this disaffected Republican group would join hands with a powerful labor body, which, at last, was ready to try its independent fortune at the polls. And so it turned out to be.

Reference has been made to the Farmer-Labor party in the election of 1920. By 1924, it had largely disintegrated. But there had appeared in its place the Conference for Progressive Political Action, backed by the powerful railroad brotherhoods. Here was a labor movement that held in it the promise of political success: it represented organized labor, was right wing in its tendencies, and was not likely to permit itself to be involved in the sort of factional disputes which had rent the Socialist party. The Conference for Progressive Political Action originally met in February, 1922; and on July 4, 1924, it offered its nomination to Senator La Follette on his own platform.

La Follette accepted, helped choose as his running mate Senator Burton K. Wheeler of Montana (who was a Democrat), and wrote a platform which gained the endorsement, at the same time, of the Socialist party and the executive council of the American Federation of Labor. This, then, was the first Presidential campaign in which organized labor had formally taken part and in which Socialists, middle-class intellectuals, farmers, and organized workers were to fight under the same banner. La Follette's platform was directed largely at monopoly, that same monopoly which had been troubling the agrarian West for the last half-century. The platform went on to promise the cleaning out of official corruption; the return of the naval oil reserves; public ownership of water power; the fixing of railroad rates on the basis of prudent investment; public ownership of railroads as the only solution to the transportation problem; tax reduction for moderate incomes only; abolition of the right of the Supreme Court to nullify acts of Congress; popular election of the federal judiciary; tariff revision downward; prohibition of gambling in agricultural futures; reconstruction of the Federal Reserve Board and the Federal Farm Loan Board to provide real public control of the nation's financial and credit facilities; adequate laws to guarantee to farmers and industrial workers the right to organize and bargain collectively; the use of a popular referendum when war threatened; revision of the Treaty of Versailles; the outlawing of war, the abolition of conscription, and the reduction of armaments. La Follette ran under various party designations; but in no states, outside of Wisconsin, North Dakota, and Minnesota, did he have state organizations of any value to help him.

Despite La Follette's presence in the campaign and the uncertainty attending the three-cornered contest, only 51.1 per cent of the eligible voters went to the polls. Coolidge's majority over his two rivals was an impressive one. His popular vote was 15,725,000, against 8,386,500 for Davis, and 4,822,900 for La Follette. The electoral vote was as follows: Coolidge 382, Davis 136, La Follette 13. Davis's vote came from the Solid South and Oklahoma; La Follette's from his native Wisconsin. In the Congressional elections, the Republican triumph was sufficiently great to insure that in the Sixty-ninth Congress the insurgents would no longer hold the balance of power.

President Coolidge's good fortune did not desert him during the full term of his second administration. The country's phenomenal prosperity continued; business had the encouraging support of the administration's officers, Secretaries Mellon and Hoover in particular; industrial conflicts, except for a series of strikes in the anthracite and bituminous coal fields, were few and unimportant; and peace and plenty reigned over the land. The President continued to receive the applause of large business groups because of the energy with which he promoted the policies of which they approved and frowned upon those they disapproved.

On August 2, 1927, four years after he had become chief executive of the United States, Coolidge fluttered the political dovecotes by issuing a cryptic statement to the press which read, in its entirety, as follows: "I do not choose to run for President in 1928." Coolidge refused to amplify his message or to deny the report of his more zealous followers that he would make the canvass if drafted by the Republican convention. His continued silence kept the important delegations from New York, Massachusetts, and Pennsylvania unpledged and prevented the growth of booms for Lowden and Dawes, both of whom had expressed themselves in favor of farm-relief legislation and both of whom, therefore, Coolidge regarded as unfriendly to the policies of his administration. It began to become increasingly apparent that Secretary of Commerce Hoover was being groomed as the heir-apparent of the administration.

The readers of portents were not to be mistaken. The Republican convention assembled at Kansas City on June 12 and, although Lowden had shown considerable preconvention strength, Hoover met with little organized opposition. He received the nomination on the first ballot, as did Senator Charles Curtis of Kansas for the Vice-Presidency. The Democrats met at Houston, Texas, on June 27, with Claude G. Bowers delivering the keynote address. Governor Alfred E. Smith's strength, despite the animosities that had been revealed at the 1924 convention, had been steadily growing over the four years, with the result that objection to his choice was slight. He was named on the first ballot and Senator Joseph T. Robinson of Arkansas was nominated to make the contest with him.

The campaign of 1928 presented many curious anomalies. For one, there was little to choose between the platforms of the two parties. The Republican campaign document praised the achievements of the Coolidge administrations, lauded protectionism, and approved the Department of State's foreign policies with respect to Mexico, Nicaragua, China, and the League of Nations. With regard to agriculture, the Republicans gave their approval to none of the Congressional panaceas for farm relief; as for Prohibition, they promised merely continued "vigorous enforcement."

The Democrats, in their turn, avoided major issues quite as successfully. Although Coolidge's do-nothing policy for agriculture was bitterly arraigned, no definite program was advanced as a promised cure. The Democrats also pledged themselves to enforce the Eighteenth Amendment. The tariff question was straddled, the platform speaking of a tariff program that would "maintain legitimate business and a high standard of wages" and that would impose duties to "permit effective competition" and "insure against monopoly."

If the dissimilarities between the two party platforms seemed negligible, the Republican and Democratic standard-bearers appeared to be as far apart as the poles. However, what seemed to be striking disparities resolved themselves into only superficial differences: on the points of heritage, training, and career, the two men furnished interesting contrasts; with regard to their social and economic views, there was in reality little to choose between them. Both had come from humble origins, Hoover having been born on an Iowa farm and Smith in New York City's slums. But from birth onward, their paths had stretched in different directions. Hoover, orphaned in childhood and befriended by well-to-do relatives, had studied engineering at Stanford University and then, during his early manhood, had quickly accumulated a fortune as a mining and railroad expert and promoter. His work had taken him into obscure byways of the globe; and, too, he was as much at home in Peking, Cape Town, and London as in his adopted state of California. He had proved himself to be a capable office chief and had shown his mettle as Belgian Relief head, Food Administrator, Chairman of the American Relief Administration, and Secretary of Commerce. In all these posts, Hoover had learned to give orders; he had never been compelled to meet stubborn opposition or to reconcile differences. Smith, on the other hand, had moved in a political environment from very childhood. He had had little formal schooling, had worked at a variety of unskilled occupations and then had become a Tammany stalwart, learning his statecraft from practical situations and his daily intercourse with his fellow beings. He had been showered with the favors of his party, and at four different times had been elected governor of New York State. He was a man of the cities and a man of the people—but he was no proletarian as Debs and even the young Bryan had been.

Governor Smith conducted a gallant fight, and the outpourings of crowds, which greeted him all over the country, attested to his personal popularity. There were, however, certain great disabilities he labored under. For one he had no economic program of dissent, having nothing in particular to offer labor and agriculture. Again, he was a "wet" as far as Prohibition was concerned, a position unquestionably abhorrent to the old Bryan country of the South and West. Further, he was a Tammanyite.

In the fourth place, he was a Roman Catholic. Finally, the golden era of prosperity stood in the way of a Republican upset, no matter how great the personal gifts of the Democratic nominee. The result was, Smith's presence in the campaign brought out the greatest vote to figure in an American election up to that time—and the Democracy suffered its most humiliating defeat. Smith lost his own state of New York as well as the southern states of Virginia, North Carolina, Tennessee, Florida, and Texas. He did not carry a single border state. He almost failed in Alabama. The Far West, which had voted for Bryan and Wilson, disowned him. His total electoral vote was 87 and consisted of only Alabama, Arkansas, Georgia, Louisiana, Mississippi, and South Carolina in the erstwhile Solid South and the largely Catholic states of Massachusetts and Rhode Island.[1] Hoover's electoral vote was 444. The popular votes were as follows: for Hoover, 21,392,000; for Smith, 15,016,000. The Seventy-first Congress, elected at the same time, also was overwhelmingly Republican.

THE ENGINEER IN POLITICS

Herbert Hoover had carried his engineering habits into his business life with great success. He was to bring these same views over into politics, and their lack of success in this sphere was at once to become apparent. He was a firm believer in American industrialism and the opponent of any sort of political or social change that might, even remotely, smack of socialism. Out of economic views such as these, the political opinions inevitably stemmed: if mankind was guided by an enlightened self-interest, if the processes of the economic life could be plainly charted and their future just as plainly predicted, if, in short, society was rational, then there was no place in it for the arts of accommodation. The facts always pointed to irrefragable conclusions: all one had to do was to collect the data, and opinions—based on prejudice, cupidity, fear—could be at once relegated to the realm of the irrational where they properly belonged. Government, therefore, was not a matter of give-and-take, of compromise, reconciliation, bargaining: government was one vast agency for gathering facts and for writing Q.E.D. after plainly-arrived-at conclusions.

Before the first half of his administration was over, Herbert Hoover was to taste the bitter dregs of defeat. Politicians were stubborn in the face of facts and demanded legislation for their local constituencies; businessmen refused to regard America's economic life as a closely integrated whole and clamored for support and tariff protection for their particular industries; and the capitalist world itself, with its supposedly self-adjusting laws of supply and demand, simply collapsed in 1930 and where there had

[1] Smith carried the great cities of New York, Boston, Cleveland, St. Louis, and San Francisco. He also ran well in Chicago, Detroit, and Philadelphia.

TWO POINTS OF VIEW

once been plenty there was soon to be destitution and gaunt poverty. The world and men, after all, were much more irrational than Herbert Hoover ever believed them to be.

President Hoover met his first setback in the political arena. He was compelled to give ear to partisan considerations in the choice of his Cabinet, with the result that astonished Americans were to see his official family not made up of highly skilled experts but of Republican party stalwarts, many of them previously unknown. The State Department was filled by Henry L. Stimson, the Treasury office by Andrew W. Mellon, the Labor office by James J. Davis. These names were familiar; the rest were not. The Senate was openly hostile toward many of the Presidential appointments. It rebelled, though unsuccessfully, at the confirmation of Charles E. Hughes for the chief justiceship of the Supreme Court; it refused to approve the naming of John J. Parker, a "lily-white" Republican of North Carolina, to the same tribunal; and it challenged, in the courts, the make-up of the Federal Power Commission.

Once more, in the Hoover administration, Republican insurgency raised its head. The insurgent bloc, led in the Senate by Norris of Nebraska, opposed the President on his tariff, waterpower, and farm-relief programs, united with Democrats to override his vetoes, and made common cause with Democratic Senators in the fights on Hughes, Parker, and many of Hoover's lesser nominations.

Finally, there came the stock market crash of October, 1929, and the catastrophic economic depression that set in with the beginning of 1930. By the spring of 1931 even administration spokesmen admitted that the total of unemployed in the country was in the neighborhood of 6,500,000 workers. Bread lines existed in all the great cities, and hundreds of thousands of families were barely subsisting on the meager doles granted them by charitable agencies. The steel industry was operating at one-third of capacity; crude-oil production had reached the lowest point since 1926; the prices of copper, silver, cotton, and other commodities almost daily touched new lows. Laissez-faire had broken down, and the forecasts of the business astrologers, which had promised such happy events when Herbert Hoover took the Presidential oath on March 4, 1929, were so many meaningless and bitter words that Americans remembered when they turned to look at the uninspired man in the White House. The electorate used the only means it had in its power to show a loss of confidence: in the Congressional elections of 1930 the American voters returned the House to Democratic control and reduced the Republican membership of the Senate to a bare plurality.

· 29 ·
Leading Legislative Problems of the Nineteen Twenties

THE TARIFF ACTS OF 1922 AND 1930

WITH the Republican party again in control of the Presidency and Congress in 1921, it was inevitable that businessmen should demand and legislators grant an immediate revision of the Democratic Tariff Act of 1913. The result was that the Sixty-seventh Congress, which Harding had called in special session immediately after his inauguration, passed an Emergency Tariff Act in May, 1921. This raised the duties on agricultural articles, wool, and sugar and devoted particular attention to the new chemical industry. Meanwhile, the House Ways and Means Committee and the Senate Finance Committee were recasting the whole tariff structure, schedule by schedule. It was soon apparent, as the debates became public, that protectionism had few real foes in either party. The reason was plain: industrialization had made giant strides during the war, nowhere greater than in the South and West, where once low tariff principles had prevailed. Therefore, it was no surprise to anyone that the Fordney-McCumber Tariff bill, when it finally emerged from the Senate Committee in April, 1922, proved to contain the highest rates in American tariff history up to that time. In rare instances only were rates cut below the duties of 1913; the general tendency was to approximate the levels of 1909 and to set prohibitory duties for the benefit of the new industries. With little genuine opposition, and then only from a few Western Progressives and a score or so of old-fashioned Southern Democrats, the new tariff bill became law on September 19, 1922.

The administrative features of the 1922 tariff were unique in two particulars: 1. the ad valorem duties were to be assessed on the foreign value of the goods or their export value at the port of shipment, whichever happened to be higher; 2. the act explicitly stated that the principle underlying American protection was to be that of the equalization of the costs of production between American products and those foreign articles entering into competition with ours. In other words, the tariff was to be a flexible one henceforth; and provision therefore was made for the creation of a Tariff Commission. This Tariff Commission was to ascertain what these differences in production costs were; was to investigate complaints of unfair practices by foreign competitors; and was to draw up new schedules of rates, as its investigations determined their necessity. To the President was given the power of proclaiming the new rates upon information furnished by the Tariff Commission. In this fashion, the Republican tariff makers could claim that their guiding thought was to protect American industry from foreign dumping and American workers from the competition of the "pauper labor" of Europe.

By 1928, dissatisfaction with the existing tariff was again general, and when the Seventy-first Congress met in special session, on President Hoover's call, the Congressional committees once more proceeded to a thorough overhauling of the protective system. Opponents of high protection, particularly those whose economic well-being depended upon the creation of a healthy foreign trade (investment bankers, importers, and automobile manufacturers were three groups in this class), hoped that the spirit of nationalism had somewhat abated and that the tariff wall would be lowered. They regarded President Hoover, because of his economic training and his interest in the stimulation of American foreign trade, as sympathetic to their point of view. Much to their amazement, they were to see the Little Americans again firmly perched in the saddle, the same disregard expressed for the maintenance of an international division of labor, and the same intention displayed to shut our doors to European wares, even in the face of threatened reprisals. And they were to see President Hoover yielding to this party. The only solace the President could offer the friends of international trade was the promise that the flexibility provision would be employed to adjust such inequalities as the new tariff act contained.

The House Ways and Means Committee reported out the Hawley bill on May 7, 1929, and on May 28, so smoothly did the organization machine run, the bill was passed by a vote of 264 to 147. Duties on farm products and on raw materials were raised; minerals received particular attention; the rates on textiles and on dyestuffs were again scaled upward; compensatory duties were placed on manufactured articles the raw materials of which were taxed. But this time the Senate was less willing to follow the House's lead and insurgent Republicans from the Far West again revolted, as they had over the Payne-Aldrich bill in 1909. Insurgent Senators first tried to restrict the Senate Finance Committee to a consideration of the agricultural schedule only; this maneuver failing, they succeeded in incorporating two radical amendments into the Smoot bill. The first provided for an export debenture, or bounty, on all farm products exported, in order to make the tariff on foodstuffs effective; the second vested the administration of the flexibility power in the hands of Congress instead of the President. Despite the protests of President Hoover, the Senate bill was passed with both these amendments and in this fashion went into conference committee.

If the President could not crack the whip over the Senate, he could over the House, with the result that the House conferees refused to accept the Senate bill. Matters were thus deadlocked until May, 1930, with neither side yielding on the debenture or Congressional flexibility. Finally, on May 19, the Senate voted to untie the hands of its conferees. How completely the Senate had broken away from Hoover's leadership may be seen in the closeness by which the act was accomplished. The vote to give up the export debenture plan was 43 to 41, with fourteen Republicans voting or paired against the resolution. The vote to place the flexibility tariff power in the hands of the President was 43 to 42, with Vice-President Curtis casting the deciding ballot for the resolution. These differences out of the way, the conference committee was able to agree on its report. On June 13, 1930, the Senate passed the Smoot-Hawley bill by a vote of 44 to 42, eleven Republicans voting against the bill and five Democrats voting for it. On the next day, the House did similarly, the vote being 222 yeas to 153 nays. On June 17, 1930, President Hoover affixed his signature and the Tariff Act of 1930 was law.

Under the new act the rates were higher than ever. In a large number of cases, the duties on raw materials ranged from 50 to 100 per cent greater than those in the 1922 schedules; generally the average ad valorem rate for all the schedules was 40.08 per cent as compared with 33.22 per cent in the 1922 Act. It is interesting to note that the tariff makers refused to pay heed to those interests that wanted no protection at all. Thus, the automobile manufacturers had to accept a duty of 10 per cent although they themselves had agitated for the placing of automobiles on the free list.

As in the 1922 Act, the Tariff Act of 1930 provided for the appointment of a Tariff Commission (expanded to six members) with power to investigate production costs and to recommend to the President the lowering or raising of rates. It was largely upon the retention of this provision, with its promise of flexibility, that President Hoover appealed for popular support for the new measure. However, the experiences with the flexibility power, as exercised by Presidents Harding and Coolidge, had been none too reassuring. Thus, from 1922 to June, 1929, Harding and Coolidge had proclaimed thirty-seven changes in rates: thirty-two of these had provided for higher duties; five for lower ones. And when, in 1924, a majority of the Commission had recommended that the sugar duty be lowered, President Coolidge had simply filed their report and done nothing. Critics pointed out, too, that the consuming public had no representation before the Commission and that the body had heretofore been a football of politics and had, indeed, been packed in the interests of high-protectionist groups.

While the Hawley-Smoot bill was still before Congress, no signs were wanting that a large and increasing body of Americans were impatient with, if not actually hostile toward, the excesses of log-rolling, bartering, and lobbying which entered into legislative tariff making. More and more people were beginning to realize that the American economic life was international in its scope and could not be confined within high Chinese walls. Indeed, while the tariff bill was still being considered in Congress, European trade associations, from every important country on the Continent, filed protests against it with American consular and diplomatic representatives. And after the Tariff Act of 1930 was signed by the President, foreign governments proceeded to enact retaliatory measures. Before 1931 closed, fully twenty-five countries either had made extensive tariff revisions, had increased specific duties, or had threatened to do so. In almost every important case, the justification advanced was the necessity for fighting the United States with her own weapons.

There could be no question, as the nineteen thirties progressed, that an important reason for the continuance of world-wide depression was to be found in the artificial barriers erected to impede the international flow of goods and services. Everywhere, economic nationalism—which meant national self-sufficiency—was being fostered by governments. And the United States had been a leader in creating such devices, of which the protective tariff was the most important.

CREATING A MERCHANT MARINE

The merchant marine, which the United States Shipping Board and the Emergency Fleet Corporation had provided the nation during the years 1917 to 1920, was owned, and in considerable measure also operated, by the government. However necessary such a "socialist" scheme might be in wartime, under normal conditions it was repugnant to the spirit of American individualism. Of course, it was being argued, the government should give every encouragement, but if we were to put our carrying trade on such a sound basis that it would meet effectively the competition of British and German shipping companies, the merchant fleet must be operated by private owners.

In line with such ideas, there were therefore enacted the Merchant Marine Act of 1920 and the Merchant Marine Act of 1928. Under both of these measures the Shipping Board and the Merchant Fleet Corporation were continued. Under the first law the Shipping Board was to dispose of the wartime merchant fleet, as quickly as possible, to private operators. Every precaution was taken to see that the ships did not fall into the hands of foreign companies. Easy terms of payment were to be granted to purchasers. The Merchant Fleet Corporation was to have these functions: it was to operate those ships it could not sell to private groups; it was to establish new shipping routes and keep ships in these services until private capital could be induced to take them over; it was to make loans to such shipping companies as were willing to operate over these new routes. To perform these tasks, the Merchant Fleet Corporation was given the use of a revolving fund of $25 million.

Between 1920 and 1928 the Shipping Board sought to interest American capital in the development of a merchant fleet that would be capable of carrying at least half of the country's overseas trade. Because American capital was timid to venture into a new field, the Shipping Board continued to lower purchase prices on its vessels and even went so far as to guarantee the losses of those operators who were willing to work the new routes. However, it became apparent that none of these new shipping companies was accumulating enough surpluses for capital replacements. The only remedy was subsidy, and this, in a measure, was offered by the Merchant Marine Act of 1928.

The law of 1928 renewed the declaration of a privately owned and operated merchant marine. It maintained the same administrative agencies. The Merchant Fleet Corporation was to continue to operate the government-owned ships until they could be disposed of, and was also given the power of replacement and repair so that the portion of the merchant fleet which was still government-owned would not become obsolete. Subsidy was provided for through three means, two of which were directly indicated and one of which was implied: 1. There was set up a revolving fund of $250 million from which construction loans up to three-fourths of the costs of building were to be made to private operators. 2. Private owners were to be given, as an encouragement to ship building and operation, long-term mail carrying contracts. 3. The price at which the Shipping Board was selling its vessels to private operators constituted an indirect subsidy. For example, from 1925 to 1930 the Shipping Board sold to ten lines 104 vessels for something less than $23 million; on the other hand, the total cost of construction for these 104 ships had been $258 million.

On December 31, 1930, there were registered under the American flag 1778 ocean-going ships of 1000 gross tons or more, of which 1345 ships were privately owned and 433 ships were still controlled by the Shipping Board's Merchant Fleet Corporation. The gross tonnage owned privately was 7,136,-746; that owned by the government, 2,462,095. The outcome of this government interest was an extraordinary increase in the American merchant marine; and we were gradually freeing ourselves from a dependence upon British bottoms for the carriage of our exports and imports.

However desirable such an outcome might be regarded (and there were some who disputed its desirability), the question inevitably presented itself: could not the government have attained the same end, at no greater cost, and at the same time have provided lower rates for shippers and better working conditions for seamen and longshoremen, had it continued to own and operate the ships it had built at such great expense? But such a consideration was given no serious attention; and in subsequent legislation, as we shall see, the United States continued, with heavy public subsidies, to support a privately owned and operated merchant marine.

THE RAILROAD PROBLEM

The Railroad Administration of 1917 to 1919 was designed to be only a war expedient, with the result that on December 24, 1919, President Wilson announced that on March 1, 1920, the railroads of the country would be restored to private management. Congress gave considerable thought to the problem and the Transportation Act of 1920, which was signed by President Wilson on February 28, turned out to be a complete overhauling of the Interstate Commerce Act. This measure reorganized the Interstate Commerce Commission. The law provided for a bipartisan board of eleven commissioners, who were to be appointed by the President with the consent of the Senate for 7-year terms.

The commission was given the power of establishing and maintaining rates which were to yield "a fair return upon the aggregate value of the railway property of the country."

The more prosperous roads were to share their profits with the less prosperous. All carriers enjoying a net railway operating income in excess of 6 per cent of their property value were to set aside half of the excess in their own reserve funds and were to turn over the other half to the Commission to be applied to a railroad contingent fund. From this contingent fund, the Commission might make loans to less fortunate carriers for capital expenditures. This was the so-called recapture clause.

The long- and short-haul clause was amended, and the rules of procedure the Commission had been employing were put into statutory form.

For the first time since its creation, the Commission was given the power to prescribe minimum rates.

The twilight zone between state and federal control was removed. The Commission was authorized to adjust rates and eliminate discriminations in those cases where persons engaged in intrastate commerce appeared to have obtained advantages over persons engaged in interstate commerce.

The commission was empowered to draw up a plan for the consolidation of the railroad lines of the country into a limited number of systems. Such combinations were to be exempt from the restrictions of the antitrust laws; were to be on economic and not on geographic bases; and were to be made with an eye to the maintenance of competition between the carriers in the existing channels of trade.

The antipooling clause of the original Act was radically amended to permit the Commission to authorize pools, for the division of traffic, if better service could be attained or economies of operation effected.

The Commission was given the right to approve the formation of the Railway Express Agency out of the four great express companies then existing.

The Commission was at last given authority to regulate the issuance of railway securities and to supervise the use to which the proceeds from their sales were to be put. After December 31, 1921, no person could be an officer or director of more than one carrier without the Commission's consent. Even stronger was the prohibition against participation by directors in the sale of securities for their roads.

Elaborate machinery for the mediation of disputes between the railroads and their employees was set up. While compulsory arbitration was discarded, attempts were made to check industrial conflict through the creation of a Railroad Labor Board. This board was to sit in consideration of disputes which had not been settled by conference between the interested parties or by hearings before local boards of adjustment. In 1926, however, the Railroad Labor Board was abolished and in its place was established a Federal Board of Mediation which was to act on disputes only when asked to do so by one or another of the parties involved.

For a time, the Commission seriously concerned itself with the preparation of a plan for that consolidation of the country's railroad systems which the Act of 1920 had authorized, but up to the present (1948) no important consolidations have been made under the terms of the Act, although a number of proposals have been advanced and debated.

In the six decades of government regulation of the railroads the wheel of fortune had taken a strange turn. In the first two-thirds of the period, the railroad managers had steadfastly opposed attempts at public control: they had, with every weapon at their command, fought valuation, rate-fixing, and supervision over security issues by the government's agency, the Interstate Commerce Commission. In the last third of the period, however, the railroad managers were to appear in the role of humble petitioners praying for protection from the competition of new rivals. For the railroads were being menaced from strange quarters. Pipeline companies were not transporting the crude petroleum alone but beginning to carry gasoline and refined oil as well; interstate bus and motor truck lines had made their appearance to carry passengers and freight, if not so quickly, certainly as comfortably, more cheaply, and often with greater mobility, for the question of terminals did not trouble them; coastal and interior waterways, steamship and barge lines were furnishing a type of competition not met with before. Larger and larger numbers of persons were traveling by passenger auto, and in the nineteen forties the airlines were beginning to break measurably into the railway business. The result was, during the nineteen twenties and thirties, a serious relative decline in the railroad freight business and an absolute decline in the railroad passenger business.

To seek relief from such unregulated competition became a leading concern of the railroad executives of the nineteen twenties and thirties, and they came to urge upon Congress a large variety of measures which, they contended, were necessary to prevent the railroad industry from suffering serious harm. Thus, regulation was not over; it was to continue and, apparently, to develop in new directions. But that the railroads should regard themselves as vulnerable and should agitate for government assistance was a development that would have amazed the antimonopolists and Grangers of the eighteen seventies, had they been endowed with the gift of peering into the future.

THE PUBLIC DEBT AND TAX REDUCTION

In 1900, the interest-bearing public debt of the United States had been $1,023,479,000, or a per capita distribution of $13.47. In 1914, the debt had been $967,953,000, or a per capita distribution of $9.88. At the end of the fiscal year June 30, 1920, as a result of the costs of the war, the public debt stood at $24,061,000,000, or a per capita distribution of $228.00. Secretary of the Treasury Mellon, aided and supported by Presidents Harding, Coolidge, and Hoover, reduced this burden 33 per cent in the decade of the twenties with the result that on June 30, 1930, the public debt stood at $16,185,000,000, which was a per capita distribution of $134.00.

Tax reduction was one of the leading preoccupations of the government during the decade of the twenties, and the Congresses of the Harding and Coolidge administrations were regularly called upon to bend their energies in this direction. At first there appeared considerable objection to Mellon's program of lifting the tax burden from the shoulders of the wealthy. Small attention was accorded to his argument that those who had to pay such a large proportion of their profits into the Treasury in the shape of income surtaxes were retarded from engaging in new industrial enterprises. But before long Congress yielded, and Democratic lawmakers joined with their Republican colleagues in enacting the administration revenue acts. In a series of such laws, passed between 1921 and 1929, the wartime taxes on income, excess profits, and corporations, as well as a great variety of excise taxes, were either repealed outright or greatly reduced. The principal beneficiaries of the Mellon program were the more prosperous elements of the population. True, some new industries made their appearance as a result of the new funds available but for the most part savings in the upper-income brackets appeared to pour into stock market speculation. Mr. Mellon's feat of lowering taxes and reducing the national debt led to all sorts of extravagant praise for his policies—he was hailed as "the greatest Secretary of the Treasury since Alexander Hamilton."

The depression of 1930 abruptly terminated the happy round and at once proved that the Treasury's policy had been woefully shortsighted. By radically diminishing surtaxes, the government had not made more private funds available for productive enterprise but had really given spur to speculation; by failing to apply itself more assiduously to the national debt's reduction through the maintenance of high income taxes in the upper brackets, it was compelled to face the fact that Americans for generations to come would be called upon to meet the costs of World War I as well as of the depression of the nineteen thirties. And the costs of World War II seemed only to pile Ossa on Pelion.

PROVIDING FOR THE WAR VETERANS

It was the hope of legislators, when they expanded the powers of the Bureau of War Risk Insurance in 1917 and made provision for the permanent care of totally disabled war veterans, as well as the sale, on easy terms, of life insurance by the government to all men under arms, that scandalous pension agitation, such as that which followed the Civil War, would be effectively prevented. But the hope was illusory. The original act had provided for hospitalization and rehabilitation treatment for those who had suffered injuries in the war; in addition, all totally disabled veterans were to receive compensation of $30 monthly, while increased allowances were made for dependents. But the compensation provisions were liberalized in 1918 and 1919. In 1921, all affairs pertaining to veterans were concentrated in a single agency known as the Veterans' Bureau. In 1924, liberalization of the existing code was further extended. The first step toward a civil disability pension law was taken in 1930, a brief twelve years after the war's end. The law provided that certain nonservice physical and mental disabilities from which war veterans were suffering on January 1, 1930, were to be held as being of service origin and such veterans were to be compensated by monthly payments ranging from $12 to $40, according to the degree of disability. Observers quite justly pointed out that once the principle of pensions for civil disabilities was accepted, the grant of service pensions pure and simple would follow as a matter of course.

At the close of World War I, a discharge bonus, totaling in all $256 million, was paid to all service men. Not content with this gift, the friends of the veterans pressed for further grants and introduced bonus bills in Congress during the period 1920 to 1924. Finally a bonus bill was passed over President Coolidge's veto on May 19, 1924. The law provided for the issuance of adjusted service certificates in the form of 20-year endowment policies. Against these certificates the veterans might borrow money from the government. The size of the certificates depended upon the length of service of their holders, with $1.25 per day being the credit for overseas service and $1.00 per day the credit for home service. Because the certificates were to bear compound interest at 4 per cent, the face value at maturity was to be, on an average, considerably more than $1000 for each veteran. In the winter of 1930, there appeared an agitation for the immediate redemption of these certificates. Against such a proposal the Hoover administration sternly set its face. Even the compromise measure —providing for the increase of the loan value of the certificates from the then-existing proportion of 22½ per cent to 50 per cent, and the reduction of the interest charge from 6 to 4½ per cent—was opposed by the President and the Secretary of the Treasury. Nevertheless, even the usually compliant House disregarded the President's wishes and in February, 1931, Congress passed the Bonus Loan bill in the form indicated. The President promptly vetoed the measure; in less than twenty-four hours both House and Senate had overridden the Presidential veto by record majorities.[1]

The Veterans' Bureau had been established to supervise the medical and hospital care of disabled veterans, provide for their rehabilitation through occupational therapy, furnish employment, and supervise payment of compensation and insurance claims. In 1930, a further step toward the centralization of activities applying to returned soldiers was taken with the consolidation of the Veterans' Bureau, the Pension Bureau, and the National Home for Disabled Volunteer Soldiers to form the single Administration of Veterans' Affairs. For the fiscal year ending June 30, 1930, the government spent close to half a billion dollars on the work of the Veterans' Bureau. These were great sums; they were to be exceeded vastly by the expenditures of the Veterans' Administration after World War II.

THE REGULATION OF POWER

For the three decades preceding the outbreak of World War I the two leading domestic questions which had engrossed the attention of the American public were the regulation of railroads and the regulation of large-scale corporate business. The problems of the rails and of corporate business still remained vexing ones: To their company, by the nineteen twenties, was added the problem of power supervision. That something had to be done, a large group of persons was agreed, for the generation of electricity for heat, light, and power had become one of the most significant and essential American industries. And this had occurred prac-

---

[1] For later veteran legislation, see below, pages 575, 654.

tically overnight. Thus, in 1902, there had been produced by water power and by fuel 4768 million kilowatt-hours of electrical energy; by 1929, 97,-352 million kilowatt-hours. In short, over the period 1902 to 1929, the production of electrical energy had increased more than twentyfold. In 1931, the electrical industry, which at the turn of the century was only in its infancy, was in possession of an investment worth $12 billion. Into the bargain, the industry was characterized by holding-company management and control, as a result of which small groups of individuals—usually associated with finance capital—were able to dominate, as a rule through minority stock ownership, vast operating properties.

The federal government, despite the fact that by 1930 from one-tenth to one-seventh of the total electric power being generated in the nation was moving across state lines and therefore lay in that twilight zone where it was amenable to no controls as to rates and services, was slow to formulate any program. Only in the case of water power produced on navigable streams were some efforts at regulation made, and even here Congress did not move until 1920. The Federal Water Power Act of that year created the Federal Power Commission, which was to consist of the Secretaries of War, Interior, and Agriculture and which was to perform its functions through the staffs of the different departments. The Federal Power Commission was invested with the following functions:

It was empowered to issue licenses to citizens of the United States for the purpose of "constructing, operating, and maintaining dams, water conduits, reservoirs, power houses, transmission lines, and other projects necessary or convenient for development and improvement of navigation." Such licenses were to apply only to contemplated projects on the navigable waters of the United States, the public lands, and Indian reservations.

It was to prescribe rules and regulations governing the accounting practices of such licensees; might examine the books and papers of those companies; and require the licensees to submit full information bearing on their assets, capitalization, and the net investment in their plants.

Licenses were to be issued for a maximum period of fifty years.

After the expiration of a license the Commission had the power of recapture of any project upon the payment to the owner of the net investment in the property plus such severance damages as might exist (i. e., damages to property dependent upon the project recaptured). If the Commission failed to exercise its rights to recapture, the licensee might ask for a renewal.

The Commission was given the right to regulate the rates which the licensee, a subsidiary corporation, or any corporation buying power from it charged for power sold across interstate or international boundaries. The Commission, similarly, was given the right to regulate security issues. The Commission also was to have jurisdiction over the rates and security issues of its licensees in those states which had not yet created their own public-utilities commissions.

By 1930, it was apparent that a Commission made up of Cabinet officers was unable to cope with the many and intricate problems that were regularly coming to its attention. The result was the creation, in June, 1930, of a full-time Federal Power Commission to have the status of the Interstate Commerce Commission and the Federal Trade Commission. This new commission was to be made up of five commissioners to be named by the President with the consent of the Senate, and was to create its own organization.

Between 1920 and 1930, the Federal Power Commission licensed 449 projects, of which 43 were in the eastern region and 406 were in the western region. The extent of the Commission's control over water power may be seen from the fact that by 1946, 40 per cent of all the horsepower capacity of hydrostations in the country was under its supervision.

During the nineteen twenties, the demand for the extension of federal jurisdiction over power companies grew. If the Hoover administration was hostile to further federal interference, the proposals for tightening up the Water Power Act, for extending governmental control over all power companies, and even for governmental operation of important water-power sites were not wanting for friends. A party in the Senate, headed by Couzens of Michigan, called for federal regulation of all interstate power corporations, with particular attention to holding companies. Another Senatorial party, headed by Norris of Nebraska, was favorably disposed toward government operation of the principal sites. The Norris group made a test case of federal operation of the Muscle Shoals plant in Alabama (on the Tennessee River), and twice, in 1928 and 1931, Congress passed resolutions providing for government operation, only to have the measures killed by the vetoes of Presidents Coolidge and Hoover.

In 1917, because of the need for nitrates in the manufacture of explosives, the government had authorized the construction of two nitrate plants at the foot of Muscle Shoals. Both plants were to be worked by the cyanamide process. To provide the electrical energy needed for these plants it was also decided to construct a series of dams on the Tennessee River. The total investment of the government at Muscle Shoals was $145 million, of which more than two-thirds went to build the nitrate plants, neither of which was used after January, 1919. From 1925 on, the station was kept in operation by the United States Corps of Engineers, and most of the power generated was sold to the Alabama Power Company for distribution in the neighboring communities. But the return from the private company was small, in fact was not much in excess of $1 million annually.

Congress, therefore, began to concern itself with the creation of a program which would call for the adequate use of both the nitrate plants and the hydroelectric station. In 1928, both houses passed the Norris-Morin resolution, which was largely the work of Senator Norris. This measure called for the completion of the various power units at Muscle Shoals and the creation of a government-owned corporation to work the nitrate properties (for the manufacture of agricultural fertilizers) and sell the surplus power. The resolution had, almost completely, the support of the South and the West; it was, on the other hand, opposed by the industrial East. On May 25 the resolution was sent to President Coolidge, who proceeded to kill it by a pocket veto.

In 1930 to 1931, the friends of government operation again were successful in the Senate and a Norris resolution, embodying substantially the provisions of the 1928 bill, was once more passed by both Houses. President Hoover was as unbending as his predecessor in his opposition to the government's engaging in the power business in competition with private enterprise. In a stinging veto message on March 3, 1931, he said: "I hesitated to contemplate the future of our institutions, of our government, and of our country if the preoccupation of its officials is to be no longer the promotion of justice and equal opportunity but is to be devoted to barter in the markets. That is not liberalism; it is degeneration."

The President's acceptance of the gage of combat indicated that the power question was to play an important part in the Presidential election of 1932 and was to be no small concern of the Franklin D. Roosevelt administrations. Indeed, out of the Muscle Shoals project the great TVA experiment was built.

· 30 ·

America in Two Hemispheres

THE UNITED STATES AND LATIN AMERICA

PRESIDENT Wilson's Mexican program had established the principle that intervention was abhorrent to American policy. After some serious errors, the Coolidge administration eventually was to build upon this foundation. In 1921, Secretary of State Hughes sought to exact pledges from Mexico that lands owned by Americans would not be confiscated, that the agrarian decrees and Article xxvii of the Mexican constitution would not be made retroactive, and that all properties seized since 1910 would be restored to their original owners. Only then would recognition be accorded. But this high-handed attitude met with a storm of protest in the United States with the result that the State Department became distinctly conciliatory and on September 3, 1923, diplomatic relations were once more restored.

But Hughes's policy, apparently, was not entirely satisfactory to his successor Frank B. Kellogg, who had followed him into the State office in 1925. Kellogg, in an unnecessarily threatening statement, charged that the new Calles government was not exercising itself to protect American lives and property rights.

The enactment of the Mexican Petroleum Law and the Alien Land Law, in December, 1925, only increased the tension that Kellogg's sharp warning had created. The first measure vested the ownership of all Mexican petroleum deposits in the Mexican nation; and offered in exchange for titles obtained prior to 1917, 50-year concessions, to be dated from the time when exploitation had first commenced. The second law carried into effect the provisions of Article xxvii of the 1917 Constitution. Kellogg once again protested on behalf of American oil interests, but the oil and land regulations were put into effect, nevertheless; although, it is to be noted, the Mexican government did not proceed to annul the titles of those companies not complying with the registration law.

Beginning with the year 1927, relations between the two countries definitely took a turn for the better. Ambassador Sheffield, who had not been particularly successful in gaining the confidence of Mexicans, was recalled in October, 1927, and in his place was sent Dwight W. Morrow, partner in J. P. Morgan and Company and personal friend of the President. Morrow exercised himself in the interest of American rights without offending the national pride of the Mexicans; at the same time, the zeal with which he and the members of his family applied themselves to gaining Mexican good will, by a close study of the problems and aspirations of the people of that land, produced an effect that was altogether gratifying. Mexicans, apparently, were appreciative, for they began at once to make sweeping concessions. In November, 1927, the Mexican Supreme Court rejected that part of the land law which limited to a term of years the titles in subsoil deposits acquired and worked before 1917. The Mexican Congress proceeded to legislate to this effect; the laws were further liberalized by decree, the claims of foreign corporations as well as of nationals being recognized. The American State Department in 1928 expressed itself as satisfied with these concessions and advised Americans that henceforth they should seek protection of their rights in the Mexican courts. In 1929, the Mexican government, which for the preceding three years had been carrying on a heated controversy with the Catholic Church and threatening to seize all church properties and secularize education, adjusted this difficulty, too, on the basis of a compromise; and in 1930 the Mexican churches were once again opened to worshipers. By this step, American Catholics, who had become bitter foes of the Mexican government and who in 1926 had joined the intervention party, were somewhat propitiated.

Events in the twenties pointed, as well, to a clarification of the country's Caribbean policy. The military intervention that had taken place in the Dominican Republic in 1916 was terminated September 18, 1924. In Haiti, the process of American withdrawal was slower. From 1922 to 1930, the Haitians were actually governed by the American occupation. In the earlier year, the loose administrative machinery set up under President Wilson was entirely recast and the island republic took on the definite form of an American protectorate. An American high commissioner was appointed to supersede the minister to Haiti, and in this official's hands was centralized control over the treaty officials and the expeditionary force. Parliamentary government was suspended, while an American bureaucracy of some two hundred and fifty persons ruled over Haiti's financial offices, its gendarmerie, its public works and its public health, agricultural, and legal activities. In 1930, however, President Hoover indicated that the American occupation would definitely terminate with the lapsing of the treaty arrangements in 1936. In fact, by 1934 the marines were out of Haiti.

In the case of Nicaragua, too, there took place the liquidation of the old policy of active American occupation. Under the watchful eye of American officials the Nicaraguan Congress in 1925 proceeded to elect a new president who was installed with the consent of the State Department. The new incumbent possessed, however, no more security than his predecessors had had, and the presence in the country of large bands of insurgents forced the Coolidge administration to take formal cognizance of the situation. In January, 1927, President Coolidge reported to Congress the reasons for our continued concern over the Nicaraguan situation. We were compelled to intervene, he said: 1. to protect American life and property; 2. to enforce the Central American treaty of 1923 under which the five Central American republics of Guatemala, Honduras, Salvador, Nicaragua, and Costa Rica had pledged themselves not to recognize any administration which had seized political control as a result of a coup d'état, "so long as the freely elected representatives of the people thereof have not constitutionally reorganized the country" (the leader of the successful revolt, or anyone intimately connected with him, could not be designated president of the new administration);[1] 3. to safeguard our canal rights in Panama and in Nicaragua; 4. to forestall interference by other powers.

The result was the dispatching of Henry L. Stimson to Nicaragua in 1927, in an effort to find a formula which would be satisfactory to the various local factions. That same year, under Stimson's guidance, an understanding was reached that was acceptable to all parties except Augusto Sandino, who took to the jungle and for the next two years carried on a desultory guerrilla warfare against the Nicaraguan government and the American expeditionary force. The warring factions (except Sandino) surrendered their arms and the elections of 1928 were held; similar elections, under the eye of American marines, were held in 1930 and again in 1932. In 1933, however, President Hoover, in line with an earlier promise, withdrew the American forces.

There was no doubt that under Presidents Coolidge and Hoover the policy inaugurated by Theodore Roosevelt and followed by Taft and Wilson, that is to say, physical occupation by armed American forces, had been terminated. It was not that postwar America was more liberal than prewar America: our State Department had merely become more realistic. It was evident to American statesmen, in the late twenties and the thirties, that American purposes in the Caribbean could be effected just as completely, with more dispatch, and certainly with less friction or awakening of outside hostility, through a compliant native officialdom. This was mature, imperialist statecraft functioning quietly, effectively, and pervasively. It tended to still opposition at home, gain the friendship of the politicians of the Caribbean lands, and silence criticism of American purposes abroad, particularly in South America.

The question of our real interest in the Caribbean requires some examination. It is to be doubted whether American public policy was gov-

[1] It should be noted that this policy extended *only* to Central America and *not* to South America.

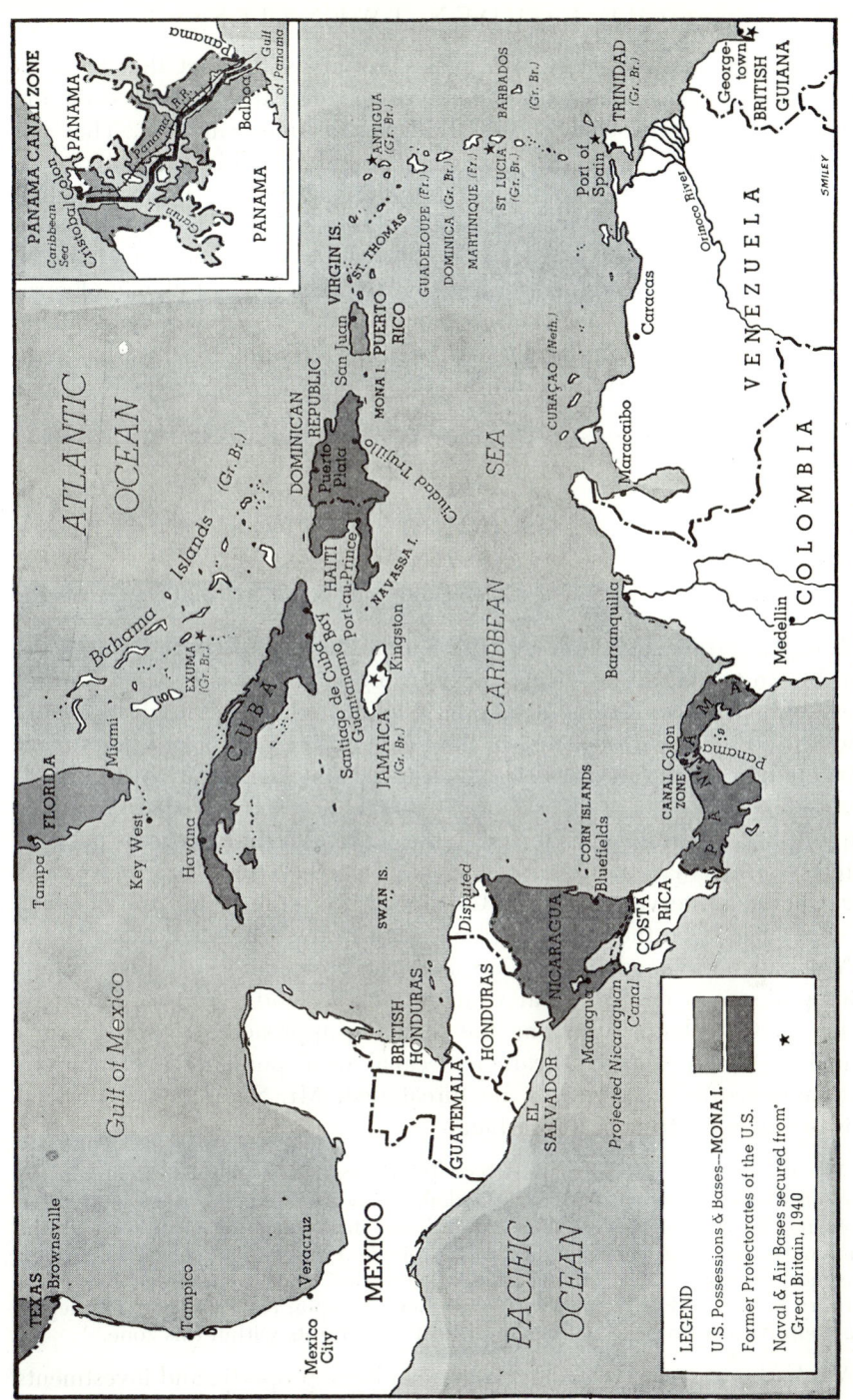

THE UNITED STATES IN THE CARIBBEAN

erned to an exclusive, or even a major, extent by the fact that financial investments of American citizens had grown so greatly in the decade and a half following the outbreak of the Spanish-American War. That our economic stake in the Caribbean countries was sizable was, of course, apparent; but that Washington was regularly exercising itself on behalf of American property rights, expending large sums of money on naval demonstrations, expeditionary forces, and the maintenance of elaborate treaty establishments, is a matter less easy to believe. The following figures indicate the nature of America's economic interest in those lands of the Caribbean in whose affairs we had been actively interfering, that is to say, the Central American countries, Haiti, and the Dominican Republic.

AMERICA'S ECONOMIC INTEREST IN THE CARIBBEAN, 1913–29

	1913	1929	Increase
Investments	$49,000,000	$218,186,000	345.3%
Imports from U.S	36,686,000	81,843,000	123.1%
Exports to U.S.	28,466,000	51,345,000	80.4%

It is plain, from such figures as these, that the increase in the American-Caribbean trade had not been nearly in proportion to the increase in investments. In other words, it may be doubted whether American capital had flowed southward because of the belief on the part of our investment bankers that here were markets which could quickly be taught to absorb or produce more goods. It is more reasonable to suppose that American capital in the Caribbean followed in the wake of a diplomatic or political interest rather than the reverse. We may say, therefore, that the reasons for American intervention in the Caribbean up to the end of the nineteen twenties had been the following, somewhat in the order indicated:

We had intervened in the Caribbean to protect our Isthmian policy. This policy was one of naval strategy entirely and revolved about the belief that the lands adjoining the seagoing approaches to the Panama Canal and the proposed Nicaraguan canal were points from which our national security could easily be threatened. Mr. Stimson had phrased this Isthmian doctrine in this fashion:

> The failure therefore of one of these [Caribbean] Republics to maintain the responsibilities which go with independence may lead directly to a situation imperilling the vital interest of the United States in its seagoing route through the Panama Canal. Out of this situation has followed our national policy—perhaps the most sensitive and generally held policy that we have—which for half a century has caused us to look with apprehension upon even the perfectly legitimate efforts of European nations to protect their rights within this zone.

We had intervened to protect American lives, property, and investments against local disorders and the depredations of armed bands.

We had landed troops upon the express invitation of the native governments.

We had intervened to preserve internal peace, to instruct the Caribbean peoples in the methods of orderly government, and to help them cope with their problems in a civilized fashion. Our motive had been in part humanitarian, in part economic, for it was fully appreciated that only through the cultivation of the arts of peace could these backward lands reach a higher industrial plane.

It may be said that in recent years this Isthmian policy has been in process of liquidation, largely because of State Department acceptance of the idea that European powers no longer were threatening American rights in the Isthmian Canal region. By the nineteen thirties American policy once more was based on the Monroe Doctrine (modified, of course, by our special rights in the Canal Zone and in the proposed Nicaraguan canal project). Indeed, the American protectorate over Cuba was ended in 1934 when President Franklin D. Roosevelt by an executive agreement terminated both the Platt Amendment and the protectorate. Similarly, in 1936, a treaty was signed between the United States and Panama under which our virtual protectorate over Panama also was surrendered.

More important as an earnest of American intentions in the Caribbean has been the repudiation of the Roosevelt corollary of the Monroe Doctrine, that policy which made the United States stand in the role of guarantor for the nations of the Western Hemisphere—that they would preserve the peace, pay their debts, and meet their obligations to European countries. In March, 1930, the State Department made public a memorandum on the Monroe Doctrine written in 1928 by J. Reuben Clark, at that time Undersecretary of State. In this document, the Monroe Doctrine was defined as possessing the following attributes: 1. It is unilateral. "The United States determines when and if the principles of the Doctrine are violated, and when and if violation is threatened. No other power of the world has any relationship to, or voice in, the implementing of the principles which the Doctrine contains." 2. "The Doctrine does not concern itself with purely inter-American relations." 3. "The Doctrine states a case of the United States versus Europe, not of the United States versus Latin America." 4. The United States has always used the Doctrine to protect Latin-American nations from the aggressions of European powers. "So far as Latin America is concerned, the Doctrine is now, and always has been, not an instrument of violence and oppression, but an unbought, freely bestowed and wholly effective guaranty of their freedom, independence, and territorial integrity against the imperialistic designs of Europe." 5. The Roosevelt corollary is not properly a part of the Doctrine itself, nor does it grow out of the Doctrine: ". . . it is not believed that this corollary is justified by the terms of the Monroe Doctrine, however much it may be justified by the application of the doctrine of self-preservation." [2]

All these developments were positive tokens of good will and were a harbinger of the time when Latin-American suspicions of "Yankee imperialism" would largely be dissipated. It was a good sign also that the policy inaugurated by Secretary Stimson was continued by Secretary Hull with the active support of President Franklin D. Roosevelt.

RENEWAL OF THE PEACE MOVEMENT

The United States had expressed its decision against entry into the League of Nations in the "solemn referendum" of 1920: and at no subsequent time was there any serious effort made to revise that verdict. Although the State Department from time to time co-operated either officially or unofficially in a number of League undertakings, the American people continued to regard the League as an instrument of Britain and France for the maintenance of the iniquitous Versailles system. During the nineteen twenties, these two countries had refused to relax their pressure on Germany; they had failed to recognize that their triumphs in North Africa, the Near East, and the Far East were making it just so much harder for the imperialist-capitalist economies of Italy and Japan to continue expanding peaceably. In the thirties these economically unappeased nations, now in the form of totalitarian states, challenged the status quo: and the League stood helpless in the face of aggression in Ethiopia, China, and Central Europe.

For a brief period, in the late nineteen twenties, the Briand-Kellogg Pact gave renewed hope for lasting peace. The pact had originated from French Premier Aristide Briand's suggestion, in April, 1927, that the United States and France enter into such a bilateral understanding; in December, Kellogg had proposed that the treaty be made multilateral and that, in time, all the nations of the world be invited to subscribe to it. Kellogg had pushed the matter with such energy that, by the summer of 1928, fourteen countries, including all the great world powers except Russia, had signified their willingness to participate along with the United States.

The treaty consisted of three articles: Article I outlawed war "as an instrument of national policy"; Article II committed the high contracting parties to settle all disputes, of whatever nature, by pacific means; Article III provided that the treaty was to go into effect as soon as the ratification of its signatories had been deposited at Washington. The convention, however, was to remain open for adherence by all the nations of the world. On January 15, 1929, the United States Senate, by a vote of 85 to 1, ratified

[2] This memorandum was in line with ideas Secretary Stimson had expressed as early as 1927.

the Kellogg Pact, and on July 29, 1929, it was proclaimed to be in force.

That the State Department meant to carry out the articles of the Pact of Paris in good faith (despite their violation by European and Asiatic signatories) was demonstrated by the fact that it proceeded to write a new group of bilateral arbitration conventions and to create the machinery for making the Bryan treaties for compulsory investigation effective. In 1928, Washington began to replace the Root conventions of 1908 to 1910 by another series which called for the arbitration of those international disputes that were justiciable in their nature. The first of these was written with France; by the middle of the thirties, a total of twenty-seven such agreements had been signed with almost all the important powers, the exceptions being Great Britain, Spain, Japan, and Russia. These new Kellogg treaties specifically exempted the following topics from arbitration: matters within the domestic jurisdiction of either of the contracting parties; matters involving the interest of third parties; matters affecting the Monroe Doctrine; matters involving the obligations of the other contracting party under the Covenant of the League of Nations.

At the same time, Secretary Kellogg began to extend the scope of the Bryan conciliation treaties. It will be remembered that Secretary Bryan had negotiated a number of treaties that called for the creation of permanent peace commissions empowered to investigate those disputes not submitted to arbitration. It was not until 1928 that the United States began giving thought to the erection of these investigating commissions or to the completion of the round of treaties. By the middle of the thirties, there existed in all some thirty-five of these agreements. Interestingly enough, Japan signed neither an arbitration nor a conciliation convention with the United States.

With Latin-American nations, the understandings reached in 1929 were even more specific. The two conventions signed at Washington provided for the following: First, compulsory arbitration of legal disputes arising out of the interpretation of treaties, questions of international law, and the existence of those facts which constituted violations of international law. Such disputes were to be submitted for arbitration to the World Court, to the Hague tribunal, or to special bodies to be created as disagreements arose. Second, the conciliation of all disputes, not submitted to arbitration, by commissions made up of members of the states involved. In cases of emergency, such differences were to be referred to committees at Washington or Montevideo, made up of diplomatic representatives accredited to those capitals. These two conventions were signed by the American government without reservation being made as to the Monroe Doctrine; they meant, in effect, that the United States was willing to forego the right of intervention and to submit all difficulties involving it and Latin-American nations to arbitration or conciliation. By the middle of the thirties the United States and sixteen other nations had ratified the conciliation convention and the United States and thirteen other nations the arbitration convention.

During the twenties, the United States moved steadily in the direction of membership in the World Court. It is interesting to note that while American opinion was indifferent toward affiliation with the League, the contrary was the case as far as participation in the World Court was concerned. In fact, from its inception in September, 1921, to the outbreak of World War II, four distinguished American jurists had sat on the tribunal.

So real was American interest in the World Court that President Harding, in February, 1923, submitted its protocol to the Senate for ratification, accompanied by a group of reservations prepared by Secretary of State Hughes. The Hughes reservations were the following: 1. adherence to the Court was not to imply the creation of a legal relationship between the United States and the League of Nations; 2. the United States was to have the right to appoint representatives to the League Council and Assembly when those bodies sat to elect judges; 3. the United States was to pay its fair share of the Court's expenses; 4. the statute of the Court was not to be amended without the consent of the United States. A fifth reservation, added by President Coolidge later, declared that none of the Court's advisory opinions was to be binding upon the United States, unless such opinions were specifically requested by us. However, the Senate was hostile, and three more years of agitation passed before finally, in January, 1926, it adopted a resolution favoring American adherence. In addition to incorporating the Hughes reservation in modified form, the resolution embodied a greatly amplified version of the Coolidge reservation. This declared that no advisory opinions could be rendered unless they were publicly given and until all the signatories to the protocol had been notified; further, the Court was not, without the consent of the United States, to "entertain any request for an advisory opinion touching any dispute or question in which the United States has or claims an interest."

In September, 1926, the forty-eight signers of the World Court protocol signified their willingness to accept the first four reservations and the first half of the fifth reservation which the Senate had outlined; to the American claim for a veto right over requests for advisory opinions touching American interests, they would not yield, however. Here the matter rested until the winter of 1929, when Elihu Root, at the invitation of the League Council, was able to work out a formula that was acceptable to World Court members and American State Department alike. The Root formula called for submission of all requests for advisory opinions to the United States; for the discussion of American objections to such opinions with the parties concerned; and for American withdrawal from the Court, without prejudice to its interests, if the other powers refused to concede that the United States had a vital national concern in the rendering of such opinions. In brief, as long as we were to be members of the World Court, the Court was to be prevented from handing down opinions affecting questions "in which the United States has or claims an interest." The Senate did not take action until January 7, 1935, and then by a vote of 52 for and 36 against (7 votes less than the necessary two-thirds), it rejected ratification. Despite its interest in peace and its concern with bilateral conventions and multilateral pacts (notably as affecting Latin America), the United States was reluctant to enter the international system that originated in the Versailles peace.

NAVAL LIMITATION

The decade of the nineteen twenties also saw an effort made to promote world peace by limitation of naval armaments. At the Washington Conference of 1921 to 1922 and at the London Conference of 1930 treaties were written that were designed to stop the competition in the building of dreadnoughts, to establish a system of ratios for capital and auxiliary ships, and to recognize that naval parity existed between the United States and Great Britain.

The call for the Washington Conference was issued by President Harding in the summer of 1921, invitations being extended to Great Britain, France, Italy, and Japan for the purpose of discussing the question of limitation of armament; and to Belgium, the Netherlands, Portugal, and China (in addition to the great powers) for the purpose of discussing questions affecting the Pacific and the Far East. The conference wrote two sets of treaties: the first group related to naval limitation; the second to matters rising out of Far Eastern questions.

The following understandings emerged from these meetings: The powers agreed to the scrapping of a number of battleships which were either afloat or still in the process of construction. They agreed to a holiday, until 1931, in the building of capital ships and settled the battleship-construction program of the United States, Great Britain, and Japan for the decade of the thirties. They also agreed to the following ratios of capital ship tonnage: 5 (United States): 5 (Great Britain): 3 (Japan): 1.67 (France and Italy). The United States, Great Britain, and Japan signed a convention in which these powers pledged themselves to the maintenance of the status quo as far as fortifications and naval bases in the Pacific Ocean were concerned. Specifically, Japan promised to limit the fortifications of certain of her islands in the Pacific; and the United States promised to do similarly as regards the Philippine and Aleutian Islands. But the conferees could come to no decision on the matter of auxiliary craft; no treaty, therefore, was drawn up.

The agreements reached with regard to the Far East were the following: First, the representatives of the United States, Great Britain, Japan, and France signed, together, a Four-Power Treaty, whose purpose was "to respect their rights in relation to their insular possessions and insular dominions in the region of the Pacific Ocean." This convention went on to stipulate that any controversies arising among the high contracting parties, which could not be settled by diplomacy, were to be submitted to joint conferences of all the signatories for their consideration and adjustment. Second, China and Japan succeeded in arriving at an agreement concerning Shantung, under which Japan consented to return the German rights in the Peninsula to China. Third, there was also signed a Nine-Power Treaty (in which the five powers were joined by Belgium, the Netherlands, Portugal, and China) that guaranteed the territorial integrity of China with continued recognition of the Open-Door principle. It was to be a widened Open Door, however, which promised equal opportunity for the industry as well as the commerce of all nations, and which pledged the powers not to seek special rights or privileges for their own nationals at the expense of the nationals of other countries. Finally, another Nine-Power Treaty established the principle of China's control over her own tariff. This convention, too, called for the creation of a commission to study the question of the abolition of the extraterritorial rights of foreigners in China. Without too much controversy, the Senate proceeded to ratify the treaties that the American delegation had signed.

In 1928, our State Department wrote a treaty with the Chinese Nationalist Government in which we agreed to accept exclusive Chinese tariff control; but we did not consent to the relinquishment of our extraterritorial rights. In a measure, therefore, we proceeded to accept the spirit of the Far Eastern settlement. Not as much could be said for the other signatories of the Nine-Power Treaty. In September, 1931, Japan invaded Manchuria and in February, 1932, she set up the puppet state of Manchukuo, completely under her domination. This was clearly in violation of the Briand-Kellogg Pact and the Nine-Power Treaty; and in a note to Japan, Secretary Stimson said so, at the same time pointing out that the United States could not recognize the new state. But the great European powers were unwilling to back up the United States.

While the subsequent Roosevelt administrations did not in so many words reaffirm the Stimson doctrine, American policy in the Far East was guided by it. In this way, a part of the work of the Washington Conference was undone in a decade; the other part, that concerned with naval limitation, too, went by the board—in this case, in a decade and a half.

We have noted that the Washington Conference failed to make any arrangements for limiting the construction of light cruisers and auxiliary naval craft. Abortive efforts were made to remedy this defect in 1924 and again in 1927. It remained for the London Conference of January to April, 1930, to formulate a three-power pact which was signed by the United States, Great Britain, and Japan, and proclaimed in force October 27, 1930.

We may sum up the achievements of the London Conference in this fashion: 1. The conference established naval parity between Great Britain and the United States, once and for all. 2. It continued the capital-ship construction holiday to the end of 1936. 3. Although it did not provide for a cessation in the building of auxiliary craft, it did fix limits on such building within a system of ratios and so tended to restrict the total of naval armament. 4. The treaty set up what was, to Japan, a satisfactory relation between American and Japanese naval strength. At the Washington Conference, the ratio of capital ships agreed upon had been 5:3. The London Conference made this 10:6 for big-gun cruisers; 10:7 for small-gun cruisers; 10:7 for destroyers; and 10:10 for submarines. 5. Under the so-called "escalator clause," any contracting party was permitted to build additional ships in any category if a nonsignatory should launch upon a new building program out of line with its relative naval position. By 1936, as will be indicated below, the treaty powers were ready to invoke the "escalator clause" because a burst of naval rearmament by Germany and Italy was disturbing the *status quo*. Indeed, on December 31, 1936, the London Treaty was a dead letter and naval disarmament a lost cause, for a new naval race was taking place all over the world.

INTERALLIED DEBTS AND REPARATION PAYMENTS

Significant among the factors making for an acrimonious isolationism among many influential American political figures during the period between the wars was the existence of a great body of inter-Allied debt which Europeans considered a contribution to the common war effort, but which numerous Americans regarded as a transaction more or less on the commercial level. During World War I, and in the two years immediately thereafter, the United States government had lent to the Allied powers a total of $10,350,000,000. It is important to note that of this amount, a total of $3,273,000,000 was lent after the Armistice. In 1922, Congress proceeded to set up machinery for the refunding of these war debts, owed us by twenty nations. Washington made it plain, however, that the conditions for refunding would be adjusted with every consideration being given the debtors' different abilities to meet their obligations. Between June, 1923, and May, 1930, seventeen of the twenty nations came to terms with us, as appears in the following table:

The Refunding of the War Loans, 1923–30

Country	Amounts of original loans	Amounts of funded debts	Average interest rates over whole period
Armenia *	$ 11,959,917	$ —	—
Austria	24,055,708	24,614,885	3.3%
Belgium	379,087,200	417,780,000	1.8%
Cuba †	10,000,000	—	—
Czechoslovakia	91,879,671	185,071,023	3.3%
Estonia	13,999,145	13,830,000	3.3%
Finland	8,281,926	9,000,000	3.3%
France	3,404,818,945	4,025,000,000	1.6%
Great Britain	4,277,000,000	4,600,000,000	3.3%
Greece	27,167,000	32,497,000	3.3%
Hungary	1,685,835	1,982,555	3.3%
Italy	1,648,034,050	2,042,000,000	0.4%
Jugoslavia	51,758,486	62,850,000	1.0%
Latvia	5,132,287	5,775,000	3.3%
Liberia †	26,000	—	—
Lithuania	4,981,628	6,432,465	3.3%
Nicaragua *	431,849	—	—
Poland	159,668,972	178,560,000	3.3%
Rumania	37,922,675	66,560,560	3.3%
Russia *	192,601,297	—	—
Total	$10,350,490,597	$11,671,953,489	2.1% ‡

* Debts unfunded.
† Debts paid.
‡ Average for all settlements.

But from what source were these interallied debts to be satisfied? Plainly, from German reparations. During the whole decade of the twenties, the Allies sought to perfect a formula that would allow the collection of the greatest possible sum from the vanquished nation and at the same time not cripple her economic and financial life. After several unworkable schemes were tried, there was evolved in 1929 the Young Plan,[3] which seemed to promise some hope of success. This called for the following: First, 37 annual payments, averaging $512,500,000, were to be made, to be followed by 22 further annual payments averaging $391,250,000. Actually, over the 59 years, Germany was to pay $27,500,000,000; but the annuities, capitalized at 5 per cent, represented a reparation

[3] So-called after the American chairman of the formulating committee, Owen D. Young.

amount totaling only $9,272,000,000. Second, of each annuity payment in the first group of 37 years, $165,000,000 was to be unconditional and to be earmarked to meet the reconstruction costs of the Allies. The conditional part was to be scaled down in proportion to any adjustments that might be made in the interallied debts. That is to say, if the United States reduced the amounts the Allies were to pay her, the Allies in turn would reduce the conditional payments to be made by Germany. In the second group of 22 annuities, there was to be no unconditional portion; therefore these entire payments were to be adjusted to the interallied debts. Third, Germany was to obtain the sums needed for the annuities from two sources; namely, from a mortgage on the German railroads, and from ordinary receipts in the governmental budget. Fourth, a Bank for International Settlements was set up to handle the reparation funds and to have certain other fiscal functions.

Thus the Young Plan definitely joined reparation payments and interallied debts together. But our State and Treasury Departments consistently refused to regard the two as inseparable, even going so far as to decline American representation on the directorate of the Bank for International Settlements. Nevertheless, the relationship existing between the interallied debts and the reparation annuities was only too apparent. The Allies had made loans to one another, usually estimated to amount to $21,613,-000,000. But in view of the liberal terms on the basis of which the intergovernmental loans had been refunded, the capitalized value had been scaled down to $10,814,000,000. On the other hand, the capitalized value of the German reparation annuities was $9,272,000,000.[4]

By 1931, it was generally recognized that the Young Plan was no more satisfactory than its predecessors: it far outran Germany's ability to pay. Then, in the middle of the year, when the whole German financial structure was threatened with ruin and it was evident that the annuity for 1931 to 1932 could not be met, President Hoover was compelled to bow before the inevitable: after an exchange of views with the principal nations affected, Washington announced the establishment of a moratorium, for a single year, on all intergovernmental debts and reparation payments. The two financial operations were now officially linked and we could col-

[4] How the Allies managed to skim what cream there was may be noted from the following. Germany paid in all on the various reparation accounts $4,470,000,000. The Allies paid to the United States, against the war debts, $2,606,000,000. On the other hand, it was made possible for Germany to finance her payments in considerable measure out of private loans which continued until 1931. Of the estimated total of $6,000,000,000 lent to Germany, $2,500,000,000 came from the United States. Under the Nazi regime, repatriation of German dollar bonds began to take place, largely through the use of blocked *Reichsmarks,* and at a discount frequently as much as 70 cents on the dollar. In other words, Americans got almost nothing when the transactions were balanced. On the other hand, Europeans got more cash out of Germany, lent her less, and into the bargain got more favorable terms in the settlement of the private-loan accounts.

lect from the Allies only as much or as little as they, in turn, could collect from Germany.

Indeed, in 1932, our former Allies made this an explicit policy when, at a conference at Lausanne, they agreed to write off 90 per cent of the German reparations due under the Young Plan, provided that "a satisfactory settlement is obtained between them [Germany's creditors] and their own creditors [the United States]." The United States took no official cognizance of this understanding; and here the matter continued to rest with "token" payments being made up to 1933 and then even these stopping.[5]

With the Nazi party in power in Germany, after midsummer 1933, and pledged as Hitler was to the termination of reparation payments, it was becoming increasingly clear that the payments on the war loans had ceased finally. Americans viewed this state of affairs with bitterness. On the one hand, our former Allies continued to expend staggering sums for rearmament purposes at the same time that they protested their inability to pay. On the other, there was the realization that the cost of "making the world safe for democracy" during the years 1914 to 1920 in considerable measure was to be borne by future generations of Americans in terms of an increased tax burden.

One thing, at any rate, the United States learned, and that was that our purse strings were not to be loosened again so easily—at any rate until the nineteen forties. In 1934, Congress passed the Johnson Act, which forbade foreign governments in default on their debts to the United States to float public issues in this country. The Neutrality legislation of 1935 to 1937, as we shall see, extended the same prohibition to belligerents, outside of the Western Hemisphere, whether or not they were in default.

RUSSIAN RELATIONS

The United States, alone among the great powers, failed to establish diplomatic relations with Russia during the nineteen twenties. Not only would the State Department not grant recognition, but it steadfastly declined to encourage trade by private individuals with the Soviets. The following influences and beliefs, as guiding Washington's Russian policy during the twenties, are to be noted particularly:

The State Department refused to consider the Communist rule in Russia as being aught but temporary. Recognition, therefore, awaited the collapse of Sovietism.

Administration officials declined to become enthusiastic about the potential significance of the Russian-American trade.

---

[5] The little country of Finland was the only one to continue the payments (she did so in full each year) on the interallied loans.

It was held at Washington that Russian labor, in particular industries, was often conscripted. According to our tariff laws, therefore, commodities produced under such conditions could not be imported by Americans. In 1931, the American Treasury Department placed an embargo on Russian lumber and pulpwood on the ground of the use of forced labor.[6]

The Soviets had repudiated the Russian state debt, had confiscated the property of American citizens, and had refused to satisfy the claims of American nationals against the Russian government. The United States had advanced $192 million to the Kerensky government (which preceded the Soviet regime), in 1917, and this debt had never been funded. American bankers, in 1916, had sold to the American investing public $75 million worth of Russian imperial bonds. These had been defaulted. In addition, Americans had claims totaling some $430 million against the Russian government for losses suffered in the revolutions of 1917 and as a result of property confiscations.[7]

There never could be friendly relations between the two nations as long as Russia carried on communist propaganda against American institutions, either through the American Communist party or through its own trade agencies.

Thus, we may say that the State Department insisted upon the presentation of tangible evidences of Russian good faith and ability to meet obligations as conditions precedent to the opening of negotiations. European governments, on the other hand, recognized first and negotiated later. Nevertheless, if official Washington was critical toward Russia, the American people certainly were interested in the Russian experiment and, beginning with the late twenties, books and reports on Russia, depicting the efforts of the Soviet governments to carry out their gigantic industrialization program, were being widely read. It is true that the State Department would neither countenance the floating of a Russian loan in this country nor give its encouragement to the extension, by Americans, of credits to the Soviets. This did not prevent American citizens and corporations, however, from entering into commercial relations with Russia at their own risk. Long-term credits were granted by outstanding American manufacturers, American technicians helped build and start off Soviet enterprises, American promoters sought to acquire concessions for the exploitation of Russian raw materials. The result was that Russian-American trade grew to considerable proportions in the late twenties. So, in 1913, American exports to Russia were worth $26,465,000; in 1930, they were worth $136,307,000. In 1913, American imports from Russia were worth $29,315,-

[6] But it would not ban the importation of manganese (needed in steel production). Thus the lines of economic necessity and political principle often cross, to the complete confusion of the latter.

[7] Of course, these claims have never been critically examined. Claims commissions would probably scale them down radically.

000; by 1930, at $24,386,000, they were almost at the prewar level. That these economic factors would ultimately have altered Old Guard Republican policy, even had there been no New Deal, is a safe assumption.

The anomalies of this situation and the fact that Japanese maneuvers in the Far East were drawing the United States and Russia together (at any rate, as far as Eastern foreign policy was concerned), prompted President Franklin D. Roosevelt to seek an accommodation. At his invitation the Russian Commissar for Foreign Affairs, Maxim Litvinoff, came to Washington; and after a series of conversations, formal diplomatic relations were declared resumed on November 16, 1933. The basis was an exchange of notes between President Roosevelt and Mr. Litvinoff.

The notes committed both governments to respect the territorial integrity of each other and not to tolerate within their borders organizations which had as their aim "the overthrow of, or bringing about by force of a change in the political or social order" of the other. (The reference here, obviously, was to the Communist, or Third International, which presumably was not to carry on its propagandist activities in the United States.) Russia waived all claims for American military activities in the eastern Siberian intervention after World War I, while other financial claims and counterclaims were to be negotiated between the new Russian ambassador to Washington and the State Department. Despite the fact that ambassadors were appointed in 1934, by 1948 the claims question still remained unsettled.

Section X

IMPERIAL AMERICA IN THE MACHINE AGE

· 31 ·

Capital and Labor

THE GROWTH OF POPULATION

BETWEEN 1871 and 1900, the population of the United States had almost doubled in size; during the thirty years from 1901 to 1930, the gain had been but a little more than 60 per cent. The slowing up of the country's population growth was a definite characteristic of the twentieth century and was due largely to the following factors: 1. the restriction of immigration; 2. the movement from the country to the cities; 3. a wider exercise of birth control, particularly by the country's urban populations. In 1900, the population of the United States was 75,994,575; in 1910, 91,972,266; in 1920, 105,710,620; in 1930, 122,775,046; in 1940, 131,669,275. The population was reckoned at 143,382,000 in January, 1948, and estimates of a population of more than 154,000,000 were made for 1950, since the birth rate had shown an extraordinary rise from the low level of the thirties. The gains in population had hardly been distributed equally in the period 1921 to 1930. In fact, more than one-fourth of the total increase was concentrated in the two states of New York and California. Each of these states had gained more than 2,000,000; Michigan, Texas, and Illinois had each gained more than 1,000,000; Florida had increased its population by one half, New Jersey by more than one-fourth, and North Carolina by one-fourth. Although the percentage increase in population in the period 1931 to 1940 was less than half of what it had been in any previous decade for the nation as a whole, the Pacific coast states increased their population by 18.8 per cent. This trend continued during the war years, when the West Coast added more than 1,500,000 to its population, principally in such centers as Los Angeles, Portland, and San Francisco.

The country had become increasingly urbanized in the almost fifty years since the opening of the new century. In 1900, 40 per cent of the population was urban (living in communities having 2500 or more inhabitants); in 1910, 45.8 per cent; in 1920, 51.4 per cent; in 1930, 56.2 per cent; in 1940, 56.5 per cent. Although the outer edges of metropolitan areas tended to grow faster than their centers in the period 1930 to 1945, America's population had been unable to resist the pull of the cities. Chief among the reasons for the great growth of our urban population were the following: the advances of industrialization; the country's large immigrant population had naturally gravitated toward the cities to join kinsmen and to take up anew the old community life of their native lands; Americans, in growing numbers, had come to demand the fuller satisfactions of living—the modern apartment houses, the amusements, educational facilities, outlets for aesthetic enjoyment, the excitement and movement of crowds—which only the cities could offer. Nothing more typified the civilization of America in the postwar era than metropolitan New York, where, within a radius of fifty miles of Manhattan Island, were closely planted 290 cities, boroughs, and villages seating a population of more than 10,000,000. These were all part of New York City's urban life: they came here to work, play, shop; they read the New York newspapers, attended the New York schools and colleges, had New York's heroes and spoke New York's slang. And what was true of metropolitan New York was also true in only less degree of nearly a score of other metropolitan centers.

Not that a countervailing tendency was not beginning to evidence itself. If the great cities were glamorous, they were also crowded and impersonal; their transportation facilities were becoming taxed well-nigh beyond endurance; their living quarters were so many huge barracks that shut out the sky and the sun and put to an end that pleasant friendliness and community of feeling which had been so characteristic of provincial America. The city dweller had a small circle of intimates, but he had no neighbors. He had his personal problems, but the affairs of his community were remote and unreal. Municipal administration had become institutionalized, along with so much of industry and commerce, and public opinion was a small still voice. By the twenties, here and there a few Americans were beginning to quit the great cities, in protest against these dehumanizing tendencies. But the movement toward a decentralizing process could not go very far because the countryside and semirural communities still failed to offer opportunities for individual advancement comparable to the metropolitan centers. Thus, despite the fact that rural America was becoming a more attractive place to live in than it had been but two decades back, flight from the metropolis generally stopped in the suburbs, where the slave of the 8:17 fondly believed he was enjoying the freedom of the country without relinquishing the advantages of the city.

THE GROWTH OF INDUSTRY

As we have seen, by 1900 the machine had become an important factor in American life. But in the three decades following, the machine was to become mightier and have a more pervasive influence—it was to produce more, furnish more comforts, conquer new domains, until by the mid-twentieth century, Americans began to regard it very much as the hallmark, the peculiar, distinguishing sign, of our whole civilization. The machine was ruthless: it broke down privacy, swept away ancient trades, destroyed skill, created technological unemployment, wasted natural resources, standardized and sometimes vulgarized taste, quickened the tempo of men's lives and brought in a crop of new psychoneurotic disorders, made warfare a horror and an inferno, constricted the size of the world until men almost everywhere were performing their daily tasks in the same way, employing their idle moments in much the same fashion, and very largely thinking the same thoughts. Yet the machine was beneficent, too: it was releasing mankind from the bitter, back-breaking labor of centuries and was making life comfortable for the toiling masses; it was producing, if only slowly, more leisure time; it was turning out more goods and raising standards of living everywhere. True, inequalities in wealth and income still existed; and periodic breakdowns, or business crises, continued to occur, during which production slowed down and large numbers of persons were thrown out of work to suffer privations and often real want. The fault, however, lay not in the machine but in the instabilities of our society.

The machine, too, made for more color and variety in our daily lives; it put amusements within the reach of all; it dressed the humblest shopgirl in clothes whose designs, at least, were the work of the smartest Paris salons. It was making life healthier and more secure against the ravages of nature; it was making Americans bolder and more certain of themselves; if it was destroying old crafts—glass blowers, weavers, cabinetmakers—it was creating new groups of artisans—radio mechanics, sanitary engineers, chauffeurs, steel construction workers. Thus the machine worked for both good and ill, and toward which side the balances tipped only a rash or a prophetic person might venture to say.

Such were the general characteristics of the period in which Americans were moving in the postwar era. What were the more particular attributes of this machine age? Between 1900 and 1929, the wealth of the country had risen from $88 billion to $361 billion, and the per capita distribution had almost tripled. There were definite signs to be read of the bettering of the national well-being: increases in savings bank deposits; the great growth of life insurance policies; the appearance and flourishing of the building and loan associations (which made home ownership possible); the great increase in school attendance; a widespread diffusion of goods once regarded as luxuries but by the end of the twenties considered part of the daily round of living (for example, the automobile, the telephone and radio, electrical lighting and household appliances, modern plumbing, and central heating). The total realized income grew from $27,100,000,000 in 1909 to $66,000,000,000 in 1922 and $84,000,000,000 in 1929. In terms of 1913 dollars, these incomes were as follows: 1909, $28,200,000,000; 1922, $40,400,000,000; 1929, $52,500,000,000. In 1929, the per capita wealth was $2977 and the per capita income was $692.

The tabulation that follows presents the data for manufacturing establishments in selected years over the period being discussed:

GROWTH OF MANUFACTURES IN THE UNITED STATES, 1899–1929 *

(In thousands)

Year	No. of establishments	Wage earners	Value of products	Value added by manufacture
1899	208	4,713	$11,407,000	$ 4,831,000
1914	273	7,024	24,217,000	9,858,000
1919	214	8,998	62,000,000	24,803,000
1921	196	6,944	43,619,000	18,327,000
1927	192	8,350	62,718,000	27,585,000
1929	207	8,743	69,417,000	31,687,000

* For 1899 and 1914, the figures relate to factories (excluding hand and neighborhood establishments), whose products were valued in excess of $500; for subsequent years, only factories whose products were valued in excess of $5000 are included.

Which were America's great industries at the end of the decade of the golden nineteen twenties? The following were the outstanding: textiles and products; machinery; steel and products; food products; paper and printing; chemicals; transportation and equipment; lumber and products; stone, glass and clay; nonferrous metals. In short, we were turning out vast quantities of capital, or producer, and consumer goods. We were happily circumstanced: thanks to our great wealth of raw materials, our great capital plant, our technological skills, and our magnificent domestic market, we were—or seemed—safe from those perils that constantly threatened the older economies of European nations. The twenties, also, had seen pioneering in new fields to employ new capital investments and create job opportunities for fresh skills and part of the workers displaced by advancing mechanization in older industries. During the twenties the radio, aviation, motion picture, natural gas, and chemical industries had suddenly appeared and as quickly grown to maturity; while the advance of the automobile and the electric-power and light industry had brought in their train a whole host of new activities and services.

The East and the Middle West continued to be the centers of industry and finance in the twentieth century, as they had been in the nineteenth,

Nevertheless, in the South and trans-Mississippi West industrialization proceeded at a more rapid pace. For the most part, both the newer regions produced consumer goods where nearness to raw materials and cheaper labor gave them comparative advantages. Thus, the South tended to concentrate on cotton textiles, rayon, tobacco products, fertilizer production, and iron manufacturing, while in the trans-Mississippi West foodstuffs, feeds, iron, and nonferrous metals predominated. However, as the century advanced, the manufactures of both regions became more generalized. Coincidentally, labor became less docile; unions began to be organized; capital fought back; and by 1930 it had become evident that neither of the newer regions was destined to skip that dark cycle of turbulence so characteristic of the industrial development of the East and Middle West.

The processes of marketing, too, had undergone a complete transformation. One might mention the following phenomena as being recent developments of our changed industrial society: 1. Installment selling. During the years 1923 to 1929, the amount of installment purchasing was estimated to be in the neighborhood of $5,000,000,000 annually. 2. The growth of the practice of hand-to-mouth buying. This had a profound effect on style changes and on the great increase of marketing costs, particularly in the expenditures for advertising. 3. The mounting volume of advertising. It was estimated that $1,500,000,000 was being expended annually during the twenties on this form of marketing. 4. The appearance of the chain store, notably in the Five-and-Ten-Cents, groceries, drugs, tobacco, and candy fields. In a number of cities studied by the Census Bureau it was found that chain stores handled from one-fourth to one-third of the total retail sales. 5. The willingness of the American buying public to experiment with and purchase new wares, on a mass scale. This was true of the radio, the use of rayons, cosmetics, novelty shoes for women, electric stokers, oil-burning furnaces, electrical refrigerators.

MASS PRODUCTION

The machine was the emblem of the time; and mass production of goods, of standardized design, uniform quality, interchangeable parts, was what flowed from the machine. Nothing was more symbolical of our era than the chassis assembly line of American automobile plants, where every process was routinized and the men performed their single functions with the precision of automatons.

To produce units in the rhythm of the machine, power was necessary, and our use of power, therefore, quadrupled in the short period after the turn of the century. After the war, America was using as much electrical energy as all the rest of the world put together. Also, standardization, under a machine economy, was a prime requisite, and the standardizing of products was pushed with a zeal that leveled all barriers before it. In a short ten years the Department of Commerce, for most of the time under the able direction of Herbert Hoover, could report that under its auspices more than one hundred plans for standardization had been adopted in as many industries, and that the estimated annual saving to the manufacturers involved was a quarter of a billion dollars. Standardization meant that further mechanization was possible, of course, but it also made easier the replacement of parts and permitted the integration of allied industries.

Our acceptance of machine production had other results. The reduction of waste and the development of new materials and products went hand in hand with simplification and standardization. The enterprisers of the twentieth century were less willing to depend upon chance and the work of individual erratic genius to blaze new trails for them and furnish other outlets for their great accumulations of capital. They subsidized scientific foundations, kept up a ceaseless round of experiments, and carried on their payrolls large staffs of laboratory workers who puzzled over problems of pure as well as applied research. There was little likelihood of raw materials failing the machine age when this constant questing for substitutes and the reduction of waste kept up its ceaseless round. One might mention the following processes and products which had come out of the laboratories of industry: the hydrogenation process for extracting gasoline from coal, oil shale, and other minerals; the cracking of gasoline; the development of sheet cellulose (cellophane) as a dustproof and waterproof wrapper; dry milk, corn syrup, cellulose sausage casings, viosterol; carbon dioxide ice; new types of steel; lacquer, laminated bakelite, rayon, pyrex (glass substitute), fabrikoid (leather substitute).

PRODUCTIVITY

Nowhere did the influence of the machine display itself more startlingly than in the increased productivity of labor in industry. Here we are brought face to face with the nature of that new industrial revolution that had set in during the nineteen tens, had been accelerated during the twenties and, indeed, was continuing at an unchecked pace during the thirties. The machines were producing more goods—and were requiring less and less manpower for their operation. Nothing has revealed this change of affairs more convincingly than the figures collected by the National Resources Board, a New Deal agency. These showed that between 1920 and 1929 the whole of manufacturing, in terms of unit-labor productivity, became 30 per cent more efficient; mining became more than 20 per cent more efficient; and steam railroading became 20 per cent more efficient.

Here was one of the crucial points on which examination of our industrial society required focusing. Greater productivity per unit of labor meant obviously the utilization of new machine techniques and therefore the creation of new investment opportunities for capital. On the other hand, greater productivity made for labor displacement. Was there not a need for so-called buffer employment while men were shifting gradually from those industries from which they were being separated to new ones in time requiring more hands? The nineteen twenties could afford to disregard the problem in view of the fact that the total of unemployed and the smaller total of disemployed as a result of technological advance were not very great.

It should be pointed out here that unemployment figures were never recorded by a public agency, and estimates had to be resorted to. That unemployment continued to exist, even in boom periods, was generally recognized. It was estimated, for example, that during the years 1922 to 1929, the average annual figure was between 2,000,000 to 2,500,000 workers. Unemployment was generally due to the seasonal characteristics of trades, the shutting down of plants, industrial disputes, and voluntary quitting. To these more or less temporary forms was added that grimmer kind already referred to—technological disemployment.

What the toll of technological disemployment was, we did not know. But that its figures were large and that the forced shifting of labor from old to new forms of employment was accompanied by great travail were generally recognized. So, from 1919 to 1929, industries employing 40 per cent of the country's wage earners were using 900,000 fewer workers. In manufacturing, in that single decade, productivity had increased 30 per cent, while the number of workers had declined 546,000; in railroad transportation, productivity had increased 20 per cent, while the number of workers had declined 253,000; in mining, productivity had increased 20 per cent, while the number of workers had declined 100,000. In the same period the country's population had increased by 7,000,000. In short, almost 8,000,000 new job seekers were compelled to look for work in lines of endeavor outside of manufacturing, the railroads, and mining. That there should be a residue, because of the excess of job seekers over new opportunities presented, was inevitable. Wesley Clair Mitchell placed this shrinkage in jobs for the years 1920 to 1927 at 650,000.

THE POSITION OF LABOR

That the upper strata of labor, as well as capital, enjoyed the fruits of the prosperity of the twenties there was ample evidence to prove. American standards of living were considerably superior, in the postwar period, to any prevailing, certainly since the Civil War; that the margin between those of America and Europe was widening was apparent as well. But the gains of the working class—in higher wages, lower hours, better working conditions—were generally confined to the so-called aristocrats of labor, that is to say, the well-organized skilled craft workers. It was no accident, therefore, that the years 1920 to 1930 were years of waning trade-union militancy; and the unskilled were compelled to fend for themselves. One finds therefore that whereas membership in American trade unions grew fairly steadily until the end of World War I, it began thenceforth to decline. Industrial disputes also decreased in numbers and duration. In 1897, there had been 447,000 American trade unionists; in 1900, 868,500; by 1914, 2,716,900; and in 1920—the all-time peak until 1937—5,110,800. By 1922, the trade unions had lost 1,000,000 members; and in 1929 the total membership was 4,330,000.

The American Federation of Labor, the outstanding federation of workers' organizations, continued during the period wedded to its philosophy of "pure and simple" unionism—of craft organizations, wage consciousness, and job monopoly. That it should lose in prestige and remain stationary in membership, during the twenties, was inevitable. The Federation continued as a congeries of craft unions: of boilermakers, bricklayers, carpenters, printers, quarry workers. These jealously clung to their jurisdictional rights and sought, in the interest of job monopoly, to limit their numbers by long apprenticeships and high initiation fees. New fields the American Federation of Labor seemed unwilling, perhaps unable, to explore.

Some of the reasons for organized labor's inability to grow in the postwar years were the following: 1. The traditional policy of voluntarism, first laid down by Samuel Gompers, which held that labor's advance could be furthered only by its own economic power. Hence, organized labor continued unwilling to organize for political action or to demand the intervention of the state in such vital matters as those pertaining to wages, hours, and social insurance 2. The adoption of a program of union-management co-operation. Voluntarism, on its other face, called for working-class militancy; and this the leadership of the American Federation of Labor eschewed. In the words of David J. Saposs, the keenest student of the problem of the period:

. . . union-management co-operation was elevated to a cardinal principle, and was substituted for belligerency as the program of voluntarism. The new procedure was to sell unionism to the employer. If he recognized the union and permitted his workers to join it, the union in turn would co-operate in setting up machinery which would co-operate with the employer in increasing his profits through reducing costs and enlarging his markets. . . . The union now became a service agency equally interested not only in its own welfare but in that of the employer.

This program, however, was successful only with lesser employers; the great mass industries refused the proffered hand of friendship. 3. Mechanization, which was destroying rapidly the skills of the old-time artisans and hence rendering the old craft distinctions obsolete. With organized labor's refusal to shift from a craft to an industrial basis, its chances for winning over the country's great body of workers became increasingly slighter. 4. Welfare capitalism (that is to say, company health, recreational, and insurance programs), which sought to give the workers at least the same benefits as were offered by the conservative unions. 5. Open-shop movements and company unions. 6. Yellow-dog contracts, as a result of which unions might be enjoined from organizing those individual workers who had signed such agreements with their employers. 7. The refusal on the part of many of the A. F. of L. unions to admit into their memberships Negro workers. 8. Labor injunctions, which placed serious obstacles in the path of unions engaged in industrial disputes. This last phenomenon we must examine at greater length.

The chief weapon against organized labor, in the armory of capital, was not violence or counterorganization so much as the use of a peculiarly American legal device, that is to say, the injunction. Appealing to federal and state courts sitting in equity (on the ground that substantive law was deficient), employers in increasing numbers, beginning with the nineties, took to suing for injunctions to prevent unions and striking workers from committing irreparable injury to their property. The courts were quick to grant the type of relief requested. Also, the process was a swift and a successful one. During the nineteen twenties, the most common forms of injunctions, sued for against workers and their representatives the trade unions, were the following: from engaging in strikes (whether local, general, or sympathetic); from assembling to act or organize for a strike; from paying strike benefits; from engaging in boycotts; from picketing; from adopting rules against the handling of goods made by nonunion labor; from making trade agreements with employers stipulating the employment of union labor only and the production of goods under union conditions; from making trade agreements for the limitation of production; from sabotaging and the use of violence.

Such procedure received the sanction of the Supreme Court, curiously enough, on the basis of its interpretation of the Sherman Antitrust Law. The Sherman Law was invoked by the federal government itself against the striking railroad workers in 1894 and Eugene V. Debs's jail sentence for contempt was upheld by the Supreme Court. It was true that the Court had not specifically rested its judgment in that instance on the Sherman Law. Nevertheless, the way was open to the general use of the injunction against strikers on the plea of irreparable property damage. In 1908, the Supreme Court definitely decided that organized labor might be regarded as a conspiracy in restraint of trade, and hence that the Sherman Law could be made to apply to its activities as well as to those of industrial monopolies. From 1908 to the end of the twenties, the Supreme Court proceeded to add to the list of labor activities that might be regarded as in restraint of trade, and therefore illegal under the antitrust laws.

Against these practices, which it regarded as a misinterpretation and a perversion of the Sherman Law, organized labor raised its voice in heated protest. It pointed out that the decisions of the federal and state courts were acting in the interests of capital when: they classified business as property; they disregarded the theoretical limitations on the issuance of injunctions (that is to say, that the plaintiffs were to enter the courts with clean hands); they deprived labor of the only effective weapons it had against capital (that is to say, the strike and the boycott) without disarming capital of its weapons (that is to say, the black list and the lockout); they employed the temporary injunction to abridge labor's constitutional rights of freedom of speech, assembly, and trial by jury.

The force of these arguments could not easily be disregarded; and the result was the writing of the Clayton Act, in 1914, to release labor from the oppression of the Sherman Law. The Clayton Act, with its plainspoken Articles 6 and 20, indeed had every appearance of promising the long-sought relief. Article 20 seemed to say that injunctions could not be issued to prevent persons from quitting work, from engaging in peaceful picketing, from carrying on primary and secondary boycotts, from collecting and paying out strike benefits, from assembling and, in fact, from doing all those things which they could legally do in times of no industrial disputes. By 1921, labor was profoundly disillusioned. Not only had the Clayton Act, the Supreme Court was to show, not freed organized labor from the weight of legal displeasure but it had even added an additional burden, to wit, that injunction proceedings could be brought against trade unions by private individuals (instead of by the federal Department of Justice alone, as under the Sherman Law).

Renewal of agitation for real protection finally resulted in 1932 in the passage by Congress and the signing by President Hoover of the Norris-La Guardia Federal Anti-injunction Law. This measure effectively stopped the misuse of the federal judicial power. The law forbade the federal courts to issue injunctions in the following situations: 1. when workers ceased or refused to perform work; 2. on a worker's becoming a member of a trade union; 3. upon the payment of strike or unemployment benefits to strikers; 4. the giving of publicity to a strike, "whether by advertising, speaking, patrolling, or by any other method not involving fraud or violence"; 5. peaceable assembly. It also outlawed yellow-dog contracts; revoked the judicial rule that union members could be held liable for damages caused by other members; changed the procedure so that orders could not issue without testimony in open court; called upon the complainant to come into court with clean hands; and required that cases of contempt of court arising out of disregard of injunctions be tried before juries.

* * *

One of the most interesting aspects of labor's history in this period was the diminishing number of industrial disputes. Records between 1906 and 1915 are lacking; within the decade and one-half 1916 to 1930, however, there was to be seen almost a steady diminution of the number of disputes and the number of workers involved in them. (This is true except for the year 1919, which was the most violent in American labor annals.) In the light of such a state of affairs there was excellent reason for the generally held belief that American organized labor constituted the most conservative workingmen's force in the world.

What was true of the industrial sector was equally true of the political. The decline of the Socialist party, to which, in the prewar era, there had been attracted a sizable body of workers, was an outstanding phenomenon of the times. The entry of the United States into the war resulted in a split in its ranks; the Russian Revolution completed the work of destruction. What was left was a small centrist group which refused to adhere to the Third (Communist) International and which looked to the attainment of a socialist state by the ballot. In 1924, the Socialist party endorsed the candidacy of La Follette; in 1928, it again put forth its own ticket in the national canvass by nominating Norman Thomas of New York. But in 1928, despite the doubling of the electorate through woman suffrage, the Socialists received only 267,400 votes, as compared with 919,800 in 1920 and 897,000 in 1912.

That certain groups of workers should grow impatient with the evolutionary tactics of the Socialist party and the business opportunism of the American Federation of Labor was not surprising. The banner of radicalism, in the first three decades of the twentieth century, was carried by two different organizations: the first was the Industrial Workers of the World (or I.W.W., as it was more generally known), which flourished from 1905 to about 1924; the second was the Communist party, which was organized in 1919 and which, in effect, inherited the revolutionary doctrines of the earlier movement.

Radical trade unionism raised its head in the West in 1905, when the I.W.W. was formed, and for a decade and a half this militant body led no fewer than 150 strikes. Because it was distrustful of all political activity and advocated the use of the methods of direct action (that is to say, the general strike and sabotage) to attain the workers' commonwealth, the I.W.W. had much in common with European syndicalism. But in reality it was an indigenous movement, growing out of a peculiarly American situation: for it had its roots and flourished in the labor camps of the western country, where the unstable conditions of employment had led to the appearance of a large body of migratory laborers. It was perfectly understandable that the job philosophy of the American Federation of Labor unions should have no appeal for these men and that they should find more to their liking the doctrines of industrial unionism and the overthrow of capitalism, the two major tenets of the I.W.W. Such were the recruits who filled the ranks of the organization. Its leading spirit was William D. Haywood, at one time an officer of the Western Federation of Miners, although in its earlier years Daniel De Leon and Eugene V. Debs also had been associated with the movement.

In 1917, the state governments began to strike at the I.W.W. through the passage of criminal syndicalist laws. In all, sixteen states, for the most part in the West, inscribed acts on their statute books to outlaw the activities of the I.W.W., and the "wobblies" (as the members were popularly called) were proceeded against with unusual severity in Arizona, California, Michigan, and Washington. In 1918, the federal government broke the back of the movement when it arrested and tried for conspiracy 113 I.W.W. leaders. Haywood and 92 others were found guilty and sentenced to jail for terms of from one to twenty years. Haywood never served his sentence but fled to Soviet Russia, and this, too, contributed to the decline of the organization. By 1924, the I.W.W. had to all intents and purposes vanished from the scene, many of the rank-and-file membership joining the Communist party.

The Communist party, as the American section of the Third (Communist) International, was organized in 1919 at Chicago. Because it was frankly a revolutionary party and openly espoused the tenets of the Russian-inspired Red International, it was proceeded against with vigor by the federal Department of Justice and up to 1924 was compelled to carry on its activities underground. In 1924, the repeal of wartime legislation and the cutting of the Department of Justice's appropriations put an end to the Red hunts of the Attorney-General's office. The Workers' party, which had been organized in 1921 to take the place of the outlawed Communist party and which advanced a more or less traditional left program of political demands, was now superseded by the Workers' (Communist) party of America. In 1928, all surface pretense was discarded and the group again took up its old title of Communist party and candidly avowed that it was the American section of the Third International. While the paid membership of the party was small—estimates, in 1948, putting it at between 7500 and 15,000—it exerted an influence far beyond the strength of its regular adherents.

The original Communist labor program called for the capture of the

A. F. of L. unions by a policy of boring from within—that is to say, the seizure of the conservative unions by Communists and their employment as a revolutionary weapon. But these tactics ended in failure. In 1929, therefore, the Communists adopted a dual-unionist program based on industrial lines, which also proved unsuccessful. The ineffectualness of the tactic here and abroad and the advent of Hitler to power in Germany—with his threat to the U.S.S.R.—caused still another shift. The U.S.S.R. began to woo the western democracies (Great Britain, France, the United States) in order to create a coalition against the fascist states (Germany, Italy, Japan). At the same time, Communist parties were instructed to surrender their intransigence and join forces with progressive, or at any rate nonreactionary, groups for the purpose of setting up so-called People's Front governments in order to check the growth of fascism at home and the advance of fascism on the continents of Europe and Asia.

The American section of the Third International, therefore, during 1935, discontinued for the time being its dual-unionist activities. On the political front, the Communist party in the United States gave up all pretense of agitating for socialism and, beginning with the Presidential election of 1936, proceeded to render President Roosevelt whole-hearted support. This was largely due to the fact that President Roosevelt, in his foreign policy, seemed to be leaning toward a program of co-operative action among the democracies against the aggressor (i. e., fascist) nations. The frankly adventurist nature of American communism was demonstrated repeatedly in the thirties and forties by the shifts in the Communist line, in each case the changes being dictated by the necessities of the U.S.S.R. So, in September, 1939, with the German-Soviet pact, the Communists attacked the war as an imperialist one; in June, 1941, with the German attack on the U.S.S.R., the Communists clamored for our participation; and in 1945, after VJ-Day, they once more turned hostile to the United States as the Russians sought quickly to establish their domination over Europe.

THE SUPREME COURT AND PROPERTY

Between the decisions of Lochner v. New York (1905) and Bunting v. Oregon (1917) the Supreme Court receded from the bold position it had taken in defense of property rights during the eighties and nineties of the preceding century, and adopted a more conciliatory attitude. It gave its approval to a great number of state and federal laws growing out of the enlarged interpretation of the police power and a more liberal reading of the Fourteenth Amendment. Statutes affecting hours of labor, pure-food codes, injuries suffered by employees, workmen's compensation, the Adamson 8-Hour Law, rate-fixing by legislatures and commissions of the services of public utilities corporations—these received the judicial imprimatur. The Supreme Court became more popular than it had been for a generation, and if its attitude toward labor was not too generous (as we have seen above), at any rate the general outcry against the Court's arrogation of power was temporarily stilled. But the peaceful interlude was a brief one and by 1930 the Court was again being fiercely attacked on the score that it was employing its prerogative of judicial review to exalt property rights at the expense of human rights. In a dozen or more significant decisions handed down between 1917 and 1927, the Court in effect choked off the right to political dissent; refused to allow labor relief against the injunctive process; and again, by invoking the Fourteenth Amendment, interfered with the states in their use of the police power to protect life, health, and morals.

In another body of decisions, in which the Court passed on the rate-making functions of state public-service commissions and the Interstate Commerce Commission, the Court sided with property, when it answered the questions, "What shall be a reasonable rate?" "What shall constitute the rate base for public utilities?" definitely in property's favor. Agitation for the regulation of the railroads, begun in the eighteen seventies, had met with a partial success in 1887 with the passage of the Interstate Commerce Commission Act. But it was not until 1920 that the abuses against which shippers had protested had finally been brought under control. In fact, thanks to the work of the elder Senator La Follette, from 1906 on, liberals in Congress had kept their eyes steadily on the single, ultimate goal: the vesting in the Interstate Commerce Commission of the power to fix rates on the basis of a physical valuation of the carriers. A part of that victory had been achieved in 1913 with the passage of the Physical Valuation Act, the final part through the passage of the Transportation Act in 1920. Beginning with 1923, however, the Supreme Court proceeded to nullify, to a large extent, the effects of this legislation when it ordered public utility commissions and the Interstate Commerce Commission to give consideration, when fixing the rate base, not merely to original cost or prudent investment but also to the reproduction cost new of the properties.[1] By taking this stand, the Supreme Court rendered the whole procedure of government regulation, so painfully built up after an agitation of almost half a century, almost futile. The following were the decisions by which this was accomplished:

In Southwestern Bell Telephone Co. v. Public Service Commission of Missouri, 1923 (262 U.S. 276), the Court held (with Brandeis and Holmes dissenting) that a rate base for a reasonable rate must take consideration of reproduction cost new and that a return of $5\frac{1}{3}$ per cent was confiscatory. The decision was based on the rule promulgated in the Smyth v. Ames case of 1898. Justice Brandeis'

---

[1] Justice Brandeis in his dissent in the O'Fallon decision in 1929 defined prudent investment as "the reasonable and necessary investment in the property."

dissent attacked the rule in these words: "The so-called rule of Smyth v. Ames is, in my opinion, legally and economically unsound.... The Constitution does not guarantee to the utility the opportunity to earn a return on the value of all items of property used by the utility or any of them.... The compensation which the Constitution guarantees an opportunity to earn is the reasonable cost of conducting the business."

In St. Louis and O'Fallon Railway Co. v. United States, 1929 (279 U.S. 461), the Court held (with Brandeis, Holmes, and Stone dissenting) that the Interstate Commerce Commission, in fixing the valuation of the railroads for the purposes of recapture as prescribed in the Transportation Act of 1920, was to give consideration to the factor of reproduction cost new.

In United Railways v. West, 1930 (280 U.S. 234), the Court held (with Brandeis, Holmes, and Stone dissenting) that the plaintiff, a Baltimore street railway company, was right in its contention that a return of 6.26 per cent was inadequate and that anything less than 7.44 per cent would be confiscatory. The Court extended the Smyth v. Ames rule by permitting the company to subtract from its net income a depreciation charge on the basis of reproduction cost new. The inclusion of the value of the company's franchise, for the calculation of the rate base, was also allowed.

The bitter fight which was launched by Senators during February 10–13, 1930, against the appointment of Charles E. Hughes, to succeed the late W. H. Taft as Chief Justice of the Court, was not a personal one, entirely. The opposition pointed to Hughes's long record, before the Supreme Court itself, in the role of advocate for some of the country's most powerful corporations and insisted that in his decisions he could not but be influenced by his close association with great wealth. For this reason the appointment was attacked by both insurgent Republicans and Democrats and in the final balloting on Hughes's confirmation eleven Republicans voted against the man who had been their party's standard-bearer in the election of 1916.

MERGERS AND ANTITRUST LEGISLATION

The movement toward consolidation, which reached such a heightened tempo in the years immediately following the close of the nineteenth century, slowed down for a little more than a decade. Roosevelt's public campaign against the trusts and the energy with which the Department of Justice under Taft and Wilson pushed prosecutions against large combinations, contributed much to check the attempted formation of monopolies. Just as important was the appearance of new fields of enterprise to welcome capital legitimately: the automobile, electrical goods, telephone, electric power and light industries.

But in the postwar period, the trend toward consolidation again evidenced itself and the vigor of the movement was perhaps even greater than the earlier one. These new combinations were frequently effected to obtain additional capital; to permit of the exploitation of the national market, instead of merely sectional or local ones; to bring about important economies, through the use of common sales agencies or capital equipment or management. Another important motive was to be found in the fact that their creation provided opportunities for promotional profits for investment bankers on the one hand and avenues into which could flow capital savings not otherwise employed in legitimate productive enterprise on the other. This was particularly true of holding companies.

It was evident, at the end of the twenties, that such super-corporations were playing a part of the first importance in the American industrial life. Many of these consolidations, or mergers, had the characteristic intention of the earlier trusts, that is to say, the achievement of monopoly control over prices, production, and the flow of new capital into plant expansion. During the twenties, business also turned to another agency to effect the same end, and through the trade associations, which began to flourish in the second decade of the century, members of the same industry were openly exchanging price, production, and credit information. Originally inclined to view such activities with suspicion, the Supreme Court on June 1, 1925, in two decisions, gave the trade associations what was tantamount to a clean bill of health.[2] The Court held, in effect, that the members of such organizations were not actually agreeing to fix prices or curtail production; therefore, it was incumbent upon the Department of Justice to prove that arising out of the open circulation of trade data there resulted an unlawful restraint of competition.

Not only did the Supreme Court relax its severity, as far as monopolies and corporate practices were concerned, but the Department of Justice and the Federal Trade Commission also became more friendly toward the methods of Big Business. This was particularly true in the postwar period. It is not to be understood that the number of prosecutions under the antitrust laws showed a falling off. The fact is, the records of the Harding, Coolidge, and Hoover administrations were every whit as impressive as those of Roosevelt, Taft, and Wilson. The difference between the prewar and postwar decades was one of attitude, largely: in the decade of the twenties, the Department of Justice refused to be alarmed by the growing size of corporations, expressed itself as being perfectly willing to offer

[2] Maple Flooring Manufacturers' Assn. v. United States, 268 U.S. 563. Cement Manufacturers' Protective Assn. v. United States, 268 U.S. 588.

By 1927, according to the Department of Commerce, there existed some one thousand of these trade associations, many of which were engaged in all of the following activities: collection of statistics, cost-accounting practice, industrial research, commercial research, simplified practice or standardization of products, publicity, trade relations, exchange of credit information, insurance, employer-employee relationships, traffic problems. It should be noted that Mr. Hoover, as Secretary of Commerce, not only gave the trade-association movement his blessing but frequently took the lead in promoting such organizations. In this institutional development the New Deal's NRA (except for its labor provisions) was clearly foreshadowed. See below, page 563.

opinions on the legalities of projected mergers, and exerted itself almost entirely in proceeding against what it deemed unlawful trade practices.

The same was true of the Federal Trade Commission. It will be recalled that the Clayton Act had placed the following specific practices under the ban: price discrimination (Section 2), exclusive contracts (Section 3), stock acquisitions by corporations (Section 7), interlocking directorates (Section 8). The Commission was soon to show that it had little faith in its ability to check such activities and during the twenties its "cease and desist" orders grew fewer and fewer. The truth is, the Commission voluntarily imposed serious limitations on its own powers. In 1925 and 1926, over the protests of a minority group (the members of which, when their terms expired, were not reappointed), the Commission indicated that it was more cordially disposed toward business: by defining closely the types of complaints it would consider; by encouraging settlements and thus checking the filing of formal complaints; by placing limitations on the publicity heretofore given to "cease and desist" orders. How narrowly the Commission was interpreting its duties may be seen from the fact that in the late twenties and early thirties, three-fourths of its "cease and desist" orders were directed against only these five unfair methods of competition: misbranding, false and misleading advertising, misrepresentation, passing off, resale price maintenance.

With practices of the following nature, whose evils certainly outweighed any of those already mentioned, there was no disposition on the part of governmental agencies to interfere: 1. the issuance of nonvoting or non-par stock by corporations, with the result that companies were controlled not by their stockholders but by inner cliques; 2. the inadequate and often unintelligible reporting methods used by corporations; 3. the development of the holding company device, particularly in the fields of the electric power and light industry, railroading, and banking. By means of the holding company, insiders were able to gain control over huge properties although they themselves possessed but small minority interests; and state commissions regulating public utilities were frustrated, inasmuch as courts held that holding companies were not utilities and therefore were not liable to control. The holding company, too, because of its great complexity, lent itself easily to manipulation, stock-watering, speculation by syndicates, and the like.

Thus, after forty years of experience, the relations between government and business, particularly Big Business, were as ill-defined as in the beginning. Monopoly controls, notably as they affected prices, struck at the very heart of the capitalist system which could function only in the climate of a free market.

· 32 ·

Three Outstanding Problems of the Twenties and Thirties

PROHIBITION

By the end of 1914, state-wide Prohibition existed in but 11 states. If local option areas were added, still there were less than half of the American people living in regions where the open sale of intoxicating liquors was prohibited. However, the demands for the curbing of the liquor traffic took on new impetus in the next five years. America's entry into World War I gave plausible justification for federal restriction on the use of grains in the making of beer and hard liquors; the appearance of the automobile and further mechanization in industry pointed up the claims of dry advocates that inebriated persons were a menace to others on public highways and in factories; the ever-growing pressure being applied on politicians by temperance societies was a force that could not be denied. By the end of 1918, the 11 dry states of four years earlier had been joined by 18 others and two-thirds of the American people were living in Prohibition areas.

With the capture of Congress by the dry forces as the second decade opened, federal action, it appeared, could not be long delayed. In 1913, both houses repassed over President Taft's veto the Webb-Kenyon Interstate Liquor Shipment Act, which forbade the transportation of liquor from wet states into dry; and in 1917, Congress adopted a resolution submitting to the states, for their ratification, a Constitutional amendment aimed at the establishment of national Prohibition under the aegis of the federal government.

In little more than a year, the legislatures of three-fourths of the states had adopted the Amendment, with the result that its proclamation followed on January 29, 1919. On January 16, 1920, Prohibition went into effect without any compensation for the owners of distilleries, breweries, saloons, and factories making bar fixtures, in short, all those persons who had had a proprietary interest in the manufacture, sale, and transportation of beers, light wines, and hard liquors. The National Prohibition Act (known generally as the Volstead Act after its sponsor), defined as an intoxicating liquor all beverages containing more than 0.5 per cent alcohol; placed under severe regulations the manufacture and sale of alcohol for industrial, medicinal, and sacramental purposes; provided for the denaturing of alcohol to prevent its conversion into beverages; and ringed around, with formidable licensing restrictions, every conceivable phase of the remaining legitimate liquor industry.

Prohibition, under the Eighteenth Amendment, had been designed to eradicate two evils, the saloon and intemperance. The saloon, with its open drinking and its encouragement to idleness and even the more criminal forms of vice, had been eliminated. But with its going there sprang up in its place a group of more vicious institutions—the "speakeasies," "beer flats," and "blind pigs"—which, being illegal, could flourish only because they were founded on an open contempt for the law by their proprietors and patrons and because they had the protection of a corrupt local officialdom. As for universal temperance, not only was that ideal never attained but it appeared, a decade after Prohibition had gone into effect, that America was drinking almost as much as it had been before 1914.

In addition, by the end of the twenties, the hostility to the Eighteenth Amendment was no longer covert. Interestingly enough, in the acrimonious debate which ensued, the opponents of Prohibition were able to take a high moral ground: Prohibition, they said, was bringing about an open contempt for all law; it was the chief reason for the flourishing of crime; it was debauching police, prosecuting authorities, and the courts; it was depriving government of important sources of revenue and filling the pockets of an undesirable element in the community. Also, the anti-Prohibition forces were increasingly making themselves heard in the national political arena. In the Congressional elections of 1930, many seats were contested solely on the wet–dry issue, and the Seventy-second Congress saw the dry forces in it considerably weakened.

It was the opinion of President Hoover's Law Enforcement Commission, in its report of January, 1931, that enforcement of Prohibition had broken down. The Commission recommended that, if after further trial, enforcement was still impossible, the Eighteenth Amendment ought to be revised to give Congress the power to "regulate or prohibit" the manufacture, sale, and transportation of intoxicating beverages.

The country's first decade of experimentation with Prohibition thus ended uncertainly. And the end of the twenties had seen opposition to Prohibition definitely emerge into the open. The effect on national politics was curious. National politicians watched the contest between wets and drys uneasily. Would they be compelled to take sides on a question that had so many elements of danger in it—for them? Would the Democratic party, to hold its urban following, have to become wet—and risk the loss of support in the agrarian South and West? Would the Republican party, to hold its farmer constituencies, have to remain dry—and lose the support of the middle classes in the great cities? While politicians pondered the question, it became increasingly evident that Americans were wearying of the debate. For citizens were beginning to understand, as the full effects of the depression of 1930 and after made themselves felt, that the Prohibition question was not really very important; indeed, it was serving only to distract attention from more serious concerns. The Prohibition discussion, in short, seemed to be very much like a red herring drawn across the trail of every vital public question with which Americans of the twenties should have been concerning themselves.

The Democrats finally took the plunge; and in their 1932 party platform they called for the legalization of beer, the repeal of the Eighteenth Amendment, the prevention of the saloon's revival, and the return of control to the states. Mr. Roosevelt's election was regarded as a mandate, with the result that steps were at once taken by Congress to repeal the unpopular amendment; also, in March, 1933, the manufacture and sale of 3.2 per cent beer was legalized. The joint resolution for repeal passed through both houses of Congress in February, 1933; by December of the same year 36 states had ratified the new (Twenty-first) Amendment and it was therefore proclaimed by the Secretary of State. The Amendment, in addition to repealing the Eighteenth, promised such states as wished to continue dry federal protection against the transportation and importation of intoxicating liquors into their areas.

The sale of liquor became immediately legal in 19 states; in the remaining, constitutional or statutory provisions prevented the dispensing of alcoholic beverages. But within the next two years, such provisions were repealed in all the states but Alabama, Georgia, Kansas, Mississippi, North Dakota, Oklahoma, and Tennessee; and Alabama joined the column of wet states in 1937. It is to be noted that even the 6 remaining were not bone-dry, for the sale of beer was permitted. By November, 1948, only Oklahoma and Mississippi remained in the dry column. The states moved so swiftly because of the insistent pressure of public opinion, on the one hand, and because new revenue sources had to be opened up in order to make possible the local carrying of the heavy relief burden resulting from the depression. The states this time, however, did not forget that the sale of liquor had to be ringed about by all sorts of regulations in order to prevent the recurrence of a dry agitation. The results were the following: in 17 states, state-monopoly systems prevail under which the sale of liquor is a public business managed by liquor-control commissions; in 28 states, central licensing bodies are invested with the responsibility of regulating the private liquor trade; and in all the jurisdictions where liquor could be sold new means were devised for taking the curse off the business.

The federal government also assumed its share of the burden by establishing the Federal Alcohol Administration to which was assigned the function—and one, incidentally, which it performed with a high degree of success—of creating proper business standards for the liquor (but not beer) industry and promoting fair-trade practices in the interests of producers and consumers.

IMMIGRATION RESTRICTION

The movement, inaugurated in the eighteen nineties, for the barring of undesirable immigrants and for the restriction of immigration on a selective basis continued with unflagging zeal into the new century. Certainly, to those who believed that America should develop a homogeneous population, the situation was a bewildering one. In the first fifteen years of the twentieth century, over 13,000,000 newcomers were admitted at American immigration stations, and even during the period of the first world war the number of immigrants was over 1,000,000. Previous to 1921, much legislation had been enacted with the aim of reducing the quantity and improving the quality of immigrants, although no one knew precisely what constituted quality. There was general agreement that criminals, political radicals, paupers, the mentally and physically diseased, and the like were undesirable. These the laws excluded. Furthermore, there was a belief—widespread among persons whose ancestors had come from the British Isles and Western Europe (the native lands of Colonial and "old" immigrants)—that the "new" immigrants (that is, those from Southern and Eastern Europe and the Levant) were somehow "inferior," if for no other reason than that they were so different in race, religion, and cultural background as to be impervious to assimilation and Americanization. The elaborate report and recommendations of the Immigration Commission (1907–11) embodied this "Nordic" conceit, albeit in objective terms and with the appearance of scientific impartiality.

The same idea characterized the demand for literacy legislation. Illiteracy had been largely eliminated in Northern and Western Europe (including the British Isles), but was still widespread in other parts of the world. Therefore, such a test would restore the balance of immigration to the older sources. Such bills, however, had been vetoed by Cleveland in 1897, by Taft in 1913, by Wilson in 1915 and again in 1917; but in the last year, Congress overrode the Presidential veto. The results of four years' inadequate trial of the literacy test seemed to be disappointing to its advocates; and, fearing that the cessation of war in Europe would again open the immigrant floodgates, these persons began to demand a more radical immigration restriction policy. The device which increasingly began to meet with favor was the quota system; and to its perfection the

Congresses of the early nineteen twenties devoted a large part of their attention.

The first immigrant quota bill was passed by the Sixty-sixth Congress in the closing days of its last session, but President Wilson's pocket veto compelled the incoming Harding administration to take up the problem anew. The result was the passage of the Emergency Quota Act of 1921. The life of the act was to be but one year. It provided that a system of quotas was to be set up for newly admitted foreign-born, under which the total of any particular nationality to be granted admission was not to exceed 3 per cent of the number of persons of that same nationality living in the United States in 1910. The basis of the system was to be land of birth, not the land of last residence, and it was to apply to all countries except those in the Western Hemisphere. Certain efforts were made to soften the sweeping character of this restrictive measure. So, the minor children of American citizens were exempted from the law, and the following groups were given preferred quota status: the wives, parents, brothers, sisters, minor children of declarants, and World War I veterans. In May, 1922, the Emergency Quota Law was re-enacted for two years more with but slight changes.

From the point of view of the selectionists, however, the results of the law were not entirely satisfactory. While the gross number of immigrants was cut sharply in the first year, it had begun to mount again by 1923 to 1924. Again, the new law, while it did succeed in checking considerably the flow from Southern and Eastern Europe, did not encourage markedly immigrants from Northern and Western Europe. In particular, there was a large increase in the number of immigrants from Canada and Mexico, who in considerable measure were made up of persons of European birth.

The new Immigration Quota Law of 1924 accepted the principle of selection on the basis of racial stock. The quota base, from July 1, 1924 to June 30, 1927, was to be 2 per cent of the foreign-born of each nationality resident in the country at the time of the 1890 census. After July 1, 1927, the quota base was to be "that proportion of 150,000 which the number of persons of a given national origin residing in the United States in 1920 bears to the country's total population in 1920."

The quota system was to apply to all countries, with the exception of Canada, Mexico, and the independent nations of Central and South America.

The minimum quota from any one country was to be 100. There were to be entirely excluded all foreign-born who were ineligible to citizenship or who were inadmissible under the Immigration Law. (This provision was aimed at the Chinese and Japanese.)

Quota preferences, up to 50 per cent of the total from any one country, were to be granted to the unmarried children (18–21 years) and to the parents and husbands of American citizens; also to skilled agriculturists, their wives, and minor children (under 16 years).

The nonquota classes were to include: the unmarried children (under 18 years) and the wives of resident American citizens; persons born in the Western Hemisphere; ministers, professors, and bona fide students under 18 years; resident aliens returning from visits abroad.

The immigration flow was to be controlled at the ports of embarkation. American consuls, by means of visas, were to certify those immigrants whom the steamship companies might transport; also, American health officers were to attest to the physical and mental fitness of quota immigrants before passage could be booked.

The 2 per cent and 1890 quota base was continued until June 30, 1929, because the so-called national-origins base was so difficult to determine. The intention was that this device should preserve the present character of the American population on the basis of ratios already existing. But the committee—the Secretaries of State, Commerce, and Labor—charged with preparing this scientific analysis of the composition of the country's population on a number of occasions frankly confessed its inability to do so; and Mr. Hoover, both as Secretary of Commerce and as President, appealed to Congress to be released from what had turned out to be an impossible mandate. Congress was adamant, however, and after the calculations had been revised a number of times, they were proclaimed by the President, reluctantly, on March 22, 1929. The new system limited the number of quota immigrants to 150,000 annually; it was particularly partial to prospective immigrants from Great Britain and Northern Ireland, did not seriously affect the comparative status of arrivals from Southern and Eastern Europe, but did lower sharply the quotas for Germany, Irish Free State, and Scandinavia.

By the end of the twenties, therefore, selective immigration had become a definite reality and the new accretions to our population were coming from those lands whose racial stocks had been prominent in settling America. The following table shows the change that took place in the character of our immigration over the period 1901 to 1940.

During the thirties, it became plain that Washington, under the wide latitude allowed it by the immigration laws, might put an end to immigration entirely. And, in fact, immigration counted for but 0.4 per cent of the nation's increase in population from 1931 to 1940. Exercising the legal right to exclude all prospective immigrants likely to become public charges, the State Department denied visas to large numbers of applicants; while the Department of Labor deported foreign-born on a wholesale scale. Also, many foreign-born, despairing of finding employment here during the years of depression and denied relief by local authorities, began to leave the country voluntarily. Not only had the tide ceased flowing; it had begun to ebb: for during 1932 to 1935, almost 140,000 more persons quit America than arrived here. And with the outbreak of World War II immigration from Europe of course almost entirely ceased. Despite the growing need for labor, after the war, there was great reluctance displayed to re-examine the country's policy. Nevertheless, the United States could not continue to argue for the relaxation of controls over the movement of goods and capital throughout the world at the same time that it was a leader in imposing barriers against the free movement of people.

IMMIGRATION BY COUNTRIES OF ORIGIN, 1901–47

(Figures in per cents)

Period	From N. & W. Europe	From S. & E. Europe	From Asia	From Canada & Newfoundland	From Mexico	From West Indies	From other countries
1901–1910	21.7	70.8	2.8	2.0	.6	1.2	.9
1911–1915	17.7	67.4	2.8	8.0	1.8	1.4	.9
1916–1920	16.3	29.3	5.4	30.3	10.7	4.6	3.4
1921–1925	26.6	37.4	3.0	20.5	8.9	2.1	1.5
1926–1930	39.7	14.5	1.3	26.3	14.6	1.5	2.2
1931–1940	42.1	23.8	0.3	20.5	4.7	0.3	1.5
1947	66.6	30.1	0.1	2.9	0.3	0.2	0.2

THE DECLINE OF AGRICULTURE

For two decades, from 1900 to 1920, the pressure on American agriculture was temporarily relieved. Mechanization on a large scale had not yet come to the farms, so that the output of farm products did not increase in proportion to the output of other consumer goods or the increase in urban population. More and more agriculture found itself in that happy position where it was being limited to the domestic market needs (at least, for cereals and meat products), without the consequent disorganizing effects of world prices. The results were therefore the following: a comparative decline in the rural and farming populations; a smaller exportable surplus of cash crops; a comparative rise in the price of farm products; and an increase in the value of the national farm plant. Between 1900 and 1910, the aggregate value of all farm property doubled; the total value of all cereals raised in the country, between 1899 and 1909, increased 79.8 per cent, while the total yield increased only 1.7 per cent; the value of all food exports declined from $545,474,000 in 1900 (39.8 per cent of total) to $369,088,000 in 1910 (19.1 per cent of total). Nothing showed more plainly the protected state of American agriculture during these few years than the index of farm prices as compared with the index for the prices of all commodities. The following tabulation presents the figures for selected years (1900 = 100):

INDEX OF FARM PRICES, 1896–1914

Year	Prices of all commodities	Farm prices
1896	82.5	78.3
1900	100.0	100.0
1905	106.3	111.6
1910	123.8	149.3
1914	125.0	149.3

The tale of the next half-decade was even more splendid, for during the years of World War I the American farmer actually became affluent. The demand of the Allies for foodstuffs and cotton, the requirements of our own mobilized forces, the needs of postwar Europe before war-torn lands could be reclaimed—these factors, during 1915 to 1920, sent prices of crops and agricultural lands dizzily upward so that farmers opened marginal and submarginal lands, using irrigation and dry farming to overcome inadequate rainfall. The money values of American farms mounted, in some regions doubling, in others trebling their prices. Lulled by a sense of security, the American farmer pushed out his horizons: he increased his improvements, bought machinery for the first time on a large scale, invested in an automobile and auto trucks, installed a telephone, electrified his house and barn, and clamored for the extension by his state and county governments of the social services—better roads, consolidated schools, county hospital and nursing units, old-age pensions, local farm bureaus, and university extension activities. To the accompaniment, of course, of an ever-mounting tax rate.

Alas, boom times were all too brief and the bubble of the farmer's content was pricked with a suddenness and completeness that left him shaken to his depths. The era of deflation, which set in toward the end of 1920, left its mark on industry and agriculture alike, but whereas industry began to recover with 1922, agriculture remained permanently depressed. Land values plunged downward until in 1929, that year of golden prosperity for industry, they were not much higher than they had been before the war; crop prices dropped until, in some instances, they were lower than they had been for almost half a century; agriculture was left with a heavy burden of debt and taxation as a result of overexpansion of acreage, improvements, and public budgets. The depression of 1930 and after merely served to sharpen the outlines of a situation that had been steadily getting bleaker as the decade of the twenties progressed. Put simply, farm prices had been deflated, while farm costs—necessaries for home and field, mortgage debt, taxes—were still highly inflated. The farm account could not be balanced. A single statistical fact tells almost the whole story of the collapse of agriculture: in terms of the prices–received—prices–paid ratio the farm dollar in 1932 was worth only 47 cents!

The efficiency of American agriculture was being hampered not only because of declines in gross and relative income. What was more serious was the fact that fixed charges were eating up a larger and larger share of the farmer's earnings so that he was compelled to divert the use of income from the improvement of his techniques to the payment of taxes and interest on mortgages. Total fixed charges absorbed 6 per cent of gross farm income in 1910 and 12 per cent in 1930: this was indeed a heavy price to pay for land ownership. Farm mortgage debt in particular had become a millstone about the necks of American agricultural producers. In 1910, the mortgage debt on American farm land and buildings made up 27.3 per cent of the value of properties; in 1920, 29.1 per cent; and in 1930, 39.6 per cent. Inability to meet mortgage payments and to pay taxes was converting many farm owners into tenants or croppers or forcing them off the land altogether to enter the industrial reserve army of America's urban population.

Nothing proved the decline of agriculture more certainly than this state of affairs: the inability of farm tenants to pull themselves up by their own bootstraps and become farm owners. Formerly, tenancy had been of the ladder variety: younger sons, grandsons, and sons-in-law, as well as immigrants, starting out as tenants, accumulated savings and in time became owners. This upward climb had now ceased. More and more tenants were remaining permanently in that inferior status and were doomed to inadequate incomes and insecurity. In 1880, 25.6 per cent of all the farms in the country were being operated by tenants; in 1930, 42.4 per cent.

Tenancy was on the increase in the great corn-hog and wheat-raising areas of the North and in the great tobacco- and cotton-raising areas of the South. Indeed, in 1930, 73 per cent of farms growing cotton were operated by tenants, of whom half were sharecroppers. In 1930, there were 725,-000 croppers in cotton, of whom half were blacks and half whites.

The unhappy effects of the growth of tenancy were to be found in economic and social maladjustments. Said a government report on this problem:

> We find the unwholesome spectacle of men, women, and children, especially among the tenant families, moving from farm to farm each year. This social erosion not only wears down the fiber of the families themselves; it saps the

resources of the entire social order. In the spring of 1935 there were more than a third (34.2 per cent) of the 2,865,000 tenant farmers of the nation who had occupied their present farms only one year. In many areas the proportion exceeded 50 per cent. White tenants move more frequently than do colored tenants. The incessant movement of tenant and cropper families and of migratory laborers from farm to farm and from community to community deprives these families of normal social participation. It lays a heavy hand upon the large numbers of rural children caught in this current, who find their schooling periodically interrupted, if not made impossible; they suffer from mental as well as economic insecurity.[1]

Equally significant as an example of decline, was the debased position of agricultural real estate. What happened to agricultural real estate is graphically indicated by the following index figures of the estimated value per acre for 1914, 1920, 1929, and 1933. (Average for 1912–1914 = 100.)

CONDITION OF AGRICULTURAL REAL ESTATE, 1914–33

	1914	1920	1929	1933
United States	103	170	116	73
East North Central States	103	161	100	62
West North Central States	103	184	112	64
East South Central States	103	199	129	79
West South Central States	104	177	136	82
Mountain States	100	151	101	69
Pacific States	106	156	142	96

Such were the outward signs of a deep-seated malady which was not a passing phase but had all the aspects of permanence. Let us see what were the reasons for the depression under which the country's agricultural interest labored in the decades of the twenties and thirties. They may be summed up in a single phrase: the foreign market contracted and the domestic market did not expand.

First, as regards the foreign situation. The great historical reason for the advance of American agriculture after the Civil War had been our debtor status. We were borrowing capital from Europe to help transform our capitalism from a merchant to an industrial base. As a result, we engaged in an heroic expansion of agriculture to permit payments on foreign borrowings and for those raw materials we ourselves could not produce. In brief, American industry was growing up behind high tariff walls with the assistance of foreign capital; and American agricultural surpluses helped make this possible.

By 1920 (as we shall see below in greater detail), the United States had become a creditor nation. But other countries, due to the staggering costs of World War I, because they were debtors, and because of the am-

[1] Special Committee on Farm Tenancy, *Farm Tenancy* [75th Congress, 1st sess., House Document No. 149] (1937).

bitions of their own capitalists, were now desperately trying to obtain foreign exchange. How help the process better than by the enlargement of their own agricultural operations? This was notably true of the newer lands—Canada, the Latin-American countries, Australasia, the Far East —which could balance their international payments only by selling in the world market those foodstuffs and fibers which we ourselves kept pouring into Europe up to the end of the first world war. What made the situation worse was the fact that European countries began to strive with considerable success for agricultural self-sufficiency. The result was a vast expansion in the production of agricultural goods throughout the world during the nineteen twenties. Between 1913 and 1932, the United States increased its area devoted to major food crops more than 10 per cent; in the same period, Europe, Canada, Argentina, and Australia increased their acreage for the same crops more than 16 per cent. As Messrs. Ezekiel and Bean pointed out in their study, *The Economic Bases for the Agricultural Adjustment Act*, "This increase in foreign competition and foreign self-sufficiency brought about a persistent decline in United States exports of food products from 1921 on, long before the 1929 collapse. The 1932–33 export volume finally shrank below prewar levels."

Thus, the wheel had turned full circle in not more than sixty years, and America in the twenties was in the position England had been in when American agricultural surpluses first appeared in the world market. *Then,* English farmers had not been able to meet the competition of American grains and meats because they were burdened with heavy rents, labor costs, and capital charges. *Now,* we could not compete with Argentinian and Australian beef growers, Canadian and Polish bacon manufacturers, Argentinian, Australian, Canadian, Russian, and Manchurian grain farmers and Indian, Chinese, Russian, and Brazilian cotton producers for exactly the same reasons. The doors of the world market were slowly swinging shut.

Second, as regards the domestic situation. The possibilities of increasing domestic consumption of agricultural goods, in order to take in the slack, were remote. The following factors may be noted: 1. Our population growth was slowing down because of immigration restriction and birth control. 2. The two decades 1910 to 1930 witnessed a profound change in dietary habits as Americans shifted from a reliance on grains and beef to a greater use of pork, vegetables, fruits, milk, and sugar. The significance of the shift lies in this fact: grains and beef are largely the products of extensive cultivation; pork products, vegetables, fruits, and milk are the products of intensive cultivation requiring less land in use and more capital expenditures. And extensive cultivation was the method of production notably of the typical American farming unit, the family farm. 3. Women were dieting and thus eating less calories. 4. Improved methods of heating homes and the growing elimination of the need for hard and back-breaking human toil also made it possible for men as well as women to dispense with foods with high caloric contents. 5. Cotton was being replaced by rayons and other chemically produced fabrics. 6. Finally, agriculture itself had become more mechanized and efficient, making it possible to produce more foods and fibers for each dollar of labor and capital expended. In fact, between 1919 and 1929, on a stationary cultivated acreage, the output of American farmers increased more than 20 per cent! There was, therefore, a surplus of farmers in the United States.

*   *   *

Governmental programs for agriculture, during the nineteen twenties, were concerned only with details. There was no effort made to come to grips with the fundamental problems of high costs, heavy fixed charges, economic and social maladjustments springing from tenancy, and contraction of the market for agricultural goods. In the late twenties, a powerful political agrarian interest sought the passage of fundamental agricultural legislation; but these pressures Presidents Coolidge and Hoover resisted. President Hoover did make an effort to cope with the question of wheat and cotton surpluses by taking them out of the market—but to no avail. The actions of government must now be passed in review.

In August, 1921, after three years of debate in Congress, there was passed and approved by President Harding the Packers and Stockyards Act. This measure, designed to aid the cattle raisers, made it unlawful for the packers to engage in unfair practices, to combine to control prices and apportion markets, and to create a monopoly. Persons engaged in the operation of stockyards or market agencies were to register with the Secretary of Agriculture, to whom they were to furnish a statement of their scale of charges. These charges, according to the Act, were to be reasonable and nondiscriminatory. The administration of the law was to be vested in the hands of the Secretary of Agriculture, who was to operate much as the Federal Trade Commission did in the case of unfair business practices, that is to say, by entertaining complaints, by holding hearings, and by issuing orders to "cease and desist." In February, 1922, the Capper-Volstead Co-operative Act received the signature of the President. This law exempted, once and for all, agricultural associations or co-operatives from attack under the Sherman Law, for by it the co-operatives were granted the rights to process, prepare, handle, and market their wares in interstate commerce. Here, too, the Department of Agriculture, and not the Federal Trade Commission, was granted the power of supervision.

In March, 1923, to the Federal Reserve Act of 1913 and the Federal Farm Loan Act of 1916, there was added the Federal Intermediate Credit Act. The purpose of this law was to make still easier the extension of credits to farmers by setting up a system of federal intermediate credit banks for the purpose of handling agricultural paper exclusively. By the Act the Federal Farm Loan Board was authorized to grant charters to twelve new institutions, to be known as the federal intermediate credit banks. These were to be established in the same cities as the federal land banks and were to have the same officers. But they were to be separate corporations. Each bank was to have a capital stock of $5 million (with the government as the only subscriber) and each bank could issue debentures up to ten times its paid-up capital and surplus. The security for these debentures was to be the agricultural paper the banks were to rediscount. This rediscounted paper was to come from state and national banks, trust companies, agricultural credit corporations, and the like, and was to consist entirely of notes, drafts, and bills of exchange whose proceeds had been used for agricultural or livestock purposes. The intermediate credit banks could also lend directly to agricultural co-operatives on notes secured by warehouse receipts and bills of lading, for a period ranging from six months to three years and up to 75 per cent of the market value of the products that were pledged as collateral.[2] Also, in order to encourage greater banking facilities in agricultural regions, the Act permitted the establishment, by private capital, of agricultural-credit corporations, which could lend money on agricultural paper, with a nine-months' maturity.

During the twenties, the outstanding proposals advanced by farmer interests for agricultural relief were the equalization-fee and export-debenture plans. These programs set it as their purpose to raise the level of domestic prices on agricultural products up to those points where the full advantages of the tariff duties on agricultural commodities could be obtained. This was to be achieved by segregating the domestic requirement from the exportable surplus. The former was to be sold at the inflated domestic price; the latter at the going world price. Under the equalization-fee scheme, the difference between the artificial domestic price and the normal world price (on the surplus) was to be borne by the farmers of each particular commodity. Under the export-debenture scheme, this difference was to be borne by the government out of customs receipts. In short, in both instances, price fixing was to be countenanced; in the case of the export-debenture scheme, the growers of staples which entered the world market were to be directly subsidized.

The McNary-Haugen bill, which incorporated the equalization-fee scheme, made its first appearance in the lower house in January, 1924, but twice failed of passage. In February, 1927, and again in May, 1928, how-

---

[2] Thus there were finally incorporated into law the essential details of the sub-treasury scheme of the Populist agitation of the eighteen nineties. But by the nineteen twenties the agrarian problem had shifted from one of credit to one of surplus production and overexpansion of plant in the face of world competition.

ever, the farmers mobilized enough strength to jam the measure through both houses; but in neither instance did they have margins large enough to override President Coolidge's veto. The export-debenture plan was first introduced in Congress in January, 1926, reintroduced in 1928, and in 1929 was added by insurgent Republican Senators to both the Smoot Tariff bill and the administration's Agricultural Marketing bill. In each case, the Senate was compelled to give way before the House's demand that the debenture plan be abandoned. Thus agriculture failed to obtain significant relief.

The Agricultural Marketing Act of 1929, which had the approval of President Hoover, rejected the price-fixing and subsidy features of the earlier agricultural proposals. It was founded on the principle of voluntary co-operation under governmental auspices: that is to say, through the operation of nationwide co-operative marketing associations, and by the exercise of self-discipline, agriculture was to be redeemed. In more detail, the provisions of the Act were: 1. There was to be established a Federal Farm Board of eight members, to be appointed by the President, with the consent of the Senate, for six years. 2. This Board was to encourage the organization and development of agricultural co-operatives. 3. A revolving fund of $500 million was set up, from which loans were to be made to the co-operatives. 4. The Board might institute advisory committees for the particular agricultural commodities, and on their application might recognize stabilization corporations. These stabilization corporations, through loans from the revolving fund, were to be enabled to control, handle, and market the surpluses of their particular commodities. 5. The Board might enter into agreements to insure the co-operatives and the stabilization corporations against loss because of price declines.

In the stimulation of co-operative marketing associations the Board, in its three years' work, met with a notable success. Through its efforts there were organized co-operatives for marketing nearly every sort of crop produced in the country. But more important than encouraging the processes of self-help was the injunction laid upon the Board of "aiding in preventing and controlling surpluses in any agricultural commodity, through orderly production and distribution, so as to maintain advantageous domestic markets and prevent such surpluses from causing undue and excessive fluctuations or depressions in prices for the commodity." In the cases of wheat and cotton, such crises in the fall of 1929 impended with the result that the Board was compelled to act. Proceeding on the assumption that the wheat crop of 1929 was a short one, and that, therefore, the market price was too low, the Board offered to lend wheat co-operatives $1.18 per bushel for all wheat held off the market. And in February, 1930, the Board created the first of its two huge stabilization agencies, the Grain Stabilization Corporation.

This organization entered the wheat market twice and in all bought some 330,000,000 bushels, the first operation being completed in the middle of 1930 and the second in the middle of 1931. Three results were apparent from these ventures by the Federal Farm Board's subsidiary. 1. Its purchases succeeded in pegging the domestic price from 20 to 30 cents above the world figure, for something like half a year. But as soon as the Grain Stabilization Corporation abandoned the market permanently in June, 1931, the price of July wheat dropped to 57 cents, the lowest for the commodity since 1896. 2. The federal government was left in possession of the whole 1930–31 carry-over, which menaced the price of the new crop. 3. What to do with the wheat surpluses? There was, apparently, nothing for the government to do but hold them. From July to November, 1931, the Federal Farm Board was able to sell abroad some 47,000,000 bushels; the rest was left on its hands to be disposed of piecemeal, while the storage charges mounted higher and higher to wipe out most of the value of the original investment.

The same procedure was repeated in the case of cotton. The Federal Farm Board lent to cotton co-operatives, for cotton held off the market, at an average price of 16 cents a pound. But cotton prices continued to drop so that here, too, resort was had to the creation of a stabilization agency. The Cotton Stabilization Corporation, formed in June, 1930, went into the market and in its efforts to sustain the price was compelled to buy the whole 1929–30 carry-over, a total of 1,319,800 bales. The price could not be supported, however, with the result, at the end of November, cotton at New York was selling for 6.75 cents a pound. The second operation, the purchase of the 1930–31 carry-over, left the Cotton Stabilization Corporation with a total supply of 3,250,000 bales in warehouses; and in 1932, cotton was selling at 5 cents. After its affairs were wound up, it was discovered that the Federal Farm Board had lost $150 million in cotton alone.

As early as the summer of 1930, perhaps because it itself had little confidence in the program, perhaps because it appreciated that it was best to have two strings to its bow, the Federal Farm Board began an intensive campaign to urge the farmer to reduce acreage. But the American grower of staples would not, or could not, reduce acreage; and the crops for 1931 to 1932 and 1932 to 1933 were as bountiful as ever. There was another ironic element in the situation: while the Federal Farm Board exhorted and cajoled, in an effort to obtain acreage reduction, the Department of Agriculture and the states, through their educational agencies and experiment stations, happily continued on their way teaching the farmers how to grow bigger and better crops! This paradoxical state of affairs continued until President Franklin D. Roosevelt took office—and, indeed, remained to plague him as well.

· 33 ·

Economic Imperialism

ORIGINS IN AMERICA

GREAT BRITAIN had been launched on her imperialist career in the third quarter of the nineteenth century; Germany had followed in the wake of Britain a couple of decades later; it was not until World War I was over that America, abandoning her traditional isolation, set out upon the same course. We had, it is true, acquired overseas possessions as a result of the Spanish-American War; but we had not become imperialist, in the modern sense, until almost twenty years had elapsed after the fall of Manila. This new American imperialism meant an awareness of the fact that the domestic economy of the nation was inextricably tied up with world economy: that our movements and our decisions were being affected, sometimes to a very marked degree, by events taking place in remote corners of the earth. This, then, was the stuff of imperialism: raw materials that were vital to our industries and that we did not ourselves produce; outlet markets that could absorb our surpluses of manufactured goods; fields of investment for our saved capital; the maintenance of peace everywhere, lest fine adjustments be disturbed to hinder the steady supply of something we needed, close a market to our wares, or stop the interest payment on a governmental or industrial bond held by American rentiers.

The United States was a mighty nation in the period following the first world war, yet we were not altogether self-sufficient, for the list of those materials for which we were dependent upon outside sources was a long one.[1] To obtain these necessities for our factories, American merchants, engineers, geologists, agronomists, and investment bankers found it necessary to keep up a persistent search. It was inevitable, therefore, that we should be interested in Bolivia because tin was mined there, in British Malaya because rubber was grown there, in Brazil because of its manganese, Peru because of its vanadium, Canada because of its wood pulp. In addition, we had things to sell and saved capital to invest. To hunt out markets for these surpluses of our factories and annual incomes became another great concern of Americans in the decade following the end of World War I. Of the sale of our industrial surpluses and the investment of

[1] For a tabulation of such raw materials, see below, page 546.

our saved capital, more will be said below. It is enough at this point to repeat that the three items of inadequate domestic raw materials, industrial surpluses, and saved capital changed our economy, made us an imperial nation, and forced us to regard with greater attention and occasionally real anxiety the progress of the rest of the world that lay beyond our thresholds.

It has been said that the consequences of the acceptance, by Americans, of their imperial destiny were serious. Whether they were to end unhappily; whether, indeed, it was possible to check our headlong career along the way once trod by Romans, Venetians, Dutchmen, and (only yesterday) Germans—these, after all, were questions for speculation only. This, however, was certain: our new-found grandeur had made us, as a people, disliked and envied; and had compelled all those interested in public questions to give thought to the implications of our wider destiny.

IMPERIALIST FOREIGN POLICY

As our industrial and financial attitudes toward the world changed with the widening of our horizons, so, though more slowly and perhaps less consciously, our political attitudes changed with them. That we had become an imperial nation, at least industrially and financially, was plain; that our foreign policy was imperial, was not so easy to prove. For one thing, unanimity did not exist because there was definite opposition by statesmen at Washington to the relinquishment of America's traditional attitude of aloofness from the rest of the world; for another, there had not yet appeared a public leader to point up the doctrine of America's imperial destiny by openly proclaiming it (as, for example, Joseph Chamberlain had done in England, the Kaiser in Germany); for still a third, party distinctions were too loosely drawn in America to permit one or the other of the major parties to identify itself with the cause of America's interest overseas. But that, sooner or later, foreign and international policies would have to conform with economic interests, was a truism which few could deny after regarding the recent histories of the British, German, and French nations. It remained for the future to clarify the details of such an American policy whose general contours one found little difficulty in outlining.

In the meanwhile, these foreign policies were being regarded by Americans as having been clearly defined: the Monroe Doctrine; the Isthmian policy, which has turned the Caribbean into an American lake; peace by arbitration; restricted immigration; the Open Door. Only the last needs some amplification. The Open-Door principle, in the decades of the twenties and thirties, meant not merely the equality of commercial opportunity enunciated by Hay; it signified, in addition, equality of financial opportunity for our investment bankers and the right to buy raw materials freely even in the face of world monopoly. So, our Department of Commerce, under Secretary Hoover, protested vigorously and often successfully when artificial means were created to inflate the prices of the following more or less monopolistically controlled commodities: long-staple cotton (Egypt), camphor (Japan), coffee (Brazil), nitrates (Chile), potash (France-Germany), mercury (Spain-Italy), rubber (British Malaya), sisal (Yucatan). And, as we shall see below, in the thirties Secretary of State Hull persisted in demanding the safeguarding of American commercial, financial, and philanthropic rights in China in the midst of the undeclared Sino-Japanese War.

The determination of the following questions still was unsettled during the twenties and thirties: 1. What was to be America's tariff policy? The "isolationists" were quite willing to shut out the wares of other peoples. The "imperialists" saw that an open exchange of goods was necessary to permit our debtors to pay interest and principal on the loans we had made to them out of our saved capital.[2] 2. What was to be our final attitude toward affiliation with the League of Nations and the World Court? The isolationists were suspicious of Europe and refused to regard its problems as our concern. The imperialists felt that only through the maintenance of peace in every corner of the globe could the delicate mechanism of American economic imperialism keep its equipoise. 3. What were we to do about the interallied or war debts? The isolationists demanded payment. The imperialists were willing to talk reduction or cancellation because they knew that these debts stood in the way of further financial operations overseas by our investment bankers. 4. To what extent might our investors abroad expect governmental assistance when their bonds or physical properties were jeopardized, or government co-operation in finding new fields for investment? The isolationists said never. The imperialists were not unaware of the fact that sooner or later government and financiers must come to an understanding, as had been the case in prewar Great Britain, France, and Germany, and was again true of postwar France and Britain. In both these countries the investment centers, as far as foreign lending was concerned, had virtually become annexes of the ministries for foreign affairs. Indeed, the American State Department had shown a definite interest in the character of the bond issues being floated by Amer-

---

[2] We have used the terms "isolationists" and "imperialists" to express states of mind that were familiar to postwar America. By the thirties the issue had not yet been clearly drawn to allow for the appearance of groups who openly supported one set of views as against the other. That is to say, there were not—yet—Little Americans as against Big Americans. The whole debate in the thirties was being clouded by the emergence of another consideration: the possibility of another world war outbreak. In this connection, those in favor of maintaining American neutrality, in such an event, approximated the position of the isolationists; while those who favored American participation in efforts to achieve world peace—even at the expense of our entering the war as soon as it started (the so-called "collective securityites")—approximated the position of the imperialists.

ican bankers, as early as 1922, and had offered to pass an opinion on the desirability of any foreign loans being taken up by American investors. Of course, this was not supervision or control, but that it was a step in that direction could not be denied.

AMERICA AS A CREDITOR NATION

We must now review briefly how our surpluses of goods and saved capital changed our whole national economy. Before World War I, we had been a debtor nation, exporting largely our agricultural wares to meet the charges on our foreign financial obligations; after the war, we became a creditor nation, exporting manufactured goods and capital and with the favorable balances forcing our economic penetration into every land on the face of the earth. Indeed, it may be said that an important key to the prosperity of the twenties was to be found exactly at this point. We had, in our foreign trade, a heavy commodity balance in our favor. On the one hand, to permit foreign nations to pay their balances, we extended them credits; and on the other, we bought from them their physical properties—their manufacturing plants, plantations, mines, public utility concessions, and the like. We may anticipate our story just a little by pointing out that when foreign peoples no longer could continue paying the services on the loans we made them, our commodity exports declined—and depression then set in on the American sector.

Although, on the basis of visible items (that is to say, exports and imports of merchandise and specie), the international payments of the United States left the country each year in possession of a favorable balance, we were actually a debtor nation until the outbreak of World War I. This was due to the fact that the invisible items in our foreign transactions—interest payments on foreign capital invested here, American tourists' expenditures abroad, immigrants' remittances, freight charges, and insurance premiums—came to more than $500,000,000 a year (average) over the eighteen years from 1896 to 1914. Some of these adverse balances we paid in gold; the residue, a credit to foreigners, was added to the investments these had accumulated in American enterprises. At the turn of the century, such investments had totaled $3,330,000,000. By the end of 1914, these holdings of foreigners had amounted to $4,500,000,000. Of course, in the same period, American capital had penetrated into Canada, Mexico, and the Caribbean lands, and these foreign interests of ours were worth in the neighborhood of $1,500,000,000. But when all transactions were balanced, the United States was still heavily a debtor nation in 1914.

All this the war changed. The warring nations of Europe needed American foodstuffs, manufactured articles, and munitions of war. They paid for these by returning here American securities, by gold shipments, and by

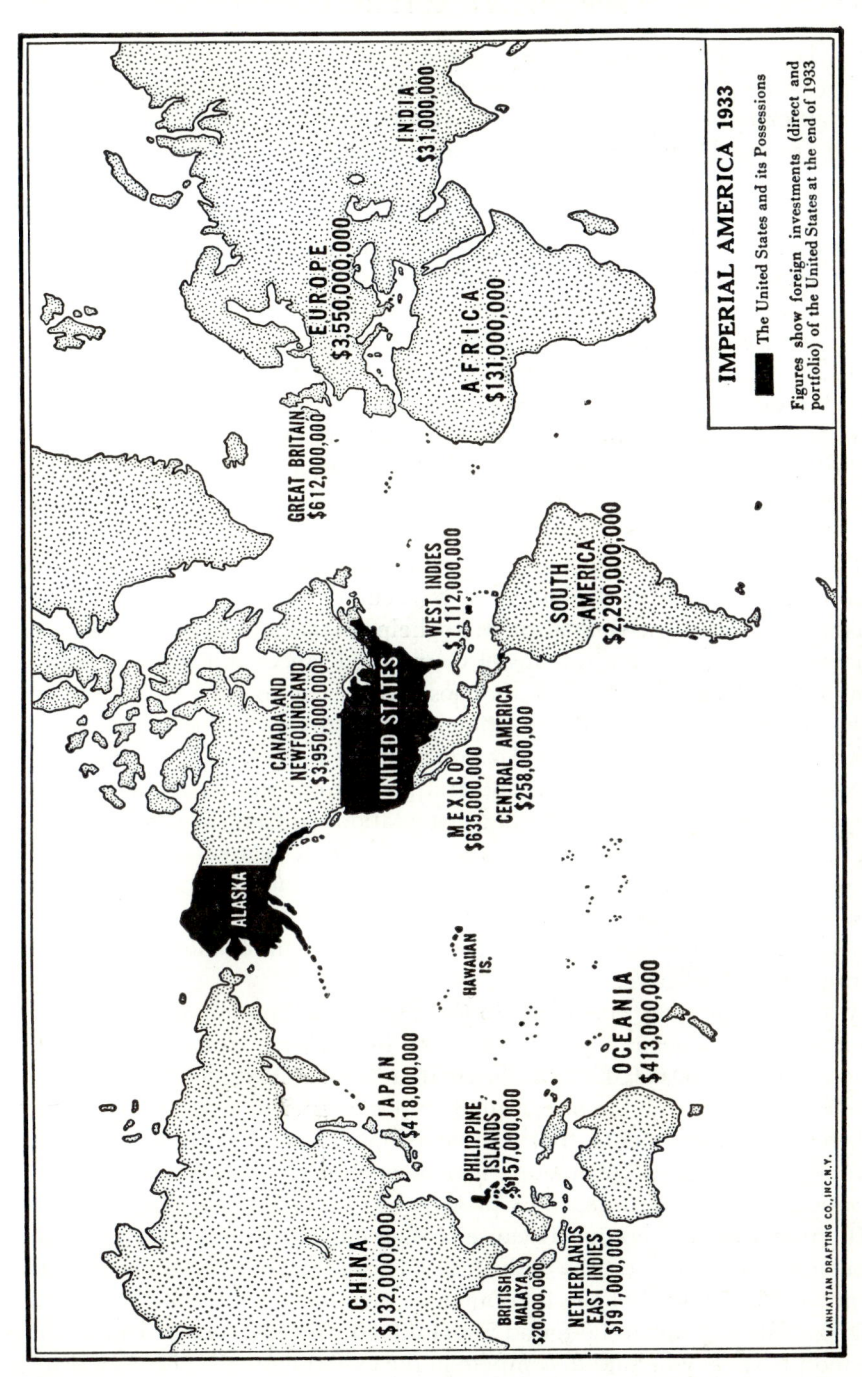

AMERICAN INVESTMENTS OVERSEAS, 1933

heavy borrowings. The result was, the end of the war period saw Europe deeply in our debt; and the subsequent years saw that debt steadily mounting, rather than otherwise. A series of circumstances contributed to the change in the balance of American international payments: our exports, particularly of manufactured goods, increased greatly; the revival of the American merchant marine reduced freight payments to foreign carriers; the restriction on foreign immigration began to cut heavily into immigrants' remittances; Europe began to pay us interest charges, instead of the reverse. In the transactions of the war years 1914 to 1918, alone, our favorable balance was almost $8,500,000,000; in each subsequent year until 1930, the balance in our favor was fully $1,000,000,000. Indeed, at the end of 1930, because there were no real offsets to counterbalance American export surpluses and the interest payments due us, the rest of the world was in our debt to the amount of $16,000,000,000, which took the form of private long-term American investments abroad in government loans and physical properties.

This, then, is what happened to the many billions of dollars making up America's favorable trade balances, particularly in the years following 1914. The capital was left abroad: to help finance the Allied cause; to rehabilitate the currency systems of Germany, France, and Italy; to maintain the Weimar Republic in the postwar years; to give Mussolini in Italy a chance to stabilize his position; to erect American branch factories in Canada, Ireland, Italy, and Scandinavia; to mine tin in Bolivia, drill oil wells in Mexico, Venezuela, and Iraq; to lay out rubber plantations in the Netherlands East Indies, banana plantations in Central America, and sugar plantations in Cuba. Thus the surplus products of the American farms, mines, and factories took us far afield and bound American destinies in a thousand-and-one intimate ties with the political stability of Latin America, Asia, and postwar Europe, and with the maintenance of capitalist institutions everywhere.

At the end of 1930, according to the Bureau of Foreign and Domestic Commerce, American private long-term investments abroad amounted roughly to $16,000,000,000. Of this, half represented direct investments, that is, ownership of factories, mines, sales agencies, and the like; and half portfolio investments, that is, ownership of foreign securities of both a public and a private character. The accompanying map shows the distribution of these investments, by principal world areas.

It is important to examine, because of their effects on domestic American economy, the nature of the industrial distribution of the direct investments. 1. Fully a fifth of the total amount invested directly in other lands ($1,534,000,000) was to be found in manufacturing enterprises, which, for the most part, may be said to compete in the export markets with American industries manned by American labor. The result was that in 1932 American manufacturers of automotive vehicles had 76 foreign units; of radios and phonographs, 31 foreign units; of telephones, 32 foreign units; of agricultural implements, 10 foreign units; of heating and ventilating equipment, 44 foreign units; of petroleum refining, 61 foreign units; of rubber manufactures, 41 foreign units. An incomplete count showed in the field of manufactures alone 1520 such branch and subsidiary plants employing more than a quarter of a million foreign workers. 2. Investments in sales organizations, worth $362,000,000. 3. Ownership of communication and transportation properties, worth $1,609,800,000. 4. Investments in oil lands, refineries, and petroleum distribution agencies, worth $1,117,900,000. (The petroleum lands were largely situated in Mexico and Venezuela, with significant holdings in Argentina, Bolivia, Columbia, Peru, Iraq, China, and Angola.) 5. Ownership of mines and smelters, worth $1,185,200,000. (Copper properties were held in Canada, Chile, Mexico, and Peru; iron mines in Cuba; nickel mines in Canada; vanadium mines in Peru; tin mines in Bolivia; nitrate deposits in Chile.) 6. Investments in agricultural lands worth $874,500,000. (In Cuba and Santo Domingo, Americans grew sugar; in other Caribbean areas, fruits; in the Far East, Brazil, and Liberia, rubber; in Mexico, guayule rubber and cattle.) 7. Investments in the paper and pulp industry, $278,900,000. 8. In miscellaneous enterprises (general merchandising, banking, ocean shipping under foreign registries, the motion-picture industry, real estate, etc.), $907,000,000.[3]

This single fact is of the utmost significance to an understanding of America's world position in the postwar era: the extraordinary capital operations were not an ephemeral phenomenon which grew out of the unprecedented prosperity of the decade of the twenties. They had become a permanent characteristic of the American capitalist-imperialist economy, as inexorable in their ebb and flow as the tides. The fact is, the depression of 1930 and after affected our position only in detail. At the end of 1936, the total of direct investments stood at $6,816,000,000, while the total of portfolio investments was at $4,741,000,000, and the grand total was $11,557,-000,000. It will be noted that the shrinkage was largely in the portfolio-investment category; and this was due to the sinking-fund operations and redemptions of dollar bonds by foreign governments.

It is significant to note, as well, that despite depression American capital investments abroad were earning very large returns. So, in 1935, the total thus credited to our account was $521,000,000, and in 1936, $568,000,000. Only one aspect of the picture had changed: the great growth of foreign-held investments in the United States, occasioned by political uncertainties in Europe. Europeans, largely, were pouring long-term and short-term capital into this country—in 1936, foreigners here possessed property

[3] In 1938, when the Bureau of Foreign and Domestic Commerce presented new figures for American direct investments abroad, it was able to report an appreciable decline in only one sector—agricultural properties. And this was due almost entirely to the poor economic position of sugar.

claims worth $7,600,000,000 [4]—in order to buy American stocks and bonds, to maintain bank balances, and to acquire direct investments. On these accounts, in 1935, we paid out to foreigners $171,000,000, and in 1936, $238,000,000. The following table presents comparative data for the twenties and thirties:

INTEREST AND DIVIDENDS PAID BY AMERICANS AND FOREIGNERS, 1921–39

Annual average	Payments by foreigners to U. S.	Payments by us to foreigners	Balance in our favor
	(In millions of dollars)		
1921–1925	$381	$138	$243
1926–1930	865	328	537
1931–1935	525	114	411
1936–1939	567	249	318

FOREIGN TRADE

America's foreign trade almost doubled between 1900 and 1914; by 1916, it had doubled again; by 1929 it was, in value, four and a half times as great as in 1900. On the other hand, the extraordinary drop in our foreign trade after 1930 was an outstanding characteristic of continued depression. The accompanying table indicates, in summary form, this situation:

EXPORTS AND IMPORTS OF MERCHANDISE, 1901–39

(Figures in thousands of dollars)

Yearly average	Total exports & imports	Total exports	Total imports	Excess of exports
1901–05	$2,426,000	$1,454,000	$ 972,000	$ 482,000
1906–10	3,124,000	1,779,000	1,345,000	434,000
1911–15	4,083,000	2,371,000	1,712,000	659,000
1916–20	9,879,000	6,521,000	3,358,000	3,163,000
1921–25	7,847,000	4,397,000	3,450,000	947,000
1926–30	8,810,000	4,777,000	4,033,000	744,000
1931–35	3,738,000	2,025,000	1,713,000	312,000
1936–39	5,468,000	3,019,000	2,449,000	570,000

The table below shows two noteworthy facts in connection with our foreign trade: the proportion of movable goods exported declined some-

[4] This was an official estimate. In 1938, unofficial estimates were putting the figure at considerably over $8,000,000,000!

what: the kinds of goods bought and sold changed significantly. The first phenomenon was due to the constant expansion of our domestic market; the second to the increasingly industrial character of our economy.

PRODUCTION OF MOVABLE GOODS AND PROPORTION EXPORTED
1899–1939

(In millions of dollars)

Year	Agricultural products	Manufactures	Mining	Freight receipts (R.R.'s)	Total	Exports U.S. merchandise	Per cent of total
1899	$ 3,355	$ 4,831	$ 600	$ 981	$ 9,767	$1,253	12.8
1914	8,165	9,675	1,450	2,082	21,372	2,071	9.7
1919	17,677	24,748	3,158	3,625	49,208	7,750	15.7
1929	11,851	31,687	4,200	4,899	52,587	5,157	9.8
1933	6,128	14,538	1,750	2,529	24,945	1,647	6.6
1935	8,010	21,700	2,600	2,831	35,141	2,243	6.4
1939	9,121	24,683	3,222	4,350	41,376	3,123	7.6

Before the turn of the century, America exported agricultural products largely and imported great quantities of manufactured and semimanufactured goods. By the opening of World War I, exports of nonagricultural wares had caught up with food and fiber products. By the twenties, these were outdistanced by manufactured goods. From 1896 to 1900, agricultural products represented 66.2 per cent of the value of our exports annually; from 1931 to 1935, the annual average had fallen to 36.8 per cent; for the period 1936 to 1939, it stood at 27.6 per cent.

The following table shows our ten leading merchandise exports on the basis of their 1939 ranking:

LEADING EXPORTS, 1926–30

(Values in millions and tenths of millions)

	average	1939
Cotton, unmanufactured	$765.7	$242.9
Machinery (inc. office appliances)	488.0	503.8
Petroleum and products	524.4	350.1
Automobile parts and accessories	406.2	253.7
Tobacco, unmanufactured	144.5	77.4
Chemicals	137.4	162.7
Iron and steel products	170.7	235.6
Fruits and nuts	122.2	83.2
Coal and coke	121.8	151.5
Copper (inc. ore manufactures)	150.0	97.1

There is a question that arises at this point: If in periods of normal trade rarely more than 10 per cent annually of our total production of movable goods was exported, could we cut ourselves off completely from the rest of the world without seriously deranging the finely adjusted mechanisms of our capitalist system? The answer was, No; for when the crude figures for movable goods were broken down, it was possible to perceive at once that some of our basic agricultural, mineral, and heavy industries, as well as a great variety of newly developed light ones, were closely bound up with the existence of a world market. The following table shows the percentage of the product of certain industries exported:

PERCENTAGE OF PRODUCT OF CERTAIN INDUSTRIES EXPORTED, 1914–39

	1914	1929	1933	1939
Tobacco leaf	47.2	41.2	39.3	13.7
Cotton	62.6	54.8	65.6	55.0
Phosphate rock	70.5	41.0	45.0	25.3
Meat products	10.5	10.2	6.6	26.7
Canned salmon	27.9	12.2	8.7	15.2
Wheat	19.7	17.9	5.4	11.1
Fresh apples	5.5	15.5	13.0	10.0
Dried fruits	19.7	46.0	39.1	25.8
Canned fruits	22.3	22.8	20.8	39.5
Gum resin	62.8	60.8	54.5	44.4
Refined mineral oils	37.9	19.6	11.9	8.2
Copper, refined	54.8	36.2	41.0	53.8
Printing and book-binding machinery	18.0	27.6	38.8	29.2
Office appliances	23.6	30.2	26.1	20.4
Agricultural implements and machinery	†	25.1	29.8	71.9 *
Automobiles	4.5	12.9	7.3	17.3
Aircraft and parts	†	11.6	30.2	42.0

† Not recorded.
* Including tractors.

Who bought our wares? Not Europe, largely, as had been the case in the second half of the nineteenth century, but the Western Hemisphere and Asia. To Europe still went our cotton, meats, and grains; to the other portions of the globe went our manufactured goods, and because this second category was becoming increasingly the more important, we were beginning to find the chief outlets for our products in the less developed countries of the earth. The following percentages show the changes that took place in our markets:

GEOGRAPHIC DISTRIBUTION OF EXPORT TRADE, 1896–1939

(Figures in per cents)

Geographic sections	1896–1900	1921–1925	1926–1930	1931–1935	1936–1939
Canada and Newfoundland	6.9	14.3	17.4	14.8	15.4
Latin North America	5.6	10.1	8.4	8.0	9.2
South America	3.1	6.8	9.4	7.0	9.5
Europe	76.7	52.7	46.8	47.4	40.1
Asia	3.9	11.3	12.0	17.3	17.0
Oceania	2.3	3.2	3.7	2.4	2.9
Africa	1.5	1.6	2.3	3.1	4.1

While we prided ourselves upon being a self-contained nation, and indeed were so to an extraordinary degree (only Russia being our equal), American industry in reality depended upon many imported articles not merely for its continued prosperity but often for its very existence. Thus, in the manufacture of steel alone we imported some forty different commodities from more than fifty countries. A great variety of other goods, from necessities like rubber tires and mica insulation to amenities like coffee, chocolates, and silk raiment were wholly dependent on the produce of other lands.

We may obtain an idea of how large a part these vital imports played in the American economy by noting the values of the more important imports for the period 1926 to 1930 (the figure given in each case is the annual average): coffee, $281,700,000; cane sugar, $207,300,000; crude rubber, $294,400,000; raw silk, $368,200,000; newsprint, $134,200,000; paper and manufactures, $151,200,000; paper base stocks, $114,500,000; tin, $88,900,000; furs and manufactures, $114,800,000; hides and skins, $118,-000,000; burlaps, $72,300,000; wool and mohair, $78,800,000; cocoa, $45,-500,000; flax, hemp, and ramie products, $44,300,000; tea, $27,000,000; nickel, $12,500,000.

The table on the next page makes the point more clearly, for it shows the percentage of our apparent consumption of certain products which was represented by imports:

DEPENDENCE OF AMERICAN INDUSTRY ON CERTAIN IMPORTS, 1925–29

Commodities imported	Imports as per cent of apparent consumption
Minerals:	
Asbestos	100.0
Graphite (amorphous)	71.8
Graphite (crystalline)	80.6
Iodine	100.0
Magnesite	51.2
Mica (sheet)	73.9
Nitrates (Chilean)	100.0
Potash	86.5
Metals:	
Antimony	100.0
Bauxite	40.2
Chrome ore	100.0
Manganese	92.1
Nickel	97.7
Platinum	95.1
Tin	100.0
Tungsten	76.1
Vanadium	63.1
Agricultural wares:	
Camphor	100.0
Cattle hides	23.1
Coconuts	100.0
Flax fiber	100.0
Flax seed	49.6
Jute	100.0
Manila fiber	100.0
Rubber	100.0
Shellac	100.0
Silk	100.0
Foods:	
Bananas	100.0
Cacao beans	100.0
Coffee	100.0
Tea	100.0
Sugar (cane and beet)	82.5

As we might expect, in view of the changed character of our imports, the sources of our foreign-bought commodities changed markedly. How little we were really dependent upon Europe the following table reveals with startling clarity.

GEOGRAPHIC DISTRIBUTION OF IMPORT TRADE, 1896–1939

(Figures in per cents)

Geographic sections	1896–1900	Yearly average 1921–1925	1926–1930	1931–1935	1936–1939
Canada and Newfoundland	5.0	11.5	11.9	13.8	14.4
Latin North America	10.3	14.9	11.4	10.3	10.1
South America	13.2	12.2	13.5	14.3	13.2
Europe	52.6	30.4	29.9	30.1	28.1
Asia	14.6	27.3	29.7	28.6	29.9
Oceania	3.1	1.6	1.3	.9	1.9
Africa	1.3	2.1	2.3	1.9	2.8

Part Three

AMERICA

AND WORLD LEADERSHIP

Part Three

Section XI

AMERICA FIGHTS DEPRESSION

· 34 ·

The New Deal

FROM AN OLD TO A NEW DEAL

BETWEEN 1922 and 1929, American productivity and investment continued their steady advance until, in the last year before the Great Depression, gross private domestic investment totaled $15 billion and the national income was reckoned at $80 billion. As Americans moved through those golden years, they beguiled themselves into believing they were living in a new day: the business cycle had been conquered. Weak spots in the economy were ignored, therefore; the powers of central banking were not called upon; and established criteria for stock prices were disregarded. Only a few heeded warning signals: the end of the building boom in the fall of 1928, oil wells producing in excess of market demand, steel and automobile production dropping. The outward movement of European capital was a clearer portent. Then, in the two weeks following October 24, 1929, the "new era" burst like a bubble: $25 billion in market values were wiped out between the September highs and the quotations of early November.

The depression of the nineteen thirties hit the United States with the fury of a cyclone. Between 1929 and 1932, the total physical output of goods was reduced 37 per cent; total labor income, 40 per cent; total property income, 31 per cent. The farmer's purchasing power was reduced 50 per cent. There were at least 15,000,000 unemployed persons. With the unprecedented collapse in prices, the burden of debt was well-nigh intolerable.

In previous downswings of the business cycle, the forces of depression had been permitted to spend themselves. Falling prices and tightening credit had been followed by a liquidation of debts and the writing-down of capital values. Costs of production dropped; surplus stocks of goods were consumed. Then credit had revived to pump new life into the system and the capital goods industries began to resume production. With the stimulation of purchasing power in this sector, the consumer-goods industries could raise their prices once more—and the cycle was ready for another upswing.

Certain barriers stood in the way of the normal movement of the cycle in the thirties. The heavy goods industries were already confronted by unused plant; prices did not decline evenly; bank credit could not easily be revived because so many banks were carrying speculative securities in their portfolios. To these obstructions, the Hoover administration added artificial ones. Despite the general assumption that the Hoover attitude was a do-nothing one, it is important to note that President Hoover formulated a program which was intended really to check the natural blood-letting process.

To help agriculture, not by sloughing off the greater part of its debt load, but by getting for it higher prices, the Federal Farm Board was set up in 1930. And to permit financial agencies and large borrowers to carry their debts, the Reconstruction Finance Corporation (RFC) was established in February, 1932. This agency, with an initial fund of $500 million at its disposal and the right to borrow more money, was to make government credits available to release the frozen assets of banks and mortgage companies and to come to the assistance of the railroads. At this point in the nation's development, wholesale bankruptcy—the usual process by which capital claims are written down—would have been attended by too much risk, for the great investors now were the institutional savers: life insurance companies, savings banks, building-and-loan associations. These held the farm and urban mortgages and the railroad and public utility securities of the country and the failure of such institutions might have been fatal to the nation's shaken economy.

The depression was in its third year when the Presidential contest of 1932 took place. The Republicans renamed President Hoover and Vice-President Curtis as their standard-bearers. The Democrats nominated Governor Franklin D. Roosevelt of New York for the Presidency and Speaker John N. Garner of Texas for the Vice-Presidency. The Socialists named Norman Thomas and the Communists William Z. Foster as their candidates.

Franklin D. Roosevelt was fifty years old at the time he was chosen. Although a Democrat, he first appeared in New York state politics as a foe of Tammany Hall in 1910, when he was elected to the New York Senate. An early supporter of Woodrow Wilson for President in 1912, his reward—at thirty-one—had been the assistant secretaryship of the Navy. In 1920, he was Cox's running mate in the forlorn contest against Harding. A year later he was stricken with infantile paralysis but, thanks to his great physical and moral courage, after seven years of almost complete invalidism he was able to fight his way back to health. He had become a close friend of Alfred E. Smith; it was Smith who prevailed upon him to make the New York gubernatorial contest in 1928 in the hope of strengthening Smith's chances of election to the Presidency. Smith lost but Roosevelt won; and during 1929 to 1932, Roosevelt was a successful, but not a great governor of a pivotal state.

Roosevelt's campaign captured the country's imagination. Beginning in the early summer of 1932, he travelled more than 25,000 miles and visited almost every state in the Union; and he talked openly and freely of fundamental economic problems. One clear-cut distinction between the position of the two candidates quickly began to emerge. Hoover attributed the depression to international factors; Roosevelt tended to stress the difficulties and faults in our own economy. Early indications promised a Democratic victory, but the results exceeded all expectations. The popular vote was 22,821,857 for Roosevelt; 15,761,841 for Hoover; 884,781 for Thomas; and 102,991 for Foster. The electoral vote was 472 to 58, Hoover carrying only the six states of Maine, New Hampshire, Vermont, Connecticut, Pennsylvania, and Delaware. The Democrats also elected heavy majorities to both houses of Congress.

As the country awaited the inauguration of the Roosevelt administration and the New Deal which it had so hopefully promised, the nation touched the depths of depression. Prices continued to drop. Local private and public agencies were finding it impossible to carry the growing load of relief, for the unemployed were estimated at from 13,600,000 to 17,000,000, and many had come to the end of their savings. The banking system began to sag and then to collapse. On the eve of Mr. Roosevelt's inauguration, the panic had reached the great financial nerve centers of the nation. March 4 saw banking operations practically at a standstill in every state and all security and commodity exchanges closed. Even with the generous aid of the Reconstruction Finance Corporation, the great credit and money organizations confessed themselves unable to continue the struggle.

Although Roosevelt had been critical of this agency, when he assumed office he did not ask for its liquidation, but made it an integral part of his own recovery program. But unlike his predecessor, he did not place almost his sole reliance upon the RFC. On March 5, he ordered every bank in the nation closed for four days and placed an embargo on the withdrawal or transfer for domestic or export use of gold or silver; on March 9, when the Seventy-third Congress met in special session, Roosevelt had ready for its consideration the Emergency Banking bill which both houses passed the very same day. The intention of the measure was to permit the sound banks to reopen and to furnish them with currency for the purpose of liquefying their assets. In addition, the Act provided that the Secretary of the Treasury could call in all gold and gold certificates in the country; and that the RFC was to be authorized to subscribe to the preferred stock, capital notes, and debentures of banks and trust companies.

The second emergency measure of the administration was the so-called Economy bill for the purpose of balancing the budget. This was to be effected in two ways: by cutting the salaries of government employees and by paring down benefit payments under the pension and veterans' compensation systems. The bill was passed by both houses and on March 20 received the President's signature. Two days later, on March 22, the President signed a bill which legalized beer and wine with an alcoholic content of 3.2 per cent by weight, largely in the interests of obtaining additional revenue. A fourth recovery act, this one designed to cope quickly with more obvious aspects of the unemployment problem, was the signing on March 31 of a bill setting up the Civilian Conservation Corps. This agency was to put to work at once on reforestation, road building, and flood control projects some 250,000 unemployed citizens who were to be housed in special camps under the supervision of army officers and paid $30 monthly. With immediate emergency questions thus out of the way, the more enduring parts of the New Deal program were now ready for submission to Congress. Before these are examined, however, it is necessary to consider the theory of reconstruction that was at the heart of the New Deal legislation.

THEORY AND TACTICS

The New Deal has been described as a revolution and, although it showed none of the violence and turbulence associated with revolutionary overthrow, it did represent a shift in political power—from big industrialists, investment bankers, and the larger farmers to the lower middle class and the workers. To this extent, it also stood for—and achieved—a more equitable distribution of the national wealth and income. Less went to the shares of the great receivers, more to the little men; a new concept of welfare thus became the basic characteristic of the American economy. As a consequence—because here the state played a positive role—the New Deal marked a sharp change in American concepts of the function of the state. The state had previously been an impartial force seeking to stand above the contests in the market place or, at most, offering mediation to preserve the principles of justice and equity. Under the New Deal, the state turned from aloofness to intervention. Hence, it imposed on the free business enterpriser all sorts of controls and regulations; it entered freely into business itself, often as competitor with private corporations; it used its great fiscal powers to redistribute wealth and income and to create new income; it committed itself to an elaborate program of social security that offered protection to a large part of the whole population against the mischances of unemployment, invalidity, and sudden death. The laissez-faire state, with only a skeletal apparatus of offices and agencies became the social-service state with a vast and intricately contrived and permanent machinery of officials and bureaucrats.

Kansas City Star, March, 1933

IT LOOKS AS IF THE NEW LEADERSHIP WERE REALLY GOING TO LEAD

Furthermore, the revolution took place despite the fact that the pivot of its operations changed. The New Deal started out by being essentially nationalist in its outlook and interests, and continued so until 1937. From 1937 on, it became increasingly internationalist. And yet the fundamental political and social philosophy remained the same. The American state was to be used for security; this could be done by reordering our domestic economy without any real concern over what was happening outside our shores—so ran the thinking and planning of the New Deal up to 1937. The American state was to be used for security; but we could not be free to handle the problems of full employment and of improving standards of living until the whole world was made safe from aggression, and freedom from want and fear could not be assured Americans unless all peoples were similarly guaranteed these rights—thus ran the philosophy of the New Deal from 1937 on. The same groups, by and large, who had supported the New Deal in its first stage followed its leadership in the second.[1]

THE BASES OF NEW DEAL POLICY

Some of the New Deal policies were understood and acted upon at once; some were adopted only to be abandoned later; some were originally primary and then were pushed into the background. Always, however, there existed the thought that the responsibility of public authority for the welfare of the people was clear and that the intervention of the state was justifiable. The bases of the New Deal policy may be put down in this fashion:

1. Capital plant at home had presumably overexpanded as far as the normal requirements for agricultural and industrial goods were concerned; investment therefore was no longer to be the exclusive concern of private banking. This theory was pushed most energetically in the field of agriculture, where limitation of production became the basis of policy. That it was also extended to industry was evident from the codes of "fair competition" written during 1933 to 1935 under the National Industrial Recovery Act. Under these, many industries, in the process of policing themselves, provided for rigorous controls over the use of existing machinery and over new-plant expansion. The idea also colored trade-union policy, for unions were allowed to impose limitations upon production through so-called feather-bed jobs, full-crew requirements, and similar devices. From this conception of overexpansion there followed the New

[1] The year 1937 has been chosen as the dividing line because it was in October, 1937, that President Roosevelt delivered his famous "quarantine" speech, in which he called upon "the peace-loving nations" to make a "concerted effort" to protect the sanctity of international treaties and to maintain "international morality." From that time on he was more and more preoccupied with the fear and certainty that a general war threatened.

Deal theory of social investment as complementary and sometimes in opposition to private investment.

2. Prices were being "managed," or they were "sticky" in significant areas of business operations. The New Deal held that this was due to monopolistic practices and to imperfect competition, that is to say, to conscious interference with the free movement of prices on the part of corporations. A bold attack on monopoly practices was therefore in order.

3. Labor had an inadequate share of the national income on the one hand, and unequal bargaining powers in industrial relations on the other. Both conditions could be remedied by compelling the legal recognition of trade unions and by legislation fixing minimum wages and maximum hours of work.

4. Business enterprises in many fields had become "overcapitalized," in the sense that their fixed charges due to capital costs were higher than would permit the concerns affected to operate profitably. Since such costs did not adjust easily and quickly to changed market conditions, the difficulties of total market adjustment were intensified. Debt revisions were therefore in order.

5. The public utilities industry, furnishing electric power and light, which was notably under corporate control, was not favorably disposed to a vast expansion program to reach potential users and isolated communities. At this point was introduced a bold piece of social engineering —the Tennessee Valley Authority.

6. The toll taken by unemployment, cyclical as well as technological (although on the later point there was much debate), was very great. There were other insecurities with which philanthropy and private savings could not cope unaided: old age, invalidity, child dependency, sudden death. Security to the American population against these perils was a prime concern of government.

7. There were dark spots in our economy: inadequate housing for low-income earners, the plight of sharecroppers and agricultural laborers, unemployed youth. Here, too, was a field for state intervention.

8. The financial mechanism of banking and credit was too powerful an agency to be left entirely in private hands. Banking had to be made at least a semipublic function, so that banking policy could lead positively in controlling the ups and downs of business fluctuations.

9. The world market was no longer functioning properly; high tariff walls, quota systems, foreign governmental controls, and the manipulations of foreign exchange prevented the usual absorption of American surpluses. Our cotton, cereals, tobacco, oil, copper were piling up in warehouses to derange markets at home. Two lines of attack were indicated: controlled production and the elimination of those blocks that were hindering the orderly processes of world trade.

PROGRAMS OF ACTION

So ran the New Deal analysis. From this there followed certain programs, of which the following were the outstanding:

1. *The restoration and maintenance of prices.* Many attacks on the problem were launched: the dollar was devalued; gold was purchased from abroad; limitations were imposed on the production of agricultural products, petroleum, and coal; codes of fair competition in industry were written to eliminate cutthroat methods. The greatest success was met with in the case of agriculture, although here crop loans and subsidies were also required for the purpose of making production control effective. Taking the economy in the large, however, the device that was really successful in pushing up prices was government spending, or pump priming.

2. *The reduction of debt.* Private debts had become unduly burdensome, notably within the context of a deflationary price situation. The New Deal sought to come to grips with this problem in two ways: by raising prices, and by writing down the face value of debt in places where price change itself could not be entirely and immediately effective. For agriculture it created a new fiscal agency (the Federal Farm Mortgage Corporation) which was to make possible the exchange of privately held agricultural long-term paper for semipublic (or public-guaranteed) paper. For home owners it created a new fiscal agency (the Home Owners' Loan Corporation) for a similar purpose. For businessmen, corporations, and municipalities, it radically changed the bankruptcy law to permit those who were insolvent to come to an understanding with their creditors quickly and at small legal cost.

3. *The revival and expansion of credit.* To pump short-term and long-term funds into enterprise, state intervention was imperative. The commercial banks, because of their nonliquidity, were not in a position to extend loans for working capital. The agencies of long-term credit—savings banks, insurance companies, trust companies, title and mortgage companies—seeing their earlier investments unproductive, feared to assume further risks. The New Deal jumped into the breach. It expanded the powers and operations of the RFC to open commercial banks and help them achieve liquidity quickly. It established virtual public control over the Federal Reserve System, so that the system could be induced by government policy to expand (and contract) credit. It obtained for the Board of Governors of the Federal Reserve System the power to lower (and raise) the minimum legal reserves required of member banks. It obtained for the same agency the right to raise (or lower) the margin requirements for security purchases, thus controlling to an extent the amount of credit flowing into brokers' loans. It used the RFC to make

direct loans to private business and to municipalities and other public corporations for housing, electric power plants and the like.

4. *The raising of the purchasing power of labor.* Labor, confronted by shrinking opportunities of employment, was forced to sell its services cheaply. Sweated industries had reappeared and child labor had increased. The key to the rehabilitation of labor was to be chiefly its own united strength. The National Labor Relations Act therefore ordered employers to bargain with the workers' own trade unions and to give up practices that prevented labor organization. Closed shops became more and more common; and also industrial practices and standards were modified and improved through labor-management co-operation. To defend those incapable of effective organization—children, women, the unskilled— minimum-wage and maximum-hour legislation and the abolition of child labor were aimed at. After several failures these objectives were achieved in the Fair Labor Standards Act of 1938.

5. *The relief of the needy, the protection of dependents, and social security.* Wholesale unemployment, illness, and invalidity, and the unrest of youth were the results of the depression. The relief of distress was an imminent public duty, and the New Deal experimented with this problem in many ways. It lent generously to the states for straight outdoor relief. It created a federal agency (the Public Works Administration) to extend credit to public and quasi-public authorities to finance long-term public construction projects. It wrote social security legislation under which direct federal appropriations and federal matching grants-in-aid were made to the states to provide for the unemployables and the permanently needy (the aged, the blind, dependent and crippled children). It devised a significant code under which, as a result of contributions largely by employers, unemployment funds were built up in the states; and also, from equal contributions by employers and workers, an insurance fund from which were to be paid annuities to workers upon retirement. It created work for the temporarily needy and unemployed in short-term projects financed by the federal government (under the Works Progress Administration).

6. *The construction of homes.* The New Deal recognized that the building of decent homes for low-income earners was an outstanding need; it therefore established an agency (the United States Housing Authority) which, with government financing and subsidies, was to assist quasi-public authorities to create low-cost housing.

7. *The protection of the investor and the saver.* To defend the property rights of the American investor, the New Deal set up the Securities and Exchange Commission and gave it wide powers to supervise the issuance of new securities by corporations, to obtain for investors adequate information about the financial practices of corporations and their directors

and officers, and to regulate the functioning of brokers and the security exchanges or markets, themselves. Similarly, the Federal Deposit Insurance Corporation was devised to guarantee deposits in savings banks accounts up to $5000.

8. *The rehabilitation of the electric power industry.* Believing that an outlet for savings and a work of social reconstruction could be achieved in an expanded electric light and power industry, the New Deal created the Tennessee Valley Authority. The stated purposes were the rehabilitation of the population of the Tennessee Valley and the establishment of an experiment in the public operation of electric light and power. Focusing its attention on this industry as an example of banking domination, the New Deal also provided for the elimination of unnecessary holding companies.

9. *The revival of foreign trade.* The decline of foreign trade was a characteristic of our unbalanced economy. The New Deal sought to revive American overseas commerce; and for this purpose it created the Export-Import Bank to finance the flow of goods and even to extend credits to foreign governments. But the New Deal was equally interested in the restoration of world trade generally. Congress was therefore prevailed upon to permit the writing of reciprocal trading agreements with foreign nations as an executive function. Through the agency of the State Department (and without Senate participation) a large number of such commercial treaties was drawn up, the net effect of which was the measurable lowering of tariff barriers. These agreements also contained most-favored-nation clauses.

10. *Pump-priming.* When private enterprise failed to respond immediately, or when business activity became sluggish, the New Deal proceeded to lend and spend. This it called "priming the pump"; in other words, the federal government boldly engaged in deficit financing in an effort to raise national income. It lent to distressed banks, railroads, insurance companies, mortgage corporations, and industrial concerns; and to farmers, home owners, the states, municipalities, and newly created public authorities. It spent—by subsidies, grants-in-aid, outright appropriations—in order to rehabilitate marginal farmers, to finance the building of ships, to tear down slums and put up low-rent housing, to furnish old-age pensions, to construct public buildings, and to provide flood control, roads, and reforestation. It gave people work; and at the same time it added to the social wealth of the nation. This meant a steady increase in the national debt, a situation which the New Deal faced with equanimity because its theory of deficit financing was based on the premises that governmental spending made for an increase in national income and that an increase in national income made greater taxation possible. The nation

was going into debt, it was true; but the debt was largely held at home and, as a result of the debt, the country's assets had been increased.

THE NEW DEAL AGENCIES

Such were the general New Deal policies and tactics designed to restore the American economy and make possible its smooth functioning, this time with more equity as far as the great masses of the country's population were concerned. A fuller description of some of the legislative enactments and the agencies set up is now in order.

Agriculture. Agriculture, because its condition was critical, received the immediate and the continuing attention of the New Deal. The goals for recovery and reform were the following: 1. The establishment of parity prices, that is, the restoration of the farmer's purchasing power to the position it had held in the years before World War I. The period of August, 1909 to July, 1914, was fixed on as the base period, the assumption being that at that time the prices farmers paid were in balance with the prices they received. 2. The establishment of parity income, a concept which later replaced the concept of parity prices. It was the intention of the Department of Agriculture to obtain for farmers the relative income, as compared with total national income, which they had been receiving in the prewar years. 3. The adjustment of farm production to meet market requirements. This meant, chiefly, adjustment to domestic consumption. Surpluses were to be held off the market by means of government loans. Justification for this attitude was subsequently found in the concept of the "ever-normal granary." 4. Soil conservation and improved land use. 5. Debt reduction and security against foreclosure at the hands of mortgagees. 6. Rural relief and rehabilitation for submarginal farmers and tenants.

The first legislative enactment to carry out the major intention of this program was the Agricultural Adjustment Act of May, 1933. Since it was assumed that agricultural distress was due to overproduction, not to underconsumption, the growers of the basic staples were to be induced to restrict plantings. As compensation, they were to receive subsidies and crop loans, with the government holding the surpluses off the market. The AAA tied together the subsidies, or so-called benefit payments, with a processing tax on millers, meat packers, cotton ginners, etc., and principally for this reason, was found unconstitutional by the Supreme Court on January 6, 1936.

To meet the high court's objections, Congress passed the temporary Soil Conservation and Domestic Allotment Act of 1936 and the Agricultural Adjustment Act of 1938. In both these measures, the justification for governmental action was found in the necessity for protecting the land resources of the nation and for encouraging the utilization of improved methods of cultivation. Again subsidies—this time directly—and crop loans were to be the basic instruments for obtaining compliance. The purpose of the commodity loans was to lay a floor below which farm prices could not fall.

Agricultural credit was almost as acute a problem as agricultural prices. To ease the farmers' debt burden, the Emergency Farm Mortgage Act of May, 1933, authorized the federal land banks to make loans on the basis of "normal" values. This was followed in 1934, by the Farm Mortgage Refinancing Act of 1934, which created the Federal Farm Mortgage Corporation under the direction of the Farm Credit Administration. The FFMC was given a revolving fund of $2 million in bonds, guaranteed as to principal and interest, which it could exchange for the bonds held by federal land banks and which it also could invest directly in farm mortgage loans. To check foreclosure of farm properties, the Federal Farm Bankruptcy Act of June, 1934, declared unconstitutional by the Supreme Court in 1935, was succeeded by the Farm Mortgage Moratorium Act. This permitted distressed farmers, with court permission, to enjoy a three-year respite against seizure. During this breathing space, the mortgagor was to retain possession upon the payment of a reasonable rental fixed by the court and could possess the farm by paying the appraised value. Creditors might demand a reappraisal or sale at auction, but for ninety days thereafter, the debtor had the right to redeem at the sales price.

The third factor of the agricultural problem, the submarginal farmer, also became the object of government concern. After a series of unsuccessful experiments with resettlement projects, the Farm Security Administration was finally set up in 1937 to devise ways and means of bringing relief to distressed small farmers and agricultural laborers; the chief method employed was rehabilitation through social-service activities.

Thus the New Deal made agriculture a charge of the state—granting subsidies and imposing varied controls over the production and prices of such staple agricultural products as cotton, tobacco, wheat, corn, and rice. In addition to supporting the purchasing power of established commercial farmers, government agencies all but assumed the task of providing the farmer with credit. Total farm debt was reduced 17 per cent, but by the end of 1937 perhaps half of agricultural long-term paper was in the possession of governmental agencies. By 1946, such agencies held about the same proportion of a relatively declining farm debt.

Industry. As in agriculture, so in industry, the New Deal tried to push revival by price-raising expedients and by the establishment of standards of competition. To this end, industry was to police itself. Despite the fact that a major commitment of American industrial policy was the Sherman

Antitrust Act, the New Deal was prepared to welcome the cartelization of American business. For this purpose, the National Industrial Recovery Act was passed in June, 1933. It set up a National Recovery Administration, under whose aegis every branch of American business was to form code authorities and these were to draft principles and practices guaranteeing "fair competition." When completed, most of these codes incorporated methods for establishing minimum prices and restricting production. In addition, the codes generally imposed the 40-hour work week as a standard, banned the labor of children under 16, and fixed minimum wages ranging from $12 to $15 a week.

By the fall of 1933, the early acquiescence of industry faded. Code violation spread. By June, 1934, a conference of leading industrialists urged that government retire to its traditional functions. While the business community attacked the NIRA as excessive state intervention, a government investigating commission concluded that the code-making process was fostering monopoly and oppressing small industrialists, distributors, and the consumer. In May, 1935, the Supreme Court found the NIRA unconstitutional on three counts: that Congress could not delegate its legislative authority to private individuals, the code authorities; that the federal government could not legislate about industrial practices if these practices did not directly affect interstate commerce; and that a national emergency did not exist.

The administration then turned back to its original assumption that administered prices in certain areas of business operations represented monopolistic practices. New and more vigorous enforcement of the antitrust laws was undertaken, therefore.

Labor. In its attempt to balance the economy, the New Deal sought to guarantee labor certain rights. The minimum standards incorporated in the NIRA codes were, in effect, a barrier to the treatment of labor as a commodity to be bought at the cheapest rate. Section 7 (a) of the law declared that employees "shall have the right to organize and bargain collectively through representatives of their own choosing," free from coercion by employers or their agents.

With this guarantee, wage earners turned to labor organization with an enthusiasm that reversed the long decline of the labor movement during the nineteen twenties. Free unions increased in membership and spread into new industries such as steel and automobile manufacturing. Industrial conflict grew as the newly invigorated labor movement demanded recognition by employers. In June, 1934, Congress passed a Labor Disputes Joint Resolution authorizing the President to establish machinery to investigate industrial conflicts arising under the NIRA. The boards might prescribe rules and conduct elections to determine representation for the purpose of collective bargaining.

The outlawing of the NIRA by the Supreme Court compelled the writing of new labor enactments. In July, 1935, Congress passed the National Labor Relations Act, which obligated employers to bargain collectively with their workers and to refrain from certain unfair practices, notably discrimination for union activity and the formation of company unions. To enforce the act, Congress provided for a National Labor Relations Board of three members. The Board was to proceed by the use of quasi-judicial powers similar to those exercised by the Federal Trade Commission in its own field. It was to determine what was to be the appropriate unit for the purposes of collective bargaining—plant, craft, employer unit—to investigate questions concerning the representation of employees, to conduct elections when the workers asked for them, and to certify the organization duly chosen by the majority of the workers voting.

In a group of five notable rulings, on April 12, 1937, the Supreme Court, by five-to-four decisions, except in one instance where interstate commerce was clearly affected, held that the NLRB might deal with employer-employee relations, even when the products of the employers were locally manufactured. The right to organize was a "fundamental right," the Court declared, and unions were essential to allow laborers to treat with their employers on a basis of equality. In 1938, six other decisions clarified the Board's powers and approved most of its procedures.

In addition to protecting the right to organize, the New Deal intervened to guard the welfare of workers who could not make effective use of union action. The Fair Labor Standards Act of 1938 established the 40-hour week, with time-and-a-half for overtime, in all of the country's industries, which were to draw up minimum wage scales in order to achieve a 40-cents an hour level. In addition, the law excluded from interstate commerce, goods manufactured by "oppressive child labor," which was defined as the employment of children under 16 or the labor of persons between 16 and 18 in hazardous occupations. The Children's Bureau of the Department of Labor was to define "hazardous occupations," and to make rules for the employment of children between 14 and 16 in occupations other than mining and manufacturing. The labor of children in agriculture was excluded from such regulation if they were beyond the school attendance age as fixed by state law. Thus, by administrative order, child labor was virtually abolished from the land.

Labor Organization. With its rights protected by government intervention, the labor movement reversed the trend of the nineteen twenties, when it had barely kept pace with population growth and made no advances in the field of basic and mass production industries. Union membership increased from 4,000,000 in 1929 to 11,000,000 at the end of the nineteen thirties. As the labor movement revived, a new force arose to challenge the leadership of the American Federation of Labor, the Committee for Industrial Organization. The apparent basis for the conflict was simple: were the unorganized workers to be formed into trade unions on craft or industrial lines? Some observers wondered whether that conflict did not actually represent fear that the older organizations, leaders, attitudes, and techniques would be swamped by the new recruits.

When the NIRA was invalidated, revolt broke loose in the A.F. of L. ranks. John L. Lewis, head of the miners, threw down the gage of battle at the 1935 convention of the A.F. of L. and although his resolution favoring industrial organization in the basic industries was defeated, he won the support of ten outstanding unions. With these he formed the CIO to work for organization on industrial lines within the Federation. Lewis' ten supporting unions were suspended in 1936. In 1937, the Federation's convention authorized the expulsion of any of the suspended unions which should refuse to return on the terms laid down.

While the Federation was pursuing its own organizing activities, the CIO pushed free unions into the hitherto closed areas of the automobile and steel industries. Organization and the sit-down strike (later outlawed by the Supreme Court in the Fansteel case) finally won the United Automobile Workers of America partial recognition from General Motors in February, 1937, after a 40-day strike. A month later, and without a strike, United States Steel recognized the CIO Steel Workers' Organizing Committee as exclusive bargaining agent for all its workers and established the 40-hour week and grievance machinery. Although the SWOC was defeated in its strikes against the "Little Steel" companies, in the spring and summer of 1937, its successes stiffened the determination of the CIO leaders against yielding to A.F. of L. insistence that they cease their "dual" and independent activity.

In 1938, nine of the ten CIO unions were expelled from the Federation and the CIO, which had been only a temporary organization, was renamed the Congress of Industrial Organizations, and established as a permanent body in October. Efforts at reunion failed, in spite of Presidential intervention in the conference of 1939. The American labor movement has continued divided, more on factional and personal grounds than on genuine differences of principle. Most amazing has been the personal conduct of Lewis. After the defeat of Wendell Willkie in 1940, Lewis retired from the Presidency of the CIO and withdrew from the organization in 1941, continuing as the head of an unaffiliated United Mine Workers until 1946, when he returned to the A.F. of L. fold; late in 1947, he once more "disaffiliated" the miners from the Federation, threatening to create a third general labor body. Despite these personal conflicts, the numerical strength of organized labor continued unimpaired. By 1948, at least 16,000,000 workers were members of unions.

Social Security. Labor organization might help raise wages; labor-standards legislation might help protect the weakest groups among working people, but neither could guard against the threat latent in old age, unemployment, and dependency. The Social Security Act of 1935 (amended in 1939) made provision for all three contingencies. Many categories of workers in establishments employing eight or more persons were to be assured retirement allowances at 65 years of age and after through an Old-Age and Survivors' Insurance program administered by the federal government. The fund was to be built up by matching contributions from workers and employers; and this contribution was initially put at 1 per cent, for each, of wages and earnings up to $3000 a year. Benefit payments were to be based on marital status, length of coverage, and the size of the over-all contributions. Dependent survivors were also to be provided for. Unemployment compensation was to be administered by the states themselves. Through the agency of a federal payroll tax of 3 per cent on payrolls, as a compulsory device, states were to be encouraged to set up their own unemployment-insurance plans, financed in large measure by drawbacks from the federal payroll tax. By 1938, every state had some form of unemployment insurance. To ease the burden of care for the needy aged, the needy blind, neglected, dependent and crippled children, the law provided for federal grants to the states, more or less on a matching basis. A Social Security Board was provided to administer most of the law's provisions. And in May, 1937, three important Supreme Court decisions validated the federal unemployment insurance tax, the old-age benefit levy, and state unemployment-insurance laws.

Works and Relief. The New Deal program for public works and relief assumed the need to stimulate recovery by government spending. Furthermore, against the Hoover dictum that relief of the needy was a local responsibility stood the fact of approaching local bankruptcy. The New Deal moved on two paths, therefore. Its program of public works attempted to stimulate private employment and the capital goods industries through RFC loans and projects undertaken by the Public Works Administration, which was established in 1933. Communities in danger of bankruptcy could find few self-liquidating projects to justify RFC loans, however, and the PWA program moved tardily for all its $3 billion in appropriations. More direct relief began with the CCC, which has already been mentioned. Nevertheless, it required a considerable length of time before a proper program was devised to care for the temporarily unemployed. In May, 1933, the Federal Emergency Relief Administration was set up; in October, 1933, the Civil Works Administration; and finally, in July, 1935, the Works Progress Administration. Care of the unemployables was gradually shifted to local home relief agencies with federal aid to states and municipalities; while the WPA provided employment, sometimes making possible additions to public plant, as a substitute for outdoor relief. Most of the WPA projects were purely of a "make-work" character, it is to be noted. Nevertheless, there were social gains because writers, artists, musicians, and workers in the theater were encouraged to continue their activities under government sponsorship.

Money and Banking. Since the New Deal was concerned from the outset with efforts to raise prices and ease the pressure of the debt burden, currency expansion and bank credit inflation became major preoccupations. In April, 1933, the United States formally went off the gold standard when an executive order stopped the free movement of gold both within and without the country. Congress gave its authorization in the Gold Repeal Joint Resolution of June, 1933, which cancelled the gold clause in all federal and private obligations. A step in the direction of increasing the amount of money in circulation was taken with the passage of the Thomas Amendment to the AAA in May, 1933. This permitted the President to issue up to $3 billion worth of United States notes; to reduce the gold content of the dollar as much as 50 per cent; and to accept silver from foreign governments on the account of the intergovernmental debts, as well as to buy American-mined silver. In January, 1934, Congress enacted the Gold Reserve Act, and under it, the President fixed the value of the dollar at 59.06 cents in terms of its old parity; in other words, the government was permitted to buy gold anywhere at $35 an ounce.

Bank-credit expansion was linked with banking reform. The Banking Act of 1933 and the Banking Act of 1935 provided for the following changes in the country's banking policy: a Federal Deposit Insurance Corporation guaranteed deposits in savings bank accounts up to $5000. Banks belonging to the Federal Reserve System were to cut themselves off from their security affiliates. The government's hold on the Federal Reserve System was greatly extended through the creation of the Board of Governors of the System, all of whom were to be appointed by the President. The Open-Market Committee was to be dominated by the Board and was to have control over the power of expanding and contracting credit. The Board of Governors was also given the right to raise (or lower) reserve requirements of member banks and to raise (or lower) margin requirements on security purchases. Credit expansion was pushed also through government loans, notably by the use of the RFC.

Another outstanding financial reform was the regulation of the security exchanges. On May 27, 1933, the President signed the Federal Securities Act which forbade public offers of new securities unless these were registered with the subsequently created Securities and Exchange Commission. The Commission was established in June, 1934, and given wide powers to obtain for investors adequate information about the financial practices of corporations, their directors and officers, and to regulate the functioning of brokers and the security exchanges. In 1935, the Commission's powers were further increased by the Public Utility Holding Companies Act, which empowered the SEC to restrict holding companies in the public utility field, thus closing a cycle in the development of corporate capitalization.

Oil, Coal, Railroads, and Shipping. The New Deal had subsidized agriculture and experimented in government support of self-regulation by industry. In the case of petroleum and bituminous coal, the invalidation of the NIRA was followed by legislation to support restriction on production in order to maintain prices. In 1935, the Connally "Hot Oil" Act excluded from interstate commerce oil produced in violation of state agreements restricting production. In 1935 and 1937, minimum-price machinery was established for the bituminous coal industry. The Supreme Court invalidated the first Bituminous Coal Conservation Act but the Guffey-Vinson Act of 1937 received its approval.

Of the truly "problem industries," railroads and shipping were among the most important, and since their welfare involved both institutional investors and national defense, government intervention seemed an obvious necessity. The railroads' most serious difficulties stemmed from the excessive debt burden due to overcapitalization (62 per cent of which constituted bonded debt) and from the existence of unnecessarily duplicating and competing systems (upon which had been superimposed the financially manipulated holding companies).

The economic solutions were simple: debt had to be squeezed out, the holding companies eliminated, and the railroads reorganized into a few comprehensive systems. The New Deal could not meet the implication of a possible elimination of $10 billion of railroad values held by institutional investors. Hence, it resorted to palliatives. The ICC permitted the railroads to raise their rates. The RFC made loans totalling $486,876,528 by 1941. In 1936, railroad holding companies were placed under the supervision of the ICC and a Federal Co-ordinator of Transportation was appointed. He was to eliminate wastes, improve the financial position of the roads, and bring about a greater degree of co-operation. In 1940, the ICC was given supervision over motor transport and another portion of the law of 1920 was repealed: in 1936, the clause allowing "recapture" of earnings above 6 per cent had been dropped; now the ICC was relieved of the duty to propose consolidations among railway systems, although its approval was required for any consolidation that might be undertaken.

In the field of shipping, the Merchant Marine Acts of 1936 and 1938 recognized that the subsidy program of the acts of 1920 and 1928 had failed. Eighty-eight per cent of the American fleet would be obsolete by 1942, and its exclusively cargo tonnage was in even worse condition. The law of 1936 vested administrative power in the United States Maritime Commission. This was to lay out the essential routes, prescribe labor conditions on subsidized vessels, and administer the three types of subsidies provided by the law. Instead of the old mail contracts, American ship operators were to receive construction differentials, operating differentials, and countervailing subsidies to meet the differences in cost between American and foreign builders and operators and also to counter the grants of foreign governments. If necessary, and if the President agreed, the United States Maritime Commission might even build a large government-owned merchant fleet either by contract or in United States Navy yards.

Power and Housing. While neither power nor housing was a "problem industry" in the sense of bituminous coal, both were national problems which the New Deal tried to attack. In May, 1933, Congress created the Tennessee Valley Authority with the stated purpose of rehabilitating the population of the Valley and establishing an experiment in the public operation of electric light and power plants. A board of directors of three persons was to be appointed by the President. The board was authorized to build dams, power plants, and transmission lines, to develop fertilizers, and to lay out a general plan for promoting the social and economic welfare of the seven states in the Tennessee Valley region.

The power program was obviously to be most important and here the New Deal entered the field of state capitalism. The TVA was to generate and sell power, with priority to public bodies and co-operatives, for the purpose—originally, at any rate—of creating a "yardstick" against which the rates and practices of private utilities could be measured. It was also to advance rural electrification by providing transmission lines to farms and villages not supplied with electricity and to help municipalities acquire their own power plants and other utility properties. In 1936, the Supreme Court declared that the government might sell and transmit the energy generated at the Wilson Dam to towns in its area. Other decisions validated PWA grants to cities for the construction of municipal power plants.

By 1938, the TVA had completed four dams and had four more under construction. Its accomplishments as regarded flood control and fertilizer production were indeed impressive. Bitter opposition to its power program continued from the private utilities which served the cities in the TVA area. In 1939, the Supreme Court curtailed that opposition by refusing to enjoin the government from distributing the power generated at its plants: The franchises of the power companies affected did not guarantee freedom from future competition, hence these companies could not halt the government's program. As a result of these decisions, the largest power companies in the region sold out to the TVA. Nevertheless, government sale of electric power was to remain subordinate to its recognized functions in aid of navigation, the conservation of natural resources, the control of floods, and the furthering of national defense. This criterion did not prove a barrier to further federal action. The nineteen thirties saw great hydroelectric developments at Grand Coulee Dam (Columbia River), Boulder (now Hoover) Dam on the Colorado, Bonneville Dam (Columbia River), and Fort Peck Dam (upper Missouri River).

In the field of power control, the Public Utility Act of 1935 enlarged the sphere of action of the Federal Power Commission, which was given authority over all utilities transmitting electricity across state lines. More important was the jurisdiction over public utility holding companies granted the SEC. It was empowered to end certain financial abuses in this field and, as soon as practicable, to limit the operations of registered holding companies to a system whose utility assets were physically interconnected and capable of being operated economically as a single co-ordinated system confined to a single area. This was the so-called "death sentence" clause. After prolonged litigation, the Supreme Court in 1939 upheld the requirement that public utility holding companies register with the SEC. In April, 1946, the Supreme Court validated the "death sentence" clause. By 1947, relations between the regulatory authority and the leading companies had improved; the industry considered that the major readjustments under the Act had been completed.

The burden of mortgage debt gave the first impulse toward New Deal intervention in the field of housing. Humanitarian concern and the need to revive the building industry added reason for continued government preoccupation with the issue. Since construction costs were particularly the victims of unsound financing and monopoly prices, both as regards materials and labor, the building industry was one of the most speculative in the country. According to Evans Clark, head of the research organization, The Twentieth-Century Fund, whereas the total value of urban real estate had increased 14 per cent from 1921 to 1929, the long-term mortgage debt rose from $9,000,000,000 to $27,600,000,000, or 208 per cent. The pressure of the topheavy debt on mortgagors became intense so that foreclosures took place, or continued to threaten, leaving financial institutions with great blocks of properties on their hands.

The Home Owners' Refinancing Act, approved June 13, 1933, and the Home Owners' Loan Act, approved April 27, 1934, set up two agencies to extend relief to home owners. The first, the Home Owners' Loan Corporation, was to serve the needs of home owners by refinancing mortgage debts; the second, the Federal Savings and Loan Associations, was to provide funds for home construction. The HOLC offered to exchange its bonds for the instruments of the mortgagee; the previous mortgages and all other liens were to be converted into a single first mortgage secured by the home and held by the corporation. Interest was to be at 5 per cent and principal was to be repaid in fifteen years, beginning with June 13, 1936.

To stimulate building, relieve financial institutions, and make the lending of money for mortgages safer, the National Housing Act of June, 1934, set up a Federal Housing Administration. The law provided a program of mutual mortgage insurance, covering first mortgages on residential property which were being amortized, and authorized national mortgage associations which might buy and sell mortgages and use these as backing for the issue of securities. The FHA was to standardize methods of construction and financing. It was authorized to guarantee or insure mortgages up to 80 per cent of the appraised value of approved houses, with interest not exceeding $5\frac{1}{2}$ per cent. The FHA was also empowered to insure loans for home modernization. In 1938, FHA mortgage insurance terms were liberalized: interest rates were lowered to 5 per cent and the maximum amortization period was extended from 20 to 25 years.

Humanitarian concern for the great number of families who lived in substandard dwellings also expressed itself in New Deal legislation. Under the National Housing Act of 1937 (amended in 1938) a United States Housing Authority was established and given a fund of $800 million out of which to make loans and grants to local communities. It was authorized to advance funds to local housing authorities, for 60 years at 3 per cent. These loans were to cover 90 per cent of the costs of construction, with the other 10 per cent provided locally. In addition, the USHA could grant an annual subsidy for the upkeep of low cost housing. The act also provided that for every new dwelling built with federal funds, at least one unsafe or unsanitary dwelling must be either repaired or eliminated.

While the New Deal program did ease the pressure of mortgage debt and give some stimulus to home building, housing remained a national problem. The cost of providing decent homes for the low-income groups continued beyond any practicable national budget.

· 35 ·
Challenges to the New Deal

THE ELECTION OF 1936

By June, 1936, when the Republican convention assembled at Cleveland, the major New Deal programs for industry and agriculture had been declared unconstitutional by the Supreme Court. The Republican platform opened with the statement, "America is in peril": the President had usurped the powers of Congress and ridden roughshod over the rights of the states; the NIRA had promoted regimentation, and the Hull tariff policies (to be discussed in detail below) had flooded the nation with foreign commodities. Restore high protection, the Republicans argued, and allow the states, by compact among themselves, to deal with problems of prices, production, and industrial relations. As their standard-bearers, the Republicans chose Alfred M. Landon, Governor of Kansas, and newspaper-owner Frank Knox of Illinois.

Roosevelt dominated the proceedings at the Democratic convention although he did not appear in person at Philadelphia. The New Deal was in a defiant mood because of Supreme Court hostility and the growing disapproval of the business community. It challenged both, and pledged the administration to a continuing fight on "the activities of malefactors of great wealth who defraud and exploit the people." President Roosevelt and Vice-President Garner were renominated by acclamation. Victory at the polls was attained as easily. Labor flocked to the defense of the Democratic ticket, particularly through CIO support for Labor's Non-Partisan League, while the Republican cause was not aided by the rallying of unreconstructed conservatives of both parties who refused to see that trade unionism and social security had come to stay. Mr. Landon, who was personally a liberal and sympathetic to many of the New Deal achievements, was put in an equivocal position and he never recovered. The President's re-election was one of the most impressive demonstrations of the popular will in American politics. He received a popular vote of 27,751,000 to Mr. Landon's 16,670,000, and he carried every state but Maine and Vermont. Of the minor parties, the Socialists polled 187,000 and the Communists 80,000 votes. With motley support from the advocates of Dr. Townsend's old-age pension plan and the demagogueries of Father Coughlin, Republican

Representative William Lemke of North Dakota won 892,000 votes for his Union party and its program of monetary inflation.

THE SUPREME COURT FIGHT

The Supreme Court's powers had not been an immediate issue in the 1936 campaign—although Mr. Landon did pledge himself to a constitutional amendment permitting greater federal control over agriculture and industry—yet in numerous cases in 1935 and 1936, the Court, sometimes in 5-to-4 decisions, had declared the methods and the objectives of much New Deal legislation beyond the scope of the federal government. Besides the National Industrial Recovery Act and the first Agricultural Adjustment Act, the Supreme Court had invalidated the Frazier-Lemke Farm Mortgage Act, the Railroad Retirement Act, the Bituminous Coal Stabilization Act, and the Municipal Bankruptcy Act. The federal government's power over taxation and commerce, the Court declared in effect, could not be extended to give federal control over production, prices, or debtor-creditor relationships. And in its decision on the New York State Minimum Wage Law, the Supreme Court denied the states any right to legislate on wages. In certain areas of economic relations, therefore, no government might constitutionally intervene: there existed a no-man's-land which public authority might not enter.

While this might well be in accord with the thinking and the intent of the Founding Fathers, it paralyzed action. President Roosevelt accepted the challenge and, in February, 1937, he presented a program for the reorganization of the Supreme Court. Justices might retire at seventy. If they did not, the President might appoint up to six additional members to supplement the nonretiring justices.

The storm that arose took the President by surprise. Party ranks were disordered, old friends deserted ancient loyalties—Governor Lehman of New York and Senator Wheeler of Montana broke with the President on the issue—and a bitter controversy raged in Congress and in the press. Historians and professors of law entered the lists with learned volumes on the nature of the legal process and the consequences of judicial review for a democracy. Charles A. Beard supported the old Jacksonian contention that Constitutional interpretation concerned Congress and the Executive as well as the Supreme Court. If Congress agreed "... with four of the Supreme Court Justices that five of the Justices have misread, misinterpreted and in substance violated the Constitution, then Congress has the civic and moral obligation to bring the Court back within the Constitution." The President's opponents, on the other hand, feared the destruction of the country's Constitutional liberties if the Supreme Court might be manipulated by Executive appointment. As one of them said, no Supreme

Court at all would be better than "a Supreme Court which is subservient to any one man." The President himself entered the oratorical arena in two public addresses in which he declared that there was "no definite assurance that the three-horse team of the American system of government will pull together" and stated frankly that he wanted "to appoint Justices who will not undertake to override Congress or legislative policy."

The President was unsuccessful because of the hostility of the Senate. His bill was reported out adversely by the Senate Judiciary Committee; a long debate ensued; and when his chief whip, Senator Robinson of Arkansas, died suddenly, the administration support collapsed. A substitute proposal was introduced and, because it pleased nobody, the Senate voted to recommit it on July 22, 1937. And so the drama ended.

Although the Presidential measure was defeated, Court decisions in the spring of 1937 treated New Deal measures with new tenderness. Thus, on March 29, the Supreme Court reversed its decision in the New York Minimum Wage case, upholding an almost similar Washington statute and expressly overruling the Adkins decision of 1923 upon which the New York case had been based. In April, the Court sustained the constitutionality of the National Labor Relations Act; in May, it held that Alabama's unemployment insurance law did not violate the Constitution; and, as the term of court drew to a close, the old-age benefit system of the Social Security Act was accepted under the general welfare clause, with only two dissents.

On June 1, 1937, at the height of the Court debate, Justice Van Devanter resigned. He was succeeded by Senator Hugo L. Black of Alabama, an enthusiastic New Dealer. Justice Sutherland, another member of the "conservative" element in the high tribunal, retired the following year. During the 1938 term, and in important decisions thereafter, the Court so broadened its definition of interstate commerce, freedom of contract, and the "due process" clause as to give New Deal legislation the stamp of constitutionality. Yet the Court stood victor, for the principle of judicial review remained intact and unrestricted; the Court's authority as an institutional force had not been surrendered.

THE RECESSION OF 1937 TO 1938

The New Deal's spending and easy-money programs and its confidence in the essential soundness of American institutions spread the processes of revival. Agriculture was the first to respond, but the country's industry was not slow to follow; so that up to midsummer of 1937 (except for a brief recession in 1934) the course of business activity moved upward. Vast sums were being poured out by the government on public works, in loans to public authorities and private enterprise, in the form of the soldiers' bonus, for relief. These were stimulating heavy goods and consumer-goods industries alike. There were other forces exerting significant influences: the administration's devaluation and credit policies were encouraging prices to rise, thus relieving considerably the burden of debt charges; business was replacing portions of obsolescent plants and machinery; more efficient industries were hastening to introduce labor-saving devices in order to reduce their wage costs; European countries and Japan, embarked on rearmament programs, were buying American raw materials and heavy goods.

Yet more than 9,000,000 people were out of work, and although industrial production was almost as high as it had been in 1929 it should have been higher; for the population of the country was larger and the rate of productivity in industry was perhaps 25 per cent greater. A number of reasons may be adduced for the lag. First, the government's spending and lending policy frightened off new business investment. Second, whereas labor had before been receiving an inadequate share of the national income, under the New Deal its share probably was too great. This increased the costs of production. Third, there was no real revival in our foreign trade, largely because of the national-economic policies pursued by most of the countries of Europe.

In August, 1937, business activity went into a sharp and steep decline. The drop in agricultural prices and in the value of the farm dollar was almost catastrophic. The Federal Reserve index of industrial production fell from 118 in May, 1937, to 76 in May, 1938. The new downswing in the business cycle was attributed to four factors: 1. Prices had been rising during 1936 to 1937 and businessmen, fearing further sharp advances, had piled up inventories. 2. In certain basic commodities, steel and building materials particularly, prices had continued sticky. 3. The Board of Governors of the Federal Reserve System had doubled reserve ratios after August, 1936, and sterilized the gold which had come into the country after dollar devaluation. There followed a contraction in bank loans and hence a decline in the volume and velocity of deposit turnover. While this was not general, some banks, notably in New York and Chicago, felt it expedient to contract their commercial loan and investment portfolios. 4. Most important, however, was the end of pump-priming as the government reduced expenditures. Whereas, as the economist Arthur Gayer pointed out, the government had added between $3 and $4 billion to the national income during 1934 to 1936; in 1937 its contribution was less than $1 billion.

To meet the onset of depression, the administration moved on two fronts: it renewed stimulation of the economy and launched an attack on the monopoly which was assumed responsible for the continued inflexibility of prices. The O'Mahoney Monopoly Inquiry Act of 1938 established a

Temporary National Economic Committee composed of three Senators, three Representatives, and representatives of the Justice, Treasury, Commerce and Agriculture Departments, the SEC, and the Federal Trade Commission. The TNEC was supposed to inquire into the general situation in order to discover the causes for prolonged depression and unemployment and to ascertain the possible relationship between depression and the existence and prevalence of monopoly controls over prices. For three years, the Committee's experts made statistical and other studies of specific problems; the Committee itself heard 552 witnesses from 95 industries. The TNEC inquiry produced a great mass of print: 17,000 pages of testimony and 43 monographic studies, but its results did not match its research. The Committee was unfortunate in composition, approach, and timing. Large and diffuse in makeup, its personnel was not animated by a common purpose. Although the inquiry was broad, it failed to examine important issues, notably the problems of measuring concentration and the relation of such concentration to productive efficiency, the distribution of income, and the mechanism of investment. Nor did the TNEC look effectively into the reasons for the failure of the antimonopoly policies of the past half-century. Finally, the TNEC lacked the colorful and energetic general counsel whose work had done so much to make previous congressional or commission investigations significant.

The Committee's recommendations included: federal charters of incorporation for enterprises doing business on a nationwide scale, enforcement of the antitrust laws, reform of patent law procedure, and tax revision in the interests of small enterprises and new businesses. Congress took action only in regard to the patent laws: like the President and the public, the legislature was more concerned with the war in April, 1941.

Investigation and legal action against monopoly were necessarily slow processes. The recession of 1937 to 1938 was an immediate fact. To promote new recovery, the administration returned to pump-priming and an easy-money policy. In June, 1938, Congress passed bills for increased expenditures on public works and relief. In addition to the appropriations requested by the President, the Senate provided $212 million to permit parity payments to growers of wheat, rice, cotton, and tobacco. Federal Reserve measures released the gold which had been sterilized after devaluation of the dollar, and lowered member bank reserve requirements. As an additional measure of stimulation, Congress authorized the RFC to make direct loans to businessmen.

SLOWING DOWN OF THE NEW DEAL

Production indexes rose as a result of the renewal of government spending in 1938, but basic economic issues remained essentially unresolved.

In the meantime, several forces were working to end the New Deal as an aggressive force in domestic policy. The first Roosevelt administration had produced notable reform measures in the fields of banking, regulation of the stock exchanges and the issue of securities, power control, and industrial relations. The second Roosevelt administration saw few such major changes except in agriculture. There, the concepts of parity income and the ever-normal granary plan helped make agriculture not merely a recognized special interest, but almost a subsidized charge of the state.

The slackening of the New Deal may be laid at the door of the international situation, which diverted administration attention from domestic issues, and to the strengthening of opposition at home. The breakdown in international order was evident by the fall of 1937. In 1938, it became clear that the New Deal had no more power to abolish the business cycle than had the "new era" which preceded it. The political alliance among western farmers, eastern labor and urban elements, and southern conservatism began to creak at the joints. The Republicans gained strength. After 1938, President Roosevelt was compelled to face the obverse of the situation which confronted Republican Chief Executives in the nineteen twenties—when Democrats and dissident Republicans united; for now southern Democrats were joining an increasing Republican minority to block further attempts at extending the New Deal.

Thus, the most notable domestic activity of the second Roosevelt administration was embodied in its expenditures rather than in new legislation, although this did include certain significant measures. The Fair Labor Standards Act of 1938 has already been mentioned. The Food, Drug, and Cosmetics Act of 1938 finally modernized the pioneer legislation of 1906 and 1911 to include new commodities and a revision of labeling requirements. In the Hatch Acts of 1939 and 1940, Congress attempted to alter political practices. The measures outlawed certain forms of intimidation and coercion; they also forbade federal employees, or state employees paid wholly or in part from federal funds, to engage in the party activities long traditional among minor government workers at both primary and general elections.

Beginning with William Howard Taft, almost every President had urged reorganization of the executive department of the federal government. The growth of government functions had produced a confusion of authority among departments, bureaus, and independent agencies. Congress failed to impose order when that entailed a diminution of patronage. Finally, in 1932, it turned the ungrateful task over to President Hoover. A Democratic Congress reversed that policy in 1933 and refused to grant President Roosevelt similar powers in 1936. By 1939, Congress changed opinions once again and passed a law much resembling the measures it had previously opposed. The Reorganization Act of 1939 authorized the

President to regroup minor government bureaus and independent agencies in the interests of efficiency, but Congress retained the power to negative his action within a 60-day period. Continuing along the same lines, the Eightieth Congress created a commission, headed by ex-President Herbert Hoover, to examine once more the possibilities of reorganization of the federal offices.

Although the New Deal made few broad advances during this period, it did continue action in certain areas. The Bituminous Coal Act of 1937, the Robinson-Patman Resale Price Maintenance Act of 1937, and the Wheeler-Lea Act of 1938 carried forward certain aspects of the policy embodied in NIRA. The first encouraged and permitted industrial price-fixing with government supervision and consent. The two latter attempted to control the plane of competition by forbidding price discrimination, loss leaders, and similar practices, even in retail trade, and by strengthening the Federal Trade Commission's power to define "unfair competition."

In one sense, the administration's task became easier after 1937. As the international situation grew more threatening, armaments expenditures bolstered the "make-work" of relief and public works as a means of priming the pump for recovery. Deficits incurred to avert or prevent depression might be questioned; deficits incurred to build up the army and fleet of the United States in a world moving glacier-like toward war seemed necessary even to a nation that meant to remain neutral. Thus, almost repeating past patterns, the New Deal, like the New Freedom, was eclipsed by war.

DEFICIT FINANCING

Rearmament expenditures needed small defending, but the cost of the "war on depression" was another matter. The Democratic platform of 1932 had advocated a balanced budget and the first New Deal Congress had actually practiced economy. Immediate needs prevented any extension of that policy. Instead, annual budgets rose until federal expenditures stood at $8,400,000,000 in 1937, when rearmament began to make an increasingly important part of federal spending. For the years 1931 to 1938, the total federal deficit was $20,000,000,000, against which might be balanced assets arising from recoverable loans and expenditures on public-works construction; these came to $12,000,000,000.

At the same time that deficits increased, so did taxes. Federal taxes in 1931 came to $2,700,000,000; in 1938, they stood at $5,900,000,000. In 1931, federal taxes represented 4.5 per cent of national income, while in 1938, the percentage was 9.5. Income, estate, gift, and corporation taxes were increased by the Revenue Act of 1935 and in 1936, as a further tax on corporations, an undistributed-profits tax was levied. Because of the great hostility engendered, this device was abandoned in the Revenue Act of

1938. In 1930, at least 95 per cent of all federal tax revenue was produced by income taxes, tobacco taxes, and customs duties; in 1938, these sources contributed 58 per cent. The New Deal developed new tax sources, notably manufacturers' excise taxes, liquor taxes (because of the repeal of Prohibition), and payroll taxes. At the same time, it is important to note that the federal government was not called upon to pay as much, proportionately, for its borrowings. The yield on United States government bonds was 3.65 per cent in the second quarter of 1929 and only 2.57 per cent in the last quarter of 1937. The rearmament program did not raise interest rates and these remained low through the period of preparation and of actual war.

The New Deal justified its fiscal program on the following grounds: Pump-priming stimulated private enterprise. Deficit financing also made additions to the national wealth because of public-works construction. Debt in itself was not pure evil so long as the carrying charges of the debt were not unduly onerous. Needless to say, there were many who questioned the New Deal fiscal theories; and an analysis—as we shall see—indicates that the New Deal did not meet with unqualified success so far as the nation's economic responses were concerned.

TOWARD A CRITIQUE OF THE NEW DEAL

Against these burdens, present and future, one may consider some of the economic consequences of the New Deal. From 1933 to 1939, the United States had a national administration pledged to act for recovery and reform. That administration undertook to redress the social balance in favor of the "forgotten man." In large measure, however, the forgotten man tended to remain forgotten unless he became part of an organized group which could bring pressure to bear in strategic political areas. Thus, the principal benefits of the AAA went to the producers of such staples as cotton, tobacco, corn, and wheat. The NLRA made it possible for trade unionists to bargain for a larger share of the product of the industries in which they worked; on the other hand, the varied plans for industrial self-regulation gave support to price maintenance rather than to increased competitive efficiency. It was impossible for the New Deal—and perhaps for any administration that intended to remain in office—to press for sharper writing down of capital claims; for a more effective squeezing out of the capital and labor stagnant in agriculture and the "problem industries"; or for a tax policy that would not impose unnecessarily heavy burdens on investment nor yet make the lower income groups bear the cost of relief through increasing taxes on consumption.

Measured in terms of achievement of objectives, the New Deal scored in unexpected fashion. It had attributed the depression following 1929 to overexpansion of capital plant, the existence of managed prices in certain industries, and the malfunctioning of world markets. In many fields, moreover, business enterprises had incurred fixed charges too great to permit prompt adjustment to changed market conditions. Privately controlled banking had failed to give positive leadership to mitigate business fluctuations. Labor received an inadequate share of the national income, partly because of its unequal bargaining power. Finally, certain factors in the economy as a whole—the human wastage of unemployment, inadequate housing for low-income groups, the position of agricultural labor, the pressure of insecurities which neither private charity nor individual savings could master—justified governmental intervention.

We have seen how the New Deal handled the last problem. On humanitarian grounds, its action was justified, but future economic consequences of social security and wage-and-hour standards could not readily be measured. Although the New Deal recognized the problem of overcapitalization, especially in regard to the railroads, it could no more secure deflation in this area than investigation, publicity, and antitrust prosecutions could change established business practice in the areas of administered prices. Privately controlled banking had not halted the wild speculation which was the final phase of the economic revival of the nineteen twenties; government-controlled banking and government aid to support cheap credit proved unable to reverse the downward trend which followed. Business had access to ample funds at low interest rates, but bank loan portfolios did not expand correspondingly.

While the New Deal had economic consequences unforeseen and perhaps undesired by its proponents, its political consequences were even more significant. The emergence of pressure groups impressed the public as well as the political scientist. Governmental response to such groups was no new phenomenon in American politics. Novel, however, was the implicit assumption that the general welfare would be promoted by the government's bestowing special favors upon an increasing number of pressure groups. The co-operation of group interests had become the ruling practice in tariff-making and the resulting impact on the general welfare had not been encouraging.

Even more important, perhaps, was the fact that the New Deal had parted completely with the nineteenth-century conception of the laissez-faire or passive state; Americans were fully launched on the experiment of state capitalism. The depression of 1930 and after had persuaded New Deal theoreticians that capitalism's progress in the United States had slowed down, if it had not ceased altogether. Now the state had to assume positive functions. Accordingly, its role as umpire was magnified and extended into other regions, as in the case of the establishment of the National Labor Relations Board and the Social Security Board. Its social-service activities were expanded, particularly in the handling of the problems of the unemployed, the unemployables, and other dependents.

Nor was this all. Under the New Deal, the state began to initiate projects and undertakings of a distinctly economic character. The national state, in short was beginning to take on, in many domains, the essential color of private enterprise. It borrowed money, not alone for the maintenance of the traditional civil and military establishments of government, but also for the purposes of buying and selling commodities, processing goods, creating electric power and light, dealing in real estate, engaging in warehousing, the banking business, and the shipping and railroading businesses. It set up corporations and corporate agencies which possessed charters, directors, assets, thousands of employees, and industrial and mercantile policies. As in big business, there were interlocking directorates and the shifting of funds.

This was a startling transformation; and it raised for many Americans disquieting problems. There were—even before World War II—at least fifty New Deal corporations and corporate agencies which were in or could go into business. Some were created by Congress, some by Presidential order, some by departmental decision alone. Often they were run by Cabinet officers who, in the nature of things, were compelled to delegate power to anonymous lesser officials. The pattern was too complex and too obscure for popular control.

To whom, in the final analysis, were these executive agencies to be responsible? To Congress? But Congress did not possess any longer a sensitive enough machinery for their surveillance. Its committee system had been laid out for a simpler day; and to keep track of all the executive agencies would require a functionary group quite as complex as that already managing the new authorities and offices. To the courts? But the courts were even less fitted than Congress for the supervision of policy-making and policy-executing bodies. To public opinion? But how was public opinion to secure accurate and reasonably uncolored information? By what tests was the worth of these new public bodies to be measured? By those of private business? But the New Deal authorities and offices did not have to enter the money market for fresh funds; they did not have to conserve assets; they were not called upon to present favorable profit-and-loss statements. Wage policies were fixed by statute and not by the competition of the market place.

How—most important of all—were the functionaries to be prevented from extending their authority? For here lay the real danger of a bureaucracy: that it tended to associate its own well-being with the general welfare. This was one of the vexing problems the New Deal had created. It was not possible to dismiss it lightly, or to seek to disguise its perils by referring to the new state as the "social-service state." Even as the nation entered upon actual war, the question of this new American bureaucracy could not be downed, and it was one of the important reasons for the increasingly critical tone that Congress took toward the President.

Reaction to these issues of executive power, legislative control, and the growth of bureaucracy became evident not only in the discussions of political scientists, but also in the arena of elections. In 1938, the Republicans increased their House membership from 89 to 172; their Senators from 15 to 23. And President Roosevelt's attempt to eliminate opposition within his own party showed that southern Democrats, at least, owed their seats to their constituents rather than to the influence of the national administration. For, of the legislators opposed by the President in Democratic primary contests and at the polls, only Representative John F. O'Connor of New York failed of election, while Senators George of Georgia, Smith of South Carolina, and Tydings of Maryland all retained their seats. The complex of American politics had not been destroyed by the undoubted magic of the Roosevelt program and personality.

Section XII
WORLD WAR II
AND ITS CONSEQUENCES

· 36 ·

The Struggle for Neutrality

THE INTERNATIONAL ECONOMIC POLICY OF THE NEW DEAL

THE foreign policy of the New Deal, like the policy of the Republican administrations which preceded it, was confronted by conflicting choices. The New World wished to remain safely isolated from the torment of the Old. Yet the pressure of events and interests pushed the United States further and further into that torment. In a sense, then, the story of the New Deal's foreign policy is the story of the conflict between popular will and the logic of facts.

That struggle is as clear in trade policy as in the attempt to keep the United States out of World War II. The United States was a creditor nation. It desired to expand foreign markets for its industries and for agricultural staples like tobacco, wheat, and cotton. Yet it acted to reserve its markets for its own producers. Economists and certain business leaders recognized the paradox, but these were a minority: the influence of the economists may be measured by the fact that the Hoover administration ignored their protest against the Smoot-Hawley tariff of 1930, although such a protest was signed by one thousand leaders in the field.

The New Deal was no more consistent than the Old. It wished to revive foreign trade, yet its action at the London Economic Conference, which met in June, 1933, prevented agreement to secure the exchange stability necessary for revival. We have seen how the deflation of 1929 to 1931 shattered the unsound financial structure of Austria and Germany and forced protective measures on England and France. The Hoover Moratorium (which linked war debts and reparations even while it denied legal validity to the act) was followed by outright default among the United States' principal debtors. England abandoned the gold standard. France imposed import quotas. Nations supplemented tariffs with rigid exchange controls and competitive currency inflation. After weeks of talk, the participants in the London Economic Conference failed to do more than make inconclusive plans for securing a measure of currency stabilization. Even these had no effect, for on July 3, 1933, President Roosevelt declared that the United States must rise from depression by way of a sound internal program rather than through international action to stabilize currency and free international trade. Although a tentative stabilization agreement with England and France was reached in 1936, the pattern of international trade had been set in new molds: the common sense of trade as an exchange at least nominally of mutual benefit all but disappeared; nations seemed to have returned to the idea of trade as a form of warfare, seeking competitive advantage by all sorts of quantitative controls and currency manipulations.

If the American position at the London Economic Conference were to be taken as definitive, the United States stood committed to economic nationalism. The facts of continued foreign investment and the success of the Hull trade pacts indicate that American policy was more complex. Although about half the United States portfolio investments were in default by 1938, private investment abroad did not cease. In 1930, the United States had $7,600,000,000 in direct and $7,800,000,000 in portfolio investments. In 1940, its foreign investments stood at $7,000,000,000 and $3,600,000,000 respectively. Even though 66 per cent of Latin-American dollar bonds were in default, Congress established a second Export-Import Bank in 1935 (the first had been created to finance trade with Russia) and this made loans to nations like Brazil, which accounted for nearly a quarter of the total private debt in default. Nor were returns from America's foreign holdings unencouraging: While the leading American corporations reported 3.8 per cent as their average return in 1938, foreign holdings averaged 5.8 per cent. If foreign investment had not entirely recovered from the crisis of the early thirties, income returns were rising.

INCOME FROM FOREIGN INVESTMENTS, 1929–39

(Millions of Dollars)

	1929	1932	1939
Direct	480	99	400
Portfolio	400	320	125

The Hull trade program, however, was concerned with outlets for goods as well as capital. Its object was to break through the barriers each nation was raising and so restore something resembling a world market. General tariff reduction was not politically practicable in the United States. Treaties for reciprocal reduction of duties had generally foundered in the Senate, where a two-thirds vote was required for ratification. Secretary of State Hull's plan avoided both dangers. The Trade Agreements

Act of 1934, which embodied most of that program, allowed the President to negotiate agreements for lowering United States tariff rates up to 50 per cent (subsequently raised to 75 per cent), if the other nation made similar concessions. During such negotiations, the United States sought to secure exchange facilities equal to those it had enjoyed in some given past year, and to have the benefit of any tariff concessions later made to third parties. This pushed the concept of flexible multilateral trade and "most-favored-nation" treatment into the constricting field of international commerce.

Certain agricultural interests stood out in opposition, declaring that, once again, tariff policy sacrificed the producer of agricultural staples to the industrialist. But Mr. Hull stuck to his last. There were triennial renewals of the Reciprocal Trade Agreements Act until 1948; the State Department negotiated understandings with 42 countries; and the measure of its success may be ascertained from the fact that during the peace years 1934 to 1939, American exports to countries in the program increased 63 per cent as against an increase of only 32 per cent to countries not participating.

In 1948, the Republican Eightieth Congress sought to end the plan, yielding to the traditional pressures of protected industries. But the outcry was too great: How could we talk of European recovery—which was linked with expanding imports to us—at the same time that we pushed tariff walls upward once more? Congress compromised, extending the act for a single year but expanding the powers of the United States Tariff Commission in those cases where further revision downward was contemplated. All this demonstrated that our responsibilities as a creditor nation were not yet universally understood.

LATIN-AMERICAN AFFAIRS

In its relations with the nations of Latin America, the United States continued along the new paths broken in the middle twenties. Theodore Roosevelt's "Big Stick" had been followed by Philander Knox's "Dollar Diplomacy," and that by the somewhat sermonizing intervention of Woodrow Wilson. In the early nineteen twenties, the United States had troops in Haiti and the Dominican Republic; its marines were chasing "bandits" in Nicaragua; and certain American interests, in oil and large landed property particularly, were eager for intervention in Mexico. The first Coolidge administration receded from this policy of preaching, pinprick, and intervention in 1924, when it withdrew our troops from the Dominican Republic. The following year, the United States made a partial withdrawal from Nicaragua. The Morrow mission to Mexico in the fall of 1927 was perhaps the greatest contribution to more cordial inter-American relations, but that did not prevent several members of the Pan-American Conference of 1928 from taking a hostile tone toward the "Colossus of the North."

The Hoover administration struck out farther along these lines. As President-elect, Mr. Hoover made a goodwill tour southward and proclaimed that in the Western Hemisphere no nation was paramount, but all were "friendly and equal states." In 1930, the State Department issued the Clark Memorandum which repudiated Theodore Roosevelt's "corollary" to the Monroe Doctrine. Said the Memorandum: the doctrine stated the position of the Americas *vis-à-vis* Europe; it was not a claim to United States hegemony in the Western Hemisphere. Action followed words, moreover. In 1932, the United States did not help American bankers establish a customs receivership when El Salvador defaulted on loan payments, even though the loan contract provided for such intervention. In 1933, the United States finally quit Nicaragua.

The new trend was named and developed by the Roosevelt administration. The first Roosevelt inaugural pledged the United States to act as a Good Neighbor toward the other American nations. That promise was kept when Cubans revolted against the Machado dictatorship in 1934; for the United States refused to intervene "to restore order" under the Platt Amendment. Indeed, the Platt Amendment itself was abrogated in 1934. United States intervention in the Caribbean was further restricted that year by the withdrawing of American marines from Haiti; and financial control over that republic came to an end in 1935. In 1936, the United States negotiated a new treaty with Panama, ending our unilateral guarantee of its independence and our right to intervene in its affairs. The treaty was ratified by the Senate in 1939.

The United States followed its diplomatic measures for conciliating Latin-American opinion with an economic and cultural program. The Hull trade agreements worked toward easing trade among the American republics. The Export-Import Bank, reorganized in 1935 and given renewed authority in 1937, as a single bank, made loans totalling $115,100,000 by 1939. When World War II broke out, the Bank was among the agencies with which the United States tried to help cushion the loss of Latin America's normal export markets. An Inter-American Advisory Commission on economic problems made studies of transportation, marketing, exchange, and production questions. Quota agreements attempted to ease the position of coffee growers in fourteen nations. Projects for increasing the production of essential war materials in Latin America sought to meet those countries' needs for new markets and the requirements of the United States rearmament program. In 1939 and again in 1941, Congress continued the Export-Import Bank and then broadened its functions to include help in "the development of the resources, the stabilization of the economies, and the orderly marketing of the products of the Western Hemisphere."

On another level, the United States attempted to counter geography and habit. Latin America was closer to the Old World than to the United States. It long had taken its intellectual guidance from Paris, Rome, and Madrid, and much of its military training from Germany. Since 1926, the United States had promoted the interchange of military missions; now, it pushed this program, even leasing over-aged and decommissioned warships to Brazil in 1937. The following year, Congress appropriated money for a cultural interchange program as well as for the dispatch of American experts in agriculture, engineering, library administration, and other technical fields.

The new role of the United States in the Western Hemisphere may be traced through the Pan-American Conferences. Although the Montevideo Conference of 1933 opened in an atmosphere of suspicion toward the United States, it closed with new confidence, largely as the result of Secretary Hull's intimations of the projected trade program and of the American delegation's readiness to bring problems into open discussion. In January, 1936, after joint action by the United States and South American governments had finally halted five years of war between Bolivia and Paraguay over the Chaco, President Roosevelt suggested a special conference to deal with the problems of maintaining the peace among American states. The conference met at Buenos Aires in December. The President himself attended and his presence had great psychological effect. The chief result of the gathering was a Declaration of Principles of Inter-American Solidarity and Co-operation. In this, the American nations proclaimed "their absolute juridical liberty, their unqualified respect for their respective sovereignties and the existence of a common democracy throughout America." Any act likely to disturb the peace justified consultation. In addition to proclaiming a common democracy, the conference accepted a set of common principles: territorial conquest was proscribed, hence no acquisition made by violence was to be recognized; "intervention by one State in the external or internal affairs of another State is condemned"; "forcible collection of pecuniary debts is illegal"; and all differences of any origin or nature should be settled by conciliation, unrestricted arbitration, or the operation of international justice. Should war occur or threaten, or intervention impend, the states of the Pan-American Union pledged themselves to consultation.

In 1938, the Eighth International Conference of American States met at Lima, Peru. Once again, American nations declared their opposition to the use of force as a means of national aggrandizement. Reflecting a growing concern with the Nazi leaders' claim to dominion over persons of German origin abroad, the Conference asserted that aliens may not claim "collectively the condition of minorities" and should not "exercise the political rights invested in them by the laws of their own countries." The Fourth Article of the Declaration of Lima implemented the agreement to consult in emergencies, by providing for meetings of American foreign ministers on the initiative of any one of them.

World War II began on September 1, 1939. On September 23, the first such emergency conference assembled at Panama. The conference reaffirmed the Lima declaration of solidarity and recommended that its member governments take "the necessary measures to eradicate from the Americas the spread of doctrines that tend to place in jeopardy the common American ideal." Most striking, however, was the Declaration of Panama, which asserted that "... there can be no justification for the interests of the belligerents to prevail over the rights of neutrals, causing disturbance and suffering to nations which by their neutrality in the conflict and their distance from the scene of events, should not be burdened with its fatal and painful consequences." The neutral American republics, therefore, were entitled to have their adjacent waters untroubled by the hostile activities of non-American belligerents. Those "adjacent waters" were defined as an area 300 miles from shoreline and stretching from Passamaquoddy Bay to the Strait of Juan de Fuca. The "Safety Belt" was not to be defended by force, however, and the warring nations showed no readiness to respect it, or even to return satisfactory reply to protests about incidents like the *Graf Spee* affair, when British cruisers fought that German battleship which was about to attack a French steamer off the Uruguay coast.

By June, 1940, the Low Countries and France had fallen, and the Western Hemisphere stood confronted by the problem of the future of French and Dutch possessions in the New World. Both the State Department and Congress informed European governments that this country would recognize no territorial transfers; but the United States did not stop with a unilateral declaration of policy. The foreign ministers assembled again, at Havana on July 21, 1940. Here, Secretary Hull proposed not a mere sharing of separate protectorates, but a collective trusteeship through an Inter-American Commission for Territorial Administration. Should areas in the Americas be threatened with a change of sovereignty as a result of war, the American nations jointly might set up a provisional administration. Any republic might take necessary emergency action, but the matter was to be brought before the Commission as soon as possible, and no administrating power was to use its position to seek economic privileges.

By 1941, when involvement in the war seemed imminent, the United States had so conciliated most of its neighbors to the southward that the hostility of the early nineteen twenties was muted into something like respect. And, to the rest of the world, the American republics had shown that great states and small could live in honorable peace and unite, on something like equal terms, when their common interest stood threatened. Certain soft spots remained, to be sure. Pan-American conferences talked of a common democratic faith, but most Latin-American governments remained dictatorships established by palace revolution. The United States and its southern neighbors might try to increase and develop inter-American trade, but the natural course of that trade lay between the eastern and western shores of the Atlantic rather than between the northern and southern portions of the Western Hemisphere. Nevertheless, American capital—slowly, it is true—was moving southward; and the prospects for transforming the economies of Latin-American peoples, and in the process raising their standards of living, seemed bright.

Such developments were for the long run; for the present, the United States could reckon the achievements of the Good Neighbor policy and be proud. Nor did that grand scheme halt at the St. Lawrence. In spite of Canada's participation in the British imperial preference system, which gave inter-Empire trade special tariff concessions, she negotiated a trade pact with the United States under the law of 1934. The Canadian government discussed issues of defense with the United States in 1937. In August, 1938, President Roosevelt, in a speech at Kingston, Ontario, declared that "... the people of the United States will not stand idly by if domination of Canadian soil is threatened by any other empire." A year later, the two countries implemented this pledge by organizing a Permanent Joint Board of Defense to study problems of securing the hemisphere's safety at the north.

Thus, whatever frictions might remain, the special linkage of United States and Latin-American interests and policy known as "Hemisphere Solidarity" was becoming a fact by 1940 to 1941; fascist infiltration into the Latin-American economy had been checked; American had replaced German and Italian interests in the principal South American airlines; and a spirit of mutual goodwill was growing. The way lay clear to an even closer co-operation among the Americas, should war touch the United States.

NEUTRAL RIGHTS AND PHILIPPINE INDEPENDENCE

In large measure, American foreign policy between 1933 and 1939 was shaped by the disillusionment following World War I. Whatever the relation between neutral rights and economic interests, the United States had also entered the war "to make the world safe for democracy," and the end-result of the struggle appeared to be depression at home and the triumph of fascism abroad. More and more Americans believed that it was economic forces which drew nations into war and that if the people were given a chance to speak their will, they never would sanction entry into another world conflict. Thus in 1937, when Representative Ludlow of Indiana proposed a Constitutional amendment denying Congress the power to declare war except after an affirmative decision at a national referendum, 73 per cent of the persons questioned in an opinion poll approved the measure. If opportunity for profit encouraged war, then the United States should forego such gains and take measures to keep its economic welfare from being tied to the needs of any belligerent. The disclosures of Senator Gerald Nye's committee investigating the munitions industry strengthened that view in 1934 and 1935; the rise of a new isolationism gave it intellectual coherence. Widespread debt default and the failure of the League of Nations to follow its scoldings of Japan and Italy with action against the invasion of China and Ethiopia further convinced the American people that the United States should take fullest advantage of the oceans that separated it from the hatreds and the problems of Europe.

In 1934, Congress passed the Johnson Act, which closed the American securities markets to nations that had defaulted on their debts. The following year, Hearst editorials, the oratory of Father Coughlin, and the diplomatic wisdom embodied in the antiforeign "crackerbarrel" philosophy of comedian Will Rogers produced a spate of telegrams which caused the Senate to defeat a resolution for United States membership in the World Court for International Justice. In 1935, too, Congress passed a law requiring the President to impose an embargo on the shipment of arms to belligerents and to prohibit Americans from travelling on belligerent ships. In 1936, these provisions were reinforced by a clause prohibiting non-American belligerents from floating loans in the United States. Unlike these temporary measures, the Neutrality Act of 1937 was intended to embody a permanent policy. The law empowered the President to proclaim the existence of a "state of war." When such condition prevailed in any area, the act required a ban on the sale of arms and forbade more than 90-day credits to belligerents. American ships might not carry implements of war. Americans might not travel on belligerent vessels nor might American merchantmen be armed. At his discretion, the President might bar American ships from transporting any goods until they had been paid for; he might deny the use of American ports as supply bases or close United States ports to belligerent submarines or armed merchantmen.

In effect, Congress had surrendered the "neutral rights" for which the United States had contended in war and in argument through the major part of its existence. Peace was more valuable than freedom to trade.

For all the sweeping character of the new neutrality policy, it allowed the President considerable discretion in actual enforcement. It was left to him to take the initial step by declaring the existence of "a state of war." When civil conflict flared in Spain in the spring of 1936, President Roosevelt made the necessary declaration and so prevented the export of American arms to Spain's legally chosen government. The Neutrality Acts were applied more flexibly in other situations. Italy invaded Ethiopia in 1935 and the arms embargo was invoked; but shipment of gasoline and oil continued, swelling American trade with Italy from the $25,000 monthly average of 1934 to the $600,000 of November, 1935. In the case of Japanese aggression against China, the United States backed and filled, unwilling to label the "China incident" a war, because that would injure the victim rather than her assailant. Yet the United States was not ready to risk use of the large discretionary power over raw material exports; here the determining factor was the fear that Japanese aggression would be shifted southward against the rich and relatively unprotected British and Dutch possessions in the Southwest Pacific.

American reluctance to be drawn into a Pacific war took shape in our Philippine policy as well. In 1933, Congress passed the Hawes-Cutting Act for Philippine independence over President Hoover's veto; but the Filipinos rejected the Act because of its unfavorable trade terms, restrictions on immigration, and continuance of military controls. The following year, the Tydings-McDuffie Act made the Philippine commonwealth completely autonomous except for foreign affairs, a limit on public debt, judicial review, American control over Philippine armed forces, and the recognition of the authority of an American High Commissioner. The Philippines were to be completely independent by July 4, 1946, however. In the interval, to ease the economic transition between colonial status and complete independence, Philippine exports were to bear an increasing portion of the United States tariff—a provision later altered to provide for a system of duty-free quotas on most Philippine exports but sugar. Defense issues were left to further negotiation. War came before the program could be carried out in its entirety, but Philippine independence was recognized in 1946. The Bell Act made some concessions to Philippine trade. Philippine exports were to enter the United States duty-free for 8 years. During the 20 years after, they would pay successive increments of 5 per cent until the full tariff was in force. Also, United States citizens were to have equal economic privileges with citizens of the Philippines; and the island government was to grant the United States land, air and naval bases.

NAVAL CONSTRUCTION

Attempts to keep the United States out of the war by foregoing neutral rights and relinquishing certain overseas possessions did not prevent a simultaneous growth of navalism. Japan invaded Manchuria in 1931 and transformed that Chinese province into the puppet state of Manchukuo. In spite of British failure to make a parallel forthright statement, the United States declared in January, 1932, that it would not recognize the legality of situations, régimes, treaties or agreements impairing its rights in China or brought about by means contrary to the Kellogg Pact of 1928. After its Lytton Commission had reported, the League of Nations, in 1933, pledged its members not to recognize Manchukuo. Japan not only survived the rebuke but attempted to force China's government to withdraw from North China. When that pressure produced not compliance but a revival of Chinese unity, Japan invaded China proper in July, 1937.

A second cause for the growth of American navalism was the definitive failure of naval disarmament in 1935. The London Conference of 1930 foreshadowed that, for its "escalator clause" allowed the signatories to ignore treaty limitations on total cruiser and destroyer tonnage in order to match building by nonsignatories. Japan denounced even this innocuous treaty in 1934. At the London Conference of December, 1935, the United States refused to retreat from the 5:5:3 ratio on capital ships and the meeting broke up in futility. The German rearmament program, Japanese and fascist aggression in 1937, and the midsummer recession all contributed to the policy embodied in the Roosevelt message of January, 1938.

This called for new naval construction on an unprecedented scale. The Naval Act of May, 1938, increased tonnage in every category. The House sponsor of the bill, replying to rising opposition said: "It is the fundamental naval policy of the United States to maintain an adequate navy in sufficient strength to guard the continental United States by affording naval protection to the coastline in both oceans at the same time...."

FASCIST AGGRESSION

By 1938, the United States stood between two fires. Americans wished to remain free of the struggles for power which were desolating Europe and the Far East; yet those guiding American foreign policy knew that fascism, as an expansive political force, held a new threat to the security of the United States. President Roosevelt attempted to waken support for a policy of international action in October, 1937, when his Chicago speech urged that the peaceable democracies "quarantine the aggressors." That found little support—in the United States or in foreign capitals. In fact, Congress showed new enthusiasm for the Ludlow Resolution, which was defeated by only a small House majority in January. The naval expansion program was adopted in 1938; on the other hand, the proposal to fortify Guam was defeated. Thus, the hopes and fears of Americans.

If it was difficult to arouse warlike sentiment against Japan, which had been the target of "Yellow Peril" demagogues for thirty years, it was even harder to create a crusading spirit against European fascism. Mussolini had long since been absorbed and digested by public opinion; his sins against civil liberties were forgiven because he "made the trains run on time." Hitler was wilier, if his brutalities were more flagrant; he both muddied and fished in the troubled waters of European politics—now ranting against the iniquities of Versailles, now holding out the promise of a "holy war" against Russian communism. All this while a timetable was being inexorably followed; its purpose was nothing less than the reestablishment of German power in Central Europe and on the Continent. In 1935, Germany rearmed and obtained the Saar by plebiscite; in 1936, the Rhineland was remilitarized and the pressure on Austria began; in 1938, Austria was annexed—and Munich occurred.

From 1920 to 1930, France and England had refused to ease the status quo for republican Germany; between 1933 and 1937, they refused to act to preserve the status quo against the onslaught of fascist Germany. By 1938, both Western Powers were too demoralized to do more than bargain in an effort to gain breathing space for rearming themselves. Thus, British Prime Minister Neville Chamberlain journeyed to Munich and returned, at the end of September, 1938, proclaiming the establishment of "peace in our time" as a consequence of the dismemberment of Czechoslovakia.

That peace rapidly passed into the War of Nerves of October, 1938–September, 1939: Although the European powers had not joined battle, they were jockeying for position in the fight to come. The German-Italian agreement of 1936—labelled the Rome-Berlin Axis on which a forthcoming "New Order" of fascist world power was to revolve—was strengthened by a consultative pact with Japan. Aggression moved at a swifter pace. In March, 1939, Czechoslovakia, which had lost its German-inhabited Sudetenland district by the Munich agreement among England, France, Germany and Italy, was invaded and partitioned by Germany. Then the Lithuanians were forced to yield Memel; and the campaign of threat against Poland began.

France and England countered with pledges of aid to Poland, Rumania, and Greece, should those nations be attacked; but the facts of geography and the precedents of recent diplomacy made the fascist powers confident that these promises would mean no more than the guarantees given Czechoslovakia. Italy invaded and seized Albania on April 7. On August 21, the Nazis cut the ground from beneath the feet of the Western Powers. For, while these were making inconclusive attempts to bring Soviet Russia into their orbit, the Nazis concluded a 10-year nonaggression pact with the Soviet Union. This was an astounding triumph: fascist Germany had an ally (for the USSR was to supply her in the event of war); Poland could be swallowed without trouble; and if hostilities broke out in the West, the danger of a two-front war was averted. In the face of all this, Britain stood fast, and turned her pledge to Poland into a formal alliance.

On September 1, 1939, Germany invaded Poland without declaring war. England presented an ultimatum demanding that the invasion be terminated by 11 A. M., September 3. A few minutes after the hour, Neville

Chamberlain turned to a London microphone and announced the end of the peace he had brought from Munich.

THE NEW PREPAREDNESS

Unlike Woodrow Wilson, President Roosevelt did not ask Americans to remain neutral in thought and deed in 1939. Americans wanted an Allied victory, but they had no desire to participate in winning it. The neutrality program would keep them uninvolved; rearmament would render them safe. One slight gesture Congress did make: in November, in special session, it yielded to the President and amended the Neutrality Act to allow the cash sale of munitions.

As the *sitzkrieg* of the winter of 1939 to 1940 quickened into the Germans' spring *blitzkrieg* attack on Belgium, the Netherlands, France, Denmark, and Norway, Americans felt less secure between their oceans. France had fallen and Western Europe lay under the Nazi power by June, 1940; England was fighting for her life. If England failed—the British fleet, which had long been reckoned as part of American naval defense, might pass into Nazi control. It was plain that the United States had to act to protect itself. The Treasury moved swiftly, ordering the impounding of French, Dutch, Danish, Belgian, and Norwegian assets and credits in the United States to keep them out of Nazi hands. The Havana Conference—under the lead of the State Department—took measures to guard the American possessions of the defeated nations.

This was only a beginning. The armaments program was stepped up, reaching appropriations of $17,600,000,000 in 1940. The Revenue Act of 1940 increased income tax rates and lowered exemptions. The RFC began to accumulate stockpiles of strategic materials and metals, and lent money to finance the construction of new plants for producing war materials. In May, 1940, the President appointed a National Defense Advisory Committee of top industrialists to co-ordinate the rearmament program. Although this body had no mandatory authority, the prestige of its members was supposed to help bring order into a confusion that increased as the War Department, the Navy Department, foreign buyers, and civilian purchasers engaged in simultaneous bidding for scarce materials and labor skills.

In January, 1941, the rearmament program entered its second phase, requiring a new concentration of productive capacity on defense needs. Reorganization of national defense plants came on January 7, 1941, as the Office for Emergency Management absorbed the functions of the National Defense Advisory Committee. The chief operating agency of the OEM was the Office of Production Management, headed by William Knudsen. The

OPM had far more authority than its predecessor, a fact which might be expected to facilitate its action. For the OPM was to speed production, supervise the flow of material into military and essential civilian services, plan the use of the available labor supply, and co-ordinate defense purchases. In March, as defense proper merged into Lend-Lease, a National Defense Mediation Board was set up under the OEM to deal with labor disputes in essential industries. In April, an Office of Price Administration was formally established; the Supply, Priorities and Allocations Board was created in August, 1941.

The materials aspect of the preparedness program had been backed by new calls upon man power. In July, 1940, the National Guard was inducted into the regular Army. In September, Congress adopted the first law for peacetime conscription in the history of the United States. Neutrality passed into a new phase that September, as the United States exchanged 50 over-aged destroyers for 99-year leases on eight British naval bases ranging from Newfoundland to Trinidad and British Guiana.

THE THIRD-TERM CONTEST

Against this background of fear, uncertainty, and a popular will equally hostile to Hitler and to war, the quadrennial battle for the Presidency seemed at once unreal and portentous. The United States was the one great nation which could afford a full and free election in 1940. The campaign was marked by a breaking of precedent. Casting aside the third-term tradition, the Democrats renominated President Roosevelt and picked his Secretary of Agriculture, Henry A. Wallace, as his running mate.

Meanwhile, earlier, the Republicans had met at Philadelphia and, disregarding the official chieftains, had permitted the rank and file to name their candidate. This was Wendell Willkie of Indiana and New York, one-time Democrat and public-utility executive, who had won wide attention as a result of his effective criticisms of the New Deal. With him was nominated Senator McNary of Oregon.

Willkie was no standpatter; with much of the New Deal he sympathized. He was opposed, however, to its inefficiency and irresponsibility, to its hostility to business, and to its willingness to build up a towering bureaucracy. On foreign policy he saw eye to eye with the President: Britain had to be aided, the Axis meant to fight us.

Despite some defections from the Democratic ranks—the larger farmers of the Middle West returned to the Republican fold, John L. Lewis supported Willkie—the political alliance effected by the New Deal stood firm. Roosevelt was triumphantly re-elected, although by a reduced majority. His popular vote was 27,243,466 against Willkie's 22,304,755; his electoral vote 449 against Willkie's 82. The Republicans carried the New England and Midwestern states—and that was all. The Democrats also won both houses of Congress.

LEND-LEASE

President Roosevelt accepted re-election as an endorsement for his determination to bring all-out aid to the Allies; but that program did not take shape in law before a final struggle for the American mind had been waged —and won. Since the middle nineteen twenties, those who wished the United States to take a positive share in world affairs in co-operation with other nations had fallen back before those who declared that America would be best advised to mind her own business. It became something of a fashion to scoff at the "idealism" of Woodrow Wilson. In fact, the Kellogg peace program helped win President Coolidge's Secretary of State the sobriquet of "Nervous Nellie." On another level, debt default, fear that American diplomats would be overreached by their European counterparts, and sheer inability to regard Europe seriously made Americans anxious to retreat into a comfortable shell. The complete press coverage of the great American dailies and weeklies, the radio, the work of groups like the Foreign Policy Association—these made it possible for Americans to be informed of what was occurring beyond their shores, far better informed than they had been before World War I. But Americans were too prosperous in the twenties and too worried by depression in the thirties to make a real effort to keep in touch with the outside world.

In consequence, isolationism had many respected advocates. War would not come, said Senator Borah in the summer of 1939. When war did come, a large number of Americans held it the nation's first duty to keep out. Herbert Hoover declared that the Allies did not need American help; their economic resources and enforcement of the blockade against Germany would force the Nazis to yield. In *A Foreign Policy for America* (1940), Charles A. Beard, the dean of American historians, defended nonintervention on the ground that the converse policy injured American interests and brought no proportionate good to the world outside. Charles A. Lindbergh took another tack: American intervention in the war was being fostered by the British, the Jews, and the Roosevelt administration. The British were certain to be defeated, hence the United States could best preserve Western civilization not by aid to a Britain which would prove ungrateful in the end, but by co-operation with a victorious Germany.

Against that view stood those who, like the Committee to Defend America by Aiding the Allies, insisted that the globe had shrunk since Thomas Jefferson set off the New World sphere of democracy from the Old World sphere of absolute government. In the world of 1939 to 1941, democratic liberty was not safe in the United States unless it was safe everywhere.

The fall of France and the battle for Britain sent the point home. When President Roosevelt urged that Congress make the United States the "arsenal of democracy," the struggle entered its final stages. The isolationists suffered from the peculiar character of the support they had gathered. For, by 1941, the isolationist camp sheltered "elder statesmen" like former President Hoover, scholars like Beard, noisy nationalists like the McCormicks and the Hearsts, and the native fascists of organizations like the White Camellia and the Christian Front. Yet not even so vigorous an interventionist as Raymond Buell of the Foreign Policy Association, long known as an advocate of greater American concern with international trade and co-operation, suggested armed action. In the same *Isolated America* (1940) which warned the United States of the consequences of fascist victory over England, Buell observed that there was no conceivable danger of the United States being attacked while Europe and Asia were at war and he concluded: "Under no circumstances should the United States again send a huge expeditionary force to Europe."

Nevertheless, the President and his friends persevered; and in March, 1941, they won legislative agreement with their contention that assistance to Britain and her allies constituted America's best defense. For in that month Congress, after weeks of debate, passed H.R. 1776, the Lend-Lease bill. By its terms, the President was authorized to sell, exchange, "lease, lend or otherwise dispose of" any defense article—including weapons, transport, machinery, food, repair service, training, and information—to any nation whose defense he deemed "vital to the defense of the United States." In payment, the United States was to receive recompense in "kind or property, or any other direct or indirect benefit which the President deems satisfactory." Congress made an initial appropriation of $7 billion and an Office of Lend-Lease Administration was set up under Edward R. Stettinius, Jr. Within hours of the law's approval, planes, guns and food were on their way to Britain and Greece.

When Lend-Lease was formally terminated in September, 1946, the full measure of American aid was revealed. Prior to VJ-Day, total Lend-Lease came to $48,600,000,000; after VJ-Day, $2,100,000,000. Against this, reverse Lend-Lease contributed only $7,800,000,000. Of the more than $50,000,000,000 in military supplies, petroleum products, industrial materials and equipment, food, and services we furnished the foes of the Axis, 62 per cent ($31,400,000,000) went to the British Empire and 22.3 per cent ($11,300,000,000) to the Soviet Union. France and China obtained lesser amounts. Thus resistance to Axis pressures was strengthened; and thus the war was won.

The tempo of war production and preparedness quickened. The reorganization of the defense effort has already been sketched. As the winter of 1940 to 1941 passed, neutrality faded into a word and the law of 1937 became a dead letter. The United States froze Axis assets and closed Nazi consulates in June—diplomatic relations had actually been suspended for months. When Hitler invaded Russia on June 22, 1941—so confident of victory was he over a Europe in which only Britain held out effectively that he was ready to risk attack on his quasi-ally—the administration extended Lend-Lease aid to the Soviet Union. In July, American troops landed in Iceland. Conscription, which had been enacted for only a single year, was renewed by the narrowest of margins in the House. By fall, American planes and ships were patrolling the Western Atlantic, and, in November, after German submarines had sunk the *Greer, Kearney,* and *Reuben James,* Congress ignored the law of 1937 and authorized the arming of American merchantmen. "Combat zones" barred to American vessels were redefined to give American ships greater freedom in carrying war supplies to the British dominions.

Thus, the neutrality policy, which had been so hopefully devised to insulate the United States from war, lay in the discard. The victory of fascism on the Continent in 1941 and the pressure of Japanese aggression in the Far East were edging the United States toward war. By November, 1941, the nation was in a tense state of semibelligerency. Only an incident was needed to push the United States into armed participation in the conflict; curiously enough the provocation came not from Germany but from Japan.

· 37 ·

The Shooting War

THE ROAD TO PEARL HARBOR

SINCE the beginning of the century, dissension among the Western Powers had been the opportunity of Japan. That dissension eased her path in the Sino-Japanese War of 1895; it helped produce the Anglo-Japanese Alliance of 1903; and it influenced Western opinion during the Russo-Japanese War of 1905. World War I enabled Japan to take over Germany's Pacific colonies and to assume a new position in the Far East.

American opposition forced some Japanese yielding, however: Japan gave way on her Twenty-One Demands upon China and she finally withdrew from Siberia. During the prosperous years of the nineteen twenties, Japan accepted the secondary status implied in the 5:5:3 ratio of the Washington Naval Disarmament Conference of 1921, but the worldwide depression which ended the decade fostered an upsurge of militarism. The attitude of the Western Powers imposed few restraints upon Japanese military leaders. Neither England nor the United States gave *de jure* recognition to the results of Japanese aggression against China—the seizure of Manchuria in 1931 and the establishment of the puppet state of Manchukuo in 1932; the claim to hegemony in China based upon the Japanese conquests following the invasion of 1937—but neither did they, through the League of Nations or by action outside the League, give effective support to any penalizing action.

Continued strife among the European Powers speeded the tempo of Japanese aggression. In July, 1937, Secretary of State Cordell Hull restated the American position: the United States stood for peace and peaceful negotiation, international law, the sanctity of treaties, and equality of commercial opportunity in the Far East. Nevertheless, American citizens were urged to leave Shanghai and those who consented were evacuated between August and October, 1937. In September, Japan bombed Chinese civilians. In October, President Roosevelt suggested a quarantine of aggressors, and the League of Nations urged the signatories of the Nine-Power Treaty to consult, as that instrument provided. Japan did not attend the ensuing Brussels conference, however, and that broke up without action. In December, when Japanese bombers sank the *Panay,* American public opinion pressed for further withdrawal in the Far East rather than for punitive measures.

During the course of 1938, the brutality of Japan's war against China stirred public sentiment sufficiently for a private boycott to cut the sale of Japanese goods in the United States. The American State Department protested against economic discrimination in China. On November 18, Japan declared that the discriminations were not deliberate, and, in any event, Japan was building a "New Order" in East Asia. The United States replied tartly: this country did not recognize the "... need or warrant for any one power to take upon itself to prescribe what shall be the terms and conditions of a 'new order' in areas not under its sovereignty and to constitute itself the repository of authority and the agent of destiny in regard thereto." In December, too, the United States opened a credit of $25 million for China and extended the monetary agreement of July, 1937, thus allowing China to sell her silver to the Treasury for American dollars.

As the European situation grew more tense, Japan increased pressure against the Western Powers in China. On July 26, 1939, the United States countered incidents like the Japanese blockade of the British concession at Tientsin by announcing the termination of the commercial treaty of 1911. Two weeks earlier, Congress had refused to replace the mandatory arms embargo of the Neutrality Act with a "cash-and-carry" provision, on the ground that there was no danger of war.

The outbreak of war in September left the United States chief defender of Western rights in the Far East, a position in which it was not always effectively seconded by Britain. The Burma Road was shut to military supplies for China and British Ambassador Craigie recalled the lapsed Anglo-Japanese Alliance in a Tokyo speech as he deplored the efforts of "interested third parties" to keep the two island empires separated. The May-Sheppard Act of May, 1940, had given the President power to halt or restrict the export of defense materials. After the Japanese joined the Rome-Berlin Axis in September, the United States imposed an embargo on the export of scrap iron to Japan and made a new loan to China.

For, in spite of retreat and maneuver in face of the Allied disasters of April-June, 1940, the Western Powers were stiffening: the Japanese, who had been balked in China, might turn southward toward the oil, tin, and rubber of British Malaya and the Netherlands Indies. During the fall and winter of 1940 to 1941, secret discussions among American, British, and Dutch representatives considered the possibilities of joint action to defend Singapore and the threatened areas. That April, the Japanese and the Russians concluded a nonaggression pact and the locus of Japanese action moved southward. She had already occupied Hainan Island during the winter of 1939 to 1940 and used the Battle of Britain as an opportunity to take over the northern portion of French Indo-China.

In July, 1941, the German-dominated regime of Marshal Henri Pétain —which, with Vichy as capital, maintained a fascist government over a truncated and defeated France—permitted the Japanese to occupy the remainder of Indo-China. Shortly afterward, the United States froze Japanese assets. On July 26, General Douglas MacArthur, formerly United States Chief of Staff, was recalled to active service and sent to the Philippines, while an American military mission left for China. All that summer—while the British reopened the Burma Road to supplies moving into China and joint American, British, Dutch, and Dominion action embargoed oil shipments to Japan—American and Japanese diplomatic representatives continued secret conferences. In August, British Prime Minister Churchill announced that his country stood behind the United States position.

That position remained what it had been since 1932: The status quo in the Pacific could be altered by peaceful negotiation alone. The sovereignty and territorial integrity of all nations must be respected, moreover, and commercial and investment opportunities in the Pacific be open to all on equal terms. Should Japan's militarists accept the American principles, they must recede from their attempt to secure dominion over East Asia, with probable loss of control over the Japanese people. A new government, with General Tojo as premier, took office on October 18. About a month later, on November 19, special envoy Saburu Kurusu arrived in the United States with new proposals: an acknowledged Japanese protectorate over China; United States help in securing supplies of oil, rubber, tin, and other raw materials for Japan; and a joint guarantee of Philippine independence. On the 21st, the Japanese Diet heard warnings of impending war. The United States replied to the Japanese proposals on the 26th, when Secretary Hull invited Japan to leave the Axis. He suggested that she withdraw from China and Indo-China, surrender her extraterritorial rights, stabilize the yen with the dollar and conclude a new trade agreement with the United States.

On the 6th of December, President Roosevelt addressed a message to Emperor Hirohito; only imperial intervention could save the peace. On the morning of December 7, the Japanese Government delivered its reply: Japanese carrier planes bombed the American base at Pearl Harbor.

Congress recognized the existence of a state of war with Japan on December 8. Germany and Italy declared war on the United States, then, and the American Congress retorted in kind. On December 10, 1941, the twenty-years' truce was over. After almost a decade of struggle for neutrality, the United States had been forced into World War II.

THE WAR IN THE FAR EAST

The Far Eastern phase of the war opened with an Allied debacle. The attack on Pearl Harbor cost the United States 5 capital ships, the bulk of its locally based aircraft, and 4575 casualties. More ominous was the fact (as revealed by subsequent inquiry) that the military and naval command at the great base had failed to maintain even ordinary vigilance. Britain's defense of Malaysia showed a similar lack of unified command and military imagination. Within six months after the attack on Pearl Harbor, the Western Powers had lost their Far Eastern fortresses: the Philippines fell after a gallant struggle in which the Filipinos bore a full share; the end of Singapore provided a grim joke as its guns lowered uselessly out to sea while Japanese armies came marching in by land. The Netherlands Indies fell after Burma and Singapore, and Japanese armies, spreading to New Guinea, New Britain, and the Solomons, posed a threat to Australia itself. On the northern rim of the Pacific, Japanese occupation of the Aleutian Islands of Attu, Kiska, and Agatu put American soil in foreign possession for the first time since the War of 1812. In an incredibly short time, the Japanese militarists had achieved their goal: They had beaten all the military forces the Western Powers could bring against them. They had driven those powers from the southwest Pacific. From Formosa to the Solomons, from Wake Island to the eastern border of India, Japanese arms ruled East Asia and its seas. The bases most useful for Western counterattack had been broken. China was immobilized, barred from Allied aid by Japanese control of her coasts, blocked off by desert and jungle and mountain from aid overland.

If the United States and Britain had had only the one enemy to meet, the task would have been stupendous. But the Pacific phase of World War II was only part of the task. Germany was the heart and head of the Axis and the two centers of counteroffensive against Germany, Britain and the Soviet Union, were fighting for very survival in the winter and spring of 1941 to 1942. Britain had been stripped of matériel by the defeats of 1940; American productivity had not achieved full strength in 1942. Yet the reeling Allies hung on doggedly in the Pacific, trying to supply China by air from India, bolstering Chinese armies with the Fourteenth Air Force of General Chennault and with General Stilwell's efforts to train a modern ground force. To cope with the issue of concentration of effort (and the lack of that had been one of the causes of the Allies' Pacific debacle) the first combined command over land, sea and air forces was organized. General Douglas MacArthur became head of the Southwest Pacific Theater of war, commanding Australian and New Zealand as well as American troops. Admiral Chester W. Nimitz was named commander-in-chief of the Pacific Fleet Area.

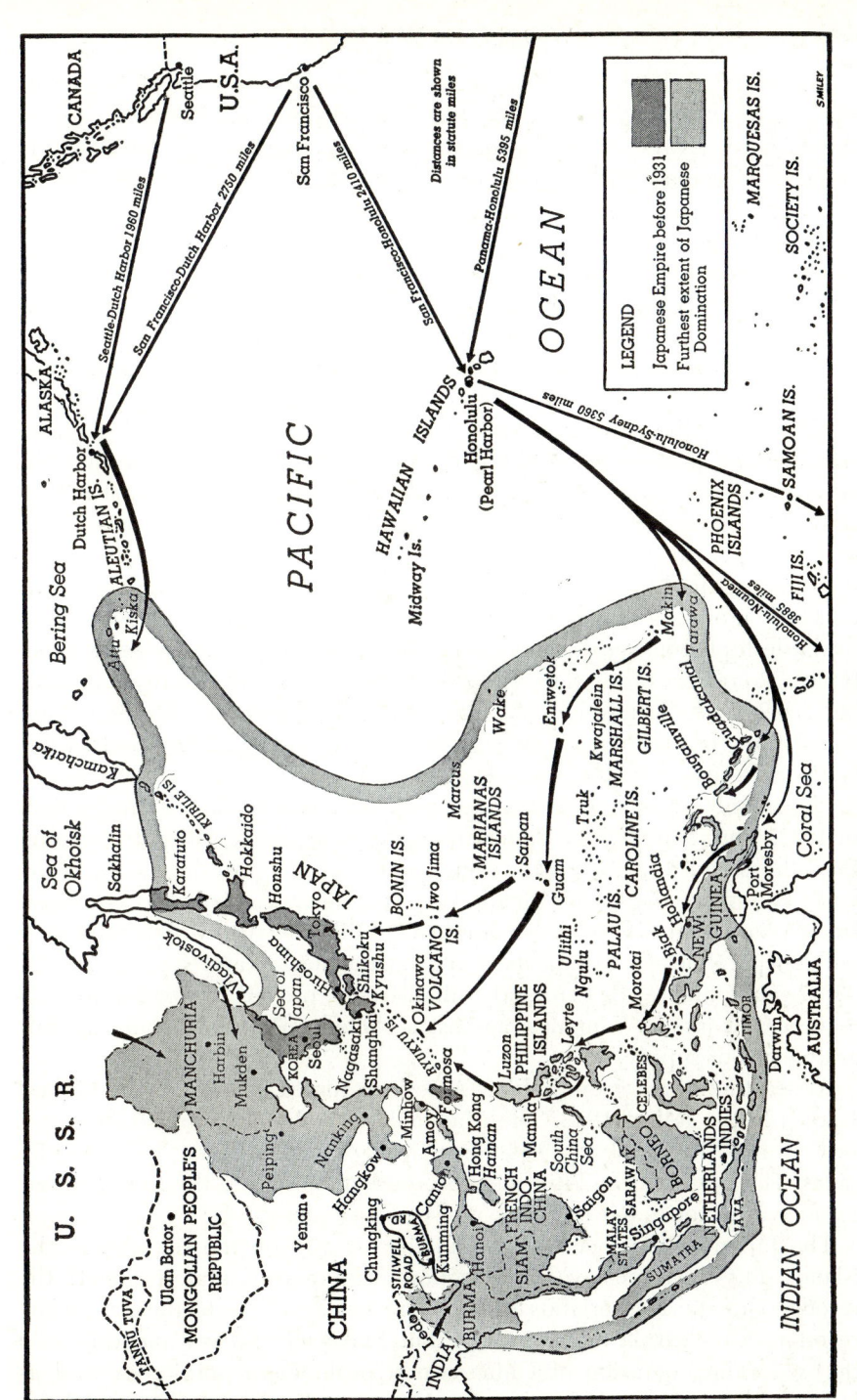

WORLD WAR II: PACIFIC PHASE

The Navy and its carrier-borne aircraft brought a note of hope into the cheerless summer of 1942. In May, the battle of the Coral Sea forced the Japanese Navy to give over the attempt to strike at Australia. In June, carrier planes of the Pacific Fleet caught a Japanese flotilla off Midway. And in August, the first fruit of unified Army-Navy action in the Pacific came with the landing on Guadalcanal and the Battle of the Bismarck Sea. The naval victory blocked Japanese reinforcements. Dogged courage held Guadalcanal and made other island campaigns possible. American and Australian troops fought up along the island ladder—the Solomons, New Britain, New Guinea, Bougainville—toward the lost riches of East Asia.

Meanwhile, the American naval building program was moving ahead rapidly. The magnitude of the program is shown by the fact that the Navy made more than $17 billion in commitments during the first half of 1942 alone. Between 1940 and 1943, the Navy had increased from 1076 to 4167 ships, exclusive of landing craft; warships had risen from 383 to 613; the time required for building an aircraft carrier was cut from three years to a little more than one year. By 1945, the American Navy had grown to 23 battleships, 20 aircraft carriers and 78 carriers of the escort and smaller types; 72 cruisers of all classes, and 738 destroyers and destroyer escorts, besides 240 submarines and the supply vessels, transports, hospital ships, and landing craft which brought its total strength to 91,209 vessels. (The Navy had 4500 craft of all types in 1940.)

Planes and ships and submarines gnawed on at Japanese supply lines in 1943. That summer the Aleutians were recaptured. Allied troops dug in on the islands they had taken and moved north toward the Asiatic mainland. To replace the Burma Road, Allied engineers carried the Ledo Road from Assam in India to Mongyu, and vital oil moved to China through a parallel pipeline. In Burma itself during the winter and spring of 1944, American, Chinese, British, and Indian troops proved it possible to fight a successful jungle campaign against a skilled enemy with only aircraft as a means of supply.

At sea the attack grew bolder. American forces landed on the Gilbert Islands in the fall of 1943. The Marshalls were bombed and then seized in February. In October, 1944, came the landing on Leyte in the Philippines. The Battle of the Philippine Sea added another to the roll of American naval victories in the Pacific phase of the war.

The Japanese had been beaten in the air and on the sea and in the islands, but their most valuable conquests remained almost intact: the resources of the Netherlands Indies were not available to the Allies; the reconquest of Burma did not mean that Malaysia's rubber and tin could be used. The liberation of China was a problem in politics as well as logistics. Direct assault against the Japanese home islands would be a costly process: Iwo Jima and the Okinawa campaign showed how dearly the Japanese would yield their land.

On August 6, 1945, an American bomber dropped the first atomic bomb on Hiroshima. On the 8th, Russia joined the war against Japan, striking at the Kwangtung army in Manchuria. American naval vessels under Admiral Halsey's command had already bombarded Japan proper. On August 9, the second atomic bomb hit Nagasaki. Japan asked for peace on August 10. On September 2, the instrument of surrender was signed, and the military phase of World War II had ended.

The Pacific phase of the war began with the shock of disillusionment; its sudden end tainted victory with a curious numbness. The Western World had solved the alchemists' problem; its scientists had transmuted matter not to gold but to unimaginable power, and the future with such power in the hands of the present rulers of men was a thing to make the heart stand still.

THE WAR IN EUROPE

Victory in Asia had been a triumph over an enemy protected by distance and the advantage of initial success. Victory in Europe presented the same problems, complicated by the dual role of the Allies as conquerors and liberators. The coalition among Britain, the Soviet Union, and the United States offered other problems still, but those remained in abeyance during the years of actual war.

At the end of 1941, when the United States entered the "shooting war," the Nazis held Western Europe from Norway to the Pyrenees: Pétain's government at Vichy was a Nazi satellite and there were those who counted Franco's neutral Spain a Nazi vassal. The defeat of Greece and of the British force in Crete in the spring of 1941 gave the Nazis effective control of the north shore of the Mediterranean. Only Malta held out as a center of British naval and air power. Along the thousand-odd miles of the Eastern Front, Russian resistance had given the military experts the lie—the best-informed quarters had counted 90 days as the effective limit of Russian ability to withstand the German attack of June, 1941—but resistance had not yet turned to counteroffensive. The American troops which landed in Northern Ireland in January, 1942, could scarcely be taken as an answer to Russia's pressure for a second front in the West. (It is important to observe that by a second front the Russians meant an offensive mounted from the Atlantic and not the Mediterranean. Churchill advocated an attack on the "soft underbelly" of the Continent—that is, through Italy and the Balkans, so that the Western Powers would be in Central Europe when peace came. Churchill was prepared to fight the war politically as well as militarily: His was a remarkable wisdom, as subsequent events were to reveal. Enough to say that Churchill was voted down, and the Russians had their way.)

Their demands grew more urgent as the Germans struck into Stalingrad and threatened the Caucasus oil fields and the Middle East beyond. And in Egypt, Rommel was driving on Cairo. During the winter of 1941 to 1942, the Germans seemed on the verge of success in a great movement to envelop the Near and Middle East. The fall of Stalingrad would free the northern arm of that envelopment. Its southern arm seemed about to grasp Egypt and the Suez Canal, for General Wavell's victory over the Italians in the spring of 1941 had been canceled when the British lost Crete and the Germans under Rommel replaced Italian commanders and troops in the African campaign.

In the spring and summer of 1942, American matériel and the military capacity of British General Montgomery retrieved the previous year's defeat in the Mediterranean area. El Alamein broke the German thrust against Egypt and the British pushed Rommel back into Tripoli. The Suez Canal was secured. Stalingrad did not fall but, instead, captured its besiegers.

The Allies could make their first counter move. On November 7, 1942, an American army under the command of General Dwight D. Eisenhower landed in French North Africa. The landing brought new problems, for France's North African possessions were commanded by men loyal to the Pétain regime, and the democratic powers must choose between sacrifice of men and matériel in fighting or the acceptance of the status quo. Military considerations prevailed, leaving liberals in the United States to squirm at the spectacle of American troops freeing French territory to be ruled by semifascist Admiral Darlan under the Nazi-modeled laws of the Pétain government. An assassin disposed of Darlan not long after, and so cut the Gordian knot. Immediately, following the invasion of North Africa, the Germans occupied the territory under Pétain's rule. Since the French fleet had been scuttled at Toulon, the last reason for deference to Vichy was gone. The Allies, therefore, declared that the French people would be left free to choose their own government after victory and, in the meantime, General Henri Giraud (who was not considered a "political" figure like General Charles de Gaulle) was recognized as head of the provisional government of French North Africa.

Between Algeria and Egypt lay the Afrika Korps and its Italian partner. The struggle for Tunisia gave American generals important lessons in the mastery of wicked terrain and in the actual conduct of large armies in mobile warfare. The lessons were costly, especially at Kasserine Pass, but the lessons were learned. Rommel's Mareth Line was outflanked by the victory of February 23–27, 1943. By midsummer, Tunisia and Tripolitania were in Allied hands together with 200,000 tons of Axis matériel and 349,-

000 prisoners. The British had driven the Italians from Eritrea, Somaliland, and Ethiopia. The Red Sea–Suez supply route was safe; the south shore of the Mediterranean secure.

American, English, and Canadian forces under Generals Patton and Montgomery moved northward in July. They made good the Sicilian landing on August 10. On the 17th, organized resistance ended. Eight days later, a palace revolution ousted Mussolini, but the German cohorts of *Der Fuehrer* rescued *Il Duce*. The Allies accepted Italian Marshal Badoglio as possessed of sufficient authority to warrant signing an armistice on September 3, 1943. Italy declared war on Germany October 13, and thereafter enjoyed the curious status of "cobelligerent." The Italian campaign was prolonged through bitter months from the Salerno landing of September 9 and the long struggle for the Anzio beachhead, until Rome fell on June 4, 1944. Nor did that end the fighting in Italy. Until May 2, 1945, when the German armies finally capitulated, American, English, and Italian Partisan forces fought on, with Canadians, New Zealanders, French, Senegalese, Poles, and even a Jewish Palestinian brigade beside them.

King Victor Emmanuel retired in favor of his eldest son Umberto on June 4, 1944. Even the scion of the House of Savoy failed to maintain himself, however. The Italian people held their first free general election since the triumph of fascism and they voted to make Italy a republic.

While Allied forces battled for Italy in 1943 to 1944, the air arm struck at German transport, industry, and strategic weapon emplacements. Night raids, daylight raids, Commando and Ranger attacks probed the German defenses. On the Eastern Front, the Russians edged forward after Stalingrad. At sea, the Battle of the Atlantic entered a new phase after the surrender of Italy removed the threat of the Italian fleet and freed naval forces to fight the U-boats.

Yet the Germans held Western Europe from Narvik to the Pyrenees; from the Vistula to the Aegean the nations lay enslaved. In April, 1942, an American mission to London, headed by American Chief of Staff General Marshall and Presidential representative Harry L. Hopkins, had planned a cross-Channel attack for the summer of 1943. Transport and assault craft were lacking, however, and that summer's threat to Egypt led to the North African campaign, which entailed postponing the invasion of Europe. After the Tunisian campaign, it seemed more than ever evident that Axis possession of the northern coast of the Mediterranean made an immediate Western Front impossible. Troops were massed for training in England, therefore, while heavy bombers delivered an intensive assault against German transport and air raids struck German supplies of oil at the Ploesti fields in Rumania.

In December, 1943, the military commanders finally decided upon the definitive opening of a Western Front which would strike the Germans directly and divert more forces from the East than the relatively few divisions drawn into Italy. General Eisenhower was appointed Supreme Commander of the new European Theater. Landing craft continued a critical problem, along with a possible Bulgarian attack on Turkey and fear of further deterioration in the position of the Chinese. During the spring of 1944, the Russian counteroffensive gathered momentum. In April, the Russians took the Tatar Pass approaches to the Balkans; in May, the Crimea was recaptured. And on June 6, the first contingents of the American invasion army landed in Normandy.

As the French had put faith in their Maginot Line along their eastern frontier, the Germans trusted their slave-built Atlantic Wall. But Yankee ingenuity outflanked that as violation of Belgian neutrality had eliminated the other. Prefabricated ports and an undersea oil pipeline made it possible to land and supply a large modern army on the mine-sown waste of "Omaha Beach" in Normandy. Beneath the shelter of a superior air force (military aircraft production rose from 19,433 in 1941 to 95,237 in 1944), the beachhead was made good and extended. On July 25, the offensive broke out of the beachhead to the Meuse. The Third Army, under General George S. Patton, Jr., with Canadian forces co-operating, wheeled to clamp a pincers about Falaise and 100,000 German troops were captured in that pocket. General Patch landed near Cannes on August 15; the Allies freed Paris on the 25th. Early in September, Allied forces turned back to reduce the Channel ports still in German hands, while other armies moved eastward. Between August 31 and September 19, 1945, St. Nazaire, Lorient, Le Havre, Dieppe, and Brest were redeemed, but Brest was too badly damaged to be of immediate use.

On October 21, the northern wing of General Omar N. Bradley's Twelfth Army Group took Aachen; the road into the Low Countries and Germany seemed open. In the United States, the business community and the economists calculated the effect of the end of the European war upon the economic structure and counted the help which the fight against Japan might give to ease the transition to peace. Von Rundstedt's Ardennes counterattack upset such calculations. In early December, 1944, American, Canadian, and British forces held a line running east of Aachen to Echternach and southward within striking distance of Saarbrücken. Four divisions of General Courtney H. Hodges' American First Army were stretched thin over the 75 miles between Mondschau and Trier. On December 16, with prolonged heavy fog to shield his movements from American air observation, von Rundstedt struck there with 24 divisions, breaking through on a 40-mile front. For tense hours, it seemed that von Rundstedt might extend his break-through to push armored forces behind the Allied lines and stab back to Antwerp, cutting the principal supply route for the Allied thrust against the Rhine.

U. S. Army Photographs

WORLD WAR II: ON THE WESTERN FRONT

The Americans rallied swiftly. Rear-line and "noncombat" troops, cooks, technicians, clerks, took up their guns and fought. The Seventh Armored Division hung on at St. Vith. At Bastogne, the remnants of 4 broken divisions refused to yield although they were completely surrounded. The fog, which had been von Rundstedt's ally, began to clear on December 23, thus freeing American aircraft to hit at his armor and supply. On the 26th, the Fourth Armored Division relieved Bastogne. The Third Army under General Patton had wheeled north from the Saar meanwhile, striking into Luxembourg on December 22. By the end of January, the front was restored. For a six-weeks' delay in the Allied offensive, the Germans had paid 220,000 casualties (110,000 prisoners) and 1400 tanks and assault guns; they had stripped themselves of strategic reserves and depleted the forces needed to ward Russian attack from the east.

By February, 1945, American and French forces were in Alsace, while the First Army finally took the Roer River dams which had helped the enemy block advance at the north. The First captured ruined Cologne on March 7 and took the Remagen Bridge. That windfall was exploited to the full and expanded into the bridgehead which served as springboard for the final offensive. On March 11, the Allies controlled the west bank of the Rhine from Nijmegen in Holland to Coblentz. Then the Saar was enveloped, destroying the German pocket there, and the Rhine offensive could be mounted.

Air preparations began on March 22. Airborne troops and then the Ninth Army under General William H. Simpson built a 25-mile bridgehead 6 miles deep in two days. The bridgeheads broadened swiftly; troops struck fast, smothering resistance all along the Western Front. By the first week in April, the Allies were over the Weser, on the way to join the Russians at Leipzig. On April 25, the Ninth and First Armies halted at the Elbe, establishing contact with the Russians at Torgau. The Third Army wheeled toward Czechoslovakia to meet the Russians in Austria and prevent German reorganization for a last-ditch guerrilla fight in a favorable mountain sector.

By May, the "shooting war" against Germany was over. The German forces in Northwestern Germany, Holland, and Denmark surrendered on the 5th. Those in Italy had yielded on the 2nd. In Austria, the Germans capitulated four days later. At Reims, on May 8, all that was left of Hitler's thousand-year Third Reich surrendered its land, sea, and air forces to the Allies.

Between October, 1940, and December 31, 1945, 15,136,424 persons were inducted into the American armed services. Total casualties, in all arms of the services were 1,068,370: 392,757 dead; 673,434 wounded; 2179 missing. Of that total, the European Theater of Operations (excluding Italy) accounted for 589,269 casualties.

The military phase of the war was a triumph over distance and the problems of supply as well as a victory over a skilled enemy gorged with conquest. During the course of the war, American commanders who scarcely deserved the name professional by European standards (so small was the United States regular Army and so far its national tradition from militarism) learned how to handle masses of men and matériel in actual battle. They mastered the technique of coalition warfare with unprecedented speed and efficiency. The Combined Chiefs of Staff, an organization set up at the Washington Conference of December, 1941, when President Roosevelt and Prime Minister Churchill and their Chiefs of Staff met and decided upon plans to pool British and American strength for victory, was able to deal with strategic problems as a whole. General George C. Marshall, Chief of Staff of the Army; Admiral Ernest J. King, Chief of Naval Operations; General Henry H. Arnold, head of the Air Forces; and Admiral William D. Leahy, the President's Chief of Staff, were the American members of the Combined Chiefs of Staff. These, with British representatives Sir John Dill and Sir Henry Maitland Wilson, contrived to avoid much of the friction and diffusion of effort that had characterized previous "grand alliances." Directly responsible to the Combined Chiefs of Staff (as these were responsible to the President and the Prime Minister) were the commanders of each of the war theaters that covered the globe. Within these areas, military leaders made considerable progress not only in unifying national efforts, but also in overcoming the interservice frictions which seem an inevitable corollary of effective team spirit within each. Out of the debacle of 1941 to 1942, the Western Allies brought the order of unified command. Only in China, where long-standing political issues complicated the torturing problems of logistics, did the organization of coalition war fail to operate effectively. And even there, the outstanding issue was met: China's independent government survived and China remained in the war.

Analyzing their own defeat, the members of the German General Staff put the principal blame on Hitler's "military imagination." That had demanded the blitzkrieg of 1940, the 1941 attack on Russia and its varied shiftings in objective, and the von Rundstedt counterattack in the Ardennes. The invasion of North Africa had caught the German generals off guard; the character of the Normandy invasion bewildered them. And in contrast to the relatively unified efforts of the Allies, the Germans had never worked with the Japanese and found themselves merely hampered by the Italians. The logic of fascism had no place for joint action among equals.

THE PEOPLES' WAR

The final precision and co-ordination of the Allied military onslaught was matched and perhaps heralded by the diplomatic aspect of the war. Joint action between Britain and the United States had been a fact since August, 1941, when President Roosevelt and Prime Minister Churchill met aboard their respective cruisers in Newfoundland's Placentia Bay to discuss the issues of war and the ends of war. At a moment when the enemy held Western Europe, had driven deep into Russia, and was harrying the Atlantic sea lanes, the spokesmen for the United States and Britain—in the so-called Atlantic Charter—announced the principles of the peace which would follow their victory. Neither party sought territorial or other gain from the conflict. Neither wished national boundaries altered without the "freely-expressed wishes of the people concerned." Both desired the restoration of sovereign rights and self-government to the vanquished nations. After victory, all nations should have access on equal terms to trade and raw materials and all should work toward collaboration in achieving the ends of improved labor standards, economic advancement, and social security. The Atlantic Charter further promised the disarmament of the aggressors and effort to secure an end to the use of force as an instrument of national policy. The United States and Britain sought a peace that would guarantee national security, freedom of the seas and assurance "that all the men in all the lands may live out their lives in freedom from fear and want."

By January, 1942, 24 nations had approved the Atlantic Charter and pledged themselves that none would conclude a separate peace. Others joined until, ultimately, 45 nations had accepted the Atlantic Charter as a statement of their principles in international intercourse.

The next great conference of the Peoples' War met at Casablanca on January 15, 1943, about two months after the landing in North Africa. This Anglo-American conference made unconditional surrender a condition of peace with the Axis and its Balkan satellites. In August, the President, the Prime Minister, and their Combined Chiefs of Staff gathered at Quebec to discuss over-all diplomatic and military strategy, particularly for the attack against Japan. That October, the foreign ministers of the three great powers met at Moscow to plan further common action against the enemy. Their November communiqué reaffirmed the unconditional surrender policy, and made the United Nations' war aims more specific. Italian fascism must end; Austria's independence must be restored; collaboration among the powers must continue after the war through a "general international organization based on the principle of the sovereign equality of all peace-loving states...."

Two conferences among heads of state followed, illustrating the unity of the war in its European and its Pacific phases. At Cairo on November 23-25, 1945, the President and the Prime Minister met with Chinese Generalissimo Chiang Kai-shek. The United States, Britain, and China declared that Japan was to lose the fruits of past aggression. Korean independence, the return of Formosa, the Pescadores, and Manchuria to China, and the loss of the mandated Pacific islands would cancel out Japan's territorial gains since 1895. The United States and Britain had renounced the extraterritorial rights and economic privileges granted them by treaty with China; in December, 1943, the United States repealed its laws excluding Chinese immigration and assigned China an annual quota of 105 immigrants.

At Tehran on November 28, the President and the Prime Minister joined with Marshal Stalin in reaffirming the policies outlined at Moscow. On December 1, the three powers declared that they recognized "fully the supreme responsibility resting upon us and all the United Nations to make a peace which will command the goodwill of the overwhelming mass of the peoples of the world and banish the scourge and terror of war for many generations."

It was almost two years later that the three powers assembled at Yalta in February, 1945. Victory over the Nazis was within grasp and the Axis satellites—Italy, Rumania, Bulgaria, Finland, and Hungary—had surrendered and specific problems of the postwar world must be faced. A secret agreement then pledged Russia to enter the war against Japan. The published agreements concerned the eastern boundary of Poland, which was set at the Curzon Line of 1919; and plans to occupy Germany, to disarm and disband her armies, and to bring war criminals to justice were prepared. The foreign ministers of the powers were to gather in regular conference to deal with later issues as they arose.

By July, 1945, when the last Big Three Conference met at Potsdam, Germany had surrendered. The general election which returned the British Labour Party to power replaced Winston Churchill with Clement Atlee as Prime Minister of Great Britain; the death of President Roosevelt had made Harry S. Truman President of the United States. Problems became more immediate as the war ended; victory made inter-Allied friction less of a luxury. Certain issues, notably the control of European waterways, had to remain unsettled. Others—such as the western boundary of Poland and Russia's absorption of Esthonia, Latvia, and Lithuania (independent as a result of World War I, but formerly in her possession)—were left in abeyance. Poland was to be provisional administrator for Silesia, part of East Prussia, Brandenburg, and Pomerania, while definitive boundary demarcation was left to the future. Peace treaties with Italy and the Balkan satellites were to be drafted first; the knottier Austrian and German treaties would be postponed. The treatment of occupied Germany was sketched in broad outline: the occupying powers were to deal with Germany as an economic unit although she was divided into four zones of administration—English, French, American, and Russian; reparations were to be paid, in kind rather than in money; war criminals were to be punished; German cartels, trusts and other monopolies were to be ended, and the German economy reorganized with stress on agriculture and peaceful industry.

THE UNITED NATIONS

The diplomatic conferences of World War II outlined the aims and some of the strategies of the Peoples' War. As important, perhaps, were their contributions to a Peoples' Peace. At Moscow, on October 30, 1943, while victory was still in the future, the foreign ministers of the United States, Great Britain, and Russia had emphasized the need to establish an international organization to assure the peace. The United States House of Representatives had already adopted the Fulbright Resolution, which approved American membership in an international peace organization. On November 5, the Senate followed the example the House had set on September 21. The form of the new society of nations was not yet decided; the fact of United States participation was all but certain.

Between August 21 and October 7, 1944, representatives of the United States, Great Britain, Russia, and China met in two sets of conferences on problems of peace and the organization of international security. The Dumbarton Oaks conversations were followed by full-scale sessions at San Francisco, where representatives of 51 nations, small and large, assembled from April 25 to June 26, 1945. These drew up the Charter of the United Nations, which provided for a new world organization with three co-ordinate branches—the Security Council, the General Assembly and the International Court of Justice.

The Charter declared the United Nations organization based on the principle of the "sovereign equality of all its members," but the Security Council is given "primary responsibility" for maintaining international peace and security. It has the right to pass upon applications for admission and to recommend that offending nations be suspended from membership. The Council has 11 members, 5 permanent—the United States, Britain, Russia, China, and France—and 6 chosen by the General Assembly for 2-year terms. In addition to general supervision over the maintenance of peace, the Council is to formulate plans for regulating armaments. Each member of the Council has one vote. Seven votes are required for affirmative action on procedural questions; on other matters, the 7 affirmative votes must include the concurring votes of the permanent members, but parties to a dispute are to refrain from voting. (This last, in effect, gave each permanent member the right of absolute veto over all nonprocedural questions.)

Upon the application of the parties to any dispute which may "endanger the maintenance of international peace and security," upon the suggestion of the General Assembly, or even upon the appeal of a nonmember state, the Council may recommend methods of adjustment, if ordinary measures fail. Upon its own initiative, the Security Council may investigate "any dispute or any situation" which might lead to international friction or further dispute. To give effect to its decisions, the Council may call upon its members to interrupt economic relations, partly or completely, to break communications by rail, sea, air, post, telegraph or radio, and even to sever diplomatic relations with the offender. If such measures fail, the Security Council may take action by land, sea, or air forces to "include demonstrations, blockade and other operations . . ." Forces for Security Council military action are to be provided by the member nations, in accordance with a separate agreement ratified by the participating states, and directed by a Military Staff Committee, consisting of the representatives of the Chiefs of Staff of the 5 permanent members.

The General Assembly includes all the members of the United Nations. It may discuss all issues within the scope of the Charter and may make recommendations on the principles of disarmament and on the problems of maintaining the peace. While the Security Council is dealing with any specific question, however, the Assembly may intervene only on the Council's request. The Assembly is also to initiate studies and make recommendations concerning the development and codification of international law, as well as the furthering of international co-operation for economic, social, cultural, educational, and public health progress, and the achievement of fundamental freedoms and human rights for all.

Security Council and General Assembly provide the U.N. with its legislature and its executive. Chapter XIV of the Charter gives it an International Court of Justice for its principal judiciary organ. The court is to consist of 15 members, no two of whom may be from the same state, who are to be elected by absolute majority in the General Assembly and in the Security Council. If any party to a cause refuses to abide by the Court's judgment, the other party may appeal to the Security Council to make recommendations or to take measures to give effect to the Court's judgment. In addition to dealing with cases brought before it by member states, the Court shall give advisory opinions on legal issues to the General Assembly, the Security Council, or any other organ of the U.N.

Among those organs, the Secretariat, the Trusteeship Council, and the Economic and Social Council are the most important. The Secretariat is charged with routine functions, with the registration and publication of treaties entered into after the Charter comes into force and even, through the Secretary General, with the responsibility to bring to the attention of the Security Council any matter that may threaten the peace.

The Trusteeship Council is to consist of the powers administering trust territories, the permanent members of the Security Council who are not acting as administrators, and a sufficient number of members elected for 3-year terms by the General Assembly to divide the Council equally among administering and nonadministering powers. The former are to submit annual reports concerning the political, economic, social, and educational advancement of the inhabitants of the trust areas. The Council is to have general supervision over the trusteeship agreements, including the reception and examination of petitions in consultation with administering authority. It may make periodic visits to the trust territories "at times agreed upon with the administering authority." Each member of the Trusteeship Council has a single vote and decision is by majority of the members present and voting. The trusteeship system is to be applied to territories under League of Nations mandate, territories detached from enemy states as a result of World War II, and territories voluntarily placed under the system, but the terms of trusteeship and the administering power are to be decided by special agreement. Areas designated as "strategic" in any trusteeship agreement shall be under the Security Council, so far as their relations with the U.N. are concerned.

As in the General Assembly, the World Court, and the Trusteeship Council, the right of veto does not exist in the Economic and Social Council. The Council is to consist of 18 members chosen by the General Assembly for 3 years and eligible for immediate re-election. It is to make or initiate studies and reports on international social, economic, cultural, and health problems. It may make recommendations to the General Assembly or its members, prepare draft conventions on issues within its field of competence, set up commissions, and hold conferences on special problems. In those technical fields where intergovernmental co-operation has been a fact, the Council will help co-ordinate effort and may increase that will to peace and international order without which the most ingeniously devised machinery is useless.

The League of Nations had been something of an afterthought in 1919; besides, national representatives had had small share in drafting its Covenant; and the people of the United States had no sense of participation in the plan. The San Francisco Conference met under the shadow of the Hiroshima explosion. A sense of urgency permeated reports of the discussion. The American delegation, at least, represented important sections of American opinion, for in addition to Secretary of State Stettinius and former Secretary Hull, President Truman appointed two Senators (Republican Arthur H. Vandenberg and Democrat Tom Connally), two Representatives (Republican Charles A. Eaton and Democrat Sol Bloom) and former Governor of Minnesota Harold Stassen and Dean Virginia C. Gildersleeve.

The U.N. Charter was signed on June 26, 1945. On July 28, after relatively mild debate, the Senate ratified the Charter by a vote of 89–2. On October 24, Russian ratification added the 29th to the nations necessary to make the U.N. a going concern. If the absence of the United States and Russia had weakened the League of Nations from its beginnings, the U.N. was not to have that problem. Whether its Charter would be an effective constitution for a peaceful world still remained to be seen.

· 38 ·

Domestic Problems of Wartime America

MOBILIZATION OF MEN AND RESOURCES

FOR the United States, World War II was a disagreeable necessity justified, beyond the demands of self-preservation, by hope that victory would make future war less likely. In uncommonly sober determination, Americans bore the dislocations of their daily living. The families of more than 15,000,000 men gave them up to the armed services with a minimum of protest; while the wives of large numbers patiently followed their husbands from army post to army post until the notice for embarkation arrived. Three and a half million people moved with war industry. Hundreds of communities in Arkansas, California, and the Gulf States learned the meaning of boom and migration: rents soared; everything from Sunday-school classrooms to chicken houses was turned into lodgings for war workers; and "trailer towns" became a new social problem as schools and other community facilities were unbearably overtaxed.

Whole patterns of American life shifted. Coastal cities dimmed out, lest glare from their lights silhouette our freighters against the sky, fair target for German U-boats. Pedestrians walked safely as gasoline rationing ended all but necessary driving. Suburbia planted spinach in its flower beds and servants disappeared into factories. "Rosie the Riveter" entered the gallery of contemporary folklore, and it was discovered that the hand which held the knitting needle was not entirely inept with the screw driver. Thrift became a patriotic duty instead of a habit that lowered the standard of living; Federal Reserve regulations checked installment buying and the use of charge accounts. No more did the "annual model" dated a year ahead fill the advertising pages of the newspapers each fall. For the first time in recent memory, the buyer stood humbly before the man with goods to sell and the "customer is always right" became a forgotten slogan. Millions of American families learned a new geography as they followed the course of battle all over the globe, and other millions found a new feeling of community with their fighting men while their blood dripped into Red Cross collection flasks for processing into plasma.

World War II was global and total: it covered the earth in three dimensions; it enveloped every aspect of the national life. The United States was faced with the need to shift production from the goods of peace to the necessities of war. It must raise and equip an army of many millions; transport those troops to the five continents and the islands of the seas; and keep them supplied thereafter. In addition, American farms and factories must maintain our own civilian population and help feed and arm our allies. The nation's economic strength must support diplomatic aims, moreover: good neighbors to the south required essential markets and imports; trade with the European neutrals must be managed so as to minimize antagonism, yet make certain that neither their resources nor our exports should serve the enemy. Morale at home must be preserved, and our own democratic liberties retained or we would lose the American Way we were fighting to keep.

This war required a mobilization more complete than any the American people had ever attempted. Peacetime conscription, through the Selective Service Act of 1940, lay the foundation for the mobilization of military man power. Local draft boards raised the men needed in the first instance, while state and federal directors were responsible for general administration. Relatively few of the men eligible had been drafted under the law between 1940 and 1941, but these were held in service for 6 months beyond the original one-year period, thus providing the nation with at least the nucleus of a mass army by December 7, 1941. After Pearl Harbor, all men between 18 and 65 were required to register. Only the 20–45 age group was considered eligible, however, and some physically fit members of this group were exempted from the draft by reason of marital status or work in essential industry. The requirements of global war soon demanded a more stringent policy. In June, 1942, Congress provided increased allowances to the dependents of men in the services, thus lessening the number of deferments. All volunteering was halted in December. The following year, the age limit was lowered to 18 and occupational deferments sharply restricted, although farm workers and "pre-Pearl Harbor fathers" retained a favored position. When the call for combat troops increased during 1942 and 1943, women were enlisted into military service. As mechanics, technicians, instructors, and clerks, they released men for fighting or necessary production. In the Army, Navy, Coast Guard, Marines, and Air Ferry Command, some 200,000 women served on the same terms as men, except that they used no weapons in combat and were volunteers, not draftees.

Military mobilization entailed a huge training program, for mechanized warfare exacts an uncommon degree of skill from its soldiers and, by European standards, ours was but an improvised army. All the tests of the psychologists were used to select men for training and all the devices of the educators were applied to give them the needed skills quickly. Since those men must also be physically and emotionally fit to deal out death and live through the mingled boredom and terror of war, tests of personality became as important as tests of verbal intelligence and manual dexterity. In addition to assigning enlisted men, the mass of conscripts (17,300,000 of the 31,000,000 registrants were examined or passed on for examination and 15,136,424 had been inducted by December, 1945) must be sifted for "officer material" because regular Army, National Guard, and Reserve Corps together could not begin to meet the need. By June 30, 1942, the first officer-training program had raised the army's officer roll to 190,662; by June, 1945, that stood at 772,511, a number larger than the total force of the Army of the United States in 1940. The Navy expanded its officer personnel from 13,149 in 1941 to 48,226 in 1945. How well the training program answered its purpose may be measured by the high command's success in solving the particularly difficult military problems of fighting a war thousands of miles from home and there defeating powerfully entrenched enemies.

Drafting men of military age and selecting those fit for actual service were only parts of the great task. Farms, factories, merchant ships, mines, lumber camps, railroads, electric plants—all these must be manned as well as the armed forces. Although women and men too old, too young or otherwise unfit for the service could function effectively on the home front, the over-all demand was so great and increased so swiftly that the process of staffing war industry may be termed a mobilization, and a mobilization of productive facilities as well as of man power. The defense program, which had been rather a side line of the economy in 1939 to 1940, took an increasingly important share of the national effort following the enactment of Lend-Lease. After Pearl Harbor, the war effort absorbed a growing share of the gross national product and demanded complete control of resources. Priorities and allocation orders for raw materials were a chief means of imposing such control. As firms manufacturing civilian goods were denied supplies, their effort could be shifted to war production. In many smaller establishments, the transition entailed serious deficits for the proprietors, unemployment for their workers, and a loss for war production as a whole. In 1940, an Office of Small Business Activities was established. The following year, a more comprehensive program undertook to make surveys, develop methods of subcontracting, and provide financing. Here, the Smaller War Plants Corporation, which was set up in 1942, proved particularly useful.

Subcontracting allowed more complete use of total industrial capacity, but in many fields capacity itself was not sufficient. In consequence of wartime needs for building planes and ships and manufacturing munitions, it was necessary to increase production of basic and raw materials.

Higher prices and subsidies raised the output of high-cost producers, particularly in copper, lead, and zinc. New plants were built to recover magnesium and bromine from the sea. Bolivian tin, once shipped to England for refining, was smelted in Texas. Aluminum and, in a lesser degree, steel capacity was increased. A new synthetic rubber industry had to be created.

Much of this expansion was government financed, through the RFC and its subsidiaries, particularly the Defense Plant Corporation. By the end of the war, this had built or equipped 2000 plants for the manufacture of such diverse items as aviation gasoline, hemp, machine tools, and medicines. In addition, it had constructed the Big and Little Inch pipelines to carry oil to the Eastern seaboard without overloading rail transport or exposing an unnecessary number of tankers to submarine attack. The new facilities were generally operated, on lease or contract, by existing private firms.

With the mobilization of tools and plants and basic materials, new problems emerged, this time in regard to man power. The census of 1940 counted the American labor force as 53,000,000, between 5,000,000 and 8,000,000 of whom were unemployed. Yet skilled labor was soon in short supply. Prolonged joblessness had weakened skills; depression meant failure to train workers in industry; and our schools were not equipped to make good that deficiency. Training programs under WPA and the National Youth Administration had tried to maintain skills in the unemployed and give skills to young people; during the early stage of rearmament, the United States Office of Education had formulated a plan of its own. However useful these efforts may have been, the need was actually met by mass production methods, reserving the skilled worker for those operations to which his skill was indispensable.

At the end of 1942, the man power problem had shifted to a new plane: shortage of numbers rather than shortage of skills. The War Manpower Commission was set up to help co-ordinate the allocation of men among the armed forces, the merchant marine, war manufactures, essential civilian production, and the farms, forests, railroads, and mines. The authority of the WMC had been limited at first, but by 1943 hiring was concentrated in the United States Employment Service. Now, workers were "frozen" in war production jobs and, in areas where the shortage was greatest, intensive pressure was applied to draw workers into essential industries without offering higher pay. A longer work week, the recall of over-age workers, the employment of women, and boys in the 14–17 age group, all helped provide necessary man power. The resultant fatigues and dilutions of skill may have operated to reduce per capita productivity, but the efficiency of war production, like the efficiency of armies, is measured by victory not economy.

MOBILIZING SCIENCE

Besides the mobilization of armed forces, industrial facilities, and workers, the United States had to mobilize brain power as well. The nation had important reservoirs of scientific strength. In Army and Navy bureaus, and agencies like the Bureau of Standards, the federal government maintained scientific services of its own. Foundations and the universities supported advanced study. Industrial laboratories concerned themselves with pure research as well as the solution of specific industrial problems. These organizations were not geared to joint action for war, however; here, as in other fields, the great need was for co-ordinated effort. In 1941, the Office of Scientific Research and Development was set up as a center for scientific mobilization. The OSRD made wide use of the contract system, thus permitting considerable freedom for scientific initiative, and its administrative liaison with the high command attempted to make military leaders familiar with the strategic possibilities of newly developed weapons.

The most striking contribution of scientific mobilization was the atomic bomb, for here military, academic, and industrial science combined to take atomic fission from the laboratory to world politics in less than five years. In 1940, Alexander Sachs, spurred by a group of scientists including exiles Enrico Fermi and Albert Einstein, called President Roosevelt's attention to the advance of German research into nuclear fission and to the progress of similar experiments at Columbia, Johns Hopkins, California, and the Carnegie Institution of Washington. Although neither the Navy nor scientific co-ordinators were especially enthusiastic in 1940, the problem was taken up and contracts awarded for further study. By 1942, after successive enlargements of program, the project had demonstrated that uranium fission did release enough energy to be significant for military purposes. Thereafter, the problem was to develop methods for securing necessary materials: uranium 235, pure graphite, and the new element, plutonium. By 1943, the Army Engineer Corps was able to take over from the scientists; pilot and production plants were built and operated by leading industrial firms under contracts which denied them patents or profit but gave them large experience in what might prove an important new field of technology. In July, 1945, the result of five-years' work exploded in a blinding flash at Los Alamos, New Mexico. Early that August, the army used the atomic bomb against the Japanese cities of Hiroshima and Nagasaki. And, even the guarded reports of the results of that attack made the world know that it soon must choose between the end of modern war or the end of modern civilization.

In addition to that notable demonstration of the effect of science on strategy, the OSRD gave the armed forces new weapons and new safeguards. It furthered the development of radar, submarine-detecting de-

ATOM BOMB PLANT IN OAK RIDGE, TENNESSEE

Acme News Pictures

vices, long range navigation aids, electrical directors of antiaircraft fire, and the proximity fuze. This last so increased the effectiveness of artillery that, until the Battle of the Bulge, it was restricted to overwater action, lest enemy education by a "dud" shell turn our own inventiveness against us. Besides these and other weapons like the portable rocket gun, the flamethrower, and improved explosives, the OSRD developed methods for deceiving enemy radar, smokes to screen operations, more efficient incendiary bombs, and new transportation equipment like the seagoing truck called the DUKW.

In the field of military medicine, OSRD made its great contribution in the fight against malaria and wound infection. Modern research had found a new and nontoxic bactericide in penicillin, but this was available only in minute quantities. The English and Canadian experts in penicillin research turned to OSRD for help in the problem of quantity production. Work began in 1943. By 1945, penicillin supplies had been so increased that the new drug was available to fight infection among civilians as well as soldiers.

During the dark months of 1941 to 1942, malaria seemed a more potent enemy than the Japanese. Quinine was the only known suppressant of the disease; but the Netherlands Indies, which was the chief source of quinine, was lost to the Allies, and the war must be fought in malaria country. By 1944, however, OSRD research had proved the chemical atabrine less toxic than feared and able to cure the more virulent type of malaria besides. In the struggle to lower the incidence of malaria, DDT, long known but only lately used, proved particularly useful against insect-borne diseases. Applied in quantity, DDT destroyed mosquitoes over large areas, lessening the threat of many tropical plagues. Dusted into clothing, it killed the lice and fleas which carry typhus and thus helped prevent epidemics which would have been particularly dangerous to armies in contact with populations driven into the filth and crowding of war-broken cities.

MOBILIZING MORALE

Plant capacity, man power, and brain power might be assembled, but mobilization could scarcely reach maximum efficiency without good morale. The chief government means for promoting such morale—aside from the visible effectiveness of the war effort and the visible justice of social policies—were the Office of Civilian Defense, the War Damage Insurance program, and the Office of War Information. Modern air war makes it necessary for the noncombatant population to protect itself against panic, fire, disease, and hunger. With local volunteers as personnel, federal and state directors of civilian defense attempted to give people the necessary information and to provide centers for help in the event of enemy action. While the efforts of volunteer air-raid precaution staffs may have been as bumbling as they were fortunately unrequired, they did impart a new sense of community to the growing isolation of American urban life.

The Office of War Information was set up in 1942 with the twin aim of protecting our own morale and undermining that of our enemies. It endeavored to support public confidence without imposing "thought control." Although the OWI was charged with ineptitude in its propaganda broadcasts overseas and with "babying" the public by withholding bad news, the agency did its work with a considerable degree of restraint and good sense. If it could not avoid the duplication of effort characteristic of wartime Washington, where every war board had its own public-relations staff competing for the attention of American readers, that very eagerness pays tribute to the effectiveness of American democracy in wartime.

Another proof of the strength of that spirit can be seen in the handling of the issue of internal enemies. World War I had set an unfortunate pattern of hysteria, but that was not followed in 1941. Even the wholesale and unnecessary removal of Japanese from the Pacific coast was accomplished with a minimum of noise and an effort at discrimination. German and Italian aliens were registered, restricted in their freedom of movement, and forbidden to own certain types of cameras, radio equipment, and firearms; but the 600,000 Italian resident aliens had their rights restored in 1942. Although 1228 Germans were interned and 20 members of the German-American Bund deprived of citizenship on the ground that their naturalization had been obtained by fraud, there was no epidemic of patrioteering. Few conscientious objectors were treated as criminals, moreover; nor did Americans fight for democracy by denying civil rights to individuals whose opinions they opposed.

ECONOMIC IMPACTS OF THE WAR

Organization. The achievements of America's mobilization can be seen as we turn from its processes to some of its effects. Over-all organization was one of the most pressing needs of the mobilization, for total war ignores the normalities of a market economy and imposes one objective: the creation of implements of war when they are needed, in the quantity they are needed, and where they are needed. Even during the rearmament period of March, 1939–November, 1941, it became evident that the defense program required a new orientation of the economy and a new degree of government control. Voluntary co-ordination through the National Defense Advisory Committee was the first measure adopted. As the defense effort gathered momentum, the Office of Production Management replaced the NDAC and, in January, 1942, was itself succeeded by the War Production Board, which was put in charge of procurement and production. Closely associated with the WPB were agencies like the Office of Defense Transportation, the Oil Administration, the Food Administration, the War Labor Board, the War Manpower Commission, and the Office of Economic Stabilization. Interagency feuding and confusion of authority continued, however. To cut through the tangle, President Roosevelt set up a new overall body in May, 1943. The Office of War Mobilization under James F. Byrnes, who retired from the Supreme Court to serve as co-ordinator of the American war effort, was to be top agency, having final authority below the President on the home front. The OWM functioned effectively (perhaps because the crucial task of converting to war production had been achieved) until it was abolished in November, 1945.

Production. Mechanized warfare requires mass production of war goods. For such production, the United States had a reasonably sufficient labor force, a sound industrial plant that could be converted to war uses, adequate amounts of power and raw materials, and a fairly efficient system of land transportation. True, machine tools were in short supply, American shipping was in no condition to meet the new demands upon it, and certain raw materials presented problems. But the chief obstacle was psychological. The defense program had proceeded upon the assumption that rearmament could be accomplished as an addition to high-level output of consumer goods. Although the Supply, Priorities, and Allocations Board had been willing to disrupt the nation's economic life for the defense program, the OPM as a whole was not ready to wrench the economy into new paths.

The shock of Pearl Harbor eased that problem. Consumer durables were eliminated from production schedules unless for Army use; the economy shifted from a peace goods-plus-armaments basis to an armament-plus-war program. Machine-tool output rose swiftly. The "impossible" goal of 50,000 military planes was approached in 1942, when production reached 47,653; in 1943 and 1944, the goal was almost doubled as military aircraft output totaled 85,405 and 95,237 planes. Shipping also was a prime need, for however the United States increased its war production, that could serve no military purpose on this side of the Atlantic. Lend-Lease to Britain and Russia, the North African campaign, assembling forces for the cross-Channel attack, maintaining our effectiveness in the Pacific combined to swell the demand for merchant ships. U-boat attacks grew perilously effective. To counter the U-boats, the Navy organized convoys and built small carriers that were amazingly effective; American scientists improved devices for submarine detection—and destruction; and American shipyards roared into activity on all coasts. In 1940, the Maritime Commission designed a standard freighter—the so-called Liberty ship—that could be turned out by mass production methods. By 1943, the United

States was building more than a million tons of shipping a month, a good deal of permanent value.

Well before this, in 1942, the crucial issue of production had shifted again, this time to basic materials. The lack of aluminum pushed government into prodding existing manufacturers to increase capacity, and even to financing new producers. Steel was more difficult, for the industry feared future overproduction as a result of plants built in wartime and such new plants would themselves require steel needed for essential production. Only relatively minor expansion occurred, therefore, and the great increase in wartime output was secured by more intensive and efficient use of existing capacity.

Rubber presented a third problem. The United States depended on imports for its supply. The Japanese victory of 1941 to 1942 cut off those imports. Without rubber, military and civilian motor transport would grind to a stop, to say nothing of the consequences to the electrical industry and the output of essential medical supplies. Stockpiles of rubber had been accumulated in 1940 and 1941, but war demand speeded depletion. Yet it was six months after Pearl Harbor before a synthetic rubber program was formulated and even longer before that was translated into production. Agricultural interests pushed for the use of alcohol as raw material; petroleum interests insisted that the Buna process was cheaper and more productive. Confusion and recriminations multiplied as the oil companies were charged with submitting to German cartel agreements and hindering prewar production of synthetic rubber in the United States in order to safeguard markets for American petroleum. A committee headed by Bernard M. Baruch surveyed the problem, then, and recommended a production goal of 1,037,000 tons of synthetic rubber in 1942. By the end of 1944, the United States was producing at the rate of 940,000 tons annually, short of the goal but greater than our total imports of crude rubber in any year before 1939. Although even this left civilian demand unsatisfied, the essential requirement was met: America's motorized army moved to victory on rubber tires.

The effectiveness of the war production effort may be seen by the movement of the Federal Reserve index. Taking 1939 as 100 (and recalling that though the 1939 level of industrial output was below that of 1929, 1939 was not a depression year) production rose as follows:

1940	125	*1942*	199	*1944*	235
1941	162	*1943*	239	*1945*	203

Thus, during World War II, output almost doubled. Over-all productivity did not increase as rapidly, for gains from the application of mass production techniques to shipbuilding and airplane manufacture were offset by lower productivity in other fields. Much of the increased output stemmed from greater use of industrial capacity and longer hours of work rather than from higher output per man-hour. Yet even that went up very considerably: with 1939 as 100, the index of man-hour output rose to 148 in 1940 and 150 in 1941.

Prices and Wages. It was natural—despite governmental controls—that prices should rise. From 1939 to the end of 1945, wholesale prices increased 37.2 per cent; during World War I they had gone up almost 100 per cent. The consumer price index, or cost of living, rose even less. With 1935 to 1939 as 100, these were the index figures for all consumer items:

1939	99.4	*1942*	116.5
1940	100.2	*1943*	123.6
1941	105.2	*1944*	125.5
		1945	128.4

Wage increases, on the other hand, were impressive. In manufacturing industries, average weekly earnings rose from $23.86 in 1939 to $44.41 in 1945 (or more than 90 per cent). In bituminous coal mining the rise was from $23.88 to $52.25 (or more than 100 per cent); in private building construction from $30.34 to $53.86 (or more than 75 per cent). The improved well-being of American workers during World War II (as contrasted with World War I) is thus revealed (only wages for workers in manufacturing industries are compared). From 1914 to 1919, *real* wages went up 7.6 per cent. From 1939 to 1945, *real* wages, on the other hand, went up 44.1 per cent. Here are the index figures for World War II:

	Average Weekly Earnings	*Consumer Prices*	*Real Wages*
1939	100.0	100.0	100.0
1941	124.0	105.8	117.2
1944	193.1	126.2	153.0
1945	186.1	129.1	144.1

Income. The war continued the process of redistribution of national income, a trend that had begun with the New Deal. The following was the percentage distribution of family-income groups by income classes:

Income Range	1935–36	1942	1945
Under $1,000	46.5	24.6	20.1
$1,000–$2,000	35.3	30.5	27.0
$2,000–$3,000	11.2	19.3	22.4
$3,000–$4,000	3.4	11.2	15.2
$4,000–$5,000	1.2	6.4	6.8
over $5,000	2.4	8.0	7.4

The changes were most impressive. By 1945, almost 50 per cent of America's families were obtaining incomes between $2,000 and $5,000; even corrected for the rise in the cost of living, this constituted an important shift. The well-being of America, in short, was based on its numerous middle class.

Considering total national income figures, the same pattern emerges in other forms. Below are figures for national income by distributive shares.

NATIONAL INCOME BY DISTRIBUTIVE SHARES, 1939–45

(billions of dollars)

	1939	1941	1944	1945
National income	72.5	103.8	182.3	182.8
Compensation of employees	47.8	64.3	121.2	122.9
Income of unincorporated enterprises				
Farm	4.5	6.9	12.4	13.5
Business and professional	6.8	13.9	22.0	23.7
Rental income of persons	3.5	4.3	6.7	7.0
Corporate profits				
Before tax	6.5	17.2	23.8	20.2
After tax	5.0	9.4	9.9	8.9
Dividends	3.8	4.5	4.7	4.8
Net interest	4.2	4.1	3.2	3.1

The following table is also of interest. It shows the disposition of personal incomes; taxes and savings reduced the inflationary pressure on goods in short supply.

DISPOSITION OF PERSONAL INCOME, 1939–45

(billions of dollars)

	1939	1941	1944	1945
Personal income	72.6	95.3	164.9	171.6
Less: Personal tax and nontax payments	2.4	3.3	18.9	20.9
Equals: Disposable personal income	70.2	92.0	146.0	150.7
Less: Personal consumption expenditures	67.5	82.3	110.4	121.7
Equals: Personal savings	2.7	9.8	35.6	29.0

Labor. The larger share of national income going to "employee compensation" indicates the improvement in the position of labor during the war. Employment increased in the high-wage rather than in the low-wage industries. Although the war produced demands for the lowering of labor standards, the 40-hour week was retained, thus adding overtime to pay envelopes. The labor movement made considerable progress, expanding its numbers and contract coverage until it counted a membership of over 13,000,000; nearly 64 per cent of the workers in manufacturing industries had the protection of collective bargaining contracts.

During the rearmament program, labor disputes in defense plants had prompted the organization of a National Defense Mediation Board in March, 1941. When the Board denied a union shop contract to the men who dug coal in the steel companies' "captive mines," the CIO labor representative withdrew and the board refused to hear complaints by CIO unions (a special arbitration panel later provided for union recognition in the mines concerned). In December, 1941, a labor-industry conference produced a no-strike pledge. Government supplemented that in January, 1942, by organizing a War Labor Board to replace the NDMB. Industrial relations moved fairly smoothly under WLB supervision, although workers were restive as regulations restricted wage rises to sums not in excess of 15 per cent, the calculated increase in living costs since 1939.

The comparatively peaceable course of labor relations was disturbed in 1943, as in 1941, by the refusal of soft coal miners to work without a satisfactory contract. Demands for wage increases lay at the root of the difficulty and the government was twice obliged to take over the bituminous coal mines in order to keep production moving. The mine strikes and the much-publicized loss of 13,500,000 man-days of working time (0.32 per cent of total time worked) helped provoke the enactment of the Smith-Connally Act over Presidential veto in June, 1943. The new wartime law imposed elaborate regulations for taking strike votes; provided for a "cooling-off" period between vote and action; authorized government seizure of struck plants needed for war work; and forbade strikes or stoppages during government operation.

Under the law, the soft coal mines were seized in the fall, and in December, 1943, when the failure of prolonged negotiations under the Railway Labor Act foreshadowed a rail strike, the railroads were taken over by the Army. The law's actual effect in suppressing strikes is uncertain: 5,000,000 fewer man-days were lost through strikes in 1944 than in 1943, but a slightly larger percentage of the labor force was involved in conflict.

Agriculture. When World War II began in 1939, the United States had a surplus of agricultural staples. The war did little to ease the pressure of that surplus on farm prices, for Britain, the chief importing belligerent, preferred to draw food and fiber supplies from Empire and Commonwealth countries and reserve dollar exchange for the purchase of American military goods. Lend-Lease and war demand brought rapid improvement after 1941. By 1943, the purchasing power of farmers had increased 49 per cent over the base period 1938–39; farm income totaled 9.3 per cent of the national income as against 7.8 per cent in 1929. With total farm population declining, farm labor cut by 900,000 persons, and no increase in acreage, farm production doubled during the war. This was made possible by good weather, good farming methods—improved seed, more machinery, and a doubled use of fertilizer—and the prospect of continued profits. The Price Stabilization Act of 1942 guaranteed the farmer parity prices for two years after the end of the war.

Economic Warfare. On July 30, 1941, well before Pearl Harbor, an Economic Defense Board had made the United States' foreign commerce an instrument in the attempt to deny the European Axis powers present supplies and future markets. After December, 1941, the American government joined Britain in more intensive economic warfare. Stock-piling of essential metals, fibers, and rubber was transformed into preclusive buying, and the Allies tried to outbid the Axis for Turkish chrome, Spanish wolfram and mercury, Portuguese wolfram, and Swedish bearings. By export licenses, control of the funds and property of the nationals of conquered countries, and general trading licenses, the Allies sought to make the neutrals themselves end or limit their trade with Germany. Through export controls, too, the United States and Britain brought pressure on the neutrals' need for Allied goods, notably petroleum. At first, responsibility for America's share in economic warfare was divided between the Commerce and State Departments. The Board of Economic Warfare succeeded, to be supplanted by an Office of Economic Warfare in 1943. This was replaced by the Foreign Economic Administration, which carried through until the end of active hostilities in September, 1945. Although military success was the most effective influence on neutral policy, the whole pattern of economic warfare during World War II indicated that while neutrals might make money in world conflicts, their rights held good only in an ever constricting circle.

Trade policy toward Latin America required a more positive approach. If hemisphere solidarity was to be more than a phrase, the United States, as the strongest economic unit, must bolster the position of its neighbors who had lost essential markets by the war. War demand made it possible to buy Latin-American hides, wool, and oil, although Congressional opposition prevented the purchase of foreign meat for use by our armed forces. Stabilization agreements eased the position of coffee producers. Since Latin America was a potential source of necessary raw materials, the RFC and its subsidiaries contracted for existing output and attempted to encourage new activities: The Rubber Development Corporation tried to help restore the production of natural rubber in South America. The Metals Reserve Company agreed to buy 18,000 tons of Bolivian tin annually for a period of 5 years; an over-all agreement with Brazil secured her entire exportable surplus of bauxite, mica, manganese, and industrial diamonds for the United States; a similar agreement made certain of Mexico's antimony. RFC money redeemed Latin-American airways from German and Italian control. In 1942, a loan to Mexico helped settle the long-standing controversy between the Mexican government and the foreign oil companies whose properties had been taken over in 1938. The Export-Import Bank, which was given wider powers and more funds in 1941, made loans to improve transport and establish new industries in Latin America. By 1943 to 1944, Warren L. Pierson, head of the agency, declared that the object of United States policy was to "decolonize" Hispanic America. In this area, at least, stress on economic power as a factor in foreign policy pointed the way to reversal of prewar trends toward a contracting foreign trade.

United States consideration for the wartime welfare of her southern neighbors produced not only a large degree of co-operation in the war effort, diplomatic and military (in February, 1942, a Joint Mexican–United States Defense Commission was set up; in May, a Joint Brazil–United States Defense Commission was established, and both nations sent armed forces to join the Allies in Italy) but also the pact of Chapultepec of March, 1945, and the Inter-American Treaty of Mutual Assistance, drawn up in August, 1947, and ratified by the United States Senate on December 8. The treaty classified itself as a regional agreement under Article 51 of the U.N. Charter, and declared that armed attack against one American state was to be considered an armed attack against all. In event of attack, there was to be consultation and assistance, but no state was required to use armed force without its consent. Significant was the provision for consultation in case of aggression other than armed attack, or in the event of "any other fact or situation" which might endanger the peace.

FISCAL ISSUES AND INFLATION

The shifts and the great increase in production made necessary by war brought proportionate dislocations in economic relationships. The sum of those dislocations implies inflation, never more serious a problem than in modern war when taxpayers, through their government, become the principal purchasers. Rising prices tend to expand production by creating incentive for higher output, drawing forth high-cost supplies, and easing the burden of debt; but such rapid price increases also encourage hoarding, excess forward buying, and concentration on speculative profit rather than increased production. The process accelerates, moreover, spreading through the entire economy. Insofar as rising prices affect consumers, they bear most heavily on fixed-income receivers and the lower income groups, which normally spend the largest share of their receipts on consumption. While such rises do tend to reduce the demand for commodities, and so have a beneficial effect, such illustration of "from him that hath not shall be taken away," is not conducive to good wartime morale.

To check unreasonable price increases, the administration formulated a program based upon the assumption that war decreases the effectiveness of the price system as a means of allocating resources and commodities. The problem required attack on two levels, direct controls and income absorption through new plans for raising revenue. Successive measures imposed new and higher taxes. Corporation tax rates and excess profits levies reached new heights during the war. Rates on personal income were also raised and exemptions lowered to reach the large portion of the national income received by those in the lower brackets. A tax of 5 per cent on gross incomes, withheld at the source, was introduced in 1942; in 1943, taxes were put on a current basis by forgiving 75 per cent of the federal tax on the previous year's income. This measure may have benefited the large taxpayer unduly, reckoning over the course of his lifetime, but it had the immediate advantage of increasing the Treasury's current receipts. As exemptions were cut and millions of new taxpayers brought onto the rolls, collection at the source was introduced and tax forms simplified.

In addition to higher corporation, excess profits, and personal income taxes, wartime revenue acts raised the rates on gifts and estates and devised new excise levies. Although the Revenue Acts of 1941, 1942, and 1943 brought rates to new high levels and reached every segment of the population with income taxes and excises, Congress did not accept the contention that taxes should pay an even greater share of war costs. In 1942, it rejected the President's request that the wartime revenue system be so adjusted as to leave no American a net income greater than $25,000. Even more significant was the persistent "freezing" of Social Security payments at 1 per cent. By 1944, the demand for higher taxes as an absorbent of purchasing power slackened: that year's tax bill repealed the gross income levy and reduced the normal tax on the first income bracket (but higher surtax rates made total payments for the group higher than before).

In 1944, taxes paid only 47 per cent of expenses. World War II, like its predecessors, was financed by borrowing. The debt limit, which had been raised from $49,000,000,000 to $69,000,000,000 in 1941, rose at the rate of $50,000,000,000 yearly. By March, 1945, the federal debt stood at $235,950,000,000. About two-thirds of this was held by banks and other institutional investors, but an active Treasury campaign put a fair portion of the six War Loans into war stamps and nonnegotiable small-denomination bonds bearing 2.9 per cent interest if held the full 10 years to maturity.

Despite the fiscal program, the rapid rise in income payments represented a threat to price stability. With the average of 1935 to 1939 as 100, the index of income payments stood at 105.4 in 1939. The movement of that index followed the pattern:

1940	113.5	1943	213.0
1941	138.0	1944	233.4
1942	174.6	1945	239.1

Hence, direct price controls were needed. At the production level, these were first exerted against demand through the system of allocations and priorities for scarce raw materials and basic commodities. In April, 1941, the President set up an Office of Price Administration and Civilian Supply (renamed the Office of Price Administration in August, when its functions were restricted to price regulation) to prevent spiraling prices, rising living costs, and inflation. Although the upward movement continued, general price regulation was not authorized until January, 1942, when Congress passed the Emergency Price Control law. In April, the OPA issued its General Maximum Price Regulation, fixing ceilings, including rents, at the March level. In October, the price control law was supplemented by a Stabilization Act, which extended control to wages. In April, 1943, an executive "Hold the Line" order authorized still tighter administration of the law.

Besides fixing prices at the wholesale and then the retail level, the OPA carried out a rationing program. Tires and gasoline were the first commodities to be rationed to consumers; sugar and coffee followed, then processed foods, meat, fats, cheese, and shoes. By March, 1943, millions of ration books had been issued and housewives learned to balance wartime budgets in terms of ration points as well as money. In June, 1943, to meet the implication of wages frozen at the October, 1942, level, Congress authorized payment of subsidies to processors of meat, dairy products, and some fruits, in order that farmers might have price incentives for larger production without such increases' spiraling up the long road to the consumer.

The stabilization program was not completely effective. Business complained of bureaucrats, forms in quintuplicate and an increasing squeeze on profits, although those had reached new heights. Agriculture considered its interests injured by renewal of the subsidy program in 1944. Labor was caught by rising income taxes, against which no credits would be allowed in postwar years, higher prices, and the limitation of wage rises to a presumed 15 per cent rise in living costs. The consumer complained of the deterioration of quality and the disappearance of goods. Nevertheless, the stabilization program did moderate wartime price dislocations as appears from previous consideration of general price trends.

THE ELECTION OF 1944

For the first time, in 1944, a President asked a fourth term in office. For the first time, too, American soldiers cast their ballots in the field. When

THAT'S OKAY, JOE—AT LEAST WE CAN MAKE BETS

the United States last held a Presidential election in wartime, in 1864, soldiers were furloughed *en masse* to return home and vote, particularly in doubtful states like Indiana. Geography did not permit that solution in 1944. As election approached, the soldier vote became an increasingly important issue. For, although men were now drafted at 18, military service would deprive many eligible voters of their rights. Extreme positions in the debate were represented by those who urged a federal ballot with uniform qualifications for all soldiers and those who wished state suffrage regulations—including the polltax and disfranchisement of Negroes—to have full sway. The discussion ran hot and long, ending in a compromise measure which became law without the President's signature. The bill provided that the states determine the eligibility of voters and the validity of their ballots. Congress recommended that the states ease registration requirements and liberalize provision for absentee voting. A federal War Ballot for United States offices was authorized if a given state agreed before July 15 and if a soldier who had applied for a state ballot by September 1 did not receive such ballot by the first of October. In addition, Congress made special provision for mailing campaign material to men in service. Twenty states accepted the federal ballot; many others simplified their registration procedure, shortened the ballot of state offices, and increased the time for receipt of absentee ballots. In consequence of the new legislation and of the services' efforts to make voting possible, over 4,000,000 soldiers applied for ballots and 2,700,000 voted, casting 5.6 per cent of the total popular vote for President.

At their 1944 convention, the Democrats renominated President Roosevelt for a fourth term and replaced Henry Wallace with Senator Harry S. Truman of Missouri as his running mate. The Republicans chose two Governors: Thomas E. Dewey of New York, who had a good record as an administrator, and John W. Bricker, who had established a reputation for economy as depression executive of Ohio. Republican campaigners stressed the danger of one-man rule, the need to preserve the private-enterprise economy against postwar continuance of the New Deal, and the desirability of introducing new blood in Washington. The Democrats charged that the influence of isolationists in the Republican party made it an unsafe guide in postwar foreign affairs, and called attention to Dewey's lack of experience in that delicate and important field. Roosevelt was re-elected with a popular vote of 25,602,505 to Dewey's 22,006,278, while the electoral count gave him 432 to Dewey's 99 votes. Several of the noisier isolationists failed of re-election to a Congress where the Democratic majority was increasingly dependent on southern votes. As important as this foreshadowing of a change in the political climate was the fact that the United States had held a free election in wartime, a political luxury no other nation felt able to enjoy.

AMERICA'S CONTRIBUTION TO THE WAR EFFORT

The war had required a mighty effort. Something more than 15,000,000 men and women were called into the country's armed services; in addition, its whole normal working force—and more—was enlisted in turning out the goods, manning the ships, providing the social services, and running the offices that a total war demands. We had done our share in assuring an Allied victory; indeed, America's part was far greater than we ourselves commonly understood or the rest of the world was prepared to recognize.

Through the fiscal year 1946, America's war expenditures had piled up to the extraordinary figure of $330,000,000,000; this exceeded the combined outlays of Great Britain and the Soviet Union. American military dead came to 392,757, the wounded to 673,434; these exceeded the casualties of the entire British Empire. Wartime aid to our Allies totaled $50,700,000,000 (against which $7,800,000,000 was to be charged for reverse Lend-Lease); without this assistance—in planes, tanks, ships, munitions, trucks, food, clothing—Russia or Britain could not have survived.

Bernard M. Baruch, writing in 1948, recalled America's contribution to a forgetting world. "We made 300,000 airplanes, more than 15,000,000 rifles and carbines, 319,000 pieces of field artillery, 86,000 tanks, 64,500 landing craft, 52,000,000 tons of merchant shipping." These flowed overseas to supply American forces or as gifts to our Allies. In the process, we mined our soil, depleted our iron and oil reserves, wore out our railroads and much of our industrial equipment. The price we paid for victory was a heavy one; it was small wonder that Europe's suspicion and hostility in the postwar frayed American tempers and led to a revival of isolationism.

What was impressive, nevertheless, was that American aid continued to go out to a war-torn world. From the middle of 1945 to the middle of 1948 American public gifts and loans—in UNRRA grants, the British loan, surplus and property credits, and the ERP—came to more than $21,000,000,000. Despite suspicions abroad and misgivings at home the American people had made its decision: it was not going to withdraw into its own shell as it did after World War I. It was the acceptance of its new role in world economic and political affairs—with the attendant dangers and responsibilities—that made the United States of the nineteen-forties really a new America.

· 39 ·

Postwar Reconstruction

PROBLEMS OF
INTERNATIONAL ECONOMIC RECONSTRUCTION

VICTORY in Europe and unexpectedly rapid victory over Japan faced a tired world with the issues of economic reconstruction. Physical damage in modern war is cataclysmic: air attack seeks out transport, power, and housing; mobile artillery extends the battle area; land mines make agriculture perilous. The German high command used destruction as an instrument of political policy, moreover; conquered Europe was forced to pay the cost of its conquest: its livestock slaughtered recklessly, seed and feed grain exhausted, soil fertility depleted by lack of fertilizer, industrial plant run down by overuse. To destruction and soil depletion must be added the consequences of slave exploitation. Even when mass extermination was not the German purpose, the population of Europe suffered in health and the distortion of normal reproduction patterns as hundreds of thousands of war prisoners were kept from their families and resistance forces took to the forests and hills.

Relief plans began as early as 1943, when UNRRA (United Nations Relief and Rehabilitation Administration) was organized. With contributions of 1 per cent of national income from each of its members, this organization sought to bring relief supplies and welfare services into liberated areas. By December 31, 1945, $3,611,900,000 had been paid or pledged, of which the United States contributed $1,350,000,000. UNRRA concluded European operations at the end of 1946; its activities in the Far East continued through the first quarter of 1947. But recovery lagged. Needs were undercalculated. Inadequate supplies of fertilizer, insufficient seed and draft animals, and unfavorable weather continued to cut Europe's grain output during 1946 and 1947. The fat shortage was not overcome. The world that had been smothered by agricultural abundance during the nineteen thirties was confronted by short crops.

The economic consequences of the German occupation of Western Europe were as serious as its effect on physical conditions, for a highly industrialized area was despoiled of the productivity with which to approach a market—even if markets were open to exchange food and raw materials for manufactures. To meet these economic dislocations, international gatherings evolved long-range plans for international economic co-operation. The Bretton Woods conferences of July, 1944 devised the International Bank for Reconstruction and Development and the International Monetary Fund. To promote world-wide currency stability without reversion to the gold standard, the members of the Fund (totaling $8,800,000,000 in gold and national currencies) agreed to establish initial parities for their currencies and to support them within 1 per cent of that level; changes were to be made only after consultation, on penalty of expulsion or exclusion from use of the Fund's resources. Although nations might control capital movements, restrictions on payments and exchange for current international account were to be considered temporary measures and the Fund could press for their removal and impose penalties for noncompliance. To ease transfer, countries were empowered to buy desired foreign exchange from the Fund with their own currencies in proportion to their respective contributions. In this way, the world (with Russia refusing to participate) tried to check those currency controls and manipulations that had contributed so much to the international economic difficulties of the nineteen thirties.

But the world sorely needed capital for development programs as well; and for this purpose Bretton Woods also established the International Bank for Reconstruction and Development. The Bank, with more than $8,300,000,000 in capital, was to guarantee securities for approved projects and even to make loans directly, after investigation and upon guarantee by the government of the country concerned. The Bank, operating on a business basis, was to raise funds in the securities markets, to charge 1–1½ per cent for its services, and to refuse backing for loans for unproductive purposes or in amounts beyond a country's power to service. Both in the Fund and the Bank, voting power was weighted according to contribution, increasing United States influence. The Bank, in 1947, found a ready American market for its first bond issue, and by midsummer 1948, had made four loans to France, the Netherlands, Denmark, and Luxembourg totaling almost $500,000,000.

The United Nations International Trade Organization was another instrumentality of potential significance; for, it was proposed through this body to break down trade barriers among countries, eliminate discriminatory practices, and encourage the international flow of capital for productive investment. After a preliminary conference at London in 1946, the chief trading nations (again with Russia refusing to attend) met at Geneva from April to August, 1947, and drafted a charter which incorporated the principles of commerce for which the United States delegation contended. Trade on the most-favored-nation basis, equal access to markets, elimination of import quotas and cartel practices, and protection for foreign investors were basic notions agreed upon by the delegates of 23 countries.

Although the draft charter was modified through 44 reservations by the major signatories and underwent serious re-examination by a full conference of 56 nations meeting at Havana in the winter of 1947 to 1948, the Geneva discussions had important results. Eighty bilateral trade agreements, incorporating tariff reductions up to 50 per cent, were concluded. Five great trading nations—the United States, France, Britain, China, and Benelux (the customs union of Belgium, the Netherlands, and Luxembourg)—agreed to the most-favored-nation principle. And Britain, Canada, and South Africa pledged themselves to free each other of obligations under the Ottawa preference agreements of 1931. This last was an important concession to the concept of freer world trade, for imperial preference had made it impossible for Empire countries to grant tariff concessions to countries outside the Empire unless those were paralleled by a percentage differential in favor of Empire exports. At Havana, it may be noted, concessions had to be made to economically underdeveloped nations, who sought time in which to work out programs of industrialization. This was a proper demand: and such countries were to have a free hand to use devices of control—tariffs, quotas—but only when these met certain limited and fixed conditions. The ITO was to supervise such situations. Thus real beginnings. They augured well for a revival of a world trading community, despite Russia's absence from the gatherings and agreements.

Other international bodies designed to further reconstruction and to break down national hostilities—in all of which the United States participated—were the following. The Food and Agriculture Organization. This was set up in November, 1945, to encourage advanced agricultural production methods and to assure a better distribution of foodstuffs. The Civil Aviation Organization. Formed in 1944, this body was created to deal with world-wide problems of commercial aviation. The World Health Organization. In 1946, this agency was established to advance public-health facilities all over the world and to help eliminate those infectious diseases which plagued notably the peoples of underdeveloped countries.

INTERNATIONAL POLITICAL PROBLEMS

After World War I, the United States had turned its back on the attempt to solve international problems in the political sphere. It did not follow that course after World War II. The Senate made the United States a member of the United Nations in 1945. Congress accepted the Bretton Woods agreements and appropriated the money needed to bring them into force. It went further in July, 1946, lending $3,750,000,000 to the British government on terms that may be considered generous in comparison with those of the postwar loans of 1919. In return, Britain agreed to permit full convertibility of the pound into dollars in the so-called sterling area—countries in the British economic sphere of influence who were Britain's creditors. The steep rise of prices in the United States, after November, 1946, and the lag in European recovery made this relative freedom of exchange a means of depleting Britain's dollar credits. Convertibility was suspended by informal agreement with the United States Treasury in the summer of 1947; and the British began to husband their resources in the United States more carefully. But by March, 1948, the British loan had been used up: the fund had been exhausted in one and a half years instead of the expected three to five. The world-wide shortage of dollars was continuing. It had become increasingly apparent that Britain—and the rest of Europe—needed more assistance. It was at this point that the concept of international co-operation began to be put under its most severe testing.

Disagreement between the United States and Britain on the one hand and Russia on the other had made its appearance early over relatively unimportant matters—the first being the drawing up of the peace treaties with Italy and the Axis satellites. The rift widened as opposing viewpoints began to manifest themselves. That rift, in fact, tended to obscure the significance of the trial of the major war criminals, a policy decided on in August, 1945. From November 30, 1945 to August 31, 1946, an International War Crimes Tribunal, with judges representing the United States, Great Britain, Russia, and France, presided over a formal trial of the 21 top military and civil leaders of Nazi Germany. Twenty-four persons (Hitler and Propaganda Minister Goebbels escaped by their presumed death during the struggle for Berlin) were indicted, but suicide, flight, and the court's decision that the head of the Krupp munitions empire was mentally and physically unfit to be held responsible for his crimes reduced the number. The defendants were charged with conspiring to wage aggressive war and with committing crimes against humanity. The opinion of the court was handed down on September 30, 1946, and sentence passed on October 1. Three defendants were acquitted, 6 given prison terms at hard labor, 12 sentenced to death by hanging. The trial established what might be a significant precedent in international law, for it declared aggressive war a crime and held the rulers of a state liable in their lives for the commission of that crime. Formal public trial for such offense might have made fitting resolution to the bleak drama of World War II. Yet the execution of 12 individuals (including the hanging of the body of Hermann Goering who contrived to commit suicide) seemed grotesquely inadequate either as punishment or as psychological purgation. The trials themselves were blurred in their effect by the rising clamor of dissension among the four great Allies.

Thus, at Potsdam in July-August, 1945, the question of control of

Europe's inland waterways had had to remain in abeyance, for the Russians rejected the American plan to have arteries like the Danube, the Dardanelles, the Rhine, and the Kiel Canal regulated by an international body, including members outside the bordering states. Then, at the meeting of foreign ministers that fall, the United States refused to agree to the awarding of $300 million in reparations from Italy to Greece, Albania, Yugoslavia, and Russia. On November 27, President Truman's Navy Day speech indicated that firmness as well as forbearance would be the keynote in American-Russian relations. From then on the United States was committed to stopping the further advance of communism.

The Moscow Conference of December, 1946, finally came up with a formula: it decided that the great powers would draft the treaties with the Axis satellites; and that these would be submitted to a conference including all the smaller states which had fought the Axis, not merely those which had participated in Balkan military operations. After prolonged controversy, the Italian and satellite treaties took acceptable form, with the United States winning most of its points: reparations demands on Italy were reduced and made payable over an 8-year period; and Russia agreed that the $100 million she was to receive in goods were to be delivered in a manner that "would not interfere with Italian reconstruction." (These treaties the Senate confirmed.) The Free Territory of Trieste—the city's population was largely Italian but its hinterland was Slav—was also created. Its governor, possessing most of the administrative and legislative power, was to be responsible to the U.N. rather than to the territory's legislature, which would be dominated by the local Yugoslav population. By the first quarter of 1948, however (after the U.N. Security Council had been unable to select a governor for Trieste), France, Britain, and the United States declared their willingness to abandon the scheme and return Trieste to Italian rule. Except for small Russian contingents in Hungary and Rumania to guard the supply line to Austria, troops were to be withdrawn ninety days after ratification of the treaties with the Axis satellites, which occurred in September, 1947; the treaties further provided that within six months an international conference was to meet to discuss problems of Danubian navigation. This last met in the summer of 1948 and ended with complete routing of the Western Powers. The Danube in other words, was to be controlled by Russia and her satellites and the effort to keep the river a great international waterway was defeated. The future of the Italian colonies was left in abeyance, but Britain controlled their administration.

As the treaties with the Axis satellites took shape, the reconstruction of Germany became the object of friction. At Potsdam, it had been agreed that Germany would be administered as an economic unit and that Russia would receive industrial plants from the British and American zones as reparations. The United States held that unification must precede reparations deliveries; when Russia refused to assent, deliveries were halted. In July, 1946, the United States offered to join its occupation zone with that of any other power and Secretary of State Byrnes observed that, "Justice, charity and mercy will make those we fear as enemies become our friends." In short, it had become apparent that Germany could not function at a lower level of production as an agricultural nation, particularly in the light of the fact that its chief farming region was in the Russian zone.

In the fall of 1946, Secretary Byrnes proposed a treaty guaranteeing the demilitarization of Germany. Germany should also have a decentralized federal government; and, unless economic unification were achieved, giving the industrialized western areas freer access to the agrarian east, the United States would support a program of greater German exports. That December, Britain and the United States combined their zones to speed up this plan; and during the following summer, the United States pushed for greater steel and coal production in the Ruhr. General George C. Marshall, who succeeded Mr. Byrnes as Secretary of State, made it clear that the United States did not intend to allow reparations payments to increase American costs of occupying Germany. Largely upon that specific issue, and because the last shred of amity had disappeared, the Foreign Ministers Council of December, 1947, adjourned *sine die* in an exchange of recriminations among Messrs. Molotov, Bevin, and Marshall.

The parting of the ways with Russia did not prevent the Western powers from going ahead with their plans. In February, 1948, the representatives of the United States, Britain, France, Belgium, the Netherlands, and Luxembourg set up a political and economic union of the three western zones of Germany. Trizonia now replaced Bizonia; it comprised two-thirds of Germany's population and industry. But it was cut off from the eastern zone and the Danubian basin, its traditional breadbasket. Germany, in short, had to be fed until such time when its industrial potential was fully restored. But it was not to be a Germany unwatched. The new state was to be under Western supervision. An international authority was to be created to control the Ruhr industries. Military occupation was to last until the peace of Europe was assured. The currency was to be stabilized and the budget balanced. Such a Germany would participate in the European Recovery Program.

Nor was this the only independent measure taken to assure the revival of Western Europe. In March, 1948, Britain, France, Belgium, the Netherlands and Luxembourg signed a treaty of mutual defense and established a joint general staff. Thus the European Western Union was started: the first step, one hoped, in the realization of that age-old dream of a federal Europe. The United States at once offered assistance; and the Senate passed a resolution giving the Union's plans to fight aggression its blessings and offered assistance (the so-called Vandenberg Resolution).

THE MARSHALL PLAN

German economic restoration was part of the larger problem of European revival. The war had taken a deadly toll of all kinds of industrial installations; and the harsh winter of 1946 to 1947 and ensuing crop failure had almost brought the economic processes to a standstill. Piecemeal aid and food supplies from America—itself confronted by shortages—could only be stopgaps; Europe had to become productive again. This thought was voiced by Secretary Marshall at Harvard on June 5, 1947: European recovery, thenceforth, was to be the goal of American foreign policy. But said he, "the initiative must come from Europe." Given an adequate program of economic rehabilitation—plus guarantees of proper public fiscal management and co-operation—and the United States would render large-scale financial assistance.

Secretary Marshall proposed that all Europe was to be included—West and East alike, Britain and France as well as Germany, Russia and her satellite states. At first, Russia was silent; Czechoslovakia and Poland—under her influence—even accepted an invitation which went out among European countries for a meeting to prepare those estimates Secretary Marshall had called for. Then the axe fell; Russia would have no part of the so-called Marshall Plan; it was, said Molotov, an "imperialist plot" to "enslave Europe." East was to be separated from West, by Russian action.

At Paris, in July, representatives from 16 European nations met, with 8 declining to come largely because of Russian pressure. These conferences produced a "Report of the Committee for European Economic Recovery." It contained: 1. a careful analysis of Europe's needs in the way of additions to and improvements of capital plant; 2. a statement of what the participating European nations were prepared to do for themselves along the lines of economic integration, increased production, and financial reform; 3. and estimates of the amount of American help that would be needed. This last was put at between $16,400,000,000 and $22,400,000,000; such assistance was to be extended over 5 years. By then, said the report, Europe would be on its own feet.

Russian denunciation became sharper as public opinion in France and England—and in the United States—swung behind the Marshall Plan. The United States refused to be swayed from its purpose; in fact, Secretary Marshall openly accepted the Russian challenge. For, in reporting to the American people on December 19, 1947, following the failure of the meeting of the Foreign Ministers Council, he could say: "It does not appear possible that paper agreement can assure a lasting peace.... The Soviet Union has recognized the situation in its frank declaration of hostility and opposition to the European Recovery Program." And on the same day,

President Truman sent to Congress the administration's proposals for the implementation of the Marshall Plan. The European Recovery Program, as it was to be called, would cost $17,000,000,000 over the period from April 1, 1948 to June 30, 1952. The Republican Congress delayed action as the country debated the momentous consequences of such a commitment. In any case, a preliminary step was taken: the voting of $522,000,000 as "interim emergency aid" to France, Italy, and Austria to help them through the winter of 1947 to 1948.

Time was running out, however: for Communist pressures on France and Italy threatened the balance in Europe which the Western powers were seeking to create. And when Czechoslovakia fell before a Communist coup in the spring of 1948, Congress was made to understand that partisan politics now really had to stop at the water's edge. It was at this point that Senator Arthur H. Vandenberg of Michigan, erstwhile isolationist but now chairman of the Foreign Relations Committee, stepped into the breach. He stood shoulder-to-shoulder with Secretary Marshall; and his support heartened other Republican colleagues with an international viewpoint in both Houses. Thus, a bipartisan foreign policy which had emerged as early as 1945, guided our relations with other countries, notably during 1947 and 1948.

In April, Congress passed an act creating the European Recovery Program. The United States committed itself to a 4-year plan of economic aid to the 16 European countries, that is to say, through June, 1952. For the first 12 months $5,300,000,000 was to be allotted. An independent Economic Co-operation Administration was to be set up. And the countries receiving aid were to pledge themselves, by treaty, to co-operate in the removal of trade barriers and the stabilization of currencies. For the same 12 months, military and financial assistance was also voted to China, Greece, and Turkey.

In June, Republican isolationists threatened the ERP when they sought to pare sharply the funds which the original act had voted. Again Senator Vandenberg intervened; and the appropriation bill, as passed, cut only $300,000,000 from the fund. President Truman made an excellent appointment in naming Paul G. Hoffman, one of the country's outstanding industrialists, head of the Economic Co-operation Administration. Western Europe took heart; it was also encouraging to observe that Marshall was right and Molotov wrong, for recovery was moving ahead rapidly in Britain, France, the Ruhr, and elsewhere. And as production rose, the stock of communism in the West declined. The support of ERP—and the adoption of a new defense program by the United States—had, for the time being at any rate, stopped the Russians in their efforts to control the whole of Europe.

THE U.N.

The cleavage between West and East was manifesting itself just as clearly within the U.N. Early in 1946, Iran protested the continued presence of Russian troops in her territory, although all foreign contingents were to have been withdrawn upon the end of military operations in Europe. Charges of bad faith, investigation, debate, and more charges were finally followed by the departure of Russian troops early in 1947. The Greek problem was more tangled. Social tensions turned the Greek constitutional monarchy into a semifascist state during the nineteen thirties. A plebiscite restored the Greek monarchy in 1945, but it did not restore order; nor were British resources equal to the costs of supporting the government against armed rebels in the hills and rebuilding the devastated land. The United States agreed to assume Britain's Greek commitments and to give Greece assistance. Meanwhile, the country continued turbulent: rebel forces—the Greek government claimed—were being aided by Yugoslavia and Albania. The U.N. appointed a commission to investigate the Greek charges, declared them reasonably well-founded, and urged all parties to seek mutual adjustment. In the Security Council, Russia supported the Yugoslav contention that it was the character of the Greek government and not outside interference which was responsible for the rebellion. Repeated use of the veto by Russia blocked action on proposals in the Council for a border committee in Greece and it was by the Assembly's action, with Russia and her Slav supporters abstaining, that such a committee was established in October, 1947. The fighting nevertheless went on; and though the Communist guerrillas were contained in a small area, their resistance continued through the summer of 1948. And then their fight began to slacken as Greece—under the direction of American missions—slowly set out on its way to recovery.

While the Greek question was returning the Balkans to their familiar role of powderkeg, atomic disarmament caused further conflict. In January, 1946, the United States offered to cease manufacturing atomic weapons and to make available its knowledge of atomic engineering if the rest of the world would first agree to international control of the sources of the raw materials of atomic energy and supervision of their subsequent use. In the same month, the U.N. General Assembly set up an Atomic Energy Commission and gave it this directive: "Proceed with the utmost dispatch [to] make specific proposals... for control of atomic energy... for the elimination from national armaments of atomic weapons and of all other major weapons adaptable to mass destruction." The Commission was established in June; it was made responsible to the U.N. Security Council and had a similar composition (including the veto power); and up to April, 1948, it and its subcommittees met several hundred times, exploring fully the involved political and technical questions that necessarily arose.

But from the beginning of the Commission's deliberations it was apparent that East and West were poles apart: not even the remote possibility of a compromise emerged. The United States, Britain, Canada, France, and China took the position that an international control system was feasible and should be established at once: for inspection, the creation of a strategic balance in the location of nuclear materials, products, and plants, even ownership. Only then would it be safe to outlaw atomic weapons. Russia and its satellites wanted to reverse the process: first prohibit atomic weapons and destroy existing stock piles; then international conventions could be drawn up. From this stand the Russians never deviated—that a program of international control constituted "an unwarranted infringement of national sovereignty." Of course it did: but so did all other plans for international co-operation. Since the nineteen thirties the world had been ruefully regarding the collapse of systems founded on pledged words alone; supervision was essential, but here the Russians, suspicious of alien inspection and foreigners in their land generally, would not yield. On this rock the Commission's efforts foundered; and in May, 1948, it adjourned *sine die* reporting to the U.N. General Assembly in September its inability to agree on a plan. An atomic race to threaten the world's peace, as had a similar naval race fifty years earlier, was presumably taking place.

Other activities in the international sphere indicated that the United States meant to play a vigorous role to hasten reconstruction and to establish the basis for a durable peace. We intervened in the Italian elections of April, 1948, to prevent that unhappy land from going down before Russian pressures. But not with troops, but with food and promise of further aid. Free elections took place: and the Communist Popular Front was overwhelmingly defeated. Italy was saved for the Western bloc. During March-May, 1948, as a result of the meeting of the ninth International Conference of American Republics at Bogotá, our ties with our Latin-American neighbors were strengthened. An Inter-American Defense Council was created; a loose constitution for an "Organization of American States"—which called for full consultation—was drawn up; and a resolution to resist Communist inroads was adopted unanimously.

On the question of Palestine we backed and filled and then adopted a clear-cut position even at the risk of antagonizing Britain. After years of debate—with the U.N. finally taking the lead (it was one of the body's important positive achievements)—the partition of Palestine into independent Jewish and Arab states was voted by the General Assembly in November, 1947. The United States and Russia both voted for the resolution; but the United States, in this case, was unclear as to how enforcement was to be achieved. The Jews proceeded to establish themselves firmly in the area allotted to them; Arab resistance—supported from Egypt, Syria, and Transjordan—led to the outbreak of guerrilla war. In March, 1948, the United States—concerned about Russian intervention—reversed itself: it asked for the suspension of partition plans and the creation of a U.N. trusteeship of "indefinite duration." Meanwhile the British had announced the surrender of their mandate as of May 15; and an invasion of Palestine by troops of the Arab League (those from Transjordan were supplied and officered from Britain) commenced. The Jews set up the Republic of Israel and proceeded to consolidate their position on the coast, suffering defeat, however, in Jerusalem at the hands of the Transjordan army.

Once more the United States reversed itself: President Truman announced the immediate recognition of the Israeli Republic. Russia did similarly. While the embargo was not lifted nor a request for credits granted, American support strengthened the determination of the Jews to resist. The U.N. again stepped in, only to see its mediator assassinated. But U.N. effort continued during 1948 and renewed fighting in Palestine was halted by another truce while negotiation see-sawed on.

Thus our course in the troubled waters of international politics in the postwar period. A policy was emerging: it was firm and nonaggressive; it aimed at peace without the sacrifice of essential interests. We would support the U.N. and help build its authority; until that time we were prepared to operate in close agreement with the other nations of the Western Powers. True, as a result of the repeated exercise of the veto by Russia in the U.N. Security Council, U.N. positive accomplishment was small. But Americans were more realistic now than they had been thirty years earlier. They were determined to co-operate and did so—in a limited sphere, because of Russian negativism—effectively. By the end of 1948, the Russians were aware of at least these two things: that their analysis of impending American economic collapse had proved false; and that Western Europe had a greater vitality than they had been prepared to realize. For a time they temporized; and there seemed to take place a truce in the so-called cold war between the East and West.

Then hostilities suddenly flared up once more; and the peace of the world hung in the balance. The Western Powers were succeeding in the rehabilitation of western Germany; they had issued a new currency for their zones in Germany and their sectors in Berlin; they were obtaining the support of the German people. The Russians met all this with a spectacular move; at the end of June, 1948, they banned all surface traffic between the western zones and Berlin. They hoped to starve Berlin and in this way force the Americans, English, and French out of the city. But they were playing for larger stakes: with the prestige of the Western Powers thus fatally weakened, Germany might be won—for communism.

The American-British countermove appeared to be a temporary makeshift; Berlin was to obtain its food and fuel from the air. The air lift turned out to be amazingly successful. Daily, hundreds of flights from the American and British zones—carrying food, fuel, medicines, passengers—were completed to Berlin; they took place despite Russian "maneuvers" over the air lanes; they succeeded in meeting the normal requirements of the blockaded city. By the end of September, American planes were delivering more than 4000 tons of supplies daily to Berlin. Every three minutes of the day a plane landed at Tempelhof Airport. The Western Powers had indicated their determination to stay on in Berlin.

It was really a portentous decision, far graver in its implications than appeared on the surface. For a willingness to resist the Russian pressure at Berlin meant a willingness to resist Russian arms. To maintain peace the United States would have to mobilize for war. In effect, in the second half of 1948, the strategic requirements of such a plan were taking shape. In what was obviously an informed article printed in *The Saturday Evening Post* on September 11, 1948, Joseph and Stewart Alsop indicated the nature of the American over-all plan. It included the following: 1. An American Army, Navy, and Air Force brought up to full peacetime strength (America's chief reliance, however, would be on its long-range air striking power); 2. a series of alliances with our Western allies; 3. the support of the defense establishments of the western European countries through military lend-lease; 4. the creation of a chain of overseas bases from which an offensive by air and sea could be launched "in decisive retaliation, the moment the first act of aggression is committed."

This meant many things—some dangerous, all fateful in their consequences. The United States was finished with isolation; the United States, through foreign alliances if need be, was committed to the defense of western Europe against further communist inroads; the United States was ready to fight at once—instead of waiting agonizing months as it mobilized while a prepared enemy captured all the strategic positions. It remained for the Russians to decide for peace or war. In such uncertainty did the world live three and one-half years after the Axis powers had been destroyed.

THE POSTWAR POLITICAL CLIMATE

After VJ-Day, the postwar political climate in the United States seemed to be veering toward that which prevailed in the nineteen twenties. War had required a great increase in executive power and unparalleled controls over economic life. It also had created proportionate resentment and weariness. War production achievement and war prosperity—it was inevitable, therefore—gave new confidence to the business community and the party which remained its political exponent. The elections of 1942 brought only slight Republican gains in Congress, but in 1944 President Roosevelt outran his ticket. The Republican Presidential slate represented the conservative wing of the party; the Democrats replaced Henry A. Wallace with Harry S. Truman as Vice-Presidential candidate. With the death of President Roosevelt in April, 1945, the New Deal lost its remaining magic and the progressive vote within both parties its most effective leader. Mr. Truman declared he meant to continue the Roosevelt program of welfare legislation and sent messages to Congress accordingly, but he chose new advisers and soon turned his talents for leadership into other channels.

In 1946, the Republicans won control of both Houses of Congress and 25 governorships besides. The Republicans regarded their victory as a mandate for the liquidation of the New Deal. In 1943, President Roosevelt himself had hinted that the task of reform had ended. A Democratic Congress shut down the remaining relief agencies. It did not re-enact the Guffey Bituminous Coal Act, with its machinery for stabilizing coal prices. It denied funds to the National Resources Planning Board, and thus eliminated that agency. The new Republican legislative regime proceeded more drastically. Though President Truman recommended that the United States Employment Service remain under federal administration until June, 1947, Congress returned it to the states immediately. The Farm Security Administration was terminated, budgets for the Interior and Agriculture Departments were cut, and Social Security coverage and minimum-wage standards were left unchanged. In 1946, wartime excess profits taxes were repealed, but Congress was unable to carry a general tax reduction over President Truman's veto in 1947. It did so, however, in 1948, purely as a political measure.

The Taft-Hartley Act, passed over Presidential veto in June, 1947, was indicative of the new trend. The law amended the Wagner Act to give final authority in investigation and enforcement not to the NLRB as a whole, but to its general counsel, and ordered that the Board follow court rules as to the admissibility of evidence. Supervisory employees were denied protection of their right to organize, and plant guards might form only unaffiliated organizations. Only unions which submitted financial reports and declared that their officers did "not belong to or support any organization that advocates the overthrow of government by force" could have cases heard by the Board or appear on the ballot in collective-bargaining elections. (This was aimed at Communist-dominated unions.) On the other hand, employers were given rights previously denied them. They were allowed to petition for elections to choose collective bargaining agents and to disseminate their views on the issue. They were to be held responsible only for action by their authorized agents. "Unfair labor practices" by unions were defined and forbidden, jurisdictional strikes,

	THE HOUSE		THE SENATE	
	Democrats	Republicans	Democrats	Republicans
1928	167	267	39	56
1930	214	220	47	48
1932	313	117	59	36
1934	322	103	69	25
1936	333	89	76	15
1938	260	172	69	23
1940	267	162	66	28
1942	222	209	57	38
1944	243	190	57	38
1946	188	246	45	51
1948	263	171	54	42

PARTY FORTUNES, 1928–48

secondary boycotts, sympathy strikes were outlawed, and the closed shop was virtually terminated. Certain feather-bedding devices were declared unfair. Further, all political contributions were banned; and unions could be sued for breach of contract. In addition to restoring the use of injunctions in labor disputes at NLRB option, the law made the federal Mediation and Conciliation Service an independent agency outside the Department of Labor. In the event of an impending industry-wide strike, the President was authorized to appoint a Board of Inquiry and to secure an injunction forbidding the strike for 60 days if the public health or safety was affected. During this period, conciliation was to be attempted and the

Board of Inquiry to make its report. Fifteen days later, the NLRB was to hold an election to determine whether the employees were prepared to accept the "final offer of settlement made by their employer as stated by him"; the injunction was to be vacated; and the President was to submit a report and recommendations to Congress.

Despite the friction common when the executive and legislative branches are held by different parties, Congress did adopt important new legislation. The Reorganization Act of 1946 attempted to improve Congressional procedure. Congressmen themselves were given higher salaries and retirement annuities. To ease the burdens of committee service, standing committees were reduced from 80 to 34 and provided with professional assistants and a Legislative Reference Service. The act also required registration of lobbyists, the adoption of a tentative legislative budget and over-all appropriation legislation, and annual adjournment by July 15.

In the areas of defense, important legislation emerged. In 1947, the National Security Act created a unified national defense establishment. A new Department of Defense was set up and an independent Air Force was provided for. President Truman asked for a Universal Military Training program. This he did not get; but Congress gave him a peacetime draft and a vastly expanded military budget. In June, 1948, a Draft Act provided for the calling up of young men between the ages of 19 and 25 for twenty-one months' service. For the fiscal year 1948, defense expenditures voted came to $9,000,000,000; for the fiscal year 1949, to $14,700,-000,000, with an authorized military strength in all branches of 2,000,000 men, and a greatly increased air arm.

The development of atomic energy for military purposes had significant legislative repercussions. The original May-Johnson bill, with its emphasis on military control, was buried in the House Rules Committee while the Senate Special Committee on Atomic Energy held hearings after November, 1945, and published its report in April, 1946. On August 1, the President signed a bill providing for a permanent Joint Congressional Committee on Atomic Energy, and an Atomic Energy Commission. This latter was to be a civilian body, although the military was to be represented and liaison maintained with military agencies. The Commission's 5 members were to be appointed by the President, with the advice and consent of the Senate, for terms of 5 years. After prolonged Senate debate, David Lilienthal, formerly head of the TVA, was finally confirmed as chairman of the new agency. The law attempted to serve three ends: national security; research and development; and checks upon possible future growth of monopoly. The act provided severe penalties against violation of secrecy rules, extending to death or life imprisonment should a jury find that information had been revealed with intent to injure the United States or benefit a foreign nation. The Commission was to engage in research on its own account and to contract for research by universities and industrial laboratories, a method which had been fruitful in wartime. Control of raw materials bearing fissionable elements was vested in the Commission and it was to license atomic-energy devices. Further, if an invention was essential to the use of fissionable materials or atomic energy, the Commission might declare its patents "affected with the public interest" and subject to licensing regulations, including general use on payment of a reasonable royalty.

The act sought both to fit the new force into the traditional governmental framework and to adapt that framework to its new tasks. Thus, the "public interest" clause attempted to secure a greater degree of latitude for the Commission, but judicial review was specifically provided for: The Commission's findings of fact were to be conclusive "if supported by substantial evidence." Like the Employment Act of 1946, the Atomic Energy Act made formal provision for liaison with Congress and advice to the President. For, when any industrial or commercial use of atomic energy had developed sufficiently for practical application, the Commission was to report to the President, giving him the facts and an "estimate of the social, political, economic and international effects" of that application. In Congress, 9 Senators and 9 Representatives were to constitute a Joint Committee on Atomic Energy. This was to make a continuing survey of the Commission and its work and to maintain close relations with it both informally and by hearings as well as by consideration of the reports the Atomic Energy Commission was to render Congress each January and July. Such detailed provision for supervision and contact indicated that political leaders had given constructive consideration not only to the problem of relations among the President, the legislature, and the executive agencies it had created, but also to the problem of the democratic direction of social change.

Like tendencies appeared in the Employment Act of 1946. This declared it the responsibility of the federal government to "promote maximum employment, production and purchasing power," as long as these were consonant with free competitive enterprise and the general welfare. For this purpose, the law established a Council of Economic Advisers to the President; this was to be made up of three members qualified by training and experience to appraise and formulate policies. The initial reports of this body—and the materials furnished the President for his own semiannual economic reports to the Congress—were so sanely drawn that the business community and the public generally listened to the advisers with respect. They were exerting a growing influence, although themselves possessing no powers.

The Eightieth Congress' record, which played such a large part in the Presidential campaign of 1948, was not unimpressive. On the score of

European recovery and in the matter of defense it had faced up to its responsibilities seriously, albeit with a good deal of prodding. On domestic issues, its performance was less commendable. It had passed a tax-reduction bill, thus further encouraging the inflationary spiral. It had antagonized labor in the badly drawn Taft-Hartley Act (which did have commendable features). It had narrowed rather than expanded the coverage of the Social Security Law. It had refused to do anything about President Truman's demands for an over-all farm program, long-range housing financing, federal aid to education, national health legislation, civil rights for Negroes, and price controls. Democratic orators made much of these derelictions; Republicans pleaded for more time to think through such important pieces of legislation. As has so frequently occurred, therefore, the outcome of the election was expected to hinge upon the personalities involved.

THE PRESIDENTIAL ELECTION OF 1948

The Republicans met at Philadelphia during June 21–25, 1948, with the leading contenders for the nomination Governor Thomas E. Dewey of New York, Senator Robert A. Taft of Ohio, former Governor Harold E. Stassen of Minnesota, Governor Earl Warren of California, and Senator Arthur H. Vandenberg of Michigan. The preconvention contest had been interesting, with Stassen, particularly, capturing the imagination of Republican youth as he took a clear-cut stand on the question of American participation in international affairs. Taft and Dewey threatened to create deep-seated antagonisms as they directed their campaigns at each other; it was hoped, by many, that Vandenberg would emerge as the compromise candidate.

The Dewey forces at Philadelphia, however, were too well organized, and Dewey received the nomination on the third ballot; Governor Warren was named for the Vice-Presidency by acclamation. No breach had occurred in the ranks of the G.O.P. and the delegates returned to their homes confident of victory after sixteen years of exile from the seats of power.

The Democrats also met at Philadelphia, during July 12–15. A heavy pall hung over the proceedings for all were convinced that the party faced defeat in the election. Democratic gloom was further deepened by the fact that General Dwight D. Eisenhower, who had become president of Columbia University, refused to permit his name to be put in nomination; and Supreme Court Justice William O. Douglas—the last hope of the New Dealers in the party—turned down a proffer of the second place. The deep-South delegates, incensed at President Truman's courageous demand for honest civil-rights legislation (including federal laws against poll taxes, lynching, discrimination in employment, and racial segregation) threatened to walk out of the hall and the Democracy. When Mr. Truman insisted that his civil-rights plan be written into the Democratic platform, the unreconstructed southerners made good their threat. The "Dixiecrats" formed the so-called States' Rights party and chose as nominees, Governor J. Strom Thurmond of South Carolina and Governor Fielding L. Wright of Mississippi.

President Truman, too, had a well-organized machine at the convention; he was nominated on the first ballot. In an effort to conciliate southerners, seventy-year-old Senator Alben W. Barkley of Kentucky was named for the Vice-Presidency.

Governor Dewey was 46, Michigan-born, and a graduate of the Columbia University Law School. He had won acclaim as a vigorous prosecutor of New York gamblers and racketeers; he had become Governor of New York in 1942, had run unsuccessfully against Roosevelt in 1944, and been re-elected to the governorship in 1946. His administrations had been highly satisfactory, although the problems facing him had not been too difficult because of the excellent financial position in which his Democratic predecessor had left New York State. Known as a reserved and cold person, Governor Dewey had succeeded in attracting the loyalty of a group of men who were personally devoted and who helped in the shaping of his ideas. On most domestic issues, he stood silent, but on international problems he had taken sides against isolationism, political and economic.

Harry S. Truman was 64, Missouri-born and bred, and a product of the hurly-burly of its Democratic politics. He had come to the Senate in 1934, had gained prominence as the head of a committee investigating war production, and had been elected Vice-President in 1944. On Roosevelt's death, on April 12, 1945, he had succeeded to the Presidency, confessing: "The whole weight of the moon and stars and all the planets fell on me." Generally, he had followed in Roosevelt's footsteps: seeking to conciliate the Russians and to support New Deal policies. The first objective he had been compelled to give up when Russian aggression indicated only too plainly that the leaders of the Kremlin wanted a disorganized Europe; the second he had pressed less energetically not because he was a conservative but because he was more at home in the company of his Missouri friends. The New Dealers therefore quit Washington.

Although Truman championed the expansion of Social Security and housing legislation and was sufficiently worried about inflation to seek greater governmental controls, some intransigent New Dealers supported the Progressive party which was organized to support the Presidential candidacy of former Vice-President Henry A. Wallace, who campaigned with Democratic Senator Glen A. Taylor of Idaho as his running mate.

The stigma of Communist domination marked Wallace's program and his campaign and ultimately cost him the bulk of the New Deal and labor support on which he had counted, for he stressed conciliation of Russia and opposed the ERP, new defense programs, and the American position on atomic energy.

Thus, the Democrats went into the 1948 campaign opposed by the "Dixiecrats," and the Wallace forces as well as the Republicans (to say nothing of perennial Socialist candidate Norman Thomas and the tickets of numerous minor parties). By August, forecasters, commentators for press and radio, and the masters of the sampling techniques of the opinion polls had so discounted President Truman's chances of re-election that many of his own party leaders gave him only perfunctory support. In face of defeatism, Southern defections, and a slender campaign purse, President Truman virtually carried on a one-man campaign, attacking the Republican Eightieth Congress for its sins of commission and omission. Particularly, he scored the refusal of its special session to take positive action to check the upward spiralling of prices, even if that should require such drastic measures as price controls, allocation of scarce materials, or even rationing. Governor Dewey sought to dissociate himself from the Eightieth Congress; he promised, in effect, that he would leave the achievements of the New Deal untouched; and he accepted the main points of the Truman foreign policy: support of the United Nations; the Marshall Plan; aid to the Western European Union and to China; and a firm policy with Russia.

As election night passed, those scanning the returns saw the incredible and refused to believe it. Not until nearly noon of the day following was the decision of the voters evident. President Truman had obtained 304 electoral votes to Dewey's 189 and Thurmond's 38 (which increased to 39 when a Tennessee elector added his pledged vote to the tally). Of the 47,332,632 votes counted that week, President Truman received 23,667,727, while Governor Dewey scored 21,542,581. Governor Thurmond polled 1,005,945; Mr. Wallace, 1,116,379. In Congressional and gubernatorial contests, the people rendered a like unexpected verdict. The Democrats won impressive majorities in House and Senate, and succeeded in replacing Republican governors even in Michigan, Connecticut, and Indiana, which stood in the Republican electoral column.

Of the factors which contributed to the startling turn of events, three appeared significant to contemporaries. President Truman's dogged fight won sympathy and votes. Governor Dewey's confidence, and his failure to come to grips with the issues raised by his opponent convinced an important segment of the electorate that there was a real difference between the forces which the opposing candidates represented. Secondly, contrary to political shibboleth, prosperity did not send the farm vote back to the

Republicans. Although Governor Dewey carried the Dakotas, Nebraska, Kansas, and Indiana, much of the Middle West voted for Truman. Thirdly, and especially important, in view of the lackadaisical attitude of many Democratic professional politicians, was the fact that organized labor finally rallied to President Truman's support. Trade unionists' votes helped defeat 50 Representatives who voted for the Taft-Hartley Act; trade unionists' leg-work did much to bring out the urban vote; and trade unionists' belief that Mr. Wallace had allied himself with Moscow alienated organized labor from the Progressive Party and helped hold states like Ohio and California for the Democrats.

The election of 1948 made Mr. Truman President in his own right and undisputed leader of his party. It demonstrated that prosperity as well as economic catastrophe could make midwestern farmers vote Democratic; that organized labor held significant political power; and that the Democrats could carry a Presidential election though the Solid South was broken and a border state like Maryland shifted to the Republican column. In brief, Americans seemed to say that the New Deal was not dead; labor had to be defended and government utilized to redistribute wealth and income and to control the economy. Moreover, Mr. Truman's international program was endorsed: isolationism (with which too many Republicans were identified) was dead. Europe must be aided and communism checked. In a way, the election was a reply to Moscow and an answer to Europe's perplexity: the American people stood four-square behind the Marshall Plan.

PROBLEMS OF RECONVERSION

The almost simultaneous ending of the European and Pacific phases of the war left the United States with armed forces totaling nearly 12,000,000 men. The demobilization program was shaped to meet the needs of security, the demands of equity, the shortage of transport, and the problems of economic equilibrium. Men were discharged as individuals, not in military units, on the basis of a point system taking into account length of service, service overseas, decorations, and dependent children. In 1944, Congress had enacted measures to ease the readjustment of able-bodied veterans to civil life as well as to care for the disabled. Discharged soldiers might legally claim the jobs they had held before being drafted. If unable to get work, they might draw unemployment compensation at $20 a week for 52 weeks. The government guaranteed 50 per cent of any loan up to $2,000 (later $4,000) a veteran might seek for home building or beginning a business. In addition, the law granted subsistence and tuition payments for periods of study equal to the time spent in the Army. The loan provisions of the "GI Bill of Rights" were liberalized the next year and eligibility for study broadened to include veterans over the 26-year age limit. Despite the meager allowances, veterans—many of them married and with families—thronged the American campuses, where their excellent scholastic performances gave a new seriousness to American higher education.

In 1944, Congress had also planned for the demobilization of industry. The Contracts Settlement Act provided for rapid action, especially as regarded small firms. Machinery for government use was to be removed as fast as possible, and invoices were to be paid for on the cost-plus-a-percentage system. Through the RFC War Assets Corporation (which became the independent War Assets Administration in March, 1946), the government acted to dispose of surplus materials in a fashion that would not glut the commercial producers' market. This was done with great efficiency and not too much loss to the government, and many small businesses operated by veterans were started as a result.

In a sense, time lost characterizes all war periods when productive work must be set aside and resources, human and material, devoted to devising the most efficient means of destruction. The uprooting is physical and psychological; its impact on education and family life has far-reaching consequences. The development of new industrial areas on the Pacific coast, in the Midwest and South, even in less urbanized areas of a state like New York, drew people from their homes, put women to work in factories, and strained community resources. The number of young people in the 14–17 age group, working full or part-time, tripled between 1940 and 1945; high-school enrollment dropped; states relaxed their laws for the protection of youth in industry or were unable to maintain standards of enforcement. By 1945, that trend was somewhat arrested: Illinois and Maine raised the minimum age for employment; Georgia, North Carolina, and Texas tightened their school-attendance laws. Migration, with its marked changes in living habits (mothers at work, often on night shifts; wartime separation of parents; the absence of the sometimes steadying influence of older brothers) crowding; and war tension—all these made for insecurity and instability among young people. The median age for juvenile delinquency brought to the attention of authorities dropped from 16 to 11 years in the war-industry areas of New York, and in the nation as a whole more than 50 per cent of burglaries and automobile thefts and a third of the robberies and larcenies were committed by persons under 21.

THE POSTWAR BOOM

The demobilization of men and industry was accompanied by the demobilization of economic controls. The War Manpower Commission was abolished after VJ-Day and the War Labor Board ceased functioning in November, 1945. Most civilian rationing was also terminated, but Congress extended OPA until June, 1946. Meanwhile, there appeared a general pressure against the price level and a sharp inflation set in, due to heavy deferred demand, a short corn crop, exports to Europe, and to the great increase in the monetary resources of the country. The greatest price rises occurred in those items entering into cost-of-living budgets—food, clothing, house furnishings—and workers therefore became restive. During the fall and winter of 1945 to 1946, there were widespread strikes in the steel, oil, automobile, packing house, and electrical industries. In each case, labor finally won increases in wages—this so-called first round coming to an increase of 18½ cents an hour; but new price rises absorbed wage increases—and nothing was gained. In fact, the year marked the culmination of the wartime truce between management and labor, the gage of battle being thrown down when the United Mine Workers declared its government contract at an end in the fall of 1946. A federal court enjoined the strike and imposed a heavy fine for contempt of court when the miners did not return immediately. The fine against the UMW was not collected, but UMW president John L. Lewis was required to pay the fine assessed against him. The strikes in basic industry, the engineers' and trainmen's strike on the railroads in May, and the prolonged tangle in the coal fields helped create a public sentiment favorable to the restrictions on organized labor imposed by the Taft-Hartley Law and by numerous state acts as well.

By November, 1946, price controls at the consumer level disappeared except for sugar and rice. During the winter and spring of 1947, materials control ended; only the ceiling on rents was retained. By October, 1947, wheat reached the level preceding the break of 1920 and the commodity price index was still rising. While the stockmarket continued relatively unstirred, even when United States Steel increased its dividend and Bethlehem announced a stock split-up, speculation on the commodity exchanges provoked the government, as a principal buyer of wheat, to press for the increase of trading margins to 33⅓ per cent. A second round of wage increases followed in the spring of 1947, this time the increase being 15 cents an hour, and a third round took place in the spring of 1948. Prices continued, in consequence, to go up.

The price rise was, in fact, the only really disturbing element in the American economy during the postwar period; otherwise, the extraordinary boom that had set in—greater indeed than the one that had followed the end of World War I—appeared to be soundly based. Even in the case of prices there were distortions that might be regarded as temporary. True, by 1948, the general price level was almost as high as the peak figure for 1920. But prices of farm products and raw materials pushed the general index up. By the end of 1947, the wholesale prices of farm products were 96.2 per cent higher than in 1926; those of raw materials were 80.9 per cent higher. On the other hand, prices of manufactured products were up only 53.7 per cent and prices of all commodities other than farm products and foods were up only 45.5 per cent.

Farmers continued the leading beneficiaries of the boom; labor was not far behind; indeed, the lower and middle middle-class groups in the population were emerging from the war with greater purchasing power, absolutely and relatively, than they had ever enjoyed previously in American history. From 1939 to 1948, the purchasing value of the farm dollar had increased more than 50 per cent; labor's *real* wages had increased almost 25 per cent. What was even more significant was the fact that a redistribution in the nation's income was occurring. During 1935 to 1936, a study of income distribution by income classes showed that only 16 per cent of all consumer units were receiving more than $2000 a year. By 1941, this proportion had mounted to 36 per cent; by 1945 it stood at 50 per cent. Put another way, the lower income classes were benefiting at the expense of the top income class. The following table shows what proportions of the nation's total income were received by the different income classes. The change in the position of the top 20 per cent will be noted.

SHARE OF NATIONAL INCOME RECEIVED BY SPENDING UNITS, 1935-36—1946 [1]

Families and Single Individuals— Annual Incomes	Percentage of Total Civilian Income Received		
	1935–36	1941	1946
Lowest fifth of income recipients	4.0	3.4	4.4
Second fifth " " "	8.7	8.7	10.6
Third fifth " " "	13.6	15.3	16.0
Fourth fifth " " "	20.5	22.0	22.1
Highest fifth " " "	53.2	50.6	46.9

As Americans regarded their world in the fourth year after the end of World War II, they had every reason to be pleased with the fruits of their dynamic economy. It was progressing technologically and diffusing welfare over a wider and wider segment of the whole population; true, it had not eliminated the danger of recession and economic downturn; but government and business knew more about fiscal controls and were more sensitive to their employment. Everywhere, in 1948, demand continued to run ahead of supply: there was enormous consumer demand at home, particularly for durable goods and housing; domestic investment

[1] The materials are derived from *The Economic Reports of the President* (New York, 1948).

in capital goods continued to increase—in fact, American industry, in many quarters, was badly short of capital; the export trade, linked with the country's foreign policy, far exceeded the ability of the world to send us goods. Too, accumulated savings, as a cushion to the inflation, were large; industrial relations were good; and the United States was guided by an improved business management and possessed new tools, plants, and techniques.

The following figures, comparing the position of the United States in 1948 with 1939, show something of the advances that had been made. In 1948, the civilian labor force was more than 61,000,000; in 1939 it had been 55,000,000. In 1948, the gross national product was being turned out at the rate of $246,500,000,000; in 1939, it had been $90,400,000,000. In 1948, the national income was at the rate of $210,000,000,000; in 1939, it had been $72,500,000,000. In 1948, personal-consumption expenditures were at the rate of $175,000,000,000; in 1939, they had been $67,500,000,000. In 1948, gross private domestic investment was at the rate of $37,000,000,000; in 1939, it had been $9,000,000,000. At the end of 1947, the Federal Reserve index of production stood at 192 (186 being the monthly average); the monthly average for 1939 had been 109. In 1947, farm income was $18,300,000,000; in 1939, it had been $4,500,000,000. In 1947, corporate profits after taxes were $18,100,000,000; in 1939, they had been $5,000,000,000. At the end of 1947, the average gross weekly earnings of factory workers was $52.69 ($49.25 being the average for the year as a whole); the average for 1939 had been $23.86. True, the country's positive trade balance was abnormal: for 1947, exports came to $19,700,000,000 and imports only to $8,500,000,000, including income on investments. But our creditor position was improving—at the beginning of 1947, the United States was a net creditor to the amount of $5,300,000,000; at the end of the year, the amount stood at $10,400,000,000—and with a change in imports for the better our investments abroad were bound to act as a stabilizer of the American economy.

All this was to the good. What distortions existed were largely to be found in the realm of monetary policy and fiscal management. In the course of financing the war, the government more than tripled the combined supply of paper money and demand deposits in the hands of the public, increasing the total from $33,000,000,000 in 1939 to $109,000,000,000 in 1947. The public debt was enormous: it stood at $259,100,000,000 at the end of 1947 as compared with $40,400,000,000 in 1939. True, the budget was smaller than it had been during the war years, federal expenditures for 1947 to 1948 being $42,500,000,000 as compared with $100,400,000,000 for 1944 to 1945 and $8,700,000,000 for 1938 to 1939. Small Treasury surpluses were being accumulated for debt redemption. But government continued a heavy spender and lender: and its subsidies, soldiers' bonuses, and farm-price support policies helped keep the inflation spiraling upward. The same was true of the activities of government credit-insuring agencies. Further, the federal tax policy, which restricted savings and therefore discouraged the accumulation of capital, tended to expand the use of bank credit, another inflationary force. Generally, economists and business leaders agreed, what was needed were the following: an increase in government fiscal surpluses (which would retire debt held by the banks and thus narrow the base for bank-credit expansion); curbs on installment credit; the purchase of more savings bonds by the consuming public; an end to the support of the market for government bonds (so that the interest rate could go up); and an increase in bank reserve requirements.

The accompanying graphs show the relationship between public debt, local and federal, and national income for pivotal years of war and depression, as well as liquid assets in the hands of individuals and business enterprises, 1940–48. Also shown is business activity, as exemplified by indexes of industrial production, freight carloadings, and farm prices paid and received. The public debt-national income chart is reprinted, with permission, from The Twentieth Century Fund study, *America's Needs and Resources* (1948). The other material is from the Board of Governors of the Federal Reserve System. (1935–39 = 100 for production and carloadings; 1910–14 = 100 for agricultural prices).

Given changes and controls along the lines mentioned above, and given a continued redistribution of the national income to achieve better balance among sections, groups, and individuals—as well as constant adjustment of prices, wages, and profits—and it was apparent that the American economic system possessed a real vitality. Basic to its maintenance was the existence of real price competition. So declared the Council of Economic Advisers in its second annual report; in these judgments many Americans concurred. Their confidence in themselves had been revived; they had traveled far since the opening of the nineteen thirties. And if they were troubled by the division between East and West in the international sphere, the great majority approved of the administration's policy of an adequate defense program and firmness in the face of Russian pressures. Americans had learned that power and responsibilities were two sides of the same coin.

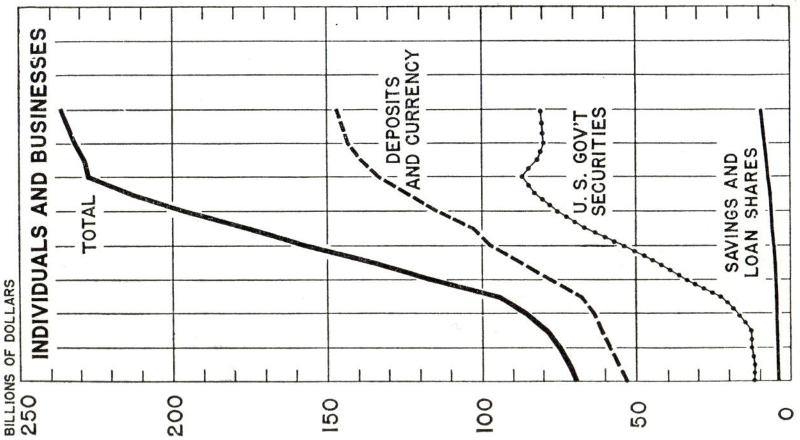

POSTWAR RECONSTRUCTION

LIQUID ASSET OWNERSHIP BY INDIVIDUALS AND BUSINESSES
1940-50

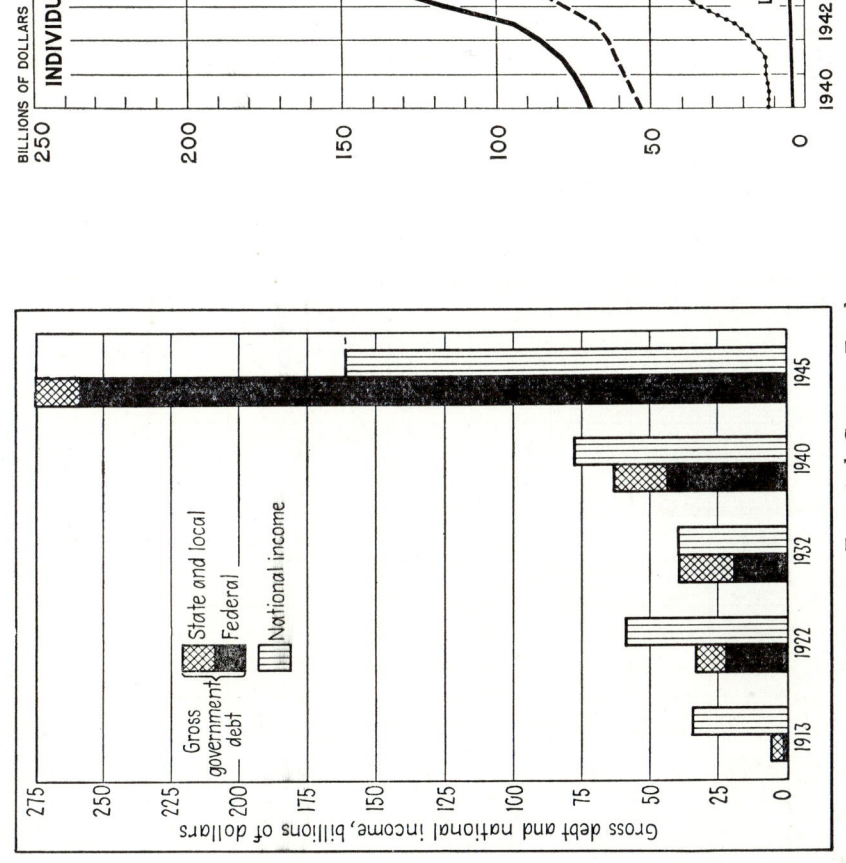

Federal Reserve Estimate

GROSS GOVERNMENT DEBT AND NATIONAL INCOME
1913, 1922, 1932, 1940 AND 1945

Twentieth Century Fund

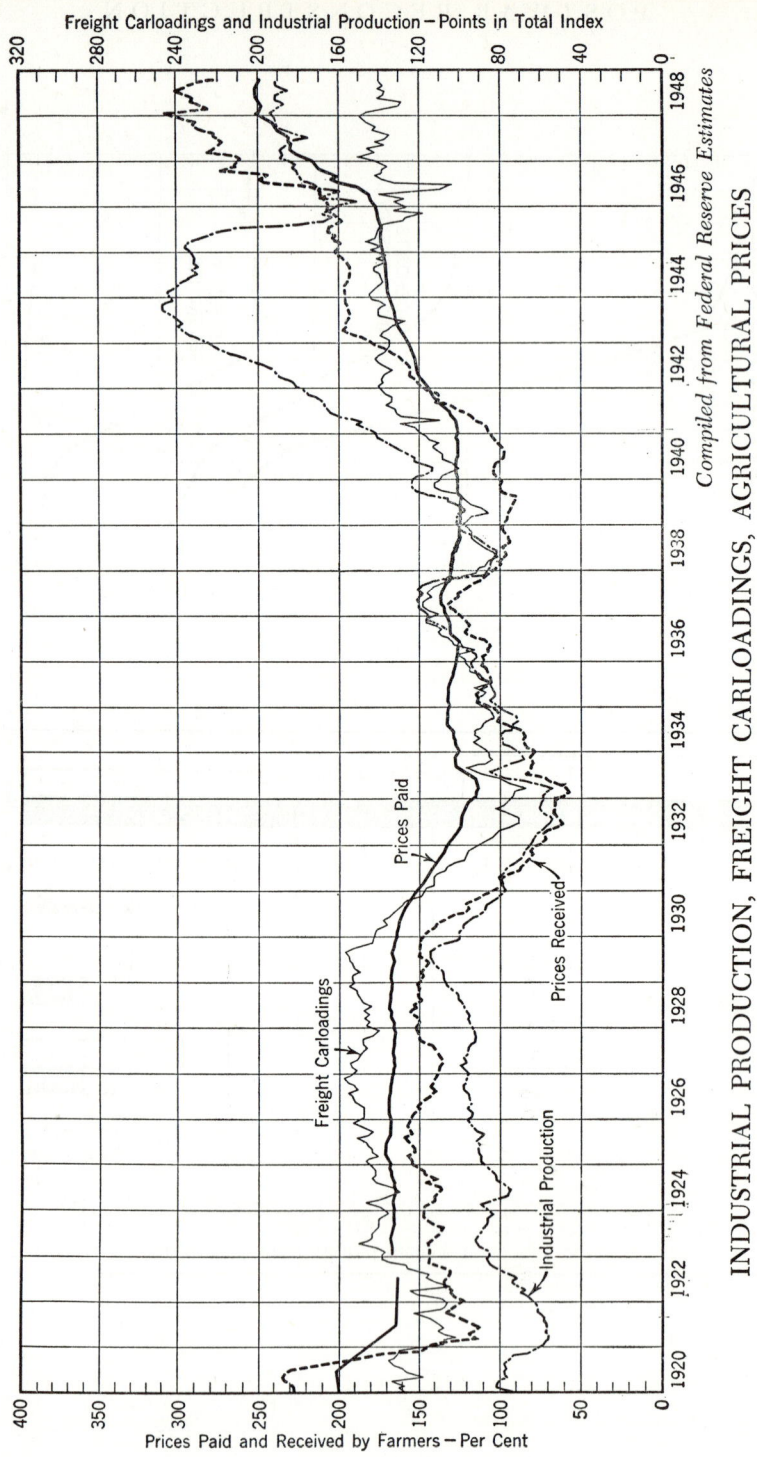

INDUSTRIAL PRODUCTION, FREIGHT CARLOADINGS, AGRICULTURAL PRICES
1920–48

Compiled from Federal Reserve Estimates

· 40 ·

Life, Learning, and the Arts Between World Wars

ASPECTS OF THE AMERICAN SCENE

DURING the nineteen twenties, the splendor of Machine-Age America was everywhere expressed. Foreigners, visiting our shores for the first time, found much to astonish them: the dazzling shops, the comfortable homes, the ever-present automobile; these seemed common characteristics to be viewed alike in the mighty metropolises and the smaller inland towns. America was standardized and America was rich. What better sign of wealth than the zeal with which her prosperous citizens vied with one another in disposing of large parts of their gains? Certainly, only a confident expectation that fortune would continue gracious could account for the munificence of American philanthropic endeavor. Well might the wealthy part with their surpluses; that their positions were secure could not be denied. Well might the toilers with hand and brain buy automobiles, radios, single-family houses, electric washing machines, and fur coats: that the Machine's happy round would never cease was the expectation of every American who was living in the wonder days of the Golden Twenties.

The "new era" collapsed in 1929, and the illiteracy, child labor, economic insecurity, and corroding poverty which had troubled only a few during the buoyant years, wakened a concern that had been all but silent, politically, since the days of the Square Deal and the New Freedom. Yet the twenties' pressures on provincialism continued. Radio and the motion picture forced a new uniformity upon America: the tag-line of a radio comedian ran from coast to coast; from coast to coast during the thirties, girls painted their lips and shaped their bodies to match the shadows that screens showed alike in New York City and a Dakota town. The physical mobility, which had marked American life since the nation's beginning, was increased by the introduction of the cheap automobile. In 1908, Henry Ford inaugurated a new era in American business when the Model T went into quantity production. By 1915, he had produced 1,000,000 cars; by 1925, his company was turning out 2,000,000 cars a year; in 1928, Model T was discontinued shortly after car number 15,000,000 was completed. He and his competitors had put America on wheels.

Travel took on a new urgency during the depression, and the driving that had once meant pleasure served the desperate search for work. The war years saw a second migration as families moved to war-industry areas and thousands of young wives followed their husbands from army camp to army camp. Mechanical entertainment, the hunt for jobs, the needs of war thrust on against the externals of provincialism. Crucial regional differences might mark social and political attitudes; in speech and dress and tastes, Americans were becoming increasingly alike.

To the foreign observer, skyscrapers and the relative absence of class differentiation in women's dress distinguished the American scene of the twenties. He noted that culture (in the sense of interest in letters and the arts) was a feminine preserve in a country where the business of man was business. American civilization suffered, the foreign observer remarked: prohibition, the absence of a varied and robust public cuisine, the fact that the intellectual was not considered fully male and adult—all could be traced to feminine domination. By the middle thirties, however, the emancipation of women had proceeded so far that middle-class women were free to be "lowbrows" if they chose. With the Nineteenth Amendment, women had won the vote; custom and technological advance freed them from corsets and the cookstove; bobbed hair took them into that male refuge, the barbershop; repeal admitted them to the last sanctum, the bar. Middle-class women were being raised to earn their livings; the middle-class wife could keep her job after marriage without much loss of status to her husband. Women had won political and educational equality; they dictated the patterns of family spending and, because of their relatively longer life-span, an increasing proportion of the nation's wealth was falling into their hands. Yet the influence of women was almost negligible in politics: the few who became governors or senators usually inherited the unexpired terms of deceased husbands; legislation in the fields of education and child care, which might be presumed of particular interest to them, made no startling advances after the achievement of suffrage; no woman became known as a political boss.

During the thirties, the American scene, which had appeared so standardized in its human aspect, began to be marked by the Dust Bowl. Unwise cultivation, heedless cutting of forests, economic pressures for continuing production of row crops like cotton tore top soil loose to blow and silt up the rivers of the Great Valley. With flood and drought, Nature completed what man's overzealousness had begun. Arkansas and Oklahoma were worst affected during the middle thirties, but through all the semiarid West battered trucks and cars rolled their loads of families seeking work and new homes, or even the casual shelter of a relief camp.

While the depression increased American mobility, it extended the new leisure of the twenties. For the American workman received part of his increased productivity in shorter working time. The last major stronghold of the 72-hour week fell in 1927, when the steel industry finally introduced the 8-hour day except in certain processes. Save for sweated trades and cotton textile mills, the 8-hour day became the rule. During the thirties, short time helped meet the unemployment problem. The 30-hour week was labor's panacea. Employers found loss of efficiency in part-time operation preferable to higher taxes or an even greater roster of the entirely unemployed. The National Industrial Recovery Act and the Fair Labor Standards Act of 1938 established the 40-hour work week as an industrial standard. Paid vacations, which had been a middle-class prerogative, reached the upper layers of workingmen in the thirties and by the early nineteen forties many union contracts incorporated either paid vacations or their equivalent.

Voluntary or involuntary, leisure gave Americans more time for recreation. Commercialized sport reached a pinnacle in 1927, when spectators paid $2,600,000 to see Gene Tunney win a rather dull prizefight, which expert publicity built into the "battle of the century." College football frequently had its most devoted audience among people who had never seen a college classroom; and professional baseball, purged of scandal and—for a time, at any rate—firmly ruled by a "czar," continued the national game of republican America. Despite the stimulus of night games, made possible by more powerful arclighting, baseball felt the competition of professional football. Basketball, too, became an important spectator sport.

Gambling found new votaries during the depression years. Legalized betting at horse and dog tracks returned with hard liquor in the early nineteen thirties, and people who had learned to take little flyers in real estate and the stockmarket contented themselves with the less costly thrill to be had at the $2 parimutuel window. The dime chain letter, the bingo parlor with its middle-aged women patrons, and the policy or "numbers racket" lottery all flourished in spite of law.

Healthier than the overdevelopment of athletic spectacle was the parallel growth of participant sports. Golf and its costumes helped free the American male from the drabness of the "business suit." Bowling came back with beer. By the late thirties, golf and tennis percolated into the upper levels of the working class. Play, once condemned as evidence of original sin or tolerated as preparation for the serious business of living, was almost rehabilitated, even for lower-class adults.

With the new leisure, the provision of entertainment became an important part of economic life. As an industry and a social force, the motion picture reached maturity during the twenties and took on new life with the introduction of sound. The films soon assimilated the disturbing element of speech, but the cost of production made artistic experiment too risky: the fairy tale for grownups still prevailed and executives played follow-the-leader. Yet producers paid hugely for successful plays and books—even if those required much "purifying" before adaptation—and spent large sums on biographical films. More interesting were demonstrations, like John Ford's in *Stagecoach,* of what intelligence could do for the "horse opera"; the development of the documentary film in the *Plow that Broke the Plains;* and the "pure movie" of the animated cartoon.

While the motion picture was drawing weekly audiences of 40 million, radio was making its entry into American life. Lee De Forest invented the audion in 1906 and broadcasting was mechanically possible. With the drone of "Alabama, 24 votes for Underwood," in 1924, Americans outside the city of assemblage first heard the public proceedings of a Presidential convention. Before the end of the decade, radio manufacturing was an important American industry; by 1945, 56 million sets were reckoned in use and the people of the United States spent nearly $720 million a year on their purchase and upkeep. Isolated broadcasting stations had consolidated into networks that could cover the nation with their programs. Broadcasting became a great industry combining the peculiar madnesses of advertising and show business. The nineteen twenties had introduced commercial broadcasting; the thirties expanded that to include public service. The approach of war turned radio from a toy into a weapon. Within limits, controversy took a new place on the air waves. News broadcasts gave a terrifying sense of immediacy to each "crisis" and it was possible to hear the D-day guns in an American living room. Radio commentators replaced newspaper editorialists as formulators of public opinion; politicians counted a "radio voice" among their candidates' assets; and teachers of diction found new sources of income.

As a transmitter, whether of news, opinion, opera or advertising, radio had proved itself: it had brought fine music into the home and won a broad public for the classics. Creatively, particularly in adult education and entertainment, it had, as yet, achieved little. Its comics were juvenile— there were a few notable exceptions; its soap operas came straight from the pulps; its children's programs combined horror with the wildly impossible. Television, rising to greater popularity with improvements in technique, was still produced for an uncritical audience more concerned with seeing an image at a distance than with the quality of what it saw. But beginning in 1948, as television suddenly began to grow into a great new industry, experimentation began to take place.

While the bulk of the entertainment provided by radio and the motion picture was candidly and deliberately puerile, the American drama reached full stature in the Machine Age. With the development of the movie and the decline of the traveling company, the commercial theater has disappeared from all but the largest communities, yet "Little Theater" groups and other organizations were producing a theater of recreative play which might be even more valuable as a builder of taste. For metropolitan audiences, more and more good plays were being written and were receiving intelligent, imaginative handling. Not the least element in the progress of the stage during the twenties was the fact that American dramatic writing belonged among the best of the creative literature of the time; indeed it stood head and shoulders above the similar efforts of the younger English and Continental playwrights. In *Craig's Wife* and the *Show-Off* and *Broadway*, the New York playgoer saw the middle-class life he lived and the strange existences which flourished on the fringes of prohibition. Maxwell Anderson and Elmer Rice were experimenting with their medium to make it show, through the life and the problems they knew, the issues of man's being. Nobel prizewinner Eugene O'Neill was the great American playwright of this period, not only to the critics but also to the large audiences which attended his plays. As his work passed from the tormented naturalism of his pictures of fo'c'sle and sea through *Anna Christie* and *The Emperor Jones* and *Strange Interlude*, it reflected the artistic and spiritual preoccupations of his time. O'Neill disregarded the classical unities and those later rules of the dramatic craft which insisted upon the presentation of pat situations whose artificial perplexities could be resolved in the space of two hours. He wrote "expressionistic" dramas to depict conflict not between men and men or men and ideas but between men and emotions.

The depression, meanwhile, had brought fresh talent to the theater. Critics opened their arms to Clifford Odets despite his Marxist outlook. Odets' earlier plays were his best, however; he has not lived up to the measure of his promise. Lillian Hellman, who depicts other segments of American life with a more acrid pen, has shown an uneven but interesting pattern of growth. In Tennessee Williams and Mary Chase, the sight of the modern world produces a peculiar variety of fantasy, much akin to that tendency in Steinbeck which has been labelled the "cult of the poor slob."

The theater itself entered on new paths during the nineteen thirties. For years, American audiences had checked their brains with their hats when they went to musical shows. *Of Thee I Sing* helped breach the tradition and create a vogue for the literate musical; *Pins and Needles* gave the form "social consciousness"; by 1948, a musical wholly without meaning or social comment was something to remark on Broadway. A depression lack of money encouraged the production of plays without scenery.

Thorton Wilder, who had won the connoisseurs by his picture of a delicately decadent society in Rome and popular success by a tale of Providence working in Peru, turned to the American scene and told of life in *Our Town*. Orson Welles gave *Julius Caesar* in modern clothes on a bare stage, and proved the play's pertinence to a dictators' time. The depression was also responsible for the first instance of government support to the theater in America. To give work relief to unemployed theatrical artisans and performers, the Federal Theater project was organized. Before it was liquidated, it had developed and popularized the living newspaper technique of dramatizing public issues; it had made T. S. Eliot's *Murder in a Cathedral* one of the most successful of modern plays in verse; and, with the *Swing Mikado*, initiated a trend that continued to bear fruit on the commercial stage.

The Machine Age, which dominated the American scene whether in smooth or faulty working, helped institutionalize the collection and dissemination of news and the creation of public opinion. By the turn of the century, Pulitzer and Hearst had found that the conduct of a newspaper could be turned into an enterprise of Big Business. And, although they did not part altogether with the traditions of personal journalism of the middle period, they plainly indicated that the future of the newspaper lay in its ceaseless adaptation to the requirements of a mechanical age. The successors of these earlier giants were commercial entrepreneurs rather than journalists. They banded newspapers together in great chains; they depersonalized editorials and toned down opinion. More and more, the American newspaper came to regard itself as an agency for informing and amusing its readers rather than as a public tribune. That it became, also, a medium in which the wares of local merchants, and to a lesser degree, those of national corporations could be hawked was in a sense inevitable, for only from advertising revenues could the modern newspaper be supported. This state of affairs, at any rate, continued to the coming of the New Deal. Then, certainly from 1936 on, many newspapers became violently partisan once more, particularly when they were opposed to President Franklin Roosevelt's policies. It did not seem to matter, however; for the election returns apparently showed that newspapers were no longer molding public opinion.

That the *World* and the New York *Journal* of the eighteen nineties had not plumbed all the possibilities of popular journalism was demonstrated by another phenomenon of the age: the picture tabloid of the twenties. On the model of the *Daily News*, with which the publishers of the Chicago *Tribune* invaded New York in 1919, these were made up of a maximum of photographs and a minimum of reading matter. Some of the tabloids became daily "confession magazines" replete with faked photographs and the "diaries" of criminals, but these either were bankrupted or tamed by the thirties.

With the decline of personal journalism, the syndicated columnist replaced the editorial writer in the shaping of public sentiment and people took their political opinions from Walter Lippmann, Samuel Grafton, Walter Winchell, or Westbrook Pegler, as they had once followed Horace Greeley or Henry Watterson or Samuel Bowles of the Springfield *Republican*. Newspapers themselves were bombarded with and often published matter colored by the "public relations counsel" of the special interest groups which played an increasingly important part in American life. While the business of running a newspaper became more and more consolidated and efficient, and newspapers improved in variety and accuracy of specialized reporting, the newspaper met competition from other sources of information. The radio had the advantage of speed and immediacy in the presentation of news, but it still lacked detailed coverage.

The years between the wars saw a decline in the number of newspapers, although circulation continued at high levels. Among magazines, the shrinkage was less in number, for pulps were launched and died without being counted by any except specialists. But mortality was high in the "quality" field: the *Century, Scribner's,* and the *Bookman* disappeared. As the tabloids had been the principal innovation in newspaper publication during the twenties, the picture magazine was the novelty of the depression decade; greatest of these were *Life* and *Look*, each with circulations running into the millions. There also appeared weekly news magazines of which *Time* and *Newsweek* were outstanding.

The twenties had condensed world culture into a 5-foot shelf of books, astoundingly advertised and sold on easy payments. The thirties further reduced the burden of appearing intellectually alert by bringing the digest magazine into new popularity. The four million circulation of the *Reader's Digest,* with editions in Spanish, Portuguese, Arabic, and Braille, won such tribute of imitation that someone proposed a "digest of digests" to keep the earnest and busy abreast of their reading.

Whether it be magazine or successor to the old-fashioned dime novel, the "comic book" splashed raw color on newsstands during the thirties, and astonished Red Cross Grey Ladies reported it favorite reading among hospitalized Navy recruits during World War II. Fantasy, crime, and sadism were major elements in the more popular comic books; but psychologists were able to assure anxious parents that reading them would not make their children particularly neurotic. By the forties, the comic-book technique was being used skillfully to tell the story of the Bible, abstract novels, and present history soundly; the educators, following Wesley, refused to let the devil have all the good tunes.

Foreign observers like André Siegfried and native critics like H. L. Mencken agreed that the Puritan tradition survived in Machine-Age America. How otherwise account for the great membership in the Protestant dissenting churches, their evangelical zeal both abroad and at home, and the crusades these regularly fostered against the saloon and intemperance, cigarette smoking, and modern "immorality"? A count in 1930 found that the total number of church communicants was in the neighborhood of 50,000,000 persons, of whom 9,200,000 were members of the Baptist Church; 9,119,000 of the Methodist Church; 2,800,000 of the Lutheran Church; and 2,670,000 of the Presbyterian Church. In certain areas of the country, the South and trans-Mississippi West, particularly, evangelical Christianity was a living force. But, by and large, it may be said that during the whole period of the early twentieth century, the influence of the country's churches was very rapidly slipping. A number of reasons might be cited for this state of affairs: Protestant Christianity, particularly in the evangelical sects, was rent by the great doctrinal struggle between the Fundamentalists, who still clung tenaciously to the literal interpretation of the Bible, and the Modernists, who had surrendered that before modern science and the evidence of biblical scholarship. The inability of the Protestant churches to resolve their differences under the head of a real denominational union was another reason for a prevailing dissatisfaction with institutional religion.

The position of Catholicism, certainly in its outward aspects, seemed to be more secure. Its numbers and its institutional life were impressive: in 1930, the Catholic population of the country was in excess of 20,000,000 persons, of whom more than 2,000,000 were children in regular attendance in parochial schools; too, the Catholic hierarchy supported a ramified system of educational plants and eleemosynary institutions, and publicly avowed an advanced program of social action (though steadfastly conservative as far as divorce and birth control were concerned). The acceptance of the leadership of Rome made the faith conspicuous; nevertheless, the Church's influence on modern living was hardly commensurate with its numbers and the apparent devotion of its members.

Those trends were not much altered by the depression or the war. Church membership was reckoned at 72,400,000 by 1945; the Catholic Church gained 4,300,000 members, the evangelical churches made about the same percentage gains, but the Presbyterian and Episcopal denominations lagged. Church attendance fell off, yet apparently Americans yearned for faith. The more spectacular cults flourished. Frank Buchman of Iowa won numerous prosperous converts to his Oxford Groups. The novels of Lloyd Douglass and Scholem Asch, books like the *Return to Religion* and *Peace of Mind* all stood high on best-seller lists. Among Protestant intellectuals, Barth and Kierkegaard rose to new esteem; there was a widespread revulsion from institutionalized efforts at improving the natural man: man was inherently evil and he could not save himself. In much religious thinking, the emphasis tended to shift from morals to belief. For in a world torn by depression and social disintegration and war, man's relation to other men seemed beyond his control; his relation to God, on the other hand, he could maintain by himself and alone. Orthodoxy became almost fashionable as men sought a "cosmic guarantee of the most deeply held human values." Thus, poets like Allen Tate and T. S. Eliot returned to Anglican traditionalism and some public figures found refuge in the bosom of Mother Church. Yet that aspect of religion which admitted man's utter impotence did not win the great body of Americans.

SCIENTIFIC ADVANCE

Where the wonders the machine performed were on all sides plainly in view, one had no cause for surprise at the large part that science played in the life of modern America. The automobile, the airplane, the radio, the motion picture were but the more apparent triumphs of mind over matter in the nineteen twenties. The achievement of the thirties lay in improving existing machines and techniques rather than in introducing entirely new industries based on applications of science. Air-conditioning did become something of a fad during the decade, but it was not sufficient to have a tonic effect on the economy. Plastics, plywood, and other specialized synthetic materials were a more important contribution, and the field was stimulated by World War II in much the same fashion as the chemical industry had benefited from World War I. Rayon became a formidable competitor to both silk and cotton in the twenties; the later thirties produced the wholly synthetic nylon fiber; the forties hinted at commercial use for fibers made of casein, chicken feathers, and even peanut and soybean protein. War demand for rubber and insulating materials hurried the development of plastics as it hastened the development of the processing of raw materials from sea water, which had begun in 1934, when bromine was first extracted on a commercial scale. Costs apart, a modern chemist could make a new material or adapt an old one to fit almost any pattern of properties presented to him.

In the field of industrial technique, the assembly line of the twenties made all the world fear America's industrial competition. That technique improved during the thirties, when the continuous strip mill was introduced into the steel industry. Applied to the manufacture of ships, guns, and planes, mass-production methods made good a lack of previous intensive war preparation. Powder metallurgy, new uses for welding, and the use of electronics in industrial testing were significant wartime contributions to technology.

Medicine and public health advanced on many fronts between the wars. Sanitation improved. Greater knowledge of nutrition and higher incomes for at least part of the population gave more Americans better diets, yet deficiency diseases like scurvy, pellagra, and xeropthalmia became widespread during the thirties and uncounted children suffered from rheumatic fever. Examination of men of draft age showed that 31.4 per cent in the first group called were unfit for service; by December, 1944, 46.9 per cent of those summoned had to be rejected. Domestic workers, the unemployed, and farmers headed the list of those unable to serve; dental and eye defects, many preventable, further lowered the level of fitness.

Medical research pressed on to good effect, nonetheless. During the late thirties, drug therapy roused new interest as French and German chemists returned to the sulfanilamides, which had been discovered in 1908. The first sulfa drug was introduced into the United States in 1936, when Long of Johns Hopkins used it in meningitis. After 1938, American chemists developed new sulfa compounds less toxic than the original. To the sulfa drugs, with their potential dangers as well as their miraculously swift action, the war years added the antibiotics, penicillin, streptomycin, and tyrothrycin. If World War II was unique in destructiveness, it was also unique in the fact that comparatively few of its soldiers died of contagious disease, infected wounds, or shock. (During the 48 months of the Civil War 43,012 American soldiers died of wounds; the World War II total was 25,493 for 44 months of fighting.)

While the new drugs and "plasma" were entering the American vocabulary, the lay public began to read of "psychosomatics." The younger generation of the twenties had discovered Freud with delight; their shocked elders before long found a fillip to gossip in psychoanalysis. The thirties replaced the fad with a more solid interest; the war brought renewed concern for the nation's mental health. The total number of patients admitted to hospitals for mental diseases increased from 82,475 in 1934 to 102,104 in 1943; mental disease and inability to meet the minimum requirements of mental tests were the leading cause for rejections among both white and Negro draftees; mental disorders were the chief reason for military discharges.

Thus far, the practical aspects of American scientific progress have been stressed here. For, although American inventors have helped create the modern world, America's contribution to scientific fundamentals has been less significant. The seminal ideas—evolution, the atomic theory, relativity, quantum theory—are European. Willard Gibbs, the greatest scientific theorist of nineteenth-century America, had more influence in Europe than in his own country. Even in 1947, with science closely linked to national defense and more than $9 billion being spent on scientific work each year, only 17 per cent went for research as against development and only a fraction of that for fundamental study. Nevertheless, American science showed increased interest and accomplishment in basic research. The foundations supported by Carnegie, Rockefeller, and Guggenheim money, the Institute for Advanced Study, the universities and technical institutes, and even certain of the great industrial companies gave facilities for work in pure science. Out of such effort came Michelson's measurement of the velocity of light, Millikan's research on cosmic rays, and Thomas Hunt Morgan's studies in the mechanism of heredity. Richly-endowed observatories helped the United States take the lead in astronomical research. By the late thirties, that had given rise to new cosmologies. Hubble pictured an ever-expanding universe ending in nothing; Millikan and Tolman a universe expanding and contracting indefinitely.

In 1945, the nonvaluative approach, which had simplified life for so many scientists, encountered the atomic bomb. Unlike artists, who were often obliged to fight censorship, the pure scientists had followed knowledge for knowledge's sake without hindrance. The inventor and industrial scientist had long known that knowledge was not power. After 1945, the pure scientist began to learn the same lesson. Secrecy shut down on research in nuclear physics soon after 1939. Tension in international relations exerted strong pressure for the continuance of that policy and even for its spread into fields like bacteriology, with its nightmarish military possibilities. Politics demands secrecy and has the power to impose it. Scientific advance rests upon community of effort through publicity. Thus, paradoxically, an age more dependent on science than any before it may be taking the first steps on the road toward a new alchemy.

EDUCATION AND THE SOCIAL DISCIPLINES

Faith in education has long been an essential article in the American secular creed. Public education had become firmly entrenched in the American scheme by the end of the nineteenth century, and the next three decades were to mark a steady progress onward. School-attendance laws raised the compulsory school-going age until, in many jurisdictions, children through the age of sixteen were called upon to attend regular sessions. Plants were modernized so that often the local public school took on all the aspects of a great athletic and social center, with fully equipped gymnasium, auditorium, swimming pool, and the like; a ceaseless experimentation was carried on in curriculums and special projects. The twenties brought child behavior clinics into public school systems; activity programs began to be introduced in the thirties. Nevertheless, despite PWA grants for school buildings and WPA provision of special teachers' projects, elementary education suffered during the depression. The war prosperity which followed entailed social dislocation, pupil crowding, and a great loss of trained staff, as industry offered higher pay and freedom from the humiliating restrictions many communities imposed on their teachers' personal lives. Surveys during the early forties measured the deterioration: trained teachers left school systems and enrollment in teacher-training schools declined. Facilities were worst in the areas which produced the largest number of children, moreover; it was becoming increasingly evident that federal aid for elementary education could not be challenged much longer.

During the nineteen twenties, secondary education made striking advances. The half-million students attending high school in the United States had grown to an army of more than three-and-one-half million by the end of the twenties. The curriculum here underwent less radical changes: formal disciplines continued the rule, largely because the high school was still regarded as preparation for entrance into college; an entirely successful course of study had not yet appeared to meet the educational needs of boys and girls who were at school not by choice but because of the requirements of school-attendance laws and the inability to obtain employment in industry. By 1939, many educators had formulated the problem of secondary education as the need to fit the majority of young people for a variety of semiskilled occupations, rather than the few quasi-crafts of "vocational education." It was also important to combine that training with a general education which would equip these young people with the ability to make reasonably intelligent decisions as citizens and a more satisfying use of their leisure. Increased high-school enrollment after 1945 pointed up existing deficiencies and called attention to the lack of trained personnel and the deterioration of plant. Nevertheless, high-school education had become part of the American way and enthusiasm for the high school basketball team was often the most genuinely unifying factor in a community.

Nothing has been more interesting to witness than the unanimity with which twentieth-century America accepted a collegiate education as a prime requisite for future success, whether the chosen career was to be in business, politics, or the professions. In 1900, but 224,000 young men and women were in attendance at colleges and universities; by 1930, their numbers had swelled to more than 900,000. Eleven per cent of World War II draftees had had college training as against 5 per cent in 1917. Following the war, there was an extraordinary increase in the numbers attending colleges, the GI Bill of Rights being particularly helpful in this regard. By 1948, more than 2,340,000 were registered. Americans looked forward to tripling this number in another generation.

The entire pattern of the higher learning in America had been critically examined meanwhile. More and more, educators encountered the problem of liberal education in the United States: by classic definition, a liberal education is one proper to a free man; by that definition, a free man is one who need not earn his living. How then were the attitudes needed by the disinterested studies that help make effectively functioning citizens in a democracy to be equated with the demands and attitudes required of a man with his living to earn? During the thirties, Robert M. Hutchins of the University of Chicago became chief spokesman for new goals in education. As against the notion that "there is nothing true unless experimental science makes it so," he held that science could teach man nothing about his real interest—values. Contrary to American shibboleth, civilization was not a standard of living or a way of life but the deliberate pursuit of a common ideal. Hence, it was necessary to stress familiarity with the tradition of Western culture as set forth in its great books. These traditionalists rejected current emphasis on emotion and will as against intellect; they stood for reasoning, not experimentation, in the determination of social goals and, against the notion that the merit of an idea or belief was less significant that the fact that it was held, they supported a known hierarchy of values.

In reply, advocates of the scientific approach observed that European universities' concentration on the classics had not saved that continent. Modern psychology showed that human relations were governed by irrational emotional forces, which could be controlled by the intellect only if that applied a critical empirical viewpoint to the study of the personality and of the social sciences. The necessary common content for education could be found more readily in scientific method than in study of any merely literary canon.

The pressure of the war years, with their absorption of students, and their emphasis on mathematics and the physical sciences, sharpened the issue of synthesis as against vocationalism in education. The traditionalists had scored usefully, meanwhile. The better technical schools insisted that their students take a certain number of courses in the humanities and the social sciences. An increasing number of colleges—following the lead of Columbia College which had inaugurated such a program in 1919—were building their curriculums about integrated courses in the social sciences, the humanities, and the physical sciences.

The social sciences had accepted the scientific approach wholeheartedly during the nineteen twenties. Through the two interwar decades, the social scientists surveyed and described the world before them. The political scientists concerned themselves less with the nature of the state and more with the processes of government and group struggles for power. The sociologists rebelled against being confused with reformers and declared that no more than the physicists were they interested in "the ultimate destiny of the human race and the justice of the existing order." A new interest in human ecology made itself evident in the work of regional students like Odum, and the National Resources Planning Board undertook elaborate studies which might serve as raw material for future synthesis. In works like Robert and Helen Lynd's *Middletown* and *Middletown in Transition,* sociologists applied the methods of cultural anthropology to the study of contemporary America.

During the nineteen twenties, American economists displayed a generous eclecticism in theory and a genuine interest in describing the real world. Thomas Nixon Carver sang dithryambs to Prohibition and permanent prosperity in *Our Present Economic Revolution* and Wesley C. Mitchell added more facts to his work in the business cycle; the institutionalists also studied property as a legal concept and showed how political and social institutions shaped and were shaped by economic facts. Nevertheless, by 1928, one eclectic observed that economics would do well to organize its material and ideas if it was "to retain the semblance of a science." The depression brought a new interest in theory. Thorstein Veblen's work won a general audience through popularizations and wider influence in academic circles. Academic economics—at least, during the thirties—was also much influenced by the ideas of the Englishman, John Maynard Keynes. Seeking stability and full employment, Keynes placed too much emphasis on oversaving. To him, the Western world seemed to be already mature. The war and its aftermath—plus the hesitancies and fumblings of the British planned economy—caused a re-examination of the new doctrine. Continued savings were needed in a world filled with poverty; and the price mechanism—given a free market—still seemed a successful tool for making and distributing goods.

While the social scientists tried to measure and describe the world about them, American historians looked back upon time gone in new awareness that the past, as seen in historical writing, both reflects and illuminates the present. American historians did useful and notable work in many fields, ranging from contributions to the *Encyclopedia of the Social Sciences* and the *Dictionary of American Biography* to participation in such cooperative historical series as *A History of American Life, The Economic History of the United States,* and *The Rise of Modern Europe.* If the interwar period produced no narrative history to rank with the writings of Parkman or Henry Adams, it gave rise to a new outlook. More and more, historians took Terence's "Nothing human is alien to me," for their watchword. Economics and the new psychology helped deepen the historian's understanding of people and events. Increasingly, he turned to manners and the work of the mind for his material, producing books like V. L. Parrington's *Main Currents in American Thought* and Charles and Mary Beard's *The Rise of American Civilization.*

In the realm of formal thinking, John Dewey ranked foremost among Americans. It was his achievement to evolve a complete system out of that pragmatism whose principles had first been laid down by Charles S. Peirce and William James. For Dewey, logic was a tool or instrument to be used in the service of society and its problems, and no thinking was real that did not grow out of experience. As he himself put it, his philosophy stemmed from the "growth of democracy—the development of the experimental methods in the sciences, evolutionary ideas in the biological sciences, and the industrial reorganization." It was natural, therefore, that he should insist that the problem before us was the employment of ideas first in our adjustments to and then in the transformation of an empirical world.

Speculative and systematic philosophy declined in spite of the fact that the traditionalists in education held pragmatism in abhorrence and preached a return to Aristotle through St. Thomas Aquinas. The mathematical work of Whitehead and Bertrand Russell aroused much interest among philosophers, and the social implications of thinking were reexamined. Of the new currents, logical positivism joined forces with Dewey's instrumentalism, while semantics filtered down to inform the lay public that words are not always what they seem.

MUSIC, PAINTING, AND ARCHITECTURE

Music in America flourished as never before during the nineteen twenties. Not only was there a sound tradition alive, but every encouragement was given the native composer. Foundations nurtured him, symphony orchestras gave him a hearing, his intentions and achievements were as seriously studied as were those of other creative artists. If musical composition, in America, still lagged behind the other arts, it could not be claimed that neglect of the composer was the explanation. Yet the situation was full of hope and, as the result of the efforts of a number of serious workers in musical forms, there was every reason to believe that a true American music was in the process of emerging. The radio had created a wide audience for the classics. Meanwhile, WPA music projects brought living musicians to another audience in the thirties. Schools paid greater attention to music, encouraging both appreciation and expression; the level of musical taste improved. Nevertheless, it was in light and popular expression that American music had its greatest vitality. American composers did respectable serious work, but when they turned to the modern idiom they found themselves unintelligible to all but the relatively thin layer of the musically sophisticated; the great new audience which still had the classics to assimilate, had no ears for them.

Modern art had had a longer time to win favor in America. Most American painters went to France at the turn of the century; and whether they left our shores or not, they could not but be influenced by the teachings of Manet and his group and then Cézanne. This was not slavish imitation but a commendable understanding of the fact that the great Frenchmen had revolutionized modern art and had freed the artist from stultification. To work honestly with materials, to express the significance of the subject rather than its outward semblance, to concern oneself with form, color, and design without regard for dead formulas: these meant release. The result was the appearance of a goodly company of painters all of whom had learned this lesson well, all of whom, nevertheless, were distinctly American. Native artists launched on the bold experiments of postimpressionism, cubism, and futurism and sought to express that "significant form," which had become so truly the keynote of all the modern arts. Before the postwar decades were over, there had emerged a large body of contemporary painters and sculptors, and a notable group of craftsmen using other materials, whose work indicated that modernism was exactly fitted to the American temper. Municipal museums acquired their work, foundations sprang up to provide the gallery space for periodic displays, great industrial companies became art patrons, and Americans themselves had enough confidence in their taste to buy pictures for their homes.

French influence was balanced by the regionalism of John Steuart Curry and Grant Wood and by use of the American industrial scene as material for formal decorative design. The thirties introduced a new factor: the government as patron. The WPA art project began in 1935 and spent $10 million before it was liquidated in 1943. The project produced no outstanding new talents, but it did galvanize the art life of the nation: 90 art centers were established in areas where no galleries existed, artists were enabled to work where they lived and, most important of all, felt themselves accepted as sound workingmen rather than mere bohemians. In 1943, Congress refused to finance the Army's plan to send artists into the active theaters of war, however. Magazines took over some War Department commitments, but the most immediately significant work was done in photography and the cartoon. Nevertheless, as the United States moved into another postwar era, its artists had a renewed appreciation of a heritage that included the early "primitives," Ryder and Eakins and Mary Cassatt, John Sloan and George Luks and George Bellows. American artists could get their training in Wisconsin or Iowa, New Mexico or New York. Meanwhile, a revived hostility to modernism livened art criticism and prevented the modern school from ossifying into a new academicism.

Architecture did not break loose from the bondage of old forms until the first decade of the twentieth-century was over. In the eighteen nineties and even earlier, Louis Sullivan had seen the possibilities of steel-frame construction and purely functional building; but for a time, his lessons were forgotten along with the Whitmanesque largeness of his spirit. As buildings soared higher (under the impulsion of high ground rents) misguided architects sought to fetter the skyscraper. New vistas were opened largely because of an accident: in the midst of World War I, to prevent the growth of a city of perpetual twilight, New York's municipal assembly passed an ordinance requiring the "setting back" of tall structures after certain heights had been reached. With the resulting treatment of the skyscraper as a series of masses, in which the sparing decoration used was made to accentuate the vertical line, a new design emerged in which form, materials, and decoration were blended together to realize to the fullest the functional nature of the building. Even more startling in its implications was the work of Frank Lloyd Wright, a pupil of Sullivan and one of the great artists of modern times. Wright built houses, hotels, factories, and pleasure gardens, ever in keeping with his own dictum that "a building should be made to grow easily from its site, shaped to harmonize with its surroundings of Nature." He experimented with materials, he created revolutionary patterns: his was an ever-fruitful talent whose many bewildering forms gained the admiration of the contemporary world.

The depression ended the development of skyscraper design for a decade, but the architect found new opportunities in public building. For the first time, structure and ornament were viewed as a whole by more than a few practitioners. While the conflict between functionalist and eclectic continued, the former was gaining ground: few architects asked to plan a public library would now imitate a Roman bath. The architects of the thirties found fresh opportunity in home design, particularly on the Pacific Coast. The pressing need for shelter may halt the movement for style in other than costly structures, but the demand for beauty in building has become part of American life.

LITERATURE BETWEEN THE WARS

While American music, painting, and architecture were achieving a new maturity in the twenties and thirties, American literature continued to grow. The novels of Upton Sinclair, Jack London, and Robert Herrick in the early years of the twentieth century marked the break with the complacencies of the Gilded Age and the subservience of American writers to European models. Here were signposts: by concerning himself with American life the American novelist had something to contribute to the world's literature. This promise was fulfilled in the works of the generation which reached maturity in the nineteen twenties. Working in obscurity for almost twenty years, fighting censorship as he added slowly to an impressive shelf his *Sister Carrie, Jennie Gerhardt, The Financier, The Titan,* and *An American Tragedy,* Theodore Dreiser was compelled to wait until the twenties for universal recognition. Beneath the lumbering of his prose lay an extraordinary capacity for pity: the weak and poor men and women who filled his pages were held chained by circumstances and if they thrashed about helplessly, finally succumbing to their baser passions, theirs was not the blame.

Steeping himself in the manners, habits, morals, and speech of middle-class America, Sinclair Lewis produced a series of social satires that were, at the same time, examples of highly skillful reporting and of real imaginative writing. *Main Street* had vulgarized its men and women, turned them into empty drums, deprived them of sensibility and the capacity for honest expression: and on them rather than on society itself Lewis visited his disdain, scorning the village as it had been scorned in E. M. Howe's *Story of a Country Town*, in *The Man That Corrupted Hadleyburg*, and in Stephen Crane's *The Monster*. In 1930, Lewis was awarded the Nobel Prize for literature, the first American to be thus honored. During the depression decade, Lewis vented his displeasure upon the youngsters because, in their hunt for new answers, they too quickly abandoned the values of their elders. In the forties, he turned on Main Street once more, flaying off another patch of skin and adding new portraits to those that made *Main Street, Babbitt, Elmer Gantry, Arrowsmith,* and *Dodsworth* a gallery of Machine-Age Americans.

Sherwood Anderson, too, dipped deeply into American life. *The Triumph of the Egg, Horses and Men,* and *Winesburg, Ohio,* collections of the short stories in which he was at his best, were moving documents of simple people, frustrated by a too-hard objective world and driven into themselves. They sought expression in subterranean ways, sometimes their impulses became overpowering, and the result was a flash of aberrant conduct. Willa Cather was perhaps the finest novelist of this group, when judged by the rules of the literary craft. Her important books, *O Pioneers! The Song of the Lark, My Antonia, The Lost Lady, Death Comes for the Archbishop,* were finely plotted and their women characters, in particular, were drawn with a warmth and understanding for which there was no equal in contemporary literature. For all that he has ceased to be fashionable, James Branch Cabell was the finest stylist of the period and its outstanding ironist. *Jurgen* and *The Cream of the Jest* showed a mastery over materials that marked the truly great comic writer.

The thirties' chief contribution was the revival of social awareness, for the most pungent critics of American life during the twenties had disclaimed responsibility for action. In thwacking prose, H. L. Mencken, for example, lambasted the "booboisie" when it interfered with its betters' enjoyment of drink or of literature, but the same club beat the reformer about the ears. And the young men who had grown up during World War I felt so deeply betrayed that they made understatement a cult and guarded themselves against any emotions but those personal enough to be made trivial. Rather than endure American life—or oppose it—many took refuge abroad.

The expatriates returned after 1933. Devaluation of the dollar made life less comfortable abroad; as exchange dropped, the Lost Generation came back from Paris, Bali, Majorca, and Capri. Coincidentally, there followed a new discovery of America. In reportage like Walter Evans' *American Photographs* and Margaret Bourke-White's *You Have Seen their Faces,* in essays like Edmund Wilson's *American Jitters* and in the regional novelists, scarcely a corner of the United States escaped creative recording. William Saroyan and Pietro di Donato used their Armenian and Italian backgrounds for something more than a curiosity of local color. Negro writers came to a new maturity, writing of their white neighbors as well as of their own people, as Richard Wright did in *Native Son*. From the Georgia of Erskine Caldwell's *Tobacco Road* to Mari Sandoz' Nebraska, and the *Late George Apley's* Boston, every aspect of America was caught in fiction. James T. Farrell (following Dreiser) worked in the great tradition of naturalism, which edged over into social criticism as it had with Zola. That criticism expressed itself also in the "proletarian" novels of Grace Lumpkin, Fielding Burke, and Thomas Bell. Less rooted in theory although equally critical of his society was John Dos Passos. Meanwhile, in the spirit of *Moby Dick,* Thomas Wolfe wrestled mightily with his America. William Faulkner depicted a Mississippi as mythical as Cabell's Poictesme in a style that recalled the lesser Elizabethans. John Steinbeck produced the decade's *Uncle Tom's Cabin* when he wrote *The Grapes of Wrath*. More complete and successful as an artist, Ernest Hemingway caught, and half-created, the image of his generation in its disillusion, its self-protecting fear of reason, and its cult of action.

American poetry had burgeoned in the decade before World War I. By the twenties, the names of Edgar Lee Masters, Carl Sandburg, Vachel Lindsay, Edwin Arlington Robinson, and Robert Frost were more than items in an American catalogue, important only because they were native. Masters' bitter, revealing flashes of Middle-Western life; Sandburg's poems in praise of millions of men toiling in wheat fields and steel mills; Lindsay's rhythmic chants; Frost's quiet lyrics that gave meaning and variety to a rural New England almost forgotten by the rushing new age; Robinson's fine, muted narratives—these, when put together, formed a complete whole. Poets like T. S. Eliot, Robinson Jeffers, Hart Crane, and Archibald MacLeish explored a new world in a new language, for the influence of Eliot and Ezra Pound, which had revitalized poetic speech, also put that speech beyond the understanding of the average educated man. In *John Brown's Body,* Stephen Vincent Benet restored narrative poetry to the list of books that "sold," but he had no successors. As the growth of fascism capped war and depression with the threat of another holocaust, some of the poets repented of their indifference to social issues. MacLeish assailed the "irresponsibles." Ezra Pound tried to win his countrymen to fascism in footling treason from whose penalty the plea of insanity rescued him. Eliot abandoned American citizenship and the twentieth century for Anglo-Catholic royalism, to which he hoped to convert at least an élite.

Literary criticism, which so readily becomes criticism of life, was in lively health between the wars, if health can be measured by heat of polemic. To the straight-speaking of Randolph Bourne, succeeded the battle between H. L. Mencken and Stuart Sherman and then the Armageddon of the "new humanism." The thirties saw a revival of sociological criticism, with the Southern agrarians arguing for a pure criticism of pure literature as part of their attack on industrialism and all its works, while Granville Hicks and V. C. Calverton spoke for the Marxists. In fact, it was Marxism that captured the imaginations of many of America's younger critics during 1932–1937. But the Moscow trials disillusioned most, quenching enthusiasm for the philosophy of the Soviet Union and damping their zest for socialism.

America had a literature in the interwar period, as she had a music and an art. In each field, Americans did good work. In no field did they approach the achievement of contemporary Europeans—Proust, Joyce, Mann, Rolland, Picasso, Sibelius. And, in literature at least, no American of these decades reached the stature of Emerson, Whitman, Mark Twain, or Henry James. Yet appreciations ripened and taste grew. There was no reason to be ashamed of American achievement.

THE LEVEL OF POPULAR TASTE

In his deft and prescient fashion, Alexis de Tocqueville set forth the problem of American civilization: was the realization of essential social and political equality to mean the triumph of mediocrity in art and thought? Many Americans were ready to give an affirmative answer, in the twenties at least. Yet the significant accomplishments in every field of creative endeavor in the interwar period prove the growth of that sound taste without which the artist cannot flourish, however lofty his genius. What was interesting in America was the fact that support for art was not the peculiar prerogative of the wealthy: a great segment of the middle class had learned what sound artistic values really were. The result showed itself particularly in the common modes of daily living. The products of the machine were finally accepted for what they were instead of being tortured into meaningless aping of obsolete techniques. Industry called upon artists like Raymond Loewy to design or redesign its goods. And from the type of the morning newspaper and the format of a paper-bound detective story to the glassware of the Five-and-Dime, from the clean-lined modern stove to the pert shop window, the objects of common life increasingly met the demand that they be well-designed, not merely decorated. Everywhere in the great cities dinginess and crowding told of Lewis Mumford's paleolithic age of industry, but across that dinginess flashed quiet motorcars and shopgirls whose costumes showed that taste was no longer limited to the wealthy.

This was achievement; yet it would be a grave error to hold that it was thoroughgoing or even enough. Too many Americans still lived in the miserable dumbbell tenements of the Gilded Age, still worked in office or factory or even on the land without a sense of security, a feeling of the permanence of most essential things. Nevertheless, there was a growing public—or rather a series of publics—for all the arts. More people went to museums and bought good prints (which could be had for not much more than the cost of a really well-bound book) and listened to the best music of the past. If *Abie's Irish Rose* was a hit play of the period, it was no worse than *East Lynne; Life with Father* (which finally outstripped *Tobacco Road* in length of run) was certainly far better. Even when a favored form of artistic expression might be crude—as the educated musician considered "swing," for example—its votaries listened critically, compared and contrasted techniques and, half-unaware, prepared themselves for broader appreciation.

On all cultural levels, taste was paving the way then. The United States was not yet a nation where the automobile mechanic diverted his leisure with creative philosophic speculation. Yet it was a land where a seamen's trade union local could hold a reasonably creditable exhibition of paintings by its members, where universities maintained "artists in residence," and where even lesser industrial cities supported symphony orchestras. In the words a forgotten contemporary may have meant for de Tocqueville: "If it be said that this system has not hitherto produced as great men [as the European aristocracies] I reply that the plan of this nation was not, and is not, to see how many *individuals* we can raise up who shall be distinguished, but to see how high, by free schools and free institutions, we can raise the great mass of population." [1]

THE NEW AMERICA

Where do we stand at the conclusion of the first half of the twentieth century? In a hundred years America had traveled far. Just before the Civil War its economy was still largely agricultural and mercantile; its affairs were of little concern to the outside world and its part in international affairs an unimpressive one; its population was homogeneous, state intervention was virtually non-existent, its working force was unorganized, its business atomistic and owner-managed.

By 1949, American agriculture, industry, and finance dominated the

[1] Todd, John, *Hints Addressed to the Young Men of the United States.* (Northampton, Mass., 1844), p. 27.

world. Our institutionalism was complex: Business was Big, so was Labor, so was the state. The changes which the decades since the Civil War had brought are graphically indicated below. National income, and value of man-hour output rose enormously, while the work-week had been cut almost in half and employment, after reaching a plateau, seemed about to begin another climb. How those decades had affected the manner in which Americans earned their livings is also shown. Particularly significant is the shrinkage in agriculture and the parallel expansion of trade and the service industries and of professional and government employment.

Once again, we are indebted to The Twentieth Century Fund for permission to use material from *America's Needs and Resources*.

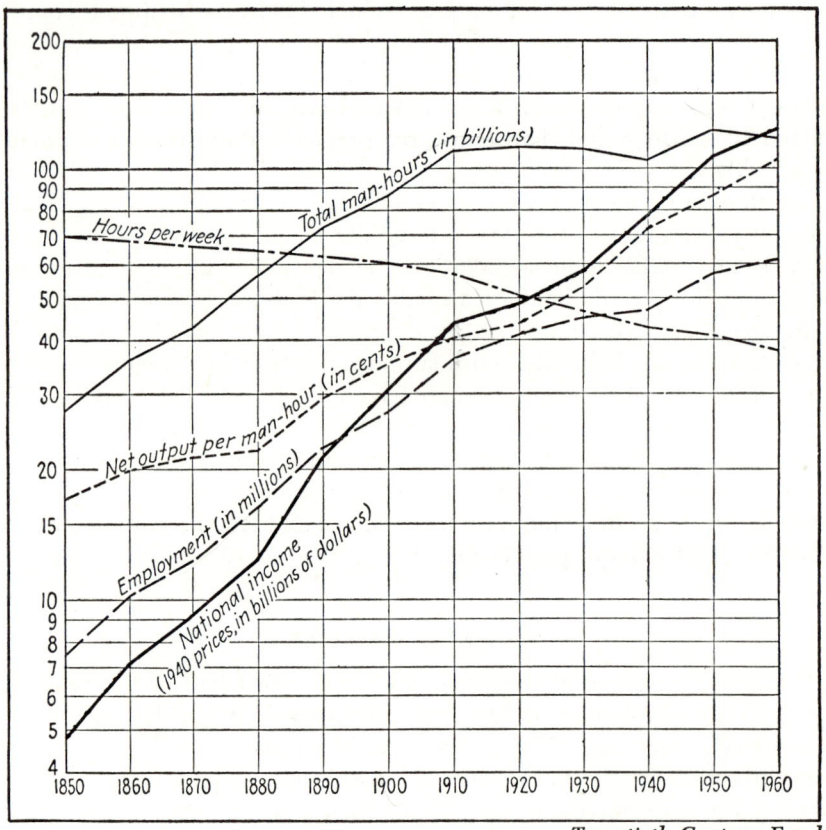

Twentieth Century Fund

TRENDS IN EMPLOYMENT, WORKING HOURS, OUTPUT PER
MAN-HOUR AND NATIONAL INCOME
1850–1960

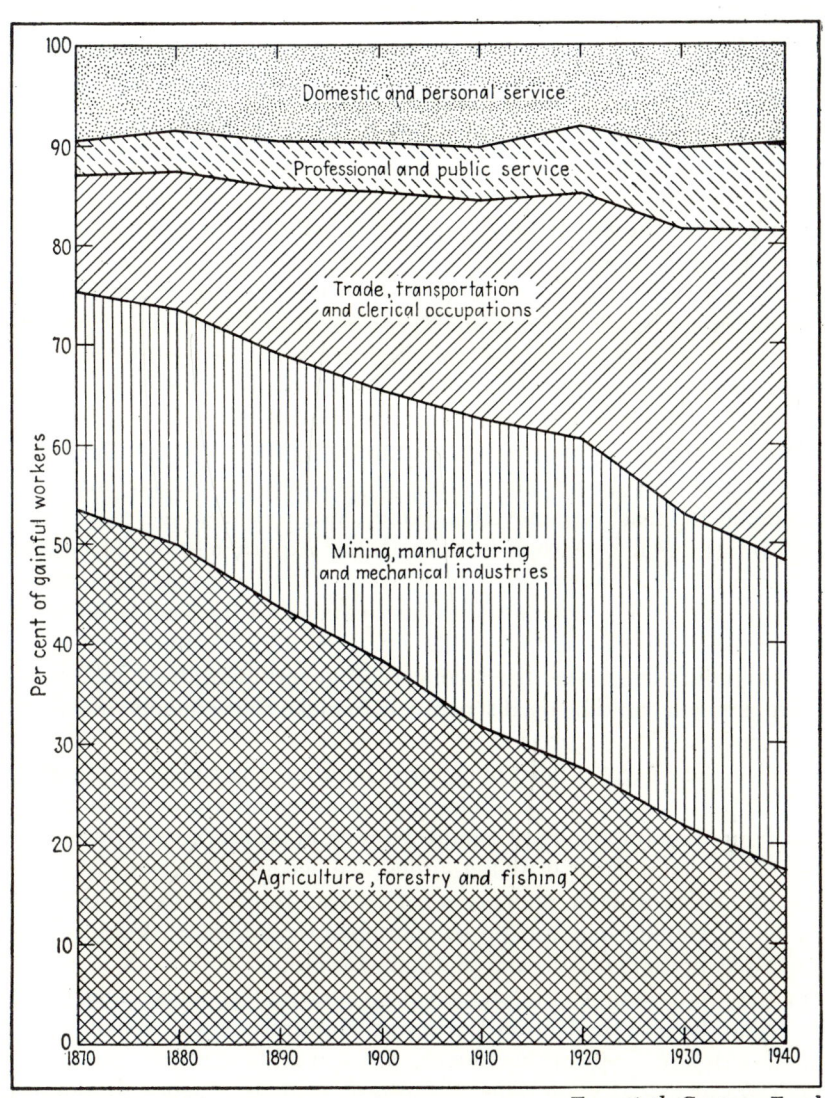

Twentieth Century Fund

**CHANGING COMPOSITION OF AMERICAN LABOR FORCE
1870–1940**

The outward shape of things everywhere had changed; not so the traditional values which had supported the American people through earlier years of uncertainty. Americans were still equalitarians, utilitarians, individualists, pragmatists. They still believed in the capacity and integrity of each person—spiritually and materially—to realize his full potentialities; they still believed in welfare; they were devoted to a deep-seated love for peace, and a willingness to let other peoples fulfill their own destinies. The preservation of individual rights, the maintenance of equality of opportunity, human betterment, a non-regimented world devoted to peace not war: these were the ideals Americans continued to accept in a world confused by a babble of ideologies.

Americans were not unaware of the instabilities of a free society: this was one of the prices freedom demanded. Pressure groups tugged and pulled—compromises had to be worked out. Redistribution of wealth and social security were proper interests of public policy—the interventionist state had to be accepted. Defense was necessary—great military budgets, with their threats of continued inflation, had to be faced. A free market system produced runaway booms and sharp depressions—a certain amount of planning, at the least contracyclical policy, was required.

But Americans had learned from the bitter experiences of the nineteen thirties. In the first place, they had learned that they could not live unto themselves alone. Their well-being was linked with the well-being of the whole world. In the second place, they had learned that monetary, credit, and fiscal policies were the direct concern of government; here, at any rate, was a tool which could be used sensitively to make the economic life a more orderly one.

The first lesson was a hard one: for it required the fullest political and economic participation in the affairs of peoples remote from our shores and alien to our thinking. And yet, could we remain secure, as we pushed upward our own standards of living, unless we accepted the world-wide indivisibility of prosperity and peace? This was the One World of which Wendell L. Willkie had spoken so courageously in 1943; Americans had come to accept that analysis and prediction as fact.

For they had come to understand how amazingly poor a great part of the world outside of the United States was. Hundreds of millions of workers labored with tools as primitive as were those in biblical times; standards of living were as low as were those of the serfs of feudal manors; millions of people annually died of starvation because of the dearth of transportation, because of floods, and because of the absence of machinery. The typical European and Asiatic peasant, using a cradle for harvesting, produced only 100 bushels of bread grain from a year's work. The typical American farmer, using a tractor-drawn combine, produced 2000 bushels. Before World

War II, the average annual income per capita produced was from $50 to $90 in most South American countries and in China; in the United States it was $525 per capita a year.

Mechanization was the key to the problem of dearth: for mechanization grew food, built roads and railroads, created water and sewage-disposal facilities, developed electricity and flood-control works, erected factories, and made possible schools, hospitals, and modern homes. But mechanization required capital; and the United States—thanks to its savings—was the only country capable of investing in great developmental projects abroad.

The cost of mechanization staggered the imagination. In the United States, capital investment per worker came to $6,000. In the Soviet Union, the cost of the change-over from primitive agriculture to industrial production—still at low levels—was $3500 per worker. If only 100,000,000 out of the 800,000,000 now gainfully employed workers throughout the world were converted into new industrial producers—laboring at manufacturing, transportation, and the service occupations—and if the investment per worker were only $2000, the cost would be $200 billion! Not all of this, of course, would have to be paid for in dollars or in other international currencies; a goodly part would be provided by domestic labor, raw materials, and internal funds.

But the contribution of the United States would be crucial. This was what Americans were facing up to; this was the new role America was assuming in the world; this was the broadening horizon. The world would be truly One World only if people could produce goods more efficiently and distribute their fruits more equitably; only if they could exchange their products and ideas freely; only if they were prepared to defend the sanctity of the individual's person and conscience; only if they were ready to develop and respect the notions of mutual regard and respect. These were the working principles of American life. Applied to the whole world, freedom, wellbeing, and security should be the realizable aspirations of all men everywhere.

Bibliography

TEXTBOOKS AND SERIES

General Texts Relating to the History of the United States Since 1865. The following *general accounts* cover the field of recent American history: Charles A. Beard, *Contemporary American History* (1914); Charles A. and Mary R. Beard, *Rise of American Civilization*, v. 2 (1927); Ray A. Billington, B. J. Loewenberg, and S. H. Brockunier, *United States; American Democracy in World Perspective* (1947); T. C. Cochran and William Miller, *Age of Enterprise* (1943); Harold U. Faulkner, *American Political and Social History* (5th. edition, 1948); J. D. Hicks, *American Nation*, 2 v. (1941); J. C. Malin, *An Interpretation of Recent American History* (1926); S. E. Morison and H. S. Commager, *Growth of the American Republic*, 2 v. (1942); D. S. Muzzey and J. A. Krout, *American History for Colleges* (1943); A. M. Schlesinger and H. C. Hockett, *Political and Social Growth of the American People*, 2 v. (1941). Among the works dealing with the United States since 1900, D. C. Dumond, *Roosevelt to Roosevelt* (1940); H. B. Parkes, *Recent America* (1941); and Harvey Wish, *Contemporary America* (1945) will be found useful.

The following texts concern themselves almost exclusively with the *economic history* of the United States and will prove valuable for purposes of supplementing the discussions of economic matters contained herein: E. L. Bogart and Ernest Kemmerer, *Economic History of the American People* (1947); D. R. Dewey, *Financial History of the United States* (rev. edition, 1928); H. U. Faulkner, *American Economic History* (5th. edition, 1943); E. C. Kirkland, *History of American Economic Life* (1940); Broadus and L. M. Mitchell, *American Economic History* (1947); F. A. Shannon, *America's Economic Growth* (1940); C. W. Wright, *Economic History of the United States* (1941).

The following texts have as their subject American *diplomatic* relations; they, too, will prove valuable as supplementary reading: R. G. Adams, *History of the Foreign Policy of the United States* (1924); T. A. Bailey, *Diplomatic History of the American People* (1946); R. J. Bartlett, *Record of American Diplomacy* (1947); S. F. Bemis, *Diplomatic History of the United States* (rev. edition, 1942); A. C. Coolidge, *United States as a World Power* (1908); C. R. Fish, *American Diplomacy* (rev. edition, 1923); W. F. Johnson, *America's Foreign Relations*, 2 v. (1916); J. H. Latané, *History of American Foreign Policy* (1927). Additional material, presented from the point of view of the individuals who shaped American foreign policy, will be found in *American Secretaries of State and Their Diplomacy* (1927–29), edited by Samuel F. Bemis; see particularly v. 7, 8, 9, and 10, which cover the activities of the Department from Seward to Hughes.

Among extended reference works, the *Dictionary of American Biography*, 21 v. (1928–44); the *Dictionary of American History*, 5 v. (1940) and the *Encyclopedia of the Social Sciences*, 15 v. (1930–35) are particularly necessary.

MORE DETAILED DISCUSSIONS. The following volumes of *The American Nation: A History* (1907–18), edited by Albert Bushnell Hart, will be found useful: v. 22, W. A. Dunning, *Reconstruction, Political and Economic, 1865–77;* v. 23, E. E. Sparks, *National Development, 1877–85;* v. 24, D. R. Dewey, *National Problems, 1885–97;* v. 25, J. H. Latané, *America as a World Power, 1897–1907;* v. 27, F. A. Ogg, *National Progress, 1907–17*. In *The Chronicles of America Series* (1918–21), edited by Allen Johnson, the following volumes present interesting discussions of special topics in recent American history: v. 32, W. L. Fleming, *Sequel to Appomattox;* v. 33, E. E. Slosson, *American Spirit in Education;* v. 34, Bliss Perry, *American Spirit in Literature;* v. 35, S. P. Orth, *Our Foreigners;* v. 37, H. Thompson, *Age of Invention,* v. 38, J. Moody, *Railroad Builders;* v. 39, B. J. Hendrick, *Age of Big Business;* v. 40, S. P. Orth, *Armies of Labor;* v. 41, J. Moody, *Masters of Capital;* v. 42. H. Thompson, *New South;* v. 43, S. P. Orth, *The Boss and the Machine;* v. 44, H. J. Ford, *Cleveland Era;* v. 45, S. J. Buck, *Agrarian Crusade;* v. 46, C. R. Fish, *Path of Empire;* v. 47, H. Howland, *Theodore Roosevelt and His Times;* v. 48, C. Seymour, *Woodrow Wilson and the World War;* v. 50, W. R. Shepherd, *Hispanic Nations of the New World. A History of American Life* (1927–46), edited by A. M. Schlesinger and D. R. Fox, stresses the social aspects in the development of the American people; the following volumes cover our period: v. 8, Allan Nevins, *Emergence of Modern America, 1865–78;* v. 9, Ida M. Tarbell, *Nationalizing of Business, 1878–98;* v. 10, A. M. Schlesinger, *Rise of the City, 1878–98;* v. 11, H. U. Faulkner, *Quest for Social Justice, 1898–1914;* v. 12, Preston W. Slosson, *Great Crusade and After, 1914–28.* The nine volumes of the *Economic History of the United States,* edited by Henry David, H. U. Faulkner, Louis M. Hacker, and others, will, when completed, present a full-scale American economic history: v. 5, Fred A. Shannon, *Farmer's Last Frontier: Agriculture, 1860–97* (1945); v. 8, George Soule, *Prosperity Decade* (1947); v. 9, Broadus Mitchell, *Depression Decade* (1947) have appeared.

Among graphic presentations of American history, *The Pageant of America* (1926 and later) edited by Ralph H. Gabriel is most detailed; see particularly: v. 3, R. H. Gabriel, *Toilers of Land and Sea;* v. 4, M. Keir, *March of Commerce;* v. 5, M. Keir, *Epic of Industry;* v. 11, S. T. Williams, *American Spirit in Letters;* v. 12, F. J. Mather, Jr. and others, *American Spirit in Art;* v. 13, T. F. Hamlin, *American Spirit in Architecture;* v. 14, O. S. Coad and E. Mims, Jr., *American Stage.* Among later presentations, the following are interesting: J. T. Adams, editor, *Album of American History,* 3. v. (1944–46), v. 3 covers the period 1853–93; Roger Butterfield, *American Past* (1947); L. M. Hacker, R. Modley, and G. R. Taylor, *United States: a Graphic History* (1937); Bellamy Partridge and Otto Bettman, *As We Were; family life in America, 1850–1900* (1946).

1: THE SMOLDERING EMBERS OF WAR

THE RECONSTRUCTION PERIOD. Excellent general discussions of various aspects of the problems of reconstruction will be found in these volumes: H. K. Beale, *Critical Year: A Study of Andrew Johnson and Reconstruction* (1930); Claude G. Bowers, *Tragic Era* (1929); C. H. Coleman, *Election of 1868* (1933); W. A. Dunning, *Essays on Civil War and Reconstruction* (1910) and *Reconstruction, Political and Economic* (1907); W. L. Fleming, *Sequel to Appomattox* (1919); G. F. Milton, *Age of Hate* (1930); *Studies in Southern History and Politics* (1914). For more detailed treatments, largely political in character, consult J. F. Rhodes, *History of the United States since the Com-*

promise of 1850, v. 6 and 7 (1906) and Ellis P. Oberholtzer, *History of the United States since the Civil War*, v. 1, 2, and 3 (1917–26). Documents illustrating the history of the period will be found in W. L. Fleming, *Documentary History of Reconstruction*, 2 v. (1906–7) and Louis M. Hacker, *Shaping of the American Tradition*, section VII (1947). Of interest for an account of the shaping of the Fourteenth Amendment is Benjamin B. Kendrick, *Journal of the Joint Committee of Fifteen on Reconstruction* (1914). The work of the Freedmen's Bureau is described in P. S. Pierce, *Freedmen's Bureau* (1904).

ANDREW JOHNSON AND THE RADICAL LEADERS. These volumes present the history of the period from the point of view of the leading actors. The Johnson biographies depict the much-maligned President in a favorable light: L. P. Stryker, *Andrew Johnson, A Study in Courage* (1929); R. W. Winston, *Andrew Johnson: Plebian and Patriot* (1929); G. H. Haynes, *Charles Sumner* (1909). R. N. Current, *Old Thad Stevens* (1942) is a sympathetic re-evaluation.

2: AFTERMATH OF VICTORY

BUSINESS SCANDALS. The following will give some notion of the nature of the business scandals that characterized the Reconstruction era: C. F. Adams, Jr., *Chapters of Erie* (1886); J. B. Crawford, *Crédit Mobilier* (1880); R. H. Fuller, *Jubilee Jim: The Life of Colonel James Fisk, Jr.* (1928); Bouck White, *Book of Daniel Drew* (1910).

RECONSTRUCTION IN THE SOUTHERN STATES. A notable series of scholarly treatises throws light on the processes of reconstruction and redemption in the individual southern states. The following will well repay examination: E. M. Coulter, *Civil War and Readjustment in Kentucky* (1926); W. W. Davis, *Civil War and Reconstruction in Florida* (1913); H. J. Eckenrode, *Political History of Virginia During Reconstruction* (1904); J. R. Ficklen, *History of Reconstruction in Louisiana Through 1868* (1910); W. L. Fleming, *Reconstruction in Alabama* (1905); J. W. Garner, *Reconstruction in Mississippi* (1901); J. G. de R. Hamilton, *Reconstruction in North Carolina* (1914); Ella Lonn, *Reconstruction in Louisiana after 1868* (1918); J. W. Patton, *Unionism and Reconstruction in Tennessee* (1934); J. S. Reynolds, *Reconstruction in South Carolina* (1905); F. B. Simkins and R. H. Woody, *South Carolina During Reconstruction* (1931); T. S. Staples, *Reconstruction in Arkansas* (1923); C. Mildred Thompson, *Reconstruction in Georgia* (1915). For Negro viewpoints, W. E. B. Du Bois, *Black Reconstruction* (1935) and A. A. Taylor, *Negro in South Carolina during the Reconstruction* (1924).

THE KU KLUX KLAN. For this subject, these books will prove useful: S. F. Horn, *Invisible Empire: the Story of the Ku Klux Klan, 1866–71* (1934); J. C. Lester and D. L. Wilson, *Ku Klux Klan* (1905).

FOREIGN AFFAIRS DURING RECONSTRUCTION. See titles cited under TEXTBOOKS AND SERIES, as well as the following: *Cambridge History of British Foreign Policy*, v. 1 and 2 (1922); W. A. Dunning, *British Empire and the United States* (1914).

3: PASSING OF THE SOUTHERN QUESTION

GRANTISM. A lively discussion of the scandals attending the Grant administrations will be found in D. C. Seitz, *Dreadful Decade, 1869–79* (1926); more sober is Allan Nevins, *Hamilton Fish: The Inner History of the Grant Administration* (1936). A modern biography is W. E. Woodward, *Meet General*

Grant (1928); a traditional one is L. A. Coolidge, *Ulysses S. Grant* (1917); W. B. Hesseltine, *Ulysses S. Grant, Politician* (1935) considers another aspect. For the Liberal Republican movement, see E. D. Ross, *Liberal Republican Movement* (1919) and Carl Schurz, *Reminiscences*, 3 v. (1909). Don C. Seitz, *Horace Greeley: Founder of the New York Tribune* (1926) and D. T. Lynch, *"Boss" Tweed: The Story of a Grim Generation* (1928), will prove useful for other aspects of the period. Particularly interesting is A. B. Paine, *Thomas Nast; His Period and His Pictures* (1904).

DISPUTED ELECTION OF 1876. The standard work on the subject is P. L. Haworth, *Hayes-Tilden Election* (rev. edition, 1927). H. C. Eckenrode, *Rutherford B. Hayes* (1930) presents Hayes in a sympathetic light. A. C. Flick, *Samuel Jones Tilden* (1939) and Allan Nevins, *Abram S. Hewitt: with Some Account of Peter Cooper* (1935) illuminate the Democratic side of the campaign. A political narrative is J. W. Burgess, *Administration of President Hayes* (1916).

THE NEW SOUTH. The following volumes treat various aspects of the South's development since reconstruction: B. W. Arnold, *History of the Tobacco Industry in Virginia from 1860-94* (1897); W. G. Brown, *Lower South in American History* (1902); C. R. Fish, *Restoration of the Southern Railroads* (1919); M. B. Hammond, *Cotton Industry* (1897); A. B. Hart, *Southern South* (1910); E. Q. Hawk, *Economic History of the South* (1934); W. B. Hesseltine, *South in American History* (1943); B. F. Lement, *Cotton Textile Industry of the Southern Appalachian Piedmont* (1933); W. H. Page, *Rebuilding of Old Commonwealths* (1902); F. B. Simkins, *Pitchfork Ben Tillman, South Carolinian* (1944); H. Thompson, *From the Cottonfield to the Cotton Mill* (1906) and *New South* (1919).

STATUS OF THE NEGRO. These books present the point of view of the white southerner: E. G. Murphy, *Problems of the Present South* (1904) and A. H. Stone, *Studies in the American Race Problem* (1908). And these represent the attitude of the Negro himself: W. E. B. Du Bois, *Souls of Black Folk* (1903); Booker T. Washington, *Story of the Negro* (1909) and *Up from Slavery* (1913). See also, C. H. Wesley, *Negro Labor in the United States, 1850-1925* (1927). Among political studies are P. Lewinson, *Race, Class, and Party* (1932) and W. F. Nowlin, *Negro in National Politics* (1931).

4: THE EMBATTLED POLITICIANS

GENERAL TREATMENTS. In addition to the volumes cited under TEXTBOOKS AND SERIES, these others may be consulted: H. T. Peck, *Twenty Years of the Republic* (1905), a stimulating historical work by an amused and literate observer; H. C. Thomas, *Return of the Democratic Party to Power in 1884* (1919); W. E. Binkley, *American Political Parties* (1943); E. E. Robinson, *Evolution of American Political Parties* (1924); E. M. Sait, *American Parties and Elections* (1927); Hannah G. Roach, "Sectionalism in Congress, 1870 to 1890," *American Political Science Review*, August, 1925; Ellis P. Oberholtzer, *History of the United States since the Civil War*, v. 4 (1931); Edward Stanwood, *History of the Presidency* (1898).

RECOLLECTIONS. The following are the memoirs of prominent personages of the period: James G. Blaine, *Twenty Years in Congress* (1884); G. F. Hoar, *Autobiography of Seventy Years*, 2 v. (1888); Hugh McCulloch, *Men and Measures of Half a Century* (1888); T. C. Platt, *Autobiography* (1910); Carl Schurz, *Reminiscences*, 3 v. (1909); John Sherman, *Recollections of Forty*

Years, 2 v. (1895). *The Education of Henry Adams: An Autobiography* (1918), is an American classic and indispensable to an understanding of the post-Civil War era.

BIOGRAPHIES. Consult these: A. R. Conkling, *Life and Letters of Roscoe Conkling;* G. F. Howe, *Chester A. Arthur* (1934); D. S. Muzzey, *James G. Blaine* (1934); Allan Nevins, *Grover Cleveland: A Study in Courage* (1932) and *Letters of Grover Cleveland* (1933); W. A. Robinson, *Thomas B. Reed, Parliamentarian* (1930); T. C. Smith, *Life and Letters of James A. Garfield*, 2 v. (1925); R. G. Caldwell, *James A. Garfield* (1931); J. A. Barnes, *John G. Carlisle* (1931).

5: THREE LEADING QUESTIONS BEFORE THE POSTBELLUM PARTIES

THE PROTECTIVE TARIFF. The economic histories cited under TEXTBOOKS AND SERIES present adequate accounts of American tariff-making. Special discussions, all of them excellent, are to be found in the following: P. Ashley, *Modern Tariff History* (1920); Thomas W. Page, *Making the Tariff in the United States* (1924); Edward Stanwood, *American Tariff Controversies in the Nineteenth Century*, v. 2 (1903); Ida M. Tarbell, *Tariff in Our Times* (1911); F. W. Taussig, *Tariff History of the United States* (rev. edition, 1931).

CIVIL SERVICE REFORM. These books give complete accounts of Civil Service reform and elaborate on the problems growing out of the federal personnel administration: Edward Cary, *G. W. Curtis* (1894); C. R. Fish, *Civil Service and the Patronage* (1904); Lewis Mayer, *Federal Service* (1922); A. B. Sageser, *First Two Decades of the Pendleton Act* (1935); D. H. Smith, *United States Civil Service Commission* (1928); S. D. Spero, *Labor Movement in a Government Industry* (1924); F. M. Stewart, *National Civil Service Reform League* (1929).

SPENDING THE SURPLUS AND REWARDING WAR VETERANS. See the economic histories cited under TEXTBOOKS AND SERIES for accounts of the problem of the Treasury surplus. Pension legislation is discussed in W. H. Glasson, *Federal Military Pensions in the United States* (1918) and J. W. Oliver, *History of Civil War Pensions* (1917).

6: RELATIONS WITH THE OUTSIDE WORLD, 1876–1896

GENERAL TREATMENTS. See the histories of American foreign relations cited under TEXTBOOKS AND SERIES. C. C. Tansill, *Foreign Policy of Thomas F. Bayard, 1885–97* (1940) and A. F. Tyler, *Foreign Policy of James G. Blaine* (1927) are good special studies. For American overseas expansion, presenting the point of view of American radicals, consult, Scott Nearing and Joseph Freeman, *Dollar Diplomacy* (1925).

THE UNITED STATES AND LATIN AMERICA. Special histories, all excellent, are the following: J. H. Latané, *United States and Latin America* (1920); Dexter Perkins, *Monroe Doctrine, 1867–1907* (1937); J. F. Rippy, *Latin America in World Politics* (rev. edition, 1931); G. H. Stuart, *Latin America and the United States* (1928).

THE UNITED STATES AND GREAT BRITAIN. The following are special treatments by prominent scholars: W. A. Dunning, *British Empire and the United States* (1914); *Cambridge History of British Foreign Policy*, v. 1 and 2 (1922); R. M. McElroy, *Pathway of Peace: An Interpretation of Some American and British Crises* (1927); R. W. Mowat, *Diplomatic Relations of Great Britain and the United States* (1925). The attitude of British travelers toward America is well presented in Allan Nevins, editor, *American Social History as Recorded by British Travelers* (1923). G. H. Payne, *England, Her Treatment of America* (1931) is an unfriendly recital of relations between the two countries by an American.

THE UNITED STATES IN THE PACIFIC. The following are special accounts, all reliable: J. M. Callahan, *American Relations in the Pacific and in the Far East, 1784–1900* (1901); Tyler Dennett, *Americans in Eastern Asia* (1922); John W. Foster, *American Diplomacy in the Orient* (1903); T. F. Millard, *America and the Far Eastern Question* (1909). See also: H. B. Morse and H. F. McNair, *Far Eastern International Relations* (1931) and Louis M. Hacker, *Shaping of the American Tradition*, section IX. For Hawaii, see: H. W. Bradley, *American Frontier in Hawaii* (1942); G. V. Burroughs, *Annexation of Hawaii* (1912); E. J. Carpenter, *America in Hawaii* (1899); R. F. Pettigrew, *Course of Empire* (1920); S. K. Stevens, *American Expansion in Hawaii, 1842–98* (1945).

THE TERRITORY OF ALASKA. Jeannette P. Nichols, *Alaska* (1924) is the standard account. J. M. Callahan, *Alaska Purchase and American Canadian Relations* (1908), and V. J. Farrar, *Annexation of Russian America to the United States* (1934) will also repay examination.

THE NEW NAVY. See the following: J. R. Spears, *History of Our Navy from its Origin to the Present Day, 1775–1897*, 4 v. (1897); E. S. Maclay, *History of the United States Navy, 1775–1901*, 3 v. (1898–1901); Bernard Brodie, *Sea Power in the Machine Age* (1945). Popular accounts are to be found in H. F. Kraft and W. B. Norris, *Sea Power in American History* (1920) and John D. Long, *New American Navy*, 2 v. (1903). In addition to the works by A. T. Mahan cited in the text, see his autobiography, *From Sail to Steam* (1907).

7: SETTLING THE CONTINENT

THE WEST AND THE FRONTIER. The classic account of the influence of the frontier on American institutions is F. J. Turner, *Frontier in American History* (1921), a collection of essays. *Turner Essays in American History* (1910) is by Turner's students and admirers. F. L. Paxson, *Last American Frontier* (1910) and *History of the American Frontier* (1924) are systematic discussions of real importance. For other aspects, see: H. E. Briggs, *Frontiers of the Northwest* (1940); Everett Dick, *Vanguards of the Frontier* (1940); W. J. Trimble, *Mining Advance into the Inland Empire* (1914).

THE PUBLIC DOMAIN. The standard history is B. H. Hibbard, *History of Public Land Policies* (1924); see also, R. M. Robbins, *Our Landed Heritage; The Public Domain, 1776–1936* (1942). Special treatments are to be found in John Ise, *United States Forest Policy* (1920) and *United States Oil Policy* (1926).

THE COW COUNTRY. E. S. Osgood, *Day of the Cattleman* (1929) is an authoritative work. See also: E. D. Branch, *Hunting of the Buffalo* (1929); J. H. Cook, *Fifty Years on the Old Frontier* (1923); E. E. Dale, *Cow Country* (1942) and *Range Cattle Industry* (1930); John A. Lomax, *Cowboy Songs* (1910); P. A. Rollins, *Cowboy* (1922); W. P. Webb, *Great Plains* (new edition, 1936).

THE INDIANS. General discussions are to be found in the following, all good: John Collier, *Indians of the Americas* (1947); Clark Wissler, *American Indian* (1922); R. Gessner, *Massacre: A Survey of Today's American Indian* (1931); L. B. Priest, *Uncle Sam's Stepchildren* (1942). The student might consult these books, as well: Frank B. Linderman, *American, the Life Story of a Great Indian, Plenty Coups, Sioux Chief* (1936); Luther Standing Bear, *My People the Sioux* (1928); O. O. Howard, *My Life and Experiences Among our Hostile Indians* (1907); T. Marquis, *Memoirs of a White Crow Indian* (1928); J. G. Neihardt, *Song of the Indian Wars* (1925); Mari Sandoz, *Crazy Horse* (1942).

THE PROBLEM OF IMMIGRATION. The best general discussions of the immigration question are to be found in these books: John R. Commons, *Races and Immigrants in America* (1907); H. P. Fairchild, *Immigrant Backgrounds* (1927) and *Immigration: A World Movement and its American Significance* (rev. edition, 1925); R. L. Garis, *Immigration Restriction* (1927); I. A. Hourwich, *Immigration and Labor* (1912); J. W. Jenks and W. J. Lauck, *Immigration Problem* (1913); Marcus L. Hansen, *Immigrant in American History* (1940); Peter Roberts, *New Immigration* (1912); E. A. Ross, *Old World in the New* (1914); G. M. Stephenson, *History of American Immigration, 1820–1924* (1926); Carl Wittke, *We Who Built America: The Saga of the Immigrant* (1940). Histories of special groups will be found in the following: K. C. Babcock, *Scandinavian Element in the United States;* T. F. Blegen, *Norwegian Migration to America, 1825–60* (1931) and *Norwegian Migration to America: the American Transition* (1940); M. R. Coolidge, *Chinese Immigration* (1909); A. B. Faust, *German Element in the United States,* 2 v. (1909); R. F. Foerster, *Italian Emigration of Our Times* (1924); W. I. Thomas and Florian Znaniecki, *Polish Peasant in Europe and America,* 5 v. (1918–20). Important documents will be found in E. Abbott, *Historical Aspects of the Immigration Problem: Selected Documents* (1926).

8: BUILDING THE RAILROADS

GENERAL TREATMENTS. Standard accounts are to be found in the following: W. S. Cunningham, *American Railroads* (1922); A. T. Hadley, *Railroad Transportation: Its History and its Laws* (1885); E. R. Johnson and T. W. Van Metre, *Principles of Railroad Transportation* (1921); Eliot Jones, *Principles of Railway Transportation* (1924); A. C. Laut, *Romance of the Rails,* 2 v. (1929); John Moody, *Railroad Builders* (1919); W. Z. Ripley, *Railway Problems* (1913) and *Railroads; Rates and Regulation* (1913). F. L. Paxson, *History of the American Frontier* (1924) discusses western phases of railroad development. Lewis Corey, *House of Morgan* (1930) is an authoritative account of the role played by J. P. Morgan in rail consolidations.

THE GREAT AMERICAN RAIL SYSTEMS. In the following biographical and scholarly works will be found standard treatments of the creation of the great rail systems: C. F. Adams, Jr., *Chapters of Erie* (1886); S. Daggett, *Chapters on the History of the Southern Pacific* (1922); J. B. Hedges, *Henry Villard and the Railways of the Northwest* (1930); G. Kennan, *E. H. Harriman* (1922); *Memoirs of Henry Villard* (1909); Oscar Lewis, *Big Four: The Story of Huntington, Stanford, Hopkins, and Crocker* (1938); E. P. Oberholtzer, *Jay Cooke, Financier of the Civil War,* 2 v. (1907); J. G. Pyle, *Life of James J. Hill,* 2 v. (1917); R. E. Riegel, *Story of the Western Railways* (1926); E. V. Smalley, *History of the Northern Pacific Railroad* (1883); A. D. H. Smith, *Commodore Vanderbilt* (1927); Nelson Trottman, *History of the Union Pacific* (1923).

CONGRESSIONAL AID TO RAILROADS. Consult: L. H. Haney, *Congressional History of Railways,* 2 v. (1910).

BIBLIOGRAPHY

9: THE NEW AGRICULTURE

GENERAL TREATMENTS. The best general history of American agriculture is to be found in the scholarly introductions, written by the editors, to the selections published in L. B. Schmidt and E. D. Ross, *Readings in the Economic History of American Agriculture* (1925). E. E. Edwards, "American Agriculture—the First 300 Years," U.S. Department of Agriculture, *Yearbook* (1940) is a good brief account. N. S. B. Gras, *History of Agriculture in Europe and America* (1925) contains a group of important chapters relating to the United States. The best special account is Fred A. Shannon, *Farmer's Last Frontier: Agriculture, 1860–97* (1945). R. M. La Follette, editor, *Making of America*, v. 5 *[Agriculture]* (1905), will be found useful. The articles in the *Encyclopedia of the Social Sciences* make a complete history of agriculture in the United States, see "Agriculture in the United States" and the cross references cited. Specialized discussions will be found in: T. N. Carver, *Principles of Rural Economics* (1911); H. N. Casson, *Romance of the Reaper* (1908); W. T. Hutchinson, *Cyrus Hall McCormick*, 2 v. (1930–35); Cyrus McCormick, *Century of the Reaper* (1931); H. W. Quitance, *Influence of Farm Machinery on Production and Labor* (1904); Leo Rogin, *Introduction of Farm Machinery in Its Relation to the Productivity of Labor in the Agriculture of the United States* (1931); Joseph Schafer, *Social History of American Agriculture* (1936); J. G. Thompson, *Wheat Growing in Wisconsin* (1909). The annual reports and *Yearbooks* of the U.S. Department of Agriculture for 1872, 1899, 1921–25, and 1940 have important articles relating to agricultural history. E. E. Edwards, *Bibliography of the History of American Agriculture*, Bibliographical Contribution 32, U.S. Department of Agriculture (1939) is a serviceable guide.

COTTON. M. B. Hammond, *Cotton Industry* (1897), is a standard account. Consult, also: R. P. Brooks, *Agrarian Revolution in Georgia, 1865–1912* (1914); C. W. Burkett and C. H. Poe, *Cotton* (1906); J. A. B. Scherer, *Cotton as a World Power* (1916); R. B. Vance, *Human Factors in Cotton Culture* (1929).

THE FARMERS' DILEMMA. Scholarly recitals of the first importance, throwing light on the bases of agrarian discontent, will be found in: S. J. Buck, *Granger Movement* (1913) and *Agrarian Crusade* (1921); John D. Hicks, *Populist Revolt: A History of the Farmers' Alliance and the People's Party* (1931). Everett Dick, *Sod-House Frontier, 1854–90* (1937) is a colorful narrative of the collapse of the western boom. F. A. Shannon, *Farmer's Last Frontier: Agriculture, 1860–97* (1945) deals with the entire problem in perspective. Contemporary accounts that will repay reading, are: A. F. Bentley, *Condition of the Western Farmer* (1893); J. R. Elliott, *American Farms* (1890); W. G. Moody, *Land and Labor in the United States* (1883); W. A. Peffer, *Farmer's Side: His Troubles and Their Remedy* (1891).

10: THE NEW INDUSTRIALISM

GENERAL TREATMENTS. In addition to the economic histories cited under TEXTBOOKS AND SERIES, consult: D. A. Wells, *Recent Economic Changes* (1889) and C. D. Wright, *Industrial Evolution of the United States* (1895), the work of competent economists living during the post-Civil War era. See also: V. S. Clark, *History of Manufactures in the United States*, v. 2 and 3 (rev. edition, 1929); B. J. Hendrick, *Age of Big Business* (1919); National Industrial Conference Board, *Graphic Analysis of the Census of Manufactures, 1849–1919* (1923). For the history of inventions, see: W. Kaempffert, editor, *Popu-*

lar History of American Invention, 2 v. (1924); H. Thompson, *Age of Invention* (1921). Malcolm MacLaren, *Rise of the Electrical Industry During the Nineteenth Century* (1943) and D. B. Steinman, *Builders of the Bridge: the Story of John Roebling and his Son* (1945) deal with particular advances. Gustavus Myers, *History of the Great American Fortunes*, 3 v. (1910) will be found interesting if considerably hostile in tone.

STEEL. J. Russell Smith, *Story of Iron and Steel* (1908) and H. N. Casson, *Romance of Steel* (1907) are good general accounts. Lewis Corey, *House of Morgan* (1930) presents a good treatment of the formation of the United States Steel Corporation; on this point, see also, section IX of Louis M. Hacker, *Shaping of the American Tradition*. Biographies of the great steelmasters will be found in Andrew Carnegie, *Autobiography* (1920); George Harvey, *Henry Clay Frick, The Man* (1928); Ida M. Tarbell, *Life of Elbert Gary* (1928).

ECONOMIC LAISSEZ-FAIRE AND THE SUPREME COURT. The following books throw important light on the role of the Supreme Court in our modern American political and economic life: R. E. Cushman, *Leading Constitutional Decisions* (1925); Benjamin B. Kendrick, *Journal of the Joint Committee of Fifteen on Reconstruction* (1914); M. C. Klinkhamer, *Edward Douglas White, Chief Justice of the United States* (1943); Gustavus Myers, *History of the Supreme Court of the United States* (1912); Carl Swisher, *Stephen J. Field, Craftsman of the Law* (1930); Charles Warren, *Supreme Court in United States History*, 3 v. (1922). For the significance of the idea of laissez-faire, see: J. R. Commons, *Legal Foundations of Capitalism* (1924); R. H. Gabriel, *Course of American Democratic Thought* (1940); C. E. Merriam, *American Political Ideas, 1867–1917* (1920). For the writing of the Fourteenth Amendment, see: H. J. Graham, "The 'Conspiracy Theory' of the Fourteenth Amendment," *Yale Law Journal*, XLVII (1938) and XLVIII (1938).

11: MONEY AND TRADE

GENERAL TREATMENTS. See the economic histories cited under TEXTBOOKS AND SERIES. The following are standard presentations: A. D. Noyes, *Forty Years of American Finance* (1909); A. B. Hepburn, *History of Coinage and Currency in the United States* (rev. edition, 1924); C. J. Bullock, *Essays on the Monetary History of the United States* (1900); Henry Clews, *Twenty-eight Years in Wall Street* (1888).

THE RESUMPTION OF SPECIE PAYMENTS. The outstanding discussion of the subject is W. C. Mitchell, *History of the Greenbacks* (1905). D. C. Barrett, *Greenbacks and Resumption of Specie Payments, 1862–79* (1931) and M. S. Wildman, *Money Inflation in the United States* (1905) are also important.

THE SILVER CONTROVERSY. Of the vast literature on this subject, the following summarize best the nature of the controversy that raged in America: F. W. Taussig, *Silver Situation in the United States* (1892); J. L. Laughlin, *History of Bimetallism in the United States* (1897); W. J. Lauck, *Causes of the Panic of 1893* (1907). For two popular treatments, see H. T. Peck, *Twenty Years of the Republic* (1905); Mark Sullivan, *Our Times: The United States*, v. 1 (1926).

FOREIGN TRADE. An exhaustive presentation will be found in E. R. Johnson and others, *History of the Domestic and Foreign Commerce of the United States*, v. 2 (1915). See also, G. M. Fisk and P. S. Pierce, *International Commercial Policies with Special Reference to the United States* (1923). Indispensable to an understanding of the whole subject of balance of international payments is C. J. Bullock and others, "Balance of Trade in the United States," *Review of*

Economic Statistics (July, 1919). For foreign capital in the United States see, Louis M. Hacker, *Shaping of the American Tradition*, section VIII.

THE AMERICAN MERCHANT MARINE. The following will prove helpful: W. L. Marvin, *American Merchant Marine* (1902); W. W. Bates, *American Marine* (1892); F. C. Bowen, *Century of Atlantic Travel, 1830–1930* (1931).

12: THE ORGANIZED WORKERS

GENERAL TREATMENTS. The standard history of American labor is John R. Commons and associates, *History of Labour in the United States*, 2 v. (1918). With this should be used John R. Commons and others, editors, *Documentary History of American Industrial Society*, v. 5–10 [1820–80] (1910–11); John R. Commons, editor, *Trade Unionism and Labor Problems* (1905). Other outstanding treatments are these: R. F. Hoxie, *Trade Unionism in the United States* (1917); Selig Perlman, *History of Trade Unionism in the United States* (1922); F. T. Carlton, *History and Progress of Organized Labor* (1920).

THE KNIGHTS OF LABOR. R. T. Ely, *Labor Movement in America* (1886) is the first authoritative account. T. V. Powderly, *Thirty Years of Labor* (1889) and *The Path I Trod* [edited by H. J. Carman, Henry David and P. H. Guthrie] (1940) are records by the order's leader. For modern accounts see, D. D. Lescohier, "Knights of St. Crispin," *University of Wisconsin Economic and Political Science Series*, v. 7, no. 1 (1910) and N. J. Ware, *Labor Movement in the United States, 1860–95* (1929).

CRAFT UNIONISM. The autobiography of Samuel Gompers, *Seventy Years of Life and Labor*, 2 v. (1895) describes the founding of the American Federation of Labor. See also, John Mitchell, *Organized Labor* (1903); Elsie Glück, *John Mitchell* (1929).

VIOLENCE. The best account of the struggles between capital and labor is Louis Adamic, *Dynamite: The Story of Class Violence in America* (1931). See E. Berman, *Labor Disputes and the President of the United States* (1924) for particular references to the railroad strikes of the seventies and the great Pullman strike. R. A. Allen, *Great Southwest Strike* (1942) deals with the railroad strikes of 1886; Almont Lindsey, *Pullman Strike* (1943) with the conflict of 1894. Henry David, *History of the Haymarket Affair* (1936) is a detailed account of the Haymarket Square explosion. J. W. Coleman, *Molly Maguire Riots* (1936), Marvin W. Schlegel, *Franklin B. Gowen: Ruler of the Reading* (1948) and J. T. Buchanan, *Story of a Labor Agitator* (1903) present other aspects of the Neanderthal period in American industrial relations.

13: AMERICAN LIFE, LETTERS, AND ART, 1865–1900

GENERAL TREATMENTS. The best discussion, in short compass, is Charles A. and Mary R. Beard, *Rise of American Civilization*, v. 2, ch. xxv (1927). An extended modern treatment is Merle Curti, *Growth of American Thought* (1943). The student should also consult: *Education of Henry Adams: An Autobiography* (1918); W. C. Ford, editor, *Letters of Henry Adams* (1930); Hamlin Garland, *Son of the Middle Border* (1917). Thomas Beer, *Mauve Decade* (1916) is a brilliant study of the eighteen nineties. A. W. Calhoun, *Social History of the American Family*, 3 v. (1917–1919) and Alma Lutz, *Created Equal: A Biography of Elizabeth Cady Stanton, 1815–1902* (1940) consider the other half of the human race; M. P. Ravenel, editor, *Half Century of Public Health* (1921), deals with impacts of urbanization.

BIBLIOGRAPHY

EDUCATION. For special treatments, see: E. P. Cubberley, *Public Education in the United States* (1919); E. W. Knight, *Influence of Reconstruction on Education in the South* (1913); E. C. Moore, *Fifty Years of American Education* (1917); Thomas Woody, *History of Women's Education in the United States*, 2 v. (1929).

RELIGION. W. W. Sweet, *Story of Religions in America* (1930) is a competent general study. C. H. Hopkins, *Rise of the Social Gospel in American Protestantism, 1865–1915* (1940); Walter Rauschenbusch, *Christianity and the Social Crisis* (1907) and A. M. Schlesinger, "A Critical Period in American Religion, 1875–1900," *Proceedings of the Massachusetts Historical Society*, LXIV (June, 1932) are significant special works.

PHILANTHROPY. A. G. Warner and others, *American Charities and Social Work* (rev. edition, 1930) is the standard discussion. Jane Addams and others, *Philanthropy and Social Progress* (1893) is a collection of papers by early leaders in the new charity. Jane Addams, *Twenty Years of Hull House* (1910) is a personal recital. For pictures of slum living, see: Jacob Riis, *How the Other Half Lives* (1890); R. A. Woods and others, *Poor in Great Cities* (1896).

JOURNALISM. The following are standard histories: W. G. Bleyer, *Main Currents of American Journalism* (1927); F. L. Mott, *American Journalism* (1941) and *History of American Magazines*, v. 3 (1930–38). See also: Rollo Ogden, editor, *Life and Letters of Edwin Lawrence Godkin*, 2 v. (1907); Don C. Seitz, *Joseph Pulitzer, His Life and Letters* (1924); J. K. Winkler, *W. R. Hearst: An American Phenomenon* (1928).

SCHOLARSHIP AND THOUGHT. H. W. Schneider, *History of American Philosophy* (1947); W. Riley, *American Thought from Puritanism to Pragmatism* (1915); and R. W. Gabriel, *Course of American Democratic Thought* (1940) are good introductions. For special aspects, see: Samuel Chuggerman, *Lester F. Ward* (1939); E. S. Dana, *Century of Science in America* (1918); E. H. Haight, and J. M. Taylor, *Vassar* (1915); Richard Hofstadter, *Social Darwinism in American Thought* (1945); Sidney Hook, *John Dewey* (1939); B. J. Loewenberg, "Darwinism Comes to America, 1858–1900," *Mississippi Valley Historical Review*, XXVIII (December, 1941); W. C. Mitchell, editor, *What Veblen Taught* (1936); R. B. Perry, *Thought and Character of William James*, 2 v. (1935); E. D. Ross, *Democracy's College* (1942); Muriel Rukeyser, *Willard Gibbs* (1942); H. E. Starr, *William Graham Sumner* (1925); Thorstein Veblen, *Higher Learning in America* (1918); C. F. Thwing, *History of Higher Education in the United States* (1906).

LITERATURE. V. L. Parrington, *Beginnings of Critical Realism in America, 1860–1920* [v. 3 of *Main Currents in American Thought* (1927–30)] is an outstanding work of sociological criticism. Oscar Cargill, *Intellectual America* (1941) deals with intellectual impacts. The writings of Van Wyck Brooks and Lewis Mumford must be read for a true understanding of the Gilded Age; see, in particular: Van Wyck Brooks, *Ordeal of Mark Twain* (1920) and *Pilgrimage of Henry James* (1925); Lewis Mumford, *Sticks and Stones* (1924) and *Brown Decades: A Study of the Arts in America, 1865–95* (1931). Matthew Josephson, *Portrait of the Artist as American* (1930) is a suggestive study. Consult also, for special topics, *Cambridge History of American Literature*, v. 3 and 4 (1917–21). Reading E. E. Howe, *Story of a Country Town;* Mark Twain, *Man That Corrupted Hadleyburg;* and Stephen Crane, *Blue Hotel* and *The Monster* will be illuminating experiences.

ART AND ARCHITECTURE. See, for this topic, the books of Lewis Mumford, mentioned above, and Suzanne La Follette, *Art in America* (1929), an admirable presentation. The following also may be consulted: S. Cheney, *New World Architecture;* C. H. Caffin, *Story of American Painting* (1905); Lorado Taft, *History of American Sculpture* (1903).

MUSIC. J. T. Howard, *Our American Music* (1931) and L. C. Elson, *History of American Music* (1925) are good presentations. W. Damrosch, *My Musical Life* (1923) and D. E. Russell, *American Orchestra and Theodore Thomas* (1927) use the biographical approach.

THE THEATER. See: H. H. Quinn, *History of American Drama from the Civil War to the Present Day* (1927) and J. R. Towse, *Sixty Years of the Theatre* (1916).

14: CURBING THE RAILROADS: THE INTERSTATE COMMERCE ACT OF 1887

SPRINGS OF WESTERN UNREST. See titles cited in Chapter IX. THE NEW AGRICULTURE, section: *The Farmers' Dilemma.*

EVOLUTION OF FEDERAL CONTROL. See Titles cited in Chapter VIII. BUILDING THE RAILROADS, section: *General Treatments* and also, 49th Congress, 1st Session, Senate *Report* No. 46; I. F. Sharfman, *Interstate Commerce Commission,* 3 v. (1931–35).

15: THE SHERMAN ANTITRUST LAW

GENERAL TREATMENTS. The following volumes are important for an understanding of the trust problem: B. J. Hendrick, *Age of Big Business* (1919); Eliot Jones, *Trust Problem in the United States* (1921); John Moody, *Masters of Capital* (1919) and *Truth about the Trusts* (1904); W. Z. Ripley, editor, *Trusts, Pools, and Corporations* (1905); H. R. Seager and Charles A. Gulick, Jr., *Trust and Corporation Problems* (1929); C. R. Van Hise, *Concentration and Control* (1912).

THE STANDARD OIL COMPANY. The following are classic accounts of the formation and early history of this monopoly: H. D. Lloyd, *Wealth Against Commonwealth* (1894); Ida M. Tarbell, *History of the Standard Oil Company,* 2 v. (1904). See also, Allan Nevins, *John D. Rockefeller,* 2 v. (1940).

THE WRITING OF THE SHERMAN ANTITRUST LAW. For special accounts, see: O. W. Knauth, *Policy of the United States Towards Industrial Monopoly* (1914); A. H. Walker, *History of the Sherman Law* (1910); Edward Berman, *Labor and the Sherman Act* (1930).

16: AGRARIAN REVOLT: GREENBACKISM, POPULISM, AND THE ELECTION OF 1896

GREENBACKISM. For special treatments, see Nathan Fine, *Labor and Farmer Parties in the United States* (1928); F. E. Haynes, *Third Party Movements since the Civil War* (1916) and *James Baird Weaver* (1919); G. H. Knowles, *Presidential Campaign of 1892* (1942); Ellis B. Usher, *Greenback Movement of 1875–84* (1911); F. P. Weberg, *Background of the Panic of 1893* (1929); M. S. Wildman, *Money Inflation in the United States* (1905).

POPULISM. An excellent discussion, covering every aspect of the question, is John D. Hicks, *Populist Revolt: A History of the Farmers' Alliance and the People's Party* (1931). See also: W. B. Bizzell, *Green Uprising: An Historical Survey of Agrarianism* (1926); S. J. Buck, *Agrarian Crusade* (1921). More detailed works, on special phases of the farmer agitation, are these: A. M. Arnett, *Populist Movement in Georgia* (1922); E. N. Barr, "The Populist Uprising," *Standard History of Kansas and Kansans,* v. 2 (1918); J. B. Clark, *Populism in Alabama*

(1927); R. C. Martin, *People's Party in Texas* (1933); F. B. Simkins, *Tillman Movement in South Carolina* (1926); C. V. Woodward, *Tom Watson: Agrarian Rebel* (1938). The following scholarly articles merit examination: Benjamin B. Kendrick, "Agrarian Discontent in the South, 1880–90," *American Historical Association Reports* (1920); Hallie Farmer, "Economic Background of Frontier Populism," *Mississippi Valley Historical Review* (March, 1924) and "Economic Background of Southern Populism," *South Atlantic Quarterly* (January, 1930); C. R. Miller, "Background of Populism in Kansas," *Mississippi Valley Historical Review* (March, 1925). The following are contemporary accounts: F. L. McVey, "Populist Movement," American Economic Association, *Economic Studies*, v. 1 (1896); W. A. Peffer, *Farmer's Side* (1891). See, also, C. A. Lloyd, *Henry D. Lloyd*, 2 v. (1912) and Louis M. Hacker, *Shaping of the American Tradition*, section IX.

THE ELECTION OF 1896. Good general discussions will be found in H. T. Peck, *Twenty Years of the Republic* (1905); E. E. Robinson, *Evolution of American Political Parties* (1924); Mark Sullivan, *Our Times: the United States*, v. 1 (1896). The following are good biographies of the leading actors in the famous campaign: Thomas Beer, *Hanna* (1929); Herbert Croly, *Marcus Alonzo Hanna* (1912); Paxton Hibben, *Peerless Leader: William Jennings Bryan* (1929); J. C. Long, *Bryan: The Great Commoner* (1928); M. R. Werner, *Bryan* (1929); C. S. Olcott, *William McKinley*, 2 v. (1916). W. J. Bryan, *First Battle* (1896) is the Democratic candidate's own story of the contest. See, also: H. L. Stoddard, *As I Knew Them* (1927); C. W. Thompson, *Presidents I've Known* (1929).

17: REPUBLICANISM TRIUMPHANT

THE MCKINLEY ADMINISTRATION. For the making of the Tariff Act of 1897, see the titles cited in Chapter V, THREE LEADING QUESTIONS BEFORE THE POSTBELLUM PARTIES, section *The Protective Tariff*. Consult, also, J. F. Rhodes, *McKinley and Roosevelt Administrations* (1922).

POLITICAL AND ECONOMIC INTERESTS IN CUBA. The standard account is L. H. Jenks, *Our Cuban Colony: A Study in Sugar* (1928). C. E. Chapman, *History of the Cuban Republic* (1927), is a political narrative. W. S. Robertson, *Hispanic-Relations with the United States* (1923) should be consulted. See also, E. F. Atkins, *Sixty Years in Cuba* (1926).

EVENTS LEADING UP TO THE WAR WITH SPAIN. E. J. Benton, *International Law and Diplomacy of the Spanish American War* (1908); F. E. Chadwick, *Relations of the United States and Spain*, 3 v. (1909–11), is the standard account. Orestes Ferrara, *Last Spanish War* (1937); W. L. Langer, *Diplomacy of Imperialism, 1890–1902*, 2 v. (1935); J. W. Pratt, *Expansionists of 1898* (1936) are special studies. A sprightly narrative, yet correct in all particulars, is Walter Millis, *Martial Spirit: A Study of Our War with Spain* (1931). See, also, Thomas Beer, *Mauve Decade* (1926); *America of Yesterday as Reflected in the Journal of John Davis Long* (1923); Louis M. Hacker, "The Holy War of 1898," *American Mercury* (November, 1930).

18: A SHORT AND GLORIOUS WAR

THE CONDUCT OF THE WAR. A history of the whole conflict, in one volume, is Walter Millis, *Martial Spirit* (1931). For the part played by the Navy, see: G. W. Dewey, *Autobiography* (1913); J. D. Long, *New American Navy*, 2 v. (1903); A. T. Mahan, *Lessons of the War with Spain* (1899). For the part played by the Army, see: Nelson A. Miles, *Serving the Republic* (1911); R. A.

Alger, *Spanish-American War* (1901); Theodore Roosevelt, *Rough Riders* (1899).

ATTITUDE OF THE EUROPEAN POWERS. See: L. B. Shippee, "Germany and the Spanish-American War," *American Historical Review* (July, 1925); B. A. Reuter, *Anglo-American Relations During the Spanish-American War* (1924).

THE PEACE OF PARIS. See, Royal Cortissoz, *Life of Whitelaw Reid* (1921); G. F. Hoar, *Autobiography of Seventy Years* (1906).

19: A WORLD THEATER

GENERAL TREATMENTS. See TEXTBOOKS AND SERIES, titles relating to American diplomatic relations. Consult, also: H. E. Barnes, *World Politics in Modern Civilization* (1930); Parker T. Moon, *Imperialism and World Politics* (1926); Scott Nearing, *American Empire* (1921); Scott Nearing and Joseph Freeman, *Dollar Diplomacy* (1925); P. S. Reinsch, *World Politics* (1900) and *Colonial Administration* (1905).

THE UNITED STATES IN THE PHILIPPINES. Discussions favorable to American occupation are W. C. Forbes, *Philippine Islands;* 2 v. (1928); Nicholas Roosevelt, *Philippines: A Treasure and a Problem* (1926); D. C. Worcester, *Philippines: Past and Present* (1914). A critical account is M. Storey and M. P. Lichauco, *Conquest of the Philippines by the United States, 1898–1925* (1926). See also, Grayson L. Kirk, *Philippine Independence* (1936) and José S. Reyes, *Legislative History of America's Economic Policy Toward the Philippines* (1923).

THE UNITED STATES IN PUERTO RICO. A good general discussion is Knowlton Mixer, *Porto Rico: History and Conditions* (1926). Victor S. Clark and others, *Porto Rico and Its Problems* (1930) is an elaborate examination of social and economic conditions. For a critical discussion of American policy, see B. W. and J. W. Diffie, *Porto Rico: A Broken Pledge* (1931). For Puerto Rico in the last two decades, see, A. D. Gayer, P. T. Homan, and E. K. James, *Sugar Economy of Puerto Rico* (1938), R. G. Tugwell, *Stricken Land* (1947), and *Puerto Rican Paradox*, by V. M. Petrullo (1947).

THE CONSTITUTION AND OUR ISLAND DEPENDENCIES. See: W. F. Willoughby, *Territories and Dependencies of the United States* (1905); W. W. Willoughby, *Constitutional Law of the United States* (1910).

THE UNITED STATES IN CUBA. The best single account is L. H. Jenks, *Our Cuban Colony* (1921). See also, H. Hagedorn, *Leonard Wood*, 2 v. (1921); G. H. Stuart, *Cuba and Its International Relations* (1921); Foreign Policy Association: Information Service Reports, "Cuba and the Platt Amendment" (April 1929) and "Problems of the New Cuba" (1935).

SECRETARY HAY AND CHINA. See the following: Tyler Dennett, *Americans in Eastern Asia* (1922) and *John Hay* (1933); F. R. Dulles, *China and America: The Story of their Relations since 1784* (1946); A. W. Griswold, *Far Eastern Policy of the United States* (1938); W. R. Thayer, *Life and Letters of John Hay*, 2 v. (1915).

20: THEODORE ROOSEVELT AND WILLIAM HOWARD TAFT

GENERAL TREATMENTS. The following are good general accounts, stressing the political aspects of the Rooseveltian era: J. H. Latané, *America as a World Power* (1907); F. A. Ogg, *National Progress* (1918); J. F. Rhodes, *McKinley and Roosevelt Administrations* (1922); E. E. Robinson, *Evolution of American Political Parties* (1924); Mark Sullivan, *Our Times*, v. 2 and 3 (1929–30).

RELATING TO ROOSEVELT. The best biography is Henry F. Pringle, *Theodore Roosevelt and His Times*, 2 v. (1920). An authorized biography is J. B. Bishop, *Theodore Roosevelt and His Times*, 2 v. (1920). See also: H. Howland, *Theodore Roosevelt and His Times* (1921); W. R. Thayer, *Theodore Roosevelt: An Intimate Biography* (1919); H. C. Lodge, *Selections from the Correspondence of Theodore Roosevelt and Henry Cabot Lodge 1884–1918*, 2 v. (1925); Theodore Roosevelt, *Autobiography* (1913); Owen Wister, *Roosevelt: The Story of a Friendship* (1930).

BIOGRAPHIES OF POLITICIANS OF THE PERIOD. See: L. A. Coolidge, *An Old-Fashioned Senator: Orville H. Platt of Connecticut* (1910); Champ Clark, *My Quarter Century of American Politics* (1920); Robert M. La Follette, *La Follette's Autobiography* (1913); N. W. Stephenson, *Nelson W. Aldrich: A Leader in American Politics* (1930). Consult, also, the following, which are the comments on the leading figures of the day by acute observers: William Allen White, *Masks in a Pageant* (1928); A. H. Kohlsaat, *From McKinley to Harding* (1923); A. W. Dunn, *From Harrison to Harding* (1922); Lincoln Steffens, *Autobiography*, 2 v. (1931).

RELATING TO TAFT. See: K. W. Heckler, *Insurgency: Personalities and Policies of the Taft Era* (1940); H. F. Pringle, *Life and Times of William Howard Taft*, 2 v. (1939); *Taft and Roosevelt: the Intimate Letters of Archie Butt*, 2 v. (1930). For the Tariff Act of 1909, see the titles cited in Chapter V. THREE LEADING QUESTIONS BEFORE THE POSTBELLUM PARTIES, section: *The Protective Tariff*; also, H. Parker Willis, "Tariff of 1909," *Journal of Political Economy* (January and March, 1910).

21: ROOSEVELTIAN POLICIES AT HOME

THE TRUST PROBLEM. See titles cited under Chapter XV. THE SHERMAN ANTITRUST ACT.

THE MONEY POWER. The best discussions of this subject are to be found in Lewis Corey, *House of Morgan* (1930); John Moody, *Masters of Capital* (1919); Louis D. Brandeis, *Other People's Money* (1914).

RAILROAD LEGISLATION. See titles cited under Chapter VIII. BUILDING THE RAILROADS, Section: *General Treatments*.

CONSERVATION. See for this topic: B. H. Hibbard, *History of Public Land Policies* (1924); Gifford Pinchot, *Fight for Conservation* (1910); C. R. Van Hise and L. Havemeyer, *Conservation of our Natural Resources* (1930).

22: THE TRIUMPH OF REFORM

GENERAL TREATMENTS. In addition to the works cited in the text, the student will find it profitable to consult the following: C. G. Bowers, *Beveridge and the Progressive Era* (1932); Herbert Croly, *Promise of American Life* (1909); B. P. De Witt, *Progressive Movement* (1915); H. U. Faulkner, *Quest for Social Justice* (1931); Louis Filler, *Crusaders for American Liberalism* (1939); F. C. Howe, *Confessions of a Reformer* (1925) and *Wisconsin: An Experiment in Democracy* (1912); C. C. Regier, *Era of the Muckrakers* (1932); Lincoln Steffens, *Autobiography*, 2 v. (1931); C. E. Merriam, *American Political Ideas, 1867–1917* (1920); Harold Zink, *City Bosses in the United States* (1930).

POLITICAL REFORM. For the operations of the new political devices, consult any standard textbook concerned with American government. C. A. Beard, *American Government and Politics* (rev. edition, 1931); A. J. Lovejoy, *La Fol-*

lette and the Establishment of the Direct Primary in Wisconsin (1941); S. P. Orth and R. E. Cushman, *American National Government* (1931).

SOCIAL AND ECONOMIC LEGISLATION. The outstanding work is J. B. Andrews and J. R. Commons, *Principles of Labor Legislation* (1927); see, also, C. C. Catt, *Woman Suffrage and Politics* (1938); W. E. Weyl, *New Democracy* (1912).

SOCIALISM IN THE UNITED STATES. A good summary will be found in Nathan Fine, *Labor and Farmer Parties in the United States* (1928). The standard history is Morris Hillquit, *History of Socialism in the United States* (1910). Consult, also, F. E. Haynes, *Social Politics in the United States* (1924); McAlister Coleman, *Eugene V. Debs* (1930); John Spargo, *Socialism* (1910); Socialist Labor Party, *Daniel De Leon, The Man and His Work* (1919).

23: ROOSEVELTIAN POLICIES ABROAD

GENERAL TREATMENTS. See the titles cited under TEXTBOOKS AND SERIES, particularly those concerned with American diplomatic relations. Henry F. Pringle, *Theodore Roosevelt* (1931) and Allan Nevins, *Henry White: Thirty Years of American Diplomacy* (1930) contain full discussions of Roosevelt and foreign affairs. Consult, also, Alfred L. P. Dennis, *Adventures in American Diplomacy, 1896–1906* (1928); Chester L. Jones, *Caribbean Interests of the United States* (1916).

ROOSEVELT IN VENEZUELA AND PANAMA. For the Venezuela episode, see H. C. Hill, *Roosevelt and the Caribbean* (1927). For detailed discussions of the Panama Canal, see the following: J. B. Bishop, *Panama Gateway* (1915); W. D. McCain, *United States and the Republic of Panama* (1937); Gerstle Mack, *Land Divided: A History of the Panama Canal and other Isthmian Canal Projects* (1946); W. F. McCaleb, *Theodore Roosevelt* (1931); H. G. Miller, *Isthmian Highway* (1929); D. C. Miner, *Fight for the Panama Route* (1940); E. T. Parks, *Colombia and the United States, 1769–1934* (1935); F. J. Rippy, *Capitalists and Colombia* (1931); M. W. Williams, *Anglo-American Isthmian Diplomacy, 1815–1915* (1916).

ROOSEVELT AND THE FAR EAST. See: T. A. Bailey, *Theodore Roosevelt and the Japanese-American Crises* (1934); G. H. Blakeslee, editor, *Japan and Japanese-American Relations* (1910); Tyler Dennett, *Theodore Roosevelt and the Russo-Japanese War* (1925); A. W. Griswold, *Far Eastern Policy of the United States* (1938); P. C. Jessup, *Elihu Root*, 2 v. (1938); P. J. Treat, *Diplomatic Relations between the United States and Japan*, 3 v. (1932–38).

DOLLAR DIPLOMACY. Special treatments, relating to American interests in China, are: Herbert Croly, *Willard Straight* (1924); H. K. Norton, *China and the Powers* (1927); J. W. Overlach, *Foreign Financial Control in China* (1919); J. G. Reid, *Manchu Abdication and the Powers, 1908–12* (1935).

NAVALISM. See titles cited under Chapter VI. RELATIONS WITH THE OUTSIDE WORLD, 1876–96, section: *The New Navy*. See also, Harold and Margaret Sprout, *Rise of American Naval Power, 1776–1918* (1939).

24: THE NEW FREEDOM

ELECTION OF 1912. Good general discussions will be found in Charles A. Beard, *Contemporary American History* (1914); F. A. Ogg, *National Progress, 1907–17* (1918); E. E. Robinson, *Evolution of American Political Parties* (1924). The parts played by the leading actors, in their own words, are set forth in: Robert M. La Follette, *Autobiography* (1913); Theodore Roosevelt,

New Nationalism (1910); Woodrow Wilson, *New Freedom* (1913). W. J. Bryan, *Tale of Two Conventions* (1912) and Champ Clark, *My Quarter Century of American Politics* (1920) tell the dramatic story of Baltimore, where Wilson received the nomination. For an amusing recital of the formation of the Progressive party, see Donald Richberg, *Tents of the Mighty* (1930). On this topic, consult also: F. E. Haynes, *Third Party Movements since the Civil War* (1916); B. P. De Witt, *Progressive Movement* (1915).

WOODROW WILSON, PRESIDENT. The authorized biography is R. S. Baker, *Woodrow Wilson, Life and Letters*, 8 v. (1927–39). The following other works may be consulted: W. E. Dodd, *Woodrow Wilson and His Work* (1921); Josephus Daniels, *Life of Woodrow Wilson* (1921) and *Wilson Era: Years of Peace, 1910–17* (1944); Charles Seymour, *Woodrow Wilson and the World War* (1921); William Allen White, *Woodrow Wilson: The Man, His Times, and His Task* (1924); D. F. Houston, *Eight Years with Wilson's Cabinet* (1926); William G. McAdoo, *Crowded Years* (1931); J. P. Tumulty, *Woodrow Wilson as I Knew Him* (1925). F. L. Paxson, *American Democracy and the World War: Pre-War Years, 1913–17* (1936) is a useful general work; Harley Notter, *Origins of the Foreign Policy of Woodrow Wilson* (1937) a special study.

THE TARIFF ACT OF 1913. For works on this topic see the books by Ashley, Page, and Taussig in the titles cited under Chapter V. THREE LEADING QUESTIONS BEFORE THE POSTBELLUM PARTIES, section: *The Protective Tariff*.

THE FEDERAL RESERVE SYSTEM. Consult the following: A. B. Hepburn, *History of Coinage and Currency in the United States* (rev. edition, 1924); Carter Glass, *Adventure in Constructive Finance* (1927); R. L. Owen, *Federal Reserve Act* (1919); E. W. Kemmerer, *A B C of the Federal Reserve System* (1918); H. L. Reed, *Development of Federal Reserve Policy* (1922); H. Parker Willis, *Federal Reserve System* (1923); P. M. Warburg, *Federal Reserve System*, 2 v. (1930).

TRUST LEGISLATION. See titles cited under Chapter XV. THE SHERMAN ANTITRUST ACT. See, also, G. C. Henderson, *Federal Trade Commission* (1924) and W. H. Taft, *Antitrust Act and the Supreme Court* (1914).

25: FOREIGN AFFAIRS IN THE WILSON ADMINISTRATIONS

WOODROW WILSON AND MEXICO. These books are standard accounts: C. W. Hackett, *Mexican Revolution and the United States, 1910–26* (1926); J. F. Rippy, *United States and Mexico* (rev. edition, 1931); J. F. Rippy and others, *Mexico* (1928). See also, J. M. Callahan, *American Foreign Policy in Mexican Relations* (1932).

WOODROW WILSON AND THE CARIBBEAN. See: W. H. Calcott, *Caribbean Policy of the United States, 1890–1920* (1942); C. L. Jones, *Caribbean Interests of the United States* (1916) and *Caribbean Backgrounds and Prospects* (1931); C. L. Jones and others, *United States and the Caribbean* (1929).

THE PEACE MOVEMENT. See the following for good summaries: Devere Allen, *Fight for Peace* (1930); K. A. Bratt, *That Next War?* (1930); Jerome Davis, *Contemporary Social Movements* (1930); F. G. Tuttle, *Alternatives to War* (1931).

AMERICAN NEUTRALITY. Indispensable to an understanding of the problems besetting the United States as a neutral are the official state papers published in U.S. Department of State, *Papers Relating to the Foreign Relations of the United States: 1914, 1915, 1916, 1917, War Supplements* (1928–31). For the European events leading up to the outbreak of World War I, the following are the standard American accounts: S. B. Fay, *Origins of the World War*, 2 v. (1928); B. E. Schmitt, *Coming of the War*, 2 v. (1930). The student should consult, too, H. E. Barnes, *Genesis of the World War* (rev. edition, 1929) and *World Politics and Modern Civilization* (1930), for the viewpoint of the leading exponent of the revisionist cause in the United States. C. Hartley Grattan, *Why We Fought* (1929), is a convenient summary of the reasons for American entry, which, though critical in tone, covers the whole ground. Alice M. Morrissey, *American Defense of Neutral Rights, 1914-17* (1939) is an academic treatment; compare, Edward Borchard and W. P. Lage, *Neutrality for the United States* (1937). The following biographies and memoirs are among the important documents of the times: Charles Seymour, editor, *Intimate Papers of Colonel House*, 4 v. (1926-28); B. J. Hendrick, *Life and Letters of W. H. Page*, 3 v. (1922-25); William Jennings Bryan, *Memoirs* (1925); J. von Bernstorff, *Memoirs* (1936) and *My Three Years in America* (1920); Stephen Gwynn, *Letters and Friendships of Sir Cecil Spring Rice* (1929). The story of the British blockade will be found in J. M. Kenworthy and G. Young, *Freedom of the Seas* (1928) and J. A. Salter, *Allied Shipping Control* (1921). For German submarine warfare, consult R. H. Gibson and M. Prendergast, *German Submarine War, 1914-18* (1931).

26: THE UNITED STATES ENTERS THE WORLD WAR

WHY WE FOUGHT. See the titles cited under the previous chapter, section, *American Neutrality*. In addition, for the significance of the part played by propaganda, consult: H. D. Lasswell, *Propaganda Technique in the World War* (1927); H. C. Peterson, *Propaganda for War* (1939); J. D. Squires, *British Propaganda at Home and in the United States from 1914 to 1917* (1935). For America's financial position during the period of neutrality, consult A. D. Noyes, *War Period in American Finance: 1908-25* (1926). For the work of the preparedness advocates, consult H. Hagedorn, *Leonard Wood*, 2 v. (1931). The following may also be examined: J. S. Bassett, *Our War with Germany* (1919); John B. McMaster, *United States in the World War*, 2 v. (1918-20); Charles Seymour, *American Diplomacy During the World War* (1934); C. C. Tansill, *America Goes to War* (1938).

MOBILIZING MEN AND MONEY. The best accounts are to be found in the biographies of the Cabinet officers directing these activities. See, Frederick Palmer, *Newton D. Baker: America at War*, 2 v. (1931) and William G. McAdoo, *Crowded Years* (1931). Consult also, E. H. Crowder, *Spirit of Selective Service* (1920). J. M. Clark, *Costs of the World War to the American People* (1931), is a scholarly reckoning.

MOBILIZING INDUSTRY AND LABOR. A convenient summary is W. F. Willoughby, *Government Organization in War Time and After* (1919). See also: B. M. Baruch, *American Industry in the War: A Report of the War Industries Board* (1941); A. M. Bing, *Wartime Strikes and their Adjustment* (1921); B. Crowell and R. F. Wilson, *How America Went to War*, 6 v. (1921); Samuel Gompers, *Seventy Years of Life and Labor*, 2 v. (1925); W. D. Hines, *War History of American Railroads* (1928).

MOBILIZING OPINION AND MORALE. For the work of the Committee on Public Information, see J. R. Mock and Cedric Larson, *Words that Won the War: The Story of the Committee on Public Information* (1940). For the treatment of conscientious objectors, see Norman Thomas, *Conscientious Objector in Amer-*

ica (1923). For the attitude toward dissenters generally, see Zechariah Chafee, Jr., *Freedom of Speech* (1921). For Wilson's wartime utterances, see R. S. Baker and W. E. Dodd, *Public Papers of Woodrow Wilson*, 6 v. (1925–27). For alien enemy property in the United States, see the section of that name in Charles P. Howland, editor, *Survey of American Foreign Relations: 1930* (1930).

27: THE OUTCOME OF THE WAR

ON THE WESTERN FRONT. The most important book on this topic is that written by the commander of the American Expeditionary Force, General John J. Pershing, *My Experiences in the World War*, 2 v. (1931). Convenient summaries are the following: U.S. War Department, *War with Germany: A Statistical Summary* (1919); T. G. Frothingham, *American Reinforcement in the World War* (1927). For the part played by the Navy, see Admiral W. S. Sims and B. J. Hendrick, *Victory at Sea;* see also, Louis Guichard, *Naval Blockade, 1914–18* (1930) and E. E. Morison, *Admiral Sims and the Modern American Navy* (1942). Excellent histories, in brief compass, of the military aspects of the entire struggle are B. H. L. Hart, *Real War* (1930) and C. J. H. Hayes, *Brief History of the Great War* (1928).

THE PEACE CONFERENCE AND THE TREATY OF VERSAILLES. The standard history is H. W. V. Temperley, editor, *History of the Peace of Paris*, 6 v. (1920–24). Paul Birdsall, *Versailles Twenty Years After* (1941) incorporates new material and a critical summation of the results of recent scholarship. J. M. Keynes, *Economic Consequences of the Peace* (1920) is a brilliant attack on the treaty and the treaty-makers. A. Tardieu, *Truth About the Treaty* (1921), presents the case for France. The leading works setting forth the positions of the American peace commissioners are the following: R. S. Baker, *Woodrow Wilson and the World Settlement*, 3 v. (1922); Robert Lansing, *Peace Negotiations: A Personal Narrative* (1921); E. M. House and C. Seymour, *What Actually Happened at Paris* (1921); Allan Nevins, *Henry White* (1930); J. T. Shotwell, *At the Paris Peace Conference* (1937).

THE REJECTION OF THE TREATY BY THE SENATE. Thomas Bailey, *Woodrow Wilson and the Lost Peace* (1944) and *Woodrow Wilson and the Great Betrayal* (1945); D. H. Fleming, *United States and the League of Nations, 1918–20* (1932); Henry Cabot Lodge, *Senate and the League of Nations* (1925).

THE COLLAPSE OF WILSONISM. Consult the following works for various aspects of the topics discussed in the text: H. K. Beale, *Are American Teachers Free?* (1936); Zechariah Chafee, Jr., *Freedom of Speech* (1921); A. G. Hays, *Let Freedom Ring* (rev. edition, 1937); Walter Lippmann, *American Inquisitors* (1928); J. M. Mecklin, *Ku Klux Klan: A Study of the American Mind* (1924); Maynard Shipley, *War on Modern Science* (1927).

28: POLITICS IN THE NINETEEN TWENTIES

POLITICIANS AND POLITICAL MOVEMENTS. James C. Malin, *United States After the World War* (1930); Preston W. Slosson, *Great Crusade and After, 1914–28* (1930); R. V. Peel and T. C. Donnelly, *The 1928 Campaign* (1931). See also, the books by Dumond, Parkes, and Wish cited under TEXTBOOKS AND SERIES. Other material will be found in S. H. Adams, *Incredible Era: The Life and Times of Warren Gamaliel Harding* (1939); Arthur Capper, *Agricultural*

Bloc (1922); Nathan Fine, *Labor and Farmer Parties in the United States, 1828–1928* (1928); Alfred Lief, *Democracy's Norris* (1939); Mark Sullivan, *Our Times*, v. 6 (1935); W. A. White, *Masks in a Pageant* (1928); Calvin Coolidge, *Autobiography* (1929); W. S. Meyers and W. H. Newton, *Hoover Administration* (1936).

29: LEADING LEGISLATIVE PROBLEMS OF THE NINETEEN TWENTIES

THE TARIFF ACTS. F. W. Taussig, *Tariff History of the United States* (rev. edition, 1931); J. M. Jones, *Tariff Retaliation* (1934).

CREATING A MERCHANT MARINE. James C. Malin, *United States After the World War* (1930); Brookings Institution, *United States Shipping Board* (1931); National Industrial Conference Board, *Merchant Marine Problem* (1929); L. W. Maxwell, *Discriminatory Duties and the American Merchant Marine* (1926); J. P. Kennedy, "Economic Survey of the American Merchant Marine," (1937) and C. N. Weems, Jr., "Rebuilding the United States Merchant Marine," (1938) both *Reports* of the Foreign Policy Association.

THE RAILROAD PROBLEM. Rogers MacVeagh, *Transportation Act, 1920: Its Sources, History and Text* (1923); D. Phillip Locklin, *Economics of Transportation* (1936); H. G. Moulton and associates, *American Transportation Problem* (1933); H. D. Wolfe, *Railroad Labor Board* (1937).

THE PUBLIC DEBT AND TAX REDUCTION. H. L. Lutz, *Public Finance* (1936); Twentieth Century Fund, *Facing the Tax Problem* (1933).

THE REGULATION OF POWER. C. O. Hardy, *Recent Growth of the Electric Light and Power Industry* (1929); H. S. Raushenbush and H. W. Laidler, *Power Control* (1928).

30: AMERICA IN TWO HEMISPHERES

GENERAL TREATMENTS. S. F. Bemis, *Diplomatic History of the United States* (rev. edition, 1942); C. A. Howland, editor, *Survey of American Foreign Relations*, 4 v. (1928–31); W. S. Myers, *Foreign Policies of Herbert Hoover, 1929–33* (1940), includes useful papers.

THE UNITED STATES AND LATIN AMERICA. J. Fred Rippy, *Latin America in World Politics* (3rd. edition, 1938); Carleton Beals, *Mexican Maze* (1931); Waldo Frank, *America Hispaña* (1931); Ernest Gruening, *Mexico and Its Heritage* (1928); M. M. Knight, *Americans in Santo Domingo* (1928); A. C. Millspaugh, *Haiti under American Control, 1915–30* (1931); L. L. Montagu, *Haiti and the United States* (1940); Harold Nicholson, *Dwight Morrow* (1935); H. L. Stimson, *American Policy in Nicaragua* (1927); A. Alvarez, *Monroe Doctrine* (1924); U.S. Department of State (prepared by J. Reuben Clark), "Memorandum on the Monroe Doctrine" (1930); Foreign Policy Association, "Trade Rivalries in Latin America" (F. P. *Reports*, v. xiii, no. 13, 1937); A. K. Weinberg, *Manifest Destiny: A Study of Nationalist Expansion in American History* (1935).

RENEWAL OF THE PEACE MOVEMENT. J. S. Bassett, *League of Nations* (1928); David Bryn-Jones, *Frank B. Kellogg* (1937); D. F. Fleming, *United States and the World Court* (1945) and *United States and World Organization, 1920–33* (1938); D. H. Miller, *Peace Pact of Paris* (1928); J. T. Shotwell, *War as an Instrument of National Policy* (1929); W. E. Rappard, *Quest for Peace* (1940).

NAVAL LIMITATION. R. L. Buell, *Washington Conference* (1922); C. G. Dawes, *Journal as Ambassador to Great Britain* (1939), has material on the abortive London Naval Conference; Yamato Ichihashi, *Washington Conference and After* (1928); Harold and Margaret Sprout, *Toward a New Order of Sea Power* (1940), deals with United States naval policy and world affairs, 1918–22; B. H. Williams, *United States and Disarmament* (1931).

INTERALLIED DEBTS AND REPARATIONS PAYMENTS. C. Bergman, *History of Reparations* (1927); C. G. Dawes, *Journal of Reparations* (1939), describes the making of the Dawes Plan; National Industrial Conference Board, *Inter-Ally Debts and the United States* (1925); H. G. Moulton and Leo Pasvolsky, *World War Debt Settlements* (1926) and *War Debts and World Prosperity* (1932).

RUSSIAN RELATIONS. W. S. Graves, *America's Siberian Adventure, 1918–20* (1930); F. L. Schuman, *American Policy toward Russia since 1917* (1928); Foreign Policy Association, "The Outlook for Soviet-American Trade," (F. P. *Reports*, v. x, no. 11, 1934) and "The Outlook for Soviet-American Relations" (F. P. *Reports*, v. ix, no. 1, 1933).

31: CAPITAL AND LABOR

GENERAL TREATMENTS. F. L. Allen, *Only Yesterday* (1931); President's Conference on Unemployment, *Recent Economic Changes*, 2 v. (1929); President's Research Committee on Social Trends, *Recent Social Trends in the United States*, 2 v. (1933); George Soule, *Prosperity Decade* (1947); H. T. Warshow, *Representative Industries in the United States* (1928); T. N. Carver, *Present Economic Revolution in the United States* (1925).

MASS PRODUCTION. Taylor Society, *Scientific Management in American Industry* (1929); James T. Adams, *Our Business Civilization* (1929); Charles A. Beard, editor, *Whither Mankind?* (1928); Stuart Chase, *Tragedy of Waste* (1925), *Men and Machines* (1929), *Prosperity: Fact or Myth* (1930); R. S. and H. M. Lynd, *Middletown* (1929); Lewis Corey, *Decline of American Capitalism* (1934); R. G. Tugwell, *Industry's Coming of Age* (1927).

THE POSITION OF LABOR. S. Perlman and P. Taft, *History of Labor in the United States, 1896–1932* (1935); C. R. Daugherty, *Labor Problems in American Industry* (rev. edition, 1938); Henry David, H. J. Carman and H. J. Lahne, editors, *Labor in Twentieth Century America* [4 volumes have appeared (1942–45)]; Edward Berman, *Labor and the Sherman Act* (1930); Felix Frankfurter and N. Greene, *Labor Injunction* (1930); P. F. Brissenden, *History of the I.W.W.* (1920); J. S. Gambs, *Decline of the I.W.W.* (1932); L. L. Lorwin, *American Federation of Labor* (1933); E. E. Witte, *Government in Labor Disputes* (1932); Leo Wolman, *Growth of American Trade Unions, 1880–1923* (1924) and *Ebb and Flow in American Trade Unionism* (1936); David J. Saposs, *Left-Wing Unionism* (1926); James Oneal, *American Communism* (1927); Paul H. Douglas and Aaron Director, *Problem of Unemployment* (1931).

THE SUPREME COURT AND PROPERTY. Charles Warren, *Supreme Court in United States History*, v. 3 (1922); J. R. Commons, *Legal Foundations of Capitalism* (1924); Louis Boudin, *Government by Judiciary* (1932); E. S. Corwin, *Twilight of the Supreme Court* (1934); Felix Frankfurter, editor, *Mr. Justice Brandeis* (1932); Max Lerner, *Mind and Faith of Justice Holmes* (1943). J. F. Pollard, *Mr. Justice Cardozo* (1935); M. R. Cohen, *Law and the Social Order* (1933); S. J. Konefsky, *Chief Justice Stone and the Supreme Court* (1945).

MERGERS AND ANTITRUST LEGISLATION. H. R. Seager and C. A. Gulick, Jr., *Trust and Corporation Problems* (1929); H. W. Laidler, *Concentration in American Industry* (1931); A. A. Berle, Jr. and G. C. Means, *Modern Corporation and*

Private Property (1932); J. C. Bonbright and G. C. Means, *Holding Company* (1932); W. J. A. Donald, *Trade Associations* (1933); Frank A. Fetter, *Masquerade of Monopoly* (1931); W. Z. Ripley, *Main Street and Wall Street* (1927); National Industrial Conference Board, *Mergers and the Law* (1929); Arthur R. Burns, *Decline of Competition* (1936); D. M. Keezer and Stacy Macy, *Public Control of Business* (1930); John T. Flynn, *Security Speculation* (1934); H. G. Moulton, *Financial Organization of Society* (rev. edition, 1938); Lewis Corey, *House of Morgan* (1930); Anna Rochester, *Rulers of America* (1936); Ferdinand Lundberg, *America's Sixty Families* (1937); Twentieth Century Fund, *Big Business: Its Growth and Its Place* (1937) and *How Profitable Is Big Business?* (1937).

32: THREE OUTSTANDING PROBLEMS OF THE TWENTIES AND THIRTIES

PROHIBITION. E. H. Cherrington, *Evolution of Prohibition in the United States* (1920); Peter Odegard, *Pressure Politics: The Story of the Anti-Saloon League* (1928); Charles Merz, *Dry Decade* (1931); Mary Earhart, *Frances Willard: From Prayers to Politics* (1944); Herman Feldman, *Prohibition: Its Economic and Industrial Aspects* (1927); National Commission on Law Observation and Enforcement, *Report on the Enforcement of the Prohibition Law in the United States* (71st Congress, 3d Session, House Document No. 722, 1931); L. V. Harrison and Elizabeth Laine, *After Repeal* (1936).

IMMIGRATION RESTRICTION. H. P. Fairchild, *Immigration: A World Movement and Its American Significance* (rev. edition, 1925); R. L. Garis, *Immigration Restriction* (1927); W. J. Lauck, *Immigration Problem* (1913); M. R. Davie, *World Immigration: With Special Reference to the United States* (1936); Manuel Gamio, *Mexican Immigration to the United States* (1930).

THE DECLINE OF AGRICULTURE. J. D. Black, *Agricultural Reform in the United States* (1930); Wilson P. Gee, *Place of Agriculture in American Life* (1930); Edwin G. Nourse, *American Agriculture and the European Market* (1924); Clara Eliot, *Farmer's Campaign for Credit* (1927); E. R. A. Seligman, *Economics of Farm Relief* (1929); Bernhard Ostrolenk, *Surplus Farmer* (1932); J. M. Goldstein, *Agricultural Crisis* (1935); Louis M. Hacker, "The Farmer is Doomed," John Day Pamphlets (1933); P. B. Sears, *Deserts on the March* (1935).

33: ECONOMIC IMPERIALISM

GENERAL AND SPECIAL TREATMENTS. Julius Klein, *Frontiers of Trade* (1929); Paul M. Mazur, *America Looks Abroad* (1930); Hiram Motherwell, *Imperial Dollar* (1929); C. F. Remer, *Foreign Investments in China* (1933); Benjamin H. Williams, *Economic Foreign Policy of the United States* (1929); Charles A. Beard, *Idea of National Interest* (1934) and *Open Door at Home* (1934); Scott Nearing and Joseph Freeman, *Dollar Diplomacy* (1925); Scott Nearing, *Twilight of Empire* (1930); Nicholas Roosevelt, *America and England?* (1930); R. W. Dunn, *American Foreign Investments* (1926); Max Winkler, *Foreign Bonds: An Autopsy* (1933) and *United States Capital in Latin America* (1928); C. Lewis and K. T. Schlotterbeck, *America's Stake in International Investments* (1938); Commission of Inquiry into National Policy, *International Economic Relations* (1934); U.S. Bureau of Foreign and Domestic Commerce, *Handbook of American Underwriting of Foreign Securities, 1914–29* (Trade Promotion Series No. 104, 1930), *A New Estimate of American Investments Abroad* (Trade Information Bulletin, No. 767, 1931), *American Direct Investments in Foreign*

Countries (Trade Information Bulletin No. 731, 1930), *American Direct Investments in Foreign Countries: 1936* (Economic Series No. 1, 1938); Brooks Emeny, *Strategy of Raw Materials* (1934).

34: THE NEW DEAL

GENERAL TREATMENTS. Charles A. Beard and George H. E. Smith, *Old Deal and the New* (1940); James A. Farley, *Jim Farley's Story: The Roosevelt Years* (1948); Louis M. Hacker, *American Problems of Today* (1938) and *Shaping of the American Tradition*, section XI; Cordell Hull, *Memoirs*, 2 v. (1948); Harold L. Ickes, *Autobiography of a Curmudgeon* (1943); Robert E. Sherwood, *Roosevelt and Hopkins: An Intimate History* (1948); Basil Rauch, *History of the New Deal, 1933–38* (1944); Arthur M. Schlesinger, *New Deal in Action, 1933–39* (1940). The London *Economist*, "The New Deal: An Analysis and an Appraisal," (October 3, 1936), gives a balanced English viewpoint. Broadus Mitchell, *Depression Decade: From New Era to New Deal* (1947), covers the entire period.

FROM AN OLD TO A NEW DEAL. The causes of the depression are discussed in their varied aspects in these books: A. A. Berle, Jr. and G. C. Means, *Modern Corporation and Private Property* (1936); Alfred M. Bernheim and M. G. Schneider, editors, *Security Markets* (1935); Evans Clark, and others, *Internal Debts of the United States* (1933); E. L. Dulles, *Depression and Reconstruction: A Study of Causes and Controls* (1936); F. W. Hirst, *Wall Street and Lombard Street* (1931); Maurice Levin and others, *America's Capacity to Consume* (1934); F. C. Mills, *Economic Tendencies in the United States* (1932); E. G. Nourse and associates, *America's Capacity to Produce* (1934); Lionel Robbins, *Great Depression* (1930). The following deal with the election of 1932: W. S. Myers and W. A. Newton, *Hoover Administration: A Documented Narrative* (1936); R. V. Peel and T. C. Donnelly, *The 1932 Campaign* (1935); F. D. Roosevelt, *Public Papers and Addresses*, 9 v. (1938–41). The early stages of the New Deal are considered in: Leonard P. Ayres, *Economics of Recovery* (1934); Ernest K. Lindley, *Halfway with Roosevelt* (1937) and *Roosevelt Revolution* (1933); J. T. Salter, editor, *American Politician* (1938); S. C. Wallace, *New Deal in Action* (1934).

THE NEW DEAL: THEORY AND TACTICS. Partisans: pro: Mordecai Ezekiel, *$2,500 a Year: From Scarcity to Abundance* (1936); F. D. Roosevelt, *Looking Forward* (1933) and *On Our Way* (1934); R. G. Tugwell, *Industrial Discipline and the Governmental Arts* (1933); H. A. Wallace, *America Must Choose* (1934) and *New Frontiers* (1934). Partisans: con: Walter Lippmann, *Method of Freedom* (1934); William MacDonald, *Menace of Recovery* (1934). Academic treatments: A. B. Adams, *National Economic Security* (1936); Brookings Institution, *Recovery Program in the United States* (1937).

THE NEW DEAL AGENCIES. AGRICULTURE. Works treating the problem as a whole include, Harold Barger and H. H. Landsberg, *American Agriculture, 1899–1939* (1942); Louis M. Hacker, *Farmer Is Doomed* (1933); C. T. Schmidt, *American Farmers in the World Crisis* (1941). The following deal with special problems: Jonathan Daniels, *Southerner Discovers the South* (1938); Carey McWilliams, *Ill Fares the Land* (1942) and *Factories in the Field* (1939); A. F. Raper and I. De A. Reid, *Sharecroppers All* (1941). The government programs are considered in Wilson Gee, *American Farm Policy* (1934); E. G. Nourse, *Marketing Agreements under the Agricultural Adjustment Act* (1935) and *Three Years of the Agricultural Adjustment Act* (1937).

INDUSTRY. The Twentieth-Century Fund studies, *Big Business: Its Growth and Its Place* (1937) and *How Profitable is Big Business?* (1937) supply background as does A. R. Burns, *Decline of Competition* (1936). Hugh S. Johnson, *Blue Eagle from Egg to Earth* (1935) is a personal account. President's Committee of Industrial Analysis, *National Recovery Administration* (1937) is a critical appraisal. G. B. Galloway, *Industrial Planning under the Codes* (1935); E. T. Grether, *Price Control under Fair Trade Legislation* (1939); L. S. Lyon and Victor Abramson, *Government and Economic Life*, 2 v. (1940) are special studies.

LABOR AND LABOR ORGANIZATION. The following deal with general problems: E. Stein and others, *Labor Problems in America* (1944); L. L. Lorwin, *American Federation of Labor* (1933); Marjorie Clark and S. Fanny Simon, *Labor Movement in America* (1938). The rise of the CIO is described in Herbert Harris, *American Labor* (1939) and *Labor's Civil War* (1940); J. R. Walsh, *CIO: Industrial Unionism in Action* (1937). The Twentieth Century Fund study, *Labor and Government* (1935) and Robert R. R. Brooks, *Unions of Their Own Choosing* (1939), discuss the background and early operation of the Wagner Act. Horace R. Cayton and G. S. Mitchell, *Black Workers and the New Unions* (1939) and H. R. Northrup, *Organized Labor and the Negro* (1944) continue the story of the Negro in industry; see, particularly, Sterling Spero and A. H. Harris, *Black Worker* (1931). Labor's position in society is illuminated by U.S. Senate, Subcommittee of the Committee on Education and Labor ("Civil Liberties Committee"), *Hearings and Report on Violations of Free Speech and Assembly and Interference with Rights of Labor"* (1936–38).

SOCIAL SECURITY. "Appraising the Social Security Program," American Academy of Political and Social Science, *Annals*, v. 202 (March, 1939); Eveline M. Burns, *Toward Social Security* (1936); Paul H. Douglas, *Social Security* (rev. edition, 1939); Lewis Merriam, *Relief and Social Security* (1946); James Parker, *Social Security Reserves* (1942).

WORKS AND RELIEF. A. D. Gayer, *Public Works in Prosperity and Depression* (1935) and H. L. Ickes, *Back to Work: The Story of PWA* (1935) deal with the works program. The "human" side of unemployment is shown in Louise V. Armstrong, *We, Too, Are the People* (1938); Eli Ginzberg and associates, *Unemployed* (1943); J. N. Leonard, *Three Years Down* (1939). The following consider special relief problems: Jacob Baker, *Government Aid . . . to Professional . . . Workers* (1936); George Biddle, *American Artist's Story* (1939); Hallie Flanagan, *Arena* (1940); Kenneth Holland and T. E. Hill, *Youth in the CCC Camps* (1942); L. L. Lorwin, *Youth Work Programs* (1941); Walker Wynne, Jr., *Five Years of Rural Relief* (1939). These may be listed among general studies of relief: J. C. Brown, *Public Relief, 1929–39* (1940); Donald S. Howard, *WPA and Federal Relief Policy* (1943); U.S. Federal Works Agency, Federal Emergency Relief Administration, *Final Statistical Report* (1942).

OIL, COAL, RAILROADS, AND SHIPPING. L. S. Lyon, *Government and Economic Life*, 2 v. (1940) is a useful general survey. See also, Fred F. Blackly and Miriam E. Oatman, *Federal Regulatory Action and Control* (1940). On the merchant marine, J. P. Kennedy, "Economic Survey of the American Merchant Marine," (1937); Foreign Policy Association, "Rebuilding the American Merchant Marine," (F. P. *Reports* v. xiii, no. 20, 1938) and R. L. Dewey, "The Merchant Marine Act of 1936," *American Economic Review*, v. XXVII, p. 239, will be useful. For the railroads, see, R. L. Dewey, "The Transportation Act of 1940," *American Economic Review*, v. XXXVI, p. 15; Joseph B. Eastman, "Report of the Federal Coordinator of Transportation," (Senate Document No. 152, 73d Congress, 2nd Session, 1934) and "Report" (House Document No. 89, 74th

Congress, 1st Session, 1935); Herbert Spero, *Reconstruction Finance Corporation Loans to the Railroads, 1932–37* (1939).

MONEY AND BANKING. B. H. Beckhard, *New York Money Market,* 4 v. (1932); W. Randolph Burgess, *Reserve Banks and the Money Market* (1936); Neal H. Jacoby and R. J. Saulnier, *Business, Finance, and Banking* (1948); H. G. Moulton, *Financial Organization of Society* (1938) deal with general issues. Problems of the early nineteen thirties are considered in Leo Pasvolsky, *Current Monetary Issues* (1933); Ferdinand T. Pecora, *Wall Street Under Oath* (1939); William H. Steiner, *Money and Banking* (1933); Twentieth Century Fund, *Debts and Recovery, 1929–37* (1938). Charles C. Chapman, *Development of American Business and Banking Thought, 1913–36* (1936) deals with the maturing of American finance. New Deal financial measures are treated in A. W. Crawford, *Monetary Management under the New Deal* (1940); Foreign Policy Association, "The United States Silver Policy," (F. P. *Reports,* v. xi, no. 13, 1935); Emanuel Stein, *Government and the Investor* (1941); R. L. Weissman, *New Federal Reserve System* (1936) and *New Wall Street* (1939). The Reconstruction Finance Corporation, *Seven-Year Report to the President and Congress* (1939) presents the results of the activities of an important agency. Esther R. Taus, *Central Banking Functions of the United States Treasury, 1789–1941* (1943) considers a special fiscal problem.

POWER AND HOUSING. David Lilienthal, *TVA: Democracy on the March* (1944); Twentieth Century Fund, *Power Industry and the Public Interest* (1944). T. R. Carskaden, *Houses for Tomorrow* (1944); James Ford and others, *Slums and Housing,* 2 v. (1936); M. W. Straus and T. Wegg, *Housing Comes of Age* (1938); Nathan Straus, *Seven Myths of Housing* (1944).

35: CHALLENGES TO THE NEW DEAL

GENERAL TREATMENTS. See Chapter XXXIV, section *General Treatments.* Also see: L. M. Hacker, *Shaping of the American Tradition,* Section XI, and Merle Fainsod and Lincoln Gordon, *Government and the American Economy* (1941).

THE ELECTION OF 1936. James A. Farley, *Behind the Ballots: the Personal History of a Politician* (1938); E. E. Robinson, *They Voted for Roosevelt: the Presidential Vote, 1932–44* (1947); F. D. Roosevelt, *Public Papers and Addresses,* 9 v. (1938–41).

THE SUPREME COURT FIGHT. E. S. Corwin, *Court over Constitution* (1938) and *Constitutional Revolution* (1941); Erik M. Erikson, *Supreme Court and the New Deal* (1941); Robert H. Jackson, *Struggle for Judicial Supremacy* (1941). See also, references on the Supreme Court in Chapter XXXI, section, *The Supreme Court and Property.*

THE RECESSION OF 1937–38. On the spending policy, see, A. E. Burns and D. S. Watson, *Government Spending and Economic Expansion* (1940); Alvin H. Hansen, *Full Recovery or Stagnation* (1938). For monopoly, consult, T. C. Blaisdell, *Federal Trade Commission* (1933); Wendell Berge, *Cartels* (1944); David Lynch, *Concentration of Economic Power* (1946).

SLOWING DOWN OF THE NEW DEAL. Harold Barger, *Outlay and Income in the United States, 1921–39* (1942); Ralph C. Epstein, *Industrial Profits in the United States* (1942); Solomon Fabricant, *Employment in Manufacturing, 1899–1939* (1942) and *Labor-Savings in American Industry* (1945); Simon Kuznets, *Commodity Flow and Capital Formation* (1938) and *National Income and Its Components,* 2 v. (1941); F. C. Mills, *Prices in Recession and Recovery*

(1936); National Resources Committee, *Technological Trends and National Policy* (1937).

Toward a Critique of the New Deal. Criticism from the left: Lewis Corey, *Decline of American Capitalism* (1934); Norman Thomas, *Choice before Us* (1934). Criticism from the study: Columbia University Commission, *Economic Reconstruction* (1934); Eli Ginzberg, *Illusion of Economic Stability* (1939); Friedrich A. Hayek, *Collectivist Economic Planning* (1935). Criticism from New Dealers disillusioned: Donald Richberg, *Rainbow* (1936) and Raymond Moley, *After Seven Years* (1939). From a political opponent: Herbert Hoover, *Addresses upon the American Road, 1933–38* (1939). The following consider the political implications of the expansion of government: G. C. S. Benson, *New Centralization* (1941); K. G. Crawford, *Pressure Boys* (1939); E. P. Herring, *Public Administration and the Public Interest* (1936); A. N. Holcombe, *New Party Politics* (1934); F. R. Kent, *Without Grease* (1936); J. L. McCamy, *Government Publicity: Its Practice in Federal Administration* (1939); John McDiarmid, *Government Corporations and Federal Funds* (1939); Nelson M. McGreary, *Development of Congressional Investigative Power* (1940); A. C. Millspaugh, *Democracy, Efficiency, Stability: An Appraisal of American Government* (1942); Thorsten Sellen and Donald Young, "Pressure Groups and Propaganda," *Annals*, Amer. Academy of Pol. and Soc. Science, v. 179 (May, 1935). Costs are counted in the Twentieth Century Fund study, *Facing the Tax Problem* (1937) and Lucius Wilmerding, *Spending Power* (1943).

36: THE STRUGGLE FOR NEUTRALITY

The International Economic Policy of the New Deal. For background material, consult, W. A. Brown, *International Gold Standard Reinterpreted*, 2 v. (1940); Paul Einzig, *World Finance, 1914–35* (1935); A. D. Gayer and C. T. Schmidt, compilers, *American Economic Foreign Policy* (1939); International Documents Service, *International Currency Experience: Lessons of the Interwar Period* (1944). The following will be useful on American investments (and see under Chapter 33): Hal Lary, "United States in the World Economy" (1943); Cleona Lewis and K. T. Schlotterbeck, *America's Stake in International Investment* (1938); J. T. Madden, Marcus Nadler, and H. C. Sauvain, *America's Experience as a Creditor Nation* (1937); R. L. Sammons and Milton Abelson, "American Direct Investments in Foreign Countries" (1942). On the reciprocal trade program, consult, G. L. Beckett, *Reciprocal Trade Agreement Program* (1941); H. B. Hinton, *Cordell Hull* (1942); J. C. Pearson, *Reciprocal Trade Agreements Program* (1942); Alonzo E. Taylor, *New Deal and Foreign Trade* (1935).

Latin-American Affairs. For general treatments, see under Textbooks and Series, section on diplomatic histories. See also, L. D. Baldwin, *Story of the Americas* (1943) and S. F. Bemis, *Latin-American Policy of the United States* (1943). For the new orientation in inter-American relations, see: A. A. Berle, Jr., *New Directions in the New World* (1940); Carnegie Endowment for International Peace, Division of International Law, *International Conferences of American States, First Supplement, 1933–40* (1940); Charles Wertenbaker, *New Doctrine for the Americas* (1941). Among books dealing with special problems, see: W. A. M. Burden, *Struggle for Airways in Latin America* (1943); John MacCormac, *Canada: America's Problem* (1941); E. W. McInnis, *Unguarded Frontier: A History of American-Canadian Relations* (1942).

Neutral Rights and Philippine Independence. Elton Atwater, *American*

Regulation of Arms Exports (1941); Edward Borchard and W. P. Page, *Neutrality for the United States* (1937); J. R. Hayden, *Philippines* (1942); J. F. Rippy, *America and the Strife of Europe* (1938); Whitney Shepardson and W. O. Scroggs, editors, *United States in World Affairs* (1940—).

NAVAL CONSTRUCTION. R. H. Albion, *Sea-Lanes in Wartime: The American Experience, 1775–1942* (1943); Forrest Davis, *Atlantic System: the Story of Anglo-American Control of the Seas* (1941); G. T. Davis, *Navy Second to None* (1940).

THE NEW PREPAREDNESS. The defense program is considered under various aspects in the following: Seymour Harris, *Economics of American Defense* (1941); A. G. Hart and associates, *Paying for Defense* (1941); H. G. Moulton, *Fundamental Issues in National Defense* (1941) and *New Philosophy of Public Debt* (1943); A. C. Pigou, *Political Economy of War* (rev. edition, 1943); U.S. Maritime Commission, *America Builds Ships* (1940). On the Lend-Lease program, see: R. G. D. Allen, "Mutual Aid between the United States and the British Empire, 1941–45," Royal Statistical Society, *Journal*, v. 109, no. 3, pp. 243–77 (1946); E. R. Stettinius, Jr., *Lend-Lease: Weapon for Victory* (1944).

THE THIRD TERM CONTEST. Spokesmen for the Republican opposition: T. E. Dewey, *Case Against the New Deal* (1940); Herbert Hoover, *Further Addresses on the American Road* (1940); Wendell Willkie, *Free Enterprise* (1940) and *This is Wendell Willkie* (1940). F. D. Roosevelt, *Public Papers and Addresses* (1938–41), presents the other side. The following books give a picture of the foreign-policy debate: C. A. Beard, *Foreign Policy for America* (1940); R. L. Buell, *Isolated America*. See also, Max Lerner, *Ideas for the Ice Age* (1941) and Harold Lavine and James Wechsler, *War Propaganda and the United States* (1940).

37: THE SHOOTING WAR

GENERAL TREATMENTS. Since World War II remains contemporary history, it is too soon for treatment in full perspective. The following are useful: for background: Winston S. Churchill, *Second World War: The Gathering Storm, 1919–39* (1948); C. G. Haines and R. J. S. Hoffman, *Origins and Background of the Second World War* (1943); Allan Nevins and Louis M. Hacker, *United States and Its Place in World Affairs* (1943); Cordell Hull, *Memoirs*, 2 v. (1948); Dexter Perkins, *America and Two Wars* (1944). Military aspects of the war are treated in: H. S. Commager, *Story of the Second World War* (1945); Edgar McInnis, *The War: An Annual Survey* (1939–45); R. W. Shugg and H. A. DeWeerd, *World War II: A Concise History* (1946); G. C. Marshall, H. H. Arnold, and E. J. King, *War Reports* (1947). S. E. Morison, *History of the United States Naval Operations in World War II* will be complete in 13 volumes (1947–). Bernard Brodie, *Guide to Naval Strategy* (1944) is useful. Francis Brown, *War in Maps* (1944) shows a global war. Waverley Root, *Secret History of the War*, 3 v. (1945–46) rides an anti-State Department hobby hard, but gives useful details.

THE ROAD TO PEARL HARBOR. T. A. Bisson, *America's Far Eastern Policy* (1945) is a general work. Backgrounds of conflict will be found in, J. G. Grew, *Ten Years in Japan* (1944); Owen Lattimore, *Manchuria: Cradle of Conflict* (1932); Nathaniel Peffer, *Prerequisites for Peace in the Far East* (1940); J. L. Stimson, *Far Eastern Crisis* (1936). Forrest Davis and E. K. Lindley, *How War Came* (1942) is a popular account; U.S. Department of State, *Peace and War*:

U.S. Foreign Policy, 1931–41 (1943) an official account. See, also, U.S. Department of State, *Papers Relating to the Foreign Relations of the U.S.: Japan, 1931–41.*

THE WAR IN THE FAR EAST. For a sampling of personal accounts, see: Theodore H. White, editor, *Stilwell Papers* (1948); John Hersey, *Hiroshima* (1946); C. P. Romulo, *I Saw the Fall of the Philippines* (1942). Strategic problems are considered in Cyril Falls, *Nature of Modern Warfare* (1941) and Lawrence Rosinger, "Strategy of the War in Asia," (F. P. *Reports,* April 16, 1943). See also, Gilbert Cant, *Great Pacific Victory from the Solomons to Tokyo* (1946).

THE WAR IN EUROPE. For a sampling of personal accounts, see: W. H. Mauldin, *Up Front* (1945); Richard Tregaskis, *Invasion Diary* (1944); Walter Karig and Welbourne Kelly, *Best from Yank* (1945). Political issues are dealt with in Herbert Hoover and Hugh Gibson, *Problems of Lasting Peace* (1942) and N. J. Spykman, *America's Strategy in World Affairs* (1942). A. C. Clifford, *Conquest of North Africa* (1943) and Alan Moorehead, *Mediterranean Front* (1942) deal with the preliminaries to the attack on "the soft underbelly of Europe." George C. Marshall, *Selected Speeches and Statements* (1945) and B. G. Wallace, *Patton and his Third Army* (1946) give partial pictures of the attack in the west. Dwight D. Eisenhower, *Crusade in Europe* (1948) is the story of the Allied commander-in-chief. For a summary of military action in Europe, see under GENERAL TREATMENTS.

THE PEOPLES' WAR. U.S. Department of State, Publication No. 2353, *Charter of the United Nations* (1945) presents the hope; No. 2774, *Making of the Peace Treaties* (1947) portrays the thorny road. H. A. Wallace, *Century of the Common Man* (1943) and W. L. Willkie, *One World* (1943) are significant.

38: DOMESTIC PROBLEMS OF WARTIME AMERICA

MOBILIZATION OF MEN AND RESOURCES. H. S. Tobin and P. W. Bidwell, *Mobilizing Civilian America* (1940) and U.S. Office of Facts and Figures, *American Preparation for War* (1942) are general treatments. The first impacts are dealt with in Pendleton Herring, *Impact of War* (1940) and W. F. Ogburn and others, *American Society in Wartime* (1943). L. B. Hershey, *Selective Service in Peacetime* (1941) and *Selective Service in Wartime* (1942, 1944, 1945) are illuminating. The war economy is described in Seymour E. Harris, *Economics of America at War* (1943); Emanuel Stein and Jules Backman, *War Economics* (1942); Emanuel Stein, J. D. Magee, and W. J. Ronan, *Our War Economy: Government—Production—Finance* (1943).

MOBILIZING SCIENCE. E. C. Andrus, D. W. Bronk, and others, *Advances in Military Medicine,* 2 v. (1948); J. D. Baxter, *Scientists Against Time* (1946); Henry DeWolf Smyth, *Atomic Energy for Military Purposes. . . .* (1945).

MOBILIZING MORALE. H. L. Childs and J. Whitton, *Propaganda by Shortwave* (1943); Merle Curti, "The American Mind in Three Wars," *Journal of the History of Ideas* (June, 1942); Carroll C. Pratt, *Psychology: The Third Dimension of War* (1942); G. B. Watson, editor, *Civilian Morale* (1942).

ECONOMIC IMPACTS OF THE WAR. ORGANIZATION. W. H. Nicholls and J. A. Vieg, *Wartime Government in Operation* (1943).

PRODUCTION. Geoffrey H. Moore, *Production of Industrial Materials in World War I and World War II* (1944); Donald M. Nelson, *Arsenal of Democracy* (1946); K. C. Stokes, *Regional Shifts in Population, Production, and Markets, 1939–43* (1943); War Production Board, *War Production in 1945* (June, 1946).

U.S. Special Committee to Study the Rubber Situation, *Report* (1942) and F. A. Howard, *Buna Rubber: The Birth of an Industry* (1947) deal with a special problem in keeping a mechanized army rolling.

PRICES AND WAGES. C. O. Hardy, *Wartime Control of Prices* (1941); Meyer Jacobstein and H. G. Moulton, *Effects of the Defense Program on Prices, Wages, and Profits* (1941); F. C. Mills, *Prices in a War Economy* (1942); U.S. Department of Labor, Bureau of Labor Statistics, *Chart Series* (1945); U.S. Office of Price Administration, *First Quarterly Report: For Period ended April 30, 1942*.

INCOME. Simon Kuznets, *National Product: War and Prewar* (1944) and *National Product in Wartime* (1945).

LABOR. Aaron Levenstein, *Labor Today and Tomorrow* (1945); S. T. Williams and Herbert Harris, *Trends in Collective Bargaining* (1945).

AGRICULTURE. U.S. Department of Agriculture, Bureau of Agricultural Economics, *Agricultural Situation* (November, 1945) and *Net Farm Income and Parity Report, 1943 and Summary for 1910–42* (July, 1944).

ECONOMIC WARFARE. Antonin Basch, *New Economic Warfare* (1941); R. W. B. Clarke, *Britain's Blockade* (1940); Paul Einzig, *Economic Warfare, 1939–40* (1940); D. L. Gordon and Royden Dangerfield, *Hidden Weapon* (1947); C. L. Leith, J. W. Furness, and Cleona Lewis, *World Minerals and World Peace* (1943); T. Reveille, *Spoil of Europe: The Nazi Technique in Political and Economic Conquest* (1941).

FISCAL ISSUES AND INFLATION. W. L. Crum, J. H. Fennelly, and L. H. Seltzer, *Fiscal Planning for Total War* (1942); U.S. Bureau of the Budget, *United States at War* (1946); U.S. Secretary of the Treasury, *Annual Report on the State of the Finances* (1940–47). See, also, references under *Prices, Income*.

39: POSTWAR RECONSTRUCTION

PROBLEMS OF INTERNATIONAL ECONOMIC RECONSTRUCTION. W. A. Brown, "The Future Economic Policy of the United States" (1943) and "The Economic Exploitation of Europe and Its Consequences," *Nature*, v. 153 (June 3, 1944); Irvin Hexner, *International Cartels* (1945); Cleona Lewis, *Debtor and Creditor Countries: 1938, 1944* (1945); E. S. Mason, *Controlling World Trade* (1945); Twentieth Century Fund, *Rebuilding the World Economy* (1947); Seymour Harris, *European Recovery Program* (1948).

INTERNATIONAL POLITICAL PROBLEMS. Quincy Wright, editor, *Foreign Policy for the United States* (1947); U.S. Department of State: Publication No. 2702, *International Control of Atomic Energy: Growth of a Policy* (1946); Pub. No. 2882, Marshall, G. C., *Harvard Commencement Address* (1947); Pub. No. 2930, *Report of the Committee on European Economic Cooperation*, v. 1 (1947); U.S. Senate, 80th Congress, 1st Session, *European Recovery Program* (1947), basic documents and background. Walter Lippmann, *Cold War* (1947) and Twentieth Century Fund, *Report on the Greeks* (1948) consider special aspects of the problem. Louis Doleirt, *United Nations* (1946) and Herman Finer, *United Nations Economic and Social Council* (1946) deal with the new world organization.

THE POSTWAR POLITICAL CLIMATE. 79th Congress, 2nd Session, "An Act for the Development and Control of Atomic Energy"; President's Advisory Commission on Universal Training, *Program for National Security* (1947); U.S. Council of Economic Advisers, *Annual Reports to the President* (1946—).

PROBLEMS OF RECONVERSION. C. C. Abbott, *Financing Business During the*

720   BIBLIOGRAPHY

Transition (1946); B. M. Baruch and J. M. Hancock, *Report on War and Postwar Adjustment Policies* (1944); Board of Governors of the Federal Reserve System, *Public Finance and Full Employment* (1945); J. M. Clark, *Demobilization of Wartime Economic Controls* (1944); M. G. de Chazeau, A. G. Hart, G. C. Means, and others, *Jobs and Markets* (1946); H. M. Groves, *Postwar Taxation and Economic Progress* (1946); C. O. Hardy, *Prices, Wages, and Employment* (1946); S. E. Harris, editor, *Economic Reconstruction* (1945); Calvin B. Hoover, *International Trade and Domestic Employment* (1945); A. D. H. Kaplan, *Liquidation of War Production* (1945); H. G. Moulton and K. T. Schlotterbeck, *Collapse or Boom at the End of the War* (1942); Theodore W. Schultz, *Agriculture in an Unstable Economy* (1945); Smaller War Plants Corporation, *Economic Concentration and World War II* (1946); J. H. Williams, *Postwar Monetary Plans and Other Essays* (1945).

THE POSTWAR BOOM. B. M. Anderson, S. H. Schlichter, and others, *Financing American Prosperity* (1946); Simon Kuznets, *National Income* (1946); C. R. Noyes, "Prospect for Economic Growth," *American Economic Review*, XXXVII (March, 1947); Twentieth Century Fund, *America's Needs and Resources* (1947).

40: LIFE, LEARNING, AND THE ARTS BETWEEN WORLD WARS

THE AMERICAN SCENE. AMERICA IN PROSPERITY. F. C. Allen, *Only Yesterday* (1931); Lawrence Greene, *Era of Wonderful Nonsense* (1939); R. S. and H. M. Lynd, *Middletown* (1929); President's Conference on Unemployment, *Recent Economic Changes*, 2 v. (1929); President's Research Committee on Social Trends, *Recent Social Trends in the United States*, 2 v. (1933); H. M. Robinson, *Fantastic Interim* (1943); Caroline Ware, *Greenwich Village, 1920-30* (1935). James T. Adams, *Our Business Civilization* (1929) [cf. F. C. Sharp and P. G. Fox, *Business Ethics* (rev. edition, 1937)]; John C. Ransom, F. L. Owsley, and others, *I'll Take My Stand* (1930); and H. E. Stearns, editor, *Civilization in America* (1922) are critiques from the viewpoint of the dependent middle class, the Southern agrarian, and the intellectual respectively. AMERICA IN DEPRESSION. See, Chapter XXXIV, section *Works and Relief*. See further, Franz Alexander, *Our Age of Unreason* (1942); F. C. Allen, *Since Yesterday* (1940); Charles A. and Mary R. Beard, *America in Midpassage* (1939); R. S. and H. M. Lynd, *Middletown in Transition* (1937); "Recent Social Trends," *American Journal of Sociology*, v. 67 (May, 1942). Among the mass of social criticism, the following repay reading: Alfred Bingham, *Insurgent America* (1936); Stuart Chase, *Economy of Abundance* (1934); Lewis Corey, *Crisis of the Middle Class* (1935); Howard Scott, *Introduction to Technocracy* (1933); George Soule, *Coming American Revolution* (1934). The expatriate and his return are presented in Malcolm Cowley, *Exile's Return: A Narrative of Ideas* (1934) and H. E. Stearns, *Rediscovering America* (1934). Henry Miller, *Air-Conditioned Nightmare* (1945) describes the backtrek of the "unreconstructed." [Cf. H. E. Stearns, editor, *America Now* (1938)]. America's "second-class citizens" are discussed in Anna de Koven, *Women in Cycles of Culture* (1941); E. R. Embree, *American Negroes* (1942); M. L. Ernst and Alexander Lindey, *Censor Marches On* (1940); Oliver La Farge, editor, *Changing Indian* (1942); Carey McWilliams, *Prejudice* (1944); Gunnar Myrdal, *American Dilemma*, 2 v. (1944).

Among general works on amusements, see F. R. Dulles, *America Learns to Play: A History of Popular Recreation, 1607-1940* (1940); R. B. Weaver, *Amusements and Sports in American Life* (1939). Aspects of the new communication are discussed in the following: A. N. Goldsmith and A. C. Lescaboura, *This Thing Called Broadcasting* (1930); K. S. Tyler, *Modern Radio* (1947); [cf. Hadley Cantril, *Invasion from Mars* (1940) for an instance of radio-generated mass hysteria]; M. D. Huettig, *Economic Control of the Motion Picture Industry* (1944); Deems Taylor, M. Peterson, B. Hale, *Pictorial History of the Movies* (1943); Margaret Thorp, *America at the Movies* (1940); J. W. Krutch, *American Drama since 1918* (1939); F. L. Mott, *American Journalism: A History of Newspapers in the United States* (1941); Roger Burlinghame, *Engines of Democracy: Inventions and Society in Mature America* (1940); R. C. Epstein, *Automobile Industry* (1928); E. D. Kennedy, *Automobile Industry* (1941); J. H. Frederick, *Commercial Air Transportation* (1942); F. C. Kelly, *Wright Brothers* (1943); W. F. Ogburn, *Social Effects of Aviation* (1946).

SCIENTIFIC ADVANCE. See also, Chapter XXXVIII, section, *Mobilizing Science*. Williams Haynes, *Men, Money and Molecules* (1936); Bernard Jaffe, *Men of Science in America* (1944) and *Outposts of Science* (1935); Wheeler McMillen, *New Riches from the Soil* (1946); A. K. Solomon, *Why Smash Atoms?* (1940); James Stokley, *Science Remakes Our World* (1946); Harold Ward, editor, *New Worlds in Medicine* (1946) and *New Worlds in Science* (1941).

EDUCATION AND THE SOCIAL DISCIPLINES. On popular education, consult, Benjamin Fine, *Our Children Are Cheated* (1947); I. L. Kandel, editor, *Twenty-Five Years of American Education* (1924); E. W. Knight, *Education in the United States* (1929); A. E. Meyer, *Development of Education in the Twentieth Century* (1940); Winston Sanford, *Illiteracy in the United States* (1930). Changes in higher education are discussed in R. F. Butts, *College Charts Its Course* (1939) and E. V. Hollis, *Philanthropic Foundations and Higher Education* (1938). The "Donnybrook of the higher learning" is exemplified in such books as: R. M. Hutchins, *Higher Learning in America* (1936) [cf. Veblen's book of the same name] and *Education for Freedom* (1943); John U. Nef, *United States and Civilization* (1942); George A. Lundberg, *Can Science Save Us?* (1947); R. S. Lynd, *Knowledge for What?: The Place of the Social Sciences in American Culture* (1939). Aspects of the social sciences themselves are discussed in such general works as, Merle Curti, *Growth of American Thought* (1943); Paul T. Homan, *Contemporary Economic Thought* (1928); R. H. Lowie, *History of Ethnological Theory* (1937); G. A. Lundberg, Read Bain, and Nils Anderson, *Trends in American Sociology* (1929); Vernon L. Parrington, *Main Currents in American Thought*, 3 v. (1927–30). Notable instances of the new currents are embodied in such books as Thurman W. Arnold, *Folklore of Capitalism* (1937); Edward Chamberlin, *Theory of Monopolistic Competition* (1938); J. M. Clark, "Past Accomplishments and Present Prospects of American Economics," *American Economic Review*, XXVI (March, 1936); John Dewey, *Logic: The Theory of Inquiry* (1936); E. E. Neff, *Poetry of History* (1947); C. K. Ogden and I. A. Richards, *Meaning of Meaning* (1936); *Proceedings of the Conferences on Science, Philosophy, and Religion*, Third Symposium (1943).

MUSIC, PAINTING, AND ARCHITECTURE. Aaron Copland, *Our New Music* (1941); L. Reis, *Composers in America* (1938); Paul Rosenfeld, *Hour with American Music* (1929); W. Sergeant, *Jazz Hot and Hybrid* (1939); H. Cahill and A. H. Barr, editors, *Art in America* (1935); Sheldon Cheyney, *Story of Modern Art* (1941); Talbot Hamlin, *Architecture: An Art for All Men* (1947); Louis H. Sullivan, *Autobiography of an Idea* (1926); Frank Lloyd Wright, *Modern Architecture* (1931) and *Autobiography* (1932).

LITERATURE BETWEEN THE WARS. Percy Boynton, *America in Contemporary*

Fiction (1940); Oscar Cargill, *Intellectual America: Ideas on the March* (1941); Harry Hartwick, *Foreground of American Fiction* (1934); Granville Hicks, *Great Tradition* (1935); Alfred Kazin, *On Native Grounds* (1942); H. E. Luccock, *American Mirror* (1940); F. O. Matthiessen, *Achievement of T. S. Eliot* (1935).

POPULAR TASTE. See, also, titles under THE AMERICAN SCENE, above. F. L. Mott, *Golden Multitudes* (1947) provides material for study of comparative taste in reading. "Symposium on Characteristics of American Culture and its Place in General Culture," American Philosophical Society, *Proceedings*, v. 83 (September, 1940) is an interesting contribution to the long-standing argument between those Americans who observe the growth of conditions favorable to the emergence of culture and those who want to see culture itself.

Index

Absentee landlordism, 184. *See also,* Tenancy.
Adams, Charles Francis, 46
Adams, Charles Francis, Jr., 228
Adams, Henry, 61, 214, 678
Addams, Jane, 208, 355, 432
Agrarian discontent, 64, 65, 184, 223, 252
Agricultural Adjustment Act of 1933 (AAA), 561
Agricultural Marketing Act of 1929, 533
Agriculture (*See also,* Farm bloc, Foreign trade): changes in production, 141-43, 148-49, 531; credit problems of, 174-75, 402-03; exports and, 139-40, 330; governmental aid to: credit, 402-03, 531; economic, 474, 531-34; education, 149-50; New Deal program for, 257, 561-62; prices, 143, 437-38, 527-28; problems of, 1870-90, 147, 151-53; 1920-40, 527-29; surplus and, 147, 531; World War I, 437-38, 527; World War II, 630-31, 659-60
Aguinaldo, Emilio, 296, 308
Alabama Claims, 40-42
Alaska: boundary settlement, 104; civil government in, 72, 104; purchase of, 42; resources, 105
Aldrich, Nelson W., 81, 83, 289, 330, 334
Aldrich-Vreeland Act of 1908, 394
Aleutian Islands, 602, 604
Algeciras Conference, 377-78
Alger, R. A., 289, 293
Allison, W. B., 81, 177, 289, 330
Altgeld, J. P., 193
American Association for Old Age Security, 363
American Federation of Labor (A.F. of L.): communist tactics in, 515; during the nineteen twenties, 467, 510-11; organization and progress to World War I, 188-89, 195-97, 201; struggle with the CIO, 565
American Sugar Refining Company, 82, 240, 283
Ames, Oakes, 30, 31
Anderson, Maxwell, 669
Anderson, Sherwood, 682
Anthony, Susan B., 205

Architecture in America, 219-20; 680-81
Arms embargo, 590
Army (*See also,* Selective Service): in Mexico, 407; in Spanish-American War, 295-98; in World War I, 444-48; in World War II, 607-11, 619-20; reorganization of, 371, 652
Army Appropriations Act of 1916, 429
Arnold, General Henry H., 611
Arthur, Chester A., 65, 68, 85
Art in America, 217-19, 679-80
Atkins, Edwin F., 283-84
Atlantic Charter, 612
Atlee, Clement, 613
Atomic bomb, 605, 622, 675
Atomic disarmament, 647
Atomic Energy Act of 1946, 652-53
Atomic Energy Commission (U.N.), 646-47
Atomic Energy Commission (U.S.), 652
Automobile in America, 665-66
Aviation: civilian, 480, 506, 673; World War I, 446; World War II, 604-08

Babcock, O. E., 42, 49
Badoglio, Marshal Pietro, 607
Balance of international payments (*See also,* Foreign trade): agriculture and, 146-47; United States as creditor, 540-42; United States as debtor, 183, 538
Ballinger, R. A., 337, 351
Bank for International Settlements, 499
Banking Acts of 1933 and 1935, 567
Banks (*See also,* Federal Reserve system, National Banking system): Chinese interests of, 377-80; closing of, 553; consolidations among, 346; failures, 552; investigation of (1912), 346; railroad financing by, 344
Baruch, Bernard M., 436, 627, 637
Bayard, Thomas F., 95, 96
Beard, Charles A., 573, 596, 597
Beard, Charles and Mary, 204, 678
Beecher, Henry Ward, 69, 207
Belknap, W. W., 49
Bell Act, 591
Bellamy, Edward, 364
Benelux, 640

723

Benét, Stephen Vincent, 683
Berger, Victor L., 365, 366, 441, 457
Bernstorff, von, 418, 420
Beveridge, Albert J., 360
Bevin, Ernest, 643
Bigelow, John, 84
Bimetallism. See, Gold Standard, Silver.
Bismarck Sea, battle of, 604
Bizonia, 643
Black, Hugo L., 574
"Black Codes," 15, 16
"Black Friday," 31, 32
Blaine, James G., 61, 66; Bering Sea dispute, 95; biographical sketch, 62-63; corruption charges, 69; dominance in Garfield Cabinet, 67; election of 1884, 64, 69, 70; of 1888, 73; of 1892, 75; Isthmian Canal, 94; Latin-American policy, 62, 92, 96; naval interests, 105; reciprocity treaties, 82; tariff, 79; Venezuelan boundary, 96
Blair, General Francis, P., 26
Bland, Richard P., 177, 180
Bland-Allison Act, 52, 177-78
Blount, J. H., 103
Board of Economic Warfare, 631
Board of Governors of the Federal Reserve System, 538, 567, 575
Bonaparte, Charles J., 84, 341
Bonanza farms, 148
Bonus, soldiers'. See, Veterans.
Booth, John Wilkes, 10
Borah, William E., 454-55, 596
Borie, Adolph E., 45
Boston police strike, 464-65
Bourbon Democracy, 54, 56
Bourke-White, Margaret, 683
Bourne, Randolph, 684
Boutwell, G. S., 35
Bowles, Samuel, 209, 671
Boycott and labor, 511
Bradley, General Omar N., 608
Branch factories, 540
Brandeis, Louis D., 355, 390
Brazil–United States Defense Commission, 632
Bretton Woods conferences, 639-40
Briand-Kellogg Pact, 492-93, 496
Bristow, Benjamin H., 49, 50, 64, 170
Brown, Gratz, 46
Brussels Conference of 1937, 599
Bryan, William Jennings: biographical sketch, 268; candidacies, 1896, 182, 261, 266-72; 1900, 304-05; 1908, 332; Colombia, 371; election of 1912, 385; imperialism, 304-05; Secretary of State, 390, 413, 493; silver champion, 180, 268

Bryan-Chamorro Treaty, 372, 411
Buchman, Frank, 672
Buell, Raymond L., 597
Burchard, S. D., 70
Burma Road, 600
Butler, General Benjamin F., 35, 48, 255
Butler-Crawford Act of 1947, 315
Byrnes, James F., 626, 643

Cairo Conference of 1943, 613
Cabell, James Branch, 682-83
Caldwell, Erskine, 683
Calverton, V. C., 684
Cameron, G. D., 35, 62, 65
Canada: defense of, 589; disputes with, 94-95, 377
Cannon, Joseph G., 89, 178, 330, 336
Capper-Volstead Co-operative Act of 1922, 531
Caribbean and the United States, 487, 490-91. See also, Imperialism.
Carlisle, John G., 76, 178, 181
Carnegie, Andrew: business methods of, 162; contribution to peace movement, 106, 412; philosophy of, 166; steel industry and, 162-64
Carnegie Steel Company, 106, 162-64, 238
Carpetbaggers, 21
Carranza, Venustiano, 402-09
Cartelization. See, NIRA.
Carver, Thomas Nixon, 678
Casablanca Conference of 1943, 612
Cassatt, A. J., 128
Cassatt, Mary, 680
Cather, Willa, 682
Catholicism, 206, 672
Cattle industry, 113-15
Cervera, Admiral, 295-97
Chaco dispute, 587
Chamberlain, Joseph, 295, 306
Chamberlain, Neville, 593
Chapultepec, pact of, 632
Chase, Mary, 669
Chase, Salmon P., 171
Chautauqua, 206
Chennault, General Claire, 602
Chiang Kai-shek, 613
Child labor, 359-61, 564
China: American interests in (1903–13), 377-80; Boxer uprising, 324-25; dismemberment of, 306, 323; immigration from, 121-22; Japanese aggression against, 496, 591-92, 599-600; role in World War II, 604, 611, 613; Washington Conference of 1922, 495
Churchill, Winston, 601, 605-06, 611-13
CIO (Committee for Industrial Organiza-

INDEX

tion; Congress of Industrial Organizations), 565, 572
Civil Aviation Organization, 640
Civil rights: during reaction after World War I, 457; for Negroes, 16, 17, 19, 33, 58, 655
Civil service, 20, 63, 84-86. *See also,* Hatch Act, Pendleton Act.
Civil War: agriculture, 28; capitalist dominance and, 10, 22, 23, 28, 32; decline of merchant marine, 185-86; effect on labor, 189; hatred aroused by, 3, 6; influence on manufacturing, 156; influence on protective tariff, 29, 78, 79; precipitating factors, 3-5; slavery and, 4-7
Civil Works Administration (CWA), 568
Civilian Conservation Corps (CCC), 554
Clark, Champ, 385
Clark, J. Reuben, 491, 586
Clayton Antitrust Act of 1914, 397-99, 512, 519
Clayton-Bulwer Treaty, 368
Cleveland, Grover, 61, 64, 68; biographical sketch, 70, 71; bond sales, 71, 181-82; civil service, 71, 86; Cuba, 284-85; election of 1884, 69; of 1892, 75; financial problems under, 76; fisheries, 95; Hawaii, 71, 77, 102-03; inflation, 71; pensions, 71, 89; public lands, 113, 226, 349; Pullman strike, 76, 200; railroad regulation, 234; repudiation of, 76, 266-67; silver, 76, 177, 180-81; tariff, 76, 81, 83; trusts, 248; Venezuela boundary dispute, 77, 97-98
Codes and Code Authorities. *See,* NIRA.
Colfax, Schuyler, 26, 30, 31
Colombia, 369-72
Colonial policy, 319. *See also,* Alaska, Hawaii, Jones Acts, Philippines, Puerto Rico.
Combined Chiefs of Staff, 611
Commodity loans, 561
Communism, 513-15, 645, 657
Concentration, industrial. *See,* Monopoly, Trusts.
Conciliation treaties of 1928, 592-93
Conference for Progressive Political Action, 467
Conkling, Roscoe, 17, 35, 62, 63, 65-68, 167-68
Conscientious objectors, 441, 625
Conscription, 595, 598, 652. *See also,* Selective Service.
Conservation, 71, 113, 331, 349-51
Contracts Settlement Act of 1944, 658
Cooke, Jay, and Company, 47, 132, 344
Coolidge, Calvin, 460; Boston police strike, 464-66; Caribbean relations, 487-88, 585; farm relief, 531, 533; Mexican relations, 409, 486-87; veterans' legislation, 482
Cooper, Peter, 254
Coral Sea, battle of, 604
Cotton Stabilization Corporation, 534
Coughlin, Father, 573, 590
Council of Economic Advisers, 654, 662
Cox, James M., 460-61
Crane, Hart, 683
Crane, Stephen, 217, 682
Credit (*See also,* Currency, Federal Reserve System, Inflation): agricultural, 402-03, 531; expansion, 558, 567
Crédit Mobilier, 30, 66, 131
Creel, George, 441
Criminal syndicalist laws, 514
Croly, Herbert, 354
Cuba: agents in the United States, 286; American economic interests in, 283-84, 322; American intervention in, 320-22; insurrection of 1895, 284-86; occupation of, 319; Platt Amendment, 319-31, 491, 587; reciprocal trade agreement, 321, 393; Ten-Years' War in, 43, 281-82; War with Spain and, 298-99
Cullom, S. M., 233
Cullom Committee, 224, 233-34
Currency (*See also,* Banks, Greenbacks, Silver): adoption of gold standard, 273; banks and, 173; devaluation of, 567; Federal Reserve System and, 395-96; specie payment, 54
Currency Act of 1900, 273, 303
Curry, John Steuart, 680
Curtis, George W., 63, 69, 84-85, 215
Czechoslovakia, 593, 645

Dana, Charles Augustus, 209
Darlan, Admiral, 606
Daugherty, Harry M., 460, 462-63
Davis, David, 51, 253
Davis, Jefferson, 12, 13
Davis, John W., 466
Dawes, Charles G., 465, 468
Day, W. R., 277, 299, 300
"Death sentence" for utility holding companies, 570
Debs, Eugene V.: opposition to World War I, 441; Pullman strike, 170, 199-200, 511; Socialist candidate for Presidency, 304-05, 330, 365, 366, 388, 461, 465
Debt (*See also,* Public debt): agricultural, 151-52; depression, 552-58; housing, 570; railroads, 568

Declaration of Lima, 588-89
Declaration of Panama, 589
Defense, Department of, 652
Defense Plant Corporation, 621
Defense program. See, Preparedness, World War II.
Deficit financing, 578-79
De Forest, Lee, 668
De Leon, Daniel, 365-66, 514
De Lôme, Dupuy, 287-88
Democratic party. In political campaigns from 1866 to 1948, see, Elections; in connection with other issues and men, see, names and topical headings.
Depew, Chauncey M., 98, 120
Depression of 1930: bank failures during, 553; causes of, 552; effects of, 551-53; onset of, 551; recession of 1937–38, 574-76; recovery programs, 552, 556-71
Dewey, D. R., 173
Dewey, Admiral George, 292, 295-96
Dewey, John, 205, 678-79
Dewey, Thomas E., 636, 654-57
Dickinson, Emily, 210-11, 216-17
Dill, Sir John, 611
Dingley, Nelson, 278
Direct primary, 355-57
Dole, Sanford B., 102-03
Dollar devaluation. See, Currency.
Dominican Republic: Grant's effort to annex, 42; intervention in, 372-74, 410; termination of occupation, 487
Donato, Pietro di, 683
Donnelly, Ignatius, 260, 305
Douglass, Lloyd, 672
Dreiser, Theodore, 681
Drew, Daniel, 127, 129, 204
Dust bowl, 666

Eakins, Thomas, 210, 217, 680
Eaton, Dorman B., 84-85
Economic Co-operation Administration, 645
Economic Defense Board, 632
Economic nationalism, 583-85. See also, Imperialism, International Trade Organization.
Economic warfare, 437, 631-32
Economy Act of 1933, 553
Eddy, Mary Baker, 207
Edmunds, George F., 65, 170, 247
Education: adult, 206; agricultural, 112, 149-50; higher, 211, 676-77; in dependencies, 314, 317; public, 205-06, 675-76; women's, 212
Eighteenth Amendment, 404, 469, 520-22

Einstein, Albert, 622
Eisenhower, Dwight D., 606, 608, 654
Elections: 1860, 10; 1866, 16, 18; 1868, 26, 27; 1870, 45; 1872, 35, 46, 47, 253; 1874, 48, 254; 1876, 50-52, 254; 1880, 66, 67, 254; 1882, 68; 1884, 69, 70, 255; 1888, 72-73; 1892, 75, 262; 1894, 76, 262-63; 1896, 264-72; 1898, 303; 1900, 304-05; 1904, 329-30; 1908, 331-32; 1910, 337; 1912, 384-85; 1914, 391; 1916, 423-24; 1918, 449; 1920, 460-62; 1924, 465-67; 1928, 468-70; 1932, 532-33; 1936, 573; 1938, 577, 582; 1944, 634-35; 1946, 650-51; 1948, 654-57
Electric power industry, 506, 569. See also, Holding companies.
Electoral Commission, 51
Eliot, Charles W., 68, 211
Eliot, T. S., 670, 673, 683, 684
Emancipation Proclamation, 7
Emergency Banking Act of 1933, 553
Emergency Farm Mortgage Act of 1933, 562
Emergency Price Control Law of 1942, 634
Employers' liability, 359. See also, Workmen's Compensation.
Employment Act of 1946, 653
Equalization fee plan, 532
Estrada Palma, Tomas, 286, 321
Europe, reconstruction of, 638-40 (See also, European Recovery Program, Marshall Plan).
European investments in the United States: balance of international payments, 183; increase of during the nineteen thirties, 541-42; rails, 127, 137, 344; reduction of during World War I, 428; size of in 1900, 183
European Recovery Program (ERP), 644-45
European Western Union, 643
Ever-normal granary, 561
Exchange controls, 584-85, 639-40
Exchange stabilization, 584, 683-84
Excise taxes: Civil War, 29; New Deal, 579; Spanish-American War, 294; World War I, 435; World War II, 633
Exports. See, Foreign trade.
Export debenture plan, 474-75
Export-Import Bank, 560, 584, 586, 632

Fair Labor Standards Act of 1938, 361, 559, 564, 577, 667
Fall, Albert B., 462-64
Far East (See also, China, Japan, Philippines): United States interest in, 323-

INDEX 727

25, 377-80; Washington Conference of 1922, 452, 495
Farm bloc, 532-33
Farm Credit Administration, 562
Farm Mortgage Moratorium Act of 1935, 562
Farm Mortgage Refinancing Act of 1934, 562
Farm Security Administration (FSA), 562, 650
Farmer-Labor party, 461, 467
Farmers' alliances, 256, 258. *See also,* Populist party.
Farrell, James T., 683
Federal Alcohol Administration, 523
Federal Co-ordinator of Transportation, 569
Federal Deposit Insurance Corporation, 560
Federal election laws, 73-74
Federal Emergency Relief Administration, 567
Federal Farm Board, 533-34, 552
Federal Farm Loan Act of 1916, 402-03
Federal Farm Loan Board of 1929–33, 532
Federal Farm Mortgage Corporation, 558
Federal Housing Administration (FHA), 571
Federal Intermediate Credit Act of 1923, 531
Federal Power Commission, 483-84, 570
Federal Reserve Board, 395-96, 428
Federal Reserve System: establishment of, 395-97; in World War I, 428; New Deal recasting of, 558, 567
Federal Savings and Loan Associations, 570
Federal Trade Commission: activity under Wilson, 400, 418; under Wilson's successors, 419; establishment of, 398-99
Federal Trade Commission Act of 1914, 397-98
Federal Water Power Act, 457, 483-84
Fermi, Enrico, 622
Fifteenth Amendment, 33
Fish, Hamilton, 41, 43, 91
Fisk, Jim, 31, 32, 45
Food Administration, 437, 626
Food and Agriculture Organization (FAO), 640
Foraker Act of 1900, 315
Forbes, Charles R., 463
Forbes, W. Cameron, 309
Ford, Henry, 665
Foreign Economic Administration, 631
Foreign investments (American): Cuba, 322; entry of American capital into international money market, 345; minor character of to World War I, 307; Philippine Islands, 312; relation to prosperity of the nineteen twenties, 538; status of in the nineteen thirties, 541-42
Foreign investments (in the United States), 137, 183-84, 541-42
Foreign Ministers Council, 642-43
Foreign trade: agriculture, 139-40, 529-30; character of American, 543-45; creditor position of United States, 540; debtor position of United States, 183, 307; depression of 1930, 476, 584; during World War I, 427; during World War II, 595, 597, 631-32, 639-40, 661; exports, 139-40, 184-85, 543-45; imports, 545-47; markets, 185, 545; reciprocal trading agreements, 585; Russia, 584; United Nations and, 639-40
Foster, William Z., 552
Four-Power Treaty, 496
Fourteenth Amendment: as political platform, 16; Roscoe Conkling and interpretation of, 167-68; interpretation of by Supreme Court, 167-68, 515-16; provisions of, 16, 166
France: Briand-Kellogg pact, 493; desire for revenge on Germany, 451; propaganda of in United States (1914–17), 426; relations with during Civil War and Reconstruction, 37; World War II, 593-94, 606, 608-10
Frankfurter, Felix, 355, 439
Freedman's Bureau, 8, 14, 15, 18, 21, 36
Freund, Ernst, 355
Freylinghuysen, F. T., 92
Frick, Henry Clay, 162, 198-99
Frost, Robert, 683
Fuel Administration, 684
Fulbright Resolution, 614
Fundamentalists, 673

Garfield, Harry A., 438
Garfield, James A., 18; assassination of, 68; biographical sketch, 65-66; Civil Service reform, 67; Crédit Mobilier, 30; Half-Breed leader, 62
Garfield, James R., 333, 341, 350, 351
Gary, Elbert H., 163-64
Gaulle, General Charles de, 606
General Maximum Price Regulation, 634
Gentlemen's Agreement, 376
George, Henry, 153, 210, 214, 634
Germany: attitude during Spanish-American War, 294, 296, 302; economic collapse of, 499, 583; Samoan Islands, 100;

INDEX

Germany (*continued*)
 Venezuela, 367-68; World War I, 419-22, 426-27, 430-31; World War II, 593, 601, 608-11, 642-43, 648-49
Gibbs, Willard, 211, 212, 674
Gilded Age, 202-03, 210, 211, 685
GI Bill of Rights, 657-58, 676
Gilman, Daniel Coit, 210, 211
Giraud, General Henri, 606
Glass, Carter, 395
Goebbels, Joseph, 641
Goering, Hermann, 641
Goethals, George Washington, 371, 436
Gold, 31-32, 181-82, 273, 575. *See also*, Currency, Economic nationalism, Foreign trade, Public debt, Silver.
Gold market, 31, 32
Gold Repeal Joint Resolution of 1933, 567
Gold Reserve Act of 1934, 567
Gold standard, 176, 264, 303, 329, 567. *See also*, Currency, Silver.
Gompers, Samuel, 195-96, 332, 465, 510
Good neighbor policy, 586
Gorgas, W. E., 319, 371
Gorman, A. P., 61, 82
Gould, Jay, 31-32, 127, 129, 131, 132, 192
Grand Army of the Republic (G.A.R.), 3, 88-89. *See also*, Veterans.
Grain Stabilization Corporation, 533
Grafton, Samuel, 671
Granger Movement, 229-230. *See also*, Agrarian discontent.
Grant, Ulysses Simpson: election of, 26, 27; estimate of, 41, 45; foreign policy, 37, 41-43; Gould as associate of, 32; impeachment of Andrew Johnson, 23, 24, 32, 44; Republican Presidential campaign of 1880, 66-68; Reconstruction policy, 27, 32, 34; scandals of administration, 48-50; suspension of habeas corpus by, 36
Great Britain: American agriculture and, 139; controversies with, 40-42, 95-99, 368-71, 414-18; Japanese aggression and, 600; naval limitation and, 497; propaganda in the United States, 425-26; relations with, 294-96, 302, 594, 595, 597, 599, 620, 630, 637, 640-41
Greece, 646
Greeley, Horace, 46, 47, 209, 671
Greenbacks, 26, 31 (*See also*, Currency); gold reserve (1893), 181; issue of, 171; legal tender cases, 172; resumption of specie payments, 172
Greenback party, 253-55
Gresham, Walter Q., 262
Guadalcanal, 604
Guffey Bituminous Coal Act, 568, 650

Haiti, 410, 487
Half-Breeds, 62, 65
Hampton Wade, 56
Hancock, General Winfield Scott, 66, 79
Hanna, Mark: election of 1896, 264-65, 270-72; of 1900, 304-05; Roosevelt's attitude toward, 327; Senator, 277; War with Spain and, 289
Harding, Warren Gamaliel: election and Presidency, 460-64; naval armaments limitation, 495; treaty for conciliation of Colombia, 371-72
Harmon, Judson, 248
Harriman, E. H., 126, 132-35, 380
Harrison, Benjamin: biographical sketch, 72; failure to enforce Sherman Act, 247-48; Treasury surplus, 73, 89
Harrison, F. B., 310-11
Havana Conference of 1939, 594
Havemeyer, H. O., 283, 321
Hawaii, 71, 100-03
Hawes-Cutting Act of 1932, 591
Hay, John, 91, 210, 270, 306; arbitration of Alaskan boundary, 377; Isthmian canal treaties, 369-71; Open Door in China, 323-25; retention of the Philippines, 300; war with Spain, 288, 294
Hay–Bunau-Varilla Treaty, 370
Hay-Herran convention, 369
Hay-Pauncefote Treaty, 368, 371
Hayes, Max S., 365, 461
Hayes, Rutherford B., 61, 64, 65; biographical sketch, 50; Civil Service reform, 85; pension bills, 52; removal of Arthur, 52, 68; silver, 178
Haywood, William D., 514
Health: mental, 674; Philippines, 314; slums and, 203-04
Hearst, William Randolph, 209-10, 286, 597, 670
Hellman, Lillian, 669
Hemingway, Ernest, 683
Hemisphere solidarity, 589
Hendricks, T. A., 64
Henry, Joseph, 212
Hepburn, A. B., 173
Hepburn Act, 237, 331, 347-48
Herrick, Robert, 681
Hicks, Granville, 684
Hill, David B., 61, 82, 258, 267, 304
Hill, James J., 132-33, 204, 328
Hiroshima, 605
Hitler, Adolf, 500, 590
Hoar, George F., 62, 66, 247, 258
Hobson, Richmond P., 297
Hodges, General Courtney H., 608
Hoffman, Paul G., 645
Holding companies: development of, 239-

INDEX

40, 517; Federal Trade Commission and, 518-19; power, 570; railroads, 568
Holmes, Justice Oliver Wendell, 377
Home Owners' Loan Corporation (HOLC), 570
Home Owners' Refinancing Act of 1933, 570
Homer, Winslow, 210, 217-18
Homestead Act, 112-13
Hopkins, Harry L., 607
Hoover, Herbert: agricultural problems, 474-75, 533; election to Presidency, 468-70; foreign trade, 185, 537; governmental reorganization, 577-78; head of Food Administration, 437; Philippines, 591; power, 484-85; prohibition, 521; reparations, 499-500; role in depression, 472, 552; tariff, 474; World War II, 596, 597
House, Colonel Edward M., 418, 429, 432
Housing, 203-04, 571
Howe, Frederic C., 355-56
Huerta, Victoriano, 406-07
Hughes, Charles Evans: fight on Supreme Court appointment of, 472, 517; League of Nations Covenant, 454; Republican candidate for President (1916), 423-25; Secretary of State, 462, 486
Hull, Cordell, 599, 601
Hull trade program, 584-86
Hutchins, Robert M., 677

Immigration, 4; changes in origin, 119, 523; Chinese, 68, 121-22; Contract Labor Law, 122-23; encouragement of, 117, 118; legislation affecting, 117, 121-23; measures restricting, 524-25; reasons for restricting, 120-21, 523
Imperialism (*See also*, Caribbean, China): Caribbean and Latin America, 538, 540-41; character of American before World War I, 306-08; election of 1900, 304-05
Imports. *See*, Foreign trade.
Income, national: during the depression of 1930 and after, 551; during World War II and postwar, 629, 660-61, 686; from 1909 to 1929, 506; under New Deal recovery, 628
Income tax (*See also*, Internal revenue): amendment permitting, 393; tariff of 1894, 82, 83, 170
Independent Republicans, 64. *See also*, Liberal Republicans, Mugwumps.
Indians, 115-17
Industrial Workers of the World (I.W.W.), 439, 457, 513-14. *See also*, Labor.
Industry (*See also*, Monopoly, Tariff, Trusts): concentration of, 162-63, 517-19; development of, 1865-1900, 157-58; growth of, 506-07; immigration and, 118; labor productivity, 508-09; mechanization, 156, 159; New Deal and, 563; World War I, 435-37; World War II, 626-27, 661, 689
Inflation, 632-34, 659-61. *See also*, Agriculture, Currency, Price Control.
Ingalls, John J., 247, 258
Ingersoll, Robert, 63, 212
Initiative and referendum, 356-57
Injunction, 332, 399, 511-12. *See also*, Labor.
Insular Cases, 318-19
Insurgent Republicans. *See*, Progressive movement.
Instrumentalism, 679
Interallied debts, 497-500
Inter-American Conference for the Maintenance of Peace, 587
Inter-American Defense Council, 647
Inter-American Treaty of Mutual Assistance of 1947, 632
Internal revenue, 49 (*See also*, Excise taxes, Income tax): Civil War excises, removal of, 29, 87; income tax, 82, 83; New Deal measures, 578-79; World War I, 435; World War II, 633
International Bank for Reconstruction and Development, 639
International Monetary Fund, 639
International Trade Organization, 639-40
International War Crimes Tribunal, 641
Interstate Commerce Act, 224, 234, 341
Interstate Commerce Commission, 234-37, 266, 328, 341, 348-49, 516, 569. *See also*, Railroads, Supreme Court.
Intervention, 386-87, 554, 580-81, 685-86, 688. *See also*, Laissez-faire, New Deal.
Intervention. *See*, Good Neighbor policy, Latin-American nations by name.
Investments. *See* Foreign investments, Industry.
Iran, 646
Isolationism, 378, 537. *See also*, Imperialism, Neutrality, World War II.
Isthmian canal: diplomacy of, 368-69; Nicaraguan project, 304, 369, 372, 379, 491; Panama Canal, 369-71
Italo-Ethiopian War, 591
Italy, 607, 647

James, Henry, 210, 216, 684
James, William, 210, 213, 678
Japan: aggression against China, 323, 496, 591, 599-600, 613; League of Nations, 591-92, 599; Pacific phase of World

Japan (*continued*)
  War II, 601-05; Pearl Harbor, 601; Theodore Roosevelt and, 375-76
Jeffers, Robinson, 683
Jefferson, Thomas, 61, 327, 596
Johnson, Andrew: biographical sketch, 11, 12; conflict with Congress, 15, 19, 20, 24; impeachment and trial of, 23, 25; Mexican policy, 37, 39; political errors of, 17, 18; reconstruction policy of, 13, 14, 26; relations with Grant, 23, 24
Johnson, Hiram W., 386, 424, 460
Johnson, Reverdy, 40
Johnson Debt Default Act of 1934, 500, 590
Joint Committee on Atomic Energy, 653
Joint Committee of Fifteen on Reconstruction, 15-16, 63
Jones Act of 1916, 310-11; of 1917, 315, 317
Juarez, Benito, 30, 39
Juvenile delinquency, 658

Kansas-Nebraska bill, 5, 6
Kasserine Pass, battle of, 606
Keating-Owen Act of 1916, 360, 404
Kellogg, Frank B., 486, 493, 596
Kellogg pacts, 492, 493
Keynes, John Maynard, 389, 443, 451, 678
King, Admiral Ernest J., 611
Knights of Labor, 189-96, 200
Knox, Philander, 333, 393; American bankers in China and, 379-80; "Dollar Diplomacy," 378, 393; efforts on behalf of Peace Movement, 413; Latin-American policy, 371, 378-79; opposition to League of Nations, 454
Knudsen, William, 594
Ku Klux Klan, 34, 36, 56, 458, 465-66
Kurusu, Saburu, 601

Labor (*See also,* A.F. of L., CIO, I.W.W., Knights of Labor, Supreme Court): antitrust laws and, 200, 399, 511-12; contrast with capital, 188; immigration and, 120-21; injunction and, 399, 511-13; legislative protection of, 122-23, 369-62, 404, 559, 564, 566, 577; organization of, 189-90, 439, 457, 510-11, 563, 579-80, 629-30; productivity of, 508-09, 628; wages, 198, 439, 510, 628
La Follette, Robert M.: biographical sketch, 336; independent candidacy, 461; influence on reform movement, 353, 355; "insurgency," 332, 334, 337, 391; railroad regulation, 347, 349, 516

La Follette Seamen's Bill of 1916, 404
Laissez-faire: American industrialism, 165-67; attacks on, 354, 580-81; enthronement of, 64, 157, 165-66; Radical reconstruction policy and, 22; Supreme Court, 168-69, 361-63, 516-17
Lamar, Lucius Q. C., 71
Land values. *See,* Agriculture.
Landon, Alfred M., 572
Lansing, Robert, 408, 417, 420, 421, 456
Latin America (*See also,* Foreign trade, Imperialism, and under countries' names): arbitration treaties, 493-94; Good neighbor policy, 585-87; propaganda in, 587; relations with, 1870 to 1900, 92-96; Theodore Roosevelt and, 372-74; World War II, 588-89, 594, 631-32
League of Nations: formulation of Covenant, 453-54; issue in 1920 campaign, 461; Republican opposition to, 454, 460, 465; unofficial dealings with, 492
Leahy, Admiral William D., 611
Ledo Road, 604
Lee, Robert E., 12
Lemke, William, 573
Lend-Lease, 565, 595, 620, 630, 637
Lerner, Max, 215
Lewis, John L., 565, 595, 659
Lewis, Sinclair, 682
Liberal Republicans, 36, 45-47, 64. See *also,* Independent Republicans, Mugwumps.
Lilienthal, David, 652
"Lily-white" Republicans, 57
Limitation of production, 561-62, 568
Lincoln, Abraham, 5, 24, 44; death of, 10; freedom from hatred, 7, 32; Reconstruction policy, 8-10
Lindbergh, Charles A., 576
Lindsay, Vachel, 683
Lippmann, Walter, 354-55, 671
Liquor control. *See,* Prohibition.
Literacy test. *See,* Immigration.
Literature in America, 215-17, 681-84
Lloyd, Henry Demarest, 214, 242, 263, 269
Lodge, Henry Cabot, 74, 330, 332, 449; American preparedness (1915–17), 429; campaign of 1884, 69; immigration restriction, 121, 123; opposition to League of Nations, 454-55; War with Spain, 299, 300
Loewy, Raymond, 684
Logan, John A., 62, 65, 69
Logical positivism, 679
London, Jack, 681

INDEX

London Conference of 1930, 497; of 1935, 592
London Economic Conference of 1933, 583-84
Long, J. D., 293
Lowden, Frank O., 460, 465, 468
Ludlow resolution, 589
Lumpkin, Grace, 684
Lusitania, 419
Lynd, Robert and Helen, 678
Lytton Commission, 592

McAdoo, William G., 390, 436, 460, 466
MacArthur, General Douglas, 601, 602
McCormick, Cyrus H., 148
McCormick, Vance C., 437
McCrary, G. W., 232-33
McDonald, John, 49
McKinley, William, 61, 74, 185; biographical sketch, 265; currency position, 178, 265-66; declaration of war on Spain, 287-91; tariff, 81, 82, 178, 265; territorial expansion, 103; trust legislation, 249
MacLeish, Archibald, 683
McNary-Haugen bill, 532-33
Macune, C. W., 256, 260
Madero, Francisco, 405-06
Mahan, Admiral A. T., 106-07, 300, 306
Malaria, 624
Manchukuo, 591, 599
Manchuria, 380, 391, 599-600
Man power. *See,* Mobilization.
Maritime Commission, 626
Marketing, changes in, 507
Marshall, General George C., 611, 643-44
Marshall Plan, 644-45, 656, 657
Marxism. *See,* Communism, Socialism.
Masters, Edgar Lee, 684
Maximilian, Archduke, 38-39
Maximum hours regulation, 361-62. *See also,* Fair Labor Standards Act of 1938, NIRA.
May-Sheppard Act of 1940, 650
Mechanization, 157, 503, 507-09, 673, 689
Mellon, Andrew, 462, 466, 468, 472, 480-81
Mencken, H. L., 672, 682, 684
Mental health. *See,* Health.
Merchant Fleet Corporation, 476-77
Merchant marine: decline of, 40, 101, 185-89; subsidies to, 186-87, 404, 477, 569
Merchant Marine Act of 1920, 457; of 1928, 476; of 1936 and 1938, 568-69
Metals Reserve Company, 631

Mexican–United States Defense Commission, 632
Mexican War, 5
Mexico: American economic interests in, 405; dispute with France concerning, 37; disorders in, 406-07; economic legislation of, 408, 486-87; pressure for intervention in, 407-08; relations with, 406-09, 431, 486-87, 585, 632
Michelson, A. A., 675
Miles, General Nelson A., 298
Miller, W. H. H., 73
Millikan, R. A., 675
Mineral production, 159-61
Minimum Wage laws, 361, 559, 564, 573
Mitchell, John, 329
Mitchell, Wesley C., 678
Mobilization (*See also,* Conscription, Selective service): industry, 435-36, 620-21, 624-28; man power, 433, 619-20
Modernists, 673
Molotov, Vyacheslav, 643, 645
Monopoly (*See also,* TNEC, Trusts): beginnings of, 20, 30; credit, 344-46; during the nineteen twenties, 419; early industrial concentration, 238, 240-41, 401; effect on prices, 557; under New Deal policies, 563
Monroe Doctrine, 38; application by Blaine, 92; Briand-Kellogg Pact, 493; Good Neighbor policy, 586; Hoover Administration and, 491; League of Nations Covenant, 454; Roosevelt Corollary of, 373, 491-92
Montgomery, General Sir Bernard, 606-07
Moore, W. H., 163
Morgan, J. P., and Company: American purchasing agent for Allied governments, 427-28; Chinese investment, 380; promoter of combinations, 344-45; railroad financing, 127, 129, 134, 344; sale of bonds for gold, 181-82; shipping industry, 187; steel industry, 163-64, 344
Morgan, Thomas Hunt, 675
Morrill, J. S., 78
Morrill Act, 112, 149, 211
Morrison, W. R., 79, 80, 235
Morrow, Dwight W., 486-87, 585
Morton, Oliver P., 35, 62
Moscow Conference of 1943, 612; of 1946, 642
Most-favored-nation treatment, 585, 639
Motion picture, 668
Muckrakers, 353-54
Mugwumps, 64, 69, 71
Mulligan letters, 69, 70

INDEX

Mumford, Lewis, 685
Munich agreement, 593
Muscle Shoals, 484-85
Music in America, 220, 679
Mussolini, Benito, 540, 592, 607

Nagasaki, 605
Napoleon III, 37-39
National Bank Act of 1863, 173, 175
National banking system, 173-75. See also, Federal Reserve System.
National Civil Service Reform League, 84-85
National Defense Advisory Committee, 594, 625
National Defense Mediation Board, 595, 630
National Housing Acts, 571
National Industrial Recovery Act (NIRA), 563, 564, 667
National Labor Relations Act of 1935, 559, 564
National Labor Relations Board (NLRB), 580, 651, 652
National Labor Union, 189-90
National Monetary Commission, 394
National Recovery Administration (NRA), 563
National Resources Planning Board, 650
National Security Act of 1947, 652
Naval armaments: expansion of, 381-83, 592; limitation of, 495-97
Navalism. See, Navy.
Navy: as colonial administrator, 410-11; building programs, 68, 105, 381-83, 591-92; development of (1880-98), 68, 73, 105-07; during Spanish-American War, 292-98; during World War I, 444, 446; during World War II, 604, 626
Negroes, 8, 14, 15, 21-23, 56-60
Neutrality: British blockade and, 414-18; campaign of 1940, 596-98; foreign investments and, 427-28; German submarine warfare and, 419-22; legislation of 1935-37, 500; Nye committee and, 590; Woodrow Wilson and, 414; World War I, 414-22; World War II, 590
Neutrality Act of 1937, 590
New Deal, 388; agencies, 561-71; agricultural program, 561-62; banking reform, 567; bureaucracy and, 581-82; cartelization, 563, 578; credit expansion, 558, 567; critique of, 579-82; currency expansion, 567, 663; economic consequences, 579-80; economic recovery, 574; emergency measures, 553-54; foreign policy, 586-89; foreign trade program, 583-85; industrial program, 563; labor organization, 563; labor standards, 559, 565; liquidation of, 577-78, 650; philosophy of, 327; power program, 569-70; public works, 568, 576; pump priming, 560-61; railroad program, 568; recession of 1937–38, 574-76; securities and exchange regulation, 567; social security, 566; Supreme Court, 561-62, 568, 573; theory of, 554-57
New Freedom, 388, 399
New leisure, 667
New Nationalism, 388
Newspapers in America. See, Press.
Nicaragua: American intervention in, 379, 411, 487-88; canal proposal, 369, 372
Nimitz, Admiral Chester W., 602
Nine-Power Treaty, 496, 599
Nineteenth Amendment, 357
Norris, Frank, 354
Norris, George W., 336, 472, 484-85
Norris-La Guardia Act of 1932, 512
Northern Securities Company, 338, 342
Nuclear fission. See, Atomic bomb.
Nye, Gerald, 590

Obregón, Alvaro, 407-09
Odets, Clifford, 669
Odum, Howard, 677
"Ohio Idea," 253-54
O'Fallon case, 517
Office for Emergency Management (OEM), 594
Office of Civilian Defense, 624
Office of Defense Transportation, 626
Office of Economic Stabilization, 626
Office of Economic Warfare, 631
Office of Lend-Lease Administration, 597
Office of Price Administration (OPA), 634
Office of Price Administration and Civilian Supply, 634
Office of Production Management (OPM), 594, 625
Office of Scientific Research and Development (OSRD), 622-23
Office of Small Business Activities, 620
Office of War Information (OWI), 625
Office of War Mobilization (OWM), 626
Oil Administration, 626
Oil scandals, 463-64
Old age pensions, 363. See also, Social Security.
Olney, Richard, 96-98, 189-90, 248, 284-85
O'Mahoney Monopoly Inquiry Act of 1938, 575
O'Neill, Eugene, 669

INDEX

Open Door policy, 323-25, 378, 536-37
Open-Market Committee. *See,* Federal Reserve Board.
Open-Market operations. *See,* Federal Reserve System.
Ottawa Preference Agreement of 1931, 640

Packers and Stockyards Act of 1921, 531
Page, Walter Hines, 390, 417, 418, 421
Painting in America, 217-18, 670-71
Palestine, 647-48
Palmer, A. Mitchell, 408, 441, 457, 460
Panama, 370-71, 491, 586
Panama Canal. *See,* Isthmian Canal.
Pan-American conferences, 92-93, 188, 587-88
Panay, sinking of, 600
Panics, financial, 47-48, 180, 331. *See also,* Depression of 1930.
Parity income, 561
Parker, Alton B., 329
Parker, Sir Gilbert, 425-26
Parker, John M., 423-24
Parrington, Vernon Louis, 678
Patch, General Alexander M., 608
Patton, General George S., Jr., 607-08, 610
Patrons of Husbandry. *See,* Granger movement.
Payne, Sereno E., 334
Peace Movement, 412-14, 453-55, 460, 465, 494-95, 592-93
Pearl Harbor, 601, 620, 626
Peck, Harry Thurston, 62
Peffer, W. A., 257-58
Pegler, Westbrook, 671
Peirce, Charles S., 213, 678
Pendleton Act, 85
Pensions. *See,* Reform movement, Social Security, Veterans.
People's party. *See,* Populist party.
Pershing, General John J., 407, 444-45
Pétain, General Henri, 601, 607
Philanthropy: during nineteen twenties, 664, 674; institutionalization of, 209; role in depression of 1930, 559
Philippine Islands (*See also,* Imperialism): acquisition of, 299-300; civil government for, 309-10; conquest of, 295, 308-09; economic importance of, 312-13; independence for, 308, 310-11, 385, 461, 466, 591; Japanese conquest of, 314, 602; liberation of, 604
Philippine Sea, battle of, 604
Philosophy in America, 212-13, 679-80
Pierson, Warren L., 632
Pinchot, Gifford, 350-51

Platt, T. C., 67
Platt Amendment, 319-20, 491, 586
Poetry in America, 216-17, 684-85
Poland, invasion of, 593
Police power, 355. *See also,* Laissez-faire, Supreme Court.
Population (*See also,* Immigration, Urbanization): growth of, 198, 503, 661; immigration and, 109; slackening in rate of increase of, 503; urbanization, 108, 504, 687; westward movement of, 109-10
Populism, 252-53, 258
Populist party: absorption by free-silver issue, 268-69; agrarian discontent and, 256-57; decline of, 303, 305, 332; election of 1892, 262; of 1894, 262-63; Farmers' Alliance and, 74, 256, 258; influence of, 352-54; labor and, 359; organization of, 257-58; program of, 256, 260-62; sectional factor in, 56
Portfolio investments. *See,* Foreign investments.
Postwar reaction, 457-58
Potsdam Conference of 1945, 613
Pound, Ezra, 683
Pound, Roscoe, 355
Powderly, Terence V., 192, 195
Power, 482-85, 569-70
Pragmatism, 355, 678-79
Pre-emption Act of 1841, 110, 113
Preparedness, 430, 594-95, 598, 649, 652
Press: development of (1860–90), 209-10; in nineteen twenties, 670; editorial influence, 671; yellow journalism, 209, 670-71; war propaganda and, 210, 425-26
Pressure groups, 580, 688
Price control, 633-34. *See also,* Inflation, OPA.
Price Stabilization Act of 1942, 634
Prices: agricultural, 147, 529, 531, 660; during World War I, 439; during World War II and postwar, 629, 659; industrial concentration and, 238-40, 244; inflexibility of, 557; monopoly, 576; New Deal efforts to raise, 558, 567; TNEC investigation and, 576
Processing taxes, 561
Production, wartime expansion of, 626-27
Progressive movement, 338, 348, 356
Progressive party, 385-88, 391, 423-24
Prohibition, 520-22, 554, 666
Protection. *See,* Tariff.
Protestantism, evangelical, 672
Proximity fuze, 624
Psychoanalysis, 674

Public debt: currency problem and, 171, 173; Mellon policy and, 480-81; National banking system and, 175; New Deal and, 578; post-Civil War controversies, 26, 27, 29; World War I, 434-35; World War II, 633, 661-63
Public lands, 111-13
Public Utility Holding Companies Act of 1935, 568
Public Works Administration (PWA), 559, 566
Puerto Rico: acquisition of, 296, 300; development of, 316-17; government of, 315, 461; problems of, 316-17
Pulitzer, Joseph, 98, 209-10, 285, 670

Quay, M. S., 72, 73, 83
Quebec Conference of 1943, 612
Quota laws. See, Immigration.

Radar, 624
Radio, 668
Railroads: abuses of, 125, 127, 129-31, 224-28; agrarian discontent and, 223; administration during World War I, 436, 478; cattlemen and, 114; consolidations, 30, 479; construction of transpacific lines, 130-33; financial problems of, 127, 129, 568; foreign investments in, 127, 137, 344; governmental aid to, 30, 120, 135-37, 344; Granger movement and, 228-30; growth of (1860-1930), 124-25; labor relations of, 190, 331, 359, 479; laws regulating: Elkins Act, 328, 347; Interstate Commerce Act, 125, 234; Hepburn Act, 237, 331, 347-48; Mann-Elkins Act, 348-49; Transportation Act of 1920, 478-79; of 1934, 568; problems, 479-80; rebates, 227-28, 241-45, 348; regulation of, 125, 228-30; speculation and, 47; Supreme Court and, 125; typical systems, 127-35
Rationing, 634
Rawlins, General John A., 43
Reagan, J. H., 233, 247
Recall of elective officials, 356
Reciprocal trade agreements. See, Foreign trade, Tariff.
Recreation, 667
Reconstruction: Congressional program for, 9, 11, 15; economic implications of, 32, 156; end of, 33-36, 52; foreign affairs in, 39-45; Grant and, 20, 21, 32, 33; Johnson's program, 13, 14; Joint Congressional Committee on, 15, 16, 63; Lincoln's program, 8-10; measures, 19-21, 33, 34; military aspects of, 19, 21; new state constitutions and, 21-23; Southern intransigence and, 14, 17, 18
Reconstruction Finance Corporation (RFC), 552, 553, 558-59, 568, 595, 621
Reed, Thomas B., 74, 89, 278, 289
Reform movement: factors influencing, 332; muckrakers 354; political and social thinkers and, 355; politics, 356-57; social and economic legislation, 358
Reid, Whitelaw, 288, 299, 300, 306
Religion in America, 207-08, 672-73
Reorganization Act of 1939, 577-78, 652
Reparations (See also, Interallied Debts): World War I, 452, 498-500; World War II, 614, 643
Republican party. In political campaigns, see, Elections; in connection with other issues and men, see, names and topical headings.
Resumption Act of 1875, 29
Revenue Act of 1935, 578; of 1940, 594; of 1941–43, 633; of 1948, 650. See also, Public debt, Taxation.
Rice, Elmer, 669
Richardson, H. H., 210, 219
Richardson, W. A., 48, 49
Robertson, W. H., 67
Robinson, Edwin Arlington, 683
Rockefeller, John D.: organizer of Standard Oil, 239, 241-45; philanthropic activity, 211
Rockefeller, William, 241, 243, 345
Roebling, John A., 210, 219
Rogers, Will, 590
Rogers Act of 1924, 86
Rome-Berlin Axis, 593
Rommel, General Ernst, 606
Roosevelt, Franklin Delano: agricultural problem and, 534; biographical sketch, 552; campaign of 1920, 461; of 1932, 432-33; of 1936, 572; of 1940, 595-96; of 1944, 636; economic nationalism, 584; fight on the Supreme Court, 573-74; foreign policy: Far East, 599, 601; Good Neighbor, 585-87; Latin America, 491; Lend-Lease, 596-97; Neutrality, 590-91, 594, 597-98; Russian, 502, 597; United Nations, 613; program for recovery, 553-54, 574; prohibition, 522, 554; role in World War II, 611-13
Roosevelt, Theodore, 63, 73; biographical sketch, 326-27; conservation of natural resources, 349-51; election of 1884, 326; of 1900, 303-05; of 1904, 329-30; of 1908, 331-32; of 1912, 383, 386-88; of 1916, 423-25; foreign policy: corol-

INDEX

lary to Monroe Doctrine, 372-73, 491-92, 587; European intervention, 375-78; Far East, 375-76; imperialism, 307-08, 367; Latin America, 367-70, 373-74; navalism, 327, 380, 382; Progressive movement and, 385-87, 423-24; railroad regulation, 328, 331; relations with Insurgent Republicans, 339; relations with William Howard Taft, 332-33, 351; role in Spanish-American War, 288, 293, 295; role in World War I, 429, 449; Sherman Antitrust Law enforcement, 328, 331, 340; Vice-Presidential nomination, 304
Root, Elihu, 303, 319, 371, 454, 494
Royce, Josiah, 213
Rubber, synthetic, 627
Rundstedt, von, 608-09, 611
Rusk, J. M., 73
Russia: Alaskan purchase, 42; American intervention in Russo-Japanese War, 374-75; friction with after World War II, 641-44, 646-49; in World War I, 431, 497-98; in World War II, 605-06, 608; nonaggression pact with Germany, 593; relations with, 1920-28, 500-01; resumption of diplomatic relations, 502
Ryder, Albert P., 211, 217-18, 680

Sachs, Alexander, 622
Salisbury, Lord, 96-97, 295, 373
Samoan Islands, 99-100
Sampson, Commodore W. T., 292, 296-97
Sandoz, Mari, 683
San Francisco Conference of 1945, 614
Santo Domingo. See, Dominican Republic.
Saposs, David J., 510
Sargent, John Singer, 218
Saroyan, William, 683
Schiff, Jacob H., 133, 345
Schley, Commodore W. W., 292, 296-97
Schurz, Carl, 45, 69, 84, 85
Schwab, C. M., 437
Science in America, 212-13; 673-75
(Dred) Scott decision, 6, 16
Scott, T. A., 128, 162
Sectional conflict, 64, 65. See also, Agrarian discontent, Civil War, Populism.
Securities and Exchange Commission (SEC), 559, 567, 619
Seidel, Emil, 366, 388
Selective Service Act of 1917, 433; of 1940, 619
Semantics, 679
Settlement house movement, 208
Seventeenth Amendment, 356, 404

Seward, William H., 6, 14, 39, 42
Seymour, Horatio, 26, 27
Shafter, General W. R., 297
Sharecroppers, 144, 528-29. See also, Tenancy.
Shepherd, A. R., 48
Sherman, John: currency policy, 54, 73, 76, 177; election of 1880, 65; Half-Breed leader, 62; pension legislation, 89; Secretary of State, 277; trust legislation, 241, 247
Sherman Antitrust Act (See also, Labor, Monopoly, Trusts): enactment, 73, 247-48; enforcement, 249-50, 328, 331, 341, 344, 400, 402; inadequacies, 340-41; labor, 200, 511-12; trade associations, 518; Supreme Court and, 250-51, 340, 342-44, 400-01, 511-12, 518
Sherman, Stuart, 684
Siegfried, André, 672
Silver: demonetization (Crime of '76), 176; campaign of 1896, 266; free coinage of, 177, 266; Greenback party and, 254; legislation: Bland-Allison Act, 52, 177; Silver Purchase Act, 73, 76, 177, 178, 180-81; Thomas Amendment, 567; panic of 1893, 180
Simpson ("Sockless Jerry"), 257-59, 263
Simpson, General William H., 610
Sims, Admiral W. S., 446
Sinclair, Upton, 354, 681
Sixteenth Amendment, 393
Slavery, 5-6
Smaller War Plants Corporation, 620
Smith, Alfred E., 466, 468-70
Smith-Connally Act of 1943, 630
Social legislation: federal under New Deal, 566, 571, 577; state in early nineteen hundreds, 358-63
Socialism: decline of, 513; development before World War I, 353, 363-66, 388, 425-26; early manifestation in labor movement, 196
Socialist Labor party, 75
Social science, 677-78
Social security, 566, 633, 654, 655
Soil Conservation and Domestic Allotment Act of 1936, 561
Soldiers' bonus, 482
Soldier vote, 636
South: agrarian movement in, 56; cultural eclipse of, 54-55; development of railroads in, 54, 134; disfranchisement of Negroes, 55-57; industrialization, 54-55, 146, 507; post-Civil War economic conditions, 14, 19, 54, 143; restoration of white control in, 35-37, 51-54; role

South (*continued*)
  in elections, 37, 471, 656-57; tenancy, 36, 144
Soviet Union (USSR). *See,* Russia.
Spain: Cuban policy of, 285; relations with United States, 43, 283-91
Spanish-American War: consequences of, 303; events preceding, 284-91; military phase of, 293-94, 295-98; treaty of Paris of 1898, 298-300; yellow press, 285-87
Speakership of House, 74, 391
Specie payments, resumption of, 172
Spencer, Herbert, 166, 212
Stabilization. *See,* Inflation.
Stabilization Act, 634
Stalin, Marshal Joseph, 613
Stalingrad, 605-06
Stalwart Republicans, 62, 65
Standardization, 507-08, 666
Standard Oil. *See,* Monopoly, Rebates, Rockefeller.
Stanton, Edwin M., 20-24, 44
Stanton, Elizabeth Cady, 205
Stassen, Harold E., 617, 654
State capitalism, 581
Steel, 124, 160-62, 551, 621, 627
Steel Workers' Organizing Committee (SWOC), 565
Steinbeck, John, 669, 683
Stephens, Uriah S., 190
Stettinius, Edward R., Jr., 597
Stevens, J. L., 102-03
Stevens, Thaddeus, 15, 78
Stewart, A. T., 45
Stilwell, General Joseph W., 602
Stimson, Henry L., 312, 472, 488, 492, 496
Stock speculation, 47-48, 331, 480, 551, 659
Strikes (*See also,* Labor): anthracite coal fields, 1902, 328-29; defense industries, 595, 630; diminishing in nineteen twenties, 468, 513; Haymarket Square, 193; Homestead (Pa.), 75, 162, 198-99; Pullman, 199-200; railroads in 1877, 190; World War I, 439, 457, 513-14; World War II, 630, 659
Subsidies. *See,* Agriculture, Housing, Merchant Marine, Price Control.
Sub-treasury plan, 256, 258
Suffrage: Fifteenth Amendment, 33; Negro, 12, 15, 19, 20, 26, 56, 57; Nineteenth Amendment, 357
Sulfa drugs, 624
Sullivan, Louis H., 210-11, 219, 680-81
Sumner, Charles, 9, 15, 40-43, 84-85
Sumner, William Graham, 213

Supply, Priorities and Allocations Board, 595, 626
Supreme Court: chastening of, 570, 574; constitutional status of dependencies, 317-19; federal child labor laws, 360; Fourteenth Amendment, 168-69, 515-16; frustration of Interstate Commerce Act, 235-37; Granger cases, 230; in 1936 election, 573; income tax law of 1894, 170; injunction in Debs case, 170, 511; labor, 200, 399, 511-12; Legal Tender cases, 172; Negro rights, 57-59; New Deal legislation, 561-62, 568, 573; property rights in the nineteen twenties, 516-17; railroad regulation, 235-37, 342, 348; Roosevelt's fight on, 573-74; Sherman Antitrust Law, 250-51, 340, 342-44, 400-01; social legislation in the states, 361-62, 515-16; Tennessee Valley Authority (TVA), 569; workmen's compensation, 359
Sylvis, W. H., 189
Synthetic rubber, 627, 673

Taft, William Howard: biographical sketch, 333; Chief Justice of Supreme Court, 361, 517; conservation policy, 351; foreign policy, 321, 378, 454; navalism, 382-83; Philippines, 309; Prohibition, 520; quarrel with Roosevelt, 351, 384; role in World War I, 439, 449; tariff policy, 335-38; trust policy, 341, 344
Taft-Hartley Act of 1947, 650, 652, 659
Tanner, James, 89
Tarbell, Ida, 354
Tariff (*See also,* Balance of international payments, Foreign trade): Civil War to 1890, 29, 75, 78-82; concessions, 280-81; Cuba, 321, 393; measures: Dingley Act, 278-81, 321, 335; emergency legislation of 1921, 473; Fordney-McCumber Act, 473-74; McKinley Act, 81, 82; Morrill Act, 78; Payne-Aldrich Act, 333-36, 385, 474; Smoot-Hawley Act, 474-76, 583; Underwood Act, 391-93, 423; Wilson-Gorman Act, 82, 83; Philippines, 312, 393; reciprocal trade agreements, 82, 337-38, 584-86; relation to American industrialization, 158, 297
Tariff Board of 1909, 335
Tariff Commission, 80, 393-94, 474-76
Taste, popular, 684-85
Taussig, F. W., 394
Taylor, Moses, 282-83

INDEX

Taxation. *See*, Internal Revenue, Revenue Acts, Tariff.
Taxes: excess-profits, 435, 480, 633, 649; excise, 29, 87, 294, 435, 480, 579, 633; income, 82, 83, 435, 580, 633
Tehran Conference of 1943, 613
Television, 668
Teller, H. H., 264, 269, 291
Temporary National Economic Committee (TNEC), 576
Tenancy, 14, 36, 144, 528-29
Tennessee Valley Authority (TVA), 557, 560, 569-70
Ten-per cent plan, 8, 9
Tenure of Office Act, 20, 23, 24
Theater in America, 220, 222, 669-70
Thirteenth Amendment, 14
Thomas Amendment, 567
Thomas, General Lorenzo, 24
Thomas, Norman, 513, 552, 656
Thomson, J. Edgar, 128, 162
Thompson, Carmi A., 311-12
Thurman, A. G., 64, 72
Thurmond, J. Strom, 655, 656
Tilden, Samuel J., 50-51, 64, 66
Tillman, Benjamin R., 55, 56, 260, 263, 267
Tojo, General Hidejeki, 601
Tolman, Richard, 675
Tocqueville, Alexis de, 684-85
Tracy, B. F., 73
Trade Agreements Act of 1934, 585
Trade Associations, 518
Trade Unions. *See*, Labor.
Transportation Act of 1920, 478-79
Treasury surplus, 73, 87-89
Treaties: arbitration, 413, 493; Axis satellite, 613, 641-42; Bryan-Chamorro, 372, 411; Clayton-Bulwer, 368; Four-Power, 496; Inter-American of Mutual Assistance, 632; Isthmian canal, 369-72, 386-89, 411; London, 497, 592; naval limitation, 495-97; Nine-Power, 496, 599; Paris, 298-99; secret, 450; trade agreements, 584-86, 639-40; Versailles, 450-56; Washington, 192, 415
Trieste, 642
Trizonia, 643
Truman, Harry S., 613, 636, 650, 654; campaign of 1948, 655-57; foreign policy of, 642, 645
Trumbull, Lyman, 46
Trusts (*See also*, Monopoly): Clayton Act, 397-99; Federal Trade Commission Act, 397-98; growth of, 238-40, 249; mergers, 517-19; prosecution of, 341-42; Sherman Antitrust Act, 247-48;

Supreme Court decisions, 250-51, 340, 342-44, 400-01; Standard Oil Company, 241-45
Twain, Mark, 210, 215-16, 684
Tweed Ring, 48
Tunney, Gene, 667
Twenty-first Amendment, 522
Tydings-McDuffie Act of 1934, 591

Underwood, Oscar W., 391, 668
Undistributed-profits tax, 578
Unemployment: depression of 1930, 551; New Deal and, 566-67, 575; Social Security Act, 566, 633; technological, 508-09
Unemployment insurance. *See*, Social Security.
Union League clubs, 14
Union Pacific Railroad, 130-31
Union-Republican party, 9, 10, 14, 15
United Automobile Workers of America, 565
United Confederate Veterans, 3
United Mine Workers, 328-29, 565, 659
United Nations: charter, 614, 617; conflict in, 646-48; organization, 614-16
United Nations war aims, 612
United Nations Relief and Rehabilitation Administration (UNRRA), 638
United States Employment Service, 650
United States Foreign Service, 85
United States Housing Authority (USHA), 559, 571
United States Maritime Commission, 569, 626
United States Shipping Board, 404, 436, 476-78
United States Steel Corporation, 165, 344, 401
Untermyer, Samuel, 344
Uranium fission, 622
Urbanization, 108, 503-04

Vandenberg, Arthur H., 616, 645, 654
Vanderbilt, Cornelius, 31, 126-27, 204
Vanderbilt, W. H., 127
Veblen, Thorstein, 210, 214-15, 678
Venezuela: boundary dispute, 77, 96-98; controversy with Germany concerning, 367-68
Veterans (*See also*, Grand Army of the Republic): Civil War, 3; pensions, 87-89; World War I, 481-82; World War II, 657-58
Veterans' Bureau, 463, 482
Villa, Francisco, 407
Villard, Henry, 132, 137

INDEX

Virgin Islands, 411
Virginius affair, 43, 283
"Visiting statesmen," 51, 66

Wade-Davis bill, 9, 11, 13
Wade-Davis Manifesto, 10
Wages, 198, 439, 628, 660. *See also,* Labor, Prices.
Wagner Act. *See,* National Labor Relations Act.
Wallace, Henry A., 595, 636, 650, 655-57
Walsh, F. P., 439
Walsh, Thomas J., 463-64
Wanamaker, John, 73
War Assets Administration (WAA), 658
War Assets Corporation, 658
War criminals, 641
War Industries Board, 435-36
War Labor Board, 439, 630, 658
War Manpower Commission, 621, 658
War of Nerves, 593
War Production Board (WPB), 625-26
War risk insurance, 434, 624
Washington Conference of 1921 to 1922, 452, 495, 599
Watson, Thomas E., 260, 269, 330, 332
Watterson, Henry, 270, 671
Wavell, General Sir Alexander, 606
Weaver, General James B., 67, 255, 260, 262
Webb-Kenyon Interstate Liquor Shipment Act of 1913, 520
Webster, Daniel, 6
Webb-Pomerene Act of 1918, 399-400
Welles, Orson, 670
West: agrarian movement in, 228-30, 252; cattle raising, 113-15; discontent in, 352; industrialization of, 507; wheat production, 141-43
Weyl, Walter, 354, 431
Weyler, Valeriano, 285-87
Wheeler, Everett P., 84
Wheeler, Burton K., 467, 573
Whiskey Ring, 49
White, Andrew D., 62, 69, 98
White, Henry, 377, 450
White, William Allen, 388, 462
White primary, 57, 59
Whitman, Walt, 210, 214
Whitney, William C., 71, 98, 106
Wickersham, G. W., 333, 341, 401
Wilder, Thornton, 670
Williams, G. H., 35
Williams, Tennessee, 669
Willkie, Wendell, 565, 595, 688
Wilson, Edmund, 683
Wilson, Henry, 30, 31

Wilson, Sir Henry Maitland, 611
Wilson, Woodrow: banking reform, 395; biographical sketch, 389-90; Caribbean policy, 410-11; concept of leadership, 390; contest with Senate, 449, 454-56; election of 1912, 388-89; of 1916, 423-25; of 1918, 449; of 1920, 460-62; Fourteen Points, 442; League of Nations, 451-56; Mexican policy, 406-09; neutrality, 414; Philippines, 310-11; preparedness, 430; prestige, 458-59, 461, 596; relations with Great Britain (1914-17), 414-18; relations with Germany, 419-22, 430-32; tariff policy, 391; trust policy, 397; Versailles, 451-56; war aims, 429-30, 442-43
Winchell, Walter, 671
Windom, William, 67, 73
Wolfe, Thomas, 683
Women: higher education, 212; influence of, 666; mothers' assistance acts, 362-63; position of, 205; protection of in industry, 361; service in World War II, 618-19; suffrage, 357
Wood, General Leonard: aspirant for Republican nomination in 1920, 460; military governor of Cuba, 319; Philippines, 311-12; preparedness (1917), 429; Spanish-American War, 297
Woodford, S. L., 289-91
Woods, Robert A., 208
Workmen's compensation, 358-59
Works Progress Administration (WPA), 559, 566-67, 670, 675, 680
World Court for International Justice, 465, 590
World Health Organization, 640
World War I: armistice, 443, 448-49; campaign in France, 444-48; causes of American entry, 425-32; civilian organization for, 435-39; mobilization, 433-35, 440-41; neutrality, 414-22; outbreak in Europe, 413-14; preparedness, 430; propaganda, 425-56; strikes, 439, 457, 464-65; Versailles Treaty, 450-56, 492
World War II: agriculture, 630-31; campaigns, 602, 604, 607-10; demobilization, 657-58; diplomatic conferences of, 612-14; economic warfare, 631-32; enemy aliens, 625; labor, 629-30; mobilization: men, 619-20; money, 633; morale, 624-25; production, 620-21, 624-25; science, 622-24, 674; neutrality, 588-91, 595-98; outbreak in Europe, 593-94; preparation, 594-95, 598; prices and profits in, 629; production, 626-27;

relations with Japan preceding, 591-92, 599-600
Wright, Frank Lloyd, 681
Wright, Richard, 683

Yalta Conference of 1945, 613
Yellow-dog contract, 511

Young Men's Christian Association (YMCA), 207
Young Plan, 498-500
Young Women's Christian Association (YWCA), 207

Zimmermann, Alfred, 431